CRIMINAL LAW

AND

PROCEDURE

SEVENTH EDITION

CRIMINAL LAW

AND

PROCEDURE

SEVENTH EDITION

DANIEL E. HALL, J.D., Ed.D.

CENGAGE
Learning®

Australia • Brazil • Mexico • Singapore • United Kingdom • United States

CENGAGE
Learning®

**Criminal Law and Procedure,
Seventh Edition**
Daniel E. Hall, J.D., Ed.D.

Senior Vice President, General Manager
for Skills and Global Product
Management: Dawn Gerrain

Product Manager: Paul Lamond

Senior Director, Development/Global
Product Management, Skills: Marah
Bellegarde

Senior Product Development Manager:
Larry Main

Senior Content Developer: Melissa Riveglia

Product Assistant: Diane E. Chrysler

Marketing Manager: Scott Chrysler

Senior Production Director: Wendy Troeger

Production Manager: Mark Bernard

Senior Content Project Manager:
Betty L. Dickson

Art Director: Heather Marshall, PMG

Senior Technology Project Manager:
Joe Pliss

Media Developer: Deborah Bordeaux

Cover image(s): Giorgio Fochesato/Getty
Images

For product information and technology assistance, contact us at
Cengage Learning Customer & Sales Support, 1-800-354-9706

For permission to use material from this text or product,
submit all requests online at **www.cengage.com/permissions**.
Further permissions questions can be e-mailed to
permissionrequest@cengage.com

Library of Congress Control Number: 2013953740

ISBN-13: 978-1-285-44881-7

ISBN-10: 1-285-44881-2

Cengage Learning
200 First Stamford Place, 4th Floor
Stamford, CT 06902
USA

Cengage Learning is a leading provider of customized learning solutions
with office locations around the globe, including Singapore, the United
Kingdom, Australia, Mexico, Brazil, and Japan. Locate your local office
at: **www.cengage.com/global**

Cengage Learning products are represented in Canada by
Nelson Education, Ltd.

To learn more about Cengage Learning, visit **www.cengage.com**
Purchase any of our products at your local college store or at our
preferred online store **www.cengagebrain.com**

Printed in the United States of America
1 2 3 4 5 6 7 18 17 16 15 14

BRIEF CONTENTS

CONTENTS

PART I
Criminal Law

Chapter 1

Chapter 2

Chapter 3

Chapter 4

Chapter 5

Chapter 16

SENTENCING AND APPEAL **582**

PREFACE

Like its six previous editions, *Criminal Law and Procedure*, 7th Edition, is a comprehensive text covering both substantive criminal law and criminal procedure. The importance of constitutional law to these fields is emphasized, as are practical insights. This book has been designed for use in undergraduate programs in both legal studies and criminal justice.

ORGANIZATION OF THE TEXT

Because I don't believe in fixing things that aren't broken and because the reviewers and users of this book have told me that it isn't broken, I have retained the original organization, content, and pedagogy in this edition. This remains a combination textbook and casebook. The cases are edited and the text written with the undergraduate student in mind. It is my hope that the writing level of this book will challenge undergraduate students without overwhelming them.

All of the pedagogical features of the earlier editions have been retained, including highlighted definitions, glossary of terms, table of cases, and a thorough index. The distinction between chapter questions and chapter problems continues in this text, the former testing content knowledge and the latter testing the students' problem-solving, critical thinking, and analytical skills.

Keeping in mind the diverse audience of students and instructors who use this text, I have designed two general methods of use. The first is as a combination text and casebook. The second method is to omit the cases and use the text alone. Both methods are possible because I do not use any case to exclusively teach a point of law. Instead, the cases are used to illustrate a point in practice and to develop the cognitive skills of students. Accordingly, if time does not permit it or the educational goals of an instructor are focused elsewhere, the cases may be omitted without losing substantive content.

The first half of the text covers substantive criminal law, and the second half of the text discusses both the constitutional dimensions of criminal procedure and the practical dimensions of the criminal justice process.

KEY FEATURES

Ethical Considerations that expose students to ethical questions in criminal law and general ethical principles and laws that apply to players in the criminal justice system.

Writing Style that challenges but does not overwhelm undergraduate students.

Key Terms that are in bold on first use and clearly defined in the margin.

Cases that reinforce content and promote the development of case analysis skills.

Sidebars that can be used to spark class discussion and student interest in issues involving the criminal justice system and criminal law.

Exhibits that reinforce textual material and help illustrate important ideas.

Web Links that highlight websites that are germane to chapter materials.

Review Questions that call for content-related answers to reinforce and retain chapter concepts.

Chapter Problems & Critical Thinking Exercises that are intended to develop critical thinking and problem-solving skills.

CHANGES IN THE SEVENTH EDITION

I have added new material and updated existing material to keep abreast of changes in both the law and the criminal justice disciplines. The changes and additions include, inter alia, the following:

- There were many important Supreme Court cases since the last edition. The law of the book has been updated through early 2013.

- Several new case excerpts were added including a trial court decision on cyber-stalking, a trial court decision on jury tampering and free speech, the revival of the Fourth Amendment property doctrine in *Jones,* the Fourth Amendment dog sniff case *Florida v. Jardines,* the Fourth Amendment DNA swab case *Maryland v. King*, the *Miranda* case *Howes v. Fields*, and the Court's decision on mandatory life sentences for juveniles, *Miller v. Alabama*. Although not new, an excerpt of *Terry v. Ohio* was added. A few case excerpts were eliminated in favor of in-text discussions. These include *Coolidge, Scarfo, Stansbury,* and *Baze.* Several cases were moved to appear closer to their in-text references.

- A note about case excerpts: To this author, there are three objectives of including judicial opinions in a textbook. The first is doctrinal: to teach the law. The second is purely cognitive: to develop a reader's analytical, and more specifically, legal reasoning skills. The third is to develop the reader's familiarity with the language and structure of legal writing. I consider all of these purposes when selecting cases, knowing that every case will not accomplish all three objectives. In addition, the importance and impact of a case, its age, the clarity of its language, and my ability to successfully edit it are considered. I have taken some liberties in my editing. Because ellipses can be distracting to the reader, many citations and footnotes were redacted without any indication in the text. The reader is advised to consult the appropriate official reporter for the complete text.

- The number of additions, edits, and deletions from the text narrative are too great to list them all. But new topics and stories and elaborations of existing material include more on punitive damages in civil law, the relationship of state and federal criminal authority, corporate criminal liability, the Penn State scandal and failure to report as crime, California Mentally Disordered Program, what amounts of reasonable suspicion in practice, the custody element of *Miranda,* the unreliability of eyewitness identification and the Court's decision in *Perry,* the recent Confrontation Clause decisions, race and sex limitations on peremptory challenges, and stories intended to provoke reader interest, such as the Cannibal Cop, the DOJ's position on the public safety exception and the Boston Bombing suspect, more on wiretaps and technology, the Wall Street trader arson and suicide, the case of a bank manager who was kidnapped, had a bomb strapped to her, and was forced to rob her bank as an example of duress, and the Treyvon Martin homicide and stand-your-ground laws.

- Crime and other data have been updated. New sidebars discussing the Fair Sentencing Act of 2010 and the New York City stop-and-frisk program were added, as was a graphic illustrating the continuum of self-defense protection (e.g. retreat, castle, stand-your-ground).

- A few subchapters have been created.

- The chapter objectives have been revised from what the reader will do in the chapter to what the reader should be able to do after completing the chapter.

Please share any ideas you have for improvement of this book with either the publisher or me. I may be reached at hallslaw@yahoo.com

ANCILLARY MATERIALS

SUPPLEMENTAL TEACHING AND LEARNING MATERIALS

Instructor Companion Site

The Online Instructor Companion Site provides the following resources:

Instructor's Manual
The Instructor's Manual has been revised to incorporate changes in the text and to provide comprehensive teaching support. The Instructor's Manual contains the following:

- Syllabus and lesson plans for each chapter
- Answers to exercises in the text
- Test Bank and answer key

PowerPoint Presentations
Customizable PowerPoint® Presentations focus on key points for each chapter. (Power-Point® is a registered trademark of the Microsoft Corporation.)

Cengage Learning Testing Powered by Cognero is a flexible, online system that allows you to:

- author, edit, and manage test bank content from multiple Cengage Learning solutions
- create multiple test versions in an instant
- deliver tests from your LMS, your classroom or wherever you want

Start right away!

Cengage Learning Testing Powered by Cognero works on any operating system or browser.

- No special installs or downloads needed
- Create tests from school, home, the coffee shop—anywhere with Internet access

What will you find?

- *Simplicity at every step.* A desktop-inspired interface features drop-down menus and familiar, intuitive tools that take you through content creation and management with ease.
- *Full-featured test generator.* Create ideal assessments with your choice of 15 types of questions (including true/false, multiple choice, opinion scale/likert, and essay). Multi-language support, an equation editor and unlimited metadata help ensure that your tests are complete and compliant.
- *Cross-compatible capability.* Import and export content into other systems.

MindTap

MindTap for Hall/Criminal Law and Procedure is a highly personalized fully online learning platform of authoritative content, assignments, and services offering you a tailored presentation of course curriculum created by your instructor. MindTap for Hall/Criminal Law and Procedure guides you through the course curriculum via an innovative learning path where you will complete reading assignments, annotate your readings, complete homework and engage with quizzes and assessments. MindTap includes a variety of web-apps known as "MindApps"—allowing functionality such as having the text read aloud to you, as well as MindApps that allow you to synchronize your notes with your personal Evernote account. MindApps are tightly woven into the MindTap platform and enhance your learning experience.

How MindTap helps students succeed?

- Use the Progress App to see where you stand at all times–individually and compared to highest performers in your class.
- ReadSpeaker reads the course material to you.
- MyNotes provides the ability to highlight text and take notes—that link back to the MindTap material for easy reference when you are studying for an exam or working on a project.

- Merriam Webster Dictionary and a glossary are only a click away.
- Flashcards are pre-created to help you memorize the key terms.

Not using MindTap in your course?

- It's an online destination housing ALL your course material and assignments . . . neatly organized to match your syllabus.
- It's loaded with study tools that help you learn the material more easily.
- To learn more go to www.cengage.com/mindtap or ask your instructor to try it out.

Please note the Internet resources are of a time-sensitive nature and URL addresses may often change or be deleted.

ACKNOWLEDGMENTS

I would like to thank the Senior Product Manager Shelley Esposito and the Senior Content Developer Melissa Riveglia, for their continued support and belief that this text.

Thanks to each of the following individuals for taking the time to review and comment on the text. The changes that resulted from their recommendations have added considerably to the organization and pedagogy of this book:

Celia L. Murray
Georgia Piedmont Technical College
Clarkston, GA

Todd Richardson
Daytona State College Daytona
Beach, FL

Robin Rossenfeld
Community College of Aurora
and Colorado Community
Colleges—Online
Aurora, CO

ABOUT THE AUTHORS

A native of Indiana, Daniel E. Hall is Professor and Chair of Justice and Community Studies, Professor of Political Science, and affiliate of Black World Studies at Miami University. He is also visiting professor of law at Sun Yat-sen University in Guangzhou, China. Previously, he served as chairperson and associate professor in the Department of Criminal Justice at the University of Toledo and Associate Professor of Criminal Justice and Legal Studies at the University of Central Florida. He has also held adjunct faculty positions at the Barry University School of Law, College of Micronesia, and the University of Evansville. He earned his B.S. at Indiana University, J.D. at Washburn University, and Ed.D. in Higher Education at the University of Central Florida. In addition to experience as a defense attorney in the United States and assistant attorney general of the Federated States of Micronesia, he has 14 years of experience teaching criminal law and procedure in higher education. He has authored a dozen journal articles and 21 books (including subsequent editions), all on public law subjects. Daniel lives in Hamilton, Ohio, with his daughters, Grace Kathryn and Eva Joan. You may email Daniel at hallslaw@yahoo.com. You are also invited to visit his personal Web site, Danielhall.org

TABLE OF CASES

PART I

CRIMINAL LAW

CHAPTER 1

INTRODUCTION TO THE LEGAL SYSTEM OF THE UNITED STATES

Chapter Outline

Federalism

Separation of Powers

The Structure of the Court System

Duties and Powers of the Judicial Branch

Comparing Civil Law and Criminal Law

The Authority of Government to Regulate Behavior

The Purposes of Punishing Criminal Law Violators
 Specific and General Deterrence
 Incapacitation
 Rehabilitation
 Retribution

Ethical Considerations: Basics on Ethics in Criminal Law

Chapter Objectives

After completing this chapter you should be able to:

- describe the basic constitutional structure of state and federal governments with an emphasis on how structure affects criminal law and criminal justice administration.

- compare and contrast federal and state authorities in criminal law.

- describe both civil and criminal law with an emphasis on their differing objectives and procedures.

- describe the third branch of government, the judiciary, including the structure of U.S. courts and the authorities and duties of courts in criminal justice.

FEDERALISM

Before one can undertake learning criminal law or criminal procedure, a basic understanding of the legal system of the United States is necessary. This can be a complex task, as criminal law and procedure are significantly influenced by federal and state constitutional law, the common law, and statutory law at both the federal and state levels. It will be easier to understand how these areas of law affect criminal law if we first explore the basic structure of American government.

The United States is divided into two sovereign forms of government—the government of the **federalism.** It is also common to refer to this division as the vertical division of power, as the national government rests above the state governments in hierarchy in those areas where the constitution grants supremacy to the federal government. The Framers of the Constitution of the United States established these two levels of government in an attempt to prevent the centralization of power, that is, too much power being vested in one group. The belief that "absolute power corrupts absolutely" was the catalyst for the division of governmental power.

In theory, the national government, commonly referred to as the *federal government,* and the state governments each possess authority over citizens, as well as over particular policy areas, free from the interference of the other government (dual sovereignty). Most crimes fall into the jurisdiction of a state court alone, but there are small zones of authority that are exclusively federal as well. In many instances, when the authorities of both a state and the federal government are implicated, the two coordinate their investigations and prosecution. This process, commonly known as cooperative federalism, is discussed more fully later in this chapter.

Determining what powers belong to the national government, as opposed to the states, is not always an easy task. The Framers of the Constitution intended to establish a limited federal government. That is, most governmental powers were to reside in the states, with the federal government being limited to the powers expressly delegated to it by the U.S. Constitution. This principle is found in the Tenth Amendment, which reads: "The powers not delegated to the United States by the Constitution, nor prohibited to it by the States, are reserved to the States respectively, or the people."

federalism

■ A system of political organization with several different levels of government (for example, city, state, and national) coexisting in the same area, with the lower levels having some independent powers.

sidebar

At trial, a *sidebar* is a meeting between the judge and the attorneys, at the judge's bench, outside the hearing of the jury. Sidebars are used to discuss issues that the jury is not permitted to hear. In this text, the sidebars will appear periodically. This periodic feature contains information relevant to the legal subject being studied.

What powers are delegated to the United States by the Constitution? There are several, including, but not limited to, the power to take the following actions:

1. Coin money, punish counterfeiters, and fix standards of weights and measures.
2. Establish a post office and post roads.
3. Promote the progress of science and useful arts by providing artists and scientists exclusive rights to their discoveries and writings.
4. Punish piracy and other crimes on the high seas.
5. Declare war and raise armies.
6. Conduct diplomacy and foreign affairs.
7. Regulate interstate and foreign commerce.
8. Make laws necessary and proper for carrying into execution other powers expressly granted in the Constitution.

The last two of these powers—the regulation of interstate commerce and the making of all necessary and proper laws—have proven to be significant sources of federal authority. Also important is the Supremacy Clause of Article VI, which provides that

> This Constitution, and the Laws of the United States which shall be made in Pursuance thereof; and all Treaties made, or which shall be made, under the Authority of the United States, shall be the supreme Law of the Land; and the Judges in every State shall be bound thereby, any Thing in the Constitution or Laws of any State to the Contrary notwithstanding.

The Supremacy Clause declares federal law, if valid, to be a higher form of law than state law. Of course, if the federal government attempts to regulate an area belonging to the states, its law is invalid and the state law is controlling. But if the federal government possesses **jurisdiction** or concurrent state and federal jurisdiction exists, federal law trumps state law. This is true when federal and state laws are in conflict and when the federal government has taken over the area to the exclusion of the states (preemption). This is not a common issue in criminal law, because state and federal laws rarely conflict; rather, they are more likely to be parallel or complementary. In such cases, a state government and the federal government have **concurrent jurisdiction** (see Exhibit 1–1).

Keep in mind that the U.S. Constitution is the highest form of law in the land. It is the federal constitution that establishes the structure of our government. You will learn later the various duties of the judicial branch of government. One duty is the interpretation (determining what written law means) of statutes and constitutions. The highest court in the United States is the United States Supreme Court. (In this text, all references to the *Court* are to the Supreme Court of the United States unless stated otherwise.) As such, that Court is the final word on what powers are exclusively federal or state, or concurrently held. However, once the Supreme Court decides that an issue is exclusively under the control of state governments, each state, through its judiciaries, has the final word on that issue.

jurisdiction

■ The geographical area within which a court (or a public official) has the right and power to operate. Or the persons about whom and the subject matters about which a court has the right and power to make decisions that are legally binding.

concurrent jurisdiction

■ Two or more jurisdictions or courts possessing authority over the same matter.

Exhibit 1–1   FEDERAL AND STATE CRIMINAL JURISDICTION

State Jurisdiction	Concurrent Jurisdiction	National (Federal) Jurisdiction
1. States may regulate for the health, safety, and morals of their citizens	1. Those acts that fall into both federal and state jurisdictions	1. Crimes that are interstate in character
2. Those acts that involve a state government, its officials and property	Examples: Bank robbery of a federally insured institution; an act of terrorism against the United States that harms an individual, state property, or individual property	2. Crimes involving the government of the United States, including its officials and property
Examples: Murder; rape; theft; driving under the influence of a drug; gambling		Examples: Murder of a federal official or murder on federal land; interstate transportation of illegal item; interstate flight of a felon

During the past 200 years, the Supreme Court has differed in its approach to federalism. Two general models can be identified, though. *Dual federalism* refers to an approach under which the states and federal government are viewed as coequals. Under this approach, the Tenth Amendment is interpreted broadly and the Commerce Clause and the Necessary and Proper Clause are read narrowly. The Tenth Amendment is interpreted as an independent source of state powers, staking out policy areas upon which the national government cannot encroach.

Another model, *hierarchical federalism,* positions the national government as superior to the state governments. Under this approach, the Commerce and Necessary and Proper Clauses are construed broadly. The Tenth Amendment becomes a truism; that is, it reserves to the states only those powers the national government does not possess. Accordingly, state jurisdiction decreases as federal jurisdiction expands.

Cooperative federalism, which is not a third jurisdictional model, but instead, a relational descriptor, is characterized by significant interaction between the states and federal government (and local forms of government) in an effort to effectively regulate and administer laws and programs. Cooperative federalism is a product of the political branches, the executive and legislative, not legal (federalism) mandate. The increased cooperation between state and federal law enforcement agencies to fight the war against drugs in the 1980s and 1990s and the war against terrorism in the 2000s are good examples of cooperative federalism. The Court has vacillated between the two jurisdictional models. The dominant approach in recent decades has been hierarchical federalism. This is not to say that the states are powerless. In fact, one policy area over which the states have maintained considerable control is criminal law. More than 90 percent of all crimes fall within the jurisdiction of the states, not the federal government. However, the sphere of federal government power in criminal law is increasing. This is because more acts are committed in, or are committed using an item that has traveled in, interstate commerce. Acts that have traditionally been state-law crimes may today be federal crimes as well, if there is an interstate component to the act. For example, if carjacking, which is the state crime of robbery, is committed with a gun that has traveled in interstate commerce, it is also a federal crime. An act that harms an individual or property invokes state jurisdiction. If the same act can be characterized as **terroristic,** as defined by federal law, then federal jurisdiction and separate federal criminal liability may exist as well. Drug trafficking, if interstate, is a violation of federal law and possibly multiple state laws. Certain violations of civil liberties also invoke concurrent federal and state jurisdiction. Which government will bring charges in these situations is more a political question than a legal one. It is not a violation of double jeopardy for an individual to be tried and punished by both federal and state governments, even for the same act because the constitutional prohibition of double jeopardy was intended to preclude two trials or punishments by the same jurisdiction, not by multiple jurisdictions.

Regardless of the expansion of federal jurisdiction, most crimes continue to fall within the exclusive jurisdiction of the states. This is because one of the responsibilities of the states is to regulate for the health and safety of its citizens. This is known as the **police power.** Most murders, rapes, and thefts are state-law crimes. A few policy areas belong exclusively to the federal government. Punishing counterfeiters is an example. Although the expansion of federal authority is likely to continue to increase as people and goods become more national and international in character, the Supreme Court has reaffirmed the central role of states in protecting people (police power) and it has conversely made it clear that a genuine connection to interstate commerce or other federal authorities must exist for the federal government to criminalize behavior.

For example, the Supreme Court invalidated the Gun-Free Zone Act of 1990 because it found no genuine connection between guns around schools and interstate commerce. Similarly, the Brady Handgun Violence Protection Act was invalidated in *Printz v. United States*[2] because it required state officials to conduct background checks on gun purchasers. The Court held that Congress was without the authority to direct local enforcement officers in this way. In yet another case favoring state authority *United States v. Morrison*[3] the Supreme Court struck down part of the Violence Against Women Act because it held that it was a state, not federal, authority to provide victims of sex crimes with civil remedies against their attackers. In another 2000 case, *Jones v. United States*[4], the Court invalidated the application of a federal arson statute to the prosecution of a man for firebombing his cousin's home. The Court rejected the United States' theory that it had jurisdiction because the home's mortgage, its insurance, and its natural gas were all purchased in interstate commerce. The Court penned that if it were to accept the government's position, "hardly a building in the land would fall outside the federal statute's domain."

However, a connection was found in the 2005 case *Gonzales v. Raich*.[5] In that case, the federal government's prohibition of the possession of marijuana was upheld, although state law allowed its possession and use for medical purposes. The interstate

terrorism

■ The definition of terrorism is the subject to ongoing debate. However, one federal statute defines it as activities that involve violence or acts dangerous to human life that are violations of law and appear to be intended to intimate or coerce a civilian population, to influence a policy of government by intimidation or coercion, or to affect the conduct of government through mass destruction, assassination, or kidnapping.[1] 18 U.S.C. §2331.

police power

■ The government's right and power to set up and enforce laws to provide for the safety, health, and general welfare of the people.

nature of marijuana production and sales made for an easy case of federal jurisdiction. In fact, the plaintiffs conceded this point. Their theory that California's law permitting limited use of marijuana should trump federal law failed, largely because the federal government had a "rational basis" to believe that the state law would undermine the intention of the federal law by providing a stream through which interstate drug trafficking could occur.

In 2010, the Court affirmed a federal statute that delegated the authority to seek civil commitment of federal sex offenders after their sentences were served to federal prosecutors. Similar state laws were previously upheld, but in the 2010 case *United States v. Comstock*,[6] the defendant complained that civil commitment was a traditional state authority and accordingly, the federal law was invalid. Relying on the Necessary and Proper Clause, the Court rejected the argument. That the statute required the federal government to give the appropriate state officials the first opportunity to file for commitment in state court also reduced the Court's concerns that state autonomy was threatened.

Local governments have not been mentioned so far. This is because the Constitution does not recognize the existence of local governments. However, state constitutions and laws establish local forms of government, such as counties, cities, and districts. These local entities are often empowered by state law with limited authority to create criminal law. These laws, usually in the form of ordinances, are discussed in Chapter 2.

The result of this division of power is that the states (as well as other jurisdictions, such as the District of Columbia), the federal government, and local governments each have a separate set of criminal laws. For this reason, you must keep in mind that the principles you will learn from this book are general in nature. It is both impossible and pointless to teach the specific laws of every jurisdiction of the United States in this textbook.

SEPARATION OF POWERS

separation of powers

■ Division of the federal government (and state governments) into legislative (lawmaking), judicial (law interpreting), and executive (law carrying out) branches.

Another division of governmental power is known as **separation of powers.** This is the division of governmental power into three branches—the executive, legislative, and judicial—making a horizontal division of power, just as federalism is the vertical division (see Exhibit 1–2). Each branch is delegated certain functions that the other two may not encroach upon. The executive branch consists of the president of the United States, the president's staff, and the various administrative agencies that the president oversees. Generally, it is the duty of the executive branch to enforce the laws of the federal government. In criminal law, the executive branch investigates alleged violations of the law, gathers the evidence necessary to prove that a violation has occurred, and brings violators before the judicial branch for disposition. The president does this through the various federal law enforcement and administrative agencies.

statute

■ A law passed by a legislature.

The legislative branch consists of the United States Congress, which creates the laws of the United States. Congressionally created laws are known as **statutes.** Finally, the judicial branch comprises the various federal courts of the land. That branch is

Exhibit 1-2   DIVISION OF GOVERNMENTAL POWER

	Legislative Branch	**Executive Branch**	**Judicial Branch**
The Government of the United States (Federal Government)	United States Congress	President of the United States	Federal Courts
State Governments	State Legislatures	Governors	State Courts

charged with the administration of justice. A more comprehensive discussion of the judicial branch follows later in this chapter.

In a further attempt to diffuse governmental power, the framers designed a system of checks and balances that prevents any one branch from exclusively controlling a function. Several checks can be found in the Constitution.

For example, Congress is responsible for making the law. This function is checked by the president, who may veto legislation. The president is then checked by Congress, which may override a veto with a two-thirds majority. The president is responsible for conducting foreign affairs and making treaties and for serving as commander in chief of the military. The Senate, however, must approve the treaties negotiated by the executive branch, and Congress has been delegated the authority to make the rules that regulate the military. In the context of criminal law, this means that Congress, state legislatures, and local councils declare what acts are criminal; for their part, the president, state governors, prosecutors, and law enforcement agencies detect and respond to criminal acts, prosecute violators, and administer judicially ordered punishments. The judicial branch interprets criminal law, oversees criminal adjudications, sentences offenders, and to a limited extent oversees the entire system of adjudication and punishment.

Through the power of judicial review, the judiciary may invalidate actions of the president or Congress that violate the Constitution. In contrast, the political branches select federal judges through the nomination (president) and confirmation (Senate) process. Unpopular judicial decisions may be changed either by statute, if the issue is one of statutory interpretation, or by constitutional amendment, if the issue is one of constitutional interpretation and Congress possess the authority to impeach federal judges.

Keep in mind that two levels of government exist, excluding local entities. Even though the U.S. Constitution does not establish three branches of government for the many states (the U.S. Constitution designs the structure of the federal government only but also demands that states have republican forms of government), all state constitutions do, in varying forms, model the federal constitution. The result is a two-tiered system with each tier split into three parts.

In this form of government, the legislature defines what acts are criminal, what process must be used to assure that a wrongdoer answers for an act, and what punishment should be imposed for the act.

The duty of the executive branch is to enforce and implement the laws created by the legislature, as well as to enforce the orders of courts. For example, if a state legislature prohibits the sale of alcohol on Sundays, it is the duty of the appropriate state law enforcement agencies—the police or the alcohol, tobacco, and firearms agents—to investigate suspected violations and take whatever lawful action is necessary to bring alleged violators to justice. Law enforcement, in the criminal law context, is accomplished through law enforcement agencies and prosecutorial agencies. At the federal level, there are many law enforcement agencies: the Federal Bureau of Investigation, Drug Enforcement Administration, United States Marshal Service, Department of Homeland Security, Immigration and Customs Enforcement, United States Secret Service, United States Coast Guard, Transportation Security Administration (including the Air Marshal Service), and Department of the Treasury are only a few. State law enforcement agencies include state departments of investigation, state police departments, and local police departments. These and other enforcement agencies are responsible for investigating criminal conduct and for gathering evidence to prove that a criminal violation has occurred. When the law enforcement agency has completed its investigation, the case is turned over to a prosecutor. The prosecutor is the attorney responsible for representing the people. The prosecutor files the formal criminal charge, or conducts a grand jury, and then sees the prosecution through to fruition. In the federal system, the prosecutor is called a United States attorney. In the states and localities, prosecutors are known as district attorneys, county attorneys, state attorneys, city attorneys, or, simply, prosecutors.

Finally, the judicial branch is charged with the administration of justice. The courts become involved after the executive branch has arrested or accused an individual of a crime as well as at certain points during criminal investigations. The duties of the judicial branch are explored further in the next section of this chapter. Lawyers, legal assistants, and law enforcement officials are likely to have significant contacts with state and federal courts; therefore, it is important to understand the structure of the court system.

THE STRUCTURE OF THE COURT SYSTEM

Within the federal and state judiciaries, a hierarchy of courts exists. All state court systems, as well as the federal court system, have at least two types of courts: trial courts and appellate courts. However, because each state is free to structure its judiciary in any manner, significant variation is found in the different court systems. What follows are general principles that apply to all states and the federal system.

trial court

■ A court that hears and determines a case initially, as opposed to an appellate court; a court of general jurisdiction.

Trial courts are what most people envision when they think of courts. A case begins at the trial court, where witnesses are heard and evidence is presented—often to a jury as well as a judge—and where verdicts and sentenced are announced. In the federal system, trial courts are known as United States District Courts. The United States is divided into 94 judicial districts, using state boundaries to establish district limits. Each state

sidebar

The court system is actually many court systems composed of the federal system and the many state systems. In 2010, approximately 104 million cases were filed in state and local trial courts, a decline from about 106 million in the two years previous according to the National Center for State Courts. Of these, 54 percent were traffic offenses, 20 percent were criminal cases, 18% were civil cases, 6 percent were domestic cases, and 2 percent were juvenile cases.

Source of state statistics: R. LaFountain, R. Schauffler, S. Strickland, and K. Holt, *Examining the Work of State Courts: An Analysis of 2010 State Court Caseloads* (National Center for State Courts 2012).

In 2012 the federal system was composed of 1 Supreme Court, 13 appellate courts, and 94 district courts. The district courts had 372,563 civil and criminal cases, a 5% decline from 2011; 1,261,140 petitions for bankruptcy were filed in federal bankruptcy courts, an astonishing 14% decline in from 2011. The regional courts of appeals didn't experience the declines of the trial courts. Total filings rose by 4% to 57,501. In 2011, 7,082 cases were filed, 79 were heard, and 78 cases terminated in the Supreme Court.

Source of federal statistics: 2012 Judicial Business of the United States Courts, Administrative Office of the United States Courts: *http://www.uscourts.gov/ uscourts/Statistics/JudicialBusiness/2012/JudicialBusinespdfversion.pdf*

constitutes at least one district, although larger states are divided into several districts. For example, Kansas has only one district, and the federal trial court located in Kansas is known as the United States District Court for the District of Kansas. California, in contrast, is made up of four districts: the Northern, Eastern, Central, and Southern Districts of California.

State trial courts are known by various names, such as district, superior, county, and circuit courts. Despite variations in name, these courts are very similar.

Appellate courts review the decisions and actions of trial courts (or lower appellate courts, as discussed later) for error. These courts do not conduct trials, but review the **briefs** submitted by the parties and examine the **record** from the trial court for mistakes, known as trial court error. Often, but not always, appellate courts will hear argument from the attorneys involved in the case under review, but witnesses are not heard nor other evidence submitted. After the appellate court has reviewed the record and examined it for error, it renders an opinion. An appellate court can reverse, affirm, or remand the lower court decision. To *reverse* is to determine that the court below has rendered a wrong decision and to change that decision. When an appellate court *affirms* a lower court, it is approving the decision made and leaving it unchanged.

appellate court

■ A higher court that can hear appeals from a lower court.

brief

■ A written document filed with a court through which a party presents a legal claim, legal theory, supporting authorities, and requests some form of relief.

record on appeal

■ A formal, written account of a case, containing the complete formal history of all actions taken, papers filed, rulings made, opinions written, etc.

In some cases, an appellate court will remand the case to the lower court. A *remand* is an order that the case be returned to the lower court and that some action be taken by the judge when the case is returned. Often this will involve conducting a new trial. For example, if an appellate court decides that a judge acted in a manner or made a decision that prevented a criminal defendant from having a fair trial, and the defendant was convicted, an appellate court may reverse the conviction and remand the case to the trial court for a new trial with instructions that the judge not act in a similar manner.

In the federal system and many states, there are two levels of appellate courts, an intermediate and highest level. The intermediate-level courts in the federal system are the United States Courts of Appeal.[7] There are 11 judicial circuits in the United States, with one court of appeal in each circuit. Additionally, there is a court of appeal for Washington, D.C., and for the Federal Circuit. Therefore, there are 13 United States Courts of Appeal in total (see Exhibit 1–3). Appeals from the district courts are taken to the circuit courts. The highest court in the country is the United States Supreme Court. Appeals from the circuit courts are taken to the Supreme Court. Also, appeals of federal issues from state supreme courts are taken to the United States Supreme Court. Although appeal to a circuit court and to a state's first appellate court (and often its second level of appeal as well) is generally a right any litigant has, the Supreme Court is not required to hear most appeals, and it does not. In recent years, the Supreme Court has denied review of approximately 97 percent of the cases appealed. Therefore, the States' Supreme Courts and federal circuit courts are often a defendant's last chance to have his or her case heard.

Many states also have intermediate-level appellate courts, as well as a high court, although a few states have only one appellate court. Most states call the high court the supreme court of that state and the intermediate level court the court of appeals. An example of an exception is New York, which has named its highest court the Court of Appeals of New York and refers to its lower-level courts as supreme courts.

In states that have only one appellate court, appeals are taken directly to that court. New Hampshire is such a state, so appeals from New Hampshire's trial courts are taken directly to the Supreme Court of New Hampshire. Note that in most instances a first appeal is an appeal of right. This means that an individual has a right to appeal, and the appellate court is required to hear the case. However, second appeals are generally not appeals of right, unless state law has provided otherwise. To have a case heard by the United States Supreme Court and most state supreme courts, the person appealing must seek **certiorari,** an order from an appellate court to the lower court requiring the record to be sent to the higher court for review. When "cert." is granted, the appellate court will hear the appeal; and when certiorari is denied, it will not.

Finally, be aware that a number of **inferior courts** exist. These are courts that fall under trial courts in hierarchy. As such, appeals from these courts do not usually go to the intermediate-level appellate courts, as described earlier, but to the trial-level court first. Municipal courts, police courts, and justices of the peace are examples of inferior

certiorari

■ (Latin) "To make sure." A request for certiorari (or "cert." for short) is like an appeal, but one that the higher court is not required to take for decision. It is literally a writ from the higher court asking the lower court for the record of the case.

inferior court

■ A court with special, limited responsibilities, such as a probate court.

Exhibit 1-3   THE 13 FEDERAL JUDICIAL CIRCUITS

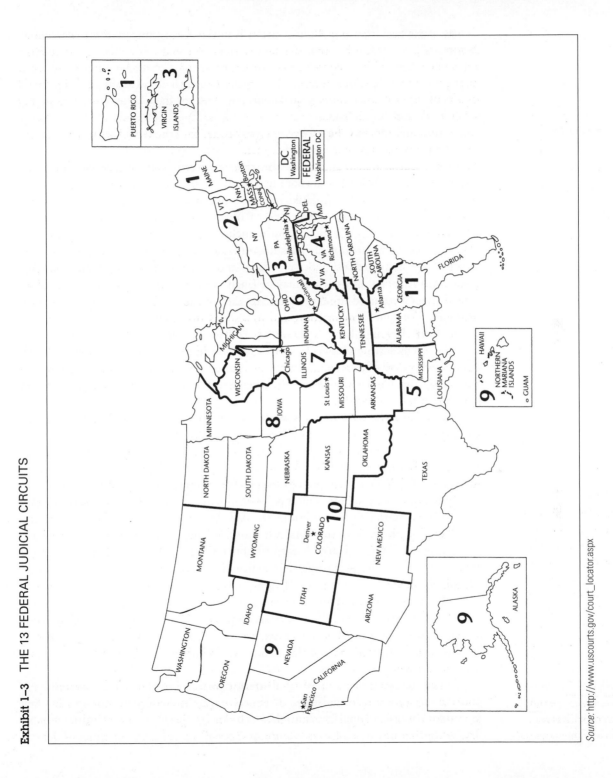

Source: http://www.uscourts.gov/court_locator.aspx

court of record

■ Generally, another term for trial court.

de novo

■ Anew. For a case to be tried again as if there had not been a prior trial.

court of general jurisdiction

■ Another term for trial court; that is, a court having jurisdiction to try all classes of civil and criminal cases except those that can be heard only by a court of limited jurisdiction.

court of limited jurisdiction

■ A court whose jurisdiction is limited to civil cases of a certain type, or that involve a limited amount of money, or whose jurisdiction in criminal cases is confined to petty offenses and preliminary hearings.

courts. An appeal from one of these courts is initially heard by a state trial-level court before an appeal is taken to a state appellate court. The federal system also has inferior courts. The United States Bankruptcy Courts are inferior courts because appeals from the decisions of these courts go to the district courts, in most cases, and not to the courts of appeals. Only after the trial court has rendered its decision may an appeal be taken to an appellate court.

Many inferior courts in the state system are not **courts of record.** No digital, audio, or stenographic recording of the trial or hearing at the inferior court is made. As such, when an appeal is taken to the trial level court, it is normally **de novo.** This means that the trial-level court conducts a new trial, rather than reviewing a record as most appellate courts do. This is necessary because there is no record to review, because the inferior court is not a court of record. Federal district courts do not conduct new trials, as all federal courts, including bankruptcy courts, are courts of record. State inferior courts have limited jurisdiction; for example, municipal courts usually hear municipal ordinance violations and only minor state law violations. The amount of money that a person may be fined and the amount of time that a defendant may be sentenced to serve in jail are also limited. Generally, no juries are used at the inferior court level.

Exhibit 1–4 is a basic diagram of the federal and state court systems. The appellate routes are indicated by lines drawn from one court to another. Later in this book you will learn how the appeals process works and how the federal and state systems interact in criminal law. Note where this diagram is located so that you may refer to it later.

Most state trial courts are known as **courts of general jurisdiction.** Courts of general jurisdiction possess the authority to hear a broad range of cases, including civil law as well as criminal. In contrast, **courts of limited jurisdiction** hear only specific types of cases. You have already been introduced to one limited jurisdiction court, municipal courts. Inferior courts, such as municipal courts, are always courts of limited jurisdiction. Some states employ systems that have specialized trial courts to handle domestic, civil, or criminal cases. These may be in the form of a separate court (e.g., Criminal Court of Harp County) or may be a division of a trial court (e.g., Superior Court of Harp County, Criminal Division). Appellate courts may also be limited in jurisdiction to a particular area of law, such as the Oklahoma Court of Criminal Appeals.

The federal government also has special courts. As previously mentioned, a nationwide system of bankruptcy courts is administered by the national government. In addition, the United States Claims Court, Tax Court, and Court of International Trade are part of the federal judiciary, and each has a specific area of law over which it may exercise jurisdiction. Often those cases over which they have jurisdiction are exclusive of district courts. However, the jurisdiction of those courts is outside the scope of this book, as they deal only with civil law. Criminal cases in federal court are heard by district courts, and criminal appeals are heard by the United States Courts of Appeals.

Exhibit 1–4   STATE AND FEDERAL COURT STRUCTURES

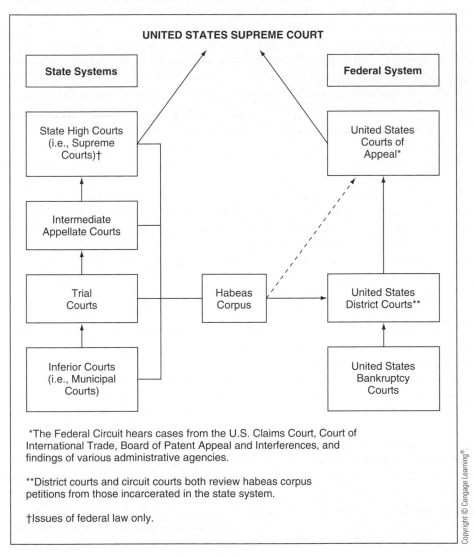

*The Federal Circuit hears cases from the U.S. Claims Court, Court of International Trade, Board of Patent Appeal and Interferences, and findings of various administrative agencies.

**District courts and circuit courts both review habeas corpus petitions from those incarcerated in the state system.

†Issues of federal law only.

DUTIES AND POWERS OF THE JUDICIAL BRANCH

Of the three branches of government, attorneys and other legal professionals have the most interaction with the judicial branch. For that reason, we single out the judicial branch for a more extensive examination of its functions.

First, it must be emphasized that all courts—local, state, and federal—are bound by the U.S. Constitution. Consequently, all courts have a duty to apply federal constitutional law. This duty is important in criminal law because it allows defendants to assert their U.S. constitutional claims and defenses in state court, where most criminal cases are heard. Of course, defendants may assert applicable state laws as well.

As previously stated, the judicial branch is charged with the administration of justice. The courts administer justice by acting as the conduit for dispute resolution. The courts are the place where civil and criminal disputes are resolved, if the parties cannot reach a resolution themselves. In an effort to resolve disputes, courts must apply the laws of the land. To apply the law, judges must **interpret** the legislation and constitutions of the nation. To *interpret* means to read the law in an attempt to understand its meaning. This nation's courts are the final word in declaring the meaning of written law. If a court interprets a statute's meaning contrary to the intent of a legislature, then the legislature may later rewrite the statute to make its intent clearer. This revision has the effect of "reversing" the judicial interpretation of the statute. The process is much more difficult if a legislature desires to change a judicial interpretation of a constitution. At the national level, the Constitution has been amended 26 times. The amendment process is found in Article V of the Constitution and requires action by the federal legislature as well as by the states. Amending a constitution is simply a more cumbersome and time-consuming endeavor than amending legislation.

The judicial branch is independent from the other two branches of government. Often, people think of the courts as enforcers of the law. Though this notion is true in a sense, it is untrue in that the judicial branch does not work with the executive branch in an attempt to achieve criminal convictions. It is the duty of the courts of this nation to remain neutral and apply the laws fairly and impartially. The U.S. Constitution establishes a judiciary system that is shielded from interference from the other two branches. For example, the Constitution prohibits Congress from reducing the pay of federal judges after they are appointed. This prevents Congress from coercing the courts into action under the threat of no pay. The Constitution also provides for lifetime appointments of federal judges, thereby keeping the judicial branch from being influenced by political concerns, which may cause judges to ignore the law and make decisions based on what is best for their political careers. Judicial independence permits courts to make decisions that are disadvantageous to the government, but required by law, without fear of retribution from the other two branches.

The need for an independent judiciary is particularly important when one considers the role courts play as the guardians of constitutional principles, including civil rights. **Judicial review** is a power held by the judicial branch that permits courts to review the actions of the executive and legislative branches, and of the states, and declare acts that are in violation of the Constitution void. Hamilton wrote of the power of judicial review, and of the importance of an independent judiciary, in the *Federalist Papers,* where he stated:

> Permanency in office frees the judges from political pressures and prevents invasions on judicial power by the president and Congress.

■ ■ ■

The Constitution imposes certain restrictions on the Congress designed to protect individual liberties, but unless the courts are independent and have the power to declare

interpret

■ Studying a document *and* surrounding circumstances to decide the document's meaning.

judicial review

■ A higher court's examination of a lower court's decision.

the laws in violation of the Constitution null and void these protections amount to nothing. The power of the Supreme Court to declare laws unconstitutional leads some to assume that the judicial branch will be superior to the legislative branch. Let us look at this argument.

Only the Constitution is *fundamental* law; the Constitution establishes the principles and structure of the government. To argue that the Constitution is not superior to the laws suggests that the *representatives of the people* are superior *to the people* and that the Constitution is inferior to the government it gave birth to. The courts are the arbiters between the legislative branch and the people; the courts are to interpret the laws and prevent the legislative branch from exceeding the powers granted it. The courts must not only place the Constitution higher than the laws passed by Congress, they must also place the intentions of the people ahead of the intentions of the representative. . . .

The landmark case dealing with judicial review is *Marbury v. Madison,* 1 Cranch 137, 2 L. Ed. 60 (1803). Chief Justice Marshall wrote the opinion for the Court and determined that, although the Constitution does not contain explicit language providing for the power of judicial review, Article III of the Constitution implicitly endows the judiciary with the authority. Although seldom used by the Supreme Court for over a hundred years following the *Marbury* decision, it is now well established that courts possess the authority to review the actions of the executive and legislative branches and to declare any law, command, or other action void if it violates the U.S. Constitution. The power is held by both state and federal courts. Any state or federal law that violates the U.S. Constitution may be struck down by either federal or state courts. Of course, state laws that violate state constitutions may be stricken for the same reason.

The power to invalidate statutes is rarely used, for two reasons. First, the judiciary is aware of how awesome the power is; consequently, courts invoke the authority sparingly. Second, many rules of statutory construction exist and have the effect of preserving legislation. For example, if two interpretations of a statute are possible, one that violates the Constitution and one that does not, one rule of statutory construction requires that the statute be construed so that it is consistent with the Constitution. Although rarely done, statutes are occasionally determined invalid. In Chapter 8 and 9, on defenses, you will learn many constitutional constraints on government behavior. These defenses often rely on the authority of the judiciary to invalidate statutes or police conduct to give them teeth.[8]

COMPARING CIVIL LAW AND CRIMINAL LAW

Criminal law exists in a larger legal framework than civil law. Understanding the context of any legal subject and its relationship to other legal subjects is important. It is common to distinguish between criminal law and civil law. While important differences exist between the two, there are also many similarities. Exhibit 1–5 compares criminal and civil law.

Exhibit 1–5   CRIMINAL AND CIVIL LAW COMPARED

	Criminal Law	Civil Law
Purposes	Retribution, deterrence, incapacitation, rehabilitation	Compensation and deterrence
Remedies	Fines, restitution, imprisonment, counseling, rehabilitation, injunctions, capital punishment	Damages and equitable relief
Parties	Government and individual defendant	Individual plaintiff and defendant (or government as individual)
Standard of Proof	Beyond a reasonable doubt	Preponderance of evidence
Burdens	Government bears burden of proof and process designed to protect rights of defendant (due process)	Plaintiff bears burden of proof and parties treated equally in process

The source of most of the dissimilarities between criminal law and civil law is the differing objectives of the two. There are many purposes of criminal law. First, it is intended to deter behavior that society has determined to be undesirable. A second purpose of criminal law is to punish those who take the acts deemed undesirable by society, specifically, to give victims and the community at large a sense of retribution. A third purpose is to incapacitate, through imprisonment, electronic monitoring, death, and other methods, offenders. Fourth, the rehabilitation of offenders is also an objective in many cases. Arguably, there is only one purpose, to prevent antisocial behavior. Under this theory, punishment is used as a tool to achieve the primary goal of preventing antisocial behavior. The purposes of punishing individuals who violate criminal laws are discussed in greater detail in Chapter 2.

In contrast, civil law has as its primary purpose the compensation of those injured by someone else's behavior. It is argued that the real purpose of civil law is the same as that of criminal law. By allowing lawsuits against individuals who have behaved in a manner inconsistent with society's rules, civil law actually acts to prevent undesirable behavior. However, prevention of bad behavior may be more the consequence of civil law than the purpose. To understand this you must know something about civil law.

Many definitions of civil law exist. This author prefers a negative definition similar such as, civil law is all law except that which is criminal law. Whatever definition you accept, many areas of law fall under the umbrella of civil law. Two of the largest categories of civil law are contract law and tort law.

Contract law is a branch of civil law that deals with agreements between two or more parties. You probably have already entered into a contract. Apartment leases, credit card agreements, and book-of-the-month club agreements are all contracts.

contract

■ An agreement that affects or creates legal relationships between two or more persons. To be a *contract,* an agreement must involve at least one promise, consideration, persons legally capable of making binding agreements, and a reasonable certainty about the meaning of the terms.

To have a **contract,** two or more people must agree to behave in a specific manner. If you violate your obligation under a contract, you have committed a civil wrong called a breach of contract. The landlord may sue you for your breach and receive **damages.** *Damages* are monetary compensation for loss.

Tort law is a branch of civil law that is concerned with civil wrongs but not contract actions. You have likely seen television ads for personal injury attorneys. These attorneys are practicing in the tort law area. A civil wrong, other than a breach of contract, is known as a **tort.** Torts are different from contracts in that the duty owed another party in contract law is created by the parties through their agreement. In tort law, the duty is imposed by the law. For example, at a party you are struck and injured by a beer bottle heaved by an intoxicated partier: A tort has been committed. The partier is known as a *tortfeasor*, which is the term used to describe one who commits a tort. Yet, why does that partier owe you a duty not to strike you with a flying beer bottle? You have not entered into a contract with the partier whereby he has promised not to harm you in this manner. The answer is that the law imposes the duty to act with caution when it is possible to injure another or cause injury to another's property. This duty is imposed upon all people at all times. The law requires that we all act reasonably when conducting our lives.

When a person fails to act reasonably and unintentionally injures another, that person is responsible for a **negligent** tort. Automobile accidents and medical malpractice are examples of negligent torts. When a person injures another intentionally, an **intentional** tort has occurred. Many intentional torts are also crimes, and this is one zone where criminal and common law coexist. If at that fraternity party you make a partier angry, and as a result he intentionally strikes you with the bottle, then he has committed both a crime and an intentional tort. Although criminal law may impose a jail sentence (or other punitive measures), tort law normally seeks only to compensate you for your injury. So, if you suffered $1,000 in medical bills to repair your broken nose, you would be entitled to that amount; but the partier cannot be sentenced to jail or otherwise be punished within the civil tort action. A separate criminal charge may be filed by the government. Although less common, tort negligence and criminal law also intersect. Extreme negligence, such as driving when drunk, that results in death or injuries can lead to both civil and criminal liabilities.

The final type of tort is the **strict liability** tort. In these situations liability exists even though the tortfeasor acted with extreme caution and did not intend to cause harm. An example of a strict liability tort is blasting. Whenever a mining or demolition company uses blasting, it is liable for any injuries or damages it causes to property, even if the company exercises extreme caution.

Damages that are awarded (won) in a lawsuit to compensate a party for actual loss are **compensatory damages.** Compensatory damages do just what the name states—compensate the injured party. However, another type of damages exists—**punitive damages.** Contrary to what you have learned so far, punitive damages are awarded in civil suits and are intended to prevent undesirable behavior by punishing those who commit outrageous acts. Punitive damages are often requested by plaintiffs in lawsuits but are rarely awarded. Do not worry if the idea of punitive damages confuses you

damages

■ Money that a court orders paid to a person who has suffered damage (a loss or harm) by the person who caused the injury (the violation of the person's rights).

tort

■ A civil (as opposed to a criminal) wrong, other than a breach of contract.

negligence

■ The failure to exercise a reasonable amount of care in a situation that causes harm to someone or something.

intentional

■ Determination to do a certain thing.

strict liability

■ The legal responsibility for damage or injury, even if you are not at fault or negligent.

compensatory damages

■ Damages awarded for the actual loss suffered by a plaintiff.

punitive damages

■ Damages that are awarded over and above compensatory damages or actual damages because of the wanton, reckless, or malicious nature of the wrong done by the plaintiff.

because it appears to be a criminal law concept. Such damages are penal in nature, and many lawyers argue that they should not be allowed because a person can end up punished twice—once when convicted and sentenced by a criminal court and again by a civil court if punitive damages are awarded.

Trial courts have considerable discretion in awarding punitive damages. There is a limit, however. In the 1996 case *BMW v. Gore,*[9] a jury verdict in actual damages of $4,000 accompanied by a punitive damages award of $4,000,000, which was reduced to $2,000,000 by the State Supreme Court, was set aside by the United States Supreme Court because it found that the plaintiff wasn't on notice, a due process requirement, that it could be penalized by such a sum. As such, the judgement was arbitrary. Because it was a civil case, not a criminal case, the court couldn't turn to the Eighth Amendment's bar on excessive fines to review the award. Instead, it held that due process, the basic fairness clause that applies to all governmental conduct and decisions, expects punitive damages awards to be reasonable, considering three factors: (1) the degree of reprehensibility of conduct, (2) the disparity between actual harm and the punitive award, and (3) a comparison of the award to similar civil or criminal penalties. What was Gore's injury? He had not been told that the car he purchased had been repainted to cover damage from acid rain. On remand, the trial court gave the plaintiff the choice between a new trial or accepting $50,000 in punitive damages.

In State Farm v. Campbell[10] a plaintiff sued an insurance company over a $50,000 liability policy. The jury awarded the plaintiff $2,600,00 and actual damages of $145,000,000 in punitive damages. The trial judge reduced the punitive award to $1,000,000. The Supreme Court, applying the *BMW* criteria, found the 9:1 ratio of actual to punitive damages excessive and remanded the case to the state court with an order to reduce the award.

In the well-known case involving the massive oil spill in Alaskan waters by one of Exxon's oil tankers, *Exxon Shipping Co. v. Baker,*[11] the jury award of $2.5 billion in punitive damages and $507 million in actual damages, a 5:1 ratio, was found to be excessive. Unlike the earlier cases, *Exxon* was not decided on due process grounds but, rather, upon maritime law. Regardless, the Court's rejection of the 5:1 ratio is instructive in all cases.

The last major case in which the Supreme Court reviewed a punitive damages award was *Phillip Morris U.S.A. v. Williams.*[12] The jury award of $821,485.50 in actual damages and $79.5 million in punitive damages—which had been reduced by the trial judge to $32 million in punitive damages—was reversed and remanded to the trial court to reduce the punitive damages figure. In addition to being excessive, the Court rejected the award because it punished the company for harm caused to third parties, people not involved in the litigation. On remand, the award was reinstated with a different theory. Phillip Morris appealed this decision to the United States Supreme Court, which denied certiorari.

Do not get the concept of punitive damages mixed up with restitution or fines, which are discussed later in this text. Those forms of punishment, which occur in criminal cases, are limited by the Eighth Amendment's prohibition of excessive fines, as well as by due process.

Finally, a few other differences between criminal law and civil law should be mentioned. First, in civil law the person who brings the lawsuit (the plaintiff) is the person who was injured. For example, suppose you are at the grocery store doing your shopping and request the assistance of a checkout person who has recently divorced a spouse who looks very much like you. The checker immediately becomes enraged and vents all of his anger for his ex-wife on you by striking you with a box of cereal, which he was checking. He has committed a possible assault and battery in both tort law (these are intentional torts) and criminal law. However, in tort law, you must sue the checker yourself to recover any losses you suffer.

In criminal law, on the other hand, the government—whether national, state, or local—is always the party that files criminal charges. Often you will hear people say that they have filed criminal charges against someone. This statement is not accurate. What they have usually done is to file a complaint; the government determines whether criminal charges are to be filed. This is because a violation of criminal law is characterized as an attack on the citizens of a state (or the federal government) and, as such, is a violation of public, not private, law. Because it is public, the decision to file—or not to file—is made by a public official, the prosecutor. So, in our example, you have to contact either the police or your local prosecutor to have a criminal action brought against the checker.

Civil cases are entitled *citizen v. citizen;* in criminal law, it is *government* (i.e., *State of Montana*) *v. citizen*. In some jurisdictions, criminal actions are brought under the name of the people. This is done in New York, where criminal cases are entitled *The People of the State of New York v. citizen*.

There is no difference between a criminal action brought in the name of the state and a criminal action brought in the name of the people of a state. All prosecutions at the national level are brought by the United States of America. Note that governments may become involved in civil disputes. For example, if the state of South Dakota enters

sidebar

ABOUT CASE NAMES, TITLES, AND CAPTIONS

Cases filed with courts are given a case title, also known as a case name. The title consists of the parties to the action. In civil cases the title is *citizen v. citizen,* for example, *Joe Smith v. Anna Smith*. In criminal actions the title is *the government v. citizen*. For example, *United States of America v. Joe Smith or State of New Mexico v. Anna Smith.*

Cases also have captions. The caption appears at the top of the title page of all documents filed with a court and includes the case name, the court name, the case number, and the name of the document being filed with the court. The illustration in Exhibit 1–6 is an example of both a criminal case caption and a civil case caption.

into a contract with a person, and a dispute concerning that contract arises, the suit will be titled either *citizen v. South Dakota* or *South Dakota v. citizen.*

The two fields also differ in what is required to have a successful case. In civil law one must show actual injury to win. If, in our grocery store example, the box of cereal missed your head and you suffered no injury (damages), you would not have a civil suit. However, a criminal action for assault or battery may still be brought, as no injury is required in criminal law. This is because the purpose of criminal law is to prevent this type of conduct, not to compensate for actual injuries.

To turn this idea around, there are many instances in which a person's negligence could be subject to a civil cause of action, but not to a criminal action. If a person accidentally strikes another during a game of golf with a golf ball, causing injury, the injured party may sue for the concussion received; but no purpose would be served by

Exhibit 1–6   SIMPLE CAPTION—CRIMINAL CASE AND CIVIL CASE

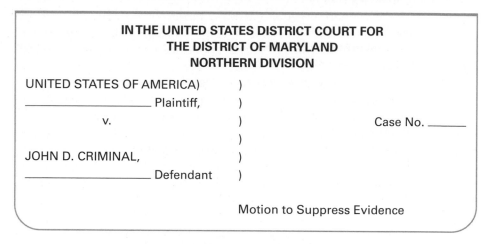

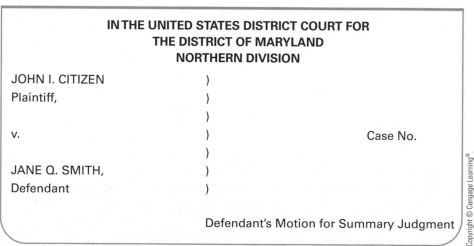

prosecuting the individual who hit the ball. No deterrent effect is achieved, as there was no intent to cause the injury. In most cases, society has made the determination (through its criminal laws) that a greater amount of **culpability** should be required for criminal liability than for civil. Criminal law is usually more concerned with the immorality of an act than is tort law. This is consistent with the goals of the two disciplines, as it is easier to prevent intentional acts than accidental ones. These concepts will be discussed later in the chapter on mens rea.

culpable

■ Blamable; at fault. A person who has done a wrongful act (whether criminal or civil) is described as "culpable."

THE AUTHORITY OF GOVERNMENT TO REGULATE BEHAVIOR

Freedom and liberty are two concepts that pervade the American political being. Most of us have learned that the longing for freedom of religious thought caused the English Puritan emigration from England to what was to become Plymouth, Massachusetts, in 1620. Later, the desire for freedom from the oppressive crown of England was the catalyst for the Declaration of Independence and the American Revolution. Finally, the fear that all governments tend to abuse their power led to the creation of a constitution that contains specific limits on governmental power and specific protections of individual rights. But what exactly is freedom? Liberty?

Freedom generally means the ability to act without interference. In a political and legal sense, it means the ability to act free from the interference of government. However, even in the freest societies, personal behavior is limited. This is because the actions of every member of society have the potential, at times, to affect other members. The total absence of government is anarchy, and few people believe that freedom results from anarchy. Without government, there would be little control over behavior. No system would exist to punish those who intentionally injure others. No system would exist to allow someone injured by the negligence of another to recover his or her losses. There would be no deterrence to wrongful behavior, other than fear of retribution from the victim. The strong and cunning would prey on the weak and unintelligent; the licentious on the decent. Although it is true that to live in such a world would be living free from government interference, it would not be a life free of oppression and arbitrary harm. Fear of sexual and other assault, fear that the strong will freely take property from others, the inability to obtain compensation for injuries, and so forth, all reduce an individual's freedom. To prevent anarchy and thereby increase freedom, people establish governments that have the authority to regulate behavior. The paradox is that too much government can be as much of a threat to freedom as too little government.

To achieve greatest freedom, a delicate balance between governmental authority and individual liberty must be struck (see Exhibit 1–7). Accordingly, individuals do not possess absolute freedom. As is commonly quipped, one person's freedom ends at the tips of the noses of other persons. While people do not possess absolute freedom, certain freedoms are protected in nearly all societies. In the United States, the Constitution establishes a zone of freedom over which government is prohibited from, or at least must have a very good reason for, regulating. The individual freedoms that comprise

Exhibit 1–7   MAXIMIZING SECURITY AND LIBERTY: THE TENSION BETWEEN FREEDOM AND THE NEED FOR GOVERNMENTAL PROTECTION

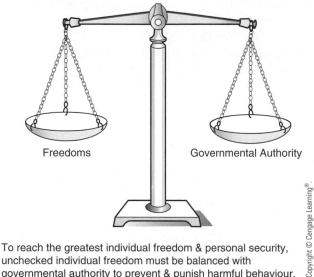

Freedoms   Governmental Authority

To reach the greatest individual freedom & personal security, unchecked individual freedom must be balanced with governmental authority to prevent & punish harmful behaviour.

civil liberties

■ Political liberties guaranteed by the Constitution and, in particular, by the Bill of Rights, especially the First Amendment.

this zone are known as individual rights, civil rights, or **civil liberties**. Said another way, civil rights are freedoms that are legally protected and enforceable.

The forefathers of the United States were sensitive to this relationship when they met in Philadelphia to draft the Constitution of the United States. Some characterize the relationship between a democratic republican form of government and its people as a contract. The people relinquish some freedoms in an effort to secure other freedoms. The preamble to the U.S. Constitution recognizes this principle. It states:

"We, the People of the United States, in order to form a more perfect union, establish justice, insure domestic tranquility, provide for the common defense, promote the general welfare, and secure the blessings of liberty to ourselves and our posterity, do ordain and establish this Constitution for the United States of America."

The concept is also found in the Declaration of Independence, where Thomas Jefferson penned:

. . . that all Men are created equal, that they are endowed by their Creator with certain unalienable Rights, that among these are Life, Liberty, and the Pursuit of Happiness— That to secure these Rights, Governments are instituted among Men, deriving their just Powers from the Consent of the Governed."

So the contract was formed. The people are to receive the benefits of an organized, fair government. The government is to establish laws designed to protect the people from one another and from other nations. In exchange, the people agree to comply with the laws created by their government. Some would argue that the duty extends to require the people to participate in the activities of the government. You have probably heard people speak of a "duty" to vote. Clearly, this is the rationale for requiring individuals to sit as jurors.

Every government is different. Some governments permit little or no political participation by the people. Others permit more. In those nations where the people are active participants, the rights and duties of individuals can vary significantly. This is because values can vary significantly from culture to culture. Hence, what one society believes to be an important freedom and protects from government interference may not be so valued by other societies.

In nearly all nations, however, governmental involvement in the affairs of people is continually increasing. This is due in part to the fact that people are becoming less independent. That is, members of society now depend on one another to provide goods and services that were once commonly self-provided. In addition, the staggering increase in world population has caused people to have much more contact with each other than they did 100 years ago. The greater the population, contact between, and dependence of people on one another, the greater the number of conflicts that will arise requiring government intervention. As the population and dependence of people increase, so does the likelihood that one person's action may affect another. A person who lives alone in a forest far from other people can scream loudly in the middle of the night without bothering anyone. This person could dispose of trash in any manner desired. If that same person lived in the middle of a city, the scream could wake people, and the improper disposal of trash could cause the spread of disease as well as create an unpleasant environment. As the number of contacts between members of a society increases, so does the number of conflicts requiring government intervention. Even if the parties involved do not desire legal intervention to resolve their conflict, society will sometimes intervene through its government to prevent unacceptable behavior. For example, society has decided that duels are not an acceptable method of resolving disputes, even if two individuals wish to use this method. The government will try to prevent such behavior from occurring. If the duel is not discovered until after the fact, then the parties involved may be punished for participating.

As the need for government involvement in the private lives of citizens increases, it becomes more difficult to protect civil liberties. Many of these liberties are contained in the first 10 amendments to our Constitution, which are commonly known as the **Bill of Rights.** As the world becomes more populated and complex, the balance between permissible government involvement in the private lives of its citizens and impermissible encroachment upon those citizens' civil liberties becomes harder to maintain. As that line becomes thinner, the duty of the defense lawyer and the legal assistant to be zealous in preparation of their defenses increases.

As previously discussed, the attempt to control people's behavior is achieved through both civil law and criminal law. Generally, society reserves only those acts that are perceived as serious moral wrongs or extremely dangerous for sanction under criminal law. Those acts that are accidental or are not serious breaches of moral duty

Bill of Rights

■ The first 10 amendments (changes or additions) to the U.S. Constitution.

are usually not criminal, but may lead to civil liability. Beliefs about what acts should be considered under each category are very subjective and often change because a problem intensifies or because the public perceives an increased problem, even though the situation may not be any different than in years before.

For example, the 1980s saw an increased effort to stop people from driving while under the influence of alcohol. Many states enacted new laws increasing the penalty for violating their DUI statutes. In addition, a few states limited police discretion by requiring that violators be arrested. The practice once exercised by many police departments of taking drunk drivers home was stopped by legislative command. At one time, it can be argued that civil law was as much of a deterrent to driving under the influence as was criminal law. Fear of civil liability for causing property damage or personal liability was as great as fear of criminal liability, because of the inconsistent and often minor penalties that followed convictions for driving under the influence. However, as public concern over alcohol-related automobile accidents increased, the focus turned to criminal law to prevent such behavior. Increased penalties, consistent arrest policies, and mandatory alcohol treatment for those convicted are now common.

The extensive media coverage given to particular cases, such as the Larry Mahoney accident,[13] have increased the public awareness that one who drives while intoxicated risks arrest, conviction, and punishment, as well as civil liability for injuries to property and person. What this example teaches is that society determines what acts will be treated as criminal based on public perceptions of morality, the importance of deterrence, and the danger posed to the public by the acts in question. Do not forget that criminal acts are often the subject of civil suits. This is not always true, as noted earlier in this chapter, when the general purposes of civil law and criminal law were discussed.

THE PURPOSES OF PUNISHING CRIMINAL LAW VIOLATORS

You have already learned that the general goal of criminal law is to prevent behavior determined by society to be undesirable. The criminal justice system uses punishment as a prevention tool. Many theories support punishing criminal law violators. Although some people focus on one theory and use it as the basis for punishment, a more accurate approach, in this author's opinion, is to recognize that many theories have merit and that when a legislature establishes the range of punishment applicable to a particular crime, many theories were involved in motivating individual legislators. It is unlikely that every member of a legislature will be motivated by the same objective. It is also unlikely that an individual legislator will be motivated by one theory only. Rather, all of the following objectives influence legislative decision making to some degree.

Specific and General Deterrence

Specific deterrence seeks to **deter** individuals already convicted of crimes from committing crimes in the future. It is a negative reward theory. By punishing Mr. X for today's crime, we teach him that he will be disciplined for future criminal behavior. The arrest and conviction of an individual show that individual that society has the capability to detect crime and is willing to punish those who commit crimes.

deter

■ To discourage; to prevent from acting.

General deterrence attempts to deter all members of society from engaging in criminal activity. In theory, when the public observes Mr. X being punished for his actions, the public is deterred from behaving similarly for fear of the same punishment. Of course, individuals will react differently to the knowledge of Mr. X's punishment. Individuals weigh the risk of being caught and the level of punishment against the benefit of committing the crime. All people do this at one time or another. Have you ever intentionally run a stoplight? Jaywalked? If so, you have made the decision to violate the law. Neither crime involves a severe penalty. That fact, in addition to the likelihood of not being discovered by law enforcement agents, probably affected your decision.

Presumably, if conviction of either crime was punished by incarceration (time in jail), then the deterrent effect would be greater. Would you be as likely to jaywalk if you knew that you could spend time in jail for such an act? Some people would; others would not. It is safe to assume, however, that as the punishment increases, so does compliance. However, one author observed that it is not as effective to increase the punishment as it is to increase the likelihood of being punished.[14] It is unknown how much either of these factors influences behavior, but it is generally accepted that they both do.

Incapacitation

Incapacitation, also referred to as restraint, is the third purpose of criminal punishment. Incapacitation does not seek to deter criminal conduct by influencing people's choices but prevents criminal conduct by restraining those who have committed crimes. Criminals who are restrained in jail or prison—or in the extreme, executed—are incapable of causing harm to the general public. This theory is often the rationale for long-term imprisonment of individuals who are believed to be beyond rehabilitation. It is also promoted by those who lack faith in rehabilitation and believe that all criminals should be removed from society to prevent the chance of repetition.

Crimes that are caused by mental disease or occur in a moment of passion are not affected by deterrence theories, because the individual does not have the opportunity to consider the punishment that will be inflicted for committing the crime before it is committed. Deterrence theories are effective only for individuals who are sufficiently intelligent to understand the consequences of their actions, are sane enough to understand the consequences of their actions, and are not laboring under such uncontrollable feelings that an understanding that they may be punished is lost.

Rehabilitation

Rehabilitation is another purpose of punishing criminals. The theory of rehabilitation is that if the criminal is subjected to educational and vocational programs, treatment and counseling, and other measures, it is possible to alter the individual's behavior to conform to societal norms. Another author noted:

> To the extent that crime is caused by elements of the offender's personality, educational defects, lack of work skills, and the like, we should be able to prevent him from committing more crimes by training, medical and psychiatric help, and guidance into law-abiding patterns of behavior. Strictly speaking, rehabilitation is not "punishment," but help to the offender. However, since this kind of help is frequently provided while the subject is in prison or at large on probation or parole under a sentence that carries some condemnation and some restriction of freedom, it is customary to list rehabilitation as one of the objects of a sentence in a criminal case.[15]

The concept of rehabilitation has come under considerable scrutiny in recent years, and the success of rehabilitative programs is questionable. However, the poor quality of prison rehabilitative programs may be the cause of the lack of success of these programs.

Retribution

Retribution, or societal vengeance, is the fifth purpose. Simply put, punishment through the criminal justice system is society's method of avenging a wrong. The idea that one who commits a wrong must be punished is an old one. The Old Testament speaks of an "eye for an eye." However, many people question the place of retribution in contemporary society. Is retribution consistent with American values? Jewish or Christian values? The question is actually moot, as there are few instances in which retribution stands alone as a reason for punishing someone who did not comply with the law. In most instances, society's desire for revenge can be satisfied while fulfilling one of the other purposes of punishment, such as incapacitation.

It has also been asserted that public retribution prevents private retribution.[16] That is, when the victim (or anyone who might avenge a victim) of a crime knows that the offender has been punished, the victim's need to seek revenge is lessened or removed. Therefore, punishing those who harm others has the effect of promoting social order by preventing undesirable conduct by victims of crimes. Retribution in such instances has a deterrent effect, as victims of crimes are less likely to seek revenge. This is a good example of how the various purposes discussed are interrelated.

Finally, consider a sociological note. Do not become so focused on criminal law as a method of social control that you forget the many other methods of control that exist.

> The criminal law is not, of course, the only weapon which society uses to prevent conduct which harms or threatens to harm these important interests of the public. Education, at home and at school, as to the types of conduct that society thinks good and bad, is an important weapon; religion, with its emphasis on distinguishing between good and evil conduct, is another. The human desire to acquire and keep the affection and respect of family, friends and associates no doubt has a great influence in deterring

most people from conduct that is socially unacceptable. The civil side of the law, which forces one to pay damages for the harmful results that one's undesirable conduct has caused to others, or which in inappropriate situations grants injunctions against bad conduct or orders the specific performance of good conduct, also plays a part in influencing behavior along desirable lines.[17]

Ethical Considerations

BASICS ON ETHICS IN CRIMINAL LAW

This feature, which appears in every chapter of this book, examines a particular ethical issue or dilemma that attorneys, judges, legal assistants, law enforcement officers, and parties confront in criminal cases.

In criminal cases, the various parties are governed by different sets of rules. Attorneys are regulated by state bar authorities. Most state bar authorities have adopted a modified version of the American Bar Association's (ABA) model rules. The ABA first issued a set of rules, the Canons of Professional Ethics, in 1908. In the 1960s, the ABA issued a new set of rules under the title Model Code of Professional Responsibility. Then, 20 years later, the Model Rules of Professional Conduct were issued. Today, it is the Model Rules that most states have adopted, typically with modifications. Accordingly, the Model Rules will be referenced in this book.

State bar authorities, not the ABA, enforce ethics rules. Typical sanctions for violations are reprimands, suspensions of the right to practice, restitution, and disbarment, which is the permanent removal from the practice of law. Additionally, judges possess the authority to discipline violations by attorneys (actually anyone appearing before the court) and contemptuous behavior with fines, temporary incarceration, and other penalties. Although not regulated by state or federal governmental authorities, paralegals are guided by the National Association of Legal Assistants and the National Federation of Paralegal Associations codes of professional conduct. More significantly, paralegals are indirectly regulated by state bars through their supervising attorneys, who are ultimately accountable for the research conducted by, and documents drafted by, their paralegals. Law enforcement officers are bound by state and federal laws and departmental rules.

Above all of these rules are the U.S. Constitution and the 50 state constitutions. Today, there is considerable constitutional case law that looks, smells, and tastes like ethics rules. Prosecuting attorneys, for example, are required to disclose evidence that tends to prove innocence to defendants. A violating prosecutor may be disciplined by a court, regardless of the bar's rules on the subject.

In each of the following chapters, a different dimension of ethics in criminal law will be explored more fully.

┌─ **Web Links** ──

Courts and Prosecutors

What follows are a few of the excellent sites providing statistical data on United States courts and prosecutors:

- *http://www.albany.edu/sourcebook/*
- *http://www.ncsconline.org* (National Center for State Courts)
- *http://www.communitycourts.org* (community courts page)

└──

Key Terms

appellate courts	culpability	police power
Bill of Rights	damages	punitive damages
briefs	de novo	record
certiorari	deter	record on appeal
civil liberties	federalism	separation of powers
compensatory damages	inferior courts	statute
concurrent jurisdiction	intentional	strict liability
contract	interpret	terroristic
court of record	judicial review	tort
courts of general jurisdiction	jurisdiction	trial courts
courts of limited jurisdiction	negligence	

Review Questions

1. What is the primary duty of the executive branch of government in criminal law?
2. Define the term "court of record."
3. Define jurisdiction, and differentiate between a court of general jurisdiction and a court of limited jurisdiction.
4. What are the goals of criminal law? Civil law?
5. Who may file a civil suit? A criminal suit? How are these different?
6. What are compensatory damages? Punitive damages?
7. Should punitive damages be permitted in civil law? Explain your position.
8. Define culpability.

Problems & Critical Thinking Exercises

1. In 1973 the United States Supreme Court handed down the famous case *Roe v. Wade,* 410 U.S. 113 (1973), wherein the Court determined that the decision to have an abortion is a private decision that is protected from government intervention, in some circumstances, by the U.S. Constitution. Suppose that a state legislature passes legislation (a state statute) that attempts to reverse the *Roe* decision by prohibiting all abortions in that state. Which is controlling in that state, the statute or the decision of the United States Supreme Court? Explain your answer.

2. Same facts as in problem 1, except the state supreme court has determined that the state constitution protects the life of fetuses from abortion, except when the life of the mother is endangered. Which is controlling when a mother seeks to have an abortion and her life is not endangered to any greater amount than the average pregnancy—the state constitutional provision protecting fetuses or the decision of the United States Supreme Court? Explain your answer.

3. Assume that the United States Supreme Court has previously determined that regulation of traffic on county roads is a power reserved exclusively to the states. In reaction to this opinion, the United States Congress enacts a statute providing that the regulation of county roads will be within the jurisdiction of the United States Congress from that date forward. Your law office represents a client who is charged with violating the federal statute that prohibits driving on all roads while intoxicated. Do you have a defense? If so, explain.

4. In theory, people can increase their "freedom" by establishing a government and relinquishing freedoms (civil liberties) to that government. Explain why this paradox is true.

5. A bomb is exploded in a crowded shopping mall, killing 50 people and injuring hundreds of others. A written message is received at the local police station claiming that the attack was perpetrated by Foreigners for a New United States (FNUS), an established organization that has as its purpose the "destruction of the government of the United States and its citizens who support their government." Agents of the Federal Bureau of Investigation, working with local police, traced the message to Terry Ist, a leader of FNUS. Terry Ist was charged, convicted, and sentenced pursuant to the following federal statute:

Terrorism

  i. Terrorist organization: The Attorney General, upon credible evidence that an organization has as a purpose to bring harm to the United States or its citizens, may declare such organization a terrorist organization by publishing notice of such declaration in the *Federal Register*.

  ii. Any individual who is a member of a terrorist organization, as declared by the Attorney General in the previous section of this law, and who causes harm to person or property with the intent of (i) intimidating or coercing a civilian population; (ii) influencing the policy of a government by intimidation or coercion; or (iii) affecting the conduct of a government by mass destruction, assassination or kidnapping is guilty of terrorism, a felony.

  iii. The government of the United States shall have exclusive jurisdiction to prosecute individuals for all crimes arising from acts of terrorism, as defined by this law herein.

After Terry Ist's conviction, the state where the bombing took place requested that Terry be turned over to it, where he was to be tried for murder and other offenses. The United States refused, citing section iii of the above law. Further, the United States Attorney filed a motion to have the case removed to federal court, along with an accompanying motion to dismiss the criminal action, asserting that section iii prohibits the state prosecution. Discuss the federalism issue, making the best case for both the state and federal governments. Conclude by explaining who should prevail and why.

To reach the greatest individual freedom & personal security, unchecked individual freedom must be balanced with governmental authority to prevent & punish harmful behaviour.

Endnotes

1. 18 U.S.C. §2331.
2. *Printz v. United States,* 521 U.S. 98 (1997)
3. *United States v. Morrison,* 529 U.S. 598 (2000)
4. *Jones v. United States,* 529 *U.S.* 848 (*2000*)
5. *Gonzales v. Raich,* 545 U.S. 1 (2005)
6. *United States v. Comstock*, 560 U.S. _____ (2010)
7. 28 U.S.C. § 41 *et seq.*
8. For more on the separation of powers and federalism, See Daniel E. Hall and John P. Feldmeier, *Constitutional Law: Governmental Power and Individual Freedoms,* 2nd ed. (Upper Saddle River, NJ: Prentice Hall Publishing, 2011), chapters 1–7. Chapter 1 contains a discussion of judicial review authority.
9. 517 U.S. 559 (1996).
10. 538 U.S. 408 (2003).
11. 554 U.S. 571 (2008).
12. 549 U.S. 346 (2007).
13. In May, 1988, Larry Mahoney, while driving under the influence of alcohol, struck a school bus, causing it to burst into flames. At the time he hit the bus, he was traveling in the wrong direction on an interstate highway. Twenty-four children and three adults died in the fire. On December 22, 1989, a Kentucky jury convicted Mr. Mahoney of second-degree manslaughter and other lesser offenses, and recommended that he be sentenced to 16 years in prison. Mahoney, who was characterized as a model prisoner, was granted early release from prison for good behavior in 1999, six years short of his sentence. "Drunken Driver Lives in Obscurity," *The Cincinnati Enquirer, May* 14, 2003.
14. *See* E. Puttkammer, *Administration of Criminal Law,* 16–17 (1953).
15. Schwartz and Goldstein, *Police Guidance Manuals* (Charlottesville: University of Virginia Press, 1968), Manual No. 3, at 21–32, reprinted in *Cases, Materials, and Problems on the Advocacy and Administration of Criminal Justice* 173 by Harold Norris (unpublished manuscript available in the Detroit College of Law library).
16. *See* Note, 78 *Colum. L. Rev.* 1249, 1247–59 (1978); LaFave and Scott, *Criminal Law* 26 (Hornbook Series, St. Paul: West, 1986).
17. LaFave and Scott at 23.

CHAPTER 2

INTRODUCTION TO CRIMINAL LAW

Chapter Objectives

After completing this chapter you should
be able to:

- identify and describe the objectives of
  criminal law and begin thinking critically
  about these objectives.
- identify and describe the various
  sources of criminal law.
- brief a judicial opinion and you should
  have begun practicing your case
  analysis skills.
- outline and explain the fundamental
  history of the U.S. legal system.
- explain the tension between social
  control and freedom.

THE DISTINCTION BETWEEN CRIMINAL LAW AND CRIMINAL PROCEDURE

In all areas of legal study, a distinction is made between substance and procedure. Substantive law defines rights and obligations. Procedural law establishes the methods used to enforce legal rights and obligations. The substance of tort law defines what a tort is and what damages an injured party is entitled to recover from a lawsuit. Substantive contract law defines what a contract is, tells whether it must be in writing to be enforceable, who must sign it, what the penalty for breach is, and other such information. The field of civil procedure sets rules for how to bring the substance of the law before a court for resolution of a claim. To decide that a client has an injury that can be compensated under the law is a substantive decision. The question then becomes how injured clients get the compensation to which they are entitled. This is the procedural question. Procedural law tells you how to file a lawsuit, where to file, when to file, and how to prosecute the claim. Such is the case for criminal law and procedure.

criminal law

■ The branch of the law that specifies what conduct constitutes crime and establishes appropriate punishments for such conduct.

criminal procedure

■ The rules of procedure by which criminal prosecutions are governed.

Criminal law, as a field of law, defines what constitutes a crime. It establishes what conduct is prohibited and what punishment can be imposed for violating its mandates. Criminal law establishes what degree of intent is required for criminal liability. In addition, criminal law sets out the defenses to criminal charges that may be asserted. Alibi, insanity, and the like are defenses and fall under the umbrella of criminal law.

Criminal procedure puts substantive criminal law into action. It is concerned with the procedures used to bring criminals to justice, beginning with police investigation and continuing throughout the process of administering justice. When and under what conditions may a person be arrested? How and where must the criminal charge be filed? When can the police conduct a search? How does the accused assert a defense? How long can a person be held in custody by the police without charges being filed? How long after charges are filed does the accused have to wait before a trial is held? These are all examples of criminal procedure questions that As you will learn in later chapters, many of the rules of criminal procedure have their roots in both the U.S. and state Constitutions. Of course, statutory law is also important in this context. Do not worry if you cannot always distinguish between a procedural question and a substantive one. There is considerable overlap between the two concepts.

The first part of this text is devoted to criminal law and the latter part to criminal procedure. In the remainder of the book, the term "criminal law" is used often. In most cases, this refers to general criminal law, including both substantive criminal law and criminal procedure.

SOURCES OF CRIMINAL LAW

Criminal law is a body of many laws emanating from many sources. Today, most American criminal law is a product of legislative enactment. That has not always been so. Further, administrative regulations now make up a much larger percentage of criminal law than in the past. It is vital to successful legal research that that you understand the sources of criminal law. As you read this section, you will begin to see why an understanding of the functions of the three branches of government is important to an understanding of all criminal law.

The Common Law

The oldest form of criminal law in the United States is the **common law.** The common law developed in England and brought to the United States by the English colonists.

> The common law, as it exists in this country, is of English origin. Founded on ancient local rules and customs and in feudal times, it began to evolve in the King's courts and was eventually molded into the viable principles through which it continues to operate. The common law migrated to this continent with the first English colonists, who claimed the system as their birthright; it continued in full force in the 13 original colonies until the American Revolution, at which time it was adopted by each of the states as well as the national government of the new nation.[1]

But what exactly is this common law? Simply stated, the common law is judge-made law. It is law that has been developed by the hands of the judges of both England and the United States. To comprehend how the common law developed, an understanding of English legal history, particularly the concepts of precedence and **stare decisis,** is important. Beginning with William the Conqueror in 1066 (Norman Conquest), the English monarchy began using law to reinforce the authority of the monarchy, to increase fairness over the existing feudal systems, to promote economic stability and development, and to unify the kingdom. Prior to 1066, all law in England was local and varied. In the early years after the Norman Conquest, the king sent his judges to hear cases throughout the nation. These judges returned to London, where they discussed their decisions. This process, along with the creation of royal courts, led to the development of rules of court and legal doctrines that would be applied in all cases. One such doctrine, intended to make the law the judges were applying consistent and predictable, holds that when a court renders a legal decision, that decision is binding on itself and its inferior courts, whenever the same issue arises again in the future.

The decision of a court is known as a **precedent.** The principle that inferior courts will comply with that decision when the issue is raised in the future is known as "stare decisis et non quieta movera" (a Latin phrase meaning "stand by precedents and do not disturb settled points"). The Supreme Court of Indiana expressed its view of stare decisis:

> Under the doctrine of stare decisis, this Court adheres to a principle of law which has been firmly established. Important policy considerations militate in favor of continuity and predictability in the law. Therefore, we are reluctant to disturb longstanding precedent which involves salient issues. Precedent operates as a maxim for judicial restraint to prevent the unjustified reversal to a series of decisions merely because the composition of the court has changed.[2]

common law

■ The legal system that originated in England and is composed of case law and statutes that grow and change, influenced by ever-changing custom and tradition.

stare decisis

■ (Latin) The doctrine that judicial decisions stand as precedents for cases arising in the future.

precedent

■ Prior decisions of the same court, or a higher court, that a judge must follow in deciding a subsequent case presenting similar facts and the same legal problem, even though different parties are involved and many years have elapsed.

Most of the early decisions were based upon feudal law. The impact, however, of having royal courts with national authority recognize a feudal legal principle, and subsequently applying that principle throughout the kingdom, was that England, for the first time in its history, had a set of laws that were *common to all,* and hence is the explanation for the name of this type of law.

> The common law, as frequently defined, includes those principles, usages, and rules of action applicable to the government and security of persons and property which do not rest for their authority upon any express or positive statute or other written declaration, but upon statements of principles found in the decisions of courts. The common law is inseparably identified with the decisions of the courts and can be determined only from such decisions in former cases bearing upon the subject under inquiry. As distinguished from statutory or written law, it embraces the great body of unwritten law founded upon general custom, usage, or common consent, and based upon natural justice or reason. It may otherwise be defined as custom long acquiesced in or sanctioned by immemorial usage and judicial decision. . . .
>
> In a broader sense the common law is the system of rules and declarations of principles from which our judicial ideas and legal definitions are derived, and which are continually expanding. It is not a codification of exact or inflexible rules for human conduct, for the redress of injuries, or for protection against wrongs, but is rather the embodiment of broad and comprehensive unwritten principles, inspired by natural reason and an innate sense of justice, and adopted by common consent for the regulation and government of the affairs of men.[3]

As stated, the common law is fluid and dynamic, changing to meet societal values and expectations. As one court stated, "The common law of the land is based upon human experience in the unceasing effort of an enlightened people to ascertain what is right and just between men."[4]

While courts (and the monarch) were responsible for making law in the early years of the common law, the situation changed with the advent of Parliament in the thirteen and fourteenth centuries. While the early Parliament had very limited authority, it eventually evolved into the general lawmaking body of England, displacing courts in the lawmaking function. Today, legislatures in all common law nations are the primary lawmakers. In the United States, the Congress of the United States is the federal lawmaker and the legislatures of the states are each responsible for making state laws. However, for reasons detailed later, courts continue to play an important role in the development of the common law.

Historically what happened in criminal law is that courts defined crimes, as there was usually no legislative enactment that determined what acts should be criminal. As time passed, established "common-law crimes" developed. First the courts determined what acts should be criminal, and then the specifics of each crime developed; what exactly had to be proved to establish guilt, what defenses were available, and what punishment was appropriate for conviction. Although there is great similarity between the common laws of the many jurisdictions in the United States, differences exist because judicial decisions of one state are not binding on other states. However, courts may look outside their jurisdictions for opinions to guide them in their decisionmaking if no court in their jurisdiction has addressed the issue under consideration. Each state, as a separate and sovereign entity, has the power to decide whether to adopt the common law, in whole or in part, or to reject it.

The 13 original states all adopted the common law. Most did so through their state constitutions. Today, only Louisiana has not adopted the common law in some form. However, for reasons you will learn later, approximately half of the states no longer recognize common-law crimes.[5] Even in those states, though, the civil common law and portions of the criminal common law (i.e., defenses to criminal charges) continue in force. Most states have expressly adopted the common law either by statute or by constitutional authority. Generally, there is no federal common law; rather, federal courts, in certain civil cases, apply the common law of the states in which they sit. For example, a U.S. district court in New Jersey will apply New Jersey common law. Even though this may appear strange to you, it is common practice for federal courts to apply state law. Further discussion of this topic is beyond the scope of this text.

Finally, be aware that common law has been modified and even abolished in some jurisdictions. The modifications to, and nullifications of, common law have come about in many different manners. In some instances, courts have decided that the common law must be changed to meet contemporary conditions or to bring the law into conformity with state or federal constitutional principles. In extreme situations, parts of the common law have been totally abolished. Because legislatures are charged with the duty of making the laws, they have the final word on the status of the common law, unless there is a state constitutional provision stating otherwise. Some legislatures have expressly given their judiciaries the authority to modify the common law, often with limitations. State legislatures are free to modify, partially abolish, or wholly abolish the common law as long as their own state constitution or the U.S. Constitution is not violated by so doing.

The common law normally is inferior to legislation. This means that if a legislature acts in an area previously dealt with by common law, the new statute controls, absent a statement by the legislature to the contrary. For example, assume that under common law adultery was a crime in State Y. The legislature of State Y can change this by simply enacting a statute that provides that adultery is not criminal. The legislature may also amend the common law by continuing to recognize common-law adultery, but change the penalty for violation. If a state constitution, statute, or judicial decision has not abrogated the common law, presume that it continues in effect.

The Principle of Legality

The question of whether common-law crimes should continue to exist is debatable. Those who favor permitting common-law crimes like that it permits courts to "fill in the gaps" left by the legislatures when those bodies either fail to foresee all potential crimes or simply forget to include a crime that was foreseen. However, a separation-of-powers question is raised by this scenario: namely, should the judicial branch actively second-guess or clean house for the legislative branch? Such conduct does appear to be the exercise of legislative authority. However, few people want intentionally dangerous or disruptive behavior not to be criminalized, and it appears to be impossible for legislatures to foresee all possible acts that are dangerous and disruptive.

Those who oppose a common law of crimes point to the concept embodied in the phrase "nullum crimen sine lege," which translates roughly to "there is no crime if there is no statute." Similarly, "nulla poena sine lege" has come to mean that "there shall be no punishment if there is no statute." These concepts, when considered in concert, insist that the criminal law must be written, that the written law must exist at the time that the accused committed the act in question, and that criminal laws be more precise than civil laws.[6] This is the *principle of legality*.

The legality principle is founded on the belief that all people are entitled to know, prior to committing an act, that the act is criminal and that punishment could result from such behavior. This is commonly referred to as *notice*. The idea is sensible, as it appears to be a rule consistent with general notions of fairness and justice, not only in the United States but for peoples around the world. Does it appear fair to you to hold individuals criminally accountable for taking an act that they could not have known was prohibited? The legality principle remedies the notice problem by requiring that written law be the basis of criminal liability, not unwritten common law. Understand that the law imposes a duty on all people to be aware of written law; thus, all people are presumed to be aware of criminal prohibitions. The *Keeler* case discusses the legality principle. Today, the principle of legality is subsumed in the right to due process (a fair process) found in the Fifth and Fourteenth Amendments to the Constitution of the United States and in the constitutions of the various states.

sidebar

HOW TO BRIEF A CASE

You are about to read the first judicial decision found in this text. Decisions of courts are often written and are commonly referred to as *judicial opinions* or *cases*. These cases are published in law reporters so they may be used as precedent. Many cases appear in this text for your education. Your instructor may also require that you read other cases, often from your jurisdiction. The cases included in your book have been edited, citations have been omitted, and legal issues not relevant to the subject discussed have been excised. There is a common method that students of the law use to read and analyze, also known as briefing, cases. Please go to Appendix C now to learn more about how to brief a case.

sidebar *(continued)*

Most judicial opinions are written using a similar format. First, the name of the case appears with the name of the court, the cite (location where the case has been published), and the year. When the body of the case begins, the name of the judge, or judges, responsible for writing the opinion appears directly before the first paragraph. The opinion contains an introduction to the case, which normally includes the procedural history of the case. This is followed by a summary of the facts that led to the dispute, the court's analysis of the law that applies to the case, and the court's conclusions and orders, if any.

Most opinions used here are from appellate courts, where many judges sit at one time. After the case is over, the judges vote on an outcome. The majority vote wins, and the opinion of the majority is written by one of those judges. If other judges in the majority wish to add to the majority opinion, they may write one or more *concurring opinions*. Concurring opinions appear after majority opinions in the law reporters. When judges who were not in the majority feel strongly about their position, they may file dissenting opinions, which appear after the concurring opinions, if any. Only the majority opinion is law, although concurring and dissenting opinions are often informative.

During your legal education you may be instructed to brief a case. Even if your instructor does not require you to brief cases, you may want to, as many students understand a case better after they have completed a brief. Here are suggestions for reading and understanding cases:

1. Read the case. On your first reading, do not take notes; simply attempt to get a *feel* for the case. Then read the case again and use the following suggested method of briefing.

2. State the *relevant* facts. Often, cases read like little stories. You need to weed out the facts that have no bearing on the subject you are studying.

3. Identify the issues. *Issues* are the legal questions discussed by the court.

4. State the applicable rules, standards, or other law, as they apply to the issues you have identified.

5. Summarize the court's decision and analysis. Why and how did the court reach its conclusion? Note whether the court affirmed, reversed, or remanded the case.

For a more thorough discussion of briefing and to read a sample brief, see Appendix C.

KEELER V. SUPERIOR COURT
Supreme Court of California   2 Cal. 3d 619, 470 P.2d 617 (1970)

In this proceeding for writ of prohibition, we are called upon to decide whether an unborn viable fetus is a "human being" within the meaning of the California statute defining murder. We conclude that the legislature did not intend such a meaning, and that for us to construe the statute to the contrary and apply it to this petitioner would exceed our judicial power and deny petitioner due process of law.

The evidence received at the preliminary examination may be summarized as follows: Petitioner and Teresa Keeler obtained an interlocutory decree of divorce on September 27, 1968. They had been married for sixteen years. Unknown to the petitioner, Mrs. Keeler was then pregnant by one Ernest Vogt, whom she had met earlier that summer. She subsequently began living with Vogt in Stockton, but concealed the fact from petitioner. Petitioner was given custody of their two daughters, aged 12 and 13 years, and under the decree Mrs. Keeler had the right to take the girls on alternate weekends.

On February 23, 1969, Mrs. Keeler was driving on a narrow mountain road in Amador County after delivering the girls to their home. She met petitioner driving in the opposite direction; he blocked the road with his car, and she pulled over to the side. He walked to her vehicle and began speaking to her. He seemed calm, and she rolled down her window to hear him. He said, "I hear you're pregnant. If you are, you had better stay away from the girls and from here." She did not reply, and he opened the car door; as she later testified, "He assisted me out of the car . . . [I]t wasn't rough at this time." Petitioner then looked at her abdomen and became "extremely upset." He said, "You sure are. I'm going to stomp it out of you." He pushed her against the car, shoved his knee into her abdomen, and struck her in the face with several blows. She fainted, and when she regained consciousness, petitioner had departed.

Mrs. Keeler drove back to Stockton, and the police and medical assistance were summoned. She had suffered substantial facial injuries, as well as extensive bruising of the abdominal wall. A Caesarian section was performed, and the fetus was examined in utero. Its head was found to be severely fractured, and it was delivered stillborn. The pathologist gave as his opinion that the cause of death was skull fracture with consequent cerebral hemorrhaging, that death would be immediate, and that the injury could have been the result of force applied to the mother's abdomen. There was no air in the fetus' lungs, and the umbilical cord was intact. . . .

The evidence was in conflict as to the estimated age of the fetus; the expert testimony on the point, however, concluded "with reasonable medical certainty" that the fetus had developed to the stage of viability, i.e., that in the event of premature birth on the date in question, it would have had a 75 percent to 96 percent chance of survival.

An information was filed charging petitioner, in count I, with committing the crime of murder. . . .

Penal Code section 187 provides: "Murder is the unlawful killing of a human being, with malice aforethought." The dispositive question is whether the fetus which petitioner is accused of killing was, on February 23, 1969, a "human being" within the meaning of the statute. If it was not, petitioner cannot be charged with its "murder". . . .

. . .

We conclude that in declaring murder to be the unlawful and malicious killing of a "human being," the Legislature of 1850 intended that term to have the settled common law meaning of a person who had been born alive, and did not intend the act of feticide—as distinguished from abortion—to be an offense under the laws of California.

. . .

KEELER V. SUPERIOR COURT (continued)

The People urge, however that the sciences of obstetrics and pediatrics have greatly progressed since 1872, to the point where, with proper medical care, a normally developed fetus prematurely born . . . is "viable" . . . since an unborn but viable fetus is now fully capable of independent life. . . . But we cannot join in the conclusion sought to be deduced: we cannot hold this petitioner to answer for murder by reason of his alleged act of killing an unborn—even though viable—fetus. To such a charge there are two insuperable obstacles, one "jurisdictional" and the other constitutional.

Penal Code section 6 declares in relevant part that "No act or omission" accomplished after the code has taken effect "is criminal or punishable, except as prescribed by this code. . . ." This section embodies a fundamental principle of our tripartite form of government, i.e., that subject to the constitutional prohibition against cruel and unusual punishment, the power to define crimes and fix penalties is vested exclusively in the legislative branch. Stated differently, there are no common law crimes in California. . . . In order that a public offense be committed, some statute, ordinance or regulation prior in time to the commission of the act, must denounce it.

▪ ▪ ▪

Applying these rules to the case at bar, we would undoubtedly act in excess of the judicial power if we were to adopt the People's proposed construction of section 187. As we have shown, the Legislature has defined the crime of murder in California to apply only to the unlawful and malicious killing of one who has been born alive. We recognize that the killing of an unborn but viable fetus may be deemed by some to be an offense of similar nature and gravity; but as Chief Justice Marshall warned long ago: "It would be dangerous, indeed, to carry the principle that a case which is within the reason or mischief of a statute, is within its provisions, so far as to punish a crime not enumerated in the statute, because it is of equal atrocity, or of kindred character, with those which are enumerated." . . . Whether to thus extend liability for murder in California is a determination solely within the province of the Legislature. For a court to simply declare, by judicial fiat, that the time has now come to prosecute under section 187 one who kills an unborn but viable fetus would indeed be to rewrite the statute under the guise of construing it. . . . to make it "a judicial function". . . "raises very serious questions concerning the principle of separation of powers."

The second obstacle to the proposed judicial enlargement of section 187 is the guarantee of due process of law. . . .

The first essential of due process is fair warning of the act which is made punishable as a crime. "That the terms of a penal statute creating a new offense must be sufficiently explicit to inform those who are subject to it what conduct on their part will render them liable to its penalties, is a well-recognized requirement, consonant alike with ordinary notions of fair play and the settled rules of law."

Do not forget that *Keeler* is an opinion of the California Supreme Court; therefore, it is not the law of all of the United States. Similar decisions have been made in other states, however.

Also note that the court determined that the common law violates "ordinary notions of fair play" and that no warning or notice was given to Keeler that his act could be defined as murder. As the court noted, these requirements are embodied in

due process

■ The *due process* clauses of the Fifth and Fourteenth Amendments to the U.S. Constitution require that no persons be deprived of life, liberty, or property without having notice and a real chance to present their side in a legal dispute.

the **due process** clauses of the U.S. Constitution and the constitutions of the many states. There are two dimensions to due process, procedural and substantive. Procedural due process, in both civil and criminal law, requires that individuals be put on notice of impending government action, be given an opportunity to be heard and to present evidence, and in some cases, benefit from other rights, such as having counsel appointed and having the case heard by a jury. Substantive due process recognizes individual rights to act or not to act. For example, privacy is not explicitly protected in the Constitution of the United States. Regardless, the Supreme Court has found an implicit right to privacy in the due process clauses' protection of liberty. Through this implicit right, the Court has invalidated laws prohibiting interracial marriage, prohibiting the use of contraception by married persons, and prohibiting women from ending pregnancies in some circumstances.

Although common law crimes are suspect when viewed through a due process lens, the United States Supreme Court has determined that states may, under some circumstances, recognize common law crimes The court in *Keeler* based its decision on the California Constitution's Due Process Clause. You should remember that the California Supreme Court is the final word on California law, and *Keeler* teaches you that the California Constitution provides more protection than the U.S. Constitution in this regard. Still, the U.S. Constitution places limits on the use of the common law by the states to create crimes. This is done primarily through the Due Process Clause and the provision prohibiting ex post facto laws. You will learn more about the Due Process and Ex Post Facto Clauses later in this book when we examine defenses to criminal charges. If states, such as California in the *Keeler* case, want to increase a defendant's rights beyond what the U.S. Constitution protects, they may do so through their own statutes or constitutions.

Other Uses of the Common Law

Even in those jurisdictions that have abandoned use of the common law to create crimes, the common law continues to be important for many reasons.

First, many statutes mirror the common law in language. That is, legislatures often simply codify the common law's criminal prohibitions. Hence, when a question arises concerning whether a particular act of a defendant is intended to fall under the intent of a criminal prohibition, the case law handed down prior to codification of the common law may answer the question. The result is that the crime remains the same but the source of the prohibition has changed. It is also possible for a legislature to change only part of a common-law definition and leave the remainder the same. If so, prior case law may be helpful when considering the unaltered portion of the definition.

Second, many of the concepts developed at the common law are still recognized. For example, the distinction between felonies and misdemeanors continues today. Although jurisdictions vary in definition, a felony is a serious crime usually punishable by more than one year in prison. A misdemeanor is less serious and usually is punishable by one year or less in jail.

Third, legislatures occasionally enact a criminal prohibition without establishing the potential penalty for violation. In such cases, courts will often look to the penalties applied to similar common law crimes for guidance.

Fourth, in addition to defining crimes, the common law established many procedures that were used to adjudicate criminal cases. These procedures most often dealt with criminal defenses. What defenses could be raised, as well as how and when, were often answered by the common law. For example, the various tests to determine if a defendant was sane when an alleged crime was committed were developed under the common law. If a legislature has not specifically changed these procedural rules, they remain in effect, even if the power of courts to create common-law crimes has been abolished.

Statutory Law

As you have already learned, the legislative branch is responsible for the creation of law. You have also learned that legislatures possess the authority to modify, abolish, or adopt the common law, in whole or in part. During the nineteenth century, the codification of criminal law began.[7] This effectively displaced the role of the judiciary in defining crimes. Today, nearly all criminal law is found in criminal codes.

Although the power of the legislative branch to declare behavior criminal is significant, there are limits. The constitutions of the United States and of the many states contain limits on such state and federal authority. Most of these limits are found in the Bill of Rights. For example, the First Amendment to the federal Constitution prohibits government, with few exceptions, from punishing an individual for exercising choice of religion and for expressing opinions and thoughts. If a legislature enacts a law that violates a constitutional provision, it is the duty of the judicial branch to declare the law void. This is the power of judicial review, previously discussed in Chapter 1. For now, you need only understand that legislatures do not have unlimited authority to create criminal law.

Ordinances

The written laws of municipalities are termed **ordinances.** Ordinances are laws enacted by city, county, and other local governments. Ordinances can be administrative or civil in nature, e.g., zoning, building, construction, and related matters). Municipalities also be empowered by state law to make criminal laws. In some instances, criminal ordinances mirror state statutes but apply to those acts that occur within the jurisdiction of the city. For example, many cities have assault and battery ordinances, just as their states have assault and battery statutes. Traffic and parking violations may also be criminal, although some cities pursue these as civil violations, which permits enabling the state to pursue criminal charge for the same act.

Ordinances may not conflict with state or federal law. Any ordinance that is inconsistent with higher law may be invalidated by a court. States limit the power of cities to punish for ordinance violations, and most city court trials are to the bench, not to a jury.

ordinance

■ A local or city law, rule, or regulation.

Administrative Law

It is likely that during your life, you have likely had to deal with several administrative agencies. Agencies are governmental units, federal, state, and local, that administer the affairs of the government. Although often lumped together, the agencies are actually of two types: social welfare and regulatory. The two names reflect the purposes behind each type. Social welfare agencies put into effect government programs. For example, in Indiana, the State Department of Public Welfare administers the distribution of public money to those deemed needy. In contrast, state medical licensing boards are regulatory, because their duty is to oversee and regulate the practice of medicine in the various states. Regulatory and administrative agencies both receive their delegation of authority from the legislative branch.

regulation

■ Law created by governmental administrative agencies.

Because legislatures do not possess the time or the expertise to write precise statutes, they often enact statutes that are very general, and in those statute grant one or more administrative agencies the authority to make more precise laws. Just as legislative enactments are known as statutes (or codes), administrative laws are known as **regulations** or rules. The extent to which a legislature may delegate its lawmaking authority, if at all, has been a continuing source of disagreement. Some scholars argue that legislatures may not grant such an important legislative function to agencies. Doing so is believed to be a violation of the principle of separation of powers, because agencies usually fall under the control of the executive branch, and the legislative branch is not permitted to delegate its powers to the executive branch, or vice versa.

In spite of these separation of powers problems, the United States Supreme Court has determined that agencies may create regulations that have the effect of law, including criminal prohibitions. The Court's opinion on how much authority may be delegated to administrative agencies has undergone a few changes over the years. In 1911, the United States Supreme Court handed down the opinion in the *Grimaud* case.

Grimaud is the law today. Agencies may be delegated penal rulemaking authority. However, the Supreme Court has said that although Congress may delegate to an agency the authority to make criminal laws, it may not delegate the responsibility of establishing penalties to an agency, with the possible exception of small fines. Congress must either set the precise penalty or set a range from which an agency can further determine the appropriate penalty.

An interesting question concerns how much guidance Congress must give an agency in its delegation. Because Congress is delegating its power to create law to an agency, it is expected to give the agency some guidance as to what it wants. This limits the discretion

sidebar

FINDING ADMINISTRATIVE REGULATIONS

Federal administrative rules are found in the Code of Federal Regulations (C.F.R.). New rules that have not yet been added to the C.F.R. may be found in the *Federal Register*. Each state has its counterpart publications. For example, in Florida they are the Florida Administrative Code and the *Florida Administrative Weekly*, respectively.

of the agency and prevents it from becoming a substitute legislature.[8] Normally, Congress must provide an intelligible principle or sufficient standards to guide an agency.[9] It takes little congressional guidance to satisfy these tests. Due to the special nature of criminal law (i.e., the deprivation to liberty that may result from a criminal conviction), defendants have argued that Congress must be more specific, or give an agency less discretion, when delegating the authority to create penal rules, as opposed to non-penal rules. The Supreme Court refused to answer that question in *Touby v. United States*.

UNITED STATES V. GRIMAUD
United States Supreme Court 220 U.S. 506 (1911)

The defendants were indicted for grazing sheep on the Sierra Forest Reserve without having obtained the permission required by the regulations adopted by the Secretary of Agriculture. They demurred on the ground that the Forest Reserve Act of 1891 was unconstitutional, insofar as it delegated to the Secretary of Agriculture power to make rules and regulations and made a violation thereof a penal offense.

. . .

From the various acts relating to the establishment and management of forest reservations it appears that they were intended "to improve and protect the forest and to secure favorable conditions to water flows." . . . It was also declared that the Secretary "may make such rules and regulations and establish such service as will insure the objects of such reservation, namely, to regulate their occupancy and use to prevent the forests thereon from destruction; *and any violation of the provisions of this act or such* rules and regulations shall be punished," as is provided in [the statute].

Under these acts, therefore, any use of the reservations for grazing or other lawful purpose was required to be subject to the rules and regulations established by the Secretary of Agriculture. To pasture sheep and cattle on the reservation, at will and without restraint, might interfere seriously with the accomplishment of the purposes for which they were established. But a limited and regulated use for pasturage might not be inconsistent with the object sought to be attained by the statute. The determination of such questions, however, was a matter of administrative detail. What might be harmless in one forest might be harmful to another. What might be injurious at one stage of timber growth, or at one season of the year, might not be so at another.

In the nature of things, it was impracticable for Congress to provide general regulations for these various and varying details of management. Each reservation had its peculiar and special features; and in authorizing the Secretary of Agriculture to meet these local conditions, Congress was merely conferring administrative functions upon an agent, and not delegating to him legislative power.

. . .

It must be admitted that it is difficult to define the line which separates the legislative power to make laws from the administrative authority to make regulations. This difficulty has often been recognized [as] referred to by Chief Justice Marshall . . . : "It will not be contended that Congress can delegate to the courts, or to any other tribunals, powers which are strictly and exclusively legislative. But Congress may certainly delegate to others, powers which the legislature may rightfully exercise itself." What

(continued)

were these non-legislative powers which Congress could exercise but which also might be delegated to others was not determined, for he said: "The line has not been exactly drawn which separates those important subjects, which must be entirely regulated by the legislature itself, from those of less interest, in which a general provision may be made, and power given to those who are to act under such general provisions to fill up the details."

From the beginning of the Government, various acts have been passed conferring upon the executive officers power to make rules and regulations—not for the government of their departments but for administering the laws which did govern. None of these statutes could confer legislative power. But when Congress had legislated and indicated its will, it could give to those who were to act under such general provisions "power to fill up the details" by the establishment of administrative rules and regulations, the violation of which could be punished by fine or imprisonment fixed by Congress, or by penalties fixed by Congress or measured by the injury done.

∎ ∎ ∎

It is true that there is no act of Congress which, in express terms, declares that it shall be unlawful to graze sheep on a forest reserve. But the statutes, from which we have quoted, declare that the privilege of using reserves for "all proper and lawful purposes" is subject to the proviso that the person shall comply "with the rules and regulations covering such forest reservation." The same act makes it an offense to violate those regulations.

∎ ∎ ∎

The Secretary of Agriculture could not make rules and regulations for any and every purpose. As to those here involved, they all regulate matters clearly indicated and authorized by Congress.

TOUBY V. UNITED STATES
United States Supreme Court   500 U.S. 160 (1991)

Petitioners were convicted of manufacturing and conspiring to manufacture "Euphoria," a drug temporarily designated as a schedule I controlled substance pursuant to § 201(h) of the Controlled Substances Act. We consider whether § 201(h) unconstitutionally delegates legislative power to the Attorney General and whether the Attorney General's subdelegation to the Drug Enforcement Administration (DEA) was authorized by statute. . . .

[T]he Controlled Substances Act (Act) . . . establishes five categories or "schedules" of controlled substances, the manufacture, possession, and distribution of which the Act regulates or prohibits. Violations involving schedule I substances carry the most severe penalties, as these substances are believed to pose the most serious threat to public safety. Relevant here, § 201(a) of the Act authorizes the Attorney General to add or remove substances, or to move a substance from one schedule to another. . . .

When adding a substance to a schedule, the Attorney General must follow specified procedures. First, the Attorney General must request a scientific and medical evaluation from the Secretary of Health and Human Services (HHS), together with a recommendation as to whether the substances should be controlled. A substance cannot be scheduled if the Secretary recommends against it. . . . Second, the

TOUBY V. UNITED STATES *(continued)*

Attorney General must consider eight factors with respect to the substance, including its potential for abuse, scientific evidence of its pharmacological effect, its psychic or physiological dependence liability, and whether the substance is an immediate precursor of a substance already controlled. . . . Third, the Attorney General must comply with notice-and-hearing provisions of the Administrative Procedure Act . . . which permit comment by interested parties. . . . In addition, the Act permits any aggrieved person to challenge the scheduling of a substance by the Attorney General in a court of appeals. . . .

It takes time to comply with these procedural requirements. From the time when law enforcement officials identify a dangerous new drug, it typically takes 6 to 12 months to add it to one of the schedules. . . . Drug traffickers were able to take advantage of this time gap by designing drugs that were similar in pharmacological effect to scheduled substances but differing slightly in chemical composition, so that existing schedules did not apply to them. These "designer drugs" were developed and widely marketed long before the Government was able to schedule them and initiate prosecutions. . . .

To combat the "designer drug" problem, Congress in 1984 amended the Act to create an expedited procedure by which the Attorney General can schedule a substance on a temporary basis when doing so is "necessary to avoid an imminent hazard to the public safety." . . . Temporary scheduling under § 201(h) allows the Attorney General to bypass, for a limited time, several of the requirements for permanent scheduling. The Attorney General need consider only three of the eight factors required for permanent scheduling. . . . Rather than comply with the APA notice-and-hearing provisions, the Attorney General need provide only a 30-day notice of proposed scheduling in the Federal Register. . . . Notice also must be transmitted to the Secretary of HHS, but the Secretary's prior approval of a proposed scheduling is not required. . . . Finally . . . an order to schedule a substance temporarily "is not subject to judicial review."

Because it has fewer procedural requirements, temporary scheduling enables the government to respond more quickly to the threat posed by dangerous new drugs. A temporary scheduling order can be issued 30 days after a new drug is identified, and the order remains valid for one year. During this 1-year period, the Attorney General presumably will initiate the permanent scheduling process. . . .

The Attorney General promulgated regulations delegating to the DEA his powers under the Act, including the power to schedule controlled substances on a temporary basis. Pursuant to that delegation, the DEA Administrator issued an order scheduling . . . "Euphoria" as a schedule I controlled substance. . . .

While the temporary scheduling order was in effect, DEA agents, executing a valid search warrant, discovered a fully operational drug laboratory in Daniel and Lyrissa Touby's home. The Toubys were indicted for manufacturing and conspiring to manufacture Euphoria. They moved to dismiss the indictment on the grounds that § 201(h) unconstitutionally delegates legislative power to the Attorney General. . . . The United States District Court for the District of New Jersey denied the motion to dismiss . . . and the Court of Appeals for the Third Circuit affirmed. . . . We granted certiorari . . . and now affirm.

The Constitution provides that "all legislative Powers herein granted shall be vested in a Congress of the United States." From this language the Court has derived the nondelegation doctrine: that Congress may not constitutionally delegate its legislative power to another Branch of government. "The nondelegation doctrine is rooted in the principle of separation of powers that underlies our tripartite system of Government." . . .

(continued)

TOUBY V. UNITED STATES *(continued)*

We have long recognized that nondelegation does not prevent Congress from seeking assistance, within proper limits, from its coordinate Branches. . . . Thus, Congress does not violate the Constitution merely because it legislates in broad terms, leaving a certain degree of discretion to executive or judicial actors. So long as Congress "lay[s] down by legislative act an intelligible principle to which the person or body authorized to [act] is directed to conform, such legislative action is not a forbidden delegation of legislative power." . . .

Petitioners wisely concede that Congress has set forth in § 201(h) an "intelligible principle" to constrain the Attorney General's discretion to schedule controlled substances on a temporary basis. . . . Petitioners suggest, however, that something more than an "intelligible principle" is required when Congress authorizes another Branch to promulgate regulations that contemplate criminal sanctions. They contend that regulations of this sort pose a heightened risk to individual liberty and that Congress must therefore provide more specific guidance. Our cases are not entirely clear as to whether or not more specific guidance is in fact required. . . . We need not resolve the issue today. We conclude that § 201(h) passes muster even if greater congressional specificity is required in the criminal context.

Although it features fewer procedural requirements than the permanent scheduling statute, § 201(h) meaningfully constrains the Attorney General's discretion to define criminal conduct. . . .

It is clear that in § 201(h) and § 202(b), Congress has placed multiple restrictions on the Attorney General's discretion to define criminal conduct. These restrictions satisfy the constitutional requirements of the nondelegation doctrine.

So, an agency may be delegated the authority to declare acts criminal. Congress must provide at least an "intelligible principle," and possibly more, when making this type of delegation. Congress may not delegate the authority to set a penalty to an agency, although it may allow the agency to set the penalty for a violation from within statutory guidelines. An agency may not, however, establish more serious penalties, such an imprisonment, even if the sentences fall within statutory limits.

While agencies may not sentence individuals to imprisonment, legislatively endorsed, noncriminal deprivations of freedom may be ordered by agencies in rare circumstances, such as during quarantines, for psychiatric evaluations and treatment, and to detain illegal immigrants.

An interesting issue that has arisen in recent years is the extent to which private parties may be delegated governmental powers. For example, in some states, fines levied by homeowner and condominium associations are enforceable in courts. While this area of law is in development and much remains to be defined, a few general principles can be deduced. First, private parties may not, or have very limited authority to, punish individuals. Second, when private parties are acting on the behalf of a government, they are bound by the same rules that apply to the government.[10]

Court Rules

Just as administrative agencies need the authority to "fill in the gaps" of legislation because statutes are not specific enough to satisfy all of an agency's needs, so do courts.

The United States Congress and all of the state legislatures have enacted some form of statute establishing general rules of civil and criminal procedure. However, to fill in the gaps left by legislatures, courts adopt **court rules,** which also govern civil and criminal processes. Although court rules deal with procedural issues (such as service of process, limits on the length of briefs and memoranda, and timing of filing) and not substantive issues, they are important. Of course, court rules may not conflict with legislative mandates. If a rule does conflict with a statute, the statute is controlling. One exception to this rule may be when the statute is unconstitutional and the rule is a viable alternative, but discussion of this situation is best left to a course on constitutional law and judicial process.

rules of court

■ Rules promulgated by the court, governing procedure or practice before it.

Most court rules are drafted under the direction of the highest court of the state and become effective by either vote of the court or presentation to the state legislature for ratification. In the federal system, the rules are drafted by the Judicial Conference under the direction of the Supreme Court and then presented to Congress. If Congress fails to act to nullify the rules, they become law. Of course, Congress may amend the rules at will. Many jurisdictions also have local rules, that is, rules created by local courts for practice in those courts. The rules cannot conflict with either statutes or higher court rules. In the federal system, district courts adopt local rules. Being familiar with the rules of the courts in your jurisdiction is imperative. If you are not, you may miss important deadlines, file incomplete documents, or have your filings stricken.

The Model Penal Code

On occasion, the **Model Penal Code** will be referenced in this text. Actually entitled *Model Penal Code and Commentaries,* it was drafted by a group of scholars and practitioners expert in criminal law while working for the American Law Institute, a private organization. The intent of the drafters of the Code was to draft a consistent, thoughtful code that could be recommended to the states for adoption. The code itself is not law until adopted by a legislature.

Model Penal Code

■ A proposed criminal code prepared jointly by the Commission on Uniform State Laws and the American Law Institute.

According to one source, by 1985, 34 states had "enacted widespread criminal-law revision and codification based on its provisions; fifteen hundred courts had cited its provisions and referred to its commentary."[11] The Model Penal Code has been included in this text, in edited form, as Appendix B. You should refer to that as the Code is discussed in the following chapters.

Constitutional Law

Finally, constitutional law is included in this list of sources of criminal law, not because it defines what conduct is criminal, but because of its significant impact on criminal law generally. In particular, the U.S. Constitution, primarily through the Bill of Rights, is responsible for establishing many of the rules governing criminal procedure. This has been especially true in the past few decades. You will become more aware of why this is true as you learn more about criminal law and procedure. Pay close attention to the dates of the cases included in this text (see Exhibit 2–1); it is likely that many were handed down in your lifetime.

Exhibit 2–1 IMPORTANT DATES IN THE HISTORY OF THE CONSTITUTION OF THE UNITED STATES

May 25, 1787	Constitutional Convention opens in Philadelphia.
September 17, 1787	Constitutional Convention closes, delegates sign the Constitution, and it is sent to the states for ratification. This is recognized as Constitution (and Citizenship) Day by federal law.
December 6, 1787	Delaware is the first state to ratify the Constitution.
June 21, 1788	New Hampshire is the ninth state to ratify, and thereby provides the requisite number of ratifying states to adopt the Constitution for the entire United States.
May 29, 1790	Rhode Island is the thirteenth (last) state to ratify the Constitution.
December 15, 1791	Bill of Rights is ratified.
December 6, 1865	Thirteenth Amendment, abolishing slavery, is ratified.
July 28, 1868	Fourteenth Amendment, providing for due process, equal protection, and privileges and immunities, is ratified.
February 3, 1870	Fifteenth Amendment, prohibiting the vote from being withheld for race, color, or previous servitude, is ratified.
May 7, 1992	The Twenty-seventh Amendment, the last to date, was ratified. Addressing the raises for members of Congress, the amendment is the last to be ratified even though it was one of the original 12 amendments to be proposed.

Although it is common for courses in constitutional law to focus on the U.S. Constitution, do not forget that each state also has its own constitution with its own body of case law interpreting its meaning. Even though the dominant source for defending civil liberties has been the U.S. Constitution, it is possible that a shift to state constitutions will occur, as the current Supreme Court is expected to be more conservative on criminal issues, which means it is less likely to extend constitutional protections. Remember, the U.S. Constitution is the highest form of law, and the states may not decrease the individual protections secured by it. States, may, however, increase civil liberties through state law. Most state constitutions mirror the federal constitution, often verbatim. In spite of this, state courts are free to interpret their constitutional provisions as providing more protection than their federal counterparts, even if identical in text. See Exhibit 2–2 for a summary of the sources of criminal law.

Exhibit 2–2 SOURCES OF CRIMINAL LAW

Source	Comment
CONSTITUTIONS	The United States and every state have a constitution. The U.S. Constitution is the supreme law of the land. Amendment of the federal Constitution requires a 2/3vote by both houses of the United States Congress and approval by 3/4 of the states or in the alternative, for 2/3 of the states to call for a constitutional convention and approval of 3/4 of the states of any suggested amendments. All existing amendments were enacted using the first method.
STATUTES	The written law created by legislatures, also known as codes. State statutes may not conflict with either their own constitution or the federal Constitution. State statutes also are invalid if they conflict with other federal law, and the federal government has concurrent jurisdiction with the states. Statutes of the United States are invalid if they conflict with the U.S. Constitution or if they attempt to regulate outside federal jurisdiction. Legislatures may change statutes at will.
COMMON LAW	Law that evolved, as courts, through judicial opinions, recognized customs, and practices. Legislatures may alter, amend, or abolish the common law at will. In criminal law, the common law is responsible for the creation of crimes and for establishing defenses to crimes.
REGULATIONS	Created by administrative agencies under a grant of authority from a legislative body. Regulations must be consistent with statutes and constitutions and may not exceed the legislative grant of power. The power to make rules and regulations is granted to "fill in the gaps" left by legislatures when drafting statutes.
ORDINANCES	Written law of local bodies, such as city councils. Must be consistent with all higher forms of law.
MODEL PENAL CODE	Written under the direction of the American Law Institute. It was drafted by experts in criminal law to be presented to the states for adoption. It is not law until a state has adopted it, in whole or in part. More than half of the states have adopted at least part of the Model Penal Code.
COURT RULES	Rules created by courts to manage their cases. Court rules are procedural and commonly establish dead-lines, lengths of filings, etc. Court rules may not con-flict with statutes or constitutions.

Ethical Considerations

DEFENDING INDIVIDUALS CHARGED WITH HORRENDOUS CRIMES

Defense attorneys are not held in the highest regard by all people, many of whom assume that a defense attorney's willingness to defend individuals charged with horrendous crimes is a reflection of the attorney's values. In actuality, this conclusion is correct, but there is a disconnect between the value that motivates an attorney to defend an individual charged with a horrendous crime and the value that many individuals apply in judging the attorney for the decision. Defense attorneys are often judged by individuals who apply personal values to them, while the attorneys must apply professional values.

The two model codes from which the states have enacted their rules that govern attorney ethics, the Model Rules of Professional Conduct and Model Code of Professional Responsibility, require attorneys to zealously represent their clients, regardless of the alleged crime. This requirement does not exist in a vacuum. The entire U.S. system of justice is built upon the idea that if you have two opposed parties, each with a loyal, zealous advocate, the truth will be unveiled to the fact finder. This *adversarial system* was developed in England and exists, in various forms, in all common-law nations.

The obligation of defense attorneys to zealously represent their clients and to maintain their clients' confidentiality is not without a price. Defense attorneys are the subject of public disdain and ridicule. In some circumstances, their professional and personal lives are injured when they are called upon to defend unpopular defendants. An example of this is the attorney featured in the case *People v. Belge,* which you will find in Chapter 10 of this book. In this case, two attorneys, Francis R. Belge and Frank H. Armani, represented a man accused of murder. During their conversations with the accused, he claimed to have committed three other murders. The attorneys confirmed two of the murders of young women by visiting the locations where his client had buried the bodies of his victims. After viewing the bodies, the attorneys discussed whether they should disclose the location of the bodies. They concluded that their duty to their client to maintain his confidence did not permit disclosure. They continuously denied knowing the location of the bodies throughout the case, even when asked by the families of the missing girls. When their client disclosed having told them, there was public outrage. Although accord was not universal, most ethics scholars agreed that the attorneys made the correct decision.

Ethical Considerations *(continued)*

But the decision came at a high price. Both men received death threats and began to carry guns. Belge was charged with the health crime of not reporting a dead body for burial (see Chapter 10), Belge's family life was injured, and his practice diminished. He ultimately moved to another state. Armani's experience was similar, but he remained in the region and his practice eventually recovered. Armani said of the decision they made:

> God only knows that this thing drove me crazy; it really bothered me. And if there was any way I could have, I would have told Mr. and Mrs. Hauck. But my hands were tied. And as a result, this thing has cost me dearly. My law practice failed. I spent nearly $40,000 defending Garrow. . . . I've lost about every friend I have. But there was nothing else I could do. Please believe that!

Unquestionably, if the attorneys had not visited the scene, they would have been correct in maintaining their client's confidence. However, the prosecutor who obtained the grand jury indictment against Belge alleged that the attorneys' presence at the crime scene changed matters. The court hearing the case, however, held that "Belge conducted himself as an officer of the Court with all the zeal at his command to protect the constitutional rights of his client. Both on the grounds of privileged communication and the interests of justice the Indictment is dismissed."

Source: Mark Gado, *Robert Garrow: The Predator,* Court TV, Crime Library, at *http://www.crimelibrary.com/serial_killers/predators/robert_garrow/1.html* (March 11, 2008).

Web Links

Findlaw

www.findlaw.com is an excellent site that contains state and federal statutory law, administrative law, and case law. In addition, FindLaw provides information on law schools, law firms, professional development, and legal news.

Key Terms

common law	due process	regulations
court rules	Model Penal Code	stare decisis
criminal law	ordinance	
criminal procedure	precedent	

Review Questions

1. What are civil liberties? Give two examples of civil liberties that are protected by the Constitution of the United States.
2. What is the common law? How do the concepts of stare decisis and precedent relate to the common law?
3. The common law is different in every state. Why?
4. What does the Latin phrase "nullum crimen sine lege" translate to? Explain the significance of that phrase.
5. Explain how the common law can violate the principle of legality.
6. State three uses the common law has in criminal law in those jurisdictions that do not permit common-law creation of crimes.
7. What is the source of most criminal law today? Where does that law come from?
8. What is an ordinance?
9. What is a regulation?
10. What is a court rule?
11. Place the following sources of law in order of authority, beginning with the highest form of law and ending with the lowest. Notice that both state and federal sources of law are included: U.S. Code, state constitutions, federal administrative regulations, ordinances, U.S. Constitution, state administrative regulations, state statutes.

Problems & Critical Thinking Exercises

1. List the various purposes for punishing criminal law violators. Using your answers from problem 2, determine if the goals of punishment can be achieved if prosecution is sought for the following acts (problems 3–5):
2. John, having always wanted a guitar, stole one from a fellow student's room while that student was out.
3. Jack suffers from a physical disease of the mind that causes him to have violent episodes. Jack has no way of knowing when the episodes will occur. However, the disease is controllable with medication. Despite this, Jack often does not take the medicine, as he finds the injections painful and inconvenient. One day, when he had not taken the medicine, Jack had an episode and struck Mike, causing him personal injury.
4. The same facts apply, as in problem 3, except there is no treatment or medication that can control Jack's behavior. He was diagnosed as having the disease years before striking Mike and has caused such an injury before during a similar violent episode.
5. Unknown to Kevin, he has epilepsy. One day while he was driving his automobile, he suffered his first seizure. The seizure caused him to lose control of his car and strike a pedestrian, inflicting a fatal injury.

Endnotes

1. 15A Am. Jur. 2d *Common Law* 6 (1976).
2. *Marsillett v. State,* 495 N.E.2d 699, 704 (Ind. 1986) (citations omitted).
3. 15A Am. Jur. 2d *Common Law* 1 (1976).

4. *Helms v. American Security Co.,* 22 N.E.2d 822 (Ind. 1986).

5. T. Gardner, *Criminal Law: Principles and Cases,* 4th ed. (Criminal Justice Series) (St. Paul: West, 1989).

6. P. Robinson, *Fundamentals of Criminal Law* (Boston: Little, Brown, 1988).

7. Today in the United Kingdom, where the common law originated, most law is created by Parliament (which dates to the 1300s), not by courts.

8. See *Schechter Poultry Corp. v. United States,* 2nd ed., 295 U.S. 495 (1935).

9. See D. Hall, *Administrative Law: Bureaucracy in a Democracy,* 5th ed., ch. 5 (Upper Saddle River, NJ: Prentice Hall, 2012).

10. For more on this subject, see D. Hall, *Administrative Law: Bureaucracy in a Democracy,* 5th ed., ch. 11 (Upper Saddle River, NJ: Prentice Hall, 2012).

11. J. Samaha, *Criminal Law,* 3rd ed. (St. Paul: West, 1990).

CHAPTER 3

THE TWO ESSENTIAL ELEMENTS

Chapter Objectives

After completing this chapter you should be able to:

- identify and define the two basic elements of most crimes, mens rea and actus reus.

- describe the evolution of mens rea and actus reus from the early common law to modernity, particularly as found in the Model Penal Code.

- be challenged to reflect on what it means to have a guilty mind, from both a psychological and a legal perspective.

- define and describe corporate and vicarious liability.

- apply and compare the historic and modern law of mens rea and actus reus to real life scenarios.
- define and apply element analysis to statutory definitions of crimes.

- read and identify the major elements of a judicial opinion.
- identify the major elements of a case brief.

MENS REA

Nearly every crime consists of two essential elements: the mental and the physical. This chapter begins by addressing the mental element and concludes by examining the physical element.

It is common to distinguish between acts that are intentional and those that occur accidentally. Everyone has caused injury to another person or another person's property accidentally. That the injury was accidental (not intended) often leads to a statement such as, "I'm sorry. I didn't mean to hurt you." In these situations, people often feel a social obligation to pay for any injuries they have caused, or to assist the injured party in other ways, but they probably do not expect to be punished criminally. As the late Supreme Court Justice Holmes stated, "Even a dog distinguishes between being stumbled over and being kicked." As this statement implies, to make such a distinction between accidental and intentional acts that injure others appears to be natural. For humans, it is consistent with common notions of fairness. Indeed many of the earliest laws known to humanity, dating back thousands of years, distinguish intentional from intentional behavior, treating the latter as less serious. Modern criminal law follows this model; that is, people are often held accountable for intentional behavior and not for accidental, even though the consequences may be the same. However, this is not always so. Under some circumstances, accidental behavior (negligent or reckless) may be the basis of criminal liability.

Mens rea is the mental part, the state of mind required to be criminally liable. It is often defined as "a guilty mind" or possessing a criminal intent. It is best defined as the state of mind required to be criminally liable for a certain act. It is sometimes the case that no intent whatsoever is required to be guilty of a crime, although most criminal laws require intent to some degree before criminal liability attaches to an act.

Mens rea is an important concept in criminal law. It is also a confusing one, largely because of the inconsistency and lack of uniformity between criminal statutes and judicial decisions. One author found 79 words and phrases in the U.S. Criminal Code used to describe mens rea.[1] Often, when courts or legislatures use the same term, they do so assuming different meanings for the term. For this reason, the drafters of the Model Penal Code attempted to establish uniform terms and definitions for those terms. The Model Penal Code approach is examined later. First, you will learn how mens rea was defined at the common law.

mens rea

■ (Latin) A state of mind that produces a crime.

Mens Rea and the Common Law

One principle under the common law was that there should be no crime if there was no act accompanied by a guilty mind. The Latin phrase that states this principle is: "actus non facit reum nisi mens sit rea." Today, under some statutes, no intent is required to be guilty of a crime. Despite this, the principle that "only conscious wrongdoing constitutes crime is deeply rooted in our legal system and remains the rule, rather than the exception."[2]

Many terms have been used to describe a guilty mind. Malicious, mischievous, purposeful, unlawful, intentional, with specific intent, knowing, fraudulent, with an evil purpose, careless, willful, negligent, and reckless are examples of terms and phrases used to describe the mental state required to prove guilt.

General, Specific, and Constructive Intent

general intent

■ The desire to commit a prohibited act but not the outcome of that act.

specific intent

■ An intent to commit the exact crime charged or the precise outcome of the act, not merely an intent to commit the act without an intention to cause the outcome.

One common law distinction is between **general intent** and **specific intent.** The distinction turns on whether the defendant intended to cause the consequences of the act. If the defendant had a desire or purpose to cause the *result* of the act, then the defendant possessed specific intent. If the defendant intended only the act, and not the result of that act, then the defendant possessed general intent. For example, Don Defendant throws a large rock at Victoria Victim, inflicting a fatal wound. If Defendant only intended to injure Victim, not kill her, then he possessed general intent. However, if Defendant threw the rock hoping it would kill Victim, then he possessed specific intent. The distinction between general and specific intent is often an important one, as many statutes require specific intent for a higher-level crime and general intent for a lower crime. In this example, many state statues would allow Defendant to be responsible to be charged with first-degree murder if he intended to kill Victim, but with second-degree murder if he only intended to injure Victim under many contemporary state statutes.

So long as a defendant intends to cause the result, it is irrelevant that the means used to achieve the result are likely to fail. For example, assume Defendant desires to cause the death of Victim. One day, while walking down a street, Defendant notices Victim far away. Defendant picks up a rock and hurls it toward Victim, hoping it will strike Victim and kill her, although because of the distance, he does not expect the rock to strike its intended target. However, all of those afternoons practicing his baseball pitch paid off, and the rock hits Victim in the head, killing her instantly. The fact that Defendant threw the rock with an intent to kill is enough to establish Defendant's specific intent. The fact that the act is unlikely to be successful is no defense.

scienter

■ (Latin) Knowingly; with guilty knowledge. [pronounce: si-*en*-ter]

Specific intent may also be proved, in some jurisdictions, by showing that the defendant possessed knowledge of a particular fact or illegality. This requirement of knowledge is known as **scienter.** Although scienter and mens rea are commonly treated as synonyms, they are not. Scienter is a specific form of mens rea. If an individual commits a crime with a scienter element while believing that the act engaged in is lawful or without the specific knowledge required, then specific intent is lacking, and only general intent can be proven.[3] Scienter often does not require proof of subjective knowledge (what was actually in the defendant's mind), but can be established if the prosecution can prove that the defendant should have known the fact in question. For example, assume that Abina recently emigrated to the United States. In her home country uniforms are common. Security guards, cab drivers, and hotel employees all wear uniforms that are difficult to distinguish from police. Not fully acclimated to the

United States, she ignored the warning of a police officer to not cross a street against a red pedestrian light. She didn't give the office much thought because she was accustomed to ignoring people in uniform. The officer approached her, threatened to arrest her, and she struck the officer in the face. She was arrested and charged with battery of a peace officer, a felony. A jury Returning to our police officer example, a jury could find that a reasonable person should have known that the individual was an officer because heshe was wearing a police uniform, for example, and find the defendant guilty of assault on a police officer, even if the jury believes that the defendant didn't subjectively know the assaulted individual was a police officer.

Consider the crime of receiving stolen property. If an individual received stolen property, but did so without knowledge that it was stolen, then no crime has been committed. For some crimes that require scienter, the absence of scienter may leave a general-intent crime. If a man strikes a person whom he believes is obstructing traffic, he has committed an assault. If he knew, or should have known, that the person was a police officer attempting to direct traffic, then he may be accountable for the higher crime of assault on a police officer. However, if the police officer was not wearing a uniform and did not announce himself as an officer, then the defendant is liable only for simple assault. Possession of burglary tools and obstruction of justice are also examples: the former requiring knowledge of the tools' character and the latter requiring knowledge of obstruction.

At common law, specific intent could be found in a third type of situation, whenever **constructive intent** could be proven. That is, although the defendant does not intend to cause the result, it is so likely to occur that the law treats the act as one of specific intent. If John fires a handgun at close range at Sally, aiming at her torso, and kills her as a result, it is possible that he could be charged with the specific-intent crime of first-degree murder, even though he only intended to injure her. This is because the possibility of killing someone under those circumstances is significant. However, liability may not exist if he had aimed at her leg and the weapon discharged improperly, causing the bullet to strike her in the torso. This is because the likelihood of killing someone with a gunshot to the leg is much less than with a gunshot to the upper body. The bullet entered the victim's torso as a result of the malfunction of the gun; it was not Defendant's desire to shoot her in the upper body. As to the amount of probability necessary to prove constructive intent, only "practical or substantial" probability is required, not absolute.[4]

Specific intent can be found in a fourth situation, whenever a defendant intends a result beyond the act taken. This refers to situations when a criminal act is uncompleted. For example, if a man attacks a woman intending to rape her, but she is able to free herself and escape, he may be charged with assault with intent to rape. To prove this charge, the prosecution must show that he assaulted the victim with the specific intent of raping her. Proving that the defendant had a specific intent to assault her is not enough to sustain the intent-to-rape charge, although it would justify a conviction for assault, a lesser crime.

Another example is the crime of breaking and entering with the intent to burglarize. Again, the prosecution must prove that the defendant intended to steal from the home after the entry and did not complete the burglary for some reason. Proving that

constructive

■ Inferred, implied, or presumed from the circumstances.

the defendant broke in and entered, but had no intent to steal, will support a conviction for breaking and entering, but not intent to commit burglary.

General intent is much easier to define, as it is simply the desire to act. In most situations, if the prosecution can show that a defendant intended to take the act that resulted in the prohibited outcome, then general intent is proved. Generally, no desire to cause a particular consequence is required. So, if you fire a gun without a desire to kill someone, but the bullet does kill a person, you possess a general intent and may be prosecuted for a general-intent homicide.

Some jurisdictions require more than simply a desire to act to prove general intent. In those states, some level of negligence must be proven. Consider the following two examples:

Rural Defendant has lived on a farm for more than 20 years. Defendant's nearest neighbor is over three miles away, and Defendant routinely target shoots in his backyard. He has never encountered anyone in the area where he shoots, and everyone who lives in the community knows of his practice. One day, while target shooting, he accidentally shoots and kills a trespasser he did not know was on his property. In the second example, Metro Defendant likes to hunt on weekends. One weekend, Metro and his friend were hunting and Metro lost sight of his friend. Eager to capture his first deer of the season, Metro fired into a bush in which he observed some movement. But Metro's friend was in the bush, and Metro's gunshot inflicted a fatal wound.

In both examples, the defendants had no desire to harm the individuals who were shot, and both possessed the intent to fire the weapon. A strict construction of general and specific intent results in both defendants committing a general-intent murder. However, In some jurisdictions, Rural may be free from liability because he appears to have been less reckless or negligent than Metro, who should have considered the possibility that it could have been his friend who was causing the disturbance in the bush.

This discussion has not exhausted the many definitions and distinctions that exist for specific and general intent. In the *Carson* case, it appears that the Court of Appeals for the District of Columbia has created a hybrid general-specific intent for the crime of cruelty to children.

JANET A. CARSON, APPELLANT V. UNITED STATES, APPELLEE
556 A.2d 1076, 1989   D.C. App. LEXIS 57 (1989)

On June 4, 1985, Janet Carson arrived home from work at about 3:45 P.M. and was informed by one of her children that a fuse needed replacement. While looking for a fuse, appellant noticed that eight dollars were missing from her dresser drawer. She called her children—thirteen-year-old Cornell, six-year-old Everett, five-year-old Angelica, and eight-year-old Charmaine Schmidt—to her bedroom; each child denied knowing anything about the missing money. At that point she went downstairs, and as she returned upstairs she picked up an electrical cord; she later testified that she routinely used the cord to discipline the children. She again asked the children about the missing money, and they again denied any knowledge of the money's disappearance. Appellant then whipped each of the children several times.

The next day at the school attended by Everett, Angelica, and Charmaine, school officials noticed marks and bruises on the children. Detective Harmon of the Metropolitan Police Department went to the school and took the three children to Children's Hospital. Everett's abrasions were cleaned and bandaged; the other two children received no treatment.

Appellant was subsequently charged with three counts of cruelty to children. . . . [Ms. Carson was convicted and sentenced to thirty days on each count, which was suspended to one year's probation. She appealed the conviction and this is the opinion of the appellate court.]

Before considering appellant's claim that the evidence was insufficient to support her conviction, we must first determine the mens rea required for conviction under D.C. Code § 22–901. We conclude that the offense is a general intent crime, which also requires a showing of malice. . . .

Section 22–901 provides in pertinent part:

Any person who shall torture, cruelly beat, abuse, or otherwise willfully maltreat any child under the age of 18 years . . . shall be deemed guilty of a misdemeanor, and, when convicted thereof, shall be subject to punishment by a fine of not more than $250, or by imprisonment for a term not exceeding 2 years, or both.

The [D.C. Jury Instructions] define the elements of the offense as follows:

1. that the defendant tortured, cruelly beat, abused or otherwise maltreated a child;
2. that at the time of the incident, the child was under the age of 18 years; and
3. that the defendant acted willfully, that is, with an evil intent or with bad purpose to maltreat

the child. It is not enough that you find that the defendant exercised bad judgement or acted unreasonably. Rather, it is necessary that you find that the defendant was motivated by an evil intent or state of mind in committing the acts which constitute the offense.

■ ■ ■

Judicial interpretation of D.C. Code § 22–901 has been limited . . . [T]he United States Court of Appeals for the District of Columbia held that the terms "abuse" and "willfully mistreat" as used in the statute "call for something worse than good intentions coupled with bad judgment," and incorporate "the requirement of an evil state of mind." . . . The cases would seem to teach that cruelty to children is something more than a general intent crime and something less than a specific intent crime.

■ ■ ■

In other contexts, this court has equated the terms "evil intent" and "malice." This court has noted that a showing of bad or evil purpose is "necessary to distinguish the mental state required for malice-based offenses from that involved in crimes the conviction for which demands proof no more than general intent or criminal negligence." Thus, if cruelty to children requires proof of something more than general intent, that something more would seem to be malice.

■ ■ ■

Having determined the mens rea required for conviction of cruelty to children, we must now determine whether the government's proof was sufficient to establish the requisite mens rea in this case. Appellant concedes that the record supports the trial court's finding of general intent. However, she argues that the government failed to prove that she acted with malice. She argues that, according to her undisputed testimony, she was motivated not

(continued)

JANET A. CARSON, APPELLANT V. UNITED STATES, APPELLEE *(continued)*

by an evil intent but, rather, by a "concern for [her] children's welfare and upbringing." At first blush, the record supports her argument as to motivation.

The government argues, however, that to find malice "all that is required [is] a conscious disregard of a known and substantial risk of the harm. . . ."

Malice is a rather slippery concept, not amenable to precise definition. . . . Simply put, we believe that a parent acts with malice when a parent acts out of a desire to inflict pain rather than out of genuine effort to correct the child, or when the parent, in a genuine effort to correct the child, acts with a conscious disregard that serious harm will result.

■ ■ ■

In this case, appellant's testimony regarding her motive was not directly contradicted. The government relied basically on the nature of the wounds and the manner of the punishment to establish malice. The government introduced pictures of the injuries sustained by the children and also pointed to the ages of the children, and the fact that appellant used an electrical cord to whip the children as evidence that appellant acted with evil intent, or at least as evidence that appellant acted with a conscious disregard that serious harm (of the nature which would flow from an evil intent) would result.

From our perspective in this court, we cannot conclude that the evidence justifies the inference that appellant acted out of a desire to inflict pain. . . .

The trial court also noted that appellant had "high standards" for her children—"she didn't want them to steal; she didn't want them to use drugs." The court found that appellant had worked hard to make a good life for herself and her children. She had left the welfare rolls and become a policewoman, "supporting all those children on her own." We echo the trial court's sentiment that appellant had a genuine and deep-felt love and concern for her children.

Further, we do not believe that the punishment was so excessive or the manner so egregious as to lead to the conclusion that appellant acted with a conscious disregard of the serious harm which would result. The mother testified that the whippings lasted perhaps a minute. As to the manner of discipline, reasonable people might disagree as to whether whipping with an electrical cord is in itself offensive or no more offensive than the use of commonly employed devices or methods used to exact discipline. We would only note that appellant testified that because the children were jumping around and that because she was eight months pregnant and therefore awkward, the cord made contact on the children's bodies where it otherwise may not have done so.

However, when the manner of punishment, the length of punishment, the nature of the injuries and the ages of the children are viewed as a whole, we cannot say that the trial court was plainly in error in concluding that appellant acted with conscious disregard of the harm which resulted. . . .

Conviction AFFIRMED.

Malum in Se and Malum Prohibitum

Often, crimes are characterized as either malum in se or malum prohibitum. If a crime is <u>inherently evil</u>, it is <u>malum in se</u>. If a crime is not evil in itself, but is only <u>criminal because declared so by a legislature</u>, then it is <u>malum prohibitum</u>. Examples of crimes that are malum in se are murder, rape, arson, and mayhem. Failure to file your quarterly tax report or to get the proper building permit are both crimes malum prohibitum.

The distinction between malum in se and malum prohibitum is used throughout criminal law, but the importance of the distinction is in how it affects intent. Crimes malum in se are treated as requiring an evil intent, and crimes malum prohibitum are not. Some crimes may be both malum in se and malum prohibitum, depending upon the degree of violation. For example, speeding "a little over the limit may be malum prohibitum, but speeding at high speed malum in se."[5] Whether an act is malum prohibitum or in se often determines what crime may be charged. This decision usually revolves around the issue of foreseeability of harm.

In the preceding example, speeding slightly over the limit is not likely to cause another's death, whereas racing through a city at 30 miles over the speed limit can foreseeably cause a fatal accident. If while driving four miles over the speed limit, the defendant strikes and kills a pedestrian who walks into the driver's path from behind another car, the act is likely to be determined malum prohibitum, and no resulting manslaughter charge will follow. However, the same may not be true if the driver is traveling at 30 miles over the speed limit when the accident occurs.

Transferred Intent

Whenever a person intends a harm, but because of bad aim or other cause, the intended harm befalls another, the intent is transferred from the intended victim to the unintended victim. This is the doctrine of **transferred intent.** If John Defendant observes a neighbor burning the American flag and in anger shoots at him, missing him but killing William, the doctrine of transferred intent permits prosecution of Defendant as if he intended to kill William.

There are limits on the doctrine of transferred intent. First, the harm that actually results must be similar to the intended harm. If the harms are substantially different, then the intent does not transfer. For example, if A throws a baseball at B's window, hoping to break it, and the ball instead hits C in the head and kills him, it cannot be said that the intent to break the window transfers to C and that A can be punished for intentionally killing C. Person A may be criminally liable for a lesser crime, such as involuntary manslaughter, depending upon the amount of negligence involved, but he is not responsible for intentionally causing C's death.

A second limitation on the doctrine is that the transfer cannot increase the defendant's liability. In other words, any defenses the defendant has against the intended victim are transferred to the unintended victim. For example, A shoots at B in self-defense

transferred intent

■ The principle that if an unintended illegal act results from the intent to commit a crime, that act is also a crime.

sidebar

Although some jurisdictions no longer distinguish between crimes malum in se and malum prohibitum, many still do. What crimes fall into each category is determined by judicial decision. Thus, the case law in your jurisdiction must be researched to determine where the crime in question falls.

but hits C, inflicting a fatal wound. Because A had a valid defense if B had been killed by the shot, then A also has a defense as to C. In this case, A has committed no crime.

In some situations a defense may only limit a person's criminal liability to a lesser charge. You will learn later that certain defenses negate specific intent, but not general intent. One such defense is intoxication. <u>Assault</u> is a <u>general-intent</u> crime, whereas assault with an intent to kill is a specific-intent crime. Intoxication may be a defense to the higher assault with an intent to kill, but not assault. So if A, while intoxicated, hurls a knife at B but hits C, A may be charged with assault because intoxication would be no defense if she hit B. Person A would have a defense against the specific-intent crime of assault with intent to kill, so the same defense is available for harm to C.

Strict Liability

At the beginning of this chapter, it was noted that some acts are criminal although no mens rea accompanies the prohibited act. These crimes are proven simply by showing that the act was committed, and <u>no particular mental state has to be proved at all</u>. This is **strict liability,** or <u>liability without fault</u>, and is an exception to the common-law requirement that there be both an evil mind and an evil act to have a crime. The term *strict liability* is not used in all jurisdictions. Further, the term also has a tort meaning. Do not confuse criminal liability without fault with tort strict liability. However, for convenience, the term "strict liability" is used in this text.

Strict liability crimes usually are minor violations, punished by fines and not incarceration. However, strict liability is permitted as the mental element, or lack thereof, for felonies and may be punished with incarceration.

Most traffic violations, such as running a stoplight and speeding, are examples of strict liability crimes. Laws intended to protect minors are often silent on knowledge of the age of the victim. Statutory rape, for example, is treated as a strict liability crime in most states; therefore, a mistaken belief, even if it is the result of a fraudulent representation of age by the victim, does not relieve the defendant of criminal responsibility for having sexual intercourse with a minor. Similarly, selling drugs or alcohol or otherwise contributing to the delinquency of minors often does not have a mens rea requirement, at least in regard to the age of the victim. It is common for crimes that are malum prohibitum to be strict liability, whereas crimes malum in se usually require proof of some mental state. It is also generally true that violation of crimes malum prohibitum is not punished as severely as violation of crimes malum in se.

Often, "public offenses" or "regulatory offenses" are strict liability. The term "regulatory" is often used because the criminal prohibition has been established by an administrative agency through rulemaking, is enforced by an administrative agency, or is part of a comprehensive regulatory scheme established by a legislature. In many cases, strict liability laws deal with potential, rather than actual, harms. For example, a murder statute can be applied only after someone has been murdered. However, many strict liability offenses deal with violations and no harm. As examples, running a stoplight, speeding, or failing to have adequate fire extinguishers in your business may or may not result in an injury. Regardless of whether harm results, you are liable for the offense.

This approach is considered regulatory because the purpose is to induce compliance (using the easy-proof standard) with the law, rather than to punish for caused harm. Increased compliance is a result of an awareness by people that violation alone means liability; hence, they are more cautious and less likely to engage in the prohibited conduct. Of course, this argument can be made to justify making all crimes strict liability. The idea of not requiring any intent for acts to be criminal is contrary to the American values of fairness and justice, and this is probably the reason that the strict liability standard has not been extended to all crimes.

Strict liability is available only for crimes defined by legislatures. With little restriction, legislatures may define an act as criminal without requiring proof of intent. However, in jurisdictions that continue to recognize common-law crimes, mens rea must be an element.

There are an increasing number of regulatory offenses in the United States. Indeed, there has been a significant in the number of strict liability crimes, both regulatory and other, in recent decades. According to one study, 40% of nonviolent federal offenses created during a two-year period had no, or weak, mens rea requirements.[6]

Strict liability crimes, particularly those that impose serious penalties, have been challenged on many grounds. Some jurists believe that the expansion of strict liability beyond infractions and regulatory violations threatens democracy itself. In constitutional terms, these concerns manifest as due process challenges, and many lower courts have stricken strict liability laws under this theory. But the United States Supreme Court has upheld strict liability statutes in most instances, affording legislatures wide latitude in defining criminality.[7] Even so, there are limits, and if a legislature eliminates proof of mens rea for a crime that has traditionally required proof of specific intent or purpose or omits mens rea for a crime that is punished severely, due process is implicated and may be the basis for invalidating the change.

In the *Morissette* case, the Supreme Court addressed the omission of mens rea for the traditional crime of converting (theft) spent bomb casings The defendant was convicted at the trial level, but the United States Supreme Court reversed the conviction.

MORISSETTE V. UNITED STATES
342 U.S. 246 (1952)

Mr. Justice JACKSON delivered the opinion of the Court.

This would have remained a profoundly insignificant case to all except its immediate parties had it not been so tried and submitted to the jury as to raise questions both fundamental and far-reaching in federal criminal law, for which reason we granted certiorari.

On a large tract of uninhabited and untilled land in a wooded and sparsely populated area of Michigan, the Government established a practice bombing range over which the Air Force dropped simulated bombs at ground targets. These bombs consisted of a metal cylinder about forty inches long and eight inches across, filled with sand and enough

(continued)

black powder to cause a smoke puff by which the strike could be located. At various places about the range signs read Danger—Keep Out—Bombing Range. Nevertheless, the range was known as good deer country and was extensively hunted.

Spent bomb casings were cleared from the targets and thrown into piles 'so that they will be out of the way.' They were not sacked or piled in any order but were dumped in heaps, some of which had been accumulating for four years or upwards, were exposed to the weather and rusting away.

Morissette, in December of 1948, went hunting in this area but did not get a deer. He thought to meet expenses of the trip by salvaging some of these casings. He loaded three tons of them on his truck and took them to a nearby farm, where they were flattened by driving a tractor over them. After expending this labor and trucking them to market in Flint, he realized $84.

Morissette, by occupation, is a fruit stand operator in summer and a trucker and scrap iron collector in winter. An honorably discharged veteran of World War II, he enjoys a good name among his neighbors and has had no blemish on his record more disreputable than a conviction for reckless driving.

The loading, crushing and transporting of these casings were all in broad daylight, in full view of passers-by, without the slightest effort at concealment. When an investigation was started, Morissette voluntarily, promptly and candidly told the whole story to the authorities, saying that he had no intention of stealing but thought the property was abandoned, unwanted and considered of no value to the Government. He was indicted, however, on the charge that he "did unlawfully, wilfully and knowingly steal and convert" property of the United States of the value of $84, in violation of 18 U.S.C. 641, 18 U.S.C.A. § 641, which provides that "whoever embezzles, steals, purloins, or knowingly converts" government property is punishable by fine and imprisonment. Morissette was convicted and sentenced to imprisonment for two months or to pay a fine of $200. The Court of Appeals affirmed, one judge dissenting ...

The contention that an injury can amount to a crime only when inflicted by intention is not a provincial or transient notion. It is universal and persistent in mature systems of law, as belief in freedom of the human will and a consequent ability and duty of the normal individual to choose between good and evil. A relationship between some mental element and punishment for a harmful act is almost as instinctive as the child's familiar exculpatory "but I didn't mean to," and has afforded the rational basis for a tardy and unfinished substitution of deterrence and reformation in place of retaliation and vengeance as the motivation for public prosecution. . . .

Crime, as a compound concept, generally constituted only from concurrence of an evil-meaning mind with an evil-doing hand, was congenial with an intense individualism and took deep and early root in American soil. As the states codified the common law of crimes, even if their enactments were silent on the subject, their courts assumed that the omission did not signify disapproval of the principle but merely recognized that intent was so inherent in the idea of the offense that it required no statutory definition.

However, [some crimes fall into a] category of another character, with very different antecedents and origins. The crimes there involved depend on no mental element but consist only of forbidden acts or omissions. . . . The industrial revolution multiplied the number of workmen exposed to injury from increasingly powerful and complex mechanisms, driven by freshly discovered sources of energy, requiring higher precautions by employers. Traffic of velocities, volumes and varieties unheard of came to subject the wayfarer to intolerable

MORISSETTE V. UNITED STATES *(continued)*

casualty risks if the owners and drivers were not to observe new cares and uniformities of conduct. Congestion of cities and crowding of quarters called for health and welfare regulations undreamed of in simpler times. Wide distribution of goods became an instrument of wide distribution of harm when those who dispersed food, drink, drugs, and even securities, did not comply with reasonable standards of quality, integrity, disclosure and care. Such dangers have engendered increasingly numerous and detailed regulations which heighten the duties of those in control of particular industries, trades, properties, or activities that affect public health, safety or welfare.

. . . Many violations of such regulations result in no direct or immediate injury to person or property but merely create the danger or probability of injury which the law seeks to minimize.

* * *

Stealing, larceny, and its variants and equivalents, were among the earliest offenses known to the law that existed before legislation [common law]. . . . State courts of last resort, on whom fall the heaviest burden of interpreting criminal law in this country, have consistently retained the requirement of intent in larceny-type offenses. If any state has deviated, the exception has neither been called to our attention nor disclosed by our research.

We hold that the mere omission from [the conversion statute] of any mention of intent will not be construed as eliminating that element from the crimes denounced.

Strict Liability and Statutory Construction

The problem addressed by the Supreme Court in *Morissette* occurs often: What is the mens rea requirement when a statute does not provide for such? That decision depends on many factors. First, the **legislative history** of the statute may indicate whether the crime was intended to have a mens rea requirement. The statements of members of legislatures while debating the law (before it became law and was a bill), reports of committees of Congress, and other related materials may indicate whether the legislature intended a mens rea requirement. Second, courts look to whether the crime existed under the common law. If so, the mens rea used under the common law may be adopted by the court. Other factors include the seriousness of the harm to the public; mens rea standards for other related crimes; the punishment imposed upon conviction; the burden that would be placed on the prosecution if mens rea were required; and rules of statutory construction.

Generally, the greater the potential harm to the public and the more difficult it is for prosecution to prove mens rea, the more likely a court is to find that strict liability is to be imposed.[8] Although not a significant factor, the amount of penalty can play a role. The greater the penalty, the more likely that some intent will be read into the statute. Also, courts will look to other related statutes for guidance. If a state legislature has consistently required proof of intent for all crimes of larceny and theft, then if a new statute is enacted dealing with a particular theft (i.e., theft of computer information),

legislative history

■ The background documents and records of hearings related to the enactment of a bill.

and that law does not specify the mental state that must be proven, the court will fill in the missing element with intent.

Finally, courts have rules that must be followed when interpreting a statute. These are known as *canons* of **statutory construction.** You previously learned one of these rules; that is, whenever a statute can be construed as either constitutional or unconstitutional, it must be read as constitutional. Some jurisdictions follow the rule, either by judicial rule (canon) or by statute, that if a criminal statute does not specifically impose strict liability, then the court is to impose a mens rea requirement. This is what the Supreme Court did in *Morrisette.* And *Troiano* is a case from New York, a state jurisdiction where such a rule is applied. See Exhibit 3–1 for examples of other canons that are applied in criminal cases.

There is an important exception to the presumption of mens rea when a statute is silent on the subject, public welfare cases. The Supreme Court has long recognized that public welfare, or regulatory, laws are often intended to impose strict liability because of the large risk that legislatures and administrative agencies are attempting to manage. In such cases, courts are not to impose mens rea when the law, statute or administrative regulation, is silent on state of mind. For example, strict liability for corporate officials

statutory construction

■ Guidelines employed by judges in the interpretation of statutes that have developed and evolved over hundreds of years.

Exhibit 3–1 EXAMPLES OF CANONS OF CONSTRUCTION THAT APPLY IN CRIMINAL CASES

Canon	Description
Narrow Construction	Criminal statutes are to be narrowly construed by courts.
Ambiguous Language	Ambiguous language in a statute is to be construed in the defendant's favor or, if too ambiguous, the statute is void.
Legislative Prerogative	Courts are to be mindful that the source of penal law should be legislatures, not courts. Criminal statutes are to be narrowly construed. This is also known as the Rule of Lenity.
Constitutionality Presumption	Statutes are presumed constitutional, and if a court can construe a statute as constitutional or unconstitutional without causing unfairness to the defendant, the statute is to be construed as constitutional.
Plain Meaning	The plain meaning of a statute shall be enforced unless the result is absurd. If absurd, the court may turn to other evidence (e.g., legislative intent) to assist in interpreting the statute.

PEOPLE V. ALICIA TROIANO
552 N.Y.S.2d 541, 1990   N.Y. Misc. LEXIS 90 (1990)

[Defendant was charged with having insufficient brakes on her car and the following facts were stipulated to by the parties:]

On May 1, 1987 at approximately 11:35 P.M. the defendant was involved in a two-car accident. . . . Defendant was the owner and operator of a 1972 Oldsmobile station wagon. . . . The driver of the other vehicle died as a result of injuries suffered in that accident. The decedent failed to yield the right of way at a stop sign at that intersection. The decedent's blood alcohol level was .10%. Both vehicles were impounded. The defendant's vehicle was inspected by Al Stern of Al's Towing Corporation, and as a result of that inspection, the instant charge was brought. [Mr. Stern testified that the defendant's right rear brake was insufficient under state law guidelines.]

The defendant testified that she had not experienced any problems with the braking system of the car. She did not hear any squeaks or other noises. She did not notice any leaking of brake fluid and was able to stop properly at a stop sign just minutes before the accident. Further, the car had been inspected in September, 1986 and had a proper inspection sticker affixed to the windshield.

The defense also called Mr. Troiano, defendant's husband, who had been employed as an automobile mechanic until 1983. Following Stern's inspection, Mr. Troiano towed the vehicle in question back to his house. He pulled off all four wheels and examined the brake shoes and lining and found the brake lining on the right rear wheel to be a little more than 1/16 of an inch at its thinnest point and, consequently adequate.

. . .

[The statute] provides in pertinent part, that "every motor vehicle, operated or driven on the highways of the State, shall be provided with adequate brakes. . . ."

The court will first deal with the question of whether the statute is one of strict liability. The plain language of [the brake statute] does not require a mens rea or a culpable mental state as an element of the crime and in reliance thereon the People have made no attempt to make a prima facie showing that defendant knew or had reason to know of the defect.

"Culpable mental state" means intentional, knowing, reckless or criminally negligent conduct. . . . If the commission of a particular offense or some material element thereof does not require a culpable mental state on the part of the actor, such an offense is one of "strict liability."

It is a well-known principle of statutory construction that absent the legislature's clear indication of an intent to impose strict liability, a statute should be construed to require mens rea. . . . [The Court determined that the defendant had to have had knowledge of the defect to be liable and that no such showing had been made. Accordingly, defendant's motion for dismissal was granted.]

who injure consumers who purchased misbranded drugs was upheld. [9] Similarly the Court refused to impute mens rea for the crime of possessing a hand grenade because of the public safety rationale of the law.[10] For a law to qualify as a public welfare statute, the harm that it seeks to prevent or control must seriously threaten health or life. In addition, the history of how the act as regulated is important. If the threat is not widespread and significant, the law will not be characterized as public welfare and a court will be more likely to impose mens rea.[11]

Another factor is implicit in the public welfare cases—the nature of the act regulated. If the act was a crime at the common law that required the government to prove state of mind, as opposed to being a recent regulatory creation, it is more likely that a court will want to impose mens rea.

Vicarious Liability

vicarious liability

■ Legal responsibility for the acts of another person because of some relationship with that person.

The term **vicarious liability** refers to situations in which one person is held accountable for the actions of another. Under vicarious liability, there is no requirement of mens rea as there is for strict liability, and in addition, there is no requirement for an act, at least not by the defendant. The person who is liable for the actions of another need not act, encourage another to act, or intend any harm at all. As is true with vicarious liability in tort law, this situation is most common between employers and employees.

Employers may be liable for the actions of their employees when criminal laws relating to the operation of the business are violated. For example, the owner of a business may be prosecuted for failure to comply with product safety regulations, even though that was a duty delegated to an employee and the owner had no knowledge that the products manufactured were substandard. Vicarious liability is often imposed on those who market food and drugs.[12] This is because of the significant public welfare interest in the quality of these products.

Corporate Liability

corporate liability

■ The liability of a corporation for the acts of its directors, officers, shareholders, agents, and employees.

Corporate liability is a form of vicarious liability. Under the common law, corporations could not be convicted of crimes. However, this is no longer the law.

Corporations, partnerships, and other organizations can be held criminally accountable for the acts of their employees and agents under traditional respondeat superior theory. Agents must be working within the scope of their employment for the company to be liable. If an employee of Starbucks strikes an enemy while on break in the parking lot of the store, the company is not liable for battery. However, if officers of a corporation send employees into a workplace knowing that it is dangerous and represent to the employees that it is safe, the company may be liable for battery to the employee, or even manslaughter, if death results.

One legal scholar identified three theories under which corporations can be found criminally liable today. The first is traditional principal-agent theory, which developed at the common law. Second, corporations should be liable for the actions of their policymakers but not their employees. The third theory holds that corporations are liable for their agents and employees when corporate policy or practices fail to prevent the crime from happening.[13]

The Model Penal Code provides for corporate liability when the agent is acting within the scope of employment. In addition, it must be shown that the corporation had a duty under the law to act, and the act was not done or the act taken by the agent was authorized, requested, commanded, performed, or recklessly tolerated by the board of directors or other high management.[14]

Today, in most jurisdictions, corporations can be held criminally liable for any act that is criminal for a natural person. This includes crimes against the person, such as rape, murder, and battery. *People v. Warner-Lambert Co.,* which appears later in this chapter, is an example of when a company was charged with negligent homicide. In a subsequent case in Illinois, a corporation was convicted of involuntary manslaughter and several of its officers were convicted of murder for the death of an employee that could have been prevented.[15] The most common criminal actions against corporations, however, are not crimes against person. They are property and regulatory crimes.[16]

Obviously, companies cannot be incarcerated, so fines are usually imposed. In some instances, **injunctions** may be imposed or a company's status may be altered, suspended, or terminated. Finally, note that corporate liability does not free the agent from criminal liability. In most cases, the agents or employees remain criminally liable for their acts. Indeed, proving corporate mens rea can be more difficult than proving individual mens rea. Two prominent cases illustrate this point.

One of the most famous cases of alleged corporate crime involved Ford Motor Company. In the late 1960s, Ford designed a new subcompact car, the Pinto. To maximize trunk space, the Pinto's fuel tank was located behind the rear axle rather than above it, which was the common design. However, this new design made the car more vulnerable to fire and explosions in rear-end accidents. Other design decisions, including lack of reinforcement of the rear of the car and a poorly designed fuel filler pipe, accentuated the risk. Following several deaths from fires resulting from rear-end collisions, civil suits were filed against Ford in different states. During discovery in one of those actions, a report that detailed the costs of correcting the problem ($11 per car, 12.5 million cars, totaling $137 million) in comparison to the costs of the expected number of deaths and injuries (180 deaths, 180 injuries, totaling $49.5 million) was produced. This and other evidence led prosecutors in Indiana to charge Ford with negligent homicide.[17]

Many civil actions also were filed by individuals who were harmed. Ultimately, Ford was not convicted of the charged crime but was found liable in several civil actions. Although an unsuccessful criminal prosecution, the Ford case continues to be prominent in discussions of corporate criminal liability because the underlying premise of the prosecution—namely, that a corporation can be charged with traditional crimes—was generally accepted.

The 2002 Enron debacle is another example. As a result of misrepresentations about Enron's financial status by Enron officers and Enron's accounting firm, Arthur Andersen, LLP, investors were not aware of Enron's financial distress. Employees and investors lost millions of dollars when the company went bankrupt in December 2001. In addition to criminal charges against Enron officials, Enron's accounting firm, Arthur Andersen, LLP, was charged with obstruction of justice for destroying Enron documents and computer files that were sought by federal authorities. The government alleged that Andersen employees destroyed files containing unfavorable information about Enron that had not been made available to investors. Andersen, a top-five accounting firm, had 85,000 employees and offices the world over at the time of its indictment. Many commentators were critical of the indictment, asserting that the focus of corporate crime should be the responsible individuals, not companies. A conviction of Andersen, it was alleged, could lead to more than a fine (as provided for by statute). Andersen faced demise by losing its Securities and Exchange status and its corporate status. This would result in 85,000 unemployed individuals, most of whom were not parties to the crime.

injunctions

■ A judge's order to a person to do or to refrain from doing a particular – thing.

Ultimately, Andersen was convicted of obstruction of justice and was sentenced to 5 years' probation and a $500,000 fine. The terms of its probation included additional fines if it committed new crimes, and the firm was required to obtain approval before it sold its assets. Andersen appealed, and in 2005 a unanimous Supreme Court set aside the conviction.[18] However, as a result of the scandal, Andersen had lost nearly all of its clients, had surrendered its license to practice before the Securities and Exchange Commission, had its license revoked in many states, its total staffing had fallen to just a few hundred, and the firm was defending against more than a hundred civil actions by the time the Supreme Court issued its decision in 2005. When this text went to press in 2014, Arthur Anderson LLP was still in business, although it surrendered its license to practice before the Securities and Exchange Commission, lost its right to practice in many states, and was conducting little accounting work.

Current Approaches to Mens Rea

The Model Penal Code and States of Mind

The drafters of the Model Penal Code chose to reject most of the common law terms when they addressed mens rea. The result is that the Model Penal Code recognizes four states of mind: purposeful; knowing; reckless; and negligent (see Exhibit 3–2).[19]

Exhibit 3–2   MENS REA UNDER THE MODEL PENAL CODE

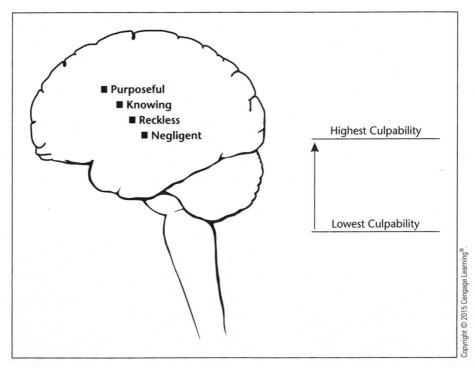

- Purposeful
- Knowing
- Reckless
- Negligent

Highest Culpability

Lowest Culpability

To act **purposely,** a defendant must have a desire to cause the result. *Purposely* most closely equates with what the common law called *specific intent.*

To act **knowingly,** a defendant must be aware of the nature of the act and be practically certain that his or her conduct will cause a particular result—which is not the defendant's objective. The difference between purposeful acts and knowing acts is that to be purposeful, one must act intending to cause the particular result. To act knowingly, the defendant must be practically certain (nearly 100% positive) that the result will occur, but the defendant is not taking the act to cause that result. For example, if a legitimate moving company owner leases a van to an illegal drug dealer knowing that the van will be used to transport drugs across the country, the owner has acted knowingly. He has not acted with purpose, because it is not the owner's objective to transport the contraband.

The third state of mind recognized by the Model Penal Code is **recklessness.** Individuals act recklessly when they consciously disregard a substantial and unjustifiable risk that the result will occur. The difference between a knowing act and a reckless act is in the degree of risk. "A person acts 'knowingly' with respect to a result if he is nearly certain that his conduct will cause the result. If he is aware only of a substantial risk, he acts 'recklessly' with respect to the result."[20] The Code says that the risk taken must be one that involves a "gross deviation from the standard of conduct that a law-abiding person would observe in the actor's situation."[21]

The final state of mind is **negligence.** The definition of negligence is similar to recklessness; that is, there must be a "substantial and unjustifiable risk" taken by the defendant. However, a person acts negligently when there is no conscious awareness of the risk, when there should have been. To act recklessly, one must take a risk that amounts to a "gross deviation from the standard of conduct that a law-abiding person would observe in the actor's situation." When defendants have acted negligently, they have failed to perceive (be aware of) the risk altogether, and that failure is a gross deviation from a law-abiding person's standard.

Element Analysis

So far, the discussion of culpable states of mind has been limited to one state of mind for each individual crime. For example, under the common law, a specific intent to kill must have been proven to establish first-degree murder. This was true of all offenses under the common law; that is, only one state of mind had to be shown. This was true even if the crime had many different elements.

Elements are the parts of a crime. The prosecution must prove all the elements of a crime beyond a reasonable doubt to gain a conviction. For example, the common-law elements of larceny were (1) the taking and carrying away (2) of personal property (3) of another (4) with an intent to steal. The prosecution has the burden of proving all four elements. If the prosecution fails to prove any element, the defendant must be acquitted. At common law, only one mental state had to be proved: intent to steal. Additionally, the prosecution had to show that the other four elements occurred without reference to mental state. This is known as *offense analysis*, as the entire offense is thought of as requiring one mental state.

---

purposely

■ Intentionally; knowingly.

knowingly

■ With full knowledge and intentionally; willfully.

recklessness

■ Indifference to consequences; indifference to the safety and rights of others. Recklessness implies conduct amounting to more than ordinary negligence.

negligence

■ Under the MPC, a defendant acts negligently when the resulting harm or material element of a crime occurs because of the defendant has taken a substantial and unjustifiable risk, even if the risk is not perceived, so long as the risk involves a gross deviation from the standard of conduct that a law-abiding person would observe.

element

■ A basic part. For example, some of the *elements* of a cause of action for battery are of an intentional, unwanted physical contact. Each of these things ("intentional," "unwanted," etc.) is one element.

The Model Penal Code (MPC), as well as some specific statutes, recognizes that the various acts of a crime may involve differing mental states. As such, each element of a crime may have a different mens rea.[22]

Assume that state law prohibits (1) notary publics (2) from notarizing documents (3) of known blood relatives (4) of the third degree or closer (degrees define closeness of family relationship). Under the Code, the first two elements appear to require no mental state—just the act of a notary notarizing a document. Hence, it would be no defense for the notary to claim that he was signing the document as a witness and not as a notary. The third element requires specific knowledge that the person for whom he notarizes the document is a blood relative. If the notary can prove that there was no reason for him to have known of the relationship, then his knowledge is negated. The last element is likely to be treated as a negligence element. It would be a valid defense for the notary to show that she made a reasonable error as to the degree of the relationship. Attempt to apply element analysis when examining penal statutes in your state or in your criminal law class.

Proving Mens Rea

At trial, the prosecution has the burden of establishing that the defendant possessed the required mental state when the act was committed. Proof of intent can be troublesome to prosecution, especially when the prosecution has to prove subjective intent. *Subjective intent* refers to the motives, intentions, and desires that were in the defendant's mind at the time the act took place. Subjective intent is a defendant's actual intent.

Objective intent is not the defendant's actual intent; rather, it is a legal imposition upon defendants of what they should have known or believed at the time the act occurred. Generally, the law imposes a reasonable person standard. That means that the defendant is expected to have known or believed what a reasonable person would have known at the time of the act. Objective intent is easier to prove than is subjective intent. This is because the prosecution does not have to probe directly into a defendant's mind to prove that an intent to harm existed; rather, all that has to be shown is that the defendant should have known that the harm would result.

In most cases, defendants do not admit to committing the acts in question. Even when defendants do admit to some acts, they commonly deny intent. For crimes that require intent, admission of the act is not enough to sustain a conviction. The question is: How does a prosecutor gain a conviction for a crime that requires showing of intent when the defendant denies possessing the required intent? The answer is by using **inferences.**

inference

■ A fact (or proposition) that is *probably* true because a true fact (or proposition) leads you to believe that the *inferred* fact (or proposition) is also true.

An *inference* is a conclusion that a judge or jury is permitted to make after considering the facts of a case. Imagine that a man walks up to another man and strikes him in the head with a hammer, using great force in his swing. The wound is fatal, and the attacker is charged with first-degree murder. To sustain a first-degree murder charge in this jurisdiction, it must be shown that the man intended to cause the victim's death. The defendant disavows such intent, admitting only that he intended to hit and injure the victim. In such a case, the jury would be permitted to infer the defendant's intent to kill the victim from the seriousness of the act. In a jurisdiction that uses the objective standard, the jury could conclude that a reasonable person would have known that the blow from a hammer would cause the victim's death, and the subjective intent of the defendant would not matter.

A **presumption** is a conclusion that must be made by a judge or jury. Most people have heard of the presumption of innocence in criminal law. This presumption is a *rebuttable presumption*. Rebuttable presumptions are conclusions that must be made by a judge or jury, unless disproven by the facts. Hence, defendants are innocent until proven guilty. *Irrebuttable presumptions* are conclusions that must be made by the judge or jury and cannot be disproved. Regardless of what the evidence shows, an irrebuttable presumption stands as a fact.

Motive

The reason a person commits a crime is **motive.** More particularly, the reason that leads a person to a desired result or particular action is motive.

Motive is different from mens rea. Motive leads to mens rea. Motive is concerned with why people act. Mens rea, in contrast, is concerned with whether a person intended to act. For example, greed is a motive for many acts. A bank robber's motive for robbing a bank is greed (or even, possibly, the challenge). The robber's mens rea is neither greed nor the emotional thrill resulting from the risk; rather, it is the intent to take money using force or threat. Said another way, the robber's mens rea (intent) is used to satisfy the motive (greed).

Motive is not an element of crimes. Therefore, prosecutors do not have to prove motive to be successful in a prosecution. As a practical matter, however, the trier of fact will want to know why the defendant committed the alleged crime. In many crimes, the motive will be apparent. Greed is easily understood and is imputed by juries to accused thieves. In other crimes, such as murder, there may be no apparent motive, and the prosecutor may need to introduce evidence explaining why a defendant would commit such a heinous crime. Was the murder motivated by greed (e.g., to gain an inheritance), or by passion (e.g., in revenge for infidelity), or by some other emotion? Usually, the prosecutor will prove motive; but in a case in which the defendant has pleaded insanity, the defendant bears the burden of providing either that there was no motive (e.g., the defendant did not want this to happen, but a mental disease or defect made her do it), or that the motive was the product of insanity (e.g., he believed the decedent was Godzilla).

A bad motive does not make an otherwise lawful act criminal. Conversely, a good motive does not excuse the commission of a crime. The issue is simply whether the prosecution has proven, beyond a reasonable doubt, that all the elements of the crime were committed.

Motive plays a role at sentencing. A good motive may justify a mitigation of sentence, whereas a bad motive may act in the reverse.

In some instances, a good motive may prevent charges from being filed at all. Police and prosecutors do not pursue some cases, even though a crime has been committed, when a person acted with good intentions. Conversely, law enforcement officials may pursue a case more passionately if the defendant acted from an evil motive. Exhibit 3–3 summarizes mens rea versus motive.

presumption

■ A presumption *of law* is an automatic assumption required by law that whenever a certain set of facts shows up, a court must automatically draw certain legal conclusions.

motive

■ The reason why a person does something.

Exhibit 3–3   MENS REA V. MOTIVE

	Mens Rea	Motive
Defined	The level of intentionality to commit an act that is required to prove a crime.	The reason a person acted.
Trial	An element of nearly all crimes that must be proven at trial beyond a reasonable doubt.	Not an element of any crime and doesn't have to be proved. However, a prosecutor may need to establish voluntariness motive in order to persuade a fact finder to convict.
Sentencing	May be considered in mitigation or aggravation.	May be considered in mitigation or aggravation.

ACTUS REUS

Earlier in this chapter you learned the Latin phrase "actus non facit reum nisi mens sit rea." The phrase expresses the common-law requirement that two essential elements must be present to have a crime: a guilty mind and a guilty act. **Actus reus** is the physical part of a crime; it is the act engaged in by the accused. An act is a physical movement. If Mrs. X shoots and kills Mrs. T, the act is pulling the trigger of the gun.

The Model Penal Code states that a "person is not guilty of an offense unless his liability is based on conduct that includes a voluntary act."[23]

Voluntariness

To be held criminally liable for one's actions, those actions must be voluntary. To be voluntary, an act must occur as a result of the actor's conscious choice. The person accused must have acted freely, or no liability attaches. The Model Penal Code requires that acts be voluntary and specifically lists the following as being involuntary:

1. reflexes and convulsions;
2. bodily movements during unconsciousness or sleep;
3. conduct during hypnosis or resulting from hypnotic suggestion; and
4. other movements that are not a product of the effort or determination of the actor.[24]

Do not confuse the concepts of mens rea and actus reus. All that is required to have an act is a choice by the defendant to act. No evil intent is required to have an act; that is a question of mens rea. Say that Jim chooses to swing his arm. As a result, he hits Tom. What intent is required to prove battery and whether Jim possessed that

actus reus

■ (Latin) An act. For example, an *actus reus* is a "wrongful deed" (such as killing a person) which, if done with mens rea, a "guilty mind" (such as *malice aforethought*), is a crime (such as *first-degree murder*).

intent are questions of mens rea. For actus reus, all that need be known is whether Jim voluntarily chose to swing his arm. His swing would be involuntary if Bill grabbed Jim's arm and moved it, causing it to strike Tom.

In the *Cogdon* case, a woman was acquitted of murdering her daughter because it was determined that her acts were not voluntary.[25] No defense of insanity was raised in this case. If it had been, the analysis would have been different. In most jurisdictions, one cannot claim lack of a voluntary act if insanity is also claimed. In those situations, the rules of the insanity defense apply See Chapter 8 for a complete discussion of insanity as a defense.

KING V. COGDON
Supreme Court of Victoria (1950)

Mrs. Cogdon was charged with the murder of her only child, a daughter called Pat, aged 19. Pat had for some time been receiving psychiatric treatment for a relatively minor neurotic condition of which, in her psychiatrist's opinion, she was now cured. Despite this, Mrs. Cogdon continued to worry unduly about her. Describing the relationship between Pat and her mother, Mr. Cogdon testified: "I don't think a mother could have thought any more of her daughter. I think she absolutely adored her." On the conscious level, there was no doubt [of] Mrs. Cogdon's deep attachment to her daughter.

To the charge of murdering Pat, Mrs. Cogdon pleaded not guilty. Her story, though somewhat bizarre, was not seriously challenged by the Crown, and led to her acquittal. She told how on the night before her daughter's death, she had dreamt that their house was full of spiders and that these spiders were crawling all over Pat. In her sleep, Mrs. Cogdon left the bed she shared with her husband, went into Pat's room, and awakened to find herself violently brushing at Pat's face, presumably to remove the spiders. This woke Pat. Mrs. Cogdon told her she was just tucking her in.

At the trial, she testified that she still believed, as she had been told, that the occupants of a nearby house bred spiders as a hobby, preparing nests for them behind the pictures on their walls. It was these spiders that in her dreams had invaded their home and attacked Pat. There had also been a previous dream in which ghosts had sat at the end of Mrs. Cogdon's bed and she had said to them, "Well, you have come to take Pattie." It does not seem fanciful to accept the psychological explanation of these spiders and ghosts as the projections of Mrs. Cogdon's subconscious hostility toward her daughter, a hostility which was itself rooted in Mrs. Cogdon's own early life and marital relationship.

The morning after the spider dream, she told her doctor of it. He gave her a sedative and, because of the dream and certain previous difficulties she had reported, discussed the possibility of psychiatric treatment. That evening, Mrs. Cogdon suggested to her husband that he attend his lodge meeting, and asked Pat to come with her to the cinema. After her husband had gone, Pat looked through the paper, not unusually found no tolerable programme, and said that as she was going out the next evening, she thought she would rather go to bed early. Later, while Pat was having a bath preparatory to retiring, Mrs. Cogdon went into her room, put a hot water bottle in the bed, turned back the bedclothes,

(continued)

KING V. COGDON *(continued)*

and placed a glass of hot milk beside the bed, ready for Pat. She then went to bed herself. There was some desultory conversation between them about the war in Korea, and just before she put out her light, Pat called out to her mother, "Mum, don't be so silly worrying about the war, it's not on our front step yet."

Mrs. Cogdon went to sleep. She dreamt that "the war was all around the house," that the soldiers were in Pat's room, and that one soldier was on the bed attacking Pat. This is all of the dream that she could later recapture. Her first "waking" memory was of running from Pat's room, out of the house

to the home of her sister who lived next door. When her sister opened the front door, Mrs. Cogdon fell into her arms crying, "I think I've hurt Pattie."

In fact, Mrs. Cogdon had, in her somnambulistic state, left her bed, fetched an axe from the wood-heap, entered Pat's room, and struck two accurate forceful blows on the head with the blade of the axe, thus killing her.

▪ ▪ ▪

At all events the jury believed Mrs. Cogdon's story . . . [Mrs. Cogdon] was acquitted because the act of killing itself was not, in law, regarded as her act at all . . .

Thoughts and Statements as Acts

Thoughts alone are not acts that can be made criminal. People may think evil thoughts, but if there is no act furthering such a thought, there is no crime.

Generally, people are also free to speak. The First Amendment to the U.S. Constitution protects freedom of speech. When the First Amendment applies, speech may not be made criminal. There are, however, limits to First Amendment protection of speech. Inciting riots, treason, solicitation, conspiracy, and causing imminent harm to others are examples of speech that may be prohibited. You will learn more about the First Amendment protection of speech later.

Personal Status as an Act

Generally, a person's status cannot be declared criminal. Illness, financial status, race, sex, and religion are examples of human conditions. Some conditions are directly related to illegal behavior. For example, being addicted to illegal narcotics is a condition that cannot be punished. This is because status is generally believed not to be an act. However, using and selling prohibited narcotics are acts and may be punished.

Vagrancy is one area over which there is a split in legal opinion. Some courts have held that vagrancy may be prohibited; others have determined that vagrancy is a condition and does not constitute a crime. One author noted that there is a "growing body of authority" holding such statutes unconstitutional.[26]

In *Robinson v. California,* [Shouldn't this info should go within endnote 27? Maybe not because it's within a feature.] the United States Supreme Court was called upon to review a California statute that made it a crime "either to use narcotics, or to be addicted to the use of narcotics." The Court reversed Robinson's conviction, and in the opinion stated:

> This statute, therefore, is not one which punishes a person for the use of narcotics, for their purchase, sale or possession, or for antisocial or disorderly behavior resulting from their administration. It is not a law which even purports to provide or require medical treatment. Rather, we deal with a statute which makes the "status" of narcotic addiction a criminal offense, for which the offender may be prosecuted "at any time before he reforms." California has said that a person can be continuously guilty of this offense, whether or not he has ever used or possessed any narcotics within the state, and whether or not he has been guilty of any antisocial behavior there.
>
> It is unlikely that any State at this moment in history would attempt to make it a criminal offense for a person to be mentally ill, or a leper, or to be afflicted with a venereal disease. A State might determine that the general health and welfare require that the victims of these and other human afflictions be dealt with by compulsory treatment, involving quarantine, confinement, or sequestration. But in the light of contemporary human knowledge, a law which made a criminal offense of such a disease would doubtless be universally thought of to be an infliction of cruel and unusual punishment in violation of the Eighth and Fourteenth Amendments. . . .
>
> We cannot but consider the statute before us as of the same category . . . . We hold that a state law which imprisons a person thus afflicted as a criminal, even though he has never touched any narcotic drug within the State or been guilty of any irregular behavior there, inflicts a cruel and unusual punishment in violation of the Fourteenth Amendment. . . . [27]

While personal status may not be criminalized, it may be subject to the regulatory authority of the state. Individuals who are mentally ill and who pose a danger to themselves or others may be civilly committed, for example. This includes the commitment of sexual predators. This topic is discussed more fully in Chapter 4.

Possession as an Act

Possession of certain items, such as narcotics or burglary tools, may be made criminal. Possession of deadly weapons is both a federal and a state crime. Following the terrorist attacks of September 11, 2001, for example, Congress made it unlawful to possess biological agents or delivery systems for biological agents that are intended to be used as weapons.[28] Possession is not, strictly speaking, an act. Possession does not involve an active body movement; rather, possession is a passive state of being. Even so, most possession laws have been upheld.

Jurisdictions differ in what is required to prove possession. Some require that actual possession be shown, whereas others allow proof of constructive possession. Constructive possession is used to extend criminal liability to those who never exercised actual possession but had dominion and control over the contraband. A person who is the owner and driver of a car may have never possessed the cocaine that his passenger is using, but the law says that the driver is in constructive possession because the dominion and control over the auto belong to the driver. In essence, the law imposes a duty on people to remove illegal items from the area over which they have dominion and control. Failure to comply with such a duty is treated as an act and can lead to criminal liability.

One problem with crimes of possession is the possibility of convicting people who had no knowledge of the existence of illegal items in an area under their dominion and control. An owner of a house has dominion and control over the guest room but may not be aware that a guest has brought illegal items into the room. Most jurisdictions have remedied this problem by requiring knowledge of the presence of the goods. The Model Penal Code also uses such a test. The Code states that possession is an act as long as the "possessor knowingly procured or received the thing possessed or was aware of his control thereof for a sufficient period to have been able to terminate his possession." Under the Code, possession can be actual or constructive. However, if constructive, the possessor must have known of the items for a period of time long enough to permit the possessor to terminate possession. So, if the owner of the house discovered the cocaine only minutes before the police arrived to search the premises, no possession could be found on the owner's behalf.

Finally, one person or many people can be in possession of items. Using the preceding example, assume that two or more people jointly owned the home in question. All of the owners could be liable, if it was determined that all had constructive possession and adequate time to remove the cocaine from the house. It is possible that fewer than all of the owners knew of the cocaine and, as such, did not have constructive possession. Each person who is alleged to have dominion and control (constructive possession) must be examined individually, and separate decisions as to their individual liability must be made.

Omissions as Acts

In 2011 allegations of sexual abuse of children by former Penn State assistant football coach Jerry Sandusky went viral. Sandusky was convicted and sentenced in 2012 to 30 to 60 years in prison for abusing many young men.[29] But this wasn't the end of the story. Several other Penn State officials were charged with crimes resulting from Sandusky's crimes, including perjury and failure to report abuse of a minor. Rape and perjury are acts. Failing to report a crime does not involve an act. It is just the opposite—failure to act. Generally, only acts are prohibited by criminal law. Rarely does criminal law require a person to act. However, in some situations, people have a duty to act, and failure to act is criminal. An **omission** is a failure to act when required to do so by criminal law.

omission

■ Failing to do something that should be done.

It is often the case that a person who may have a moral duty to act does not have a legal duty to act. In most instances, people do not have a legal duty to assist one another in times of need. It would not be criminal in most jurisdictions for an excellent swimmer to watch another drown. Nor would it be criminal to watch another walk into a dangerous situation, such as a bank robbery in progress, if the observer had no connection with the criminal event. There are exceptions to this rule. To be liable for a failure to act, a person must have a "duty" to act. The duty to act can come about in many different ways.

At common law, several exceptions to the "no duty to assist people in danger" rule evolved. Many of these are discussed in the following paragraphs. Bear in mind that many legislatures have codified one or more of these exceptions. In those instances, the duty is imposed by statute and not the common law.

Duty Imposed by Statute

Under the common law, in most instances people had no duty to assist others whose lives were in danger. Today, criminal statutes may impose liability for failure to assist someone in danger. A few states have enactments that directly change the common-law rule and require people to assist others who are in danger. However, even in those jurisdictions, rescue need not be attempted if the rescuer's life would thereby be endangered. Imposing criminal liability for not rescuing someone in danger of losing life or limb continues to be the exception and not the rule. However, no legal reason prevents all jurisdictions from requiring people to rescue one another when there is no danger associated with the rescue.

Setting aside the common law doctrine that one doesn't have a duty to act, many contemporary statutes impose a duty to act in specific circumstances. The Penn State sex abuse crimes are an example. At one point, a Penn State employee witnessed a rape of a youth by Sandusky in Penn State's showers. The employee reported the incident to Joe Paterno, who was Penn State's football coach at the time. Paterno is alleged to have passed on the report to his superiors, Tim Curley and Gary Schultz. Pennsylvania law required knowledge of sexual abuse by an employee to be reported to the "person in charge," who had an obligation to pass the report along to "authorities." Questions were raised about whether Paterno reported all that he knew, whether he should have reported the incident to authorities, and whether Curley and Schultz made the required reporting to authorities. At the time of this writing in 2013, the two men were awaiting trial for perjury and failure to report.

Failing to report child abuse is one of many examples of omissions as crimes today. State and federal laws require businesses that store or dispose of toxic materials to file certain documents, taxpayers are required to file tax returns, drivers of automobiles involved in accidents are required to stop at their accident scenes, and some states require individuals to report wild animals that are loose.

Some states go further than others in creating statutory obligations that did not exist at the common law. For example, Ohio criminalizes the failure to report any felony that has, or is being, committed. The same law requires health care professionals to report stab wound, gunshot wounds, and burn injuries that appear to be the result of violence.[30]

Duty by Relationship

A duty to assist another can be created by the existence of a personal relationship. The most common examples are parent-to-child and spouse-to-spouse. In such personal relationships, a level of dependence exists that gives rise to criminal liability for failure to assist the party who is in danger. There is no bright-line rule for determining if a duty is owed. The more that one party becomes dependent upon another party or the parties become dependent upon one another, the more likely that a duty to assist is created.

Generally, any time a joint enterprise is undertaken by two or more parties, it can be assumed that a duty to assist one another during that enterprise is created. For example, if two people decide to go river rafting, they must rescue one another during that rafting trip, provided that the rescuer is not endangered by attempting the rescue.

In the parent–child relationship, a parent can be guilty of manslaughter if the child dies as a result of the parent's failure to seek medical attention for the child when the child is sick, or for failing to pull the child out of a pool when the child is drowning. The same would be true of a spouse. If a wife permitted her husband to die when she could have saved his life by summoning medical attention, she could be criminally liable. In addition, it has been held that employers owe a duty to assist their employees. For example, the master of a ship must attempt to rescue a seaman who has fallen overboard.??

Duty by Contract

A duty to act can be created in a third way—by contract. For example, physicians are hired to care for the health of their patients. If a doctor watches as a patient slowly dies, doing nothing to save the patient's life when there were measures that could have been taken, the doctor is liable for homicide. The same is true of a lifeguard. The lifeguard is hired to save those who are drowning, and if a lifeguard sits and watches a swimmer drown when the swimmer could have been saved, the lifeguard is liable for homicide.

Remember, the general rule is that people owe no duty to rescue others. So, if an expert swimmer happens to be on the beach when another person is drowning, the expert swimmer can watch the person drown without risking criminal liability.

Assumption of Duty

Even though the general rule is that people do not have a duty to rescue strangers, it is possible, either expressly or by one's actions, to make an *assumption of duty*. The assumption is express if it is stated orally or in writing. Assumption is different from duty premised on contract, in that assumptions are gratuitous. If Sidney is at a pool and agrees to care for another's child, Sidney has assumed the duty expressly. If the child falls into the pool, and Sidney takes no action to save the child, Sidney is liable for murder if the child drowns.

It is possible through one's actions to assume the duty to rescue someone. Assume that Sidney is now at a lake. One person, David, is swimming, and three other people are relaxing on the beach. David begins to scream for help. Sidney jumps up and dives into the water to rescue David. Halfway out to David, she changes her mind and returns to shore. By the time she returns to shore, it is too late for someone else to make the swim to David, and David dies. In this case, Sidney assumed the duty of the rescue by beginning the rescue attempt. However, whether Sidney is liable for murder depends on what condition the drowning person was left in after Sidney changed her mind. If Sidney's actions caused the other three people on the beach to fail to attempt a rescue, Sidney's actions left David in a worse condition than he would have been in had Sidney not begun the rescue. However, if Sidney's actions did not prevent anyone else from attempting a rescue, Sidney's action did not put David in a worse situation and Sidney is not liable for murder, even if the other person fails in the rescue attempt.

Finally, note that we can easily change this last example into an express assumption. All that has to be added is a statement by Sidney to the others on the beach that she will swim out and rescue David. Such a statement, if it caused others to forgo a rescue attempt, is an express assumption of duty.

Creating Danger

Any time a person creates the circumstance that endangers a stranger, a duty to save the stranger is created. This is true whether the danger was caused intentionally or negligently. So, if an arsonist sets fire to a house that is believed to be empty and is discovered not to be, the arsonist must attempt to save anyone inside. If not, the arsonist is also a murderer. The same would be true of a negligently caused fire. If an electrician begins a fire in a home and does nothing to warn the inhabitants, the electrician is also liable for murder.

Causation

Some acts are criminal even though the prohibited result does not occur. For example, it is a crime to lie when testifying in court (the crime of perjury). Assume that the purpose of the lie is to deceive the jury and change the outcome of the case. Even if no juror—or anyone else, for that matter—believes the lie and the purpose is not achieved, it is a crime. Causation is not an issue in such crimes.

For crimes that do require a particular result, the act must be the "cause" of the result. In criminal law, two forms of causation exist: factual and legal. If either of these "causes" is missing, then a defense as to the intent of the crime exists. Even if so, the actor may be convicted of a lower, non-intent crime.

An act is the *cause in fact* of the result if the result would not have occurred unless the act occurred. This is known as the *sine qua non* test, which means that "but for" the conduct, the harm would not have resulted.

Legal cause must also be proved. Legal causation focuses on the degree of similarity between the defendant's intended result and the actual result. It also examines the similarity between the intended manner used to bring about a result and the actual manner that caused the result. Generally, the greater the similarity between the purpose and the result, and the manner intended and the manner that actually caused the result, the more likely that the defendant is the legal cause. Legal cause is also commonly referred to as **proximate cause.** *Proximate* means "nearly, next to, or close." In the context of criminal causation, it refers to the relationship between the act and the result. The result must be a consequence of the act, not a coincidence. A happening is proximately caused by an act if a reasonable person would have foreseen and expected the result. This is called **foreseeability.**

legal cause

■ The proximate cause of an injury; probable cause; cause that the law deems sufficient.

foreseeable

■ The degree to which the consequences of an action *should* have been anticipated, recognized, and considered beforehand. *Not* hindsight.

proximate cause

■ The "legal cause" of an accident or other injury (which may have several actual causes). The *proximate cause* of an injury is not necessarily the closest thing in time or space to the injury, and not necessarily the event that set things in motion, because "proximate cause" is a legal, not a physical concept.

Most problems raised in this area involve legal causation, not factual causation. This is because, to prove factual causation, it must be shown that the defendant's action set into motion the events that led to the prohibited result. The question that should be asked is, had the defendant not acted, would the result have happened? If the answer is no, then the defendant is the factual cause. Determining legal causation is more troublesome, however.

Let us examine a few examples. Hank shoots Mark, intending to kill him. Mark dies from the gunshot wound. Hank is the factual cause of the murder because it was his conduct that caused Mark to die. To state it another way, "but for" Hank's act, Mark would not have died." Hank is also the legal cause of Mark's death because the resulting death is identical to Hank's intention.

Now assume that Hank intended only to injure Mark, not to kill him. Accordingly, he shot Mark in the arm. Mark then contacted a hospital, which dispatched an ambulance. The paramedics who arrived to assist Mark negligently administered a dangerous medication, which caused his death. Hank continues to be the factual cause of Mark's death, because if he had not injured Mark, the medical attention that ended Mark's life would not have been necessary. However, Hank is not the legal cause of Mark's death. This is because the result greatly differs from Hank's intent. There is not enough similarity between Hank's purpose when he shot Mark (to cause an injury) and the resulting harm (Mark's death).

intervening cause

■ A cause of an accident or other injury that will remove the blame from the wrongdoer who originally set events in motion.

Note that it is common for legal cause to be lacking when an **intervening cause** exists, as it does in the previous example. An *intervening cause* is a happening that occurs after the initial act and changes the outcome. Intervening causes function to block the connection between an act and the result, because the intervening cause changes what would have been the result if the result had flowed freely from the act. Intervening causes can negate or lower criminal liability for the particular result. However, lower crimes may continue to be punishable. In the preceding example, the intervening cause is the negligent medical care of the paramedics. Hank's intent was not to cause Mark's death, and, as such, he was not the legal cause of Mark's death. Of course, Hank may also have a mens rea defense.

Assume that Hank shot Mark intending to kill him, but because Hank is a poor shot, he only injured Mark. As before, the paramedics who treat Mark negligently administer the wrong medication and cause his death. Again, Hank is the factual cause of Mark's death. Whether he is the legal cause is debatable. Even though the intended result occurred, it occurred in a manner entirely unintended. If the manner in which the result occurs differs significantly from the manner that was intended, the defendant may not be liable. This appears consistent with common notions of fairness: Why should Hank be liable for murder when at least part of the blame belongs to the paramedics? Courts are split on this issue. Some would find that Hank is liable for intent murder, whereas others would hold Hank liable for a lower murder.

If a victim suffers the intended injury while attempting to avoid the injury, the defendant is liable for the crime, even though the manner is entirely different than intended. So if Mark is struck and killed by a bus while running from Hank, who intends to stab Mark to death, Hank is considered both the legal and the factual cause of

Mark's death. There is a limit to this theory; that is, there must be some nexus between the unintended manner and the act. If a reasonable person would not have expected the result to occur, the defendant is not liable. So, if Mark was not killed by a passing bus but, rather, by a hit on the head by a piano accidentally dropped by movers, Hank is not the legal cause of his death. This is true even though Mark would not have happened to be under the piano if he were not running from Hank.

In the rare instance where two events happen simultaneously, and both could be the legal cause of the outcome, both are treated as the legal cause. This is true even if only one event was the actual cause. For example, if two people shoot a victim at the same moment, both are liable for murder. However, it is possible that only one actually caused the death. If it is not possible to determine which bullet was the actual cause of death, both people are liable. If it can be determined which bullet was responsible for killing the victim, the other party is relieved of responsibility for murder (although not attempted murder).

Even though the preceding examples dealt with purposeful crimes, remember that the principle applies to all crimes that require a particular result. The result need not be one that comes about purposefully or intentionally. Crimes of recklessness and negligence may require a specific result to be criminal. Reckless homicide requires that the behavior that is reckless actually cause a death.

The Model Penal Code also requires that the conduct in question be the actual result or cause of the result. Section 2.03 of the Model Penal Code also, if a particular result is necessary to prove a crime, the "element is not established unless the actual result is a probable consequence of the actor's conduct." Further, the Code states that the crime is not proven if the actual result is different from the defendant's purpose, unless:

1. The resulting harm is the same; however it occurred to the wrong person or thing (transferred intent).
2. The actual harm is not as great or as serious as intended.
3. The actual harm involves the same kind of injury or harm as intended and is not *too remote or accidental* in its occurrence to have a bearing on the actor's liability.

These requirements apply to all levels of culpability under the Code—that is, purposeful, knowing, reckless, and negligent—and must be adjusted accordingly. So, if the crime is one of recklessness or negligence, then the Code's criteria should be viewed in light of risks and probable results and not purpose.

The phrase "too remote or accidental" is the Code's proximate cause requirement. It is the same as discussed earlier, except that the drafters of the Code chose not to use the phrase "proximate cause." In *People v. Warner-Lambert Co.,* a company and some of its officers were indicted for manslaughter and negligent homicide. The charges stemmed from an industrial accident at one of Warner-Lambert's plants. The high court of New York dismissed the indictments, finding that the defendants were not the proximate cause of the plant employees' deaths because the explosion that caused their deaths was not foreseeable.

PEOPLE V. WARNER-LAMBERT CO. D
51 N.Y.2d 295, 414 N.E.2d 660 (1980), cert. denied, 450 U.S. 1031 (1981)

On the day on which the explosion occurred, Freshen-Up gum, which is retailed in the shape of a square tablet with a jelly-like center, was being produced at the Warner-Lambert plant by a process in which filled ropes of the gum were passed through a bed of magnesium stearate (MS), a dry, dustlike lubricant which was applied by hand, then into a die-cut punch (a Uniplast machine) which was sprayed with a cooling agent (liquid nitrogen), where the gum was formed into the square tablets. Both the MS (normally an inert, organic compound) and the liquid nitrogen were employed to prevent the chicle from adhering to the sizing and cutting machinery, the tendency to adhere being less if a dry lubricant was used and the punch was kept at a low temperature. The process produced a dispersal of MS dust in the air and an accumulation of it at the base of the Uniplast machine and on overhead pipes; some also remained ambient in the atmosphere in the surrounding area.

Both MS and liquid nitrogen are considered safe and are widely used in the industry. In bulk, MS will only burn or smolder if ignited; however, like many substances, if suspended in the air in sufficient concentration the dust poses a substantial risk of explosion if ignited. . . . Liquid nitrogen is highly volatile, is easily ignited and, if ignited, will explode. Among possible causes of such ignition of either liquid oxygen or ambient MS are electrical or mechanical sparks.

• • •

There was proof that an inspection of the plant by Warner-Lambert's insurance carrier in February, 1976, had resulted in advice to the insured that the dust condition in the Freshen-Up gum production area presented an explosion hazard and that the MS concentration was above the [low point where explosion could occur], together with recommendations for installation of a dust exhaust system and modification of electrical equipment to meet standards for dust areas. Although a variety of proposals for altering the dust condition were considered by the individual defendants in consultations and communications with each other and some alterations in the MS application were made, both ambient and settled MS dust were still present on November 21, 1976.

• • •

The issue before us, however, is whether defendants could be held criminally liable for what actually occurred, on theories of reckless or negligent conduct, based on the evidence submitted to this Grand Jury, viewed in the light most favorable to the People. The focus of our attention must be on the issue of culpability, taking into account the conduct of the defendants and the factors of foreseeability and of causation, all of which in combination constitute the ultimate amalgam on which criminal liability may or may not be predicated.

First, we look at the evidence as to the actual event or chain of events which triggered the explosion—evidence which may only be characterized as hypothetical and speculative. . . . The prosecution hypothesizes that under what it describes as "the most plausible of theories," the initial detonation was attributable to mechanical sparking. . . .

Another explanation for the initial explosion was offered by an expert called by the prosecution who hypothesized that liquid oxygen . . . dripped onto settled MS dust at the base of the Uniplast, became trapped there, and then, when subjected to the impact caused by a moving metal part, reacted violently, causing ignition of already dispersed MS.

Viewed most favorably to the People, the proof with respect to the actual cause of the explosion is speculative only, and as to at least one of the major hypotheses—that involving oxygen liquefaction—there was no evidence that the process was foreseeable or known to any of the defendants. In sum, there was no proof sufficient to support a finding that defendants foresaw or should have foreseen the physical cause of the explosion. This being so, there was not legally sufficient evidence to establish the offenses charged or any lesser included offense.

The "Year-and-a-Day Rule"

At common law, a person could not be charged with murder if the victim did not die within one year and one day after the act took place. The rule was one of causation. It was developed to prevent a conviction for murder at a time in history when medical science could not precisely determine the actual cause of a person's death. If a person lived for more than a year and a day after being injured by a defendant's acts and then died, it was assumed that medical science could not pinpoint the exact cause of death and that to hold the defendant liable would be unjust. It is questionable, in light of the advances in medicine, whether the rule should continue to exist. It has been abolished in many states. In *Rogers v. Tennessee* (2001) the Supreme Court reviewed a conviction in Tennessee that was allowed to stand because the Tennessee courts announced the abrogation of the rule in the case. The court was asked to invalidate the conviction as *ex post facto* and contrary to due process.

ROGERS V. TENNESSEE
532 U.S. 451 (2001)

This case concerns the constitutionality of the retroactive application of a judicial decision abolishing the common law "year-and-a-day rule." At common law, the year-and-a-day rule provided that no defendant could be convicted of murder unless his victim had died by the defendant's act within a year and a day of the act. . . . The Supreme Court of Tennessee abolished the rule as it had existed at common law in Tennessee and applied its decision to petitioner to uphold his conviction. The question before us is whether, in doing so, the court denied petitioner due process of law in violation of the Fourteenth Amendment.

Petitioner Wilbert K. Rogers was convicted in Tennessee state court of second-degree murder. According to the undisputed facts, petitioner stabbed his victim, James Bowdery, with a butcher knife on May 6, 1994. One of the stab wounds penetrated Bowdery's heart. During surgery to repair the wound to his heart, Bowdery went into cardiac arrest, but was resuscitated and survived the procedure. As a result, however, he had developed a condition known as "cerebral hypoxia," which

results from a loss of oxygen to the brain. Bowdery's higher-brain functions had ceased, and he slipped into and remained in a coma until August 7, 1995, when he died from a kidney infection (a common complication experienced by comatose patients). Approximately 15 months had passed between the stabbing and Bowdery's death, which, according to the undisputed testimony of the county medical examiner, was caused by cerebral hypoxia "secondary to a stab wound to the heart." . . .

Based on this evidence, the jury found petitioner guilty under Tennessee's criminal homicide statute. The statute, which makes no mention of the year-and-a-day rule, defines criminal homicide simply as "the unlawful killing of another person, which may be first degree murder, second degree murder, voluntary manslaughter, criminally negligent homicide or vehicular homicide." . . . Petitioner appealed his conviction to the Tennessee Court of Criminal Appeals, arguing that, despite its absence from the statute, the year-and-a-day rule persisted as part of the common law of Tennessee and, as such, precluded his conviction.

(continued)

ROGERS V. TENNESSEE *(continued)*

The Court of Criminal Appeals rejected that argument and affirmed the conviction. The court held that Tennessee's Criminal Sentencing Reform Act of 1989 (1989 Act), which abolished all common law defenses in criminal actions in Tennessee, had abolished the rule. The court also rejected petitioner's further contention that the legislative abolition of the rule constituted an *ex post facto* violation, noting that the 1989 Act had taken effect five years before petitioner committed his crime. . . .

The Supreme Court of Tennessee affirmed on different grounds. The court observed that it had recognized the viability of the year and a day rule in Tennessee in *Percer v. State*, 118 Tenn. 765, 103 S.W. 780 (1907), and that, "[d]espite the paucity of case law" on the rule in Tennessee, "both parties . . . agree that the . . . rule was a part of the common law of this State." Turning to the rule's present status, the court noted that the rule has been legislatively or judicially abolished by the "vast majority" of jurisdictions recently to have considered the issue. The court concluded that, contrary to the conclusion of the Court of Criminal Appeals, the 1989 Act had not abolished the rule. After reviewing the justifications for the rule at common law, however, the court found that the original reasons for recognizing the rule no longer exist. Accordingly, the court abolished the rule as it had existed at common law in Tennessee. The court disagreed with petitioner's contention that application of its decision abolishing the rule to his case would violate the *Ex Post Facto* Clauses of the State and Federal Constitutions. Those constitutional provisions, the court observed, refer only to legislative Acts. . . .

Although petitioner's claim is one of due process, the Constitution's *Ex Post Facto* Clause figures prominently in his argument. The Clause provides simply that "[n]o State shall . . . pass any . . . ex post facto Law" (Art. I, § 10, cl. 1). The most well-known and oft-repeated explanation of the scope of the Clause's protection was given by Justice Chase, who long ago identified, in dictum, four types of laws to which the Clause extends:

> 1st. Every law that makes an action done before the passing of the law, and which was innocent when done, criminal; and punishes such action. 2d. Every law that aggravates a crime, or makes it greater than it was, when committed. 3d. Every law that changes the punishment, and inflicts a greater punishment, than the law annexed to the crime, when committed. 4th. Every law that alters the legal rules of evidence, and receives less, or different, testimony, than the law required at the time of the commission of the offense, in order to convict the offender.

Strict application of *ex post facto* principles [to courts] would unduly impair the incremental and reasoned development of precedent that is the foundation of the common law system. The common law, in short, presupposes a measure of evolution that is incompatible with stringent application of *ex post facto* principles. It was on account of concerns such as these that *Bouie* restricted due process limitations on the retroactive application of judicial interpretations of criminal statutes to those that are "unexpected and indefensible by reference to the law which had been expressed prior to the conduct in issue." Bouie v. City of Columbia, ...

We believe this limitation adequately serves the common law context as well. It accords common law courts the substantial leeway they must enjoy as they engage in the daily task of formulating and passing upon criminal defenses and interpreting such doctrines as causation and intent, reevaluating and refining them as may be necessary to bring the common law into conformity with logic and common sense. It also adequately respects the due process concern with fundamental fairness and protects against vindictive or arbitrary judicial lawmaking by safeguarding defendants against unjustified and unpredictable breaks with prior law.

ROGERS V. TENNESSEE (continued)

Accordingly, we conclude that a judicial alteration of a common law doctrine of criminal law violates the principle of fair warning, and hence must not be given retroactive effect, only where it is "unexpected and indefensible by reference to the law which had been expressed prior to the conduct in issue." . . .

Turning to the particular facts of the instant case, the Tennessee court's abolition of the year-and-a-day rule was not unexpected and indefensible. The year-and-a-day rule is widely viewed as an outdated relic of the common law. Petitioner does not even so much as hint that good reasons exist for retaining the rule, so we need not delve too deeply into the rule and its history here. Suffice it to say that the rule is generally believed to date back to the thirteenth century, when it served as a statute of limitations governing the time in which an individual might initiate a private action for murder known as an "appeal of death"; that by the eighteenth century, the rule had been extended to the law governing public prosecutions for murder; that the primary and most frequently cited justification for the rule is that thirteenth-century medical science was incapable of establishing causation beyond a reasonable doubt when a great deal of time had elapsed between the injury to the victim and his death; and that, as practically every court recently has noted to have considered the rule as to render it without question obsolete. . . . For this reason, the year-and-a-day rule has been legislatively or judicially abolished in the vast majority of jurisdictions recently to have addressed the issue. . . .

[The Court then discussed the small number of Tennessee cases that mention the Rule and concluded that in no case did the Supreme Court of Tennessee ever apply the Rule.]

In short, there is nothing to indicate that the Tennessee court's abolition of the rule in petitioner's case represented an exercise of the sort of unfair and arbitrary judicial action against which the Due Process Clause aims to protect. Far from a marked and unpredictable departure from prior precedent, the court's decision was a routine exercise of common law decisionmaking in which the court brought the law into conformity with reason and common sense. It did so by laying to rest an archaic and outdated rule that had never been relied upon as a ground of decision in any reported Tennessee case.

The judgement of the Supreme Court of Tennessee is accordingly affirmed.

Concurrence

In this chapter you have learned that there are two primary components of crimes—the mental and the physical. Although a showing of mens rea is not required for every crime, there must be a showing of some act or omission for all crimes.

For crimes that have both a mental and a physical element, an additional requirement of concurrence must be proved. *Concurrence* is the joining of mens rea and the act. The mens rea must be the reason that the act was taken. Stated another way, the mental state must occur first and set into motion the act. For example, Sandira hates Andy and desires to see him dead. Because of this feeling, Sandira waits for Andy to leave the house one night and runs him down with her car. In such a case, Sandira's mens rea set into motion the act that caused Andy's death. Now imagine that Sandira accidentally kills Andy in an auto accident. After the accident, she exclaims his happiness over Andy's demise. In this case, the mens rea occurred after the act. It was not the catalyst for the act that killed Andy, and, as such, there was no concurrence.

The mere fact that the mental state happens before the act does not mean that there is concurrence. There must be a connection between the intent and the act; the mens rea must set the act into motion. So if Doug forms the desire to kill Andy today but takes no action to further the desire, he cannot be charged with murder a year later when he accidentally shoots Andy while hunting.

As stated by the Court of Appeals of Indiana:

> Unless statutorily stated otherwise, it is black letter law that in order to constitute a crime "criminal intent" . . . must unite with an overt act, and they must concur in point of time. There must be a criminal act or omission as well as criminal intent. A felonious intent unconnected with an unlawful act constitutes no crime. . . . A person can only be punished for an offense he has committed and never for an offense he may commit in the future. A crime cannot be predicated upon future acts or upon contingencies or the taking effect of some future event.[31]

Ethical Considerations

OVERZEALOUS REPRESENTATION

In the Chapter 2's Ethical Considerations feature, you learned that attorneys have an obligation to zealously represent clients. But how far can an attorney take this obligation? What if a defense attorney intentionally hides the evidence of a client's crime from the government? This is precisely what happened in *In Re Ryder*. The attorney in that case hid the gun that his client used in a robbery, along with the stolen cash. Interestingly, the attorney had previously been a federal prosecutor!

Well, there is a limit to zealous representation. The Model Rules qualify the zealous representation requirement to behavior that is *within the bounds of the law*. In the case of the attorneys in the Chapter 2 feature, their decision not to disclose the location of the buried victims of their client's murders was held to be ethical. Because the ethical obligation not to disclose client communications trumped the administrative violation of not reporting the location of human remains. An attorney, however, may notintentionally mislead a court or fabricate evidence. Advising or coaching witnesses to testify falsely—known as the crime of suborning perjury—is also overzealous conduct. Harboring a client fugitive, filing false documents with a court, allowing evidence within one's control to spoil without notifying the opposing party or court, harassing and bribing

Ethical Considerations *(continued)*

jurors and witnesses, and destroying or hiding evidence, as occurred in *In Re Ryder* are other examples of excessively zealous conduct.

Be aware that while defense attorneys and prosecutors both share an obligation to zealously represent their clients, they have different constitutional missions. For the defense attorneys, the constitutional mission is the same as their general ethical obligation. For prosecutors, however, the duty is to seek justice. Accordingly, prosecutors are not to focus exclusively on obtaining convictions. Instead, they are to continuously reflect on whether justice is served by their decisions and actions. You will learn later in this book how this obligation creates obligations for the prosecutors that do not exist for defense attorneys.

Web Links

American Bar Association

The American Bar Association's home page *http:www.abanet.org* has considerable law-related information, including criminal law, legal education, and legal ethics topics. It also contains links to other sources of legal information.

Key Terms

actus reus

constructive intent (to match specific intent]

corporate liability

elements

foreseeability

inferences

injunctions

intervening cause

knowingly

legal cause

legislative history

mens rea

motive

negligence

omission

presumption

proximate cause

purposely

recklessness

scienter

specific intent

statutory construction

strict liability

strict liability crimes

transferred intent

vicarious liability

Review Questions

1. In criminal law, causation is broken down into two forms. Name and briefly describe each.
2. Can a person be prosecuted for failing to save a stranger from danger? Why or why not?
3. What is concurrence?
4. What is an omission?
5. The Model Penal Code recognizes four types of mens rea. Name and briefly describe each.
6. What is vicarious liability?
7. What is a rebuttable presumption? An irrebuttable presumption?
8. Can corporations and other associations be guilty of crimes?
9. Distinguish mens rea from motive.

Problems & Critical Thinking Exercises

1-6. Many prisoners in the state and federal correctional systems are held at minimum-security "farms." Only inmates considered not to be dangerous are housed at these facilities because of the minimal security. In fact, in many cases it is possible for inmates to simply walk off. Of course, most do not leave the premises, because to do so results in an increased sentence (either due to a conviction for escape or a decrease in "good time") and a likelihood that the sentence will be spent in prison rather than the more desirable farm. Despite this practice, prisoners of these facilities do escape. Problems 1 through 6 present several different sets of facts involving a fictitious inmate, Spike Vincelli. Read each problem and discuss the defenses, if any, that Spike may have against a charge of escape. Discuss each in light of the following two statutes:

Statute I
It shall be unlawful for any person committed to any correctional facility to escape from that facility. Escape is defined as passing beyond the borders of a facility with an intent to never return or being lawfully beyond the borders of the facility and not returning when required to do so with an intent to never return. Violation of this statute constitutes a felony.

Statute II
It shall be unlawful for any person committed to any correctional facility to leave the premises of the facility. Leaving is defined as passing over the boundary lines of the facility. Violation of this statute constitutes a misdemeanor.

1. On June 21, Spike Vincelli received a telephone call from a hospital informing him that his mother had been involved in a serious accident. That evening, Spike left to see his mother, intending to return in the morning.
2. On June 21, Spike Vincelli had his first epileptic seizure. The seizure caused Spike to fall outside the boundary line surrounding the facility.
3. On June 21, Spike Vincelli decided that he was bored with living on the farm. That night he walked off the premises and fled for a friend's house 300 miles away, intending never to return.
4. On June 21, Spike Vincelli became involved in a fight with Ben Ichabod. In a fit of rage, Ben picked Spike up and threw him over the fence surrounding the farm. Spike was caught outside the fence by a guard before Spike had an opportunity to return.

5. In early April, Spike Vincelli decided that he was going to escape. He developed a plan that called for him to leave in July and meet his brother, who was passing through the area. As part of the plan, Ben Ichabod, a fellow inmate, was enlisted to pick Spike up off the ground and throw him over the fence that surrounded the facility. However, Ben, who is not very bright, threw Spike over the fence on June 21.

6. On June 21, Spike Vincelli became involved in a fight with Ben Ichabod. Ben, in a fit of rage, picked Spike up and threw him over the fence surrounding the facility. While outside the fence, Spike became overcome with a sense of freedom and ran from the facility.

7. Fred failed to show up for a date he had made with Penni. Penni, who was angered by Fred's actions, decided to vent her anger by cutting the tires of Fred's automobile. However, Penni did not know what make of automobile Fred drove and mistakenly cut the tires of a car owned by Fred's neighbor, Stacey. Penni is now charged with the "purposeful destruction of personal property." Penni claims that her act was not purposeful because she did not intend to cut the tires of Stacey's car. Discuss this defense.

8. William, an experienced canoeist, was hired by a Boy Scout troop to supervise a canoe trip. While on the trip, two boys fell out of their canoe and began to drown. William watched as the boys drowned. Is William criminally liable for the deaths?

9. Sherri, who was near bankruptcy, decided to burn her house down and make an insurance claim for the loss. Sherri started the fire, which spread to a neighbor's house located 20 feet from Sherri's home. Unknown to Sherri, her neighbor was storing massive quantities of dynamite in the home. The fire at the neighbor's house spread to the room where the explosives were being stored, and the resulting explosion caused such vibrations that a construction worker one block away fell off a ladder and subsequently died from the fall. Sherri is charged with arson and murder. She has pled guilty to arson but maintains that she is not liable for the death of the worker. Is she correct?

10. The following statute was enacted by State Legislature:

    It shall be unlawful for any person to be a pedophile. Pedophilia is defined as a condition where a person over the age of 17 years possesses a sexual desire for a person under the age of 8 years.

    While attending a group therapy session, Jane admitted that she had sexual interest in boys under 8 years of age. A member of the group contacted the local police and reported Jane's statement. Jane was subsequently arrested and charged with violating the quoted statute. Discuss her defenses, if any.

11. Ashley, Amy, and Karen are roommates in college. They occupy a four-bedroom apartment, and all share in the bills and household duties. One weekend, a friend of Karen's, Janice, came to visit. Janice arrived on Thursday and was scheduled to stay until Monday. She stayed in the extra bedroom. On Thursday evening, Ashley discovered, while she was watching Janice unpack, that Janice had a significant amount of cocaine in one suitcase. Later that night, Ashley discussed this matter with Karen, who stated, "I'm sure she does—why does it matter to you?" Ashley immediately confronted Janice and told her that she would have to remove the cocaine from the premises or Ashley would call the police. Janice picked up the suitcase, carried it to her car, and placed it in the trunk. The next morning, when Karen learned what Ashley had done, Karen encouraged Janice to bring the suitcase back into the apartment. On Sunday morning, the police arrived with a warrant to search the apartment. The search uncovered the suitcase in the extra bedroom. Later, at the police station, the suitcase was opened and the drugs were discovered. All four women were charged with possession. Do Amy, Ashley, or Karen have a defense? The jurisdiction where they live applies the Model Penal Code.

12. In some nations, vicarious criminal liability is much broader than in the United States. For

example, parents may be vicariously liable for the criminal acts of their children until the children reach adulthood. Should such laws be adopted in the United States? Explain your answer.

13. Develop your own fact scenarios, one demonstrating specific intent and another demonstrating general intent. Explain why each is an example of specific intent or general intent.

14. Using the two fact scenarios you created in problem 13, change the facts so the general-intent crime becomes a specific-intent crime and the specific-intent crime becomes a general-intent crime.

Endnotes

1. J. Goldstein, et al., *Criminal Law: Theory and Process* (New York: Free Press, 1974).

2. 21 Am. Jur. 2d, *Criminal Law* 129 (1981).

3. *See United States v. Birkenstock*, 823 F.2d 1026 (7th Cir. 1987); *United States v. Pompanio,* 429 U.S. 10 (1976).

4. LaFave & Scott, *Criminal Law* (Hornbook Series, St. Paul: West, 1986), at 217.

5. LaFave & Scott at 34.

6. Gary Fields and John R. Emshwiller, *As Federal Crime List Grows, Threshold of Guilt Declines, The Wall Street Journal*, September 27, 2011.

7. *See Lambert v. California*, 355 U.S. 225 (1957), in which the United States Supreme Court found that a strict liability statute was violative of the due process clause of the United States Constitution.

8. LaFave & Scott at 244–45.

9. *United States v. Dotterweich,* 320 U.S. 277 (1943).

10. *United States v. Freed,* 401 U.S. 601 (1971).

11. For a thorough discussion of mens rea and public welfare rationale see J. Manly Parks, The Public Welfare Rationale: Defining Mens Rea in RCRA, 18 Wm. & Mary Envtl. L.& Pol'y Rev. 219 (1993), http://scholarship.law.wm.edu/wmelpr/vol18/iss1/6

12. *United States v. Dotterweich,* 320 U.S. 277 (1943).

13. Jeffrey P. Cogin, *Corporations Can Kill Too: After Film Recovery, Are Individuals Accountable for Corporate Crimes*, Loyola of Los Angeles Law Review 19 (1986): 1411, 1413-1414, http://digitalcommons.lmu.edu//llr/vol19/iss4/12

14. Model Penal Code § 2.07 deals with liability of corporations and unincorporated associations.

15. For more on the original cases, see Cogin, *infra*. For the reversals, see *People v. O'Neil, 194 Ill. App.3d 79,* 550 N.E.2d 109 (1990). The convictions of the individuals were reversed and remanded for retrial on appeal. The defendants pled guilty to involuntary manslaughter to avoid retrial. William Presecky, *2 Bosses*

Plead Guilty in 83 Death of Plant Worker, Chicago Tribune, September 8, 1993, http://articles.chicagotribune.com/1993-09-08/news/9309080122_1_charles-kirschbaum-job-related-death-film-recovery-systems

16. *See* Jeffrey S. Parker, "Criminal Sentencing Policy for Organizations: The Unifying Approach of Optimal Penalties," 26 *Am. Cr. Law R.* 513 (1989).

17. For more on this case, see Francis T. Cullen, William J. Maakestad, and Gray Cavender, *Corporate Crime under Attack: The Ford Pinto Case and Beyond* (Cincinnati: Anderson Publishing, 1987). See also G. Schwartz, "The Myth of the Ford Pinto Case," 43 *Rutgers Law R.* 1013 (1991).

18. Arthur Andersen v. United States, 544 U.S. 696 (2005)

19. Model Penal Code § 2.02, General Requirements of Culpability.

20. Kaplan & Weisberg, *Criminal Law* (Boston: Little, Brown, 1986).

21. Model Penal Code § 2.02(2)(c).

22. The Model Penal Code actually recognizes three "objective elements" that may have differing culpability levels. Those are circumstance, result, and conduct. Also, the Code provides, at § 2.02(4), that one mental state shall apply to an entire offense, unless a contrary intent is plain.

23. Model Penal Code § 2.01.

24. *Id.*

25. *King v. Cogdon* (Vict. 1950).

26. A. Loewy, *Criminal Law*, 2nd ed. (Nutshell Series) (St. Paul: West, 1987).

27. *Robinson v. California,* 370 U.S. 660 (1962).

28. Model Penal Code §2.01(4).

29. Tim Rohan, *Sandusky Gets 30 to 60 Years For Sexual Abuse, New York Times,* October 8, 2012, http://www.nytimes.com/2012/10/10/sports/ncaafootball/penn-state-sandusky-is-sentenced-in-sex-abuse-case.html

30. O.R.C. sec. 2921.22.

31. *Gebhard v. State*, 484 N.E.2d 45, 48 (Ind. Ct. App. 1985).

CHAPTER 4

CRIMES AGAINST THE PERSON

Chapter Outline

Chapter Objectives

After completing this chapter you should be able to:

- list, explain, and compare the elements of common law and contemporary crimes against the person, such as murder, rape, and assault.

- list, explain, and compare the common defenses to charges of crimes against the person, such as self-defense.

- identify and analyze contemporary legal issues concerning death and suicide.

- identify the material facts and legal issues in 1/3 of the cases you read.

STUDYING CRIMES

In the next three chapters you will learn about many crimes. It would be impossible to include a discussion of all crimes. The federal government and each city and state have their own unique laws. What follows is a discussion of the major crimes recognized, in some form, in most jurisdictions. The crimes have been categorized as crimes against the person, crimes against property, and crimes against the public. Although it is common to make these distinctions, do not concern yourself with understanding why these classifications have been made; they are used only for organizational purposes. In a sense, all crimes are offenses against the public in the United States. That is why the public prosecutes crimes, and private individuals may not. Also, any offense "against property" is actually injuring a person, not the property. A stolen iPod set does not long to be returned to its rightful owner. However, the rightful owner does feel wronged and desires the return of the stolen item. In a sense, the classifications are often accurate in that they describe the focus of the criminal conduct. The focus of a thief's act is property; hence, a crime against property. The focus of a rapist's attack is a human; hence, a crime against a person.

All of the following crimes have been broken into parts. Each part of a crime is an **element** of that crime. At trial, every element of a crime must be proven beyond a reasonable doubt by the prosecution. If any element is not proven beyond a reasonable doubt, the accused must be found not guilty. The rule requires that each element be proved individually. That is, if a crime consists of six elements, and a jury is convinced that five have been proven, but cannot say that the sixth has been proven beyond a reasonable doubt, then there must be a not-guilty verdict. This is true even if the jury was solidly convinced that all the other elements were true and generally believed that the defendant committed the crime. Later you will learn more about the standard for determining guilt beyond a reasonable doubt.

Finally, you may notice that, often, if one crime has been proven, all the elements of a related lesser crime can also be proved. For example, if a defendant is convicted of murdering someone with a hammer, he has also committed a battery of the victim. In such circumstances, the lesser offense merges into the greater offense. This is the **merger** doctrine. Under this doctrine, both crimes may be charged; but if the defendant is convicted of the more serious crime, the lesser is absorbed by the greater, and the defendant is not punished for both. If acquitted of the greater charge, the defendant may be convicted of the lesser.

element

■ A basic part. For example, some of the *elements* of a cause of action for battery are an intentional, unwanted physical contact. Each of these things ("intentional," "unwanted," etc.) is one "element."

merger of offenses

■ When a person is charged with two crimes (based on exactly the same acts), one of which is a lesser included offense of the other. The lesser crime *merges* because, under the prohibition against double jeopardy, the person may be tried for only one crime.

HOMICIDE

Homicide is the killing of one human being by another. Not all homicides are crimes. It is possible to cause another person's death accidentally, that is, accompanied by no mens rea. For example, if a bridge builder lost her balance and fell against a coworker, causing the coworker to fall to his death, no crime has been committed, but there has been a homicide.

Criminal homicide occurs when a person takes another's life in a manner proscribed by law. The law proscribes more than intentional killings. Under the Model Penal Code, purposeful, knowing, negligent, and reckless homicides may be punished.

sidebar

CRIME STATISTICS

There are many different ways to measure crime. Some methods, such as observation and experimentation, are impractical, or even more, immoral. The federal bureau of investigation collects crime data from police departments all over the United States. These data are compiled and reported yearly under the title *Uniform Crime Reports*. Although a good comprehensive source of crime data since 1929, UCR data have some flaws. The most significant flaw concerns underreporting. Many crimes are not reported to the police. Even when a crime is reported, most police agencies report only the most serious offense committed. Hence, many crimes go unreported by individuals and police agencies. Also, because UCR data are aggregate data, no detail about the number of victims, offenders, or offenses per incident are provided. To remedy some of these problems, there is an ongoing effort to redesign the ucr system. This effort, known as the National Incident-based Reporting System (NIBRS), asks local law enforcement officers to move beyond aggregate data to providing information about each criminal incident.

Since 1991, colleges and universities that receive federal monies have been required to collect statistics on campus crime. The Campus Security Act requires that the collected data be made available to current and prospective faculty, staff, and students.

The second major system of crime data collection is the National Crime Victimization Survey, administered by the U.S. Census Bureau on behalf of the U.S. Department of Justice. The NCVS is a large random survey of U.S. households. Respondents are asked whether they have been victimized by one or more of the listed violent and nonviolent crimes. The NCVS touts an impressive 95 percent response rate to its survey. The NCVS has its flaws as well. Some victims, particularly of certain crimes, are reluctant or ashamed to report the crime. Also, some people may not know that they have been victimized (e.g., embezzlement or fraud).

UCR data are often used in this text. For additional information, NCVS data should be examined. Also, most local and state law enforcement agencies and courts have data available that are not provided by either the UCR or NCVS, such as data on arrests and crimes not included in the UCR or NCVS systems.

Sources: The FBI's UCR reports can be found in many locations, including *http://www.fbi.gov/ucr/ucr.htm*. NCVS data can be found in many locations, including *http://www.ojp.usdoj.gov/bjs*

Exhibit 4–1 CRIME CLOCK 2011

2011 CRIME CLOCK STATISTICS

A Violent Crime occurred every	**26.2 seconds**
One Murder every	36.0 minutes
One Forcible Rape every	6.3 minutes
One Robbery every	1.5 minutes
One Aggravated Assault every	42.0 seconds
A Property Crime occurred every	**3.5 seconds**
One Burglary every	14.4 seconds
One Larceny-theft every	5.1 seconds
One Motor vehicle Theft every	44.1 seconds

Copyright © Cengage Learning®.

Source: US FBI, Uniform Crime Reports (2012)

The mens rea part of homicide is important. The determination of what mens rea was possessed by the defendant (actually, what mens rea can be proven by the prosecution) will usually determine what crime may be punished. At common law, various forms of murder were developed. This is where we begin.

Homicide and the Common Law

Initially, at common law, all murders were punished equally: the murderer was executed.[1] Over time, the value of proportional punishment developed and homicides were eventually divided into murder and manslaughter with differentiated punishment. Manslaughter was punished by incarceration, not death.

Murder, at common law, was defined as (1) the unlawful killing of a (2) human being with (3) malice aforethought. It was the requirement of malice aforethought that distinguished murder from manslaughter. Although malice aforethought was defined differently among the states, the following types of homicide became recognized as murder under the common law:

1. When the defendant intended to cause the death of the victim.
2. When the defendant intended to cause serious bodily harm, and death resulted.

3. When the defendant created an unreasonably high risk of death that caused the victim's death, regardless of the defendant's mens rea. This was known as "depraved-heart murder."
4. When the doctrine of felony-murder was applicable.

All criminal homicides that did not constitute murder were treated as manslaughter. Today, nearly every jurisdiction further divides murder into degrees, and most divide manslaughter into voluntary and involuntary. Few jurisdictions rely on the common-law definition of malice aforethought. However, many states continue to recognize felony-murder.

The Felony-Murder Doctrine

Cole Allen Wilkins committed a burglary of a home that was under construction. He loaded several appliances stolen during the burglary into the bed of a pickup truck. Sixty-two miles away from the burglarized home, a stove that Wilkins' had loaded into the truck fell onto the interstate. Wilkins left the stove on the road, and later a driver was killed when he swerved into the path of an oncoming vehicle in an attempt to avoid hitting the stove. Wilkins was charged and convicted of a crime that developed a long time ago, first-degree felony murder. You will learn more about his appeal in a moment, after you are introduced to this old crime.

At common law, one who caused an unintended death during the commission (or attempted commission) of any felony was guilty of murder. This became known as **felony-murder.** Under the early common law all felonies were punished by death. Generally, most of the crimes that were felonies under the common law posed a threat to human life. This threat was one justification for the harshness of the rule. However, as the common law developed, many new crimes were created, many of which did not involve serious threat to human life. For this reason the felony-murder doctrine was very harsh, as it applied to all felonies regardless of their relative dangerousness to human life. In time, courts began to limit the application of the rule to specified felonies—those perceived as posing the largest threat to human life. It was common to apply the rule to rape, mayhem, arson, kidnapping, and robbery.

For example, Grace and Eva decided to rob the First National Bank. They agreed to use whatever amount of violence is necessary to carry out the robbery. During the robbery a bank teller summoned the police by use of a silent alarm. As Grace and Eva were leaving the bank, the police shouted to them, ordering their surrender. Grace then fired a shot from her gun and fatally wounded a police officer. Using the felony-murder rule, both Grace and Eva are criminally liable for the death of the police officer, even though Eva did not fire the weapon or conspire with Grace to kill the officer.

The felony-murder rule acts to impute the required mens rea to the defendant and to create a form of vicarious liability between cofelons. The rule imputes mens rea because it applies in situations of unintended death; however, murder in the first degree is a specific-intent crime. The rationale is that one who engages in inherently dangerous crimes should be aware of the high risk to human life created by the crime. Vicarious liability is also imposed in some states; that is, all the individuals involved in the perpetration of the crime may be criminally liable for the resulting death.

Wrong!

felony-murder rule

■ The principle that if a person (even accidentally) kills another while committing a felony, then the killing is murder.

Today, most states have felony-murder statutes. Generally, the following requirements must be proven to establish a felony-murder:

1. The defendant must have been engaged in the commission, or attempted commission, of a named felony, and
2. during the commission, or attempted commission, of that felony a death occurred, and
3. there is a causal connection between the crime and the death.

In most jurisdictions the legislature has specified the crimes that must be committed, or attempted, for the rule to apply. A few jurisdictions have limited the application of the rule to crimes that were felonies at common law, and others have limited the rule to felonies that involve a threat to human life.

To satisfy the second requirement, it must be determined when the commission of the crime began and when it concluded. This appears to be an easy task, and it is in most cases, but in some instances it is not clear. Suppose that a robber knew that a large sum of money was being transferred between a bank and an armored car at a particular time and intended to steal the money during that transfer. Also assume that on the day of the robbery, the traffic was heavier than anticipated by the robber and, in an effort to arrive at the bank on time, the robber ran a stop sign. While passing through the intersection, the robber struck another vehicle, killing the driver. Was this death during the commission, or attempted commission, of the robbery? What if a police officer were to chase an individual from the scene of a felony and get shot 15 minutes and one mile away from the scene of the crime? Is this during the commission, or attempted commission, of the felony? It is likely that no felony-murder would be found in the first example, because the death was too far removed from actual commission of the crime. The result would be different if the robber struck and killed the motorist while fleeing from the police immediately after commission of the holdup. This answers the second question. Courts have generally held that deaths that occur during the flight of a felon are "during the commission of the felony." However, the chase must be immediate, and the rule does not apply if there is a gap between the time the crime occurred, or was attempted, and the time the chase begins. The third element can be troublesome. In many ways this requirement is similar to the causation requirement discussed in Chapter 3 regarding actus reus. That is, the commission, or attempted commission, of the felony must be the legal cause (proximate cause) of the death. The death must be a "consequence, not coincidence" of the act; the resulting death must have been a foreseeable consequence of the act. So, if a patron of a store suffers a heart attack during a robbery, which was precipitated by the crime, the robbers are guilty of felony-murder if the patron dies. However, if a patron who is unaware of an ongoing robbery suffers a heart attack and dies, the robbers are not liable for the death. The mere fact that the death and the crime occurred simultaneously does not mean that the robbers were the legal cause of the death.

Returning to Defendant Wilkins and the stolen stove, he won reversal of his conviction in 2013 because the Supreme Court of California found the nexus between the death of the motorist and the burglary to be too distant in time and lacking in nexus.[2]

In some states, the act that causes the death of the victim need not be taken by one of the perpetrators of the crime. For example, if Grace and Eva become involved in a shoot-out with the police after they rob the First National Bank, and the police accidentally shoot an innocent bystander, then Grace and Eva are guilty of felony-murder. This is because they began the series of events that led to the death of the bystander. However, if a police officer (or another) kills one of many felons who are jointly involved in the commission of the crime, it is generally held that the other felons are not guilty of felony-murder.[3]

Although the felony-murder rule does impose vicarious liability between cofelons, this aspect is limited. If a defendant can prove that he did not commit the act that caused the death; did not authorize, plan, or encourage the act of his cofelon; and had no reason to believe that his cohort would commit the act, he has a defense to felony-murder in some jurisdictions. Note that the rules concerning parties (principals and accomplices) to crimes may create liability independent of the felony-murder rule. (See Chapter 7 for a discussion of parties to crimes.)

Finally, note that in most jurisdictions that continue to recognize felony-murder, the murder is treated as first-degree murder for the purpose of sentencing. Other statutes provide that felony-murders that occur during named felonies are to be treated as first-degree murder and that murders during "all other felonies" are to be treated as second-degree murder. Even if the statute that creates this "all other felony" category does not expressly state that the felony must involve a danger to human life, it is common for courts to impose the requirement.

In the *Losey* case, a defendant appealed his conviction of involuntary manslaughter and aggravated burglary. The Ohio Court of Appeals applied a statute that read, "No person shall cause the death of another as a proximate result of the offender's committing or attempting to commit a felony." The statute named the crime involuntary manslaughter. The case is interesting from a causation perspective. Read the case and decide for yourself if the defendant should be punished for the death that occurred.

STATE V. LOSEY
23 Ohio App. 3d 93, 491 N.E.2d 379 (1985)

Defendant testified that he approached a house located at 616 Whitehorne Avenue shortly after 11:00 P.M. on November 25, 1983; that he knocked at the front door and, upon receiving no response, forced open the door and proceeded to attempt to remove a bicycle. His friend, who had been waiting outside, yelled that a car was slowly approaching. The defendant then placed the bicycle beside the front door and departed, leaving the front door open behind him. James Harper, the owner of 616 Whitehorne Avenue, testified that he heard a noise at approximately 1:00 A.M. Shortly thereafter, his mother, with whom he resided, appeared at his bedroom door inquiring about the noise. They proceeded together to the living room, whereupon they discovered the open front door and the bicycle standing near the

(continued)

STATE V. LOSEY *(continued)*

door. James Harper stated that he told his mother to go back to her bedroom while he went to check the rest of the house. After so checking, he returned to the living room and was calling the police when his mother appeared in the hallway looking very upset and then collapsed. He called an emergency squad, which attempted to revive Mrs. Harper for almost an hour when the squadmen pronounced her dead. Prior to the burglary, Mrs. Harper had returned from bingo at approximately 10:00 P.M. that evening and had gone to bed. Based on these facts, the trial court found defendant guilty of aggravated burglary and involuntary manslaughter.

■ ■ ■

The doctor's testimony established that defendant's conduct was a cause of Mrs. Harper's death in the sense that it set in motion events which culminated in her death. However, it still must be determined whether defendant was legally responsible for her death—whether the death was the proximate result of his conduct. It is not necessary that the accused be in a position to foresee the precise consequence of his conduct; only that the consequence be foreseeable in the sense that what actually transpired was natural and logical in that it was within the scope of the risk created by his conduct. . . .

By the same token, in this case, the causal relationship between defendant's criminal conduct and Mrs. Harper's death was not too improbable, remote, or speculative to form a basis for criminal responsibility. Although the defendant did not engage in loud or violent conduct calculated to frighten or shock, his presence was nevertheless detected by Mrs. Harper. . . . [Conviction affirmed.]

Misdemeanor Manslaughter

Similar to the felony-murder rule, one may be guilty of misdemeanor manslaughter if a death results from the commission of a misdemeanor, not a felony. Conviction of misdemeanor manslaughter results in liability for manslaughter, often involuntary manslaughter, and not murder.

Just as the felony-murder doctrine has been limited in recent years, so has the crime of misdemeanor manslaughter. This is due largely to the significant increase in the creation of nonviolent crimes by legislatures and administrative bodies. Many states require that the misdemeanor be *malum in se*, and crimes that are *malum prohibitum* cannot be a basis for misdemeanor manslaughter. Requiring that the misdemeanor have a mens rea element is another limitation; that is, strict liability crimes may not be the basis for misdemeanor manslaughter. There is a trend to reject the misdemeanor manslaughter rule (as there is with the felony-murder rule) and require that one of the four types of culpability recognized by the Model Penal Code (purposeful, knowing, negligent, or reckless) be present before imposing liability.

Statutory Approaches to Homicide

Although the common law recognized only one form of murder, most states now divide murder into degrees; most often into first and second degrees. **First-degree murder** is the highest form of murder and is punished more severely than second-degree murder. **Second-degree murder** is a higher crime than manslaughter.

first-degree murder

■ The highest form of homicide. The killing of another person with malice and premeditation, cruelty, or done during the commission of a major felony is typically murder in the first degree.

second-degree murder

■ Murder without premeditation.

First- and Second-Degree Murder

For a murder to be of the first degree, the highest crime, it must be shown that the homicide was willful, deliberate, and premeditated. Generally, first-degree murder applies whenever the murderer has as a goal the death of the victim. *Willful,* as used in first-degree murder, is a specific-intent concept. To be willful, the defendant must have specifically intended to cause the death.

Deliberate is usually defined as "a cool mind, not acting out of an immediate passion, fear, or rage." The term *premeditated* means "to think beforehand." Similar to *deliberate*, it eliminates impulsive acts from the grasp of first-degree murder. It is commonly said that there must be a gap in time between the decision to kill and the actual act. Of course, the length of the gap is the critical issue. Most courts hold that the gap in time must be "appreciable." Again, this term does little to define the length of time. The fact is that courts differ greatly in how they define *appreciable*. There are many reported cases where a lapse of only seconds was sufficient.[4] Some courts have held that all that need be shown is that the defendant had adequate time to form the intention before taking the act; the length of time is not determinative of the question.[5]

In *State v. Snowden*, the defendant appealed his conviction of first-degree murder, claiming that he lacked premeditation. As such, he should have been convicted of second-degree murder, not first-degree. Decisions such as this obscure the difference between first- and second-degree murder. Do you agree with the Idaho Court that there can be premeditation even if there is "no appreciable space of time between the intention to kill and the act of killing"? Note that the facts of this case did not require mention of the prior case where it was held that "no appreciable" time has to be shown. The fact that the autopsy evidenced that the murder occurred after the victim suffered torture would justify a murder conviction under the statute.

STATE V. SNOWDEN
79 Idaho 266, 313 P.2d 706 (1957)

Defendant Snowden had been playing pool and drinking in a Boise pool room early in the evening. With a companion, one Carrier, he visited a club near Boise, then went to nearby Garden City. There the two men visited a number of bars, and defendant had several drinks. Their last stop was the HiHo Club.

Witnesses related that while defendant was in the HiHo Club he met and talked to Cora Lucyle Dean. The defendant himself said he hadn't been acquainted with Mrs. Dean prior to that time, but he had "seen her in a couple of the joints up town." He danced with Mrs. Dean while at the HiHo Club. Upon departing from the tavern, the two left together.

In statements to police officers, that were admitted to evidence, defendant Snowden said after they left the club Mrs. Dean wanted him to find a cab and take her back to Boise, and he refused because he didn't feel he should pay her fare. After some words, he related:

> She got mad at me, so I got pretty hot and I don't know whether I back handed her there or not. And,

we got calmed down and decided to walk across to the gas station and call a cab.

They crossed the street, and began arguing again. Defendant said: "She swung and at the same time she kneed me again. I blew my top."

Defendant said he pushed the woman over beside a pickup truck which was standing near a business building. There he pulled his knife—a pocket knife with a two-inch blade—and cut her throat.

The body, which was found the next morning, was viciously and sadistically cut and mutilated. An autopsy surgeon testified the voice box had been cut, and that this would have prevented the victim from making any intelligible cry. There were other wounds inflicted while she was still alive—one in her neck, one in her abdomen, two in the face, and two on the back of the neck. The second neck wound severed the spinal cord and caused her death. There were other wounds all over the body, and her clothing had been cut away. The nipple of her right breast was missing. There was no evidence of sexual attack on the victim; however, some of the lacerations were around the breasts and vagina of the deceased. . . .

[M]urder is defined by statute as follows:

All murder which is perpetrated by means of poison, or lying in wait, torture, or by any other kind of willful, deliberate and premeditated killing, or which is committed in the perpetration of, or attempt to perpetrate arson, rape, robbery, burglary, kidnapping, or mayhem, is murder in the first degree. All other murders are of the second degree.

The defendant admitted taking the life of the deceased.

The principal argument of the defendant pertaining to [the charge of premeditated murder] is that the defendant did not have sufficient time to develop a desire to take the life of the deceased, but rather his action was instantaneous and a normal reaction to the physical injury which she dealt him. . . .

There need be no appreciable space of time between the intention to kill and the act of killing. They may be as instantaneous as successive thoughts of the mind. It is only necessary that the act of killing be preceded by a concurrence of will, deliberation, and premeditation on the part of the slayer, and, if such is the case, the killing is murder in the first degree.

In the present case, the trial court had no other alternative than to find the defendant guilty of willful, deliberate, and premeditated killing with malice aforethought in view of the defendant's acts in deliberately opening up a pocket knife, next cutting the victim's throat, and then hacking and cutting until he had killed Cora Lucyle Dean. . . .

Note that the statute mentioned in *Snowden* to describe first-degree murder is used by many jurisdictions. Those murders that result from poisoning, follow torture, or are traditional felony-murders are often designated first-degree murder. Following the attacks of September 11, 2001, some states amended their statutes to include deaths resulting from terrorist activity in the classification of first degree murders.[6] Second-degree murder is commonly given the negative definition "all murders that are not of the first degree are of the second." Second-degree murders differ from first in that the defendant lacked the specific intent to kill or lacked the premeditation and deliberation element of first-degree murder.

HOMICIDE IN THE UNITED STATES

There was one murder in the United States every 36 minutes in 2011. A total of 14,612 people were murdered or the subject of a nonnegligent manslaughter in 2011, a 10% decrease from 2002. This was 4.7 of every 100,000 persons in the United States. Most people are murdered with guns, primarily handguns. Knives, poisons, fists, and other weapons are also used to commit homicides.

Source: Uniform Crime Reports, U.S. Department of Justice, Federal Bureau of Investigation, 2012.

Intent to Do Serious Bodily Harm and the Deadly Weapon Doctrine

One method of reducing a murder from the first-degree to the second-degree is by proving that the defendant did not intend to kill but only intended to cause the victim serious bodily harm. Note that if the defendant intended less than serious bodily harm, the crime is either manslaughter or a form of reckless or negligent homicide.

In this area, inferences are important. Juries (or judges, if the court is acting as the finder of fact) are permitted to view the facts surrounding the murder and determine what the defendant's state of mind was when the act occurred. A jury may conclude from the facts that the defendant did intend to cause the death of the victim and convict the defendant of first-degree murder. If a jury concludes that the defendant did not intend to cause the death of the victim, but that the defendant did intend to cause serious bodily injury, then the crime is second-degree murder.

A related inference used in murder cases is the *deadly weapon doctrine*. This rule permits juries to infer that a defendant intended to kill his or her victim if a **deadly weapon** was used in the killing. Being an inference, this conclusion does not have to be drawn; it is a decision for the fact finder. If a jury were to conclude that a defendant's use of a deadly weapon indicated that murder was intended, then a first-degree murder conviction would be warranted. So, if Gwen intended only to injure Fred by shooting him, but Fred died because of the wound, then a jury could convict Gwen of first-degree murder. Of course, the jury could reject the inference if they believed that Gwen did not intend to kill Fred, and in that case either second-degree murder (if her intent was to inflict serious bodily injury) or manslaughter would be appropriate.

Any device or item may be a deadly weapon if, from the manner used, it is calculated or likely to produce death or serious bodily injury.[7] The Model Penal Code defines a deadly weapon as "any firearm, or other weapon, device, instrument, material, or substance, whether animate or inanimate, which in the manner it is used or is intended to be used is known to be capable of producing death or serious bodily injury."[8] Under these definitions, some items that are not normally considered deadly may be deadly weapons if their use is calculated to cause serious bodily injury or death. The opposite is also true; some items that are normally considered deadly may not be, if used

deadly weapon

■ Any instrument likely to cause serious bodily harm under the circumstances of its actual use. Such things as a fan belt used to choke a man and a fire used to burn an occupied house have been called *deadly weapons* by courts.

Exhibit 4–2   CIRCUIT COURT/CRIMINAL DIVISION

```
                              CIRCUIT COURT
STATE OF WISCONSIN          CRIMINAL DIVISION        MILWAUKEE COUNTY
- - - - - - - - - - - - - - - - - - - - - - - - - - - - - - - - - - -
STATE OF WISCONSIN, Plaintiff                       INFORMATION

          vs.                          CRIME(S):
                                       See Charging Section Below
Jeffrey L. Dahmer    05/2[?]60         STATUTE(S) VIOLATED
924 N. 25th St.                        See Charging Section Below
Milwaukee, WI                          COMPLAINING WITNESS:
                                       Donald Domagalski
               Defendant,              CASE NUMBER:
                                       F-912542
- - - - - - - - - - - - - - - - - - - - - - - - - - - - - - - - - - -
```

I, E. MICHAEL MC CANN, DISTRICT ATTORNEY FOR MILWAUKEE COUNTY, WISCONSIN,
HEREBY INFORM THE COURT THAT THE ABOVE NAMED DEFENDANT IN THE COUNTY OF
MILWAUKEE, STATE OF WISCONSIN,

COUNT 01: FIRST DEGREE MURDER

COUNT 12: FIRST DEGREE INTENTIONAL HOMICIDE

on or about June 30, 1991, at **924 North 25th Street**, City and County of
Milwaukee, did cause the death of another human being, Matt Turner a/k/a
Donald Montrell, with intent to kill that person contrary to Wisconsin
Statutes section 940.01(1).

Upon conviction of each count of First Degree Intentional Homicide and each
count of First Degree Murder, Class A Felonies, the penalty is life
imprisonment.

DATED   E. MICHAEL MC CANN
                                       DISTRICT ATTORNEY

_____9/10/91_____   E. Michael McCann
                                       District Attorney

                                           Jeffry T. Dahmer
                                              9.10.91

  Jeffry T. Dahmer 9.10.91
  x The statement on page   (3)
  I is accurate as it applies
  to this pg
        Jeffry T. Dahmer
             9.10.91
```

*Source:* http://law2.umkc.edu/faculty/projects/ftrials/mcveigh/mcveighcertif.html
```

in a manner that does not pose a threat of serious harm or death. Hence, a bowling ball may be transformed from a recreational device into a deadly weapon when it is used to crush a person's skull. A gun, probably the most obvious example of a deadly device, may not be deemed deadly if used to hit someone over the head. A person's hands and feet are not normally deadly weapons. However, if it can be shown that the victims were significantly smaller than the defendants or that the defendants were especially expert in the use of their hands to cause injury, then the hands may constitute deadly weapons.

In the *Labelle* case, the inference created by the deadly weapon doctrine was used to affirm a trial court conviction of attempted murder.

LABELLE V. STATE
550 N.E.2d 752 (Ind. 1990)

Appellant waived his right to a jury trial and was tried to the court and found guilty of attempted murder . . . and carrying a handgun without a license. . . .

The evidence produced at trial which tended to support the determination of guilt shows that members of the Outlaws motorcycle gang, who refer to themselves as "brothers," sometimes frequent the Beehive Tavern in Indianapolis. On February 2, 1987, appellant was a patron of the Beehive. He asked Oliphant, the bartender and co-owner of the bar, whether the Outlaws had come into the bar before, and Oliphant informed him that they had. Appellant remained at the Beehive until closing time and returned the next night. By 11:00 P.M., at least three employees and several patrons were in the bar. Three members of the Outlaws, including the victim, Allen Mayes, were there shooting pool. Sometime after 11:00, appellant threw a beer can at the stage, whereupon Oliphant asked him to leave, and appellant spat in his face. Oliphant testified, "[appellant said] that we're going to a funeral[,] to get my brothers together because we were going to a funeral. . . . [Appellant] told me I wasn't worth killing but a few of them—a few people in here were. And he proceeded to walk out the door." Oliphant stated that the three Outlaws were standing by the bar about ten feet from the door as he followed appellant out and that they were in roughly the same place when he came back in. Two or three minutes later, a shot rang out and Mayes was struck in the neck by a bullet and fell to the floor.

Fifteen to twenty minutes after the shooting, appellant was found under a truck which was parked across the street from the Beehive. A crowd which included the victim's two companions stood outside the bar and watched as appellant was being placed under arrest, and one of the Beehive's managers testified that appellant shouted at the two men, "Scumbags, you tell your brothers the angels are on their way[.] I got your brother."

The door to the bar has a diamond-shaped window, which is taped to leave unobstructed only a two- or three-inch peephole. Looking into the bar from the outside, the peephole is approximately five feet, seven inches off the ground. Police found a bullet hole in the taped area to the right of the peephole. . . . [the police] searched the underneath side of the truck and found a .38 caliber revolver on the transmission brace, above the approximate spot appellant's head had been when he was under the truck. . . . [The medical expert] testified that, based on test results, it was his opinion that the bullet in Mayes's neck was from a .38 caliber weapon. . . .

Appellant also claims that there was insufficient evidence of intent to kill to support a conviction for attempted murder. . . . This court held there [in a previous case] that intent may be inferred from the use of a deadly weapon in a manner likely to cause injury or death and upheld the conviction. This Court has repeatedly upheld convictions for murder and attempted murder where the State sought to carry its burden of proof on the issue of intent by producing evidence that the defendant fired a gun in a crowd or at a group of people.

Appellant conceded in his testimony that he did fire a shot at the Beehive, but maintained that he was trying to hit a light over the door to the bar. He testified that he could not see into the bar because of the tape on the window and his distance from the door and that he had no intention of shooting any person, but intended only to aggravate Oliphant. . . .

State of mind can be established by the circumstances surrounding an incident. Appellant questioned the bartender the night before the shooting as to whether the Outlaws frequented the Beehive. . . . The eye-level location of the peephole and the proximity of the bullet hole to it would support an inference that the shot was fired into this inhabited barroom in a manner calculated to strike anyone standing at the bar in the upper body or head. This constitutes utilization of a deadly weapon in a manner likely to cause injury or death. There was sufficient evidence to support the trial court's verdict.

The judgement of the trial court is affirmed.

Communicable Diseases and Murder

Communicable diseases, such as acquired immunodeficiency syndrome (AIDS) and anthrax, raise interesting criminal law situations. First, the intentional transmission of a disease can be criminal. For example, passing a disease to another, if intentional, is either attempted murder, if the disease is not passed to the victim, or murder, if the disease is successfully passed to, and causes the death of, the victim. This was what happened following the September 11, 2001, terrorist attacks on the World Trade Center and Pentagon. One week after the attacks, letters containing deadly anthrax spores were mailed to two U.S. senators and several media outlets. Five people were killed and many more were injured. The attacks led to the largest bioterrorism investigation in U.S. history. The key suspect in the case committed suicide in 2008, as the filing of charges against him became imminent. Although no one was ever charged, the highly contagious nature of the material and the obvious intentionality of the act would have easily supported a high mens rea homicide charge.[9]

Second, the unintentional but criminally negligent or reckless passing of such a disease may also be criminal under negligent manslaughter statutes. Sharing a needle with another, knowing that it has been used by an HIV-infected individual, falls into this category, as does the passing of the disease by a prostitute who knows of her infection to a client.

Third, due to the nature of the disease, it is often not discovered until long after it is contracted, and death may not occur for many years. This poses problems in jurisdictions that continue to follow the year-and-a-day rule or other similar rules.

Fourth, in some situations, defendants have claimed that, because of the low probability of infecting another person, it is a factual impossibility to commit murder using AIDS. Fifth, AIDS may be characterized as a deadly weapon, and therefore, a charge of assault may be elevated to assault with a deadly weapon. Similarly, attacks leading to death may be treated as murder under the deadly weapon doctrine.

In most states, preexisting laws (e.g., murder, attempted murder, and intentional transmission of venereal disease) are relied upon to prosecute AIDS-related crimes. However, a few states have enacted statutes specifically directed at the intentional or negligent transmission of AIDS.

Manslaughter

manslaughter

■ A crime, less severe than murder, involving the wrongful but nonmalicious killing of another person.

At common law, murder was an unlawful killing with malice aforethought. **Manslaughter** was an unlawful killing without malice aforethought. Just as was the case with murder, the common law did not divide manslaughter into degrees. Whenever the states began codifying homicides, it was common for manslaughter to be divided into degrees, commonly referred to as voluntary and involuntary, although a few jurisdictions used first- and second-degree language. Today, many jurisdictions continue to recognize two forms of manslaughter.

The important fact is that manslaughter is a lesser crime than murder; accordingly, it is punished less severely. It is a lesser crime because some fact or facts exist that make the defendant less culpable than a murderer in the eyes of the law. The most common fact that mitigates a defendant's culpability is the absence of a state of mind that society has decided should be punished as murder. Even though society has decided that, because of such extenuating circumstances, a defendant should not be punished as a murderer, it has also decided that some punishment should be inflicted.

Provocation

provocation

■ An act by one person that triggers a reaction of rage in a second person. *Provocation* may reduce the severity of a crime.

Provocation of the defendant by the victim can reduce a homicide from murder to manslaughter. In jurisdictions that grade manslaughter, a provoked killing is treated as the higher manslaughter, whether that provoked killing is called first-degree or voluntary.

The theory of provocation, also known as "heat-of-passion manslaughter," is that a defendant was operating under such an anger or passion that it was impossible for the defendant to have formed the desire to kill, which is required for both first- and second-degree murder. The defense of provocation applies to instances in which people act without thinking, and their impulsive act is the result of the victim's behavior.

Again, an objective test is used when examining the defense of provocation. To prove provocation, it must be shown that the provoking act was so severe that a reasonable person may also have killed. It does not require that a reasonable person would have killed, only that a reasonable person would have been so affected by the act that homicide was possible. A few states have enumerated the acts that may function to negate intent to kill (and reduce the homicide to manslaughter) in their manslaughter statutes. Any act not included may not be used by a defendant to reduce a murder charge.

Catching one's spouse in the act of adultery is an example of an act that is considered adequate provocation to reduce any resulting homicide to manslaughter. This rule applies only to marriages and not to other romantic relationships. Generally, serious assaults (batteries) may constitute adequate provocation.

If two people are engaged in "mutual combat," then any resulting death may be reduced from murder to voluntary manslaughter. The key to this defense is mutuality. If it can be shown that the victim did not voluntarily engage in the fight, then the defense of mutual combat is not applicable, and the defendant is responsible for murder.

It is widely held that words and gestures are never adequate provocation. This is true regardless of how vile or vicious a statement or gesture is to the defendant. However, some recent cases have distinguished statements that are informational from those that are not. In such situations, if a statement provides information of an act, and that act would be sufficient provocation, if witnessed, then the statement may also be provocation.

In the *Schnopps* case, the trial judge refused to instruct the jury on the alternative of manslaughter, as opposed to murder. The trial judge followed the rule that statements are never adequate provocation. The appellate court reversed the judge, holding that the statements made by the defendant's wife directly before he killed her may have been adequate provocation for a jury to find voluntary manslaughter and not murder.

Usually, when claiming adultery as provocation, one must actually have caught his or her spouse in the act. Also, the general rule is that words are not adequate provocation. What did the court do in the *Schnopps* case? It appears that the court attempted to sidestep those rules, in a manner that would permit the benefit of the defense without changing the rules. It did this by holding that in adulterous situations, an admission of adultery to one's spouse, when uttered for the first time, is as shocking as finding one's spouse engaged in the act.

COMMONWEALTH V. SCHNOPPS
383 Mass. 178, 417 N.E.2d 1213 (1981)

On October 13, 1979, Marilyn R. Schnopps was fatally shot by her estranged husband George A. Schnopps. A jury convicted Schnopps of murder in the first degree, and he was sentenced to the mandatory term of life imprisonment. Schnopps claims that the trial judge erred by refusing to instruct the jury on voluntary manslaughter. We agree. We reverse and order a new trial. . . .

Schnopps testified that his wife had left him three weeks prior to the slaying. He claims that he first became aware of the problems in his 14-year marriage at a point about six months before the slaying.

According to the defendant, on that occasion he took his wife to a club to dance, and she spent the evening dancing with a coworker. On arriving home, the defendant and his wife argued over her conduct. She told him that she no longer loved him and that she wanted a divorce. Schnopps became very upset. He admitted that he took out his shotgun during the course of this argument, but he denied that he intended to use it. . . . [The defendant and his wife continued to have marital problems for the next few months.]

On the day of the killing, Schnopps had asked his wife to come to their home and talk over their

(continued)

marital difficulties. Schnopps told his wife that he wanted his children at home, and that he wanted the family to remain intact. Schnopps cried during the conversation and begged his wife to let the children live with him and to keep their family together. His wife replied, "No, I am going to court, you are going to give me all the furniture, you are going to get the Hell out of here, and you won't have nothing." Then, pointing to her crotch, she said, "You will never touch this again, because I have got something bigger and better for it."

On hearing those words, Schnopps claims that his mind went blank, and that he went "berserk." He went to a cabinet and got out a pistol he had bought the day before, and he shot his wife and himself. . . . [Schnopps lived and his wife died.]

Schnopps argues that "[t]he existence of sufficient provocation is not foreclosed absolutely because a defendant learns of a fact from oral statements rather than from personal observation," and that a sudden admission of adultery is equivalent to a discovery of the act itself, and is sufficient evidence of provocation.

Schnopps asserts that his wife's statements constituted a "peculiarly immediate and intense offense to a spouse's sensitivities." He concedes that the words at issue are indicative of past as well as present adultery. Schnopps claims, however, that his wife's admission of adultery was made for the first time on the day of the killing and hence the evidence of provocation was sufficient to trigger jury consideration of voluntary manslaughter as a possible verdict.

The Commonwealth quarrels with the defendant's claim, asserting that the defendant knew of his wife's infidelity for some months, and hence the killing did not follow immediately upon the provocation. Therefore, the Commonwealth concludes, a manslaughter instruction would have been improper. The flaw in the Commonwealth's argument is that conflicting testimony and inferences from the evidence are to be resolved by the trier of fact, not the judge.

Withdrawal of the issue of voluntary manslaughter in this case denied the jury the opportunity to pass on the defendant's credibility in the critical aspects of his testimony. The portion of Schnopps' testimony concerning provocation created a factual dispute between Schnopps and the Commonwealth. It was for the jury, not the judge, to resolve the factual issues raised by Schnopps' claim of provocation.

Reversed and remanded for new trial on the manslaughter issue.

Finally, the defense will not be available if there was a sufficient "cooling-off" period. That is, if the time between the provocation and the homicide was long enough for a defendant to regain self-control, then the homicide will be treated as murder and not manslaughter.

Imperfect Self-Defense and Defense of Others

If Aryana harms Ita while defending herself from Ita's attack, Aryana is said to have acted in self-defense. Self-defense, when valid, normally works to negate criminal liability entirely. So, if Aryana kills Ita to avoid serious bodily harm or death, she has committed an excused homicide. What happens if Aryana was incorrect in her belief that her life was endangered by Ita? This is known as an imperfect self-defense and does not negate culpability entirely. It may, however, reduce liability. Thus, Aryana may be liable only for voluntary manslaughter and not murder. For Aryana to be successful in her claim, she must prove that she had a good-faith belief that her life was in danger and that the killing appeared to be necessary to protect herself.

A person may also have an imperfect self-defense when an excessive amount of force is used as protection. So, if Aryana was correct in her belief that she needed to use force for her protection, but used excessive force, she receives the benefit of reduced liability. Again, there must be a reasonable, although incorrect, belief that the amount of force used was necessary.

The concept of self-defense is extended to the defense of others. So, if Aryana kills Ita while defending Thea and Haris from apparent imminent harm, Aryana is no more liable than if she were defending herself. Just as with an imperfect self-defense, if individuals have a mistaken, but reasonable, belief that another is in danger, and they kill as a result of that belief, they are responsible for voluntary manslaughter rather than murder. Also, if one uses deadly force when a lesser amount of force would have been sufficient to stay the attack, liability is limited to manslaughter, provided that the belief that deadly force was necessary was reasonable under the circumstances.

Involuntary Manslaughter

The lowest form of criminal homicide in most jurisdictions is involuntary manslaughter, sometimes named second-degree manslaughter. In most instances involuntary manslaughter is a form of negligent or reckless manslaughter.

You have already learned the misdemeanor manslaughter rule. In jurisdictions that recognize the rule, the person who commits the misdemeanor that results in an unintended death is responsible for the lowest form of criminal homicide.

Involuntary manslaughter also refers to negligent homicide, vehicular homicide, and similar statutes that punish for unintended, accidental deaths. The classic vehicular homicide is when a motorist runs a red light, strikes another car, and causes the death of the driver or passenger of that automobile. Some states, such as Illinois, make vehicular homicide a separate crime from involuntary manslaughter and impose a lesser punishment for vehicular homicide.[10]

Be aware that many states now have specific statutes dealing with deaths caused by intoxicated drivers. Often the punishment is greater if the death is the result of a drunk or otherwise impaired driver.

The term *negligent* has a different meaning in criminal law than in civil law. In tort law, any unreasonable act that causes an injury creates tort liability. In criminal law, more must be shown. The risk taken by the defendant must be high and pose a threat of death or serious bodily injury to the victim. In addition, some jurisdictions require that the defendant be aware of the risk before liability can be imposed. Of course, knowledge can be inferred from the defendant's actions. Some jurisdictions do not require knowledge of the risk (scienter).

The Model Penal Code Approach to Homicide

The Model Penal Code states, "A person is guilty of criminal homicide if he purposely, knowingly, recklessly, or negligently causes the death of another human being."[11] The Code then classifies all criminal homicides as murder, manslaughter, or negligent homicide. This is done by taking the four mens rea elements (purposeful, knowing, reckless, and negligent) and setting them into one of the classifications. There is some overlap; for example, under some conditions a reckless homicide is murder, and under other conditions it is manslaughter. Let us look at the specifics of the Code.

It is unsurprising that, all purposeful and knowing homicides are murder under the Model Penal Code. Additionally, a reckless homicide is murder when committed "under circumstances manifesting extreme indifference to the value of human life." The Code then incorporates a "felony-murder" type rule, by stating that recklessness and indifference to human life are presumed if the accused was engaged in the commission or attempted commission of robbery, rape, arson, burglary, kidnapping, or felonious escape. So, if the accused are involved in one of those crimes, and a death results, they may be charged with murder under the Code. Note that the Code creates only a presumption of recklessness and indifference, which may be overcome at trial. Murder is the highest form of homicide, and the Code declares it to be a felony of the first degree.

Manslaughters are felonies of the second degree under the Code. All reckless homicides, except those previously described, are manslaughters. As at common law, the Code contains a provision that reduces heat-of-passion murders to manslaughter. Specifically, the Code states that a homicide, which would normally be murder, is manslaughter when it is

committed under the influence of extreme mental or emotional disturbance for which there is reasonable explanation or excuse. The reasonableness of such explanation or excuse shall be determined from the viewpoint of a person in the actor's situation under the circumstances he believes them to be.

Last, negligent homicides are entitled just that. They are felonies of the third degree.

Life, Death, and Homicide

The actus reus of murder and manslaughter is the taking of a human life. Determining when life begins and ends can be a problem in criminal law, especially when dealing with fetuses.

At common law it was not a crime to destroy a fetus, unless it was "born alive." To be born alive, the fetus must leave its mother's body and exhibit some ability to live independently. Some courts have required that the umbilical cord be cut and that the fetus show its independence thereafter before it was considered a human life. Breathing and crying are both proof of the viability of the child.

Today, many states have enacted feticide statutes that focus on the viability of the fetus. Once it can be shown that the fetus is viable—that is, could live independently if it were born—then anyone who causes its death has committed feticide. Of course, this does not apply to abortion. Since the United States Supreme Court decision in *Roe v. Wade*, 410 U.S. 113 (1973), a woman possesses a limited right to abort a fetus she carries. Thus, states may not prohibit abortions that are protected under that decision. The primary purpose of feticide statutes is to punish individuals who kill fetuses without the mother's approval, as occurred in the *Keeler* case (see Chapter 2).

At the other end of the life continuum is death. Medical advances have made the determination of when death occurs more complex than it was only years ago. For a long time, people were considered dead when they ceased breathing and no longer had a heartbeat. Today, artificial means can be used to sustain both heart action and respiration. That being so, should one be free of criminal homicide in cases where the victim is being kept "alive" by artificial means and there is no reasonable hope of recovery? Should a physician be charged with murder for "pulling the plug" on a patient who has irreversible brain damage and is in a coma? Using the respiration and heart-function test, it would be criminal homicide to end such a treatment. However, many states now use brain death, rather than respiration and heartbeat, to determine when life has ended. In states that employ a brain death definition, it must be shown that there is a total cessation of brain function before legal death exists. The importance of defining death is illustrated by the *Fierro* case.

STATE V. DAVID FIERRO
124 Ariz. 182, 603 P.2d 74 (1979)

The facts necessary for a resolution of this matter on appeal are as follows Between 8 and 9 o'clock on the evening of 18 August 1977, Victor Corella was given a ride by Ray Montez and his wife Sandra as they were attempting to locate some marijuana. In the vicinity of 12th Street and Pima, Ray Montez heard his name called from another car. He stopped his car, walked over to the other car and saw that the passenger who had called his name was the defendant Fierro. Defendant told Ray Montez that his brother in the "M," or "Mexican Mafia," had instructed the defendant to kill Corella. Ray Montez told defendant to do it outside the car because he and his wife "did not want to see anything."

Montez returned to his car. Defendant followed and began talking with Corella. Corella got out of the car. Montez started to drive away when defendant began shooting Corella. Corella was shot once in the chest and four times in the head. Following the shooting, Corella's body was taken to the emergency room at Maricopa County Hospital. His blood pressure was very low due to secondary bleeding from the gunshot wound to the chest area. Surgery was performed in an effort to control the bleeding. He was then taken to the surgical intensive care unit, where a follow-up examination and evaluation revealed that he had suffered brain death. Corella was maintained on support systems for the next three days while follow-up studies were completed which confirmed the occurrence of brain death. The supportive measures were terminated and he was pronounced dead on 22 August 1977. . . .

(continued)

STATE V. DAVID FIERRO *(continued)*

CAUSE OF DEATH

At the trial, Dr. Hugh McGill, a surgical resident at the Maricopa County Hospital, testified that:

> After surgery he was taken to the intensive-care unit. He was evaluated by a neurosurgeon who felt there was nothing we could do for his brain, he had brain death. He remained somewhat stable over the next two or three days. We had follow-up studies that confirmed our impression of brain death and because of that supportive measures were terminated and he was pronounced dead, I believe, on the 22nd. . . .

Defendant initially argues that the termination of support systems by attendant doctors three days after Corella suffered "brain death" was the cause of Corella's death [and as such, he could not be responsible for Corella's death]. . . .

By the phrase "unchanged by human action" in Drury, we meant human action that changes or breaks the chain of natural events and of itself causes the death of the victim. In the instant case, the removal of life support systems did not change nor alter the natural progression of the victim's physical condition from the gunshot wounds in the head to his resulting death. There was no change "by human action." . . .

In the instant case, the body of the victim was breathing, though not spontaneously, and blood was pulsating through his body before the life support mechanisms were withdrawn. Because there was an absence of cardiac and circulatory arrest, under the common-law rule, he would not have been legally dead. Under the Harvard Medical School test and Proposal of the National Conference of Commissioners on Uniform State Laws, he was, in fact, dead before the life supports were withdrawn as he had become "brain" or "neurologically" dead prior to that time.

We believe that while the common-law definition of death is still sufficient to establish death, the [brain death test] is also a valid test for death in Arizona. In the instant case, expert testimony was received, which showed that the victim suffered irreversible "brain death" before the life supports had been withdrawn. In effect, the doctors were just passively stepping aside to let the natural course of events lead from brain death to common-law death. In either case, the victim was legally dead for the purpose of the statute. . . .

Suicide

Successful suicide was a crime under the common law of England. The property owned by the one who committed suicide was forfeited to (taken by) the Crown. In early American common law, attempted suicide was a crime, usually punished as a misdemeanor. Today suicide is not treated as a crime. However, it is possible to restrain and examine individuals who have attempted to commit suicide under civil psychiatric commitment laws.

It continues to be criminal to encourage or aid another to commit suicide. In most situations such a commission is treated as murder. Assisting suicide may be treated as murder, or, as in Michigan, it may be a separate crime that is punished less severely.

The most well-known suicide cases involve Dr. Jack Kevorkian of Michigan. Dr. Kevorkian, a physician, assisted 20 terminally ill persons in committing suicide between 1990 and 1994, earning him the nickname Dr. Death.

Dr. Kevorkian's license to practice medicine was suspended in 1991 for his behavior, and criminal charges have been filed against him on several occasions. The first three cases were dismissed because the statute under which he was charged was held unconstitutional.

The Michigan legislature enacted a law in February 1993 that provided for as much as 4 years' imprisonment and a $2,000 fine for providing the physical means by which another attempts or commits suicide or participates in a physical act by which another attempts or commits suicide. The person charged must have had knowledge that the other person intended to commit suicide.[12]

In 1999 Dr. Kevorkian allowed the news program *60 Minutes* to nationally broadcast his act of assisting Thomas Youk to die. However, Dr. Kevorkian went further than he had in previous cases. Rather than providing a machine to the patient that could assist in death, Dr. Kevorkian administered a lethal injection to Mr. Youk. He then challenged Michigan prosecutors to charge him again. They did, and Dr. Kevorkian was convicted of murder and sentenced to 10 to 25 years in prison. He was paroled in 2007 after serving 8 years in prison and died 4 years later.

While Dr. Kevorkian may have gone too far in committing euthanasia, his first three acquittals suggest that there is public support for physician-assisted suicide. In 1997 Oregon enacted the Death With Dignity Act. This law, which decriminalizes physician-assisted suicide under certain circumstances, is the first law of its type in U.S. history.[13] Whether other states will follow Oregon's lead remains to be seen. It will take individual state action to pave the way for physician-assisted suicide, however, since the Supreme Court handed down *Washington v. Glucksberg* (1997).[14] In *Glucksberg* the Court found that terminally ill patients do not possess a privacy or due process right in having physicians assist them in committing suicide. Accordingly, state action is required to recognize the right.

Corpus Delicti

Corpus delicti is a Latin phrase that translates as "the body of a crime." Prosecutors have the burden of proving the corpus delicti of crimes at trial. Every crime has a corpus delicti. It refers to the substance of the crime. For example, in murder cases the corpus delicti is the death of a victim and the act that caused the death. In arson, the corpus delicti is a burned structure and the cause of the fire.

A confession of an accused is never enough to prove corpus delicti. There must be either direct proof or evidence supporting a confession.

In murder cases the corpus delicti can usually be proved by an examination of the victim's corpse. After an autopsy a physician is usually prepared to testify that the alleged act either did, or could have, caused the death. In some instances, the body of a victim cannot be located. Such "no body" cases make the job of the prosecution harder. Even so, if evidence—such as blood stains and discovered personal effects—establishes that the person is dead, then murder may be proven. Of course, the prosecution must also show that the defendant caused the death. So, if a defendant confesses to a murder, or makes other incriminating statements, and no other evidence is found, then no

corpus delicti

■ (Latin) "The body of the crime." The material substance upon which a crime has been committed; for example, a dead body (in the crime of murder) or a house burned down (in the crime of arson).

corpus delicti exists, and the defendant cannot be convicted. However, if blood matching the victim's is discovered where the defendant stated the murder occurred, then a murder conviction can be sustained.

ASSAULT AND BATTERY

assault

■ An intentional threat, show of force, or movement that could reasonably make a person feel in danger of physical attack or harmful physical contact. It can be a crime or tort.

battery

■ An intentional, unconsented to, physical contact by one person (or an object controlled by that person) with another person. It can be a crime or a tort.

Assault and **battery** are two different crimes, although they commonly occur together. As with homicide, all states have made assaults and batteries criminal by statute.

A *battery* is an intentional touching of another that is either offensive or harmful. The mens rea element varies among the states; however, most now provide for both intentional and negligent battery. Of course, negligence in criminal law involves a greater risk than in civil law. To be negligent in criminal law, there must be a disregard of a high risk of injury to another; in tort law, one need only show a disregard of an ordinary risk. The Model Penal Code provides for purposeful, knowing, and reckless batteries. In addition, if one uses a deadly weapon, negligence may give rise to a battery charge. Otherwise, negligence may not provide the basis for a battery conviction.

The actus reus of battery is a touching. An individual need not touch someone with his or her actual person to commit a battery. Objects that are held are considered extensions of the body. If Sherry strikes Doug with an iron, she has battered him even though her person never came into contact with his. Likewise, items thrown at another are extensions of the person who took the act of propelling them into the air. If Doug were to injure Sherry with a knife he threw at her, then he has battered her.

A touching must be either offensive or harmful to be a battery. Of course, any resulting physical injury is proof of harm. The problem arises when one touches another in a manner found offensive to the person being touched, but there is no apparent physical injury. For example, a man who touches a woman's breast without her consent has committed a battery because the touching is offensive. If a person touches another in an angry manner, a battery has been committed, even though the touching was not intended to injure the party and in fact does no harm.

There are two varieties of assault. First, when a person puts another in fear or apprehension of an imminent battery, an assault has been committed. For example, if Gary attempts to strike Terry, but Terry evades the swing by ducking, Gary has committed an assault. The rule does not require that the victim actually experience a physical blow; apprehension of an impending battery is sufficient. Apprehension is simply an expectation of an unwanted event. Also, the threat must be imminent to rise to the level of an assault. A threat that one will be battered in the future is not sufficient. So, if Terry told Gary that he was "going to kick the shit out of him in one hour," there is no assault.

Because an apprehension by the victim is required, there is no assault under this theory if the victim was not aware of the assault. For example, if X swings his arm at Y intending to scare Y, but Y has her back turned and does not see X's behavior, then there is no assault. This is not true of batteries. If X strikes Y, a battery has been committed, regardless of whether Y saw the punch coming.

The second type of assault is an attempted battery. This definition remedies the problem just discussed. Any unsuccessful battery is an assault, regardless of the victim's knowledge of the act. Of course, it must be determined that the act in question would have been a battery if it had been completed.

To prove battery, it must be shown that a contact was made. Making contact is not necessary to prove an assault. However, it is possible to have both an assault and a battery. If John sees Henry swing the baseball bat that strikes John, there has been an assault and battery. However, due to the doctrine of merger, the defendant will be punished only for the higher crime of battery.

Aggravated Assault and Battery

Under special circumstances, an assault or battery can be classified as aggravated. If aggravated, a higher penalty is imposed. The process of defining such crimes as more serious than simple assaults and batteries varies. Statutes may call such crimes aggravated assault or battery; or they may refer to specific crimes under a special name, such as assault with intent to kill; or they may simply use the facts at the sentencing stage to enhance (increase) the sentence; or they may refer to such crimes as a higher assault, such as felony assault rather than misdemeanor assault. In any event, the following facts commonly aggravate an assault or battery.

The assault is aggravated if the assault or battery is committed while the actor is engaged in committing another crime. So, if a man batters a woman while possessing the specific intent to rape her, he has committed an aggravated battery. This is true regardless of whether the rape was completed. If a defendant is stopped before he has committed the rape, but after he has assaulted or battered the victim, there has been an aggravated battery. Hence the crime may be titled "assault with intent to commit rape" or "assault with intent to murder."

It is also common to make assault and battery committed on persons of some special status more serious. Law enforcement officers or other public officials often fall into this category. Of course, the crime must relate to the performance or status of the officer to be aggravated. For example, if an off-duty police officer is struck by an angry neighbor over a boundary dispute, the battery is not aggravated. Examples of other protected classes of individuals are minors and the mentally disabled.

The extent of injury to the victim may also lead to an increased charge. Usually a battery may be aggravated if the harm rises to the level of "serious bodily injury." Some statutes specifically state that certain injuries aggravate the crime of battery, such as the loss of an eye. Mayhem, a related crime, is discussed next.

MAYHEM

mayhem

■ The crime of violently, maliciously, and intentionally giving someone a serious permanent wound. In some states, a type of aggravated assault. Once, the crime of permanently wounding another (as by dismemberment) to deprive the person of fighting ability.

Mayhem, originally a common-law crime, is the crime of intentionally dismembering or disfiguring a person. The crime has an interesting origin. In England, all men were to be available to fight for the king. It was a serious crime to injure a man in such a manner as to make him unable to fight. Early punishments for mayhem were incarceration, death, and the imposition of the same injury that had been inflicted on the victim. Originally, only dismemberment that could prevent a man from fighting for the king was punished as mayhem. As such, cutting off a man's leg or arm was punishable, whereas cutting off an ear was not. Of course, causing a disfigurement was not mayhem.

Today, both disfigurement and dismemberment fall under mayhem statutes. Many jurisdictions specifically state what injuries must be sustained for a charge of mayhem. Causing another to lose an eye, ear, or limb are examples, as is castration.

Some states no longer have mayhem statutes. They have chosen to treat such crimes as aggravated batteries.

SEX CRIMES

This section deals with crimes that involve sex. Keep in mind that crimes such as assault and battery may be sexually motivated. For example, if a man touches a woman's breast, he has committed a battery (provided that the touching was unwelcome).

The term "sex crimes" actually encompasses a variety of sexually motivated crimes. Rape, sodomy, incest, and sexually motivated batteries and murders are included. Obscenity, prostitution, abortion, distribution of child pornography, and public nudity are examples of other sex-related offenses.

Although certain offenses are universally prohibited, other offenses vary among the states. For example, rape is criminal in all states, but prostitution is not.

Rape

rape

■ The crime of imposing sexual intercourse by force or otherwise without legally valid consent.

At common law, the elements of **rape** were (1) sexual intercourse with (2) a woman, not the man's wife (3) committed without the victim's consent and by using force. Many problems were encountered with this definition. First, the common-law definition required that the rapist be a man. Hence, women and male minors could not be convicted of rape. Also, the *marital rape exception* provided that men could not be convicted of raping their wives. Similarly, a man could not be charged with battering his wife if the battery was inflicted in an effort to force sex. This exception was founded upon the theory that when women married they consented to sex with their husbands upon demand. Additionally, many courts wrote that to permit a woman to charge her husband with such a crime would lead to destruction of the family unit. Finally, the last requirement, with force and without consent, led many courts to require victims to resist the attack to the utmost and to continue to resist during the rape.

States have changed the common-law definition of rape to remedy these problems. First, most states have worded their statutes to permit minors and women to be charged with rape. While there are few cases of women actually raping men, or other women, there are several cases where women have been convicted as principals to the crime.[15] The Model Penal Code is gender neutral regarding all sex crimes except rape.[16]

The marital rape exception has been abolished in most states. A few states have retained the rule in modified form; Ohio, for example, provides immunity to a husband except when he is separated from his wife.[17]

Finally, the last requirement has changed significantly. A person need not resist to the extent required under the common law. What is required now is proof that the victim did resist. However, a victim need not risk life or serious bodily injury in an attempt to prevent the rape. So, if a woman simply tells a man on a date, "I don't want

sidebar

RECIDIVISM BY SEXUAL OFFENDERS

Special legislation dealing with sexual predators can be found as early as 1930. In recent years, states have enacted laws requiring treatment after release from prison, monitoring after release, castration as part of sentences, and civil commitment of offenders after release. One reason sexual offenders receive so much attention is the apparent inability to treat and reform them. The recidivism rate of sexual offenders is much higher than that of those who commit other crimes. One study found that rapists and child molesters reported that they had committed five or more sexual offenses for which they had not been arrested. As many as 50 percent of all sexual offenders will reoffend after being released from prison. Within three years of release, 7.7 percent of rapists commit another rape. Nearly one-third of rapists commit some form of violent crime within three years of release.

Contrary to a prevailing myth, a sex offender's likelihood of reoffending does not diminish with age. Some experts believe what is critical is identifying potential sex offenders at an early age. Research has shown that the level of violence committed by sex offenders increases as their acts go undiscovered.

Source: Steven I. Friedland, "On Treatment, Punishment, and the Civil Commitment of Sex Offenders," 70 *U. Colo. L. Rev.* 73 (1999).

to," there has been inadequate resistance. The result would be different if the man produced a gun and told the woman he would kill her if she resisted.

So, the elements of rape, under new statutes, are (1) sexual intercourse (2) with another against that person's will or without that person's consent and (3) by the use of force or under such a threat of force that a reasonable person would have believed that resistance would have resulted in serious bodily harm or death.

Note that one element has not changed—namely, the definition of sexual intercourse. Generally, the contact must be penis-vagina; anal sex, fellatio, and other acts are usually punished under sodomy statutes. The requirement is the same today as it was under the common law. The "slightest penetration" of the woman's vulva is sufficient. The man need not ejaculate.

Some states grade rape according to the extent of injuries that the victim received and whether the victim knew the rapist. The Model Penal Code punishes rape as a felony in the second degree, unless serious bodily injury occurs or the victim was not a social companion of the rapist, in which case the rape is of the first degree.

Nonforcible Rape

statutory rape

■ The crime of having sexual intercourse with a person under a certain state-set age, regardless of consent.

Under some circumstances, one may commit a rape even though the other party consented to the sexual contact. So-called **statutory rape** is such a crime. The actus reus of statutory rape is sexual intercourse with someone under a specified age, commonly 16. The purpose of the law is to protect those the law presumes are too young to make a mature decision concerning sex. Hence, consent is not relevant. So, a rape has occurred when a girl under age 16 consents to sexual intercourse with a male aged 18 or older.

In most states, statutory rape is a strict liability crime. The act of having sex with someone below the specified age is proof alone of guilt. No showing of mens rea is required. A few states impose a knowledge requirement. In those states, if the accused can convince the jury that there was reason to believe that the other party was "of age," then the accused is acquitted. For example, if a 15-year-old girl tells a boy that she is 17, she indeed looks 17, and she shows the boy a falsified identification bearing that age, he would have a defense to statutory rape.

In many states, only females are protected by statutory rape laws. If a boy of 15 years has sex with a girl of 17 years, the law will not punish her as they would the boy if the ages were turned around. It has been alleged that such treatment is violative of the Equal Protection Clause of the U.S. Constitution. The United States Supreme Court has rejected that claim by reasoning that a goal of such statutes is the prevention of teenage pregnancy. Because females can be impregnated, states have a legitimate interest in prosecuting males who have sex with females who are under the age of consent.[18] Using this analysis a state may prosecute males only, as females cannot impregnate young men or women. However, many acts by adult females (or adult males to young males) may be prosecuted under another law, such as child molestation or criminal deviate conduct.

Similar to statutory rape, having sex with those who are incapable of consenting due to mental or emotional disability is also rape.

Sodomy

Sodomy has traditionally been defined as noncoital sex with a member of the opposite sex, sex with a member of the same sex, or sex with an animal. Many statutes now include sodomy in "criminal deviate conduct" statutes. Sodomy is prohibited in most states; and in most jurisdictions fellatio, cunnilingus, bestiality, homosexual activity, anal sex, and sometimes masturbation are included. There is substantial disagreement concerning whether such acts should be prohibited between consenting adults. Those who support sodomy laws usually do so for religious reasons. Those who oppose such laws contend that two adults should be permitted to engage in any sexual conduct they desire, provided that no one is injured. In any event, one practical problem exists; enforcement of sodomy laws is nearly impossible. Determining what sexual acts people engage in privately is not an easy task. Additionally, law enforcement appears to have no incentive to enforce such laws when there appears to be no resulting injury, and there is substantial noncompliance with many sodomy laws, such as fellatio and cunnilingus.

Those who oppose enforcement of sodomy laws between consenting adults do not oppose punishment of those who force acts of sodomy on others. At common law, a man had to have penile-vulva contact to commit rape. If a man forced oral or anal sex on a woman, he committed sodomy. Sodomy was also punished severely. Some states continue to prohibit sodomy, even in marriage. And the Supreme Court upheld such laws until 2003, when it found the prohibition of sex, in any form, between consenting adults in private to be violative of the inherent right to privacy found in the Due Process Clauses in *Lawrence v. Texas*.[19]

Rape Shield Laws

So-called **shield laws** were enacted in the 1970s and 1980s in an effort to protect rape victims from harassment by defense attorneys at trial. Before such laws existed, defense attorneys often would use evidence of a victim's prior sexual conduct to infer that the victim

sodomy

■ A general word for an "unnatural" sex act or the crime committed by such act. While the definition varies, *sodomy* can include oral sex, anal sex, homosexual sex, or sex with animals.

shield laws

■ A state law that prohibits use of most evidence of a rape (or other sexual crime) victim's past sexual conduct at trial.

had consented to the act. It is thought that the humiliation of the rape itself, matched with the threat of harassment at trial, accounted for the nonreporting of many rapes.

To protect victims from unwarranted abuse at trial, rape shield laws were enacted. Evidence of prior sexual conduct, except with the defendant, is not permitted at trial. Also, evidence of a victim's reputation in the community is inadmissible.

Incest

Sex between family members is *incest*, which is a crime. Generally, law enforcement is concerned with abuse of children, although it is also a crime for two consenting adult family members to engage in sex. Often, when an adult family member is involved with a child, other statutes, such as child molestation laws, will also apply.

---

sidebar

DO CIVIL LAW NATIONS BETTER PROTECT VICTIMS OF SEX CRIMES?

The United States is of the Common Law tradition because of its roots in England, where the common law originated. Other examples of Common Law nations include Angola, Australia, Belize, and New Zealand. Many nations fall into the Civil Law tradition, including Angola, France, Italy, Germany, Mexico, Costa Rica, and Venezuela. Common Law nations employ different versions of an adversarial and accusatorial form of adjudicating cases. Civil Law nations employ inquisitorial forms of adjudication. Adversarial forms emphasize truth through contest, that is, two competing parties developing the facts and competing to persuade the court that their versions of the truth are correct. Adversarial systems also highly value the rights of criminal defendants. Inquisitorial systems are less confrontational and more concerned with the truth than with protecting the rights of defendants. So, adversarial systems emphasize both factual and legal guilt, the latter reflecting an expectation that police and prosecutors respect the rights of a defendant in the process. Inquisitorial systems put a premium on factual guilt.

When operationalized, the adversarial system is more adversarial because the rights of a defendant to confront the accusers, to cross-examine witnesses, and to have a public jury trial are paramount and the process is punctuated by specific activities, such as pretrial evidentiary hearings, trial, and sentencing. Trials are highly technical, and rules of evidence are designed to keep unreliable, duplicative, and illegally obtained evidence from juries. Victims possess few or no rights. In inquisitorial systems, on the other hand, a case progresses as a continuous investigation wherein a dossier (case file) is prepared. Both the state and the defendant contribute

sidebar *(continued)*

to development of the dossier. There are few rules of evidence, and it is the dossier that is reviewed for the guilt/innocence determination at trial.

Testifying to a crime can be difficult for anyone, but it is particularly different for many victims of sex crimes. In the past, rape victims in adversarial trials were subjected to harassing cross-examination by defense attorneys, often intended to call their sexual character into question. Although many states in the United States have enacted rape shield laws intended to limit the breadth of what may be examined (e.g., the sexual history of a victim may be explored only if directly relevant), the adversarial system demands that accusers be physically present and subject to examination, in public trials. In the United States this demand in embodied in the Sixth Amendment to the Constitution of the United States and the constitutions of all of the states.

The inquisitorial system, on the other hand, permits written statements (hearsay and inadmissible in the United States) of victims to be included in the dossier. For this reason, at least one scholar has posited that inquisitorial systems are less traumatic to victims of sex crimes.[20] Of course, this reason transcends sex crime victims to all victims, as well as to nonvictim witnesses who are intimidated by courtrooms and defendants.

Inquisitorial systems offer another advantage to victims. They permit victims to directly participate in the process. In many inquisitorial nations, victims are allowed to have counsel and to sue, in the same proceeding, their victims. In adversarial systems, victims must file a separate civil lawsuit to recover any damages resulting from the crime.

The actus reus of incest is intercourse, or other sexual conduct, between family members. Normally, incest laws parallel marriage laws for a definition of *family*. That is, if two people are permitted to marry under state law, then they are also permitted to engage in sex, regardless of marriage. It is common for states to prohibit marriage of individuals of first cousin affinity and closer.

If the incestuous party is a parent, courts often attempt to seek family counseling and therapy rather than incarceration. However, in extreme situations criminal penalties can be severe, and civil remedies allow removal of the child from the home, as well as termination of parental rights.

Sex Offenses Against Children

Most states have a number of statutes specifically aimed at protecting children from sexual abuse and exploitation. Indiana has five statutes that directly pertain to sexual activity with children. Those statutes are as follows:

Indiana Code § 35-42-4-3 Child Molesting

(a) A person who, with a child under twelve (12) years of age, performs or submits to sexual intercourse or deviate sexual conduct commits child molesting, a Class B felony. However, the offense is a Class A felony if it is committed by using or threatening the use of deadly force, or while armed with a deadly weapon, or if it results in serious bodily injury.

(b) A person who, with a child under twelve (12) years of age, performs or submits to any fondling or touching, of either the child or the older person, with intent to arouse or to satisfy the sexual desire of either the child or the older person, commits child molesting, a Class C felony. However, the offense is a Class A felony if it is committed by using or threatening the use of deadly force, or while armed with a deadly weapon.

(c) A person sixteen (16) years of age or older who, with a child of twelve (12) years of age or older but under sixteen (16) years of age, performs or submits to sexual intercourse or deviate sexual conduct commits child molesting, a Class C felony. However, the offense is a Class A felony if it is committed by using or threatening the use of deadly force, or while armed with a deadly weapon.

(d) A person sixteen (16) years of age, or older who, with a child twelve (12) years of age or older but under sixteen (16) years of age, performs or submits to any fondling or touching, of either the child or the older person, with intent to arouse or to satisfy the sexual desires of either the child or the older person, commits child molesting, a Class D felony. However, the offense is a Class B felony if it is committed by using or threatening the use of deadly force, or while armed with a deadly weapon.

(e) It is a defense that the accused person reasonably believed that the child was sixteen (16) years of age or older at the time of the conduct.

(f) It is a defense that the child is or has ever been married.

Indiana Code § 35-42-4-4 Child Exploitation

(b) Any person who knowingly or intentionally:

(1) manages, produces, sponsors, presents, exhibits, photographs, films, or videotapes any performance or incident that includes sexual conduct by a child under sixteen (16) years of age; or

(2) disseminates, exhibits to another person, offers to disseminate or exhibit to another person, or sends or brings into Indiana for dissemination or exhibition matter that depicts or describes sexual conduct by a child under sixteen (16) years of age; commits child exploitation. . . .

(c) A person who knowingly or intentionally possesses:

(1) a picture;

(2) a drawing;

(3) a photograph;

(4) a negative image;

(5) undeveloped film;

(6) a motion picture;

(7) a videotape; or

(8) any pictorial representation; that depicts sexual conduct by a child who is, or appears to be, less than sixteen (16) years of age and that lacks serious literary, artistic, political or scientific value commits possession of child pornography. . . .

Indiana Code § 35-42-4-5 Vicarious Sexual Gratification

(a) A person eighteen (18) years of age or older who knowingly or intentionally directs, aids, induces, or causes a child under the age of sixteen (16) to touch or fondle himself or another child under the age of sixteen (16) with intent to arouse or satisfy the sexual desires of a child or the older person commits vicarious sexual gratification. . . .

(b) A person eighteen (18) years of age or older who knowingly or intentionally directs, aids, induces, or causes a child under the age of sixteen (16) to:

(1) engage in sexual intercourse with another child under sixteen (16) years of age;

(2) engage in sexual conduct with an animal other than a human being; or

(3) engage in deviate sexual conduct with another person . . . commits vicarious sexual gratification. . . .

Indiana Code § 35-42-4-6 Child Solicitation

A person eighteen (18) years of age or older who knowingly or intentionally solicits a child under twelve (12) years of age to engage in:

(1) sexual intercourse;

(2) deviate sexual conduct; or

(3) any fondling or touching intended to arouse or satisfy the sexual desires of either the child or the older person; commits child solicitation. . . .

Indiana Code § 35-42-4-7 Child Seduction

(e) If a person who is:

(1) at least eighteen (18) years of age; and

(2) the guardian, adoptive parent, adoptive grandparent, custodian . . . of a child at least sixteen (16) years of age but less than eighteen (18) years of age; engages in sexual intercourse or deviate sexual conduct with the child, the person commits child seduction. . . .

Note that statutory rape falls under the child molestation statute in Indiana. Also, the defense of a good-faith and reasonable belief that a child is of statutory age is recognized by statute.

The number of people charged with committing sex crimes against children is increasing. Many of those charged are nonbiological guardians. This trend has led to statutes such as Ind. Code § 35-42-4-7, "Child seduction," which was added to Indiana's sex offenses statutes in 1987.

Megan's Laws, Commitment, and Castration

In New Jersey in 1994, Megan Kanka, a 7-year-old girl, was kidnapped, raped, and murdered by a recidivist sex offender who had been released from prison. In response, New Jersey enacted what has become known as Megan's Law. The statute requires sex offenders to register with local law enforcement agencies. These agencies, in turn, make the registration information available to the public.

Today, every state has some form of Megan's Law.[21] In some states, registration is required and the information is not generally available. In other states, the public may request the information. And in others, law enforcement officials are required to disseminate the information. The rapid adoption of such laws by the states is due in part to the federal government. In 1996 a federal statute became effective that encouraged the states to adopt such laws and threatened loss of federal funds to those states that did not participate.[22]

In addition to registration and notification laws, some states have turned to civil or regulatory law to control sex offenders. Kansas law, for example, provides for the civil commitment of sexual predators who are "mentally abnormal" or suffer a "personality disorder," who lack control over their behavior, and who pose a danger to others. The law may be applied to any individual who meets these standards, regardless of whether charged, convicted, or previously punished. The Supreme Court found this law constitutional in *Kansas v. Hendricks* (1997).[23]

Subsequently in the 2002 case *Kansas v. Crane*,[24] the Court again reviewed the Kansas law against a challenge that it violates due process to require anything less than total loss of control. The Court rejected this theory while reaffirming the *Hendricks* requirement of some loss of control.

A similar Washington state statute was upheld by the Supreme Court in *Seling v. Young* (2001).[25] The Court reasoned that the law is not criminal in nature, it is regulatory, and there is a long history of civil detention of individuals who are both mentally ill and dangerous. Federal law also provides for the civil commitment of sex offenders who are released from federal prison. The Supreme Court upheld the law against federalism challenges in 2010 in *United States v. Comstock*.[26]

Critics allege that these laws are unconstitutional efforts by states to bypass the criminal justice system by using civil commitment to punish sexual offenders. They also contend that individuals are not being punished for their actual behaviors but for their status. While the Supreme Court rejected these claims in the *Hendricks* case, it also emphasized that only individuals who are both mentally ill and dangerous may be committed and that the state must prove these elements in an adversarial hearing by at least clear and convincing evidence.

California has one of the most aggressive offender mental illness programs in the nation. The California Mentally Disordered Offender program (MDO) requires all corrections inmates to be screened for illness. If illness is found, inmates receive treatment while in prison. At the end of a prison term, an inmate is examined, and if determined to have a severe mental disorder that poses a danger to others, treatment is ordered as a condition of parole. Treatment is residential until an offender is determined to be no longer dangerous. Parolees in the MDO program are entitled to annual review and a hearing to determine dangerousness.

So-called chemical castration is also used to control sex offenders. Drugs such as Depo-Provera are used to inhibit the sex drive and sexual function of male sex offenders. Actual surgical castration is provided for by Texas law in lieu of taking the drugs. Texas leaves the choice to the offender. Castration is criticized for not addressing the underlying motivation of sex crimes—the need to control others. It is argued that castration will only lead to the commission of some other form of violent crime.[27]

KIDNAPPING AND FALSE IMPRISONMENT

Kidnapping

Kidnapping was a misdemeanor at common law, although it was regarded as a very serious crime, often resulting in life imprisonment. Felonies were often punished by death at the early common law. Today kidnapping is a felony and carries a harsh penalty in most states. Additionally, if the kidnapping takes the victim across state lines, the crime is a violation of the Federal Kidnapping Act.[28] The federal government, usually the Federal Bureau of Investigation, may become involved in any kidnapping 24 hours after the victim has been seized, by virtue of the Federal Kidnapping Act, which creates a presumption that the victim has been transported across state lines after that period of time.[29]

The elements of kidnapping are (1) the unlawful (2) taking and confinement and (3) asportation of (4) another person (5) by use of force, threat, fraud, or deception.

The taking of the victim must be unlawful. Thus, arrests made by police officers while engaged in their lawful duties are not kidnappings. Neither is it kidnapping for a guardian to take a ward from one place to another, as long as the action is lawful. However, when officers, or others, act completely without legal authority, they may not be shielded from liability.

There must be a taking and confinement. Confinement is broadly construed. If Pat puts a gun to Craig's back and orders him to walk a half mile to Pat's home, there has been a confinement. Generally, there must be a restriction of the victim's freedom to take alternative action.

This taking and confinement must occur as a result of threat, force, fraud, or deception. Of course, Pat's gun in the example is ample threat to satisfy this requirement. Deception may also be used to gain control over the victim. For example, if Jon convinces his estranged wife to enter a house under the pretense of discussing their marital difficulties and then locks the door, he has fraudulently gained control over her.

Finally, there must be an asportation of the victim. *Asportation* means movement. The issue of the amount of movement necessary to meet this requirement is the most controversial question concerning kidnapping as a crime. The Model Penal Code and

kidnapping

■ Taking away and holding a person illegally, usually against the person's will or by force.

most states now hold that if the kidnapping is incidental to the commission of another crime, there is insufficient asportation; some courts speak in terms of a movement of a "substantial distance."[30] To be incidental, a kidnapping must simply be a product of an intent to commit another crime. If a bank robber orders a teller to move from her window to the safe to fill a bag with money, four of the elements of kidnapping are present; however, the third element, asportation, has not been established because the movement was only incidental to the robbery. The result may be different if the teller was ordered to move to the safe for the purpose of raping her. The issue of substantial distance was raised in *Commonwealth v. Hughes*. In that case the court focused on whether the movement substantially increased the risk of harm to the victim.

Many statutes specifically state that if the acts of asportation and confinement occur in furtherance of named crimes, then there is a kidnapping. Such statutes commonly include kidnapping for ransom, political reasons, rape, and murder. It is also common to upgrade kidnappings for these reasons. One type of kidnapping that is usually graded low is the taking of a child by a parent in violation of a court order.

Parental Kidnapping

With a dissolution of marriage comes the separation of property owned by the couple, as well as a custody order if the couple has children. Often, costly and bitter custody disputes are also the result of divorce. In recent years "childnapping," or kidnapping of one's own child in violation of a custody order, has received much public attention.

---

sidebar

AMBER ALERTS

In 1996 Amber Hagerman, age 9, was kidnapped while riding her bicycle. Her abductor murdered her. In response, local news agencies, concerned citizens, and local law enforcement agencies partnered to create a public notification system of abducted children. Because time is critical in child abduction cases, the system is intended to provide expeditious and widespread notification of abductions. At the initiation of President George W. Bush, Congress enacted a national Amber Alert system in 2003. Although named for Amber Hagerman, AMBER is also an acronym for America's Missing: Broadcast Emergency Response. Today, all 50 states are participants in the system and various methods of disseminating the alerts are used, including radio, telephone, television, leaflets, and websites. Beginning in 2012, a national wireless system was established to text, free of charge, Amber Alerts to wireless users. The U.S. Department of Justice reports that hundreds of children have been recovered as a result of the AMBER system.

COMMONWEALTH V. HUGHES
399 A.2d 694 (Pa. Super. Ct. 1979)

The appellant approached the victim, Ms. Helfrich, who was seated on a park bench.] Appellant asked Ms. Helfrich if she wanted to go for a ride or smoke some marijuana with him. When Ms. Helfrich refused, appellant left. Minutes later, the appellant returned, placed a sharp kitchen knife to her throat, and stated, "I think you are going for a ride." Appellant forced Ms. Helfrich to walk to his car one and one-half blocks away and threatened to kill her if she resisted. Once in the car, he drove around the Media area in a reckless manner for approximately two miles and stopped his car in an abandoned lot surrounded by trees. He then forced Ms. Helfrich into the wooded area where he raped her. . . .

"A person is guilty of kidnapping if he unlawfully removes another a substantial distance, under the circumstances, from the place where he is found or if he unlawfully confines another for a substantial period in a place of isolation" . . . .

The framers of the Model Penal Code were aware of the experience of other jurisdictions when they drafted the model kidnapping statute. They recognized that "[w]hen an especially outrageous crime is committed there will be a public clamor for the extreme penalty and it is asking too much of public officials and juries to resist such pressures" . . . . To combat the undesirable situation of charging kidnapping to obtain a higher permissible sentence, the framers of the Model Penal Code drafted the kidnapping statute restrictively. . . . The drafters made explicit their "purpose to preclude kidnapping convictions based on trivial changes of location having no bearing on the evil at hand."

Drawing from the experience of other jurisdictions, the comments to the Model Code, and the fact that the Pennsylvania statute is similar to the Model Penal Code statute of kidnapping, it is clear to us that the legislature intended to exclude from kidnapping the incidental movement of a victim during the commission of a crime which does not substantially increase the risk of harm to the victim.

Turning to the case at hand, we find that the movement of the victim was not a trivial incident to the other crime charged. Although the victim was removed only a distance of 2 miles, the wooded area to which she was brought was in an isolated area, seemingly beyond the aid of her friends and police. Under the circumstances, two miles is a substantial enough distance to place the victim in a completely different environmental setting removed from the security of familiar surroundings. (In addition, the movement itself seriously endangered the victim as she was subject to a knife poised at her throat and to the reckless driving of appellant. At one point, appellant drove onto a one-way street in the wrong direction.) . . . Accordingly, the conviction is sustained.

Due to the rise in the number of such acts, new statutes specifically aimed at parental kidnapping have been adopted. The federal government entered this arena in 1980 by enacting the Parental Kidnapping Prevention Act.[31] Although this statute does not concern itself with criminal sanctions for childnapping, it does require that all states respect child custody orders of other states. That is, a person cannot escape a court order concerning custody of the child by kidnapping the child and fleeing to another jurisdiction. Interestingly, the federal government has left the actual punishment of parental kidnapping to the states. The federal kidnapping act specifically excludes such acts from its reach. Thus, kidnapping by a parent must be punished in a state court.

This may occur in the state from which the child is taken or in any state where the parent takes the child.

Kidnapping of one's own child is often punished less severely than other kidnappings. This is sensible because many childnappings do not create a risk to the child's welfare; rather, they are the result of an overzealous, loving parent or a parent who is trying to hurt the other parent. Obviously, the crime should be punished because of the harm to the custodial parent, but the crime does not have the same evil motive a kidnapping with an intent to rape or murder does.

False Imprisonment

false imprisonment

■ The unlawful restraint by one person of the physical liberty of another.

The crime of **false imprisonment** is similar to kidnapping, and in fact all kidnappings involve a false imprisonment. The opposite is not true. Not all false imprisonments are kidnappings. A false imprisonment occurs when (1) one person (2) interferes (3) with another's liberty (4) by use of threat or force (5) without authority. The primary distinction between the two crimes is the absence of asportation as an element of false imprisonment.

Today, some states have one statute that encompasses both false imprisonment and kidnapping. Such statutes are drafted so that the crime is graded, often elevating the crime if the motive is ransom, rape, serious bodily injury, or murder.

STALKING

stalking

■ The crime of repeatedly following, threatening, or harassing another person in ways that lead to a legitimate fear of physical harm. Some states define *stalking* more broadly as any conduct with no legitimate purpose that seriously upsets a targeted person, especially conduct in violation of a protective order.

In recent years, **stalking** has been the subject of considerable media, public, and legislative attention. Public awareness of stalking increased when prominent public figures who were the victims of stalkers, including politicians, actors, and law enforcement officials, began to speak out.

Stalking posed unique problems to law enforcement officials, prosecutors, and judges. Before 1990, no state had a law specifically aimed at combating stalking. Therefore, preexisting criminal laws, such as assault, battery, and threats, as well as the use of restraining orders, were relied upon in dealing with stalkers. But these laws proved ineffective. Often there is no assault, battery, or provable threat until the victim has been injured or murdered. Even when one of these crimes could be proven, sentences were short. Restraining orders also proved to give victims little protection.

In response to the growing public interest in stalking, California enacted the nation's first stalking law in 1990. By 1993, another 46 states had enacted similar laws.[32]

Stalking laws vary in their elements, but most include a list of acts that satisfy the actus reus of the crime. These include following, harassing, threatening, lying in wait, or conducting surveillance of another person. Usually, one act does not amount to stalking; rather, there must be a pattern or scheme of acts. The first statutes had as a mens rea element a specific intent to cause emotional distress, or to invoke fear of bodily injury or death. However, this has proven ineffective, as stalkers, who are often suffering from emotional or mental illness, often do not have a specific intent to cause fear or harm, even though either or both of these are likely to result. Many states, such as Washington, have remedied this by lowering the mens rea to actual or constructive knowledge. As long as the stalker should have known that the victim would suffer distress or fear, the mens rea satisfies this breed of stalking law. Through these laws, the police may intercede before violence occurs.

Even before stalking laws, many states criminalized harassment. Personal harassment, telephone harassment, and other specific forms of harassment are commonly included in these laws. However, as mentioned earlier, these statutes were not effective in stopping stalkers, primarily because of the short sentences violators usually received.

Cyberstalking

A new type of stalker has emerged in the recent past, the cyberstalker. **Cyberstalking** is the crime of using communication technology to transmit obscene, abusive, or harassing language intended to harass or threaten another person. Because of the impersonal and seemingly anonymous nature of electronic communications, it is both easier and safer to harass other persons than it has been in the past. In recent years, stalking using another person's identity has increased. Known as "spoofing," this crime has two victims: the individual receiving the messages and the individual whose identity has been stolen.

Both state and federal statutes exist that criminalize cyberstalking. For example, the Communications Decency Act, 47 U.S.C. § 223(a)(1)(A), provides for criminal prosecution of any person who "by means of a telecommunications device knowingly makes, creates, or solicits, and initiates the transmission of any comment, request, suggestion, proposal, image, or other communication which is obscene, lascivious, filthy, or indecent, with the intent to annoy, abuse, threaten or harass another person." Another federal statute, 18 U.S.C. § 875(c), makes it a federal crime to "transmit [ ] in interstate or foreign commerce any communication containing any threat to kidnap any person or any threat to injure the person of another." Other federal and state laws that were originally intended to apply to telephone harassment may apply as well.

The federal government extended its reach over stalking in 18 U.S.C. §2261(A) to include "harassment" and the use of computers to commit stalking. That statute makes criminal the act "to kill, injure, harass, or place under surveillance with intent to kill, injure, harass, or intimidate, or cause substantial emotional distress to a person" using "mail, any interactive computer service, or any facility of interstate or foreign commerce. . . ."

However, any time speech is criminalized, there is a First Amendment free speech issue. Statute 47 U.S.C. § 223(a)(1)(A) and similar statutes have been challenged as overbroad because they prohibit not only obscene speech, which clearly may be regulated, but also "indecent" speech that is intended to annoy. The jury is still out on this question.[33]

Although the Supreme Court has not spoken on the issue, lower courts have. In *United States v. Cassidy,* a federal trial court found the defendant's offensive tweeting to be protected by the First Amendment's free speech guarantee.

Cyberstalking

■ Cyberstalking is the crime of using communication technology to transmit obscene, abusive, or harrassing language intended to harass or threaten another person.

UNITED STATES V. CASSIDY
814 F. Supp.2d 574 (D.C. District of Maryland 2011)

The Indictment in this case alleges that the Defendant, William Lawrence Cassidy, violated a federal stalking statute, 18 U.S.C. § 2261A(2)(A), when, with the intent to harass and cause substantial emotional distress to a person in another state, he used an interactive computer service to engage in a course of conduct that caused substantial emotional distress to a person whose initials are A.Z. by posting messages on www.Twitter.com and other Internet websites. . . .

[According to the FBI agent who investigated] A.Z. is an enthroned tulku or reincarnate master who was enthroned in 1988 as a reincarnate llama. Following the enthronement ceremony, the Supreme Head of this particular Sect of Buddhism renamed the center where A.Z. taught as Kunzang Odsal Palyou Changchub Choling ("KPC" or the "Center"). KPC was designated as the Supreme Head's seat in the West, and A.Z. is believed by members of the KPC to be the only American-born female tulku. . . .

[According to the FBI agent] Defendant, who was then known as William Sanderson, befriended one of the monks of the KPC in 2007; he claimed he was also a Buddhist American tulku and expressed an interest in meeting A.Z. Those close to A.Z. encouraged her to meet with Defendant. Thereafter, A.Z. invited Defendant to join her at her retreat in Arizona and Defendant asked to ride alone with her in her vehicle. While in the vehicle, Defendant proposed to A.Z., and she declined. He also asked her to pretend they were married. A.Z. confided in Defendant and shared details of her personal life, including the sexual abuse she had endured as a child and particulars of the failed relationship with her ex-husband. In response, Defendant asked A.Z. if she wanted him to kill her ex-husband, and A.Z. requested that her ex-husband not be harmed.

[The FBI agent's] affidavit also alleges that when Defendant claimed to have Stage IV Lung Cancer, members of the KPC took care of him, as if these were his final days. At that time, it came to light that Defendant's real name was William Cassidy. KPC members and A.Z. also began to notice that Defendant's conduct was inconsistent with this Sect's teachings. For example, he would gossip even though the Sect considers gossip offensive. These incidents led A.Z. to investigate Defendant's lineage to assess whether he was in fact a tulku.

Despite these concerns, however, KPC promoted Defendant in February 2008 to the position of Chief Operating Officer of KPC. Defendant held this position for only 2 weeks. On February 23, 2008, A.Z. learned that Defendant was never a tulku and confronted him. Defendant immediately left the retreat, taking with him a Buddhist nun, Nydia Alexandra. The [FBI agent's] affidavit asserts that, in the wake of his departure, the Defendant used Twitter and logs to harass KPC and A.Z. . . . [The court explained that tweets and blogs are not messages to specific individuals. They are the equivalent of a colonial bulletin board.] . . . the Twitter account "Vajragurl" frequently posts tweets.

As of July 5, 2010, over 350 tweets were posted on "Vajragurl" that allegedly were directed at A.Z. KPC believes that all but a few hundred of the alleged 8,000 tweets on the "Vajragurl" account pertain to A.Z. and KPC. [Defendant posted these posts anonymously and, while critical of A.Z. when written about her directly, they were not threatening. There were many disturbing posts concerning violence that were not specifically directed at A.Z., and when read in conjunction with the posts specifically about A.Z., her sect, and beliefs, were offensive or harassing to her.]

Defendant's tweets and blog postings have caused A.Z. substantial emotional distress. She fears for her own safety and that of her fellow KPC members. As a result of the alleged harassment,

UNITED STATES V. CASSIDY *(continued)*

A.Z. has not left her house for a year and a half, except to see her psychiatrist. A.Z. was in such fear for her safety that she did not go to an October 2010 retreat. . . .

[T]he First Amendment protects speech even when the subject or manner of expression is uncomfortable and challenges conventional religious beliefs, political attitudes or standards of good taste. . . . Indeed, the Supreme Court has consistently classified emotionally distressing or outrageous speech as protected, especially where that speech touches on matters of political, religious, or public concern. This is because "in public debate our own citizens must tolerate insulting, and even outrageous, speech in order to provide 'adequate' 'breathing space' to the freedoms protected by the First Amendment'" . . . .

Even though numerous court decisions have made a point to protect anonymous, <u>uncomfortable</u> speech and extend that protection to the Internet, not all speech is protected speech. There are certain "well-defined and narrowly limited classes of speech" that remain unprotected by the First Amendment. . . . [I]t is clear that the Government's Indictment is directed at protected speech that is not exempted from protection by any of the recognized areas just described. First, A.Z. is a well-known religious figure who goes by the names Alyce Zeoli or Catherine Burroughs. Martha Sherrill, a *Washington Post* journalist wrote a critical nonfiction book about A.Z. entitled *The Buddha from Brooklyn* (Random House 1st ed. 2000). Second, although in bad taste, Mr. Cassidy's tweets and blog posts about A.Z. challenge her character and qualifications as a religious leader. And, while Mr. Cassidy's speech may have inflicted substantial emotional distress, the Government's Indictment here is directed squarely at protected speech: anonymous, uncomfortable Internet speech addressing religious matters.

Tellingly, the Government's Indictment is not limited to categories of speech that fall outside of First Amendment protection – obscenity, fraud, defamation, true threats, incitement or speech integral to criminal conduct. Because this speech does not fall into any of the recognized exceptions, the speech remains protected. . . .

Here, A.Z. had the ability to protect her "own sensibilities simply by averting" her eyes from the Defendant's blog and not looking at, or blocking his tweets. [The court distinguished posts from telephone calls, which are directed at specific individuals.]

[The court dismissed the indictment against Defendant.]

CIVIL RIGHTS AND HATE CRIMES

The federal and state governments have enacted laws criminalizing acts that encroach upon an individual's civil liberties. It is a crime against the United States for <u>two or more</u> persons to conspire to injure, oppress, threaten, or intimidate a person for exercising a federally secured right.[34]

In addition, any person acting pursuant to state law or authority (under color of law) who deprives a person of a federally secured right due to alienage, race, or color is guilty of a federal civil rights crime.[35] Because of the "color of law" requirement, defendants are usually state or local officials. It was under this statute that the police officers who beat Rodney King in Los Angeles were tried and convicted in federal court.

CRIME IN THE UNITED STATES

There were 6,222 reported incidents involving 7,254 hate crimes in the United States in 2011. Of these crimes, 47% were racially motivated, 20% were motivated by religious beliefs, 21% by sexual orientation, 12% by ethnicity, 1% by disability, and a few were attributable to multiple factors. Most of these crimes were committed against the person, with intimidation and assault being the most common offense. A sizeable minority of hate offenses were committed against property, private and public.

Source: Uniform Crime Reports, Hate Crime Statistics, U.S. Department of Justice, Federal Bureau of Investigation, 2012.

sidebar

In addition to criminal remedies, victims may seek civil remedies under a separate civil rights statute.[36] States have similar civil rights laws.

So-called hate crimes laws have become popular in recent years. By 1993, 49 states had enacted hate crimes statutes.[37] Although commonly referred to as hate crime laws, most of these statutes do not actually declare an act criminal; rather, they are sentence enhancements for crimes in which the motive was the victim's race, ethnicity, religion, or other factor.

Florida's hate crime law reads as follows:

Evidencing prejudice while committing offense; enhanced penalties

(1) The penalty for any felony or misdemeanor shall be reclassified as provided in this subsection if the commission of such felony or misdemeanor evidences prejudice based on the race, color, ancestry, ethnicity, religion, sexual orientation, or national origin of the victim:

  (a) A misdemeanor of the second degree shall be punishable as if it were a misdemeanor of the first degree.
  (b) A misdemeanor of the first degree shall be punishable as if it were a felony of the third degree.
  (c) A felony of the third degree shall be punishable as if it were a felony of the second degree.
  (d) A felony of the second degree shall be punishable as if it were a felony of the first degree.

[The statute then provides for civil remedies to victims in subsection 2.]

(3) It shall be an essential element of this section that the record reflect that the defendant perceived, knew, or had reasonable grounds to know or perceive that the victim was within the class delineated herein.[38]

Hate crimes laws have been attacked on First Amendment grounds as violating a person's right to expression. Clearly, a statute that makes a person's beliefs, and the expression of those beliefs, criminal is unconstitutional. But the Supreme Court has upheld statutes that enhance sentences when otherwise prohibited acts are taken because of a prejudicial motive. For example, a state cannot make it illegal to hate a particular ethnic group. Further, with few exceptions (e.g., fighting words), the state may not regulate a person's First Amendment right to express hatred of a particular group. But if the person's beliefs motivate a criminal act, such as a trespass or battery, then the sentence for that crime may be enhanced. See Chapter 9 for a more thorough review of the First Amendment aspects of hate crime legislation.

Ethical Considerations

CAN AN OUTSPOKEN RACIST JOIN THE BAR?

Matthew F. Hale graduated from the Southern Illinois University School of Law in 1988 and passed the Illinois bar exam in the same year. However, he was not admitted to membership because the Illinois Bar authority questioned whether he was morally fit to be an attorney. Like all bar authorities, the Illinois Bar requires more than competence, as proved by passing the bar exam, to join the bar. It also requires good moral character and fitness. Hale's character was questioned by the Committee on Character and Fitness of the Illinois Bar because he was discovered to be a vocal and vehement racist. This was the first time since 1950 that the Illinois Bar had denied the admission of an applicant because of moral character. In that case, the applicant was denied admission because he was alleged to be a communist, and he refused to respond to an inquiry about his support for the Communist Party when asked by the Bar. Although he went on to be a law professor, Hale lost his appeal, eventually at the Supreme Court of the United States; therefore, he never obtained admission to the Illinois Bar.

At Hale's appeal of the decision of the Committee on Character and Fitness to an appeals panel of the Bar, examples of the depth of his hatred for black people and Jewish people and his disruptive and disrespectful protests were presented, as well as evidence that he lied to the Bar, had been arrested for assault and battery, failed to disclose a minor conviction in his application, and evidence that he had been suspended by his undergraduate college (Bradley University) for violating its policies, including referring to a member of the University community as "Jew Boy." Also, he wrote the following response to a woman who supported affirmative action:

Your comments appearing in the Saturday, July 22nd issue of *The Journal Star* were as pathetic as they were asinine. When in the hell are people of your ilk

(continued)

Ethical Considerations (continued)

going to face the fact that the nigger race is inferior in intellectual capacity. And I underline inferior. You have examples all around you, and yet you continue to cling to the misbegotten equality myth, which is not only destroying our universities but also our whole country. Is it going to take your rape at the hands of a nigger beast or your murder before you become aware of the problem. . . . I'm looking forward to the day when our people's eyes are opened and when people who believe in the equality myth no longer have any power to promote this garbage to others.

The appellate panel also discovered that one of Hale's past girlfriends had obtained a protective order against him because of his verbal abuse. His membership in the World Church of the Creator (WCOTC) was also significant. The doctrine of the church, which he led for a time as its Pontifex Maximus, asserts that the Jewish race is inferior, is an enemy of the church, and called for the destruction of all Jews. The church's beliefs about all nonwhites were similar. Although not emphasized by Hale for fear of turning away white member prospects, WCOTC doctrine also assaulted Christianity. Significant to the Bar was the church's requirement that Hale put his race above all other loyalties. Through his role as Pontifex Maximus, he preached racial hatred to both congregants and others.

Although Hale insisted that he could separate his beliefs from his duties as an attorney, he lost on appeal. The Bar concluded that he was not fit for a variety of reasons. One rule, for example, requires attorneys not to discriminate against those in the legal system because of sex, race, religion, or national origin. The Bar reaffirmed his First Amendment right to hold and express his racist beliefs—but not as an officer of the court. His beliefs were likely not enough to justify his exclusion from the Bar. It was the combination of the extremity of his beliefs when accompanied with his apparent disregard for the law, as evinced by his prior conduct, that excluded him from membership.

Two days after Hale's appeal was denied, a member of WCOTC began a two-day shooting spree. He ultimately killed two and injured nine people. He focused his deeds on racial minorities. The shooter committed suicide at the end of his killing spree. Hale indicated that the shooter was angry about the Bar's decision and said other violence could occur if he was not admitted to the Bar. Later, law enforcement officers would acquire a recording of Hale laughing about the spree and the lives that were taken.

Eventually, Hale also lost his appeal to the Illinois Supreme Court, and he was never admitted to the Bar. Subsequently, the WCOTC found

Ethical Considerations *(continued)*

itself embroiled in a trademark battle with another church that claimed WCOTC had stolen its name. Enraged at the judge in the case for ordering the WCOTC to stop using the name, Hale planned the judge's murder. The plot was discovered before the judge was harmed, and Hale was charged with soliciting the murder of the judge. He was convicted of soliciting the murder (and three counts of obstruction of justice) and sentenced to 40 years in prison in 2005.

Sources: Emelie East, "The Case of Matthew F. Hale: Implications for First Amendment rights, social mores and the direction of bar examiners in an era of intolerance of hatred," 13 *Geo. J. Legal Ethics* 741 (2000); the process and the Hale quote are from this source.

Anti-Defamation League (*http://www.adl.org/learn/ext_us/Hale.asp? xpicked=2&item=6*); the information on the trademark case and Hale's conviction are from this source.

⌐ Web Links

Legislative Information

Washburn Law School maintains a comprehensive site that includes state and federal legislative information. Enter through http://www.washlaw.edu. The U.S. Library of Congress also has legislative information on its page at *http://thomas.loc.gov.*

Key Terms

assault	felony-murder	rape
battery	first-degree murder	second-degree murder
corpus delicti	kidnapping	shield laws
cyberstalking	manslaughter	sodomy
deadly weapon	mayhem	stalking
element	merger of offenses	statutory rape
false imprisonment	provocation	

Review Questions

1. What is the primary distinction between first- and second-degree murder?
2. What is felony-murder?
3. What is the difference between an assault and a battery?
4. What is the marital rape exception?
5. John caught his wife having sex with another man. In a fit of rage, he killed his wife. What crime has been committed?
6. What is meant by the phrase "imperfect self-defense"?
7. What is the primary distinction between false imprisonment and kidnapping?
8. Under the common law, if a person cut another's limb off, what crime was committed?
9. Give an example of a nonforcible rape.
10. What was the common-law definition of murder?

Problems & Critical Thinking Exercises

1. State statute reads: "Any act of 1. sexual intercourse 2. with another person 3. against that person's will and 4. by use of force or under such a threat of force that resistance would result in serious bodily injury or death, is rape." Explain how this statutory definition of rape differs from the common-law definition.

2. On May 5, Mark and Sam, who had been neighbors for three years, argued over Sam's construction of a ditch, which diverted water onto Mark's property. Mark told Sam to stop construction of the ditch or he "would pay with his life." The following day, Mark and Sam met again in Sam's garage. Within minutes Mark became very angry and cut Sam's leg with an ax he found in Sam's garage. After cutting Sam he panicked and ran home. Sam attempted to reach a telephone to call for help, but the cut proved fatal.

    Mark has been charged with first-degree murder. He claims that he had no intent to kill Sam; rather, he only intended to hit him on the leg with the dull, flat side of the axe in an effort to scare Sam. Discuss the facts and explain what crimes could be proved and why.

3. On July 1, 2013, Jeff shot Megan during a bank robbery. Megan remained on life-support systems until September 4, 2014. At that time the systems were disconnected and she ceased breathing. On June 15, 2014, her physician had declared her brain dead. It was not until September 4, 2014, that her family decided to stop the life-support system. Jeff is charged with murder. Discuss any defenses he may have.

4. Penelope and Brenda had been enemies for years. One evening Penelope discovered that Brenda had attempted on many occasions to "pick up" Penelope's boyfriend. Penelope told a friend that she was "going to fix Brenda once and for all—that she was going to mess her face up bad." That evening Penelope waited for Brenda outside her home and attacked her with a knife. Penelope slashed her in the face four times and cut off one ear. Brenda reported the event to the police, who have turned it over to the county prosecutor's office. As the office legal assistant, you have been assigned the task of determining what crime can be charged.

5. State Statute reads: "It shall be a felony for any person to purposefully, knowingly, or recklessly cause the death of another person by the use of poison or other toxins." Eddie Farmer spread a toxic insecticide on his crops, which eventually

mixed with rainwater and made its way into his neighbor's well. The insecticide was new, but it had been recommended by other farmers who had used it successfully. His neighbor's seven-year-old son, Mikey, died from the poisons in the water. Eddie has been charged with violating the state statute. Is he liable?

6. One evening after a play Tracy was approached by a woman who pointed a pistol at her and ordered her to "give me all your money and jewelry." Tracy removed her jewels and handed them over, but told the robber that her money was in her purse, which was in the trunk of her car. The robber asked her where her car was parked, and Tracy pointed to a car 30 feet away. Tracy was then ordered to go to the automobile, remove the purse, and give it to the robber. She complied, and the woman ran off. The thief was eventually captured and tried for aggravated robbery and kidnapping. She was convicted of both and has appealed the kidnapping conviction. What do you think her argument would be to reverse the kidnapping conviction?

7. Do you believe that prostitution and solicitation of prostitution are victimless crimes? If so, does the threat of AIDS and other communicable diseases change your decision?

8. Make your best argument in support of legalizing (decriminalizing) prostitution.

9. Consider your life experiences. Have you ever committed a technical stalking (such as repeatedly seeking the affection of an uninterested person)?

Endnotes

1. A. Loewy, *Criminal Law*, 2d ed. (Nutshell Series; St. Paul: West, 1987).
2. ***People v. Wilkins, Case*** No. S190713, Supreme Court of California (March 7, 2013).
3. *See Commonwealth v. Redline*, 391 Pa. 486, 137 A.2d 472 (1958).
4. *See* LaFave & Scott, *Criminal Law* § 7.7 (Hornbook Series; St. Paul: West, 1986).
5. *State v. Corn*, 278 S.E.2d 221 (N.C. 1981).
6. *See*, for example, N.Y. Penal Law § 125.27(a)(xiii).
7. *Labelle v. State*, 550 N.E.2d 752 (Ind. 1990); *see also* LaFave & Scott at § 7.2(b).
8. Model Penal Code § 210.0(4).
9. The Federal Bureau of Investigation's prime suspect in the case committed suicide before he was charged. A microbiologist with a Ph.D. from the University of Cincinnati, Bruce Ivins had been employed by the United States Army Medical Research Institute of Infectious Diseases. See *http://www.fbi.gov/about-us/history/famous-cases/anthrax-amerithrax/amerithrax-investigation*
10. *See* Ill. Rev. Stat. ch. 38, para. 9–3.
11. The Model Penal Code addresses homicide at § 210.0 *et seq.*
12. Mich. Comp. Laws Ann. § 752.1027.
13. Robert Hardaway, Miranda Peterson, and Cassandra Mann, "The Right to Die and the Ninth Amendment: Compassion and Dying After *Glucksberg* and *Vacco*," 7 *George Mason L. Rev.* 313 (1999).

14. 521 U.S. 702 (1997).

15. *See* 65 Am. Jur. 2d *Rape* 28 (1976).

16. Model Penal Code § 213.

17. Ohio Rev. Code § 2907.

18. *Michael M. v. Superior Court*, 450 U.S. 464 (1981).

19. The Court upheld a sodomy law in *Bowers v. Hardwick*, 478 U.S. 186 (1986) but explicitly reversed that decision in *Lawrence v. Texas*, 539 U.S. 558 (2003).

20. Louise Elaine Ellison (July 1997), *A Comparative Study of Rape Trials in Adversarial and Inquisitorial Criminal Justice Systems,* Dissertation: University of Leeds, Faculty of Law.

21. Steven I. Friedland, "On Treatment, Punishment, and the Civil Commitment of Sex Offenders," 70 *U. Colo. L. Rev.* 73 (1999).

22. 42 U.S.C. § 14071.

23. 117 S. Ct. 2072 (1997).

24. 534 U.S. 407 (2002).

25. 531 U.S. 250 (2001).

26. 560 U.S. 126 (2010).

27. Jean Peters-Baker, "Challenging Traditional Notions of Managing Sex Offenders: Prognosis Is Lifetime Management," 66 *U. Mo. at Kansas City L. Rev.* 629 (1997).

28. 18 U.S.C. § 1201.

29. 18 U.S.C. § 1201(b).

30. Model Penal Code § 212.1.

31. 28 U.S.C. § 1738A.

32. Karen Brooks, "The New Stalking Laws: Are They Adequate to End Violence?" 14 *Hamline J. Pub. L. & Pol'y.* 259 (1993).

33. *ApolloMedia v. Reno*, 19 F. Supp. 2d 1081 (1998), aff'd, 119 S. Ct. 1450 (1999); and *ACLU v. Reno* 521 U.S. 844 (1997).

34. 18 U.S.C. § 241.

35. 18 U.S.C. § 242.

36. 42 U.S.C. § 1983.

37. *People v. Superior Court*, 15 Cal. App. 4th 1593, 1599 (1993).

38. Fla. Stat. Ann. § 775.085.

CHAPTER 5

CRIMES AGAINST PROPERTY AND HABITATION

Chapter Outline

Arson

Burglary

Theft Crimes

Ethical Considerations: The Ineffective Assistance of Counsel

Chapter Objectives

After completing this chapter you should be able to:

- list the elements of historic and contemporary crimes involving property and habitation, such as arson, burglary, and larceny.

- identify the crimes of arson, burglary, and larceny in given fact scenarios.

- describe how computers and the Internet have given rise to new ways to commit old crimes and how the law is changing to deal with these developments.

- identify the material facts and legal issues in one-third of the cases you read, and describe the court's analyses and conclusions in the cases.

ARSON

Michael Marin, former Wall Street trader, Yale University School of Law graduate, and believed-to-be a millionaire, called the Phoenix, Arizona emergency line on July 5, 2009, to report that his estate mansion was ablaze. He reported having escaped the fire by wearing scuba gear to avoid the inhalation of smoke, and scaling down a rope ladder from the second floor. Later it was discovered that Marin was broke and unable to pay his bills. Police also discovered, thanks in part to a well-trained canine, that the fire was set intentionally. Marin was charged with arson and convicted in 2012. Moments after the verdict was read, Marin was seen on a court television monitor taking a drink from a sports bottle. He collapsed and died. Subsequent testing revealed that he ingested the poison cyanide. Oddly, the day Marin set fire to his home is the day of the greatest number of arsons in U.S. history, according to one source.[1]

arson

■ The malicious and unlawful burning of a building.

Arson is a crime against property. In addition, it is a crime against habitation. Crimes against habitation developed because of the importance of peoples' homes. In England and the United States, the concept that a "man's home is his castle" has great influence. A home is not merely property but, rather, a refuge from the rest of the world. As such, special common-law crimes developed that sought to protect this important sanctuary. Arson and burglary are such crimes.

At common law, arson was defined very narrowly. It was the (1) malicious (2) burning of a (3) dwelling house of (4) another. This definition was so narrowly construed that owners could burn their own property with an intent to defraud their insurers and not be guilty of arson, because they did not burn the dwelling of another.[2] In addition, the structure burned had to be a *dwelling,* which was defined as a structure inhabited by people. This definition did include outhouses and the area directly around the home (*curtilage*), as long as the area was used frequently by people. However, the burning of businesses and other structures was not arson.

To be a burning, the dwelling must actually sustain some damage, although slight damage was sufficient. If the structure is simply charred by the fire, there is a burning. However, if the structure is only smoke-damaged or discolored by the heat of a fire that never touched the building, there is no arson. Finally, causing a dwelling to explode is not arson, unless some of the dwelling is left standing after the explosion and is then burned by a fire caused by the explosion.

At common law, *malice* was the mens rea of arson. As was true of murder at common law, *malice* meant evil intent. However, an intentional or extremely reckless burning would suffice.

Today, the definition of arson has been broadened by statute in most, if not all, states. It is now common to prosecute owners of property for burning their own buildings, if the purpose was to defraud an insurer or to cause another injury. Be aware that the fraud may constitute a separate offense: defrauding an insurance carrier. Also, the structure burned need not be a dwelling under most statutes, though most statutes aggravate the crime if a dwelling is burned. Although the common law did not recognize explosions as a burning, the Model Penal Code and most statutes do.[3]

sidebar

CRIME IN THE UNITED STATES

In 2011, a total of 52,333 arsons were reported. There were 18 offenses per 100,000 residents in that year.

Source: Crime in the United States, U.S. Department of Justice, Federal Bureau of Investigation, 2012.

The mens rea for arson under the Model Penal Code is purposeful and reckless. If a person starts a fire or causes an explosion with the purpose of destroying the building or defrauding an insurer, a felony of the second degree has been committed. It is a felony of the third degree to purposely start a fire or cause an explosion and thereby recklessly endanger a person or structure.[4] Note that under the Model Penal Code the fire need not touch the structure, as was required by the common law. Setting the fire is enough to satisfy the burning requirement.

Arson is often graded. The burning of dwellings is usually the highest form of the crime. The burning of uninhabited structures is usually the next highest form of arson, and arson of personal property, if treated as arson, is the lowest.

BURGLARY

The (1) breaking and entering (2) of another's dwelling (3) at night (4) for the purpose of committing a felony once inside, was **burglary** at common law. A burglary, or entry of a dwelling, may be for the purpose of theft, rape, murder, or another felony. For that reason, burglary is a crime against habitation, as well as against property and person.

burglary

■ Unlawfully entering the house of another person with the intention of committing a felony (usually theft).

sidebar

CRIME IN THE UNITED STATES

In 2011 there was a total of slightly fewer than 2.2 million burglaries and attempted forcible entries to structures in the United States. Of all the property crimes in 2011 in the United States, 24% were burglaries. Unlike many crimes, burglary is on the rise, the 2009 rate being 1.7% higher than the 2002 rate. Of all burglaries, 75% percent are of residences. Most residential burglaries occur during the day, while most nonresidential burglaries occur at night.

Source: Crime in the United States, U.S. Department of Justice, Federal Bureau of Investigation, 2012.

The first element, the actus reus, a breaking, can be satisfied by either an actual break-in or by a constructive breaking. If one enters a dwelling by simply passing through an open door or window (a trespass), there is no breaking. Generally, there has to be some act by the defendant to change the condition of the house so as to gain entry. For example, opening an unlocked door or window is a breaking, while passing through an open door or window is not a breaking. Of course, picking a lock and breaking a window or door are breakings.

A burglar may also gain entry by a constructive breaking. A constructive breaking occurs when one uses fraud or force to gain entry. So, if a burglar poses as a telephone repair worker to gain entry, then the breaking element has been satisfied. The same is true if the owner consents to the burglar's entry under threat or the use of force.

Once the breaking occurs, there must be an entry of the home. The burglar does not need to fully enter the structure; an entry occurs if any part of the burglar's body enters the house. So, the individual who breaks a window and reaches in to grab an item has entered the house.

Modern statutes have eliminated the breaking requirement, although most still require some form of "unlawful entry." Because trespasses, frauds, and breakings are unlawful, they satisfy modern statutory requirements.

The second element required is that the breaking and entry be of another person's dwelling. As with arson, at common law the structure had to be a dwelling. The person who lives in the dwelling does not have to be the owner, only an occupant. As such, rental property is included. Interestingly, at least one court has held that churches are dwellings, regardless of whether a person actually resides in the church, premised on the theory that churches are God's dwellings.[5] The dwelling had to belong to another person, so one could not burglarize one's own property. No jurisdiction continues to require that the structure be a dwelling. Most statutes now refer to all buildings or other structures.[6] However, if the structure burglarized is a dwelling, most states punish the crime more severely than if it was another type of building.

Exhibit 5–1

Actual breaking through the door

Entry through a closed unlocked door is considered a breaking

Entry through an open door is not a breaking

Gaining entry by threatening or coercing occupant to open door is a constructive breaking

Gaining entry through fraud is a constructive breaking

The third element was that the burglary occur at night. Although this is no longer an element of burglary, many states do aggravate the crime if it happens at night.

The fourth element is that the person entering must have as a purpose the commission of a felony once inside. This is the mens rea of the crime. If the person's intent is only to commit a misdemeanor, there is no burglary. If Jay's intent is to murder Mark, there is a burglary. It is not a burglary if Jay's intent is to punch Mark in the nose.

Of course, many breakings and enterings with an intent to commit a burglaries are not completed. A burglar may be caught by surprise by someone who was not known to be inside and flee from the property. It also happens that burglars are caught in the act by occupants who return to the building. In any event, what is important is that the intended felony need not be completed. All that needs to be proven is that the accused entered with an intent to commit a felony. As is always true, proving a person's subjective mental state is nearly impossible. Thus, juries are permitted to infer intent from the actions of the defendant. A jury did just that in the *Lockett* case.

Some statutes now provide that intent to commit any crime is sufficient, whether misdemeanor or felony. However, many continue to require an intent to commit either felony or any theft.

STATE OF ILLINOIS V. GERRY LOCKETT
196 Ill. App. 3d 981, 554 N.E.2d 566 (1990)

Gerry Lockett was charged with residential burglary, convicted after a jury trial, and sentenced to 8 years imprisonment. . . .

At about 3:00 A.M. on November 27, 1987, Allan Cannon entered his apartment, which he shared with his sister. Cannon noticed a broken window in his sister's bedroom. He then saw a man, whom he did not know, standing about six feet away from him in the apartment hallway. The only light came from the bathroom off the hallway. The man said to Cannon, "I know your sister." Cannon fled the apartment to call the police from the nearby El station. Outside his apartment, Cannon saw the man running down an alley. Cannon described the man to police as a dark black man with curly hair, about 5'5" weighing about 200 pounds.

Cannon returned to his apartment and noticed that his bicycle had been placed on his bed, and that his sister's baby clothes, which had been packed in bags, had been thrown all over. Although the apartment was in a general state of disarray, which Cannon admitted was not uncommon, nothing had been taken. . . .

Lockett also argues, without merit, that the evidence could not support an inference of his intent to commit a theft. But when Cannon entered his apartment, he found a broken window and later noticed a rock and broken glass on the floor, indicating that the window had been broken from outside. Cannon also discovered contents of the apartment had been rearranged and thrown about. Even assuming that Lockett was, as he said, an acquaintance of Cannon's sister, and that the Cannons, as defense counsel implied, were less than diligent housekeepers, Lockett's presence, without permission, in the dark, empty apartment, at 3 A.M., supported the jury's inference of intent to commit a theft.

In summary, most jurisdictions have changed burglary in such a way that the following elements are common: (1) an unlawful entry (2) of any structure or building (3) for the purpose of committing a felony or stealing from the premises (4) once inside.

As mentioned, burglary may be graded and higher penalties imposed if the act occurred at night; involved a dwelling or was perpetrated at a dwelling that was actually inhabited at the time of the crime; or was committed by a burglar with a weapon. See Exhibit 5–1 for a summary illustration of burglary.

THEFT CRIMES

Introduction to Theft Crimes

There are many types of theft. It is theft to take a pack of gum from a grocery store and not pay for it; for a lawyer to take a client's trust fund and spend it on personal items; for a bank officer to use a computer to make a paper transfer of funds from a patron's account to the officer's with an intent to later withdraw the money and abscond; and to hold a gun on a person and demand that property and money be surrendered. However, they are all fundamentally different crimes.

Some thefts are more violative of the person, such as robbery, and others are more violative of a trust relationship, such as an attorney absconding with a client's money. The crimes also differ in the methods by which they are committed. A robbery involves an unlawful taking. Embezzlement, however, involves a lawful taking with a subsequent unlawful conversion.

Larceny was the first theft crime. It was created by judges as part of the common law. The elements of larceny were very narrow and did not cover most thefts. Larceny began as one crime, but developed into many different crimes. This was not a fluid, orderly development, for two reasons. First, when larceny was first created, well over 600 years ago, the purpose of making it criminal was more to prevent breaches of the peace (fights over possession of property) than to protect ownership of property. Larceny did not prohibit fraudulent takings of another's property. The theory was that an embezzlement or other theft by trick was less likely to result in an altercation (breach of the peace) between the owner and the thief, because the owner would not be aware of the theft until after it was completed. Using this theory, many courts were reluctant to expand the scope of larceny. Second, at early common law, larceny was punishable by death. For this reason, some judges were reluctant to expand its reach.[7]

Eventually, two other theft crimes were created, embezzlement and false pretenses. Despite the creation of these crimes, many theft acts continued to go unpunished because they fell into the cracks that separated the elements of the three common-law theft crimes. Some courts attempted to remedy this problem by broadening the definitions of the three crimes. However, computers, electronic banking, and other technological advances have led to new methods of stealing money and property, posing problems not anticipated by the judges who created the common-law theft crimes. Some states have changed their definitions of larceny, false pretenses, and embezzlement to be more contemporary. Other states have simply abandoned the common-law crimes and have enacted consolidated theft statutes. The common-law theft crimes, modern consolidated theft statutes, and the Model Penal Code approach to theft are discussed here.

sidebar

CRIME IN THE UNITED STATES

The United States Department of Justice includes the following as larceny for the purpose of the Uniform Crime Reporting Program: shoplifting, pocket-picking, purse-snatching, thefts from automobiles, thefts of motor vehicles, and all other thefts of personal property that occur without the use of force. The program shows that there were 6.2 million reported larcenies in the United States in 2011. This represents 1,977 thefts per 100,000 people, a decrease of 19 percent from 2002. Of all property crimes, 68% were thefts. The average loss for a victim was $987 with over $6 billion dollars in total loss to all victims of larceny. Motor vehicle parts are the most common items stolen. In addition, over 715,000 automobiles were stolen in 2011, or 230 per 100,000 people, a 43% decline since 2002.

Source: Crime in the United States, United States Department of Justice, Federal Bureau of Investigation, 2012.

Larceny

At common law the elements of **larceny** were (1) the trespassory taking (2) and carrying away (*asportation*) (3) of personal property (4) of another (5) with an intent to permanently deprive the owner of possession. The actus reus of larceny was the taking and carrying away of personal property of another. The mens rea was the intent to permanently deprive the owner of possession.

To have had a common-law larceny, there must have been a "taking" of property. A taking alone would not have sufficed; the taking must have been unlawful or trespassory. That is, the property must be taken by the defendant without the owner's consent. This element is concerned only with the method that the defendant used in acquiring possession. For example, if Mandy takes Sean's wallet from his hand, she has committed a taking. However, if Sean were to give Mandy his wallet with the understanding that she is to return it at a specified time, there is no unlawful taking when she does not return it; she lawfully acquired possession of the wallet. Taking property from another without that person's consent was a trespass under the common law, but failing to return property was not.

In an effort to protect employers (masters) from theft by their employees (servants), the theory of *constructive possession* was created. This theory held that when an employee received actual possession of the employer's property as part of the job, the employer maintained "constructive possession" while the employee had custody of the property. If this theory had not been developed, employees would have been free to steal property entrusted to them, as larceny required a trespassory taking. Of course, if an employee took property that was not under his or her care, there was a trespassory taking.

larceny

■ Stealing of any kind. Some types of larceny are specific crimes, such as *larceny by trick* or grand larceny.

Interestingly, the theory of constructive possession was never extended to other relationships. This led to the creation of a new crime—embezzlement.

Once the taking has been effected, the defendant must carry away the property. This carrying away is called *asportation*. Generally, any asportation, even slight movement, will satisfy this requirement. The term *asportation* is deceiving, as not all property has to be "carried away" to satisfy this requirement. Riding a horse away will satisfy the requirement, as will driving another's automobile. Most states have done away with the asportation requirement by statute.

Third, the item stolen must be personal property. Land and items attached to land (e.g., houses) are considered real property. Theft of such property was not larceny. All other property is personal property. Objects that are movable property are personal property. In the early years of larceny, there was a further requirement that the item stolen be tangible personal property. Tangible personal property includes most items, such as automobiles, books, electronic equipment, and the like. Documents, such as stocks, bonds, and promissory notes, which represent ownership of something, are considered intangible property. It was not larceny to steal intangible personal property. Under modern statutes, most states have broadened theft to include all types of property.

The fourth element is that the personal property taken and carried away must be owned by another. One cannot steal from oneself. However, the rule was extended to prohibit prosecution of a partner for taking partnership assets and joint tenants from taking each other's things; also, because husband and wife were one person under the common law, it was not possible for spouses to steal from one another.

Finally, the mens rea element: It is required that the defendant intend to permanently deprive the owner of possession of the property. In short, to be a thief one must have an intent to steal. If Jack takes Eddie's lawn mower, intending to return the mower when he has completed his mowing, he has not committed larceny, as he did not possess an intent to permanently deprive Eddie of his possession of the mower. Also, the accused must intend to deprive an owner (or possessor) of property to be guilty of larceny. If an accused had a good-faith belief that he had lawful right to the property, the requisite mens rea did not exist, and there was no larceny.

Although proving "an intent to permanently deprive the owner of possession" is the common method of proving the mens rea of larceny, it is not the only method. Courts have held that if the property is held so long that it causes the owner to lose a significant portion of its value, a larceny has occurred. Some cases have held that if the property is taken with an intent to subject the property to substantial risk, there is a larceny. Of course, the intent must exist at the time of taking. To illustrate this last method, imagine a thief who steals a plane intending to use it in a daredevil show. In such a case the thief is subjecting the property to a substantial risk, and even though the intent was to return the plane when the show was over, there is a larceny.

Embezzlement

The definition of larceny left a large gap that permitted people in some circumstances to steal from others. That gap was caused by requiring a trespassory taking of the property. For various reasons, people entrust money and property to others. The intent is not to transfer ownership (title), only possession. A depositor of a bank gives possession of money to the bank; a client may give an attorney money to hold in a trust account; a stockbroker may keep an account with a client-investor's money in it. In all of these situations, the money is taken lawfully; there is no trespassory taking. So, what happens if the person entrusted with the money *converts* (steals) it after taking lawful possession? At the early common law, it was not a crime. However, the thief could have been sued for recovery of the stolen money.

This theory was carried to an extreme in a case in which a bank teller converted money handed to him by a depositor to himself, by placing the money in his own pocket. It was held that there was no larceny, because the teller acquired the money lawfully. The court also determined that there was no larceny under the theory of constructive possession, because the employer (bank) never had possession of the money. If the teller had put the money in the drawer and then taken it, the bank would have had constructive possession, and he would have committed larceny. The result was that the teller was guilty of no crime.[8] Unsatisfied with this situation, the English Parliament created a new crime: **embezzlement.**

The elements of embezzlement are (1) conversion (2) of personal property (3) of another (4) by one who has acquired lawful possession (5) with an intent to defraud the owner.

To prove embezzlement, the prosecution must first show that an act of **conversion** occurred. Conversion is the unauthorized control over property with an intent to permanently deprive the owner of its possession or which substantially interferes with the rights of the owner.

As was the case with larceny, only tangible personal property was included. Today, nearly all forms of personal property may be embezzled. Also, the property had to belong to another. One could not embezzle one's own property.

The element that distinguished embezzlement from larceny was the taking requirement. Whereas larceny required a trespassory taking, embezzlement required lawful acquisition. Accountants, lawyers, bailees, executors of estates, and trustees are examples of those who can commit embezzlement.

To satisfy the mens rea requirement of embezzlement, it must be shown that the defendant possessed an "intent to defraud." Mere negligent conversion of another's property is not embezzlement. Because the mens rea requirement is so high, bona fide claims of mistake of fact and law are valid defenses. If an accountant makes an accounting error and converts a client's money, there is no embezzlement. This is a mistake of fact. If a friend you loaned money to keeps the money with the mistaken belief that he is allowed to in order to offset damage you caused to his property last year (when the law requires that he sue you for the damage), there is no embezzlement. This is a mistake of law and negates the intent required, as does a mistake of fact.

Embezzlement is prohibited in all states. Some states have retained the name *embezzlement;* others have named it theft and included it in a consolidated theft statute. Embezzlement, which occurs in interstate commerce, federally insured banks, and lending institutions, or involves officers and agents of the federal government, is also made criminal by the statutes of the United States.[9] Statute 18 U.S.C. § 641 is

embezzlement

■ The fraudulent and secret taking of money or property by a person who has been trusted with it. This usually applies to an employee's taking money and covering it up by faking business records or account books.

conversion

■ Any act that deprives an owner of property without that owner's permission and without just cause.

the embezzlement of public monies, property, and records statute. Violation of that provision, if the property embezzled has a value of $100 or greater, results in a fine of up to $10,000 and 10 years in prison. The remainder of that statute deals with embezzlement of nonpublic property that occurs in interstate commerce or by federal officials. The penalties vary for each provision.

False Pretenses

At common law, it was not larcenous to use lies (false representations) to gain ownership of property. For example, if Brogan were to sell Sean a ring containing glass, while representing to Sean that the ring contained a diamond, it was not larceny under the early common law, even though Brogan knew that the ring contained glass. The early judges believed strongly in the concept of *caveat emptor,* which translates as "let the buyer beware."

false pretenses

■ A lie told to cheat another person out of his or her money or property. It is a crime in most states, though the precise definition varies.

As it had done with embezzlement, Parliament decided to make such acts criminal. It did so by creating the crime of **false pretenses**. The elements of false pretenses are (1) a false representation of (2) a material present or past fact (3) made with knowledge that the fact is false (4) and with an intent to defraud the victim (5) thereby causing the victim to pass title to property to the actor.

To prove the first element, it must be shown that the actor made a false representation. This representation may be made orally or by writing, or may be implied by one's actions. The law does not require that people disclose all relevant information during a business transaction—*caveat emptor* still exists in that regard. The law does, however, require that any affirmative statements (or implications from actions) be true. So, if a buyer fails to ask if property has a lien against it, there is no false pretense if the seller does not inform the buyer of such. The opposite is true if the buyer inquires about existing liens and encumbrances and is told there are none.

The false representation must be important to the transaction. If the statement is important, the law says that it is *material*. Generally, a representation is material if it would have had an impact on the victim's decisionmaking had the victim known the truth at the time the transaction took place. For example, if Connie represents to Pam that the lighter in a used car she is selling works, when it does not, she has not committed false pretenses. However, if she states to Pam that the automobile recently had its engine replaced, that would be material and she would be liable for false pretenses if she knew that the statement was untrue.

The fact conveyed by the actor must not only be material, but it must also concern a present fact or past fact. In this context, *present* refers to the time of the transaction. Statements of expected facts, promises, predictions, and expectations cannot be the basis of false pretenses. So, if Aaron buys an automobile from Kathy and promises to pay her in 6 months, it is no crime if he fails to pay because he loses his source of income during that period. To permit breaches of such promises to be criminal would be the same as having a debtor's prison, which is not recognized in the United States. The same is not true if Aaron made the promise but had no intent of paying the debt. Some states treat this as false pretenses under the theory that his state of mind at the time of the sale was fraudulent. Some states do not treat his action as criminal and place the burden on Kathy to seek her own remedy in a civil cause of action. It is also necessary that the representation be one of fact. Accordingly, opinions are not included. Of course, the line between fact and opinion is often unclear.

It must also be proved that the defendant knew the statement was false. An unintentional misrepresentation is not sufficient to establish this element in most jurisdictions, although most jurisdictions will find knowledge if the lower mens rea standard, recklessness, is proved.

The defendant must have the additional mens rea of "intent to defraud." As with other theft crimes, if persons have a bona fide belief that a particular property belongs to them, there is a defense. In addition to intending to defraud the victim, it must also be shown that the victim was defrauded. Hence, if the victim was aware of the falsity of the statement and entered into the bargain anyway, there has been no crime.

Finally, the misrepresentation must be the cause of the victim passing title to property to the defendant. *Title* is ownership. Transferring possession to the defendant is not adequate. However, causing one to transfer possession of property by use of fraud was a type of larceny, known as *larceny by trick*. Just as with larceny and embezzlement, only tangible personal property was included within the grasp of the prohibition at early common law. Today, false pretenses usually includes all property that is subject to the protection of larceny—in most instances, this includes all personal property.

Fraudulent Checks

Related to the crime of false pretenses is the crime of acquiring property or money by writing a check (draft) from an account that has insufficient funds to cover the draft. The act appears to fall into the category of false pretenses. Some theorize that a check is a promise of future payment, and, accordingly, the check does not meet the "representation of present or past fact" requirement of false pretenses. Courts have rejected that theory and held that at the time one drafts a check, a representation is made that there are adequate funds in the account to pay the amount drafted.

Today, most states have bad-check statutes. Conviction of these laws, for the most part, results in a less serious punishment than conviction on false pretenses.[10] Three common material elements are found in bad-check statutes. First, the mens rea may be proven by showing either an intent to defraud the payee or knowledge that there were insufficient funds in the account. Second, the check must be taken in exchange for something of value; third, there must have been insufficient funds in the account.

Mail Fraud

Another crime related to false pretenses is mail fraud.[11] Mail fraud is a crime against the United States, because the mail system is run by a federal agency. Using the U.S. mail system with an intent to defraud another of money or property is mail fraud. The intended victim need not be defrauded; the act of sending such mails with the intent to defraud is itself criminal.

Mail fraud has become increasingly important in recent years, because it often is the foundation of a RICO count.

■ (19 U.S.C. 1961). A
broadly applied 1970
federal law that creates
certain "racketeering
offenses" that include
participation in various
criminal schemes and
conspiracies, and that
allows government seizure
of property acquired in
violation of the act.

Racketeer Influenced and Corrupt Organizations Act

Another federal statute that deals with fraud is the **Racketeer Influenced and Corrupt Organizations Act**, commonly known as RICO.[12] The United States Congress enacted RICO in the early 1970s in an attempt to curb organized crime.

Judicial interpretation of RICO has led to much controversy in recent years. Some people contend that the effect of court opinions has been to extend the prohibition of RICO beyond Congress's original intent. Today, all businesses, not just traditional organized crime, are subject to RICO.

To establish a RICO violation, the United States must prove that the (1) defendant received money or income (2) from a pattern of racketeering activity and (3) invested that money in an enterprise (business), (4) which is in interstate commerce or affects interstate commerce.

The second element is the key to proving a RICO violation. The term *pattern* means "two or more acts," referred to as the predicate acts. Those acts must fall into the definition of a "racketeering activity." The statute provides a list of state and federal crimes that are considered to be racketeering. Murder, kidnapping, extortion, and drug sales and transportation are examples of the state crimes included in the list. Mail fraud, wire fraud, "white slave traffic" or the transport of women across state boundaries for immoral purposes, securities fraud, and bribery are a few examples of the federal crimes included. Mail fraud is often the basis of a RICO violation, because the mails are often used by such enterprises.

For example, the Supreme Court announced in a 1994 decision that RICO could apply to a coalition of antiabortion groups that were alleged to have conspired, through a pattern of racketeering, to shut down abortion clinics.[13] In that case, extortion, including alleged threats of assault, was used to satisfy this element.

Violation of RICO can result in serious criminal penalties. In addition, victims of such activity may sue civilly and receive treble damages, costs, and attorney fees. RICO also provides for **forfeiture** of property in criminal proceedings. *Forfeiture* is the taking of property and money of a defendant by the government. Many crimes have forfeiture provisions. A forfeiture is not the same as a fine. Forfeitures and fines are both levied as punishment, but the focus of a fine is generally to hurt a defendant's pocketbook. Forfeitures are specifically aimed at getting the property or money connected to the crime for which the individual was convicted. So, in a RICO situation, a convicted party could stand to lose the enterprise itself, as well as all profits from that activity.

However, many aspects of civil RICO are identical to criminal RICO. One such aspect is the pattern requirement. Whether the case is civil or criminal, a pattern of racketeering must be proven. The United States Supreme Court addressed the pattern question because the various appellate courts of the United States were divided on how to define that phrase. In *H.J., Inc. v. Northwestern Bell Telephone Co.*, 492 U.S. 229 (1989), the Supreme Court defined a pattern as more than one predicate act that are related to one another and the facts pose a threat of continued racketeering activity. *H.J.* is also a good illustration of how "legitimate businesses" are subject to RICO.

forfeiture

■ A deprivation of money, property, or rights, without compensation, as a consequence of a default or the commission of a crime.

Forgery

Another crime related to fraud is **forgery**. *Forgery* is the (1) making of (2) false documents (or the alteration of existing documents making them false) (3) and passing the document (4) to another (5) with an intent to defraud.

The purpose of forgery statutes is both to prevent fraud and to preserve the value of written instruments. These functions are important because if forgery were to become common, people would no longer trust commercial documents, such as checks and contracts. The effect that would have on commerce is obvious.

The actus reus of forgery is the making of the document. That involves the actual writing and drafting of the document, as well as passing the document (*uttering*) to a potential victim. The mens rea of forgery is knowledge of the falsity of the document and an intent to defraud.

In many jurisdictions, forgery and uttering are separate crimes. In those states one must only make the false instrument and possess an intent to defraud. The defendant need not present the document (utter) to the victim. That act, when accompanied with an intent to defraud, is the crime of *uttering*.

forgery

■ Making a fake document (or altering a real one) with intent to commit a fraud.

Receiving Stolen Property

Not only is it a crime to steal another's property, but it is also a crime to receive property that one knows is stolen, if the intent is to keep that property. In essence, one who buys or receives as a gift property that is known to be stolen is an accessory (after the fact) to the theft. Although the law applies to anyone who violates its prohibitions, the primary focus of law enforcement is *fences*, people who purchase stolen property with the intent of reselling the property for a profit. They act as the retailers of stolen property, with the thieves acting as suppliers.

The elements of **receiving stolen property** are (1) receiving property (2) that has been stolen (3) with knowledge of its stolen character (4) with an intent to deprive the owner of the property.

Receipt of the property may be shown by showing either actual possession or constructive possession of the property. Constructive possession occurs any time the defendant has control over the property, even though the defendant does not have actual possession. For example, if one makes arrangements for stolen property to be delivered to one's home, there is receipt once the property is in the house, even if the defendant was not present when the property was delivered. Receiving includes not only purchases of stolen property but also other transfers, such as gifts.

The property in question must have been stolen. In this context, stolen property includes that property acquired from larcenies, robberies, embezzlement, extortion, false pretenses, and similar crimes.

The final two elements deal with the mens rea of the crime of receiving stolen property. It is necessary that the defendant knew of the property's stolen character at the time of acquiring the property. Actual knowledge that the property was stolen is required. However, if it can be proven that the defendant had a subjective belief that the goods were stolen, but lacked absolute proof of that fact, the crime has still been

receiving stolen property

■ The criminal offense of getting or concealing property known to be stolen by another.

committed. The fact that a reasonable person would have known that the property was stolen is not enough to convict for receiving stolen property. If persons receive property under a bona fide belief that they have claim to the property, they are not guilty of receiving stolen property, even though that belief was unfounded.

The last element requires that the receiver of the property intends to deprive the owner of the property. Of course, if a defendant intends to keep the property, then this requirement is met. The language of the crime is broader, however, and includes any intent to deprive the owner of the use, ownership, or possession of the property. Thus, if one receives the property intending to destroy it or to give it as a gift, this element has been satisfied.

Not only do the states prohibit receiving stolen property, but the federal government also makes it a crime to receive stolen property that has traveled in interstate commerce or to receive stolen property while on lands controlled by the United States.[14]

Robbery

robbery

■ The illegal taking of property from the person of another by using force or threat of force.

The material elements of **robbery** are (1) a trespassory taking (2) and carrying away (asportation) (3) of personal property (4) from another's person or presence (5) using either force or threat (6) with an intent to steal the property.

Robbery is actually a type of assault mixed with a type of larceny. Because of the immediate danger created by the crime of robbery, it is punished more severely than either larceny or simple assault. Robbery was a crime under the common law and is a statutory crime in all states today.

The elements of trespassory taking—asportation, intent to steal, and that the property belongs to another—are the same as for larceny. However, robbery also requires that the property be taken from the victim's person or presence. So property taken from another's hands, off another's body, or from another's clothing is taken from the person. Property that is taken from another's presence, but not from the person, also qualifies. For example, if a bank robber orders a teller to stand back while the thief empties the cash drawer, there has been a robbery. The states differ in their definitions of "from another's presence," but it is generally held that property is in a victim's presence any time the victim is in control of the property. This is true in the bank robbery example, as the teller was exercising control over the cash drawer at the time of the robbery.

It is also necessary that the crime be committed with the use of force or threat. This element is the feature that most distinguishes robbery from larceny. As far as force is concerned, if any force is used beyond what is necessary to simply take the property, there is robbery. For example, it is larceny, not robbery, if a pickpocket steals a wallet free of the owner's knowledge. Only the force necessary to take the wallet was used. It is robbery, however, if the victim catches the pickpocket, and an altercation ensues over possession of the wallet. The same result is true when dealing with purse snatchers. If the snatcher makes a clean grab and gets away without an altercation, it is larceny from the person. If the victim grabs the bag and fights to keep it, then it is robbery. A threat of force may also satisfy this requirement. So, if the robber states to the victim, "Give me your wallet or I'll blow your head off," there is a robbery, even though there was no physical contact.

In most jurisdictions, the threatened harm must be immediate; threats of future harm are not adequate. It is also possible that the threat will be to someone else, such as a family member. The thief who holds a man's wife and threatens to harm her if the man does not give up his money is not free from the charge of robbery just because the person giving up the money is not the one threatened.

The mens rea of robbery is the specific intent to take the property and deprive the owner of it. As with the other theft crimes, a good-faith, but incorrect, claim of right to the property is a defense. In *Richardson v. United States*, 403 F.2d 574 (D.C. Cir. 1968), a defendant's claim of right to money was a gambling debt. The trial court did not permit the illegal debt to be used as a defense, but the appellate court reversed. It stated in its opinion that:

> The government's position seems to be that no instruction on a claim of right is necessary unless the defendant had a legally enforceable right to the property he took. But specific intent depends upon a state of mind, not upon a legal fact. If the jury finds that the defendant believed himself entitled to the money, it cannot properly find that he had the requisite specific intent for robbery.

Robbery is a crime pursuant to state law, and the United States has also prohibited certain robberies. Robbery of a federally insured bank is an example.[15]

Robbery is usually, if not always, graded. Robbery is graded higher if it results in serious injury to the victim or is committed using a deadly weapon.

Extortion

Extortion is more commonly known as *blackmail*. Extortion is similar to robbery because both acts involve stealing money under threat. However, the threat in a robbery must be of immediate harm. Extortion involves a threat of future harm. At common law, extortion applied only against public officers. Today, extortion is much broader. The elements of extortion are (1) the taking or acquisition of property (2) of another (3) using a threat (4) with an intent to steal the property. In a few jurisdictions, the

extortion

■ To compel, force, or coerce; for example, to get a confession by depriving a person of food and water. To get something by illegal threats of harm to person, property, or reputation. The process is called *extortion*.

---

sidebar

CRIME IN THE UNITED STATES

Robbery is defined as the "taking or attempting to take anything of value from the care, custody, or control of a person or persons by force or threat of force or violence and/or by putting the victim in fear." During 2011, there 354,396 robberies were reported under this definition. The number of robberies decreased 21% from 2007.

Source: Uniform Crime Reports, U.S. Department of Justice, Federal Bureau of Investigation, 2012.

extortionist must actually receive the property, whereas others require only that the threat be made.

A threat of future physical harm satisfies the threat element, as do threats to injure another's reputation, business, financial status, or family relationship. As in the case of robbery, the threat may be directed at one person and the demand for property made on another. For example, if a thief states to John, "Give me $100,000 or I will kill your wife," he is an extortionist, even though he has not threatened John.

The threatened conduct itself need not be illegal to be extortion. For example, if Stacy tells Lisa that she is going to inform the authorities of Lisa's involvement in illegal drug trade unless Lisa pays her $10,000, she is an extortionist, even though informing the police of the activity is not only legal but is encouraged by society.

The federal government has made it a crime for federal officers to extort the public, to be involved in an extortion that interferes with interstate commerce, and to extort another by threatening to expose a violation of federal law.

The *Dioguardi* case deals with extortion in the labor relations area. In most situations it is proper for unions and employees to threaten to picket an employer. In this case the threats were not part of usual labor–management relations; they were made with the purpose of extorting corporate money. Accordingly, the threats were found to be extortion, not protected labor activity.

PEOPLE V. DIOGUARDI
8 N.Y.2d 260, 203 N.Y.S.2d 870 (1960)

The Appellate Division has reversed defendants' convictions for extortion and conspiracy to commit extortion, dismissed the indictment, and discharged them from custody. In addition to the conspiracy count, the indictment charged defendants with extorting $4,700 from the officers of two corporations. Said corporations were nonunion, conducted a wholesale stationery and office supply business in Manhattan, did an annual business of several million dollars, and their stock was wholly owned by a family named Kerin. Anthony Kerin, Sr., president and "boss" of the Kerin companies, made all the important corporate decisions. The other two corporate officers were his son Kerin, Jr., and one Jack Shumann.

Defendant McNamara, the alleged "front man" in the extortive scheme, was an official of Teamster's Local 295 and 808, as well as a member of the Teamster's Joint Council. Defendant Dioguardi, the immediate beneficiary of the payments and the alleged power behind the scene, was sole officer of Equitable Research Associates, Inc.—a *publishing house*, according to its certificate of incorporation, a *public relations concern*, according to its bank account and the Yellow Pages of the telephone directory, a *labor statistics concern*, according to its office secretary and sole employee, and a *firm of labor consultants*, according to its business card. . . .

[During late 1955 and early 1956 various unions were attempting to unionize Kerin's business. The two primary unions involved in this attempt were both locals of the Teamsters. Eventually, one union began picketing the business while the other was on the premises handing out literature.]

The appearance of the picket line—which truck drivers from two companies refused to cross—thoroughly alarmed the Kerin officers, since they

PEOPLE V. DIOGUARDI *(continued)*

were in an "extremely competitive business," and a cessation of incoming or outgoing truck deliveries for as short a period as two weeks would effectively force them out of business.

• • •

McNamara assured Kerin, Sr. that his troubles could be ended, and *would be,* if he did three things: (1) "joined up" with McNamara's local 295, (2) paid $3,500 to Equitable to defray the "out-of-pocket" expenses incurred by the various unions that had sought to organize the companies, and (3) retained Equitable as labor consultant at $100 per month for each company for the period of the collective bargaining contract. . . . McNamara repeatedly assured Kerin, Sr. that the picketing would stop immediately and the companies would be guaranteed labor peace if his program were accepted.

Kerin, Sr., stated that he was not adverse to having his employees organized by local 295, if it was a good honest union, and that he could "accept

the idea of a hundred dollars a month as a retainer fee for labor counsel and advise." He protested against the proposed payment of $3,500, however, as an "extraordinary charge" that sounded "like a holdup," to which McNamara replied: "It may seem that way to you, Mr. Kerin, but that is the amount of money that these unions that have sought to organize you . . . have expended, and *if we are going to avoid further trouble and further difficulties, it is my suggestion that you pay that to the Equitable Associates."*

• • •

Upon the proof in this record, a jury could properly conclude that defendants were guilty of extortion—cleverly conceived and subtly executed, but extortion nonetheless. The essence of the crime is obtaining property by a wrongful use of fear, induced by a threat to do an unlawful injury. It is well-settled law in this State that fear of economic loss or harm satisfies the ingredient of fear necessary to the crime.

Consolidated Theft Statutes

The distinctions among the three common-law crimes of theft, larceny, embezzlement, and false pretenses are often hard to draw. This fact, matched with the belief that there is no substantive difference between stealing by fraud or by quick use of the hands, has led many jurisdictions to do away with the common-law crimes of larceny, false pretenses, and embezzlement and to replace them with a single crime named theft. Exactly what crimes are included in such statutes differs, but larceny, false pretenses, and embezzlement are always included. Many jurisdictions also add one or more of the following: fraudulent checks, receiving stolen property, and extortion.

These statutes often use the language of the common law in defining theft. For example, Florida's statute reads:

A person is guilty of theft if he knowingly obtains or uses, or endeavors to obtain or to use, the property of another with intent to, either temporarily or permanently:
(a) Deprive the other person of a right to the property or a benefit therefrom or Appropriate the property to his own use or to the use of any person not entitled thereto.[16]

This statute includes the three common-law theft crimes. The primary change of consolidated theft statutes is that prosecutors no longer need to charge which specific crime has occurred. At trial, if the jury decides that a defendant has committed a larceny and not an embezzlement, they can convict. At common law, if the defendant was charged with embezzlement, not larceny, the jury would be forced to acquit if they determined that the defendant committed larceny rather than embezzlement.

Robbery is usually not included in consolidated theft statutes because of its significant threat of harm. Consolidation usually includes only misappropriations of property that do not pose serious risks to life.

Of course, those crimes that are included in consolidation statutes are not always punished equally. Grading of such offenses based on the amount of property appropriated, the nature of the theft, and the type of property stolen is common.

Identity Theft

It is possible to steal a person's identity as well as a person's property. The advent of the computer has made identity theft more common. Identity theft occurs whenever an individual uses a victim's name, social security number, e-mail address, or other identifying items in an effort to represent himself or herself as the victim. The mens rea of most identity theft statutes is an intention either to gain something of value through the deceit or to commit any other crime. This is the text of the Washington identity theft statute:

RCW 9.35.020 Identity theft.

(1) No person may knowingly obtain, possess, use, or transfer a means of identification or financial information of another person, living or dead, with the intent to commit, or to aid or abet, any crime.

(2) (a) Violation of this section when the accused or an accomplice uses the victim's means of identification or financial information and obtains an aggregate total of credit, money, goods, services, or anything else of value in excess of one thousand five hundred dollars in value shall constitute identity theft in the first degree. Identity theft in the first degree is a class B felony.

   (b) Violation of this section when the accused or an accomplice uses the victim's means of identification or financial information and obtains an aggregate total of credit, money, goods, services, or anything else of value that is less than one thousand five hundred dollars in value, or when no credit, money, goods, services, or anything of value is obtained shall constitute identity theft in the second degree. Identity theft in the second degree is a class C felony.

(3) A person who violates this section is liable for civil damages of five hundred dollars or actual damages, whichever is greater, including costs to repair the victim's credit record, and reasonable attorneys' fees as determined by the court.

(4) In a proceeding under this section, the crime will be considered to have been committed in any locality where the person whose means of identification or

financial information was appropriated resides, or in which any part of the offense took place, regardless of whether the defendant was ever actually in that locality.

(5) The provisions of this section do not apply to any person who obtains another person's driver's license or other form of identification for the sole purpose of misrepresenting his or her age.

(6) In a proceeding under this section in which a person's means of identification or financial information was used without that person's authorization, and where there has been a conviction, the sentencing court may issue such orders as are necessary to correct a public record that contains false information resulting from a violation of this section.

An offender may be charged and convicted of both identity theft and the underlying crime. The defendant in the following case was convicted under the Washington statute. On appeal she alleged that her conviction of both identity theft and forgery put her in double jeopardy.

STATE V. BALDWIN
45 P.3d 1093 Wash. App. Div. 1, 2002.

Jeanne Baldwin was found guilty of three counts of identity theft and two counts of forgery. The trial court imposed an exceptional sentence premised on the crimes being "major economic offenses" because Baldwin had utilized a complicated scheme to purchase a home and several automobiles with the stolen identities. Baldwin's central argument is that her convictions for both identity theft and forgery violate double jeopardy principles. We disagree, and affirm because the offenses involved different victims.

I

Baldwin, representing herself as "Kaytie Allshouse," purchased a house, forging Allshouse's name to two deeds of trust. The first deed of trust secured the interest of an institutional lender, Global Holdings; the second, subordinate, deed was in favor of the sellers, Diane Masin and David Swadberg. The deeds secured payment of $45,500, and $6,500, respectively.

Two months later, Baldwin rented a mailbox at the Mail Room, a mailbox-rental outlet in Everett. Baldwin presented herself as "Monica Schultz" and produced a Washington driver's license bearing that name. She signed Schultz's name to the mailbox application and began receiving mail in some fifteen other names. Baldwin later rented a mailbox from Jerald Landwehr at Cascade Storage, another mailbox-rental outlet. Baldwin again rented under a false name, this time as "Carol Hopey." She produced two pieces of identification, including a Washington driver's license. Baldwin told Landwehr the mailbox was for "Econo Accounting," and a number of her "employees" would be receiving mail. Letters and packages in a number of names were received at that mailbox.

Meanwhile, a U.S. postal inspector acting on a complaint placed a thirty-day mail cover on the Cascade Storage box address. Under a mail cover, all

(continued)

mail to a specific address is recorded by postmark, addressee, sender, and class of mail. The mail cover revealed mail in numerous names being sent to the rented box. The inspector then contacted a Detective who investigates financial crimes for the Snohomish County Sheriff's Office.

The detective traced the telephone number listed on the Cascade Storage rental paperwork to Baldwin. His suspicions that Baldwin had stolen Hopey's identity were confirmed when Cascade Storage manager Jerald Landwehr picked Baldwin's picture out of a photomontage.

As the detective and inspector proceeded to attempt to locate and call individuals whose names had been gleaned from the Cascade Storage mail cover, they learned the Everett Police Department had been independently investigating allegations of similar multiple name use at the Mail Room in Everett. The detective showed the same photomontage to the Mail Room's manager who immediately picked out Baldwin's picture. . . .

■ ■ ■

A search of the Granite Falls property yielded a wallet containing a Washington driver's license in the name of "Kaytie Allshouse" bearing Baldwin's picture, and two VISA cards, also in the name of "Kaytie Allshouse." The search also uncovered vehicle titles and registrations for four different vehicles in the names of "Kaytie Allshouse" and "Carol Hopey," and auto insurance policies or cards in the names of "Kaytie Allshouse," "Carol Hopey," and "Monica Schultz." Officers also found a social security card for "Kaytie Allshouse" as well as homeowner's insurance correspondence and a utility bill, all addressed to "Kaytie Allshouse" at the Granite Falls address.

Baldwin was charged with six counts: (1) theft of Kaytie Allshouse's identity; (2) theft of Monica Schultz's identity; (3) theft of Carol Hopey's identity; (4) forgery of a deed in Allshouse's name; (5) forgery

of Allshouse's name on an adjustable rider; and (6) forgery of a junior deed in Allshouse's name.

At trial, Kaytie Allshouse testified that she did not sign her name to the two trust deeds on the Granite Falls property. When asked how she felt about finding that someone had used her name to buy a house, she stated, "I don't want this in my name. It's not mine. I do not own it. . . . I just can't afford it. I don't want it." Likewise, Hopey testified she did not know Baldwin, had never lived in Snohomish County, had never rented a private mailbox, and had given no one permission to use her name. The jury found Baldwin guilty on all counts except the alleged forgery of the adjustable rate rider. . . .

Baldwin next contends that separate convictions and punishments for counts 1, 4, and 6 twice expose her to jeopardy. Her contention fails because each offense, as charged, includes elements not included in the other and each offense includes different victims.

The double jeopardy clause is not violated if the Legislature specifically authorizes multiple punishments. Washington applies the "same evidence" test to determine legislative intent. By this test, a defendant cannot be convicted of offenses that are identical both in fact and in law. The convictions stand, however, if there is an element in each offense which is not included in the other, and if proof of one offense would not necessarily also prove the other. . . .

Proof of theft of identity does not ipso facto prove forgery. Forgery requires the making, completion, or alteration of a written instrument. Theft of identity, on the other hand, requires use of a means of identification with the *intent* to commit an unlawful act. Thus, a jury could find Baldwin guilty of theft of identity, but not forgery. Because the elements of the two crimes are not the same, there is a strong presumption that the Legislature authorized multiple punishments for the same crime.

STATE V. BALDWIN *(continued)*

In addition to the three crimes not being the same in law, they are not the same in fact. As noted in *State v. McJimpson*, two crimes may not be the same in fact even though they arose from the same transaction. The court in *McJimpson* held that because each offense harmed a different victim, they were not the same in fact. Thus, the two offenses were not the same offense under the "same evidence" test. The same reasoning applies to this case. Baldwin was not subjected to double jeopardy because counts 1, 4 and 6 each has different victims.

Nor are we persuaded by Baldwin's assertion that the convictions for theft of identity and forgery merge. The merger doctrine applies only when the Legislature has clearly indicated that to prove a particular degree of a crime, "the State must prove not only that a defendant committed that crime . . . but that the crime was accompanied by an act which is defined as a crime elsewhere in the criminal statutes. . . . " It is relevant only when a crime is "elevated to a higher degree by proof of another crime proscribed elsewhere in the criminal code."

Here, neither of these crimes are crimes of degree; thus, neither crime elevates the other. Baldwin counters that to be convicted of identity theft, the State had to prove forgery. She claims that forgery is therefore an element of and merely incidental to the central crime of theft of identity, thus merging the two offenses. This "lesser included" offense argument fails because the State was not required to prove forgery in order to convict of theft of identity. Accordingly, the two crimes do not merge. . . . [Conviction affirmed].

The federal government also has an **identity theft** statute, the Identity Theft and Assumption Deterrence Act of 1998 (Identity Theft Act). Specifically, the Act[17] makes it a federal crime when anyone

> knowingly transfers or uses, without lawful authority, a means of identification of another person with the intent to commit, or to aid or abet, any unlawful activity that constitutes a violation of Federal law, or that constitutes a felony under any applicable State or local law.

identity theft

■ The act of assuming another person's identity by fraud.

The Model Penal Code Consolidation

The Model Penal Code contains a comprehensive consolidation of theft offenses.[18] Provided that a defendant is not prejudiced by doing so, the specification of one theft crime by the prosecution does not prohibit a conviction for another. So if defendants are specifically charged with larceny, they may be convicted of false pretenses or embezzlement by a jury.

The Code recognizes the following forms of theft:

1. Theft by taking (includes common-law larceny and embezzlement).
2. Theft by deception (includes common-law false pretenses).
3. Theft by extortion.

4. Theft of property known to be mislaid, misdelivered, or lost, and no reasonable attempt to find the rightful owner is made.
5. Receiving stolen property.
6. Theft of professional services by deception or threat.
7. Conversion of entrusted funds.
8. Unauthorized use of another's automobile.

The Code declares that thefts are felonies of the third degree if the amount stolen exceeds $500 or if the property stolen is a firearm, automobile, airplane, motorcycle, motorboat, or other vehicle; and, in cases of receiving stolen property, if the receiver of the property is a fence, then it is a felony of the third degree regardless of the value of the property. The Code makes all unauthorized uses of automobiles misdemeanors.

Because the crime of robbery involves a danger to people, it is treated as a separate crime.[19] If during the commission of a theft the defendant inflicts serious bodily injury upon another, threatens serious bodily injury, or threatens to commit a felony of the first or second degree, there is a robbery. It is a felony of the second degree unless the defendant attempts to kill or cause serious bodily injury, in which case it is a felony of the first degree.

Forgery is also treated as a separate offense.[20] Forgery is treated as a felony of the second degree if money, securities, postage stamps, stock, or other documents issued by the government are involved. It is a felony of the third degree if the forged document affects legal relationships, such as wills and contracts. All other forgeries are misdemeanors.

Destruction of Property

Every year a significant amount of financial loss is the result of destruction of property. Arson accounts for much of this total, but not all. Most states have statutes making the destruction of another's property criminal. These laws may be part of the statute covering arson or may be a separate section of the criminal code.

malicious (criminal) mischief

■ The criminal offense of intentionally destroying another person's property.

Destruction of property, commonly called **criminal mischief**, is normally a specific-intent crime and includes all types of destruction that affect the value or dignity of the property. For example, defacing a Jewish tombstone by painting a swastika on it would be criminal mischief, even though the paint can be removed and the tombstone is left physically unharmed.

Mischief is often graded so that the most heavily penalized offenses against public property are those resulting in damage in excess of a stated dollar amount or involving a danger to human life. The most serious mischiefs are usually low-grade felonies, and the rest are misdemeanors. For example, the Kentucky mischief statutes read:

Ky. Rev. Stat. § 512.020

(1) A person is guilty of criminal mischief in the first degree when, having no right to do so or any reasonable ground to believe that he has such right, he intentionally or wantonly defaces, destroys, or damages any property causing pecuniary loss of $1,000 or more.

(2) Criminal mischief in the first degree is a Class D felony.

Ky. Rev. Stat. § 512.030

(1) A person is guilty of criminal mischief in the second degree when, having no right to do so or any reasonable ground to believe that he has such a right, he intentionally or wantonly defaces, destroys, or damages any property causing pecuniary loss of $500 or more.

(2) Criminal mischief in the second degree is a Class A misdemeanor.

Ky. Rev. Stat. § 512.040

(1) A person is guilty of criminal mischief in the third degree when:

(a) Having no right to do so or any reasonable ground to believe that he has such right, he intentionally or wantonly defaces, destroys, or damages any property; or

(b) He tampers with property so as knowingly to endanger the person or property of another.

(2) Criminal mischief in the third degree is a Class B misdemeanor.

At common law, hairline distinctions existed among the three crimes against property: larceny, embezzlement, and false pretenses. Today, statutes in most states have consolidated theft crimes so that the focus is now on whether a theft occurred, not whether the correct crime has been charged. These consolidation statutes include larceny, false pretenses, and embezzlement. Although it varies, often such statutes will also include receiving stolen property, various forms of fraud, and extortion. Robbery and forgery are treated as separate crimes.

Arson and burglary are separate crimes because they involve more than a threat to property. At common law, only residences were protected by arson and burglary laws. As noted at the beginning of the chapter, because of the sanctity that our culture attaches to dwellings and because of the danger to human life created by arson and burglary, these crimes received special attention. Today, arson and burglary have been broadened to include more than just dwellings.

In addition to criminal remedies for these crimes, victims often have civil remedies available. As previously discussed, victims are responsible for filing and proving such a civil case. However, a prior admission of guilt (or conviction) may prevent defendants from relitigating their innocence in a civil trial.

Computer Theft Crimes

Computer-related crimes are costly and are on the rise. According to a report issued in 2008 by the Computer Security Institute, 50% of the respondent corporations reported having experienced virus attack, 44% reported insider abuse, 29% reported unauthorized access, 42% reported laptop theft, 27% experienced an attack specifically targeted at it or a small number of like organizations, 17% theft/loss of data, 13% system penetration, 6% website defacement, 2% sabotage, among other offenses. The total costs of these crimes is in the hundreds of billions of dollars each year.[21]

Computer crimes take two general forms. First, computers can be the target of a crime. Theft of hardware and software is an example. Destruction and vandalism of computers is another crime where the computer is itself the target of an unlawful act. Viruses are also used to destroy computer programs.

A second form of computer crime involves using a computer as a tool in the commission of a crime. Violating privileges by improperly obtaining confidential information, threat and harassment through cyberspace, and the illegal distribution of obscenities fall into this category. Computers can also be used to steal. Obtaining illegal entry into a bank's computer records from a personal computer in order to steal money is an example, as is using another person's personal identification number and bank card to access an automatic teller machine.

Many computer-related crimes are punishable without special computer crimes laws. Existing penal laws such as theft, larceny, and criminal mischief may include computer activity. For example, stealing funds from a bank through a computer can usually be prosecuted under existing theft laws if a special computer theft statute has not been enacted. Similarly, criminal mischief statutes could be used to prosecute the intentional destruction of computer programs by viruses.

In addition to existing laws, the federal government and 49 states had enacted special legislation to deal with computers and crimes by 1998. The Federal Counterfeit Access Device and Computer Fraud and Abuse Act became law in 1984 and was amended in 1986 by the Computer Fraud and Abuse Act. That law prohibits:

1. A knowing, unauthorized access to information contained in a federal interest computer.
2. An intentional, unauthorized access to financial information held by a financial institution or credit agency.
3. An intentional, unauthorized access of a computer of the United States that would affect the government's operation of the computer.
4. Thefts of property by use of computer as a result of a knowing and intentional scheme to defraud.
5. Knowingly altering, damaging, or destroying information within a federal interest computer or preventing the authorized use of such a computer.
6. Knowingly trafficking in any password without authorization if the trafficking affects interstate commerce or is used by or for the U.S. government.

Some of these crimes are misdemeanors, and others are felonies. The federal government regulated computer crime further through the Computer Abuse Amendments Act of 1994.[22] This statute criminalizes the transmission of any data intended to cause damage to a computer used by the federal government or a financial institution. It also prohibits "trafficking in passwords" that provide access to government computers or that interfere with interstate or foreign commerce.

In addition, there is a federal electronic espionage statute. Statute 18 U.S.C. § 1831 protects corporate propriety information. It reads, in part:

In General—

Whoever, intending or knowing that the offense will benefit any foreign government, foreign instrumentality, or foreign agent, knowingly—

(1) steals, or without authorization appropriates, takes, carries away, or conceals, or by fraud, artifice, or deception obtains a trade secret;

(2) without authorization copies, duplicates, sketches, draws, photographs, downloads, uploads, alters, destroys, photocopies, replicates, transmits, delivers, sends, mails, communicates, or conveys a trade secret;

(3) receives, buys, or possesses a trade secret, knowing the same to have been stolen or appropriated, obtained, or converted without authorization;

(4) attempts to commit any offense described in any of paragraphs (1) through (3); or

(5) conspires with one or more other persons to commit any offense described in any of paragraphs (1) through (3), and one or more of such persons do any act to effect the object of the conspiracy, shall, except as provided in subsection (b), be fined not more than $500,000 or imprisoned not more than 15 years, or both.

The private sector expends considerable resources in the prevention and detection of computer crimes. Law enforcement agencies have been forced to hire investigators and consultants with computer expertise to effectively investigate claims and educate the public in preventing computer crimes. As computer use and dependence increase, so will computer crimes.

BRIGGS V. MARYLAND
704 A.2d 904 (Md. Ct. App. 1998)

Terry Dewain Briggs appeals his conviction for the crime of unauthorized access to computers, in violation of Maryland Code. . . . The primary issue raised in this case is the meaning of the statutory requirement of access "without authorization" as used in § 146. The question we must answer is whether an employee who is entitled to use an employer's computer system in connection with employment duties, but who exceeds the scope of that authorization, is acting in a manner proscribed by Article 27, § 146. Briggs contends that his conduct did not come within the prohibition of the statute. We agree, and accordingly, shall reverse.

In November, 1994, the Scarborough Group, Inc. (Scarborough), a medium-sized securities investment company, hired Terry Briggs as a computer programmer and system administrator. Briggs, a twenty-three-year-old computer specialist, was hired to program and design software to maintain the company computer system. As part of his job responsibilities, he entered data in the computer system and placed passwords on the files to secure the data. The management

(continued)

of the entire computer system was entrusted to Briggs. Following a dispute on July 24, 1995, about the terms of his employment contract, Briggs resigned as an employee of the company. Shortly after Briggs left the company, Scarborough realized that some of its computer files were secured with passwords known only to Briggs. Scarborough and Briggs were unable to resolve the situation. Scarborough filed a civil suit against Briggs, and also contacted the Anne Arundel County police.

The State charged Briggs in a two-count criminal information: count one, theft of computers, in violation of Article 27, § 342(a) (1) and, count two, unauthorized access to computers, in violation of Article 27, § 146(c) (2). At trial, Scarborough contended that Briggs changed the passwords two days before the meeting about Brigg's employment contract, and put them in a subdirectory named "ha-ha he-he," dated July 22, 1995 by the computer. Scarborough maintained that Briggs never had permission to place the company files in a directory and to protect the file with passwords, without anyone else in the company having access to the passwords. Although he denied any knowledge about "ha-ha he-he," Briggs admitted that he placed passwords on company files months earlier as part of his job in securing files, but that he had difficulty remembering the passwords because so much time had passed. Briggs suggested that Scarborough filed criminal charges against him in order to discredit him as a government witness in a Securities and Exchange Commission investigation that Briggs had initiated alleging that certain activities at Scarborough violated federal security regulations. Briggs maintained that the computer date on the password subdirectory had been changed to incriminate him.

The State alleged that Briggs intentionally and willfully and without authorization accessed a computer system to interrupt the operation of the computer system and computer services. In his motion for judgement of acquittal, Briggs argued that he was not guilty as a matter of law (that the statute did not apply to his activities) and as a matter of fact (that he was fulfilling his employment responsibilities). Briggs reasoned that Article 27, § 146 was not intended to apply to authorized computer users who, arguably, used their positions to cause harm to their employers by misusing the computer. The State argued that Briggs was guilty of unauthorized access, because although Briggs was authorized to access the computer system, he was not authorized to access the system in such a way as to interrupt the operation of the computer services of the system. The trial court denied Briggs's motion for judgement of acquittal, and the jury found Briggs guilty of unauthorized access to computers in violation of Article 27, § 146(c)(2)(i). The court sentenced Briggs to one year incarceration, with all but two days suspended, two years supervised probation, 150 hours of community service, and a fine of $500. The court also ordered him to cooperate with Scarborough and required him to release any remaining password information and client files. Briggs noted a timely appeal to the Court of Special Appeals. We granted certiorari on our own motion before consideration by that court.

Appellant argues before this Court that Article 27, § 146 criminalizes the conduct of an individual who intentionally and willfully accesses a computer without authorization and is inapplicable to conduct that can be characterized as only exceeding authorized access. He concludes that the statute is inapplicable on its face because, as part of his employment, he was authorized to access the computer system. The purpose of the statute, Appellant continues, was to deter unauthorized users from breaking into computer systems, i.e., to prevent "hackers" from gaining unauthorized access. Briggs distinguishes operating a computer system

BRIGGS V. MARYLAND (continued)

without authorization from exceeding authorized access by using the computer in an improper manner. He concludes that application of this statute to his conduct is contrary to legislative intent.

The State contends that even though access for other activities may have been authorized, a person, whether he is an employee, "hacker," or otherwise, violates the statute when that person "intentionally, willfully, and without authorization" accesses a computer system or any part of a computer system to cause the malfunction or interrupt the operations of the computer system or any part of that system. The State maintains that there was sufficient evidence to support the verdict because Briggs did not have authority to place passwords on the files without anyone else in the company having those passwords, and that he did so with the intent of interrupting the operation of the computer system. . . .

We need not address Appellant's factual argument that he was authorized to place passwords on Scarborough's computer system, because we find the second element dispositive and hold that Appellant's access to the computer was not "without authorization" within the meaning of the statute. When faced with a question of statutory construction, we look first to the plain meaning of the words of the statute, with the goal to ascertain and effectuate legislative intent.

We give the words of the statute their ordinary and natural meaning. If the language of the statute is plain and clear and expresses a meaning consistent with the statute's apparent purpose, no further analysis is ordinarily required. On the other hand, if the language of the statute is ambiguous or unclear, "we must consider 'not only the literal or usual meaning of the words but their meaning and effect in light of the setting, the objectives and purpose of the enactment,' in our attempt to discern the construction that will best further the legislative objectives or goals."

The statute prohibits unauthorized access of a computer, computer network, or computer systems. "Access" is defined in the statute "to instruct, communicate with, store data in, retrieve data from, or otherwise make use of equipment including . . . computers." § 146 (a) (9). "Without authorization" modifies the word "access." Therefore, the unlawful act is unauthorized access. "Authorization" is not defined in the statute. Turning to dictionary definitions of "authorize," we find that *Black's Law Dictionary* 133–34 (6th ed. 1990) defines "authorize" to mean "[t]o empower; to give a right or authority to act. To endow with authority or effective legal power, warrant, or right. To permit a thing to be done in the future." (Citation omitted.) Similarly, *Webster's New International Dictionary*, Unabridged 186 (2d ed. 1950) defines "authorize" to mean "to clothe with authority or legal power; to give right to act; to make legal; to legalize; to give authoritative permission to or for; to justify." The testimony at trial that Briggs had authority to enter data in the computer and to place passwords on the files to secure the data establishes that he was authorized, under the statute, to "instruct, communicate with, store data in, retrieve data from and to make use of computer data equipment and other data processing equipment." . . .

The plain language of the statute suggests that if an employee were initially permitted to "instruct," "communicate with," "store data in," or "retrieve data from" the computer system, then that employee's access would be authorized. The statute makes no reference to authorized users who exceed the scope of their authority. If the Legislature intended the statute to cover employees who exceeded the scope of their authority or who misused their authority, it could have done so explicitly. We conclude that the intent of the General Assembly was to criminalize the misuse of computers or computer networks by those whose initial access was unauthorized. [Judgement of conviction reversed.]

On the other side, computer technology has advanced law enforcement in some respects. The *Briggs* case is an illustration of the application and complexity of computer crimes.

National Crime Information Center

■ Computerized records of criminals, warrants, stolen vehicles, etc.

The **National Crime Information Center** (NCIC) is used by law enforcement agencies nationwide in the reporting and detection of wanted persons. Computers are used to organize and manage case files. Graphics programs are used to recreate crimes and to project a fugitive's appearance after donning a disguise or after having aged. These are but a few of the uses computers play in law enforcement. The use of computers by law enforcement raises interesting search and privacy questions. This topic is discussed in Chapter 12.

Ethical Considerations

THE INEFFECTIVE ASSISTANCE OF COUNSEL

Criminal defendants are entitled to the effective assistance of counsel. So, what is the remedy for convictees who believe that their defense counsel committed professional malpractice? First, convictees may appeal their conviction. Second, the attorney may be sued in civil court for malpractice. Third, convictees may file a complaint with the bar authority. However, the standard of proof for convictees is high and, accordingly, most do not prevail.

To get a conviction remanded for new trial because of ineffective counsel in most jurisdictions, convictees must show that the representation was extremely inadequate, and as a consequence, the appellants were convicted. As plaintiffs in malpractice suits (where money damages, but not remand or reversal of the conviction, are sought), convictees have a similar expectation. They must obtain appellate relief from the conviction because of the ineffective assistance of counsel or must prove their innocence, separate from the criminal court judgement. This is commonly known as the exoneration rule because the bar is so high to prove criminal malpractice that few cases are filed. The trend is toward adoption of the exoneration rule in the states.

The final avenue of remedy for a victim of criminal malpractice is to file a complaint against a convictee with the bar authority. The exoneration rule is not applied in such cases. As such, malpractice that was not the cause of a conviction may be disciplined. In such cases, a plaintiff-convictee must prove incompetence or that another specific ethical rule (e.g., confidentiality) was violated.

For more on criminal malpractice, see Johanna M. Hickman, "Recent Developments in the Area of Criminal Malpractice," 18 Geo. *J. Legal Ethics.* 797 (2005).

┌───┐

Web Links

Crime Data

Two excellent sites will provide a huge amount of data on crime. Reports on crime-related issues may also be found in these locations. The first is the National Institute of Justice, at http://www.ojp.usdoj.gov/nij/, and the second is the Bureau of Justice Statistics, at http://www.ojp.usdoj.gov/bjs/. Both are U.S. Department of Justice offices

└───┘

Key Terms

arson

burglary

conversion

criminal mischief

embezzlement

extortion

false pretenses

forfeiture

forgery

identity theft

larceny

National Crime Information Center

Racketeer Influenced and Corrupt Organizations Act

receiving stolen property

robbery

Review Questions

1. What is "constructive breaking," when referring to the crime of burglary?

2. Define larceny.

3. What is criminal mischief?

4. Embezzlement is often punished more severely than simple larceny. Why?

5. What does the acronym RICO represent? What are the basic elements of RICO?

6. What are "fences?" At common law, what crime do fences commit?

7. How is destruction of a building by explosion treated by the Model Penal Code? At common law?

8. Brogan runs by a woman on the street and grabs her purse as he passes her. The purse is easily pulled from her arm, and Brogan's intent is to keep the contents. What crime has been committed?

9. Brogan runs by a woman on the street and grabs her purse as he passes her. The woman catches the strap and fights to keep the purse; however, the strap breaks, and Brogan is successful. He keeps the contents of the purse. What crime has been committed?

10. What is the difference between forgery and uttering?

Problems & Critical Thinking Exercises

1. Arson is quite different today than it was at common law. What are the major differences?

2. Burglary is quite different today than it was at common law. What are the major differences?

3. Doug and Sherri are an elderly couple who are retired and residing in Florida. Both have suffered substantial physical deterioration, including vision loss and poor memory. Ned, who had coveted their 1962 Corvette for years, told the couple that they should trust him with their financial affairs, including giving him title to their vehicle. He told the two that he would drive them to the places they needed to go, but that state law required that his name appear on the title of the car, as he would be the sole driver. Doug and Sherri complied with his request, believing that his statement concerning Florida law was correct.

    Subsequently, the couple created a trust account and named Ned as trustee. The purpose of the account was to provide Ned with a general fund from which he was to pay the household bills. Ned withdrew all the money and placed it into his personal account. When this occurred, the couple contacted Ned, who claimed to know nothing of the account. Sherri contacted the local prosecutor, who conducted an investigation. Through that investigation, it was discovered that Ned held title to the Corvette.

    You work for the prosecutor. Your assignment is to determine what crimes have been committed, if any. Your state has no theft statute, but recognizes common-law theft crimes.

4. Gary and Paige were friends until they discovered that they shared an interest in Tracy. After Paige won her affection, Gary became enraged and took a key and ran it down the side of Paige's car. He then poured gasoline over the car and set it on fire. Gary has been arrested. What crimes should be charged?

5. Kevin was walking down the sidewalk that passed in front of Sean's home. As he passed Sean's house, he looked in a front window and noticed a carton of soft drinks sitting in the kitchen. As he was thirsty, Kevin broke the front window and crawled into Sean's house. Once inside, he poured himself a glass of cola and sat down at the dining room table. While seated at the table, he picked up a ring with a value in excess of $1,000, and put it into his pocket. When he finished his drink, he placed the empty glass in the sink and left. He later sold the ring and bought a stereo with the proceeds. What crimes have been committed, using common-law theft crimes?

6. Brogan has an affair with Janice, who is married. After Janice ends the affair, Brogan threatens to tell Janice's husband about their sexual involvement unless Janice pays Brogan $5,000. Janice complies. What crime has been committed?

7. Penni is working the night shift at a local convenience store when Craig and Guido come in. Craig states to Penni, "Give us all the money in the register and we will not hurt you. Give us any trouble and we will knock the #?!@ out of you!" Penni complies. What crime has been committed? What if they had been brandishing weapons?

8. Discuss what crimes you think should be included in consolidated theft statutes and why. Explain why particular crimes should be left out of such a statute.

Endnotes

1. Davenport, P., *Michael Marin, Ex-Wall Street Trader, Took Cyanide After Arson Guilty Verdict*. Huffington Post, July 27, 2012, found at http://www.huffingtonpost.com/2012/07/27/michael-marin-cyanide_n_1710731.html and *Arson in America*: The odd tale of Michael Marin, IndependentMail.com (April 23, 2013).
2. 5 Am. Jur. 2d *Arson* 2 (1962).
3. Model Penal Code § 220.1.
4. Model Penal Code § 220.1(1) and (2).
5. *People v. Richards*, 108 N.Y. 137, 15 N.E. 371 (1988).
6. LaFave & Scott, *Criminal Law* 797 (Hornbook Series; St. Paul: West, 1986).
7. A. Loewy, *Criminal Law*, 2d ed. (Nutshell Series; St. Paul: West, 1987).
8. *Bazeley's Case,* 2 East P.C. 571 (Cr. Cas. Res. 1799); *see* LaFave & Scott, *Criminal Law* § 8.1 (Hornbook Series; St. Paul: West, 1986).
9. 18 U.S.C. § 641 *et seq.*
10. LaFave & Scott, *Criminal Law* § 8.9 (Hornbook Series; St. Paul: West, 1986).
11. 18 U.S.C. § 1341.
12. 18 U.S.C. § 1961 *et seq.*
13. *N.O.W. v. Scheidler*, 114 S. Ct. 798 (1994).
14. 18 U.S.C. § 2311 *et seq.*
15. 18 U.S.C. § 2113.
16. Fla. Stat. Ann. § 812.012 *et seq.*
17. 18 U.S.C. § 1028.
18. Model Penal Code § 223 *et seq.* deals with theft offenses.
19. *Id.* § 222.1.
20. *Id.* § 224.1.
21. 2008 Computer Crime and Security Survey, Computer Security Institute (2008), http://gocsi.com/sites/default/files/uploads/CSIsurvey2008.pdf
22. 18 U.S.C. §§ 1029–30.

CHAPTER 6

CRIMES AGAINST THE PUBLIC

Chapter Objectives

After completing this chapter, you should be able to

- describe historic and contemporary crimes against the public, including crimes against the public order, against the administration of government, against public morality, and against the environment.

- critically examine and discuss the laws of terrorism, especially those laws enacted in response to the September 11, 2001, attacks on the United States.

- explain the tension between national security and freedom and how the war on terror confounds the historic distinction between the law of war and criminal law

- explain what role that morality has, and what you believe it should play, in penal law.

- identify the material facts and legal issues in one-third of the cases you read and describe the court's analyses and conclusions in the cases.

DEFINING A "CRIME AGAINST THE PUBLIC"

Chapters 4 and 5 were concerned with crimes that victimize individuals or entities, such as corporations and other business organizations. This chapter examines crimes that do not have individual victims. These are crimes involving the public welfare, social order, and society's morals. Many, if not most, of these crimes are malum prohibitum in nature, not malum in se.

Historically religion has played a role in the "criminalization" of "victimless" crimes. Of course, religious groups do not dictate such policy—this would violate the First Amendment's Establishment Clause. Religion does, however, influence the moral values of the members of a society. In the United States this influence is predominantly Christian. This is the reason that some acts that directly harm no one are prohibited.

Some critics call for an end to "victimless crimes." Despite this opposition, many victimless crimes exist and are likely to continue to be prohibited. However, in a democracy such as the United States, it is important to avoid an unwarranted infringement of civil liberties. The more a law is premised upon a moral judgement, the greater the scrutiny of, and reasons justifying, such laws should be.

Some of the crimes discussed here bear directly upon the administration of government and justice and less upon moral determinations. For example, contempt of court is a crime against the public, and the premise of its prohibition is the theory that if society punishes offenders, others will comply with court orders, and the administration of justice will be enhanced. Prostitution is an example of a crime that is prohibited more for moral reasons than any other.

The crimes included in this chapter have been divided into five subsections: crimes against public morality; crimes against the public order; crimes against the administration of government; crimes against sovereignty and security; and crimes against the environment.

CRIMES AGAINST PUBLIC MORALITY

Prostitution and Solicitation

prostitution

■ A person offering her (in most states, his or her) body for sexual purposes in exchange for money. A crime in most states.

Often said to be the oldest profession, **prostitution** is prohibited in every state except Nevada, where each county is given the authority to determine whether it should be permitted.

Prostitution is defined as (1) providing (2) sexual services (3) in exchange for compensation. In a few states, only intercourse is included in the definition of sexual services. In most states, however, sexual services include sodomy, fellatio, cunnilingus, and the touching of another's genitals. The Model Penal Code includes homosexual and other deviate sexual conduct in its definition of sexual activity.[1]

The service must be provided in exchange for compensation. The person who is sexually promiscuous, but unpaid, goes unpunished. Compensation normally means money, but it can come in any form. Thus, the prostitute who accepts legal services from a lawyer in exchange for sexual services has received compensation. Where prostitution is illegal, it is common for prostitutes to use businesses, such as massage parlors and escort services, as fronts.

Solicitation is a related crime. Any person who engages in selling sex, buying sex, or attempting to buy sex is guilty of solicitation. Note that a prostitute may be guilty of both solicitation and prostitution, if the prostitute makes the first contact with the buyer. There need not be the actual sale of sex for solicitation—only an attempt to sell sexual services. The clients of prostitutes, when prosecuted, are charged with solicitation.

The Model Penal Code states that "[a] person commits a violation if he hires a prostitute to engage in sexual activity with him, or if he enters or remains in a house of prostitution for the purpose of engaging in sexual activity."[2]

Those who promote prostitution (*pimps*) are usually punished more severely than prostitutes and customers. The Model Penal Code makes knowingly promoting prostitution a felony of the third degree if a child under 16 years of age is prostituted; the defendant's wife, child, or other ward is prostituted; the defendant forces or encourages another to engage in prostitution; or the defendant owns, controls, or manages a house of prostitution. In all other cases promotion is a misdemeanor.

Nearly all sex-for-hire cases fall under state jurisdiction. However, the federal government may be involved in prosecution when a prostitute is transported in interstate commerce, or any other person is transported in interstate commerce for an immoral purpose.[3]

Deviate Sexual Conduct

Rape and related crimes were discussed in Chapter 4. That chapter focused on sexual behavior that results in harm to a victim. This discussion is different, as there is usually no victim other than society as a whole. Deviate sexual conduct has many definitions, but most states include fellatio, cunnilingus, anal sex, and all homosexual activity within the grasp of their deviate sexual statutes. Therefore, consenting adults, married or not, may be prosecuted for participating in such sexual activity under many older statutes.

The foundation of the prohibition of sodomy and related acts is morality. Adherents of many religions, including Christianity, believe that all sex other than vaginal intercourse between a man and woman is deviate. The reality is that many, if not most, people engage in sex that satisfies the definition of deviate sex. For this reason, many people argue that such acts are normal and should not be prohibited. Others argue that it does not matter if the behavior is normal or deviate—that sex between two consenting adults is private and involves no victims and, as such, is of no concern of the government. Regardless such laws continue to exist. Further, they have survived constitutional challenges in many instances.

Despite continued prohibition of sodomy, and related acts, in many states, the laws are seldom enforced. One reason is that law enforcement officials have shown a reluctance to enforce such laws, often because crimes perceived as more serious are time-demanding and leave little manpower and resources to enforce victimless crimes. In addition, there simply is the problem of discovering violations. Most sexual conduct occurs privately, and thus the police rarely discover violations independently. Of course, those who participate in prohibited sexual conduct are not likely to report their sex partners' acts to law enforcement. But it is possible for officers to discover violations, and several cases where it has happened have resulted in arrests, convictions, and appellate review.

In 1982, a local police officer discovered Michael Hardwick engaged in consensual oral sex with another man in Hardwick's bedroom. The officer was in the house to serve a warrant on Hardwick. The officer arrested both men for violating Georgia's sodomy statute. Although the prosecutor declined to file charges, Hardwick sued the Georgia attorney general, seeking an order of the court enjoining enforcement of the sodomy law. The case made its way to the Supreme Court of the United States, where the law was upheld. Hardwick's theory was that the right to privacy, found implicit in the Fourteenth Amendment's due process guarantee, shielded private consensual sexual conduct from governmental regulation. The Court rejected this argument, holding that the nation's long moral history of revulsion and prohibition of same-sex sodomy outweighed Hardwick's privacy concerns. The decision of the Court was 5–4. Justice Powell voted with the majority, and after his retirement he stated that he regretted his vote in the case. This is not the end of the story, however. In 1998, the Georgia Supreme Court found the statute to be violative of the privacy protections in the Georgia Constitution.[4] Then, the United State Supreme Court revisited the issue in *Lawrence v. Texas*.

LAWRENCE V. TEXAS
539 U.S. 558 (2003)

Justice Kennedy delivered the opinion of the Court.

Liberty protects the person from unwarranted government intrusions into a dwelling or other private places. In our tradition the State is not omnipresent in the home. And there are other spheres of our lives and existence, outside the home, where the State should not be a dominant presence. Freedom extends beyond spatial bounds. Liberty presumes an autonomy of self that includes freedom of thought, belief, expression, and certain intimate conduct. The

(continued)

LAWRENCE V. TEXAS *(continued)*

instant case involves liberty of the person both in its spatial and more transcendent dimensions.

The question before the Court is the validity of a Texas statute making it a crime for two persons of the same sex to engage in certain intimate sexual conduct.

In Houston, Texas, officers of the Harris County Police Department were dispatched to a private residence in response to a reported weapons disturbance. They entered an apartment where one of the petitioners, John Geddes Lawrence, resided. The right of the police to enter does not seem to have been questioned. The officers observed Lawrence and another man, Tyron Garner, engaging in a sexual act. The two petitioners were arrested, held in custody overnight, and charged and convicted before a Justice of the Peace.

The complaints described their crime as "deviate sexual intercourse, namely anal sex, with a member of the same sex (man)." The applicable state law is Tex. Penal Code Ann. § 21.06(a) (2003). It provides: "A person commits an offense if he engages in deviate sexual intercourse with another individual of the same sex." The statute defines "[d]eviate sexual intercourse" as follows:

> "(A) any contact between any part of the genitals of one person and the mouth or anus of another person; or
> "(B) the penetration of the genitals or the anus of another person with an object." § 21.01(1).

The petitioners exercised their right to a trial *de novo* in Harris County Criminal Court. They challenged the statute as a violation of the Equal Protection Clause of the Fourteenth Amendment and of a like provision of the Texas Constitution. Tex. Const., Art. 1, § 3a. . . . [The defendant lost on appeal. The appellate court relied on *Bowers v. Hardwick* in analyzing the federal issue.]

The Court began its substantive discussion in *Bowers* as follows: "The issue presented is whether the Federal Constitution confers a fundamental right upon homosexuals to engage in sodomy and hence invalidates the laws of the many States that still make such conduct illegal and have done so for a very long time." That statement, we now conclude, discloses the Court's own failure to appreciate the extent of the liberty at stake. To say that the issue in *Bowers* was simply the right to engage in certain sexual conduct demeans the claim the individual put forward, just as it would demean a married couple were it to be said marriage is simply about the right to have sexual intercourse. The laws involved in *Bowers* and here are, to be sure, statutes that purport to do no more than prohibit a particular sexual act. Their penalties and purposes, though, have more far-reaching consequences, touching upon the most private human conduct, sexual behavior, and in the most private of places, the home. The statutes do seek to control a personal relationship that, whether or not entitled to formal recognition in the law, is within the liberty of persons to choose without being punished as criminals.

This, as a general rule, should counsel against attempts by the State, or a court, to define the meaning of the relationship or to set its boundaries absent injury to a person or abuse of an institution the law protects. It suffices for us to acknowledge that adults may choose to enter upon this relationship in the confines of their homes and their own private lives and still retain their dignity as free persons. When sexuality finds overt expression in intimate conduct with another person, the conduct can be but one element in a personal bond that is more enduring. The liberty protected by the Constitution allows homosexual persons the right to make this choice.

Having misapprehended the claim of liberty there presented to it, and thus stating the claim to be whether there is a fundamental right to engage in consensual sodomy, the *Bowers* Court said: "Proscriptions against that conduct have ancient roots." In academic writings, and in many of

LAWRENCE V. TEXAS *(continued)*

the scholarly *amicus* briefs filed to assist the Court in this case, there are fundamental criticisms of the historical premises relied upon by the majority and concurring opinions in *Bowers*. We need not enter this debate in the attempt to reach a definitive historical judgement, but the following considerations counsel against adopting the definitive conclusions upon which *Bowers* placed such reliance.

At the outset it should be noted that there is no longstanding history in this country of laws directed at homosexual conduct as a distinct matter. Beginning in colonial times there were prohibitions of sodomy derived from the English criminal laws passed in the first instance by the Reformation Parliament of 1533. The English prohibition was understood to include relations between men and women as well as relations between men and men. See, *e.g.*, *King* v. *Wiseman,* 92 Eng. Rep. 774, 775 (K. B. 1718) (interpreting "mankind" in Act of 1533 as including women and girls). Nineteenth-century commentators similarly read American sodomy, buggery, and crime-against-nature statutes as criminalizing certain relations between men and women and between men and men. See, *e.g.*, 2 J. Bishop, *Criminal Law* § 1028 (1858); 2 J. Chitty, *Criminal Law* 47–50 (5th Am. ed. 1847); R. Desty, *A Compendium of American Criminal Law* 143 (1882); J. May, *The Law of Crimes* § 203 (2d ed. 1893). The absence of legal prohibitions focusing on homosexual conduct may be explained in part by noting that according to some scholars the concept of the homosexual as a distinct category of person did not emerge until the late nineteenth century. See, *e.g.*, J. Katz, *The Invention of Heterosexuality* 10 (1995); J. D'Emilio & E. Freedman, *Intimate Matters: A History of Sexuality in America* 121 (2d ed. 1997) ("The modern terms *homosexuality* and *heterosexuality* do not apply to an era that had not yet articulated these distinctions"). Thus early American sodomy laws were not directed

at homosexuals as such but instead sought to prohibit nonprocreative sexual activity more generally. This does not suggest approval of homosexual conduct. It does tend to show that this particular form of conduct was not thought of as a separate category from like conduct between heterosexual persons.

Laws prohibiting sodomy do not seem to have been enforced against consenting adults acting in private. A substantial number of sodomy prosecutions and convictions for which there are surviving records were for predatory acts against those who could not or did not consent, as in the case of a minor or the victim of an assault. As to these, one purpose for the prohibitions was to ensure there would be no lack of coverage if a predator committed a sexual assault that did not constitute rape as defined by the criminal law. Thus the model sodomy indictments presented in a 19th-century treatise, see 2 Chitty, *supra,* at 49, addressed the predatory acts of an adult man against a minor girl or minor boy. Instead of targeting relations between consenting adults in private, 19th-century sodomy prosecutions typically involved relations between men and minor girls or minor boys, relations between adults involving force, relations between adults implicating disparity in status, or relations between men and animals.

To the extent that there were any prosecutions for the acts in question, 19th-century evidence rules imposed a burden that would make a conviction more difficult to obtain even taking into account the problems always inherent in prosecuting consensual acts committed in private. Under then-prevailing standards, a man could not be convicted of sodomy based upon testimony of a consenting partner, because the partner was considered an accomplice. A partner's testimony, however, was admissible if he or she had not consented to the act or was a minor, and therefore incapable of consent. See, *e.g.*, F. Wharton, *Criminal Law* 443 (2d ed. 1852); 1 F. Wharton, *Criminal*

(continued)

LAWRENCE V. TEXAS *(continued)*

Law 512 (8th ed. 1880). The rule may explain in part the infrequency of these prosecutions. In all events that infrequency makes it difficult to say that society approved of a rigorous and systematic punishment of the consensual acts committed in private and by adults. The longstanding criminal prohibition of homosexual sodomy upon which the *Bowers* decision placed such reliance is as consistent with a general condemnation of nonprocreative sex as it is with an established tradition of prosecuting acts because of their homosexual character.

The policy of punishing consenting adults for private acts was not much discussed in the early legal literature. We can infer that one reason for this was the very private nature of the conduct. Despite the absence of prosecutions, there may have been periods in which there was public criticism of homosexuals as such and an insistence that the criminal laws be enforced to discourage their practices. But far from possessing "ancient roots," *Bowers*, 478 U.S., at 192, American laws targeting same-sex couples did not develop until the last third of the 20th century. The reported decisions concerning the prosecution of consensual, homosexual sodomy between adults for the years 1880–1995 are not always clear in the details, but a significant number involved conduct in a public place. It was not until the 1970s that any State singled out same-sex relations for criminal prosecution, and only nine States have done so. . . . Over the course of the last decades, States with same-sex prohibitions have moved toward abolishing them. In summary, the historical grounds relied upon in *Bowers* are more complex than the majority opinion and the concurring opinion by Chief Justice Burger indicate. Their historical premises are not without doubt and, at the very least, are overstated. . . .

It must be acknowledged, of course, that the Court in *Bowers* was making the broader point that for centuries there have been powerful voices to condemn homosexual conduct as immoral.

The condemnation has been shaped by religious beliefs, conceptions of right and acceptable behavior, and respect for the traditional family. For many persons these are not trivial concerns but profound and deep convictions accepted as ethical and moral principles to which they aspire and which thus determine the course of their lives. These considerations do not answer the question before us, however. The issue is whether the majority may use the power of the State to enforce these views on the whole society through operation of the criminal law. "Our obligation is to define the liberty of all, not to mandate our own moral code. . . .

In our own constitutional system the deficiencies in *Bowers* became even more apparent in the years following its announcement. The 25 States with laws prohibiting the relevant conduct referenced in the *Bowers* decision are reduced now to 13, of which 4 enforce their laws only against homosexual conduct. In those States where sodomy is still proscribed, whether for same-sex or heterosexual conduct, there is a pattern of nonenforcement with respect to consenting adults acting in private. The State of Texas admitted in 1994 that as of that date it had not prosecuted anyone under those circumstances. . . .

Two principal cases decided after *Bowers* cast its holding into even more doubt. In *Planned Parenthood of Southeastern Pa. v. Casey*, 505 U.S. 833 (1992), the Court reaffirmed the substantive force of the liberty protected by the Due Process Clause. The *Casey* decision again confirmed that our laws and tradition afford constitutional protection to personal decisions relating to marriage, procreation, contraception, family relationships, child rearing, and education. In explaining the respect the Constitution demands for the autonomy of the person in making these choices, we stated as follows:

LAWRENCE V. TEXAS *(continued)*

"These matters, involving the most intimate and personal choices a person may make in a lifetime, choices central to personal dignity and autonomy, are central to the liberty protected by the Fourteenth Amendment. At the heart of liberty is the right to define one's own concept of existence, of meaning, of the universe, and of the mystery of human life. Beliefs about these matters could not define the attributes of personhood were they formed under compulsion of the State."

Persons in a homosexual relationship may seek autonomy for these purposes, just as heterosexual persons do. The decision in *Bowers* would deny them this right.

The second post-*Bowers* case of principal relevance is *Romer v. Evans*, 517 U.S. 620 (1996). There the Court struck down class-based legislation directed at homosexuals as a violation of the Equal Protection Clause. *Romer* invalidated an amendment to Colorado's constitution which named as a solitary class persons who were homosexuals, lesbians, or bisexual either by "orientation, conduct, practices or relationships . . . and deprived them of protection under state antidiscrimination laws. We concluded that the provision was "born of animosity toward the class of persons affected" and further that it had no rational relation to a legitimate governmental purpose. . . .

The foundations of *Bowers* have sustained serious erosion from our recent decisions in *Casey* and *Romer*. When our precedent has been thus weakened, criticism from other sources is of greater significance. In the United States criticism of *Bowers* has been substantial and continuing, disapproving of its reasoning in all respects, not just as to its historical assumptions. . . The courts of five different States have declined to follow it in interpreting provisions in their own state constitutions parallel to the Due Process Clause. . . .

To the extent *Bowers* relied on values we share with a wider civilization, it should be noted that the reasoning and holding in *Bowers* have been rejected elsewhere. The European Court of Human Rights has followed not *Bowers* but its own decision in *Dudgeon v. United Kingdom*. . . . Other nations, too, have taken action consistent with an affirmation of the protected right of homosexual adults to engage in intimate, consensual conduct.

The doctrine of *stare decisis* is essential to the respect accorded to the judgements of the Court and to the stability of the law. It is not, however, an inexorable command. . . .

Bowers was not correct when it was decided, and it is not correct today. It ought not to remain binding precedent. *Bowers v. Hardwick* should be and now is overruled.

The present case does not involve minors. It does not involve persons who might be injured or coerced or who are situated in relationships where consent might not easily be refused. It does not involve public conduct or prostitution. It does not involve whether the government must give formal recognition to any relationship that homosexual persons seek to enter. The case does involve two adults who, with full and mutual consent from each other, engaged in sexual practices common to a homosexual lifestyle. The petitioners are entitled to respect for their private lives. The State cannot demean their existence or control their destiny by making their private sexual conduct a crime. Their right to liberty under the Due Process Clause gives them the full right to engage in their conduct without intervention of the government. "It is a promise of the Constitution that there is a realm of personal liberty which the government may not enter." The Texas statute furthers no legitimate state interest which can justify its intrusion into the personal and private life of the individual. . . .

Marriage, Contraception, and Abortion

Marriage is a state-coopted institution. States regulate marriage in a number of ways. All states specify how many people may marry, two in each union, who may marry (no close relatives), who has the authority to perform the marriage ceremony, when couples may marry (some states require a waiting period and/or blood tests), and the payment of a fee for the issuance of a license. Additionally, states and the federal government have built marriage into their tax schemes. There are limits, however, to the regulation of marriage. For example, for many years states prohibited and criminalized marriages between people of different races. As you will read in Chapter 9, the Supreme Court invalidated these laws as violating one's right to liberty, as protected by due process. Similarly, criminal prohibitions of the use of contraceptives and early term abortions were invalidated.

Due process and equal protection are evolving values and rights. Although a federalism and not a deviate sexual conduct case, the Supreme Court's 2013 decision *United States v. Windsor*, which invalidated a provision of the Defense of Marriage Act, contains sweeping equal protection and due process language that can be interpreted as foreshadowing a decision securing a right to same sex marriage in the near future. These topics are discussed more fully in Chapter 9.

Indecent Exposure and Lewdness

Indecent exposure, or the exposure of one's "private parts" in public, was a common-law misdemeanor. Today, the crime is usually criminalized by state statute or local ordinance.

Most indecent exposure laws require (1) an intentional exposure (2) of one's private parts (3) in a public place. In some jurisdictions, it is required that the exposure be done in an "offensive manner."

In 1991, the United States Supreme Court examined a public nudity statute in the context of nude barroom dancing. In *Barnes v. Glen Theater, Inc.,*[5] the Court upheld an Indiana statute that required dancers to wear pasties and G-strings. Although the court found that nude dancing was expressive conduct, it determined that states may require the dancers to cover their genitals. The court did say that erotic performances were protected by the First Amendment, provided the dancers wear a scant amount of clothing. The Court upheld the law because it determined that the state's objective was not to regulate expression, but to regulate for order and morality. Further, the Court held that the interference with expression was minimal.

The Model Penal Code prohibits public indecency. The Code goes further with a provision proscribing all lewd acts that the defendant knows are likely to be observed by others who would be "affronted or alarmed" by the acts.[6]

Obscenity

Congress shall make no law respecting the establishment of religion, or prohibiting the free exercise thereof; *or abridging the freedom of speech,* or of the press; or the right of the people peaceably to assemble, and to petition the Government for a redress of grievances.

This is the First Amendment to the U.S. Constitution. Most, if not all, states have a similar provision in their constitutions. The italicized portion represents the only protection of speech in the Constitution. Because it is brief and broad, it is dependent upon a great amount of interpretation to give it meaning. Also, because of its brevity and broadness, courts often interpret it differently. Even the Supreme Court has changed its interpretation of the clause, in particular areas, on several occasions. Freedom of speech encompasses far more than will be examined in this chapter. What will be discussed here is the extent of governmental power to regulate conduct that it deems to be indecent. Specifically, this section addresses sexually explicit materials, including films, books, and erotic dancing. It is well established that the term *speech,* as used in the First Amendment, means more than spoken utterances. It includes all forms of expression.

Both the federal and state governments regulate conduct, speech, books, movies, and other forms of expression that are believed to be "obscene." State governments are the most involved with regulating obscenity, due to general police power (the power to regulate for the health, welfare, and safety of citizens). However, the federal government is also involved; for example, it has criminalized sending obscene materials through the mail.[7]

Not all indecencies may be criminalized. Simply because something strikes one person as indecent does not mean that it should be prohibited. People have differing values, and to allow governments to prohibit all conduct (or other things) that is found offensive by some member of society would be to allow our government to criminalize all aspects of life. In addition, people perceive things differently. For example, in 1990 the Cincinnati Arts Center was charged with obscenity for displaying photographs taken by a respected artist, Robert Mapplethorpe. Included in the photos were depictions of nude children. The prosecutor contended that the pictures were obscene. A jury did not agree. The Arts Center and its director were acquitted, and many of the jurors commented that the testimony of art experts convinced them that the pictures had serious artistic value and were not obscene.[8]

It is important that the First Amendment be flexible and tolerant of new ideas and methods of expression. Simply because the majority of citizens would not see value in a form of expression does not mean it has no value. If the opposite were true, then expression aimed at particular minority groups could be censored. This is not to say that there is no limit on the freedom of expression. When considering sexually oriented expression, that line is drawn when the expression becomes obscene.[9]

Obscenity has proven to be an elusive concept for the Supreme Court. Through a series of decisions, from 1957 to the present, the Court has attempted to define *obscenity*. The famous quotation from Justice Potter Stewart -"I shall not today attempt further to define [obscenity]; and perhaps I could never succeed in intelligibly doing so. But I know it when I see it."—*Jacobellis v. Ohio,*[10] is a testament to the difficulty in defining such a concept. It also reflects what many people believe—that they may not be able to define obscenity, but they recognize it when they see it.

In *Roth v. United States,*[11] it was held that because it lacks redeeming social importance, obscenity is not protected by the First Amendment. The Court then established a test for determining whether something was obscene, and, as such, not protected by the First Amendment. That test was "whether to the average person, applying contemporary community standards, the dominant theme of the material taken as a whole appeals to prurient interest." In addition, the material had to be "utterly without redeeming social value." Simply because "literature is dismally unpleasant, uncouth, and tawdry is not enough to make it 'obscene.'"[12]

In 1973 the Supreme Court reexamined the *Roth* obscenity test in *Miller v. California*.[13] In *Miller* the Court rejected the requirement that the material be "utterly without redeeming social value" and lowered the standard to lacking "serious literary, artistic, political, or scientific value." The test under *Miller* has three parts:

1. The average person, applying contemporary community standards, would find that the work, taken as a whole, appeals to the prurient interest and
2. the work must depict or describe, in a patently offensive manner, sexual conduct specifically defined by the applicable state law, and
3. the work, when taken as a whole, must lack serious literary, artistic, political, or scientific value.

The *Miller* test makes it easier for states to regulate sexual materials. An "average person" has been equated with a reasonable person, as used in tort law.[14] The material must appeal to "prurient interest." Materials that have a tendency to excite a lustful, "shameful or morbid interest in nudity, sex or excretion" meet the prurient interest element.[15] Material that provokes normal, healthy, sexual desires is not obscene because it does not appeal to prurient interest.[16]

The Court gave examples in *Miller* of "patently offensive" materials that included depictions or descriptions of "ultimate sex acts, normal or perverted, actual or simulated . . . of masturbation, excretory functions, and lewd exhibition of the genitals."

One area where the states have substantially more power to regulate obscenity is when minors are involved. The Court has held that all child pornography is unprotected because of the special need to protect children from exploitation.[17] Similarly, governments may prohibit the distribution and sale of erotic materials to minors, even if such materials are not obscene.[18] Also, in *Osborne v. Ohio*,[19] the Supreme Court held that a person may be convicted for possession of child pornography in the home. This is an exception to the general rule that a person may possess obscene material in the home.

As mentioned in *Miller,* governments may control the time, place, and manner of expression. Accordingly, certain restrictions may be valid that deal with expression in certain places, such as establishments that sell alcohol. (Chapter 8 addresses constitutional defenses to criminal accusations and discusses other time, place, and manner issues.)

One place where the authority of the government to regulate sexually explicit materials is lessened is in homes. In many respects, the law reflects the attitude that a "man's home is his castle" and deserves special protection. Thus, the United States Supreme Court struck down the conviction of a man for possession of obscene materials in his home.[20] However, as previously mentioned, a person is not privileged to possess child pornography in the home.

The Model Penal Code makes it a misdemeanor to knowingly or recklessly do any of the following:[21]

1. Sell, deliver, or provide (or offer to do one of the three) any obscene writing, picture, record, or other obscene representation.
2. Present or perform in an obscene play, dance, or other performance.
3. Publish or exhibit obscene materials.
4. Possess obscene materials for commercial purposes.
5. Sell or otherwise commercially distribute materials represented as obscene.

The Code presumes that anyone who distributes obscene materials in the course of business has done so knowingly or recklessly.

Material is considered obscene under the Code if "considered as a whole, its predominant appeal is to prurient interest, that is, a shameful or morbid interest, in nudity, sex, or excretion, and if in addition it goes substantially beyond customary limits of candor in describing or representing such matter." Note that the Code's definition is similar to the Supreme Court's definition. The Code does add the requirement that the material go beyond "customary limits of candor." The Code makes it an affirmative defense that the obscene material was possessed for governmental, scientific, educational, or other justified causes. It also is not a crime for a person to give such materials to personal associates in noncommercial situations. The Code focuses on punishing commercial dissemination of obscene material.

Obscenity is a complex area of law. Many different criminal prohibitions exist throughout the states and federal government that focus on the sale, distribution, and possession of sexually oriented materials, performance of erotic dance, and public nudity. So long as minors are not involved, the activity is protected unless it is obscene. To determine whether pornography is obscene (hardcore), one must apply the three-part *Miller* test. The states are free to regulate if children are involved, either as participants in the erotic materials (or performance) or as buyers of erotic materials, even if the material is not obscene.

In 2010, the Supreme Court invalidated a federal statute that regulated films that depicted animal cruelty on First Amendment grounds.

UNITED STATES V. STEVENS
(559 U.S. 460 (2010))

[The federal statute in question] establishes a criminal penalty of up to five years in prison for anyone who knowingly "creates, sells, or possesses a depiction of animal cruelty," if done "for commercial gain" in interstate or foreign commerce. A depiction of "animal cruelty" is defined as one "in which a living animal is intentionally maimed, mutilated, tortured, wounded, or killed," if that conduct violates

(continued)

UNITED STATES V. STEVENS *(continued)*

federal or state law where "the creation, sale, or possession takes place." In what is referred to as the "exceptions clause," the law exempts from prohibition any depiction "that has serious religious, political, scientific, educational, journalistic, historical, or artistic value."

The legislative background of [the law] focused primarily on the interstate market for "crush videos." According to the House Committee Report on the bill, such videos feature the intentional torture and killing of helpless animals, including cats, dogs, monkeys, mice, and hamsters. Crush videos often depict women slowly crushing animals to death "with their bare feet or while wearing high heeled shoes," sometimes while "talking to the animals in a kind of dominatrix patter" over "[t]he cries and squeals of the animals, obviously in great pain." Apparently these depictions "appeal to persons with a very specific sexual fetish who find them sexually arousing or otherwise exciting." The acts depicted in crush videos are typically prohibited by the animal cruelty laws enacted by all 50 States and the District of Columbia. . . .

This case, however, involves an application of [the law] to depictions of animal fighting. Dogfighting, for example, is unlawful in all 50 States and the District of Columbia. . . .

Stevens moved to dismiss the indictment, arguing that [the law] is facially invalid under the First Amendment. The District Court denied the motion. It held that the depictions subject to §48, like obscenity or child pornography, are categorically unprotected by the First Amendment. . . .

The First Amendment provides that "Congress shall make no law . . . abridging the freedom of speech." "[A]s a general matter, the First Amendment means that government has no power to restrict expression because of its message, its ideas, its subject matter, or its content. . . .

"From 1791 to the present," however, the First Amendment has "permitted restrictions upon the content of speech in a few limited areas," and has never "include[d] a freedom to disregard these traditional limitations." These "historic and traditional categories long familiar to the bar,"—including obscenity, defamation, fraud, incitement, and speech integral to criminal conduct,—are "well-defined and narrowly limited classes of speech, the prevention and punishment of which have never been thought to raise any Constitutional problem."

The Government argues that "depictions of animal cruelty" should be added to the list. . . .

The Government contends that "historical evidence" about the reach of the First Amendment is not "a necessary prerequisite for regulation today," and that categories of speech may be exempted from the First Amendment's protection without any long-settled tradition of subjecting that speech to regulation. Instead, the Government points to Congress's 'legislative judgment that . . . depictions of animals being intentionally tortured and killed [are] of such minimal redeeming value as to render [them] unworthy of First Amendment protection,' and asks the Court to uphold the ban on the same basis. The Government thus proposes that a claim of categorical exclusion should be considered under a simple balancing test: "Whether a given category of speech enjoys First Amendment protection depends upon a categorical balancing of the value of the speech against its societal costs."

As a free-floating test for First Amendment coverage, that sentence is startling and dangerous. The First Amendment's guarantee of free speech does not extend only to categories of speech that survive an ad hoc balancing of relative social costs and benefits. The First Amendment itself reflects a judgement by the American people that the benefits of its restrictions on the Government outweigh the costs. . . .

When we have identified categories of speech as fully outside the protection of the First

UNITED STATES V. STEVENS *(continued)*

Amendment, it has not been on the basis of a simple cost-benefit analysis. In *Ferber*, for example, we classified child pornography as such a category. We noted that the State of New York had a compelling interest in protecting children from abuse, and that the value of using children in these works (as opposed to simulated conduct or adult actors) was *de minimis*. But our decision did not rest on this "balance of competing interests" alone. We made clear that *Ferber* presented a special case: The market for child pornography was "intrinsically related" to the underlying abuse, and was therefore "an integral part of the production of such materials, an activity illegal throughout the Nation."

Our decisions in *Ferber* and other cases cannot be taken as establishing a freewheeling authority to declare new categories of speech outside the scope of the First Amendment. . . .

[The Court then found the law to be too broad. Not only could crush videos be prosecuted under the law, but bull fights, hunting, and other protected speech could as well.] Our construction of [the law] decides the constitutional question; the Government makes no effort to defend the constitutionality of [the law] as applied beyond crush videos and depictions of animal fighting. It argues that those particular depictions are intrinsically related to criminal conduct or are analogous to obscenity (if not themselves obscene), and that the ban on such speech is narrowly tailored to reinforce restrictions on the underlying conduct, prevent additional crime arising from the depictions, or safeguard public mores. But the Government nowhere attempts to extend these arguments to depictions of any other activities—depictions that are presumptively protected by the First Amendment but that remain subject to the criminal sanctions of [the law].

Nor does the Government seriously contest that the presumptively impermissible applications of [the law] (properly construed) far outnumber any permissible ones. However "growing" and "lucrative" the markets for crush videos and dogfighting depictions might be, they are dwarfed by the market for other depictions, such as hunting magazines and videos, that we have determined to be within the scope of [the law]. We therefore need not and do not decide whether a statute limited to crush videos or other depictions of extreme animal cruelty would be constitutional. We hold only that [the law] is not so limited but is instead substantially overbroad, and therefore invalid under the First Amendment.

Regulating the Internet

The ability of the World Wide Web to penetrate every home and community across the globe has both positive and negative implications—while it can be an invaluable source of information and means of communication, it can also override community values and standards, subjecting them to whatever more may or may not be found online. . . . [T]he Internet is a challenge to the sovereignty of civilized communities, States, and nations to decide what is appropriate and decent behavior.[22]

According to Internetworldstats.com, Internet use around the world exceeded 2.4 billion users in 2012. The greatest number of users are found in Asia, followed by Europe and North America. However, the greatest penetration is in North America, followed by Oceana/Australia and Europe. Evincing that the Internet is becoming a worldwide phenomenon, the greatest growth in users between 2000 and 2012 was in the Middle East, Africa, Latin America, and Asia. Some commentators believe it is reshaping the political identity of people all over the world. Others believe it is a great social equalizer, tearing down class, education, and economic barriers. Still others are concerned about the negative social impact the Internet may present. Many of the barriers that are being destroyed were in place to protect those individuals who are not capable or mature enough to protect themselves. To protect these people, state legislatures and Congress have acted to regulate the Internet.

Obscene and harmful information has been the primary source of regulation, although commercial transactions, gambling, and other subjects are also regulated. In 1998, 16 million children under the age of 18 were using the Internet. Over 6 million of the children using the Internet were under the age of 13. Simultaneous to the growth in child use of the Internet has been a growth in adult sites. In 1998, it was estimated that there were more than 30,000 adult sites on the Internet and that as much as 70 percent of all Web traffic was unsuitable for children.[23] The first major national attempt to protect children from adult-oriented information on the Internet was the Communications Decency Act of 1996.[24] This statute limited the transmission of "obscene" and "indecent" materials to children. However, this statute was held unconstitutional by the Supreme Court in *Reno v. ACLU* (1997).[25] "The Supreme Court held that the law was overbroad because it prohibited both protected speech (indecent materials) and unprotected speech (obscene materials)." Obscene material, as defined by *Miller* and other cases, may be regulated but indecent material may not. In addition, the Court found that the law was overbroad because it limited access, both adult and juvenile. While it is lawful to limit the access of children to indecent materials (even if not obscene), the law limited the access of everyone because under current technology there is not a way to create zones that children cannot enter. In real space, it is possible to create such zones. Adult bookstores, for example, are zones where children may not enter.

Congress attempted again to protect children from the dangers of the Internet in 1998 through the Child Online Protection Act.[26] This law limited regulation to material that is harmful to minors. The law specifically incorporates the *Miller* test into its definition of what is prohibited. In a narrowly drafted decision, the Supreme Court upheld this law in 2002.[27] The court made it clear, however, that other constitutional issues may need to be examined in an attempt to correct the error of the Communications Decency Act. It remains to be seen if this law is constitutional.

In addition to shielding minors from adult content, Congress and the states have attempted to protect children from being used in sexually explicit films. While there is no question that the use of children can be criminalized, as can the possession of child pornography itself, modern technology has changed the landscape considerably. Today, it is possible to have genuine photos of children and alter them to make it appear as if they are nude or engaged in sexual conduct. Photos of adults can be merged with those of children, and other computer graphic techniques can be employed to create virtual child pornography.

In the Child Pornography Prevention Act of 1996, Congress prohibited not only images of actual children in pornography but also "virtual" images created with the use of computers. As was true of the Communications Decency Act, the Supreme Court found the law to be contrary to First Amendment principles in *Ashcroft v. Free Speech Coalition.*

ASHCROFT V. FREE SPEECH COALITION
535 U.S. 234 (2002)

We consider in this case whether the Child Pornography Prevention Act of 1996 (CPPA), 18 U.S.C. § 2251 *et seq.*, abridges the freedom of speech. The CPPA extends the federal prohibition against child pornography to sexually explicit images that appear to depict minors but were produced without using any real children. The statute prohibits, in specific circumstances, possessing or distributing these images, which may be created by using adults who look like minors or by using computer imaging. The new technology, according to Congress, makes it possible to create realistic images of children who do not exist. . . .

By prohibiting child pornography that does not depict an actual child, the statute goes beyond *New York v. Ferber*, 458 U.S. 747 (1982), which distinguished child pornography from other sexually explicit speech because of the State's interest in protecting the children exploited by the production process. As a general rule, pornography can be banned only if obscene, but under *Ferber*, pornography showing minors can be proscribed whether or not the images are obscene under the definition set forth in *Miller v. California*, 413 U.S. 15 (1973). *Ferber* recognized that "[t]he *Miller* standard, like all general definitions of what may be banned as obscene, does not reflect the State's particular and more compelling interest in prosecuting those who promote the sexual exploitation of children." . . .

The principal question to be resolved, then, is whether the CPPA is constitutional where it proscribes a significant universe of speech that is neither obscene under *Miller* nor child pornography under *Ferber*.

I

Before 1996, Congress defined child pornography as the type of depictions at issue in *Ferber*, images made using actual minors. 18 U.S.C. § 2252 (1994 ed.). The CPPA retains that prohibition at 18 U.S.C. § 2256(8)(A) and adds three other prohibited categories of speech, of which the first, § 2256(8)(B), and the third, § 2256(8)(D), are at issue in this case. Section 2256(8)(B) prohibits "any visual depiction, including any photograph, film, video, picture, or computer or computer-generated image or picture" that "is, or appears to be, of a minor engaging in sexually explicit conduct." The prohibition on "any visual depiction" does not depend at all on how the image is produced. The section captures a range of depictions, sometimes called "virtual child pornography," which include computer-generated images, as well as images produced by more traditional means. For instance, the literal terms of the statute embrace a Renaissance painting depicting a scene from classical mythology, a "picture" that "appears to be, of a minor engaging in sexually explicit conduct." The statute also prohibits Hollywood movies, filmed without any child actors, if a jury believes an actor "appears to be" a minor engaging in "actual or simulated . . . sexual intercourse." § 2256(2).

These images do not involve, let alone harm, any children in the production process; but Congress decided the materials threaten children in other, less direct, ways. Pedophiles might use the materials to encourage children to participate in sexual activity. "[A] child who is reluctant to engage in sexual activity with an adult, or to pose for sexually explicit photographs, can sometimes be convinced by viewing depictions of other children 'having fun' participating in such activity." Congressional Findings, note (3) following § 2251. Furthermore, pedophiles might "whet their own sexual appetites" with the pornographic images, "thereby increasing the creation and distribution

(continued)

ASHCROFT V. FREE SPEECH COALITION (continued)

of child pornography and the sexual abuse and exploitation of actual children." Under these rationales, harm flows from the content of the images, not from the means of their production. In addition, Congress identified another problem created by computer-generated images: Their existence can make it harder to prosecute pornographers who do use real minors. As imaging technology improves, Congress found, it becomes more difficult to prove that a particular picture was produced using actual children. To ensure that defendants possessing child pornography using real minors cannot evade prosecution, Congress extended the ban to virtual child pornography.

Section 2256(8)(C) prohibits a more common and lower tech means of creating virtual images, known as computer morphing. Rather than creating original images, pornographers can alter innocent pictures of real children so that the children appear to be engaged in sexual activity. Although morphed images may fall within the definition of virtual child pornography, they implicate the interests of real children and are in that sense closer to the images in *Ferber*. Respondents do not challenge this provision, and we do not consider it.

Respondents do challenge § 2256(8)(D). Like the text of the "appears to be" provision, the sweep of this provision is quite broad. Section 2256(8)(D) defines child pornography to include any sexually explicit image that was "advertised, promoted, presented, described, or distributed in such a manner that conveys the impression" it depicts "a minor engaging in sexually explicit conduct." One Committee Report identified the provision as directed at sexually explicit images pandered as child pornography. ("This provision prevents child pornographers and pedophiles from exploiting prurient interests in child sexuality and sexual activity through the production or distribution of pornographic material which is intentionally pandered

as child pornography"). The statute is not so limited in its reach, however, as it punishes even those possessors who took no part in pandering. Once a work has been described as child pornography, the taint remains on the speech in the hands of subsequent possessors, making possession unlawful even though the content otherwise would not be objectionable.

Fearing that the CPPA threatened the activities of its members, respondent Free Speech Coalition and others challenged the statute. . . .

The First Amendment commands, "Congress shall make no law . . . abridging the freedom of speech." The government may violate this mandate in many ways, but a law imposing criminal penalties on protected speech is a stark example of speech suppression. The CPPA's penalties are indeed severe. A first offender may be imprisoned for 15 years. § 2252A(b)(1). A repeat offender faces a prison sentence of not less than 5 years and not more than 30 years in prison. While even minor punishments can chill protected speech, this case provides a textbook example of why we permit facial challenges to statutes that burden expression. With these severe penalties in force, few legitimate movie producers or book publishers, or few other speakers in any capacity, would risk distributing images in or near the uncertain reach of this law. The Constitution gives significant protection from overbroad laws that chill speech within the First Amendment's vast and privileged sphere. Under this principle, the CPPA is unconstitutional on its face if it prohibits a substantial amount of protected expression. See *Broadrick v. Oklahoma*, 413 U.S. 601, 612 (1973).

The sexual abuse of a child is a most serious crime and an act repugnant to the moral instincts of a decent people. Congress also found that surrounding the serious offenders are those who flirt with these impulses and trade pictures and written accounts of sexual activity with young children.

Congress may pass valid laws to protect children from abuse, and it has. The prospect of crime, however, by itself does not justify laws suppressing protected speech. . . .

As a general principle, the First Amendment bars the government from dictating what we see or read or speak or hear. The freedom of speech has its limits; it does not embrace certain categories of speech, including defamation, incitement, obscenity, and pornography produced with real children. . . .

The CPPA prohibits speech despite its serious literary, artistic, political, or scientific value. The statute proscribes the visual depiction of an idea—that of teenagers engaging in sexual activity—that is a fact of modern society and has been a theme in art and literature throughout the ages. Under the CPPA, images are prohibited so long as the persons appear to be under 18 years of age. 18 U.S.C. § 2256(1). This is higher than the legal age for marriage in many States, as well as the age at which persons may consent to sexual relations.

Both themes—teenage sexual activity and the sexual abuse of children—have inspired countless literary works. William Shakespeare created the most famous pair of teenage lovers, one of whom is just 13 years of age. See Romeo and Juliet, act I, sc. 2, l. 9 ("She hath not seen the change of fourteen years"). In the drama, Shakespeare portrays the relationship as something splendid and innocent, but not juvenile. The work has inspired no less than 40 motion pictures, some of which suggest that the teenagers consummated their relationship. *E.g.*, Romeo and Juliet (B. Luhrmann director, 1996). Shakespeare may not have written sexually explicit scenes for the Elizabethan audience, but were modern directors to adopt a less conventional approach, that fact alone would not compel the conclusion that the work was obscene.

Contemporary movies pursue similar themes. Last year's Academy Awards featured the movie, Traffic, which was nominated for Best Picture. . . . The film portrays a teenager, identified as a 16-year-old, who becomes addicted to drugs. The viewer sees the degradation of her addiction, which in the end leads her to a filthy room to trade sex for drugs. The year before, American Beauty won the Academy Award for Best Picture. . . . In the course of the movie, a teenage girl engages in sexual relations with her teenage boyfriend, and another yields herself to the gratification of a middle-aged man. The film also contains a scene where, although the movie audience understands the act is not taking place, one character believes he is watching a teenage boy performing a sexual act on an older man.

Our society, like other cultures, has empathy and enduring fascination with the lives and destinies of the young. Art and literature express the vital interest we all have in the formative years we ourselves once knew, when wounds can be so grievous, disappointment so profound, and mistaken choices so tragic, but when moral acts and self-fulfillment are still in reach. Whether or not the films we mention violate the CPPA, they explore themes within the wide sweep of the statute's prohibitions. If these films, or hundreds of others of lesser note that explore those subjects, contain a single graphic depiction of sexual activity within the statutory definition, the possessor of the film would be subject to severe punishment without inquiry into the work's redeeming value. This is inconsistent with an essential First Amendment rule: The artistic merit of a work does not depend on the presence of a single explicit scene. For this reason, and the others we have noted, the CPPA cannot be read to prohibit obscenity, because it lacks the required link between its prohibitions and the affront to community standards prohibited by the definition of obscenity.

[I]n *Osborne v. Ohio*, 495 U.S. 103 (1990), the Court ruled that these same interests justified a ban

(continued)

ASHCROFT V. FREE SPEECH COALITION *(continued)*

on the possession of pornography produced by using children. "Given the importance of the State's interest in protecting the victims of child pornography," the State was justified in "attempting to stamp out this vice at all levels in the distribution chain." . . . Osborne also noted the State's interest in preventing child pornography from being used as an aid in the solicitation of minors. . . . The Court, however, anchored its holding in the concern for the participants, those whom it called the "victims of child pornography." . . . It did not suggest that, absent this concern, other governmental interests would suffice. . . .

In contrast to the speech in *Ferber*, speech that itself is the record of sexual abuse, the CPPA prohibits speech that records no crime and creates no victims by its production. Virtual child pornography is not "intrinsically related" to the sexual abuse of children, as were the materials in *Ferber*. While the Government asserts that the images can lead to actual instances of child abuse, . . . the causal link is contingent and indirect. The CPPA, for reasons we have explored, is inconsistent with *Miller* and finds no support in *Ferber*. The Government seeks to justify its prohibitions in other ways. It argues that the CPPA is necessary because pedophiles may use virtual child pornography to seduce children. There are many things innocent in themselves, however, such as cartoons, video games, and candy, that might be used for immoral purposes, yet we would not expect those to be prohibited because they can be misused. The Government, of course, may punish adults who provide unsuitable materials to children, see *Ginsberg v. New York*, 390 U.S. 629 (1968), and it may enforce criminal penalties

for unlawful solicitation. The precedents establish, however, that speech within the rights of adults to hear may not be silenced completely in an attempt to shield children from it. . . .

The Government submits further that virtual child pornography whets the appetites of pedophiles and encourages them to engage in illegal conduct. This rationale cannot sustain the provision in question. The mere tendency of speech to encourage unlawful acts is not a sufficient reason for banning it. . . .

The Government next argues that its objective of eliminating the market for pornography produced using real children necessitates a prohibition on virtual images as well. Virtual images, the Government contends, are indistinguishable from real ones; they are part of the same market and are often exchanged. In this way, it is said, virtual images promote the trafficking in works produced through the exploitation of real children. The hypothesis is somewhat implausible. If virtual images were identical to illegal child pornography, the illegal images would be driven from the market by the indistinguishable substitutes. Few pornographers would risk prosecution by abusing real children if fictional, computerized images would suffice.

In sum, § 2256(8)(B) covers materials beyond the categories recognized in *Ferber* and *Miller*, and the reasons the Government offers in support of limiting the freedom of speech have no justification in our precedents or in the law of the First Amendment. The provision abridges the freedom to engage in a substantial amount of lawful speech. For this reason, it is overbroad and unconstitutional.

States also have laws regulating the Internet. Of course, these laws must be crafted to avoid First Amendment and state-law free speech barriers. Additionally, the interstate character of the Internet can create jurisdictional problems for states. In *American Library Association v. Pataki* (S.D. N.Y. 1997),[28] a New York statute that regulated the Internet in much the same manner as the federal Communications Decency Act was invalidated not on First Amendment grounds but on jurisdictional grounds. The federal court that heard the case ruled that New York was without the authority to regulate conduct outside its borders. Congress responded to the *Free Speech Coalition* decision by enacting an amended version of the law that was invalidated. The new statute, known as PROTECT, criminalizes soliciting, distributing, promoting, or presenting images with the belief, or that is intended to cause another to believe, that they are depictions of minors. To avoid the overbreadth problem of *Free Speech Coalition*, PROTECT did not include a ban on all virtual child pornography. The Court found the subtle distinction between banning all virtual child pornography and those depictions intended to convince others that they are actual minors adequate to uphold the law in *United States v. Williams*.[29]

Due to the plethora of cases addressing pornography and obscenity, it is strongly recommended that thorough research be conducted. There is a good chance that precedent with similar facts may be found. Beware, however, that this is an issue that often leaves courts split. Be sure that the opinions you find reflect the law of your jurisdiction.

CRIMES AGAINST THE PUBLIC ORDER

Crimes against the public order are crimes that involve **breaches of the peace**. The phrase *breaches of the peace* refers to all crimes that involve disturbing the tranquility or order of society. Breaches of the peace as a crime has its roots in early English common law. In England, breaches of the peace by individuals were criminal, as were breaches by groups.

Three groups of breaches were recognized; all were punished as misdemeanors. If three or more people met with an intention of causing a disturbance, they committed the common-law offense of unlawful assembly. If the group took some action in an attempt to breach the peace, they were guilty of rout; if they were successful, the crime was riot.

Today, all jurisdictions prohibit breaches of the peace in some form by statute. The names of statutory crimes include disorderly conduct, unlawful assembly, riot, inciting violence, unlawful threat, and vagrancy.

Riot and Unlawful Assembly

Most states now have legislation that prohibits groups of people from meeting with the purpose of committing an unlawful act or committing a lawful act in an unlawful manner. This crime may be named unlawful assembly or riot. A group, or "assembly," is a specified minimum number of people, often three or five. Some jurisdictions continue to recognize the distinctions between unlawful assembly, rout, and riot.

The Model Penal Code recognizes two related crimes: riot and failure to disperse. Both crimes require an assembly of two or more persons who are behaving in a disorderly manner. If the purpose of the assembly is to commit a crime (felony or misdemeanor), to coerce public officials to act or not act, or if a deadly weapon is used, then the crime is riot.[30]

breachs of the peace

■ A vague term for any illegal public disturbance; sometimes refers to the offense known as "disorderly conduct." It is defined and treated differently in different states.

Failure to disperse occurs when a law enforcement officer, or other official, orders the members of a group of three or more to disperse, and someone refuses. The disorderly conduct that the assembly is engaged in must be "likely to cause substantial harm or serious inconvenience, annoyance, or alarm," before an officer may order the group to disperse. This provision is included because the freedoms to associate and assemble are protected by the First Amendment to the U.S. Constitution, and such activity may be regulated only when it poses a threat to person, property, or society.

Most jurisdictions punish these crimes as misdemeanors. However, they may be elevated to felony if committed with a dangerous weapon, if someone is injured as a result of the activity, or if law enforcement officers are obstructed from performing their duties. The Model Penal Code makes rioting a felony of the third degree and failure to disperse a misdemeanor.

Disturbing the Peace

As mentioned, individuals may also commit crimes against the public order. Disturbing the peace is such a crime. This crime is also known as disorderly conduct, threat, excessive noise, and affray. In essence, any time the public order or tranquility is unreasonably interrupted by an individual, disturbance of the peace has occurred. States may have one law that encompasses all such acts or separate statutes for each.

Disturbances may occur in hundreds of forms. One may disturb the peace by making loud noises in a residential area at midnight, by attempting to cause fights with others, or by encouraging others to engage in similar conduct. Statutes often also prohibit indecent language and gestures.

These statutes are often broadly worded and are vague. As such, they are often attacked as being unconstitutional. The defenses of overbreadth and vagueness are discussed in Chapter 8 on defenses and are not covered here. One defense that will be examined is the First Amendment right to free speech and its relationship to offensive words and gestures.

As you have learned, the First Amendment protects all forms of expression. This protection prohibits government from making expression criminal. However, exceptions to the First Amendment have been created. Words that have a likelihood of causing a riot are such an exception. That is, even though the words are expression, they may be punished. The reason is obvious: riots lead to property damage, personal injuries, and sometimes death. As such, the interest of the government to control such behavior outweighs the First Amendment interest.

fighting words

■ Speech that is not protected by the First Amendment to the U.S. Constitution because it is likely to cause violence by the person to whom the words are spoken.

The **fighting words** doctrine is another exception. The Supreme Court has defined *fighting words* as those that inflict injury, tend to incite an immediate breach of the peace, or by their nature will cause a violent reaction by a person who hears them.[31] Laws that regulate speech that may be regulated, such as fighting words, must be drafted narrowly; that is, only the conduct intended must be prohibited. If a law is drawn so broadly that both fighting words and legitimate speech are criminalized, it is unconstitutional and void.

The defendant in the *Witucki* case was convicted of disorderly conduct. The court found that his speech was unprotected because he used fighting words.

CITY OF LITTLE FALLS V. EDWIN GEORGE WITUCKI
295 N.W.2d 243 (Minn. 1980)

On December 11, 1978, a Morrison County Court jury found defendant guilty of disorderly conduct in violation of Little Falls, Minnesota, Ordinances. . . .

At approximately 11:00 P.M. on September 19, 1978, defendant Edwin George Witucki and a few of his friends entered the West Side Bar in Little Falls, Minnesota. Just outside the building defendant found a cat which he carried into the building and placed on the bar. Pursuant to defendant's request, one bartender served the cat some beef jerky and a shotglass of cream and served defendant a drink.

About five minutes later, the other bartender, Paula Erwin, told defendant to take the cat outside. He refused. She told him he was cut off from being served until the cat was removed. He responded, "I let you slip once too many times, I'm not going to let you slip again." Erwin, for the third time, told defendant to remove the cat. He responded by saying, "Hey, Butch, I don't have to take any of your crap." She then turned to return to the other end of the bar, and Witucki called her a "black-haired witch," a "cocksucker," and a "son-of-a-bitch."

When asked at trial about her reaction to the words, Erwin testified, "I didn't care for them very well. It scared me. There was nothing I could do about it. There were no guys around so I thought the best thing for me to do, because I was really mad at the time, was just to walk away from him." She also testified that calling the police or any sort of violent action on her part would not be wise or safe because he might wait for her outside after hours and because he was much larger than she and there were no men around to help her.

■ ■ ■

The question is, did defendant's words in the circumstances in which they were uttered constitute "those personally abusive epithets which, when addressed to the ordinary citizen, are as a matter of common knowledge, inherently likely to provoke violent reaction." . . .

In *In re S.L.J.* the appellant was a fourteen-year-old girl who yelled "fuck you pigs" at two police officers. . . . The court noted that although "no ordered society would condone the vulgar language" and although "her words were intended to, and did, arouse resentment in the officers, the constitution requires more before a person can be convicted for mere speech." The court held that where the words were spoken in retreat by a small teenage girl who was between fifteen and thirty feet from the two police officers sitting in their squad car, "there was no reasonable likelihood that [the words] would tend to incite an immediate breach of the peace or to provoke violent reaction by an ordinary, reasonable person.

In *Cohen v. California*, 403 U.S. 15, 91 S.Ct. 1780, 29 L. Ed. 2d 284 (1971), the defendant wore a jacket on which the words "Fuck the Draft" were plainly visible. The words were not directed against the person of any possibly offended person; they were directed against the draft.

The instant case is readily distinguishable from both *In re S.L.J.* and *Cohen v. California*. Unlike the defendant's language in *Cohen*, Witucki's language was directed at and was intended to be about a person, namely Erwin. The abusive language hurled by defendant at Erwin could readily be found by a jury to be inherently likely to incite violence. Defendant was not, as in *Cohen*, merely expressing a controversial political opinion in a vulgar way; he was directly insulting and intimidating an innocent person.

■ ■ ■

The fact that the words used by appellant are vulgar, offensive, and insulting, and that their use is condemned by an overwhelming majority of citizens

(continued)

does not make them punishable under the criminal statutes of this state unless they fall outside the protection afforded to speech by the First Amendment.

■ ■ ■

Defendant's speech in this case is not a "trifling and annoying instance of individual distasteful abuse of a privilege." He addressed such abusive, vulgar, insulting and obscene language toward the bartender that his language was properly found to be within the fighting words category of unprotected speech. . . . [Conviction affirmed.]

Incitement/Advocacy of Unlawful Conduct

Whenever one person, acting independently, encourages another to commit an unlawful act or intends to cause a riot, the crimes of incitement of unlawful behavior or incitement of riot may be charged. Unlike riot, which requires a group, one person may commit this crime. Unlike disturbing the peace, it may be committed in a peaceful manner.

However, because the First Amendment applies, such statutes must be narrowly drawn. In fact, only speech that creates a **clear and present danger** may be controlled. The United States Supreme Court has said that "incitement of imminent lawless action" may be regulated.[32] Anything less may not be regulated. Hence, merely advocating unlawful conduct in the abstract is protected. Advocating future unlawful conduct is also protected, as it poses no imminent threat.

clear and present danger

■ A test of whether or not speech may be restricted or punished. It may be if it will probably lead to violence soon or if it threatens a serious, immediate weakening of national safety and security.

Threats

Finally, in the speech arena, threats are addressed. Threat statutes may make threatening individuals, groups, or even property, criminal. Threats to harm people are similar to assaults. However, threat is broader, as it often protects property and the people at large. The purpose of threat statutes is to preserve public order, and the purpose of assault statutes is to protect individuals.

For example, if a defendant were to call in a bomb threat to a public office, there would be no assault, but there is a threat. A person may be guilty of threat by making the prohibited statements, even if untrue. So, if a defendant makes a bomb threat, but has placed no bomb in the building, a crime has been committed. Threats are misdemeanors in most jurisdictions and are punished less severely than assaults. In the *Thomas* case, the defendant was convicted under the Kentucky threat statute.

Vagrancy and Panhandling

Vagrancy, as a criminal law issue, has received considerable attention. Most states and municipalities have statutes that forbid vagrancy. At common law, a *vagrant* was one who wandered from place to place with no means of support, except the charity of others. At one time, in early English law, vagrancy applied to disorderly persons, rogues (a dishonest wanderer), and vagabonds (a homeless person with no means of support).

THOMAS V. COMMONWEALTH OF KENTUCKY
574 S.W.2d 903 (Ky. Ct. App. 1978)

The case for the Commonwealth was based solely on the testimony of Gladys Thomas. Mrs. Thomas on direct examination stated that on the Friday before she went to swear out the warrant that she was in her front yard cutting weeds with a butcher knife when appellant came out of the house, hit her across the back with his hand, laughed and ran into a barber shop next door. Appellant then came back laughing and hit her across the back with a belt and then ran into a liquor store about three doors down from the house. Appellant continued to aggravate Mrs. Thomas until she asked him to go and get her a coke. Mrs. Thomas then testified thusly:

> So, we went about an hour, an hour and a half after my mom left and he came in and said, "I told you to get ready to go," and I said, "I'm not going," and he grabbed me by the hair of the head and threw me against the refrigerator and said, "you are going or I will kill you and prove self-defense. This is one time everything is on my side. So, just get dressed and let's go somewhere and show everybody what a happy family we are."

Next, Mrs. Thomas gave testimony concerning the circumstances surrounding the threat which is the basis for the charge against appellant:

> So, on Wednesday, he came in and he said, "I will come home. I'm coming home." I said, "you can't. You absolutely cannot. I went and applied for welfare," and he said, "I have to tell the man, Mr. Clark, that I'm here or I'll be in trouble." One thing led to another and he jumped in the middle of the floor and said, "you and Brenda have got me against the wall. You're going to get me in trouble. I will cut both your heads off before I go back." Those are almost the exact words. And I looked around and the little girl was standing right in the screen door.

On cross-examination, Mrs. Thomas testified that this threat was made in the late afternoon and that on the next morning, on July 15, 1976, she sent and got a warrant.

[The applicable Kentucky statute] provides thusly:

A person is guilty of terroristic threatening when:

(a) He threatens to commit any crime likely to result in death or serious bodily injury to another person or likely to result in substantial property damage to another person; or

(b) He intentionally makes false statements for the purpose of causing evacuation of a building, place of assembly, or facility of public transportation.

(c) Terroristic threatening is a Class A misdemeanor.

This court believes that [this statute] is not unconstitutionally vague and overbroad since the conduct proscribed, "threaten[ing] to commit a crime likely to result in death or serious physical injury" is not protected under either the Kentucky or U.S. Constitutions. Further, the language of the statute is sufficiently explicit to put the average citizen on notice as to the nature of the conduct so proscribed.

This court is aware of the recent decision in *U.S. v. Sturgill*, 563 F.2d 307 (6th Cir. 1977), which invalidated [another Kentucky statute] on the basis that it was unconstitutionally overbroad. [The invalidated statute] provides: "A person is guilty of harassment when with intent to harass, annoy or alarm another person he: (b) In a public place, makes an offensively coarse utterance, gesture, or display, or addresses abusive language to any person present."

In *Sturgill*, the court held that in order for a statute, which punishes spoken words only, to withstand an attack on its constitutionality, it must be first authoritatively interpreted by the state courts

(continued)

THOMAS V. COMMONWEALTH OF KENTUCKY *(continued)*

as not interfering with speech protected by the First Amendment.

This case can be distinguished from *Sturgill*, in that the language is proscribed under [the terroristic threatening statute] is clearly without constitutional protection under the First Amendment. . . .

Certainly, [the terroristic threat statute] does not apply in the case of idle talk or jesting. The defendant's

intent to commit the crime of "terroristic threatening" can be plainly inferred from the defendant's own words and the circumstances surrounding them. All the statute requires is that the defendant threaten "to commit any crime likely to result in death or serious physical injury to another person or likely to result in substantial property damage to another person."

[Conviction] Affirmed.

Beginning in the 1880s, it was common in the United States for statutes to prohibit a wide range of behavior as vagrancy. These statutes were drafted broadly to allow law enforcement officers considerable discretion in their enforcement. This discretion was used to control the "undesirables" of society. Many statutes made the status of being homeless, a gambler, and a drug addict a crime.

Today, states may not make personal status, such as drug addiction or alcoholism, a crime. The United States held that doing so violates the Eighth Amendment's prohibition of cruel and unusual punishment.[33] However, until 1972, people found undesirable by the police could be arrested under broadly worded vagrancy statutes for "wandering," or walking around a city, because this was an act, not a status. This situation ended in 1972 when the United States Supreme Court handed down *Papachristou v. City of Jacksonville,* 405 U.S. 156 (1972). The Court announced in that case that vagrancy statutes that prohibit walking around, frequenting liquor stores, being supported by one's wife, and similar behavior, to be "too precarious for a rule of law" and violative of the Due Process and Cruel and Unusual Clauses of the Constitution.

The result of *Papachristou* has been more narrowly drawn vagrancy statutes. Today such laws focus on more particularized behavior, and in many instances a mens rea element has been added. This addition prevents simple acts, such as walking at night, from being criminal. For example, a vagrancy law may prohibit "loitering or standing around with an intent to gamble," or "loitering or standing in a transportation facility [e.g., bus station] with the intent of soliciting charity."

In recent years panhandling (begging) has increasingly become a problem for most cities. Panhandlers often choose to congregate in and near public transportation egresses and ingresses, because of the large number of people who use such facilities. Because panhandlers are sometimes aggressive and intimidating to patrons of such facilities, some jurisdictions have chosen to prohibit begging at public transportation sites.

As the number of homeless persons grows in the United States, so will the problems associated with vagrancy and panhandling. Examine statutes and ordinances that prohibit such activities with an awareness that they must be drawn carefully to avoid a

First Amendment speech problem. Also be aware that other constitutional provisions may be implicated, such as the First Amendment's freedom of association and the Due Process and Equal Protection Clauses of the Fifth and Fourteenth Amendments.

Crimes Involving Firearms

A discussion of the regulation of firearms properly begins with the Second Amendment to the U.S. Constitution, which reads:

> A well regulated Militia, being necessary to the security of a free State, the right of the people to keep and bear Arms, shall not be infringed.

Despite the tireless efforts of firearms lobbyists to convince the nation that the Second Amendment was intended to protect the individual's right to possess arms, the Supreme Court of the United States as well as nearly all lower courts that have heard this issue have concluded that the Amendment is intended to preserve a collective right, the right to have a well-regulated militia. The second half of the clause, to keep and bear arms, is interpreted as conjunctive with the first half of the clause, which provides for a well-regulated militia.

In a 1939 Supreme Court decision, *United States v. Miller*,[34] a defendant who had been charged under a federal law prohibiting possession of short-barreled shotguns and rifles challenged the law as violating his Second Amendment right to possess a firearm. The Court stated:

> The Constitution as originally adopted granted to the Congress power—"To provide for calling forth the Militia to execute the Laws of the Union, suppress Insurrections and repel Invasions; To provide for organizing, arming, and disciplining, the Militia, and for governing such Part of them as may be employed in the Service of the United States, reserving to the States respectively, the Appointment of the Officers, and the Authority of training the Militia according to the discipline prescribed by Congress." U.S.C.A. Const. art. § 8. With obvious purpose to assure the continuation and render possible the effectiveness of such forces the declaration and guarantee of the Second Amendment were made. It must be interpreted and applied with that end in view.
>
> The Militia which the States were expected to maintain and train is set in contrast with Troops which they were forbidden to keep without the consent of Congress. The sentiment of the time strongly disfavored standing armies; the common view was that adequate defense of country and laws could be secured through the Militia—civilians primarily, soldiers on occasion.
>
> The signification attributed to the term Militia appears from the debates in the Convention, the history and legislation of Colonies and States, and the writings of approved commentators. These show plainly enough that the Militia comprised all males physically capable of acting in concert for the common defense. 'A body of citizens enrolled for military discipline.' And further, that ordinarily when called for service these men were expected to appear bearing arms supplied by themselves and of the kind in common use at the time.

The Supreme Court affirmed this interpretation of the Second Amendment in the 1980 case *United States v. Lewis*.[35] The Court did not pass on the question if the Second Amendment establishes an individual right, as opposed to connecting the right to arms to the militia right, again until 2008 when it invalidated a Washington, D.C., ordinance forbidding the possession of handguns in the home in *District of Columbia v. Heller*, 554 U.S. The Court explicitly found an independent, individual right to possess arms under the Second Amendment for the first time.

However, Washington, D.C., is federal territory. As such, *Heller* did not address whether the Second Amendment's right to possess firearms applies against the states. Indeed, several cases from the late 1800s stood for the principle that the Second Amendment, whatever its meaning, only limited federal authority. The Supreme Court accepted *certiorari* in a case involving state regulation of arms only a year following the *Heller* decision and issued a decision in 2010.

MCDONALD V. CHICAGO
561 U.S. 3025 (2010)

Two years ago, in *District of Columbia v. Heller*, 554 U.S. (2008), we held that the Second Amendment protects the right to keep and bear arms for the purpose of self-defense, and we struck down a District of Columbia law that banned the possession of handguns in the home. The city of Chicago (City) and the village of Oak Park, a Chicago suburb, have laws that are similar to the District of Columbia's, but Chicago and Oak Park argue that their laws are constitutional because the Second Amendment has no application to the States. We have previously held that most of the provisions of the Bill of Rights apply with full force to both the Federal Government and the States. Applying the standard that is well established in our case law, we hold that the Second Amendment right is fully applicable to the States.

Otis McDonald, Adam Orlov, Colleen Lawson, and David Lawson (Chicago petitioners) are Chicago residents who would like to keep handguns in their homes for self-defense but are prohibited from doing so by Chicago's firearms laws. A City ordinance provides that "[n]o person shall . . . possess . . . any firearm unless such person is the holder of a valid registration certificate for such firearm." The Code then prohibits registration of most handguns, thus effectively banning handgun possession by almost all private citizens who reside in the City. . . .

Several of the Chicago petitioners have been the targets of threats and violence. For instance, Otis McDonald, who is in his late seventies, lives in a high-crime neighborhood. He is a community activist involved with alternative policing strategies, and his efforts to improve his neighborhood have subjected him to violent threats from drug dealers. Colleen Lawson is a Chicago resident whose home has been targeted by burglars. . . .

Petitioners argue that the Chicago and Oak Park laws violate the right to keep and bear arms for two reasons. Petitioners' primary submission is that this right is among the "privileges or immunities of citizens of the United States" and that the narrow interpretation of the Privileges or Immunities Clause adopted in the *Slaughter-House Cases* should now be rejected. As a secondary argument, petitioners contend that the Fourteenth Amendment's Due Process Clause "incorporates" the Second Amendment right. . . .

MCDONALD V. CHICAGO *(continued)*

[The Court chose to analyze the case under the Fourteenth Amendment's Due Process Clause and not the Privileges and Immunities Clause because of the long history of not applying the Privileges and Immunities Clause to the states. It then reviewed the legal standard for applying one of the rights from the Bill of Rights against the states (called incorporation). For a right to apply against the states, it must be found fundamental to an ordered liberty.]

. . . . Self-defense is a basic right, recognized by many legal systems from ancient times to the present day, and in *Heller*, we held that individual self-defense is "the *central component* " of the Second Amendment right. . . .

Heller makes it clear that this right is "deeply rooted in this Nation's history and tradition." *Heller* explored the right's origins, noting that the 1689 English Bill of Rights explicitly protected a right to keep arms for self-defense, and that by 1765, Blackstone was able to assert that the right to keep and bear arms was "one of the fundamental rights of Englishmen."

Blackstone's assessment was shared by the American colonists. As we noted in *Heller*, King George III's attempt to disarm the colonists in the 1760's and 1770's "provoked polemical reactions by Americans invoking their rights as Englishmen to keep arms."

The right to keep and bear arms was considered no less fundamental by those who drafted and ratified the Bill of Rights. "During the 1788 ratification debates, the fear that the federal government would disarm the people in order to impose rule through a standing army or select militia was pervasive in Antifederalist rhetoric." . . . Thus, Antifederalists and Federalists alike agreed that the right to bear arms was fundamental to the newly formed system of government.

Evidence from the period immediately following the ratification of the Fourteenth Amendment only confirms that the right to keep and bear arms was considered fundamental. In an 1868 speech addressing the disarmament of freedmen, Representative Stevens emphasized the necessity of the right: "Disarm a community and you rob them of the means of defending life. Take away their weapons of defense and you take away the inalienable right of defending liberty." "The fourteenth amendment, now so happily adopted, settles the whole question." . . .

The right to keep and bear arms was also widely protected by state constitutions at the time when the Fourteenth Amendment was ratified. In 1868, 22 of the 37 States in the Union had state constitutional provisions explicitly protecting the right to keep and bear arms. . . . .

In *Heller*, we held that the Second Amendment protects the right to possess a handgun in the home for the purpose of self-defense. Unless considerations of *stare decisis* counsel otherwise, a provision of the Bill of Rights that protects a right that is fundamental from an American perspective applies equally to the Federal Government and the States. We therefore hold that the Due Process Clause of the Fourteenth Amendment incorporates the Second Amendment right recognized in *Heller*. The judgement of the Court of Appeals is reversed, and the case is remanded for further proceedings.

Possession, Sale, and Transfer Laws

McDonald and *Heller* apply to possession of handguns in the home. There is nothing in those decisions to limit the authority of government to require the registration of firearms, background checks prior to firearms purchases, or to more thoroughly regulate larger and more dangerous firearms, or the possession of any firearm outside of the home.

One of the most common forms of weapons regulation is possession. Both federal and state laws prohibit a variety of possession-related offenses. These include improper possession of a weapon that is otherwise permitted, e.g., concealed possession; possession of altogether prohibited weapons, e.g., machine guns; and possession by certain classes of persons, e.g., possession by ex-felons, aliens, fugitives, mental incompetents, individuals who were dishonorably discharged from the military, those under stalking-related court orders, and individuals convicted of misdemeanor domestic violence. The possession of firearms is also prohibited in certain areas designated by statute. Near schools, in public buildings, in airports, in national and state parks, and on airplanes are examples.

One of the most significant federal firearms statutes is the National Firearms Act.[36] Enacted in reaction to the organized crime problem of the 1930s, this law prohibited the sale and possession of automatic weapons (machine guns). Another important federal law is the Gun Control Act of 1968. Among its many provisions are a prohibition of mail order guns and the prohibition of the possession, transfer, or receipt of firearms by felons, aliens, and certain other persons. Many of the limitations of the Gun Control Act were repealed or reduced in the Firearm Owners Protection Act of 1986,[37] such as lifting the ban on the interstate sales of long guns and the use of the U.S. Post Office mail to ship ammunition. The federal Brady Handgun Violence Prevention Act of 1993—named for President Ronald Reagan's White House Press Secretary James Brady, who was shot during an attempted assassination of the president—requires all federally licensed gun dealers to conduct background checks of firearms purchasers to ensure that purchasers do not fall into one of the categories of ineligible buyers under the Gun Control Act of 1968. Records checks are now being implemented through the National Instant Background Check System (NICS). Another federal statute, the Violent Crime Control and Law Enforcement Act of 1994, prohibits the sale of semiautomatic weapons and large ammunition magazines. Additionally, the Bureau of Alcohol, Tobacco, Firearms and Explosives, the federal agency charged with enforcing federal gun laws, has promulgated a large set of regulations interpreting and further regulating firearms.

Firearms Use Laws

Many jurisdictions forbid the discharge of firearms in urban areas, absent good cause. Arizona's unlawful discharge statute (A.R.S. § 13-3107) reads:

(A) A person who with criminal negligence discharges a firearm within or into the limits of any municipality is guilty of a class 6 felony. . . .

(C) This section does not apply if the firearm is discharged:

(1) As allowed pursuant to the provisions of Chapter 4 of this title.

(2) On a properly supervised range.

(3) In an area recommended as a hunting area by the Arizona game and fish department, approved and posted as required by the chief of police, but any such area may be closed when deemed unsafe by the chief of police or the director of the game and fish department.

(4) For the control of nuisance wildlife by permit from the Arizona game and fish department or the U.S. fish and wildlife service.

(5) By special permit of the chief of police of the municipality.

(6) As required by an animal control officer in the performance of duties as specified in section 9-499.04.

(7) Using blanks.

(8) More than one mile from any occupied structure as defined in section 13-3101.

(9) In self-defense or defense of another person against an animal attack if a reasonable person would believe that deadly physical force against the animal is immediately necessary and reasonable under the circumstances to protect oneself or the other person.

Other law forbids the use of certain weapons for hunting and fishing. For example, shotguns may not be permitted in the hunting of certain game. Some statues prohibit "aiming," "pointing," and otherwise threatening people with firearms.

The use of a weapon in the commission of a crime is sometimes a separate crime from the underlying offense. Nearly all jurisdictions require or permit enhancement of sentences for crimes committed while in possession of a firearm.

Registration and Licensing

In addition to background checks, many states require guns to be registered. In some instances, licenses must be obtained to carry or use weapons.

The National Firearms Act[38] requires national registration of all firearms manufactured or transferred in the United States, and it prohibits the sale of automatic weapons (machine guns).

Drug and Alcohol Crimes

Crimes that involve the use of narcotics and alcohol may be classified in many ways. In one sense, such activity offends many people in society and appears to be an offense against the public morality. Whenever a pimp uses a young woman's drug addiction to induce her to become involved in prostitution, it appears to be a crime against an individual. In the states, drug and alcohol crimes are universally regulated, although definitions and punishments vary considerably.

Drug and alcohol crimes are included in this section because of their impact on the order of society. Alcohol-related driving accidents are the cause of many fatalities. Drug addiction often is the cause of other crimes, such as theft, assaults, and prostitution. Police report that a number of domestic problems are caused by alcohol and drugs and that much of the violence directed toward law enforcement officers is drug related. Large cities, such as Detroit and Washington, D.C., have experienced a virtual drug boom, which has led to increased assaults, batteries, and drug-related homicides. Many addicts, desperate for a "fix," steal for drug money.

Drug and alcohol use are also expensive. Corporate America has recently awakened to the expenses associated with employee drug use. Employees who use drugs have high absenteeism and low productivity. Decreased performance caused by drug use can be costly, in both human and dollar terms. This is true especially in positions that require great concentration or pose risks to others, such as that of commercial pilots.

In addition to business expenses, the high cost of rehabilitation can disable a family financially, and the price of drug-abuse detection and prosecution is high.

Alcohol Crimes

Let it not be mistaken, alcohol is a drug. However, the law treats alcohol differently than it does other drugs. Alcohol may be legally possessed, consumed, and sold, subject only to a few restrictions. Narcotics, on the other hand, are significantly restricted. Their sale, possession, and consumption are limited to specific instances, such as for medical use. The federal government, as well as every state, has statutes that spell out what drugs are regulated.

There are many alcohol-related crimes. Public drunkenness laws make it criminal for a person to be intoxicated in a public place. This crime is a minor misdemeanor and rarely prosecuted, as many law enforcement agencies have a policy of allowing such persons to "sleep it off" and then releasing them.

All states have a minimum age requirement for the sale or consumption of alcohol. Those below the minimum age are minors. Any minor who purchases or consumes alcohol is violating the law. Additionally, any adult who knowingly provides alcohol to a minor is also guilty of a crime, commonly known as contributing to the delinquency of a minor.

Merchants holding liquor licenses may be subject to criminal penalties for not complying with liquor laws, such as selling alcohol on holidays, Sundays, or election day, as well as for selling alcohol to minors. A merchant who violates liquor laws may also suffer the civil penalty of revocation of liquor license.

Alcohol and automobiles have proven to be a deadly and expensive combination. All states have laws that criminalize driving while under the influence of alcohol or drugs. Driving while under the influence of alcohol or drugs, driving while intoxicated, and driving with an unlawful blood-alcohol level are the names of these crimes.

These statutes are generally of two genres. One type of law generally prohibits the operation of a motor vehicle while under the influence of any drug, including alcohol. To prove this charge, the quantity of the drug or alcohol in the defendant's system is not at issue; the defendant's ability to operate the vehicle safely is. In such cases, field sobriety tests are often required of the suspect. These are tests that the suspect usually performs at the location where the police made the stop. Coordination, spatial relations, and other driving-related skills are tested by field sobriety tests.

The second type of law prohibits driving a motor vehicle any time a person's blood-alcohol level is above a stated amount. The states vary in the quantity required, although 8 hundredths of a percent (0.08) and 10 hundredths of a percent (0.10) are common. The effect of these laws is that an irrebuttable presumption is created. The law presumes that anyone with the stated blood-alcohol level or above cannot safely operate a motor vehicle. Under such statutes, evidence that a person can safely operate a motor vehicle with a blood-alcohol level greater than the maximum allowed is not permitted.

In recent years drunk driving has received considerable public and legislative attention. The result has been stricter laws and greater punishment for offenders. The once-common police practice of driving drunk drivers home is virtually nonexistent today.

First offenses are usually misdemeanors. Second or third offenses are felonies. In many jurisdictions, there has been a move toward alcohol treatment rather than incarceration. This often involves house arrest, alcohol treatment, and defensive driving education. Also, while in these programs, convicted persons are commonly required to submit to periodic blood or urine screening.

For first-time offenders, these programs have many advantages over prison. First, the focus is on curing the alcohol problem. If successful, the possibility of repetition is eliminated. Second, convicted persons are often permitted to continue to work and maintain family relationships. Finally, the cost of administration of alcohol programs is lower than the cost of incarceration. The value of such programs for repeat offenders is questionable, and in many jurisdictions jail time is required as early as a second conviction.

Drug Crimes

Unlike possession of alcohol, possession of other drugs is a crime. Every state and the federal government has enacted some variation of the Uniform Controlled Substance Act, a model act (similar to the Model Penal Code) drafted by the Commissioners on Uniform Laws. These statutes establish schedules of drugs that categorize drugs based on their danger, potential for abuse, and medical benefits. These factors then determine a drug's allowed usage. For example, one schedule exists for drugs that may not be used under any condition, and another schedule permits use for medical and research purposes only. There are three basic drug crimes: possession, sales/distribution, and use.

Possession of prohibited drugs is a crime. Of course, actual possession is sufficient actus reus, but some jurisdictions also make constructive possession criminal. Constructive possession permits conviction of those people who exercise dominion and control over property where the illegal drug is located, even though the person has no "actual physical possession" of the prohibited narcotic. However, the Model Penal Code[39] and most jurisdictions require knowledge that the drug was present before culpability is imposed. As such, if a guest stays in Robert's home, Robert is not criminally liable for any drugs the guest has stowed away, unless Robert is aware of their presence. Once Robert becomes aware, he must see that the drugs are removed within a reasonable time or risk a possession charge.

First-time conviction of possession, if the quantity is small, is a misdemeanor and normally results in probation. In many states, if a person pleads guilty, submits to a term of probation, and successfully completes the probation, then no adjudication of guilt is entered; so, no record of conviction exists. Probation terms usually include drug counseling, periodic drug testing, and no other arrests during the period. This type of procedure is known as *deferred sentencing or suspended imposition of sentence*. See Chapter 16 for a discussion of sentencing.

The sale or distribution of prohibited drugs is the second primary drug offense. Generally, it is punished more severely than possession. Not only are sales prohibited, but any "delivery" or "distribution" of drugs is also illegal. "Possession with an intent to deliver or sell" is similar to simple possession, except a mens rea of intending to sell must be proven. Possession with an intent to sell or deliver is punished more severely than possession; often, such possession is punished equally with actual sale or delivery.

The quantity of the drug involved affects the level of punishment for both possession and sale/distribution offenses. Other factors, such as selling to minors, may aggravate the sentence.

Unauthorized use of a controlled substance is also a crime. The mens rea is knowing use. So, if a person takes a pill containing a controlled substance that someone—who represented it to be an aspirin—gives him or her, there is no crime. Of course, the taking must be voluntary. If a person is forced down and injected with an illegal drug, he or she has committed no crime.

Recall from the earlier discussion of actus reus that addiction to controlled substances may not be made criminal. The United States Supreme Court has held that criminalizing a person's status as an addict is cruel and unusual punishment, as prohibited by the Eighth Amendment to the U.S. Constitution.[40] It is permitted, however, to punish a person for the act of taking a controlled substance.

sidebar

DRUG COURTS

Drug cases began to clog court dockets in the 1980s. As a result, legislators, judges, and others searched for alternatives to deal with drug offenders. One alternative that has proven to be popular is the drug court. The first drug court opened in Miami, Florida, in 1989. By 1997, there were 161 programs in existence in 38 states, the District of Columbia, and Puerto Rico. Forty percent of those courts were in Florida and California. Additionally, nearly every state without a drug court was in the process of developing one.

As the name implies, the drug court hears only drug cases. In most drug courts, only non-violent drug offenders are eligible for admission. The time of admission varies between programs. In some courts, the offender is deferred into the program. If the offender successfully completes the program, no conviction results. In others, offenders are channeled into the program after a plea of guilty or postconviction.

The drug court specializes in the treatment and monitoring of drug offenders. All programs have a treatment component, although the form of treatment varies significantly among programs. In addition, drug court programs are characterized by intensive monitoring. Participants are required to submit to daily or weekly drug screenings, and they are required to frequently appear in court. Many programs also use a system of "graduated sanctions" to punish participants who fail to meet program requirements.

The data concerning the success of drug programs are not clear. Unfortunately, one study indicates that 48 percent of the participants do not successfully complete their programs. It is too early to know the degree to which these programs decrease recidivism as compared to processing individuals through other courts, but at least one researcher has found that graduated sanctions programs may be successful in this regard.

Sources: Drug Courts: Overview of Growth, Characteristics, and Results Report of the General Accounting Office (GAO/GGD 97–106), July 31, 1997; and Adele Harrell, U.S. Department of Justice, National Institute of Justice (1998).

RICO and CCE

You have already learned that the Racketeer Influenced and Corrupt Organizations Act (RICO) was enacted to fight organized crime in all its forms. Another federal statute, Continuing Criminal Enterprise (CCE),[41] was enacted specifically to combat drug trafficking. The statute is aimed at prosecuting the people at the top of the drug-dealing and smuggling pyramid, and, accordingly, it has become known as the "Drug Kingpin statute."

A person engages in a criminal enterprise if (1) he is an administrator, organizer, or other leader (2) of a group of five or more people (3) who are involved in a series of drug violations. A *series* of violations means three or more drug convictions.[42]

Conviction of CCE results in stern punishment. A general violation receives 20 years to life in prison. Second convictions carry 30 years to life. If a person is determined to be a "principal leader," the amount of drugs involved was enormous, or the enterprise made $10 million or more in one year from drugs, then life imprisonment is mandatory. Fines may also be imposed. Also, the statute provides for imprisonment or death when murder results from the enterprise.[43]

Finally, the Comprehensive Forfeiture Act of 1984[44] applies to both RICO and CCE violations. This statute permits the government to seize property and money that is used in the commission of the crimes and that is a product of the crimes. So, if a drug dealer uses a boat to smuggle drugs, the boat can be seized, even though it may have been purchased with "honest" money. Any items acquired with drug money may be seized, as can bank accounts and trusts.

Possession of Drug Paraphernalia

Another tool in the government's arsenal against drug use are laws that prohibit the sale, use, and possession of drug paraphernalia. These laws are often aimed at retailers who sell the devices that are used to take drugs. Needles, roach clips, and specialized pipes are examples of the type of paraphernalia that are proscribed.

These laws have been challenged on many fronts. One challenge asserts that such laws are vague because they do not adequately describe what is proscribed. In addition, it has been asserted that these laws are overly broad because they include devices that may be used for both legitimate and illegal purposes.[45] These issues were considered by the United States Supreme Court in the 1994 case, *Posters 'N' Things, Ltd. v. United States.*[46] In this case the Court held that a law proscribing items "primarily intended" or "designed for" drug use was neither too vague nor overly broad and, accordingly, found it constitutional.

CRIMES AGAINST THE ADMINISTRATION OF GOVERNMENT

Perjury

Perjury was a crime at common law and continues to be prohibited by statute in all states.

perjury

■ Lying while under oath, especially in a court proceeding. It is a crime.

The basic elements of perjury are (1) the making of a (2) false statement (3) with knowledge that it is false (4) while under oath. To gain a conviction, the prosecution has the tough burden of proving the mens rea: that the person who made the statement knew that it was false. As with other crimes, juries are permitted to infer a defendant's knowledge from surrounding facts.

In addition, the statement must be made while under oath. Be aware that this requirement includes far more than testifying in court. Most laws cover all statements made before a person authorized to administer oaths. Therefore, perjury laws apply to people who sign affidavits before notary publics and appear as witnesses before a court reporter (e.g., for deposition), a grand jury, and all others who have the authority to administer oaths. For those individuals who have a religious objection to "swearing," the law permits an affirmation. This is simply an acknowledgment by the witness that the testimony he or she renders is truthful. The law treats an affirmation in the same manner as it does an oath.

Some jurisdictions require that the false statement be "material," or important to the matter. This requirement prevents prosecutions for trivial matters. Some jurisdictions have defined *materiality* as any matter that may affect the outcome of a case. If a statement is not material, even if untrue, then a perjury conviction is not permitted.

subornation of perjury

■ The crime of asking or forcing another person to lie under oath.

A related crime is **subornation of perjury**. This crime occurs when one convinces or procures another to commit perjury. One who commits subornation is treated as a perjurer for the purpose of sentencing.

In addition to being a crime in every state, perjury has been made criminal by statute in the United States. 18 U.S.C. § 1621 reads:

> Whoever (1) having taken an oath before a competent tribunal, officer, or person, in any case in which a law of the United States authorizes an oath to be administered, that he will testify, declare, depose, or certify truly . . . is true, willfully and contrary to such oath states or subscribes any material matter which he does not believe to be true. . . .

Of course, truth is a complete defense to a charge of perjury. What is truthful is not always easy to determine, and in most questionable cases prosecutors choose not to pursue the matter. This decision is largely due to the mens rea element.

sidebar

THE PROBLEMS OF PRESIDENT CLINTON: A CASE STUDY IN CRIMES AGAINST THE PUBLIC

One of the most public cases of crimes against the public occurred in the late 1990s. For several years independent Counsel Kenneth Starr investigated President William J. Clinton and many of his associates for activities that transpired before and after Clinton assumed the presidency. In December 1998 the House of Representatives of the United States impeached President Clinton after receiving a referral from Mr. Starr. The House issued a two-count impeachment alleging both perjury and obstruction of justice.

In the impeachment, the president was accused of committing perjury to a grand jury. The House alleged that Mr. Clinton lied about the nature of his relationship with a White House intern, Monica Lewinsky. He was also accused of lying about a prior perjury he committed in a deposition in a sexual harassment action filed by Paula Jones, who had been an employee of the State of Arkansas when Mr. Clinton was governor of that state. In addition, he was charged directly with perjury in the Paula Jones sexual harassment lawsuit, with suborning perjury in that case, and with obstructing justice in that case.

Perjury can be a tricky affair because language can be a tricky affair. Proving perjury requires actual knowledge of falsity, materiality, and an oath. The mens rea is the difficult part, as demonstrated in the Clinton case. In response to questions concerning whether he had sexual relations with Ms. Lewinsky, Mr. Clinton answered in the negative. Later, it was discovered that these answers were true using Mr. Clinton's definition of sex, which he narrowly defined as intercourse. He later admitted to having oral and other forms of sexual contact with Ms. Lewinsky. Mr. Clinton also used semantics to evade disclosing other facts. For example, he relied on distinctions in tense when responding to certain questions. Mr. Clinton responded to one question by stating "[I]t depends on what the meaning of the word 'is' is. If the, if he, if is means is and never has been, that is not, that is one thing. If it means there is none, that was a completely true statement."

Another problem prosecutors faced in the Clinton case was his inability to recall facts. In response to many details, the president answered that he was unable to remember; or he would provide a qualified answer (e.g., I believe, but I'm not sure). In such cases, a prosecutor must prove that the witness did know the answer in order to prove perjury—a very difficult task.

Concerning the obstruction of justice charges, Mr. Starr alleged that Mr. Clinton attempted to retrieve gifts he had given to Ms. Lewinsky in an attempt to prevent them from falling into the hands of investigators. In addition, Mr. Starr accused the president of attempting to coach witnesses into testifying in a certain manner. For example, his secretary testified that the president met with her, told her that there were several things she needed to know, and that he had been asked about Monica Lewinsky in deposition the day before. He then posed these questions and statements to the secretary: "You were always there when she was there, right? We were never really alone. Monica came on to me, and I never touched her, right? You can see and hear everything, right?"

(continued)

On February 12, 1999, the Senate of the United States voted 45 to 55 in favor of conviction on the perjury count and 50–50 on the obstruction of justice count, in both cases falling short of the 67 votes necessary to convict and remove the president. Because Kenneth Starr (as well as many constitutional scholars) was of the opinion that a president must be impeached and removed before a criminal action may be filed against the president, Mr. Starr did not file criminal charges against Mr. Clinton. Mr. Clinton may now be charged and tried for both the perjury and obstruction allegations. In 1999, the trial judge in the Paula Jones case held Mr. Clinton in contempt of court for "giving false, misleading and evasive answers that were designed to obstruct the judicial process. . . . Simply put, the president's deposition testimony regarding whether he had ever been alone with Ms. Lewinsky was intentionally false, and his statements regarding whether he had ever engaged in sexual relations with Ms. Lewinsky likewise were intentionally false, notwithstanding tortured definitions and interpretations of the term 'sexual relations.'" The court ordered Mr. Clinton to pay plaintiff's expenses resulting from efforts to disprove his statements, as well as related court costs.

Source: for contempt information: http://www.foxnews.com/news/packages/president/side0414a99.sml

Bribery

bribery

■ The offering, giving, receiving, or soliciting of anything of value in order to influence the actions of a public official.

As is true of perjury, **bribery** was a crime at English common law. Actually, bribery was initially a violation of biblical law, because it was wrong to attempt to influence judges, who were considered to be God's earthly representatives. Eventually, the crime was recognized by the courts of England.

Today, bribery is a statutory crime in the states and in the United States. The essential elements of the crime are (1) soliciting or accepting (2) anything of value (3) with the purpose of (4) violating a duty or trust. Two primary forms of bribery are that of a public official and commercial bribery.

As mentioned, bribery began as a prohibition of influencing a judge. The crime was eventually extended to include bribery of all public officials and public servants. Statutes make it bribery to be the one accepting or giving the "thing of value." Hence, if a corporate official gives a public official money in exchange for awarding a contract to the company, both the corporate officer and the public official have committed bribery.

Most bribery statutes declare that unsuccessful offers are bribes. Thus, if the public official rejects the offer of the corporate officer, there is still a bribery violation. The offer need not be of money in exchange for a favor; anything of value is sufficient. Automobiles, tickets to a St. Louis Cardinals game, and a promise of sexual favors all satisfy this requirement.

The offer must be made to a *public official or servant*. Both terms are defined broadly. Further, the offeror must be seeking to influence the official in a matter over which the official has authority. Most courts have held that whether the officer actually had the authority to carry out the requested act is not dispositive; the issue is whether the offeror believes that the official possesses the authority. Awarding of government contracts, setting favorable tax assessments, and overlooking civil and criminal violations are examples of corrupt acts.

The offer alone makes the offeror guilty of bribery. For the public official to be convicted, there must be an acceptance. This usually means that the official does the requested act; however, it is widely held that an acceptance is all that is necessary to support a conviction.

Bribery has been extended beyond the public affairs realm to commercial life. Whenever a person who is engaged in business activities breaches a duty or trust owed to someone (or something, such as a business organization) in exchange for something of value, bribery has been committed.

The Model Penal Code declares that commercial bribery is a misdemeanor. The Code applies to people in specific positions, such as lawyers, accountants, trustees, and officers of corporations.[47] Anyone who makes an offer to someone in one of these positions to violate the trust or duty created by the position is guilty of bribery. Of course, any person holding such a position who accepts such an offer is also guilty of bribery. The Code specifically states that any person who holds himself or herself out to the public to be in the business of appraising the value of services or commodities is guilty of bribery if he or she accepts a benefit to influence the decision or appraisal. Knowing that one is violating the trust is the mens rea under the Code.

If a seller for the Widgcom Company were to offer the purchasing agent of Retailers, Inc., money in exchange for receiving the contract to supply Retailers with Widgets for the next year, commercial bribery has occurred. A corporate officer who accepts free personal air travel in exchange for buying all corporate airline tickets from the same airline has committed bribery.

Finally, note that there are statutes that prohibit "throwing" athletic contests for pay. That is, any player, coach, owner, or official who accepts a benefit to cause one participant to win or lose commits bribery. These laws often apply to both professional and amateur sports.

Tax Crimes

You have likely heard the quip, "In life, only two things are certain, death and taxes." Tax revenues are the lifeblood of government. In the United States, people are taxed at the federal, state, and local levels (county, municipal, and school district taxes). These taxes come in many forms, including income tax, gift and estate tax, sales tax, and excise taxes. Tax laws apply to individuals, estates, and business entities.

All taxing authorities have statutes that impose both civil and criminal penalties for violation of tax laws. Common violations of tax laws are tax evasion, failing to file a required tax return, filing a fraudulent return, and unlawful disclosure of tax information. These are not the only crimes related to taxes, however, as shown by the applicable federal statutes, which embody 16 tax-related crimes.[48]

Tax evasion involves paying less tax than required or underreporting one's income with the intent of paying less tax. The federal statute covering tax evasion reads:

26 U.S.C. § 7201 Attempt to evade or defeat tax

Any person who willfully attempts in any manner to evade or defeat any tax imposed by this title or the payment thereof shall, in addition to other penalties provided by law, be guilty of a felony and, upon conviction thereof, shall be fined not more than $100,000 ($500,000 in the case of a corporation), or imprisoned not more than 5 years, or both, together with the costs of prosecution.

Tax fraud, a crime closely related to evasion, involves using fraud or false statements to avoid a tax obligation. This crime may occur in many ways, including falsifying statements that are provided to a revenue agency, such as fraudulent receipts used for deductions. Filing false tax returns is also a form of tax fraud.

Failure to file a required tax return is also criminal. The relevant federal statute reads:

26 U.S.C. § 7203 Willful failure to file return, supply information, or pay tax

Any person required under this title to pay any estimated tax or tax, or required by this title or by regulations made under authority thereof to make a return, keep any records, or supply any information, who willfully fails to pay such estimated tax or tax, make such return, keep such records, or supply such information . . . [shall] be guilty of a misdemeanor and, upon conviction thereof, shall be fined not more than $25,000 ($100,000 in the case of a corporation), or imprisoned not more than 1 year, or both, together with the costs of prosecution.

Note that § 7203 applies to anyone who is required to file a tax return, pay a tax, or supply information. Therefore, this provision can be the basis of a prosecution of an employer who pays his or her employees in cash and makes no report to the Internal Revenue Service. Likewise, although some entities are not taxed, such as partnerships, they are required to file informational returns, and failure to do so violates this provision.

Tax evasion, filing fraudulent tax returns, and the unauthorized disclosure of information are crimes of commission. That is, an affirmative act is required to commit these crimes.

Failing to file a required return, or other information, is an act of omission. Proving such crimes requires not proof of an illegal act but that a required act was not taken. The quoted statutes require willful violations. Negligence in preparing a tax return or in filing the return is not criminal. However, such errors may lead to civil penalties.

The willfulness requirement was considered by the Supreme Court in *Cheek v. United States.*

---

tax evasion

■ The deliberate nonpayment or underpayment of taxes that are legally due. Criminal tax evasion has higher fines than civil fraud and the possibility of a prison sentence upon the showing of "willfulness."

tax fraud

■ The deliberate nonpayment or underpayment of taxes that are legally due.

Tax laws require the disclosure of all income and profits. This includes income from illegal sources. Gamblers are required to report their winnings, prostitutes their income, and drug dealers the profits derived from their sales. Failure to report income from illegal acts is the same as failure to report legally earned income. Because requiring people to report income from illegal activities raises a self-incrimination problem, tax laws require that all information obtained be kept confidential. Tax officials are not permitted to disclose such information to law enforcement authorities, and to do so is *unlawful disclosure*. The privilege against self-incrimination is discussed more thoroughly in Chapter 8.

Obstruction of Justice

Obstruction of justice refers to any number of unlawful acts. As a general proposition, any act that interferes with the performance of a public official's duties obstructs justice. However, the crime is most commonly associated with law enforcement and judicial officials.

CHEEK V. UNITED STATES
498 U.S. 192 (1991)

Willfulness, as construed by our prior decisions in criminal tax cases, requires the Government to prove that the law imposed a duty on the defendant, that the defendant knew of this duty, and that he voluntarily and intentionally violated this duty. We deal first with the case where the issue is whether the defendant knew of the duty purportedly imposed by the provision of the statute or regulation he is accused of violating, a case in which there is no claim that the provision at issue is invalid. In such a case, if the Government proves actual knowledge of the pertinent legal duty, the prosecution, without more, has satisfied the knowledge component of the willfulness requirement. But carrying this burden requires negating a defendant's claim of ignorance of the law or a claim that because of a misunderstanding of the law, he had a good-faith belief that he was not violating any of the provisions of the tax laws. This is so because one cannot be aware that the law imposes a duty upon him and yet be ignorant of it, misunderstand the law, or believe that the duty does not exist. In the end, the issue is whether, based on all the evidence, the Government has proved that the defendant was aware of the duty at issue, which cannot be true if the jury credits a good-faith misunderstanding and belief submission, whether or not the claimed belief or misunderstanding is objectively reasonable.

In this case, if Cheek asserted that he truly believed that the Internal Revenue Code did not purport to treat wages as income, and the jury believed him, the Government would not have carried its burden to prove willfulness, however, unreasonable a court might deem such a belief. . . .

We thus disagree with the Court of Appeals' requirement that a claimed good-faith belief must be objectively reasonable if it is to be considered as possibly negating the Government's evidence purporting to show a defendant's awareness of the legal duty at issue. Knowledge and belief are characteristically questions for the fact finder.

The types of acts that fall under such statutes include tampering with witnesses or jurors, interfering with police officers, destroying evidence needed for a court proceeding, and intentionally giving false information to a prosecutor in an effort to hinder a prosecutorial effort. However, obstruction statutes are drafted broadly, thereby permitting creative prosecutions. For example, it is common for women who are physically abused by their husbands to contact the police during a violent episode and demand the husband's arrest, usually in an effort to get the man out of the house. Once the husband is arrested, many women lose interest in prosecuting and often refuse to testify against their husbands in court. In such a case, a prosecutor could charge the wife with obstruction of justice because of her refusal to testify.

Resisting arrest is a similar crime. At common law, one could resist an unlawful arrest. Although a few jurisdictions have retained this rule, this is not presently the law in most jurisdictions. Most states have followed the Model Penal Code approach, which prohibits even moderate resistance to any arrest.[49] It is a wise rule, considering the remedies that are available if a police officer makes an unlawful arrest. If the arrest is unlawful, but in good faith, the arrestee will be released either at the police station or after the first judicial hearing. If the arrest was unlawful and made maliciously, the arrestee not only will be released but also has a civil cause of action for false imprisonment and violation of civil rights.

Contempt

Failure to comply with a court order is contemptuous, as is taking any act with the purpose of undermining a court's authority or intending to interfere with its administration and process. Although statutes provide for contempt, it is widely accepted that the contempt power is inherent.

contempt

■ A willful disobeying of a judge's command or official court order. Contempt can be *direct* (within the judge's notice) or *indirect* (outside the court and punishable only after proved to the judge). It can also be *civil contempt* (disobeying a court order in favor of an opponent) or *criminal contempt*.

Contempt is broken down into direct and indirect criminal contempt and direct and indirect civil contempt. *Direct contempt* refers to acts that occur in the presence of the judge. Although contempt usually occurs in the courtroom, the judges' chambers and office area are included. *Indirect contempt* refers to actions taken outside the presence of a court but that are violative of a court order.

Criminal contempt is levied to punish a person for violating a court order. Civil contempt, in contrast, does not have punishment as its purpose. It is intended to coerce a person into complying with a court order. For example, if Mary refuses to testify at a trial despite an order to testify, the judge may order her confined until she complies. Once she testifies, she is free. It is often said that civil contemnors hold the keys to their jail cells, whereas criminal contemnors do not. In theory, one who has been held in civil contempt can be punished for criminal contempt after complying with the court order. In practice this punishment seldom occurs, presumably because judges and prosecutors feel that the civil punishment imposed is adequate.

The contempt power is significant. Indirect criminal contemnors are entitled to all the protections of other criminal defendants, such as a right to a trial, assistance of counsel, and proof beyond a reasonable doubt. Direct criminal contemnors have no such rights, as the act took place in the presence of a judge. However, any sentence imposed may be appealed and reviewed for fairness.

Civil contemnors have few rights. They do not possess the rights of those accused of crimes, because civil contempt is not considered a criminal action. In most instances they enjoy no right to appeal. A civil contemnor holds his or her own key; he or she must comply with the court's order. Of course, if an appellate court determines that the underlying order is unlawful, the civil contemnor is released. However, the individual may be charged with criminal contempt for failure to comply with the order before it was held unlawful by an appellate court. The fact that a court order may be nullified at some future date does not justify noncompliance. Court orders must be obeyed to assure the orderly administration of justice.

sidebar

TWO CASES OF CONTEMPT

Contempt of court orders are common in domestic law cases. One case, which received considerable media attention, involved Dr. Elizabeth Morgan, who refused to obey a court order to disclose the location of her child, Heather, claiming that her ex-husband had molested the child. The judge ordered that she disclose the location of the child so her ex-husband could exercise his court-ordered visitation rights. She refused, and the judge ordered that she be incarcerated until she disclosed the child's whereabouts. Dr. Morgan spent a total of 759 days in jail and was released only after an act of Congress limited the amount of time a civil contemnor could spend in jail to one year.

A case from Houston, Texas, teaches that the contempt power of judges is powerful. Houston attorney John O'Quinn was found in criminal contempt by a federal district judge for sleeping in a jury room. The basis for the contempt citation was an order from the judge that O'Quinn (and others) "stay out of the facilities up here on this floor unless you get prior permission." The Fifth Circuit Court of Appeals reversed the conviction, finding that the judge's order was too vague. However, this is a good example of the breadth of the contempt power; had the judge's order been more specific, it would have been upheld.

Source: "A Hard Case of Contempt," *Time,* Sept. 18, 1989; "A Mother's 759 Days of Defiance," *U.S News & World Report,* Oct. 9, 1989.

Legislatures also have the power to cite for contempt. Legislatures, usually through committees, conduct hearings and other proceedings when considering bills and amendments to statutes. The contempt power serves the same function for legislatures that it does for courts. It furthers the orderly performance of legislative duties. Refusal to testify before a legislative body (usually a committee) or to produce documents or other items, and disruption of a proceeding are examples of legislative contempt. Persons charged with legislative contempt possess the same rights as defendants charged with other crimes. In most instances, legislative bodies refer contempt cases to prosecutors, rather than adjudicating such cases themselves.

CRIMES AGAINST SOVEREIGNTY AND SECURITY

In the last section you read about crimes that interfere with public administration. Those crimes may—but not necessarily—be intended to destroy the government or to make a political statement. This section examines the very serious crimes of treason, sedition, espionage, and terrorism.

Treason

The United States has had law dealing with treason since its earliest years. The only crime mentioned in the Constitution is treason. Article III, section 3 reads:

> Clause 1: Treason against the United States, shall consist only in levying War against them, or in adhering to their Enemies, giving them Aid and Comfort. No Person shall be convicted of Treason unless on the Testimony of two Witnesses to the same overt Act, or on Confession in open Court.
>
> Clause 2: The Congress shall have Power to declare the Punishment of Treason, but no Attainder of Treason shall work Corruption of Blood, or Forfeiture except during the Life of the Person attainted.

Congress implemented Clause 1,[50] and the resulting elements of the offense are as follows:

1. A person who owes an allegiance to the United States,
2. *Levies* war or *Adheres* to an enemy of the United States and
3. commits an overt act and
4. possesses treasonable intent.

Interestingly, one does not have to be a citizen of the United States to commit treason. Persons living in the United States owe allegiance to the nation and may be charged with treason. Generally, speech is not an overt act, except when state secrets are revealed to an enemy. To satisfy the mens rea requirement, one must intend to betray the United States. Clause two requires two witnesses to the treasonous act. The two witnesses may testify to separate acts, so long as they support the same act of treason.

Sedition and Espionage

Sedition has been recognized as a crime since the first days of the Constitution. The Alien and Seditions Acts of the late eighteenth century made it a crime to write false, scandalous, or malicious stories about the government; increased the residency period required to become a citizen; and increased the president's authority to deport dangerous aliens.

The provisions of the sedition laws prohibiting free speech were controversial, and many prominent Americans opposed them—including Thomas Jefferson and James Madison. After the law expired by its own sunset provision, Congress reimbursed the paid fines for all those who had been convicted under its authority.[51]

Today there are several sedition laws, including a prohibition of seditious conspiracies to overthrow the government;[52] the Logan Act, which prohibits individuals from corresponding with foreign governments in relation to disputes such governments may have with the United States; and a prohibition of recruiting members of the U.S. armed forces to act against the United States.[53]

Many forms of espionage and subversive activities are made criminal in the federal statutes.[54] Most of these require either an intention or reason to believe the United States will be injured and an overt act in furtherance of the crime.

Terrorism

Prior to September 11, 2001, there were many terrorism statutes. Post-9/11, there are many more. This section examines a few of the federal statutes defining terrorism crimes. Other issues, such as the rights of detainees in the War on Terror and electronic eavesdropping in a post-9/11 environment, are discussed later in this book.

Recent acts of terrorism, however, have been the catalyst to new terrorism and sedition laws. The Foreign Intelligence Surveillance Act of 1978 (FISA) delegated substantial authority to federal law enforcement officials. FISA provided for secret court orders authorizing surveillance (without probable cause) of non-U.S. persons. The objective of such orders is not to build cases for criminal prosecution, but to gather foreign intelligence.

In 1995 Timothy McVeigh, with accomplices, bombed the federal building in Oklahoma City, Oklahoma, killing 167 people, including several children, and injuring over 600 others.[55] It would be the worst act of terror, in terms of loss of life, in modern United States until the attacks of September 11, 2001. McVeigh was eventually executed for the deaths resulting from the bombing. See Exhibit 6-1 for a copy of McVeigh's death certificate. Unhappy with the lack of rights of the victims during the trial of McVeigh and with the right of defendants to repeated habeas corpus appeals on the same subjects, Congress, with President Clinton's approval, enacted the Antiterrorism and Effective Death Penalty Act of 1996. Through this statute habeas corpus relief was limited, inter alia, by requiring petitions to be filed within one year and limiting the number of petitions that may be filed in any one case. The Act also requires victim compensation and requires courts to provide closed-circuit television access to victims in instances where the venue of trial is changed from the location of the crime.

Following the September 11 attacks, the Uniting and Strengthening America by Providing Appropriate Tools Required to Intercept and Obstruct Terrorism Act of 2001 was enacted. This law is commonly known as the Patriot Act. The Patriot Act was reauthorized, with amendments, in 2006. The Patriot Act changed existing law (including the Omnibus Crime Control and Safe Streets Act of 1968) in many ways, including the following:

- Federal law enforcement authority to monitor e-mail and other forms of communication was expanded. Examples include treating stored voice-mail messages like e-mail, not as telephone conversations. E-mail enjoys less protection than telephone conversations do.
- Federal court authority to issue pen register and trap orders (devices used to determine the origin of electronic communications) was broadened to include the entire nation.

Exhibit 6–1 OFFICIAL COPY, VIGO COUNTY HEALTH DEPARTMENT CERTIFICATE OF DEATH

Vigo County, Indiana Health Department Death Certificate for Timothy McVeigh, who was executed for the 1995 bombing of the Murrah Federal Building in Oklahoma City, OK.

ATTENTION ESTATE: The Social Security # is being requested by this state agency in order to pursue its statutory responsibility. Disclosure is voluntary and there will be no penalty for refusal.

Local No. ...... 599 ....

OFFICIAL COPY
VIGO COUNTY HEALTH DEPARTMENT
CERTIFICATE OF DEATH

THE RECORDS IN THIS SERIES ARE CONFIDENTIAL PER IC 16-37-1-10

TYPE/PRINT IN PERMANENT BLACK INK

DECEDENT

1. DECEASED—NAME (First, Middle, Last): Timothy James McVeigh
2. SEX: Male
3a. TIME OF DEATH: 7:14 A.M
3b. DATE OF DEATH (Month, Day, Yr): June 11, 2001
4. *SOCIAL SECURITY NUMBER: 129-58-4709
5a. AGE—Last Birthday (Years): 33
5b. UNDER 1 YEAR: Months / Days
5c. UNDER 1 DAY: Hours / Minutes
6. DATE OF BIRTH (Mo, Day, Yr): April 23, 1968
7. BIRTHPLACE (City and State or Foreign Country): Lockport, NY
8a. WAS DECEDENT A U.S. VETERAN?: Yes
8b. YEAR LAST SERVED IN U.S. ARMED FORCES?: 1991
9a. PLACE OF DEATH (Check only one. See instructions): HOSPITAL ☐ Inpatient ☐ ER/Outpatient ☐ DOA; OTHER ☐ Nursing Home ☒ Other (Specify) ☐ Residence — U S Penitentiary
9b. FACILITY NAME (If not institution, give street and number): U S Penitentiary, 4200 Bureau Road
9c. CITY, TOWN, OR LOCATION OF DEATH: Terre Haute
9d. COUNTY OF DEATH: Vigo
10. MARITAL STATUS (Specify): Never Married
11. SURVIVING SPOUSE (If wife, give maiden name): N/A
12a. DECEDENT'S USUAL OCCUPATION (Give kind of work done during most of working life. Do not use retired): Soldier
12b. KIND OF BUSINESS/INDUSTRY: US Army
13a. RESIDENCE—STATE: New York
13b. COUNTY: Niagara
13c. CITY, TOWN, OR LOCATION: Lockport
13d. STREET AND NUMBER: 6289 Campbell Blvd
13e. ZIP CODE: 14094
13f. INSIDE CITY LIMITS: ☐ No ☒ Yes
13g. ON A FARM?: ☒ No ☐ Yes
14. CITIZEN OF WHAT COUNTRY?: USA
15. WAS DECEDENT OF HISPANIC ORIGIN? ☒ No ☐ Yes (If yes, specify Cuban, Mexican, Puerto Rican, etc.)
16. RACE—American Indian, Black, White, etc. (Specify): White
17. DECEDENT'S EDUCATION (Specify only highest grade completed): Elementary/Secondary (0-12): 12; College (1-4 or 5+):

PARENTS

18. FATHER'S NAME (First, Middle, Last): William McVeigh
19. MOTHER'S NAME (First, Middle, Maiden Surname): Mildred Noreen Hill

INFORMANT

20a. INFORMANT'S NAME (Type/Print): Robert Nigh
20b. MAILING ADDRESS (Street and Number or Rural Route Number, City or Town, State, Zip Code): 2 West 6th St Tulsa, OK 74119
20c. Relationship: Attorney

DISPOSITION

21a. METHOD OF DISPOSITION: ☐ Burial ☒ Cremation ☐ Removal from State ☐ Entombment ☐ Donation ☐ Other (Specify)
21b. DATE AND PLACE OF DISPOSITION (Name of cemetery, crematory, or other place): June 11, 2001 Terre Haute Crematory
21c. LOCATION—City or Town, State: Terre Haute, IN
22a. EMBALMER'S NAME: No Embalming
22b. EMBALMER'S LICENSE NO.: N/A
23. WAS DEATH REPORTED TO CORONER? ☐ No ☒ Yes
24a. SIGNATURE OF FUNERAL DIRECTOR: [signature]
24b. LICENSE NUMBER (of Licensee): FD09200035
25. NAME, ADDRESS, AND LICENSE NUMBER OF FUNERAL HOME: Mattox Ryan Funeral Home 602 S 7th Street Terre Haute, IN 4780 FH19900001

CAUSE OF DEATH

26. PART I. Enter the diseases, injuries, or complications that caused the death. Do not enter nonspecific terms, such as cardiac or respiratory arrest, shock, or heart failure. List only one cause on each line. — Approximate Interval Between Onset and Death

IMMEDIATE CAUSE (Final disease or condition resulting in death) a. Lethal Injection
DUE TO (OR AS A CONSEQUENCE OF):
Conditions, if any, which gave rise to the immediate cause, stating the underlying cause last. b.
DUE TO (OR AS A CONSEQUENCE OF): c.
DUE TO (OR AS A CONSEQUENCE OF): d.

PART II. Other significant conditions - Conditions contributing to death but not previously stated in Part I
27. WAS DECEDENT PREGNANT OR 90 DAYS POSTPARTUM? (Yes or no): NO
28a. WAS AN AUTOPSY PERFORMED? (Yes or no): NO
28b. WERE AUTOPSY FINDINGS AVAILABLE PRIOR TO COMPLETION OF CAUSE OF DEATH? (Yes or no): NO

CERTIFIER

29a. CERTIFIER (Check only one)
☐ CERTIFYING PHYSICIAN To the best of my knowledge, death occurred at the time, date, and place, and due to the cause(s) as stated
☐ HEALTH OFFICER On the basis of examination and/or investigation, in my opinion, death occurred at the time, date, and place, and due to the cause(s) as stated
☒ CORONER On the basis of examination and/or investigation, in my opinion, death occurred at the time, date, and place, and due to the cause(s) and manner as stated
29b. SIGNATURE AND TITLE OF CERTIFIER: Susan S. Amos, MD Vigo County Coroner
29c. MEDICAL LICENSE NO: 01031117
29d. DATE SIGNED (Month, Day, Year): June 11, 2001
30. NAME AND ADDRESS OF PERSON WHO COMPLETED CAUSE OF DEATH (ITEM 26) (Type/Print): Susan Amos Coroner 501 Hospital Lane Terre Haute, IN 47802

HEALTH OFFICER

31. HEALTH OFFICER'S SIGNATURE: [signature], MD
32. DATE FILED (Month, Day, Year): JUN 11 2001

33. MANNER OF DEATH: ☐ Natural ☐ Pending Investigation ☐ Accident ☐ Suicide ☐ Could not be Determined ☒ Homicide
34a. DATE OF INJURY (Month, Day, Year): June 11, 2001
34b. TIME OF INJURY: 7:14 A.M.
34c. INJURY AT WORK? (Yes or no): No
34d. DESCRIBE HOW INJURY OCCURRED: Judicial Execution by Lethal injection
34e. PLACE OF INJURY—At home, farm, street, factory, office building, etc. (Specify): U.S. Penitentiary
34f. LOCATION (Street and Number or Rural Route Number, City or Town, State): 4200 Bureau Rd. Terre Haute, IN
34g. DATE PRONOUNCED DEAD (Month, Day, Year): June 11, 2001
34h. MOTOR VEHICLE ACCIDENT? (Yes or no) If yes, specify driver, passenger, pedestrian, etc.: No

SDH06-004 State Form 10110 (R5/1-99)

Source: http://law2.umkc.edu/faculty/projects/ftrials/mcveigh/mcveighcertif.html

- Prior to the Patriot Act, law enforcement officers did not have to establish probable cause to obtain a court order to a telephone company to trace (using pen register/traps). Because the content of telephone conversations was not being intruded upon, law enforcement officers were only required to show that the data are "relevant to an ongoing investigation." The Patriot Act extended this procedure to obtaining a record of Web addresses a suspect visits, even though identification of a Web address also identifies content.

- The Patriot Act authorizes "roving wiretaps." A roving wiretap is authorization to move a wiretap from one telephone or form of communication to another in order to follow the communications of the person under surveillance.

- Several new crimes were created, including money laundering of cybercrime and terrorism, overseas use of fraudulent U.S. credit cards, terrorist attacks on mass transit, and harboring terrorists, and it increased the penalties for counterfeiting.

- The Attorney General of the United States was delegated greater authority to deport suspected alien terrorists.

- Law enforcement agencies were given the authority to share grand jury and wiretap information that constitutes "foreign intelligence" with intelligence agencies. Previously, this action was not permitted.

Also in response to the September 11 attacks, President Bush issued Military Order 1. This order empowered the Secretary of Defense to detain members of al Qaeda who have participated in, or planned, terrorist activity. The order also provided for military tribunals for terrorists with a two-thirds majority of each commission required for conviction. The Secretary of Defense then issued Military Commission Order 1, which was an elaboration of the responsibilities and authorities issued by President Bush in Military Order 1. This order established the procedures for implementing President Bush's order. For example, it permits the imposition of the death sentence, mandates a secret vote of the military judges, and allows for forfeiture of the property of those convicted.

In 2002, Congress created the Department of Homeland Security (DHS) through the Homeland Security Act. DHS is headed by a secretary, a cabinet-level officer. DHS is charged with preventing and responding to terrorism and with overseeing the other responsibilities of the agencies under DHS supervision. Much of the federal government's arsenal in the war on terror was consolidated under DHS. The Federal Emergency Management Agency, U.S. Coast Guard, Customs, Border Patrol, Secret Service, Transportation Security Administration, and Citizenship and Immigration Services (previously Immigration and Naturalization Service) are all units reporting to DHS. In total, DHS has nearly 200,000 employees under its umbrella.

These new laws are not without their critics. The most common criticism is that civil liberties are being lost in the effort to increase national security. To these critics, two threats are posed by terrorism. The first is terrorism. The second is the possible overreaction to terrorism. Proponents of these new laws believe that terrorism is substantially different from other crime and that the loss of some freedoms is needed to maintain security.

The Crimes of Terrorism

The Federal Terrorism statute, 18 U.S.C. § 2331, defines international terrorism as follows:

(1) the term "international terrorism" means activities that—

    (A) involve violent acts or acts dangerous to human life that are a violation of the criminal laws of the United States or of any State, or that would be a criminal violation if committed within the jurisdiction of the United States or of any State;

    (B) appear to be intended—

        (i) to intimidate or coerce a civilian population;

        (ii) to influence the policy of a government by intimidation or coercion; or

        (iii) to affect the conduct of a government by mass destruction, assassination, or kidnapping; and

    (C) occur primarily outside the territorial jurisdiction of the United States, or transcend national boundaries in terms of the means by which they are accomplished, the persons they appear intended to intimidate or coerce, or the locale in which their perpetrators operate or seek asylum;

(2) the term "national of the United States" has the meaning given such term in section 101(a)(22) of the Immigration and Nationality Act;

(3) the term "person" means any individual or entity capable of holding a legal or beneficial interest in property;

(4) the term "act of war" means any act occurring in the course of—

    (A) declared war;

    (B) armed conflict, whether or not war has been declared, between two or more nations; or

    (C) armed conflict between military forces of any origin; and

(5) the term "domestic terrorism" means activities that—

    (A) involve acts dangerous to human life that are a violation of the criminal laws of the United States or of any State;

    (B) appear to be intended—

        (i) to intimidate or coerce a civilian population;

        (ii) to influence the policy of a government by intimidation or coercion; or

        (iii) to affect the conduct of a government by mass destruction, assassination, or kidnapping; and

    (C) occur primarily within the territorial jurisdiction of the United States.

Another statute, 18 U.S.C. § 2332, prohibits the following acts:

(a) Prohibited acts.—

(1) **Offenses.**—Whoever, involving conduct transcending national boundaries and in a circumstance described in subsection (b)—

    (A) kills, kidnaps, maims, commits an assault resulting in serious bodily injury, or assaults with a dangerous weapon any person within the United States; or

(B) creates a substantial risk of serious bodily injury to any other person by destroying or damaging any structure, conveyance, or other real or personal property within the United States or by attempting or conspiring to destroy or damage any structure, conveyance, or other real or personal property within the United States; in violation of the laws of any State, or the United States, shall be punished as prescribed in subsection (c).

(2) **Treatment of threats, attempts and conspiracies.**—Whoever threatens to commit an offense under paragraph (1), or attempts or conspires to do so, shall be punished under subsection (c).

(b) Jurisdictional bases.—

(3) **Circumstances.**—The circumstances referred to in subsection (a) are—

(A) the mail or any facility of interstate or foreign commerce is used in furtherance of the offense;

(B) the offense obstructs, delays, or affects interstate or foreign commerce, or would have so obstructed, delayed, or affected interstate or foreign commerce if the offense had been consummated;

(C) the victim, or intended victim, is the U.S. government, a member of the uniformed services, or any official, officer, employee, or agent of the legislative, executive, or judicial branches, or of any department or agency, of the United States;

(D) the structure, conveyance, or other real or personal property is, in whole or in part, owned, possessed, or leased to the United States, or any department or agency of the United States;

(E) the offense is committed in the territorial sea (including the airspace above and the seabed and subsoil below, and artificial islands and fixed structures erected thereon) of the United States; or

(F) the offense is committed within the special maritime and territorial jurisdiction of the United States.

(2) **Co-conspirators and accessories after the fact.**—Jurisdiction shall exist over all principals and co-conspirators of an offense under this section, and accessories after the fact to any offense under this section, if at least one of the circumstances described in subparagraphs (A) through (F) of paragraph (1) is applicable to at least one offender.

(c) Penalties . . .

Yet another definition of terrorism can be found in the Homeland Security Act, 6 U.S.C. § 101(15):

(15) The term "terrorism" means any activity that—

(A) involves an act that—

(i) is dangerous to human life or potentially destructive of critical infrastructure or key resources; and

(ii) is a violation of the criminal laws of the United States or of any State or other subdivision of the United States; and

(B) appears to be intended—

(i) to intimidate or coerce a civilian population;

(ii) to influence the policy of a government by intimidation or coercion; or

(iii) to affect the conduct of a government by mass destruction, assassination, or kidnapping.

In an attempt to strike at terrorist organizations, federal law authorizes the Secretary of State to designate any foreign group of two or more persons that commit terrorist activities or plan or prepare to commit terrorist activities. Once designated, those who support the organization are in violation of federal law, noncitizens who are members of these organizations are immediately deportable, and the financial resources of the organizations may be seized by the United States.

Additionally, other federal statutes address specific acts of terrorism, such as bioterrorism; bombing public places; attacking mass transportation systems; harboring terrorists; supporting and financing terrorism, terrorist organizations, and nations that support terrorism; and using weapons of mass destruction. For example, 18 U.S.C. § 2332(a) prohibits the use of a weapon for mass destruction

(1) against a national of the United States while such national is outside of the United States;

(2) against any person or property within the United States, and the mail or any facility of interstate or foreign commerce is used in furtherance of the offense; such property is used in interstate or foreign commerce or in an activity that affects interstate or foreign commerce; any perpetrator travels in or causes another to travel in interstate or foreign commerce in furtherance of the offense; or the offense, or the results of the offense, affect interstate or foreign commerce, or, in the case of a threat, attempt, or conspiracy, would have affected interstate or foreign commerce;

(3) against any property that is owned, leased or used by the United States or by any department or agency of the United States, whether the property is within or outside of the United States; or

(4) against any property within the United States that is owned, leased, or used by a foreign government. *Weapon of mass destruction* is defined as "any destructive device as defined in this law, any weapon that is designed or intended to cause death or serious bodily injury through the release, dissemination, or impact of toxic or poisonous chemicals, or their precursors, any weapon involving a biological agent, toxin, or vector (as those terms are defined in section 178 of this title), any weapon that is designed to release radiation or radioactivity at a level dangerous to human life."

Following the tragic attacks of September 11, 2001, Zacarias Moussaoui was charged with being the intended twentieth hijacker. Moussaoui could not board any of the hijacked flights on September 11 because he was in federal custody. Exhibit 6-2 is an excerpt of his indictment.

Exhibit 6–2   INDICTMENT OF THE TWENTIETH HIJACKER IN THE SEPTEMBER 11, 2001, ATTACKS ON THE UNITED STATES

IN THE UNITED STATES DISTRICT COURT FOR THE EASTERN DISTRICT OF VIRGINIA ALEXANDRIA DIVISION

UNITED STATES OF AMERICA	)	CRIMINAL NO:
	)	
-v-	)	Conspiracy to Commit Acts of Terrorism Transcending National Boundaries
	)	(18 U.S.C. §§ 2332b(a)(2) & (c))
ZACARIAS MOUSSAOUI,	)	(Count One)
a/k/a "Shaqil,"	)	
a/k/a "Abu Khalid al Sahrawi,"	)	Conspiracy to Commit Aircraft Piracy
	)	(49 U.S.C. §§ 46502 (a)(1)(A) and (a)(2)(B))
Defendant.	)	(Count Two)
	)	
	)	Conspiracy to Destroy Aircraft
	)	(18 U.S.C. §§ 32(a)(7) & 34)
	)	(Count Three)
	)	
	)	Conspiracy to Use Weapons of Mass Destruction
	)	(18 U.S.C. § 2332a(a))
	)	(Count Four)
	)	
	)	Conspiracy to Murder United States Employees
	)	(18 U.S.C. §§ 1114 & 1117)
	)	(Count Five)
	)	
	)	Conspiracy to Destroy Property
	)	(18 U.S.C. §§ 844(f), (i), (n))
	)	(Count Six)

DECEMBER 2001 TERM AT ALEXANDRIA INDICTMENT

THE GRAND JURY CHARGES THAT:

<u>COUNT ONE</u>

(Conspiracy to Commit Acts of Terrorism Transcending National Boundaries)

<u>Background: al Qaeda</u>

1. At all relevant times from in or about 1989 until the date of the filing of this Indictment, an international terrorist group existed which was dedicated to opposing non-Islamic governments with force and violence. This organization grew out of the "mekhtab al khidemat" (the "Services Office") organization which had maintained offices in various parts of the world, including Afghanistan, Pakistan (particularly in Peshawar), and the United States. The group was founded by Usama Bin Laden and Muhammad Atef, a/k/a "Abu Hafs al Masry,"

(continued)

Exhibit 6–2 (continued)

together with "Abu Ubaidah al Banshiri," and others. From in or about 1989 until the present, the group called itself "al Qaeda" ("the Base"). . . .

2. Bin Laden and al Qaeda violently opposed the United States for several reasons. First, the United States was regarded as an "infidel" because it was not governed in a manner consistent with the group's extremist interpretation of Islam. Second, the United States was viewed as providing essential support for other "infidel" governments and institutions, particularly the governments of Saudi Arabia and Egypt, the nation of Israel, and the United Nations organization, which were regarded as enemies of the group. Third, al Qaeda opposed the involvement of the United States armed forces in the Gulf War in 1991 and in Operation Restore Hope in Somalia in 1992 and 1993. In particular, al Qaeda opposed the continued presence of American military forces in Saudi Arabia (and elsewhere on the Saudi Arabian peninsula) following the Gulf War. Fourth, al Qaeda opposed the United States Government because of the arrest, conviction and imprisonment of persons belonging to al Qaeda or its affiliated terrorist groups or those with whom it worked. For these and other reasons, Bin Laden declared a jihad, or holy war, against the United States, which he has carried out through al Qaeda and its affiliated organizations.

3. One of the principal goals of al Qaeda was to drive the United States armed forces out of Saudi Arabia (and elsewhere on the Saudi Arabian peninsula) and Somalia by violence. Members of al Qaeda issued *fatwahs* (rulings on Islamic law) indicating that such attacks were both proper and necessary.

4. Al Qaeda functioned both on its own and through some of the terrorist organizations that operated under its umbrella, . . .

7. Since at least 1989, until the filing of this Indictment, Usama Bin Laden and the terrorist group al Qaeda sponsored, managed, and/or financially supported training camps in Afghanistan, which camps were used to instruct members and associates of al Qaeda and its affiliated terrorist groups in the use of firearms, explosives, chemical weapons, and other weapons of mass destruction. In addition to providing training in the use of various weapons, these camps were used to conduct operational planning against United States targets around the world and experiments in the use of chemical and biological weapons. . . .

The September 11 Hijackers

9. On September 11, 2001, co-conspirators Mohammed Atta, Abdul Alomari, Wail al-Shehri, Waleed al-Shehri, and Satam al-Suqami hijacked American Airlines Flight 11, bound from Boston to Los Angeles, and crashed it into the North Tower of the World Trade Center in New York. (In this Indictment, each hijacker will be identified with the flight number of the plane he hijacked.)

10. On September 11, 2001, co-conspirators Marwan al-Shehhi, Fayez Ahmed, a/k/a "Banihammad Fayez," Ahmed al-Ghamdi, Hamza al-Ghamdi, and Mohald al-Shehri hijacked United Airlines Flight 175, bound from Boston to Los Angeles, and crashed it into the South Tower of the World Trade Center in New York.

Exhibit 6–2   (continued)

11. On September 11, 2001, co-conspirators Khalid al-Midhar, Nawaf al-Hazmi, Hani Hanjour, Salem al-Hamzi, and Majed Moqed hijacked American Airlines Flight 77, bound from Virginia to Los Angeles, and crashed it into the Pentagon.

12. On September 11, 2001, co-conspirators Ziad Jarrah, Ahmed al-Haznawi, Saaed al-Ghamdi, and Ahmed al-Nami hijacked United Airlines Flight 93, bound from Newark to San Franscisco, and crashed it in Pennsylvania.

The Defendant

13. ZACARIAS MOUSSAOUI, a/k/a "Shaqil," a/k/a "Abu Khalid al Sahrawi," was born in France of Moroccan descent on May 30, 1968. Before 2001 he was a resident of the United Kingdom. MOUSSAOUI held a masters degree from Southbank University in the United Kingdom and traveled widely.

The Charge

16. From in or about 1989 until the date of the filing of this Indictment, in the Eastern District of Virginia, the Southern District of New York, and elsewhere, the defendant, ZACARIAS MOUSSAOUI, a/k/a "Shaqil," a/k/a "Abu Khalid al Sahrawi," with other members and associates of al Qaeda and others known and unknown to the Grand Jury, unlawfully, wilfully and knowingly combined, conspired, confederated and agreed to kill and maim persons within the United States, and to create a substantial risk of serious bodily injury to other persons by destroying and damaging structures, conveyances, and other real and personal property within the United States, in violation of the laws of States and the United States, in circumstances involving conduct transcending national boundaries, and in which facilities of interstate and foreign commerce were used in furtherance of the offense, the offense obstructed, delayed, and affected interstate and foreign commerce, the victim was the United States Government, members of the uniformed services, and officials, officers, employees, and agents of the governmental branches, departments, and agencies of the United States, and the structures, conveyances, and other real and personal property were, in whole or in part, owned, possessed, and leased to the United States and its departments and agencies, resulting in the deaths of thousands of persons on September 11, 2001.

Overt Acts

In furtherance of the conspiracy, and to effect its objects, the defendant, and others known and unknown to the Grand Jury, committed the following overt acts:

MOUSSAOUI Trains at Al Qaeda Training Camp

14. In or about April 1998, ZACARIAS MOUSSAOUI was present at the al Qaeda-affiliated Khalden Camp in Afghanistan.

* * *

MOUSSAOUI Inquires About Flight Training

34. On or about September 29, 2000, ZACARIAS MOUSSAOUI contacted Airman Flight School in Norman, Oklahoma using an e-mail account he set up on September 6 with an internet service provider in Malaysia.

(continued)

Exhibit 6–2 (continued)

35. In or about October 2000, ZACARIAS MOUSSAOUI received letters from Infocus Tech, a Malaysian company, stating that MOUSSAOUI was appointed Infocus Tech's marketing consultant in the United States, the United Kingdom, and Europe, and that he would receive, among other things, an allowance of $2500 per month.

<u>MOUSSAOUI Comes to the United States</u>

46. Between on or about February 26, 2001, and on or about May 29, 2001, ZACARIAS MOUSSAOUI attended the Airman Flight School in Norman, Oklahoma, ending his classes early.

<u>MOUSSAOUI Contacts a Commercial Flight School</u>

51. On or about May 23, 2001, ZACARIAS MOUSSAOUI contacted an office of the Pan Am International Flight Academy in Miami, Florida via e-mail.

<u>Hijackers Open Bank Accounts</u>

52. In Summer 2001, Fayez Ahmed (#175), Saeed al-Ghamdi (#93), Hamza al-Ghamdi (#175), Waleed al-Shehri (#11), Ziad Jarrah (#93), Satam al-Suqami (#11), Mohald al-Shehri (#175), Ahmed al-Nami (#93), and Ahmed al-Haznawi (#93) each opened a Florida Sun Trust bank account with a cash deposit.

<u>MOUSSAOUI Inquires About Aerial Application of Pesticides</u>

53. In or about June 2001, in Norman, Oklahoma, ZACARIAS MOUSSAOUI made inquiries about starting a crop dusting company.

<u>MOUSSAOUI Purchases Flight Training Equipment</u>

56. On or about June 20, 2001, ZACARIAS MOUSSAOUI purchased flight deck videos for the Boeing 747 Model 400 and the Boeing 747 Model 200 from the Ohio Pilot Store.

<u>MOUSSAOUI Pays for Flight Lessons</u>

60. On or about July 10 and July 11, 2001, ZACARIAS MOUSSAOUI made credit card payments to the Pan Am International Flight Academy for a simulator course in commercial flight training.

<u>MOUSSAOUI Purchases Knives</u>

68. On or about August 3, 2001, ZACARIAS MOUSSAOUI purchased two knives in Oklahoma City, Oklahoma.

<u>MOUSSAOUI Travels from Oklahoma to Minnesota</u>

70. On or about August 9 and August 10, 2001, ZACARIAS MOUSSAOUI was driven from Oklahoma to Minnesota.

<u>MOUSSAOUI Takes Commercial Flying Lessons in Minnesota</u>

71. On or about August 10, 2001, in Minneapolis, Minnesota, ZACARIAS MOUSSAOUI paid approximately $6,300 in cash to the Pan Am International Flight Academy.

Exhibit 6–2 (continued)

72. Between August 13 and August 15, 2001, ZACARIAS MOUSSAOUI attended the Pan Am International Flight Academy in Minneapolis, Minnesota, for simulator training on the Boeing 747 Model 400.

<u>MOUSSAOUI Possesses Knives and Other Items</u>

73. On or about August 16, 2001, ZACARIAS MOUSSAOUI possessed, among other things:

- two knives;

- a pair of binoculars;

- flight manuals for the Boeing 747 Model 400;

- a flight simulator computer program;

- fighting gloves and shin guards;

- a piece of paper referring to a handheld Global Positioning System receiver and a camcorder;

- software that could be used to review pilot procedures for the Boeing 747 Model 400;

- a notebook listing German Telephone #1, German Telephone #2, and the name "Ahad Sabet;"

- letters indicating that MOUSSAOUI is a marketing consultant in the United States for Infocus Tech;

- a computer disk containing information related to the aerial application of pesticides; and

- a hand-held aviation radio.

<u>MOUSSAOUI Lies to Federal Agents</u>

74. On or about August 17, 2001, ZACARIAS MOUSSAOUI, while being interviewed by federal agents in Minneapolis, attempted to explain his presence in the United States by falsely stating that he was simply interested in learning to fly.

<u>Final Preparations for the Coordinated Air Attack</u>

76. On or about August 22, 2001, Fayez Ahmed (#175) used his VISA card in Florida to obtain approximately $4,900 cash, which had been deposited into his Standard Chartered Bank account in UAE the day before.

77. On or about August 22, 2001, in Miami, Florida, Ziad Jarrah (#93) purchased an antenna for a Global Positioning System ("GPS"), other GPS related equipment, and schematics for 757 cockpit instrument diagrams. (GPS allows an individual to navigate to a position using coordinates pre-programmed into the GPS unit.)

(continued)

Exhibit 6–2   (continued)

78. On or about August 25, 2001, Khalid al-Midhar and Majed Moqed purchased with cash tickets for American Airlines Flight 77, from Virginia to Los Angeles, California, scheduled for September 11, 2001.

79. On or about August 26, 2001, Waleed al-Shehri and Wail al-Shehri made reservations on American Airlines Flight 11, from Boston, Massachusetts, to Los Angeles, California, scheduled for September 11, 2001, listing a telephone number in Florida ("Florida Telephone #1") as a contact number.

80. On or about August 27, 2001, reservations for electronic, one-way tickets were made for Fayez Ahmed and Mohald al-Shehri, for United Airlines Flight 175, from Boston, Massachusetts, to Los Angeles, California, scheduled for September 11, 2001, listing Florida Telephone Number #1 as a contact number.

81. On or about August 27, 2001, Nawaf al-Hazmi and Salem al-Hazmi booked flights on American Airlines Flight 77.

82. On or about August 28, 2001, Satam al-Suqami purchased a ticket with cash for American Airlines Flight 11.

83. On or about August 28, 2001, Mohammed Atta and Abdulaziz Alomari reserved two seats on American Airlines Flight 11, listing Florida Telephone #1 as a contact number.

84. On or about August 29, 2001, Ahmed al-Ghamdi and Hamza al-Ghamdi reserved electronic, one-way tickets for United Airlines Flight 175.

85. On or about August 29, 2001, Ahmed al-Haznawi purchased a ticket on United Airlines Flight 93 from Newark, New Jersey, to San Francisco, California, scheduled for September 11, 2001.

86. On or about August 30, 2001, Mohammed Atta (#11) purchased a utility tool that contained a knife.

87. On or about September 3, 2001, in Hamburg, Germany, Ramzi Bin al-Shibh, using the name "Ahad Sabet," received approximately $1500 by wire transfer from "Hashim Ahmed" in UAE.

88. On or about September 4, 2001, Mohammed Atta (#11) sent a FedEx package from Florida to UAE.

89. On or about September 5, 2001, Ramzi Bin al-Shibh traveled from Dusseldorf, Germany, to Madrid, Spain, and did not return to Germany.

90. On or about September 6, 2001, Satam al-Suqami (#11) and Abdulaziz Alomari (#11) flew from Florida to Boston.

<u>The September 11, 2001 Terrorist Attacks</u>

100. On or about September 11, 2001, the hijackers possessed a handwritten set of final instructions for a martyrdom operation on an airplane using knives.

Exhibit 6–2 (continued)

101. On or about September 11, 2001, Mohammed Atta (#11) and Abdulaziz Alomari (#11) flew from Portland, Maine to Boston, Massachusetts.

102. On or about September 11, 2001, Mohammed Atta (#11) possessed operating manuals for the Boeing 757 and 767, pepper spray, knives, and German travel visas.

103. On or about September 11, 2001, Ziad Jarrah (#93) possessed flight manuals for Boeing 757 and 767 aircraft.

104. On or about September 11, 2001, Mohammed Atta, Abdul Aziz Alomari, Satam al-Suqami, Waleed M. al-Shehri, and Waleed al-Shehri hijacked American Airlines Flight 11, a Boeing 767, which had departed Boston at approximately 7:55 A.M. They flew Flight 11 into the North Tower of the World Trade Center in Manhattan at approximately 8:45 A.M., causing the collapse of the tower and the deaths of thousands of persons.

105. On or about September 11, 2001, Hamza al-Ghamdi, Fayez Ahmed, Mohald al-Shehri, Ahmed al-Ghamdi, and Marwan al-Shehhi hijacked United Airlines Flight 175, a Boeing 767, which had departed from Boston at approximately 8:15 A.M. They flew Flight 175 into the South Tower of the World Trade Center in Manhattan at approximately 9:05 A.M., causing the collapse of the tower and the deaths of thousands of persons.

106. On or about September 11, 2001, Khalid al-Midhar, Majed Moqed, Nawaf al-Hazmi, Salem al-Hazmi, and Hani Hanjour hijacked American Airlines Flight 77, a Boeing 757, which had departed from Virginia bound for Los Angeles, at approximately 8:10 A.M. They flew Flight 77 into the Pentagon in Virginia at approximately 9:40 A.M., causing the deaths of 189 persons.

107. On or about September 11, 2001, Saeed al-Ghamdi, Ahmed al-Nami, Ahmed al-Haznawi, and Ziad Jarrah hijacked United Airlines Flight 93, a Boeing 757, which had departed from Newark, New Jersey bound for San Francisco at approximately 8:00 A.M. After resistance by the passengers, Flight 93 crashed in Somerset County, Pennsylvania at approximately 10:10 A.M., killing all on board.

<u>COUNT TWO</u>

(Conspiracy to Commit Aircraft Piracy)

1. The allegations contained in Count One are repeated.

2. From in or about 1989 until the date of the filing of this Indictment, in the Eastern District of Virginia, the Southern District of New York, and elsewhere, the defendant, ZACARIAS MOUSSAOUI, a/k/a "Shaqil," a/k/a "Abu Khalid al Sahrawi," and other members and associates of al Qaeda and others known and unknown to the Grand Jury, unlawfully, wilfully and knowingly combined, conspired, confederated and agreed to commit aircraft piracy, by seizing and exercising control of aircraft in the special aircraft jurisdiction of the United States by force, violence, threat of force and violence, and intimidation, and with wrongful intent, with the result that thousands of people died on September 11, 2001.

(continued)

Exhibit 6–2   (continued)

Overt Acts

3. In furtherance of the conspiracy, and to effect its illegal objects, the defendant, and others known and unknown to the Grand Jury, committed the overt acts set forth in Count One of this Indictment, which are fully incorporated by reference.

(In violation of Title 49, United States Code, Sections 46502(a)(1)(A) and (a)(2)(B).)

COUNT THREE

(Conspiracy to Destroy Aircraft)

1. The allegations contained in Count One are repeated.

2. From in or about 1989 until the date of the filing of this Indictment, in the Eastern District of Virginia, the Southern District of New York, and elsewhere, the defendant, ZACARIAS MOUSSAOUI, a/k/a "Shaqil," a/k/a "Abu Khalid al Sahrawi," and other members and associates of al Qaeda and others known and unknown to the Grand Jury, unlawfully, wilfully and knowingly combined, conspired, confederated and agreed to willfully destroy and wreck aircraft in the special aircraft jurisdiction of the United States, and to willfully perform acts of violence against and incapacitate individuals on such aircraft, so as likely to endanger the safety of such aircraft, resulting in the deaths of thousands of persons on September 11, 2001.

Overt Acts

3. In furtherance of the conspiracy, and to effect its illegal objects, the defendant, and others known and unknown to the Grand Jury, committed the overt acts set forth in Count One of this Indictment, which are fully incorporated by reference.

(In violation of Title 18, United States Code, Sections 32(a)(7) and 34.)

COUNT FOUR

(Conspiracy to Use Weapons of Mass Destruction)

1. The allegations contained in Count One are repeated.

2. From in or about 1989 until the date of the filing of this Indictment, in the Eastern District of Virginia, the Southern District of New York, and elsewhere, the defendant, ZACARIAS MOUSSAOUI, a/k/a "Shaqil," a/k/a "Abu Khalid al Sahrawi," and other members and associates of al Qaeda and others known and unknown to the Grand Jury, unlawfully, wilfully and knowingly combined, conspired, confederated and agreed to use weapons of mass destruction, namely, airplanes intended for use as missiles, bombs, and similar devices, without lawful authority against persons within the United States, with the results of such use affecting interstate and foreign commerce, and against property that was owned, leased and used by the United States and by departments and agencies of the United States, with the result that thousands of people died on September 11, 2001.

Exhibit 6–2 (continued)

<u>Overt Acts</u>

3. In furtherance of the conspiracy, and to effect its illegal objects, the defendant, and others known and unknown to the Grand Jury, committed the overt acts set forth in Count One of this Indictment, which are fully incorporated by reference.

(In violation of Title 18, United States Code, Section 2332a(a).)

<u>COUNT FIVE</u>

(Conspiracy to Murder United States Employees)

1. The allegations contained in Count One are repeated.

2. From in or about 1989 until the date of the filing of this Indictment, in the Eastern District of Virginia, the Southern District of New York, and elsewhere, the defendant, ZACARIAS MOUSSAOUI, a/k/a "Shaqil," a/k/a "Abu Khalid al Sahrawi," and other members and associates of al Qaeda and others known and unknown to the Grand Jury, unlawfully, wilfully and knowingly combined, conspired, confederated and agreed to kill officers and employees of the United States and agencies and branches thereof, while such officers and employees were engaged in, and on account of, the performance of their official duties, and persons assisting such employees in the performance of their duties, in violation of Section 1114 of Title 18, United States Code, including members of the Department of Defense stationed at the Pentagon.

<u>Overt Acts</u>

3. In furtherance of the conspiracy, and to effect its illegal objects, the defendant, and others known and unknown to the Grand Jury, committed the overt acts set forth in Count One of this Indictment, which are fully incorporated by reference.

(In violation of Title 18, United States Code, Sections 1114 and 1117.)

<u>COUNT SIX</u>

(Conspiracy to Destroy Property of the United States)

1. The allegations contained in Count One are repeated.

2. From in or about 1989 until the date of the filing of this Indictment, in the Eastern District of Virginia, the Southern District of New York, and elsewhere, the defendant, ZACARIAS MOUSSAOUI, a/k/a "Shaqil," a/k/a "Abu Khalid al Sahrawi," and other members and associates of al Qaeda and others known and unknown to the Grand Jury, unlawfully, wilfully and knowingly combined, conspired, confederated and agreed to maliciously damage and destroy, by means of fire and explosives, buildings, vehicles, and other real and personal property used in interstate and foreign commerce and in activities affecting interstate and foreign commerce, and buildings, vehicles, and other personal and real property in whole and in part owned and possessed by, and leased to, the United States and its departments and

(continued)

Exhibit 6–2   (continued)

agencies, and as a result of such conduct directly and proximately caused the deaths of thousands of persons on September 11, 2001, including hundreds of public safety officers performing duties as a direct and proximate result of the said damage and destruction.

<u>Overt Acts</u>

3. In furtherance of the conspiracy, and to effect its illegal objects, the defendant, and others known and unknown to the Grand Jury, committed the overt acts set forth in Count One of this Indictment, which are fully incorporated by reference.

(In violation of Title 18, United States Code, Sections 844(f), (i), and (n).)

_____
FOREPERSON

_____
MICHAEL CHERTOFF

ASSISTANT ATTORNEY GENERAL

_____
PAUL J. McNULTY

UNITED STATES ATTORNEY EASTERN DISTRICT OF VIRGINIA

_____
MARY JO WHITE

UNITED STATES ATTORNEY SOUTHERN DISTRICT OF NEW YORK

PUBLICATION DATE:

January 15, 2002

DATE:

20020115

Source: http://www.justice.gov/ag/moussaouiindictment.htm

Finally, remember that terrorists are subject to all the "traditional" penal laws of the states and nation. Terrorists that steal can be prosecuted for larceny and those that kill can be prosecuted for murder. States also have terrorism laws, similar to the federal laws discussed below.

sidebar

CRIME IN THE UNITED STATES

Prosecutions for terrorism reached a high in the year following the attacks of September 11, 2001: 355 cases of international terrorism were filed in FY 2002, with the number falling to 41 prosecutions in 2006. At 162, domestic terrorism cases were also at a high in 2002, with that figure dropping to 104 in 2006. Since 2001, the crime of financing terrorism has existed. The number of these cases pending at any one time varies from over 30 to none.

The United States Counterterrorism Center reports that in 2008 there were approximately 12,000 terrorist incidents in the world resulting in nearly 17,000 deaths and 38,000 injuries and kidnappings. Vast amounts of property damage and financial losses also resulted from terrorism. The vast majority of the incidents occurred in the near east, Afghanistan, Pakistan, and Iraq. Violence against noncombatants in the Democratic Republic of the Congo and Somalia was also high. The perpetrators of the attacks were unknown in most cases. For those incidents where responsibility was claimed, the Taliban was the group that most frequently asserted responsibility. While no individual was killed in a terrorist incident in the United States in 2008, 33 citizens of the United States were killed abroad by terrorists, 21 of those in Iraq.

Sources: Syracuse University TRAC at *http://trac.syr.edu/index.html* and 2008 Report on Terrorism (April 30, 2009), United States National Counterterrorism Center.

CRIMES AGAINST THE ENVIRONMENT

With the modernization of the United States has come a threat to the environment. The air and water that people depend upon for sustenance have become polluted. Many species of flora and fauna have been lost, and many more are threatened.

Modernization threatens the environment in several ways. In the process of "developing" land, habitats are lost. Also, the use of dangerous chemicals and toxins has become commonplace. In many industries, toxic by-products of manufacturing are common. Toxic wastes and substances pose use, transportation, and disposal problems. The release of dangerous substances into the air or into water endangers public health and safety. It is estimated that air pollution kills 14,000 people annually and that 100,000 workers die annually from exposure to toxins.[56] The world's increased population aggravates the problem. Greater numbers of people place greater stress on natural systems. Resources are depleted faster and nature's cleansing process becomes strained and less effective.

While regulating for the environment has grown considerably in recent decades, the first major federal environmental law was the Refuse Act of 1899, a law that prohibits, with criminal penalties, dumping refuse into waterways.[57] It continues in effect today. Today there is a large body of environmental law that, to some extent, addresses many of the Nation's environmental problems. The federal government's policy is to create and maintain conditions in which man and nature can exist in productive harmony. Both the federal and state governments play a role in regulating the environment, although the federal government has the larger part currently. The federal government's role in regulating the environment dates back to at least 1899, when Congress enacted a statute making it a crime to discharge pollutants into navigable waters.

Several federal administrative agencies are charged with overseeing the enforcement and administration of environmental laws, including the Environmental Protection Agency, Coast Guard, Department of the Interior, Occupational Health and Safety Commission, and Department of Justice. Federal law provides for administrative, civil, and criminal sanctions on environmental law violators.

There are two classes of environmental laws. One class of laws is intended to further the public health and safety. The Clean Air Act, the Clean Water Act, and similar statutes are examples of this type of environmental regulation. A second class of laws is intended to protect the environment itself, for its aesthetic, recreational, and other values. The Endangered Species Act is an example of a conservation law. Of course, many laws serve both objectives.

Until recently, environmental offenses were not usually treated as criminal; rather, they were viewed as civil or administrative infractions. The federal government relied almost exclusively on administrative and civil processes to enforce environmental laws. Fines were the most common penalty sought by the government against offenders.

The belief that environmental violations are serious and should be prosecuted as criminal offenses is a recent development. For example, one of the most notorious environmental cases was that of the Love Canal neighborhood in Niagara Falls, New York, where it was discovered in 1978 that the improper disposal of toxins was causing death and illness to local residents. An entire community was forced to relocate to escape the danger—yet not one person was prosecuted in the Love Canal case.

The fear of another Love Canal—or an accident like the one involving Union Carbide in Bhopal, India, where 2,000 people were killed and 200,000 people were injured—and the dangers posed by other environmental wrongs led Congress to strengthen environmental laws. The measures included added criminal sanctions. Relying on civil remedies alone had proved ineffective. Individuals were not being held accountable, and corporations found it more cost-effective to violate the law and pay any fines than to comply with the law.

Therefore, although most violations continue to be handled through civil and administrative proceedings, the number of environmental criminal cases is increasing. Of the 500 largest corporations in the United States, one-fourth have been convicted of an environmental crime or have been subject to civil penalties for violating environmental laws.[58] The Department of Justice has a special division charged with prosecuting environmental law crimes.

Unlike at common law, today business entities, such as corporations, may be charged with crimes. Fines and dissolution of a corporation are examples of the penalties that may be imposed. Charging corporations for environmental violations is common. Of course, individuals may also be charged with violating environmental laws, and corporate employees may be charged for actions taken on behalf of a corporation. It is not a defense for an employee to claim that he or she was following a supervisor's directive, nor may it be a defense for the supervisor to claim that he or she is innocent because he or she delegated performance of the act to an employee.

Some environmental crimes are strict liability. Others, and of course those that can be punished with jail time, require some mens rea, usually a knowing violation.

Several federal environmental laws contain criminal sanctions. The most significant of these laws are the Clean Water Act; the Clean Air Act; the Comprehensive Environmental Response, Compensation, and Liability Act; the Resource Conservation and Recovery Act; the Occupational Safety and Health Act; the Toxic Substances Control Act; the Federal Insecticide, Fungicide, and Rodenticide Act; the Emergency Planning and Community Right-to-Know Act; and the Endangered Species Act. All statutes are examples of regulation for the public health, except for the final statute, which is a conservation law. These laws provide for administrative and civil remedies and procedures, in addition to criminal sanctions.

Clean Water Act

The Clean Water Act (CWA)[59] regulates the discharge of pollutants into the nation's navigable waters. The CWA establishes a scheme of permits and reporting. The contamination of water with a pollutant, without a permit or exceeding the limits of a permit, is criminal under the Clean Water Act.

Both negligent and knowing acts are criminalized and may be punished with fines and imprisonment. A knowing act is punished more severely than a negligent act. Offenders who have acted negligently may be sentenced to one year in prison, whereas knowing offenders may be sentenced to three years in prison.[60] Fines may also be imposed for both, in addition to any civil remedies.

Also, the CWA contains a "knowing endangerment" provision. If a person violates the CWA with knowledge that the violation "places another person in imminent danger of death or serious bodily injury," the offender may be sentenced to up to 15 years in prison, and significant fines may be imposed.

Finally, false reporting under the Act is criminal and may be punished by up to two years in prison, in addition to a fine.

Clean Air Act

The goal of the Clean Air Act (CAA) is to preserve air quality. It does this by regulating emissions of dangerous substances into the air.

Similar to the CWA in its criminal aspects, the CAA criminalized negligent and knowing violations of its mandates, punishing the latter more severely.[61] Further, it contains knowing endangerment and false reporting provisions.

Comprehensive Environmental Response, Compensation, and Liability Act

The Comprehensive Environmental Response, Compensation and Liability Act (CERCLA) is commonly known as *Superfund*. The purpose of CERCLA is to identify and clean up existing hazardous waste sites.

Any person who knowingly falsifies or destroys any required record or who fails to report a spill of hazardous materials may be punished with fines and imprisonment.[62]

Resource Conservation and Recovery Act

The Resource Conservation and Recovery Act (RCRA) is similar to CERCLA in that they regulate the same subject matter: hazardous materials. However, CERCLA is an after-the-fact regulation intended to clean up existing sites, whereas RCRA is intended to regulate the day-to-day use, storage, transportation, handling, and disposal of hazardous materials.

There are no negligent violations under RCRA; rather, the mens rea for conviction of its prohibitions is knowledge. For example, the knowing transportation of hazardous waste to an unlicensed facility; the knowing treatment, storage, or disposal of hazardous waste without a permit; and the knowing violation of a permit are criminal and may be punished with both imprisonment and fines. As with the CWA and the CAA, knowingly endangering another enhances the punishment for a violation of RCRA.[63]

Occupational Safety and Health Act

The Occupational Safety and Health Act (OSHA) regulates the work environment of the American worker. The objective of the law is to create safe working conditions. There is a plethora of regulations enforcing this mandate.

Any employer who causes the death of an employee as a result of noncompliance with OSHA may be prosecuted and sentenced to imprisonment and a fine. Of course, the employer may also be liable under other criminal laws, such as negligent manslaughter.

Additionally, OSHA requires employers to notify their employees of potential exposure to dangerous chemicals and to provide information and resources to protect the employees. Failure to notify employees of this risk is a criminal omission under OSHA. False reporting is also a crime under this statute.

Toxic Substances Control Act

The Toxic Substances Control Act (TSCA) is the most comprehensive federal law concerning dangerous substances. The Environmental Protection Agency (EPA) is delegated considerable authority under the TSCA to regulate the sale, manufacture, development, processing, distribution, and disposal of toxic substances. Under the TSCA, the EPA is empowered to ban, or otherwise control, the production and distribution of chemicals. Asbestos and radon are examples of chemicals that the EPA has heavily regulated under the TSCA.

Any person who knowingly or willfully violates the TSCA concerning the manufacture, testing, or distribution of a chemical may be punished with both a fine and imprisonment. Also, false reporting, failing to maintain records, and failing to submit records as required by law are criminal acts under the TSCA.[64]

Federal Insecticide, Fungicide, and Rodenticide Act

Chemicals that are lethal to pests may also be lethal or at least harmful to humans. In addition to being inhaled, pesticides find their way into human drinking water and food.

The Federal Insecticide, Fungicide, and Rodenticide Act (FIFRA) delegates to the EPA the task of regulating the manufacture, sale, distribution, and use of these chemicals. Some chemicals are forbidden; there are limits on the use of others. There are labeling and reporting requirements.

Knowing violations of any of FIFRA's requirements are criminal and may be punished with fines and imprisonment.[65]

Emergency Planning and Community Right-to-Know Act

Bhopal, India; Chernobyl; and closer to home, Three Mile Island—all three are reminders that accidents happen, or that the actions of one person, such as a terrorist, can cause a tragedy of enormous proportion. In both the Chernobyl and Bhopal incidents, there was no planning or preparation for an accident.

The purpose of the Emergency Planning and Community Right-to-Know Act is to better prepare the community in which a facility is sited for disaster and to inform the community about emissions of hazardous substances by the facility. The Act requires facilities that use or produce chemicals to report both accidental and routine releases of substances into the air or water. Further, facilities are required to provide local officials (e.g., hospitals) with information about the chemicals used.

Knowing or willful failure to give notice of a release may be punished by both imprisonment and a fine.

Endangered Species Act

The Endangered Species Act (ESA)[66] and the Marine Mammal Protection Act represent a different form of environmental law from those discussed so far. The purpose of these laws is not to protect the public health; rather, the intent is to preserve the integrity of the environment itself.

The ESA establishes a program of conservation of threatened and endangered species of plants and animals and the habitats where they are found. The law is coadministered by the Departments of Interior, Commerce, Agriculture, and Justice.

The ESA prohibits the sale, taking, possession, importation, and exportation of endangered species and the products of those species. Violations of the law are punishable by both fines and imprisonment.

Marine Mammal Protection Act

Similar to the ESA, the Marine Mammal Protection Act (MMPA)[67] is intended to protect and conserve marine mammals. The taking of such creatures without a permit by a U.S. flag vessel while on the high seas is a crime. The taking, possession, and trade of animals protected under the law is prohibited within the United States unless a permit has been obtained. Fines and imprisonment may be imposed on violators.

These are but a few of the federal environmental laws. Also, many states have similar laws. In some instances, the states have been delegated the authority to enforce federal law. Environmental laws affect every person, not just businesses that use or trade in hazardous materials.

Because of overpopulation, high-density urbanization, industrialization, resource exploitation, and technological advances, every person has a duty to be environmentally aware, and the laws of the nation impose environmental obligations on the individual. The proper disposal of trash, car batteries, and motor oil, and the regulation of hunting and fishing, are examples of environmental laws that affect the daily lives of members of the public.

Ethical Considerations

THE SPECIAL OBLIGATIONS OF PROSECUTORS

As discussed in Chapter 5, prosecutors hold a special place in the criminal justice system. A prosecutor's overarching obligation is to justice and his client is the people. Both ethics rules and the Constitution impose obligations on prosecutors that are not equally borne by defense counterparts. The ABA Model Rules of Professional Conduct even have a rule (Rule 3.8) dedicated to prosecuting attorneys.

Although rare, serious violations of the standards by prosecutors occur. In 2006, an exotic dancer claimed that she had been sexually assaulted by several members of the Duke University lacrosse team. The allegation resulted in serious racial tensions because the accuser was black and the three accused students were white. Even though the DNA of several individuals was found on the accuser, none of the DNA matched the students. The prosecutor in the case, Mike Nifong, along with an employee of the testing site, made the decision not to provide the results to the defense.

After zealously prosecuting the men and insisting in numerous interviews that they were guilty, Nifong eventually filed a motion to dismiss the charges. Subsequently, the North Carolina bar filed an ethics complaint against Nifong, alleging prosecutorial misconduct.

The first charge against Nifong was for his decision not to provide exculpatory evidence to the defense (note that defense counsel is not required to disclose incriminating evidence to the prosecutor in most

Ethical Considerations *(continued)*

circumstances). The disclosure of exculpatory evidence by prosecutors is required by bar rules and by the Supreme Court's decision in *Brady v. Maryland*, 373 U.S. 83 (1963).

Nifong was also charged with misusing pretrial publicity. It appears that he was not shy when in the media spotlight. He gave many interviews with local and national news agencies. In these interviews, he made false allegations about racial epithets rendered by the defendants; he spoke in detail about the facts, as he knew them; and he expressed his personal opinion about the defendants and their guilt. North Carolina's rule concerning pretrial publicity is similar to Rule 3.6 of the Model Rules of Professional Conduct. It states that "[a] lawyer who is participating or has participated in the investigation or litigation of a matter shall not make an extrajudicial statement that the lawyer knows or reasonably should know will be disseminated by means of public communication and will have a substantial likelihood of materially prejudicing an adjudicative proceeding in the matter." The rule continues by excepting specific facts from its prohibition. None of those exceptions covered the kind of statements made by Nifong.

Ultimately, the bar found that Nifong should have known that his statements would prejudice the case. He was also found to have misled the court on several occasions. This included several instances when he stated to the court, or to opposing counsel in discovery, that he knew of no exculpatory evidence, even though he knew about the exculpatory DNA results. In 2007 Mr. Nifong was disbarred for his actions, and he resigned as district attorney.

Web Links

The Internal Revenue Service's website contains information on tax law, compliance and filing (including updated forms that may be downloaded), tax statistics, and other information. *http://www.irs.ustreas.gov*

Key Terms

breachs of the peace	fighting words	subornation of perjury
bribery	perjury	tax evasion
clear and present danger	prostitution	tax fraud
contempt		

Review Questions

1. Andy approaches Roberta, who is standing on a street corner, and offers her $50 for sex. Roberta, an undercover vice officer, arrests Andy. What crime should he be charged with?

2. Is there a constitutional right to engage in homosexual conduct between mature, consenting adults?

3. When may a state regulate material that is thought to be sexually repulsive? What constitutional provision hinders governments from regulating such expression?

4. What are fighting words? Are they protected by the First Amendment?

5. Is proof that a driver's blood-alcohol level exceeded the statutory maximum the only way to prove that a driver was under the influence? Is it a valid defense for driver-defendants to claim that they could drive safely, even though their blood-alcohol level exceeded the amount allowed by statute?

6. What are the elements of Continuing Criminal Enterprise, and who is the statute aimed at?

7. What are the basic elements of bribery? The Model Penal Code recognizes two types of bribery. Name the two.

8. Distinguish criminal contempt from civil contempt. Do the same for direct contempt and indirect contempt.

9. Is this statement true? "Perjury is a law that applies only to judicial proceedings." Explain your answer.

10. What are the elements of indecent exposure?

11. What are the elements of treason?

12. Identify two ways that the Patriot Act of 2001 expanded the authority of federal officials to address terrorism.

Problems & Critical Thinking Exercises

1. Are the following statutes constitutional? Explain, if not.

   Statute One: Loitering

   Any person who loiters in a place in an unusual manner for longer than 15 minutes and reasonably causes a person to be concerned for their safety must identify himself to police when requested. Any person who refuses to identify himself under these circumstances or takes flight when approached by a police officer is guilty of loitering.

   Statute Two: Loitering

   Any person who continually loiters in public parks without apparent employment or who lives off the handouts of others is guilty of loitering.

2. State law prohibits "hardcore pornography." Among the many prohibitions of the law is a provision making it a felony to possess or sell materials that are known to depict bestiality (sex between a human and an animal). Sam, a local adult bookstore owner, sold to Herb a magazine entitled *Wild on the Farm*. The magazine was sealed, and its contents were not visible. The magazine was delivered to Sam in error, part of a large shipment of magazines and books.

   During a raid on Sam's establishment, the local police discovered the sales ticket reflecting Herb's purchase, his name, and his address. The police then obtained a search warrant for Herb's home and found the magazine during their search. Sam and Herb have both been charged with violating the state's obscenity law. Should they be convicted? Explain your answer.

3. Do you believe that acts that harm no one, but that most members of society find immoral, should be criminalized? Explain your position.

4. How has bribery been changed since it has become a statutory crime?

5–7. Classify each of the following as direct or indirect contempt and civil or criminal contempt.

5. During a personal injury trial, Noah told the judge to "kiss my ass" and then threw an apple, striking the judge in the head.

6. During a union dispute, a judge ordered striking employees back to work. They refused to comply with the order and the judge ordered that each employee pay $50 per day until he or she returned to work.

7. Jon received a court order to tear down a fence he had constructed. The order was served by a sheriff. Immediately after the sheriff handed the order to him, Jon screamed, "Forget that idiot judge, I'm not tearing down the fence!" Jon never removed the fence, and the judge had him arrested and ordered him to remain in jail until he agreed to comply with the order.

8. Consider and discuss this statement:

Possession and use of drugs or alcohol should not be a crime. The only dangers presented from these substances arise when a person works, drives, or conducts some activity that requires the full use of the senses, while under their influence. Criminal statutes should be narrow and proscribe only the harm sought to be prevented. No harm is created by use in controlled environments, such as in the home. Accordingly, statutes should only proscribe engaging in certain undertakings while under the influence of alcohol or drugs.

9. Do you believe terrorists should be considered criminals (and handled by the criminal justice system) or combatants (and handled by the military)? Does it matter if the accused is a U.S. citizen?

Endnotes

1. Model Penal Code § 251.2(1).
2. Model Penal Code § 251.2(5).
3. 18 U.S.C. § 2421.
4. *Powell v. Georgia,* 270 Ga. 327, 510 S.E.2d 18 (1998).
5. 501 U.S. 560 (1991).
6. Model Penal Code § 251.1.
7. 18 U.S.C. § 1461.
8. Anderson, "Mapplethorpe Photos on Trial," *A.B.A. J.* 28 (Dec. 1990).
9. There are other limits on First Amendment freedoms. Some of these are discussed in Chapter 8, in the constitutional defenses section. For more on the First Amendment, see Daniel E. Hall and John P. Feldmeier, *Constitutional Values: Governmental Powers and Individual Liberties,* chs 10 and 11 (Upper Saddle River, NJ: Pearson Prentice Hall, 2009).
10. 378 U.S. 184 [1964]).
11. 354 U.S. 476 (1957).

12. *Manual Enterprises, Inc. v. Day*, 370 U.S. 478 (1962) (opinion by Justice Harlan).
13. 413 U.S. 15 (1973).
14. 50 Am. Jur. 2d *Lewdness, Indecency, etc.* 7 (1970).
15. *See Roth v. United States*, 354 U.S. 476, 487, n. 20 (1957).
16. *United States v. Guglielmi*, 819 F. 2d 451 (4th Cir. 1987).
17. *See New York v. Ferber*, 458 U.S. 747 (1982).
18. See Capitol News Co. v. Metropolitan Government, 562 S.W.2d 430 (Tenn. 1978).
19. 494 U.S. 103 (1990).
20. *Stanley v. Georgia*, 394 U.S. 557 (1969).
21. Model Penal Code § 251.4.
22. 143 *Cong. Rec.* E1633 (Sept. 3, 1997).
23. Timothy Zick, "Congress, The Internet, and The Intractable Pornography Problem: The Child Online Protection Act of 1998," 32 *Creighton L. Rev.* 1147 (1999).
24. 110 Stat. 56.
25. 521 U.S. 844 (1997).
26. 47 U.S.C. § 231.
27. *Ashcroft v. ACLU* (2002).
28. 969 F. Supp. 160 (S.D. N.Y. 1997).
29. 553 U.S. 285 (2008).
30. Model Penal Code § 250.1.
31. *Champlinsky v. New Hampshire,* 315 U.S. 568 (1942).
32. *Brandenburg v. Ohio*, 395 U.S. 444 (1969).
33. See Chapter 3 on personal status as an act.
34. 307 U.S. 174 (1939).
35. 445 U.S. 55 (1980).
36. 26 U.S.C. § 5801 *et seq*
37. 18 U.S.C. sec. 921.
38. Id.
39. Model Penal Code § 2.01(4).
40. *Robinson v. California*, 370 U.S. 660 (1962).
41. 21 U.S.C. § 848
42. *United States v. Brantley*, 733 F.2d 1429 (11th Cir. 1984).
43. 21 U.S.C. § 848(e).
44. 21 U.S.C. § 853(a).
45. Kenneth Johnson, "The Constitutionality of Drug Paraphernalia Laws," 81 *Columbia L. Rev.* 581 (1981).

46. *Posters 'N' Things, Ltd. v. United States*, 511 U.S. 513 (1994).

47. Model Penal Code § 224.8.

48. 26 U.S.C. § 7201 *et seq.*

49. Model Penal Code § 3.04(2)(a)(i).

50. 18 U.S.C. § 2381.

51. *See* 70 Am. Jur. 2d 70.

52. 18 U.S.C. § 2384.

53. 18 U.S.C. § 2389.

54. 18 U.S.C. § 792, *et seq.*, and 50 U.S.C. § 783.

55. See Oklahoma Department of Health, *Summary of Reportable Injuries in Oklahoma: Oklahoma City Bombing Injuries*, http://web.archive.org/web/20080110063748/ http://www.health.state.ok.us/PROGRAM/injury/Summary/bomb/OKCbomb.htm, retrieved January 10, 2011.

56. Michael Norton, Federal Environmental Criminal Law Enforcement in the 1990's 1 (ALI-ABA, C868, 1993).

57. 33 USC § 407.

58. Id.

59. 33 U.S.C. § 1319(a).

60. 33 U.S.C. § 1319(c).

61. 42 U.S.C. § 7413.

62. 42 U.S.C. § 9603.

63. 42 U.S.C. § 6928.

64. 15 U.S.C. §§ 2614–15.

65. 7 U.S.C. § 136i–1(d).

66. 16 U.S.C. §§ 1531–1543.

67. 16 U.S.C. §§ 1361–1384, 1401–7.

CHAPTER 7

PARTIES AND INCHOATE OFFENSES

Chapter Outline

Parties to Crimes

Inchoate Crimes
  Attempt
  Conspiracy
  Solicitation

Ethical Considerations: Judges Have
  Rules Too

Chapter Objectives

After completing this chapter, you should
be able to:

- identify and describe the roles of the
  various participants to crimes in both
  common law and contemporary legal
  terms.

- identify the various participants to
  crimes in given fact scenarios.

- explain relative culpability of the
  participants to a crime.

- explain the culpability for unsuccessful
  attempts to commit a crime.

- identify the elements of, and contract,
  attempt, conspiracy, and solicitation.

- apply attempt, conspiracy, and
  solicitation to fact scenarios.

- identify the material facts and legal
  issues in one-half of the cases you read,
  and describe the court's analyses and
  conclusions in the cases.

PARTIES TO CRIMES

Not all crimes are committed by only one person. Not all planned crimes are completed. This chapter examines the two topics of group criminal responsibility and uncompleted crimes. Those who participate in a crime are referred to as *parties*. Uncompleted crimes are referred to as *inchoate crimes*.

At common law, there were four parties to crimes: principals in the first degree; principals in the second degree; accessories before the fact; and accessories after the fact.

A **principal** in the first degree is the participant who actually committed the proscribed act. For example, three people (A, B, and C) agree to rob a grocery store. A enters the store, points a gun at a checker, and demands that money be placed in a bag. A is a principal in the first degree.

A principal in the second degree is a party who aids, counsels, assists, or encourages the principal in the first degree during commission of the crime. A party must be present during a crime to be a principal in the second degree. However, constructive presence is sufficient. Whenever a party is physically absent from the location of the crime, but aids from a distance, that party is a principal in the second degree. So, if B, from our hypothetical case, waits in the getaway car outside the store, B is a principal in the second degree. First-degree and second-degree principals are punished equally. Principals in the second degree are also referred to as *accomplices,* as are accessories before the fact.

Anyone who aids, counsels, encourages, or assists in the preparation of a crime, but is not physically present during the crime, is an **accessory** before the fact. If C, an expert in bank security, assisted in planning the robbery, then C is an accessory before the fact. The primary distinction between a principal in the second degree and an accessory before the fact is the lack of presence during the crime of an accessory before the fact.

At common law, accessories could not be convicted until the principals were convicted. In addition, procedural rules made it more difficult to convict accessories than principals. These rules are no longer the law. Statutes commonly group principals in the first and second degree together with accessories before the fact and punish all equally.

The mens rea of an accomplice (before and during a crime) is usually intentional (specific) in common-law terms, or knowing or purposeful in Model Penal Code language. Negligent and reckless acts do not make a person a principal in the second degree or an accessory.

Accessories after the fact continue to be treated differently. A person is an accessory after the fact if (1) aid, comfort, or shelter is provided to a criminal (2) with the purpose of assisting the criminal in avoiding arrest or prosecution (3) after the crime is committed (4) and the accessory was not present during commission of the crime. D is an accessory after the fact, if A and B flee to D's house and D hides A and B from the police. It is possible to be an accessory both before and after the fact. Hence, if C were to hide A and B from the police, C would be an accessory both before and after the fact. Accessories after the fact are not punished as severely as the other three classifications of parties (Exhibit 7–1).

principal

■ A person directly involved with committing a crime, as opposed to an accessory.

accessory

■ A person who helps to commit a crime without being present. An accessory before the fact is a person who, without being present, encourages, orders, or helps another to commit a crime. An accessory after the fact is a person who finds out that a crime has been committed and helps to conceal the crime or the criminal.

Exhibit 7–1   PARTIES TO A BURGLARY

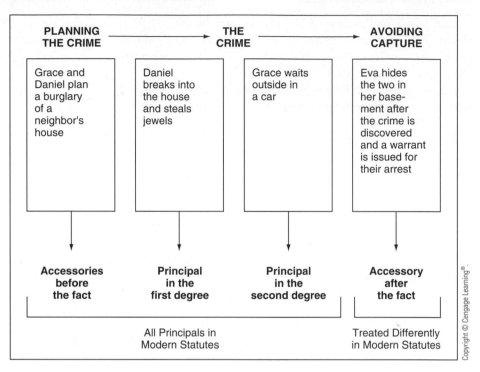

The mental state required to prove that a person was an accessory after the fact is twofold: It must be shown first that the defendant was aware of the person's criminal status (scienter) and second that the defendant intended to hinder attempts to arrest or prosecute the criminal.

INCHOATE CRIMES

Not all planned crimes are completed. Because of the danger posed by substantial planning, accompanied by an intent to carry out a plan, some uncompleted crimes may be punished.

By punishing inchoate acts, the deterrent purpose of the criminal justice system is furthered. If the rule were otherwise, law enforcement officials would have no incentive to intervene in a criminal enterprise before it is completed. By punishing attempt, conspiracy, and solicitation, an officer may prevent a planned criminal act from occurring without risking losing a criminal conviction.

Attempt

The reasons planned crimes are not always successful are numerous. In some instances, law enforcement intervention prevents completion of a crime. If a police officer stops Penny from shooting Tom moments before she commits the act, should she be free from criminal liability because she was not successful? The law answers that question in the negative, calling such uncompleted crimes *attempt*.

Attempt was not a crime at early common law; however, attempt cases do appear later in English common law. The first cases began to appear in the late 1700s and early 1800s.[1] Many of the early cases have been traced to an English court that is no longer in existence, the Star Chamber. Today, attempt is recognized in the United States by all states.

The purpose of attempt laws is to deter people from planning to commit crimes; to punish those who intended to commit a crime, but were unsuccessful; and to encourage law enforcement officers to prevent unlawful activity. The last may appear obvious; however, if it were not for making attempts illegal, police would have an incentive to permit illegal acts, so as to be able to punish the wrongdoer.

There are essentially three elements to all attempts. One, the defendant must intend to commit a crime. Two, the defendant must act in furtherance of that intent. Three, the crime is not completed.

First, the mens rea element: The defendant must intend to take some act that amounts to a crime; in common-law language, specific intent, and under the Model Penal Code, knowingly or purposefully. Some statutes specifically identify what crime must be intended, whereas others simply refer to an intent to commit any felony. In any event, the accused must intend to commit some specific crime, such as murder, rape, or theft.

The second element, the actus reus of attempt, can be problematic. The problem revolves around this question: how close to completion of the intended crime must a defendant come to be guilty of attempt? It is well established that thoughts alone do not establish a crime; mere preparation without anything further does not amount to the crime of attempt. The failing student who sits at home and contemplates how to "do in" his or her criminal law instructor commits no crime. It is not until the student goes further that he or she can be liable for attempt.

Various tests are used to determine if an act is close enough to completion to permit an attempt conviction. The four commonly used tests are proximity, res ipsa loquitur, probable desistance, and the Model Penal Code's "substantial steps" test.

The *proximity test* examines what acts have been taken and what acts are left to be taken to complete the crime. Justice Holmes said that there "must be a dangerous proximity to success."[2]

The *res ipsa loquitur test* (also called the *unequivocality test*) looks at crimes individually and finds an act, a certain point in time, which indicates that the defendant has "no other purpose than the commission of that specific crime."[3] For example, most courts have held that once a defendant hires another to commit a crime, attempt has been committed. The step of hiring the person who will complete the crime crosses the line between mere preparation and illegal act.

The third test, *probable desistance,* focuses on the likelihood that the defendant would have followed through with the crime had the opportunity existed. The foundation of the theory is that all people may plan illegal acts at some time in life, but that there is a point where most stop. Any person who passes this line of demarcation has exhibited that the crime would have been completed, had the situation permitted. Critics have attacked this test, claiming that the determination of such a line, if it exists, is arbitrary.

attempt

■ An effort to commit a crime that goes beyond preparation and that proceeds far enough to make the person who did it guilty of an "attempt crime." For example, if a person fires a shot at another in a failed effort at murder, the person is guilty of *attempted murder*.

The Model Penal Code uses a *substantial step* to completion test.[4] That is, one is guilty of attempt if substantial steps have been taken toward commission of a crime. The Code specifically states that the conduct in question must "strongly corroborate" the actor's criminal purpose. The Code goes further and lists acts that may constitute attempts, provided that they "strongly corroborate" an intent to commit a crime. That list includes:

1. Lying in wait or searching for the intended victim.
2. Enticing or seeking to entice the intended victim to go to the place where the crime will be committed.
3. Investigating the location where the crime is to be committed.
4. Unlawfully entering a structure where the crime is to be committed.
5. Possession of materials necessary to complete the crime, provided that the tools are specially designed for the commission of the crime.
6. Possession, collection, or fabrication of materials to be used in the crime, near the scene of the crime, when the materials serve no lawful purpose.
7. Soliciting someone to commit a crime.

Keep in mind that different results are possible if these tests are applied to the same facts. In the *Murray* case, discussed later in this chapter, the line between preparation and attempt is examined. Do you agree with the court?

Regardless of which test is applied, if a defendant has a change of heart and does not complete the crime, even after crossing the line, abandonment may be a valid defense.

Of course, the abandonment must be voluntary. Generally, any reason that causes a defendant to desist, other than the defendant's independent decision not to complete the crime, falls outside the defense. A criminal who chooses not to rob a store because a police officer arrives at the scene moments before the planned act was to occur is not entitled to the defense of abandonment.

legal impossibility

■ A person who is unable to commit a crime because of legal impossibility cannot be convicted of a crime he or she intends or attempts.

Two other defenses that arise in the context of attempt are legal and factual impossibility. **Legal impossibility** refers to the situation when a defendant believes that his or her acts are illegal when they are not.

If defendants commit an act while believing it illegal when it is actually lawful, they are not liable. The law of attempt does not punish one for attempting to do a lawful thing, even if the person had an evil mind.

Factual impossibility refers to situations when people attempt to commit a crime, but it is impossible to do so. For example, John breaks into his friend's school locker to steal property, but discovers that the locker is empty. Distraught by the situation, John decides to relax by smoking marijuana. Unknown to John, the cigarette contains no marijuana or other illegal drug. John has made two factual errors. In both instances John could be convicted because factual impossibility is not a defense. This rule is justified by the fact that the defendant possessed the required mens rea and took all the acts necessary to commit the offense. The crime was not fully completed only because of an extraneous fact unknown to the defendant.

sidebar

PRISONERS IN THE UNITED STATES

The number of people in prison or on probation or parole in the United States in 2011 was just shy of 1.6 million, almost 2% lower than in 2010. Much of this decline was attributable to the California Public Safety Realignment program. The objective of this program was to reduce the population in California prisons by more than 100,000 prisoners, as ordered by a federal court (affirmed by the U.S. Supreme Court in 2011) to address overcrowding. About 492 people per 100,000 were incarcerated in the United States in 2011. Violent offenders comprised the largest group of inmates in state prisons, with property and drug offenders coming in second and third in nearly identical numbers.

Source: Prisoners in 2012, Bureau of Justice Statistics, Office of Justice Programs.

PEOPLE V. MURRAY
15 Cal. 160 (1859)

The evidence in this case entirely fails to sustain the charge against the defendant of an attempt to contract an incestuous marriage with his niece. It only discloses declarations of his determination to contract the marriage, his elopement with the niece for that avowed purpose, and his request to one of the witnesses to go for a magistrate to perform the ceremony. It shows very clearly the intention of the defendant, but something more than mere intention is necessary to constitute the offense charged. Between preparation for the attempt and the attempt itself, there is a wide difference. The preparation consists of devising or arranging the means or measures necessary for the commission of the offense; the attempt is the direct movement toward the commission after the preparation is made. To illustrate: a party may purchase and load a gun, with the declared intention to shoot his neighbor; but until some movement is made to use the weapon upon the person of his intended victim, there is only preparation and not attempt. For the preparation, he may be held to keep the peace; but he is not chargeable with any attempt to kill. So, in the present case, the declarations, and elopement, and request for a magistrate, were preparatory to the marriage; but until the officer was engaged, and the parties stood before him, ready to take the vows appropriate to the contract of marriage, it cannot be said, in strictness, that the attempt was made. The attempt contemplated by the statute must be manifested by acts that would end in the consummation of the particular offence, but for the intervention of circumstances independent of the will of the party. [Conviction reversed.]

In the *Haines* case, a defendant appealed his conviction for attempted murder. He alleged that because of factual improbability, he did not take a "substantial step" toward completing a murder.

The Indiana Court of Appeals rejected factual impossibility (leaving open the issue of inherent factual impossibility) as a defense and rejected the factual assertion that AIDS cannot be transmitted through spitting and throwing blood on a person. Further, the court found that the acts of spitting and throwing blood on a person by a person with AIDS are substantial steps toward the commission of murder, thereby supporting an attempted murder conviction.

STATE V. HAINES
545 N.E.2d 834 (Ind. Ct. App. 1989)

On August 6, 1987, Lafayette, Indiana, police officers John R. Dennis (Dennis) and Brad Hayworth drove to Haines' apartment in response to a radio call of a possible suicide. Haines was unconscious when they arrived and was lying face down in a pool of blood. Dennis attempted to revive Haines and noticed that Haines' wrists were slashed and bleeding. When Haines heard the paramedics arriving, he stood up, ran toward Dennis, and screamed that he should be left to die because he had AIDS. Dennis told Haines they were there to help him, but he continued yelling and stated he wanted to [infect Dennis with the disease.] Haines told Dennis that he would "use his wounds" and began jerking his arms at Dennis, causing blood to spray into Dennis' mouth and eyes. Throughout the incident, as the officers attempted to subdue him, Haines repeatedly yelled that he had AIDS, that he could not deal with it, and that he was going to make Dennis deal with it.

Haines also struggled with emergency medical technicians Dan Garvey (Garvey) and Diane Robinson, threatening to infect them with AIDS, and began spitting at them. When Dennis grabbed Haines, Haines scratched, bit, and spit at him. At one point, Haines grabbed a blood-soaked wig and struck Dennis in the face with it. This caused blood again to splatter onto Dennis' eyes, mouth, and skin. When Dennis finally handcuffed Haines, Dennis was covered with blood. He also had scrapes and scratches on his arms and a cut on his finger that was bleeding.

When Haines arrived at the hospital, he was still kicking, screaming, throwing blood, and spitting at Dennis, Garvey, and another paramedic. . . . Haines again announced that he had AIDS and that he was going to show everyone else what it was like to have the disease and die. At one point Haines bit Garvey on the upper arm, breaking the skin. . . .

Haines was charged with three counts of attempted murder. At trial, medical experts testified that the virus could be transmitted through blood, tears, and saliva. They also observed that policemen, firemen, and other emergency personnel are generally at risk when they are exposed to body products. One medical expert observed that Dennis was definitely exposed to the HIV virus and others acknowledged that exposure of infected blood to the eyes and the mouth is dangerous, and that it is easier for the virus to enter the bloodstream if there is a cut in the skin.

Following a trial by jury, Haines was convicted of three counts of attempted murder on January 14, 1988. On February 18, 1988, Haines moved for judgment on the evidence as to the three counts of -attempted -murder, which the trial court granted.

The trial court did enter judgment of conviction on three counts of battery as a class D felony. Haines was -ordered to serve a two-year sentence on each count to run consecutively.

The only issue before us is whether the trial court erred in granting Haines' motion for judgment on the evidence and vacating the three counts of attempted murder.

PARTIES' CONTENTIONS

The State maintains that the trial court erred in granting Haines' motion for judgment on the evidence because the trial judge misconstrued the requirements of proof necessary to constitute a substantial step in accordance with the law of attempt. Haines responds that his conduct did not constitute a substantial step toward murder as charged, because all evidence relating to the AIDS virus was introduced by the defense which led only to an inference in favor of Haines.

CONCLUSION

The trial court erred in granting Haines' motion for judgment on the evidence.

This appeal presents a novel question in Indiana.

■ ■ ■

Contrary to Haines' contention that the evidence did not support a reasonable inference that his conduct amounted to a substantial step toward murder, the record reflects otherwise. At trial, it was definitely established that Haines carried the AIDS virus, was aware of the infection, believed it to be fatal, and intended to inflict others with the disease by spitting, biting, scratching, and throwing blood. . . . His biological warfare with those attempting to help him is akin to a sinking ship firing on its rescuers.

Haines misconstrues the logic and effect of our attempt statute. . . .

"It is no defense that, because of a misapprehension of the circumstances, it would have been impossible for the accused person to commit the crime attempt". . . . [O]ur supreme court observed:

> It is clear that section (b) of our statute rejects the defense of impossibility. It is not necessary that there be a present ability to complete the crime, nor is it necessary that the crime be factually possible. When the defendant has done all that he believes necessary to cause the particular result, regardless of what is actually possible under existing circumstances, he has committed an attempt. . . .

In accordance with [the statute], the State was not required to prove that Haines' conduct could actually have killed. It was only necessary for the State to show that Haines did all that he believed necessary to bring about an intended result, regardless of what was actually possible. . . . Haines repeatedly announced that he had AIDS and desired to infect and kill others. At the hospital, Haines was expressly told by doctors that biting, spitting, and throwing blood was endangering others.

While [the statute] rejects the defense of impossibility, some jurisdictions provide for the dismissal of a charge or reduction in sentence on the basis of "inherent impossibility" if the defendant's conduct was so inherently unlikely to result or culminate in the commission of a crime. . . .

While we have found no Indiana case directly on point, the evidence presented at trial renders any defense of inherent impossibility inapplicable in this case. . . .

In addition to Haines' belief that he could infect others, there was testimony by physicians that the virus may be transmitted through the exchange of bodily fluids. . . .

From the evidence in the record before us, we can only conclude that Haines had knowledge of his disease and that he unrelentingly and unequivocally

(continued)

STATE V. HAINES (continued)

sought to kill the persons helping him by infecting them with AIDS, and that he took a substantial step towards killing them by his conduct, believing that he could do so, all of which was more than a mere tenuous, theoretical, or speculative "chance" of transmitting the disease. From all of the evidence before the jury, it could have concluded beyond a reasonable doubt that Haines took a substantial step toward the commission of murder.

Thus, the trial court improperly granted Haines' motion for judgment on the evidence. . . . The trial court's judgment is reversed with instructions to reinstate the jury's verdict and resentence Haines accordingly.

Conspiracy

In 2013 Gilberto Valle was convicted of conspiracy. But this was not an ordinary conspiracy case. Valle was a husband, father of an infant, and New York City police officer when arrested. He also became widely known as Cannibal Cop. Valle was convicted of conspiracy to kidnap. The plans included rape, torture, and eating women and children. One of the intended victims was Valle's wife. Fearing for her life after discovering the plot, she reported him to authorities.

Another intended victim was the daughter of one of Valle's co-conspirators, Michael Van Hise. Van Hise wrote to a third co-conspirator that he was preserving his 3-year-old stepdaughter until she was old enough to rape and hang to death, prompting one of his co-conspirators to write that the plan was "hot" and asked to be involved if "that would be turn-on" for Van Hise. Van Hise also offered his nieces as potential victims. The visioning and planning for the crimes occurred primarily, but not exclusively, online. Valle and his co-conspirators were charged - and convicted in federal court with conspiracy to commit kidnapping and Valle was also charged with misusing the National Crime Information Center, a federal law enforcement database, to obtain information about his intended victims. Gilberto Valle Guilty: "Cannibal Cop" Guilty of Conspiring to Kidnap and Eat Women. Huffington Post. August 12. 2013.

conspiracy

■ A crime that may be committed when two or more persons agree to do something unlawful (or to do something lawful by unlawful means). The -agreement can be inferred from the persons' actions.

Conspiracy is (1) an agreement (2) between two or more persons (3) to commit an unlawful act or a lawful act in an unlawful manner. The agreement is the actus reus of the crime, and the intent to commit an unlawful act or a lawful act in an unlawful manner is the mens rea.

In some jurisdictions, the agreement alone satisfies the actus reus. In others, some act must be taken in furtherance of the objective of the agreement. Although at least one jurisdiction requires the conspirators to take "substantial steps" to be liable for conspiracy, most require less; often proof of an "overt act" will sustain a conviction. Hence, although mere preparation is not sufficient to impose liability for attempt, it is sufficient in many jurisdictions to prove conspiracy.

In the case of Valle, the so-called Cannibal Cop, prosecutors asserted that he committed the overt acts required by federal law to establish conspiracy by (1) discussing the crimes with others; (2) accessing and researching restricted law enforcement databases to identify victims; (3) traveling to meet one potential victim; (4) researching how to drug and abduct women leading to the creation of a document entitled "Abducting and Cooking [victim]: A Blueprint," and (5) communicating, by e-mail and instant messaging, his co-conspirators about "kidnapping, cooking and eating body parts" of the victims with detailed plans for two intended victims.[5]

Naturally, a conspiracy requires more than one person who must join in the agreement. One limitation on this rule is the **concert of action rule (Wharton's Rule)**. Under this rule, two people cannot be charged with conspiracy when the underlying offense itself requires two people. For example, gambling is a crime that requires the acts of at least two people. Wharton's Rule prohibits convictions of both gambling and conspiracy. Adultery and incest are other examples. This is not true of murder, as murder can be committed by one person. Wharton's Rule is limited, however, to two people. So if three people agree to gamble, a conviction of gambling and conspiracy to commit gambling is permitted.

The mens rea of conspiracy has two aspects. First, conspirators must have an intent to enter into an agreement. Second, conspirators must possess a specific intent to commit some unlawful objective. That objective must be to commit an unlawful act or a lawful act in an unlawful manner. The language of conspiracy speaks of doing unlawful acts, not necessarily criminal. This is important because some acts, when taken by an individual, may lead to civil, but not criminal, liability. However, when the same acts are taken by a group, the law of conspiracy makes them criminal. This is common in the area of fraud.

The mens rea requirement of conspiracy is strict. Contrary to the general rule, mistake of law and fact are often accepted defenses. It is a defense for a party to have been under the mistaken belief that the group's actions and objectives were legal. This is because the conspiracy must be corrupt; the parties must have had an evil purpose for their union.

What if a party withdraws from the conspiracy while it is ongoing? As a general rule, withdrawal is not a defense, because the crime was complete when the parties entered into the agreement. However, if the jurisdiction requires an agreement plus an overt act or substantial steps, and the withdrawal is made before those acts occur, there is no criminal liability on behalf of the withdrawn party. To determine when withdrawal occurred, courts look to the defendants' actions. Withdrawal is effective at the time the acts would have conveyed to a reasonable person, standing in a co-conspirator's shoes, that they were abandoning the conspiracy. Additionally, the withdrawal must occur within a time that permits the other parties to abandon the objective. A last-second withdrawal, when it is too late to stop the wheels from turning, is not a defense. The Model Penal Code recognizes voluntary withdrawal as an affirmative defense.[6]

A few procedural issues are unique to conspiracy. As a whole, these rules favor prosecution. First, conspiracy is considered a crime, independent of any crime that is the objective of the conspiracy. If Amy and Ashley conspire to murder Elsa, they have committed two offenses: murder and conspiracy to murder. It is not a violation of the Fifth Amendment's double jeopardy prohibition to punish both crimes (cumulative punishment). Conspiracy to commit a crime and the commission of that crime do

concert of action rule

■ The rule that, unless a statute specifies otherwise, it is not a conspiracy for two persons to agree to commit a crime if the definition of the crime itself requires the participation of two or more persons. Also called *Wharton Rule* and *concerted action rule*.

not merge into one. This is why conspiracy can be inchoate; it can be charged in cases where the objective is not met. If Amy and Ashley are not successful in their murderous plot, they are still liable for conspiracy to murder. One exception to the general rule of cumulative punishments is Wharton's Rule, discussed earlier.

Prosecutors must show an agreement between two or more parties to prove conspiracy. This creates some difficulties at trial. One difficulty concerns whether alleged co-conspirators should be tried together or separately. Because the United States Supreme Court has approved trial of all parties either at the location where the agreement was entered into or at any location where an act in furtherance of the conspiracy occurred, defendants are usually tried together.[7] It is possible for a defendant to be tried in a location where he or she has never been, and some argue that this practice is unconstitutional. In addition, critics argue that trying defendants together creates an increased likelihood of conviction because a form of "guilt by association" occurs in jurors' minds.

Another procedural irregularity is the **co-conspirator hearsay rule**. **Hearsay** is an out-of-court statement. Although hearsay evidence is normally inadmissible at trial, the co-conspirator exception permits the statements of one party that are made out of court to be admitted. The rule is limited to statements made during planning and commission of the conspiracy; statements made after it is completed are inadmissible.

Because two people (or more) are required to have a conspiracy, if only two people are charged, and one is acquitted, then the other cannot be punished. For example, Edgar and Robert are charged and tried together for conspiring to rob a bank. If the jury acquits one, the other must also be acquitted. At least two people must be convicted. So, if a group of people are charged, and the jury acquits all but two, the convictions stand.

Finally, be aware that many statutes deal with conspiracies, even though they are not named so. You have already examined two federal conspiracy statutes, the Racketeer Influenced and Corrupt Organizations Act and Continuing Criminal Enterprise. In recent years there has been a rise in the number of conspiracy filings. This is largely the result of RICO and related statutes and because of the procedural advantages that prosecutors have, as discussed earlier.

Solicitation

You have already encountered **solicitation** in the discussion of prostitution. But solicitation is much broader than attempting to engage someone in prostitution. Solicitation is the (1) encouraging, requesting, or commanding (2) of another (3) to commit a crime.

Solicitation is a specific-intent crime: The person must intend to convince another to commit an offense. Although the crime may be prostitution, it can be any crime in most jurisdictions. A few states limit the pool to felonies. The actus reus of the crime is the solicitation.

The crime is different from attempt, because the solicitation itself is a crime, and no act to further the crime need be taken. Of course, if Gwen asks Tracy to kill Jeff, and the deed is completed, then Gwen is an accessory before the fact of murder, as well as a solicitor.

---

co-conspirator's rule

■ The principle that statements by a member of a proven conspiracy may be used as evidence against any of the members of the conspiracy.

hearsay

■ A statement about what someone else said (or wrote or otherwise communicated). *Hearsay evidence* is evidence, concerning what someone said outside of a court proceeding, that is -offered in the proceeding to prove the truth of what was said. The *hearsay rule* bars the admission of hearsay as evidence to *prove the hearsay's truth* unless allowed by a hearsay exception.

solicitation

■ Asking for; enticing; strongly requesting. This may be a crime if the thing being urged is a crime.

Ethical Considerations

JUDGES HAVE RULES TOO

On December 16, 2000, Diana Jimenez struck another automobile while driving under the influence of alcohol. Two people were killed in the accident. Jimenez was charged inter alia with driving under the influence (DUI) manslaughter. Jimenez retained James Henson as her attorney. Henson had recently lost a reelection bid for county judge and was in his final weeks as a judge when he accepted a retainer of $15,000 and began representing Jimenez. During the course of his representation, Judge Henson suggested to his client on several occasions that she should consider returning to Colombia, her home, to avoid prosecution. She did not do this and later testified at Judge Henson's disciplinary hearing. Subsequently, Judge Henson was elected judge of a circuit court.

Judge Henson was charged with violating Florida's Rules of Professional Conduct for attorneys and for violating the Code of Judicial Conduct. Specifically, Judge Henson was found to have violated the provisions barring judges from practicing law and maintaining high standards of integrity, as well as the lawyer's prohibitions on recommending or suggesting to a client a dishonest or illegal act. Judge Henson was found to have violated these provisions, and he was removed from his post as circuit judge.

The ABA Model Code of Judicial Conduct, like its counterpart Model Rules of Professional Conduct for attorneys, has been adopted, in some form, in nearly every jurisdiction.

Web Links

GPO Gate

The U.S. Government Printing Office maintains a site with information of all three branches of the federal government. This includes the U.S. Code, Federal Register, and Code of Federal Regulations, among others. Direct access to the GPO site is at *http://www.gpoaccess.gov/index.html*

Key Terms

accessory
attempt
co-conspirator hearsay rule
concert of action rule

conspiracy
hearsay
legal impossibility
principal

solicitation
Wharton's Rule

Review Questions

1. Distinguish a principal in the first degree from a principal in the second degree. Which is punished more severely?

2. A person who helps principals prepare to commit a crime but is not present during the commission, is called what?

3. Has Jan committed attempted murder if she decides to kill her sister and mentally works out the details of when, how, and where?

4. What are the elements of conspiracy?

5. What is hearsay? What is the co-conspirator hearsay rule?

6. What is meant by the phrase "inchoate crimes?"

7. What is the difference between solicitation and attempt?

Problems & Critical Thinking Exercises

1-3. Use the following facts to answer problems 1 through 3: Abel and Baker were inmates sharing a cell in state prison. During their stay, they planned a convenience store robbery for after their release. They decided which store to rob, when they would rob it, and what method they would use. Having frequented the store on many occasions, Abel knew that the store had a safe and that the employees did not have access to its contents. Neither Abel nor Baker had any experience with breaking into safes and decided to seek help.

Accordingly, they sought out "Nitro," a fellow inmate who was a known explosives expert. They requested his assistance and promised to pay him one-third of the total recovery. He agreed. However, he would be able only to teach the two how to gain entry to the safe, because he was not scheduled for release until after the day they had planned for the robbery. He added that he owned a house in the area and that it would be available for them to use as a "hide-out until the heat was off."

The two were released as planned and drove to the town where the store was located. As instructed by Nitro, the two went to a store and purchased the materials necessary to construct an explosive, which was to be used to gain entry to the safe. That evening, Abel and Baker went to the convenience store with their homemade explosive. They left the car they were traveling in and went to the rear of the store to gain entry through a back door. However, as they entered the alley behind the store, they encountered a police officer. The officer, suspicious of them, examined their bag and discovered the bomb. Abel and Baker escaped from the officer and stayed in Nitro's house for 3 days before being discovered and arrested.

1. What crimes has Abel committed?

2. What crimes has Baker committed?

3. What crimes has Nitro committed?

4. John and Tyrone have a fight in a bar. Tyrone returns home, climbs into bed, and suffers a fatal heart attack. John, still angry from the earlier fight, climbs through a window into Tyrone's room and shoots Tyrone twice in the head. Has John committed a murder? Attempted murder? Explain your answer.

Endnotes

1. See *Rex v. Scofield,* Cald. 397 (1784) and *Rex v. Higgins,* 2 East 5 (1801).
2. *Hyde v. United States*, 225 U.S. 347 (1912).
3. Turner, "Attempts to Commit Crimes," 5 *Cambridge L.J.* 230, 236 (1934).
4. Model Penal Code § 5.01.
5. These elements are a composition of the overt acts that could be found in M. Bowman, *NYPD 'Cannibal Cop' Guilty of Kidnapping Conspiracy,* March 12, 2013, Lawyers.com found at http://blogs.lawyers.com/2013/03/nypd-cannibal-cop-guilty/ and FBI Press Release, *Manhattan U.S. Attorney Announces Arrest of New York City Police Officer for Kidnapping Conspiracy and Illegally Accessing Federal Law Enforcement Database*, October 25, 2012.
6. Model Penal Code § 5.03.
7. *Hyde v. United States*, 225 U.S. 347 (1912).

CHAPTER 8

FACTUAL AND STATUTORY DEFENSES

Chapter Objectives

After completing this chapter you should
be able to:

- define, recite the elements of, and apply
  to factual scenarios common factual
  defenses to criminal accusations, such
  as alibi.

- define, recite the elements of, and apply
  to factual scenarios common statutory
  defenses to criminal accusations, such
  as the insanity defense.

- critically discuss these defenses.

- identify the material facts and legal
  issues in one-half of the cases you read
  and describe the court's analyses and
  conclusions in these cases.

"DEFENSE" DEFINED

Criminal defendants usually claim that they are innocent of the charges against them. A defendant's reason for asserting that he is innocent is called a *defense*. Defenses can be factual: "I didn't do it!" They can also be legal: "I did it, but the case was filed after the statute of limitation had run." Many defenses have been developed under the common law; however, many others have been created by legislation. Finally, some defenses find their origin in the constitutions of the states and federal government. Some defenses are complete (perfect); that is, if they are successful, the defendant goes free. Other defenses are partial; the defendant avoids liability on one charge but may be convicted of a lesser offense.

This chapter examines several factual and statutory defenses. Chapter 9 discusses constitutional defenses.

AFFIRMATIVE DEFENSES

There is a special class of defenses known as **affirmative defenses.** Affirmative defenses go beyond a simple denial; they raise special or new issues that, if proven, can result in an acquittal or lesser liability. Defenses that raise the question of a defendant's mental state to commit a crime (e.g., insanity and intoxication), whether justification or excuse existed to commit the crime (e.g., self-defense), and alibi fall into the affirmative defenses class.

As a general rule, criminal defendants may sit passively during trial, as the prosecution bears the burden of proving the government's allegations. In all instances, **burden of proof** refers to two burdens, the burden of production and the burden of persuasion. Because it is not practical to require prosecutors to prove that every defendant was sane, was not intoxicated, or did not have justification to use force, the burdens for affirmative defenses are different than for other defenses. First, defendants have the duty of raising all affirmative defenses. In some cases, this means that defendants must inform the prosecutor of their intention to raise the defense early in the process. At trial this means that defendants must produce some evidence to support the defense. This is known as the **burden of production.**

After defendants have met the burden of production, the **burden of persuasion** then must be met. There is a split among the states; some require the defendant to carry this burden, whereas others require it of the prosecution. If defendants have the burden, they must convince the fact finder that the defense is true. Defendants must prove this by a preponderance of evidence. In jurisdictions that require prosecutors to disprove an affirmative defense, there is again a split as to the standard of proof required. Some require proof by a preponderance, and others require proof beyond a reasonable doubt.

Some of the defenses covered in this chapter are affirmative defenses. It is necessary to research local law to determine which procedure is followed in a particular jurisdiction and what defenses are considered "affirmative".

affirmative defense

■ A defense that is more than a simple denial of the charges. It raises a new matter that may result in an acquittal or a reduction of liability. It is a defense that must be affirmatively raised, often before trial or it is lost.

burden of proof

■ The requirement that to win a point or have an issue decided in your favor in a lawsuit, you must show that the weight of evidence is on your side rather than "in the balance" on that question.

burden of going forward (production)

■ The requirement that one side in a lawsuit produce evidence on a particular issue or risk losing on that issue.

burden of persuasion

■ The requirement that to win a point or have an issue decided in your favor in a lawsuit you must show that the weight of evidence is on your side, rather than "in the balance" on that question.

INSANITY

Few aspects of criminal law have received as much public attention as the insanity defense. The defense has also been the subject of considerable scholarly research and discussion. Some critics charge that the defense should not be available. Others criticize not the availability of such a defense but the particular tests employed to determine sanity. Despite its critics, insanity is recognized by nearly all jurisdictions as a defense. At least four states—Montana, Kansas, Utah, and Idaho—have abolished the insanity defense.[1] In 1994, the United States Supreme Court denied certiorari in a case challenging the abolition of the defense as violative of due process.

In reality, insanity is a mens rea defense. If a defendant was insane at the time of the crime, it is unlikely that the requisite mens rea existed. It is generally held that one who is insane is incapable of forming a rational purpose or intent. In fact, in most jurisdictions defendants may put on evidence to establish that insanity prevented the requisite mens rea from being formed. This is the defense of **diminished capacity.** It is a direct attack on the mens rea element of the crime, separate from the defense of insanity. If successful, the result could be conviction of a lesser, general-intent crime. However, a few states have made defendants choose between the insanity defense and the assertion of lack of mens rea due to insanity.

The theory underlying the defense of insanity is that no purpose of criminal law is served by subjecting insane persons to the criminal justice system. Because they have no control over their behavior, they cannot be deterred from similar future behavior. Similarly, no general deterrence will occur, as others suffering from a mental or physical disease of the mind are not likely to be deterred. The one purpose that may be served, incapacitation, is inappropriate if the defendants no longer suffer from a mental disease, or if the disease is now controlled. If the defendants continue to be dangerous, there is no need to use the criminal justice system to remove them from society, because this can be accomplished using civil commitment.

diminished capacity

■ The principle that having a certain recognized form of *diminished mental capacity* while committing a crime should lead to the imposition of a lesser punishment or to lowering the degree of the crime.

sidebar

TWINKIES, WITCHCRAFT, PMS, AND MORE

Some interesting insanity-related defenses have been raised by defendants. Although some are in the nature of full insanity defenses, most are asserted as diminished-capacity defenses.

One of the most famous is the so-called Twinkie defense, raised by a defendant in California who was charged with murdering a mayor and another official. He claimed that his large consumption of white sugar, primarily through snack foods, caused him to have a diminished capacity. The defense was successful in reducing the crime from murder to manslaughter. He was

sidebar *(continued)*

sentenced to a short prison term and committed suicide after his release. The California legislature responded to the decision by barring diminished-capacity defenses in future cases.

In addition to the Twinkie defense, all of the following have been pleaded by defendants in support of either an insanity defense or a diminished-capacity defense: premenstrual syndrome, involuntary subliminal television intoxication, brainwashing syndrome, and posttraumatic stress disorder. One defendant even asserted a witchcraft defense, claiming that witchcraft made him do it.

Many states have followed California's lead and eliminated the diminished-capacity defense. Others require defendants to choose between asserting insanity or diminished capacity.

Something that must be remembered is that criminal law has its own definition of insanity. Other areas of law (e.g., civil commitment) use different tests, as do other professions (e.g., psychiatry). Each jurisdiction is free to use whatever test it wishes to determine insanity. Three tests are used to determine sanity in the criminal law context: M'Naghten; irresistible impulse; and the Model Penal Code. A fourth test, the Durham, is no longer used in any jurisdiction but is mentioned because of its historical significance.

M'Naghten

In 1843 Daniel M'Naghten was tried for killing the British prime minister's secretary. M'Naghten was laboring under the paranoid delusion that the prime minister was planning to kill him, and he killed the minister's secretary, believing him to be the prime minister. The jury found M'Naghten not guilty by reason of insanity.[2] The decision created controversy, and the House of Lords asked the justice of the Queens Bench to state what the standards for acquittal on the grounds of insanity were.[3] Those standards were attached to the decision and set forth the following standard, known as the **M'Naghten rule.**

1. At the time that the act was committed
2. the defendant was suffering from a defect of reason, from a disease of the mind, that caused
3. the defendant to not know
   a. the nature and quality of the act taken or
   b. that the act was wrong.

M'Naghten rule

■ A principle employed in some jurisdictions for determining whether criminal defendants had the capacity to form criminal intent at the time they committed the crime of which they are accused. The M'Naghten rule is also referred to as the M'Naghten test or the right-wrong test.

The M'Naghten, or right-wrong, test is that used by most jurisdictions today. First, the defendant must have suffered from a disease of the mind at the time the act occurred. *Disease of the mind* is not clearly defined, but it appears that any condition that causes one of the two events from the third part of the test satisfies this element. That is, any disease of the mind that causes a defendant to not know the quality of an act or that an act is wrong is sufficient. In at least one case, extremely low intelligence was found adequate.[4]

The phrase "the defendant must not know the nature and quality of the act" simply means that the defendant did not understand the consequences of his or her physical act. The drafters of the Model Penal Code gave the following illustration: A man who squeezes his wife's neck, believing it to be a lemon, does not know the nature and quality of his actions.[5]

What is meant by "wrong," as used in the M'Naghten test? Courts have defined it two ways. One asks whether the defendant knew that the act was legally wrong, and the other asks whether the defendant knew that the act was morally wrong.

Irresistible Impulse

irresistible impulse

■ The loss of control due to insanity that is so great that a person cannot stop from committing a crime.

Under the M'Naghten test, defendants who knew that their actions were wrong, but could not control their behavior because of a disease of the mind, are not insane. This has led a few jurisdictions, which follow M'Naghten, to supplement the rule. These states continue to follow the basic rule but add that defendants are not guilty by reason of insanity if a disease of the mind caused the defendants to be unable to control their behavior. This is true even if the defendants understood the nature and quality of the act or knew that the behavior was wrong. This is known as **irresistible impulse.**

Irresistible impulse tests can be found in American cases as far back as 1863.[6] Of course, the largest problem with implementing the irresistible impulse test is distinguishing acts that can be resisted from those that cannot.

Durham

Durham rule

■ The principle, used in *Durham v. U.S.* (214 F.2d. 862 (1954)), that defendants are not guilty of a crime because of insanity if they were "suffering from a disease or defective mental condition at the time of the act and there was a causal connection between the condition and the act."

In 1871 the New Hampshire Supreme Court rejected the M'Naghten test and held that a defendant was not guilty because of insanity if the crime was the "product of mental disease." No other jurisdictions followed New Hampshire's lead until 1954, when the District of Columbia Court of Appeals handed down *Durham v. United States,* 214 F.2d 862 (D.C. Cir. 1954). Generally, the **Durham rule** requires an acquittal if defendants would not have committed the crime if they had not been suffering from a mental disease or mental defect.

Durham was overturned in 1972 by the District of Columbia Court of Appeals in favor of a modified version of the Model Penal Code test.[7] Today, Durham is not used by any jurisdiction.

The Model Penal Code Test

The Model Penal Code contains a definition of insanity similar to, but broader than, the M'Naghten and irresistible impulse tests. This test is also referred to as the *substantial capacity test.* The relevant section of the Code reads[8]:

A person is not responsible for criminal conduct if at the time of such conduct as a result of mental disease or defect he lacks substantial capacity either to appreciate the criminality [wrongfulness] of his conduct or to conform his conduct to the requirements of law.

The Code is similar to M'Naghten in that it requires that mental disease or defect impair a defendant's ability to appreciate the wrongfulness of his or her act. The final line, "conform his conduct to the requirements of law," incorporates the irresistible impulse concept.

The Code's approach differs from the M'Naghten and irresistible impulse test in two important regards: First, the Code requires only substantial impairment, whereas M'Naghten requires total impairment of the ability to know the nature or wrongfulness of the act. Second, the Code uses the term *appreciate,* rather than *know.* The drafters of the Code clearly intended more than knowledge, and, as such, evidence concerning the defendant's personality and emotional state are relevant.

The Model Penal Code test has been adopted by a few jurisdictions. The federal courts used the test until Congress enacted a statute that established a test similar to the M'Naghten test.[9] That statute places the burden of proving insanity, by clear and convincing evidence, on the defendant.

Guilty But Mentally Ill (GBMI)

In 1981 John Hinckley attempted to assassinate President Ronald Reagan. The president was seriously wounded and his press secretary, James Brady, suffered permanent brain injury. It was later learned that Hinckley committed the act to impress a movie actress he had never met. At trial, Hinckley was found not guilty by reason of insanity. There was both public and legislative backlash to the decision and to the insanity defense. As a result, legislators throughout the nation moved to abolish or limit the scope of the insanity defense. Today, four states—Idaho, Montana, Utah, and Kansas—have abolished the defense altogether.[10]

Rather than abolishing the defense, other states sought to limit or alter its impact. One such measure was the establishment of the Guilty But Mentally Ill (GBMI) verdict. Pennsylvania's GBMI statute reads, in part, that a "person who timely offers a defense of insanity in accordance with the Rules of Criminal Procedure may be found 'guilty but mentally ill' at trial if the trier of facts finds, beyond a reasonable doubt, that the person is guilty of an offense, was mentally ill at the time of the commission of the offense and was not legally insane at the time of the commission of the offense."[11] As you can see, the GBMI verdict is a finding of mental illness at the time of the crime, but not insanity as defined by the applicable legal test. Unlike a defendant who is not guilty by reason of insanity, a defendant who is GBMI is both punished and treated. The defendant is sentenced as any other offender for the crime, but in addition the state provides mental health treatment.

Procedures of the Insanity Defense

Insanity is an affirmative defense. In the federal system and in many states, defendants must provide notice to the court and government that insanity will be used as a defense at trial. These statutes usually require that the notice be filed a certain number of days before trial. This notice provides the prosecution with an opportunity to prepare to rebut the defense prior to trial.

In most instances, lay testimony is not adequate to prove insanity; psychiatric examination of defendants is necessary. The judge presiding over the case will appoint a psychiatrist or psychologist, who will conduct the exam and make the findings available to the judge. Often defendants wish to have a psychiatrist of their own choosing perform an examination. This is not a problem if the defendant can afford to pay for the service. In the case of indigent defendants who desire an independent mental examination, statutes often provide reimbursement from the government for independent mental examinations up to a stated maximum. In the federal system, trial courts may approve up to $1,000 in defense-related services. Defendants who seek reimbursement for greater expenses must receive approval from the chief judge of the circuit.[12]

As with all affirmative defenses, the defendant bears the burden of production at trial. Generally, the defendant must present enough evidence to create some doubt of sanity. The states are split on the issue of persuasion. Some require that the prosecution disprove the insanity claim, usually beyond a reasonable doubt. In other jurisdictions the defendant bears the burden of persuasion, usually by preponderance of the evidence. One exception is federal law, which requires the defendant to prove insanity by the higher standard—clear and convincing evidence.[13]

Disposition of the Criminally Insane

Contrary to popular belief, those adjudged insane by a criminal proceeding are not immediately and automatically released. In most jurisdictions, after a defendant has been determined "not guilty by reason of insanity," the court (the jury in a few states) must make a determination of whether the person continues to be dangerous. If so, commitment is to be ordered. If the defendant is determined not to be dangerous, then release follows. A few jurisdictions have followed the Model Penal Code approach,[14] which requires automatic commitment following a finding of not guilty by reason of insanity. This is the rule in the federal system.[15]

In theory, those committed have a right to be treated for their mental disease. In fact, due to lack of funds, security concerns, and overcrowding problems in facilities, adequate treatment is often not provided.

Once a committed person is no longer a danger, release is granted. The determination of dangerousness is left to the judge, not hospital administrators or mental health professionals—an often-criticized practice. Patients, doctors, government officials, and even the judge can begin the process of release. Some states provide for periodic reviews of the patient's status in order to determine the propriety of release. The relevant federal statute reads, in part:[16]

> When the director of the facility in which an acquitted person is hospitalized . . . determines that the person has recovered from his mental disease or defect to such an extent that his release, or his conditional release under a prescribed regimen of medical, psychiatric, or psychological care or treatment, would no longer create a substantial

risk of bodily injury to another person or serious damage to property of another, he shall promptly file a certificate to that effect with the clerk of the court that ordered the commitment . . . The court shall order a discharge of the acquitted person or, on the motion of the attorney for the government or on its own motion, shall hold a hearing [to determine if the patient is dangerous].

At that hearing, the defendant has the burden of proving by clear and convincing evidence that a risk to people or property is not created by release.

Finally, some states have a "guilty but mentally ill" verdict. Juries may return such a verdict when the defendant's illness does not rise to the level of negating culpability but treatment should be provided in addition to incarceration (see Exhibit 8–1).

sidebar

IMPACT OF THE INSANITY DEFENSE

In spite of the popular media attention it receives and the strong feelings it engenders, the insanity defense is not widely asserted and rarely results in not guilty verdicts. One author notes that defense is raised in only 1 percent of felony cases in the United States, and it succeeds in only about 25 percent of the cases in which it is asserted. This computes to about 300 insanity pleas per state per year.[17] Another researcher examined nearly 1 million cases and found that insanity was claimed in about one in a thousand cases and was successful in 29% of the time. It was discovered than when successful, it was rare for the jury to make the decision. In most cases the decision was a product of negotiation among the defendant, police, and prosecutor.[18] Other researchers also have found that the vast majority of the individuals who assert insanity suffer from a mental illness that is so serious that prosecutors support pleas of not guilty by reason of insanity or guilty but mentally ill. In a study of criminal cases in Tennessee, researchers found that 7% of defendants were referred for mental examination, and of that 7%, 19% subsequently asserted the insanity defense, and of that number, the prosecutors supported the pleas in 72% of the cases (less than 1% of all cases).[19]

Insanity at the Time of Trial

The United States Supreme Court has held that a defendant who is insane at the time of trial may not be tried.[20] The Court found that the Due Process Clauses of the Fifth and Fourteenth Amendments require that defendants be able to assist in their defense and understand the proceeding against them.

The test for determining insanity in this context is different from that discussed earlier. Insanity exists when defendants lack the capacity to understand the proceedings or assist in their defense. This simply means that defendants must be rational, possess the ability to testify coherently, and be able to meaningfully discuss their cases with their

Exhibit 8–1   INSANITY AND CRIMINAL PROCEDURE

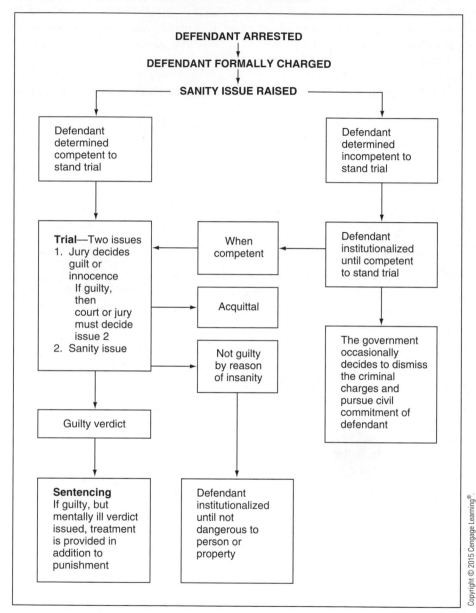

DEFENDANT ARRESTED

↓

DEFENDANT FORMALLY CHARGED

↓

SANITY ISSUE RAISED

Defendant determined competent to stand trial

Defendant determined incompetent to stand trial

Trial—Two issues
1. Jury decides guilt or innocence
   If guilty, then court or jury must decide issue 2
2. Sanity issue

When competent

Defendant institutionalized until competent to stand trial

Acquittal

The government occasionally decides to dismiss the criminal charges and pursue civil commitment of defendant

Not guilty by reason of insanity

Guilty verdict

Sentencing
If guilty, but mentally ill verdict issued, treatment is provided in addition to punishment

Defendant institutionalized until not dangerous to person or property

lawyers. The burden of establishing incompetence is placed on the defendant in many jurisdictions. While this procedure comports with due process, requiring the defendant to establish incompetence by clear and convincing evidence does not. In *Cooper v. Oklahoma* (1996),[21] the Supreme Court held that the burden of proof can be placed on the defendant but that the standard of proof cannot exceed preponderance of evidence.

If defendants are unable to stand trial because they are insane, they are usually committed until they are competent. Many statutes have mandatory commitment of defendants determined incompetent to stand trial. However, indefinite confinement is unconstitutional, based solely upon a finding of incompetence to stand trial. Generally, the Supreme Court has held that a lengthy (18 months or longer) detention (awaiting competence to stand trial) is tantamount to punishment and violative of the Due Process Clause.[22] In such cases, there must be a separate finding of dangerousness to continue to hold such persons.

A mistrial is to be declared in the event that a defendant becomes incompetent during a trial, and defendants who are sane at trial but become insane before sentencing should be sentenced to a psychiatric facility.

Last, the Supreme Court has held that a person who has become insane after being sentenced to death may not be executed until his or her sanity is regained.[23] The constitutional basis of the Court's decision was the Eighth Amendment's prohibition of cruel and unusual punishment. Thurgood Marshall penned, "It is no less abhorrent today than it has been for centuries to exact in penance the life of one whose mental illness prevents him from comprehending the reasons for the penalty or its implications."[24] Similarly, the Court has held that mentally retarded individuals may not be executed.[25]

Although not a defense, the issue of insanity during imprisonment and at the time of release is important. See Chapter 4 for a discussion of civil commitment of sex offenders and the dangerously mentally ill after release from prison.

DURESS AND NECESSITY

On September 5, 2012, the manager of a bank in Los Angeles, California, arrived at work shortly before opening, went to the vault and filled a bag with cash, proceeded to the back door, and threw the bag into the street, where two people were waiting and absconded with the money. Did the manager commit a crime? No. The night before the robbery, she was kidnapped by the two robbers. The morning of the robbery, they strapped a device to her chest, telling her that it was a bomb and that they would detonate it if she didn't comply with their directions. The device was removed by police and proved not be a bomb.[26]

Although the elements of theft may be satisfied, the manager acted under **duress**, a legal defense. To prove duress, one must show (1) that he or she was threatened (2) and that the threat caused a reasonable belief (3) that the only way of avoiding serious personal injury or death to oneself or others (4) was to commit the crime. Duress was recognized at common law and continues to be a statutory defense today.

First, it must be shown that a threat was made. Second, the threat must create a reasonable fear of immediate serious bodily harm or death. This fear must be reasonable; that is, even if the person making the threat had no intention of following through, the defense is still valid if a reasonable person would have thought the threat was real. Hence, even if bank robber never intended to kill Terry, she has the defense of duress. Terry need not be the one threatened for her to be able to claim duress. So, if bank robber threatened

duress

■ Unlawful pressure on what a person would not otherwise have done. It includes force, threats of violence, physical restraint, etc.

to kill a customer unless Terry complied, Terry could claim duress. The fear must not only be reasonable, but it must also be of serious bodily injury or death. If bank robber exclaims, "Put the money in the bag or I'll smack you across the face," the threatened danger is not sufficient to support the defense of duress. In addition, the threat of harm must be imminent or immediate. Threats of future harms are not adequate duress.

One limitation that is recognized nearly everywhere is that murder is not justified by duress. This rule is criticized, rightfully so, because it does not account for those situations where taking one life may save many more.

It is no defense to a crime to claim that one was only carrying out the orders of a superior, such as an employer or military superior. This issue was addressed in *United States v. Calley*.

The Court mentioned that the order's illegality was "apparent upon even cursory evaluation by a man of ordinary sense and understanding." What if an order appears to be legal and the person who follows it has a reasonable belief of its legality? In such cases, the defense of duress does applies.[27]

necessity

■ Often refers to a situation that requires an action that would otherwise be illegal or expose a person to tort liability.

Necessity is similar to duress. However, whereas duress is created by human pressures, necessity comes about by natural forces. When people are confronted with two choices, both causing harm, they choose the lesser harm. If they do, they may have the defense of necessity to the act taken. For example, a person may be justified in breaking into someone's cabin to avoid freezing to death. Or a captain of a ship may be justified in a trespassory use of another's dock, if setting ashore is necessary to save the ship and its passengers.

Necessity is a broad and amorphous concept. As a general proposition, it applies anytime a person is confronted with the task of choosing between two or more evils. The harm avoided need not be bodily injury; it can also be harm to property. Of course, choosing property over life is never justified. Finally, if an alternative existed that involved less harm than the chosen act, the defense is invalid.

Duress and necessity are complete defenses. When valid, they result in acquittal of all related charges.

UNITED STATES V. CALLEY
46 C.M.R. 1131 (1975)

[D]uring midmorning on 16 March 1968 a large number of unresisting Vietnamese were placed in a ditch on the eastern side of My Lai and summarily executed by American soldiers.

[PFC] Meadlo gave the most graphic and damning evidence. He had wandered back into the village alone after the trial incident. Eventually, he met his fire team leader, Specialist Four Grzesik. They took seven or eight Vietnamese to what he labeled a "ravine," where Lieutenants Calley, Sledge, and Dursi and a few other Americans were located with what he estimated as seventy-five to a hundred Vietnamese. Meadlo remembered also that Lieutenant Calley told him, "We got another job to do, Meadlo," and that the appellant started shoving people into the ravine and shooting them. Meadlo,

UNITED STATES V. CALLEY *(continued)*

in contrast to Dursi, followed the directions of his leader and himself fired into the people at the bottom of the "ravine." Meadlo then drifted away from the area but he doesn't remember where.

Specialist Four Grzesik found PFC Meadlo, crying and distraught, sitting on a small dike on the eastern edge of the village. He and Meadlo moved through the village, and came to the ditch, in which Grzesik thought were thirty-five dead bodies. Lieutenant Calley walked past and ordered Grzesik to take his fire team back into the village and help the following platoon in their search. He also remembered that Calley asked him to "finish them off," but he refused.

Specialist Four Turner saw Lieutenant Calley for the first time that day as Turner walked out of the village near the ditch. Meadlo and a few other soldiers were also present. Turner passed within fifteen feet of the area, looked into the ditch and saw a pile of approximately twenty bodies covered with blood. He saw Lieutenant Calley and Meadlo firing from a distance of five feet into another group of people who were kneeling and squatting in the ditch . . . .

Of the several bases for his argument that he committed no murder at My Lai because he was void of mens rea, appellant emphasized most of all that he acted in obedience to orders . . . .

An order of the type appellant says he received is illegal. Its illegality is apparent upon even cursory evaluation by a man of ordinary sense and understanding . . . .

We find no impediment to the findings that appellant acted with murderous mens rea, including premeditation.

USE-OF-FORCE DEFENSES

A homicide on February 26, 2012, in Florida focused the Nation's attention on several criminal justice problems, including race, the role of citizens in preventing and responding to crime, and the law of self-defense. George Zimmerman, a Hispanic 28-year-old community watch leader, shot and killed Treyvon Martin, a 17-year-old African American male. Zimmerman was charged with Martin's homicide, Zimmerman asserted self-defense.[28]

On the night of the shooting, Martin was visiting with his father and his father's fiancée. While watching television, Martin left the home to walk to a convenience store. Martin trespassed through Zimmerman's neighborhood during his walk. Zimmerman observed Martin in the neighborhood during Martin's return from the store. Finding his presence suspicious, Zimmerman followed him, called the police, is alleged to have ignored a suggestion to discontinue the pursuit by the police dispatcher, and confronted and shot Martin. Zimmerman was charged with second degree murder, tried by jury, and acquitted.

Claims that Zimmerman had a racial motivation for pursuing Martin contributed to making the incident a national cause célèbre. As it too often the case, there was a media frenzy and a prejudicial rush to judgement. Of the many social and legal questions that the Treyvon Martin homicide raised, one concerns the nature of self-defense. The defense varies between the states.

All states permit the use physical force against others in specific circumstances. Self-defense, defense of others, defense of property, and use of force to make arrests fall into this area. Self-defense, defense of others, and defense of property, when successful, are complete defenses. Imperfect self-defense (including defense of another) does not lead to acquittal; however, it does reduce murder to manslaughter.

Self-Defense

self-defense

■ Physical force used against a person who is threatening the use of physical force or using physical force.

To prove **self-defense,** it must be shown that the actor (1) was confronted with an unprovoked, (2) immediate threat of bodily harm, (3) that force was necessary to avoid the harm, (4) and that the amount of force used was reasonable.

One who initiates an attack on another cannot claim self-defense, as a general proposition. There are two exceptions to this rule. First, if attackers are met with excessive force in return, they may defend themselves. For example, Mike attacks Norm with his fists, and in defense Norm uses a deadly weapon. In such a circumstance, Mike may also use deadly force to protect himself. Second, if an attacker withdraws from the attack and is pursued by the intended victim, then he or she may claim self-defense. Suppose Randy attacks Sue with an intent to sexually assault her. After he grabs her, she displays a gun, and he runs. If Sue follows after him, intending to cause him harm, then he would be privileged to use force to defend himself.

battered woman syndrome

■ Continuing abuse of a woman by a spouse or lover, and the resulting physical or psychological harm.

The threat of harm must be immediate in most jurisdictions. Threat of future harm does not justify using force against another. To satisfy this requirement, the harm must be one that will occur unless force is used, and no other means of avoiding the harm exists. However, this principle is occasionally stretched. For example, some jurisdictions have permitted a jury to be instructed on the **battered woman syndrome** defense. Under this defense, a woman who is constantly abused by her husband may be justified in using force at a time when she is not strictly in "immediate danger." The theory is that women in such circumstances have two choices: either wait for their husbands to kill them or strike first in a form of offensive self-defense. Critics of this defense contend that because other remedies are available, such as leaving the husband and obtaining a court order restraining him from bothering her, there is no immediate danger.

Finally, the force used to defend oneself must be reasonable. It would be unreasonable to knife a person who is attempting to slap one's hand. Deadly force may be used to defend against an attack that threatens serious bodily injury or death. Deadly force may not be used to defend against other attacks.

Retreat, Castle, and Stand-Your-Ground

retreat to the wall

■ The doctrine that before a person is entitled to use deadly force in self defense, he or she must attempt to withdraw from the encounter by giving as much ground as possible.

Many states require that a person retreat from an attack, if possible, before using deadly force. This is known as the **retreat to the wall doctrine** or simply the **retreat doctrine.** But there are exceptions.

The first exception is when retreating poses a danger to the victim of the attack. Another is for police officers, who are not required to retreat when performing their lawful duties. The Model Penal Code has a retreat provision that recognizes these exceptions:

The use of deadly force is not justifiable . . . [if] the actor knows that he can avoid the necessity of using such force without complete safety by retreating or by surrendering possession of a thing to a person asserting a claim of right thereto or by complying with a demand that he abstain from any action which he has no duty to take, except that (1) the actor is not obliged to retreat from his dwelling or place of work, unless he was the initial aggressor.[29]

The Code provides that public officials need not retreat during the performance of their duties. There is no duty to retreat rather than using nondeadly force.

Also, notice that the Code requires not only retreat, but that "thing[s]" be surrendered and one comply with another's demands before deadly force is used. Of course, one can later use civil law to recover unlawfully taken items or to recover for complying with a demand that caused damage. The aggressor will be liable both civilly and criminally for such unlawful demands.

Most states, for example, do not require one to retreat from his or her home. This is known as the **castle doctrine.** The castle doctrine dates to the old common law. Indeed the phrase "A man's home is his castle" is of ancient English origin. The castle doctrine reflects the idea that the home is a very special place, a venue that is inviolable by outsiders and where the residents can feel their safest and live free from intrusion.

There are different versions of the castle doctrine between the states where it is recognized. Castle doctrine statutes commonly include one or more of the following:

1. Repeal of the common law retreat doctrine for lawful residents of homes who use deadly force against an intruder into the home.
2. The creation of a presumption that intruders are a threat to life or limb.
3. Immunity from criminal and civil liability for residents of homes who use deadly force on intruders.

As to the first of these, there are common exceptions. For example, deadly force may not be used against people who have a lawful right to be on the premises. Police officers and family members are examples. This isn't to say that an ex-wife can't use deadly force against a homicidal ex-husband who happens to be a police officer. The statutes typically deny the castle doctrine defense to residents who use deadly force against individuals they should reasonably know are lawfully entering the premises.

Another variation on the home element of the castle doctrine is the inclusion of more than homes in its grasp. For example, Ohio has extended the castle doctrine to include automobiles. The applicable statute provides that "Every person accused of an offense is presumed innocent until proven guilty beyond a reasonable doubt, and the burden of proof for all elements of the offense is upon the prosecution. The burden of going forward with the evidence of an affirmative defense, and the burden of proof, by a preponderance of the evidence, for an affirmative defense, is upon the accused."[30]

A minority, but growing number of states, have so-called **stand-your-ground** laws.[31] Florida, the location of the Zimmerman shooting of Martin, is such a state.

Castle Doctrine

■ An exception to the Retreat Doctrine, one has no obligation to retreat from his or her home before using deadly force to repel an intruder.

stand-your-ground

■ A law that enables a person to use deadly force to repel an attack without first retreating.

Stand-your-ground laws are essentially the extension of the castle doctrine to public spaces. A victim of an attack that threatens life or limb in any space, not just the home or car, does not have a duty to retreat, even if a safe retreat is available. Florida's law provides, in part:

> (3) A person who is not engaged in an unlawful activity and who is attacked in any other place where he or she has a right to be has no duty to retreat and has the right to stand his or her ground and meet force with force, including deadly force if he or she reasonably believes it is necessary to do so to prevent death or great bodily harm to himself or herself or another or to prevent the commission of a forcible felony.

As the second dimension, reasonable force, states vary between requiring the use of deadly force to be objectively reasonable to creating a presumption of reasonable fear of life or limb by intruders in the home. The difference between the two is procedural. If the former, the law permits the use of deadly force without retreat but the person who used the force may bear the burden of proving to the jury that her fear was reasonable. If the latter, the law presumes the fear was reasonable and the burden falls to the state to prove it was unreasonable. Florida shifts the burden to the state to prove that the fear was unreasonable:

> (1) A person is presumed to have held a reasonable fear of imminent peril of death or great bodily harm to himself or herself or another when using defensive force that is intended or likely to cause death or great bodily harm to another if:
>
> (a) The person against whom the defensive force was used was in the process of unlawfully and forcefully entering, or had unlawfully and forcibly entered, a dwelling, residence, or occupied vehicle, or if that person had removed or was attempting to remove another against that person's will from the dwelling, residence, or occupied vehicle; and
>
> (b) The person who uses defensive force knew or had reason to believe that an unlawful and forcible entry or unlawful and forcible act was occurring or had occurred.
>
> * * *
>
> (4) A person who unlawfully and by force enters or attempts to enter a person's dwelling, residence, or occupied vehicle is presumed to be doing so with the intent to commit an unlawful act involving force or violence.[32]

The third dimension of most castle doctrine statutes is the creation of civil liability for individuals who use deadly force in a manner recognized by the statutes. Of course, liability may be found if the person using force is found to have acted outside the protection of the castle doctrine statute, e.g., used force unreasonably.

United States' law of self-defense has evolved considerably since the old common law and the variation between the states is considerable. See Exhibit 8–2 for a continuum of the right to use deadly force as a form of self-defense.

Exhibit 8–2   DEADLY FORCE CONTINUUM

Least Protection		Self-Defense		Greatest Protection
Retreat to Wall	Castle Doctrine	Castle Doctrine Plus	Castle Doctrine Enhanced	Stand-Your-Ground
Duty to retreat, even in the home, before using deadly Force	Deadly Force may be used by residents of homes against intruders without first retreating. Person using deadly force may have to prove it was reasonable.	The use of deadly force by the resident of a home is presumed reasonable, unless the victim had fight to enter premises.	Castle Doctrine is extended to cars or other venues.	Deadly Force may be used to repel an attacker in any location without first retreating, so long as reasonable attacker threatens life or limb.

Defense of Others

It is also a justified use of force to defend another. The rules are similar to that of self-defense: There must be a threat of immediate danger to the other person; the perception of threat must be reasonable; the amount of force used must be reasonable; and deadly force may be used only to repel a deadly attack.

At common law, one was privileged to defend only those with whom a special relationship existed, such as parent and child. Today, most jurisdictions permit any person to use force to protect another.

What happens when a person uses force to defend another who is *not* privileged to use force? For example, Perry is an undercover police officer attempting to arrest Norm, who is resisting. Randa observes what is happening and comes to Norm's defense, believing that Norm was being unlawfully attacked. There is a split of authority concerning this problem. Some jurisdictions limit the authority of the defender to use force to the privilege held by the person being attacked. Because Norm was not privileged to use force against the police officer, Randa is guilty of assault. Other states, however, use an objective test. Under such a test, if a reasonable person standing in Randa's shoes would have believed that force was justified, then he or she would be acquitted.

Defense of Property and Habitation

At common law and by legislative enactment today, one may use force to defend property. As with defending oneself, only reasonable force may be used. Because property is not as valuable as life, deadly force may not be used to protect property. Thus, one must allow another to take or destroy property before killing to defend it. No force is reasonable if other methods of protecting the property were available. So, if one has ample time to seek assistance from the police or the courts, force would be unreasonable. In contrast, if an enemy appears at one's house and begins to destroy a car in the driveway, force would be permitted to protect the vehicle. Actors must have a reasonable belief that their property is in danger of trespass or destruction and that the force used was necessary to defend the property.

The basic rules concerning defense of property also apply to defense of habitation: One must have a reasonable belief that the property is threatened; only reasonable force may be used to protect the property; and other non-violent remedies must be utilized before resorting to force. However, one difference between dwellings and other property is that deadly force may be used, under some circumstances, to protect one's home.

In early common law, the security of the home was as important as life itself. Therefore, people were permitted to use deadly force against any forcible intruder after warning the person not to enter. Today the rule has been narrowed, and statutes now commonly require that the occupant must believe that the intruder intends to commit a felony once inside before deadly force may be used.

The Model Penal Code allows the use of deadly force if either (1) the intruder is attempting to take the dwelling (with no legal claim to do so) or (2) the intruder is there to commit a crime (arson, burglary, theft) and has threatened deadly force or poses a substantial risk to those inside.[33]

This provision of the Code incorporates a self-defense concept. Remember, the rules of self-defense apply in the home also. So, any time a person's life (or another's) is threatened, deadly force may be used.

Some people choose to protect their property with manmade devices, such as electric fences and spring guns. Others have used natural protection, such as dogs and snakes. Whichever is used, the rules are the same. If the device employs nondeadly force, it is likely to be lawful. An electric fence that does not have sufficient electric current to kill is a justified use of force.

However, the result is often different when one uses deadly force. There are two perspectives on the use of deadly traps to protect property. One permits the use of deadly force so long as those who set the trap would have been permitted to use such force themselves, if they had been present. So, if a murderer gains entry to a house and is killed by a spring gun, the occupant is not criminally liable because he or she would have been privileged to use deadly force against the murderer. The second perspective, adopted by the drafters of the Model Penal Code, rejects the use of deadly traps in all instances.[34] This position is sound, as deadly traps do not discriminate between the dangerous and the nondangerous. The occupant who sets such a trap is simply lucky if the intruder is a criminal and not a firefighter responding to a blaze in the home.

Imperfect Self-Defense

The so-called imperfect self-defense is actually a mens rea defense. It applies to situations when people cannot make a successful self-defense (or defense of another) claim, but because they lacked malice aforethought (or purpose), the crime should not be murder but, rather, manslaughter. The defense applies only to homicides and is not recognized everywhere.

As stated, a person must have a reasonable belief that he or another is in danger of serious bodily injury or death before deadly force may be used. What if a person possesses a good-faith but unreasonable belief? Self-defense is unavailable, but because there is no malicious intent, purpose, or malice aforethought (depending on the jurisdiction's definition of murder), the crime is reduced to manslaughter. The defense is available in a second situation: whenever people who initiates an attack using nondeadly force later justifiably the use deadly force to defend themselves.

Arrests

Sometimes it is necessary for law enforcement officers to use force to execute their duties and to defend themselves. When a police officer uses force in defense of another's attack, the rules of self-defense that you have already learned apply. In addition, because the use of force is an integral part of law enforcement, it is often justified. However, a person making an arrest does not have an unlimited right to use force against an arrestee. This section examines a person's right to resist an unlawful arrest, the so-called citizen's arrest, and arrests by law enforcement officers.

Resisting Unlawful Arrests

In some states, people may use force to resist an unlawful arrest. The amount of force is usually limited to nondeadly, although some jurisdictions permit one to use deadly force. Of course, if a person uses force against a lawful arrest, he or she is fully liable for whatever crime results (assault, battery, or murder), as well as for resisting a lawful arrest.

The rule permitting force to resist an unlawful arrest evolved during a time when arrestees were detained for long periods before appearing before a court, jail conditions were extremely poor, and no civil remedies existed for unlawful arrests. In light of these harsh facts, public policy was best served by permitting people to resist unlawful arrests.

Today, many jurisdictions have adopted an approach closer to the Model Penal Code's, which prohibits any resistance to an arrest by a law enforcement officer. This is the sensible approach, as the reasons for permitting resistance no longer exist: Arrestees must be promptly brought before judges and released if there is no probable cause. When available, bail is set immediately. Also, federal law now permits civil suits against law enforcement officers for violation of a person's civil rights. Prohibiting resistance advances two important public policy objectives: First, it fosters obedience to police, and, second, it reduces violence.

Arrests by Law Enforcement Officers

A law enforcement officer is privileged to use reasonable force to apprehend criminals and to prevent those incarcerated from escaping. At common law, police could use all but deadly force to arrest misdemeanants and deadly force to arrest felons. This latter rule was justified by the fact that all felons were put to death at early common law.

In 1974 a Memphis, Tennessee, police officer shot and killed a 15-year-old male who was fleeing a burglary. The boy had stolen 40 dollars. The family of the deceased boy sued the police department in federal court for violating his constitutional rights. The case ended up before the United States Supreme Court.

In *Tennessee v. Garner,* 471 U.S. 1 (1985), the Court held that the use of deadly force by a police officer is a "seizure" under the Fourth Amendment. Accordingly, the test used to determine whether the use of deadly force is proper is the Fourth Amendment's test: reasonability. The Court then held that the use of deadly force is reasonable only when the person fleeing is a dangerous felon. This finding invalidated the laws of many states that permitted the use of deadly force to stop all fleeing felons, including those who posed no threat to life or limb, such as thieves, extortionists, and those who tendered bad checks. The Court did not state what standard must be applied in cases of nondeadly force. Some courts applied a due process standard, others the Fourth Amendment's reasonableness standard.

In 1989 the Court handed down *Graham v. Connor,* 490 U.S. 386 (1989) in which the standard was set for all preconviction seizures, deadly and nondeadly. Through that decision, the Court held that all seizures are to be evaluated under the Fourth Amendment objective reasonableness standard. Specifically the Court held that courts must review challenged use of force from the perspective of a reasonable officer at the time the force was applied.

High-speed police chases have received considerable public attention in recent years because they pose a threat not only to the police officer and the person fleeing, but to the general public. Whether *Garner* applied to these chases was not known until 2007.

Finally, note that police officers are often put into positions where they must defend themselves, such as during an arrest. The same rules discussed earlier concerning self-defense apply in these situations, with one exception: Police officers are not required to retreat. Thus, if a police officer is involved in an arrest that involves escalating violence, the police officer may have to use deadly force to defend against the criminal's attack.

SCOTT V. HARRIS
550 U.S. 372 (2007)

Justice Scalia delivered the opinion of the Court.

We consider whether a law enforcement official can, consistent with the Fourth Amendment, attempt to stop a fleeing motorist from continuing his public—endangering flight by ramming the motorist's car from behind. Put another way: Can an officer take actions that place a fleeing motorist at risk of serious injury or death in order to stop the motorist's flight from endangering the lives of innocent bystanders?

I

In March 2001, a Georgia county deputy clocked respondent's vehicle traveling at 73 miles per hour on a road with a 55-mile-per-hour speed limit. The deputy activated his blue flashing lights indicating that respondent should pull over. Instead, respondent sped away, initiating a chase down what is in most portions a two-lane road, at speeds exceeding 85 miles per hour. The deputy radioed his dispatch to report that he was pursuing a fleeing vehicle, and broadcast its license plate number. Petitioner, Deputy Timothy Scott, heard the radio communication and joined the pursuit along with other officers. In the midst of the chase, respondent pulled into the parking lot of a shopping center and was nearly boxed in by the various police vehicles. Respondent evaded the trap by making a sharp turn, colliding with Scott's police car, exiting the parking lot, and speeding off once again down a two-lane highway.

Following respondent's shopping center maneuvering, which resulted in slight damage to Scott's police car, Scott took over as the lead pursuit vehicle. Six minutes and nearly 10 miles after the chase had begun, Scott decided to attempt to terminate the episode by employing a "Precision Intervention Technique ('PIT') maneuver, which causes the fleeing vehicle to spin to a stop." Having radioed his supervisor for permission, Scott was told to " '[g]o ahead and take him out.' " *Harris v. Coweta County*, 433 F.3d 807, 811 (CA11 2005). Instead, Scott applied his push bumper to the rear of respondent's vehicle. As a result, respondent lost control of his vehicle, which left the roadway, ran down an embankment, overturned, and crashed. Respondent was badly injured and was rendered a quadriplegic.

Respondent filed suit against Deputy Scott and others under Rev. Stat. § 1979, 42 U.S.C. § 1983, alleging, *inter alia*, a violation of his federal constitutional rights, *viz.* use of excessive force resulting in an unreasonable seizure under the Fourth Amendment. In response, Scott filed a motion for summary judgment based on an assertion of qualified immunity. The District Court denied the motion, finding that "there are material issues of fact on which the issue of qualified immunity turns which present sufficient disagreement to require submission to a jury." On interlocutory appeal, the United States Court of Appeals for the Eleventh Circuit affirmed the District Court's decision to allow respondent's Fourth Amendment claim against Scott to proceed to trial (citation omitted). Taking respondent's view of the facts as given, the Court of Appeals concluded that Scott's actions could constitute "deadly force" under *Tennessee v. Garner*, 471 U.S. 1 (1985), and that the use of such force in this context "would violate [respondent's] constitutional right to be free from excessive force during a seizure. Accordingly, a reasonable jury could find that Scott violated [respondent's] Fourth Amendment rights." The Court of Appeals further concluded that "the law as it existed [at the time of the incident], was sufficiently clear to give reasonable law enforcement officers 'fair notice' that ramming a vehicle under these circumstances was unlawful." The Court of Appeals thus concluded that Scott was not entitled to qualified immunity. We granted certiorari, 549 U.S. __ (2006), and now reverse . . . .

II

In resolving questions of qualified immunity, courts are required to resolve a "threshold question: Taken in the light most favorable to the party asserting the injury, do the facts alleged show the officer's conduct violated a constitutional right? This must be the initial inquiry." *Saucier v. Katz*, 533 U.S. 194, 201 (2001). If, and only if, the court finds a violation of a constitutional right, "the next, sequential step is to ask whether the right was clearly established . . . in light of the specific context of the case." Although this ordering contradicts "[o]ur policy of avoiding unnecessary adjudication of constitutional issues," we have said that such a departure from practice is "necessary to set forth principles which will become the basis for a [future] holding that a right is clearly established." We therefore turn to the threshold inquiry: whether Deputy Scott's actions violated the Fourth Amendment.

(continued)

III

A

The first step in assessing the constitutionality of Scott's actions is to determine the relevant facts. As this case was decided on summary judgment, there have not yet been factual findings by a judge or jury, and respondent's version of events (unsurprisingly) differs substantially from Scott's version. When things are in such a posture, courts are required to view the facts and draw reasonable inferences "in the light most favorable to the party opposing the [summary judgment] motion." In qualified immunity cases, this usually means adopting (as the Court of Appeals did here) the plaintiff's version of the facts.

There is, however, an added wrinkle in this case: existence in the record of a videotape capturing the events in question. There are no allegations or indications that this videotape was doctored or altered in any way, nor any contention that what it depicts differs from what actually happened. The videotape quite clearly contradicts the version of the story told by respondent and adopted by the Court of Appeals (citation omitted). For example, the Court of Appeals adopted respondent's assertions that, during the chase, "there was little, if any, actual threat to pedestrians or other motorists, as the roads were mostly empty and [respondent] remained in control of his vehicle." Indeed, reading the lower court's opinion, one gets the impression that respondent, rather than fleeing from police, was attempting to pass his driving test:

"[T]aking the facts from the non-movant's viewpoint, [respondent] remained in control of his vehicle, slowed for turns and intersections, and typically used his indicators for turns. He did not run any motorists off the road. Nor was he a threat to pedestrians in the shopping center parking lot, which was free from pedestrian and vehicular traffic as the center was closed. Significantly, by the time the parties were back on the highway and Scott rammed [respondent], the motorway had been cleared of motorists and pedestrians allegedly because of police blockades of the nearby intersections."

The videotape tells quite a different story. There we see respondent's vehicle racing down narrow, two-lane roads in the dead of night at speeds that are shockingly fast. We see it swerve around more than a dozen other cars, cross the double-yellow line, and force cars traveling in both directions to their respective shoulders to avoid being hit. We see it run multiple red lights and travel for considerable periods of time in the occasional center left-turn-only lane, chased by numerous police cars forced to engage in the same hazardous maneuvers just to keep up. Far from being the cautious and controlled driver the lower court depicts, what we see on the video more closely resembles a Hollywood-style car chase of the most frightening sort, placing police officers and innocent bystanders alike at great risk of serious injury.

At the summary judgment stage, facts must be viewed in the light most favorable to the non-moving party only if there is a "genuine" dispute as to those facts. Fed. Rule Civ. Proc. 56(c). As we have emphasized, "[w]hen the moving party has carried its burden under Rule 56(c), its opponent must do more than simply show that there is some metaphysical doubt as to the material facts . . . . Where the record taken as a whole could not lead a rational trier of fact to find for the nonmoving party, there is no 'genuine issue for trial . . . . [T]he mere existence of some alleged factual dispute between the parties will not defeat an otherwise properly supported motion for summary judgment; the requirement is that there be no genuine issue of material fact." When opposing parties tell two different stories, one of which is blatantly contradicted by the record, so that no reasonable jury could believe it, a court should not adopt that

SCOTT V. HARRIS *(continued)*

version of the facts for purposes of ruling on a motion for summary judgment.

That was the case here with regard to the factual issue whether respondent was driving in such fashion as to endanger human life. Respondent's version of events is so utterly discredited by the record that no reasonable jury could have believed him. The Court of Appeals should not have relied on such visible fiction; it should have viewed the facts in the light depicted by the videotape.

B

Judging the matter on that basis, we think it is quite clear that Deputy Scott did not violate the Fourth Amendment. Scott does not contest that his decision to terminate the car chase by ramming his bumper into respondent's vehicle constituted a "seizure." "[A] Fourth Amendment seizure [occurs] . . . when there is a governmental termination of freedom of movement through means intentionally applied." It is also conceded, by both sides, that a claim of "excessive force in the course of making [a] . . . 'seizure' of [the] person . . . [is] properly analyzed under the Fourth Amendment's 'objective reasonableness' standard." *Graham v. Connor*, 490 U.S. 386, 388 (1989). The question we need to answer is whether Scott's actions were objectively reasonable.

Respondent urges us to analyze this case as we analyzed Garner, 471 U.S. 1. We must first decide, he says, whether the actions Scott took constituted "deadly force." (He defines "deadly force" as "any use of force which creates a substantial likelihood of causing death or serious bodily injury," *id.*, at 19.) If so, respondent claims that *Garner* prescribes certain preconditions that must be met before Scott's actions can survive Fourth Amendment scrutiny: (1) The suspect must have posed an immediate threat of serious physical harm to the officer or others; (2) deadly force must have been necessary to

prevent escape; and (3) where feasible, the officer must have given the suspect some warning. Since these *Garner* preconditions for using deadly force were not met in this case, Scott's actions were per se unreasonable.

Respondent's argument falters at its first step; *Garner* did not establish a magical on/off switch that triggers rigid preconditions whenever an officer's actions constitute "deadly force." *Garner* was simply an application of the Fourth Amendment's "reasonableness" test, to the use of a particular type of force in a particular situation. *Garner* held that it was unreasonable to kill a "young, slight, and unarmed" burglary suspect, 471 U.S., at 21, by shooting him "in the back of the head" while he was running away on foot, and when the officer "could not reasonably have believed that [the suspect] . . . posed any threat," and "never attempted to justify his actions on any basis other than the need to prevent an escape". Whatever *Garner* said about the factors that might have justified shooting the suspect in that case, such "preconditions" have scant applicability to this case, which has vastly different facts. "*Garner* had nothing to do with one car striking another or even with car chases in general . . . . A police car's bumping a fleeing car is, in fact, not much like a policeman's shooting a gun so as to hit a person." Nor is the threat posed by the flight on foot of an unarmed suspect even remotely comparable to the extreme danger to human life posed by respondent in this case. Although respondent's attempt to craft an easy-to-apply legal test in the Fourth Amendment context is admirable, in the end we must still slosh our way through the factbound morass of "reasonableness." Whether or not Scott's actions constituted application of "deadly force," all that matters is whether Scott's actions were reasonable.

(continued)

In determining the reasonableness of the manner in which a seizure is effected, "[w]e must balance the nature and quality of the intrusion on the individual's Fourth Amendment interests against the importance of the governmental interests alleged to justify the intrusion." *United States v. Place*, 462 U.S. 696, 703 (1983). Scott defends his actions by pointing to the paramount governmental interest in ensuring public safety, and respondent nowhere suggests this was not the purpose motivating Scott's behavior. Thus, in judging whether Scott's actions were reasonable, we must consider the risk of bodily harm that Scott's actions posed to respondent in light of the threat to the public that Scott was trying to eliminate. Although there is no obvious way to quantify the risks on either side, it is clear from the videotape that respondent posed an actual and imminent threat to the lives of any pedestrians who might have been present, to other civilian motorists, and to the officers involved in the chase. See Part III-A, *supra*. It is equally clear that Scott's actions posed a high likelihood of serious injury or death to respondent—though not the near certainty of death posed by, say, shooting a fleeing felon in the back of the head or pulling alongside a fleeing motorist's car and shooting the motorist. So how does a court go about weighing the perhaps lesser probability of injuring or killing numerous bystanders against the perhaps larger probability of injuring or killing a single person? We think it appropriate in this process to take into account not only the number of lives at risk, but also their relative culpability. It was respondent, after all, who intentionally placed himself and the public in danger by unlawfully engaging in the reckless, high-speed flight that ultimately produced the choice between two evils that Scott confronted. Multiple police cars, with blue lights flashing and sirens blaring, had been chasing respondent for nearly 10 miles, but he ignored their warning to stop. By contrast, those

who might have been harmed had Scott not taken the action he did were entirely innocent. We have little difficulty in concluding it was reasonable for Scott to take the action that he did.

But wait, says respondent: Couldn't the innocent public equally have been protected, and the tragic accident entirely avoided, if the police had simply ceased their pursuit? We think the police need not have taken that chance and hoped for the best. Whereas Scott's action—ramming respondent off the road—was certain to eliminate the risk that respondent posed to the public, ceasing pursuit was not. First of all, there would have been no way to convey convincingly to respondent that the chase was off, and that he was free to go. Had respondent looked in his rear-view mirror and seen the police cars deactivate their flashing lights and turn around, he would have had no idea whether they were truly letting him get away, or simply devising a new strategy for capture. Perhaps the police knew a shortcut he didn't know, and would reappear down the road to intercept him; or perhaps they were setting up a roadblock in his path. Given such uncertainty, respondent might have been just as likely to respond by continuing to drive recklessly as by slowing down and wiping his brow (citation omitted).

Second, we are loath to lay down a rule requiring the police to allow fleeing suspects to get away whenever they drive so recklessly that they put other people's lives in danger. It is obvious the perverse incentives such a rule would create: Every fleeing motorist would know that escape is within his grasp, if only he accelerates to 90 miles per hour, crosses the double-yellow line a few times, and runs a few red lights. The Constitution assuredly does not impose this invitation to impunity-earned-by-recklessness. Instead, we lay down a more sensible rule: A police officer's attempt to terminate a dangerous high-speed car chase that threatens the lives of innocent

SCOTT V. HARRIS *(continued)*

bystanders does not violate the Fourth Amendment, even when it places the fleeing motorist at risk of serious injury or death.

The car chase that respondent initiated in this case posed a substantial and immediate risk of serious physical injury to others; no reasonable jury could conclude otherwise. Scott's attempt to terminate the chase by forcing respondent off the road was reasonable, and Scott is entitled to summary judgment. The Court of Appeals' decision to the contrary is reversed.

Arrests by Citizens

At common law, private citizens were privileged to arrest those who committed a felony or misdemeanor (which amounted to a breach of the peace) in their presence. Some jurisdictions have retained this rule, and others have changed it by statute.

In jurisdictions that have changed the rule, it is common to permit so-called citizens' arrests any time probable cause exists to believe that the person has committed a felony. In most jurisdictions a citizen may not arrest a misdemeanant unless the person making the arrest witnessed the crime. Even in such cases, only certain misdemeanors may lead to such an arrest.

The reason for these rules is to provide citizens who make such arrests with immunity from civil and criminal prosecution. However, the citizen must be privileged to make the arrest and, even when privileged, a reasonable amount of force must be used.

In some jurisdictions, a private person making an arrest may use deadly force only when the person is in fact a felon. The jurisdictions employing this rule are split: Some permit the use of deadly force by private citizens to arrest for any felony and others only for specific felonies (e.g., murder and rape). These jurisdictions are similar in one important regard. The person against whom the deadly force is used must have *in fact* committed the crime. A reasonable, but incorrect, belief that the person has committed a crime is not a defense. So, if Pat kills Sam while attempting to arrest Sam for a crime he did not commit, Pat is liable for manslaughter, even though she had a reasonable belief that he committed the crime. Some states have followed the Model Penal Code approach, which prohibits the use of deadly force by private persons in all circumstances.[35]

The results are different if a private person is assisting a law enforcement officer. In fact, many states have statutes that require citizens to assist police officers upon order. In such cases, the private party is privileged to use whatever force is reasonable. In addition, a private person responding to a police officer's order to assist in an arrest is privileged, even if the police officer was exceeding his or her authority and had no cause to make the arrest. In such instances, the police officer may be liable for both his or her own actions and the actions of the private party summoned. Of course, there are limits to the rule. For example, a private person who obeys a police officer's order to strike an already apprehended and subdued criminal would not be privileged.

INFANCY

At common law, it was a complete defense to a charge that the accused was a child under the age of seven at the time the crime was committed. It was irrebuttably presumed that children under seven were incapable of forming the requisite mens rea to commit a crime. A rebuttable presumption of incapacity existed for those between 7 and 14 years of age. The presumption could be overcome for those between 7 and 14 if the prosecution could prove that the defendant understood that the criminal act was wrong.

Few minors are charged with crimes today. This is the result of the advent of the juvenile court systems in the United States. Currently each state has a juvenile court system that deals with juvenile delinquency and neglected children.

Statutes vary, but it is common for juvenile courts to possess exclusive jurisdiction over criminal behavior of juveniles. However, some states give concurrent jurisdiction to criminal courts and juvenile courts. If concurrent, the juvenile court usually must waive jurisdiction before the criminal court can hear the case. Determining who is a juvenile also differs, with some jurisdictions utilizing a method similar to the common law (irrebuttable and rebuttable presumptions) and others simply setting an age cutoff, such as 14 or 16.

The purpose of the juvenile justice system differs from that of the criminal justice system. Whereas criminal law has punishment as one of its major purposes, the purpose of the juvenile system is not to punish but to reform the delinquent child.

INTOXICATION

In this context, *intoxication* refers to all situations in which a person's mental or physical abilities are impaired by drugs or alcohol. It is generally said that voluntary intoxication is a defense if it has the effect of negating the required mens rea. In common-law language, this means that if intoxication prevents a defendant from being able to form a specific intent, then the crime is reduced to a similar general-intent crime. For the crime of murder, intoxication is a defense if it prevents the defendant from forming the premeditation, deliberation, or purposeful element. In such cases, the charge is reduced from first-degree to second-degree murder. Not all states recognize voluntary intoxication as a defense. The question whether a defendant has a due process right to have an intoxication defense heard by a jury was answered in the negative by the Supreme Court in the 1996 case *Montana v. Engelhoff*.[36] The Court's rationale for rejecting the right focused on the scientific ambiguity of the impact of intoxication on mens rea and the lack of consensus among the states in recognizing the defense.

In the rare case of involuntary intoxication in jurisdictions that permit the defense, the defendant is relieved of liability entirely. To be successful with such a claim, the defendant is required to show that the intoxication had the same effect as insanity. In jurisdictions using the M'Naghten test for insanity, a defendant is required to prove that the intoxication prevented him or her from knowing right from wrong.

MISTAKE

People may be mistaken in two ways. First, one may believe that some act is legal when it is not. This is a mistake of law. Second, a person may not understand all the facts of a given situation. This is a mistake of fact. As a general proposition, mistake of fact is a defense, and mistake of law is not. However, many exceptions to each rule have been developed. A few of these exceptions are noted here.

Mistake of fact is a defense whenever it negates the mens rea aspect of a crime. For example, an intent to steal another's property is an element of theft. If an attorney picks up a briefcase believing it to be his or hers when it is actually someone else's, it is not theft. The mistake negates the intent to steal. To be valid, mistakes must be made honestly and in good faith.

Although honest mistakes of fact usually constitute a defense, there are exceptions. One exception is obvious: strict liability crimes, as there is no requirement of mens rea to negate.

In some instances, an honest but unreasonable mistake of fact may not eliminate culpability entirely; however, it may reduce the crime. The imperfect self-defense previously discussed falls into this category.

We have all heard, if not quipped, "Ignorance of the law is no excuse." As a general rule, this statement is true. There are two situations in which a person can make a mistake of law. The first occurs when an individual is unaware that his or her actions are prohibited by statute: "I didn't know it was against the law not to file a tax return!" The second occurs when a person takes an act, under the color of a legal right and in good faith, only to find out later that the act was illegal. For example, a landlord may have a reasonable, but mistaken, belief that she has a right to take possessions from a tenant's house to satisfy a delinquent rent debt.

For the most part, unawareness that an act is illegal is not a defense. The law presumes that everyone knows what is legal and what is not. Mistakes that fall into the second group act to negate mens rea and are more likely to be successful. The landlord in the example would not be guilty of larceny because of the mistake. Another example of such a defense is when a person has a reasonable, but mistaken, belief that he or she has the authority to take a person into custody. Therefore, officers who arrest people in good faith, but without probable cause, are not guilty of kidnapping or criminal confinement.

Another exception to the rule that mistake of law is no defense exists when a person relies on statutes, judicial opinions, or certain administrative decisions that later turn out to be wrong. The rule is sound for two reasons. First, as a matter of public policy, it is not wise to prosecute people for acting in conformity with the law. The result would be individual interpretation of all laws and disregard for those statutes, regulations, or judicial decisions believed incorrect. Second, as a matter of due process, it appears that no notice has been provided that compliance with the law will be punished.

Finally, one defense that is not accepted is reliance on the advice of counsel. If a lawyer advises a client that a particular act is legal when it is not, the client will be liable for the crime if the act is taken.

ENTRAPMENT Don't worry

To what extent should police officers be permitted to encourage someone to commit a crime? This question underlies the defense of **entrapment.** Entrapment occurs when law enforcement officers encourage a person to commit a crime with the intent of arresting and prosecuting that person for the commission of that crime.

Perjury traps are another form of entrapment. Perjury traps are committed by prosecutors whenever they inquire of a witness as to matters that are tangential or peripheral to an investigation in order to catch the witness in perjury.[37]

Entrapment is a defense of recent development, although all states and the federal government recognize some form of the defense today. There is no constitutional basis for the entrapment defense, so each jurisdiction is free to structure the defense in any manner. Of course, a state may also do away with the defense, although none have done so. This is a sound policy decision, as most people would agree that there must be some limit on police conduct. However, where the line should be drawn is debated. Currently two tests are used to determine whether a defendant was entrapped: the subjective and objective tests.

The test used in the federal system and most widely used by the states is the subjective test. The test attempts to distinguish between those who are predisposed to commit crime from those who are not. The test is subjective; the defendant's mental state at the time of the encouragement is imperative. A defendant is predisposed if he or she is ready to commit the crime and is only awaiting the opportunity. The Supreme Court has said that the subjective test is designed to draw a line between the "unwary innocent and the unwary criminal."[38]

Under the subjective approach, evidence of the defendant's criminal record may be relevant to show predisposition. For example, drug convictions may evidence a predisposition to enter into future drug purchases or sales.

The second method of determining whether a person was entrapped is objective. The Model Penal Code[39] adopts this approach, as do a minority of states. The objective approach does not focus on the particular defendant's predisposition, but asks whether the police conduct creates a "substantial risk that an offense will be committed by persons other than those who are ready to commit it."[40]

The defendant's actual state of mind is not relevant to this inquiry, and, accordingly, evidence of a defendant's criminal history is irrelevant. Under this approach, defendants may be acquitted even though they were predisposed to commit the crime. Suppose a police officer offers a prostitute $150,000 for sex. The prostitute would have agreed had the officer offered $50. Using the subjective approach, the prostitute would be convicted because she was predisposed to engage in prostitution. However, in jurisdictions using the objective test, she may have been entrapped, as women who do not normally sell sex might be encouraged to do so for $150,000.

In many states entrapment may not be used to defend against crimes involving violence to people, such as battery and murder. The Model Penal Code also takes this view.

ALIBI AND CONSENT

Alibi and consent are two factual defenses. An **alibi** is a claim by a defendant that he or she was not present at the scene of the crime at the time it was committed. Whenever defendants assert an alibi, they are simply refuting the government's factual claims. Alibi is an affirmative defense, and defendants are usually required to give the government notice of the alibi claim prior to trial. Alibi notice laws have been approved by the Supreme Court.[41] Of course, the government must prove the elements of the crime (e.g., presence at the crime) beyond a reasonable doubt. This means that the defendant bears no burden in an alibi defense.

Victim **consent** is a defense to some crimes, such as rape or larceny. That is, if a person consents to sex or to give you his property, there is no crime. Consent is, however, not a defense to many crimes, such as statutory rape, incest, child molestation, battery, and murder.

alibi

■ (Latin) "Elsewhere"; the claim that at the time a crime was committed a person was somewhere else. [pronounce: *al*-eh-bi]

consent

■ Voluntary and active agreement.

STATUTES OF LIMITATION

Many crimes must be prosecuted within a specified time after being committed. A **statute of limitation** sets the time limit. If prosecution is initiated after the applicable statute has expired, the defendant is entitled to a dismissal.

Statutes vary in length; and serious crimes, such as murder, have no limitation. Generally, the higher the crime in the jurisdiction's classification system, the longer the statute. Statutes begin running when the crime occurs; however, statutes may be tolled in some situations. *Tolling* refers to stopping the clock. The time during which a defendant is a fugitive is commonly tolled. For example, assume that the limitation on felony assault is 6 years. The assault was committed on June 1, 2009. Normally, prosecution would have to be started by June 1, 2015. However, if the defendant was fugitive from June 1, 2009, to June 1, 2010, then the statute would be tolled, and the new date of limitation would be June 1, 2016. There is no limit to how long a tolling period may run.

In 2005, a defendant in New York was tried for the second time for one of a series of rapes he committed in 1970s. He became known as the Silver Springs rapist at the time of the attacks. His first trial had occurred 33 years earlier. It concluded with a hung jury, after which he fled the jurisdiction. This tolled the clock on the statute of limitation. While he was a fugitive, incriminating DNA evidence was recovered and DNA science developed into a reliable prosecution tool. He was eventually discovered and apprehended when he applied to purchase a gun in Georgia. He was extradited from Georgia to New York, where his DNA sample was collected. His sample not only connected him to the rapes in New York but to rapes in other states where DNA evidence existed. He was convicted at his second trial. Interestingly, the case caught the public's attention and was a catalyst to a change in statute of limitations law in New York. Today, there is no limitation in rape cases.[42]

statute of limitation

■ Federal and state statutes prescribing the maximum period of time during which various types of civil actions and criminal prosecutions can be brought after the occurrence of the injury or the offense.

At common law there were no statutes of limitations, and they do not appear to have a constitutional underpinning. They are purely legislative creations. This being so, legislatures are free to alter or abolish statutes of limitation. If there is no limitation fixed, prosecution may occur any time after the crime.

Sometimes a prosecution for a serious crime may begin after the statute on a lesser included crime has expired. For example, battery is a lesser included crime of aggravated battery. Assume that aggravated battery has a 6-year statute and battery 3 years. In most jurisdictions, a prosecutor may not circumvent the 3-year statute by charging aggravated battery and including the lesser battery offense in the information or indictment. After the time has run out on the lesser offense, but not on the more serious offense, the defendant is either convicted of the greater offense or acquitted, but can no longer be convicted on the lesser offense. However, at least one jurisdiction does not follow this rule.[43]

Ethical Considerations

PLAYING BOTH SIDES OF THE FENCE

Raleigh George Spain pled guilty and was convicted of burglary of a dwelling in a Texas Court in 1976. He was sentenced to 10 years' probation. Later, he violated the terms of his probation by committing the offenses of failing to report to his probation officer, changing his residence without notifying his probation officer, and failing to pay required fees. As a consequence, the district attorney filed a petition to revoke Spain's probation. He was found in violation of the terms of his probation at hearing, his probation was revoked, and he was sentenced to the remaining eight years of his term of imprisonment.

This case would not be noteworthy except for one fact: The prosecuting attorney had been the defense counsel in the trial court. On appeal the revocation was reversed. The Court stated:

This duty to avoid a conflict of interest has long been imposed on the prosecutors of this State . . . .

Section 1.2 of the American Bar Association's Standards Relating to the Prosecution Function and the Defense Function provides that

(a) A prosecutor should avoid the appearance or reality of a conflict of interest with respect to his official duties.

(b) A conflict of interest may arise when, for example, . . .

(iii) a former client or associate is a defendant in a criminal case.

The commentary to this section states:

. . . When a conflict of interest may arise the prosecutor should recuse himself and make appropriate arrangements for the handling of the particular matter

Ethical Considerations (continued)

by other counsel . . . It is of the utmost importance that the prosecutor avoid participation in a case in circumstances where any implication of partiality may cast a shadow over the integrity of his office.

When a district attorney prosecutes someone whom he previously represented in the same case, the conflict of interest is obvious and the integrity of the prosecutor's office suffers correspondingly. Moreover, there exists the very real danger that the district attorney would be prosecuting the defendant on the basis of facts acquired by him during the existence of his former professional relationship with the defendant. Use of such confidential knowledge would be a violation of the attorney-client relationship and would be clearly prejudicial to the defendant. *See Gajewski v. United States*, 321 F.2d 261 (8th Cir. 1963). The prosecutor in this case should never have initiated or participated in the revocation proceedings.

When an appointed counsel has an actual conflict of interest, a defendant is denied his right of effective representation, without the necessity of a showing of specific prejudice . . . . We likewise conclude that when a prosecutor proceeds against a defendant whom he formerly represented as defense counsel in the same case, no specific prejudice need be shown by the defendant.

We hold that Article 2.01, *supra*, has been violated, and petitioner has been denied due process of law under the Fourteenth Amendment to the Constitution of the United States and Article I, Section 19 of the Texas Constitution.

As this case illustrates, ethical violations by prosecutors can transcend the applicable code of conduct; they can lead to constitutional, often due process, violations.

See *Ex parte Spain*, 589 S.W.2d 132 (Tex.Cr.App., 1979) and *Ex parte Morgan*, 616 S.W.2d 625 (Tex.Cr.App., 1981).

Web Links

International and Comparative Law

Several sites contain government, law, and justice information from many nations and international organizations from around the globe.

At *http://www.lawresearch.com* you will find both United States and foreign government legal information. Hieros Gamos claims to have descriptions and laws from all the nations of the world. It is an excellent site full of text and graphics. The URL is *http://www.hg.org/index.html*

Constitutions of nations can be found in the following locations:

http://confinder.richmond.edu/

http://www.findlaw.com/01topics/06constitutional/03forconst/index.html

Key Terms

affirmative defenses

alibi

battered woman syndrome

burden of persuasion

burden of production

burden of proof

castle doctrine

consent

diminished capacity

duress

Durham rule

entrapment

irresistible impulse

M'Naghten rule

necessity

retreat to the wall doctrine /
   retreat doctrine

self-defense

stand-your-ground

statute of limitation

Review Questions

1. What are affirmative defenses? How do affirmative defenses differ from other defenses?

2. What are the elements of the M'Naghten test for insanity? Irresistible impulse? Model Penal Code?

3. What must be proven to support a claim of self-defense?

4. What is the retreat doctrine?

5. What is imperfect self-defense? When is it applicable?

6. When may a law enforcement officer use deadly force to stop a fleeing suspect?

7. What is entrapment? What are the two tests used to determine if a defendant was entrapped?

8. May an insane defendant be tried? If not, what standard is used to determine whether the defendant is insane?

9. What is a statute of limitations?

10. Distinguish legal from factual impossibility, and state whether a person is criminally culpable in both circumstances.

Problems & Critical Thinking Exercises

1. Should law enforcement be permitted to encourage children to engage in criminal activity with the purpose of arresting and prosecuting the child? Should law enforcement be permitted to use family and friend relationships to induce another to engage in criminal activity with the purpose of arresting and prosecuting the family member or friend? How about preying on another's drug or alcohol addiction?

2. Ira stabbed his good friend, inflicting a fatal wound. At trial, a psychiatrist testified that Ira could not control his behavior, as he has a brain tumor that causes him to act violently. The doctor also testified that the condition did not impair Ira's ability to know what he was doing or that it was wrong. Assume that the jury believes the psychiatrist's explanation. Would Ira be convicted in a jurisdiction that uses the M'Naghten test? The irresistible impulse test? The Model Penal Code?

3. Jane was attacked by an unknown man. She was able to free herself and ran to a nearby house, with the man chasing close behind. She screamed and knocked at the door of the house.

The occupants of the house opened the door, and she requested refuge. The occupant refused, but Jane forced her way into the house. To gain entry, Jane had to strike the occupant. Once inside, she used the telephone to contact the police, who responded within minutes. At the insistence of the occupants of the house, Jane has been charged with trespass and battery. Does she have a defense?

4. Gary and Gene were both drinking at a bar. Gary became angered after Gene asked Gary's wife to dance. Gary walked up to Gene and struck him in the face. Gene fell to the floor, and as he was returning to his feet Gary hit him again. In response, Gene took a knife out of his pocket and attacked Gary with it. Gary then shot Gene with a gun he had hidden in his coat. The injury proved fatal. What crime has Gary committed?

Endnotes

1. See Henry F. Fradella, "From Insanity to Beyond Diminished Capacity: Mental Illness and Criminal Excuse in the Post-Clark Era," 18 U. *Fla. J. L. & Pub. Pol'y* 7, 28 (2007); and Samuel J. Brakel, "Searching for the Therapy in Therapeutic Jurisprudence," 33 *New Eng. J. on Crim. & Civ. Confinement* 455, fn82 (2007).

2. *M'Naghten's Case,* 8 Eng. Rep. 718 (H.L. 1843).

3. LaFave & Scott, *Criminal Law* § 4.2A(a)(Hornbook Series, St. Paul: West, 1986).

4. *State v. Johnson,* 290 N.W. 159 (Wis. 1940).

5. Model Penal Code, Tent. Draft 4, at 156.

6. LaFave & Scott at § 4.2(d).

7. *United States v. Brawner,* 471 F.2d 969 (D.C. Cir. 1972).

8. Model Penal Code § 4.01(1).

9. 18 U.S.C. § 17.

10. Justine A. Dunlap, "What's Competence Got To Do With It: The Right Not To Be Acquitted by Reason of Insanity," 50 *Okla. L. Rev.* 495 (1997).

11. 18 Pa. C.S.A. § 314.

12. 18 U.S.C. § 3006A(e)(3).

13. 18 U.S.C. § 17.

14. Model Penal Code § 4.08.

15. 18 U.S.C. § 4243(a).

16. 18 U.S.C. § 4243(f).

17. Angela Paulsen, Limiting the Scope of State Power to Confine Insanity Acquittees: *Foucha v. Louisiana, 28 Tulsa L.J,* 537 (1993).

18. Callahan, L., Steadman, H., McGreevy, M., Robbins, P. (1991) "The Volume and Characteristics of Insanity Defense Pleas: An Eight-State Study," *Bulletin of the American Academy of Psychiatry and the Law,* 19(4): 331 – 338.

19. Conner, K. (2006) Factors in a Successful Use of the Insanity Defense, *Internet Journal of Criminology*.

20. *Dusky v. United States,* 362 U.S. 402 (1960).

21. 517 U.S. 348.

22. *Jackson v. Indiana,* 406 U.S. 715 (1972).

23. *Ford v. Wainwright,* 477 U.S. 399 (1986).

24. *Id.* at 417.

25. *Atkins v. Virginia,* 122 S. Ct. 2242 (2002).

26. Winton, R., Quinones, S., Blankstein, A., Bank robbers use bomb to coerce East L.A. bank manager, *Los Angeles Times,* September 5, 2012, found at http://articles.latimes.com/2012/sep/05/local/la-me-bank-bomb-20120906

27. *See* LaFave & Scott at § 5.3(g).

28. See New York Times: Times Topics at www.nytimes.com and search for Treyvon Martin.

29. Model Penal Code § 3.04(2)(b)(ii).

30. O.R.C. §2901.05.

31. There are 21 states with stand-your-ground laws, according to the National Conference of State Legislatures; found on May 10, 2013, at http://www.ncsl.org/issues-research/justice/self-defense-and-stand-your-ground.aspx

32. Fla. Stat. §776.012.

33. Model Penal Code § 3.06(d).

34. Model Penal Code § 3.06(5).

35. Model Penal Code § 3.07(2)(b)(ii).

36. 518 U.S. 37 (1996).

37. *See Vermont v. Tonzola,* 621 A.2d 243 (Vt. 1993).

38. *Sherman v. United States,* 356 U.S. 369 (1958).

39. Model Penal Code § 2.13.

40. Model Penal Code § 2.13(2).

41. *Williams v. Florida,* 399 U.S. 78 (1970).

42. Sources: Emily Jane Goodman, "State Removes Statute of Limitations for Rape Cases," *Gotham Gazette: New York City News and Policy,* June 2006; Fox News, November 10, 2005, and Julia Preston, "After Thirty-Two Years, Clothing Yields A DNA Key to Dozens of Rapes," *New York Times,* New York Region, April 27, 2005.

43. 21 Am. Jur. 2d 225 (1990); *State v. Borucki,* 505 A.2d 89 (Me. 1986).

CHAPTER 9

CONSTITUTIONAL DEFENSES

Chapter Outline

Introduction
Double Jeopardy
Self-Incrimination and Immunity
Due Process and Equal Protection
Vagueness and Overbreadth
Analyzing Constitutional Claims
Ex Post Facto and Bills of Attainder
First Amendment and Religion
First Amendment and Speech
Privacy and Other Unenumerated Rights
Privileges and Immunities
Ethical Considerations: *Are Federal Prosecutors Subject to State Ethics Rules?*

Chapter Objectives

After completing this chapter, you should be able to:

- identify and describe specific rights discussed in the chapter, such as freedom from double jeopardy, to speak, to practice one's religion, from the establishment of a religion by the government, to privacy, to be treated equally, and to substantive and procedural due process.

- identify and explain the landmark Supreme Court cases featured in the chapter.

- apply the basic principles learned in the chapter to fact scenarios.

- identify the material facts and legal issues in two-thirds of the cases you read, and describe the court's analyses and conclusions in these cases.

INTRODUCTION

By its nature, a constitutional right is also a constitutional defense. After all, a right is something that may be asserted by person without suffering reprisal from the government. Inherently, a right stands as a limit on government. So, when a government interferes with speech, one defense may be the protection of speech itself. A variety of defenses arise from rights secured by the U.S. Constitution. Most of these rights are found in the first nine, as well as the Thirteenth, Fourteenth, and Fifteenth Amendments. You have already learned a few of these, such as the First Amendment's protection of expression. In addition, many rights that are procedural, such as the right to a speedy trial, are discussed later. A few critical defenses have been chosen for discussion in this chapter. The big dogs of criminal procedure, the Fourth, Fifth, and Sixth Amendments, are not examined in this chapter because they receive considerable attention in the chapters that follow.

Be aware that each state has its own constitution, which may provide greater protection than the U.S. Constitution. During this discussion you may want to refer to the U.S. Constitution, which is reprinted as Appendix A of this text.

DOUBLE JEOPARDY

double jeopardy clause

■ A second prosecution by the same government against the same person for the same crime (or for a lesser included offense) once the first prosecution is totally finished and decided. This is prohibited by the U.S. Constitution.

The Fifth Amendment to the U.S. Constitution provides that "no person shall be subject for the same offense to be twice put in jeopardy of life or limb." The principle of not punishing someone twice for the same act can be found as far back as Blackstone's *Commentaries* in the 1700s.[1] The **Double Jeopardy Clause** applies only to criminal proceedings.

There are actually two prohibitions in the Double Jeopardy Clause. The clause prevents: (1) a second prosecution for the same offense and (2) a second punishment for the same offense.

Often the legal question in double jeopardy cases is whether a prior "jeopardy" occurred. It is generally held that a person has been put in jeopardy once a plea of guilty has been entered and accepted by a court. An unapproved plea will not suffice, and a subsequent prosecution will not be prohibited by the Double Jeopardy Clause. In jury trials, jeopardy attaches once a jury has been selected and sworn. States treat bench trials differently, although the prevailing view is that jeopardy attaches when the first witness has been sworn.

Once jeopardy attaches, the defendant may not be tried again. However, there are a few exceptions. A defendant may be retried if the first trial was terminated by a properly declared mistrial. Mistrials may be declared for a variety of reasons. Death of the trial judge or one of the participating attorneys would likely result in a mistrial. If a witness blurts out an answer to a question before the judge has an opportunity to sustain an objection to the question, and the answer is extremely prejudicial, a mistrial may be declared. The causes of a mistrial are endless. Note that the mistrial must be proper. That is, if an appellate court later determines that a mistrial should not have been declared, the defendant has been put into jeopardy. It is always proper to retry a defendant whose prior trial was declared a mistrial upon the defendant's motion. If a defendant objects to a government motion for a mistrial, there must be a "manifest necessity" (darn good reason) for the mistrial.[2]

It is also not a violation of the Fifth Amendment to prosecute a defendant who was previously charged but whose charges were dismissed prior to jeopardy attaching. Additionally, if a defendant appeals a conviction and prevails, the defendant may be retried, unless the appellate court finds that insufficient evidence exists to retry the defendant. However, if defendants are acquitted on a serious charge and convicted on a lesser and then prevail on appeal, they may be retried only on the lesser. It is violative of the Fifth Amendment to retry the defendant on the more serious offense. Whether a defendant may be retried following government appeals has been an issue in many cases. Clearly, the government may not win a new trial following an acquittal. However, a conviction may be reinstated by an appellate court if a trial court's order setting aside the conviction is found invalid.[3] But an appellate court may not order a new trial where the trial judge entered a judgement of acquittal following a hung jury.[4] The outcomes in this area of law are dependent upon what judgement is first entered by the trial court. If it is a conviction, then an appellate court may tamper with trial judge reversals of convictions. If it is an acquittal, then double jeopardy bars acting further against the accused.

The Supreme Court has also held that double jeopardy does not bar correcting a sentence on appeal or rehearing because such a procedure is not retrial of an "offense." However, the outcome may be different if resentencing results in the application of the death penalty.[5]

The Fifth Amendment only forbids retrial for the same offense. Determining whether two acts constitute the same offense is not always an easy task. Two offenses are the same unless one requires proof of a fact that the other does not.[6] This is the "same evidence test." The civil law concept of collateral estoppel, or the preclusion of relitigating the same issue, applies in criminal cases as well. The Supreme Court first announced this in *Ashe v. Swenson*.

ASHE V. SWENSON
397 U.S. 436 (1970)

Sometime in the early hours of the morning of January 10, 1960, six men were engaged in a poker game in the basement of the home of John Gladson at Lee's Summit, Missouri. Suddenly three or four masked men, armed with a shotgun and pistols, broke into the basement and robbed each of the poker players of money and various articles of personal property. The robbers—and it has never been clear whether there were three or four of them—then fled in a car belonging to one of the victims of the robbery. Shortly thereafter the stolen car was discovered in a field, and later that morning three men were arrested by a state trooper while they were walking on a highway not far from where the abandoned car had been found. The petitioner was arrested by another officer some distance away.

(continued)

ASHE V. SWENSON (continued)

The four were subsequently charged with seven separate offenses—the armed robbery of each of the six poker players and the theft of the car. In May 1960 the petitioner went to trial on the charge of robbing Donald Knight, one of the participants in the poker game. At the trial the State called Knight and three of his fellow poker players as prosecution witnesses. Each of them described the circumstances of the holdup and itemized his own individual losses. The proof that an armed robbery had occurred and that personal property had been taken from Knight as well as from each of the others was unassailable. The testimony of the four victims in this regard was consistent both internally and with that of the others. But the State's evidence that the petitioner had been one of the robbers was weak. Two of the witnesses thought that there had been only three robbers altogether, and could not identify the petitioner as one of them. Another of the victims, who was the petitioner's uncle by marriage, said that at the "patrol station" he had not positively identified each of the other three men accused of the holdup, but could say only that the petitioner's voice "sounded very much like" that of one of the robbers. The fourth participant in the poker game did identify the petitioner, but only by his "size and height, and his actions."

The cross-examination of these witnesses was brief, and it was aimed primarily at exposing the weakness of their identification testimony. Defense counsel made no attempt to question their testimony regarding the holdup itself or their claims as to their losses. Knight testified without contradiction that the robbers had stolen from him his watch, $250 in cash, and about $500 in checks. His billfold, which had been found by the police in the possession of one of the three other men accused of the robbery, was admitted in evidence. The defense offered no testimony and waived final argument.

The trial judge instructed the jury that if it found that the petitioner was one of the participants in the armed robbery, the theft of 'any money' from Knight would sustain a conviction (citation omitted). He also instructed the jury that if the petitioner was one of the robbers, he was guilty under the law even if he had not personally robbed Knight (citation omitted). The jury—though not instructed to elaborate upon its verdict—found the petitioner "not guilty due to insufficient evidence." . . .

Six weeks later the petitioner was brought to trial again, this time for the robbery of another participant in the poker game, a man named Roberts. The petitioner filed a motion to dismiss, based on his previous acquittal. The motion was overruled, and the second trial began. The witnesses were for the most part the same, though this time their testimony was substantially stronger on the issue of the petitioner's identity. For example, two witnesses who at the first trial had been wholly unable to identify the petitioner as one of the robbers, now testified that his features, size, and mannerisms matched those of one of their assailants. Another witness who before had identified the petitioner only by his size and actions now also remembered him by the unusual sound of his voice. The State further refined its case at the second trial by declining to call one of the participants in the poker game whose identification testimony at the first trial had been conspicuously negative. The case went to the jury on instructions virtually identical to those given at the first trial. This time the jury found the petitioner guilty, and he was sentenced to a 35-year term in the state penitentiary. . . .

"Collateral estoppel" is an awkward phrase, but it stands for an extremely important principle in our adversary system of justice. It means simply that when an issue of ultimate fact has once been determined by a valid and final judgment, that issue

ASHE V. SWENSON (continued)

cannot again be litigated between the same parties in any future lawsuit. Although first developed in civil litigation, collateral estoppel has been an established rule of federal criminal law at least since this Court's decision more than 50 years ago. . . .

Straightforward application of the federal rule to the present case can lead to but one conclusion. For the record is utterly devoid of any indication that the first jury could rationally have found that an armed robbery had not occurred, or that Knight had not been a victim of that robbery. The single rationally conceivable issue in dispute before the jury was whether the

petitioner had been one of the robbers. And the jury by its verdict found that he had not. The federal rule of law, therefore, would make a second prosecution for the robbery of Roberts wholly impermissible.

The ultimate question to be determined . . . is whether this established rule of federal law is embodied in the Fifth Amendment guarantee against double jeopardy. We do not hesitate to hold that it is (citation omitted). For whatever else that constitutional guarantee may embrace, it surely protects a man who has been acquitted from having to "run the gantlet" a second time. . . .

The Double Jeopardy Clause is fully applicable to the states through the Fourteenth Amendment. However, the clause does not prevent second punishments for the same offense by different sovereigns. For example, a person who robs a federally insured bank may be prosecuted by both the state where the bank resides and the United States. This is true even though the offenses arise from the same acts. Although the Double Jeopardy Clause does not prohibit two sovereigns from prosecuting for the same offense, many states prohibit this by statute. In practice, and sometimes by policy, most prosecutors do not pursue a defendant who has been previously prosecuted in another jurisdiction for the same crime. The Model Penal Code incorporates this approach in certain circumstances.[7] Municipalities are not independent beings; they owe their existence not to the Constitution of the United States, but to a state. Accordingly, prosecutions by cities are treated as being brought by the state, and it is a violation of the Double Jeopardy Clause for a state and city to punish one for the same offense.

SELF-INCRIMINATION AND IMMUNITY

The Fifth Amendment also states that no person "shall be compelled in any criminal case to be a witness against himself." The following passage explains why the framers of the Constitution included a privilege against self-incrimination.

Perhaps the best-known provision of the Fifth Amendment is the clause against forced "self-incrimination," whose origin goes back to England where persons accused of crimes before ecclesiastical courts were forced to take an ex officio oath. That is, they had to swear to answer all questions even if the questions did not apply to the case at trial. This requirement was later adopted by the Court of Star Chamber. One of the victims of the Court was a printer and book distributor named John Lilburne, charged in 1637 with treason for importing books "that promoted Puritan dissent." Lilburne told his accusers, "I am not willing to answer to you any more of these questions because I see you go about by this examination to ensnare me. For seeing the things for which I am imprisoned cannot be proved against me, you will get other material out of my examination; and therefore if you will not ask me about the thing laid to my charge, I shall answer no more. . . . I think by the law of the land, that I may stand upon my just defense." Lilburne was convicted, fined, whipped, pilloried, gagged, and imprisoned until he agreed to take the oath. . . .

One notorious instance of forced self-incrimination in the American colonies occurred in the Salem witch trials. In 1692, Giles Corey, an elderly Massachusetts farmer, was accused of witchcraft. He knew whether he pleaded guilty or not guilty he would be convicted and executed and his property confiscated. So to assure that his heirs inherited his property, he refused to plead and thus could not be convicted. The judges ordered him strapped to a table, and stones were loaded upon his chest to force the plea out of him. Corey's final words were "more weight." Then his chest caved in.[8]

John Bradshaw, John Lilburne's attorney, stated it best when he said that "It is contrary to the laws of God, nature and the kingdom for any man to be his own accuser."

Generally, the Fifth Amendment prohibits the government from compelling people to testify when incrimination is possible. Most people have heard of "pleading the Fifth." However, if immunity from prosecution is granted to a witness, he or she may be compelled to testify. If a witness refuses to testify because of the fear of self-incrimination, the government may offer the witness immunity from prosecution so that the testimony may be compelled. There are two types of immunity: transactional and derivative use.

transactional immunity

■ Freedom from prosecution for all crimes related to the compelled testimony, so long as the witness tells the truth.

Transactional immunity shields witnesses from prosecution for all offenses related to their testimony. For example, if a witness testifies concerning a robbery, the government may not prosecute the witness for that robbery, even though the government may have evidence of guilt independent of the witness's testimony. Transactional immunity gives more protection to the witness than is required by the Constitution, so when it is granted, a witness may be ordered to testify.

use immunity

■ Freedom from prosecution based on the compelled testimony and on anything the government learns from following up on the testimony.

The minimum immunity that must be provided a witness to overcome a Fifth Amendment claim is derivative **use immunity.** This prohibits the government from using the witness's testimony or any evidence derived from that testimony to prosecute the witness. However, all evidence that is independently obtained may be used against the witness.

Use immunity only prohibits the government from using the witness's testimony against him or her. Statutes that provide only for use immunity are unconstitutional, as derivative use is the minimum protection required by the Fifth Amendment.

States vary in how immunity is granted. Some permit the prosecutor to give the immunity; others require both the request of the prosecutor and the approval of the trial judge.

A person may also waive the Fifth Amendment privilege against self-incrimination. Generally, once a person testifies freely, the privilege is waived as to the subject discussed during the same proceeding. A witness (or defendant) may not testify selectively concerning a subject. It is often said that testifying to a fact waives to the details. This principle prevents witnesses from testifying only to the information beneficial to one party and then refusing to testify further, even though they may have omitted important facts. However, witness may not be compelled to testify if there is a chance of incriminating themselves beyond the original testimony.

The fact that a witness may waive the Fifth Amendment privilege against self-incrimination on one occasion does not mean it is waived forever. First, a defendant (or witness) may speak to the police during the investigative stage and later refuse to testify at trial, provided such testimony may be incriminating. Second, it is generally held that a person who testifies before a grand jury without claiming the Fifth does not waive the right to raise the defense at trial. Third, even within the same proceeding a person may invoke the Fifth Amendment privilege against self-incrimination if the two hearings are separate and distinct. For example, a defendant may testify at a suppression hearing without waiving the privilege not to testify at trial.

Finally, the Fifth Amendment applies to all proceedings, whether civil, criminal, or administrative.[9] Therefore, a person called to testify in a civil proceeding may invoke the Fifth Amendment's privilege and refuse to testify.

DUE PROCESS AND EQUAL PROTECTION

The Fifth Amendment to the U.S. Constitution prohibits the government from depriving a person of life, liberty, or property without due process of law. This amendment acts to constrain the power of the federal government. You have previously learned that the Fourteenth Amendment has similar language and constrains the power of state governments.

The Fourteenth Amendment expressly requires the states to extend equal protection of the laws to the people. There is no express equal protection clause in the Fifth Amendment, but the Supreme Court has found it to be implied in the Due Process Clause. Equal protection concerns classifications and discrimination.

Discrimination is not inherently evil. Students discriminate between professors, possibly due to grading policy or teaching skill, when deciding what courses to enroll in. Governments also discriminate and make classifications, most of which are sensible and acceptable. For example, those who commit homicides are divided into groups: murderers, manslaughterers, and those who are excused or justified in killing. When classifications are based upon meaningful criteria (e.g., mens rea), the law is valid. However, our society has decided that certain classifications are improper and violative of equal protection. A classification between those who exercise a constitutional right and those who do not, if it results in prosecution or increased punishment for the former, is unconstitutional. Classifications based on race, religion, gender, and other immutable conditions are suspect and possibly violative of equal protection.

These clauses are important to criminal law and particularly to criminal procedure. Due process requires the government to treat people fairly; therefore, whenever a law or other governmental action appears to be unfair, there is a due process issue. In a sense, due process is a safety net, protecting the individual when another specific constitutional provision does not.

Due process has two aspects, substantive and procedural. The protection of privacy discussed later in this chapter is an example of substantive due process. On the procedural side, due process is the constitutional source of the **principle of legality**, which requires that criminal laws (and punishments) be written and enacted before an act may be punished. This is a notice concept. It would be unfair to announce that an act is illegal, or increase its punishment, after that act has been committed. You will learn later in this chapter that overly broad or vague laws may be violative of due process.

Through the Fourteenth Amendment's Due Process Clause, most of the provisions of the Bill of Rights, which initially applied only against the federal government, have been extended to the states. Today, the Fourth Amendment's right to be free from unreasonable searches and seizures, the Fifth Amendment's right to be free from self-incrimination, the Sixth Amendment's right to counsel at critical stages of criminal adjudications, and the Eighth Amendment's prohibition of cruel and unusual punishment are among the many rights that are now available to defendants in state courts.

In some instances, due process or equal protection increases the scope of a right found in the Bill of Rights. For example, the Sixth Amendment's right to counsel is limited to the critical stages of criminal proceedings. Appeals are not critical stages, and therefore the Sixth Amendment does not mandate counsel. But the Supreme Court has held that if a state provides for felony appeals by right, then the Equal Protection Clause requires that indigent defendants receive appointed counsel. To hold otherwise would unfairly discriminate against the indigent.[10]

Although the Fourteenth Amendment is the source of the incorporation of most of the Bill of Rights, its importance extends further. Any time an issue of fairness surfaces, due process should be examined. If the issue concerns one of improper classifications, equal protection law should be considered. The Supreme Court stated of substantive due process:

> The inescapable fact is that adjudication of substantive due process claims may call upon the Court in interpreting the Constitution to exercise that same capacity which by tradition courts always have exercised: reasoned judgment. Its boundaries are not susceptible of expression as a simple rule. That does not mean we are free to invalidate state policy choices with which we disagree: yet neither does it permit us to shrink from the duties of our office. As Justice Harlan observed: "Due process has not been reduced to any formula: its content cannot be determined by reference to any code. The best that can be said is that through the course of this Court's decisions it has represented the balance which our Nation, built upon postulates of respect for liberty of the individual, has struck between that liberty and the demands of organized society."

principle of legality

■ The procedural side of due process, which requires that criminal laws (and punishments) be written and enacted before an act may be punished.

VAGUENESS AND OVERBREADTH

The Due Process Clauses of the Fifth and Fourteenth Amendments to the U.S. Constitution are the foundation of the void-for-vagueness and overbreadth doctrines.

A statute is void for **vagueness** whenever "men of common intelligence must necessarily guess at its meaning and differ as to its application."[11] As to the meaning of a statute, confusion among lower courts, resulting in varying interpretations, is evidence of vagueness.[12] The Supreme Court has held that uncertain statutes do not provide notice of what conduct is forbidden and are violative of due process. The Court has also found statutes that permit arbitrary or discriminatory enforcement void. That is, if the police or courts are given unlimited authority to decide who will be prosecuted, the statute is invalid.

It is under the void-for-vagueness doctrine that many vagrancy laws have been attacked. If not for the doctrine, legislatures could draft statutes so that nearly everyone would be engaged in criminal activity at one time or another, and police and prosecutors would have the unfettered discretion to decide who to arrest and prosecute.

A closely related doctrine is **overbreadth.** A statute is overbroad if it includes within its grasp not only unprotected activity but also activity protected by the Constitution. For example, in one case a city ordinance made it illegal for "one or more persons to assemble" on a sidewalk and conduct themselves in an annoying manner. The United States Supreme Court found that the law was unconstitutional not only because it made unprotected activity illegal (fighting words or riotous activity) but also because it included activity that is protected by the First Amendment's free assembly and association provisions.[13] It is possible for a statute to be clear and precise (not vague) but overbroad.

vagueness doctrine

■ The rule that a criminal law may be unconstitutional if it does not clearly say what is required or prohibited, what punishment may be imposed, or what persons may be affected. A law that violates due process of law in this way is *void for vagueness.*

overbreadth doctrine

■ A law will be declared void for *overbreadth* if it attempts to punish speech or conduct that is protected by the Constitution and if it is impossible to eliminate the unconstitutional part of the law without invalidating the whole law.

ANALYZING CONSTITUTIONAL CLAIMS

The United States Supreme Court has developed standards of judicial review for claims that constitutional rights are violated. The first standard is generally known as strict scrutiny. A court applies the strict scrutiny test in one of two circumstances: (1) when the government burdens a fundamental right; and (2) when the government groups people into suspect classes.

As the first of the two, nearly all the rights found in the Constitution are "fundamental," and as such, laws that limit or set them aside are tested by the strict scrutiny test. Remember these standards as you read about the rights—e.g., speech, religion—discussed in this chapter. For the second condition to apply, the government must classify people by race, national origin, or religion.

Laws or actions that burden a fundament right or have a suspect classification are invalid unless the government can demonstrate *compelling governmental interest.*

The government must also show that the law is narrowly tailored to achieve its objectives; that is, it is not overly broad.

Laws that don't encroach upon individual rights and don't classify along suspect lines are tested under an easier standard. They are valid if *rationally related to a legitimate government objective.* There is a third standard that applies to classifications based upon sex and when certain rights are at issue. This standard falls between strict scrutiny and rational relationship: Laws are valid if they are *substantially related to a legitimate governmental objective.* Most—but not all—laws tested under strict scrutiny fail and most laws—but not all—survive review under the rational relationship test.

EX POST FACTO AND BILLS OF ATTAINDER

Article I of the U.S. Constitution prohibits the state and federal governments from enacting both ex post facto laws and bills of attainder.

An **ex post facto law** is one that (1) makes an act illegal after the act was taken, (2) increases the punishment or severity of a crime after it occurred, and (3) changes the procedural rules so as to increase the chances of conviction after the crime occurs. In short, a government may not make criminal law retroactive, if doing so is detrimental to the defendant. However, changes that benefit a defendant may be applied retroactively. So, if a legislature increases the prosecution's burden of proof after a defendant has committed a crime, but before trial, the legislature may make the change applicable to the defendant. The clause advances the notice theory (due process) and prevents malicious legislative action from being taken against a particular person.

A **bill of attainder** is a legislative act punishing a person without a judicial trial. This provision reinforces the concept of separation of powers. It is the duty of the legislative branch to make the laws, and it is the duty of the judicial branch to determine who has violated those laws. Alexander Hamilton, in support of the prohibition of bills of attainder, wrote:

> Nothing is more common than for a free people, in times of heat and violence, to gratify momentary passions by letting into the government principles and precedents which afterwards prove fatal to themselves. Of this kind is the doctrine of disqualification, disfranchisement, and banishment by acts of the legislature. The dangerous consequences of this power are manifest. If the legislature can disfranchise any number of citizens at pleasure by general descriptions, it may soon confine all the votes to a small number of partisans, and establish an aristocracy or an oligarchy; if it may banish at discretion all those whom particular circumstances render obnoxious, without hearing or trial, no man can be safe, nor know when he may be the innocent victim of a prevailing faction. The name of liberty applied to such a government would be a mockery of common sense.[14]

In a few instances, however, Congress may act in a judicial role. Congress may punish those who disrupt its functions for contempt. In addition, Congress is authorized by the Constitution to conduct impeachment hearings of the president, federal judges, and other federal officers and to discipline its own members.

---

ex post facto law

■ (Latin) After the fact. An *ex post facto* law is one that retroactively attempts to make an action a crime that was not a crime at the time it was done, or a law that attempts to reduce a person's rights based on a past act that was not subject to the law when it was done.

bill of attainder

■ A legislative act pronouncing a person guilty (usually of treason) without a trial and sentencing the person to death and attainder. This is now prohibited by the U.S. Constitution.

FIRST AMENDMENT AND RELIGION

The First Amendment contains many protections, including freedom of the press; freedom to choose and practice a religion; freedom of speech; and freedom to peaceably assemble. Although the First Amendment is directly applicable only against the national government, the Fourteenth Amendment extends its prohibitions to the states. The Amendment reads:

> Congress shall make no law respecting an establishment of religion, or prohibiting the free exercise thereof; or abridging the freedom of speech, or of the press; or the right of the people peaceably to assemble, and to petition the government for a redress of grievances.

Concerning freedom of religion, the First Amendment states that "Congress shall make no law respecting an establishment of religion, or prohibiting the free exercise thereof." The Free Exercise Clause is of the most importance in criminal law. The freedom to believe is, of course, absolute. Any law prohibiting a certain religious belief is void. However, the Supreme Court has held that some religious practices may be regulated.

To determine whether a specific religious act may be criminalized, the governmental interest in regulating the behavior is balanced against the First Amendment infringement. If the governmental interest is greater than the infringement, then a state may regulate the conduct. For example, it has been held that the Mormon practice of polygamy may be regulated.[15] Also, a parent who depends upon prayer to save a dying child may be charged with manslaughter for failing to seek competent medical care. In this instance the state's interest in protecting the child's life outweighs the parent's interest in practicing his or her religion in such a manner.

On the other side, the California Supreme Court disallowed the conviction of a member of the Native American Church for possession of peyote, a drug made from cactus. The court found that peyote was an important part of worship in the Native American Church, and, as such, California's interest in regulating the use of the drug was outweighed by the drug's religious significance.[16] Note that the United States Supreme Court took the opposite view concerning the use of peyote in *Department of Human Resources v. Smith*, 494 U.S. 872 (1990), wherein the Court stated that

> [T]he right of free exercise does not relieve an individual of the obligation to comply with a valid and neutral law of general applicability on the ground that the law proscribes (or prescribes) conduct that his religion prescribes (or proscribes).

Note further that Congress reacted to this decision by exempting the use of peyote by Native Americans from the Controlled Substance Act. In the *Hialeah* case, the Supreme Court invalidated several ordinances that prohibited the adherents of Santeria from sacrificing animals as part of their religious rites.

CHURCH OF LUKUMI BABALU AYE, INC. V. HIALEAH
508 U.S. 520 (1993)

This case involves practices of the Santeria religion, which originated in the nineteenth century. When hundreds of thousands of members of the Yoruba people were brought as slaves from eastern Africa to Cuba, their traditional African religion absorbed significant elements of Roman Catholicism. The resulting syncretion, or fusion, is Santeria, "the way of the saints." The Cuban Yoruba express their devotion to spirits, called *orishas*, through the iconography of Catholic saints, Catholic symbols are often present at Santeria rites, and Santeria devotees attend the Catholic sacraments. . . .

The Santeria faith teaches that every individual has a destiny from God, a destiny fulfilled with the aid and energy of orishas. The basis of the Santeria religion is the nurture of a personal relation with the orishas, and one of the principal forms of devotion is an animal sacrifice. . . . The sacrifice of animals as part of religious rituals has ancient roots. . . . Animal sacrifice is mentioned throughout the Old Testament . . . and it played an important role in the practice of Judaism before destruction of the second Temple in Jerusalem. . . . In modern Islam, there is an annual sacrifice commemorating Abraham's sacrifice of a ram in the stead of his son. . . .

According to Santeria teaching, the orishas are powerful but not immortal. They depend for survival on the sacrifice.

Santeria adherents faced widespread persecution in Cuba, so the religion and its rituals were practiced in secret. The open practice of Santeria and its rites remains infrequent. . . . The religion was brought to this Nation most often by exiles from the Cuban revolution. The District Court estimated that there are at least 50,000 practitioners in South Florida today.

Petitioner Church of Lukumi Babalu Aye, Inc. (Church), is a not-for-profit corporation organized under Florida law in 1973. The Church and its congregants practice the Santeria religion. The president of the Church is petitioner Ernesto Pichardo, who is also the Church's priest and holds the religious title of Italero, the second highest in the Santeria faith. In April 1987, the Church leased land in the city of Hialeah, Florida, and announced plans to establish a house of worship as well as a school, cultural center, and museum. Pichardo indicated that the Church's goal was to bring the practice of the Santeria faith, including its ritual of animal sacrifice, into the open.

The Church began the process of obtaining utility service and receiving the necessary licensing, inspection, and zoning approvals. Although the Church's efforts at obtaining the necessary licenses and permits were far from smooth . . . it appears that it received all needed approvals by early August 1987.

The prospect of a Santeria church in their midst was distressing to many members of the Hialeah community, and the announcement of the plans to open a Santeria church in Hialeah prompted the city council to hold an emergency public session on June 9, 1987. [The city council enacted ordinance] 87–66, which noted the "concern" expressed by residents of the city "that certain religions may propose to engage in practices which are inconsistent with public morals, peace or safety," and declared that "[t]he City reiterates its commitment to a prohibition against any and all acts of any and all religious groups which are inconsistent with public morals, peace or safety." Next, the council approved an emergency ordinance, Ordinance 87–40, that incorporated in full, except as to penalty, Florida's animal cruelty laws. . . . Among other things, the incorporated state law subjected to criminal punishment "[w]hoever . . . unnecessarily or cruelly . . . kills any animal."

CHURCH OF LUKUMI BABALU AYE, INC. V. HIALEAH *(continued)*

[In September 1987, the city council adopted three additional ordinances prohibiting owning or possessing an animal for purpose of sacrifice and regulating the slaughtering of animals.] Violations of each of the four ordinances were punishable by fines not exceeding $500 or imprisonment not exceeding 60 days, or both.

Following enactment of these ordinances, the Church and Pichardo filed this action pursuant to 42 U.S.C. § 1983 in the United States District Court for the Southern District of Florida. Named as defendants were the city of Hialeah and its mayor and members of its city council in their individual capacities. [The defendants prevailed at the trial and appellate levels.] . . .

The city does not argue that Santeria is not a "religion" within the meaning of the First Amendment. Nor could it. Although the practice of animal sacrifice may seem abhorrent to some, "religious beliefs need not be acceptable, logical, consistent, or comprehensible to others in order to merit First Amendment protection. . . . Given the historical association between animal sacrifice and religious worship . . . petitioners' assertion that animal sacrifice is an integral part of their religion "cannot be deemed bizarre or incredible." . . . Neither the city nor the courts below, moreover, have questioned the sincerity of petitioners' professed desire to conduct animal sacrifices for religious reasons. We must consider petitioners' First Amendment claim.

In addressing the constitutional protection for free exercise of religion, our cases establish the general proposition that a law that is neutral and of general applicability need not be justified by a compelling governmental interest even if the law has the incidental effect of burdening a particular religious practice. . . . Neutrality and general applicability are interrelated, and, as becomes apparent in this case, failure to satisfy one requirement is a likely indication that the other has not been satisfied. A law failing to satisfy these requirements must be justified by a compelling governmental interest and must be narrowly tailored to advance the interest. These ordinances fail to satisfy the [constitutional] requirements. . . .

There are, of course, many ways of demonstrating that the object or purpose of a law is the suppression of religion or religious conduct. To determine the object of a law, we must begin with its text, for the minimum requirement of neutrality is that a law not discriminate on its face. A law lacks facial neutrality if it refers to a religious practice without a secular meaning discernable from the language or context. Petitioners contend that three of the ordinances fail this test of facial neutrality because they use the words "sacrifice" and "ritual," words with strong religious connotations. . . . We agree that these words are consistent with the claim of facial discrimination, but the argument is not conclusive. The words "sacrifice" and "ritual" have a religious origin, but current use admits also of secular meanings. . . .

We reject the contention advanced by the city . . . that our inquiry must end with the text of the laws at issue. Facial neutrality is not determinative. The Free Exercise Clause, like the Establishment Clause, extends beyond facial discrimination. The Clause "forbids subtle departures from neutrality." . . . The Free Exercise Clause protects against governmental hostility which is masked, as well as overt. "The Court must survey meticulously the circumstances of governmental categories to eliminate, as it were, religious gerrymanders." . . .

The record in this case compels the conclusion that suppression of the central element of the Santeria worship service was the object of the ordinances. First, though the use of the words "sacrifice" and "ritual" does not compel a finding

(continued)

CHURCH OF LUKUMI BABALU AYE, INC. V. HIALEAH (continued)

of improper targeting of the Santeria religion, the choice of these words is support for our conclusion. . . . [One of the ordinances] recited that "residents and citizens of the City of Hialeah have expressed their concern that certain religions may propose to engage in practices which are inconsistent with public morals, peace or safety," and "reiterate[d]" the city's commitment to prohibit "any and all [such] acts of any and all religious groups." No one suggests, and on this record it cannot be maintained, that city officials had in mind a religion other than Santeria.

It becomes evident that these ordinances target Santeria sacrifice when the ordinances' operation is considered. Apart from the text, the effect of a law in its real operation is strong evidence of its object. To be sure, adverse impact will not always lead to a finding of impermissible targeting. . . .

It is a necessary conclusion that almost the only conduct subject to [the ordinances] is the religious exercise of Santeria Church members. The texts show that they were drafted in tandem to achieve this purpose. . . . [One of the ordinances] prohibits the sacrifice of animals but defines sacrifice as "to unnecessarily kill . . . an animal in a public or private ritual or ceremony not for the primary purpose of food consumption." The definition excludes almost all killings of animals except for religious sacrifice, and the primary purpose requirement narrows the proscribed category even further, in particular by exempting Kosher slaughter. . . .

The net result of the gerrymander is that few if any killings of animals are prohibited other than Santeria sacrifice, which is proscribed because it occurs during a ritual or ceremony and its primary purpose is to make an offering to the orishas, not food consumption. Indeed, careful drafting ensured that, although Santeria sacrifice is prohibited, killings that are no more necessary or humane in almost all other circumstances are unpunished.

Operating in similar fashion [is another ordinance] which prohibits the "possess[ion], sacrifice, or slaughter" of an animal with the inten[t] to use such animal for food purposes." This prohibition, extending to the keeping of an animal as well as the killing itself, applies if the animal is killed in "any type of ritual." . . . The ordinance exempts, however, "any licensed [food] establishment" with regard to "any animals which are specifically raised for food purposes," if this activity is permitted by zoning and other laws. This exception, too, seems intended to cover Kosher slaughter. Again, the burden of the ordinance, in practical terms, falls on Santeria adherents but almost no others. . . .

We also find significant evidence of the ordinances' improper targeting of Santeria sacrifice in the fact that they proscribe more religious conduct than is necessary to achieve their stated ends. . . .

The legitimate governmental interests in protecting the public health and preventing cruelty to animals could be addressed by restrictions stopping far short of a flat prohibition of all Santeria sacrificial practice. If improper disposal, not the sacrifice itself, is the harm to be prevented, the city could have imposed a general regulation on the disposal of organic garbage. It did not do so. Indeed, counsel for the city conceded at oral argument that, under the ordinances, Santeria sacrifices would be illegal even if they occurred in licensed, inspected, and zoned slaughterhouses. . . . Thus, these broad ordinances prohibit Santeria sacrifice even when it does not threaten the city's interest in the public health. . . .

Respondent claims that [the ordinances] advance two interests: protecting the public health and preventing cruelty to animals. The ordinances are underinclusive for those ends. They fail to prohibit nonreligious conduct that endangers these interests in a similar or greater degree than Santeria sacrifice does. The underinclusion is substantial, not

CHURCH OF LUKUMI BABALU AYE, INC. V. HIALEAH *(continued)*

inconsequential. Despite the city's proffered interest in preventing cruelty to animals, the ordinances are drafted with care to forbid few killings but those occasioned by religious sacrifice. Many types of animal deaths or kills for nonreligious reasons are either not prohibited or approved by express provision. For example, fishing . . . is legal. Extermination of mice and rats within a home is also permitted. Florida law incorporated by [the ordinances] sanctions euthanasia of "stray, neglected, abandoned, or unwanted animals . . . and the use of live animals "to pursue or take wildlife or to participate in any hunting." . . .

The ordinances are underinclusive as well with regard to the health risk posed by consumption of uninspected meat. Under the city's ordinances, hunters may eat their kill and fisherman may eat their catch without undergoing governmental inspection. . . .

A law burdening religious practice that is not neutral or not of general application must undergo the most rigorous of scrutiny. To satisfy the commands of the First Amendment, a law restrictive of religious practice must advance "interests of the highest order" and must be narrowly tailored in pursuit of those interests . . . The compelling interest standard [applies].

. . . As we have discussed . . . all four ordinances are overbroad or underinclusive in substantial respects. . . .

Respondent has not demonstrated, moreover, that, in the context of these ordinances, its governmental interests are compelling. . . .

The Free Exercise Clause commits government itself to religious tolerance, and upon even slight suspicion that proposals for state intervention stem from animosity to religion or distrust of its practices, all officials must pause to remember their own high duty to the Constitution and to the rights it secures. Those in office must be resolute in resisting importunate demands and must ensure that the sole reasons for imposing the burdens of law and regulation are secular. Legislators may not devise mechanisms, overt or disguised, designed to persecute or oppress a religion or its practices. The laws here in question were enacted contrary to these constitutional principles and they are void. Reversed.

Smith can be distinguished from *Hialeah* because *Smith* involved a law of general applicability. That is, use of the drugs, including peyote, was generally prohibited to everyone. Clearly, the laws were not enacted solely to regulate religious worship. However, in the *Hialeah* case, the Court determined that the regulation was intended to target the Santeria's religious practices. Congress and the White House responded to the Supreme Court's decisions voiding religious practices that are prohibited by laws of general applicability. First, Native American use of peyote as a religious ritual was specifically exempted from The Controlled Substance Act. Second, the Religious Freedom Restoration Act was enacted.[17] Through this statute, courts are required to apply the strict scrutiny test when applying statutes of generally applicability to religious practices. So, a government must demonstrate both a compelling reason and that there is no less restrictive way to accomplish the governmental objective. The new standard was applied in the following 2006 case.

GONZALES V. O CENTRO ESPIRITA BENEFICENTE UNIAO DO VEGETAL
546 U.S. 418 (2006)

CHIEF JUSTICE ROBERTS DELIVERED THE OPINION OF THE COURT

A religious sect with origins in the Amazon Rainforest receives communion by drinking a sacramental tea, brewed from plants unique to the region, that contains a hallucinogen regulated under the Controlled Substances Act by the Federal Government. The Government concedes that this practice is a sincere exercise of religion, but nonetheless sought to prohibit the small American branch of the sect from engaging in the practice, on the ground that the Controlled Substances Act bars all use of the hallucinogen. The sect sued to block enforcement against it of the ban on the sacramental tea, and moved for a preliminary injunction.

It relied on the Religious Freedom Restoration Act of 1993, which prohibits the Federal Government from substantially burdening a person's exercise of religion, unless the Government "demonstrates that application of the burden to the person" represents the least restrictive means of advancing a compelling interest. 42 U.S.C. § 2000bb—1(b). The District Court granted the preliminary injunction, and the Court of Appeals affirmed. We granted the Government's petition for certiorari. Before this Court, the Government's central submission is that it has a compelling interest in the *uniform* application of the Controlled Substances Act, such that no exception to the ban on use of the hallucinogen can be made to accommodate the sect's sincere religious practice. We conclude that the Government has not carried the burden expressly placed on it by Congress in the Religious Freedom Restoration Act, and affirm the grant of the preliminary injunction. . . .

O Centro Espírita Beneficente Uniã do Vegetal (UDV) is a Christian Spiritist sect based in Brazil, with an American branch of approximately 130 individuals. Central to the UDV's faith is receiving communion through *hoasca* (pronounced "wass-ca"), a sacramental tea made from two plants unique to the Amazon region. One of the plants, *Psychotria viridis*, contains dimethyltryptamine (DMT), a hallucinogen whose effects are enhanced by alkaloids from the other plant, *Banisteriopsis caapi*. DMT, as well as "any material, compound, mixture, or preparation, which contains any quantity of [DMT]," is listed in Schedule I of the Controlled Substances Act. § 812(c), Schedule I(c).

In 1999, United States Customs inspectors intercepted a shipment to the American UDV containing three drums of *hoasca*. A subsequent investigation revealed that the UDV had received 14 prior shipments of *hoasca*. The inspectors seized the intercepted shipment and threatened the UDV with prosecution.

The UDV filed suit against the Attorney General and other federal law enforcement officials, seeking declaratory and injunctive relief. The complaint alleged, *inter alia,* that applying the Controlled Substances Act to the UDV's sacramental use of *hoasca* violates RFRA. . . .

The Government's second line of argument rests on the Controlled Substances Act itself. The Government contends that the Act's description of Schedule I substances as having "a high potential for abuse," "no currently accepted medical use in treatment in the United States," and "a lack of accepted safety for use . . . under medical supervision," 21 U.S.C. § 812(b (1), by itself precludes any consideration of individualized exceptions such as that sought by the UDV. The Government goes on to argue that the regulatory regime established by the Act—a "closed" system that prohibits all use of controlled substances except as authorized by the Act itself. . . . Under the Government's view, there is no need to assess the particulars of the UDV's use or weigh the impact of an exemption for that specific use, because the

GONZALES V. O CENTRO ESPIRITA BENEFICENTE UNIAO DO VEGETAL *(continued)*

Controlled Substances Act serves a compelling purpose and simply admits of no exceptions. . . .

RFRA, and the strict scrutiny test it adopted, contemplate an inquiry more focused than the Government's categorical approach. RFRA requires the Government to demonstrate that the compelling interest test is satisfied through application of the challenged law "to the person"—the particular claimant whose sincere exercise of religion is being substantially burdened. Under the more focused inquiry required by RFRA and the compelling interest test, the Government's mere invocation of the general characteristics of Schedule I substances, as set forth in the Controlled Substances Act, cannot carry the day. It is true, of course, that Schedule I substances such as DMT are exceptionally dangerous. Nevertheless, there is no indication that Congress, in classifying DMT, considered the harms posed by the particular use at issue here—the circumscribed, sacramental use of *hoasca* by the UDV. . . .

And in fact an exception has been made to the Schedule I ban for religious use. For the past 35 years, there has been a regulatory exemption for use of peyote—a Schedule I substance—by the Native American Church. See 21 CFR § 1307.31 (2005). In 1994, Congress extended that exemption to all members of every recognized Indian Tribe. See 42 U.S.C. § 1996a(b)(1). Everything the Government says about the DMT in *hoasca*—that, as a Schedule I substance, Congress has determined that it "has a high potential for abuse," "has no currently accepted medical use," and has "a lack of accepted safety for use . . . -under medical supervision," 21 U.S.C. § 812(b)(1)—applies in equal measure to the mescaline in peyote, yet both the Executive and Congress itself have decreed an exception from the Controlled Substances Act for Native American religious use of peyote. If such use is permitted in the face of the congressional findings in § 812(b)(1) for hundreds of thousands of Native Americans practicing their faith, it is difficult to see how those same findings alone can preclude any consideration of a similar exception for the 130 or so American members of the UDV who want to practice theirs. . . . [Therefore, the application of the Controlled Substances Act to UDV's religious use of hoasca is invalidated.]

Determining whether an act is a genuine exercise of religious beliefs is not always easy. The practices of one religion may appear unusual, or even bizarre, to another. But this is not determinative. The *Hodges* case both illustrates the sensitivity with which our society treats religion and stands as an example of an activity that is not a religion, although the opinion does not contain the latter finding, for reasons you will see.

How does a court distinguish between fraudulent and bona fide religious practices? First, it must be determined that the defendant is asserting a religious belief, not a personal or philosophical belief. Several factors are considered. How well established is the religion in the world? If a defendant is the only adherent, or one of only a few followers, of a religion, it is less likely to be deemed legitimate. How old is the religion? For how long has the defendant practiced the religion? What is the nature of the practice in question? How important is the practice to the religion? Once it is determined that a religious practice is being regulated by the State, then the State's interest in regulating the defendant's conduct must be weighed against the defendant's First Amendment interest. If the State's interest is compelling, then the conduct may be regulated.

STATE V. HODGES
695 S.W.2d 171 (Tenn. 1985)

In January, 1983, defendant was charged in a multiple count indictment with tampering with utility metering devices. His lawyer appeared before the trial judge on February 22, 1983, asking for a trial date for the misdemeanors with which defendant was charged. The trial judge informed defendant's counsel on that occasion that he would not "put up with [defendant's] foolishness" and if "he comes in here dressed like a chicken, I am going to order him out of here under guard."

On June 28, 1983, defendant appeared for trial, with the same counsel, and to say that he was dressed "like a chicken" as the trial judge had anticipated, is a mild description of the outrageous attire in which defendant barely covered himself. [In a footnote the court described his appearance. The "defendant appeared for trial dressed in a grossly shocking and bizarre attire, consisting of brown and white fur tied around his body at his ankles, loins and head, with a like vest made out of fur, and complete with eye goggles over his eyes. He had colored his face and chest with a very pale green paint for coloring. He had what appeared to be a human skull dangling from his waist and in his hand he carried a stuffed snake. . . .] (T)he so-called vest consisted of two pieces of fur that covered each arm but did not meet in front and back, leaving defendant's chest and back naked to his waist. His legs were also naked from mid-way between his knee and waist to his ankles. He appeared to be carrying a military gas mask and other unidentifiable ornaments."

The trial judge first addressed defendant's attorney and asked him to have his client appear in proper clothes. Defendant's attorney responded by informing the court that defendant wished to exercise his right of "freedom of expression." The trial judge then directed his remarks to defendant and ordered him to put on "regular clothes" for the trial scheduled that day. The trial judge sought a yes or no answer, but defendant responded with the following assertion:

> "This is a spiritual attire and it is my religious belief and I have never worn anything else in court but this when I am on trial."

Whereupon, the trial judge found him to be in contempt of court, revoked his bond, and ordered him committed to jail for ten days or until he agreed to appear for trial in proper clothes.

Defendant's counsel asked the court to allow him to "build a record for appeal" which was denied. Motions were filed the following day, June 29, 1983, on behalf of defendant for a new trial, for reconsideration of the finding of contempt, and for bail pending appeal. At the hearing held the same day, defense counsel again sought an evidentiary hearing on the issue of defendant's religious belief which was again denied. . . . The court of Criminal Appeals reversed the contempt adjudication, holding that the trial judge erred in failing to inquire into the "nature and sincerity of appellant's beliefs, the denomination of his religion, its origin, organization and the length of time which appellant has espoused it."

We agree that the trial judge erred in failing to inquire into the religious belief of defendant and in failing to allow a full record to be developed for appeal. However, we think the intermediate court's instructions on remand, quoted above, may be misleading and not entirely in conformity with United States Supreme Court opinions.

A Rhode Island litigant appeared in court wearing a white, knitted skull cap and the trial judge ordered him to remove it or leave the courtroom and refused to consider the litigant's claim that he was a Sunni Muslim, that he was wearing a prayer cap that was a religious symbol of that sect, that indicated that the wearer was in constant prayer. . . . On appeal, the Supreme Court of Rhode Island accurately summarized the first amendment principle enunciated by the United States Supreme Court applicable where a religious belief or practice collides with a state law or regulation, as follows:

> Despite the exalted status so rightly afforded to religious beliefs and activities that are motivated and embody those beliefs, the freedom of an individual to practice his religion does not enjoy absolute immunity from infringement by the state. Individuals have been subject to mandatory inoculations despite religious objections to such medical care. . . . Thus while the freedom to hold religious beliefs and opinions is absolute, the freedom to act in harmony with these religious beliefs and opinions is not beyond state regulation where such restriction serves the public interest by promoting public health and safety or preserving order. We must then accommodate the right to exercise the religious freedoms safeguarded by the first amendment with the right of the state to regulate those individual freedoms for the sake of societal interests. The problem is one of balance and degree—the courts are called upon to determine when the societal interest becomes so important as to justify an incursion by the state into religious activity that is otherwise protected by the free exercise clause of the first amendment. . . .

After discussion of the United States Supreme Court's application of the balancing test to the facts . . . the Supreme Court of Rhode Island continued as follows:

> We believe that because petitioner claimed that his act was protected by the free exercise clause, in order to justifiably curtail the exercise of the alleged right the trial justice should have first allowed petitioner to display the sincerity of his religious belief, and then should have . . . [balanced] petitioner's first amendment right with the interest of the court in maintaining decorum in its proceedings by regulating dress in the courtroom. . . .

Thus, the threshold inquiry is whether or not the religious belief or practice asserted qualifies for the protection of the free exercise clause of the first amendment. The record in this case, though meager, clearly indicates that that issue may be decisive, particularly if it proves to be true that defendant is the sole adherent to his asserted religious belief and practice. . . .

Although a determination of what is a "religious" belief or practice entitled to constitutional protection may present a most delicate question, the very concept of ordered liberty precludes allowing every person to make his own standards of matters of conduct in which society as a whole has important interests. . . .

Paraphrasing an additional observation of the Court that involved Thoreau's isolation at Walden Pond, the Court made it clear that a belief which is philosophical and personal rather than religious, does not rise to the demands of the free exercise clause of the first amendment. . . .

Only beliefs rooted in religion are protected by the Free Exercise Clause, which, by its terms, gives special protection to the exercise of religion. . . . The determination of what is a "religious" belief or practice is more often than not a difficult and delicate task. . . . However, the resolution of that question is not to turn upon a judicial perception of the particular belief or practice in question; religious beliefs need not be acceptable, logical, consistent, or comprehensible to others in order to merit First Amendment protection.

One can, of course, imagine an asserted claim so bizarre, so clearly nonreligious in motivation, as not to be entitled to protection under the First Amendment. . . .

This case is clearly illustrative of what Mr. Justice Jackson had in mind when he said, "The price of freedom of religion or of speech or of the press is that we must put up with, and even pay for, a good deal of rubbish." . . .

The judgment of the Court of Criminal Appeals is affirmed and this case is remanded to the trial court for further proceedings consistent with this opinion.

FIRST AMENDMENT AND SPEECH

The First Amendment also protects speech. Refer to the text of the First Amendment, which provides that "Congress shall make no law . . . abridging the freedom of speech." In spite of the plain language of this clause, several words mean something different than what is plain. First, the clause limits the authority of Congress, but in reality it limits all three branches of the federal government. Because the Amendment has been incorporated, state and local governments are prohibited from abridging free speech as well. Second, the term speech is used. Regardless, the Supreme Court has held that more than the spoken word is protected. All forms of expression, nonverbal, artistic, written, and visual, are protected by the Free Speech Clause. Third, as is true of all the amendments, there are exceptions – even though not recognized by the text of the Amendment. As you already learned, any law that burdens speech must be narrowly tailored and it must be supported by a compelling governmental interest. Underlying the First Amendment's protection of speech is the philosophical belief that a free market of ideas will advance both democracy and a society's development. The price of free market speech is the protection of provocative, annoying, offensive, and insulting speech.

You have already learned that fighting words and those words that create a clear and present danger or the likelihood of imminent lawlessness may be regulated because the government has a compelling interest in preventing these dangers. Although the lawlessness and clear and present danger exceptions commonly refer to violence, there are examples of speech that may be prohibited because it creates a likelihood of imminent non-violent lawlessness. Encouraging jurors to not follow the law during deliberations is an example. The Julien Heicklin case illustrates the line between protected speech and jury tampering.

UNITED STATES V. JULIAN HEICKLIN
(Order Dismissing Indictment, U.S. District Court, S.D. NY April 19, 2012)

Kimba M. Wood, USDJ:

On November 18, 2010, a grand jury indicted Julian Heicklen, charging him with attempting to influence the actions or decisions of a juror of a United States Court, in violation of 18 U.S.C. § 1504, a federal jury tampering statute. The Indictment states that, from October 2009 through May 2010, in front of the entrance to the United States Court for the Southern District of New York (the "Courthouse"), Heicklen distributed pamphlets that advocated jury nullification. . . .

Heicklen advocates passionately for the right of jurors to determine the law as well as the facts. The Government states that, in advocating these views, Heicklen has on several occasions stood outside the entrance to the Courthouse, holding a sign reading "Jury Info" and distributing pamphlets from the Fully Informed Jury Association ("FIJA").

UNITED STATES V. JULIAN HEICKLIN *(continued)*

(Government's Memorandum of Law in Opposition to Defendant's Motions ("Govt.'s Mem.") at 1.) The pamphlets state that a juror has not just the responsibility to determine the facts of a case before her on the basis of the evidence presented, but also the power to determine the law according to her conscience.

In opposition to Heicklen's motion, the Government quotes an excerpt of a transcript of a recorded conversation that it alleges Heicklen had with an undercover agent from the Federal Bureau of Investigation ("FBI"), in which the agent specifically identified herself as a juror; the agent was not actually a juror. The Government alleges that Heicklen handed that "juror" a FIJA pamphlet and a single-sided, typewritten handout. The handout states in relevant part that "[i]t is not the duty of the jury to uphold the law.

It is the jury's duty to see that justice is done." The FIJA pamphlet is entitled "A Primer for Prospective Jurors" and contains 13 questions and answers for jurors regarding what FIJA characterizes as jurors' rights and responsibilities. . . .

The Court understands the statute [under which the defendant was charged] to contain three elements:

1. that the defendant knowingly attempted to influence the action or decision of a juror of a United States court;

2. that the defendant knowingly attempted to influence that juror (a) upon an issue or matter pending before that juror, or pending before the jury of which that juror is a member; or (b) pertaining to that juror's duties; and

3. that the defendant knowingly attempted to influence that juror by writing or sending to that juror a written communication in relation to such issue or matter. . . .

The statute thus prohibits a defendant from trying to influence a juror upon any case or point in dispute before that juror by means of a written communication in relation to that case or that point in dispute. It also prohibits a defendant from trying to influence a juror's actions or decisions pertaining to that juror's duties, but only *if* the defendant made that communication in relation to a case or point in dispute before that juror. The statute therefore squarely criminalizes efforts to influence the outcome of a case, but exempts the broad categories of journalistic, academic, political, and other writings that discuss the roles and responsibilities of jurors in general, as well as innocent notes from friends and spouses encouraging jurors to arrive on time or to rush home, to listen closely or to deliberate carefully, but with no relation to the outcome of a particular case. Accordingly, the Court reads the plain text of the statute to require that a defendant must have sought to influence a juror through a written communication in relation either to a specific case before that juror or to a substantive point in dispute between two or more parties before that juror.

Although "political speech by its nature will sometimes have unpalatable consequences, . . . in general, our society accords greater weight to the value of free speech than to the dangers of its misuse." The First Amendment reflects "a profound national commitment to the principle that debate on public issues should be uninhibited, robust, and wide-open." "Indeed, the Amendment exists so that this debate can occur—robust, forceful, and contested. It is the theory of the Free Speech Clause that 'falsehood and fallacies' are exposed through 'discussion,' 'education,' and 'more speech.'" That is because "speech concerning public affairs is more than self-expression; it is the essence of self-government." . . .

(continued)

UNITED STATES V. JULIAN HEICKLIN (continued)

Decisions applying the clear and present danger test articulated in *Bridges* and *Wood* have consistently held that speech may be restricted only if that speech "is directed to inciting or producing" a threat to the administration of justice that is both "imminent" and likely to materialize. . . .

The relevant cases establish that the First Amendment squarely protects speech concerning judicial proceedings and public debate regarding the functioning of the judicial system, so long as that speech does not interfere with the fair and impartial administration of justice. In *Wood*, the Supreme Court held that even speech to a grand juror may be protected by the First Amendment if it does not present a clear and present danger to the functioning of the courts (370 U.S. at 395). At the same time, the First Amendment does not create a right to influence juries outside of official proceedings because "[d]ue process requires that the accused receive a trial by an impartial jury free from outside influences." . . .

Based upon the plain meaning of the text of 18 U.S.C. § 1504, reinforced by relevant judicial interpretations and the doctrine of constitutional avoidance, the Court holds that a person violates the statute only when he knowingly attempts to influence the action or decision of a juror upon an issue or matter pending before that juror or pertaining to that juror's duties by means of written communication made in relation to *a specific case pending before that juror* or in relation to *a point in dispute between the parties before that juror*. . . .

Heicklen's alleged actions do not violate 18 U.S.C. § 1504. The Indictment alleges that Heicklen "distributed pamphlets urging jury nullification, immediately in front of an entrance to the United States District Court of the Southern District of New York."

Both pamphlets discuss the role of juries in society and urge jurors to follow their conscience regardless of instructions on the law. Heicklen's pamphlets self-evidently pertain to a "juror's duties," satisfying the requirements for liability under the second element of 18 U.S.C. § 1504. To satisfy the requirements for liability under the third element of 18 U.S.C. § 1504, however, the pamphlets must have been written or distributed in relation to an "issue or matter" pending before that juror. The two pamphlets do not relate to an "issue" pending before a juror, because a juror's duties are not a point in dispute between the parties to a suit.

Understanding "matter" to mean "case," the pamphlets could trigger liability under the statute's third element if they were distributed in relation to a particular case pending before a juror. But unlike in [a prior case], there is no allegation that Heicklen distributed the pamphlets in relation to a specific case. Indeed, the Government concedes that it "does not allege that the defendant targeted a particular jury or a particular issue."

The Court's holding merely maintains the existing balance that federal courts have found between freedom of speech and the administration of justice. Attempts to tamper with a jury in order to influence the outcome of a trial or a grand jury proceeding are still clearly prohibited under 18 U.S.C. § 1503 and 18 U.S.C. § 1504. Efforts to distribute leaflets to jurors in the immediate vicinity of courthouses may still be sanctioned through reasonable time, place, and manner restrictions such as those promulgated pursuant to 40 U.S.C. § 1315 and 41 C.F.R. § 102-74.415(c). The Court declines to stretch the interpretation of the existing statute prohibiting communications with a juror in order to cover speech that is not meant to influence the actions of a juror with regard to a point in dispute before that juror or the outcome of a specific case before that juror. For the foregoing reasons, the Defendant's motion to dismiss the Indictment is GRANTED.

Slanderous and libelous statements also fall outside the protection of the First Amendment. Fighting words, obscenity, some threats, and slanderous and libelous words are all content-based doctrines; that is, the substance of what is being said is regulated. There is a huge body of First Amendment free speech law. The application of the First Amendment to regulations of obscenity and the Internet are discussed in Chapter 6. You may want to refresh yourself with the content of that chapter before continuing. See Exhibit 9–1 for an illustration of the limits of free expression.

In some instances, a state may regulate speech, not because of its content, but by its time, place, and manner of being expressed. Here, a balancing of interests is conducted: does the government's interest in enforcing the statute outweigh the First Amendment interest? For example, it is unlawful to stand in the middle of the street to make a speech. The interest in maintaining a safe, consistent flow of traffic outweighs the First Amendment interest. However, the result would be different if a state attempted to prohibit all speeches made in a public place. Such a statute would be overbroad, as it includes not only activity that the state may regulate (standing in traffic), but also lawful activity. Commercial speech is also protected by the First Amendment, but is subject to greater control than other speech, particularly political speech.

Not only is the actual spoken word protected: Expression of ideas through acts is also protected, although to a lesser degree than pure speech. Picketing is an example of protected expression, as is flag burning.

TEXAS V. GREGORY LEE JOHNSON
491 U.S. 397 (1989)

After publicly burning the American flag as a means of political protest, Gregory Lee Johnson was convicted of desecrating a flag in violation of Texas law. This case presents the question whether his conviction is consistent with the First Amendment. We hold that it is not.

While the Republican National Convention was taking place in Dallas in 1984, respondent Johnson participated in a political demonstration dubbed the "Republican War Chest Tour." As explained in literature distributed by the demonstrators and in speeches made by them, the purpose of this event was to protest the policies of the Reagan administration and of certain Dallas-based corporations. The demonstrators marched through the Dallas streets, chanting political slogans and stopping at several corporate locations to stage "die-ins" intended to dramatize the consequences of nuclear war. On several occasions they spray-painted the walls of buildings and overturned potted plants, but Johnson himself took no part in such activities. He did, however, accept an American flag handed to him by a fellow protester who had taken it from a flag pole outside one of the targeted buildings.

The demonstration ended in front of Dallas City Hall, where Johnson unfurled the American flag, doused it with kerosene, and set it on fire. While the flag burned, the protesters chanted, "America, the red, white, and blue, we spit on you." After the demonstrators dispersed, a witness to the flag-burning collected the flag's remains and buried them in his backyard. No one was physically injured

(continued)

or threatened with injury, though several witnesses testified that they had been seriously offended by the flag-burning. . . .

Johnson was convicted of flag desecration for burning the flag rather than for uttering insulting words. That fact somewhat complicates our consideration of his conviction under the First Amendment. We must first determine whether Johnson's burning of the flag constituted expressive conduct, permitting him to invoke the First Amendment. . . . If his conduct was expressive, we next decide whether the State's regulation is related to the suppression of free expression. If the State's regulation is not related to expression, then the less stringent standard . . . for regulations of noncommunicative conduct controls. . . . If it is, then we are outside of the *O'Brien* test, and we must ask whether this interest justifies Johnson's conviction under a more demanding standard. . . .

The First Amendment literally forbids the abridgment only of "speech," but we have long recognized that its protection does not end at the spoken or written word. While we have rejected "the view that an apparently limitless variety of conduct can be labeled 'speech' whenever the person engaging in the conduct intends thereby to express an idea," . . . we have acknowledged that conduct may be "sufficiently imbued with elements of communication to fall within the scope of the First and Fourteenth Amendments." . . .

In deciding whether particular conduct possesses sufficient communicative elements to bring the First Amendment into play, we have asked whether "[a]n intent to convey a particularized message was present, and [whether] the likelihood was great that the message would be understood by those who viewed it." . . . Hence, we have recognized the expressive nature of students' wearing of black armbands to protest American military involvement in Vietnam . . . of a sit-in by blacks in a "whites only" area to protest segregation. . . .

The expressive, overtly political nature of this conduct was both intentional and overwhelmingly apparent. At his trial, Johnson explained his reasons for burning the flag as follows:

"The American Flag was burned as Ronald Reagan was being nominated as President. And a more powerful statement of symbolic speech, whether you agree with it or not, couldn't have been made at that time. It's quite a just position [juxtaposition]. We had new patriotism and no patriotism." In these circumstances, Johnson's burning of the flag was conduct "sufficiently imbued with elements of communication." . . .

In order to decide whether the *O'Brien* test applies here, therefore, we must decide whether Texas has asserted an interest in support of Johnson's conviction that is unrelated to the suppression of expression. If we find that an interest asserted by the State is simply not implicated on the facts before us, we need not ask whether *O'Brien* applies. . . . The State offers two separate interests to justify his conviction: preventing breaches of the peace, and preserving the flag as a symbol of nationhood and national unity. We hold that the first interest is not implicated on this record and that the second is related to the suppression of expression. . . .

The State's position, therefore, amounts to a claim that an audience that takes serious offense at particular expression is necessarily likely to disturb the peace and that the expression may be prohibited on this basis. Our precedents do not countenance such a presumption. On the contrary, they recognize that a principal "function of free speech under our system of government is to invite dispute. It may indeed best serve its high purpose when it induces a condition of unrest, creates dissatisfaction with conditions as they are, or even stirs people to anger." . . .

The State also asserts an interest in preserving the flag as a symbol of nationhood and national unity. . . .

TEXAS V. GREGORY LEE JOHNSON *(continued)*

Johnson was not, we add, prosecuted for the expression of just any idea; he was prosecuted for his expression of dissatisfaction with the policies of this country, expression situated at the core of our First Amendment values. . . .

Moreover, Johnson was prosecuted because he knew that his politically charged expression would cause "serious offense." If he had burned the flag as a means of disposing of it because it was dirty or torn, he would not have been convicted of flag desecration under the Texas law; federal law designates burning as the preferred means of disposing of a flag "when it is in such condition that it is no longer a fitting emblem for display." . . .

If there is a bedrock principle underlying the First Amendment, it is that the Government may not prohibit the expression of an idea simply because society finds the idea itself offensive or disagreeable. . . .

We are tempted to say, in fact, that the flag's deservedly cherished place in our community will be strengthened, not weakened, by our holding today. Our decision is a reaffirmation of the principles of freedom and inclusiveness that the flag best reflects, and of the conviction that our toleration of criticism such as Johnson's is a sign and source of our strength. . . .

The way to preserve the flag's special role is not to punish those who feel differently about these matters. It is to persuade them that they are wrong. . . . And, precisely because it is our flag that is involved, one's response to the flag-burner may exploit the uniquely persuasive power of the flag itself. We can imagine no more appropriate response to burning a flag than waving one's own, no better way to counter a flag-burner's message than by saluting the flag that burns, no surer means of preserving the dignity even of the flag that burned than by—as one witness here did—according its remains a respectful burial. We do not consecrate the flag by punishing its desecration, for in doing so we dilute the freedom that this cherished emblem represents. . . . Justice Kennedy, concurring.

I write not to qualify the words Justice Brennan chooses so well, for he says with power all that is necessary to explain our ruling. I join his opinion without reservation, but with a keen sense that his case, like others before us from time to time, exacts its personal toll. This prompts me to add to our pages these few remarks.

The case before us illustrates better than most that the judicial power is often difficult in its exercise. We cannot here ask another branch to share responsibility, as when the argument is made that a statute is flawed or incomplete. For we are presented with a clear and simple statute to be judged against a pure command of the Constitution. The outcome can be laid at no door but ours.

The hard fact is that sometimes we must make decisions we do not like. We make them because they are right, right in the sense that the law and the Constitution, as we see them, compel the result. And so great is our commitment to the process that, except in the rare case, we do not pause to express distaste for the result, perhaps for fear of undermining a valued principle that dictates decision. This is one of those rare cases.

Our colleagues in dissent advance powerful arguments why respondent may be convicted for his expression, reminding us that among those who will be dismayed by our holding will be some who have had the singular honor of carrying the flag into battle. And I agree that the flag holds a lonely place of honor in an age when absolutes are distrusted and simple truths are burdened by unneeded apologetics.

With respect to those views, I do not believe the Constitution gives us the right to rule as the dissenting members of the Court urge, however painful this judgment is to announce. . . . It is poignant but fundamental that the flag protects those who hold it in contempt.

First Amendment free exercise of speech claims also arise in the context of hate crime legislation. Such legislation either makes it illegal to express prejudicial opinions or enhances the penalty for a crime that is motivated by prejudice. The former is unconstitutional. As to the latter, most states enhance the penalties for crimes such as trespass, assault, battery, and harassment if the motive of the crime was the victim's race, religion, color, or other characteristic.

Two Supreme Court opinions, only one year apart, set the limits of hate crime laws. Both are excerpted here. In the first, the Court held an ordinance unconstitutional. In the second, the Court upheld the law.

Exhibit 9–1   THE LIMITS OF FIRST AMENDMENT FREE SPEECH

Threats/fighting words

Advocacy of violence/
disturbing the peace

Free Expression Regulations

Time, manner, and place
restrictions on public speech

Child pornography/
indecent exposure

R.A.V. V. CITY OF ST. PAUL
505 U.S. 377 (1992)

In the predawn hours of June 21, 1990, petitioner and several other teenagers allegedly assembled a crudely-made cross by taping together broken chair legs. They then allegedly burned the cross inside the fenced yard of a black family that lived across the street from the house where petitioner was staying. Although this conduct could have been punished under any number of laws, one of the two provisions under which respondent city of St. Paul chose to charge petitioner (then a juvenile) was the St. Paul-Motivated Crime Ordinance, which provides:

> "Whoever placed on public property or private property a symbol, object, appellation, characterization or graffiti, including, but not limited to, a burning cross or Nazi swastika, which one knows or has reasonable grounds to know arouse anger, alarm or resentment in others on the basis of race, color, creed, religion or gender commits disorderly conduct and shall be guilty of a misdemeanor."

Petitioner moved to dismiss this count on the ground that the St. Paul ordinance was substantially overbroad and impermissibly content-based and therefore facially invalid under the First Amendment. The trial court granted this motion, but the Minnesota Supreme Court reversed. That court rejected petitioner's overbreadth claim because, as construed in prior Minnesota cases . . . the modifying phrase "arouses anger, alarm or resentment in others" limited the reach of the ordinance to conduct that amounts to "fighting words," . . . and therefore the ordinance reached only expression "that the first amendment does not protect." . . . The court also concluded that the ordinance was not impermissibly content-based because, in its view, "the ordinance is a narrowly tailored means toward accomplishing the compelling governmental interest in protecting the community against bias-motivated threats to public safety and order." . . .

Assuming, arguendo, that all of the expression reached by the ordinance is proscribable under the "fighting words" doctrine, we nonetheless conclude that the ordinance is facially unconstitutional in that it prohibits otherwise permitted speech solely on the basis of the subjects the speech addresses. . . .

The proposition that a particular instance of speech can be proscribable on the basis of one feature (e.g., obscenity) but not on the basis of another (e.g., opposition to the city government) is commonplace, and has found application in many contexts. We have long held, for example, that nonverbal expressive activity can be banned because of the action it entails, but not because of the ideas it expresses—so that burning the flag in violation of an ordinance against outdoor fires could be punishable, whereas burning a flag in violation of an ordinance against dishonoring the flag is not. . . .

Similarly, we have upheld reasonable "time, place, or manner" restrictions, but only if they are "justified without reference to the content of the regulated speech." . . . And just as the power to proscribe particular speech on the basis of a noncontent element (e.g., noise) does not entail the power to proscribe it on the basis of a content element; so also, the power to proscribe it on the basis of one content element (e.g., obscenity) does not entail the power to proscribe it on the basis of other content elements.

In other words, the exclusion of "fighting words" from the scope of the First Amendment simply means that, for purposes of that Amendment, the unprotected features of the words are, despite their verbal character, essentially a "nonspeech" element of communication. Fighting words are thus analogous to a noisy sound truck: Each is, as Justice Frankfurter recognized, a "mode of speech," . . . both can be used to convey an idea; but neither has, in and of itself, a claim upon the First Amendment.

(continued)

R.A.V. V. CITY OF ST. PAUL *(continued)*

As with the sound truck, however, so also with fighting words: The government may not regulate use based on hostility—or favoritism—towards the underlying message expressed. . . .

Applying these principles to the St. Paul ordinance, we conclude that, even as narrowly construed by the Minnesota Supreme Court, the ordinance is facially unconstitutional. Although the phrase in the ordinance, "arouses anger, alarm or resentment in others," has been limited by the Minnesota Supreme Court's construction to reach only those symbols or displays that amount to "fighting words," the remaining, unmodified terms make clear that the ordinance applies only to "fighting words" that insult, or provoke violence, "on the basis of race, color, creed, religion or gender." Displays containing abusive invective, no matter how vicious or severe, are permissible unless they are addressed to one of the specified disfavored topics. Those who wish to use "fighting words" in connection with other ideas—to express hostility, for example, on the basis of political affiliation, union membership, or homosexuality—are not covered.

The First Amendment does not permit St. Paul to impose special prohibitions on those speakers who express views on disfavored subjects. . . .

In its practical operation, moreover, the ordinance goes even beyond mere content discrimination, to actual viewpoint discrimination. Displays containing some words—odious racial epithets, for example—aspersions upon a person's mother, for example—would seemingly be usable ad libitum in the placards of those arguing in favor of racial, color, etc. tolerance and equality, but could not be used by the speaker's opponents. One could hold up a sign saying, for example, that all "anti-catholic bigots" are misbegotten; but not that all "papists" are, for that would insult or provoke violence "on the basis of religion." St. Paul has no such authority to license one side of a debate to fight freestyle, while requiring the other to follow Marquis of Queensbury Rules. . . .

Let there be no mistake about our belief that burning a cross in someone's front yard is reprehensible. But St. Paul has sufficient means at its disposal to prevent such behavior without adding the First Amendment to the fire. . . .

WISCONSIN V. MITCHELL
508 U.S. 476 (1993)

Respondent Todd Mitchell's sentence for aggravated battery was enhanced because he intentionally selected his victim on account of the victim's race. The question presented in this case is whether this penalty enhancement is prohibited by the First and Fourteenth Amendments. We hold that it is not.

On the evening of October 7, 1989, a group of young black men and boys, including Mitchell, gathered at an apartment complex in Kenosha,

Wisconsin. Several members of the group discussed a scene from the motion picture "Mississippi Burning," in which a white man beat a young black boy who was praying. The group moved outside and Mitchell asked them: "Do you all feel hyped up to move on some white people?" . . . Shortly thereafter, a young white boy approached the group on the opposite side of the street where they were standing. As the boy walked by, Mitchell said:

"You all want to fuck somebody up? There goes a white boy: go get him." . . . Mitchell counted to three and pointed in the boy's direction. The group ran towards the boy, beat him severely, and stole his tennis shoes. The boy was rendered unconscious and remained in a coma for four days.

After a jury trial in the Circuit Court for Kenosha County, Mitchell was convicted of aggravated battery. . . . That offense ordinarily carries a maximum sentence of two years imprisonment. . . . But because the jury found that Mitchell had intentionally selected his victim because of the boy's race, the maximum sentence for Mitchell's offense was increased to seven years under a [Wisconsin statute]. That provision enhances the maximum penalty for an offense whenever the defendant "[i]ntentionally selects the person against whom the crime . . . is committed . . . because of race, religion, color, disability, sexual orientation, national origin or ancestry of that person." . . .

The Circuit Court sentenced Mitchell to four years' imprisonment for the aggravated battery. . . .

Mitchell unsuccessfully sought postconviction relief in the Circuit Court. Then he appealed his conviction and sentence, challenging the constitutionality of Wisconsin's penalty-enhancement provision on First Amendment grounds. The Wisconsin Court of Appeals rejected Mitchell's challenge, but the Wisconsin Supreme Court reversed. The Supreme Court held that the statute "violates the First Amendment directly by punishing what the legislature has deemed to be offensive thought." . . . It rejected the State's contention "that the statute punishes only the conduct of intentional selection of a victim." According to the court, "[t]he statute punishes the 'because of' aspect of the defendant's selection, the reason the defendant selected the victim, the motive behind the selection." . . .

The Supreme Court also held that the penalty-enhancement statute was unconstitutionally overbroad. It reasoned that, in order to prove that a defendant intentionally selected his victim because of the victim's protected status, the State would often have to introduce evidence of the defendant's prior speech, such as racial epithets he may have uttered before the commission of the offense. . . .

We granted certiorari because of the importance of the question presented and the existence of a conflict of authority among the states' high courts on the constitutionality of statutes similar to Wisconsin's penalty-enhancement provision. . . . We reverse. . . .

Mitchell argues (and the Wisconsin Supreme Court held) that the statute violates the First Amendment by punishing offenders' bigoted beliefs.

Traditionally, sentencing judges have considered a wide variety of factors in addition to evidence bearing on guilt in determining what sentence to impose on a convicted defendant. . . . [T]he defendant's motive for committing the offense is one important factor. . . . Thus, in many states the commission of a murder, or other capital offense, for pecuniary gain is a separate aggravating circumstance under the capital-sentencing statute. . . .

But it is equally true that a defendant's abstract beliefs, however obnoxious to most people, may not be taken into consideration by a sentencing judge. . . . In [*Dawson v. Delaware*, 503 U.S. 159 (1992)] the State introduced evidence at a capital-sentencing hearing that the defendant was a member of a white supremacist prison gang. Because "the evidence proved nothing more than [the defendant's] abstract beliefs," we held that its admission violated the defendant's First Amendment rights. . . . In so holding, however, we emphasized that "the Constitution does not erect a per se barrier to the admission of evidence concerning one's beliefs and associations at sentencing simply because those beliefs and associations are protected by the First Amendment. . . . Thus, in *Barclay v. Florida*,

(continued)

WISCONSIN V. MITCHELL *(continued)*

463 U.S. 939 (1983) . . . we allowed the sentencing judge to take into account the defendant's racial animus towards his victim. The evidence in that case showed that the defendant's membership in the Black Liberation Army and desire to provoke a "race war" were related to the murder of a white man for which he was convicted. . . . Because "the elements of racial hatred in [the] murder" were relevant to several aggravating factors, we held that the trial judge permissibly took his evidence into account in sentencing the defendant to death. . . .

Mitchell suggests that *Dawson* and *Barclay* are inapposite because they did not involve application of a penalty-enhancement provision. But in *Barclay* we held that it was permissible for the sentencing court to consider the defendant's racial animus in determining whether he should be sentenced to death, surely the most severe "enhancement" of all. And the fact that the Wisconsin Legislature has decided, as a general matter, that bias-motivated offenses warrant greater maximum penalties across the board does not alter the result here. For the primary responsibility for fixing criminal penalties lies with the legislature. . . .

Mitchell argues that the Wisconsin penalty-enhancement statute is invalid because it punishes the defendant's discriminatory motive, or reason, for acting. But motive plays the same role under the Wisconsin statute as it does under federal and state antidiscrimination laws, which we have previously upheld against constitutional challenge. . . . Title VII, for example, makes it unlawful for an employer to discriminate against an employee "because of such individual's race, color, religion, sex, or national origin." . . . In [another case] we rejected the argument that Title VII infringed employers' First Amendment rights. Nothing in our decision last Term in *R.A.V.* compels a different result here. That case involved a First Amendment challenge to a municipal ordinance prohibiting the use of "'fighting words' that insult or provoke violence, on the basis of race, color, creed, religion or gender." . . .

Finally, there remains to be considered Mitchell's argument that the Wisconsin statute is unconstitutionally overbroad because of the "chilling effect" on free speech. Mitchell argues (and the Wisconsin Supreme Court agreed) that the statute is "overbroad" because evidence of the defendant's prior speech or associations may be used to prove that the defendant intentionally selected his victim on account of the victim's protected status. Consequently, the argument goes, the statute impermissibly chills free expression with respect to such matters by those concerned about the possibility of enhanced sentences if they should in the future commit a criminal offense covered by the statute. We find no merit in this contention.

The sort of chill envisioned here is far more attenuated and unlikely than that contemplated in traditional "overbreadth" cases. We must conjure up a vision of a Wisconsin citizen suppressing his unpopular bigoted opinions for fear that if he later commits an offense covered by the statute, these opinions will be offered at trial to establish that he selected his victim on account of the victim's protected status, thus qualifying him for penalty-enhancement. To stay within the realm of rationality, we must surely put to one side minor misdemeanor offenses covered by the statute, such as negligent operation of a motor vehicle . . . for it is difficult, if not impossible, to conceive of a situation where such offenses would be racially motivated. We are left, then, with the prospect of a citizen suppressing his bigoted beliefs for fear that evidence of such beliefs will be introduced against him at trial if he commits a more serious offense against person or property. This is simply too speculative a hypothesis to support Mitchell's overbreadth claim.

The First Amendment, moreover, does not prohibit the evidentiary use of speech to establish the elements of a crime or to prove motive or intent.

WISCONSIN V. MITCHELL *(continued)*

Evidence of a defendant's previous declarations or statements is commonly admitted in criminal trials subject to evidentiary rules dealing with relevancy, reliability, and the like. Nearly half a century ago, . . . we rejected a contention similar to that advanced by Mitchell here. Haupt was tried for the offense of treason, which, as defined by the Constitution, may depend very much on proof of motive. To prove that the acts in question were committed out of "adherence to the enemy" rather than "parental solicitude," . . . the Government introduced evidence of conversations that had taken place long prior to the indictment, some of which consisted of statements showing Haupt's sympathy with Germany and Hitler and hostility towards the United States. We rejected Haupt's argument that this evidence was improperly admitted. While "[s]uch testimony is to be scrutinized with care to be certain the statements are not expressions of mere proper appreciation of the land of birth," we held that "these statements . . . clearly were admissible on the question of intent and adherence to the enemy." . . .

For the foregoing reasons, we hold that Mitchell's First Amendment rights were not violated by the application of the Wisconsin penalty-enhancement provision in sentencing him. The judgment of the Supreme Court of Wisconsin is therefore reversed, and the case is remanded for further proceedings not inconsistent with this opinion.

R.A.V. and *Mitchell* establish that while bigoted expressions themselves may not be prohibited (legislation aimed at content), bigotry as a motive may be considered at sentencing to enhance a penalty (legislation aimed at the motive of content). The Court pointed out in *R.A.V.* that the conduct itself could be punished under content neutral laws, such as open burning. Such laws apply to all outside burning, not just those that are the product of a (racial) opinion or belief. The Court upheld the sentence enhancement in *Mitchell* because it didn't criminalize the motive. Instead, a content neutral behavior was criminalized. Because of the long history of allowing motives of all sorts to be considered at sentencing, the law was upheld.

Subsequently, in a 2003 decision, *Virginia v. Black*, the Supreme Court upheld a Virginia statute that criminalized cross burning. The Supreme Court did not overrule *R.A.V.* Rather, it distinguished the Virginia statute from the challenged law in *R.A.V.* The distinguishing characteristic was Virginia's requirement that the burning occur with an intent to intimidate. There was no such element in the challenged law in *R.A.V.* The Court analogized intimidating cross burning to threatening speech, which it had previously determined could be regulated.[18]

PRIVACY AND OTHER UNENUMERATED RIGHTS

Unlike some state constitutions, the U.S. Constitution does not expressly protect privacy. Many of the expressly stated rights in the Bill of Rights protect privacy, such as the Fourth Amendment, which has been interpreted as applying to searches that encroach upon a person's reasonable expectation to privacy.

The issue is whether the Constitution protects privacy to a greater extent than through its express provisions. Stated another way, is there an independent and inherent privacy right in the Constitution? If so, what is the textual source of that right?

The Supreme Court answered the former question affirmatively in 1965 in *Griswold v. Connecticut.*[19] In that case, a Connecticut statute that prohibited the use of contraceptives, even by married couples, was held unconstitutional as invasive of a right to privacy.

As to the second issue, the source of the right, the Court found that the right to privacy grows out of the First, Fourth, Fifth, Ninth, and Fourteenth Amendments. Justice Douglas, writing for the Court, found the right to privacy to be a "penumbra" of these expressly protected rights. The Court stressed that the First Amendment's right to association protected the marriage relationship and that the intimate subject sought to be regulated was especially protected. The Court stated that

> [Prior case law] suggests that specific guarantees in the Bill of Rights have penumbras, formed by emanations from those guarantees that help give them life and substance. . . . Various guarantees create zones of privacy. The right of association contained in the penumbra of the First Amendment is one, as we have seen. The Third Amendment in its prohibition against the quartering of soldiers "in any house" in time of peace without the consent of the owner is another facet of that privacy. The Fourth Amendment explicitly affirms the "right of the people to be secure in their persons, houses, papers, and effects, against unreasonable searches and seizures." The Fifth Amendment in its Self-Incrimination Clause enables the citizens to create a zone of privacy which government may not force him to surrender to his detriment. The Ninth Amendment provides: "The enumeration in the Constitution, of certain rights, shall not be construed to deny or disparage others retained by the people." . . .
>
> The present case, then, concerns a relationship lying within the zone of privacy created by several fundamental constitutional guarantees. . . .
>
> We deal with a right to privacy older than the Bill of Rights—older than our political parties, older than our school system. Marriage is a coming together for better or worse, hopefully enduring, and intimate to the degree of being sacred. It is an association that promotes a way of life, not causes; a harmony in living, not political faiths; a bilateral loyalty, not commercial or social projects. Yet it is an association for as noble a purpose as any involved in our prior decisions.

Note that Justice Douglas found that the right to privacy was a penumbra of other fundamental, express rights. He did not find the right to privacy to be an independent constitutional right. This is because he believed that the Fourteenth Amendment was intended to extend the rights found in the Bill of Rights to the states, but that it was not intended to create independent rights. This principle is known as *total incorporation.*

Privacy has also been an issue in abortion cases. Abortion cases are complicated by a competing interest that did not exist in *Griswold,* that is, the interest of the state in protecting the fetus. In 1973 the Supreme Court handed down the landmark decision of *Roe v. Wade,* in which the Court declared that the right to privacy protects a woman's right to elect to abort a fetus in some situations.[20]

Specifically, the Court adopted a trimester analysis wherein the state's authority to regulate abortion increases as the pregnancy lengthens. During the first trimester, states could not regulate abortion procedures. During the second trimester, states could regulate abortions insofar as necessary to protect the health and life of the woman. Finally, states could protect the fetus during the third trimester, including proscribing abortion, except in cases in which abortion was necessary to protect the life or health of the mother. The Court decided that governmental interest in protecting fetuses during the third trimester was compelling because fetuses are viable at that time.

The trial court found Roe's right to privacy in the Ninth Amendment, but the Supreme Court refused to rely on the Ninth Amendment alone. Rather, the Court found the right to privacy to stem from the Fourteenth, Ninth, and other amendments.

The *Roe v. Wade* decision was the subject of intense political and legal controversy during the 1980s and 1990s. Certiorari was sought in several abortion-related cases during this period; so-called right-to-life groups believed that, with a more conservative Court than had existed since the *Roe v. Wade* decision issued, the chances of reversing the decision were good. The Court granted certiorari in several abortion-related cases, but the cardinal principle announced in *Roe v. Wade* was reaffirmed again and again: The decision whether to abort a fetus is, in some circumstances, so private and intimate that it is protected by the Constitution from governmental intrusion. This situation occurred in *Casey v. Planned Parenthood*, wherein the Court also rejected the trimester analysis.

CASEY V. PLANNED PARENTHOOD OF SOUTHEASTERN PENNSYLVANIA
505 U.S. 833 (1992)

Liberty finds no refuge in a jurisprudence of doubt. Yet 19 years after our holding that the Constitution protects a woman's right to terminate her pregnancy in its early stages, the respondents as amicus curiae, the United States, as it has done in five other cases in the last decade, again asks us to overrule *Roe*. . . .

At issue in these cases are five provisions of the Pennsylvania Abortion Control Act of 1982 as amended in 1988 and 1989. . . . The Act requires that a woman seeking an abortion give her informed consent prior to the abortion procedure, and specifies that she be provided with certain information at least 24 hours before the abortion is performed. For a minor to obtain an abortion, the Act requires the informed consent of one of her parents, but provided for [a] judicial bypass option if the minor does not wish to or cannot obtain a parent's consent. Another provision of the Act requires that, unless certain exceptions apply, a married woman seeking an abortion must sign a statement indicating that she has notified her husband of her intended abortion. . . .

Before any of these provisions took effect, the petitioners, who are five abortion clinics and one physician representing himself as well as a class of physicians who provide abortion services, brought this suit seeking declaratory and injunctive relief. Each provision was challenged as unconstitutional on its face. . . .

(continued)

CASEY V. PLANNED PARENTHOOD OF SOUTHEASTERN PENNSYLVANIA (continued)

After considering the fundamental constitutional questions resolved by *Roe*, principles of institutional integrity, and the rule of stare decisis, we are led to conclude this: the essential holding of *Roe v. Wade* should be retained and once again reaffirmed.

It must be stated at the outset and with clarity that *Roe's* essential holding, the holding we reaffirm, has three parts. First is a recognition of the right of the woman to choose to have an abortion before viability and to obtain it without undue interference from the State. Before viability, the State's interests are not strong enough to support a prohibition of abortion or the imposition of a substantial obstacle to the woman's effective right to elect the procedure. Second is a confirmation of the State's power to restrict abortions after fetal viability, if the law contains exceptions for pregnancies which endanger a woman's life or health. And third is the principle that the State has legitimate interests from the outset of the pregnancy in protecting the health of the woman and the life of the fetus that may become a child. These principles do not contradict one another; and we adhere to each.

Constitutional protection of the woman's decision to terminate her pregnancy derives from the Due Process Clause of the Fourteenth Amendment. It declares that no State shall "deprive any person of life, liberty, or property, without due process of law." The controlling word in the case before us is "liberty." . . . We have held that the Due Process Clause of the Fourteenth Amendment incorporates most of the Bill of Rights against the States. . . . It is tempting, as a means of curbing the discretion of federal judges, to suppose that liberty encompasses no more than those rights already guaranteed to the individual against federal interference by the express provisions of the first eight amendments to the Constitution. . . . But of course this Court has never accepted that view. It is also tempting, for the same reason, to suppose that the Due Process Clause protects against government interference by other rules of

law when the Fourteenth Amendment was ratified. . . . But such a view would be inconsistent with our law. It is a promise of the Constitution that there is a realm of personal liberty which the government may not enter. We have vindicated this principle before. Marriage is mentioned nowhere in the Bill of Rights and interracial marriage was illegal in most States in the 19th century, but the Court was no doubt correct in finding it to be an aspect of liberty protected against state interference by the substantive component of the Due Process Clause. . . . Neither the Bill of Rights nor the specific practices of States at the time of the adoption of the Fourteenth Amendment marks the outer limits of the substantive sphere of liberty which the Fourteenth Amendment protects. . . .

Our law affords constitutional protection to personal decisions relating to marriage, procreation, contraception, family relationships, child rearing, and education. . . . These matters, involving the most intimate and personal choices a person may make in a lifetime, choices central to personal dignity and autonomy, are central to the liberty protected by the Fourteenth Amendment. At the heart of liberty is the right to define one's own concept of existence, of meaning, of the universe, and of the mystery of human life. Beliefs about these matters could not define the attributes of personhood were they formed under compulsion of the State.

The consideration begins our analysis of the woman's interest in terminating her pregnancy but cannot end it, for this reason: though the abortion decision may originate within the zone of conscience and belief, it is more than a philosophic exercise. Abortion is a unique act. It is an act fraught with consequences for others: for the woman who must live with the implications of her decision; for the persons who perform and assist in the procedure; for the spouse, family and society which must confront the knowledge that these procedures exist, procedures some deem nothing short of an act of

CASEY V. PLANNED PARENTHOOD OF SOUTHEASTERN PENNSYLVANIA (continued)

violence against innocent human life; and depending on one's beliefs, for the life or potential life that is aborted: Though abortion is conduct, it does not follow that the State is entitled to proscribe it in all instances. That is because the liberty of the woman is at stake in a sense unique to the human condition and so unique to the law. The mother who carries a child to full term is subject to anxieties, to physical constraints, to pain that only she must bear. . . .

No evolution of legal principle has left *Roe's* doctrinal footings weaker than they were in 1973. No development of constitutional law since the case was decided has implicitly or explicitly left *Roe* behind as a mere survivor of obsolete constitutional thinking. . . .

We have seen how time has overtaken some of *Roe's* factual assumptions: advances in maternal health care allow for abortions safe to the mother later in pregnancy than was true in 1973 . . . and advances in neonatal care have advanced viability to a point somewhat earlier. . . . But these facts go only to the scheme of the limits on the realization of competing interests, and the divergences from the factual premises of 1973 have no bearing on the validity of *Roe's* central holding, that viability marks the earliest point at which the State's interest in fetal life is constitutionally adequate to justify a legislative ban on nontherapeutic abortions. The soundness or unsoundness of that constitutional judgment in no sense turns on whether viability occurs at 23 to 24 weeks. . . . Whenever it may occur, the attainment of viability may continue to serve as the critical fact, just as it has done since *Roe* was decided; which is to say that no change in *Roe's* factual underpinnings has left its central holding obsolete, and none supports an argument for overruling it. . . .

Only where a state regulation imposes an undue burden on a woman's ability to make this decision does the power of the State reach into the heart of the liberty protected by the Due Process Clause. . . .

The very notion that the State has a substantial interest in potential life leads to the conclusion that not all regulations must be deemed unwarranted. Not all burdens on the right to decide whether to terminate a pregnancy will be undue. . . .

A finding of undue burden is a shorthand for the conclusion that a state regulation has the purpose or effect of placing a substantial obstacle in the path of a woman seeking an abortion of a nonviable fetus. A statute with this purpose is invalid. . . .

Although the Court reaffirmed the right to privacy in the abortion context, it also rejected the trimester analysis in favor of an "undue interference" test. That is, a regulation is invalid if it unduly interferes with a woman's choice. Also, the Court reaffirmed the *Roe* holding that until a fetus is viable outside of the mother's womb, a state may not prohibit its abortion. Further, even after viability, abortion is permitted to save the life or health of the mother.

The Court examined the Pennsylvania statute and concluded that:

1. Requiring information concerning abortions and abortion procedures to be distributed to patients before the procedure is performed is not unduly burdensome.

2. Mandating 24-hour waiting periods between receipt of the information and performance of the procedure is not unduly burdensome.

3. Requiring parental consent (with a judicial bypass) by minor girls is not unduly burdensome.

4. Requiring spousal notification by married women is unduly burdensome, and therefore, invalid.[21]

The right to privacy applies outside the abortion context as well. For example, as the Court stated in *Casey*, the right to engage in an interracial marriage is also protected by the Fourteenth Amendment.[22] In *Eisenstadt v. Baird*,[23] the Supreme Court invalidated a statute that prohibited the sale and distribution of contraceptives to unmarried persons. The Court stated in that opinion, "If the right of privacy means anything, it is the right of the individual, married or single, to be free from unwarranted governmental intrusion into matter so fundamentally affecting a person as the decision whether to bear or beget a child."

These are a few examples of how the power of the state to regulate conduct is limited by the right to privacy. Today, courts are likely to rely on the Fourteenth Amendment as the source of the right to privacy. Arguably, the privacy right has its roots in other amendments as well, such as the Ninth Amendment, which declares that the enumeration in the Constitution of certain rights shall not be construed as denying or disparaging others retained by the people. Although this amendment appears to be an independent source of rights, probably with natural rights origins, it has received little attention by the courts, and standing alone has never been relied upon by the Supreme Court to establish an unenumerated right.

The Supreme Court refused to extend the right to privacy to include a right for consenting adults to engage in "deviate sexual" behavior in its 1986 decision *Bowers v. Hardwick*,[24] where it upheld a Georgia statute that criminalized sodomy. But the Court reversed itself seven years later in *Lawrence v. Texas*[25] (see Chapter 6 for more on this subject).

PRIVILEGES AND IMMUNITIES

Article IV, sec. 2 commands that "The Citizens of each State shall be entitled to all Privileges and Immunities of Citizens in the several States." The purpose of the clause is to prevent states from discriminating against citizens of other states. The clause applies only to the most fundamental of rights, and even then a state may overcome the prohibition if it can demonstrate a compelling reason.

Once a viable source of individual rights, the reach of clause has been severely limited by the Supreme Court, which has increasingly turned to the Fourteenth Amendment's Due Process Clause to protect unenumerated rights. One of the few rights protected by the Privileges and Immunities Clause is the right to travel freely between the states. The right to travel abroad is subject to reasonable restrictions and regulations[26] because of national security and foreign affairs concerns.

The Fourteenth Amendment contains a sister clause that forbids states from abridging the privileges or immunities of citizens of the United States. While the Fourth Amendment's Privileges and Immunities Clause forbids states from discriminating against each other's citizens, the Fourteenth Amendment's Privileges or

Immunities Clause forbids the states from abridging any person, local or not, from exercising federally secured rights.

Any time a statute conflicts with a constitutionally protected activity, the statute will fail unless the government has a compelling interest. The defenses discussed in this chapter are only a few of the many constitutional defenses. Most, but not all, criminal constitutional defenses appear in the Bill of Rights.

Nor does this chapter exhaust all the nonconstitutional defenses that may be asserted. Do not forget that each state is free to design its criminal law in any manner it wishes, so long as its design is consonant with the U.S. Constitution. The most common factual, legislative, and constitutional substantive law defenses have been discussed. Many procedural defenses are examined in later chapters of this text.

Ethical Considerations

ARE FEDERAL PROSECUTORS SUBJECT TO STATE ETHICS RULES?

In 1992, a federal grand jury indicted Joseph McDade for bribery. Four years later, he was acquitted on all charges. He claimed that during his prosecution, federal prosecutors violated well-established state ethics rules, including the no-contact rule. In both civil and criminal law, there is a general prohibition of counsel having direct contact with an opposing party without the consent and, if desired, presence of opposing counsel. In criminal cases, this rule is predicated upon the theory that without defense counsel, defendants could be subject to duress or overreaching by prosecutors. The rule applies to direct contact by attorneys or contact through agents and informants of prosecutors.

Even though this rule can be found in the ABA's Model Code of Professional Responsibility and exists in every state, the United States Department of Justice has resisted its application in federal prosecutions. Both the attorneys general of George H. W. Bush (Richard Thornburgh) and Bill Clinton (Janet Reno) were of the opinion that federal prosecutors are not subject to such state rules. Feeling persecuted and angry, McDade wanted to change the law—and he was in a better than average position to do so. McDade was a U.S. congressman (and attorney) from Pennsylvania (he served from 1962 to 1999). Following his acquittal, he proposed the Citizens Protection Act, a law that applies state ethics rules to federal prosecutors. The CPA further makes it clear that federal court rules also limit the authority of federal prosecutors. McDade testified at hearing about the law, lobbied his colleagues and the public, and eventually was successful in getting it enacted.

Sources: Brenna K. DeVaney, "The 'No-Contact' Rule: Helping or Hurting Criminal Defendants in Plea Negotiations," 14 *Geo. J. Legal Ethics* 933 (2001); and Fred C. Zacharias and Bruce A. Green, "The Uniqueness of Federal Prosecutors," 88 *Geo. L.J.* 207 (2000).

┌───┐

Web Links

Comparative Criminal Justice

At the World Factbook of Criminal Justice Systems, you will find descriptions of the legal and criminal justice systems of many nations of the world. http://bjs.ojp.usdoj.gov/content/pub/html/wfcj.cfm

The United States Department of Justice's National Institute of Justice and Bureau of Justice Statistics both offer some comparative justice information. *http://www.ojp.usdoj.gov/nij/* and *http://www.ojp.usdoj.gov/bjs/*

└───┘

Key Terms

bill of attainder

Double Jeopardy Clause

ex post facto law

overbreadth

principle of legality

transactional immunity

use immunity

vagueness

Review Questions

1. Differentiate overbreadth from vagueness. Give an example of each.

2. Differentiate a bill of attainder from an ex post facto law.

3. May racially derogatory statements be made criminal? May racial motives be used to enhance the punishment for crimes such as assault and battery?

4. Is a right to privacy specifically expressed in the U.S. Constitution?

5. Through what amendment are rights incorporated and applied against the states?

6. May religious beliefs be regulated by the state? May religious practices be regulated by the state?

7. Which of the following is protected by the First Amendment's Free Speech Clause?

   a. A public flag burning in protest of a recently enacted law.

   b. An advertisement for potato chips found on a billboard.

   c. The placing of a hand over one's heart while the national anthem is played.

Problems & Critical Thinking Exercises

1. Senator Bob Kerry of Nebraska was initially outraged by the *Texas v. Johnson* flag-burning decision. However, he later stated, "I was surprised to discover . . . [that the decision was] reasonable, understandable and consistent with those values which I believe have made America wonderful." Do you agree with Senator Kerry? Explain your position.

2. State law requires that all children between the ages of 5 and 16 years attend an approved school. Defendants have been charged with violating the

statute, as they do not permit their children to attend school. The defendants are Mennonites and claim that it would violate their First Amendment right to freely exercise their religion. The defendants teach their children in a manner consistent with their religious teachings. Should they be convicted?

3. Do you believe that a person should be subjected to two prosecutions, by different sovereigns, for the same offense? Consider specifically the prosecution

of the Los Angeles police officers who arrested and beat Rodney King. They were acquitted of assault and battery in state court. Federal civil rights charges were brought in apparent reaction to the acquittal. In your opinion, is this proper? Support your answer.

4. Do you believe that the federal Constitution implicitly protects privacy? Support your conclusion. If so, name one right not mentioned in this text that you believe is protected.

Endnotes

1. David S. Rudstein, "Brief History of the Fifth Amendment Guarantee Against Double Jeopardy," 14 *Wm & Mary Bill of Rts. J.* 193, 204 (2005).

2. *Arizona v. Washington*, 434 U.S. 497 (1978).

3. *United States v. Dreitzler*, 577 F.2d 539 (9th Cir. 1978).

4. *United States v. Martin Linen Supply Co.*, 430 U.S. 564 (1977).

5. *See Monge v. California*, 524 U.S. 721 (1998).

6. *Blockburger v. United States*, 284 U.S. 299 (1932).

7. Model Penal Code § 1.10.

8. Passage taken from a 1991 calendar prepared by the Commission on the Bicentennial of the United States Constitution, Washington, D.C.

9. *Pillsbury v. Conboy*, 459 U.S. 248 (1983).

10. *Douglas v. California*, 372 U.S. 353 (1963).

11. *Connally v. General Construction Co.*, 269 U.S. 385 (1926).

12. *United States v. Cardiff*, 344 U.S. 174 (1952).

13. *Coates v. Cincinnati*, 402 U.S. 611 (1971).

14. See *United States v. Brown*, 381 U.S. at 444 (quoting John C. Hamilton, *History of the Republic of the United States* 34 (1859), who is *quoting* Alexander Hamilton).

15. *Reynolds v. United States*, 98 U.S. 145 (1878).

16. *People v. Woody*, 61 Cal. 2d 716, 394 P.2d 813 (1965).

17. 42 U.S. sec. 2000bb.

18. 538 U.S. 343 (2003).

19. 381 U.S. 479 (1965). The Supreme Court noted in *Roe v. Wade*, 410 U.S. 113 (1973), that the right to privacy may have been recognized by the Court as early as 1891, in *Union Pacific Railroad v. Botsford*, 141 U.S. 250 (1891), in which it held that a plaintiff in a tort action could not be compelled to submit to a medical examination because it would have been an invasion of privacy.

20. 410 U.S. 113 (1973).

21. *See also Webster v. Reproductive Health Services*, 492 U.S. 490 (1989).

22. *Loving v. Virginia*, 388 U.S. 1 (1967).

23. 405 U.S. 438 (1972).

24. 478 U.S. 186 (1986).

25. 539 U.S. 558 (2003).

26. *Zemel v. Rusk*, 381 U.S. 1 (1965).

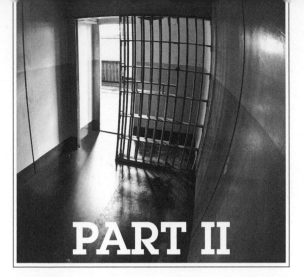

PART II

CRIMINAL PROCEDURE

CHAPTER 10

INTRODUCTION AND PARTICIPANTS

Chapter Outline

Criminal Procedure Defined

A Common-Law, Adversarial, and Accusatorial System

The Due Process Model

The Participants

Law Enforcement Officers
Prosecutors
Judges
Defense Attorneys
Victims

Liability of Governments and Their Officials

Ethical Considerations: Attorney Compensation

Chapter Objectives

After completing this chapter, you should be able to:

- explain the common-law, adversarial nature of the U.S. criminal justice systems.
- think critically about the due process and crime control models of criminal justice.
- describe the role and the ethics considerations of major players in the criminal justice system: law enforcement officers, defense attorneys, prosecutors, victims, and judges.
- describe the basic liability that government officials can incur when performing their duties.
- identify the material facts and legal issues in two-thirds of the cases you read and describe the court's analyses and conclusions in the cases.

CRIMINAL PROCEDURE DEFINED

The second section of this text addresses criminal procedure. *Criminal procedure*, as a field of law, describes the methods used in bringing an alleged criminal to justice. To state it another way, criminal procedure puts substantive criminal law into action.

Each state and the federal government has its own procedural rules. In some instances, the variation is significant. For the purpose of this text, most references will be to federal procedure. Many federal procedural rules can be found in the U.S. Code. A good number of procedures are judicially created (and approved by Congress) and are found in the Federal Rules of Criminal Procedure (Fed. R. Crim. P.). Finally, the constitutions of the national government and the states play a major role in defining procedures of criminal adjudications.

What follows is a discussion of the constitutional aspects of criminal procedure; the process, from investigation to appeal; searches and seizures; arrests; confessions and admissions; and the right to counsel.

A COMMON-LAW, ADVERSARIAL, AND ACCUSATORIAL SYSTEM

The colonists brought with them the common law of England. Today all states, except Louisiana, which is of the civil law family, are of the common law family.

adversary system

■ The system of law in the United States. The judge acts as the referee between opposite sides (between two individuals, between the state and an individual, etc.) rather than acting as the person who also makes the state's case or independently seeks out evidence.

In addition to being common law in nature, the legal system is **adversarial.** Adversarial adjudications resemble sporting events. There are two opposing parties and a neutral umpire. In criminal adjudications, these roles are played by the defendant, prosecutor, and judge. The judge in criminal adjudications is a passive participant, usually becoming involved only as needed by the parties or as required by law. Of course, the approach of judges varies; and some are more proactive than others. A pure adversarial system is not employed in the United States, and judges are expected to supervise the proceedings to assure fairness. The adversary system is built upon the theory that the truth is more likely to be discovered when there are two competing parties, each conducting its own investigation of the facts, asserting differing theories of fact and law, and each presenting its own case to the court.

sidebar

WHY LOUISIANA IS DIFFERENT

As you learn the law, you will learn that the law of Louisiana is often different from the rest of the states because, unlike the rest of the colonies, which were founded by the English (who imported the common law), Louisiana was

---

sidebar *(continued)*

founded by the French. In 1712 French emperor Louis XIV issued a Charter for the development of Louisiana with an order requiring the application of French law, also known as civil law. But for the period between 1762 and 1800, when the territory was under the control of the Spanish, French law applied. In 1803 the United States took possession of the territory. The first territorial legislature of Louisiana chose to retain the civil law.

So, how is civil law different from common law? As you have learned, the common law developed through judicial pronouncements, in response to specific disputes. The civil law, which was born in France, is more "legislative" and less "judicial." The legislative code is the primary source of law, not judicial decisions. Even more, judges have less authority to interpret and expand the meaning of the law in civil-law nations. The procedures of the two families of law are also different. Many historians cite the year 529 as marking the birth of the civil law. In that year, Roman emperor Justinian issued his famous Corpus Juris Civilis. In 1804, Napoleon issued his own legal code, which has been the foundation for many codes still in existence, including Louisiana's Code. There are four major legal families recognized by contemporary comparativists: common, civil, Islamic, and socialist. This author includes a fifth—traditional and transitional law.

Even though it is a member of the civil law family, Louisiana is equally bound by the United States Constitution and, accordingly, its law has much in common with the other states.

Also, in the common law, judges are expected to remain impartial, neutral, and detached. This is believed to increase the fairness of the proceedings. In civil law jurisdictions, on the other hand, judges sometimes develop an opinion or theory, which may limit their consideration of alternatives and accordingly, limit the facts that are sought and the theories that are advanced. In the adversarial system, the parties are largely responsible for development of the case—that is, discovery of the evidence and, accordingly, the issues of law as well.

The adversarial system has its critics. Opponents contend that the truth is not found because the system encourages the opposing parties to present distorted, misleading, and sometimes untruthful accounts of the facts. The fact finder, who is not part of the investigative process, is often left to choose between polarized versions of the same event. The adversarial system is also challenged as being unfair because it assumes two equally competent competing parties. However, because of differences in the abilities of counsel and the respective powers of the parties, this premise is questionable.

In addition to being adversarial, the criminal justice system is accusatorial. This means that the government, as the accuser, bears the burden of proving a defendant's guilt.

If the government fails in its burden, then a defendant is entitled to a directed verdict or a judgement of acquittal. The accusatorial nature of the system extends beyond placing the burden of proof on the government at trial. The entire process is designed to minimize the risk of convicting an innocent person. The philosophy that it is better to free several guilty persons than to convict one innocent person is a major theme of the U.S. criminal justice system. Accordingly, the system is designed so that the accused enjoys several advantages, the most critical one being the presumption of innocence; the freedom from self-incrimination, the right to a jury trial, and the right to counsel are others.

The fact that a defendant enjoys a few advantages does not mean that the defendant has the advantage on whole. The government, state or federal, can commit substantial resources to a prosecution.

THE DUE PROCESS MODEL

Criminal justice systems are commonly characterized as falling on a continuum that is bracketed by the *crime control* and the *due process models*. The repression, detection, and efficient prosecution of crime is central to the crime control model. Failure to detect and successfully prosecute criminals is perceived as a failure of government. This failure leads to a loss of individual liberties because citizens live in constant fear of, and are actually subject to, criminal conduct. A secondary consequence is a loss of confidence in government by the public, thereby further hindering its ability to detect and prevent crime. Prosecution in such systems tends to be bureaucratic, that is, a form of "assembly-line" justice. Some civil law and socialist law nations tend toward the crime control model.

The due process model places a premium on the integrity of individual rights and the fairness of process, as well as factual guilt. Efficiency (speed, cost, identifying an punishing offenders) is secondary. The balance is different in crime control systems. Factual guilt and efficiency are emphasized. *Factual guilt* refers to whether a defendant has in fact committed a crime. *Legal guilt* is concerned not only with factual guilt, but also with whether the defendant's rights have been observed and respected by the government in the processes of investigation and prosecution. It is possible, under the due process model, to have sufficient evidence to prove a defendant factually guilty; but because of a civil rights violation, the defendant must be declared legally not guilty. The due process model has little tolerance for conviction of the innocent; the crime control model equally abhors crimes going unsolved and defendants unpunished. Investigation and adjudication of defendants is less efficient and more costly under the due process model than under the crime control model.

This is a simplification of the two models.[1] No system falls squarely into either of the two models, although most systems can be generally characterized as adhering to the principles of one more than the other. The United States follows the due process model. Individual rights and fair procedures are the hallmark of the U.S. system of criminal justice. All individuals are innocent until proven guilty. The process itself presumes innocence, and deprivations of liberties are sharply limited and regulated before guilt is found.

Exhibit 10-1 CRIME CONTROL AND DUE PROCESS MODELS COMPARED

Model/Point on Continuum		
	Crime Control	**Due Process**
Philosophy	Discovering, apprehending, and punishing offenders, and deterring crime, is a priority. Civil liberties are protected, but not to the extent they jeopardize social control.	Discovering, apprehending, and punishing offenders is balanced against civil liberties. In some instances, civil liberties will prevail and crimes will go unpunished.
Process	Mechanistic; efficiency is a high priority. The criminal justice system is a machine through which the government processes its cases.	Cumbersome; efficiency is not a high priority. The criminal justice system is not so much a machine but a maze through which the government must navigate to secure a conviction.
Conviction Standard	Actual guilt of accused is required for conviction. Government's burdens of proof and production are less than in systems emphasizing due process.	Legal and factual guilt are required for conviction. Government has high burdens of production and proof.

Copyright © Cengage Learning®.

Also, as the severity of the government's intrusions or deprivations increases, so must the evidence of guilt. For example, less evidence is required to establish probable cause to support a search of an automobile than to bind a defendant over to trial. This is because binding a defendant over to trial entails greater losses of liberty (possible pretrial detention and the cost and humiliation of being publicly tried) than does the search. You will learn many procedures that support the conclusion that the United States adheres to the due process model. Attempt to identify these characteristics as you read the following chapters. Chapters 11 through 16 examine the basic procedures and constitutional aspects of bringing criminals to justice. First, however, you must become familiar with the participants in this process.

THE PARTICIPANTS

Besides the accused and witnesses, there are six primary participants in criminal adjudications: law enforcement officers, prosecutors, judges, defense attorneys, victims, and jurors. What follows is a discussion of all these participants except jurors. Jurors are discussed later.

Law Enforcement Officers

The front line of law enforcement in the United States is what the public commonly refers to as the *police*. Law enforcement officers exist at the national, state, and local levels.

Federal law enforcement agencies include the Federal Bureau of Investigation, the Drug Enforcement Administration, Customs, the Coast Guard, U.S. Marshals, the Secret Service, and the Bureau of Alcohol, Tobacco, and Firearms, to name only a few.

Each state has a police department, and many have a counterpart to the FBI, such as the Kansas Bureau of Investigation (KBI). In addition, within each state, county sheriffs and municipal police departments enforce the laws of the state as well as the laws of their locality. There are more than 20,000 local law enforcement agencies in the United States. This includes 12,502 local police departments; 3,086 sheriffs' offices; 49 state police departments; and more than 700,000 sworn police officers and 300,000-plus civilian personnel. In addition, there were 105,000 federal officers who carry weapons and are authorized to make arrests in the 50 states and District of Columbia in 2004. Three-fourths of these officers work in the Department of Homeland Security. An additional 1,500 officers work in U.S. territories. Additional officers are stationed in foreign nations.[2]

Discretion

Law enforcement personnel are expected to keep the peace, investigate possible wrongdoing, enforce the laws, and further crime prevention. Although it is generally held that the police must enforce the laws, it is also recognized that not all the laws can be or should be enforced. Consequently, officers exercise much discretion when performing their daily duties. Deciding whether to conduct an investigation, whether to arrest an offender, or whether a search is necessary all usually fall within the individual officer's discretion. However, the conduct of police officers must comply with constitutional, statutory, and departmental policy standards.

Ethics

As is true of prosecutors and defense attorneys, the police officer's paramount ethical code is the Constitution. Police officers have a legal and ethical obligation to keep themselves within constitutional limits when performing their duties.

More specifically, the International Association of Chiefs of Police (IACP) has formulated a set of ethical principles intended to guide the law enforcement officer in the performance of his or her duties. The IACP has issued two ethics documents, the "Law Enforcement Code of Ethics" and the "Police Code of Conduct." The Code of Ethics is a general statement of ethical responsibility that may be used as an oath of office.

The Code of Ethics recognizes that police officers hold a special public trust and that they have an obligation not to violate that trust.

Although substantially the same, the Police Code of Conduct is more specific than the Code of Ethics. The Code of Conduct prohibits discriminatory treatment of individuals based upon status, sex, religion, political belief, or aspiration; the unnecessary use of force; the infliction of cruel, degrading, or inhuman treatment; violation of confidences, except when necessary in the performance of duties or as required by law; bribery; the acceptance of gifts; refusals to cooperate with other law enforcement officials; and other unreasonable and inappropriate behavior. The Code of Conduct further qualifies the necessary force requirement by stating that force should be used "only with the greatest restraint and only after discussion, negotiation and persuasion have been found to be inappropriate or ineffective."

Officers are expected to behave in a manner that inspires confidence and respect for law enforcement officials. Further, police officers are to attempt to obtain maximum public cooperation and to enforce all laws with courtesy, consideration, and dignity. Although the IACP has no enforcement authority, the codes do provide an excellent standard for adoption by law enforcement agencies, as well as by individual officers.

For the remainder of this book, references to police or law enforcement officers are to any one of the previously mentioned agencies.

Prosecutors

Prosecutors are also central to the administration of justice. *Prosecutors* are government attorneys responsible for prosecuting violators. This role includes preparing and filing documents; engaging in pretrial activity, such as discovery; and appearing in court. Prosecutors often also act as legal counsel to law enforcement officers, rendering advice on the law of searches, seizures, arrests, surveillance techniques, and similar matters. Prosecutors appear at grand jury hearings, where they present evidence and assist the jury in other ways. Finally, in some jurisdictions, prosecutors act in a supervisory capacity as the head of a law enforcement agency, such as the Attorney General of the United States, who is the head of the Department of Justice.

At the federal level, the highest law enforcement official and prosecutor is the attorney general, who undergoes the presidential nomination and senatorial confirmation process. The attorney general is a cabinet member who heads the Department of Justice.

Within each judicial district is one U.S. attorney, a subordinate of the attorney general, who also is selected through the nomination and confirmation process. U.S. attorneys, with the aid of several assistant U.S. attorneys (AUSAs), are responsible for most federal prosecutions. In rare cases, however, another attorney from the Department of Justice may travel to a district to handle a case. Federal law also provides for the appointment of an independent counsel (special prosecutor) when government officials are suspected of violating the law.

Similar to the federal government, each state has an attorney general. The states vary in the structure of their prosecutorial agencies, but most have locally elected prosecutors, who may be titled *prosecutor, district attorney,* or *state attorney*. The degree to which these individuals answer to the state attorney general differs greatly. Additionally, local forms of government have attorneys. In some localities, these attorneys prosecute ordinance violations.

Prosecutorial Discretion

Prosecutors enjoy considerable discretion in the performance of their duties. The decision whether to prosecute an individual is one aspect of prosecutorial **discretion.** This decision must be made by a prosecutor in most cases. In a small number of cases, however, the prosecutor may not be in a position to make this decision, such as when a traffic ticket acts as the charging instrument and the case proceeds directly to court

discretion /

■ The power to act within general guidelines, rules, or laws, but without either specific rules to follow or the need to completely explain or justify each decision or action.

nolle prosequi

■ (Latin) The ending of a criminal case because the prosecutor decides or agrees to stop prosecuting. When this happens, the case is "nolled," "nollied," or "nol. prossed."

without the prosecutor's involvement. However, most cases are initiated directly by a prosecutor, grand jury, or, as is usually the case, the police (through the arrest and complaint procedure). A case may not proceed under a complaint; rather, the prosecutor must file an information (or an indictment issued by a grand jury), which replaces the complaint. If a prosecutor refuses, or files a **nolle prosequi,** the case proceeds no further.

There are two general reasons that discretion must be exercised. First, the prosecutor's ethical obligation requires that he or she seek justice, not convictions. Prosecutors are not to maintain a prosecution simply because there is a probability of prevailing. Rather, the totality of the facts must be examined, and it must be determined that a prosecution will further justice. The justice obligation continues through the entire adjudicative process.

Economics is the second reason prosecutors cannot pursue every case. The resources of the prosecutor and law enforcement agencies are limited. Not every case can be prosecuted, because there are inadequate investigators, police officers, prosecutors, and other resources. Prosecutors must prioritize cases for prosecution. The decision whether to prosecute is influenced by many factors. The facts of the case; the accused's criminal, social, and economic history; the likelihood of success; the cost of prosecution, including the probable time investment; public opinion; the seriousness of the crime; the desires of the victims; police expectations and desires; political concerns; and whether the prosecution will further the administration of justice are all considered.

Although prosecutorial discretion is broad, it is not absolute. First, the authority to file a nolle prosequi, or dismissal, may be limited. The further along a case is in the process, the more involved the court becomes in the decision. Generally, the decision not to prosecute before the formal charge (information or indictment) is filed is left to the prosecutor without judicial intervention. However, a small number of states require judicial approval of nolle prosequi decisions.

Once the formal charge has been filed, judicial approval of dismissal is the rule rather than the exception. This is true in the federal system, which also requires leave of court to dismiss complaints.[3]

Second, decisions to prosecute that are motivated by improper criteria may violate equal protection. The Fourteenth Amendment prohibits each state from taking actions that "deny to any person within its jurisdiction the equal protection of the laws." Although the Fifth Amendment does not contain this language, the Supreme Court has interpreted the Fifth Amendment's Due Process Clause as requiring equal protection of the laws. A claim that it is unfair to prosecute a person because other known violators are not prosecuted will not be successful, unless it can be shown that the accused has been singled out for an improper reason.

Generally, three elements must be shown to establish improper, discriminatory prosecution: first, that other people similarly situated were not prosecuted; second, that the prosecutor intentionally singled out the defendant; third, that the selection was based upon an arbitrary classification. As the Supreme Court stated in *Oyler v. Boles,*[4] for there to be an equal protection violation, it must be shown that "the selection was *deliberately* based upon an unjustified standard." What is an unjustified standard? Prosecutions based upon race, religion, and gender are examples. A prosecution intended to punish an individual for exercising a constitutional right is also improper. The Supreme Court discusses selective prosecution in *United States v. Armstrong* (1996).

UNITED STATES V. ARMSTRONG
517 U.S. 456 (1996)

OPINION

Chief Justice Rehnquist delivered the opinion of the Court.

In this case, we consider the showing necessary for a defendant to be entitled to discovery on a claim that the prosecuting attorney singled him out for prosecution on the basis of his race. We conclude that respondents failed to satisfy the threshold showing: They failed to show that the Government declined to prosecute similarly situated suspects of other races.

In April 1992, respondents were indicted in the United States District Court for the Central District of California on charges of conspiring to possess with intent to distribute more than 50 grams of cocaine base (crack) and conspiring to distribute the same, in violation of 21 U.S.C. §§ 841 and 846 (1988 ed. and Supp. IV), and federal firearms offenses. For three months prior to the indictment, agents of the Federal Bureau of Alcohol, Tobacco, and Firearms and the Narcotics Division of the Inglewood, California, Police Department had infiltrated a suspected crack distribution ring by using three confidential informants. On seven separate occasions during this period, the informants had bought a total of 124.3 grams of crack from respondents and witnessed respondents carrying firearms during the sales. The agents searched the hotel room in which the sales were transacted, arrested respondents Armstrong and Hampton in the room, and found more crack and a loaded gun. The agents later arrested the other respondents as part of the ring.

In response to the indictment, respondents filed a motion for discovery or for dismissal of the indictment, alleging that they were selected for federal prosecution because they are black. In support of their motion, they offered only an affidavit by a "Paralegal Specialist," employed by the Office of the Federal Public Defender representing one of the respondents. The only allegation in the affidavit was that, in every one of the 24 § 841 or § 846 cases closed by the office during 1991, the defendant was black. Accompanying the affidavit was a "study" listing the 24 defendants, their race, whether they were prosecuted for dealing cocaine as well as crack, and the status of each case.

The Government opposed the discovery motion, arguing, among other things, that there was no evidence or allegation "that the Government has acted unfairly or has prosecuted nonblack defendants or failed to prosecute them." The District Court granted the motion. It ordered the Government (1) to provide a list of all cases from the last three years in which the Government charged both cocaine and firearms offenses, (2) to identify the race of the defendants in those cases, (3) to identify what levels of law enforcement were involved in the investigations of those cases, and (4) to explain its criteria for deciding to prosecute those defendants for federal cocaine offenses.

The Government moved for reconsideration of the District Court's discovery order. With this motion it submitted affidavits and other evidence to explain why it had chosen to prosecute respondents and why respondents' study did not support the inference that the Government was singling out blacks for cocaine prosecution. The federal and local agents participating in the case alleged in affidavits that race played no role in their investigation. An Assistant United States Attorney explained in an affidavit that the decision to prosecute met the general criteria for prosecution, because

"there was over 100 grams of cocaine base involved, over twice the threshold necessary for a ten year mandatory minimum sentence; there were multiple sales involving multiple defendants, thereby indicating a fairly substantial crack cocaine ring; . . . there

(continued)

UNITED STATES V. ARMSTRONG (continued)

were multiple federal firearms violations intertwined with the narcotics trafficking; the overall evidence in the case was extremely strong, including audio and videotapes of defendants; . . . and several of the defendants had criminal histories including narcotics and firearms violations."

The Government also submitted sections of a published 1989 Drug Enforcement Administration report which concluded that "large-scale, interstate trafficking networks controlled by Jamaicans, Haitians and Black street gangs dominate the manufacture and distribution of crack."

In response, one of respondents' attorneys submitted an affidavit alleging that an intake coordinator at a drug treatment center had told her that there are "an equal number of caucasian users and dealers to minority users and dealers." Respondents also submitted an affidavit from a criminal defense attorney alleging that in his experience many nonblacks are prosecuted in state court for crack offenses, and a newspaper article reporting that federal "crack criminals . . . are being punished far more severely than if they had been caught with powder cocaine, and almost every single one of them is black."

The District Court denied the motion for reconsideration. When the Government indicated it would not comply with the court's discovery order, the court dismissed the case.

A divided three-judge panel of the Court of Appeals for the Ninth Circuit reversed, . . . A selective-prosecution claim is not a defense on the merits to the criminal charge itself, but an independent assertion that the prosecutor has brought the charge for reasons forbidden by the Constitution. Our cases delineating the necessary elements to prove a claim of selective prosecution have taken great pains to explain that the standard is a demanding one. These cases afford a "background presumption," that the showing necessary to obtain discovery should itself be a significant barrier to the litigation of insubstantial claims.

A selective-prosecution claim asks a court to exercise judicial power over a "special province" of the Executive. The Attorney General and United States Attorneys retain "broad discretion" to enforce the Nation's criminal laws. They have this latitude because they are designated by statute as the President's delegates to help him discharge his constitutional responsibility to "take *Care that the Laws be* faithfully executed." U.S. Const., Art. II, § 3; see 28 U.S.C. §§ 516, 547. As a result, "the presumption of regularity supports" their prosecutorial decisions and, "in the absence of clear evidence to the contrary, courts presume that they have properly discharged their official duties." In the ordinary case, "so long as the prosecutor has probable cause to believe that the accused committed an offense defined by statute, the decision whether or not to prosecute, and what charge to file or bring before a grand jury, generally rests entirely in his discretion."

Of course, a prosecutor's discretion is "subject to constitutional constraints." One of these constraints, imposed by the equal protection component of the Due Process Clause of the Fifth Amendment, is that the decision whether to prosecute may not be based on "an unjustifiable standard such as race, religion, or other arbitrary classification." A defendant may demonstrate that the administration of a criminal law is "directed so exclusively against a particular class of persons . . . with a mind so unequal and oppressive" that the system of prosecution amounts to "a practical denial" of equal protection of the law.

In order to dispel the presumption that a prosecutor has not violated equal protection, a criminal defendant must present "clear evidence to the contrary." We explained in Wayte why courts are "properly hesitant to examine the decision whether to prosecute." Judicial deference to the decisions of these executive officers rests in part on

UNITED STATES V. ARMSTRONG (continued)

an assessment of the relative competence of prosecutors and courts. "Such factors as the strength of the case, the prosecution's general deterrence value, the Government's enforcement priorities, and the case's relationship to the Government's overall enforcement plan are not readily susceptible to the kind of analysis the courts are competent to undertake." It also stems from a concern not to unnecessarily impair the performance of a core executive constitutional function. "Examining the basis of a prosecution delays the criminal proceeding, threatens to chill law enforcement by subjecting the prosecutor's motives and decision making to outside inquiry, and may undermine prosecutorial effectiveness by revealing the Government's enforcement policy." The requirements for a selective-prosecution claim draw on "ordinary equal protection standards." The claimant must demonstrate that the federal prosecutorial policy "had a discriminatory effect and that it was motivated by a discriminatory purpose." To establish a discriminatory effect in a race case, the claimant must show that similarly situated individuals of a different race were not prosecuted. This requirement has been established in our case law since *Ah Sin v. Wittman*, 198 U.S. 500, 49 L. Ed. 1142, 25 S. Ct. 756 (1905). Ah Sin, a subject of China, petitioned a California state court for a writ of habeas corpus, seeking discharge from imprisonment under a San Francisco County ordinance prohibiting persons from setting up gambling tables in rooms barricaded to stop police from entering. He alleged in his habeas petition "that the ordinance is enforced 'solely and exclusively against persons of the Chinese race and not otherwise.'" We rejected his contention that this averment made out a claim under the Equal Protection Clause, because it did not allege "that the conditions and practices to which the ordinance was directed did not exist exclusively among the

Chinese, or that there were other offenders against the ordinance than the Chinese as to whom it was not enforced."

The similarly situated requirement does not make a selective-prosecution claim impossible to prove. Twenty years before *Ah Sin*, we invalidated an ordinance, also adopted by San Francisco, that prohibited the operation of laundries in wooden buildings. The plaintiff in error successfully demonstrated that the ordinance was applied against Chinese nationals but not against other laundry-shop operators. The authorities had denied the applications of 200 Chinese subjects for permits to operate shops in wooden buildings, but granted the applications of 80 individuals who were not Chinese subjects to operate laundries in wooden buildings "under similar conditions." We explained in *Ah Sin* why the similarly situated requirement is necessary:

> "No latitude of intention should be indulged in a case like this. There should be certainty to every intent. Plaintiff in error seeks to set aside a criminal law of the State, not on the ground that it is unconstitutional on its face, not that it is discriminatory in tendency and ultimate actual operation as the ordinance was which was passed on in the *Yick Wo* case, but that it was made so by the manner of its administration. This is a matter of proof, and *no fact should be omitted to make it out completely*, when the power of a Federal court is invoked to interfere with the course of criminal justice of a State." 198 U.S. at 508 (emphasis added).

Although *Ah Sin* involved federal review of a state conviction, we think a similar rule applies where the power of a federal court is invoked to challenge an exercise of one of the core powers of the Executive Branch of the Federal Government, the power to prosecute. . . .

Having reviewed the requirements to prove a selective-prosecution claim, we turn to the showing

(continued)

necessary to obtain discovery in support of such a claim. If discovery is ordered, the Government must assemble from its own files documents which might corroborate or refute the defendant's claim. Discovery thus imposes many of the costs present when the Government must respond to a prima facie case of selective prosecution. It will divert prosecutors' resources and may disclose the Government's prosecutorial strategy. The justifications for a rigorous standard for the elements of a selective-prosecution claim thus require a correspondingly rigorous standard for discovery in aid of such a claim.

The parties, and the Courts of Appeals which have considered the requisite showing to establish entitlement to discovery, describe this showing with a variety of phrases, like "colorable basis," "substantial threshold showing," "substantial and concrete basis," or "reasonable likelihood," Brief for Respondents Martin et al. 30. However, the many labels for this showing conceal the degree of consensus about the evidence necessary to meet it. The Courts of Appeals "require some evidence tending to show the existence of the essential elements of the defense," discriminatory effect and discriminatory intent.

In this case we consider what evidence constitutes "some evidence tending to show the existence" of the discriminatory effect element. The Court of Appeals held that a defendant may establish a colorable basis for discriminatory effect without evidence that the Government has failed to prosecute others who are similarly situated to the defendant. We think it was mistaken in this view. The vast majority of the Courts of Appeals require the defendant to produce some evidence that similarly situated defendants of other races could have been prosecuted, but were not, and this requirement is consistent with our equal protection case law. As the three-judge panel explained, "'selective prosecution' implies that a selection has taken place."

The Court of Appeals reached its decision in part because it started "with the presumption that people of *all* races commit *all* types of crimes—not with the premise that any type of crime is the exclusive province of any particular racial or ethnic group." It cited no authority for this proposition, which seems contradicted by the most recent statistics of the United States Sentencing Commission. Those statistics show: More than 90 percent of the persons sentenced in 1994 for crack cocaine trafficking were black, United States Sentencing Comm'n, 1994 Annual Report 107 (Table 45); 93.4 percent of convicted LSD dealers were white, and 91 percent of those convicted for pornography or prostitution were white. Presumptions at war with presumably reliable statistics have no proper place in the analysis of this issue.

The Court of Appeals also expressed concern about the "evidentiary obstacles defendants face." But all of its sister Circuits that have confronted the issue have required that defendants produce some evidence of differential treatment of similarly situated members of other races or protected classes. In the present case, if the claim of selective prosecution were well founded, it should not have been an insuperable task to prove that persons of other races were being treated differently than respondents. For instance, respondents could have investigated whether similarly situated persons of other races were prosecuted by the State of California and were known to federal law enforcement officers, but were not prosecuted in federal court. We think the required threshold—a credible showing of different treatment of similarly situated persons—adequately balances the Government's interest in vigorous prosecution and the defendant's interest in avoiding selective prosecution.

In the case before us, respondents' "study" did not constitute "some evidence tending to show the existence of the essential elements of" a selective-prosecution claim. The study failed to identify

---

UNITED STATES V. ARMSTRONG *(continued)*

individuals who were not black and could have been prosecuted for the offenses for which respondents were charged, but were not so prosecuted. This omission was not remedied by respondents' evidence in opposition to the Government's motion for reconsideration. The newspaper article, which discussed the discriminatory effect of federal drug sentencing laws, was not relevant to an allegation of discrimination in decisions to prosecute. Respondents' affidavits, which recounted one attorney's conversation with a drug treatment center employee and the experience of another attorney defending drug prosecutions in state court, recounted hearsay and reported personal conclusions based on anecdotal evidence. The judgment of the Court of Appeals is therefore reversed, and the case is remanded for proceedings consistent with this opinion.

It is so ordered.

To determine whether a classification is proper, equal protection analysis must be employed. Most decisions are tested under the rational relationship test. That is, if the decision to prosecute is rationally related to a legitimate governmental objective, it is valid. If a decision is based upon race or religion, or in retaliation for a person's exercise of a right, the decision is tested under the strict scrutiny test and is invalid unless it can be shown to further a compelling governmental interest. Finally, a few classifications, such as those based upon gender, are tested under a standard less demanding than strict scrutiny but more demanding than the rational relationship test. Such laws must bear a substantial relationship to a legitimate governmental interest. In reality, claims of selective enforcement are rarely successful.

Ethics

All attorneys are bound by ethical rules. Two sets of rules are used in the United States: the Model Code of Professional Responsibility and the Model Rules of Professional Conduct. The two are similar, and every state has adopted some form of these rules. Ethical violations may result in discipline by the bar, an offended court, or both. Common sanctions include private and public reprimands, suspension, and disbarment. Under court rules and rules of procedure, other sanctions, such as monetary penalties, may be assessed. Also, all courts possess the authority to punish for contempt.

Prosecutors have special ethical responsibilities. You have already learned that the mission of the prosecutor is to achieve justice. The Model Code of Professional Responsibility states that the "responsibility of a public prosecutor differs from that of the usual advocate; his duty is to seek justice, not merely to convict."[5]

Prosecutors have an ethical obligation to be sure that a prosecution is warranted and to seek dismissal immediately upon discovering that one is not. Prosecutors are not to trump up charges to increase their power during plea negotiations. Prosecutors are only to request a fair sentence from a court. Of course, prosecutors may not use perjured or falsified evidence to obtain a conviction. In addition, you will learn later in this text that prosecutors have a constitutional duty to disclose exculpatory evidence.[6] Evidence that mitigates the degree of an offense or reduces a sentence must also be disclosed.[7] Further, prosecutors are not to avoid pursuing evidence because it may damage the government's case or assist the defendant.[8] Through discovery rules, prosecutors have a duty to disclose other evidence prior to or during trial. In short, prosecutors have an obligation to deal with defendants fairly.

On the other side, prosecutors have an obligation to pursue a prosecution when the facts of the case demand it. At trial, unless a prosecutor becomes convinced that the accused is innocent, the prosecutor is to zealously pursue a conviction.

Judges

Judges are not executive branch officials, as are prosecutors and law enforcement officers. Judges are part of the judiciary, a separate and independent branch of government. Generally, the judiciary is responsible for the resolution of disputes and the administration of justice. In regard to criminal law, judges are responsible for issuing warrants, supervising pretrial activity, presiding over hearings and trial, deciding guilt or innocence in some cases, and passing sentence on those convicted.

Having a fair and impartial party make these determinations is an important feature of the U.S. criminal justice system, and is mandated by the Constitution in many instances, as you will learn in the following chapters. A judge has the obligation to remain unbiased, fair, and impartial in all cases before the bar.

Ethics

Like attorneys, judges are subject to a code of ethics. Most states have enacted the Code of Judicial Conduct. Judges are to be fair and impartial.[9] In criminal cases, judges must be sensitive to defendants' rights and be careful not to imply to a jury that a defendant is guilty.

Defense Attorneys

Because of the complexity of the legal system and the advantage of having an advocate, competent legal counsel has become an important feature of the American system of criminal justice. The Sixth Amendment to the Constitution provides that all persons have a right to be represented by counsel in criminal cases. Today, indigent defendants have a right to counsel in all cases that may result in incarceration. Counsel for indigent defendants may be appointed from the private bar or, as is the case in most jurisdictions, a public defender will be assigned. Public defenders are provided to defendants at no cost. Regarding professional responsibility, defense counsel—whether a paid private defender or a public defender—owes his or her client the same loyalty and zeal in representation.

Ethics

Defense attorneys have high, and sometimes morally challenging, ethical responsibilities. Unlike the prosecutor, whose duty is to see that justice is achieved, the defense attorney must zealously represent the accused, within the bounds of the law,[10] regardless of innocence or guilt.

This obligation is the cause of some public disrespect for the legal profession. Attorneys are perceived as hired guns, not as advocates of civil liberties. Defense lawyers are frequently asked how they can defend people they know are guilty. There are two responses to this inquiry. First, defense attorneys often do not know whether their clients are in fact guilty, as this question is rarely asked. Second, defense attorneys are not defending the actions that the defendant is accused of committing; rather, defense attorneys are defending the rights of the accused, specifically, the right to have the government prove its case beyond a reasonable doubt using lawfully obtained evidence. In defending the rights of one person against governmental oppression, the rights of all the people are defended.

This approach, which is a vital part of the U.S. criminal justice system, is often misunderstood by the public. The defense attorney who fulfills this constitutional and ethical mission is often the source of public animosity and ridicule.

Communications between attorneys and clients are confidential and privileged. Attorneys are generally prohibited from disclosing those communications.[11] In the *Belge* case, an attorney was indicted for not revealing a client's privileged communication and was the subject of considerable public disdain. The indictment was dismissed in the interests of justice, namely, preservation of the attorney-client privilege. However, the court could do nothing to restore the attorney's good reputation and standing in his community.

Belge turned on the fact that the crimes had already occurred and the defendant posed no threat. An attorney is allowed, but not required, to report a client's intention to commit a crime.[12] Therefore, if a client informs his counsel that he intends to kill a witness if he is released on bond, the attorney may disclose this information without breaching any ethical obligations.

PEOPLE V. BELGE
372 N.Y.S.2d 798 (1975)

In the summer of 1973 Robert F. Garrow, Jr. stood charged in Hamilton County with the crime of murder. The defendant was assigned two attorneys, Frank H. Armani and Francis R. Belge. A defense of insanity had been interposed by counsel for Mr. Garrow. During the course of the discussions between Garrow and his two counsel, three other murders were admitted by Garrow, one being in Onondaga County. On or about September of 1973 Mr. Belge conducted his own investigation based upon what his client had told him and with the assistance of a friend the location of the body of Alicia Hauck was found in Oakwood Cemetery in Syracuse. Mr. Belge personally inspected the body and was satisfied, presumably, that this was Alicia Hauck that his client had told him he murdered.

This discovery was not disclosed to the authorities, but became public during the trial of Mr. Garrow in June of 1974, when, to affirmatively establish the defense of insanity, these three other murders

(continued)

PEOPLE V. BELGE *(continued)*

were brought before the jury by the defense in the Hamilton County trial. Public indignation reached the fever pitch; statements were made by the District Attorney of Onondaga County relative to the situation and he caused the Grand Jury of Onondaga County, then sitting, to conduct a thorough investigation. As a result of this investigation Frank Armani was No Billed by the Grand Jury, but [an i]ndictment . . . was returned against Francis R. Belge, Esq., accusing him of having violated [the public health law], which, in essence, requires that a decent burial be accorded the dead, and . . . requires anyone knowing of the death of a person without medical attendance, to report the same to the proper authorities. Defense counsel moved for dismissal of the Indictment on the grounds that a confidential, privileged communication existed between him and Mr. Garrow, which should excuse the attorney from making full disclosure to the authorities. The National Association of Criminal Defense Lawyers, as Amicus Curiae . . . succinctly stated the issue in the following language:

> "If this indictment stands, the attorney-client privilege will be effectively destroyed. No defendant will be able to freely discuss the facts of his case with his attorney. No attorney will be able to listen to those facts without being faced with the Hobson's choice of violating the law or violating his professional code of Ethics."

Initially in England the practice of law was not recognized as a profession and certainly some people are skeptics today. However, the practice of learned and capable men appearing before the Court on behalf of a friend or an acquaintance became more and more demanding. Consequently, the King granted a privilege to certain of these men to engage in such practice. There had to be rules governing their duties. These came to be known as "Canons." The King has, in this country, been substituted by a democracy, but the "Canons" are with us today, having been honed and refined over the years to meet the changes of time. Most are constantly being studied and revamped by the American Bar Association and by the bar associations of the various states. While they are, for the most part, general by definition, they can be brought to bear in a particular situation. Among those is the [rule that] confidential communications between an attorney and his client are privileged from disclosure . . . as a rule of necessity in the administration of justice. . . .

The effectiveness of counsel is only as great as the confidentiality of its client-attorney relationship. If the lawyer cannot get all the facts about the case, he can only give his client half of a defense. . . .

When the facts of the other homicides became public, as a result of the defendant's testimony to substantiate his claim of insanity, "Members of the public were shocked at the apparent callousness of these lawyers with the public interest and with simple decency." A hue and cry went up from the press and other news media suggesting that the attorneys should be found guilty of such crimes as obstruction of justice or becoming an accomplice after the fact. From a layman's standpoint, this certainly was a logical conclusion. However, the constitution of the United States of America attempts to preserve the dignity of the individual and to do that guarantees him the services of an attorney who will bring to the bar and to the bench every conceivable protection from the inroads of the state against such rights as are vested in the constitution for one accused of a crime. Among those substantial constitutional rights is that a defendant does not have to incriminate himself. His attorneys were bound to uphold that concept and maintain what has been called a sacred trust of confidentiality.

The following language of the brief of the Amicus Curiae further points up the statements just made: "The client's Fifth Amendment rights cannot

PEOPLE V. BELGE *(continued)*

be violated by his attorney. . . . Because the discovery of the body of Alicia Hauck would have presented 'a significant link in the chain of evidence tending to establish his guilt' . . . Garrow was constitutionally exempt from any statutory requirement to disclose the location of the body. And Attorney Belge, as Garrow's attorney, was not only equally exempt, but under a positive stricture precluding such disclosure. Garrow, although constitutionally privileged against a requirement to compulsory disclosure, was free to make such a revelation if he chose to do so. Attorney Belge was affirmatively required to withhold disclosure. The criminal defendant's self-incrimination rights become completely nugatory if compulsory disclosure can be exacted through his attorney." . . .

It is the decision of this Court that Francis R. Belge conducted himself as an officer of the Court with all the zeal at his command to protect the constitutional rights of his client. Both on the grounds of a privileged communication and the interests of justice the Indictment is dismissed.[13]

Attorneys are generally obligated to represent criminal defendants when appointed by a court or upon request by a bar association. However, an attorney may be excused for compelling reasons. In no event is belief in a defendant's guilt or disgust with the alleged acts compelling.[14]

An interesting ethical dilemma is presented when a defense attorney knows (or has a strong belief) that either the client or one of the defense witnesses has given or intends to give false testimony. On the one hand, the attorney is an officer of the court and thus prohibited from defrauding the court. On the other hand, the defense attorney has an obligation to the client. There is a split in the jurisdictions concerning how this situation is to be handled. There are three possibilities. First, the most preferable, the defense attorney dissuades the client from committing perjury. Second, the attorney moves to withdraw from the case, keeping the reason secret. Third, the attorney discloses the client's intention to commit perjury to the court. The law in each jurisdiction must be examined to determine which of these options is permitted or preferred.

Defense attorneys are sometimes asked to represent co defendants. This can create a conflict of interest for a defense attorney if the defendants have conflicting or antagonistic defenses. Because of the inherent dangers of representing co defendants, many defense attorneys refuse joint representation. It is a violation of a defendant's Sixth Amendment right to the assistance of effective counsel to have a lawyer with divided loyalties.

Finally, trial counsel for criminal defendants have an obligation to continue on appeal unless new counsel is retained or the court has authorized withdrawal. This is different from civil cases, where there is no general obligation to continue after trial.

Legal Assistants

Legal assistants are employed by both prosecutors and defense attorneys, with the latter being more common.[15] In the defense context, legal assistants may be asked to perform several tasks, including conducting initial interviews, conducting legal research, preparing drafts of motions and other documents, maintaining and organizing files, acting as a contact with incarcerated clients, assisting in preparing the defendant and other witnesses for trial, and preparing the defendant for the presentence investigation interview. Some paralegals are called upon to conduct investigations.

As employees of attorneys, legal assistants must also follow ethical guidelines and responsibilities. Although no state has yet established mandatory certification of legal assistants, and therefore there is no enforceable set of ethics rules, the National Federation of Paralegal Organizations and the National Association of Legal Assistants (NALA) have promulgated Codes of Ethics.

The NALA Code states that, first, legal assistants may not engage in the practice of law.[16] This includes rendering legal advice, establishing an attorney-client relationship, setting fees, and appearing in court on behalf of a client. Although some administrative agencies permit legal assistants to represent clients at hearings, this is never so in criminal law. The unauthorized practice of law is both criminal and unethical. Further, legal assistants are to act prudently in determining the extent to which a client may be assisted without the presence of a lawyer.[17] Finally, it is imperative that the attorney directly supervise the legal assistant's work in criminal law.[18]

Second, all employees of an attorney are bound by the confidentiality rule.[19] All communications made by a client to a legal assistant fall within the scope of the attorney-client privilege and may not be disclosed by the legal assistant.

Third, legal assistants must be careful not to suborn perjury when preparing the client and witnesses for trial. Instructing a witness in effective techniques, including dress and personal appearance, and methods of responding to inquiries (e.g., answer directly, honestly, and as succinctly as possible; look at the jury during your response) is proper. Suggesting, urging, encouraging, or directing a witness to lie or mislead a court is suborning perjury.

Fourth, legal assistants are bound through their attorney-supervisors by the American Bar Association's Model Rules of Professional Conduct and Model Code of Professional Responsibility.[20]

Victims

Recall that the legal victim of crimes is the government. That is why criminal prosecutions are brought in the name of the government. However, most crimes have another victim, the victim-in-fact. This is the person assaulted, battered, raped, or robbed. Victims affect criminal adjudications in a number of ways.

First, law enforcement officers may decline to make an arrest or conduct an investigation if the victim is disinterested in having the matter pursued. Second, the prosecutor may file a nolle prosequi, if there has been an arrest, or otherwise refuse to proceed with a prosecution if that is the victim's desire. Third, if the matter proceeds to trial, the victim may be required to testify at both pretrial hearings and trial. A victim may choose to attend even if his or her testimony is not required. Fourth, the victim may participate in the sentencing portion of the trial. As you will learn, statements concerning how a victim and a victim's family have been affected may be considered by judge and jury when passing sentence. Restitution is also made a condition of some sentences.

Victims' rights have received considerable attention since the mid-1980s. Victims' rights organizations have strenuously—and successfully—lobbied to introduce both state constitutional amendments and legislation concerning victims' rights. For example, the Arizona Constitution was amended to include a "Victims' Bill of Rights." Through that amendment and its enabling legislation, crime victims are allowed to participate in the initial appearance, be heard on conditions of release, be present at all court proceedings, confer with the prosecutor concerning disposition of the case, refuse a defense interview or other discovery request, provide an impact statement for sentencing, receive restitution and other damages, receive notice of probation modifications of the perpetrator, and receive notice of parole or death of the perpetrator.[21]

Rape shield legislation is another form of victims' rights laws. Rape shield laws exclude from trial evidence of a rape victim's sexual history (except evidence of sexual history with the accused) and reputation in the community. These laws were enacted to protect the rape victim from embarrassing, harassing, and intimidating inquiries.

In most jurisdictions, victims' rights are a matter of statutory, not constitutional, law. Change came quickly in this area. In 1982, only 4 states had victims' bills of rights. That number increased to 44 by 1987. In 1982, only 8 states allowed the use of **victim impact statements** at sentencing. By 2013, the number of states permitting victim impact evidence to be considered by sentencing judges and juries increased to 50 and 32 states now provide for victims rights in their constitutions.[22]

victim impact statement

■ At the time of sentencing, a statement made to the court concerning the effect the crime has had on the victim or on the victim's family.

In addition to laws providing for victim participation in court proceedings, laws have been enacted for the protection of both victims and witnesses. These laws provide for the relocation of a witness or victim whose cooperation with an investigation or prosecution endangers his or her life. The federal law is well known. It provides for relocation of the victim or witness and his or her immediate family at taxpayer expense. Further, the United States provides the family with a new identity.[23]

Victims are likely to have civil remedies against perpetrators under traditional civil law theories. Intentional tort actions for assault, battery, invasion of privacy, and conversion are examples.

Finally, *victim assistance organizations* are available in many jurisdictions. Some are independent, not-for-profit corporations, and others are governmental entities. These organizations provide information, counseling, and other assistance to victims. Also, most states have enacted *victim compensation programs*. In many instances restitution proves inadequate, such as when the perpetrator is indigent. In these instances, a victim can request compensation from a state victim compensation fund. These programs reimburse victims for medical expenses and, sometimes, loss of income. Generally, they do not compensate victims for property losses.

LIABILITY OF GOVERNMENTS AND THEIR OFFICIALS

Government officials, including law enforcement officers, prosecutors, and judges, are not above the law. Violation of an individual's rights by an official, even if during the performance of official duties, may lead to civil and criminal liability.[24] It is not in society's best interest, however, to create an environment where officials are threatened with civil or criminal liability for every incorrect decision and action, especially when they act in good faith and after thoughtful consideration of alternatives and repercussions. In such a world, civil authorities would be afraid to act and government would be paralyzed. Therefore, the laws governing liability of government officials are designed to provide remedies only for acts that are outrageous, malicious, shocking, or in clear violation of established rights.

States have laws that may provide remedies to the victims of improper governmental conduct. A police officer who commits an unjustified assault, battery, or false imprisonment may be liable under traditional tort and criminal law theories. These and other actions may lead to civil and criminal liability under state civil rights laws. In addition, violations of federally secured rights by state or federal officers can result in both civil and criminal prosecutions under federal civil rights statutes.[25] It was under these laws that several Los Angeles police officers were prosecuted for violating the civil rights of Rodney King in 1993. Similarly, a prosecutor who violates a person's civil rights may be liable under federal law,[26] or a similar state law, or under a state tort theory. In fewer instances, judges may also be liable for their actions.

The civil liability of officials is limited by immunity doctrines. Immunities developed at common law, and the United States Supreme Court, has determined that Congress did not intend to abolish these immunities when it enacted the civil rights acts.[27] Therefore, governmental officials may assert immunity as a defense if sued under the federal civil rights statutes.

There is a judicial immunity. Any action that is judicial in nature is shielded by *absolute immunity*. Because it is absolute, a government official is free from both suit and liability when performing judicial functions. Issuing orders (including warrants) and presiding over hearings are examples of judicial acts.

Most judicial acts are performed by judges, but not all. Prosecutors perform quasi-judicial acts and are shielded with absolute immunity for the performance of these acts. Appearing in court (including ex parte warrant application hearings) and complying with court orders are considered quasi-judicial acts. The Supreme Court has held, in *Van de Kamp v. Goldstein*, 555 U.S.—(2009) that this immunity extends to the supervisory and training functions of prosecutors when the functions in question are intimately associated with the judicial phase of a case. So, failure to supervise or properly train junior prosecutors in trial rules is immunized conduct. Other, more administrative conduct, such as recruitment, hiring, and awarding contracts is not shielded. Similar to prosecutors, police officers are shielded with absolute immunity when enforcing court orders (including warrants) and when testifying in court but not when performing non judicial tasks.

In other situations, another form of immunity may apply. A person entitled to *qualified immunity* is free from liability but not necessarily free from suit. That means that the process of establishing nonliability may involve a greater commitment of time, energy, and money by a defendant. Under absolute immunity, issues of malice, intent, or the nature of the right alleged to be violated are immaterial, because the defendant is immune regardless. In contrast, whether an official acted with malice or whether the alleged right violated was clearly established at law are material in the qualified immunity case. Under some laws, an official is liable only if malice is shown, or, as required by federal law, a plaintiff can prove that a clearly established right was violated.

So, under federal law, although prosecutors are absolutely immune from civil liability for quasi-judicial acts, such as appearing in court and filing charges, they enjoy only a qualified immunity when performing other acts, such as rendering legal advice to law enforcement officers.[28] Similarly, judges are protected by qualified immunity when performing nonjudicial but work-related functions, such as making personnel decisions.[29] Police officers are shielded by qualified immunity when conducting investigations, making warrantless searches or seizures, and engaging in administrative and personnel matters.

Finally, the government itself may be sued in some circumstances. A serious obstacle, which must be overcome to establish governmental liability, is **sovereign immunity.** The doctrine of sovereign immunity holds that the government is immune from lawsuits. Therefore, governments must consent to be sued. This is true of both state and federal governments. Most states have abolished sovereign immunity to some degree, some by statute, and a few by judicial decision.

The federal government has consented to be sued under several laws. Through the Federal Tort Claims Act (FTCA),[30] the United States has waived immunity from suit for a number of torts. In 1974, the statute was amended to permit suits based upon assault, battery, false imprisonment, false arrest, abuse of process, or malicious prosecution committed by federal law enforcement officers.

States may not be sued directly under federal civil rights statutes, nor may the federal government. However, local forms of government may be sued under federal civil rights laws if the acts alleged to have violated the plaintiff's civil rights were committed pursuant to an ordinance, regulation, policy, or decision of the locality.[31]

sovereign immunity

■ The government's freedom from being sued. In many cases, the U.S. government has waived immunity by a statute such as the Federal Tort Claims Act; states have similar laws.

Ethical Considerations

ATTORNEY COMPENSATION

Generally, attorneys get paid in one of several different ways. Salary, hourly, fixed, contingency, and court ordered are the most common methods. The first, salary, is common in corporations, not-for-profit, public service, and government settings. The attorney is hired, full- or part-time, and is paid salary and benefits regardless of time invested or success. The second, hourly, is common in simple transaction cases, such as negotiating a contract or drafting a legal document. It is also common when attorneys provide single-visit or transaction legal advice. Attorneys bill hours differently. Some record every minute of time spent on a case. This

(continued)

Ethical Considerations *(continued)*

includes research, writing, investigation, and time with the client (including e-mail, telephone, or fax). Clients who pay hourly are often asked to provide a deposit, known as a retainer, from which the attorney draws compensation and expenses. Regardless of the form of compensation, clients typically are responsible for expenses. These include filing fees, discovery costs, exhibit production expenses, and other non-attorney expenses.

Fixed fees are often offered for classes of cases where an attorney has considerable experience and can predict the total time investment. A simple divorce case and the drafting of a will are examples. Fixed fee arrangements typically do not include expenses. So, the client will pay both the fixed fee and the expenses of litigation.

Attorneys may, in certain cases, accept contingency payment. Under a contingency fee arrangement, the attorney is paid only if there is a recovery. In most cases, the fee equals a percentage of the total recovery. Many states limit the percentage an attorney may recover, and that amount varies by the size of the recovery and the effort of the attorney. In some states, for example, the contingency fee increases as a case proceeds through litigation (pretrial, trial, appeal). With a few exceptions, clients remain responsible for litigation expenses. Contingency fee arrangements are beneficial to low-income clients who might not otherwise be able to prosecute legitimate claims.

The final form of payment is the statutorily ordered payment. In specific types of cases, such as some federal civil rights cases, the law requires losing defendants to pay the attorney's fees and costs of prevailing plaintiffs. In such cases, the court hearing the case determines the amount owed and issues an order for payment. While losing parties in some other nations are expected to pay the attorneys' fees and litigation expenses of their opponents, this is not the norm in the United States, where each party is expected to pay his or her own fees. This deviation from the American rule exists to encourage civil rights clients who could not otherwise afford to prosecute their cases, either because they lack the resources to hire an attorney or because the recovery is expected to be less than attorneys' fees and costs, to seek relief.

In criminal cases, contingency fee arrangements are not allowed. Instead, clients typically pay hourly or fixed fees. Attorneys in the United States have long provided free services, known as pro bono, to low-income clients. This is done in criminal as well as civil cases.

22. See National Center for Victims of Crime website, policy pages at victimsofcrime.org.

23. Victim and Witness Protection Act, 18 U.S.C. § 224.

24. For a more thorough discussion of governmental liability, including the liability of government officials, *see* Daniel E. Hall, *Administrative Law: Bureaucracy in Democracy*, 4th ed. (Upper Saddle River, NJ: Pearson Prentice Hall, 2009).

25. *See* 42 U.S.C. § 1983; 18 U.S.C. § 241 *et seq.*

26. *See* 42 U.S.C. § 1983.

27. *See Burns v. Reed*, 111 S. Ct. 1934 (1991); *Pierson v. Ray*, 386 U.S. 547 (1967).

28. *See* Daniel Hall, *Administrative Law: Bureaucracy in Democracy*, 4th ed., ch. 11 (Upper Saddle River, NJ: Pearson Prentice Hall, 2009), for a discussion of prosecutorial immunity.

29. *Id.*

30. 28 U.S.C. §§ 1291, 1346, 1402, 1504, 2110, 2401–2402, 2411–2412, -2671–2678, and 2680.

31. *Monell v. Department of Social Services*, 436 U.S. 658 (1978). *Also see* Hall, *Administrative Law*, ch. 11, *supra*, fn. 28.

CHAPTER 11

CONSTITUTIONAL ASPECTS OF CRIMINAL PROCEDURE

Chapter Outline

Chapter Objectives

After completing this chapter, you should be able to:

- identify and describe the major provisions in the Constitution of the United States and its amendments that apply in the criminal context.

- explain why the U.S. Constitution's prominence in criminal justice has increased in recent decades.

- define, identify the landmark cases, and explain the underlying theory and rationale of the exclusionary rule, fruit of the poisonous tree, and related doctrines.

- describe the authority of the states to increase individual liberties through their constitutions and describe the relationship of federal and state constitutional and statutory law in this context.

- identify the material facts and legal issues in two-thirds of the cases you read, describe the courts' analyses and conclusions in the cases, and demonstrate the ability to synthesize and think critically about the law of the subject.

INTRODUCTION

Criminal justice is a policy subject that belongs largely to the states. Nearly 95 percent of all criminal prosecutions occur in state courts. Not only do the states conduct most criminal prosecutions, but each state is free, with few limitations, to design its criminal justice system in any manner it chooses. This was especially true in the early years of the United States. For the most part, the national government did not involve itself in state criminal law for 150 years.

This situation began to change in the 1950s, with significant changes occuring in the 1960s. Today the United States plays a major role in defining the rights of criminal defendants in state prosecutions, as well as federal. The source of federal involvement is the U.S. Constitution, and two developments account for its increased role in state criminal law. First, the reach of the Constitution has been extended to the states through what is known as *incorporation*. Second, the rights found in the Bill of Rights have significantly expanded.

INCORPORATION

Prior to the adoption of the Fourteenth Amendment, the Bill of Rights guarantees were interpreted by the Supreme Court as restricting the authority of the federal government only. The history of the amendments on the subject was so clear that Chief Justice Marshall opined that the question was one of great importance but could be decided without difficulty in the 1833 decision *Barron ex rel. Tiernan* v. *Mayor of Baltimore*, 7 Pet. 243 (1833). Accordingly, fundamental rights in the U.S. Constitution, such as the right to counsel and the right to be free from unreasonable searches and seizures, were guaranteed to a defendant only when prosecuted in federal court. If a state did not have a constitutional or statutory provision granting the right, the defendant was not entitled to its protection when prosecuted in state court.

In 1868 the Fourteenth Amendment to the U.S. Constitution was adopted. One objective of the Fourteenth Amendment is to protect certain civil liberties from state action. Section One of that amendment reads:

> All persons born or naturalized in the United States, and subject to the jurisdiction thereof, are citizens of the United States and of the State wherein they reside. No State shall make or enforce any law which shall abridge the privileges or immunities of citizens of the United States; nor shall any State deprive any person of life, liberty, or property, without due process of law; nor deny to any person within its jurisdiction the equal protection of the laws.

The language of the Fourteenth Amendment is similar to that found in the Fifth Amendment, insofar as they both contain a Due Process Clause. It is through the Due Process Clause and the Equal Protection Clause that the powers of the states are limited. However, what is meant by *due process* has been the subject of great debate among jurists and Supreme Court justices.

Note that the language of the Fourteenth Amendment does not include any of the specific guarantees found in the Bill of Rights, except that it requires the states to afford due process whenever depriving a person of life, liberty, or property. Thus, one of the most important issues raised in the context of the Fourteenth Amendment is whether it includes the rights found in the Bill of Rights, such as the rights to counsel, to freedom of the press, to freedom of speech, to be free from self-incrimination, to be free of unreasonable searches and seizures, and to be free from cruel and unusual punishments. That is, does the requirement that states treat citizens with fairness (due process) mean that states must provide juries in criminal trials, be reasonable when searching persons and homes, etc.? Today, the idea that the Fourteenth Amendment is a vehicle for the application of the Bill of Rights against the states is known as incorporation. Eleven years after the adoption of the Fourteenth Amendment the Supreme Court answered the incorporation question in the negative.[1] But the Court slowly changed its position. The first right to be incorporated was the Fifth Amendment's Takings Clause, in 1897.[2] The first application of incorporation in a criminal case occurred in 1925.[3] In the years that followed, several theories concerning which rights applied to the states developed.

At one extreme is the *independent content approach*. Under this theory, the Fourteenth Amendment's Due Process Clause does not include any right found in the Bill of Rights; that is, due process does not overlap with the Bill of Rights. Rather, due process has an independent content, and none of the rights secured in the Bill of Rights apply against the states. The Supreme Court has never adopted this position.

At the other extreme is *total incorporation*. Proponents of total incorporation, who included Supreme Court Associate Justice Black, argue that the entire Bill of Rights is incorporated by the Fourteenth Amendment and that all the rights contained therein may be asserted by defendants in both state and federal courts. The incorporation occurs automatically, as the proponents of this position believe that the drafters of the Fourteenth Amendment intended to incorporate the entire Bill of Rights. Under this approach, however, the Due Process Clause was limited to recognizing rights contained in the Bill of Rights. Another group of jurists have been labeled *total incorporation plus,* because they contend that the Due Process Clause not only incorporates the Bill of Rights but also secures additional independent rights. Neither of these positions has been adopted by the Supreme Court.

Another position, which was held by the Supreme Court until the 1960s, is known as *fundamental fairness*. Those rights that are "fundamental" and "essential to an ordered liberty" are incorporated through this approach. The fundamental fairness doctrine held that no relationship existed between the Bill of Rights and those deemed fundamental, although the rights recognized under the fundamental fairness doctrine may parallel rights recognized by the Bill of Rights.

The Supreme Court rejected the fundamental fairness doctrine in the 1960s and replaced it with the *selective incorporation doctrine*. Similar to the fundamental fairness doctrine, a right is incorporated under this doctrine if it is both fundamental and essential to the concept of ordered liberty. Like the fundamental fairness approach, independent rights are also recognized under selective incorporation analysis.

However, the two approaches differ in two major respects. First, under the fundamental fairness approach, cases were analyzed case by case. That is, it was possible to have essentially the same facts with different outcomes under the fundamental fairness

Exhibit 11–1 INCORPORATION PROCESS

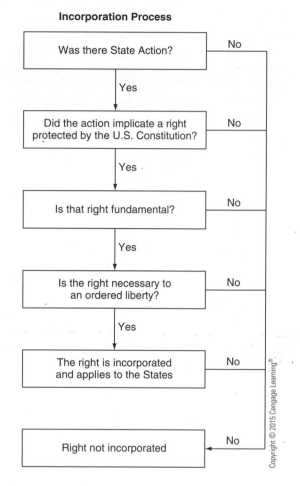

Incorporation Process

doctrine. Critics charged that the approach was too subjective. Under the selective incorporation method, blanket rules are established to act as precedent for all similar cases in the future. In addition, the entire body of precedent interpreting a federal amendment becomes applicable to the states as a result of an amendment's incorporation. Exhibit 11–1 shows the incorporation process.

Second, selective incorporation gives special attention to the rights contained in the Bill of Rights. A right secured by the Bill of Rights is more likely to be protected by the Fourteenth Amendment's Due Process Clause than are other rights. Selective incorporation continues to be the approach of the Supreme Court today.

Nearly the entire Bill of Rights has been incorporated under the selective incorporation doctrine. The right to grand jury indictment has not been incorporated,[4] nor has the right to a jury trial in civil cases, nor the Eighth Amendment's right to be free from excessive bail or fines. The right to bear arms was incorporated in 2010, the most

Exhibit 11–2 THE BILL OF RIGHTS AND INCORPORATION

Right	Status
First Amendment speech	Incorporated in *Gitlow v. New York*, 268 *U.S. 652* (1925)
First Amendment—religion	Incorporated in *Everson v. Board of Education,* 330 *U.S. 1* (1947) and *Cantwell v. Connecticut*, 310 *U.S. 296* (1940)
First Amendment press	Incorporated in *Near v. Minnesota*, 283 *U.S. 697* (1931)
First Amendment assembly	Incorporated in *DeJonge v. Oregon*, 299 *U.S. 353* (1937)
First Amendment grievances	Incorporated in *Edwards v. South Carolina*, 372 U.S. 229 (1963)
Second Amendment—arms	Incorporated in *McDonald v. Chicago*, 561 *U.S.3025 (2010)*
Third Amendment	Not incorporated (lower courts have held that it is incorporated)
Fourth Amendment	Incorporated. Different requirements incorporated through several cases, including *Mapp v. Ohio*, 367 *U.S. 643* (1961)
Fifth Amendment—grand jury	Not incorporated
Fifth Amendment—self incrimination	Incorporated in *Malloy v. Hogan*, 378 *U.S. 1* (1964)
Fifth Amendment—double jeopardy	Incorporated in *Benton v. Maryland*, 395 *U.S. 784* (1969)
Fifth Amendment takings	Incorporated in *Chicago, Burlington & Quincy Railroad Co. v. City of Chicago*, 166 U.S. 226 (1897)
Fifth Amendment—due process	Fourteenth Amendment contains due process clause
Sixth Amendment—counsel	Incorporated in *Gideon v. Wainwright*, 372 *U.S. 335* (1963)
Sixth Amendment—public trial	Incorporated in *In re Oliver*, 333 *U.S. 257* (1948)
Sixth Amendment—jury trial	Incorporated in several cases upholding right to impartial jury, number of jurors, etc.
Sixth Amendment—speedy trial	Incorporated in *Klopfer v. North Carolina*, 386 *U.S. 213* (1967)
Sixth Amendment—confront accusers	Incorporated in *Pointer v. Texas*, 380 *U.S. 400* (1965)
Sixth Amendment—compulsory process	Incorporated
Sixth Amendment—notice of charge	Incorporated
Seventh Amendment	Not incorporated
Eighth Amendment—cruel punishments	Incorporated in *Robinson v. California*, 370 *U.S. 660* (1962)
Eighth Amendment—excessive bail/fines	Not incorporated (dicta in Supreme Court opinions indicate that it will be if the Court hears the issue)
Ninth Amendment	Has never been used by Supreme Court to establish a right, although it has been cited as support for incorporated rights
Tenth Amendment	Not applicable

recent right to be recognized as fundamental. Exhibit 11–2 contains a chart of rights that have been incorporated.[5] Once incorporated, a right applies against the states to the extent and in the same manner as it does against the United States. Also, several independent due process rights have been declared. You will learn many of these in the following chapters.

EXPANSION OF RIGHTS

Another major development in the area of constitutional criminal procedure has been the expansion of many rights. The language of the Constitution is concise. It refers to "unreasonable searches and seizures," "due process," "equal protection," "speedy and public trial," and so on. No further definition or explanation of the meaning of these provisions is provided. The process of determining the meaning of such phrases is known as *constitutional interpretation*. It is possible to make each right ineffective by reading it narrowly. The opposite is also true.

During the 1960s, many rights found in the Bill of Rights were expanded by court decisions. *Expansion* refers to extending a right beyond its narrowest reading. The effect of expansive interpretation is to increase defendants' rights. An example of an expansive interpretation is the *Miranda v. Arizona* decision, 384 U.S. 436 (1966). Although the language of the Fifth Amendment does not explicitly state that a defendant must be advised of the right to remain silent, to have the assistance of counsel, and so forth, the Court now requires that such admonishments be given because of an expanded interpretation of the Fifth Amendment.

Another example of expanded individual rights is the right to privacy. No explicit constitutional language provides for a right to privacy. However, the Supreme Court has found a right to privacy to be implicit in the Constitution. The Court has held that the right to privacy protects a woman's right to abortion, in some circumstances,[6] and a couple's right to use contraceptives,[7] among many other rights. Many more expansions will be discussed later.

EXCLUSIONARY RULE

Another important constitutional development was the creation of the **exclusionary rule.** The rule is simple: Evidence that is obtained by an unconstitutional search or seizure is inadmissible at trial.

The rule was first announced by the Supreme Court in 1914.[8] However, at that time the rule had not been incorporated, and therefore the exclusionary rule did not apply to state court proceedings. This changed in 1961 when the Supreme Court declared that evidence obtained in violation of the Constitution could not be used in state or federal criminal proceedings. The case was *Mapp v. Ohio*.

exclusionary rule

■ "The exclusionary rule" often means the rule that illegally gathered evidence may not be used in a criminal trial. The rule has several exceptions, such as when the evidence is used to impeach a defendant's testimony and when the evidence was gathered in a good-faith belief that the process was legal.

MAPP V. OHIO
367 U.S. 643 (1961)

Appellant stands convicted of knowingly having had in her possession and under her control certain lewd and lascivious books, pictures, and photographs in violation [of Ohio law]. . . .

On May 23, 1957, three Cleveland police officers arrived at appellant's residence in that city pursuant to information that "a person [was] hiding out in the home, who was wanted for questioning in connection with a recent bombing." . . .

Upon their arrival at that house, the officers knocked on the door and demanded entrance but appellant, after telephoning her attorney, refused to admit them without a search warrant. They advised their headquarters of the situation and undertook a surveillance of the house.

The officers again sought entrance some three hours later when four or more additional officers arrived on the scene. When Miss Mapp did not come to the door immediately, at least one of the several doors to the house was forcibly opened and the policemen gained admittance. Meanwhile Miss Mapp's attorney arrived, but the officers, having secured their own entry, and continuing in their defiance of the law, would permit him neither to see Miss Mapp nor to enter the house. It appears that Miss Mapp was halfway down the stairs from the upper floor to the front door when the officers, in this highhanded manner, broke into the hall. She demanded to see the search warrant. A paper, claimed to be a warrant, was held up by one of the officers. She grabbed the "warrant" and placed it in her bosom. A struggle ensued in which the officers recovered the piece of paper and as a result of which they handcuffed appellant because she had been "belligerent" in resisting their official rescue of the "warrant" from her person. Running roughshod over appellant, a policeman "grabbed" her,

"twisted [her] hand," and she "yelled [and] pleaded with him" because "it was hurting." Appellant, in handcuffs, was then forcibly taken upstairs to her bedroom where the officers searched a dresser, a chest of drawers, a closet and some suitcases. They also looked into a photo album and through personal papers belonging to the appellant. The search spread. . . . The obscene materials for possession of which she was ultimately convicted were discovered in the course of that widespread search.

At the trial no search warrant was produced by the prosecution, nor was the failure to produce one explained or accounted for. At best, "There is, in the record, considerable doubt as to whether there ever was any warrant for the search."

We hold that all evidence obtained by searches and seizures in violation of the Constitution is, by that same authority, inadmissible in a state court.

Since the Fourth Amendment's right of privacy has been declared enforceable against the States through the Due Process Clause of the Fourteenth, it is enforceable against them by the same sanction of exclusion as it used against the Federal Government. . . .

Moreover, our holding that the exclusionary rule is an essential part of both the Fourth and Fourteenth Amendments is not only the logical dictate of prior cases, but it also makes very good sense. There is no war between the Constitution and common sense. Presently, a federal prosecutor may make no use of evidence illegally seized, but a State's attorney across the street may, although he supposedly is operating under the enforceable prohibitions of the same Amendment. Thus the State, by admitting evidence unlawfully seized, serves to encourage disobedience to the Federal Constitution which it is bound to uphold.

The exclusionary rule has been the subject of intense debate. There is no explicit textual language establishing the rule in the Constitution. For that reason, critics contend that the Supreme Court exceeded its authority by creating it; that it is the responsibility of the legislative branch to make such laws.

On the other side is the argument that without the exclusionary rule, the Bill of Rights is ineffective. Why have constitutional standards if there is no method to enforce them? For example, why require that the officers in the *Mapp* case have a search warrant, yet permit them to conduct a warrantless search and use the evidence obtained against the defendant? These questions go to the purpose of the exclusionary rule: it discourages law enforcement personnel from engaging in unconstitutional conduct.

The Court has been criticized for creating such a rigid, single-remedy approach to police misconduct. In fact, most nations, including those in the Western world who share a legal heritage with the United States, do not employ the rule. Instead, they attempt to deter police misconduct in ways that have lesser social expense (e.g., releasing a dangerous individual back into the public as can occur following the suppression of key evidence in the United States). Administrative discipline, civil liability, and personal criminal liability for offending officers are examples of alternatives. Indeed, the Court has begun to soften the exclusionary rule, as evinced in the *Hudson* case.

HUDSON V. MICHIGAN
547 U.S. 1096 (2006)

Justice Scalia delivered the opinion of the Court, except as to Part IV.

We decide whether violation of the "knock-and-announce" rule requires the suppression of all evidence found in the search.

Police obtained a warrant authorizing a search for drugs and firearms at the home of petitioner Booker Hudson. They discovered both. Large quantities of drugs were found, including cocaine rocks in Hudson's pocket. A loaded gun was lodged between the cushion and armrest of the chair in which he was sitting. Hudson was charged under Michigan law with unlawful drug and firearm possession.

This case is before us only because of the method of entry into the house. When the police arrived to execute the warrant, they announced their presence, but waited only a short time—perhaps "three to five seconds," before turning the knob of the unlocked front door and entering Hudson's home. Hudson moved to suppress all the inculpatory evidence, arguing that the premature entry violated his Fourth Amendment rights. . . .

The common-law principle that law enforcement officers must announce their presence and provide residents an opportunity to open the door is an ancient one. . . . [In a prior case] we were asked whether the rule was also a command of the Fourth Amendment. Tracing its origins in our English legal heritage . . . we concluded that it was.

We recognized that the new constitutional rule we had announced is not easily applied. *Wilson* and cases following it have noted the many situations in

(continued)

HUDSON V. MICHIGAN *(continued)*

which it is not necessary to knock and announce. It is not necessary when "circumstances presen[t] a threat of physical violence," or if there is "reason to believe that evidence would likely be destroyed if advance notice were given," *id.*, at 936, or if knocking and announcing would be "futile," *Richards v. Wisconsin,* 520 U.S. 385, 394 (1997). We require only that police "have a reasonable suspicion . . . under the particular circumstances" that one of these grounds for failing to knock and announce exists, and we have acknowledged that "[t]his showing is not high."

When the knock-and-announce rule does apply, it is not easy to determine precisely what officers must do. How many seconds' wait are too few? Our "reasonable wait time" standard, see *United States v. Banks,* 540 U.S. 31, 41 (2003), is necessarily vague. *Banks* (a drug case, like this one) held that the proper measure was not how long it would take the resident to reach the door, but how long it would take to dispose of the suspected drugs—but that such a time (15 to 20 seconds in that case) would necessarily be extended when, for instance, the suspected contraband was not easily concealed. . . . Happily, these issues do not confront us here. From the trial level onward, Michigan has conceded that the entry was a knock-and- announce violation. The issue here is remedy. . . .

Suppression of evidence, however, has always been our last resort, not our first impulse. The exclusionary rule generates "substantial social costs," *United States v. Leon,* 468 U.S. 897, 907 (1984), which sometimes include setting the guilty free and the dangerous at large. We have therefore been "cautio[us] against expanding" it. . . .

We did not always speak so guardedly. Expansive dicta in *Mapp,* for example, suggested wide scope for the exclusionary rule. ("[A]ll evidence obtained by searches and seizures in violation of the Constitution is, by that same authority, inadmissible

in a state court") was to the same effect. But we have long since rejected that approach. . . .

In other words, exclusion may not be premised on the mere fact that a constitutional violation was a "but-for" cause of obtaining evidence. Our cases show that but-for causality is only a necessary, not a sufficient, condition for suppression. . . .

Quite apart from the requirement of unattenuated causation, the exclusionary rule has never been applied except "where its deterrence benefits outweigh its 'substantial social costs,'" . . . The costs here are considerable. In addition to the grave adverse consequence that exclusion of relevant incriminating evidence always entails (viz., the risk of releasing dangerous criminals into society), imposing that massive remedy for a knock-and-announce violation would generate a constant flood of alleged failures to observe the rule. . . . The cost of entering this lottery would be small, but the jackpot enormous: suppression of all evidence, amounting in many cases to a get-out-of-jail-free card. Courts would experience as never before the reality that "[t]he exclusionary rule frequently requires extensive litigation to determine whether particular evidence must be excluded." Unlike the warrant or *Miranda* requirements, compliance with which is readily determined (either there was or was not a warrant; either the *Miranda* warning was given, or it was not), what constituted a "reasonable wait time" in a particular case . . . is difficult for the trial court to determine and even more difficult for an appellate court to review.

Another consequence of the incongruent remedy Hudson proposes would be police officers' refraining from timely entry after knocking and announcing. As we have observed, see *supra,* at 3, the amount of time they must wait is necessarily uncertain. If the consequences of running afoul of the rule were so massive, officers would be inclined to wait longer than the law requires—producing preventable violence against officers in some cases, and the destruction of evidence in many others. . . .

Next to these "substantial social costs" we must consider the deterrence benefits, existence of which is a necessary condition for exclusion. It is not, of course, a sufficient condition: "[I]t does not follow that the Fourth Amendment requires adoption of every proposal that might deter police misconduct." . . . To begin with, the value of deterrence depends upon the strength of the incentive to commit the forbidden act. Viewed from this perspective, deterrence of knock-and-announce violations is not worth a lot. Violation of the warrant requirement sometimes produces incriminating evidence that could not otherwise be obtained. But ignoring knock-and-announce can realistically be expected to achieve absolutely nothing except the prevention of destruction of evidence and the avoidance of life-threatening resistance by occupants of the premises—dangers which, if there is even "reasonable suspicion" of their existence, *suspend the knock-and-announce requirement anyway.* Massive deterrence is hardly required.

It seems to us not even true, as Hudson contends, that without suppression there will be no deterrence of knock-and-announce violations at all. Of course even if this assertion were accurate, it would not necessarily justify suppression. Assuming (as the assertion must) that civil suit is not an effective deterrent, one can think of many forms of police misconduct that are similarly "undeterred." When, for example, a confessed suspect in the killing of a police officer, arrested (along with incriminating evidence) in a lawful warranted search, is subjected to physical abuse at the station house, would it seriously be suggested that the evidence must be excluded, since that is the only "effective deterrent"? And what, other than civil suit, is the "effective deterrent" of police violation of an already-confessed suspect's Sixth Amendment rights by denying him prompt access to counsel? Many would regard these violated rights as more significant than the right not to be intruded upon in one's nightclothes—and yet nothing but "ineffective" civil suit is available as a deterrent. And the police incentive for those violations is arguably greater than the incentive for disregarding the knock-and-announce rule.

We cannot assume that exclusion in this context is necessary deterrence simply because we found that it was necessary deterrence in different contexts and long ago. That would be forcing the public today to pay for the sins and inadequacies of a legal regime that existed almost half a century ago. . . .

Dollree Mapp could not turn to 42 U.S.C. § 1983 for meaningful relief; *Monroe v. Pape,* which began the slow but steady expansion of that remedy, was decided the same Term as *Mapp.* It would be another 17 years before the § 1983 remedy was extended to reach the deep pocket of municipalities. Citizens whose Fourth Amendment rights were violated by federal officers could not bring suit until 10 years after *Mapp,* with this Court's decision in *Bivens v. Six Unknown Fed. Narcotics Agents,* 403 U.S. 388 (1971).

Hudson complains that "it would be very hard to find a lawyer to take a case such as this," but 42 U.S.C. § 1988(b) answers this objection. Since some civil-rights violations would yield damages too small to justify the expense of litigation, Congress has authorized attorney's fees for civil-rights plaintiffs. This remedy was unavailable in the heydays of our exclusionary-rule jurisprudence, because it is tied to the availability of a cause of action. . . .

Another development over the past half-century that deters civil-rights violations is the increasing professionalism of police forces, including a new

(continued)

HUDSON V. MICHIGAN *(continued)*

emphasis on internal police discipline. Even as long ago as 1980 we felt it proper to "assume" that unlawful police behavior would "be dealt with appropriately" by the authorities . . . we now have increasing evidence that police forces across the United States take the constitutional rights of citizens seriously. There have been "wide-ranging reforms in the education, training, and supervision of police officers."

In sum, the social costs of applying the exclusionary rule to knock-and-announce violations are considerable; the incentive to such violations is minimal to begin with, and the extant deterrences against them are substantial—incomparably greater than the factors deterring warrantless entries when *Mapp* was decided. Resort to the massive remedy of suppressing evidence of guilt is unjustified.

When it applies, the exclusionary rule prevents the admission into evidence of any item, confession, or other thing that was obtained by law enforcement officers in an unconstitutional manner.

The evidence must be obtained by the police in an unlawful manner. However, if a private citizen working on his or her own obtains evidence illegally and then turns it over to the police, it may be admitted.[9] People hired or authorized to assist the police are considered agents of the government, and therefore the exclusionary rule applies to their actions.

The exclusionary rule does not apply to pretrial matters. A defendant may not challenge a grand jury indictment because the grand jury considered illegally obtained evidence. The defendant's remedy is at trial. In most cases, but not all, evidence obtained illegally may be used at sentencing.

Another important exception to the exclusionary rule allows the government to use illegally seized evidence to rebut statements made by a defendant.[10] The government may not use the evidence if the defendant does not "open the door." That is, the government may use the evidence if the defense refers to it in its case.

Most exclusionary rule issues are resolved prior to trial by way of a motion to suppress, or exclude, evidence. In some instances the motion may be made at the moment the prosecutor attempts to introduce such evidence at trial. This is known as a *contemporaneous objection*.

sidebar

THE EXCLUSIONARY RULE IN PRACTICE

Few topics in criminal procedure are as controversial and divisive as the exclusionary rule. Clearly the public perception of the rule is that it is a device that frees the guilty, allowing murderers, rapists, and other miscreants to continue their carnage because of technicalities. Whether constraining the government to constitutional procedures should be characterized as "technical" is for each individual to decide.

sidebar *(continued)*

In spite of its reputation, the exclusionary rule is not responsible for opening the door for countless criminals. In fact, less than 0.02 percent of all felony arrests in the United States are not prosecuted because of exclusionary rule problems. Davies, "A Hard Look at What We Know (And Still Need to Learn) About the 'Costs' of the Exclusionary Rule," 1983 *A.B.F. Research* J. 611, 635, cited in *Commonwealth v. Edmunds,* 526 Pa. 374 (1991). The total number of cases not prosecuted and unsuccessfully prosecuted that are attributable to the exclusionary rule is estimated at between 0.6 percent and 2.35 percent. *Id.*

In another study of federal cases, searches and seizures were conducted in 30 percent of the prosecutions, and 11 percent of all defendants filed motions to suppress on Fourth Amendment grounds. Motions to suppress were granted in only 1.3 percent of the total number of cases, and half of the defendants who were successful in having evidence suppressed were convicted. In cases not prosecuted, exclusionary rule problems were the cause in only 0.4 percent. Report of the Comptroller General, Impact of the Exclusionary Rule on Federal Criminal Prosecutions (1979).

FRUIT OF THE POISONOUS TREE

The exclusionary rule applies to *primary evidence,* that is, evidence that is the direct result of an illegal search or seizure. It is possible that such primary evidence may lead the police to other evidence. For example, suppose a special agent of the Federal Bureau of Investigation searches a home in violation of the Fourth Amendment. The agent discovers on the homeowner's computer a plan to rob a federally insured bank. The plan includes a list of supplies that are needed and where they are hidden. Two of the items, a gun and a mask, are buried under a tree in a public park. The agent leaves the home, drives to the park, and digs up the items. Because the items were in a public space, the agent didn't need to obtain a warrant to search for them. But because they were found as a consequence of the illegal search, both the primary evidence (the plan) and the secondary or derivative evidence (the gun and mask) are inadmissible at trial. Such secondary evidence is known as **fruit of the poisonous tree.** Generally, evidence that is "tainted" by the prior illegal conduct is inadmissible. The rule does not make all evidence later obtained by law enforcement inadmissible. In some instances, evidence may be admissible because the connection between the illegally seized evidence and the subsequently obtained evidence is marginal, or as the Supreme Court has stated it, "the causal connection . . . may have become so attenuated as to dissipate the taint."[11]

fruit of the poisonous tree doctrine

■ The rule that evidence gathered as a *result* of evidence gained in an illegal search or questioning cannot be used against the person searched or questioned even if the later evidence was gathered lawfully.

Exceptions

Several exceptions to the exclusionary rule (and fruit of the poisonous tree) exist. First, such evidence is admissible at court hearings where determinations of guilt are not made, such as grand jury proceedings, pretrial hearings, and sentencing, for example. Also, if a defendant opens the door by referring to such evidence, a prosecutor may refer to it as well in rebuttal or to impeach the testimony of a defendant. This was the case in *Kansas v. Ventris* (2009),[12] where a confession was obtained illegally by a government informant. While such evidence could not be admitted at trial to prove guilt, the Supreme Court held that it could be used to impeach the defendant's testimony that he didn't commit the crime. The Court found the deterrent effect on police by excluding the evidence at trial to prove guilt was adequate and that the exclusion didn't need to extend to rebutting the defendant's testimony. In the Court's words, "[O]nce the defendant testifies inconsistently, denying the prosecution 'the traditional truth-testing devices of the adversary process,' is a high price to pay for vindicating the right to counsel at the prior stage. On the other hand, preventing impeachment use of statements taken in violation of *Massiah* would add little appreciable deterrence for officers, who have an incentive to comply with the Constitution, since statements lawfully obtained can be used for all purposes, not simply impeachment."

Another situation in which illegally obtained evidence may be admitted is when an independent source exists. An **independent source** must be an alternative, unconnected, and legal pathway to the same evidence. Consider the preceding bank robbery example. If a co-conspirator in the robbery also told the police where the money is, it is admissible regardless of the illegal confession, so long as the co-conspirator's admission was lawfully obtained.

Evidence that would be inevitably discovered by law enforcement may be admitted. This doctrine is similar to the independent source doctrine. However, police must actually obtain evidence from an untainted, lawful source to invoke the independent source doctrine. The **inevitable discovery doctrine** holds that evidence that is the fruit of an illegal search, seizure, or arrest may be admitted if it is probable that the evidence would have been obtained lawfully at a later date.

Another limitation of the fruits doctrine is the admissibility of secondary or derivative evidence in cases where suspects have not been given *Miranda* warnings but have made voluntary statements leading to the seizure of secondary or derivative evidence. You will learn more about *Miranda* and this exception later.

Because the Constitution's individual rights only limit governmental authority, evidence that is obtained illegally by private individuals and turned over to law enforcement may be admitted. Of course, the individual who illegally obtained the evidence may be prosecuted for the underlying offense, e.g. trespass or theft. If the private individual was asked or encouraged to find the evidence by the government, the evidence will be excluded under agency doctrine (although not an employee, the individual was acting as an agent of the government).

independent source

■ The general rule that if new evidence can be traced to a source completely apart from the illegally gathered evidence that first led to the new evidence, it may be used by the government in a criminal trial.

inevitable discovery rule

The principle that even if criminal evidence is gathered by unconstitutional methods, the evidence may be admissible if it definitely would have come to light anyway.

STANDING

A defendant must have **standing** before he or she may successfully have evidence suppressed. There are two aspects to standing. First, the person challenging the evidence must have an adversarial interest in the proceeding. Basically, only defendants in criminal cases may challenge evidence as seized in violation of the Fourth Amendment. A defendant's mother may not intervene in the criminal case and attempt to have evidence suppressed because her Fourth Amendment rights were violated by an illegal search and seizure—even if the claim is true. A mother lacks standing to make the claim.

The second aspect concerns the defendant's interest in the area searched or thing seized. A defendant must have a reasonable expectation of privacy to a place or thing before he or she can have it excluded at trial. To say it another way, the defendant's constitutional rights must have been violated before evidence will be suppressed. Therefore, the defendant may not assert his mother's right to be free from illegal searches and seizures.

Note that in *Simmons v. United States*, [13](1968), the Supreme Court held that a defendant may testify at a suppression hearing without waiving the right not to testify at trial and that any testimony given at a suppression hearing by a defendant may not be used against him or her at trial.

Simmons eliminated the quandary many defendants had: Should they give incriminating evidence during a suppression hearing in hopes of having the evidence excluded? Of course, if the suppression claim was unsuccessful, then a defendant faced the incriminating testimony at trial. This put many defendants in a position of having to choose one right or another: the right to be free from self-incrimination versus the right to have illegally seized evidence excluded from trial. The Supreme Court held that defendants should be free from such dilemmas.

During the 1960s and early 1970s, many jurists predicted that the Supreme Court would become so involved with criminal procedure that it would, in effect, write its own "constitutional criminal procedure code." This prediction has not proven to be true; however, many areas of criminal procedure are greatly influenced by Supreme Court decisions. It is common to refer to the expansion of individual rights and the extension of those rights to the states as the *constitutionalization* of criminal procedure.

In recent years, though, there appears to be a trend away from expansive interpretation. This is largely because the composition of the Supreme Court is more conservative than it was during the 1960s. Some believe that the trend of increasing individual rights was hindering law enforcement and welcome regression. Those who believe strongly in the rights of the individual point out that the Framers intended to create an inefficient government, in favor of protecting liberties, and proclaim that it is better to free several guilty persons than to imprison one innocent person.

standing

■ A person's right to bring (start) or join a lawsuit or to raise a particular issue because he or she is directly affected by the issues raised.

STATE CONSTITUTIONS AND THE "NEW FEDERALISM"

Each state has its own constitution. State constitutions typically differ from the U.S. Constitution in several ways. Most are longer than the U.S. Constitution. This is often a consequence of greater elaboration of governmental structures, often including how local forms of government are to be created and organized. Short of demanding a republican form of government, the federal Constitution is silent about the internal organization of state governments. State constitutions also typically provide more details about the organization of state government than the U.S. Constitution does about the federal government. It is also common for state constitutions to have more amendments than the federal Constitution. This is because amendment is easier in most states. In many, amendment can occur through public referendum. This leads to another difference between state and federal constitutions. Because state constitutions are easier to amend, they are more likely to address specific issues, and they are more likely to be internally inconsistent than is the federal Constitution.

One area where the two are very similar is in their respective bills of rights. Most states' bills of rights are identical, or nearly identical, in language to the national Constitution's Bill of Rights. There are exceptions, however. For example, several states protect privacy explicitly, while the federal Constitution does not. The Supreme Court has held, however, that there is an implicit right to privacy in several of the provisions of the U.S. Constitution, most notably, the Fourth Amendment and the due process clauses of the Fifth and Fourteenth Amendments. States that explicitly protect privacy include Alaska, Arizona, California, Hawaii, Illinois, Louisiana, Montana, and Washington, D.C., while the federal Constitution does not and only recently was the right held to be implicit in several provisions found in the Bill of Rights. California's right, found in Art. I, § 1, reads:

> All people are by nature free and independent and have inalienable rights. Among these are enjoying and defending life and liberty, acquiring, possessing, and protecting property, and pursuing and obtaining safety, happiness, and privacy.

Montana's Constitution, at Art. II, § 10, provides that

> The right of individual privacy is essential to the well-being of a free society and shall not be infringed without the showing of a compelling state interest.

Until recently, state constitutions have not played an important role in defining civil liberties. This is because both state and federal courts have looked almost exclusively to the national Constitution to answer questions concerning civil liberties, particularly in criminal cases. It is also due to the tendency of state courts to interpret state constitutional rights as identical to those secured by the national Constitution.

Increasingly, this is not the case. During the past two decades, commentators, judges, and attorneys have exhibited a renewed interest in state constitutional law. Concerned that the Supreme Court of the United States was backing away from the protections recognized by the Court in the 1960s, former Justice William Brennan of the United States Supreme Court urged states and their courts to turn to their own constitutions to protect liberties.[14]

The resurgence in state constitutional law is known as "New Federalism." State constitutions can be an independent source of civil liberties. Of course, a state constitution cannot be used to limit or encroach on a federally secured right, but it can be used to extend the scope of a right. This trend was buttressed by the Rehnquist and early Roberts Court decisions favoring dual sovereignty, for example, limited federal authority and more expansive state authority.

In several instances, state courts have determined that their state constitutions protect criminal defendants to a greater extent than does the national Constitution. The Supreme Court of Pennsylvania strongly asserted that its state's constitution has its own meaning separate and independent from the federal Constitution. In a 1991 case, that Court stated:

> [T]he decisions of the [U.S. Supreme] Court are not, and should not be, dispositive of questions regarding rights guaranteed by counter-part provisions of State Law. Accordingly, such decisions are not mechanically applicable to state law issues, and state court judges and members of the bar seriously err if they so treat them. Rather, state court judges, and also practitioners, do well to scrutinize constitutional decisions by federal courts, for only if they are found to be logically persuasive and well-reasoned, paying due regard to precedent and the policies underlying specific constitutional guarantees, may they properly claim persuasive weight as guide posts when interpreting counter-part state guarantees.[15]

The California courts have taken a similar approach. Even if a provision's interpretation parallels national law, the courts favor citing state law over federal law.

Whether a state court depends on state or federal law in defining a right determines what court has the final word on the subject. If a right is founded upon federal law, the Supreme Court of the United States is the final arbiter. If a right is founded upon state law, the highest court of the state is the final arbiter, again assuming that no federal right is encroached upon by the state decision. This problem normally arises when one person's exercise of a right affects another person's rights. For example, if a state court were to find that a fetus has a right to life in every instance, the decision would be void as violative of the federally secured right to privacy held by the mothers to elect abortions in some circumstances.

If a state court relies upon federal law when defining a right, the possibility of reversal by a federal court, usually the Supreme Court, exists. This is what occurred in California concerning the use of peyote, a drug made from cactus, by Native Americans. The Supreme Court of California decided in 1965 that the use of peyote by Native Americans during religious ceremonies was protected by the U.S. Constitution's First Amendment free exercise of religion clause.[16] That decision was not disturbed until 1990, when the Supreme Court of the United States decided that the regulation of peyote as a drug was a reasonable burden upon the First Amendment[17] and therefore overruled the 1965 California decision. Although the defendant asserted both the federal and state free exercise guarantees, the California Supreme Court relied entirely upon federal law in making its decision.

Although there has been an increase in the number of state courts that have turned to their own constitutions to protect liberties since Justice Brennan issued his famous challenge, the response hasn't been as significant as many civil libertarians had hoped. But examples of state rights expanding beyond their federal counterparts exist and even when state courts rely on federal law, it is more common today than before to cite state law as well, thereby providing an alternative basis upon which a reviewing court can affirm a decision protecting a liberty.

The *Leon* case, issued by the Supreme Court of the United States, recognized a good-faith exception to the exclusionary rule; the *Edmunds* decision, by the Supreme Court of Pennsylvania, expressly rejects the good-faith exception in state prosecutions.

As another example, several states have not followed the Supreme Court's lead in allowing statements made in violation of *Miranda* to be used by the prosecution in impeachment of a defendant.[18] These are but a few of the many instances in which a right has received greater protection under state law than under federal law.[19]

UNITED STATES V. LEON
468 U.S. 897 (1984)

[Facially valid warrants were issued by a state judge. The searches conducted under the warrants produced narcotics and other evidence of narcotics violations.]

The respondents . . . filed motions to suppress the evidence seized pursuant to the warrant. The District Court held an evidentiary hearing and, while recognizing that the case was a close one, . . . granted the motions to suppress in part. It concluded that the affidavit was insufficient to establish probable cause. . . . In response to a request from the Government, the court made clear that Officer Rombach had acted in good faith. . . . [This decision was affirmed on appeal before the court of appeals.]

The Government's petition for certiorari expressly declined to seek review of the lower courts' determinations that the search warrant was unsupported by probable cause and presented only the question "[w]hether the Fourth Amendment exclusionary rule should be modified so as not to bar the admission of evidence seized in reasonable, good-faith reliance on a search warrant that is subsequently held to be defective." . . .

[T]he exclusionary rule is designed to deter police misconduct rather than to punish the errors of judges and magistrates. . . .

If exclusion of evidence obtained pursuant to a subsequently invalidated warrant is to have any deterrent effect, therefore, it must alter the behavior of the individual law enforcement officers or the policies of their departments. One could argue that applying the exclusionary rule in cases where the police failed to demonstrate probable cause in the warrant application deters future inadequate presentations or "magistrate shopping" and thus promotes the ends of the Fourth Amendment. Suppressing evidence obtained pursuant to a technically defective warrant supported by probable cause also

UNITED STATES V. LEON *(continued)*

might encourage officers to scrutinize more closely the form of the warrant and to point out suspected judicial errors. We find such arguments speculative and conclude that suppression of evidence obtained pursuant to a warrant should be ordered only on a case-by-case basis and only in those unusual cases in which exclusion will further the purposes of the exclusionary rule.

We conclude that the marginal or nonexistent benefits produced by suppressing evidence obtained in objectively reasonable reliance on a subsequently invalidated search warrant cannot justify the substantial costs of exclusion. We do not suggest, however, that exclusion is always inappropriate in cases where an officer has obtained a warrant and abided by its terms. . . . [A]n officer's reliance on the magistrate's probable-cause determination and on the technical sufficiency of the warrant he issues must be objectively reasonable . . . and it is clear that in some circumstances the officer will have no reasonable grounds for believing that the warrant was properly issued.

COMMONWEALTH V. EDMUNDS
526 Pa. 374 (1991)

[Defendant who was convicted in the Court of Common Pleas, Criminal Division, of possession of marijuana and related offenses, appealed. The Superior Court affirmed the conviction.]

The issue presented to this court is whether Pennsylvania should adopt the "good faith" exception to the exclusionary rule as articulated by the United States Supreme Court in the case of *United States v. Leon*, 468 U.S. 897, 104 S. Ct. 3405, 82 L. Ed. 2d 677 (1984). We conclude that a "good faith" exception to the exclusionary rule would frustrate the guarantees embodied in Article I, Section 8, of the Pennsylvania Constitution. Accordingly, the decision of the Supreme Court is reversed. . . .

The trial court held that the search warrant failed to establish probable cause that the marijuana would be at the location to be searched on the date it was issued. The trial court found that the warrant failed to set forth with specificity the date upon which the anonymous informants observed the marijuana. . . . However, the trial court went on to deny the defendant's motion to suppress the marijuana. Applying the rationale of *Leon*, the trial court looked beyond the four corners of the affidavit, in order to establish that the officers executing the warrant acted in "good faith" in relying upon the warrant to conduct the search. . . .

We must now determine whether the good-faith exception to the exclusionary rule is properly part of the jurisprudence of this Commonwealth, by virtue of Article 1, Section 8 of the Pennsylvania Constitution. In concluding that it is not, we set forth a methodology to be followed in analyzing future state constitutional issues which arise under our own Constitution. . . .

This Court has long emphasized that, in interpreting a provision of the Pennsylvania Constitution, we are not bound by the decisions of the United States Supreme Court which interpret similar (yet distinct) federal constitutional provisions. . . . [T]he federal constitution establishes certain minimum levels which are "equally applicable to the [analogous] state constitutional provision." . . . However, each state has the power to provide broader

(continued)

COMMONWEALTH V. EDMUNDS *(continued)*

standards, and go beyond the minimum floor which is established by the federal Constitution. . . .

Here in Pennsylvania, we have stated with increasing frequency that it is both important and necessary that we undertake an independent analysis of the Pennsylvania Constitution, each time a provision of that fundamental document is implicated. . . .

The recent focus on the "New Federalism" has emphasized the importance of state constitutions with respect to individual rights and criminal procedure. As such, we find it important to set forth certain factors to be briefed and analyzed by litigants in each case hereafter implicating a provision of the Pennsylvania constitution. The decision of the United States Supreme Court in *Michigan v. Long*, 463 U.S. 1032, 103 S. Ct. 3469, 77 L. Ed. 2d 1201 (1983), now requires us to make a "plain statement" of the adequate and independent state grounds upon which we rely, in order to avoid any doubt that we have rested our decision squarely on Pennsylvania jurisprudence. Accordingly, as a general rule it is important that litigants brief and analyze at least the following four factors:

1. Text of the Pennsylvania constitutional provision;

2. History of the provision, including Pennsylvania case-law;

3. Related case-law from other states;

4. Policy considerations, including unique issues of state and local concern, and applicability within modern Pennsylvania jurisprudence.

Depending on the particular issue presented, an examination of related federal precedent may be useful as part of the state constitutional analysis, not as binding authority, but as one form of guidance. . . . Utilizing the above four factors, and having reviewed *Leon*, we conclude that a "good faith"

exception to the exclusionary rule would frustrate the guarantees embodied in Article I, Section 8 of our Commonwealth's Constitution. . . .

The United States Supreme Court in *Leon* made clear that, in its view, the sole purpose for the exclusionary rule under the 4th Amendment [to the Constitution of the United States] was to deter police misconduct. . . . The *Leon* majority also made clear that, under the Federal Constitution, the exclusionary rule operated as "a judicially created remedy designed to safeguard Fourth Amendment rights generally through its deterrent effect, rather than a personal constitutional right of the party aggrieved." . . .

[T]he exclusionary rule in Pennsylvania has consistently served to bolster the twin aims of Article I, Section 8, to wit, the safeguarding of privacy and the fundamental requirement that warrants shall only be issued upon probable cause. . . .

The linch-pin that has been developed to determine whether it is appropriate to issue a search warrant is the test of probable cause. . . . It is designed to protect us from unwarranted and even vindictive incursions upon our privacy. It insulates from dictatorial and tyrannical rule by the state, and preserves the concept of democracy that assures the freedom of citizens. This concept is second to none in its importance in deliniating [*sic*] the dignity of the individual living in a free society. . . .

Whether the United States Supreme Court has determined that the exclusionary rule does not advance the 4th Amendment purpose of deterring police conduct is irrelevant. Indeed, we disagree with the Court's suggestion in *Leon* that we in Pennsylvania have been employing the exclusionary rule all these years to deter police corruption. We flatly reject this notion. . . . What is significant, however, is that our Constitution has historically been interpreted to incorporate a strong right to privacy, and an equally strong adherence to the requirement of

COMMONWEALTH V. EDMUNDS *(continued)*

probable cause under Article I, Section 8. Citizens in this Commonwealth possess such rights, even where a police officer in "good faith" carrying out his or her duties inadvertently invades the privacy or circumvents the strictures of probable cause.

To adopt a "good faith" exception to the exclusionary rule, we believe, would virtually emasculate those clear safeguards which have been carefully developed under the Pennsylvania Constitution over the past 200 years.

As mentioned earlier, state laws may not reduce federally secured rights. Similarly, state laws may not enlarge federally secured rights. They may, through state law, enlarge rights also protected by federal law. In the following case, decided in 2008, the distinction that was just drawn was at issue.

VIRGINIA V. MOORE
Supreme Court of the United States (2008)

Justice Scalia delivered the opinion of the Court.

We consider whether a police officer violates the *Fourth Amendment* by making an arrest based on probable cause but prohibited by state law.

On February 20, 2003, two City of Portsmouth police officers stopped a car driven by David Lee Moore. They had heard over the police radio that a person known as "Chubs" was driving with a suspended license, and one of the officers knew Moore by that nickname. The officers determined that Moore's license was in fact suspended, and arrested him for the misdemeanor of driving on a suspended license, which is punishable under Virginia law by a year in jail and a $2,500 fine. The officers subsequently searched Moore and found that he was carrying 16 grams of crack cocaine and $516 in cash.

Under state law, the officers should have issued Moore a summons instead of arresting him. Driving on a suspended license, like some other misdemeanors, is not an arrestable offense except as to those who "fail or refuse to discontinue" the violation, and those whom the officer reasonably believes to be likely to disregard a summons, or

likely to harm themselves or others. The intermediate appellate court found none of these circumstances applicable, and Virginia did not appeal that determination. . . .

[Moore was charged and convicted of possession of cocaine with an intent to distribute. His conviction was reversed by the Virginia court of appeals and Virginia Supreme Court because it found that the Fourth Amendment prohibited the search incident to arrest because Virginia law didn't authorize the arrest.]

In a long line of cases, we have said that when an officer has probable cause to believe a person committed even a minor crime in his presence, the balancing of private and public interests is not in doubt. The arrest is constitutionally reasonable. . . .

Our decisions counsel against changing this calculus when a State chooses to protect privacy beyond the level that the *Fourth Amendment* requires. We have treated additional protections exclusively as matters of state law. In *Cooper* v. *California, 386 U.S. 58* (1967), we reversed a state court that had held the search of a seized vehicle to be in violation

(continued)

UNITED STATES V. ARMSTRONG *(continued)*

of the *Fourth Amendment* because state law did not explicitly authorize the search. We concluded that whether state law authorized the search was irrelevant. States, we said, remained free "to impose higher standards on searches and seizures than required by the Federal Constitution," but regardless of state rules, police could search a lawfully seized vehicle as a matter of federal constitutional law. . . .

In *California* v. *Greenwood, 486 U.S. 35* (1988), we held that search of an individual's garbage forbidden by California's Constitution was not forbidden by the *Fourth Amendment*. "[W]hether or not a search is reasonable within the meaning of the *Fourth Amendment*," we said, has never "depend[ed] on the law of the particular State in which the search occurs." While "[i]ndividual States may surely construe their own constitutions as imposing more stringent constraints on police conduct than does the Federal Constitution," *ibid.*, state law did not alter the content of the *Fourth Amendment*. . . .

We have applied the same principle in the seizure context. *Whren* v. *United States, 517 U.S. 806* (1996), held that police officers had acted reasonably in stopping a car, even though their action violated regulations limiting the authority of plainclothes officers in unmarked vehicles. We thought it obvious that the *Fourth Amendment's* meaning did not change with local law enforcement practices—even practices set by rule. While those practices "vary from place to place and from time to time," *Fourth Amendment* protections are not "so variable" and cannot "be made to turn upon such trivialities." . . .

If we concluded otherwise, we would often frustrate rather than further state policy. Virginia chooses to protect individual privacy and dignity more than the *Fourth Amendment* requires, but it also chooses not to attach to violations of its arrest rules the potent remedies that federal courts have applied to *Fourth Amendment* violations. Virginia does not, for example, ordinarily exclude from criminal trials evidence obtained in violation of its statutes. Moore would allow Virginia to accord enhanced protection against arrest only on pain of accompanying that protection with federal remedies for *Fourth Amendment* violations, which often include the exclusionary rule. States unwilling to lose control over the remedy would have to abandon restrictions on arrest altogether. This is an odd consequence of a provision designed to protect against searches and seizures. . . .

Finally, linking *Fourth Amendment* protections to state law would cause them to "vary from place to place and from time to time. . . .

We conclude that warrantless arrests for crimes committed in the presence of an arresting officer are reasonable under the Constitution, and that while States are free to regulate such arrests however they desire, state restrictions do not alter the *Fourth Amendment's* protections.

Moore argues that even if the Constitution allowed his arrest, it did not allow the arresting officers to search him. We have recognized, however, that officers may perform searches incident to constitutionally permissible arrests in order to ensure their safety and safeguard evidence. . . .

The Virginia Supreme Court may have concluded that *Knowles* required the exclusion of evidence seized from Moore because, under state law, the officers who arrested Moore should have issued him a citation instead. This argument might have force if the Constitution forbade Moore's arrest, because we have sometimes excluded evidence obtained through unconstitutional methods in order to deter constitutional violations. But the arrest rules that the officers violated were those of state law alone, and as we have just concluded, it is not the province of the *Fourth Amendment* to enforce state law. That Amendment does not require the exclusion of evidence obtained from a constitutionally permissible arrest.

Ethical Considerations

SHOULD JUDGES FOLLOW PUBLIC OPINION?

The Framers of the United States Constitution were fearful of centralized authority. James Madison penned, in *Federalist* No. 47, that the "[a]ccumulation of all power, legislative, executive and judiciary in the same hands, whether hereditary, self-appointed, or elective, may justly be pronounced the very definition of tyranny." Accordingly, the Framers designed a government with diffused and checked authorities. Laws are made by Congress, but the president has to endorse them before they become effective. A presidential veto, however, can be overridden by a two-thirds vote. The president is the chief executive of government and commander in chief of the military. But Congress establishes government agencies, gives them their charge, and funds them. Similarly, Congress declares war, funds the military, and makes the rules that govern the military. Both of these branches are political. The president, through the electoral college; and Congress, through direct election, are elected and accountable to the people.

The third branch of government is different. The framers intended to have a federal judiciary that is insulated from political forces. To accomplish this, federal judges are endowed with lifetime tenure after appointment, which requires nomination by the president and confirmation by the Senate. Once appointed, they cannot have their pay reduced; and they leave office only through death, retirement, or impeachment. In this sense, our federal courts are counter-majoritarian. Justice Jackson said it well:

> The very purpose of the Bill of Rights was to withdraw certain subjects from the vicissitudes of political controversy, to place them beyond the reach of majorities and officials and to establish them as legal principles to be applied by the courts. One's right to life, liberty, and property, to free speech, a free press, freedom of worship and assembly, and other fundamental rights may not be submitted to vote; they depend on the outcome of no elections.

This independence allows judges to be faithful to the law, even when their decisions are unpopular with elected officials or the public. This also advances the Model Code of Judicial Conduct canon requiring judges to avoid even the appearance of impropriety. Another canon states that judge shall not be swayed by partisan interests, public opinion, or fear of criticism.

While federal judges are well insulated from political forces, at least after appointment, judges in some state courts enjoy less independence.

(continued)

Ethical Considerations (continued)

This is because judges are elected in most states. The method of election varies. Some are partisan, others nonpartisan, and in others, retention elections are held. In the latter, there are no opposing candidates. Whether a judge should be retained is asked. If a judge is not retained, then an appointment or election is held to determine the successor.

John Fabian documents several instances where the electoral process was used to remove a judge who made a correct legal judgment that was politically unpopular. His examples involve highly contentious issues, such as the death penalty. He also gives examples of judges who appeared to have catered to public opinion and political ambitions in their campaigns as well as examples of elected officials who exploited electoral vulnerabilities of judges. Individuals who support the notion that judges should reflect majoritarian views find nothing wrong in judges responding to public opinion or bowing to political pressures. Whether elected judges can maintain judicial integrity, avoid the appearance of impropriety, and remain fair in the cases they hear is a genuine issue in a system that requires their election and reelection.

Source: John Fabian, "The Paradox of Elected Judges: Tension in the American Judicial System," 15 *Geo. J. Legal Ethics* 155 (2001).

For more on the politics of federal judicial appointments and the relationship between public opinion and federal judicial decisions, see Lee Epstein and Jeffrey A. Segal, *Advice and Consent: The Politics of Judicial Appointments* (Oxford University Press 2005), and Cass Sunstein, *Are Judges Political? An Empirical Analysis of the Federal Judiciary* (Brookings Institution Press 2006).

Web Links

Metasearching the World Wide Web

Savvy Search at *http://www.search.com/* is a multiengine search tool. Savvy Search claims that your search terms are run through 12 search engines at one time, thus increasing total hits between 200% and 800% and relevant hits by 60%. This should enhance searches in any subject, including law and justice.

Key Terms

exclusionary rule

fruit of the poisonous tree

independent source

inevitable discovery doctrine

standing

Review Questions

1. What is selective incorporation? Total incorporation? Which reflects current law?

2. Name three rights that have been incorporated and one that has not.

3. What is the exclusionary rule?

4. Give an example of when evidence would be fruit of the poisonous tree.

5. Name three exceptions to the fruit of the poisonous tree doctrine.

6. What is the "New Federalism" in the context of constitutional law?

Problems & Critical Thinking Exercises

1. The Constitution of the United States significantly affects all criminal law. Why is that so when more than 95 percent of all prosecutions occur in state courts?

2. Do you believe that evidence that has been obtained by law enforcement in an unconstitutional manner should be inadmissible at trial? Explain your position.

3. England does not employ the exclusionary rule. Rather, police officers are subject to civil liability for illegal searches. Is this a satisfactory remedy that should be employed in the United States? Can you think of alternative remedies?

Endnotes

1. *United States v. Cruikshank,* 92 U.S.w42 (1876).

2. *Chicago, Burlington & Quincy Railroad Co. v. City of Chicago,* 166 U.S. 226 (1897).

3. *Gitlow v. New York,* 268 U.S. 652 (1925).

4. *Hurtado v. California,* 110 U.S. 516 (1884).

5. *McDonald v. Chicago,* 561 U.S. __ (2010).

6. *Roe v. Wade,* 410 U.S. 113 (1973).

7. *Griswold v. Connecticut,* 381 U.S. 479 (1965).

8. The rule, as it applied in federal courts, was announced in *Weeks v. United States,* 232 U.S. 383 (1914). However, it appears that the rule was applied in at least one case prior to that date. See LaFave & Israel, Criminal Procedure 78 (Hornbook Series) (St. Paul: West, 1985).

9. *Burdeau v. McDowell,* 256 U.S. 465 (1921).

10. *Walder v. United States,* 347 U.S. 62 (1954); *United States v. Havens,* 446 U.S. 620 (1980).

11. *Nardone v. United States,* 308 U.S. 338 (1939).

12. 556 U.S. 586 (2009).

13. 390 U.S. 377.

14. William J. Brennan, Jr., *State Constitutions and the Protection of Individual Rights,* 90 Harv. L. Rev. 489 (1977).

15. *Commonwealth v. Ludwig,* 527 Pa. 472, 478 (1991).

16. *People v. Woody,* 61 Cal. 2d 716, 394 P.2d 813 (1965).

17. *Department of Human Resources v. Smith,* 494 U.S. 872 (1990).

18. See *People v. Disbrow,* 16 Cal. 3d 101, 545 P.2d 272 (1976) (California law); *State v. Santiago,* 53 Haw. 254, 492 P.2d 657 (1971) (Hawaii law); *Commonwealth v. Triplett,* 462 Pa. 244, 341 A.2d 62 (1975) (Pennsylvania law).

19. *See* Joseph Cook, *Constitutional Rights of the Accused,* 2d ed., § 1:8, n.16 (Lawyers Cooperative, 1989) for a more thorough list.

CHAPTER 12

SEARCHES, SEIZURES, AND ARRESTS

Chapter Objectives

After completing this chapter, you should be able to:

- explain the history of property/ trespass law and privacy interests as the underlying principles in the law of searches and seizures

- describe the requirements for the issuance of search and arrest warrants.

- identify, explain, and in some cases identify the landmark cases of, the many exceptions to the probable cause and warrant requirements.

- specifically explain search and seizure law as it is applied to homes, automobiles, and other locations.

- apply the law of search and seizure to specific facts scenarios.

- identify and provide examples of how technological advances has challenged the Fourth Amendment.

- critically examine recent developments intended to curb drugs and terrorism.

Identify the material facts and legal issues in nearly all of the cases you read, describe the courts' analyses and conclusions in the cases, and demonstrate the ability to synthesize and think critically about the law of the subject.

THE FOURTH AMENDMENT

Searches, seizures, and arrests are vital aspects of law enforcement. Because they involve significant invasions of individual liberties, limits on their use can be found in the constitutions, statutes, and other laws of the states and federal government.

The most important limitation is the Fourth Amendment of the U.S. Constitution, Indeed the Fourth Amendment is the most important constitutional provision in criminal law. It reads:

> The right of the people to be secure in their persons, papers and effects, against unreasonable searches and seizures, shall not be violated, and no warrants shall issue but upon probable cause, supported by oath or affirmation, and particularly describing the place to be searched and the persons or things to be seized.

First, note that while the Amendment is a single sentence, not divided into clauses by periods or semicolons, it has been interpreted as having separate clauses. The baseline clause that applies to all searches and seizures is the requirement of reasonableness. Additional clauses require that some searches and seizures be supported by probable cause, but can be warrantless; other searches and seizures can occur only if supported by probable cause and upon a warrant. In this chapter you will learn when each of these standards applies.

Several remedies are available to the defendant whose Fourth Amendment rights have been violated by the government. First, in a criminal prosecution he or she may invoke the exclusionary rule. Second, he or she may have a civil action against the offending officer under a civil rights statute, under constitutional tort theory,[1] or under traditional state tort theory. Third, individuals can request criminal prosecution by state and federal authorities for civil rights violations, assault, battery, trespass, or other criminal violations by officers. Finally, harmed individuals can complain to an officer's department or other officials (e.g. some state officials have the authority to revoke a police officer's peace officer status), seeking administrative discipline.

Note that the protections in the Bill of Rights apply only against the government. Evidence obtained by a private citizen, acting on his or her own, is not subject to the exclusionary rule. So, if Ira's neighbor illegally enters and searches his house, discovers evidence of a crime, and turns that evidence over to law enforcement, it may be used at trial. Of course, the result would be different if the neighbor was working under the direction of a government official.

Privacy and Property

The first question that must be answered in all Fourth Amendment cases is whether the Amendment applies at all. As mentioned above, the Framers of the Constitution only intended to limit *governmental authority* through the Bill of Rights. Accordingly, it must be determined if the act in question was taken under authority of law. In the criminal context this translates to acts by law enforcement officers, both police and prosecutors, in most instances. However, any person who acts on the government's behalf is subject to the constraints of the Constitution. For example, a private individual who has access to another's private computer is a governmental agent if asked by police to access records on that computer.

The determination that it is the government that has acted is in most cases easy, but it doesn't end the analysis. The Fourth Amendment applies to *searches* and *seizures*. Not all interactions between police and the public amount to searches or seizures under the Fourth Amendment.

Until 1967 the Fourth Amendment had been interpreted to protect "areas." For a search to occur, law enforcement officers had to intrude upon or physically trespass upon the property of the defendant. *Olmstead v. United States*[2] is often used as an illustration, if not as the landmark case, on this point.[3] The Court decided in *Olmstead*, handed down in 1928, that a wiretap of Olmstead's phones did not constitute a search because no physical intrusion, or trespass, of Olmstead's property occurred during the installation of the wiretap devices. Another example of the Court's physical trespass test is *Goldman v. United States,*[4] where the placement of a "detectaphone" against a wall to listen to conversations in an adjacent room did not violate the Fourth Amendment because there was no physical trespass into the room where the conversation occurred.

However, the Court changed direction in 1967 when it decided that the capture of a person's communication is itself a search, invoking the Fourth Amendment. The case, *Berger v. New York,*[5] involved a state statute that permitted warrantless wiretaps up to two months in length when officers had reasonable suspicion to believe that the wiretap would yield evidence of crime. The Court found the statute unconstitutional because of the trespass committed by the police, the extended time of the eavesdropping, the absence of a warrant issued by a neutral magistrate, the lack of probable cause, and because the statute enabled broad searches, violating the Fourth Amendment's particularly requirements.

In 1967 the rule for determining whether a search occurred changed in *Katz v. United States*. In *Katz,* the Supreme Court held that the Fourth Amendment protects people, not places. The Court established a two-part test to determine if the Fourth Amendment is implicated. First, an individual must have a subjective expectation to privacy. Second, that expectation must be objectively reasonable. The *Katz* "reasonable expectation of privacy" test continues to be the method of determining whether a search or seizure has occurred. Consistent with *Katz,* the Supreme Court has defined a search as "when an expectation of privacy that society is prepared to consider reasonable is infringed." In the same opinion the court defined a *seizure* as a "meaningful interference with an individual's possessory interest" in property.[6]

If there is no invasion of a reasonable expectation of privacy, there is no search. For example, a police officer's observations made from a public place, such as a sidewalk, are not searches, even if they are of the inside of a house through a window. Observing the exterior of an automobile, including a license plate, is not a search, nor is a dog sniff of an item or person.[7]

KATZ V. UNITED STATES
389 U.S. 347 (1967)

The petitioner was convicted in the District Court for the Southern District of California under an eight-count indictment charging him with transmitting wagering information by telephone from Los Angeles to Miami and Boston, in violation of a federal statute. At trial the Government was permitted, over the petitioner's objection, to introduce evidence of the petitioner's end of telephone conversations, overheard by FBI agents who had attached an electronic listening and recording device to the outside of the public telephone booth from which he had placed his calls. In affirming his conviction, the Court of Appeals rejected the contention that the recordings had been obtained in violation of the Fourth Amendment, because "[t]here was no physical entrance into the area occupied by [the petitioner]." We granted certiorari in order to consider the constitutional questions thus presented.

The petitioner has phrased those questions as follows:

  A. Whether a public telephone booth is a constitutionally protected area so that evidence obtained by attaching an electronic listening and recording device to the top of such booth is obtained in violation of the right to privacy of the user of the booth.

  B. Whether physical penetration of a constitutionally protected area is necessary before a search and seizure can be said to be violative of the Fourth Amendment to the United States Constitution.

We decline to adopt this formulation of the issues. In the first place, the correct solution of Fourth Amendment problems is not necessarily promoted by incantation of the phrase "constitutionally protected area." Secondly, the Fourth Amendment cannot be translated into a general constitutional "right to privacy." That Amendment protects individual privacy against certain kinds of governmental intrusion, but its protections go further, and often

have nothing to do with privacy at all. Other provisions of the Constitution protect personal privacy from other forms of governmental invasion. But the protection of a person's *general* right to privacy—his right to be left alone by other people—is, like the protection of property and of his very life, left largely to the law of the individual States.

Because of the misleading way the issues have been formulated, the parties have attached great significance to the characterization of the telephone booth from which the petitioner placed his calls. The petitioner has strenuously argued that the booth was a "constitutionally protected area." The Government has maintained with equal vigor that it was not. But this effort to decide whether or not a given "area," viewed in the abstract, is "constitutionally protected" deflects attention from the problem presented by this case. For the Fourth Amendment protects people, not places. What a person knowingly exposes to the public, even in his own home or office, is not a subject of Fourth Amendment protection. . . . But what he seeks to preserve as private, even in an area accessible to the public, may be constitutionally protected. . . .

The Government stresses the fact that the telephone booth from which the petitioner made his calls was constructed partly of glass, so that he was as visible after he entered it as he would have been if he had remained outside. But what he sought to exclude when he entered the booth was not the intruding eye—it was the uninvited ear. He did not shed his right to do so simply because he made his calls from a place where he might be seen. No less than an individual in a business office, in a friend's apartment, or in a taxicab, a person in a telephone booth may rely upon the protection of the Fourth Amendment. One who occupies it, shuts the door behind him, and pays the toll that permits him to place a call is surely entitled to assume that

KATZ V. UNITED STATES *(continued)*

the words he utters into the mouthpiece will not be broadcast to the world. To read the Constitution more narrowly is to ignore the vital role that the public telephone has come to play in private communication.

The Government contends, however, that the activities of its agents in this case should not be tested by Fourth Amendment requirements, for the surveillance technique they employed involved no physical penetration of the telephone booth from which the petitioner placed his calls. It is true that the absence of such penetration was at one time thought to foreclose further Fourth Amendment inquiry . . . for that Amendment was thought to limit only searches and seizures of tangible property . . . we have since departed from the narrow view on which that decision rested. Indeed, we have expressly held that the Fourth Amendment governs

not only the seizure of tangible items, but extends as well to the recording of oral statements, overheard without any "technical trespass under . . . local property law." *Silverman v. United States*, 365 U.S. 505, 511. Once this much is acknowledged, and once it is recognized that the Fourth Amendment protects people—and not simply "areas"—against unreasonable searches and seizures, it becomes clear that the reach of that Amendment cannot turn upon the presence or absence of a physical intrusion into any given enclosure.

We conclude that the underpinnings of [prior decisions] have been so eroded by our subsequent decisions that the "trespass" doctrine there enunciated can no longer be regarded as controlling. . . .

[The Court then held that the warrantless search was conducted in violation of the Fourth Amendment.]

It was believed by many scholars, judges, and attorneys that the *Katz* privacy test replaced the property test. Then came *Jones v. United States* in 2012, the most important Fourth Amendment case in years. Although the decision was unanimous, the justices split in their reasoning. What follows are excerpts from the majority opinion and one of the two concurring opinions.

JONES V. UNITED STATES
565 U.S. ___ (2012)

Justice Scalia delivered the opinion of the Court.

We decide whether the attachment of a Global-Positioning-System (GPS) tracking device to an individual's vehicle, and subsequent use of that device to monitor the vehicle's movements on public streets, constitutes a search or seizure within the meaning of the Fourth Amendment.

In 2004 respondent Antoine Jones, owner and operator of a nightclub in the District of Columbia, came under suspicion of trafficking in narcotics and was made the target of an investigation by a joint FBI and Metropolitan Police Department task force. Officers employed various investigative techniques, including visual surveillance of the nightclub,

(continued)

installation of a camera focused on the front door of the club, and a pen register and wiretap covering Jones's cellular phone.

Based in part on information gathered from these sources, in 2005 the Government applied to the United States District Court for the District of Columbia for a warrant authorizing the use of an electronic tracking device on the Jeep Grand Cherokee registered to Jones's wife. A warrant issued, authorizing installation of the device in the District of Columbia and within 10 days.

On the 11th day, and not in the District of Columbia but in Maryland, agents installed a GPS tracking device on the undercarriage of the Jeep while it was parked in a public parking lot. Over the next 28 days, the Government used the device to track the vehicle's movements, and once had to replace the device's battery when the vehicle was parked in a different public lot in Maryland. By means of signals from multiple satellites, the device established the vehicle's location within 50 to 100 feet, and communicated that location by cellular phone to a Government computer. It relayed more than 2,000 pages of data over the 4-week period.

[Jones moved to suppress the data because it was obtained without a valid warrant. The motion was granted in part, much of the data was admitted, he was tried, convicted, charged and convicted on additional counts, and sentenced to life in prison.]

The Fourth Amendment provides in relevant part that "[t]he right of the people to be secure in their persons, houses, papers, and effects, against unreasonable searches and seizures, shall not be violated." It is beyond dispute that a vehicle is an "effect" as that term is used in the Amendment. We hold that the Government's installation of a GPS device on a target's vehicle, and its use of that device to monitor the vehicle's movements, constitutes a "search."

It is important to be clear about what occurred in this case: The Government physically occupied private property for the purpose of obtaining information. We have no doubt that such a physical intrusion would have been considered a "search" within the meaning of the Fourth Amendment when it was adopted. . . .

The text of the Fourth Amendment reflects its close connection to property, since otherwise it would have referred simply to "the right of the people to be secure against unreasonable searches and seizures"; the phrase "in their persons, houses, papers, and effects" would have been superfluous.

Consistent with this understanding, our Fourth Amendment jurisprudence was tied to common-law trespass, at least until the latter half of the 20th century. *Kyllo v. United States*, 533 U. S. 27, 31 (2001); Kerr, *The Fourth Amendment and New Technologies: Constitutional Myths and the Case for Caution*, 102 Mich. L. Rev. 801, 816 (2004). Thus, in Olmstead v. United States, 277 U. S. 438 (1928), we held that wiretaps attached to telephone wires on the public streets did not constitute a Fourth Amendment search because "[t]here was no entry of the houses or offices of the defendants," . . .

Our later cases, of course, have deviated from that exclusively property-based approach. In Katz v. United States, 389 U. S. 347, 351 (1967), we said that "the Fourth Amendment protects people, not places," and found a violation in attachment of an eavesdropping device to a public telephone booth. Our later cases have applied the analysis of Justice Harlan's concurrence in that case, which said that a violation occurs when government officers violate a person's "reasonable expectation of privacy."

The Government contends that the Harlan standard shows that no search occurred here, since Jones had no "reasonable expectation of privacy" in the area of the Jeep accessed by Government agents (its underbody) and in the locations of the Jeep on the public roads, which were visible to all. But we need not address the Government's contentions, because Jones's Fourth

JONES V. UNITED STATES *(continued)*

Amendment rights do not rise or fall with the Katz formulation. . . .

As explained, for most of our history the Fourth Amendment was understood to embody a particular concern for government trespass upon the areas ("persons, houses, papers, and effects") it enumerates. Katz did not repudiate that understanding. Less than two years later the Court upheld defendants' contention that the Government could not introduce against them conversations between other people obtained by warrantless placement of electronic surveillance devices in their homes. The opinion rejected the dissent's contention that there was no Fourth Amendment violation "unless the conversational privacy of the homeowner himself is invaded." "[W]e [do not] believe that Katz, by holding that the Fourth Amendment protects persons and their private conversations, was intended to withdraw any of the protection which the Amendment extends to the home. . . ."

More recently, in Soldal v. Cook County, 506 U. S. 56 (1992), the Court unanimously rejected the argument that although a "seizure" had occurred "in a 'technical' sense" when a trailer home was forcibly removed, id., at 62, no Fourth Amendment violation occurred because law enforcement had not "invade[d] the [individuals'] privacy, "Katz, the Court explained, established that "property rights are not the sole measure of Fourth Amendment violations," but did not "snuf[f] out the previously recognized protection for property." . . .

The concurrence begins by accusing us of applying "18th-century tort law." That is a distortion. What we apply is an 18th-century guarantee against unreasonable searches, which we believe must provide at a minimum the degree of protection it afforded when it was adopted. The concurrence does not share that belief. It would apply exclusively Katz's reasonable-expectation-of-privacy test, even when that eliminates rights that previously existed.

The concurrence faults our approach for "present[ing] particularly vexing problems" in cases that do not involve physical contact, such as those that involve the transmission of electronic signals. We entirely fail to understand that point. For unlike the concurrence, which would make Katz the exclusive test, we do not make trespass the exclusive test. Situations involving merely the transmission of electronic signals without trespass would remain subject to Katz analysis.

CONCURRING OPINION BY JUSTICE SOTOMAYOR

[Note: Jones raised the question whether the long-term monitoring of his movements constituted a search. The Court didn't answer this question because it found the placement of the GPS device on the vehicle was a search. Justice Sotomayor wrote this concurring opinion agreeing with the outcome but expressing concern about the monitoring question.]

I join the Court's opinion because I agree that a search within the meaning of the Fourth Amendment occurs, at a minimum, "[w]here, as here, the Government obtains information by physically intruding on a constitutionally protected area." In this case, the Government installed a Global Positioning System (GPS) tracking device on respondent Antoine Jones' Jeep without a valid warrant and without Jones' consent, then used that device to monitor the Jeep's movements over the course of four weeks. The Government usurped Jones' property for the purpose of conducting surveillance on him, thereby invading privacy interests long afforded, and undoubtedly entitled to, Fourth Amendment protection. . . .

Of course, the Fourth Amendment is not concerned only with trespassory intrusions on property. Rather, even in the absence of a trespass, "a Fourth Amendment search occurs when the government violates a subjective expectation of privacy that society recognizes as reasonable. . . .

(continued)

JONES V. UNITED STATES (continued)

Nonetheless, as Justice Alito notes, physical intrusion is now unnecessary to many forms of surveillance. With increasing regularity, the Government will be capable of duplicating the monitoring undertaken in this case by enlisting factory- or owner-installed vehicle tracking devices or GPS-enabled smartphones. . . .

As Justice Alito incisively observes, the same technological advances that have made possible nontrespassory surveillance techniques will also affect the Katz test by shaping the evolution of societal privacy expectations. Under that rubric, I agree with Justice Alito that, at the very least, "longer term GPS monitoring in investigations of most offenses impinges on expectations of privacy."

In cases involving even short-term monitoring, some unique attributes of GPS surveillance relevant to the Katz analysis will require particular attention. GPS monitoring generates a precise, comprehensive record of a person's public movements that reflects a wealth of detail about her familial, political, professional, religious, and sexual associations. . . .

[Disclosed in [GPS] data . . . will be trips the indisputably private nature of which takes little imagination to conjure: trips to the psychiatrist, the plastic surgeon, the abortion clinic, the AIDS treatment center, the strip club, the criminal defense attorney, the by-the-hour motel, the union meeting, the mosque, synagogue or church, the gay bar and on and on"). The Government can store such records and efficiently mine them for information years into the future. And because GPS monitoring is cheap in comparison to conventional surveillance techniques and, by design, proceeds surreptitiously, it evades the ordinary checks that constrain abusive law enforcement practices: "limited police resources and community hostility."

Awareness that the Government may be watching chills associational and expressive freedoms. And the Government's unrestrained power to assemble data that reveal private aspects of identity is susceptible to abuse. The net result is that GPS monitoring—by making available at a relatively low cost such a substantial quantum of intimate information about any person whom the Government, in its unfettered discretion, chooses to track—may "alter the relationship between citizen and government in a way that is inimical to democratic society."

I would take these attributes of GPS monitoring into account when considering the existence of a reasonable societal expectation of privacy in the sum of one's public movements. I would ask whether people reasonably expect that their movements will be recorded and aggregated in a manner that enables the Government to ascertain, more or less at will, their political and religious beliefs, sexual habits, and so on. . . .

More fundamentally, it may be necessary to reconsider the premise that an individual has no reasonable expectation of privacy in information voluntarily disclosed to third parties. This approach is ill suited to the digital age, in which people reveal a great deal of information about themselves to third parties in the course of carrying out mundane tasks. People disclose the phone numbers that they dial or text to their cellular providers; the URLs that they visit and the e-mail addresses with which they correspond to their Internet service providers; and the books, groceries, and medications they purchase to online retailers. Perhaps, as Justice Alito notes, some people may find the "tradeoff" of privacy for convenience "worthwhile," or come to accept this "diminution of privacy" as "inevitable," and perhaps not. I for one doubt that people would accept without complaint the warrantless disclosure to the Government of a list of every Web site they had visited in the last week, or month, or year. But whatever the societal expectations, they can attain constitutionally protected status only if our Fourth Amendment jurisprudence ceases to treat secrecy

---

JONES V. UNITED STATES (continued)

as a prerequisite for privacy. I would not assume that all information voluntarily disclosed to some member of the public for a limited purpose is, for that reason alone, disentitled to Fourth Amendment protection.

Resolution of these difficult questions in this case is unnecessary, however, because the Government's physical intrusion on Jones' Jeep supplies a narrower basis for decision. I therefore join the majority's opinion.

The Court had occasion just a year later to apply the property test to a police dog sniff at the front door of a person's home in *Florida v. Jardines.*

FLORIDA V. JARDINES 569 U.S. ___(2013)
Justice Scalia delivered the opinion of the Court.

• • •

In 2006, Detective William Pedraja of the Miami-Dade Police Department received an unverified tip that marijuana was being grown in the home of respondent Joelis Jardines. One month later, the Department and the Drug Enforcement Administration sent a joint surveillance team to Jardines' home. Detective Pedraja was part of that team. He watched the home for fifteen minutes and saw no vehicles in the driveway or activity around the home, and could not see inside because the blinds were drawn. Detective Pedraja then approached Jardines' home accompanied by Detective Douglas Bartelt, a trained canine handler who had just arrived at the scene with his drug-sniffing dog. The dog was trained to detect the scent of marijuana, cocaine, heroin, and several other drugs, indicating the presence of any of these substances through particular behavioral changes recognizable by his handler.

Detective Bartelt had the dog on a six-foot leash, owing in part to the dog's "wild" nature, and tendency to dart around erratically while searching. As the dog approached Jardines' front porch, he apparently sensed one of the odors he had been trained to

detect, and began energetically exploring the area for the strongest point source of that odor. As Detective Bartelt explained, the dog "began tracking that airborne odor by . . . tracking back and forth," engaging in what is called "bracketing," "back and forth, back and forth." Detective Bartelt gave the dog "the full six feet of the leash plus whatever safe distance [he could] give him" to do this—he testified that he needed to give the dog "as much distance as I can." And Detective Pedraja stood back while this was occurring, so that he would not "get knocked over" when the dog was "spinning around trying to find" the source.

After sniffing the base of the front door, the dog sat, which is the trained behavior upon discovering the odor's strongest point. Detective Bartelt then pulled the dog away from the door and returned to his vehicle. He left the scene after informing Detective Pedraja that there had been a positive alert for narcotics.

On the basis of what he had learned at the home, Detective Pedraja applied for and received a warrant to search the residence. When the warrant was executed later that day, Jardines attempted to

(continued)

FLORIDA V. JARDINES 569 U.S. ___ (2013) *(continued)*

flee and was arrested; the search revealed marijuana plants, and he was charged with trafficking in cannabis. . . .

The Fourth Amendment provides in relevant part that the "right of the people to be secure in their persons, houses, papers, and effects, against unreasonable searches and seizures, shall not be violated." The Amendment establishes a simple baseline, one that for much of our history formed the exclusive basis for its protections: When "the Government obtains information by physically intruding" on persons, houses, papers, or effects, "a 'search' within the original meaning of the Fourth Amendment" has "undoubtedly occurred." United States v. Jones . . . By reason of our decision in *Katz v. United States*, 389 U. S. 347 (1967), property rights "are not the sole measure of Fourth Amendment violations," *Soldal v. Cook County*, 506 U. S. 56, 64 (1992)—but though Katz may add to the baseline, it does not subtract anything from the Amendment's protections "when the Government does engage in [a] physical intrusion of a constitutionally protected area,"

That principle renders this case a straightforward one. The officers were gathering information in an area belonging to Jardines and immediately surrounding his house—in the curtilage of the house, which we have held enjoys protection as part of the home itself. And they gathered that information by physically entering and occupying the area to engage in conduct not explicitly or implicitly permitted by the homeowner.

The Fourth Amendment "indicates with some precision the places and things encompassed by its protections": persons, houses, papers, and effects. Fourth Amendment does not, therefore, prevent all investigations conducted on private property; for example, an officer may (subject to Katz) gather information in what we have called "open fields"—even if those fields are privately owned—because such fields are not enumerated in the Amendment's text.

But when it comes to the Fourth Amendment, the home is first among equals. At the Amendment's "very core" stands "the right of a man to retreat into his own home and there be free from unreasonable governmental intrusion." This right would be of little practical value if the State's agents could stand in a home's porch or side garden and trawl for evidence with impunity; the right to retreat would be significantly diminished if the police could enter a man's property to observe his repose from just outside the front window.

We therefore regard the area "immediately surrounding and associated with the home"—what our cases call the curtilage—as "part of the home itself for Fourth Amendment purposes. . . .

While the boundaries of the curtilage are generally "clearly marked," the "conception defining the curtilage" is at any rate familiar enough that it is "easily understood from our daily experience." Here there is no doubt that the officers entered it: The front porch is the classic exemplar of an area adjacent to the home and "to which the activity of home life extends. . . .

Since the officers' investigation took place in a constitutionally protected area, we turn to the question of whether it was accomplished through an unlicensed physical intrusion. While law enforcement officers need not "shield their eyes" when passing by the home "on public thoroughfares," an officer's leave to gather information is sharply circumscribed when he steps off those thoroughfares and enters the Fourth Amendment's protected areas. In permitting, for example, visual observation of the home from "public navigable airspace," we were careful to note that it was done "in a physically nonintrusive manner. . . .

"[O]ur law holds the property of every man so sacred, that no man can set his foot upon his neighbour's close without his leave." As it is undisputed that the detectives had all four of their feet and all four of their companion's firmly planted on the

FLORIDA V. JARDINES 569 U.S. ___(2013) *(continued)*

constitutionally protected extension of Jardines' home, the only question is whether he had given his leave (even implicitly) for them to do so. He had not. . . .

A license may be implied from the habits of the country," notwithstanding the "strict rule of the English common law as to entry upon a close." We have accordingly recognized that "the knocker on the front door is treated as an invitation or license to attempt an entry, justifying ingress to the home by solicitors, hawkers and peddlers of all kinds." This implicit license typically permits the visitor to approach the home by the front path, knock promptly, wait briefly to be received, and then (absent invitation to linger longer) leave. Complying with the terms of that traditional invitation does not require fine-grained legal knowledge; it is generally managed without incident by the Nation's Girl Scouts and trick-or-treaters. Thus, a police officer not armed with a warrant may approach a home and knock, precisely because that is "no more than any private citizen might do."

But introducing a trained police dog to explore the area around the home in hopes of discovering incriminating evidence is something else. There is no customary invitation to do that. An invitation to engage in canine forensic investigation assuredly does not inhere in the very act of hanging a knocker. To find a visitor knocking on the door is routine (even if sometimes unwelcome); to spot that same visitor exploring the front path with a metal detector, or marching his bloodhound into the garden before saying hello and asking permission, would inspire most of us to—well, call the police. The scope of a license—express or implied—is limited not only to a particular area but also to a specific purpose. Consent at a traffic stop to an officer's checking out an anonymous tip that there is a body in the trunk does not permit the officer to rummage through the trunk for narcotics. Here, the background social norms that invite a visitor to the front door do not invite him there to conduct a search. . . .

The government's use of trained police dogs to investigate the home and its immediate surroundings is a "search" within the meaning of the Fourth Amendment.

The use of simple technology to enhance the senses has been held not to be a search. For example, a police officer may use a flashlight to look into a stopped car. However, the area where the enhancement is used, the sophistication of the technology, and the threat to privacy must all be considered. This was the issue in *Kyllo,* where the Supreme Court invalidated warrantless use of thermo-imaging on a home.

Every case presents different (and often unique) facts. Accordingly, the determination of whether a defendant's expectation to privacy is reasonable is fact sensitive. However, there are Supreme Court cases holding, as a matter of law, whether an expectation to privacy is reasonable in a given context. As an illustration, let us consider whether a person has a reasonable expectation to privacy in another person's property.

It should first be mentioned that the law distinguishes between commercial property and other private property. Generally, there is less legal right to privacy in commercial premises than in dwellings.[8]

KYLLO V. UNITED STATES
533 U.S. 27 (2001)

This case presents the question whether the use of a thermal-imaging device aimed at a private home from a public street to detect relative amounts of heat within the home constitutes a "search" within the meaning of the Fourth Amendment.

In 1991 Agent William Elliott of the United States Department of the Interior came to suspect that marijuana was being grown in the home belonging to petitioner Danny Kyllo, part of a triplex on Rhododendron Drive in Florence, Oregon. Indoor marijuana growth typically requires high-intensity lamps. In order to determine whether an amount of heat was emanating from petitioner's home consistent with the use of such lamps, at 3:20 A.M. on January 16, 1992, Agent Elliott and Dan Haas used an Agema Thermovision 210 thermal imager to scan the triplex. Thermal imagers detect infrared -radiation, which virtually all objects emit but which is not visible to the naked eye. The imager converts radiation into images based on relative warmth—black is cool, white is hot, shades of gray connote relative differences; in that respect, it operates somewhat like a video camera showing heat images. The scan of Kyllo's home took only a few minutes and was performed from the passenger seat of Agent Elliott's vehicle across the street from the front of the house and also from the street in back of the house. The scan showed that the roof over the garage and a side wall of petitioner's home were relatively hot compared to the rest of the home and substantially warmer than neighboring homes in the triplex. Agent Elliott concluded that petitioner was using halide lights to grow marijuana in his house, which indeed he was. Based on tips from informants, utility bills, and the thermal imaging, a Federal Magistrate Judge issued a warrant authorizing a search of petitioner's home, and the agents found an indoor growing operation involving more than 100 plants. Petitioner was indicted on one count of manufacturing marijuana. . . .

The Fourth Amendment provides that "[t]he right of the people to be secure in their persons, houses, papers, and effects, against unreasonable searches and seizures, shall not be violated." "At the very core" of the Fourth Amendment "stands the right of a man to retreat into his own home and there be free from unreasonable governmental intrusion." . . .

In assessing when a search is not a search, we have applied somewhat in reverse the principle first enunciated in *Katz v. United States,* (1967). Katz involved eavesdropping by means of an electronic listening device placed on the outside of a telephone booth—a location not within the catalog ("persons, houses, papers, and effects") that the Fourth Amendment protects against unreasonable searches. We held that the Fourth Amendment nonetheless protected Katz from the warrantless eavesdropping because he "justifiably relied" upon the privacy of the telephone booth. As Justice Harlan's oft-quoted concurrence described it, a Fourth Amendment search occurs when the government violates a subjective expectation of privacy that society recognizes as reasonable. . . .

The present case involves officers on a public street engaged in more than naked-eye surveillance of a home. We have previously reserved judgment as to how much technological enhancement of ordinary perception from such a vantage point, if any, is too much. While we upheld enhanced aerial photography of an industrial complex in *Dow Chemical,* we noted that we found "it important that this is *not* an area immediately adjacent to a private home, where privacy expectations are most heightened. . . .

The Government maintains, however, that the thermal imaging must be upheld because it detected "only heat radiating from the external surface of the house," Brief for United States 26. The dissent makes this its leading point, contending that there is a fundamental difference between what it calls

KYLLO V. UNITED STATES *(continued)*

"off-the-wall" observations and "through-the-wall surveillance." But just as a thermal imager captures only heat emanating from a house, so also a powerful directional microphone picks up only sound emanating from a house—and a satellite capable of scanning from many miles away would pick up only visible light emanating from a house. We rejected such a mechanical interpretation of the Fourth Amendment in *Katz,* where the eavesdropping device picked up only sound waves that reached the exterior of the phone booth. Reversing that approach would leave the homeowner at the mercy of advancing technology—including imaging technology that could discern all human activity in the home. While the technology used in the present case was relatively crude, the rule we adopt must take account of more sophisticated systems that are already in use or in development.

Where, as here, the Government uses a device that is not in general public use, to explore details of the home that would previously have been unknowable without physical intrusion, the surveillance is a "search" and is presumptively unreasonable without a warrant.

Since we hold the Thermovision imaging to have been an unlawful search, it will remain for the District Court to determine whether, without the evidence it provided, the search warrant issued in this case was supported by probable cause—and if not, whether there is any other basis for supporting admission of the evidence that the search pursuant to the warrant produced.

So, what about homes? In *Minnesota v. Olson* (1990) the Supreme Court held that an overnight guest may possess a reasonable expectation to privacy in the host's home.[9] Expanding on the reasoning in *Olson,* the defendant in *Minnesota v. Carter* (1998) asserted that a short-term guest in another's home should also be protected by the Fourth Amendment.

MINNESOTA V. CARTER
525 U.S. 83 (1998)

Chief Justice Rehnquist delivered the opinion of the Court.

Respondents and the lessee of an apartment were sitting in one of its rooms, bagging cocaine. While so engaged they were observed by a police officer, who looked through a drawn window blind. The Supreme Court of Minnesota held that the officer's viewing was a search which violated respondents' Fourth Amendment rights. We hold that no such violation occurred.

James Thielen, a police officer in the Twin Cities' suburb of Eagan, Minnesota, went to an apartment building to investigate a tip from a confidential informant. The informant said that he had walked by the window of a ground-floor apartment and had seen people putting a white powder into bags. The officer looked in the same window through a gap in the closed blind and observed the bagging operation for several minutes. He then notified headquarters, which began preparing affidavits for a search warrant while he returned to the apartment building. When two men left the building in a previously identified Cadillac, the police stopped the car. Inside were respondents Carter and Johns. As the

(continued)

MINNESOTA V. CARTER *(continued)*

police opened the door of the car to let Johns out, they observed a black zippered pouch and a handgun, later determined to be loaded, on the vehicle's floor. Carter and Johns were arrested, and a later police search of the vehicle the next day discovered pagers, a scale, and 47 grams of cocaine in plastic sandwich bags.

After seizing the car, the police returned to Apartment 103 and arrested the occupant, Kimberly Thompson, who is not a party to this appeal. A search of the apartment pursuant to a warrant revealed cocaine residue on the kitchen table and plastic baggies similar to those found in the Cadillac. Thielen identified Carter, Johns, and Thompson as the three people he had observed placing the powder into baggies. The police later learned that while Thompson was the lessee of the apartment, Carter and Johns lived in Chicago and had come to the apartment for the sole purpose of packaging the cocaine. Carter and Johns had never been to the apartment before and were only in the apartment for approximately 2½ hours. In return for the use of the apartment, Carter and Johns had given Thompson one-eighth of an ounce of the cocaine.

Carter and Johns were charged with conspiracy to commit controlled substance crime in the first-degree and aiding and abetting in a controlled substance crime in the first degree, in violation of [Minnesota statute]. They moved to suppress all evidence obtained from the apartment and the Cadillac, as well as to suppress several post arrest incriminating statements they had made. They argued that Thielen's initial observation of their drug packaging activities was an unreasonable search in violation of the Fourth Amendment and that all evidence obtained as a result of this unreasonable search was inadmissible as fruit of the poisonous tree. The Minnesota trial court held that since, unlike the defendant in *Minnesota v. Olson,* 495 U.S. 91, 109 L. Ed. 2d 85, 110 S. Ct. 1684 (1990), Carter and Johns were not overnight social guests but

temporary out-of-state visitors, they were not entitled to claim the protection of the Fourth Amendment against the government intrusion into the apartment. The trial court also concluded that Thielen's observation was not a search within the meaning of the Fourth Amendment. After a trial, Carter and Johns were each convicted of both offenses. The Minnesota Court of Appeals held that the respondent Carter did not have "standing" to object to Thielen's actions because his claim that he was predominantly a social guest was "inconsistent with the only evidence concerning his stay in the apartment, which indicates that he used it for a business purpose—to package drugs." *Minnesota v. Carter,* 545 N.W.2d 695, 698 (1996). In a separate appeal, the Court of Appeals also affirmed Johns' conviction, without addressing what it termed the "standing" issue. A divided Minnesota Supreme Court reversed, holding that respondents had "standing" to claim the protection of the Fourth Amendment because they had " 'a legitimate expectation of privacy in the invaded place.'". . .

The Minnesota courts analyzed whether respondents had a legitimate expectation of privacy under the rubric of "standing" doctrine, an analysis which this Court expressly rejected 20 years ago in *Rakas* 439 U.S. at 139–140. In that case, we held that automobile passengers could not assert the protection of the Fourth Amendment against the seizure of incriminating evidence from a vehicle where they owned neither the vehicle nor the evidence. Central to our analysis was the idea that in determining whether a defendant is able to show the violation of his (and not someone else's) Fourth Amendment rights, the "definition of those rights is more properly placed within the purview of substantive Fourth Amendment law than within that of standing." Thus, we held that in order to claim the protection of the Fourth Amendment, a defendant must demonstrate that he personally has an expectation of privacy in the place searched, and that his expectation is reasonable;

i.e., one which has "a source outside of the Fourth Amendment, either by reference to concepts of real or personal property law or to understandings that are recognized and permitted by society." The Fourth Amendment guarantees: "The right of the people to be secure in their persons, houses, papers, and effects, against unreasonable searches and seizures, shall not be violated, and no Warrants shall issue, but upon probable cause, supported by Oath or affirmation, and particularly describing the place to be searched, and the persons or things to be seized." The Amendment protects persons against unreasonable searches of "their persons [and] houses" and thus indicates that the Fourth Amendment is a personal right that must be invoked by an individual. But the extent to which the Fourth Amendment protects people may depend upon where those people are. We have held that "capacity to claim the protection of the Fourth Amendment depends . . . upon whether the person who claims the protection of the Amendment has a legitimate expectation of privacy in the invaded place."

The text of the Amendment suggests that its protections extend only to people in "their" houses. But we have held that in some circumstances a person may have a legitimate expectation of privacy in the house of someone else. In *Minnesota v. Olson,* 495 U.S. 91, 109 L. Ed. 2d 85, 110 S. Ct. 1684 (1990), for example, we decided that an overnight guest in a house had the sort of expectation of privacy that the Fourth Amendment protects. We said:

> "To hold that an overnight guest has a legitimate expectation of privacy in his host's home merely recognizes the everyday expectations of privacy that we all share. Staying overnight in another's home is a long-standing social custom that serves functions recognized as valuable by society. We stay in others' homes when we travel to a strange city for business or pleasure, we visit our parents, children, or more

distant relatives out of town, when we are in between jobs, or homes, or when we house-sit for a friend. . . .

> "From the overnight guest's perspective, he seeks shelter in another's home precisely because it provides him with privacy, a place where he and his possessions will not be disturbed by anyone but his host and those his host allows inside. We are at our most vulnerable when we are asleep because we cannot monitor our own safety or the security of our belongings. It is for this reason that, although we may spend all day in public places, when we cannot sleep in our own home we seek out another private place to sleep, whether it be a hotel room, or the home of a friend." 495 U.S. at 98–99.

In *Jones v. United States,* (1960), the defendant seeking to exclude evidence resulting from a search of an apartment had been given the use of the apartment by a friend. He had clothing in the apartment, had slept there " 'maybe a night,' " and at the time was the sole occupant of the apartment. But while the holding of *Jones*—that a search of the apartment violated the defendant's Fourth Amendment rights—is still valid, its statement that "anyone legitimately on the premises where a search occurs may challenge its legality," *id.* at 267, was expressly repudiated in *Rakas v. Illinois,* 439 U.S. 128, 58 L. Ed. 2d 387, 99 S. Ct. 421 (1978). Thus an overnight guest in a home may claim the protection of the Fourth Amendment, but one who is merely present with the consent of the householder may not.

Respondents here were obviously not overnight guests, but were essentially present for a business transaction and were only in the home a matter of hours. There is no suggestion that they had a previous relationship with Thompson, or that there was any other purpose to their visit. Nor was there anything similar to the overnight guest relationship in *Olson* to suggest a degree of acceptance into the household. While the apartment

(continued)

MINNESOTA V. CARTER (continued)

was a dwelling place for Thompson, it was for these respondents simply a place to do business.

Property used for commercial purposes is treated differently for Fourth Amendment purposes than residential property. "An expectation of privacy in commercial premises, however, is different from, and indeed less than, a similar expectation in an individual's home." If we regard the overnight guest in *Minnesota v. Olson* as typifying those who may claim the protection of the Fourth Amendment in the home of another, and one merely "legitimately on the premises" as typifying those who may not do so, the present case is obviously somewhere in between. But the purely commercial nature of the transaction engaged in here, the relatively short period of time on the premises, and the lack of any previous connection between respondents and the householder, all lead us to conclude that respondents' situation is closer to that of one simply permitted on the premises. We therefore hold that any search which may have occurred did not violate their Fourth Amendment rights.

Because we conclude that respondents had no legitimate expectation of privacy in the apartment, we need not decide whether the police officer's observation constituted a "search." The judgment of the Supreme Court of Minnesota is accordingly reversed, and the cause is remanded for proceedings not inconsistent with this opinion.

It is so ordered. . . .

DISSENT

Justice Ginsburg, with whom Justice Stevens and Justice Souter join, dissenting.

The Court's decision undermines not only the security of short-term guests, but also the security of the home resident herself. In my view, when a homeowner or lessor personally invites a guest into her home to share in a common endeavor, whether it be for conversation, to engage in leisure activities, or for business purposes licit or illicit, that guest should share his host's shelter against unreasonable searches and seizures. . . .

Do people enjoy the right to privacy in hotels? The purpose of the premises and the nature of the use of the premises must be considered in Fourth Amendment analysis. Because hotels are intended to provide individuals with safety and comfort when away from home, hotel guests may have a reasonable expectation to privacy. Several factors are considered when determining whether an individual possesses a reasonable expectation to privacy in a hotel room, including whether the defendant is a registered guest and if not, what his or her relationship to the registered guest is, whether the defendant paid any of the hotel charges, and the total time the defendant spent in the room.

Just as not all expectations to privacy are recognized at law, not all touchings of property by police amount to a search, because they do not represent a "meaningful interference" with a property interest. As to when physical contact of an "effect" by a law enforcement officer becomes a search, the Supreme Court has drawn a strict line in favor of preserving privacy. In *Bond v. United States*,[10] for example, a border patrol officer's quick squeeze of a bus passenger's soft luggage was determined to be a search, even though there was considerable evidence that passengers commonly touched each other's luggage in a manner no less intrusive than that of the border patrol officer's.

Probable Cause

Probable Cause Defined

The Fourth Amendment requires the existence of **probable cause** before warrants are to be issued. When a warrant is first obtained, the probable cause determination is made by a judge. In cases where a police officer acts without a warrant, the officer makes that determination. In both cases, as you will see, probable cause is required.

Probable cause is the minimum amount of evidence necessary for a search, seizure, or arrest to be proper under the Fourth Amendment. There is no one universal definition of probable cause. In fact, the definition of probable cause differs depending on the context. In all situations, it is more than mere suspicion and less than the standard required to prove a defendant guilty at trial (beyond a reasonable doubt). As the Supreme Court has expressed, probable cause is present when the trustworthy facts within the officer's knowledge are sufficient in themselves to justify a "person of reasonable caution" in the belief that seizable property would be found or that the person to be arrested committed the crime in question.[11]

Probable cause, while elastic itself, is one of many levels of proof that are used in criminal law. Reasonable suspicion is expected to support temporary detentions and frisks, beyond a reasonable doubt is the standard for convictions, clear and convincing evidence and preponderance of the evidence are both required to establish some specific facts that arise during pretrial and trial proceedings. The only standard to have a precise numerical setting is preponderance of evidence, which is quantified as more likely true than not or 51% confidence. Otherwise, the standards do not have precise levels of confidence. We only know how they related to one another, e.g., beyond a reasonable doubt conveys higher confidence in the truth of guilt than preponderance while reasonable suspicion represents less confidence than the preponderance standard. See Exhibit 12–1 for a visual depiction of the relationships between these standards.

When making the probable cause determination, an officer may rely on his or her own observations, hearsay evidence, and statements of witnesses, victims, and other law enforcement officers. The fact that evidence will be inadmissible at trial does not exclude it from the probable cause determination.

probable cause

■ The U.S. Constitutional requirement that law enforcement officers present sufficient facts to convince a judge to issue a search warrant or an arrest *warrant,* and the requirement that no warrant should be issued unless it is more likely than not that the objects sought will be found in the place to be searched or that a crime has been committed by the person to be arrested.

Exhibit 12–1   STANDARDS OF PROOF

Standards of Proof

	Frisks; Stops	Arrests Searches	Standard of proof in civil cases	Required to prove specific facts and in other circumstances	Required for conviction and punishment	
0%			**51%**		**100%**	
Confidence						**Confidence**
	Reasonable suspicion	Probable cause	Preponderance of evidence	Clear & convincing evidence	Beyond a reasonable doubt	

Sources: Used to Establish Probable Cause.

However, innuendo or conjecture that is not supported by facts may not be considered. Although the evidence does not have to rise to the level of being admissible at trial, it must have some credibility.

It is common for the police to depend on information from informants to obtain a search warrant. An *informant* is a person who has knowledge concerning a crime because of his or her involvement in crime. The reliability of such information (and whether it should be the basis of a warrant) is hotly debated.

In *Aguilar v. Texas,* 378 U.S. 108 (1964), the Supreme Court established a two-prong test for the use of such information (usually hearsay) when making a warrant determination. First, the affidavit had to contain information about the basis for the informant's information. This permitted the issuing judge to determine whether the informant's allegations were well founded.

Second, the officer had to provide the judge with reasons for believing that the informant was reliable. This could be done, for example, by showing that the informant had been truthful in the past.

In *Illinois v. Gates,* 462 U.S. 213 (1983), the Court reversed position and adopted a "totality of the circumstances" test, thereby overruling *Aguilar.* However, the Court did not abandon the two prongs of *Aguilar.* Although the two prongs are no longer determinative, they continue to be important factors when examining the totality of the circumstances. The Court stated that:

> The task of the issuing magistrate is simply to make a practical, commonsense decision whether, given all the circumstances set forth in the affidavit before him, including the "veracity" and the "basis of knowledge" of persons supplying hearsay information, there is a fair probability that contraband or evidence of a crime will be found in a particular place. (*Gates* at 233)

This test does not require that the officer name the informant in the application for the warrant. All that is required is that the magistrate be given enough information to make his or her own determination concerning the credibility and reliability of the informant. The law of this area was discussed fully in the Supreme Court's opinion in *Florida v. J.L.* (2000).

FLORIDA V. J.L.
529 U.S. 266 (2000)

The question presented in this case is whether an anonymous tip that a person is carrying a gun is, without more, sufficient to justify a police officer's stop and frisk of that person. We hold that it is not.

I

On October 13, 1995, an anonymous caller reported to the Miami-Dade Police that a young black male standing at a particular bus stop and wearing a plaid shirt was carrying a gun. . . . So far as the record reveals, there is no audio recording of the tip, and nothing is known about the informant. Sometime after the police received the tip—the record does not say how long—two officers were instructed to respond. They arrived at the bus stop about six minutes later and saw three black males "just hanging out [there]." One of the three, respondent J.L., was wearing a plaid shirt. Apart from the tip, the officers had no reason to suspect any of the three of illegal conduct. The officers did not see a firearm, and J.L. made no threatening or otherwise unusual movements. One of the officers approached J.L., told him to put his hands up on the bus stop, frisked him, and seized a gun from J.L.'s pocket. The second officer frisked the other two individuals, against whom no allegations had been made, and found nothing.

J.L., who was at the time of the frisk "10 days shy of his 16th birth [day]," was charged under state law with carrying a concealed firearm without a license and possessing a firearm while under the age of 18. He moved to suppress the gun as the fruit of an unlawful search, and the trial court granted his motion. The intermediate appellate court reversed, but the Supreme Court of Florida quashed that decision and held the search invalid under the Fourth Amendment. Anonymous tips, the Florida Supreme Court stated, are generally less reliable than tips from known informants and can form the basis for reasonable suspicion only if accompanied by specific indicia of reliability, for example, the correct forecast of a subject's " 'not easily predicted' " movements. The tip leading to the frisk of J.L., the court observed, provided no such predictions, nor did it contain any other qualifying indicia of reliability. Two justices dissented. The safety of the police and the public, they maintained, justifies a "firearm exception" to the general rule barring investigatory stops and frisks on the basis of bare-boned anonymous tips.

Seeking review in this Court, the State of Florida noted that the decision of the State's Supreme Court conflicts with decisions of other courts declaring similar searches compatible with the Fourth Amendment. We granted certiorari, and now affirm the judgment of the Florida Supreme Court.

II

Our "stop and frisk" decisions begin with *Terry v. Ohio,* (1968). This Court held in *Terry*:

"[W]here a police officer observes unusual conduct which leads him reasonably to conclude in light of his experience that criminal activity may be afoot and that the persons with whom he is dealing may be armed and presently dangerous, where in the course of investigating this behavior he identifies himself as a policeman and makes reasonable inquiries, and where nothing in the initial stages of the encounter serves to dispel his reasonable fear for his own or others' safety, he is entitled for the protection of himself and others in the area to conduct a carefully limited search of the outer clothing of such persons in an attempt to discover weapons which might be used to assault him."

In the instant case, the officers' suspicion that J.L. was carrying a weapon arose not from any observations of their own but solely from a call made from an unknown location by an unknown caller. Unlike a tip from a known informant whose reputation can be assessed and who can be held responsible if her allegations turn out to be fabricated, anonymous tip alone seldom demonstrates the informant's basis of knowledge or veracity. As we have recognized, however, there are situations in which an anonymous tip, suitably corroborated, exhibits "sufficient indicia of reliability to provide reasonable suspicion to make the investigatory stop." The question we here confront is whether the tip pointing to J.L. had those indicia of reliability.

In *White,* the police received an anonymous tip asserting that a woman was carrying cocaine and predicting that she would leave an apartment building at a specified time, get into a car matching a particular description, and drive to a named motel. Standing alone, the tip would not have justified a *Terry* stop. Only after police observation showed that the informant had accurately predicted the

(continued)

FLORIDA V. J.L. *(continued)*

woman's movements, we explained, did it become reasonable to think the tipster had inside knowledge about the suspect and therefore to credit his assertion about the cocaine. Although the Court held that the suspicion in *White* became reasonable after police surveillance, we regarded the case as borderline. Knowledge about a person's future movements indicates some familiarity with that person's affairs, but having such knowledge does not necessarily imply that the informant knows, in particular, whether that person is carrying hidden contraband. We accordingly classified *White* as a "close case."

The tip in the instant case lacked the moderate indicia of reliability present in *White* and essential to the Court's decision in that case. The anonymous call concerning J.L. provided no predictive information and therefore left the police without means to test the informant's knowledge or credibility. That the allegation about the gun turned out to be correct does not suggest that the officers, prior to the frisks, had a reasonable basis for suspecting J.L. of engaging in unlawful conduct: The reasonableness of official suspicion must be measured by what the officers knew before they conducted their search. All the police had to go on in this case was the bare report of an unknown, unaccountable informant who neither explained how he knew about the gun nor supplied any basis for believing he had inside information about J.L. If *White* was a close case on the reliability of anonymous tips, this one surely falls on the other side of the line.

Florida contends that the tip was reliable because its description of the suspect's visible attributes proved accurate: There really was a young black male wearing a plaid shirt at the bus stop. The United States as *amicus curiae* makes a similar argument, proposing that a stop and frisk should be permitted "when (1) an anonymous tip provides a description of a particular person at a particular location illegally carrying a concealed firearm, (2) police

promptly verify the pertinent details of the tip except the existence of the firearm, and (3) there are no factors that cast doubt on the reliability of the tip. . . ." These contentions misapprehend the reliability needed for a tip to justify a *Terry* stop.

An accurate description of a subject's readily observable location and appearance is of course reliable in this limited sense: It will help the police correctly identify the person whom the tipster means to accuse. Such a tip, however, does not show that the tipster has knowledge of concealed criminal activity. The reasonable suspicion here at issue requires that a tip be reliable in its assertion of illegality, not just in its tendency to identify a determinate person. . . .

A second major argument advanced by Florida and the United States as *amicus* is, in essence, that the standard *Terry* analysis should be modified to license a "firearm exception." Under such an exception, a tip alleging an illegal gun would justify a stop and frisk even if the accusation would fail standard pre-search reliability testing. We decline to adopt this position.

Firearms are dangerous, and extraordinary dangers sometimes justify unusual precautions. Our decisions recognize the serious threat that armed criminals pose to public safety; *Terry's* rule, which permits protective police searches on the basis of reasonable suspicion rather than demanding that officers meet the higher standard of probable cause, responds to this very concern. But an automatic firearm exception to our established reliability analysis would rove too far. Such an exception would enable any person seeking to harass another to set in motion an intrusive, embarrassing police search of the targeted person simply by placing an anonymous call falsely reporting the target's unlawful carriage of a gun. Nor could one securely confine such an exception to allegations involving firearms. . . .

Finally, the requirement that an anonymous tip bear standard indicia of reliability in order to

STATE V. SNOWDEN *(continued)*

justify a stop in no way diminishes a police officer's prerogative, in accord with *Terry,* to conduct a protective search of a person who has already been legitimately stopped. We speak in today's decision only of cases in which the officer's authority to make the initial stop is at issue. In that context, we hold that an anonymous tip lacking indicia of reliability of the kind contemplated in *Adams* and *White* does not justify a stop and frisk whenever and however it alleges the illegal possession of a firearm.

The judgement of the Florida Supreme Court is affirmed.

Probable cause may be established by an animal as well as a human. Dogs can be trained to discover bombs, drugs, and people. At borders, dogs are used to sniff vehicles for the presence of illegal aliens. At airports, dogs are used to detect explosives. Many police departments depend upon dogs to detect drugs and track fugitives.

The Supreme Court has stated that the act of having a dog sniff a person or thing is not a search.[12] The question then becomes whether a dog's indication (a dog alert) that contraband is present is probable cause to issue a warrant or to pursue a warrantless search or seizure. That is the issue the Tenth Circuit Court of Appeals addressed in the *Ludwig* case.

UNITED STATES V. LUDWIG
10 F. 3d 1523 (10th Cir. 1993)

[The trial court granted a motion to suppress evidence, finding that a warrantless search of a car trunk, based upon probable cause established by a dog alert indicating that drugs were present in the vehicle, was violative of the Fourth Amendment.]

The United States appeals the denial of its motion to reconsider the district court's suppression order. The government argues that the challenged dog sniff of Keith Ludwig's car was not a search under the Fourth Amendment, and that no warrant was required to search the car after the dog alerted. We agree and reverse.

At about 11:15 P.M. on December 12, 1992, Joel Nickles, a Border Patrol agent at the permanent checkpoint near Truth or Consequences, New Mexico, walked a trained narcotics dog through the parking lot of the nearby Super 8 Motel to see if the dog would find any contraband. . . . Less than a week earlier the motel manager had given the Border Patrol permission to walk dogs through the motel parking lot for this purpose. . . .

As Nickles and the dog were walking through the lot, the dog pulled Nickles over to Keith Ludwig's Chevrolet Impala and alerted to the trunk, indicating that illegal drugs were in the trunk. . . . Around half an hour later Border Patrol agents began surveillance of the car, which continued through the night until Ludwig first approached his car the next morning at 10:00 A.M.

Agent Phillip Sanchez, who had been surveilling the car, approached Ludwig five minutes later and identified himself. Ludwig acknowledged that the car was his, but denied the agent's request

(continued)

UNITED STATES V. LUDWIG (continued)

to inspect the car and look in the trunk. Sanchez then directed Nickles to have the dog sniff the car again, and the dog again alerted to the trunk. When Ludwig refused to open the trunk, Sanchez took the keys from the ignition, opened the trunk, and found several large bags of marijuana. Ludwig was indicted for possession with intent to distribute less than fifty kilograms of marijuana. . . .

Ludwig also suggests that the dog sniffs of his car were unreasonable searches because the agents had no reason to suspect that there were drugs in his car. . . .

Regardless of whether Ludwig subjectively expected that the drugs in his trunk would be smelled, society does not recognize that expectation as legitimate. . . .

Ludwig suggests that dog sniffs are not as reliable as courts often assume, and therefore, the dog alert does not give the agents probable cause to open and search Ludwig's trunk. . . .

Probable cause means that "there is a fair probability that contraband or evidence of a crime will be found in a particular place." . . . Although Ludwig cites several cases of mistaken dog alerts, a dog alert usually is at least as reliable as many other sources of probable cause and is certainly reliable enough to create a "fair probability" that there is contraband.

The Tenth Circuit's ruling is the generally accepted rule. An alert by a properly trained dog furnishes probable cause. However, if the police are aware that a particular dog commonly errs, its alerts may not establish probable cause.

Good-Faith Reliance on a Warrant

acting in good faith w/ warrant

Judges can differ in opinion. Judges can make mistakes. What happens if a judge finds that probable cause exists and accordingly issues a warrant, only to have the probable cause finding reversed later? Should the evidence discovered during the search be excluded?

The Supreme Court has answered this question in the negative. The Court found, in *United States v. Leon,* 468 U.S. 897 (1984), that the exclusionary rule does not apply to evidence seized by a police officer, acting in good-faith reliance on the warrant, while executing a facially valid warrant. The Court stated:

> We conclude that the marginal or nonexistent benefits produced by suppressing evidence obtained in objectively reasonable reliance on a subsequently invalidated search warrant cannot justify the substantial costs of exclusion. We do not suggest, however, that exclusion is always inappropriate in cases where an officer has obtained a warrant and abided by its terms. . . . [A]n officer's reliance on the magistrate's probable-cause determination and on the technical sufficiency of the warrant he issues must be objectively reasonable . . . and it is clear that in some circumstances the officer will have no reasonable grounds for believing that the warrant was properly issued.

The Court found that exclusion of evidence when an officer is relying on a judicially issued warrant would not advance the objective of the exclusionary rule; it would not deter future police misconduct.

For *Leon* to apply, an officer's reliance must be in good faith. An officer who misleads a judge in order to obtain a warrant is not acting in good faith. Further, the warrant must be facially valid. If a reasonable officer should know that a warrant is facially defective, then any evidence obtained under it must be excluded. Examples of facially invalid warrants include unsigned warrants, warrants that contain an inadequate description of the place or thing to be searched or seized, failure of the magistrate to require the supporting affidavit to be under oath, and such a lack of evidence that an officer could not in reasonable, good faith believe that probable cause exists. An officer may, however, rely on a warrant that contains mere technical and typographical errors, unless the errors are so fundamental that they render some element of the warrant (e.g., description) defective.

Leon is applicable only to searches and seizures that occur pursuant to warrants. An officer's good-faith, but mistaken, belief that probable cause exists to conduct a warrantless search or to make a warrantless seizure does not justify the admission of evidence obtained as a result thereof. As discussed previously in this text, several state courts have refused to follow the *Leon* holding when interpreting their state constitutions.

The *Leon* reasoning has been extended to a court official's negligent false report to police that a warrant exists[13] and to situations in which police officers act in good faith reliance upon a statute.[14] The same standards apply as in *Leon;* that is, the statute relied upon must be facially valid.

SEARCHES AND SEIZURES

The Warrant Requirement

Depending upon the circumstances, a search may be conducted with or without a warrant. The Supreme Court has expressed that there is a strong preference for the use of warrants, when possible, over warrantless actions.[15] The warrant preference serves an important purpose: it protects citizens from overzealous law enforcement practices.

> The presence of a search warrant serves a high function. Absent some grave emergency, the Fourth Amendment has interposed a magistrate between the citizen and police. This was done not to shield criminals nor to make the home a safe haven for illegal activities. It was done so that an objective mind might weigh the need to invade the privacy in order to enforce the law. The right of privacy was deemed too precious to entrust to the discretion of those whose job is the detection of crime and the arrest of criminals.[16]

Accordingly, a search conducted pursuant to a valid search warrant is per se reasonable. Warrantless searches are permitted only in special circumstances, and it is the responsibility of the government to prove that the facts of the case fit into one of the exceptions to the warrant requirement.

To give this preference some "teeth," the Supreme Court, in *Aguilar v. Texas,* 378 U.S. 108, 111 (1964), announced that, "when a search is based upon a magistrate's, rather than a police officer's determination of probable cause," reviewing courts are to accept lesser competent evidence than if the officer made the determination personally, so long as there was a "substantial basis" for the magistrate's decision. To say it another way, less evidence is required to sustain a search if a warrant was obtained prior to the search.

"Reviewing courts" are referred to because the determination that probable cause exists by a magistrate when issuing a warrant is not final. A defendant may later attack any evidence seized pursuant to a warrant through a motion to suppress. As stated, determinations by a magistrate are less likely to be overturned than those made by police officers.

The Supreme Court created an exception to the rule that evidence must be suppressed if seized pursuant to an invalid warrant in *United States v. Leon,* 468 U.S. 897 (1984), wherein it held that evidence seized by an officer who executed a search warrant with a good-faith belief that the warrant was valid will not be excluded, even though the warrant is later determined invalid. If a warrant is facially invalid, then any fruits of a search thereof must be excluded, because an officer cannot in good faith believe that such a warrant is valid. Of course, if an officer uses false information to convince the magistrate that probable cause exists, the good-faith exception does not apply. The same is true if an officer knows that the magistrate issuing the warrant is not neutral and detached.

Requirements for Obtaining a Warrant

The Fourth Amendment enumerates the requirements that must be met before a warrant can be issued. It is the responsibility of the law enforcement officer requesting the warrant to establish these elements to the judge making the warrant determination. The form application for search warrant used in the federal courts appears in Exhibit 12–2.

First, the evidence presented must establish probable cause to believe that within the area to be searched, the items sought will be found. Second, there must be probable cause to believe that the items sought are connected to criminal activity.

Third, the area to be searched and any item to be seized must be described with particularity. The amount of specificity required varies from case to case. A warrant that authorizes a police officer to search a particular home for "unauthorized contraband" clearly violates the Fourth Amendment, whereas a warrant authorizing a search of the same home for a "nine-inch knife with an ivory handle" is valid, provided the warrant is valid in all other respects (probable cause, etc.).

Warrants for the seizure of items that are illegal in themselves do not have to be as particular as others. For example, a warrant to search for a book must be more specific than one for drugs. The description "book" is clearly insufficient, whereas a warrant to search for "cocaine" probably is sufficient.

As to location, a street address is normally sufficient. If there is no street address, the warrant should describe the location, owner, color, and architectural style of the property. Of course, any additional information that aids in describing property should be included. If the building to be searched is an apartment building or similar multiunit structure, the specific subunit to be searched must be stated in the warrant.

Fourth, the facts that are alleged to establish probable cause must be "supported by Oath or affirmation." In the typical case, this means that the government will produce one or more affidavits to prove that a warrant is justified. Note that the sample application for a search warrant (Exhibit 12–2) provides space for a supporting affidavit.

Exhibit 12–2   APPLICATION AND AFFIDAVIT FOR SEARCH WARRANT

AO 106 (Rev. 5/85) Affidavit for Search Warrant _____

UNITED STATES DISTRICT COURT

_____ DISTRICT OF _____

In the Matter of the Search of

(Name, address or brief description of person or property to be searched)

**APPLICATION AND AFFIDAVIT
FOR SEARCH WARRANT**

CASE NUMBER:

I _____ being duly sworn depose and say:

I am a(n) _____ and have reason to believe

(Official Title)

that ☐ on the person of or ☐ on the premises known as (name, description and/or location)

in the _____ District of _____ there is now concealed a certain per son or property, namely (describe the person or property)

which is (give alleged grounds for search and seizure under Rule 41(b) of the Federal Rules of Criminal Procedure)

in violation of Title _____ United States Code, Section(s) _____
The facts to support the issuance of a Search Warrant are as follows:

Continued on the attached sheet   ☐ Yes   ☐ No
and made a part hereof.

_____

Signature of Affiant

Sworn to before me, and subscribed

in my presence

_____ at   _____

Date   City and State

_____   _____

Name and Title of Judicial Officer   Signature of Judicial Officer

Source: http://www.uscourts.gov/uscourts/FormsAndFees/Forms/AO106.pdf

Finally, the warrant must be issued by a neutral and detached magistrate. Although judges are most commonly given the authority to issue warrants, a state may grant this authority to others. However, the Supreme Court has stated that the person authorized must be neutral and detached and be capable of determining whether probable cause exists.

Thus, a state law permitting a state's attorney general, who had investigated the crime and would later be responsible for its prosecution, to issue a warrant was invalid.[17] In another case, a court clerk was found sufficiently detached, neutral, and capable to issue a warrant because the clerk worked for a court and was under the supervision of a judge.[18] See Exhibit 12–3 for the federal application for search warrant.

Scope of Warrants

Warrants may be issued to search and seize any item that constitutes evidence of a crime, is the fruit of a crime, is contraband, or is used to commit a crime.[19] A warrant may be issued to search or seize any place or property, whether belonging to a suspected criminal or an innocent third party. A warrant may be prospective. That is, it may be written to be executed when a triggering event occurs. An anticipatory warrant of this nature must comply with the probable cause and particularity requirements of the Fourth Amendment. For example, a warrant to search a suspect's home at the time a package of child pornography was delivered was upheld. The package was ordered by the suspect from an undercover officer and the warrant described it, limited execution of the warrant to when the package was received and taken into the home, and described the suspect's home. The application for the warrant detailed how the suspect had ordered the items.[20]

The particularity requirement acts to limit the breadth of a search. If an officer searches beyond the scope of a warrant, the exclusionary rule will make the fruits from the forbidden area inadmissible at trial.

In some circumstances the particularity requirement is heightened. For example, because of the importance of protecting the press from government intrusion, warrants to search newsrooms or similar areas must be drafted with "particular exactitude."[21] The same is true if a search will probe into confidential information, such as client records of attorneys and physicians.

As a general proposition, a warrant to search premises does not authorize the police to search the occupants of the premises.[22] Of course, a search may be conducted if an independent basis exists justifying the action. Generally, the occupants of an area to be searched may be detained until the search is complete. However, occupants cannot be detained for an "unduly prolonged" period of time.[23] Once the evidence sought is found or the threat of loss or destruction of evidence by an occupant has passed, he or she should be released.

Executing Warrants

The warrant may direct a particular officer or an entire unit of police officers to conduct the search. The language of the warrant itself contains the duties of the officers executing the warrant, as well as their limitations.

Exhibit 12–3 SEARCH WARRANT UPON ORAL TESTIMONY

AO 93A (Rev. 5/85) Search Warrant Upon Oral Testimony

UNITED STATES DISTRICT COURT

_____ DISTRICT OF _____

In the Matter of the Search of

(Name, address or brief description of person or property to be searched)

SEARCH WARRANT UPON ORAL TESTIMONY

CASE NUMBER:

To _____ and any Authorized Officer of the United States

Sworn oral testimony has been communicated to me by _____
                                                              Affiant

that h on the person of or h on the premises known as (name, description and/or location)

in the _____ District of _____ there is now concealed a certain person or property, namely (describe the person or property)

I am satisfied that the circumstances are such as to make it reasonable to dispense with a written affidavit and that there is probable cause to believe that the property or person so described is concealed on the person or premises above described and that grounds for application for issuance of the search warrant exist as communicated orally to me in a sworn statement which has been recorded electronically, stenographically, or in longhand and upon the return of the warrant, will be transcribed, certified as accurate and attached hereto.

YOU ARE HEREBY COMMANDED to search on or before _____
                                                                    Date

the person or place named above for the person or property specified, serving this warrant and making the search (in the daytime — 6:00 AM to 10:00 PM) (at anytime in the day or night as I find reasonable cause has been established) and if the person or property be found there to seize same, leaving a copy of this warrant and receipt for the person or property taken, and prepare a written inventory of the person or property seized and promptly return this warrant to _____
as required by law.   U.S. Judge or Magistrate

_____ at _____ _____

Date and Time Issued   City and State

_____   _____

Name and Title of Judicial Officer   Signature of Judicial Officer

I certify that on _____ at _____
                          Date   Time

_____ orally authorized the
          U.S. Judge or Magistrate

(continued)

Exhibit 12–3   *(continued)*

AO 93A (Rev. 5/85) Search Warrant Upon Oral Testimony

issuance and execution of a search warrant conforming to all the foregoing terms.

_____   _____   _____

Name of affiant   Signature of affiant   Exact time warrant executed

RETURN		
DATE WARRANT RECEIVED	DATE AND TIME WARRANT EXECUTED	COPY OF WARRANT AND RECEIPT FOR ITEMS LEFT WITH
INVENTORY MADE IN THE PRESENCE OF		
INVENTORY OF PERSON OR PROPERTY TAKEN PURSUANT TO THE WARRANT		

CERTIFICATION

I swear that this inventory is a true and detailed account of the person or property taken by me on the warrant.

_____

Subscribed, sworn to, and returned before me this date.

_____   _____

U.S. Judge or Magistrate   Date

Source: http://www.uscourts.gov/uscourts/FormsAndFees/Forms/AO093A.pdf

As a general proposition, warrants are to be executed during the day. This is because a nighttime search is considered to be more intrusive than a daytime search[24] and because the probability of resistance is greater at night.

To conduct a nighttime search, a specific request for a warrant authorizing such must be made. To receive a warrant permitting a nighttime search, an officer must present the magistrate with facts evidencing the necessity for a nighttime search, usually including proof that a daytime search will not be successful. An anticipated nighttime delivery of illegal goods justifies a nighttime warrant, as does a concern that evidence of a crime will be destroyed in the night.

Most states have statutes requiring that warrants be executed within a specific amount of time after issuance. Warrants issued under federal law must be executed within 10 days of issuance.[25]

In all cases, the search must be conducted when there is probable cause. If an officer fails to execute a warrant before probable cause has dissipated, then any resulting search is violative of the Fourth Amendment, and the fruits thereof are subject to the exclusionary rule. This is true even if the search is conducted within the period of time set by law.

At the premises of a search, the police must knock and announce their purpose before entering the premises. This is true whether entry is gained through the use of force or not. However, to prevent the destruction of evidence or injury to the officers, judges may issue "no-knock" warrants if the facts indicate that one or the other is likely to occur. The decision to issue a no-knock warrant must be based on the evidence. The Supreme Court has ruled that blanket exceptions to the knock-and-announce rule are violative of the Fourth Amendment. Instead, judges and police must make no-knock decisions based on the facts of each case.

RICHARDS V. WISCONSIN
520 U.S. 385 (1997)

Justice Stevens delivered the opinion of the Court.

In *Wilson v. Arkansas,* (1995), we held that the Fourth Amendment incorporates the common-law requirement that police officers entering a dwelling must knock on the door and announce their identity and purpose before attempting forcible entry. At the same time, we recognized that the "flexible requirement of reasonableness should not be read to mandate a rigid rule of announcement that ignores countervailing law enforcement interests and left "to the lower courts the task of determining the circumstances under which an unannounced entry is reasonable under the Fourth Amendment."

In this case, the Wisconsin Supreme Court concluded that police officers are never required to knock and announce their presence when executing a search warrant in a felony drug investigation. In so doing, it reaffirmed a pre-*Wilson* holding and concluded that *Wilson* did not preclude this *per se* rule. We disagree with the court's conclusion that the Fourth Amendment permits a blanket exception to the knock-and-announce requirement for

(continued)

RICHARDS V. WISCONSIN (continued)

this entire category of criminal activity. But because the evidence presented to support the officers' actions in this case establishes that the decision not to knock and announce was a reasonable one under the circumstances, we affirm the judgment of the Wisconsin court.

On December 31, 1991, police officers in Madison, Wisconsin, obtained a warrant to search Steiney Richards's hotel room for drugs and related paraphernalia. The search warrant was the culmination of an investigation that had uncovered substantial evidence that Richards was one of several individuals dealing drugs out of hotel rooms in Madison. The police requested a warrant that would have given advance authorization for a "no-knock" entry into the hotel room, but the magistrate explicitly deleted those portions of the warrant.

The officers arrived at the hotel room at 3:40 A.M. Officer Pharo, dressed as a maintenance man, led the team. With him were several plainclothes officers and at least one man in uniform. Officer Pharo knocked on Richards's door and, responding to the query from inside the room, stated that he was a maintenance man. With the chain still on the door, Richards cracked it open. Although there is some dispute as to what occurred next, Richards acknowledges that when he opened the door he saw the man in uniform standing behind Officer Pharo. He quickly slammed the door closed and, after waiting two or three seconds, the officers began kicking and ramming the door to gain entry to the locked room. At trial, the officers testified that they identified themselves as police while they were kicking the door in. When they finally did break into the room, the officers caught Richards trying to escape through the window. They also found cash and cocaine hidden in plastic bags above the bathroom ceiling tiles.

Richards sought to have the evidence from his hotel room suppressed on the ground that the officers had failed to knock and announce their presence prior to forcing entry into the room. The trial court denied the motion, concluding that the officers could gather from Richards's strange behavior when they first sought entry that he knew they were police officers and that he might try to destroy evidence or to escape. . . . The judge emphasized that the easily disposable nature of the drugs the police were searching for further justified their decision to identify themselves as they crossed the threshold instead of announcing their presence before seeking entry. . . . Richards appealed the decision to the Wisconsin Supreme Court and that court affirmed. . . .

In reaching this conclusion, the Wisconsin court found it reasonable—after considering criminal conduct surveys, newspaper articles, and other judicial opinions—to assume that all felony drug crimes will involve "an extremely high risk of serious if not deadly injury to the police as well as the potential for the disposal of drugs by the occupants prior to entry by the police."

We recognized in *Wilson* that the knock-and-announce requirement could give way "under circumstances presenting a threat of physical violence," or "where police officers have reason to believe that evidence would likely be destroyed if advance notice were given." It is indisputable that felony drug investigations may frequently involve both of these circumstances. The question we must resolve is whether this fact justifies dispensing with case-by-case evaluation of the manner in which a search was executed.

The Wisconsin court explained its blanket exception as necessitated by the special circumstances of today's drug culture, and the State asserted at oral argument that the blanket exception was reasonable in "felony drug cases because of the convergence in a violent and dangerous form of commerce of weapons and the destruction of drugs." But creating exceptions to the knock-and-announce rule based on the "culture" surrounding

RICHARDS V. WISCONSIN (continued)

a general category of criminal behavior presents at least two serious concerns.

First, the exception contains considerable overgeneralization. For example, while drug investigation frequently does pose special risks to officer safety and the preservation of evidence, not every drug investigation will pose these risks to a substantial degree. . . .

A second difficulty with permitting a criminal category exception to the knock-and-announce requirement is that the reasons for creating an exception in one category can, relatively easily, be applied to others. Armed bank robbers, for example, are, by definition, likely to have weapons, and the fruits of their crime may be destroyed without too much difficulty. If a *per se* exception were allowed for each category of criminal investigation that included a considerable—albeit hypothetical—risk of danger to officers or destruction of evidence, the knock-and-announce element of the Fourth Amendment's reasonableness requirement would be meaningless.

Thus, the fact that felony drug investigations may frequently present circumstances warranting a no-knock entry cannot remove from the neutral scrutiny of a reviewing court the reasonableness of the police decision not to knock and announce in a particular case. Instead, in each case, it is the duty of a court confronted with the question to determine whether the facts and circumstances of the particular entry justified dispensing with the knock-and-announce requirement.

In order to justify a "no-knock" entry, the police must have a reasonable suspicion that knocking and announcing their presence, under the particular circumstances, would be dangerous or futile, or that it would inhibit the effective investigation of the crime by, for example, allowing the destruction of evidence. This standard—as opposed to a probable cause requirement—strikes the appropriate balance between the legitimate law enforcement

concerns at issue in the execution of search warrants and the individual privacy interests affected by no-knock entries. . . .

Although we reject the Wisconsin court's blanket exception to the knock-and-announce requirement, we conclude that the officers' no-knock entry into Richards's hotel room did not violate the Fourth Amendment. We agree with the trial court, and with Justice Abrahamson, that the circumstances in this case show that the officers had a reasonable suspicion that Richards might destroy evidence if given further opportunity to do so.

The judge who heard testimony at Richards's suppression hearing concluded that it was reasonable for the officers executing the warrant to believe that Richards knew, after opening the door to his hotel room the first time, that the men seeking entry to his room were the police. Once the officers reasonably believed that Richards knew who they were, the court concluded, it was reasonable for them to force entry immediately given the disposable nature of the drugs. In arguing that the officers' entry was unreasonable, Richards places great emphasis on the fact that the magistrate who signed the search warrant for his hotel room deleted the portions of the proposed warrant that would have given the officers permission to execute a no-knock entry. But this fact does not alter the reasonableness of the officers' decision, which must be evaluated as of the time they entered the hotel room. At the time the officers obtained the warrant, they did not have evidence sufficient, in the judgment of the magistrate, to justify a no-knock warrant. Of course, the magistrate could not have anticipated in every particular the circumstances that would confront the officers when they arrived at Richards's hotel room. These actual circumstances—petitioner's apparent recognition of the officers combined with the easily disposable nature of the drugs—justified the officers' ultimate decision to enter without first announcing their presence and authority.

After a search is completed, the officers are required to inventory items seized. Federal rules require that the owner of the property be given a receipt for the goods taken.[26] Property unlawfully taken must be returned to the owner, unless it is unlawful in itself, such as drugs. In the 2006 case *Hudson v. Michigan,* 547 U.S. 586 (2006), the Supreme Court decided that the remedies for violations of the knock and announce requirement do not exclude exclusion of any evidence obtained following an unannounced entry. The Court found that the societal costs of such a remedy outweigh the benefits. Other remedies, such as civil suits against the officers, were found by the Court to be adequate to preserve the right.

Exceptions to the Probable Cause and Search Warrant Requirements

Although the general rule is that a warrant must be obtained before a search may be undertaken, there are many exceptions. The exceptions to the warrant requirement are sometimes referred to as **exigent circumstances.**

Consent Searches

A voluntary **consent** to a search obviates the warrant requirement. A person may consent to a search of his or her person or property. The scope of the search is limited by the person consenting. Absent special circumstances, a consent to search may be terminated at any time by the person giving consent.

A person's consent must be voluntary. All of the circumstances surrounding the consent are examined to determine whether the consent was voluntary. There is no requirement that police officers inform a person that he or she may refuse to consent.[27]

Courts examine the totality of the circumstances when determining whether a consent was voluntary. The following factors are considered, but none are dispositive:

1. The suspect's knowledge of the right to refuse.
2. The age, intelligence, and language skills of the suspect.
3. The degree of cooperation exhibited by the suspect.
4. The suspect's attitude about the likelihood of discovering contraband during the search.
5. The length of detention.
6. The nature of the detention, including the nature of the questions and whether police intimidated the suspect or coerced the statements.[28]

Police must respect any limitations placed on a suspect's consent. So, if a suspect indicates that police may search the family room of a house, but no more, any evidence discovered in another room of the house would be excluded. Also, consent may be revoked anytime before the search is completed. Prosecutors bear the burden of establishing that consents are voluntary by a preponderance of the evidence.

Of course, a defendant who is threatened or coerced into consenting has not voluntarily consented. It is not coercion for persons to be told that if they do not consent,

---

exigent circumstances

■ A situation where law enforcement officers must act so quickly to prevent the destruction of evidence, the successful flight of a suspect, or serious injury or death to any person, that there isn't time to obtain a warrant. Warrantless searches that occur when exigent circumstances exist are valid.

consent

■ Voluntary and active agreement.

a warrant will be obtained authorizing the desired search. It is coercion for officers to tell persons that if they do not consent to a search, a warrant will be obtained and the officers will ransack their home.[29]

Consent is invalid if it is obtained by a mistaken belief that the officer had a legal right to conduct the search. For example, if Officer Frisk tells Patty Pat-Down that he has a warrant, or that the law does not require that he have one, and she acquiesces, the search is invalid if he had no warrant or legal right to conduct the search.

The same is true when officers use fraud or deceit to obtain consent. For example, in one case a defendant was arrested and interrogated. He gave no incriminating information during the questioning. The following day the officers went to the home of the defendant and told his wife that he had confessed to the crime and had sent the police to seize the contraband. Based upon these statements, the defendant's wife consented to a search by the officers. The state court found that this tactic led to an involuntary consent and that the evidence seized was inadmissible at trial.[30]

The facts of that case raise another issue: third-party consent. This arises often in cases where many people share a single dwelling or room, such as families, fraternities, and dormitories. In *United States v. Matlock* (1974),[31] the Supreme Court found that a third party may consent as long as the parties share access, control, and use of the property. If coinhabitants section off a dwelling, with each tenant having exclusive control over a specific area, then only the tenant using an area may consent. If closets, desks, or similar areas are reserved for one person's private use, only that person may consent. Also, if coinhabitants are both present, either one may refuse consent for a search. If, however, police remove the coinhabitant from the premises before consent is refused, then the remaining coinhabitant's consent is adequate.[32]

Having a property interest in property does not give one a right to consent to a search of the property. The Supreme Court has said that neither landlords nor hotel managers may consent to the search of their tenants' rooms.[33] They may have a property interest, but the privacy interest rests with the tenants.

Stop and Frisk

Two of the most important exceptions to the probable cause and warrant requirements are the stop and frisk. On October 31, 1963, a Cleveland, Ohio, police detective observed three men standing on a street corner. Suspicious of the men, the detective positioned himself to watch their behavior. After some time the officer concluded that the men were "casing a job, a stick-up."

The officer approached the men, identified himself, and asked them to identify themselves. After the men "mumbled something," the officer grabbed one of the men and conducted a frisk, or a patdown, of the man's clothing. The officer felt a pistol in the man's coat pocket. He removed the gun from his coat and then patted down the other two men. Another gun was discovered during those frisks.

The officer testified that he conducted the frisks because he believed the men were carrying weapons. The first man frisked was defendant Terry. At trial he was convicted of carrying a concealed weapon and was subsequently sentenced to one to three years in prison. His appeal made it to the United States Supreme Court.

TERRY V. OHIO
392 U.S. 1 (1968)

MR. CHIEF JUSTICE WARREN delivered the opinion of the Court.

This case presents serious questions concerning the role of the Fourth Amendment in the confrontation on the street between the citizen and the policeman investigating suspicious circumstances.

Petitioner Terry was convicted of carrying a concealed weapon and sentenced to the statutorily prescribed term of one to three years in the penitentiary. Following the denial of a pretrial motion to suppress, the prosecution introduced in evidence two revolvers and a number of bullets seized from Terry and a codefendant, Richard Chilton, by Cleveland Police Detective Martin McFadden. At the hearing on the motion to suppress this evidence, Officer McFadden testified that, while he was patrolling in plain clothes in downtown Cleveland at approximately 2:30 in the afternoon of October 31, 1963, his attention was attracted by two men, Chilton and Terry, standing on the corner of Huron Road and Euclid Avenue. He had never seen the two men before, and he was unable to say precisely what first drew his eye to them. However, he testified that he had been a policeman for 39 years and a detective for 35, and that he had been assigned to patrol this vicinity of downtown Cleveland for shoplifters and pickpockets for 30 years. He explained that he had developed routine habits of observation over the years, and that he would "stand and watch people or walk and watch people at many intervals of the day." He added: "Now, in this case, when I looked over, they didn't look right to me at the time."

His interest aroused, Officer McFadden took up a post of observation in the entrance to a store 300 to 400 feet away from the two men. "I get more purpose to watch them when I seen their movements," he testified. He saw one of the men leave the other one and walk southwest on Huron Road, past some stores. The man paused for a moment and looked in a store window, then walked on a short distance, turned around and walked back toward the corner, pausing once again to look in the same store window. He rejoined his companion at the corner, and the two conferred briefly. Then the second man went through the same series of motions, strolling down Huron Road, looking in the same window, walking on a short distance, turning back, peering in the store window again, and returning to confer with the first man at the corner. The two men repeated this ritual alternately between five and six times apiece—in all, roughly a dozen trips. At one point, while the two were standing together on the corner, a third man approached them and engaged them briefly in conversation. This man then left the two others and walked west on Euclid Avenue. Chilton and Terry resumed their measured pacing, peering, and conferring. After this had gone on for 10 to 12 minutes, the two men walked off together, heading west on Euclid Avenue, following the path taken earlier by the third man.

By this time, Officer McFadden had become thoroughly suspicious. He testified that, after observing their elaborately casual and oft-repeated reconnaissance of the store window on Huron Road, he suspected the two men of "casing a job, a stick-up," and that he considered it his duty as a police officer to investigate further. He added that he feared "they may have a gun." Thus, Officer McFadden followed Chilton and Terry and saw them stop in front of Zucker's store to talk to the same man who had conferred with them earlier on the street corner. Deciding that the situation was ripe for direct action, Officer McFadden approached the three men, identified himself as a police officer and asked for their names. At this point, his knowledge was confined to what he had observed. He was not acquainted with any of the three men by name or by sight, and he had received no information

TERRY V. OHIO *(continued)*

concerning them from any other source. When the men "mumbled something" in response to his inquiries, Officer McFadden grabbed petitioner Terry, spun him around so that they were facing the other two, with Terry between McFadden and the others, and patted down the outside of his clothing. In the left breast pocket of Terry's overcoat, Officer McFadden felt a pistol. He reached inside the overcoat pocket, but was unable to remove the gun. At this point, keeping Terry between himself and the others, the officer ordered all three men to enter Zucker's store. As they went in, he removed Terry's overcoat completely, removed a .38 caliber revolver from the pocket and ordered all three men to face the wall with their hands raised. Officer McFadden proceeded to pat down the outer clothing of Chilton and the third man, Katz. He discovered another revolver in the outer pocket of Chilton's overcoat, but no weapons were found on Katz. The officer testified that he only patted the men down to see whether they had weapons, and that he did not put his hands beneath the outer garments of either Terry or Chilton until he felt their guns. So far as appears from the record, he never placed his hands beneath Katz' outer garments. Officer McFadden seized Chilton's gun, asked the proprietor of the store to call a police wagon, and took all three men to the station, where Chilton and Terry were formally charged with carrying concealed weapons.

On the motion to suppress the guns, the prosecution took the position that they had been seized following a search incident to a lawful arrest. The trial court rejected this theory, stating that it "would be stretching the facts beyond reasonable comprehension" to find that Officer McFadden had had probable cause to arrest the men before he patted them down for weapons. However, the court denied the defendants' motion on the ground that Officer McFadden, on the basis of his experience,

. . . had reasonable cause to believe . . . that the defendants were conducting themselves suspiciously, and some interrogation should be made of their action.

Purely for his own protection, the court held, the officer had the right to pat down the outer clothing of these men, who he had reasonable cause to believe might be armed. The court distinguished between an investigatory "stop" and an arrest, and between a "frisk" of the outer clothing for weapons and a full-blown search for evidence of crime. The frisk, it held, was essential to the proper performance of the officer's investigatory duties, for, without it, "the answer to the police officer may be a bullet, and a loaded pistol discovered during the frisk is admissible." [They were convicted, sentenced, and lost their appeal before the Supreme Court of Ohio.]

We would be less than candid if we did not acknowledge that this question thrusts to the fore difficult and troublesome issues regarding a sensitive area of police activity—issues which have never before been squarely presented to this Court. Reflective of the tensions involved are the practical and constitutional arguments pressed with great vigor on both sides of the public debate over the power of the police to "stop and frisk"—as it is sometimes euphemistically termed—suspicious persons.

On the one hand, it is frequently argued that, in dealing with the rapidly unfolding and often dangerous situations on city streets, the police are in need of an escalating set of flexible responses, graduated in relation to the amount of information they possess. For this purpose, it is urged that distinctions should be made between a "stop" and an "arrest" (or a "seizure" of a person), and between a "frisk" and a "search." Thus, it is argued, the police should be allowed to "stop" a person and detain him briefly for questioning upon suspicion that he may be connected with criminal activity. Upon

(continued)

TERRY V. OHIO *(continued)*

suspicion that the person may be armed, the police should have the power to "frisk" him for weapons. If the "stop" and the "frisk" give rise to probable cause to believe that the suspect has committed a crime, then the police should be empowered to make a formal "arrest," and a full incident "search" of the person. This scheme is justified in part upon the notion that a "stop" and a "frisk" amount to a mere "minor inconvenience and petty indignity," which can properly be imposed upon the citizen in the interest of effective law enforcement on the basis of a police officer's suspicion.

On the other side, the argument is made that the authority of the police must be strictly circumscribed by the law of arrest and search as it has developed to date in the traditional jurisprudence of the Fourth Amendment. It is contended with some force that there is not -- and cannot be -- a variety of police activity which does not depend solely upon the voluntary cooperation of the citizen, and yet which stops short of an arrest based upon probable cause to make such an arrest. The heart of the Fourth Amendment, the argument runs, is a severe requirement of specific justification for any intrusion upon protected personal security, coupled with a highly developed system of judicial controls to enforce upon the agents of the State the commands of the Constitution. . . .

Our first task is to establish at what point in this encounter the Fourth Amendment becomes relevant. That is, we must decide whether and when Officer McFadden "seized" Terry, and whether and when he conducted a "search." There is some suggestion in the use of such terms as "stop" and "frisk" that such police conduct is outside the purview of the Fourth Amendment because neither action rises to the level of a "search" or "seizure" within the meaning of the Constitution. We emphatically reject this notion. It is quite plain that the Fourth Amendment governs "seizures" of the person

which do not eventuate in a trip to the stationhouse and prosecution for crime—"arrests" in traditional terminology. It must be recognized that, whenever a police officer accosts an individual and restrains his freedom to walk away, he has "seized" that person. And it is nothing less than sheer torture of the English language to suggest that a careful exploration of the outer surfaces of a person's clothing all over his or her body in an attempt to find weapons is not a "search." Moreover, it is simply fantastic to urge that such a procedure performed in public by a policeman while the citizen stands helpless, perhaps facing a wall with his hands raised, is a "petty indignity." It is a serious intrusion upon the sanctity of the person, which may inflict great indignity and arouse strong resentment, and it is not to be undertaken lightly. . . .

In this case, there can be no question, then, that Officer McFadden "seized" petitioner and subjected him to a "search" when he took hold of him and patted down the outer surfaces of his clothing. We must decide whether, at that point, it was reasonable for Officer McFadden to have interfered with petitioner's personal security as he did. And, in determining whether the seizure and search were "unreasonable," our inquiry is a dual one -- whether the officer's action was justified at its inception, and whether it was reasonably related in scope to the circumstances which justified the interference in the first place. . . .

If this case involved police conduct subject to the Warrant Clause of the Fourth Amendment, we would have to ascertain whether "probable cause" existed to justify the search and seizure which took place. However, that is not the case. We do not retreat from our holdings that the police must, whenever practicable, obtain advance judicial approval of searches and seizures through the warrant procedure, *see, e.g., Katz v. United States* . . . or that, in most instances, failure to comply with the warrant requirement can

TERRY V. OHIO *(continued)*

only be excused by exigent circumstances. But we deal here with an entire rubric of police conduct -- necessarily swift action predicated upon the on-the-spot observations of the officer on the beat -- which historically has not been, and, as a practical matter, could not be, subjected to the warrant procedure. Instead, the conduct involved in this case must be tested by the Fourth Amendment's general proscription against unreasonable searches and seizures. . . .

Nonetheless, the notions which underlie both the warrant procedure and the requirement of probable cause remain fully relevant in this context. In order to assess the reasonableness of Officer Mc-Fadden's conduct as a general proposition, it is necessary "first to focus upon the governmental interest which allegedly justifies official intrusion upon the constitutionally protected interests of the private citizen," for there is . . .

. . . no ready test for determining reasonableness other than by balancing the need to search [or seize] against the invasion which the search [or seizure] entails.

And, in justifying the particular intrusion, the police officer must be able to point to specific and articulable facts which, taken together with rational inferences from those facts, reasonably warrant that intrusion. The scheme of the Fourth Amendment becomes meaningful only when it is assured that, at some point, the conduct of those charged with enforcing the laws can be subjected to the more detached, neutral scrutiny of a judge who must evaluate the reasonableness of a particular search or seizure in light of the particular circumstances. And, in making that assessment, it is imperative that the facts be judged against an objective standard: would the facts available to the officer at the moment of the seizure or the search "warrant a man of reasonable caution in the belief" that the action

taken was appropriate? Anything less would invite intrusions upon constitutionally guaranteed rights based on nothing more substantial than inarticulate hunches, a result this Court has consistently refused to sanction. And simple

"good faith on the part of the arresting officer is not enough." . . . If subjective good faith alone were the test, the protections of the Fourth Amendment would evaporate, and the people would be "secure in their persons, houses, papers, and effects," only in the discretion of the police.

Applying these principles to this case, we consider first the nature and extent of the governmental interests involved. One general interest is, of course, that of effective crime prevention and detection; it is this interest which underlies the recognition that a police officer may, in appropriate circumstances and in an appropriate manner, approach a person for purposes of investigating possibly criminal behavior even though there is no probable cause to make an arrest. It was this legitimate investigative function Officer McFadden was discharging when he decided to approach petitioner and his companions. He had observed Terry, Chilton, and Katz go through a series of acts, each of them perhaps innocent in itself, but which, taken together, warranted further investigation. There is nothing unusual in two men standing together on a street corner, perhaps waiting for someone. Nor is there anything suspicious about people in such circumstances strolling up and down the street, singly or in pairs. Store windows, moreover, are made to be looked in. But the story is quite different where, as here, two men hover about a street corner for an extended period of time, at the end of which it becomes apparent that they are not waiting for anyone or anything; where these men pace alternately along an identical route, pausing to stare in the

(continued)

same store window roughly 24 times; where each completion of this route is followed immediately by a conference between the two men on the corner; where they are joined in one of these conferences by a third man who leaves swiftly, and where the two men finally follow the third and rejoin him a couple of blocks away. It would have been poor police work indeed for an officer of 30 years' experience in the detection of thievery from stores in this same neighborhood to have failed to investigate this behavior further.

The crux of this case, however, is not the propriety of Officer McFadden's taking steps to investigate petitioner's suspicious behavior, but, rather, whether there was justification for McFadden's invasion of Terry's personal security by searching him for weapons in the course of that investigation. We are now concerned with more than the governmental interest in investigating crime; in addition, there is the more immediate interest of the police officer in taking steps to assure himself that the person with whom he is dealing is not armed with a weapon that could unexpectedly and fatally be used against him. Certainly it would be unreasonable to require that police officers take unnecessary risks in the performance of their duties. American criminals have a long tradition of armed violence, and every year in this country many law enforcement officers are killed in the line of duty, and thousands more are wounded. Virtually all of these deaths and a substantial portion of the injuries are inflicted with guns and knives.

In view of these facts, we cannot blind ourselves to the need for law enforcement officers to protect themselves and other prospective victims of violence in situations where they may lack probable cause for an arrest. When an officer is justified in believing that the individual whose suspicious behavior he is investigating at close range is armed and presently dangerous to the officer or to others, it would

appear to be clearly unreasonable to deny the officer the power to take necessary measures to determine whether the person is, in fact, carrying a weapon and to neutralize the threat of physical harm. . . .

The scope of the search in this case presents no serious problem in light of these standards. Officer McFadden patted down the outer clothing of petitioner and his two companions. He did not place his hands in their pockets or under the outer surface of their garments until he had felt weapons, and then he merely reached for and removed the guns. He never did invade Katz' person beyond the outer surfaces of his clothes, since he discovered nothing in his pat-down which might have been a weapon. Officer McFadden confined his search strictly to what was minimally necessary to learn whether the men were armed and to disarm them once he discovered the weapons. He did not conduct a general exploratory search for whatever evidence of criminal activity he might find.

We conclude that the revolver seized from Terry was properly admitted in evidence against him. At the time he seized petitioner and searched him for weapons, Officer McFadden had reasonable grounds to believe that petitioner was armed and dangerous, and it was necessary for the protection of himself and others to take swift measures to discover the true facts and neutralize the threat of harm if it materialized. The policeman carefully restricted his search to what was appropriate to the discovery of the particular items which he sought. Each case of this sort will, of course, have to be decided on its own facts. We merely hold today that, where a police officer observes unusual conduct which leads him reasonably to conclude in light of his experience that criminal activity may be afoot and that the persons with whom he is dealing may be armed and presently dangerous, where, in the course of investigating this behavior, he identifies himself as a policeman and makes reasonable

TERRY V. OHIO *(continued)*

inquiries, and where nothing in the initial stages of the encounter serves to dispel his reasonable fear for his own or others' safety, he is entitled for the protection of himself and others in the area to conduct a carefully limited search of the outer clothing of such persons in an attempt to discover weapons which might be used to assault him. Such a search is a reasonable search under the Fourth Amendment, and any weapons seized may properly be introduced in evidence against the person from whom they were taken.

----

sidebar

NEW YORK CITY STOP AND FRISK

New York City is home to a large and controversial stop and frisk program. Relying on the law established in *Terry,* New York established a program of aggressively stopping individuals who are suspected of criminality. Included in the program is Operation Clean Halls, a practice that enables owners of apartment houses and managers of public housing units to invite police into the public spaces of their buildings and to stop people who are suspected of criminality, including trespass. The program is large. More than 3,000 private housing units were enrolled in the program and over 600,000 people were stopped in 2011 alone. The program was challenged as violative of the Fourth Amendment and because of the disproportionate number of minorities stopped, as violative of equal protection as well. A federal district court found the program unconstitutional in 2012 and litigation was ongoing when this book went to press.[34]

Officers are not given carte blanche to stop and frisk. Although probable cause is not required, officers must have a "reasonable suspicion" that the person to be stopped has committed, is committing, or is about to commit a crime. The officer's suspicion must be supported by "specific and articulable facts which, taken together with rational inferences from those facts, reasonably warrant that intrusion."[35] An officer's intuition alone is not enough suspicion to support a *Terry* seizure. When reviewing an officer's reasonable suspicion decision, a court is to examine the "totality of the circumstances" as known to the officer. Facts that may not be admissible at trial may be considered.[36]

In *Terry,* the facts that the Court found established reasonable cause included the officer's personal observation of the defendant and another man pacing near a business, repeatedly looking into the business's window, and briefly encountering and conferring with a third man. In addition, the Court noted that the detective who stopped Terry had 39 years' experience in policing, and the officer testified that in his experience the men appeared to be "casing" the business. While the Court stressed that an officer's intuition alone is insufficient to establish reasonable cause, it can be relied upon in conjunction with specific facts to support a temporary detention. Another example of how much evidence is required to establish reasonable suspicion can be found in the 2000 Supreme Court case *Illinois v. Wardlow*. In *Wardlow* a defendant, who was in a high crime area, took flight immediately upon seeing police officers. The Court stated that even though a person's presence in a high crime area is not enough to establish reasonable suspicion, that fact combined with the defendant's unprovoked flight is enough.[37]

Not all contacts between an officer and a citizen amount to a seizure. A seizure occurs anytime a reasonable person believes that he or she is not free to leave. There need not be an attempt to leave. A person may feel restrained by physical contact from a police officer, tone of voice, threatening language, or the threatening presence of many officers.[38]

Mere questioning of a citizen by a police officer does not rise to the level of a detention. However, if the interrogation becomes accusatory or its duration lengthy, the Fourth Amendment may come into play. A Texas statute that required an individual to comply with a police officer's order to identify himself, even though there was no basis to believe criminal activity was afoot, was held unconstitutional by the Supreme Court in 1979.[39] The Court held that the Fourth Amendment prohibits the police from temporarily detaining a person and demanding identification without at least a reasonable suspicion to believe the individual has committed, or is engaged in committing, a crime. However, if a *Terry* stop is justified, a statute may require the individual to produce identification and if refused, the individual may be arrested, charged, and convicted for the refusal. In the 2004 decision *Hiibel v. Sixth Judicial District,* 544 U.S. 177 (2004), the Court stated:

> Obtaining a suspect's name in the course of a *Terry* stop serves important government interests. Knowledge of identity may inform an officer that a suspect is wanted for another offense, or has a record of violence or mental disorder. On the other hand, knowing identity may help clear a suspect and allow the police to concentrate their efforts elsewhere. Identity may prove particularly important in cases such as this, where the police are investigating what appears to be a domestic assault. Officers called to investigate domestic disputes need to know whom they are dealing with in order to assess the situation, the threat to their own safety, and possible danger to the potential victim. . . . Petitioner argues that the Nevada statute circumvents the probable cause requirement, in effect allowing an officer to arrest a person for being suspicious. According to petitioner, this creates a risk of arbitrary police conduct that the Fourth Amendment does not permit. Brief for Petitioner 28–33. These are familiar concerns; they were central to the opinion in *Papachristou,* and also to the decisions limiting the operation of stop and identify statutes in *Kolender* and *Brown*. Petitioner's concerns are met by the requirement that a *Terry* stop must be justified at its inception and "reasonably related in scope to the circumstances which justified" the initial stop. 392 U.S., at 20. Under these

principles, an officer may not arrest a suspect for failure to identify himself if the request for identification is not reasonably related to the circumstances justifying the stop.

A motorist may be temporarily detained under *Terry*. Also, the Supreme Court has said that once a person is lawfully pulled over and probable cause exists to believe a crime, including a traffic violation, has occurred, he or she may be ordered out of the vehicle, even though there is no reason to believe that the driver is a threat. See later in this chapter for a more thorough discussion of automobiles and the Fourth Amendment.

In addition to requiring reasonable suspicion, the *Terry* Court also stated that stops are to "last no longer than is necessary," and the investigative methods employed during the stop should be the "least intrusive means reasonably available to verify or dispel the officer's suspicion in a short period of time." If an officer detains a person longer than necessary, the investigatory detention turns into a full seizure (arrest), and the probable cause requirement of the Fourth Amendment commences.

It is not always easy to distinguish stops from arrests. But the determination is important because of the varying legal standards, reasonable suspicion and probable cause. *Florida v. Royer*, 460 U.S. 491 (1983), provides an example of the distinction between an investigatory detention and an arrest. The defendant, a suspected drug dealer, was questioned in a public area of an airport. After a few minutes he was taken 40 feet to a small police office, where he consented to a search of his luggage. The Court concluded that the search was the product of an illegal arrest, as less intrusive methods of investigation were available. As alternatives, the Court mentioned that the officers could have used narcotics dogs to inspect the luggage or could have immediately requested consent to search the defendant's luggage. The act of requiring the defendant to accompany the officers to a small room 40 feet away transformed the detention from a *Terry* stop to an arrest, which was violative of the Fourth Amendment because it was not supported by probable cause. In another case from a federal appellate court, that the police drew their guns on, and handcuffed, a driver and its occupant did not convert the *Terry* stop into a full seizure requiring probable cause. But the court acknowledged that the distinction between full seizures and *Terry* stops is often hard to draw.[40]

The fact that there has been a lawful stop does not itself justify a frisk. The purpose behind permitting investigatory stops is the advancement of crime detection and prevention. Frisks, on the other hand, are permitted to protect officers and others from the person stopped.

To conduct a frisk, an officer must have a reasonable belief that the person is armed and dangerous. Again, the officer must be able to point to facts to support this conclusion. An officer may draw on his or her experience as a police officer in making the decision. Again, however, intuition (suspicion not supported by any facts) alone is not adequate.

Full searches require probable cause. A *Terry* frisk requires less, and, accordingly, the permitted intrusion is less. The search must be limited to the outer clothing. A search of interior clothing or pockets is improper.

If the defendant is in an automobile, the officer may search those areas within the person's immediate control.[41] Once any lawful stop of a vehicle is made, the driver may be ordered out of the vehicle. However, to frisk an occupant of a vehicle, the *Terry* standard must be met.

If during a patdown an officer feels an item that may be a weapon, then the officer may reach into the clothing of the citizen to seize the item. Any item seized, whether a weapon, contraband, or other item associated with a crime, may be used as evidence.

If the officer does not feel an item that may be a weapon, the search can go no further. If the officer feels evidence of another crime, the intrusion may continue under the "plain feel" doctrine.

Plain Feel

You have learned both the plain view doctrine and the *Terry* exception to the warrant and probable cause requirements of the Fourth Amendment. The plain feel doctrine is the product of their joining. That is, what happens when an officer who is conducting a *Terry* patdown discovers, through the sense of touch, not a weapon, but contraband? May this information be used to establish probable cause allowing a more intrusive search? This question was answered in *Minnesota v. Dickerson,* 508 U.S. 366 (1993), where the Supreme Court held that evidence felt during a *Terry* frisk may be used to establish probable cause to support retrieving item, as long as the incriminating character of the evidence is immediately apparent.

The rules set out in *Terry* apply. First, stops must be supported by reasonable suspicion. Second, patdowns may be conducted only when an officer possesses a reasonable suspicion based on specific and articulable facts that the suspect may be armed and dangerous. Third, the patdown must be limited. Exploration of the clothing beyond what is necessary to determine dangerousness is not permitted, unless probable cause to believe that there is contraband is created through the officer's sense of touch.

Plain View

plain view doctrine

■ The rule that if police officers see or come across something while acting lawfully, that item may be used as evidence in a criminal trial even if the police did not have a search warrant.

Another exception to the warrant requirement is the **plain view doctrine.** Under this rule, a warrantless seizure of evidence by an officer who is lawfully in a position to see the evidence is valid.

A large body of cases discusses the plain view doctrine. From those cases it can be gleaned that for a seizure to be lawful under the doctrine, the following must be shown: (1) the officer must lawfully be in an area (2) from which the object to be seized is in plain view, and (3) the officer does in fact see the item; (4) there is probable cause to believe the object is connected to a crime, and (5) the officer has a right to access the object itself.

First, the officer must be in a place where he or she has a right to be. An officer, as is true of anyone, has a right to be in public places. Thus, evidence seen in a public park, on the street, or in a business open to the public may be seized without a warrant.

Evidence located on private property is different. As a general rule, the police have no right to enter private property to seize evidence that was in plain view from a public area. In such cases the officer is expected to obtain a warrant; the officer's observation provides the requisite probable cause. However, if an exception applies, such as preventing the destruction of the evidence, the officer may immediately seize the evidence.

If an officer is on private property for a lawful reason, then the officer may seize evidence in plain view without first obtaining a warrant. There are many reasons that an officer may be in a position to see evidence. Many of these were discussed in *Coolidge.* An officer who has to enter a home to execute an arrest warrant is not expected to overlook illegal objects in plain sight. The same is true if the officer is executing a search warrant, is in hot pursuit, is responding to an emergency, or is conducting a stop and frisk.

An officer who sees evidence because he or she has gone beyond the scope of the law enforcement right violates the Fourth Amendment, and the plain view doctrine will not support a seizure. For example, if an officer has a warrant to search a defendant's garage, any evidence obtained from the defendant's home, even if in plain view, may not be used at trial.

Second, the evidence seized must be in plain sight or plain view. Only the senses of sight and touch may be used to establish plain view. Use of the sense of touch is discussed later. Of course, whether an item is in plain sight depends on the scope of the officer's authority. An officer who has a search warrant authorizing the search of a closet for a gun may seize cocaine lying on the floor of the closet. The same is not true if the warrant did not authorize a search of the closet. In any case, the item must be plainly visible from a place where the officer has a right to be.

If an officer moves something with the intent of gaining a better vantage of the item, it is not in plain view. In one case, the movement of a stereo to record its serial number was considered an illegal search because the officers were on the premises for another reason. The Court noted in that case that merely observing the stereo, which was in plain view, was legal. If the serial number had been visible without moving the stereo, then recording its number would not have been violative of the Fourth Amendment. But moving the stereo constituted a "new invasion" of the defendant's rights.[42]

Officers may use mechanical or electrical aids in seeing evidence, so long as they are in a place they have a right to be and they are not conducting a search (encroaching on someone's right to privacy). Flashlights and binoculars are examples of such aids.

Third, the officer must see the item. In *Coolidge,* the Court stated that

> . . . the discovery of evidence in plain view must be inadvertent. The rationale of the exception to the warrant requirement, as just stated, is that a plain-view seizure will not turn an initially valid (and therefore limited) search into a "general" one, while the inconvenience of procuring a warrant to cover an inadvertent discovery is great. But where the discovery is anticipated, where the police know in advance that location of the evidence and intend to seize it, the situation is altogether different. The requirement of a warrant imposes no inconvenience whatever.[43]

In Horton v. California, 496 U.S. 128 (1990), the Supreme Court reversed itself in part by eliminating inadvertence as a requirement of plain view. The Court recognized that discoveries will be inadvertent in most instances but found requiring inadvertence unworkable. In *Horton,* an officer sought a search warrant for both the proceeds of a robbery and the weapons used during the robbery. The warrant was issued, but only for the proceeds. During the search, the officer discovered the weapon, as expected, in plain view. The Court held that even though expected, the gun was properly seized.

Fourth, the officer must have probable cause to believe that the object is subject to seizure, or, as the Court stated in *Horton,* the incriminating character of the object must be immediately apparent. *Contraband* (an item that is illegal itself, such as drugs) can be seized, as can property that is used to commit crimes, has been used in a crime, or has been stolen.

Fifth, the officer must be located such that he or she had a legal right to access the object. If not, the officer must obtain a warrant.

Search Incident to Arrest and the Protective Sweep

Two search issues arise during and immediately following an arrest. First, may officers search the arrestee's person without first obtaining a warrant? Second, may officers search the arrestee's home, apartment, or other structure where the defendant is arrested?

The issue of searching the defendant's person was addressed in *United States v. Robinson,* 414 U.S. 260 (1973), in which the Court held that, after a lawful arrest, the defendant's person may be fully searched without first obtaining a warrant. The Court held that to require officers to obtain a warrant would needlessly endanger their lives and would increase the possibility of evidence being destroyed by the defendant. Search incident to arrest includes a search of the defendant's clothing. There is no probable cause requirement for a search incident to arrest.

The second issue concerns searching the area where the defendant is arrested. The premier case in this area is *Chimel v. California.*

CHIMEL V. CALIFORNIA
395 U.S. 752 (1969)

This case raises basic questions concerning the permissible scope under the Fourth Amendment of a search incident to a lawful arrest.

The relevant facts are essentially undisputed. Late in the afternoon of September 13, 1965, three police officers arrived at the Santa Ana, California, home of the petitioner with a warrant authorizing his arrest for the burglary of a coin shop. The officers knocked on the door, identified themselves to the petitioner's wife, and asked if they might come inside. She ushered them into the house, where

they waited 10 to 15 minutes until the petitioner returned home from work. When the petitioner entered the house, one of the officers handed him the arrest warrant and asked for permission to "look around." The petitioner objected, but was advised that "on the basis of the lawful arrest," the officers would nonetheless conduct the search. No search warrant had been issued.

Accompanied by the petitioner's wife, the officers then looked through the entire three-bedroom house, including the attic, the garage,

CHIMEL V. CALIFORNIA *(continued)*

and a small workshop. In some rooms the search was relatively cursory. In the master bedroom and sewing room, however, the officers directed the petitioner's wife to open drawers and "to physically remove contents of the drawers from side to side so that [they] might view items that would have come from [the] burglary." After completing the search, they seized numerous items—primarily coins, but also several medals, tokens, and a few other objects. The entire search took between 45 minutes and an hour. . . .

When an arrest is made, it is reasonable for the arresting officer to search the person arrested in order to remove any weapons that the latter might seek to use in order to resist arrest or effect his escape. Otherwise, the officer's safety might well be endangered, and the arrest itself frustrated. In addition, it is entirely reasonable for the arresting officer to search for and seize any evidence on the arrestee's person in order to prevent its concealment or destruction. And the area into which an arrestee might reach in order to grab a weapon or evidentiary items must, of course, be governed by

a like rule. A gun on a table or in a drawer in front of one who is arrested can be as dangerous to the arresting officer as one concealed in the clothing of the person arrested. There is ample justification, therefore, for a search of the arrestee's person and the area "within his immediate control"—construing that phrase to mean the area from within which he might gain possession of a weapon or destructible evidence.

There is no comparable justification, however, for routinely searching any room other than that in which an arrest occurs—or, for that matter, for searching through all the desk drawers or other closed or concealed areas in the room itself. Such searches, in the absence of well-recognized exceptions, may be made only under the authority of a search warrant. . . .

Application of sound Fourth Amendment principles to the facts of this case produces a clear result. . . . The scope of the search was . . . "unreasonable" under the Fourth and Fourteenth Amendments, and the petitioner's conviction cannot stand.

Reversed.

Chimel significantly changed the law, as before *Chimel* was decided officers had the authority to search a much greater area as incident to arrest. The "within the defendant's immediate control" test continues to be the governing law. As with any other lawful search and seizure, any evidence obtained may be used to prosecute the defendant.

A related concept, the protective sweep, was given constitutional recognition in *Maryland v. Buie*, 494 U.S. 325 (1990). A *protective sweep* is a brief and limited warrantless search of an arrestee's home, which is permitted if the defendant is arrested therein. The purpose of the protective sweep is to check the house for other persons who may pose a danger to the arresting officers. See later in this chapter for an extended discussion of searches incident to arrest and protective sweeps.

Finally, "when a policeman has made a lawful custodial arrest of the occupant of an automobile, he may, as a contemporaneous incident of that arrest, search the passenger compartment of that automobile," including the contents of any containers found in that area.[44]

Preservation of Evidence

In some instances evidence may be destroyed before a warrant can be obtained. In such cases an officer may make a warrantless search and seizure.

Although the typical case involves the destruction of evidence, the preservation-of-evidence theory also has been applied to evanescent evidence (evidence that may vanish on its own). For example, in one case a defendant, who was arrested for drunk driving, was subjected to a warrantless blood alcohol test. The Court concluded that the warrantless test was reasonable under the Fourth Amendment.

> The officer in the present case, however, might reasonably have believed that he was confronted with an emergency, in which the delay necessary to obtain a warrant, under the circumstances, threatened "the destruction of evidence." . . . We are told that the percentage of alcohol in the blood begins to diminish shortly after drinking stops, as the body functions to eliminate it from the system. Particularly in a case such as this, where time had to be taken to bring the accused to the hospital and to investigate the scene of the accident, there was no time to seek out a magistrate and secure a warrant. Given these special facts, we conclude that the attempt to secure evidence of blood-alcohol content in this case was an appropriate incident to petitioner's arrest.[45]

So, any evidence that may be destroyed, intentionally or not, before a warrant can be obtained, can be the foundation of a warrantless search and seizure under the preservation-of-evidence exception to the Fourth Amendment's warrant requirement. See Chapter 13 for more on this subject.

Emergency Responses and Hot Pursuit

One of the many responsibilities of being a police officer is to respond to emergencies and to assist those in danger. Police officers are permitted to enter areas protected by the Fourth Amendment without a warrant if there is an emergency. For example, an officer may respond to cries for help from within a home or may enter a building that is on fire to assist firefighters. While the cause for entry must be genuine, it need not rise to the level of threatening life. In *Brigham City v. Stuart,* 547 U.S. 398 (2006), warrantless police entry of a home, following an announcement that they were entering, to quell a fight between four adults and a juvenile was upheld. During the fight, the juvenile punched one of the adults in the face, causing him to spit blood into a sink. The Court found that the officers were objectively reasonable in assuming the adult might need assistance and that the fight could escalate, leading to more serious injuries. Of course, once inside, any evidence in plain view may be seized. Also, officers may remedy any immediate problems, secure the premises, and then obtain a warrant before proceeding further, provided that no exigent circumstances justify a continued presence and search.

It has been argued that the government has such a great interest, especially in murder cases, in having immediate access to crime scenes that the Fourth Amendment warrant requirement should be dispensed with. The Supreme Court rejected that position in *Mincey v. Arizona,* 437 U.S. 385 (1978), in which a warrantless four-day search of an apartment where a police officer was murdered was held violative of the Fourth Amendment.

Similar to the emergency exception is the hot pursuit exception. An officer who is chasing a suspect does not have to end the pursuit at the door of a home or business.

The normally unlawful entry into the structure is permitted to catch the defendant. Again, once inside, the plain view exception applies.

Open Fields

The open fields doctrine is not, technically, an exception to the search warrant requirement. That is because, to be an exception to the Fourth Amendment warrant requirement, the Fourth Amendment must apply to the conduct of the officers. The Supreme Court has held that the "open fields" around one's home are not protected by the Fourth Amendment, so officers are free to intrude upon such areas without first obtaining a warrant. In addition, officers will not be liable for trespass if they make such an intrusion while performing a lawful duty.[46]

Open fields are not protected, due to the language of the Fourth Amendment itself: "The right of the people to be secure in their persons, houses, papers, and effects. . . ." The Supreme Court has found that this language extends the Fourth Amendment's protection only to a person's home and the curtilage of that home.

Curtilage is the area directly around one's home. It is treated as part of the home, as the Court has recognized that a person's privacy interest does not end at the front door of the home. Determining whether an area is curtilage, and protected, or an open field, and unprotected, can be troublesome. In *United States v. Dunn*,[47] the high Court held that a barn located 60 yards from a house was not within the curtilage, even though a fence enclosed the barn. In that opinion, the Court stated four factors that should be considered when making an open fields determination:

1. The proximity of the area claimed to be curtilage from the home.
2. Whether the area enclosed is enclosed with the home.
3. The nature of the use of the area.
4. The attempts of the residents to keep the area private.

The proximity of the area in question to the home, the fact that it is enclosed by fencing, that it is commonly used by the residents, and that the residents have taken measures to assure privacy in the area, all increase the probability that the area will be determined to be curtilage. The issue is whether the residents have a reasonable expectation of privacy in the area.

The advent of aerial surveillance has made it possible for law enforcement officers to see what were once remote areas. The question in the Fourth Amendment context is: Do people have a reasonable expectation of privacy in areas observable from aircraft?

One federal district court outlined five factors to be considered when examining the validity of aerial surveillance:

1. The height of the aircraft.
2. The size of the objects viewed.
3. The nature of the use of the area.
4. The number of flights over the area.
5. The frequency and duration of the aerial surveillance.[48]

Structures, even though in an open field, may be protected if it appears that one took measures to assure privacy.[49] However, the fact that an area is curtilage does not mean that a warrantless aerial observation is unreasonable. In a 1986 case, the Supreme Court upheld an aerial observation of a backyard that was surrounded by a fence and not visible from the street.[50] In another twist of facts, a Wisconsin court upheld a trespassory installation of cameras in an open field by police. The images of the defendants growing marijuana were admitted at trial.[51]

The impact that the 2012 *Jones* decision, reinstating the property test for a search, will have on the open fields doctrine remains to be seen. The rationale underlying the open fields doctrine is that there is no reasonable expectation to privacy in an open field. But if the government intrudes, trespasses, into a defendant's fields, *Jones* may demand a different result.

Finally, although the Fourth Amendment speaks of "houses," its protection extends to businesses and other structures as well. However, it is likely that the expectation of privacy will be less stringent in a business than in a dwelling.

Border Searches and Profiles

It is a long-standing principle of international and U.S. law that a nation's authority to protect itself is at its zenith at its borders. For this reason, searches at the borders of the United States do not require probable cause. In fact, no suspicion is required whatsoever. This rule applies to searches of both luggage and persons.[52] It also applies to vehicles that cross the border. For example, border agents may remove, inspect, and reassemble a car's gas tank with no suspicion of wrongdoing.[53] However, border searches must comply with the reasonableness requirement of the Fourth Amendment.[54]

For a strip search to be conducted, a customs official must have a "real suspicion" that illegality is afoot. As for more invasive searches, such as cavity searches, more suspicion is required. A customs official must be aware of a "clear indication" of illegality before such searches are conducted. Further, these searches must be conducted in a private and medically safe environment. A *clear indication* is less than probable cause, but more than either the *Terry* reasonable suspicion or the border strip-search "real suspicion" standards.

The border search exception to the Fourth Amendment actually extends beyond the border. For example, first arrival ports in the United States of international flights are treated as borders for purposes of the Fourth Amendment. Roadblock-style checkpoints miles from a border intended to discover illegal aliens have been approved,[55] but the authority to search is more limited than at the border. Officers may not search the occupants of the vehicles stopped at these checkpoints without probable cause.[56] Random stops of vehicles away from the border must be supported by reasonable suspicion, because they are treated as *Terry* detentions.

Customs officials commonly use profiles to determine who to detain and search. A *profile* is an established set of criteria that are believed to indicate a probability that a person is involved in illegal activity. For example, a person who makes frequent trips between the United States and Colombia (a nation noted for its drug production and exportation), who carries little or no luggage, who has paid for airline tickets with cash, whose visits to Colombia are for short periods of time (e.g., 48 hours), and who behaves nervously at the customs desk, would meet a drug courier profile. Similar profiles have been used to stop motorists in Florida suspected of transporting and trafficking drugs.

Two issues are raised by profiles: first, whether a profile may be used to establish a reasonable suspicion, thereby permitting a *Terry* stop; and second, whether profiles justify searches.

As to the first question, the answer is yes. However, a profile must be reasonable. Courts examine the totality of the circumstances when examining the validity of a profile. Although no one factor in a profile may justify a temporary detention, the whole picture may. Although race may be a factor in the decision, the Supreme Court held in *United States v. Brignoni-Ponce,* 422 U.S. 873 (1975), that race alone does not establish reasonable suspicion, even if the detention occurs near the Mexican border and the occupants appear to be of Mexican ancestry. The Court enumerated factors that may be taken into account:

1. The characteristics of the area, including the proximity to the border, the usual patterns of traffic on the road, and experience with alien traffic.
2. Information concerning recent illegal border crossings in the area.
3. The driver's behavior, such as erratic driving and obvious attempts to evade officers.
4. The type of vehicle, such as a station wagon with large compartments, which are frequently used for transporting concealed aliens.
5. Whether the vehicle appears heavily loaded or has an extraordinary number of occupants.
6. Whether passengers are attempting to hide.
7. The characteristics of persons living in Mexico, including mode of dress and hair styles.
8. Other meaningful factors in light of the officers' experiences in detecting illegal aliens.

This list is not exclusive, and profiles vary depending upon the situation. Nevertheless, the *Brignoni-Ponce* decision provided a basis upon which law enforcement agencies can create profiles and courts can adjudge the validity of those profiles.

This leads to the second question: May profiles be used to justify searches? Recall that at borders no suspicion is necessary to conduct general searches of persons and things. However, to conduct body searches a "real suspicion" must exist, and to conduct more invasive searches there must be a "clear indication" of some illegality. Although a profile may satisfy the real suspicion test, it does not, acting alone, justify more invasive searches.

Outside the border areas, profiles may be used to conduct *Terry* stops, but no more. To conduct a frisk of the persons detained, a reasonable belief as to dangerousness must exist. Probable cause is required if a full search of a person, vehicle, or other things is conducted.

Finally, although profiles may be used to support detentions, they may not be used at trial to establish guilt.[57]

---

sidebar

THE RACIAL PROFILING CONTROVERSY

In recent years the use of race as a factor in law enforcement and corrections officer's decision making has been the subject of considerable controversy. Many scholars and commentators have asserted that it is common for police officers to stop black motorists simply because of their skin color. This phenomenon has become known as "driving while black." In addition to traffic stops, race is often used as a factor to determine whose bags or person should be searched in airports and at borders.

Racial profiling was already the subject of considerable debate when the United States was attacked on September 11, 2001, by 19 Muslim terrorists. Several hijackings in the 1970s and 1980s, the 1993 World Trade Center bombing, the 1996 bombing of a U.S. military site in Saudi Arabia, the bombings of two U.S. embassies in 1996, the attack on the U.S.S. *Cole* in 2000, and other attacks on U.S. citizens and interests were all committed by Muslim extremists. In the wake of these events, many people called for increased scrutiny of people who appeared to be of Arab descent or who appeared to be Muslim. Others contended that such profiling was inherently wrong.

In an effort not to engage in "racial profiling," the United States Secretary of Transportation, Norman Mineta, ordered that race not be used as a factor by airport security officers when making decisions to search baggage or persons. This policy had many critics, who contended that ethnicity and dress were legitimate characteristics given the nature of threat to the United States.

The Supreme Court of the United States has found a middle ground. The Court has held that race, ethnicity, religion, skin color, and similar characteristics may not be the sole basis upon which a person is searched or seized. However, the Court held in *United States v. Brignoni-Ponce* (1975) that race may be one of many factors law enforcement officers may consider when stopping motorists or conducting border searches, provided that race can be connected with criminality in the particular circumstances in which the officers are operating.

Source: David A. Harris, "The Stories, The Statistics, and the Law: Why Driving While Black Matters," 84 *Minnesota Law Review* 265 (1999).

Automobiles and Roadblocks

Privacy in automobiles is protected by the Fourth Amendment. However, the Supreme Court has not extended full Fourth Amendment protection to the occupants of automobiles. The Court's rationale for decreased protection is twofold. First, due to the mobile nature of automobiles, evidence can disappear quickly. Second, automobiles are used on the public roads where they and their occupants are visible to the public; thus, an occupant of an automobile has a lesser expectation of privacy than does the occupant of a home.

Stops

Of course, a motorist may be stopped if an officer has probable cause. In addition, a *Terry* stop may be made if there is reasonable suspicion that an occupant has committed a crime or that contraband will be found. As discussed earlier, *Terry* stops must be limited in duration and reasonable in method, and a frisk of the occupant is permissible only if the officer possesses a reasonable belief that the individual may have a weapon. If a stop is arbitrary, e.g. not supported by reasonable suspicion, probably cause, or for another legitimate road safety or traffic management reason, it violates the Fourth Amendment, as found in the Prouse case.

DELAWARE V. PROUSE
440 U.S. 648 (1979)

At 7:20 P.M. on November 30, 1976, a New Castle County . . . patrolman in a police cruiser stopped the automobile occupied by respondent. The patrolman smelled marihuana smoke as he was walking toward the stopped vehicle, and he seized marihuana in plain view on the car floor. Respondent was subsequently indicted for illegal possession of a controlled substance. At a hearing on respondent's motion to suppress the marihuana seized as a result of the stop, the patrolman testified that prior to stopping the vehicle he had observed neither traffic or equipment violations nor any suspicious activity, and that he made the stop only in order to check the driver's license and registration. The patrolman was not acting pursuant to any standards, guidelines, or procedures pertaining to document spot checks, promulgated by either his department or the State Attorney General. Characterizing the stop as "routine," the patrolman explained, "I saw the car in the area and wasn't answering any complaints, so I decided to pull them off." The trial court granted the motion to suppress, finding the stop and detention to have been wholly capricious and therefore violative of the Fourth Amendment. . . .

The Delaware Supreme Court affirmed. . . .

But the State of Delaware urges . . . these stops are reasonable under the Fourth Amendment because the State's interest in the practice as a means of promoting public safety upon its roads more than outweighs the intrusion entailed. Although the record discloses no statistics concerning the extent of the problem of highway safety, in Delaware or in the Nation as a whole, we are aware of danger to life and property posed by vehicular traffic and the difficulties that even a cautious and experienced driver may encounter. We agree that the States have a vital interest in ensuring that only those qualified to do so are permitted to operate motor vehicles, that these vehicles are fit for safe operation, and hence that licensing, registration, and vehicle inspection requirements are being observed. . . .

(continued)

The question remains, however, whether in the service of these important ends the discretionary spot check is a sufficiently productive mechanism to justify the intrusion upon Fourth Amendment interests which stops entail. On the record before us, that question must be answered in the negative. Given the alternative mechanisms available, both those in use and those that might be adopted, we are unconvinced that the incremental contribution to highway safety of the random spot check justifies the practice under the Fourth Amendment.

The foremost method of enforcing traffic and vehicle safety regulations, it must be recalled, is acting upon observed violations. Vehicle stops for traffic violations occur countless times each day; and on these occasions, licenses and registration papers are subject to inspection and drivers without them will be ascertained. Furthermore, drivers without licenses are presumably the less safe drivers whose propensities may well exhibit themselves. . . .

Much the same can be said about the safety aspects of automobiles as distinguished from drivers. Many violations of minimum vehicle-safety requirements are observable, and something can be done about them by the observing officer, directly and immediately. Furthermore, in Delaware, as elsewhere, vehicles must carry and display current license plates, which themselves evidence that the vehicle is properly registered; and, under Delaware law, to qualify for annual registration a vehicle must pass the annual safety inspection and be properly insured. . . .

The marginal contribution to roadway safety possibly resulting from a system of spot checks cannot justify subjecting every occupant of every vehicle on the roads to a seizure—limited in magnitude compared to other intrusions but nonetheless constitutionally cognizable—at the unbridled discretion of law enforcement officials. To insist neither upon an appropriate factual basis for suspicion directed at a particular automobile nor upon some other substantial and objective standard or rule to govern the exercise of discretion "would invite intrusions upon constitutionally guaranteed rights based on nothing more substantial than inarticulable hunches. . . ." This kind of standardless and unconstrained discretion is the evil the Court has discerned when in previous cases it has insisted that the discretion of the official in the field be circumscribed, at least to some extent. . . ."

Accordingly, we hold that except in those situations in which there is at least articulable and reasonable suspicion that a motorist is unlicensed or that an automobile is not registered, or that either the vehicle or an occupant is otherwise subject to seizure for violation of law, stopping an automobile and detaining the driver in order to check his driver's license and the registration of the automobile are unreasonable under the Fourth Amendment. This holding does not preclude the State of Delaware or other States from developing methods for spot checks that involve less intrusions or that do not involve unconstrained exercise of discretion. Questioning of all oncoming traffic at roadblock-type stops is one possible alternative. We hold only that persons in automobiles on public roadways may not for that reason alone have their travel and privacy interfered with at the unbridled discretion of police officers. The judgment below is affirmed.

Fourth Amendment issues also arise in the context of roadblocks, which are used by law enforcement officers in two situations. First, roadblocks assist in the apprehension of a particular suspect. Second, in serving the regulatory function of protecting the public from unsafe drivers, officers may stop vehicles to determine if the car satisfies the state's safety requirements, whether the driver is properly licensed, and whether the vehicle is properly registered. Regarding the former, reasonable suspicion is required before a stop can be made. As to the latter, temporary regulatory detentions are permitted so long as they are both objectively random and reasonable. That is, the police must use an objective system in deciding what automobiles will be stopped. Every car, or every tenth car, or some similar method is permissible.

---

sidebar

DRONES

The use of unmanned aerial vehicles by the U.S. military is widely known. The military has used drones for surveillance, in combat, and to execute terrorists. Drones are attractive surveillance and fighting weapons because they are fast, inexpensive, they can survey and record images and tracks persons and objects from a great distances using cameras, thermal detection devices, radars and other equipment, and because they don't require a human pilot, they pose little risk to life. Drones can be as small as an insect and as large as a jet. For all their benefits, they also pose a serious threat to privacy. For this reason, the use of drones by police and other government agencies for criminal surveillance, to monitor borders, and for other purposes, as well as by private individuals, has begun to garner the public's attention.

Many people are concerned that an impending loosening of federal restrictions (2015) coupled with the low cost of drones will lead to a proliferation of the vehicles. The Federal Aviation Administration has predicted that 30,000 drones will be flying in the United States before 2023.[58] In response to the threat to privacy, many states have preemptively enacted laws restricting their use. By September 2013 nine states had laws restricting the use of drones. Most of those laws restricted use by law enforcement only, one restricted use by both private persons and law enforcement, and one state restrict individual use but not police use.[59]

Use by police raises Fourth Amendment concerns that the courts will have to address in the years to come. Existing Fourth Amendment law defining aerial searches by traditional aircraft and defining open fields and curtilage may prove outdated when examined in the context of drones.

The Supreme Court has also upheld roadblocks intended to discover drunk drivers. *Michigan State Police v. Sitz* (1990)[60] upheld a highway sobriety checkpoint program where 126 vehicles passed through the checkpoint, the average delay for each vehicle was 25 seconds, and 2 intoxicated drivers were arrested. The Court found that the stops were seizures under the Fourth Amendment, but that they were reasonable. In support of this conclusion, the Court stressed that the stops were of limited duration; that drunk drivers are a serious problem in the nation, and accordingly Michigan had a compelling interest in performing the sobriety checks; that all stops were governed by objective guidelines; that the guidelines required all vehicles to be stopped, thereby preventing arbitrary decisions by individual officers; that all officers were fully uniformed, thereby lessening motorists' concerns; and finally, that data support the conclusion that sobriety checkpoints are effective in apprehending drunk drivers. In the 2000 Supreme Court decision, *City of Indianapolis v. Edmond,* the Court invalidated systematic stops of cars intended to intercept illegal drugs.

CITY OF INDIANAPOLIS V. EDMOND
531 U.S. 32 (2000)

In *Michigan Dept. of State Police v. Sitz,* 496 U.S. 444 (1990), and *United States v. Martinez-Fuerte,* 428 U.S. 543 (1976), we held that brief, suspicionless seizures at highway checkpoints for the purposes of combating drunk driving and intercepting illegal immigrants were constitutional. We now consider the constitutionality of a highway checkpoint program whose primary purpose is the discovery and interdiction of illegal narcotics.

In August 1998, the city of Indianapolis began to operate vehicle checkpoints on Indianapolis roads in an effort to interdict unlawful drugs. The city conducted six such roadblocks between August and November that year, stopping 1,161 vehicles and arresting 104 motorists. Fifty-five arrests were for drug-related crimes, while 49 were for offenses unrelated to drugs. The overall "hit rate" of the program was thus approximately nine percent.

The parties stipulated to the facts concerning the operation of the checkpoints by the Indianapolis Police Department (IPD) for purposes of the preliminary injunction proceedings instituted below. At each checkpoint location, the police stop a predetermined number of vehicles. Approximately 30 officers are stationed at the checkpoint. Pursuant to written directives issued by the chief of police, at least one officer approaches the vehicle, advises the driver that he or she is being stopped briefly at a drug checkpoint, and asks the driver to produce a license and registration. The officer also looks for

signs of impairment and conducts an open-view examination of the vehicle from the outside. A narcotics-detection dog walks around the outside of each stopped vehicle.

The directives instruct the officers that they may conduct a search only by consent or based on the appropriate quantum of particularized suspicion. The officers must conduct each stop in the same manner until particularized suspicion develops, and the officers have no discretion to stop any vehicle out of sequence. The city agreed in the stipulation to operate the checkpoints in such a way as to ensure that the total duration of each stop, absent reasonable suspicion or probable cause, would be five minutes or less.

The affidavit of Indianapolis Police Sergeant Marshall DePew, although it is technically outside the parties' stipulation, provides further insight concerning the operation of the checkpoints. According to Sergeant DePew, checkpoint locations are selected weeks in advance based on such considerations as area crime statistics and traffic flow. The checkpoints are generally operated during daylight hours and are identified with lighted signs reading, "NARCOTICS CHECKPOINT___MILE AHEAD, NARCOTICS K-9 IN USE, BE PREPARED TO STOP." Once a group of cars has been stopped, other traffic proceeds without interruption until all the stopped cars have been processed or diverted for further processing. Sergeant DePew also stated

(continued)

that the average stop for a vehicle not subject to further processing lasts two to three minutes or less.

Respondents James Edmond and Joell Palmer were each stopped at a narcotics checkpoint in late September 1998. Respondents then filed a lawsuit on behalf of themselves and the class of all motorists who had been stopped or were subject to being stopped in the future at the Indianapolis drug checkpoints. . . .

The Fourth Amendment requires that searches and seizures be reasonable. A search or seizure is ordinarily unreasonable in the absence of individualized suspicion of wrongdoing. While such suspicion is not an "irreducible" component of reasonableness, *Martinez-Fuerte,* 428 U.S., at 561, we have recognized only limited circumstances in which the usual rule does not apply. For example, we have upheld certain regimes of suspicionless searches where the program was designed to serve "special needs, beyond the normal need for law enforcement." We have also allowed searches for certain administrative purposes without particularized suspicion of misconduct, provided that those searches are appropriately limited. We have also upheld brief, suspicionless seizures of motorists at a fixed Border Patrol checkpoint designed to intercept illegal aliens, and at a sobriety checkpoint aimed at removing drunk drivers from the road. In addition, in *Delaware v. Prouse,* 440 U.S. 648, 663 (1979), we suggested that a similar type of roadblock with the purpose of verifying drivers' licenses and vehicle registrations would be permissible. In none of these cases, however, did we indicate approval of a checkpoint program whose primary purpose was to detect evidence of ordinary criminal wrongdoing.

In *Martinez-Fuerte,* we entertained Fourth Amendment challenges to stops at two permanent immigration checkpoints located on major United States highways less than 100 miles from the Mexican border. We noted at the outset the particular context in which the constitutional question arose, describing in some detail the "formidable law enforcement problems" posed by the northbound tide of illegal entrants into the United States. . . . In *Martinez-Fuerte,* we found that the balance tipped in favor of the Government's interests in policing the Nation's borders. . . .

In *Sitz,* we evaluated the constitutionality of a Michigan highway sobriety checkpoint program. The *Sitz* checkpoint involved brief suspicionless stops of motorists so that police officers could detect signs of intoxication and remove impaired drivers from the road. Motorists who exhibited signs of intoxication were diverted for a license and registration check and, if warranted, further sobriety tests. This checkpoint program was clearly aimed at reducing the immediate hazard posed by the presence of drunk drivers on the highways, and there was an obvious connection between the imperative of highway safety and the law enforcement practice at issue. The gravity of the drunk driving problem and the magnitude of the State's interest in getting drunk drivers off the road weighed heavily in our determination that the program was constitutional. In *Prouse,* we invalidated a discretionary, suspicionless stop for a spot check of a motorist's driver's license and vehicle registration. The officer's conduct in that case was unconstitutional primarily on account of his exercise of "standardless and unconstrained discretion." We nonetheless acknowledged the States' "vital interest in ensuring that only those qualified to do so are permitted to operate motor vehicles, that these vehicles are fit for safe operation, and hence that licensing, registration, and vehicle inspection requirements are being observed." Accordingly, we suggested that "[q]uestioning of all oncoming traffic at roadblock-type stops" would

(continued)

be a lawful means of serving this interest in highway safety. We further indicated in *Prouse* that we considered the purposes of such a hypothetical roadblock to be distinct from a general purpose of investigating crime. . . . Not only does the common thread of highway safety thus run through *Sitz* and *Prouse,* but *Prouse* itself reveals a difference in the Fourth Amendment significance of highway safety interests and the general interest in crime control. . . .

It is well established that a vehicle stop at a highway checkpoint effectuates a seizure within the meaning of the Fourth Amendment. The fact that officers walk a narcotics-detection dog around the exterior of each car at the Indianapolis checkpoints does not transform the seizure into a search. Just as in *Place,* an exterior sniff of an automobile does not require entry into the car and is not designed to disclose any information other than the presence or absence of narcotics. Like the dog sniff in *Place,* a sniff by a dog that simply walks around a car is "much less intrusive than a typical search." Rather, what principally distinguishes these checkpoints from those we have previously approved is their primary purpose.

As petitioners concede, the Indianapolis checkpoint program unquestionably has the primary purpose of interdicting illegal narcotics. . . .

We have never approved a checkpoint program whose primary purpose was to detect evidence of ordinary criminal wrongdoing. Rather, our checkpoint cases have recognized only limited exceptions to the general rule that a seizure must be accompanied by some measure of individualized suspicion. We suggested in *Prouse* that we would not credit the "general interest in crime control" as justification for a regime of suspicionless stops (440 U.S., at 659, n.18). Consistent with this suggestion, each of the checkpoint programs that we have approved

was designed primarily to serve purposes closely related to the problems of policing the border or the necessity of ensuring roadway safety. Because the primary purpose of the Indianapolis narcotics checkpoint program is to uncover evidence of ordinary criminal wrongdoing, the program contravenes the Fourth Amendment.

Petitioners propose several ways in which the narcotics-detection purpose of the instant checkpoint program may instead resemble the primary purposes of the checkpoints in *Sitz* and *Martinez-Fuerte.* Petitioners state that the checkpoints in those cases had the same ultimate purpose of arresting those suspected of committing crimes. Securing the border and apprehending drunk drivers are, of course, law enforcement activities, and law enforcement officers employ arrests and criminal prosecutions in pursuit of these goals. If we were to rest the case at this high level of generality, there would be little check on the ability of the authorities to construct roadblocks for almost any conceivable law enforcement purpose. Without drawing the line at roadblocks designed primarily to serve the general interest in crime control, the Fourth Amendment would do little to prevent such intrusions from becoming a routine part of American life.

Petitioners also emphasize the severe and intractable nature of the drug problem as justification for the checkpoint program. There is no doubt that traffic in illegal narcotics creates social harms of the first magnitude. The law enforcement problems that the drug trade creates likewise remain daunting and complex, particularly in light of the myriad forms of spinoff crime that it spawns. The same can be said of various other illegal activities, if only to a lesser degree. But the gravity of the threat alone cannot be dispositive of questions concerning what means law enforcement officers may employ to pursue a given purpose. Rather,

(continued)

CITY OF INDIANAPOLIS V. EDMOND (continued)

in determining whether individualized suspicion is required, we must consider the nature of the interests threatened and their connection to the particular law enforcement practices at issue. We are particularly reluctant to recognize exceptions to the general rule of individualized suspicion where governmental authorities primarily pursue their general crime control ends.

Nor can the narcotics-interdiction purpose of the checkpoints be rationalized in terms of a highway safety concern similar to that present in *Sitz.* The detection and punishment of almost any criminal offense serves broadly the safety of the community, and our streets would no doubt be safer but for the scourge of illegal drugs. Only with respect to a smaller class of offenses, however, is society confronted with the type of immediate, vehicle-bound threat to life and limb that the sobriety checkpoint in *Sitz* was designed to eliminate.

Petitioners also liken the anticontraband agenda of the Indianapolis checkpoints to the antismuggling purpose of the checkpoints in *Martinez-Fuerte*. . . .

The primary purpose of the Indianapolis narcotics checkpoints is in the end to advance "the general interest in crime control," We decline to suspend the usual requirement of individualized suspicion where the police seek to employ a checkpoint primarily for the ordinary enterprise of investigating crimes. We cannot sanction stops justified only by the generalized and ever-present possibility that interrogation and inspection may reveal that any given motorist has committed some crime.

Of course, there are circumstances that may justify a law enforcement checkpoint where the primary purpose would otherwise, but for some emergency, relate to ordinary crime control. For example, as the Court of Appeals noted, the Fourth Amendment would almost certainly permit an appropriately tailored roadblock set up to thwart an imminent terrorist attack or to catch a dangerous criminal who is likely to flee by way of a particular route. . . .

Petitioners argue that our prior cases preclude an inquiry into the purposes of the checkpoint program. For example, they cite *Whren v. United States,* 517 U.S. 806 (1996), and *Bond v. United States,* 529 U.S. 334 (2000), to support the proposition that "where the government articulates and pursues a legitimate interest for a suspicionless stop, courts should not look behind that interest to determine whether the government's 'primary purpose' is valid." These cases, however, do not control the instant situation.

It goes without saying that our holding today does nothing to alter the constitutional status of the sobriety and border checkpoints that we approved in *Sitz* and *Martinez-Fuerte,* or of the type of traffic checkpoint that we suggested would be lawful in *Prouse.* The constitutionality of such checkpoint programs still depends on a balancing of the competing interests at stake and the effectiveness of the program. When law enforcement authorities pursue primarily general crime control purposes at checkpoints such as here, however, stops can only be justified by some quantum of individualized suspicion.

Our holding also does not affect the validity of border searches or searches at places like airports and government buildings, where the need for such measures to ensure public safety can be particularly acute. Nor does our opinion speak to other intrusions aimed primarily at purposes beyond the general interest in crime control. Our holding also does not impair the ability of police officers to act appropriately upon information that they properly learn during a checkpoint stop justified by a lawful primary purpose, even where such action may

(continued)

CITY OF INDIANAPOLIS V. EDMOND *(continued)*

result in the arrest of a motorist for an offense unrelated to that purpose. Finally, we caution that the purpose inquiry in this context is to be conducted only at the programmatic level and is not an invitation to probe the minds of individual officers acting at the scene.

Because the primary purpose of the Indianapolis checkpoint program is ultimately indistinguishable from the general interest in crime control, the checkpoints violate the Fourth Amendment. The judgment of the Court of Appeals is accordingly affirmed.

Although systematic roadblocks are proper, discretionary spot checks are not. In the *Prouse* case, the Supreme Court held that arbitrary stops of automobiles by law enforcement officers violate the Fourth Amendment.

Finally, note that profiles are used by some law enforcement agencies to establish a reasonable suspicion to stop motorists. For example, drug courier profiles are used in Florida, and illegal alien profiles are used by the Border Patrol. See earlier in this chapter for a more thorough discussion of the use of profiles. The Supreme Court has also held that the validity of a stop is determined by whether probable cause exists to believe a traffic violation has occurred, not the motives of the police. In *Whren v. United States* (1996),[61] the Court rejected a defendant's claim that a police officer who stops an individual who has violated a traffic law with the genuine purpose of investigating another crime (e.g., drug possession) has violated the Fourth Amendment, so long as the officer had probable cause to believe the driver has committed a traffic offense.

Searches

Where the Fourth Amendment's mandates have been reduced is in the context of the warrant requirement. In *Carroll v. United States,* 267 U.S. 132 (1925), it was announced that a warrantless search of a vehicle stopped on a public road is reasonable, provided the officer has probable cause to believe that an object subject to seizure will be found in the vehicle. The existence of probable cause is the key to the search, and no exigency has to exist for a police officer to conduct such a warrantless search.[62] This authority has been extended to permit the search to continue after the vehicle is impounded.[63] The Supreme Court has also validated warrantless seizures of vehicles when probable cause exists to believe the vehicle itself is forfeitable because the automobile had been used to traffic drugs.[64]

The sticky question in this area is the scope of the search. Generally, an officer is given the scope that a magistrate would have if a warrant were sought. Thus, if an officer has probable cause to believe that a shotgun used in a crime will be found in a car, a search of the glove box is improper. The opposite would be true if the item sought was a piece of jewelry, such as a ring.

Officers may also search closed items found in the vehicle, provided probable cause exists to believe an item sought may be contained therein.[65] The same rules apply as previously discussed. Rifling through a suitcase found in a car in search of a stolen painting that is larger than the suitcase is unreasonable and violative of the Fourth Amendment. Once the sought-after item is found, the search must cease.

An automobile may be searched incident to the arrest of its driver. This includes situations where arrestees have exited their cars, were immediately arrested, and the car is still within a reasonable proximity of the location of the arrest.[66] The purpose of this exception is to protect officers and others from hidden weapons. Accordingly, if a driver has been arrested and can no longer access the automobile, a warrantless search is not justified.

ARIZONA V. GANT
556 U.S. ___ (2009)

On August 25, 1999, acting on an anonymous tip that the residence at 2524 North Walnut Avenue was being used to sell drugs, Tucson police officers Griffith and Reed knocked on the front door and asked to speak to the owner. Gant answered the door and, after identifying himself, stated that he expected the owner to return later. The officers left the residence and conducted a records check, which revealed that Gant's driver's license had been suspended and there was an outstanding warrant for his arrest for driving with a suspended license.

When the officers returned to the house that evening, they found a man near the back of the house and a woman in a car parked in front of it. After a third officer arrived, they arrested the man for providing a false name and the woman for possessing drug paraphernalia. Both arrestees were handcuffed and secured in separate patrol cars when Gant arrived. The officers recognized his car as it entered the driveway, and Officer Griffith confirmed that Gant was the driver by shining a flashlight into the car as it drove by him. Gant parked at the end of the driveway, got out of his car, and shut the door. Griffith, who was about 30 feet away, called to Gant, and they approached each other, meeting 10 to 12 feet from Gant's car. Griffith immediately arrested Gant and handcuffed him.

Because the other arrestees were secured in the only patrol cars at the scene, Griffith called for backup. When two more officers arrived, they locked Gant in the backseat of their vehicle. After Gant had been handcuffed and placed in the back of a patrol car, two officers searched his car: One of them found a gun, and the other discovered a bag of cocaine in the pocket of a jacket on the backseat.

Gant was charged with two offenses—possession of a narcotic drug for sale and possession of drug paraphernalia (*i.e.*, the plastic bag in which the cocaine was found). He moved to suppress the evidence seized from his car on the ground that the warrantless search violated the Fourth Amendment. Among other things, Gant argued that *Belton* did not authorize the search of his vehicle because he posed no threat to the officers after he was handcuffed in the patrol car and because he was arrested for a traffic offense for which no evidence could be found in his vehicle. When asked at the suppression hearing why the search was conducted, Officer Griffith responded: "Because the law says we can do it. . . .

In *Chimel*, we held that a search incident to arrest may only include "the arrestee's person and the area 'within his immediate control'—construing that phrase to mean the area from within which he might gain possession of a weapon or destructible

(continued)

ARIZONA V. GANT *(continued)*

evidence." That limitation, which continues to define the boundaries of the exception, ensures that the scope of a search incident to arrest is commensurate with its purposes of protecting arresting officers and safeguarding any evidence of the offense of arrest that an arrestee might conceal or destroy. If there is no possibility that an arrestee could reach into the area that law enforcement officers seek to search, both justifications for the search-incident-to-arrest exception are absent and the rule does not apply. . . .

Although it does not follow from *Chimel*, we also conclude that circumstances unique to the vehicle context justify a search incident to a lawful arrest when it is "reasonable to believe evidence relevant to the crime of arrest might be found in the vehicle. . . .

Police may search a vehicle incident to a recent occupant's arrest only if the arrestee is within reaching distance of the passenger compartment at the time of the search or it is reasonable to believe the vehicle contains evidence of the offense of arrest. When these justifications are absent, a search of an arrestee's vehicle will be unreasonable unless police obtain a warrant or show that another exception to the warrant requirement applies. The Arizona Supreme Court correctly held that this case involved an unreasonable search. Accordingly, the judgment of the State Supreme Court is affirmed.

For the search incident to arrest to apply, the arrestee must not only have access to the space, but there must actually be an arrest. A warrantless search of an automobile after issuing a traffic ticket to the driver is violative of the Fourth Amendment— even though the officer could have arrested the driver and then searched the car incident to the arrest.[67] Note that *Gant* contains a second important principle; it authorizes warrantless searches, even if the driver doesn't have access to the automobile, if officers have reason to believe the evidence that is the subject of the arrest will be found inside. May the occupants of a vehicle be searched incident to a proper search of the vehicle? The answer is no[68]—but if an officer has probable cause to believe that one of the occupants has hidden the item sought on his or her person, a search of that occupant is permissible. Or, if an officer has a reasonable belief that one of the occupants may be armed, a frisk of the outer clothing is permitted to ensure officer safety.[69]

Occupants

Concerning the occupants of lawfully stopped cars, the Supreme Court has held that both driver and passengers may be ordered to exit the car without cause to believe they hold contraband, a threat to the officer, or act out of fear of flight. The Court held that it may be done routinely to protect the safety of police officers.[70]

Inventory Searches

Police officers may impound vehicles whenever the driver or owner is arrested. *Impoundment* means towing the vehicle to a garage or parking lot for storage.

Although the decision to impound a vehicle is generally left to the discretion of the police officer, an officer may not refuse a less intrusive manner of caring for the vehicle. For example, if a husband and wife are riding together, and the husband is arrested for drunk driving, the wife is to be permitted to drive the vehicle home, provided she is capable.

Once impounded, an inventory search may be conducted. The purpose of an inventory search is to protect the owner of the vehicle from vandalism, protect the safety of the officers and others, and protect the police department from claims of theft.

Because inventory searches are not conducted with an intent to discover evidence, there is no requirement of probable cause. If the facts of a case show that the police impounded a vehicle for the purpose of searching it, the search is improper.

Inventory searches are limited in scope. Although it is reasonable to search unlocked glove compartments and trunks, it is unreasonable under the Fourth Amendment if they are locked. A search of a vehicle's seats, floor area, and dashboard are routine. The Supreme Court has also stated that closed items found in impounded vehicles are subject to inventory searches.[71]

To avoid arbitrary inventory searches, police departments are expected, if not required, to establish an inventory search policy and procedure. All items discovered during an inventory search are to be recorded. See Exhibit 12–4 for a summary of the most prominent Supreme Court Fourth Amendment cases in the motor vehicle context.

Prisoners

The law generally distinguishes between pretrial detainees and convictees. The former includes individuals who have been arrested but not convicted. Because pretrial detainees have not been convicted, they may not be punished or rehabilitated. Instead the objective of their detention is to ensure their appearance at trial. Because they have not been convicted, pretrial detainees are not protected by the Eighth Amendment's prohibition of cruel and unusual punishments. But they are protected by due process.[72] In some instances the protections mirror one another. In others they do not.

Local jails, which commonly house both pretrial detainees and convictees sentenced to a year or less, must, at times, distinguish in the treatment of the two populations. The most obvious difference is that pretrial detainees may not be subjected to forms of punishment, such as a program of hard labor or shaming. Another example concerns legal materials. In order for pretrial detainees to properly prepare for trial, they have greater privacy rights to their papers, and access to counsel, than do convictees. Of course jailers must maintain order, prevent escapes, and provide for the safety of everyone in the jail setting. Rules that advance these objectives may be applied to all inmates, pretrial and convictees. Whether pretrial detainees can be subjected to systematic but suspicionless strip searches at the time of first admission to a facility was the question in the 2012 case *Florence v. Board of Chosen Freeholders*.[73]

Albert Florence and his family were stopped by the police for a traffic offense committed by his wife, who was driving their vehicle. Police checked both Florence and his wife for warrants. The computer database erroneously indicated that there was an outstanding arrest warrant for Florence. He was arrested, transported to a jail, booked, and subjected to a strip search. Unable to secure his immediate release he was still in jail six days later when he moved to a second jail, where another strip search was conducted. Florence sued under 42 U.S.C. §1983 alleging that suspicionless searches of persons

Exhibit 12–4   SUMMARY OF FOURTH AMENDMENT ISSUES AND AUTOMOBILES

SUBJECT	CASE
Stops and Arrests	
Stops may not be arbitrary.	*Delaware v. Prouse* (1979)
Stops may occur without suspicion if systematic.	*Michigan v. Sitz* (1990)
The motives of police are not relevant when determining if a stop is lawful.	*Whren v. United States* (1996)
The issue is whether there is probable cause to believe a traffic violation has occurred.	
States may delegate the discretion to arrest for misdemeanors, including traffic violations, to police.	*Atwater v. City of Lago Vista* (2001)
Systematic stops to intercept illegal drugs violate Fourth Amendment.	*Indianapolis v. Edmond* (2000)
Occupants	
Drivers and passengers are seized when pulled over, and therefore they may challenge the stop and search.	*Brendlin v. California* (2007)
Drivers of lawfully stopped auto mobiles may be ordered out without specific cause.	*Pennsylvania v. Mimms* (1977)
Occupants of lawfully stopped auto mobiles may be ordered out without specific cause.	*Maryland v. Wilson* (1997)
Occupants of automobiles may not be searched as incident to lawful search of automobiles—probable cause to believe sought item will be found on person required.	*United States v. DiRe, 332 U.S. 581* (1948)
Drivers and occupants may be frisked if officer has reasonable belief of dangerousness	*Arizona v. Johnson* (2009)
Searches	
Warrantless search of automobile valid if probable cause exists to believe item sought will be found in automobile. No exigency required if probable cause exists.	*Carroll v. United States* (1925) *Maryland v. Dyson* (1999)
Warrantless searches of closed container in automobile valid if probable cause exists to believe item sought will be found in container.	*California v. Acevedo* (1991) *New York v. Class* (1986)
Entry into lawfully stopped vehicle to read the VIN legitimate.	

Exhibit 12–4 *(continued)*

Warrantless search of personal item in automobile (e.g., purse) valid if there is probable cause to search for an item that may be concealed there.	*Wyoming v. Houghton* (1999)
Warrantless search of automobile invalid if probable cause exists to search container in automobile only.	*California v. Acevedo* (1991)
Warrantless search of recent occupant arrestee's automobile that is within his or her control is valid.	*Thornton v. United States* (2004)
Warrantless search of automobile of suspect arrested in an officer's cruiser invalid because car was outside of his control; warrantless search of car valid if reasonable belief evidence that is subject of arrest will be found within.	*Arizona v. Gant* (2009)
Warrantless search of automobile by officer who issued ticket but chose not to arrest driver is violative of the Fourth Amendment.	*Knowles v. Iowa* (1998)
Inventory searches of automobiles including containers—are valid if systematic.	*Colorado v. Bertine, 479 U.S. 367* (1987)
Properly framed profile may be used to stop an automobile, but searches and arrests require more.	*United States v. Brignoni-Ponce* (1975)
Automobile may be seized without a warrant if probable cause exists to belifeve it is contraband.	*Florida v. White* (1999)

charged with minor misdemeanors violated due process and the Fourth Amendment. The Court rejected Florence's claim in a decision exhibiting substantial deference to corrections authorities:

> Maintaining safety and order at (detention) institutions requires the expertise of correctional officials, who must have substantial discretion to devise reasonable solutions to the problems they face" . . . (T)he seriousness of an offense is a poor predictor of who has contraband."

Although a small number of pretrial detainees are housed in prisons, most inmates of these facilities are convictees. The Fourth Amendment is not fully applicable in prisons, for three reasons. First, security concerns outweigh privacy concerns. Second, loss of privacy is considered by our society to be an attribute of confinement and punishment. Third, inmates generally do not have reasonable expectations of privacy.

Hence, the Fourth Amendment is not implicated in the search of an inmate's cell, as there is no reasonable expectation of privacy in that area. The Supreme Court stated:

> A prison "shares none of the attributes of privacy of a home, an automobile, an office, or a hotel room." . . . We strike the balance in favor of institutional security, which we have noted is "central to all other correctional goals." . . . A right of privacy in traditional Fourth Amendment terms is fundamentally incompatible with the close and continual surveillance of inmates and their cells required to ensure institutional security and internal order. We are satisfied that society would insist that the prisoner's expectation of privacy always yield to what must be considered the paramount interest in institutional security. We believe that it is accepted by our society that "[l]oss of freedom of choice and privacy are inherent incidents of confinement."[74]

Although the Fourth Amendment does not apply to searches of inmates' cells, it does apply to searches of their persons. However, the probable cause and warrant requirements are dispensed within the prison context. Rather, they are tested by the Fourth Amendment's reasonableness provision. Prisoners may be searched without any particular suspicion if the search is part of a routine system. Analogous to roadblocks, if the custodians search every prisoner, or every other prisoner, or use some other system, no suspicion is required. Prisoners may also be searched without suspicion if they have recently come into contact with visitors. In *Bell v. Wolfish*[75] the Supreme Court held that strip searches of prisoners, conducted after they have contact with visitors or upon their return to the institution from outside, are permissible even without individualized suspicion. Otherwise, individual searches of inmates are allowed only when an officer has a reasonable suspicion that the inmate possesses contraband.

Although searches of inmates' cells are not included within the grasp of the Fourth Amendment, repeated searches intended to harass an inmate may be violative of the Eighth Amendment's prohibition of cruel and unusual punishment, as may searches of an inmate's person.

Probationers and Parolees

Because probationers and parolees have a lessened expectation to privacy, searches of their persons, effects, and homes do not have to be supported by probable cause. Nor do searches have to be attended by a warrant. In 1987 the Court approved a state policy that empowered a probation officer to search the homes of a probationer if "reasonable grounds" existed to believe contraband would be found.[76] In *United States v. Knights,* [77] the rule concerning searches of probationers was announced. The Court held that warrantless searches of probationers are reasonable so long as reasonable suspicion exists. The Court left open the question of searches without reasonable suspicion where a probationer consents to such searches at the time of sentencing.

In 2006, this decision was extended to parolees in *Samson v. California*,[78] where the Supreme Court held that the Fourth Amendment does not prohibit suspicion-less, warrantless searches of parolees. On the continuum of punishment, the Court noted, a parolee enjoys less privacy than probationers and only slightly more than prisoners. Significant to the Court in *Samson* was the consent of the parolees, who were given the option of remaining in prison; the large number of parolees at large; the interest of the state in monitoring parolees for reintegration; and recidivism. The Court pointed to the likelihood of recidivism, as opposed to the general population, in its *Knights* opinion as further support for the decision to subject probationers to greater oversight.

Administrative Searches

Although outside the content of this text, be aware that so-called administrative searches often require less than probable cause and a warrant to be conducted. This is largely because the purpose of such searches is not to detect and punish criminals. Instead, it is to protect the public from health and welfare threats, the violation of which are typically punished with fines, the disciplining of a license, or a similar noncriminal sanction. For example, warrantless inspections of restaurants, groceries, other highly regulated industries, public school students, and the work areas of public employees must be reasonable under the Fourth Amendment, even though probable cause is not required for any of them.

In most instances, the Fourth Amendment's reasonableness requirement is satisfied in the administrative context if there is either (1) reasonable suspicion or (2) a comprehensive regulatory scheme in place. If the latter, the scheme shall define the authority of inspectors, define the inspection itself, and provide a rationale for the inspection.[79]

ARREST

One of the most serious interferences with a person's liberty is to be physically seized by a government. Equally, arrest plays an important role in effective law enforcement.

Because of the significant impact arrest has on a person's life, the right to arrest is limited by the Fourth Amendment.

Defining Arrest

Generally, an *arrest* is a deprivation of freedom by a legal authority. As you have already learned, seizures by the police take two primary forms. First, at the lower end of the spectrum is the *Terry v. Ohio* seizure. Such seizures occur whenever a person reasonably believes that he or she is not free to leave. In addition, the seizure must be as brief as possible and be of limited intrusion to the person detained. The Court addressed the question whether passengers of vehicles are seized during traffic stops in the 2007 case *Brendlin v. California*.

BRENDLIN V. CALIFORNIA
551 U.S. 249 (2007)

Justice Souter delivered the opinion of the Court.

When a police officer makes a traffic stop, the driver of the car is seized within the meaning of the Fourth Amendment. The question in this case is whether the same is true of a passenger. We hold that a passenger is seized as well and so may challenge the constitutionality of the stop.

I

Early in the morning of November 27, 2001, Deputy Sheriff Robert Brokenbrough and his partner saw a parked Buick with expired registration tags. In his ensuing conversation with the police dispatcher, Brokenbrough learned that an application for renewal of registration was being processed. The officers saw the car again on the road, and this time Brokenbrough noticed its display of a temporary operating permit with the number "11," indicating it was legal to drive the car through November. The officers decided to pull the Buick over to verify that the permit matched the vehicle, even though, as Brokenbrough admitted later, there was nothing unusual about the permit or the way it was affixed. Brokenbrough asked the driver, Karen Simeroth, for her license and saw a passenger in the front seat, petitioner Bruce Brendlin, whom he recognized as "one of the Brendlin brothers." He recalled that either Scott or Bruce Brendlin had dropped out of parole supervision and asked Brendlin to identify himself (footnote omitted). Brokenbrough returned to his cruiser, called for backup, and verified that Brendlin was a parole violator with an outstanding no-bail warrant for his arrest. While he was in the patrol car, Brokenbrough saw Brendlin briefly open and then close the passenger door of the Buick. Once reinforcements arrived, Brokenbrough went to the passenger side of the Buick, ordered him out of the car at gunpoint, and declared him under arrest. When the police searched Brendlin incident to arrest, they found an orange syringe cap on his person. A patdown search of Simeroth revealed syringes and a plastic bag of a green leafy substance, and she was also formally arrested. Officers then searched the car and found tubing, a scale, and other things used to produce methamphetamine.

Brendlin was charged with possession and manufacture of methamphetamine, and he moved to suppress the evidence obtained in the searches of his person and the car as fruits of an unconstitutional seizure, arguing that the officers lacked probable cause or reasonable suspicion to make the traffic stop. He did not assert that his Fourth Amendment rights were violated by the search of Simeroth's vehicle, but claimed only that the traffic stop was an unlawful seizure of his person. The trial court denied the suppression motion after finding that the stop was lawful and Brendlin was not seized until Brokenbrough ordered him out of the car and formally arrested him. Brendlin pleaded guilty, subject to appeal on the suppression issue, and was sentenced to four years in prison.

The California Court of Appeal reversed . . . By a narrow majority, the Supreme Court of California reversed. . . .

A person is seized by the police and thus entitled to challenge the government's action under the Fourth Amendment when the officer, " 'by means of physical force or show of authority,' " terminates or restrains his freedom of movement. Thus, an "unintended person . . . [may be] the object of the detention," so long as the detention is "willful" and not merely the consequence of "an unknowing act." A police officer may make a seizure by a show of authority and without the use of physical force, but there is no seizure without actual submission; otherwise, there is at most an

BRENDLIN V. CALIFORNIA *(continued)*

attempted seizure, so far as the Fourth Amendment is concerned.

When the actions of the police do not show an unambiguous intent to restrain or when an individual's submission to a show of governmental authority takes the form of passive acquiescence, there needs to be some test for telling when a seizure occurs in response to authority, and when it does not. The law is settled that in Fourth Amendment terms a traffic stop entails a seizure of the driver "even though the purpose of the stop is limited and the resulting detention quite brief." And although we have not, until today, squarely answered the question whether a passenger is also seized, we have said over and over in dicta that during a traffic stop an officer seizes everyone in the vehicle, not just the driver. . . . The State concedes that the police had no adequate justification to pull the car over, but argues that the passenger was not seized and thus cannot claim that the evidence was tainted by an unconstitutional stop. We resolve this question by asking whether a reasonable person in Brendlin's position when the car stopped would have believed himself free to "terminate the encounter" between the police and himself. We think that in these circumstances any reasonable passenger would have understood the police officers to be exercising control to the point that no one in the car was free to depart without police permission.

A traffic stop necessarily curtails the travel a passenger has chosen just as much as it halts the driver, diverting both from the stream of traffic to the side of the road, and the police activity that normally amounts to intrusion on "privacy and personal security" does not normally (and did not here) distinguish between passenger and driver. An officer who orders one particular car to pull over acts with an implicit claim of right based on fault of some sort, and a sensible person would not expect a police officer to allow people to come and go freely from the physical focal point of an investigation into faulty behavior or wrongdoing. If the likely wrongdoing is not the driving, the passenger will reasonably feel subject to suspicion owing to close association; but even when the wrongdoing is only bad driving, the passenger will expect to be subject to some scrutiny, and his attempt to leave the scene would be so obviously likely to prompt an objection from the officer that no passenger would feel free to leave in the first place.

It is also reasonable for passengers to expect that a police officer at the scene of a crime, arrest, or investigation will not let people move around in ways that could jeopardize his safety. In *Maryland v. Wilson*, 519 U.S. 408 (1997), we held that during a lawful traffic stop an officer may order a passenger out of the car as a precautionary measure, without reasonable suspicion that the passenger poses a safety risk. In fashioning this rule, we invoked our earlier statement that " '[t]he risk of harm to both the police and the occupants is minimized if the officers routinely exercise unquestioned command of the situation.' " What we have said in these opinions probably reflects a societal expectation of "'unquestioned [police] command'" at odds with any notion that a passenger would feel free to leave, or to terminate the personal encounter any other way, without advance permission. . . .

Brendlin was seized from the moment Simeroth's car came to a halt on the side of the road, and it was error to deny his suppression motion on the ground that seizure occurred only at the formal arrest. It will be for the state courts to consider in the first instance whether suppression turns on any other issue. The judgment of the Supreme Court of California is vacated, and the case is remanded for further proceedings not inconsistent with this opinion.

Any seizure that extends beyond the *Terry* standard is an arrest. A *Terry* investigatory detention may be transformed into an arrest if the person is detained for an unreasonable length of time or the police use intrusive investigatory tactics. Whether an officer intends to arrest is not dispositive, nor is an announcement to the citizen that he or she is or is not under arrest. The totality of the facts will determine whether the intrusion amounts to an arrest under the Fourth Amendment.

The requirements for a *Terry* stop were discussed previously in this chapter. The following is a discussion of the Fourth Amendment requirements for arrest.

The Warrant Preference

Searches must be conducted pursuant to a valid warrant, unless an exception to the warrant requirement can be shown. Arrests are quite different. Rather than a requirement for a warrant, in most instances, there is simply a preference for one. The "informed and deliberate determinations of magistrates empowered to issue warrants . . . are to be preferred over the hurried action of officers."[80] As is the case with warrantless searches, probable cause determinations by magistrates will be supported on appeal with less evidence than those made by police officers.

Notwithstanding the preference, most arrests are made without first obtaining a warrant. The authority to make warrantless arrests has a long history. Under the common law, a law officer could arrest whenever he had reasonable grounds to believe that a defendant committed a felony. Misdemeanants who breached the peace could be arrested without warrant if the crime was committed in the presence of an officer.

United States v. Watson, 423 U.S. 411 (1976), was the case in which the Supreme Court recognized that warrantless arrests in public places, based upon probable cause, did not violate the Fourth Amendment. There is no constitutional requirement that an officer obtain a warrant to effect an arrest in a public place—even if the officer has adequate time to get the warrant prior to making the arrest. However, the Fourth Amendment does require that probable cause exist before an arrest can be made.

For a warrantless arrest in a public place to be upheld, it must be shown that the officer who made the arrest (1) had probable cause to believe that a crime was committed, and (2) that the person arrested committed that crime. As with searches and seizures, probable cause can be established in a number of ways: statements from victims and witnesses, personal knowledge and observations of the officer, reliable hearsay, and informant tips.

Most, if not all, states permit officers to arrest without a warrant if there is probable cause to believe that the suspect committed a felony. States vary in their treatment of misdemeanors, but most permit warrantless arrest only for a misdemeanor committed in an officer's presence. Some states have a broader rule that permits the arrest of a misdemeanant, even if the crime was not committed in the presence of an officer, provided there is both probable cause and an exigent circumstance.

An officer's determination of probable cause may later be attacked by the defendant. If the officer was wrong, then the defendant may be successful in obtaining his or her freedom or suppressing any evidence that is the fruit of the illegal arrest.

When an officer does seek an arrest warrant, the requirements previously discussed concerning search warrants apply. That is, the warrant must be issued by a neutral and detached magistrate upon a finding of probable cause, supported by oath or affirmation. See Exhibit 12–5 for the formal federal arrest warrant.

Arrests in Protected Areas

So far the discussion of arrests has been confined to arrests made in public. If the arrest is to be made in an area protected by the Fourth Amendment, such as a person's home, a warrant must be obtained, unless an exception exists.

Exhibit 12–5   WARRANT FOR ARREST

AO 442 (Rev. 5/85) Warrant for Arrest _____

UNITED STATES DISTRICT COURT

_____ DISTRICT OF _____

UNITED STATES OF AMERICA

V.

WARRANT FOR ARREST

CASE NUMBER:

To: The United States Marshal
and any Authorized United States Officer

YOU ARE HEREBY COMMANDED to arrest _____
Name

and bring him or her forthwith to the nearest magistrate to answer a(n)

☐ Indictment ☐ Information ☐ Complaint ☐ Order of Court ☐ Violation Notice

☐ Probation Violation Petition

charging him or her with (brief description of offense)

in violation of Title _____ United States Code, Section(s) _____

Name of Issuing Officer	Title of Issuing Officer
Signature of Issuing Officer	Date and Location

(By) Deputy Clark

Bail fixed at $ _____   by _____
Name of Judicial Officer

(continued)

Exhibit 12–5 *(continued)*

RETURN		
This warrant was received and executed with the arrest of the above-named defendant at _____		
DATE RECEIVED	NAME AND TITLE OF ARRESTING OFFICER	SIGNATURE OF ARRESTING OFFICER
DATE OF ARREST		

THE FOLLOWING IS FURNISHED FOR INFORMATION ONLY:

DEFENDANT'S NAME: _____

ALIAS: _____

LAST KNOWN RESIDENCE: _____

LAST KNOWN EMPLOYMENT: _____

PLACE OF BIRTH: _____

DATE OF BIRTH: _____

SOCIAL SECURITY NUMBER: _____

HEIGHT: _____ WEIGHT: _____

SEX: _____ RACE: _____

HAIR: _____ EYES: _____

SCARS, TATTOOS, OTHER DISTINGUISHING MARKS: _____

_____

_____

FBI NUMBER: _____

COMPLETE DESCRIPTION OF AUTO: _____

_____

INVESTIGATIVE AGENCY AND ADDRESS: _____

_____

_____

Source: http://www.uscourts.gov/uscourts/FormsAndFees/Forms/AO442.pdf

In *Payton v. New York,* 445 U.S. 573 (1980), it was held that a valid arrest warrant implicitly carries with it a limited right to enter the suspect's home to effect the arrest, provided there is reason to believe the suspect is within. Under *Payton,* the search must be limited to areas where the suspect may be hiding. Because the entry is lawful, any evidence discovered in plain view may be seized.

Arrest warrants do not authorize entry into the private property of third persons. In the absence of consent or exigent circumstances, a search warrant must be obtained before a search of a third person's home or property may be conducted.[81]

The warrant requirement is obviated if the occupant gives consent to the search. Exigent circumstances, such as hot pursuit, also justify warrantless entries into homes to effect an arrest.

Misdemeanor Arrests

The authority of law enforcement officers to arrest in cases where probable cause exists to believe an individual has committed a felony is clear. Similarly, the authority to arrest misdemeanants who breach the peace has been clear since the early common law. However, whether the arrest authority extends to minor misdemeanors was not addressed by the Supreme Court until 2001.

ATWATER V. CITY OF LAGO VISTA, ET AL.
532 U.S. 318 (2001)

In Texas, if a car is equipped with safety belts, a front-seat passenger must wear one, Tex. Tran. Code Ann. § 545.413(a) (1999), and the driver must secure any small child riding in front. Violation of either provision is "a misdemeanor punishable by a fine not less than $25 or more than $50." Texas law expressly authorizes "any peace officer [to] arrest without warrant a person found committing a violation" of these seatbelt laws, § 543.001, although it permits police to issue citations in lieu of arrest.

In March 1997, Petitioner Gail Atwater was driving her pickup truck in Lago Vista, Texas, with her 3-year-old son and 5-year-old daughter in the front seat. None of them was wearing a seatbelt. Respondent Bart Turek, a Lago Vista police officer at the time, observed the seatbelt violations and pulled Atwater over. According to Atwater's complaint (the allegations of which we assume to be true for present purposes), Turek approached the truck and "yelled" something to the effect of "we've met before" and "you're going to jail." He then called for backup and asked to see Atwater's driver's license

and insurance documentation, which state law required her to carry. When Atwater told Turek that she did not have the papers because her purse had been stolen the day before, Turek said that he had "heard that story two-hundred times."

Atwater asked to take her "frightened, upset, and crying" children to a friend's house nearby, but Turek told her, "you're not going anywhere." As it turned out, Atwater's friend learned what was going on and soon arrived to take charge of the children. Turek then handcuffed Atwater, placed her in his squad car, and drove her to the local police station, where booking officers had her remove her shoes, jewelry, and eyeglasses, and empty her pockets. Officers took Atwater's "mug shot" and placed her, alone, in a jail cell for about one hour, after which she was taken before a magistrate and released on $310 bond.

Atwater was charged with driving without her seatbelt fastened, failing to secure her children in seatbelts, driving without a license, and failing to provide proof of insurance. She ultimately

(continued)

ATWATER V. CITY OF LAGO VISTA, ET AL. *(continued)*

pleaded no contest to the misdemeanor seatbelt offenses and paid a $50 fine; the other charges were dismissed.

Atwater and her husband, petitioner Michael Haas, filed suit in a Texas state court under 42 U.S.C. § 1983 against Turek and respondents City of Lago Vista and Chief of Police Frank Miller. So far as concerns us, petitioners (whom we will simply call Atwater) alleged that respondents (for simplicity, the City) had violated Atwater's Fourth Amendment "right to be free from unreasonable seizure," . . . [the plaintiffs lost in the trial court, prevailed before a three-judge panel in the appellate court, and subsequently, the full appellate court sitting en banc reversed the three-judge panel.]

We granted certiorari to consider whether the Fourth Amendment, either by incorporating common-law restrictions on misdemeanor arrests or otherwise, limits police officers' authority to arrest without warrant for minor criminal offenses. We now affirm.

The Fourth Amendment safeguards "the right of the people to be secure in their persons, houses, papers, and effects, against unreasonable searches and seizures." In reading the Amendment, we are guided by "the traditional protections against unreasonable searches and seizures afforded by the common law at the time of the framing," since "an examination of the common-law understanding of an officer's authority to arrest sheds light on the obviously relevant, if not entirely dispositive, consideration of what the Framers of the Amendment might have thought to be reasonable." Thus, the first step here is to assess Atwater's claim that peace officers' authority to make warrantless arrests for misdemeanors was restricted at common law (whether "common law" is understood strictly as law judicially derived or, instead, as the whole body of law extant at the time of the framing).

Atwater's specific contention is that "founding-era common-law rules" forbade peace officers to make warrantless misdemeanor arrests except in cases of "breach of the peace," a category she claims was then understood narrowly as covering only those nonfelony offenses "involving or tending toward violence." . . .

We begin with the state of pre-founding English common law and find that, even after making some allowance for variations in the common-law usage of the term "breach of the peace," the "founding-era common-law rules" were not nearly as clear as Atwater claims; on the contrary, the common-law commentators (as well as the sparsely reported cases) reached divergent conclusions with respect to officers' warrantless misdemeanor arrest power. Moreover, in the years leading up to American independence, Parliament repeatedly extended express warrantless arrest authority to cover misdemeanor-level offenses not amounting to or involving any violent breach of the peace. . . .

On one side of the divide there are certainly eminent authorities supporting Atwater's position. In addition to Lord Halsbury, quoted in *Carroll,* James Fitzjames Stephen and Glanville Williams both seemed to indicate that the common law confined warrantless misdemeanor arrests to actual breaches of the peace.

Sir William Blackstone and Sir Edward East might also be counted on Atwater's side, although they spoke only to the sufficiency of breach of the peace as a condition to warrantless misdemeanor arrest, not to its necessity. Blackstone recognized that at common law "the constable . . . hath great original and inherent authority with regard to arrests," but with respect to nonfelony offenses said only that "he may, without warrant, arrest any one for breach of the peace, and carry him before a justice of the peace." Not long after the framing of the

(continued)

Fourth Amendment, East characterized peace officers' common-law arrest power in much the same way: "A constable or other known conservator of the peace may lawfully interpose upon his own view to prevent a breach of the peace, or to quiet an affray. . . ." The great commentators were not unanimous, however, and there is also considerable evidence of a broader conception of common-law misdemeanor arrest authority unlimited by any breach-of-the-peace condition. . . . We thus find disagreement, not unanimity, among both the common-law jurists and the text-writers who sought to pull the cases together and summarize accepted practice. Having reviewed the relevant English decisions, as well as English and colonial American legal treatises, legal dictionaries, and procedure manuals, we simply are not convinced that Atwater's is the correct, or even necessarily the better, reading of the common-law history. . . .

A second, and equally serious, problem for Atwater's historical argument is posed by the "divers Statutes," M. Dalton, Country Justice ch. 170, § 4, p. 582 (1727), enacted by Parliament well before this Republic's founding that authorized warrantless misdemeanor arrests without reference to violence or turmoil. Quite apart from Hale and Blackstone, the legal background of any conception of reasonableness the Fourth Amendment's Framers might have entertained would have included English statutes, some centuries old, authorizing peace officers (and even private persons) to make warrantless arrests for all sorts of relatively minor offenses unaccompanied by violence. The so-called "nightwalker" statutes are perhaps the most notable examples. From the enactment of the Statute of Winchester in 1285, through its various readoptions and until its repeal in 1827, night watchmen were authorized and charged "as . . . in Times past" to "watch the Town continually all Night, from the Sun-setting unto the Sun-rising" and were directed that "if any Stranger do pass by them, he shall be arrested until Morning. . . ."

Nor were the nightwalker statutes the only legislative sources of warrantless arrest authority absent real or threatened violence, as the parties and their *amici* here seem to have assumed. On the contrary, following the Edwardian legislation and throughout the period leading up to the framing, Parliament repeatedly extended warrantless arrest power to cover misdemeanor-level offenses not involving any breach of the peace. . . .

An examination of specifically American evidence is to the same effect. Neither the history of the framing era nor subsequent legal development indicates that the Fourth Amendment was originally understood, or has traditionally been read, to embrace Atwater's position.

Nor does Atwater's argument from tradition pick up any steam from the historical record as it has unfolded since the framing, there being no indication that her claimed rule has ever become "woven . . . into the fabric" of American law. The story, on the contrary, is of two centuries of uninterrupted (and largely unchallenged) state and federal practice permitting warrantless arrests for misdemeanors not amounting to or involving breach of the peace. . . .

Finally, both the legislative tradition of granting warrantless misdemeanor arrest authority and the judicial tradition of sustaining such statutes against constitutional attack are buttressed by legal commentary that, for more than a century now, has almost uniformly recognized the constitutionality of extending warrantless arrest power to misdemeanors without limitation to breaches of the peace. . . .

Small wonder, then, that today statutes in all 50 States and the District of Columbia permit warrantless misdemeanor arrests by at least some

(continued)

ATWATER V. CITY OF LAGO VISTA, ET AL. *(continued)*

(if not all) peace officers without requiring any breach of the peace, as do a host of congressional enactments. . . .

Accordingly, we confirm today what our prior cases have intimated: the standard of probable cause "applies to all arrests, without the need to 'balance' the interests and circumstances involved in particular situations." If an officer has probable cause to believe that an individual has committed even a very minor criminal offense in his presence, he may, without violating the Fourth Amendment, arrest the offender. . . .

The Court of Appeals's en banc judgment is affirmed.

Search Incident to Arrest and the Protective Sweep

As you learned earlier in this chapter, an officer may fully search an arrestee as incident to arrest. In addition, the area within the arrestee's immediate control may also be searched. The scope of a search incident to arrest, however, is limited to areas where a weapon might be obtained by the person arrested. Clearly, a search of any room other than the one where a defendant is being held is not supported by the doctrine of search incident to arrest.

The search-incident-to-arrest doctrine does not consider the possibility that other potentially dangerous persons may be present, but out of sight, when an arrest is made. Must police take the risk that no other dangerous persons are on the premises when making a lawful arrest? This question was answered by the Supreme Court in *Maryland v. Buie.*

It is important to note that the protective sweep may not be automatically conducted by the police, unlike a search incident to arrest. An officer must have a reasonable belief, supported by specific and articulable facts, that a dangerous person may be hiding in the home, before a protective sweep may be conducted. There need not be a belief of dangerousness to conduct a search incident to arrest.

A protective sweep must be limited to searching those areas where a person might be hiding. How far this will be permitted to go remains to be seen. Justice Brennan, dissenting in *Buie,* made this statement:

> Police officers searching for potential ambushers might enter every room including basements and attics, open up closets, lockers, chests, wardrobes, and cars; and peer under beds and behind furniture. The officers will view letters, documents and personal effects that are on tables or desks or are visible inside open drawers; books, records, tapes, and pictures on shelves; and clothing, medicines, toiletries and other paraphernalia not carefully stored in dresser drawers or bathroom cupboards. While perhaps not a "full-blown" or "top-to-bottom" search . . . a protective sweep is much closer to it than to a "limited patdown for weapons" or a "frisk" [as authorized by *Terry v. Ohio*].

MARYLAND V. BUIE
494 U.S. 325 (1990)

A "protective sweep" is a quick and limited search of a premises, incident to an arrest and conducted to protect the safety of police officers or others. It is narrowly confined to a cursory visual inspection of those places in which a person might be hiding. In this case we must decide what level of justification is required by the Fourth and Fourteenth Amendments before police officers, while effecting the arrest of a suspect in his home pursuant to an arrest warrant, may conduct a warrantless protective sweep of all or part of the premises. . . .

On February 3, 1986, two men committed an armed robbery of a Godfather's Pizza restaurant in Prince George's County, Maryland. One of the robbers was wearing a red running suit. The same day, Prince George's County police obtained arrest warrants for respondent Jerome Edward Buie and his suspected accomplice in the robbery, Lloyd Allen. Buie's house was placed under police surveillance.

On February 5, the police executed the arrest warrant for Buie. They first had a police department secretary telephone Buie's house to verify that he was home. The secretary spoke to a female first, then to Buie himself. Six or seven officers proceeded to Buie's house. Once inside, the officers fanned out through the first and second floors. Corporal James Rozar announced that he would "freeze" the basement so that no one could come up and surprise the officers. With his service revolver drawn, Rozar twice shouted into the basement, ordering anyone down there to come out. When a voice asked who was calling, Rozar announced three times: "this is the police, show me your hands." Eventually, a pair of hands appeared around the bottom of the stairwell and Buie emerged from the basement. He was arrested, searched, and handcuffed by Rozar. Thereafter, Detective Joseph Frolich entered the basement "in case there was someone else" down there. . . . He noticed a red running suit lying in plain view on a stack of clothing and seized it.

The trial court denied Buie's motion to suppress the running suit, stating in part: "The man comes out from a basement, the police don't know how many other people are down there." . . .

It goes without saying that the Fourth Amendment bars only unreasonable searches and seizures. . . . Our cases show that in determining reasonableness, we have balanced the intrusion on the individual's Fourth Amendment interests against its promotion of legitimate governmental interests. . . . Under this test, a search of the house or office is generally not reasonable without a warrant issued on probable cause. There are other contexts, however, where the public interest is such that neither a warrant nor probable cause is required. . . .

The *Terry* case is most instructive for present purposes. There we held that an on-the-street "frisk" for weapons must be tested by the Fourth Amendment's general proscription against unreasonable searches because such a frisk involves "an entire rubric of police conduct—necessarily swift action predicated upon the on-the-spot observations of the officer on the beat—which historically has not been, and as a practical matter could not be, subjected to the warrant procedure." . . .

The ingredients to apply the balance struck in *Terry* and *Long* are present in this case. Possessing an arrest warrant and probable cause to believe Buie was in his home, the officers were entitled to enter and to search anywhere in the house in which Buie might be found. Once he was found, however, the search for him was over, and there was no longer that particular justification for entering any rooms that had not yet been searched.

(continued)

MARYLAND V. BUIE *(continued)*

That Buie had an expectation of privacy in those remaining areas of his house, however, does not mean such rooms were immune from entry. In *Terry* and *Long* we were concerned with the immediate interest of the police officers in taking steps to assure themselves that the persons with whom they were dealing were not armed with or able to gain immediate control of a weapon that could unexpectedly and fatally be used against them. In the instant case, there is an analogous interest of the officers in taking steps to assure themselves that the house in which the suspect is being or has just been arrested is not harboring other persons who are dangerous and who could unexpectedly launch an attack. The risk of danger in the context of an arrest in the home is as great as, if not greater than, it is in the on-the-street or roadside investigatory encounter. . . .

We should emphasize that such a protective sweep, aimed at protecting the arresting officers, if justified by the circumstances, is nevertheless not a full search of the premises, but may extend only to a cursory inspection of those spaces where a person may be found. The sweep lasts no longer than is necessary to dispel the reasonable suspicion of danger and in any event no longer than it takes to complete the arrest and depart from the premises. . . .

The Fourth Amendment permits a properly limited protective sweep in conjunction with an in-home arrest when the searching officer possesses a reasonable belief based on specific and articulable facts that the area to be swept harbors an individual posing a danger to those on the arrest scene.

Executing Arrest Warrants

Arrest warrants may be executed at the officer's discretion, whether day or night. However, common sense dictates that warrants be served at a reasonable hour, unless an exigency exists.

In *Ker v. California,* 374 U.S. 23 (1963), an unannounced entry into a person's home was found to be violative of the Fourth Amendment. Therefore, the general rule is that officers must knock and announce their reason for being there. A number of exceptions to this rule have been recognized, including

1. When the safety of the police or others will be endangered by the announcement.
2. When the announcement will allow those inside to destroy evidence or escape.
3. When the occupants know the purpose of the officers.

The Court has said that the knock-and-announcement requirement applies whether the police gain entry by force or not. It is not important whether the police gain entry through using a key, opening an unlocked door, smashing a window, or breaking a door down. Police may obtain no-knock warrants in exceptional circumstances.

Illegal Arrests

Does the exclusionary rule apply to people as it does to things? That is, should a defendant be excluded from trial because he or she has been arrested unlawfully? Generally, the Supreme Court has answered no.[82] Therefore, the fact that a defendant is kidnapped has no bearing on whether the criminal proceeding will continue.

There may be an exception to this rule. If the conduct of the government is outrageous, shocking, and a gross invasion of a defendant's constitutional rights, he or she may be set free. This is known as a *Toscanino* case, named after the defendant in a Supreme Court case involving such a claim.

UNITED STATES V. TOSCANINO
500 F.2d 267 (2d Cir. 1974)

Francisco Toscanino appeals from a narcotics conviction entered against him in the Eastern District of New York. . . .

Toscanino does not question the sufficiency of the evidence or claim any error with respect to the conduct of the trial itself. His principal argument . . . is that the entire proceedings in the district court against him were void because his presence within the territorial jurisdiction of the court had been illegally obtained. . . . He offered to prove the following:

"On or about January 6, 1973 Francisco Toscanino was lured from his home in Montevideo, Uruguay by a telephone call. This call has been placed by or at the direction of Hugo Campos Hermedia. Hermedia was at that time and still is a member of the police in Montevideo, Uruguay. . . .

"The telephone call ruse succeeded in bringing Toscanino and his wife, seven months pregnant at the time, to an area near a deserted bowling alley in the City of Montevideo. Upon their arrival there Hermedia together with six associates abducted Toscanino. This was accomplished in full view of Toscanino's terrified wife by knocking him unconscious with a gun. . . .

"At no time had there been any formal or informal request on the part of the United States or the government of Uruguay for the extradition of Francisco Toscanino nor was there any legal basis to justify this rank criminal enterprise. . . .

"Later that same day Toscanino was brought to Brasilia. . . . For seventeen days Toscanino was incessantly tortured and interrogated. Throughout this entire period the United States government and the United States Attorney for the Eastern District of New York . . . did in fact receive reports as to its progress. . . . [Toscanino's] captors denied him sleep and all forms of nourishment for days at a time. Nourishment was provided intravenously in a manner precisely equal to an amount necessary to keep him alive. Reminiscent of the horror stories told by our military men who returned from Korea and China, Toscanino was forced to walk up and down a hallway for seven or eight hours at a time. When he could no longer stand he was kicked and beaten but all in a manner contrived to punish without scarring. When he could not answer, his fingers were pinched with metal pliers. Alcohol was flushed into his eyes and nose and other fluids . . . were forced up his anal passage. Incredibly, these agents of the United States government attached electrodes to Toscanino's earlobes, toes, and genitals. Jarring jolts of electricity were shot throughout his body, rendering him unconscious for indeterminate periods of time but again leaving no physical scars. . . .

[Toscanino was eventually drugged and brought to the United States to stand trial.]

Since *Frisbie,* the Supreme Court in what one distinguished legal luminary describes as a "constitutional revolution," . . . has expanded the interpretation of "due process." No longer is it limited to the guarantee of "fair" procedure at trial. In an effort to deter police misconduct, the term has been extended to bar the government from realizing directly the fruits of its own deliberate and unnecessary lawlessness in bringing the accused to trial. . . .

Accordingly, we view due process as now requiring a court to divest itself of jurisdiction over the person of a defendant where it has been acquired as the result of the government's deliberate, unnecessary and unreasonable invasion of the accused's constitutional rights.

Later, the Second Circuit Court of Appeals reiterated that the *Toscanino* reasoning applies only to situations in which the government's conduct is both shocking and outrageous, as was true of the allegations in *Toscanino*.[83] Be aware that not all courts have followed the Second Circuit's lead. Rather than deal with the thorny legal issue, most courts factually distinguish their cases from *Toscanino*. The Supreme Court has not yet addressed the issue.

Even though a defendant's person may not be excluded because of an illegal arrest, the evidence obtained pursuant to that arrest may be. For example, if there is a causal connection between an illegal arrest and a subsequent confession, then the statement must be excluded.[84] Or, if evidence is obtained through a search incident to an illegal arrest, it must also be suppressed. In short, any evidence obtained as a result of an illegal arrest must be excluded, unless an independent basis for its discovery can be shown by the government.

Analyzing Fourth Amendment Problems

Search and seizure problems can be complex. This area of the law is highly fact-sensitive. It is also an area where one must be careful and precise in analysis. Often search and seizure issues will be numerous in a single case, with all of the issues interrelated and interdependent.

Fourth Amendment analysis is ordered and sequential (Exhibit 12–6). In many instances, the validity of a search or seizure will depend on the validity of an earlier search or seizure. Therefore, if the government fails at an earlier stage, it may likely fail again later. For example, the police arrest Barry Burglar and conduct a search incident to arrest. During that search they discover burglar tools and other evidence of the alleged burglary. If it is determined that the arrest was invalid, then the fruits of the search incident to arrest must be suppressed. If the evidence discovered from the search led to other evidence, it may also be excluded.

Often officers obtain evidence in stages—each stage increasing the governmental interest in crime prevention, and concurrently increasing the officer's suspicion—thereby permitting a greater invasion of a person's privacy.

Even though search and seizure laws can be complex, do not forget to use common sense when analyzing Fourth Amendment issues. The exceptions to the search warrant requirement are not surprising (Exhibit 12–7); common sense tells a person that an officer may continue to pursue a fleeing murderer into the suspect's home without first obtaining a warrant. Similarly, it is not shocking that illegally obtained evidence may not be used to convict a defendant.

Two important, sometimes competing, policy objectives are at play in Fourth Amendment problems: crime detection and prevention versus the citizen's right to be free from intrusive governmental behavior. Consider these concerns when contemplating Fourth Amendment problems.

Exhibit 12–6   FOURTH AMENDMENT ANALYSIS

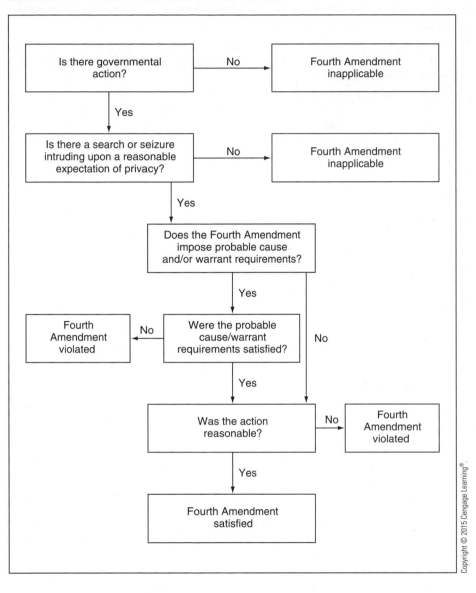

Exhibit 12–7 SUMMARY OF WARRANT RULES AND EXCEPTIONS

SEARCHES

RULE: Pursuant to the Fourth and Fourteenth Amendments, in both federal and state cases, a warrant to search must be obtained, unless one of the following exceptions is established.

EXCEPTIONS and LIMITATIONS:

1. Consent
2. *Terry* frisks
3. Plain view
4. Plain feel
5. Incident to arrest
6. Preservation of evidence
7. Emergencies and hot pursuit
8. Borders
9. Motor vehicles
10. Vehicle inventories
11. Prisoners, probationers, and parolees
12. Protective sweeps
13. Open fields
14. Administrative inspections

ARRESTS

RULE: The Fourth and Fourteenth Amendments govern arrests by both federal and state officials. Arrests in public areas may be warrantless. Arrests made in the home or other property of the defendant must be supported by either an arrest warrant or a search warrant for the defendant's person. Arrests in the homes or other property of third parties must be supported by a search warrant authorizing the search for the defendant at the particular property.

Ethical Considerations

POLICE ETHICS

Law enforcement officers are bound by departmental rules and local, state, and federal laws. The Constitution itself plays a role in defining police ethics. For example, the exclusionary rule is both an evidentiary rule and an ethical directive.

Ethical Considerations *(continued)*

In addition to the above laws, the International Association of Chiefs of Police has promulgated a model policy of ethical standards. Although not binding, these standards are widely recognized by police agencies as good guidance.

The model policy provides, inter alia, that officers:

- shall obey the law.
- shall not behave in unbecoming ways.
- shall respect other officers, be truthful, cooperate with internal investigations, and not interfere with investigations.
- shall report any convictions to their superior.
- shall not harass, intimidate, or demean others.
- shall adhere to use-of-force policies and respect civil rights.
- shall not be under the influence of alcohol or drugs while on duty or in a public place at any time.
- shall not accept gifts or gratuities or otherwise financially benefit from their position, except to receive compensation.
- shall not use their official powers to resolve personal disputes.
- shall not commence a personal relationship with the target of an investigation and other specific individuals.
- shall follow state law concerning political activities. Where silent, officers shall not engage in political activities, including campaigning, soliciting support, or posting notices, while on duty or in uniform.

Web Links

News

The home page at *http://www.newspapers.com* provides links to many newspapers in the United States and abroad.

Key Terms

consent

exigent circumstances

plain view doctrine

probable cause

Review Questions

1. In what way did *Katz v. United States* change Fourth Amendment law?

2. What are the basic requirements for obtaining a search warrant?

3. Stacey is a suspect in an embezzlement investigation. The police believe that she has hidden evidence in her neighbor's house, without the neighbor's consent. The neighbor will not consent to a search. Can the police obtain a search warrant for the non-suspect's home?

4. What is the plain view doctrine?

5. What is curtilage? Open fields? Why are the concepts important in criminal law?

6. Distinguish a stop from an arrest; a frisk from a search.

7. A police officer is approached by a man on the street who tells the officer that he was just robbed. The man points out the robber, who is standing in a park just across the street. Must the officer obtain a warrant to make the arrest?

8. A police officer is approached by a man on the street who tells the officer that he was just robbed. Although he did not see where the robber fled, he knew the assailant's name and address, as the two men "grew up together." The officer and the victim went to the police station and completed an incident report. After a telephone call to one of suspect's neighbors, they learned that he was at home. Must the officer obtain a warrant to make the arrest?

9. The same facts as in question 7, except that the victim points to a fleeing suspect. The officer chases the suspect to a house, where the officer sees the suspect enter with the use of a key. Must the officer end the chase and obtain a warrant?

10. What is a protective sweep?

Problems & Critical Thinking Exercises

1. Tommy Transmitter planned to burglarize a local audio/video dealer. On the night he intended to commit the burglary, Tommy was observed standing in an alley behind the shop by a police officer. It was 11:50 P.M. on a June evening, and Tommy was wearing a pair of jeans, tennis shoes, and a shirt.

   After 5 minutes, the officer approached Tommy and asked him "what he was doing in the alley at such a late hour." Tommy responded that he lived only a few blocks away, was suffering from insomnia, and had decided to take a walk. He produced identification that confirmed that he lived a short distance from the store. The officer then grabbed Tommy, swung him around, pushed him against the wall of the store, and "frisked him." After feeling a hard object in Tommy's back pocket, the officer reached in and discovered a small 3 X 3-inch container full of locksmith tools. He then arrested Tommy for possession of burglary tools and conducted a search incident to arrest. During that search, he discovered a diagram of the audio/video store hidden in Tommy's pants.

   Tommy was subsequently charged with attempted burglary and possession of burglary tools. He has filed a motion to suppress the tools and diagram, as well as a motion to dismiss. Should the motions be granted? Discuss.

2–5. Assume that officers have a valid search warrant for the defendant's apartment. The warrant specifies that the officers may search for stolen stereos. May the officers do the following?

2. Search the defendant's desk drawers in his study?

3. Search the defendant's closets in his bedroom?

4. Search the defendant's body?

5. Seize a transparent bag of cocaine found lying on the defendant's dining room table?

6. Do you agree with Justice Brennan that the protective sweep goes beyond the *Terry v. Ohio* decision? Explain your position.

7. In *United States v. Leon*, the Supreme Court created a good-faith exception to the probable cause requirement of the Fourth Amendment. Under *Leon*, evidence seized in good faith pursuant to a search warrant is admissible at trial, even though it is later determined that probable cause was lacking. Should this exception be extended to warrantless searches when an officer has a good-faith belief that probable cause exists?

8. Do you believe that the exclusionary rule is required under the Fourth Amendment? Can you think of any alternatives to the rule?

Endnotes

1. *Bivens v. Six Unknown Named Agents,* 403 U.S. 388 (1971).

2. 277 U.S. 438 (1928).

3. Interestingly, one scholar believes that no trespass test ever existed, even though he, like his contemporaries, taught and wrote about it. Believing it true but unimportant because it had been replaced by the privacy test, he only researched the question and came to his conclusion after the trespass test was "revived" in the 2012 *Jones* decision. See Orin S. Kerr, *The Curious History of Fourth Amendment Searches,* Supreme Court Review, *George Washington University Law Review,* March 26, 2013, available at http://papers.ssrn.com/sol3/papers.cfm?abstract_id=2154611

4. 316 U.S.129 (1942).

5. 388 U.S. 41(1967).

6. *United States v. Jacobsen,* 466 U.S. 109, 113 (1984).

7. See, for example, *United States v. Place,* 462 U.S. 696 (1983).

8. *New York v. Burger,* 482 U.S. 691 (1987).

9. *Minnesota v. Olson,* 495 U.S. 91 (1990).

10. 529 U.S. 334 (2000).

11. *Carroll v. United States,* 267 U.S. 132 (1934).

12. *United States v. Place,* 462 U.S. 696 (1983). A dog sniff of a person or thing, assuming no more intrusion, is not a search under the Fourth Amendment because no reasonable expectation of privacy has been violated. See also *Illinois v. Caballes,* 543 U.S. 405 (2005).

13. *Herring v. United States,* 555 U.S. 135 (2009).

14. See *Michigan v. DeFillippo,* 443 U.S. 31 (1979); *Illinois v. Krull,* 480 U.S. 340 (1987).

15. *Beck v. Ohio,* 379 U.S. 89 (1964).

16. *McDonald v. United States,* 335 U.S. 451, 455–56 (1948).

17. *Coolidge v. New Hampshire,* 403 U.S. 443 (1971).

18. *Shadwick v. Tampa,* 407 U.S. 345 (1972).

19. Fed. R. Crim. P. 41(b).

20. *United States v. Grubbs,* 547 U.S. 90 (2006).

21. *Zurcher v. Stanford Daily,* 436 U.S. 547 (1978).

22. *Ybarra v. Illinois,* 444 U.S. 85 (1979).

23. *Michigan v. Summers,* 452 U.S. 692 (1981).

24. *Jones v. United States,* 357 U.S. 493 (1958).

25. Fed. R. Crim. P. 41(c)(1).

26. Fed. R. Crim. P. 41(d).

27. *Schneckloth v. Bustamonte,* 412 U.S. 218 (1973).

28. *See* Jeremy Calsyn et al., "Investigation and Police Practices: Warrantless Searches and Seizures," 86 *Geo. L.J.* 1214, 1249–51 (1998).

29. *United States v. Kampbell,* 574 F.2d 962 (8th Cir. 1978).

30. *Commonwealth v. Wright,* 190 A.2d 709 (Pa. 1963).

31. 415 U.S. 164.

32. *Georgia v. Randolph,* 547 U.S. 103, 126 U.S. 1515 (2006).

33. For a discussion of landlord–tenant situations, *see Stoner v. California,* 376 U.S. 483 (1964).

34. NYPD patrols inside private buildings; residents say they are unfairly stopped. Fox News, found at http://www.foxnews.com/us/2013/03/11/nypd-program-patrols-inside-private-buildings-residents-say-theyre-unfairly/ and also http://www.nyclu.org/news/judge-finds-nypd-routinely-makes-unconstitutional-street-stops-outside-clean-halls-buildings

35. *Terry,* 392 U.S. at 21.

36. *United States v. Arvizu,* 122 S. Ct. 744 (2002).

37. *Illinois v. Wardlow,* 528 U.S. 119 (2000).

38. *United States v. Mendenhall,* 466 U.S. 544 (1980), and *United States v. Drayton,* 536 U.S. 194 (2002).

39. *Brown v. Texas,* 443 U.S. 47 (1979).

40. *United States v. Johnson,* No. 09-2245, 2010 U.S. App. LEXIS (3rd Cir. Decided January 27, 2010).

41. *Michigan v. Long,* 463 U.S. 1032 (1983).

42. *Arizona v. Hicks,* 480 U.S. 321 (1987).

43. 403 U.S. at 470–71.

44. *New York v. Belton,* 453 U.S. 454 (1981).

45. *Schmerber v. California,* 384 U.S. 757, 770–71 (1966).

46. *Oliver v. United States,* 466 U.S. 170 (1984).

47. 480 U.S. 294 (1987)

48. *United States v. Bassford,* 601 F. Supp. 1324, 1330 (D. Mass. 1985).

49. *United States v. Broadhurst,* 612 F. Supp. 777 (C.D. Cal. 1985).

50. *California v. Ciraolo,* 476 U.S. 207 (1986).

51. Timothy Lee, Police Allowed to Install Cameras on Private Property Without Warrant, May 12, 2013, found at http://arstechnica.com/tech-policy/2012/10/police-allowed-to-install-cameras-on-private-property-without-warrant/

52. *United States v. Ramsey,* 431 U.S. 606 (1977).

53. *United States v. Flores-Montano,* 541 U.S. 149 (2004).

54. *See* Torcia, *Wharton's Criminal Evidence* § 733 (13th ed.) (New York: Lawyers Co-operative, 1986 Supp.).

55. *United States v. Martinez-Fuerte,* 428 U.S. 543 (1976).

56. *United States v. Ortiz,* 422 U.S. 891 (1975).

57. *See United States v. Hernandez-Cuartas,* 717 F.2d 552 (11th Cir. 1983).

58. Richard M. Thompson, II. *Drones in Domestic Surveillance Operations: Fourth Amendment Implications and Legislative Responses.* Congressional Research Service. April 3, 2013. Can be found at http://www.a51.nl/storage/pdf/R42701.pdf

59. Liebelson, D. *Map: Is Your State a No-Drone Zone? Mother Jones,* September 30, 2013. Can be found at http://www.motherjones.com/politics/2013/09/map-are-drones-illegal-your-state

60. 496 U.S. 444.

61. 517 U.S. 806 (1996).

62. *Maryland v. Dyson,* 527 U.S. 465 (1999).

63. *Florida v. White,* 526 U.S. 559 (1999).

64. *Chambers v. Mahoney,* 399 U.S. 42 (1970).

65. *United States v. Ross,* 456 U.S. 798 (1982).

66. See *Thornton v. U.S.,* 541 U.S. 615 (2004).

67. *Knowles v. Iowa,* (1998).

68. *United States v. DiRe,* 332 U.S. 581 (1948).

69. *Arizona v. Johnson,* 555 U.S. ___ (2009).

70. *Pennsylvania v. Mimms,* 434 U.S. 106 (1977), and *Maryland v. Wilson,* 117 S. Ct. 882 (1997).

71. *Colorado v. Bertine,* 479 U.S. 367 (1986).

72. *Bell v. Wolfish,* 441 U.S. 520 (1979).

73. 566 U.S. ___ (2012).

74. *Hudson v. Palmer,* 468 U.S. 517 (1984).

75. Bell infra.

76. *Griffin v. Wisconsin,* 483 U.S. 868 (1987).

77. 534 U.S. 112 (2001)

78. 547 U.S. 843 (2006).

79. For more on this topic, see Daniel E. Hall, *Administrative Law: Bureaucracy in a Democracy,* 4th ed. (Upper Saddle River, NJ: Prentice Hall, 2009).

80. *Aguilar v. Texas,* 378 U.S. 108, 110–11 (1964).

81. *Stealgald v. United States,* 451 U.S. 204 (1981).

82. *Frisbie v. Collins,* 342 U.S. 519 (1952).

83. *United States ex rel. Lujan v. Gengler,* 510 F.2d 62 (2d Cir.), *cert. denied,* 421 U.S. 1001 (1975).

84. *Taylor v. Alabama,* 457 U.S. 687 (1982).

CHAPTER 13

INTERROGATION, ELECTRONIC SURVEILLANCE, AND OTHER POLICE PRACTICES

Chapter Outline

Interrogations, Confessions, and Admissions
Voluntariness Requirement
McNabb-Mallory Rule
Miranda
Sixth Amendment
Electronic Surveillance
Governing Statutes
Wiretaps
Tracking Devices
Stored Communications and Subscriber Records
Pen Registers and Trap Devices
National Security Surveillance
Pretrial Identification Procedures
Eyewitness Identification
Photographs
Forensic Identification Procedures
Exclusion of Improper Identifications
Ethical Considerations: Legal Advice as War Crime?

Chapter Objectives

After completing this chapter, you should be able to:

- describe the law, including the major constitutional cases, of interrogations, confessions, and admissions, including the important constitutional limitations upon governmental authority to extract confessions and admissions. You should be able to apply this law to fact scenarios.

- list and describe the federal statutory law of electronic surveillance and apply that law to fact scenarios.

- explain the law, including major constitutional cases, of lineups and apply that law to fact scenarios.

- explain the law, including the major constitutional cases, of scientific identification procedures and apply that law to fact scenarios.

- think critically about recent developments and controversies concerning the use of eyewitness identification, electronic surveillance, and other procedures.
- describe the major provisions of FISA, including who is subject to FISA, when surveillance orders are required and not required, and the role of FISC. Identify the material facts and legal issues in nearly all of the cases you read, describe the courts' analyses and conclusions in the cases, and demonstrate the ability to synthesize and think critically about the law of the subject.

INTERROGATIONS, CONFESSIONS, AND ADMISSIONS

interrogation

■ Questioning by police, especially of a person suspected or accused of a crime. A *custodial interrogation* involves a restraint of freedom, so it requires a *Miranda* warning. A routine *investigatory interrogation* involves no restraint and no accusation of a crime.

confession

■ A voluntary statement by a person that he or she is guilty of a crime.

admission

■ A voluntary statement that a fact or a state of events is true.

Questioning witnesses and suspects is a commonly used law enforcement tool. An **interrogation** occurs whenever officers question a person they suspect has committed a crime. A **confession** is a statement made by a person claiming that he or she has committed a crime. If a person asserts certain facts to be true, which are inculpatory, but do not amount to a confession, he or she has made an **admission.**

Voluntariness Requirement

As was true at common law, all confessions must be made voluntarily. This is required by the Due Process Clauses of the Fifth and Fourteenth Amendments. The totality of the circumstances must be examined when making the voluntariness determination.

Police officers do not have to physically coerce a confession for it to be involuntary. Mental or emotional coercion by law enforcement also violates a defendant's due process rights. The Supreme Court has held that a defendant's silence during questioning by police without an affirmative declaration of the exercise of the right to be free from self-incrimination may be admitted as evidence of guilt.[1] An exception to this rule is at trial. Concerned that a defendant's refusal to take the stand is so prejudicial that it violates the privilege against self-incrimination, prosecutors are forbidden from calling defendants to testify and from commenting on their silence to juries.

Involuntary confessions are to be excluded at trial. For years, the admission of a coerced confession resulted in an automatic reversal of conviction. This was changed in *Arizona v. Fulminante* (1991),[2] wherein the Supreme Court decided that a conviction is not to be automatically reversed because a coerced confession was admitted at trial. Rather, the Court held that if the prosecution can show beyond a reasonable doubt that the trial court error was harmless, the conviction is to be affirmed. That is, if there was sufficient other evidence to sustain the conviction, then it stands.

McNabb-Mallory Rule

A rule developed at the common law that required officers to present arrestees to judicial officers quickly after arrest. The rule was codified by the United States Congress, and the United States Supreme Court supplemented the statutes by imposing exclusion of confessions for violations. Congress modified the Court's decisions by statute.

As a matter of evidence law, admissions or confessions are admissible, even through hearsay, as statements against interest.[3] However, the use of interrogations, confessions, and admissions to prove guilt is controversial. The United States Supreme Court has recognized that admissions are highly suspect when relied upon alone to obtain a confession. The Court stated, in *Escobedo v. Illinois* (1964),[4] that a "system of criminal law enforcement which comes to depend on the 'confession' will, in the long run, be less reliable and more subject to abuses than a system which depends on extrinsic evidence independently" obtained through other law enforcement practices.

At common law, confessions and admissions could be used freely, as long as they were made voluntarily. The early basis for excluding involuntary confessions was the Due Process Clauses of the Fifth and Fourteenth Amendments.[5] Eventually, federal defendants could seek to have confessions suppressed if they were not taken before a magistrate promptly after arrest. This was known as the McNabb-Mallory rule, named for two Supreme Court cases.[6] The rule was not constitutionally based. Instead, the Court announced the rule in its supervisory role over the nation's federal courts. While the rule of quick presentment of arrestees to judges had existed at common law and had been codified by Congress, there was no remedy for violations. Accordingly, the Court held that confessions that occurred after unreasonable delays should be excluded. Congress reacted to McNabb-Mallory and Miranda by enacting a statute that permits the admission of a confession so long as it was voluntarily given. Another section provides that regardless of any delay in presenting a suspect to a judge, a confession shall be admitted if obtained within 6 hours of arrest. In *Corley v. United States,* 556 U.S.—(2009) it was held that if there is a delay in presenting a suspect to a judge longer than 6 hours, the old McNabb-Mallory exclusionary rule applies if a delay is found to be unreasonable.

Today, interrogations, confessions, and admissions are governed by these rules, as well as two broader rights: the Fifth Amendment right to be free from self-incrimination and the Sixth Amendment right to counsel.

Miranda

By virtue of popular television and films, the Supreme Court case *Miranda v. Arizona,* or at least the "Miranda" warnings that are a product of that case, is one of the best known judicial decisions of our time.

MIRANDA V. ARIZONA
384 U.S. 436 (1966)

[The Supreme Court consolidated appeals from several individuals who had been convicted at trials where their confessions were entered into evidence. Ernesto Miranda, for whom the case is named, was arrested for rape and kidnapping. He was interrogated at a police station. He was not advised of his constitutional rights, he never requested to see an attorney, and he never refused to discuss the allegations with the officers. He only had contact with the police during the interrogation. After two

(continued)

MIRANDA V. ARIZONA *(continued)*

hours he signed a written confession to the rape. He also attested to the voluntariness of his confession in the document. He was convicted, appealed, and lost in Arizona's appellate courts. Chief Justice Earl Warren delivered the Court's opinion.]

The cases before us raise questions that go to the roots of our concepts of American criminal jurisprudence: the restraints society must observe consistent with the Federal Constitution in prosecuting individuals for crime. More specifically, we deal with the admissibility of statements obtained from an individual who is subjected to custodial police interrogation and the necessity for procedures which assure that the individual is accorded his privilege under the Fifth Amendment to the Constitution not to be compelled to incriminate himself. . . .

Our holding will be spelled out with some specificity in the pages which follow but briefly stated it is this: the prosecution may not use statements, whether exculpatory or inculpatory, stemming from custodial interrogation of the defendant unless it demonstrates the use of procedural safeguards effective to secure the privilege against self-incrimination. By custodial interrogation, we mean questioning initiated by law-enforcement officers after a person has been taken into custody or otherwise deprived of his freedom of action in any significant way. As for the procedural safeguards to be employed, unless other fully effective means are devised to inform accused persons of their right of silence and to assure a continuous opportunity to exercise it, the following measures are required. Prior to any questioning, the person must be warned that he has a right to remain silent, that any statement he does make may be used as evidence against him, and that he has a right to the presence of an attorney, either retained or appointed. The defendant may waive effectuation of these rights, provided the waiver is made voluntarily, knowingly, and intelligently. If, however, he indicates in

any manner and at any stage of the process that he wishes to consult with an attorney before speaking there can be no questioning. Likewise, if the individual is alone and indicates in any manner that he does not wish to be interrogated, the police may not question him. The mere fact that he may have answered some questions or volunteered some statements on his own does not deprive him of the right to refrain from answering any further inquiries until he has consulted with an attorney and thereafter consents to be questioned.

The constitutional issue we decide in each of these cases is the admissibility of statements obtained from a defendant questioned while in custody or otherwise deprived of his freedom of action in any significant way. In each, the defendant was questioned by police officers, detectives, or a prosecuting attorney in a room in which he was cut off from the outside world. In none of these cases was the defendant given a full and effective warning of his rights at the outset of the interrogation process. In all of the cases, the questioning elicited oral admissions, and in three of them, signed statements as well, which were admitted at their trials. They all thus share salient features— incommunicado interrogation of individuals in a police-dominated atmosphere, resulting in self-incriminating statements without full warnings of constitutional rights.

An understanding of the nature and setting of this in-custody interrogation is essential to our decisions today. The difficulty in depicting what transpires at such interrogations stems from the fact that in this country they have largely taken place incommunicado. From extensive factual studies undertaken in the early 1930s . . . it is clear that police violence and the "third degree" flourished at that time. In a series of cases decided by the Court long after those studies, the police resulted to physical brutality—beating, hanging, whipping—and to

MIRANDA V. ARIZONA (continued)

sustained and protracted questioning incommunicado in order to extort confessions. . . .

Again we stress that the modern practice of in-custody interrogation is psychologically rather than physically oriented. As we have stated before, ". . . this court has recognized that coercion can be mental as well as physical, and that the blood of the accused is not the only hallmark of an unconstitutional inquisition.". . .

The circumstances surrounding in-custody interrogation can operate very quickly to overbear the will of one merely made aware of his privilege [against self-incrimination] by his interrogators. Therefore, the right to have counsel present at the interrogation is indispensable to the protection of the Fifth Amendment privilege under the system we delineate today. Our aim is to assure that the individual's right to choose between silence and speech remains unfettered throughout the interrogation process. A once-stated warning, delivered by those who will conduct the interrogation, cannot itself suffice to that end among those who most require knowledge of their rights. A mere warning given by the interrogators is not alone sufficient to accomplish that end. Prosecutors themselves claim that the admonishment of the right to remain silent without more "will benefit only the recidivist and the professional." Even preliminary advice given to the accused by his own attorney can be swiftly overcome by the secret interrogation process. . . .

Thus, the need for counsel to protect the Fifth Amendment privilege comprehends not merely a right to consult with counsel prior to questioning, but also to have counsel present during any questioning if the defendant so desires.

The presence of counsel at the interrogation may serve several significant subsidiary functions as well. If the accused decides to talk to his interrogators, the assistance of counsel can mitigate the dangers of trustworthiness. With a lawyer present the likelihood that the police will practice coercion is reduced, and if coercion is nevertheless exercised the lawyer can testify to it in court. The presence of a lawyer can also help to guarantee that the accused gives a fully accurate statement to the police and that the statement is rightly reported to the prosecution.

[Miranda's case was remanded, he was retried, his confession was excluded, and he was again convicted. Although sentenced to twenty to thirty years in prison, he was paroled in 1972. Subsequently, he found himself in trouble on several occasions, one leading to revocation of his parole. He spent another year in prison, was released, and was stabbed to death in bar room fight in 1976. Several Miranda Warning Cards, which he had been autographing and selling, were found on his person at the time of his death. The man alleged to have killed Miranda was arrested, read his Miranda rights, invoked his right to remain silent, was released, and fled. The Miranda murder was never prosecuted.]

Although *Miranda* concerns the rights of suspects to counsel in certain circumstances, it is not a Sixth Amendment right to counsel case. The right of a suspect to counsel at this early stage in the process rests upon the Fifth Amendment's right to be free from self-incrimination. Simply stated, the Court found that to meaningfully implement the right to be free from self-incrimination, suspects must be informed of both their right to remain silent and to the assistance of legal counsel before they are questioned.

The Warnings

The heart of the *Miranda* decision is the warnings. These are

1. The right to remain silent.
2. Any statements made may be used against the defendant to gain a conviction.
3. The right to consult with a lawyer and to have a lawyer present during questioning.
4. For the indigent, a lawyer will be provided without cost.

The warnings are to be read to all persons in custody who are to be interrogated. The law does not presume that any person, including an attorney, knows these rights. The warnings should be presented in a timely manner and read at such a speed that the arrestee can gain a full understanding of their import.

Specific language need not be used, as long as the defendant is fully and effectively apprised of each right. For example, the Court approved the following language against the defendant's claim that it conveyed the idea that he had a right to speak to his attorney before questioning but not during questioning.

> "You have the right to talk to a lawyer before answering any of our questions" and "[y]ou have the right to use any of these rights at any time you want during this interview."

The words, the Court found, "were not the *clearest possible* formulation of *Miranda*'s right-to-counsel advisement, they were sufficiently comprehensive and comprehensible when given a commonsense reading."[7]

Many law enforcement agencies have made it a policy to record (video/audio or audio only) the giving of the warnings and any waiver of rights to eliminate any question concerning whether the warnings were given and whether coercion was used to gain a waiver.

Custodial Interrogation

Not all questioning by law enforcement officers must be preceded by the *Miranda* warnings. A defendant must be "in custody" and "interrogated" by police before *Miranda* has effect. This is known as the "custodial interrogation" requirement.

The Court used the phrase "taken into custody or otherwise deprived of his freedom of action in any significant way" to define the custody element of *Miranda*. An objective test is used to determine if a suspect is in custody, the suspect's and interrogating officer's subjective beliefs about the status of the suspect are not dispositive.[8] This includes the officer's opinions about whether the suspect committed the crime and whether the individual is in custody. The test to determine if a person is in custody for *Miranda* is objective—whether a reasonable person would have felt free to leave. Although a statement by a police officer to a suspect that he is not under arrest is not dispositive, it may be considered. Of course, a person is in custody if an officer announces that an arrest is being made or that the person is not free to leave. The Court made it clear that the in-custody element may be satisfied anywhere. The defendant need not be at the police station to be in custody.

Typically a brief encounter between a citizen and a police officer is not a custodial situation. All of the surrounding facts must be considered in making the custody determination. The location of the interrogation is very important. There is a greater chance of finding a person in custody if the questioning took place in a police station or prosecutor's office rather than the suspect's home or in public. The presence of other persons during the interrogation decreases the odds of the suspect being in custody. The Court found the fact that the suspects in *Miranda* were "cut off from the outside world" troubling. The length and intensity of the questioning are also relevant.

The Supreme Court found age to be a factor in a case where police interrogated a 13-year-old boy enrolled in special education classes outside the presence of his guardians and without *Mirandizing* him. The Court concluded that the child's age and maturity impacted his perception of whether he was free to leave, as well as his ability to develop sound judgement.[9]

Determining whether a prisoner is in custody for purposes of *Miranda* is somewhat confounding. This was the issue in the *Howes* case.

HOWES V. FIELDS
565 U.S. ___ (2012)

Justice Alito delivered the opinion of the Court.

■ ■ ■

While serving a sentence in a Michigan jail, Randall Fields was escorted by a corrections officer to a conference room where two sheriff's deputies questioned him about allegations that, before he came to prison, he had engaged in sexual conduct with a 12-year-old boy. In order to get to the conference room, Fields had to go down one floor and pass through a locked door that separated two sections of the facility. Fields arrived at the conference room between 7 p.m. and 9 p.m. and was questioned for between five and seven hours.

At the beginning of the interview, Fields was told that he was free to leave and return to his cell. Later, he was again told that he could leave whenever he wanted. The two interviewing deputies were armed during the interview, but Fields remained free of handcuffs and other restraints. The door to the conference room was sometimes open and sometimes shut.

About halfway through the interview, after Fields had been confronted with the allegations of abuse, he became agitated and began to yell. Fields testified that one of the deputies, using an expletive, told him to sit down and said that "if [he] didn't want to cooperate, [he] could leave." Fields eventually confessed to engaging in sex acts with the boy. According to Fields' testimony at a suppression hearing, he said several times during the interview that he no longer wanted to talk to the deputies, but he did not ask to go back to his cell prior to the end of the interview.

When he was eventually ready to leave, he had to wait an additional 20 minutes or so because a corrections officer had to be summoned to escort him back to his cell, and he did not return to his cell until well after the hour when he generally retired. At no time was Fields given Miranda warnings or advised that he did not have to speak with the deputies.

The State of Michigan charged Fields with criminal sexual conduct. Relying on Miranda, Fields

(continued)

moved to suppress his confession, but the trial court denied his motion. [He was convicted and sentenced to 10 to 15 years in prison.]

As used in our Miranda case law, "custody" is a term of art that specifies circumstances that are thought generally to present a serious danger of coercion. In determining whether a person is in custody in this sense, the initial step is to ascertain whether, in light of "the objective circumstances of the interrogation," a "reasonable person [would] have felt he or she was not at liberty to terminate the interrogation and leave. And in order to determine how a suspect would have "gauge[d]" his "freedom of movement," courts must examine "all of the circumstances surrounding the interrogation." Relevant factors include the location of the questioning, its duration, statements made during the interview, the presence or absence of physical restraints during the questioning, and the release of the interviewee at the end of the questioning. . . .

Determining whether an individual's freedom of movement was curtailed, however, is simply the first step in the analysis, not the last. Not all restraints on freedom of movement amount to custody for purposes of Miranda. We have "decline[d] to accord talismanic power" to the freedom-of-movement inquiry, and have instead asked the additional question whether the relevant environment presents the same inherently coercive pressures as the type of station house questioning at issue in Miranda. "Our cases make clear . . . that the freedom-of-movement test identifies only a necessary and not a sufficient condition for Miranda custody."

There are at least three strong grounds for [the conclusion that prisoners will not feel in custody]. First, questioning a person who is already serving a prison term does not generally involve the shock that very often accompanies arrest. In the paradigmatic Miranda situation—a person is arrested in his home or on the street and whisked to a police station for questioning—detention represents a sharp and ominous change, and the shock may give rise to coercive pressures. A person who is "cut off from his normal life and companions," and abruptly transported from the street into a "police-dominated atmosphere," may feel coerced into answering questions.

By contrast, when a person who is already serving a term of imprisonment is questioned, there is usually no such change. "Interrogated suspects who have previously been convicted of crime live in prison." For a person serving a term of incarceration, we reasoned in Shatzer, the ordinary restrictions of prison life, while no doubt unpleasant, are expected and familiar and thus do not involve the same "inherently compelling pressures" that are often present when a suspect is yanked from familiar surroundings in the outside world and subjected to interrogation in a police station.

Second, a prisoner, unlike a person who has not been sentenced to a term of incarceration, is unlikely to be lured into speaking by a longing for prompt release. When a person is arrested and taken to a station house for interrogation, the person who is questioned may be pressured to speak by the hope that, after doing so, he will be allowed to leave and go home. On the other hand, when a prisoner is questioned, he knows that when the questioning ceases, he will remain under confinement.

Third, a prisoner, unlike a person who has not been convicted and sentenced, knows that the law enforcement officers who question him probably lack the authority to affect the duration of his sentence. . . .

In short, standard conditions of confinement and associated restrictions on freedom will not necessarily implicate the same interests that the Court sought to protect when it afforded special safeguards to persons subjected to custodial interrogation. Thus, service of a term of imprisonment,

HOWES V. FIELDS *(continued)*

without more, is not enough to constitute Miranda custody. . . .

When a prisoner is questioned, the determination of custody should focus on all of the features of the interrogation. These include the language that is used in summoning the prisoner to the interview and the manner in which the interrogation is conducted. An inmate who is removed from the general prison population for questioning and is "thereafter . . . subjected to treatment" in connection with the interrogation "that renders him 'in custody' for practical purposes . . . will be entitled to the full panoply of protections prescribed by Miranda.". . .

The record in this case reveals that respondent was not taken into custody for purposes of Miranda. To be sure, respondent did not invite the interview or consent to it in advance, and he was not advised that he was free to decline to speak with the deputies. The following facts also lend some support to respondent's argument that Miranda's custody requirement was met: The interview lasted for between five and seven hours in the evening and continued well past the hour when respondent generally went to bed; the deputies who questioned respondent were armed; and one of the deputies, according to respondent, "[u]sed a very sharp tone,". . .

These circumstances, however, were offset by others. Most important, respondent was told at the outset of the interrogation, and was reminded again thereafter, that he could leave and go back to his cell whenever he wanted ("I was told I could get up and leave whenever I wanted"). Moreover, respondent was not physically restrained or threatened and was interviewed in a well-lit, average-sized conference room, where he was "not uncomfortable." He was offered food and water, and the door to the conference room was sometimes left open. "All of these objective facts are consistent with an interrogation environment in which a reasonable person would have felt free to terminate the interview and leave."

Because he was in prison, respondent was not free to leave the conference room by himself and to make his own way through the facility to his cell. Instead, he was escorted to the conference room and, when he ultimately decided to end the interview, he had to wait about 20 minutes for a corrections officer to arrive and escort him to his cell. But he would have been subject to this same restraint even if he had been taken to the conference room for some reason other than police questioning; under no circumstances could he have reasonably expected to be able to roam free. And while respondent testified that he "was told . . . if I did not want to cooperate, I needed to go back to my cell," these words did not coerce cooperation by threatening harsher conditions. ("I was told, if I didn't want to cooperate, I could leave"). Returning to his cell would merely have returned him to his usual environment.

Taking into account all of the circumstances of the questioning—including especially the undisputed fact that respondent was told that he was free to end the questioning and to return to his cell—we hold that respondent was not in custody within the meaning of Miranda.

In addition to being in custody, a defendant must be subjected to an interrogation before *Miranda* applies. Clearly, interrogation includes questioning by law enforcement officers, but this is not all. In *Rhode Island v. Innis,* 446 U.S. 291 (1980),[10] the Supreme Court held that any "functional equivalent" to express questioning is also interrogation. That is, all actions or words by police officers that can reasonably be expected to elicit an incriminating response are interrogation.

The nature of the information elicited is not relevant; the *Miranda* court stated that the decision applies to both inculpatory and exculpatory statements. Accordingly, *Miranda* is effective whether a defendant confesses or simply makes an admission.

Waiver

A defendant may waive the right to have the assistance of counsel and/or to remain silent. The waiver must be made voluntarily and knowingly. In *Miranda,* the Supreme Court said that the "heavy burden" of proving that a defendant made a knowing and voluntary waiver rests with the prosecution; courts are to presume no waiver.

In determining whether there has been a waiver, the totality of the circumstances is considered. The actions of the police, as well as the defendant's age, intelligence, and experience, are all relevant to this inquiry.

An express waiver, preferably written or recorded, is best for the prosecution. Although more difficult for prosecutors to defend, unrecorded verbal waivers are also valid. On the other hand, a suspect who knowingly and voluntary speaks to police following the Miranda warnings waives the right to counsel.

In the same case, *Berghuis v. Thompkins* (2010), the Court held that police do not have an obligation to obtain a waiver of Miranda following the warnings. Instead, they may begin an interrogation and must stop only if the suspect unambiguously invokes the right to remain silent or asks for an attorney. Further, silence by a suspect after receiving the warnings is not the same as an invocation of the rights. If a suspect's statement is ambiguous or equivocal, the police may continue the interrogation.

Exceptions to *Miranda*

Not every communication between a police officer and a suspect amounts to an interrogation under *Miranda*. First, volunteered statements are not the product of interrogation. The *Miranda* decision explicitly states that officers are under no duty to interrupt a volunteered confession in order to read a confessor his or her *Miranda* rights.

Second, routine questions that are purely informational, and normally do not lead to incriminating responses, need not be preceded by a reading of the *Miranda* warnings. Questions about one's name, age, address, and employment, for example, are not treated as interrogation. So, a statute that requires individuals who have been legitimately arrested or detained by police to produce identification is valid because a person's name, standing alone, is not incriminating in most circumstances.[11]

Third, questions made by officers in the interest of public safety need not be preceded by a *Miranda* warning. In one case, a woman told two police officers that she had just been raped by a man carrying a gun and that the rapist had gone into a nearby grocery. The officers went to the store and arrested the man. However, he did not have the gun on his person. One of the police officers asked the arrestee where the gun was, and the arrestee responded by indicating the location where the gun was hidden in the store. The Supreme Court decided that, despite the fact that the question was interrogation and the defendant had not been Mirandized, the evidence could be used at trial. The Court recognized that in such situations, when there is a danger to the officers or the public, officers must be permitted to extinguish the public threat.

Thus, the relatively rigid *Miranda* rules are relaxed when there is a public safety exigency that was the impetus of a brief and limited interrogation designed to meet that exigency.[12]

The public safety exception came into full focus following the bombings at the 2013 Boston Marathon. The government announced that it would invoke the public safety exception and not immediately Mirandize the suspect Dzhokhar Tsarnaev. The decision was guided by a U.S. Department of Justice Memorandum entitled *Custodial Interrogation for Public Safety and Intelligence-Gathering Purposes of Operational Terrorists Inside the United States*.[13] The memorandum advises federal agents who arrest terrorist suspects to:

(1) If applicable, agents should ask any and all questions that are reasonably prompted by an immediate concern for the safety of the public or the arresting agents without advising the arrestee of his Miranda rights.

(2) After all applicable public safety questions have been exhausted, agents should advise the arrestee of his Miranda rights and seek a waiver of those rights before any further interrogation occurs, absent exceptional circumstances described below.

(3) There may be exceptional cases in which, although all relevant public safety questions have been asked, agents nonetheless conclude that continued unwarned interrogation is necessary to collect valuable and timely intelligence not related to any immediate threat, and that the government's interest in obtaining this intelligence outweighs the disadvantages of proceeding with unwarned interrogation.

The determination whether particular unwarned questions are justified on public safety grounds must always be made on a case-by-case basis based on all the facts and circumstances. In light of the magnitude and complexity of the threat often posed by terrorist organizations, particularly international terrorist organizations, and the nature of their attacks, the circumstances surrounding an arrest of an operational terrorist may warrant significantly more extensive public safety interrogation without Miranda warnings than would be permissible in an ordinary criminal case. Depending on the facts, such interrogation might include, for example, questions about possible impending or coordinated terrorist attacks; the location, nature, and threat posed by weapons that might post an imminent danger to the public; and the identities, locations, and activities or intentions of accomplices who may be plotting additional imminent attacks.

Tsarnaev was apprehended in a national manhunt that involved shoot-outs, the murder of a police officer, and a lock down (public transit and schools were closed and residents were asked to lock themselves at home) of a city. Tsarnaev was injured during the ordeal and taken to hospital where law enforcement officers conducted unMirandized interrogations of the suspect from the time of his arrest until his first appearance before a judge 16 hours later. The judge Mirandized Tsarnaev during the hearing, at which time he stopped talking.[14] No doubt asking Tsarnaev if other explosives had been built or hidden, whether he had hidden or mislaid any weapons during the manhunt, or any question concerning the immediate public safety. But it is not clear that questions beyond these matters, even if related to his alleged terrorist crimes, fall into the public safety exception. The case against Tsarnaev was in its early stages at the time of writing of this edition, so it remains to be seen whether the unMirandized interrogations will result in exclusion of, or a prosecutorial decision to not offer into evidence, his statements.

Fourth, related to the public safety exception is spontaneous questioning by police. If a question is asked spontaneously, such as in response to an emergency, there is no interrogation. For example, if an officer were to return to a room where he has placed two arrestees to find one dead, it would not be an interrogation if the officer were to excitedly utter, "Who killed this man?"

Fifth, the *Miranda* warnings do not have to be given by undercover officers because there is no custody, no "police-dominated atmosphere."[15] However, once criminal charges have been filed, undercover officers may not be used to extract information from a defendant.[16]

Sixth, the Supreme Court has determined that *Miranda* warnings do not have to be recited during routine traffic stops, even though an interrogation occurs. The Court concluded that although traffic stops are seizures for Fourth Amendment purposes, they are not custodial for Fifth Amendment purposes. The "noncoercive aspect of ordinary traffic stops prompts us to hold that persons temporarily detained pursuant to such stops are not 'in custody' for the purposes of *Miranda*." This includes answering field sobriety questions.[17]

Multiple Interrogations and Reinterrogation

Miranda clearly states that once a defendant invokes the right to remain silent, whether before or during questioning, the interrogation must stop.

Once a defendant states that he or she wants counsel present; the interrogation must cease until the defendant's attorney is available. If the defendant's attorney is not available, the police are to respect the defendant's right to remain silent and not question him or her until the attorney arrives. However, ambiguous references to an attorney do not invoke a suspect's right to be free of questioning. A suspect's request must be clear enough that a reasonable officer would believe that the suspect wanted to see counsel.[18] A defendant's invocation must be unambiguous and in the 2010 case *Berghuis v. Thompkins* the Supreme Court made it clear that silence during a long interrogation is not an invocation of the Fifth Amendment right to remain silent. So, a Mirandized suspect who remained silent for a long period and then made a single short admission was unsuccessful in having the admission excluded.

Under very limited circumstances, police officers may reattempt to interrogate a defendant who has invoked the right to remain silent. Although multiple attempts to interrogate an arrestee about the same crime are not permitted, it has been determined that a second interrogation about a separate and unrelated crime may be valid.[19]

Reinterrogations when a long period of time has passed between the two, with intervening circumstances, are permitted. In *Maryland v. Shatzer*, a 2010 Supreme Court case, a prisoner who was interrogated by police about a new crime invoked his Miranda rights, resulting in a cessation of the interrogation and the investigation was closed. The case was reopened 3 years later, the prisoner was interrogated after waiving his *Miranda* rights, and his incriminating statements were used to gain a conviction for sexual child abuse. He later asserted that his initial invocation of *Miranda* should have carried forward to the interrogation 3 years later. The Court rejected the theory, finding that his return to the general population of the prison and the 3-year period constituted a break in *Miranda* custody.

Miranda clearly stated that once an accused has invoked the right to counsel, the police are prohibited from interrogating him or her until he or she has conferred with counsel. *Miranda* did not answer this question: May police reinterrogate a defendant without counsel present once the defendant has consulted with a lawyer? The answer is found in *Minnick v. Mississippi*. *Minnick* makes it clear that once an accused has asserted a right to counsel, all police-initiated interrogations must occur with defense counsel present.

MINNICK V. MISSISSIPPI
498 U.S. 146 (1990)

To protect the privilege against self-incrimination guaranteed by the Fifth Amendment, we have held that the police must terminate interrogation of an accused in custody if the accused requests the assistance of counsel. *Miranda v. Arizona*, 384 U.S. 436, 474 (1966). We reinforced the protections of *Miranda* in *Edwards v. Arizona*, 451 U.S. 477, 484–485 (1981), which held that once the accused requests counsel, officials may not reinitiate questioning "until counsel has been made available" to him. The issue in the case before us is whether *Edwards* protection ceases once the suspect has consulted with an attorney.

Petitioner Robert Minnick and fellow prisoner James Dyess escaped from a county jail in Mississippi and, a day later, broke into a mobile home in search of weapons. In the course of the burglary they were interrupted by the arrival of the trailer's owner, Ellis Thomas, accompanied by Lamar Lafferty and Lafferty's infant son. Dyess and Minnick used the stolen weapons to kill Thomas and the senior Lafferty. Minnick's story is that Dyess murdered one victim and then forced Minnick to shoot the other. Before the escapees could get away, two young women arrived at the mobile home. They were held at gunpoint, then bound by hand and foot. Dyess and

Minnick fled in Thomas' truck, abandoning the vehicle in New Orleans. The fugitives continued to Mexico, where they fought, and Minnick then proceeded alone to California. Minnick was arrested in Lemon Grove, California, on a Mississippi warrant, some four months after the murders.

The confession at issue here resulted from the last interrogation of Minnick while he was held in the San Diego jail, but we first recount the events which preceded it. Minnick was arrested on Friday, August 22, 1986. Petitioner testified that he was mistreated by local police during and after the arrest. The day following the arrest, Saturday, two FBI agents came to the jail to interview him. Petitioner testified that he refused to go to the interview, but was told he would "have to go down or else.". . . The FBI report indicates that the agents read petitioner his *Miranda* warnings, and that he acknowledged he understood his rights. He refused to sign a rights waiver form, however, and said he would not answer "very many" questions. Minnick told the agents about the jail break and the flight, and described how Dyess threatened and beat him. Early in the interview, he sobbed "[i]t was my life or theirs," but otherwise he hesitated to tell what happened at the trailer. The agents reminded him he

(continued)

MINNICK V. MISSISSIPPI (continued)

did not have to answer questions without a lawyer present. According to the report, "Minnick stated, 'Come back Monday when I have a lawyer,' and stated that he would make a more complete statement then with his lawyer present.". . .

After the FBI interview, an appointed attorney met with petitioner. Petitioner spoke with the lawyer on two or three occasions, though it is not clear from the record whether all of these conferences were in person.

On Monday, August 25, Deputy Sheriff J.C. Denham of Clarke County, Mississippi, came to the San Diego jail to question Minnick. Minnick testified that his jailers again told him he would "have to talk" to Denham and that he "could not refuse.". . . Denham advised petitioner of his rights, and petitioner again declined to sign a rights waiver form. Petitioner told Denham about the escape and then proceeded to describe the events at the mobile home. . . .

Minnick was tried for murder in Mississippi. He moved to suppress all statements given to the FBI or other police officers, including Denham. The trial court denied the motion with respect to petitioner's statements to Denham, but suppressed his other statements. Petitioner was convicted on two counts of capital murder and sentenced to death.

On appeal, petitioner argued that the confession to Denham was taken in violation of his rights to counsel under the Fifth and Sixth Amendments. The Mississippi Supreme Court rejected the claims. . . .

The Mississippi Supreme Court relied on our statement in *Edwards* that an accused who invokes his right to counsel "is not subject to further interrogation by the authorities until counsel has been made available to him. . . ." 451 U.S., at 484–485. We do not interpret this language to mean, as the Mississippi court thought, that the protection of *Edwards* terminates once counsel has consulted with the suspect. In context, the requirement that counsel be "made available" to the accused refers to more than an opportunity to consult with an attorney outside the interrogation room.

In *Edwards*, we focused on *Miranda's* instruction that when the accused invokes his right to counsel, the "interrogation must cease until an attorney is *present* during custodial interrogation. . . . " 451 U.S., at 482 (emphasis added). In the sentence preceding the language quoted by the Mississippi Supreme Court, we referred to the "right to have counsel *present* during custodial interrogation.". . .

In our view, a fair reading of *Edwards* and subsequent cases demonstrates that we have interpreted the rule to bar police-initiated interrogation unless the accused has counsel with him at the time of questioning. Whatever the ambiguities of our earlier cases on this point, we now hold that when counsel is requested, interrogation must cease, and officials may not reinitiate interrogation without counsel present, whether or not the accused has consulted with his attorney.

Another twist on multiple interrogations was introduced by the police practice of eliciting a confession without the benefit of *Miranda* warning, following that confession with the warning, and then attempting to elicit the confession again. Apparently, there are two factors at play. First, *Miranda* prevents some suspects from confessing. Second, once a suspect confesses, the gates have been opened and he or she is likely to repeat the confession, even if the *Miranda* warnings are interposed. With this knowledge, police across the nation began seeking confessions they knew were inadmissible, only to then Mirandize their suspects in hope of obtaining a second confession (see Exhibit 13–1). This practice was invalidated as violating the Fifth Amendment in *Missouri v. Seibert*, 542 U.S. 600 (2004),[20] where the Court wrote:

> Strategists dedicated to draining the substance out of Miranda cannot accomplish by training instructions [what this Court said] Congress could not do by statute. Because the question-first tactic effectively threatens to thwart *Miranda's* purpose of reducing the risk that a coerced confession would be admitted, and because the facts here do not reasonably support a conclusion that the warnings given could have served their purpose, [the defendant's] postwarning statements are inadmissible.

Exhibit 13–1 SUMMARY OF SIGNIFICANT MIRANDA CASES

Rule	Case
Suspects in custody and subject to an interrogation must be advised of their rights to remain silent, that statements may be used to prove guilt at trial, to the assistance of counsel, and for the indigent, counsel must be provided.	*Miranda v. Arizona* (1966)
A suspect is in custody if a reasonable person would have believed he or she was not free. The subjective beliefs of the suspect and officers are immaterial.	*Stansbury v. CA* (1994)
Volunteered statements, responses to routine questions, and responses to questions concerning immediate public safety do not have to follow *Miranda* warnings to be admissible.	
Questioning by undercover officers does not need to be *Mirandized*.	*Illinois v. Perkins* (1990)
Suspect silence is not an invocation of *Miranda*; a suspect's invocation must be unambiguous.	*Berghuis v. Thompkins* (2010)
Reinterrogation for the same crime after a suspect has invoked and consulted with an attorney can only occur with suspect's attorney present.	*Minnick v. Mississippi* (1990)
Interrogation of suspect for separate and unrelated crime after suspect invoked *Miranda* for different crime is permitted, subject to *Miranda* again.	*Michigan v. Mosely* (1975)
Police technique of eliciting non-*Mirandized* confessions followed by *Miranda* warnings and reinterrogation invalid.	*Missouri v. Seibert* (2004)
A break in custody allows reinterrogation without the presence of counsel, even if *Miranda* previously invoked.	*Maryland v. Shatzer* (2010)
The age and maturity of a minor are factors in custody determinations.	*JBD v. North Carolina* (2010)
Precise words not required for warnings so long as rights are communicated.	*Florida v. Powell* (2010)
Prisoners not automatically in Miranda custody; separate custodial determination is made.	*Howes v. Fields* (2012)

Violating Miranda

Any statement obtained in violation of *Miranda* is inadmissible at trial to prove guilt. The defendant ordinarily raises the issue prior to trial through a motion to suppress.

Although statements that are illegally obtained may not be admitted to prove a defendant's guilt, the Supreme Court has said that statements that violate *Miranda* may be admitted, under certain circumstances, to impeach the defendant.[21] So, if a defendant's testimony at trial is different from an earlier confession that was suppressed as violative of *Miranda,* the confession may be admitted to rebut the defendant's in-court testimony. Also, the question concerning the application of the fruits of the poisonous tree doctrine to evidence obtained as a result of a non-Mirandized confession was open for many years. The presumption of many scholars and the decisions of many lower courts was that consequential evidence should be excluded. A minority of lower courts disagreed. The Supreme Court resolved this issue in,[22] where it held that physical fruits of a non-Mirandized confession are not to be suppressed at trial. Justice Thomas, writing for the majority, penned:

> [T]he core protection afforded by the Self-Incrimination Clause is a prohibition on compelling a criminal defendant to testify against himself at trial. . . . The Clause can-not be violated by the introduction of nontestimonial evidence obtained as a result of voluntary statements. . . . It follows that police do not violate a suspect's constitutional rights (or the *Miranda* rule) by negligent or even deliberate failures to provide the suspect with the full panoply of warnings prescribed by *Miranda.* Potential violations occur, if at all, only upon the admission of unwarned statements into evidence at trial. And, at that point, "[t]he exclusion of unwarned statements . . . is a complete and sufficient remedy" for any perceived *Miranda* violation. . . . Thus, unlike unreasonable searches under the Fourth Amendment or actual violations of the Due Process Clause or the Self-Incrimination Clause, there is, with respect to mere failures to warn, nothing to deter. There is therefore no reason to apply the "fruit of the poisonous tree" doctrine. . . . But *Dickerson's* characterization of *Miranda* as a constitutional rule does not lessen the need to maintain the closest possible fit between the Self-Incrimination Clause and any judge-made rule designed to protect it. And there is no such fit here. Introduction of the nontestimonial fruit of a voluntary statement, such as respondent's Glock, does not implicate the Self-Incrimination Clause. The admission of such fruit presents no risk that a defendant's coerced statements (however defined) will be used against him at a criminal trial. In any case, "[t]he exclusion of unwarned statements . . . is a complete and sufficient remedy" for any perceived *Miranda* violation. . . .

The Court's decision has been interpreted by some state courts as a retraction of a constitutional right, regardless of the Court's treatment of it as something else. The Ohio Supreme Court, for example, held that fruits resulting from unwarned statements are to be excluded. In its 2006 decision, *State v. Farris*,[23] that court stated

The Ohio Constitution "is a document of independent force. In the areas of individual rights and civil liberties, the U.S. Constitution, where applicable to the states, provides a floor below which state court decisions may not fall. As long as state courts provide at least as much protection as the United States Supreme Court has provided in its interpretation of the federal Bill of Rights, state courts are unrestricted in according greater civil liberties and protections to individuals and groups". . . . In general, when provisions of the Ohio Constitution and U.S. Constitution are essentially identical, we should harmonize our interpretations of the provisions, unless there are persuasive reasons to do otherwise. . . . To hold that the physical evidence seized as a result of unwarned statements is inadmissible, we would have to hold that section 10, Article I of the Ohio Constitution provides greater protection to criminal defendants than the Fifth Amendment to the U.S. Constitution. We so find here.

Only evidence obtained as the direct result of statements made in custody without the benefit of a Miranda warning should be excluded. We believe that to hold otherwise would encourage law-enforcement officers to withhold Miranda warnings and would thus weaken section 10, Article I of the Ohio Constitution. In cases like this one, where possession is the basis for the crime and physical evidence is the keystone of the case, warning suspects of their rights can hinder the gathering of evidence. When physical evidence is central to a conviction and testimonial evidence is not, there can arise a virtual incentive to flout Miranda. We believe that the overall administration of justice in Ohio requires a law-enforcement environment in which evidence is gathered in conjunction with Miranda, not in defiance of it. We thus join the other states that have already determined after Patane that their state constitutions' protections against self-incrimination extend to physical evidence seized as a result of pre-Miranda statements.

Sixth Amendment

Miranda has effect as soon as a person is in custody and is subject to interrogation. This can occur long before or directly before the filing of a formal charge. Once the adversary judicial proceeding has begun, the primary source of protection changes from the Fifth Amendment (*Miranda*), which continues in effect though, to the Sixth Amendment.

The reading of the *Miranda* warnings is sufficient for protecting a defendant's Sixth Amendment rights, so police, courts, or prosecutors are not required to inform a defendant of the independent Sixth Amendment right, although it is often done. In practice, the Sixth Amendment and Fifth Amendment rights are nearly identical, although small differences in their application exist.[24]

ELECTRONIC SURVEILLANCE

A perennial challenge for law enforcement in a free republic is to stay current with, if not ahead of, the changes in the way people steal from and hurt one another. Generally, law enforcement is more reactive in a free society. In the past, this meant that a new problem would arise, often involving loss or injury to a few people. Law enforcement would react to the new threat and often, because the threat of harm was proven, public support for law enforcement intervention had developed. Of course, the precise contours of the solution would be debated but over time, a law enforcement method would develop. However, the landscape is different today. The rapidly evolving technology of the current age poses a new problem for law enforcement. Today, using new, personally developed technology, an individual can quickly cause greater harm than ever before. Even more, if the old reactive model is applied, the precise technology used to commit the crime can be changed by the time the problem is identified and law enforcement begins to develop a solution. In regards to terrorism, the old reactive model may not be adequate. Some scholars and law enforcement officials argue that a new model needs to be developed—a model that focuses more on prevention and less on detection and prosecution. As you will see, however, the new model that is advocated by many reflects a shift in the due process/crime control continuum in the direction of crime control.

An example of this shift is in the use of electronic surveillance. Many forms of electronic surveillance are used by law enforcement agencies. Wiretaps and highly sensitive microphones are examples. When the Supreme Court first addressed the issue of wiretapping, it concluded that there was no Fourth Amendment protection because there was no trespass into a constitutionally protected physical area. This changed when the Court issued the *Katz* decision, which advanced the idea that the Fourth Amendment protects people, not places. Now, if a person has a justifiable expectation of privacy, the Fourth Amendment applies.

Despite the constitutional aspect of using such devices, this area of law is highly regulated by federal statutory law. Due to a complex statutory scheme and because the technology is changing so rapidly, this area of law is murky, to say the least. What appears here is a basic overview of the law of electronic surveillance. The landmark statute in this area of the law is Title III of the Omnibus Crime Control Act and Safe Streets Act of 1968. See Exhibits 13–2 and 13–3.

Governing Statutes

Title III of the Omnibus Crime Control Act and Safe Streets Act of 1968[25] is a federal statute that regulates the use of electronic surveillance. It is also known as Title III and the Federal Wiretap Act. The Wiretap Act has been amended on several occasions. Four significant amendments resulted from the Electronic Communications Privacy Act of 1986, which included what is known at the Stored Communications Act, and the Uniting and Strengthening America by Providing Appropriate Tools Required to Intercept and Obstruct Terrorism Act of 2001 (USA Patriot Act) and the Federal Intelligence Surveillance Act of 1978 (FISA) and the FISA Amendments Act of 2008. These laws permit the states to enact similar legislation. State laws may not lessen, although they may increase, the requirements for obtaining a warrant and they must mimic the federal laws in other ways. Today, most states have such legislation. Federal law requires state officials to report their wiretap and other electronic surveillance to the federal government for purposes of monitoring and the prevention of abuse. Exhibit 13–2 summarizes the requirements to conduct electronic surveillance.

The Wiretap Act prohibits wiretapping, bugging, or other electronic surveillance of a conversation when the parties to that conversation possess a reasonable expectation of privacy. Violation of the act may result in civil and criminal penalties. Evidence obtained

Exhibit 13–2 SUMMARY OF REQUIREMENTS TO CONDUCT ELECTRONIC SURVEILLANCE

Form of Surveillance	Requirements for Governmental Surveillance	Remedies for Violations
Wiretap	Super-warrant	Criminal and civil. Except for e-mail, illegally obtained evidence is excluded at trial. Service providers are exempt when acting in course of employment.
Tracking device	Warrant supported by probable cause	Traditional liability
Stored communication	*180 days or less:* Warrant supported by probable cause. *181 days or more:* Notice to subscriber, administrative subpoena, and specific and articulable facts with reasonable grounds to believe data sought will be relevant and material to ongoing investigation.	Criminal (lesser penalties than for Wiretap Act) and civil. Service providers absolutely immune for violations. No suppression of illegally obtained evidence in criminal proceedings.
Pen register/ Trap and trace	Government certifies relevance to investigation. Court to issue order without independent judgement of relevance.	No civil or criminal remedies. No suppression of illegally obtained evidence.

in violation of the act is excluded at trial. The suppression provision does not, however, apply to e-mail.

The statute permits states to enact their own electronic surveillance laws; however, those laws cannot provide less protection of individual rights than the federal statute. A state may, however, provide greater protection of individual rights through its surveillance law than does the federal statute. The USA Patriot Act amended existing surveillance statutes.

When the Fourth Amendment and these statutes are viewed as a whole, electronic and wire surveillance can be divided into four categories, each with a different level of privacy protection. They are

1. Wiretaps
2. Tracking devices
3. Stored communications and subscriber information
4. Pen registers and trap devices

Exhibit 13–3 EXAMPLES OF PATRIOT ACT CHANGES OF WIRE AND
ELECTRONIC SURVEILLANCE

Pre–Patriot Act	Post–Patriot Act
Warrants to intercept telephone conversation were limited to specific crimes.	List expanded to include terrorism, chemical weapons, and computer crimes.
It was unclear whether a warrant or the lesser subpoena was required to retrieve voice mail.	Administrative subpoena but not warrant required.
Pen registers and trap devices	Similar technology may be applied to e-mail; court orders have national, not district, authority.
Warrants had to specify the communications carrier.	Roving wiretaps that do not specify a carrier are permitted. The order follows the target, who may use multiple ISPs, cable companies, and cell phone carriers.
Foreign intelligence gathering was allowed, but limited.	Governmental authority to gather foreign intelligence was broadened.
Federal law protects the privacy of educational and library records.	Authority of government to obtain educational and library records that are sought in terrorism or foreign intelligence investigation is broadened.

Copyright © Cengage Learning®.

Wiretaps

Law enforcement officers may not intercept telephone conversations or the content of other electronic messages (e.g., e-mail) without first obtaining court approval.[26] The Wiretap Act requires more than the Fourth Amendment for this form of surveillance. This stance reflects the belief held by Congress that telephone conversations fall within a special zone of privacy. The high standards for issuing a wiretap warrant have led to it being dubbed a "super-warrant." The Act limits court approval only for certain crimes. Espionage, treason, murder, kidnapping, robbery, extortion, drug crimes, and bribery of public officials are included in that list. The Patriot Act expanded the list to include chemical weapons offenses, using weapons of mass destruction, financing terrorism that transcends U.S. borders, conducting financial transactions with nations that support terrorism, and material support of terrorist organizations. In recent years, most of the wiretaps issued have been requested by state officials for drug crimes.

To obtain a wiretap order, a high-level official in the U.S. Department of Justice must either apply or authorize an application for an order. Additionally, Title III empowers states to designate high-level prosecutors who may apply for a wiretap order. Such designations must appear in statute. Most states have designated their elected prosecutors and state attorneys general. The application, which shall be supported by oath or affirmation, must contain the following[27]:

1. The identity of the official applying for the order and the official authorizing the application.
2. Evidence establishing probable cause to believe that the person whose communication is to be intercepted has committed, is committing, or is about to commit one of the named crimes.
3. Evidence establishing probable cause to believe that the communication to be intercepted concerns the crime.
4. A statement that other normal investigative procedures have been tried and failed, or that no other procedure is available.
5. The time period during which the interception will occur.
6. A full description of the location where the interception will take place.
7. A statement reflecting all prior attempts to obtain a similar order for any of the same places or persons.

Wiretap applications may be made to federal judges, or if authorized by state statute, to state criminal courts. If the judge grants the application, the order must specify the person whose communication is to be intercepted, the location of the interception, the nature of the communication to be intercepted, the crime involved, and the duration of the interception. Because of the ongoing nature of such investigations, wiretap orders are sealed. In all cases, the surveillance is to cease once the desired information has been seized (recorded). After the interception has ended, the recording is to be given to the judge who issued the order, for safekeeping. See the sidebar for data on the number of wiretap orders issued between 1999 and 2001.

Execution of Wiretap Warrants

The statute provides that all communications intercepted shall, if possible, be recorded. The method of recording is to protect against editing and other alterations. The purpose of this requirement is obvious: to preserve the integrity of the evidence.

The statute also requires that all interceptions of irrelevant information be minimized. Said another way, if an officer intercepting a conversation knows that it is unrelated to the investigation, the interception is to cease. The minimization requirement is no more than a codification of the Fourth Amendment's reasonableness requirement.

Of course, determining whether an interception is related to the offense under investigation is not always easy, and courts tend to defer to the judgement of the intercepting officer in close cases. The following factors are considered by a reviewing court when a claim is made that interceptions were not properly minimized:

1. The percentage of calls that were related to the investigation. The lower the percentage, the greater the likelihood that the government did not properly minimize its interceptions.
2. The number of calls that were one-time only.

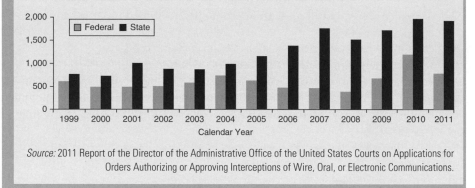

sidebar

NUMBER OF WIRETAP ORDERS, 1999 TO 2011

There were 2,732 wiretap authorizations in 2011. Most were issued at the state level for portable devices (cell, pages, etc.), and 85% were for drug crimes. The average length of original wiretap authorizations was 28 days with extensions raising the average to 42 days, data were collected on an average of 113 people per order, and 23% of the intercepted communications were incriminating. Twelve of the intercepted messages were encrypted. All were decoded. Intercepts are costly, averaging nearly $50,000 each. But many wiretaps resulted in criminal forfeitures valued in the millions of dollars; 3,547 people who had communications intercepted were arrested, 465 were convicted, and many cases were pending when the data were reported.

Source: 2011 Report of the Director of the Administrative Office of the United States Courts on Applications for Orders Authorizing or Approving Interceptions of Wire, Oral, or Electronic Communications.

3. The length of the calls intercepted. The shorter the calls, the less opportunity the government had to determine whether the interception was proper.

4. The nature of the calls. The more ambiguous the call, the greater the government's interest in prolonging its interception.[28]

Other factors may also be important to the inquiry. For example, if a known co-conspirator makes frequent calls, interception of all the calls is probably valid, even though the majority of conversations do not concern the conspiracy. Each case must be examined on its own facts to determine whether Title III or the Fourth Amendment has been violated.

Implicit in court orders under this statute is the authority to enter premises to install listening devices. Courts have held that it would be nonsensical to give an officer the authority to conduct surveillance, but not to enter the premises of the defendant to install the necessary device. The court order does not have to specifically give this authority; it is implicit in the order itself. Of course, where an officer may go depends on the facts of each case.

The statute authorizes judges to order third parties, such as telephone company personnel, to assist law enforcement officers in executing an electronic surveillance order. Third parties must be compensated for their assistance.

Within 90 days after the expiration of the order, the target of a wiretap order, who is not always the criminal suspect, must be sent notice and an inventory of what was tapped. Judges have the discretion to order that notices also be sent to third parties whose communications were intercepted. Some states, such as California, require that the order itself also be provided. In cases where an ongoing investigation would be jeopardized by the notice, the government may apply to the issuing court for an extension of time to send it.

Exceptions to the Wiretap Act

In a number of situations, a court order is not required to intercept an electronic communication. Several exceptions are discussed here.

First, be aware that the act tracks the privacy aspect of the *Katz* decision; that is, only communications for which a person has a reasonable expectation of privacy are protected. Because Title III does not expand the privacy protection aspect of the Fourth Amendment, decisions concerning whether a person has a reasonable expectation of privacy under the Fourth Amendment are applicable to Title III.

Second, any employee of a communications company who intercepts an incriminating communication while engaged in the normal course of employment (i.e., maintenance) may disclose such information to the authorities, and it may be used at trial.

Third, officers need not obtain a court order when engaged in certain national security investigations.

Fourth, in emergency situations, when an officer does not have time to obtain a court order, the interception may begin immediately, but an application must be made within 48 hours. If the judge determines that there was no emergency justifying a warrantless tap, then any evidence obtained must be suppressed. However, the statute excludes unlawfully obtained e-mail from the suppression rule.

Finally, parties to conversations or e-mail exchanges may consent to surveillance. So, law enforcement officers and individuals working with law enforcement can record or allow others to listen or read their communications without the consent of the other party.

Tracking Devices

It is possible today to use electronic and mechanical devices to track and record the movement of people and things. Law enforcement authority to place a tracking device is lower than for wiretaps, but higher than for stored communication and pen registers. Warrants for tracking devices may be issued upon the standard Fourth Amendment finding of probable cause.

An interesting question concerns the relevant standard to apply when the government wants to use cell phone data to track the whereabouts of its possessor. That is the issue addressed in the following opinion.

IN RE APPLICATION FOR PEN REGISTER
AND TRAP/TRACE DEVICE WITH CELL SITE AUTHORITY
U.S. District Court, S.D. Texas, MAGISTRATE NO. H-05-557M (Oct. 14, 2005)

As part of an ongoing criminal investigation, the government seeks a court order compelling a cell phone company to disclose records of a customer's cell phone use. Among the records sought is "cell site data," which reveals the user's physical location while the phone is turned on. By order dated September 2, 2005, the court granted the application in large part, authorizing the continued used of a pen register/trap and trace device and disclosure of certain customer records including historical cell site data. However, the order denied access to prospective cell site information, for reasons explained more fully in this opinion.

The underlying order and application have been sealed at the government's request, in order not to jeopardize the ongoing criminal investigation. This opinion will not be sealed, because it concerns a matter of statutory interpretation which does not hinge on the particulars of the underlying investigation. The issue explored here has serious implications for the balance between privacy and law enforcement, and is a matter of first impression in this circuit as well as most others. Following its standard practice in this district, the government has combined its request for subscriber records with an application to install a pen register and trap/trace device on the target phone. Basically, a pen register is a device or process which records the telephone numbers of outgoing calls; the trap and trace device captures the telephone numbers of incoming calls. Among the most commonly used law enforcement techniques (footnote omitted), a pen/trap order authorizes real-time electronic monitoring of a telephone user's calls (excluding content) for a limited duration, typically 60 days.

To assist this monitoring effort, the government seeks access to subscriber records maintained by the phone company pursuant to 18 U.S.C. § 2703(c).

Among the records sought is "the location of cell site/sector (physical address) at call origination (for outbound calling), call termination (for incoming calls), and, if reasonably available, during the progress of a call." Also sought is information regarding the strength, angle, and timing of the caller's signal measured at two or more cell sites, as well as other system information such as a listing of all cell towers in the market area, switching technology, protocols, and network architecture. Armed with this information, collectively known as "cell site data," investigators are often able to locate suspects and fugitives. . . .

The issue presented here is what legal standard the government must satisfy to compel disclosure of such prospective or "real-time" cell site data. More particularly, is this location information merely another form of subscriber record accessible upon a showing of "specific and articulable facts" under 18 U.S.C. § 2703(d), as the government contends? Or does this type of surveillance require a more exacting standard, such as probable cause under Federal Rule of Criminal Procedure 41?

1. TECHNOLOGY

Unavoidably, some familiarity with cell phone technology is necessary to address this issue. A cell phone is a sophisticated two-way radio with a low-power transmitter that operates in a network of cell sites (footnote omitted). "Cell" refers to geographic regions often illustrated as hexagons, resembling a bee's honeycomb; a "cell site" is where the radio transceiver and base station controller are located (at the point three hexagons meet). Cell phones and base stations communicate with each other on frequencies called channels. Two frequencies are paired to create a channel; one for transmitting, one for receiving. Channels that carry only cell system data are called control channels. The control channel is a frequency shared by the phone and the base station to communicate information for setting up calls and channel changing when the user moves from one cell to another. By comparison, voice channels are those paired frequencies which handle a call's traffic, be it voice or data, as well as signaling information about the call itself. The cell site sends and receives traffic from the cell phones in its geographic area to a mobile telecommunications switching office, which handles all phone connections and controls all base stations in a given region.

When a cell phone is powered up, it acts as a scanning radio, searching through a list of control channels for the strongest signal. The cell phone re-scans every seven seconds or when the signal strength weakens, regardless of whether a call is placed. The cell phone searches for a five-digit number known as the System Identification Code assigned to service providers. After selecting a channel, the cell phone identifies itself by sending its programmed codes which identify the phone, the phone's owner, and the service provider. These codes include an Electronic Serial Number (a unique 32-bit number programmed into the phone by the manufacturer), and a Mobile Identification Number, a 10-digit number derived from the phone's number.

The cell site relays these codes to the mobile telecommunications switching office in a process known as registration. . . .

It should be emphasized that cell site data transmitted during the registration process "are not dialed or otherwise controlled by the cellular telephone user." This registration process automatically occurs even while the cell phone is idle. Moving from one service area to another triggers the registration process anew. The cell site can even initiate registration on its own by sending a signal to the cell phone causing the phone to transmit and identify itself.

When the switching office gets an incoming call, it sends a "page" to the cell phone over the control channel. When the cell phone responds, the switching office assigns a voice channel to carry the actual conversation; at that point the control channel drops off. The speaker's voice is converted into electronic digits (*i.e.* a series of 1s and 0s), which are then compressed for transmission over the voice channel.

In summary, a cell phone is (among other things) a radio transmitter that automatically announces its presence to a cell tower via a radio signal over a control channel which does not itself carry the human voice. By a process of triangulation from various cell towers, law enforcement is able to track the movements of the target phone, and hence locate a suspect using that phone (footnotes omitted). . . .

3. PROSPECTIVE CELL SITE DATA AS TRACKING INFORMATION

Our analysis begins with the tracking device category, which appears at first glance to provide the most likely fit for cell site location monitoring. In its first opinion dealing with the ECPA, the Fifth Circuit cautioned that rigorous attention must be paid to statutory definitions when interpreting this complex statute: "Understanding the Act requires understanding and applying its many technical terms as defined by the Act, as well as engaging in painstaking, methodical analysis."

The ECPA's definition of tracking device is concise and straight-forward:

> As used in this section, the term "tracking device" means an electronic or mechanical device which permits the tracking of the movement of a person or thing.

(continued)

IN RE APPLICATION FOR PEN REGISTER AND TRAP (continued)

18 U.S.C. § 3117(b). Aside from its welcome brevity, the definition is striking for its breadth. Note that a device is covered even though it may not have been intended or designed to track movement; it is enough if the device merely "permits" tracking. Nor does the definition suggest that a covered device can have no function other than tracking movement. Finally, there is no specification of how precise the tracking must be. Whether from room to room, house to house, neighborhood to neighborhood, or city to city, this unqualified definition draws no distinction.

The government contends that this interpretation of "tracking device" is too expansive, and points to the Senate Report on the ECPA which contained a glossary of technological terms defining "electronic tracking devices" as one-way radio "homing" devices. But even if this glossary definition accurately depicted the Senate's working understanding of the term in 1986, that definition never made it into the United States Code. So, if the government is correct that the glossary definition is narrower than § 3117(b), the only permissible inference is that Congress intended "tracking device" to have the broader meaning. Far from supporting the government's position, the glossary definition undermines it.

By adopting the broader language, Congress may simply have been anticipating future advances in tracking technology. Such advances have indeed come to pass:

> Tracking devices have progressed a long way. Most agencies now have sophisticated tracking devices that use cell site towers or satellites. . . . These types of tracking devices are usually monitored from the law enforcement agency's office. Through the use of computers, a signal is sent to the tracking device (it is pinged), and the tracking device responds. The signal is picked up using cellular telephone cell sites or satellites. The location of the tracker, and therefore the vehicle, is determined through triangulation and a computer monitor at the agency office shows the location of the vehicle on a map. These tracking devices are very accurate, and can differentiate between a vehicle traveling on an interstate highway or the feeder (service) road. The tracking devices will also provide the direction of travel and the speed the vehicle is traveling.

. . . Thus, even traditional tracking devices such as beepers on vehicles are now monitored via radio signals using the very same cell phone towers used to transmit cell site data. Given this convergence in technology, the distinction between cell site data and information gathered by a tracking device has practically vanished. While Congress may not have known back in 1986 that a cell phone would come to be used as a tracking device, the broad language of § 3117(b) certainly left open that possibility.

While the cell phone was not originally conceived as a tracking device, law enforcement converts it to that purpose by monitoring cell site data. As with a tracking device, this process is usually surreptitious and unknown to the phone user, who may not even be on the phone. . . .

The government resists categorizing cell site data in the hands of service providers as information from a tracking device, because it is does not provide "detailed" location information. This argument is unpersuasive. . . .

The government posits a slippery slope of adverse consequences unintended by Congress if cell phones could be classified as tracking devices under § 3117(b). For example, the government notes that land-line phones, computers, and even credit cards can sometimes reveal the user's location, and these things have never been considered tracking devices. But learning a credit card user's location at the point of purchase is far different from continuously monitoring a person's movement from place to place in real time.

IN RE APPLICATION FOR PEN REGISTER AND TRAP *(continued)*

In the same vein, the government argues that such a broad interpretation of § 3117(b) "would eviscerate privacy protection under the Wiretap Act and the SCA for most communications now deemed electronic communications." This argument rests on a fallacy—i.e., that classifying cell site data as tracking information means that a cell phone must be regarded solely as a tracking device for all purposes, so that any form of communication from a cell phone *ipso facto* becomes a communication from a tracking device. Such reasoning ignores the multi-functional nature of the modern cell phone. This device delivers many different types of communication: live conversations, voice mail, pages, text messages, e-mail, alarms, internet, video, photos, dialing, signaling, etc. The legal standard for government access depends entirely upon the type of communication involved. Congress has decreed the highest protection for the contents of live conversations acquired via wiretap, intermediate protection for stored electronic communications, and the least protection for telephone numbers dialed. The legal threshold for each type of communication is different, notwithstanding that a cell phone transmits them all. It would surely make no sense to impose the wiretap requirements upon a pen/trap application merely because the cell phone can be used to intercept live conversations; it makes no more sense to impose the tracking device requirements for access to other types of cell phone communications unrelated to physical location.

Ironically, it is the government's position that threatens to undermine the federal statutory scheme for electronic surveillance. As we have seen, a cell phone can readily be converted by law enforcement to function as a tracking device, employing much the same technology as the modern beeper or transponder. Under the government's theory, law enforcement could simply install cell phones in place of the beepers currently underneath vehicles and inside drum barrels, and eliminate forever the need to obtain a Rule 41 search warrant for tracking surveillance. As explained more fully in the next part, this would violate congressional intent by collapsing the barriers between the distinct categories of electronic surveillance erected by Congress in the ECPA.

A word about the Fourth Amendment implications of cell site tracking is in order here. The government contends that probable cause should never be required for cell phone tracking because there is no reasonable expectation of privacy in cell site location data, analogizing such information to the telephone numbers found unprotected in *Smith v. Maryland*, 442 U.S. 735 (1979). The Sixth Circuit rejected that analogy in *United States v. Forest*, 355 F.3d 942, 951–52 (6th Cir. 2004). Unlike dialed telephone numbers, cell site data is not "voluntarily conveyed" by the user to the phone company. As we have seen, it is transmitted automatically during the registration process, entirely independent of the user's input, control, or knowledge. Sometimes, as in *Forest*, cell site data is triggered by law enforcement's dialing of the particular number. For these reasons the Sixth Circuit was persuaded that *Smith* did not extend to cell site data, but rejected the defendant's constitutional claim on the narrower ground that the surveillance took place on public highways, where there is no legitimate expectation of privacy. Further support for a recognizable privacy interest in caller location information is provided by the Wireless Communication and Public Safety Act of 1999. This legislation authorized the deployment of a nation-wide 9-1-1 emergency service for wireless phone users, called "Enhanced 9-1-1." Section 5 of the bill amended the Telecommunications Act to extend privacy protection for the

(continued)

call location information of cell phone users . . . In other words, location information is a special class of customer information, which can only be used or disclosed in an emergency situation, absent express prior consent by the customer. Based on this statute, a cell phone user may very well have an objectively reasonable expectation of privacy in his call location information. . . .

4. PROSPECTIVE CELL SITE DATA AND OTHER ECPA SURVEILLANCE CATEGORIES

Having concluded that prospective cell site data is properly categorized as tracking device information under § 3117, the question arises whether such data may not also be obtainable under other provisions of the ECPA. In other words, do the four broad categories of the ECPA overlap, such that location information obtainable from a § 3117 tracking device is simultaneously obtainable under the Wiretap Act, the SCA, or the Pen/Trap Statute? The answer to this question is clearly "no."

Two of the categories may be discarded at the outset. The minimal pen/trap standard does not authorize access to cell site data; Congress made that much clear in the Communications Assistance to Law Enforcement Act of 1994 ("CALEA"):

> [W]ith regard to information acquired solely pursuant to the authority for pen registers and trap and trace devices (as defined in section 3127 of Title 18), such call-identifying information shall not include any information that may disclose the physical location of the subscriber (except to the extent that the location may be determined from the telephone number).

47 U.S.C. § 1002(a)(2) (footnote omitted; emphasis supplied).

Nor is the super-warrant wiretap standard applicable here, because the government is not seeking to intercept the contents of a phone user's communication. Cell site data does not reflect the "contents" of a communication as that term is defined by the

Wiretap Act. For the same reason, the first two parts of the SCA authorizing disclosure of the contents of stored communications do not apply, because the SCA incorporates the same definition of "contents." The only remaining possibility for prospective cell site data is the SCA subscriber records category under § 2703(c). The government's application understandably invokes this authority, with its lesser "specific and articulable facts" threshold. However, neither the text nor the structure of the SCA supports the government's contention.

Carefully reviewing the language of the SCA . . . we find no mention of cell site data in the laundry list of basic subscriber information contained in § 2703(c)(2). The list does include "address," but this plainly refers to the subscriber's nominal residence for billing or contact purposes, rather than the physical location(s) where the mobile phone is used. In order to be accessible under the SCA, therefore, cell site data must fit within the broader category of transactional information referred to in § 2703(c)(1):

> (c) Records concerning electronic communication service or remote computing service.— (1) A governmental entity may require a provider of electronic communication service or remote computing service to disclose a record or other information pertaining to a subscriber or customer of such service (not including the contents of communications).

The SCA does not define the term "record or other information pertaining to a subscriber or customer of such service," nor has any reported case interpreted the phrase. The legislative history is only slightly more helpful, noting that "the information involved is information about the customer's use of the service."

However, the ECPA does define other terms within § 2703(c)(1). The records to be disclosed must pertain to the subscriber's use of the provider's

IN RE APPLICATION FOR PEN REGISTER AND TRAP *(continued)*

electronic communication service (footnote omitted). The term "electronic communication service" is defined as "any service which provides to users thereof the ability to send or receive *wire or electronic communications*." 18 U.S.C. §§ 2510(15), 2711(1) (emphasis added). The issue now becomes whether tracking device information, such as prospective cell site data, may constitute a record pertaining to "wire or electronic communications," as those terms are defined by the ECPA. If not, then access to such information is not authorized under the SCA.

Here at last the statute ceases to be so murky, yielding more definitive answers. Tracking device information such as cell site data is plainly not a form of electronic communication at all. "Electronic communication" is defined as follows:

[A]ny transfer of signs, signals, writing, images, sounds, data, or intelligence of any nature transmitted in whole or in part by a wire, radio, electromagnetic, photo electronic or photo optical system that affects interstate or foreign commerce, but does not include—

. . .

(C) any communication from a tracking device (as defined in section 3117 of this title); . . .

18 U.S.C. § 2510(12)(C) (emphasis supplied). By virtue of this tracking device exclusion (footnote omitted), no communication from a tracking device can be an electronic communication. Real-time location monitoring effectively converts a cell phone into a tracking device, and therefore cell site data communicated from a cell phone is not an electronic communication under the ECPA.

The definition of "wire communication" does not contain a similarly explicit tracking device exclusion, but the answer is the same nevertheless. "Wire communication" is defined to mean a

communication containing the human voice. Cell site data is not a wire communication under this definition because it does not involve the transfer of the human voice at any point along the path between the cell phone and the cell tower. Although voice communications obviously do take place over a cell phone, this is accomplished on a channel or frequency entirely *separate* from the control channel that transmits the cell site data necessary to set up the call. In fact, while the phone is on, cell site data is constantly transmitted over the control channel, even when the phone is not in use. To summarize, a communication from a tracking device, such as cell site data, is neither an electronic nor a wire communication under the ECPA, and so it does not fall within the range of covered services provided by an "electronic service provider." And since a subscriber does not use the phone to track his own movements in real time, prospective cell site data appears to be unrelated to any *customer* (as opposed to law enforcement) use of the provider's services. Thus, painstaking and methodical analysis of the SCA's technical terms offers no support for treating prospective cell site data as a transactional record under § 2703(c)(1) (footnote omitted).

Even more compelling is the structural argument against allowing access to prospective cell site data under the SCA. Unlike other titles of the ECPA, which regulate methods of real-time surveillance, the SCA regulates access to records and communications in storage. As implied by its full title ("Stored Wire and Electronic Communications and Transactional Records Access"), the entire focus of the SCA is to describe the circumstances under which the government can compel disclosure of existing communications and transaction records in the hands of third party service providers. Nothing in the SCA contemplates a new form

(continued)

of ongoing surveillance in which law enforcement uses co-opted service provider facilities.

Unlike wiretap and pen/trap orders, which are inherently prospective in nature, § 2703(d) orders are inherently retrospective. This distinction is most clearly seen in the duration periods which Congress mandated for wiretap and pen/trap orders. Wiretap orders authorize a maximum surveillance period of 30 days, which begins to run no later than 10 days after the order is entered. Pen/trap orders authorize the installation and use of a pen register for a period "not to exceed sixty days." By contrast, Congress imposed no duration period whatsoever for § 2703(d) orders. Likewise, Congress expressly provided that both wiretap orders and pen/trap orders may be extended by the court for limited periods of time. There is no similar provision for extending § 2703(d) orders. Pen/trap results are ordinarily required to be furnished to law enforcement "at reasonable intervals during regular business hours for the duration of the order." The wiretap statute authorizes periodic reports to the court concerning the progress of the surveillance. Again, nothing resembling such ongoing reporting requirements exists in the SCA.

Another notable omission from § 2703(d) is sealing of court records. Wiretap orders and pen/trap orders are automatically sealed, reflecting the need to keep the ongoing surveillance under wraps. The SCA does not mention sealing. Pen/trap orders must also direct that the service providers not disclose the existence of the order to third parties until otherwise ordered by the court. Section 2705(b) of the SCA authorizes the court to enter a similar non-disclosure order, but only upon a showing of possible adverse consequences, such as "seriously jeopardizing an investigation or unduly delaying a trial." Taken together, the presence of these provisions in other titles of the ECPA and their corresponding absence from the SCA cannot simply be dismissed as a coincidence or congressional absent-mindedness. Pen registers and wiretaps are surveillance techniques for monitoring communications yet to occur, requiring prior judicial approval and continuing oversight during coming weeks and months; § 2703(d) permits access to customer transaction records currently in the hands of the service provider, relating to the customer's past and present use of the service. Like a request for production of documents under Federal Rule of Civil Procedure 34, § 2703(d) contemplates the production of existing records, not documents that may be created at some future date related to some future communication. That is the most obvious explanation why the SCA makes no mention of surveillance periods, extensions, periodic reporting, or sealing. If Congress had not intended the SCA to be retrospective in nature, it would have included the same prospective features it built into the wiretap and pen/trap statutes.

6. CONCLUSION

[T]here is simply no reason to believe that Congress intended to treat location monitoring of cell phones as an exceptional type of electronic surveillance. While Congressional enactments are sometimes difficult to decipher, employing such a three-rail bank shot to create a new category of electronic surveillance seems almost perverse. Had Congress truly intended such an outcome, there were surely more direct avenues far less likely to confound and mislead judicial inquiry.

Denial of the government's request for prospective cell site data in this instance should have no dire consequences for law enforcement. This type of surveillance is unquestionably available upon a traditional probable cause showing under Rule 41. On the other hand, permitting surreptitious conversion of a cell phone into a tracking device without probable cause raises serious Fourth Amendment

---

IN RE APPLICATION FOR PEN REGISTER AND TRAP *(continued)*

concerns, especially when the phone is monitored in the home or other places where privacy is reasonably expected. Absent any sign that Congress has squarely addressed and resolved those concerns in favor of law enforcement, the far more prudent course is to avoid an interpretation which risks a constitutional collision.

Judge Orenstein's opinion was the first word on this topic; this opinion will undoubtedly not be the last. It is written in the full expectation and hope that the government will seek appropriate review by higher courts so that authoritative guidance will be given the magistrate judges who are called upon to rule on these applications on a daily basis.

In 2011 the Department of Justice continued to advocate that the Fourth Amendment doesn't apply because there is not reasonable expectation to privacy in the location data because individuals consent to have the data transmitted from their phones. Consequently, federal law enforcement officers routinely seek location data as well as other records. There have been challenges and several federal court decisions subsequent to the Texas case you read have been issued on the questions; whether the Patriot Act authorizes warrantless "real time" monitoring of the location of cell phones and if so, whether this is consonant with the Fourth Amendment. In the meantime, the advent of global positioning system technology in cell phones has made it even easier to track the whereabouts of individuals carrying phones loaded with gps programs.[29] Congress has not specifically addressed the subject and the Supreme Court has not heard the issue.

Stored Communications and Subscriber Records

The Stored Communications Act[30] amendment to Title III authorizes government access to information stored by telecommunications, cable, and Internet provider companies. This includes voice mail and e-mail.

The Stored Communications Act differentiates between information stored for less than 6 months and information stored for longer periods. The greater protection is afforded to communications stored less than 6 months. If 180 days or less, a warrant, supported by probable cause is required. If 181 days or longer, either a warrant supported by probable cause or in the alternative, notice must be provided to the subscriber; a court order, administrative, or trial or grand jury subpoena must be issued; and there must be specific and articulable facts showing that reasonable grounds exist to believe the data sought are relevant and material to an ongoing investigation.

The statute also requires a communications provider to give the government access to client information, including name, address, telephone address, session information, and means of payment data (e.g., credit card number). Probable cause and a warrant are not required for this disclosure. Instead, the requirement is for specific and articulable facts supporting a reasonable belief that the records sought are relevant to an ongoing investigation. In counterintelligence and terrorism investigations, the government can obtain stored information simply by certifying that the records are relevant to the investigation.

Violators of the Stored Communications Act are subject to both civil and criminal penalties, although the prison terms and fines are lesser than for violations of the Wiretap Act. Unlike the Wiretap Act, data obtained in violation of the Stored Communications Act are admissible in a criminal prosecution of the accused. Service providers who violate the Stored Communications Act are shielded with absolute immunity from liability. This provision is substantially different from the "acting in the normal course of employment" immunity for violations of the Wiretap Act.

Pen Registers and Trap Devices

A pen register is a device that is attached to a telephone line to record the numbers of outgoing calls. A trap and trace device records the numbers of incoming calls. Neither of these devices records or accesses the content of telephone conversations. Because they do not access content, they are not governed by the Fourth Amendment or by the 1968 Title III act. Further, the Supreme Court had held that a person does not possess a privacy interest in the numbers that he or she dials.[31] Even though not required by the Fourth Amendment, the 1986 ECPA[32] requires federal and state law enforcement officers to obtain a court order to install such a device. However, the standard for issuance of the order is relatively low. An officer only needs to certify that the information likely to be obtained is "relevant" to an ongoing criminal investigation. The court to which the application for the order is made does not make an independent decision. Once certified, the court must issue the order. The statute specifically authorizes ex parte issuance of such orders.

Because the Act was adopted before the advent of e-mail, the legal requirements for identifying the recipients and senders of e-mail was unknown until 2001. The Patriot Act answered this question by expanding the definition of pen registers to include computer software that records identifying information of e-mail, such as Internet Protocol addresses. Further, the authority of court orders for computer information was expanded to include the entire nation. Previously, such orders could be executed only in the federal district where they were issued. Given the national nature of Internet communications, law enforcement officials often had to seek multiple warrants during a single investigation.

In recent years, the Federal Bureau of Investigation has done just that. In June 2007, the FBI obtained a court order to send spyware (CIPAV) to a computer used by a person who had been sending bomb threats to a school near Olympia, Washington. The attempt was successful, resulting in the arrest and conviction of a juvenile who had been a student at the school. CIPAV, an acronym for computer and Internet protocol address verifier, was created by the FBI. How CIPAV works is not precisely known. But it appears to imbed software in a suspect's computer that then reports identifying information back to the FBI.

Another FBI program, Carnivore, has been the subject of some controversy. Carnivore is a computer wiretap system. The system requires a hardware installation at a suspect's Internet service provider (ISP). Once installed, it can detect and filter all e-mail correspondence to and from a computer. Civil libertarians were concerned that the program would be installed without court order and that there would be no genuine filtering of messages for those related to possible criminal conduct. The FBI reports that it is no longer using Carnivore in favor of a similar program, Digital Collection System 1000 (DCS1000).

Yet another type of program used by the FBI has begun to attract attention—key logger systems (KLS). These programs record the keystrokes a computer enters. The FBI uses such programs to gain access to computer files that are password protected, especially those that are encrypted.

In 2001, a new FBI KLS program, Magic Lantern, is reported to have the ability to remotely record key strokes, using e-mail or other transmissions to enter a suspect's computer.

Another interesting development during the George W. Bush administration was the assertion that the president possesses, pursuant to the commander-in-chief authority of Article II and Congressional authorization to use force to respond to the 9/11 attacks, the authority to order wiretaps without seeking FISA approval. In 2006, a U.S. district court held otherwise; and before the Sixth Circuit Court of Appeals heard the case, President Bush withdrew the assertion and agreed to use the established FISA procedure.[33]

National Security Surveillance

In 2013 Edward Snowden, an employee of the National Security Agency (NSA), the lead U.S. agency responsible for collecting foreign intelligence and for securing U.S. intelligence systems, disclosed sensitive information to the press. The United States charged him with espionage and theft of government property, he fled the United States, and he was eventually awarded temporary asylum by Russia.[34] His case became an international media sensation, provoking discussions around the world about data collection by governments, about democratic governance (privacy v. national security), international relations, and about the specific information that was disclosed, much of it embarrassing to the United States. But Snowden's case wasn't the first to raise the questions about information collection in the post-9/11 United States. There were other disclosures and discoveries, by federal government employees and others, that caused many people to worry about the erosion of privacy and abuses of power by federal officials. Indeed, the Department of Justice acknowledged that the NSA collected private data in violation of the law, although rarely.[35] As you will see below, at least one federal court has also found that the NSA violated national security law in its collection of data on U.S. persons in its Terrorist Surveillance Program.

Earlier you learned some of the criminal laws of national security, laws of sedition, treason, and terrorism. National security is receiving special attention in this book because the rise in the terror threat in the United States has resulted in greater surveillance and detention authority by federal officials and because there has been a rapid increase in technology that enables surveillance into nearly every corner of life and mind.

National security law is highly complicated, spanning criminal law, administrative law, and constitutional law. The most significant legislation is the Foreign Intelligence Surveillance Act of 1978 (FISA).[36] FISA regulates the collection of foreign intelligence by government officers, whether through wiretaps, pen registers, trap devices, and other electronic means, The 1978 FISA Act, which was enacted in response to intelligence gathering by the President Nixon administration, was substantively amended by the United and Strengthening America by Providing Appropriate Tools Required to Intercept and Obstruct Terrorism Act of 2001 (aka Patriot Act) and again in 2007 and 2008. These amendments widened the authority of federal officials to gather intelligence, often without court order.

Balancing the need for oversight and for secrecy, Congress provided in FISA for the establishment of the Foreign Intelligence Surveillance Court (FISC) and the Foreign Intelligence Act Court of Review (FISC). These courts are staffed by Article III federal judges who are appointed to the courts by the Chief Justice of the United States Supreme Court. FISC has the responsibility of issuing surveillance orders and reporting on its activities to Congress. FISCR acts as FISC's appellate court. FISCR's decisions may be appealed to the Supreme Court of the United States. In the interests of national security, both courts meet in secret. Although its hearings and deliberations are secret, the membership of the courts and their annual reports to Congress are available to the public. Select FISC orders, particularly those interpreting FISA, have been made public. In addition to FISC's reports, the Department of Justice issues an annual report to Congress summarizing its FISA activities, including its applications for FISC orders, surveillance conducted without FISC order, and summaries of surveillance conducted.

FISA, and many judicial decisions that predated FISA, is constructed around the idea that the Fourth Amendment distinguishes standard criminal cases from national security cases. Criminal investigations are aimed at preventing, discovering, and punishing crime, typically targeting persons in the United States, while national security cases are aimed at preventing attack and protecting the political, economic, social interests of the United States through surveillance of foreign governments and their agents. At the highest levels, the distinction is clear. Closer to the ground, in individual cases, it is more difficult to discern. The legal distinction is significant.

In an attempt to preserve the balance between privacy of U.S. persons and the need to gather data threatening the security of the Nation, FISA initially authorized the United States to "spy" on two targets: foreign powers and agents of foreign powers. Foreign governments, officers of foreign governments, and entities doing the work of foreign governments are all foreign powers. Agents of foreign powers include anyone, except U.S. citizens and permanent residents, who act on behalf of foreign governments in clandestine information gathering in the United States. So the original FISA applied to foreign governments and their spies.

Through the Patriot Act and other amendments to FISA, the definition of foreign power has been expanded to include groups engaged in international terrorism, foreign political groups that are not substantially composed of U.S. persons, and entities not substantially composed of U.S. persons engaged in the international proliferation of weapons of mass destruction. Agents of foreign powers have also been expanded to include non-U.S. persons engaged in international terrorism or the international proliferation of weapons of mass destruction, even if unconnected to a foreign power.

FISA applies to the collection of foreign intelligence. The provisions of FISA authorizing the United States to collect data apply only if it can be shown that the data relate to, or are necessary to prevent, attacks or other grave hostile acts upon the United States by a foreign power or agents of foreign powers, the proliferation of weapons of mass destruction, spying on the United States, espionage, or are needed to advance foreign affairs or the security of the Nation.

Generally an FISC order is required for the federal government to conduct foreign intelligence surveillance. FISC must find that probable cause exists to believe that the target of the surveillance is a foreign power or an agent of a foreign power and that the form of communication to be intercepted is in the foreign powers control. Business records orders are easier for the government to obtain. The government only has to show that the records are relevant to an ongoing investigation.

During ordered surveillance, FISA requires the Attorney General to "minimize" the acquisition, retention, and dissemination of records about U.S. persons. In cases where intelligence officers and law enforcement officers are working together, a "wall" must be created, keeping records acquired during foreign surveillance from criminal investigators. That evidence must be obtained by criminal investigators by other means.

There are two instances where an FISC order is not required for surveillance. The president may authorize surveillance if the Attorney General certifies, under oath, that the communication devices to be monitored belong to foreign powers or that it is "technical intelligence" from a foreign power being sought. The law is clear that U.S. persons are not to be targets: "There is no substantial likelihood that the surveillance will acquire the contents of any communication to which a U.S. person is a party." Additionally, the Attorney General is to minimize and report these activities. Since an amendment to FISA in 1995, the president is also authorized to order the intrusion of physical spaces controlled by foreign governments in order to collect intelligence. FISC has the same authority.

The 1978 version of FISA required that *the purpose of foreign surveillance* be the collection of foreign intelligence. In a highly criticized change, the Patriot Act softened *the purpose* requirement to *significant purpose*, thereby permitting the government to have other primary objectives, such as gathering criminal evidence.

Generally, the president is authorized, through the Attorney General, to college foreign intelligence information from foreign governments for as long as a year. If the target is an agent of a foreign government, the Attorney General must petition FISC for an order.

FISA also empowers the government to obtain data from third parties, typically communication companies. In some instances, third parties have voluntarily provided information or access to their systems for the government to collect data. In others, the government has obtained FISC orders. In recent years third-party authority has been scrutinized in the context of metadata, or non content information. An example of metadata is the government's collection of phone numbers dialed but not the content of those conversations. In its review of an application for an order to capture a huge amount of "telephony metadata," FISC ruled in 2013 that such intelligence gathering is analogous to the phone records sought in *Smith v. Maryland*.[37] In that case the Supreme Court held that when an individual dials a phone number he is transmitting the data to a third party, the telephone company, and as a consequence loses his privacy in the number he dialed. For this reason the acquisition of the number dialed, but not the content of the call, does not raise implicate the Fourth Amendment. FISC held that this conclusion is not changed because of the size of the data request.[38] The amendments to the FISA mentioned earlier empowered the Foreign Intelligence Surveillance Court to review and approve programs that collect metadata, in addition to individual orders of surveillance.

One particularly controversial authority created by the Patriot Act is the National Security Letter. Without subpoena, the government is empowered to demand non-content data from Internet service providers, communication companies, and businesses about their clients. Again, non content data include web sites visited, telephone numbers called, and e-mail addresses. Thousands, in some years tens of thousands, of NSLs have been issued yearly since 9/11. NSLs come with a "gag" order. That is, the recipient of the NSL is ordered, under criminal penalty, to not disclose to anyone, including the client who is named in the NSL, that the letter has been received. A federal district judge found this and other provisions of the NSL law to be contrary to the First Amendment's protection of free speech and the Fourth Amendment in 2013.[39]

FISC is aimed at foreign governments and its agents, abroad. As you can see, the authority of the United States to spy on U.S. persons abroad is limited to when U.S. persons are acting as foreign agents and when engaged in terrorism. If the United States wants to conduct a search within the United States, the Fourth Amendment and Title III rules you have already learned apply, even if the underlying offense is a violation of a national security law. If the government acquires otherwise protected information during an otherwise legitimate surveillance, the information is to be destroyed unless the contents indicate a threat of serious bodily harm or death to any person.

An extended discussion of national security law is beyond the scope of a criminal law and procedure text. Be aware, however, that many other statutes, executive orders, and judicial decisions exist defining this rapidly evolving area of law.

PRETRIAL IDENTIFICATION PROCEDURES

Law enforcement officers use a variety of techniques to identify a person as a criminal, such as eyewitness identifications, fingerprinting, blood tests, and, recently, deoxyribonucleic acid (DNA) tests. The use of any of these procedures raises certain constitutional issues, such as the right to be free from self-incrimination and the right to counsel.

There is also another concern: reliability. Eyewitness identification, though powerful, has a few inherent problems. First, each person will testify to his or her perception of an event, and people often perceive the same event differently. Second, not every person will use the same language to describe what was witnessed. Third, a witness may simply have a faulty memory and unintentionally testify to an untruth. Fourth, for a variety of reasons, a witness may intentionally lie.

Scientific testing may also prove to be invalid or unreliable. How accurate is the test when performed properly? Was the test performed properly in this case? Is the evidence tested actually the defendant's? These types of questions are asked of expert witnesses who testify to the results of scientific testing. This discussion begins with eyewitness identification procedures.

Eyewitness Identification

An eyewitness' identification of an offender is often a key piece of evidence in criminal cases. It is generally regarded that eyewitness testimony is one of the most persuasive forms of evidence that can be presented to jurors.

Fairness in Identification

There are two competing values concerning the reliability of evidence at trial. The first concerns the nature of the jury trial. The system is constructed around the jury as the finder of fact. In the extreme, jurors should hear all evidence and be trusted to distinguish between the reliable and unreliable. The other value is one of fair process, as enshrined in the due process clauses. Due process demands that seriously unreliable evidence with withheld from a jury.

The Supreme Court has issued several decisions that are intended to establish the balance of these competing values. In *Stoval v. Denno,* 388 U.S. 293 (1967), the Supreme Court found that the Due Process Clauses of the Fifth and Fourteenth Amendments prohibit identifications that are so *unnecessarily suggestive* that there is a real chance of misidentification. In addition to being impermissibly suggestive, an identification must be *unreliable* to be excluded.[40] *Wade* illustrates these concepts as applied to lineups.

UNITED STATES V. WADE
338 U.S. 218 (1967)

The question here is whether courtroom identifications of an accused at trial are to be excluded from evidence because the accused was exhibited to the witness before trial at a post-indictment lineup conducted for identification purposes without notice to and in the absence of the accused's appointed counsel.

The federally insured bank in Eustace, Texas, was robbed on September 21, 1964. A man with a small strip of tape on each side of his face entered the bank, pointed a pistol at the female cashier and the vice president, the only persons in the bank at the time, and forced them to fill a pillowcase with

(continued)

UNITED STATES V. WADE (continued)

the bank's money. The man then drove away with an accomplice who had been waiting in a stolen car outside the bank. On March 23, 1965, an indictment was returned against respondent, Wade, and two others for conspiring to rob the bank, and against Wade and accomplice for the robbery itself.

Wade was arrested on April 2, and counsel was appointed to represent him on April 26. Fifteen days later an FBI agent, without notice to Wade's lawyer, arranged to have the two bank employees observe a lineup made up of Wade and five or six other prisoners and conducted in a courtroom of the local county courthouse. Each person in the line wore strips of tape such as allegedly worn by the robber and upon direction each said something like "put the money in the bag," the words allegedly uttered by the robber. Both bank employees identified Wade in the lineup as the bank robber.

At trial, the two employees, when asked on direct examination if the robber was in the courtroom, pointed to Wade. The prior lineup identification was then elicited from both employees on cross examination. . . . But the confrontation compelled by the State between the accused and the victim or witnesses to a crime to elicit identification evidence is peculiarly riddled with innumerable dangers and variable factors which might seriously, even crucially, derogate from a fair trial. The vagaries of eyewitness identification are well-known; the annals of criminal law are rife with instances of mistaken identification. . . . The identification of strangers is proverbially untrustworthy. . . . A major factor contributing to the high incidence of miscarriage of justice from mistaken identification has been the degree of suggestion inherent in the manner in which the prosecution presents the suspect to witness for pretrial identification. A commentator has observed that "[t]he influence of improper suggestion upon identifying witnesses probably accounts for more miscarriages of justice than any other single

factor—perhaps it is responsible for more such errors than all other factors combined.". . . Suggestion can be created intentionally or unintentionally in many subtle ways. And the dangers for the suspect are particularly grave when the witness' opportunity for observation was insubstantial, and thus his susceptibility to suggestion the greatest.

> Moreover, "[i]t is a matter of common experience that, once a witness has picked out the accused at the lineup, he is not likely to go back on his word later on, so that in practice the issue of identity may (in the absence of other relevant evidence) for all practical purposes be determined there and then, before the trial.". . .

What facts have been disclosed in specific cases about the conduct of pretrial confrontations for identification illustrate both the potential for substantial prejudice to the accused at that stage and the need for its revelation at trial. A commentator provides some striking examples:

> In a Canadian case . . . the defendant had been picked out of a lineup of six men, of which he was the only Oriental. In other cases, a black-haired suspect was placed among a group of light-haired persons, tall suspects have been made to stand with short nonsuspects, and, in a case where the perpetrator of the crime was known to be a youth, a suspect under twenty was placed in a lineup with five other persons, all of whom were forty or over.

Similarly, state reports, in the course of describing prior identifications admitted as evidence of guilt, reveal numerous instances of suggestive procedures, for example, that all in the lineup, but the suspects were known to the identifying witness, that the other participants in a lineup were grossly dissimilar in appearance to the suspect, that only the suspect was required to wear distinctive clothing which the culprit allegedly wore. . . .

UNITED STATES V. WADE *(continued)*

Since it appears that there is grave potential for prejudice, intentional or not, in the pretrial lineup, which may not be capable of reconstruction at trial, and since presence of counsel can often avert prejudice and assure a meaningful confrontation at trial, there can be little doubt that for Wade the post--indictment lineup was a critical stage of the prosecution at which [he] was [entitled to counsel]. . . .

[The Court then concluded that in-court identifications must be excluded if they follow a lineup at which a defendant is not permitted counsel, unless the in-court identification has an independent origin.]

Evidence is not automatically excluded even when police employ an identification procedure that is unnecessarily suggestive. Instead the trial court is to make an independent determination whether the process was unreliable, e.g. created a *substantial likelihood of misidentification*. If so, the identification is to be excluded. When making the substantial likelihood of misidentification decision, a court is to examine the "totality of the circumstances" surrounding the identification. Examples of impermissibly suggestive were mentioned in the *Wade* opinion. For example, if a witness states that a white male committed a crime, it would be improper to exhibit four black men and one white man in a lineup.

Wade, Stoval, and these other decisions defining this area of law were issued in the 1970s. Subsequently a wealth of research in human memory has called the reliability of eyewitness identification into question. The problems of unconscious bias, blurred memory, the ways memories are stored and retrieved, and the phenomena of reconstructed memory make memory fallible and often unreliable.

The advent of forensic identification procedures that are highly accurate, such as DNA testing, have been used to establish the innocence of many people whose convictions were proven, often largely, by eyewitness identification. Eyewitness identification played a role in the conviction of as many as 75% of convictions that were overturned through DNA testing.[41] The problem of wrongful convictions, because of eyewitness misidentification and other causes, is so acute that a non profit group formed to raise funds, provide legal defense, and support research. The Innocence Project reports that more than 250 people have been exonerated using DNA testing since 1989.[42]

Consequently many people have called for a more critical review of eyewitness testimony than required by the 1970s decisions. The Court rejected this position in *Perry v. New Hampsire* (2012). The defendant in this case urged the Court to modify the test from requiring proof police created a suggestive situation to any suggestive circumstance, police created or not. The defendant pointed to the large number of studies that demonstrate the unreliability of eyewitness identifications in support of his position. Rejecting the proposition the Court found that (1) one of the purposes of the unnecessarily suggestive rule it had created was to deter police misconduct and that extending the protection in the manner suggested would not achieve this goal; (2) juries should be trusted to determine the reliability of evidence in all but the most extreme cases; (3) trial judges have the authority, both constitutionally and through rules of evidence, to exclude evidence that is misleading or prejudicial; and (4) the trial judge instructed the jury in how to evaluate the reliability of the eyewitness testimony.

Lineups and Showups

A **lineup** is where the police exhibit a group of people, among whom is the suspect, to a witness or victim for identification as the criminal. A one-man **showup** is an exhibition of one person to a witness or victim for identification as the criminal.

In practice, police first conduct a lineup and then, if the suspect is identified, the witness is asked at trial to testify that he or she identified the perpetrator of the crime at the lineup. Therefore, if the initial identification is faulty, the subsequent in-court identification is also faulty. Even if the witness is asked to identify anew the perpetrator of the crime, such an identification is tainted by the witness's earlier identification.

One-man showups, obviously, are more suggestive of guilt than lineups are. As such, they should be used with caution. Generally, a one-man showup should occur soon after the crime (minutes or hours). If there is time to organize a lineup, this is the preferable method of identification procedure.

The Right to Counsel

Wade mandates that counsel be provided at pretrial lineups and showups. For years it was unknown whether this meant all pretrial lineups and showups or just those after the Sixth Amendment attaches. *Kirby v. Illinois,* (1972)[43] resolved this dispute by requiring counsel only after initiation of "adversary judicial proceedings—whether by way of formal charge, preliminary hearing, indictment, information, or arraignment."

Self-Incrimination

It is not violative of the Fifth Amendment's privilege against self-incrimination for a defendant to be compelled to appear in a lineup. The privilege against selfincrimination applies to "testimony" and not to physical acts, such as walking, gesturing, measuring, or speaking certain words for identification purposes.[44] If a defendant has changed in appearance, he or she may be made to shave, to don a wig or hairpiece, or wear a certain article of clothing.

The question under the Fifth Amendment is whether the act requested is "communicative." If so, then the defendant may not be compelled to engage in the act. If not, the opposite is true.

Photographs

Today, witness identification through photo arrays are more common than lineups. The due process test discussed earlier applies to the use of photos; that is, the event must not be impermissibly suggestive and unreliable. The showing of one picture is likely to be determined improper, absent an emergency. As is true of lineups, the people

lineup

■ A group of persons, placed side by side in a line, shown to a witness of a crime to see if the witness will identify the person suspected of committing the crime. A *lineup* should not be staged so that it is suggestive of one person.

showup

■ A pretrial Identification procedure in which only one suspect and a witness are brought together.

in the photos should be similar in appearance. Also, a "mug shot" (a picture taken by law enforcement agencies after arrest) of the accused should not be mixed with ordinary photos of nonsuspects. Nor should the photos be presented in such a manner that the defendant's picture stands out.

The Supreme Court has determined that there is no right to counsel at a photo identification session, either before initiation of the adversary judicial proceeding or thereafter.

Forensic Identification Procedures

Law enforcement officials may use scientific methods of identification to prove that a defendant committed a crime. Fingerprinting, blood tests, genetic tests (deoxyribonucleic acid, or DNA, testing), voice tests, and handwriting samples are examples of such techniques.

Such tests are not critical stages of the criminal proceedings, and, accordingly, there is no right to counsel. There is also no right to refuse to cooperate with such testing on Fifth Amendment grounds, because the defendant is not being required to give testimony. However, if a test involves an invasion of privacy, then the Fourth Amendment requires probable cause before the procedure may be forced on an unwilling defendant.

Confrontation and Cross-examination Clause issues are raised when forensic experts testify as to what other experts have found or analyzed. See Chapter 15 for a more thorough discussion of these issues.

Validity and Reliability

Scientific evidence must be reliable before it may be introduced at trial. In a landmark case, *Frye v. United States,* 293 F. 1013 (D.C. Cir. 1923), it was held that scientific techniques must be generally accepted as valid and reliable by the scientific community to be admissible. *Frye* was the law from 1923 until the Supreme Court issued *Daubert v. Merrell Dow Pharmaceuticals,* 113 S. Ct. 2786 (1993). *Daubert* changed the standard of admissibility from acceptance in the scientific community to scientific validity. Under this new standard, the trial judge is required to make a preliminary determination that the proffered evidence is valid before it may be presented to a jury. In making this decision, the trial judge is to consider the following factors:

1. Whether the evidence or theory has, or can be, tested.
2. Whether it has been reviewed and tested by other scientists.
3. Whether the method has been published and the quality of the publication(s) in which it is found.
4. Whether its error rate and other potential defects are known.
5. Whether standards and protocols for its use have been established.
6. Whether its use is widely accepted in the relevant scientific community.

Techniques that are experimental and not highly reliable are not admissible. A few common scientific techniques are discussed here. Note that the results of a specific test may be denied admission, even if the scientific basis of the testing is valid, if the test is administered incorrectly. Further, scientific testing also raises Fourth, Fifth, Sixth, and Fourteenth Amendment issues, some of which are discussed later.

Fingerprinting

A fingerprint consists of several identifiable characteristics, such as loops, arches, whorls, islands, and bifurcations. The arrangement, frequency, and design of these features are among the many characteristics used to distinguish prints from one another. See Exhibit 13–4. Although it is common to state that every person has a unique set of prints, there is a possibility of duplication. However, the odds of that occurring have been estimated to be as low as one in 64 billion.[45]

Fingerprint identification is a highly accurate science and is universally accepted by federal and state courts.[46] Federal and state law enforcement agencies, as well as international agencies, possess libraries of fingerprints. Through the use of computers, fingerprints lifted from crime scenes, weapons, and other objects can be matched to a particular individual's fingerprints in a matter of minutes. Lifted prints may be matched to a print already on file or to a print taken from a suspect.

Exhibit 13–4 A FINGERPRINT

© Seth Joel/Digital Vision/Getty Images

The taking of fingerprints does not implicate the Fifth Amendment, because the accused is not compelled to give testimony. Further, it is not a search to take a suspect's fingerprints. This being so, neither probable cause nor a warrant is required to take the suspect's prints. Courts have analogized fingerprints to physical characteristics such as hair and eye color. Because it is not an invasion of a reasonable expectation to privacy (search) for an officer to visually observe a defendant, courts have reasoned that it is not an invasion of privacy to observe and record a suspect's fingerprints.

Blood Testing

Blood testing is commonly employed and universally accepted by courts in the United States. Although the science of blood testing is generally beyond scrutiny, individual blood tests are not. Laboratories make mistakes, and both the defense and the prosecution may challenge a particular test.

Securing a suspect's blood is different from rolling a fingerprint. The process of withdrawing blood involves a bodily invasion and the possibility of pain and infection. Therefore, a person's expectation of privacy is higher when the government seeks blood rather than fingerprints. Whether the government possesses the authority to compel a suspect to undergo a blood test was the subject of *Schmerber v. California*.

Schmerber stands for the principle that the withdrawal of blood, as well as other bodily intrusive procedures, constitutes a search under the Fourth Amendment. Probable cause is required, as is a warrant, unless exigent circumstances, such as those in *Schmerber,* justify bypassing the warrant requirement. In addition, such procedures must be conducted in a safe, discrete, medical environment.

SCHMERBER V. CALIFORNIA
384 U.S. 757 (1966)

Petitioner was convicted in Los Angeles Municipal Court of the criminal offense of driving an automobile while under the influence of intoxicating liquor. He had been arrested at a hospital while receiving treatment for injuries suffered in an accident involving the automobile that he was apparently driving. At the direction of a police officer, a blood sample was then withdrawn from petitioner's body by a physician at the hospital. The chemical analysis of this sample revealed a percent by weight of alcohol in his blood at the time of the offense which indicated intoxication, and the report of this analysis was admitted in evidence at trial. . . .

II. THE PRIVILEGE AGAINST SELF-INCRIMINATION CLAIM

. . . We . . . must now decide whether the withdrawal of the blood and admission in evidence of the analysis involved in this case violated petitioner's privilege. We hold that the privilege protects an accused only from being compelled to testify against himself, or otherwise provide the State with evidence of a testimonial or communicative nature, and that the withdrawal of blood and use of the analysis in question in this case did not involve compulsion to these ends. . . .

(continued)

SCHMERBER V. CALIFORNIA *(continued)*

IV. THE SEARCH AND SEIZURE CLAIM

The overriding function of the Fourth Amendment is to protect personal privacy and dignity against unwarranted intrusion by the State. . . .

The values protected by the Fourth Amendment thus substantially overlap those the Fifth Amendment helps to protect. . . .

Because we are dealing with intrusions into the human body rather than with state interferences with property relationships or private papers—"house, papers, and effect"—we write on a clean slate. . . .

In this case, as will often be true when charges of driving under the influence of alcohol are pressed, these questions arise in the context of an arrest made by an officer without a warrant. Here, there was plainly probable cause for the officer to arrest petitioner and charge him with driving an automobile while under the influence of intoxicating liquor. The police officer who arrived at the scene shortly after the accident smelled liquor on petitioner's breath, and testified that petitioner's eyes were "bloodshot, watery, sort of a glassy appearance." The officer saw petitioner again at the hospital, within two hours of the accident. There he noticed similar symptoms of drunkenness. He thereupon informed petitioner "that he was under arrest and that he was entitled to the services of an attorney, and that he could remain silent, and that anything he told me would be used against him in evidence.". . .

Although the facts which established probable cause to arrest in this case also suggested the required relevance and likely success of a test of petitioner's blood for alcohol, the question remains whether the arresting officer was permitted to draw these inferences himself, or was required instead to procure a warrant before proceeding with the test. Search warrants are ordinarily required for searches of dwellings, and, absent an emergency, no less could be required where intrusions of the human body are concerned. . . . The importance of informed, detached and deliberate determinations of the issue whether or not to invade another's body in search of evidence of guilt is indisputable and great.

The officer in the present case, however, might reasonably have believed that he was confronted with an emergency, in which the delay necessary to obtain a warrant, under the circumstances, threatened "the destruction of evidence.". . . We are told that the percentage of alcohol in the blood begins to diminish shortly after drinking stops, as the body functions to eliminate it from the system. Particularly in a case such as this, where time had to be taken to bring the accused to a hospital and to investigate the scene of the accident, there was no time to seek out a magistrate and secure a warrant. . . .

Finally, the records show that the test was performed in a reasonable manner. Petitioner's blood was taken by physician in a hospital environment according to accepted medical practices. We are thus not presented with the serious questions which would arise if a search involving use of a medical technique, even of the most rudimentary sort, were made by other than medical personnel or in other than a medical environment—for example, if it were administered by police in the privacy of the stationhouse. To tolerate searches under these conditions might be to invite an unjustified element of personal risk of infection and pain.

The Supreme Court refused to create a per se rule out of the *Schmerber* decision in the 2013 case *Missouri v. McNeely*. In that case, Missouri argued that the inherently evanescent nature of alcohol justified, per *Schmerber,* the routine warrantless drawing the blood of drivers who refuse to submit to breath testing and where police have probable cause to believe the drivers have been driving while intoxicated. The Court penned

It is true that as a result of the human body's natural metabolic processes, the alcohol level in a person's blood begins to dissipate once the alcohol is fully absorbed and continues to decline until the alcohol is eliminated. . . . But it does not follow that we should depart from careful case-by-case assessment of exigency and adopt the categorical rule proposed by the State and its amici. In those drunk-driving investigations where police officers can reasonably obtain a warrant before a blood sample can be drawn without significantly undermining the efficacy of the search, the Fourth Amendment mandates that they do so.

The context of blood testing is different in critical respects from other destruction-of-evidence cases in which the police are truly confronted with a "'now or never'" situation. In contrast to, for example, circumstances in which the suspect has control over easily disposable evidence, BAC evidence from a drunk-driving suspect naturally dissipates over time in a gradual and relatively predictable manner. Moreover, because a police officer must typically transport a drunk-driving suspect to a medical facility and obtain the assistance of someone with appropriate medical training before conducting a blood test, some delay between the time of the arrest or accident and the time of the test is inevitable regardless of whether police officers are required to obtain a warrant.

The State's proposed per se rule also fails to account for advances in the 47 years since Schmerber was decided that allow for the more expeditious processing of warrant applications, particularly in contexts like drunk-driving investigations where the evidence offered to establish probable cause is simple. The Federal Rules of Criminal Procedure were amended in 1977 to permit federal magistrate judges to issue a warrant based on sworn testimony communicated by telephone. As amended, the law now allows a federal magistrate judge to con- sider "information communicated by telephone or other reliable electronic means." Fed. Rule Crim. Proc. 4.1. States have also innovated. Well over a majority of States allow police officers or prosecutors to apply for search warrants remotely through various means, including telephonic or radio communication, electronic communication such as e-mail, and video conferencing. And in addition to technology-based developments, jurisdictions have found other ways to streamline the warrant process, such as by using standard-form warrant applications for drunk-driving investigations.

The extent of the intrusion in to the body, the medical risk of the intrusion, and the likelihood of the evidence being lost to delay are all factors in the decision whether a warrant must be obtained. In *Cupp v. Murphy*, for example, the warrantless scraping of blood from the fingernail of an accused murderer was upheld by the Supreme Court because it involved no medical risk and the risk of destruction of the evidence was large.[47]

But the opposite conclusion was reached in *Winston v. Lee,*[48] where the Supreme Court employed the analysis outlined in *Schmerber* and concluded that a defendant accused of armed robbery could not be compelled to undergo surgery to remove a bullet from his chest. The Court held that the suspect's interest in his health and bodily privacy outweighed the government's interest in obtaining the evidence. Also important to the Court was the fact that the government had other evidence to prove the defendant's guilt. This lowered the government's interest in having the bullet removed. If the bullet had been critical to the government's case, the result might have been different.

DNA Testing

Deoxyribonucleic acid (DNA) is a complex compound with two strands that spiral around one another, forming a double helix. Within the helix are molecules, called *nucleotide bases,* that connect the strands. There are four bases, identified by the letters A, T, G, and C. The A base of one strand attaches to the T base of its counterpart strand. In the same manner, the G base of one strand connects to the C base of the opposing strand. There are more than 3 billion base pairs in human DNA. However, only 3 million of these differ from person to person. The precise vertical ordering of these pairs determines a person's genetic code. See Exhibit 13–5.

Exhibit 13–5   A DNA STRAND

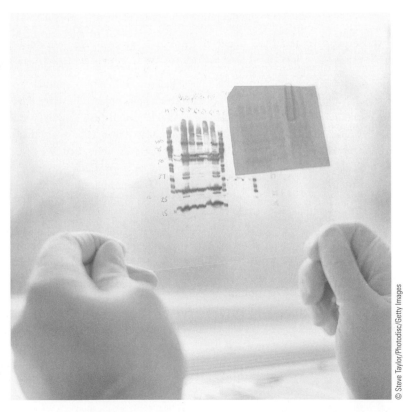

© Steve Taylor/Photodisc/Getty Images

Through biological specimens, such as hair, blood, tissue, and semen, evidence from crime scenes can be compared with specimens from suspects. This testing is known as **DNA printing** or *genetic fingerprinting*. DNA printing compares the codes and determines if they are from the same individual. DNA testing is sophisticated, and if properly performed, nearly conclusively establishes identity. The possibility of a chance match, assuming perfect testing, has been estimated to be 1 in 3 trillion.[49]

DNA has proven to be an effective weapon for both prosecutors and defendants. In recent years, several convicted felons have used DNA testing to prove their innocence and secure their release. This has occurred, for example, in rape cases where blood and semen were used as prosecution evidence, but DNA testing was unavailable. After their conviction, and from prison, these men used DNA testing to establish their innocence and set aside their verdicts. Prosecutors are increasingly relying on DNA evidence to prove their cases. DNA evidence was first used in a criminal prosecution in the United States in 1987. Forty-two percent of prosecutors reported having used DNA evidence by 1994, and the number rose to 68 percent by 2001. DNA evidence is most commonly used in sexual assault and murder cases. Overall, conviction rates in cases where prosecutors have introduced DNA evidence are high.

DNA testing is not perfect. The testing method is sophisticated, and errors can be made. For instance, methodology was hotly contested in the O. J. Simpson murder trial of 1995. Further, interpretations of test results differ. It is, therefore, imperative that a reliable laboratory be selected. Further, in some cases, the defense and prosecution may have independent DNA testing conducted. Despite the possibility of error (false positive and false negative findings), courts have generally held that DNA evidence is sufficiently reliable for admission into evidence. The parties may, of course, challenge the accuracy of a particular DNA test.[50]

In recent years the federal government and several states have enacted legislation concerning the use of DNA in criminal proceedings. For example, Congress authorized the creation of a national DNA database (CODIS) in 1994. Ironically, however, the statute did not authorize the collections of samples; CODIS remained unused until 2000, when federal law was changed to require the collection of samples from all individuals convicted of federal crimes.

Today, statutes in all 50 states authorize state and local officials to collect DNA samples from individuals convicted of terrorism, violent, sexual, and some property crimes. These samples are entered in CODIS. In 2006, the federal DNA Fingerprint Act of 2005 became effective.[51] This law expands collection of DNA samples to include individuals arrested and detained by federal authorities. However, DNA samples are to be destroyed and records expunged for individuals whose cases have been dismissed.

In many states and the federal government, another recent change in law has been the use of DNA evidence to toll the applicable statute of limitation. In such jurisdictions, law enforcement may use the DNA fingerprint in lieu of a name to file the charge and obtain an arrest warrant for the individual identified by the DNA. Once the warrant is issued, the statute of limitation is tolled. A few states, including Colorado, have gone so far as to automatically toll the statute after a suspect has been identified by DNA evidence.[52]

DNA printing

■ Comparing body tissue samples (such as blood, skin, hair, or semen) to see if the genetic materials match. The process is used to identify criminals by comparing their DNA with that found at a crime scene, and it is used to identify a child's parent. Most states allow its use as evidence.

An open question is whether police must have probable cause or obtain a warrant before conducting non invasive **DNA** tests, such as cheek swabs. Similarly, the question whether one has a right to counsel at pretrial non invasive **DNA** testing hasn't been answered by the Supreme Court. At least one state court has determined that only reasonable suspicion is required, no warrant must be obtained, and there is no right to counsel during **DNA** cheek swabs.[53]

The practice of systematically taking DNA samples from felony arrestees was challenged and decided by the Supreme Court in *Maryland v. King* (2013). The Supreme Court upheld the practice because of the many benefits of the testing, the reliability and validity of the science, and the minimal invasion of a cheek swab.

Voice Tests

Compelling a suspect to speak for the purposes of audio identification is not violative of the Fifth Amendment's prohibition against compelled self-incrimination. This is because the purpose in compelling the statements is identification, not to secure testimony. Again, the voice is considered a physical characteristic that is readily observable to the ordinary person; accordingly, it is not a search under the Fourth Amendment to compel a suspect to speak.

Voice is also at issue whenever a party intends to introduce audio records that purport to be a particular individual's, such as the defendant. For example, assume John is charged with murdering Henry. The police have in their possession a tape from John's telephone answering machine. The tape contains a threat to Henry's life that the government claims was made by John. To prove that John made the threat, the prosecutor plans to introduce voice spectrographic identification evidence.

This test involves a comparison of the recording and a voice sample provided by the defendant. It compares the complex sound waves of the two for similarity. The accuracy of voice spectrographics is questionable, and therefore this type of evidence is not universally accepted by courts. In some jurisdictions, admissibility is prohibited, whereas in others the decision is left to the trial judge.

Polygraph Tests

Polygraph testing, also known as lie detection testing, measures a subject's physical responses, such as heartbeat, blood pressure, and perspiration, during questioning. This is not a new concept. The Chinese monitored the heartbeat of suspects as long as 4,000 years ago. If a suspect's heartbeat increased during a response, he was presumed to have lied. Until recently, courts have held that the results of polygraph evidence are too unreliable to be admitted at trial, unless the parties have stipulated to admission. Today, however, a few jurisdictions permit the introduction of polygraph evidence if it is determined reliable. That is, polygraph evidence is not automatically excluded, but may be if found to be unreliable in a specific case. In *United States v. Scheffer* (1998),[54] the Supreme Court held that defendants do not have a right to introduce the results of a polygraph examination over the objection of the prosecution and where evidentiary rules preclude polygraph results. The Court found that the right of defendants to present evidence has been limited historically to that which is reliable. The Court found that the scientific community is divided on the reliability of polygraph exams and asserts; the results of such exams may be excluded at trial.

In addition to the issue of reliability, a Fifth Amendment self-incrimination issue surfaces when a prosecutor seeks an order requiring a defendant to undergo a polygraph examination. The Supreme Court has stated in dictum,[55] and the lower courts have similarly ruled directly, that lie detector tests involve communications and, accordingly, that the Fifth Amendment applies. Defendants may refuse to respond to questions when the answers may be incriminating, and *Miranda*-type warnings should be given before the test begins, assuming that custody exists. Further, a prosecutor may not refer to a defendant's refusal to submit to polygraph testing at trial.

Chain of Custody

To assure that physical evidence discovered during an investigation remains unchanged and is not confused with evidence from other investigations, police must maintain the **chain of custody.** The officer who discovered the evidence must mark it; and all subsequent contacts with the evidence, such as by forensics officers, must be recorded. This creates a record known as the chain of custody. Chain-of-custody records must be kept from the time the evidence is seized until it is introduced at trial. Breaks in the chain of custody may result in exclusion of the evidence at trial.

In some instances, evidence may be admitted even though the chain of custody has been broken. If evidence is easily identified by a witness, such as its owner, then proving the chain of custody may not be necessary. This may also be true if an item is unique and can be precisely identified by its characteristics (e.g., serial and model numbers). Even in these cases, chain of custody is sometimes required, and the best practice is for the police to maintain a chain in every instance.

The burden of establishing the chain of custody rests with the party seeking admission. The standard of proof is characterized differently among the states, but usually amounts to a preponderance of the evidence. In some jurisdictions, proof of police policy, custom, and practice may be used to prove chain of custody.

chain of custody

■ The chronological list of those in continuous possession of a specific physical object. A person who presents physical evidence (such as a gun used in a crime) at a trial must account for its possession from time of receipt to time of trial in order for the evidence to be "admitted" by the judge. It must thus be shown that the *chain of custody* was unbroken.

Exclusion of Improper Identifications

The consequences of not providing counsel during an identification procedure after the adversary judicial proceeding has begun were discussed in *Wade*. First, testimony about an illegal identification must be excluded at trial. Second, in-court identifications may be excluded if tainted by the pretrial identification. However, if the government can show, by clear and convincing evidence, that an in-court identification has a source independent of the illegal pretrial identification, then it is to be allowed. The *Wade* Court said the following factors are to be considered when making the taint or no taint determination:

1. The prior opportunity to observe the criminal act.
2. The difference between a witness's pre-lineup description and actual description of an accused.
3. Whether the witness identified another person as the criminal before the lineup.

4. Whether the witness identified the accused by photograph prior to the lineup.

5. Whether the witness was unable to identify the accused on a previous occasion.

6. The lapse of time between the crime and the identification.

In most cases, a court will find an independent source for an in-court identification and will allow a witness to identify the defendant during trial, while prohibiting mention of the pretrial identification.

The same rules apply to identifications that are impermissibly suggestive and unreliable. They must be excluded, as must the fruits thereof, unless an independent basis for an in-court identification can be shown.

Ethical Considerations

LEGAL ADVICE AS WAR CRIME?

In response to a request from White House Counsel at that time (and soon to be attorney general) Roberto Gonzales, two Department of Justice attorneys—John Yoo, deputy assistant attorney general, and Jay S. Bybee, assistant attorney general (soon to be U.S. district judge)—drafted a memorandum in 2002 addressing questions the Central Intelligence Agency had concerning interrogation methods that may be used in the war on terror. Specifically, the definition of torture was sought. The memo, commonly known as the "torture memo," defined torture as

> Physical pain [the] equivalent in intensity to the pain accompanying serious physical injury, such as organ failure, impairment of bodily function, or even death. . . . We conclude that the statute, taken as a whole, makes plain that it prohibits only extreme acts.

The memo went on to conclude that to qualify as mental torture, treatment "must result in significant psychological harm of significant duration, e.g., lasting for months or even years."

Many scholars and commentators have criticized the memo, alleging that it was not well reasoned and because it was relied on by the White House, abuses of detainees of the war on terror resulted. Yoo, who has been a vocal defender of the memo, contends that the definition was largely driven by Congress' definition of torture, which developed when it ratified the United Nations Convention Against Torture.

Some scholars have moved beyond criticizing Bybee and Yoo for their analysis; instead, they claim the authors violated their ethical responsibilities as lawyers in rendering the opinion. So much so, some have charged—including Milan Markovic—they were reckless and complicit in war crimes. According to Markovic, that they did not torture anyone themselves is not dispositive. Recklessness is the mens rea of aiding and

Ethical Considerations *(continued)*

abetting the international war crime of abusing detainees. He contends that the International Criminal Court, of which the United States is not a member, as well as other nations, has jurisdiction to try the men.

It is highly unlikely that either attorney will be charged, domestically or abroad. It is also unlikely that their bar memberships will be challenged. However, as international accountability grows, these questions will occur more frequently, and the attorney's role and responsibilities in public international law will likely change.

See Milan Markovic, "Can Lawyers Be War Criminals?" 20 *Geo. J. Legal Ethics* 347 (2007); John Yoo, *The Powers of War and Peace* (Chicago: University of Chicago Press, 2005); and John Yoo, "Behind the 'torture memos,'" *UCBerkeleyNews*, January 4, 2005 *http://www.berkeley.edu*

Web Links

National Constitution Center

The National Constitution Center has information on the Constitution, educational resources, and links to related websites. *http://www.constitutioncenter.org*

Access an interactive eBook, chapter-specific interactive learning tools, including flash cards, quizzes, and more in your paralegal CourseMate, accessed through *www.CengageBrain.com*.

Key Terms

admission	DNA printing	showup
chain of custody	interrogation	
confession	lineup	

Review Questions

1. List the rights included in the *Miranda* warnings. When must they be read to a defendant?

2. What happens if an officer fails to read a defendant his or her rights before obtaining a confession?

3. Is it a violation of the Federal Wiretap Law (Title III of the Omnibus Crime Control and Safe Streets Act) for Gary to allow law enforcement officers to listen to a telephone conversation between himself and Terry without Terry's knowledge? If so, what happens if Terry makes incriminating statements?

4. Does a defendant have a right to counsel at a lineup? If so, what is the source of that right?

5. Does a defendant have a right to counsel at a photograph identification session? If so, what is the source of that right?

6. Why must law enforcement officers obtain a court order to intercept a telephone conversation using traditional line phones and not a conversation using a cordless phone?

7. What is chain of custody?

8. Assume that a prosecutor wants a defendant to submit to genetic testing to compare the defendant's DNA with that of hair found on a victim. Does the defendant have a Fourth Amendment challenge? A Fifth?

Problems & Critical Thinking Exercises

1. While on patrol, Officer Norman heard a scream from the backyard of a house. The officer proceeded to the back of the house, where he observed two people—a badly beaten victim and a young man (Tom) standing over her. Shocked by the sight of the victim, the officer exclaimed, "What happened here?" Tom responded, "I killed her and threw the baseball bat over the fence." Officer Norman restrained the young man, called for an ambulance, and retrieved the bat. While waiting for the ambulance to arrive, Officer Norman asked the young man what his motive was for injuring the woman. Tom explained his motive to the officer. The officer never Mirandized Tom. A motion to suppress the statement, "I killed her and threw the baseball bat over the fence," as well as the statement explaining his motive, has been filed. Additionally, Tom claims that the bat should be excluded because it is a fruit of an illegal interrogation. What should be the outcome? Explain your answer.

2. An officer has made application for a court order approving electronic surveillance of Defendant. The order is granted, stating: "From June 1 to June 7, Officer X, having established probable cause, is granted the authority to intercept the wire communications of Defendant." The officer proceeded to enter Defendant's house, without a warrant, to install the listening device. Eventually, a recording is made of Defendant discussing his illegal activities with a friend. Defendant is arrested, charged, and has filed a motion to suppress the interception. Defendant asserts that the entry into his house was illegal. Discuss.

3. Why are the rules concerning the admissibility of confessions more stringent than for other forms of evidence?

4. Do you believe that it is self-incrimination to give blood, hair, and other such items that might prove one's guilt?

5. Describe a pretrial identification which you believe is unduly suggestive. Explain why it is too suggestive of guilt.

Endnotes

1. *Salinas v. Texas* 570 U.S. __ (2013).
2. 499 U.S. 279.
3. Fed. R. Evid. 804(b)(5).
4. 378 U.S. 478.
5. *Brown v. Mississippi*, 295 U.S. 278 (1936).

6. *McNabb v. United States*, 318 U.S. 332 (1943), and *Mallory v. United States*, 354 U.S. 449 (1957).

7. *Florida v. Powell*, 559 U.S. 50 (2010).

8. *Stansbury v. California*, 511 U.S. 318 (1994).

9. *J.D.B. v. North Carolina*, 564 U.S. __ (2011).

10. 446 U.S. 291 (1980).

11. See *Hiibel v. Sixth Judicial District*, 542 U.S. 177 (2004).

12. *New York v. Quarles,* 467 U.S. 649 (1984).

13. Found at http://www.nytimes.com/2011/03/25/us/25miranda-text.html (May 16, 2013).

14. *Boston bombing suspect stops talking after being read Miranda rights.* Associated Press, April 15, 2013. Found at http://www.nj.com/news/index.ssf/2013/04/boston_bombing_suspect_stops_t.html

15. *Illinois v. Perkins,* 496 U.S. 292 (1990).

16. *Massiah v. United States*, 377 U.S. 201 (1964).

17. *Pennsylvania v. Bruder,* 488 U.S. 9 (1988).

18. *Davis v. United States*, 512 U.S. 452 (1994).

19. *Michigan v. Mosley,* 423 U.S. 96 (1975).

20. 542 U.S. 600 (2004)

21. *Oregon v. Haas,* 420 U.S. 714 (1975).

22. 542 U.S. 630 (2004).

23. 109 Ohio St. 3d 519 (2006).

24. See *Montejo v. Louisiana*, 556 U.S. __ (2009).

25. 18 U.S.C. § 2510 *et seq.*

26. Although the U.S. Supreme Court has not fully addressed the e-mail issue, see *United States v. Councilman*, 418 F.3d67 (1st Cir. 2005).

27. 18 U.S.C. § 2518.

28. *Scott v. United States,* 436 U.S. 128 (1978).

29. See, for example, In the Matter of the Application of the USA for An Order Directing A Provider of Electronic Communication Service to Disclose Records, U.S. Ct. App., 3rd Cir. No. 08–4227 (Sept. 7, 2010).

30. 18 U.S.C. §§ 2701 *et. seq.*

31. *Smith v. Maryland,* 442 U.S. 735 (1979).

32. 18 U.S.C. § 2511.

33. *ACLU et al. v. National Security Agency, et al.*, Case No. 06-CV-10204 (2006).

34. Max Ehrenfreund, Asylum for NSA Leaker Edward Snowden a Challenge to U.S.–Russia Relations. *Wall Street Journal*, August 2, 2013. Can be found at Washingtonpost.com

35. Eva Perez and Shiobhan Gorman, NSA Exceeds Legal Limits in Eavesdropping Program. *Wall Street Journal,* April 16, 2013. Found athttp://online.wsj.com/news/articles/SB123985123667923961

36. 50 U.S.C. sec. 36 et seq. and 36 U.S.C. sec 1801 et seq.

37. 442 U.S. 735 (1979).

38. *In Re Application of the FBI for an Order, Amended Memorandum Opinion.* Foreign Intelligence Surveillance Court. Docket No. 13-109. August 29, 2013.

39. Ellen Nakashima, *FBI Surveillance Tool Ruled Unconstitutional. Washington Post,* March 15, 2013. Can be found by searching Washingtonpost.com

40. *Manson v. Braithwaite,* 432 U.S. 98 (1977).

41. *Eyewitness Identification: a policy review.* Found at innocenceproject.org

42. Innocenceproject.org.

43. 406 U.S. 682.

44. *Schmerber v. California,* 384 U.S. 757 (1966).

45. Braun, "Quantitative Analysis and the Law: Probability Theory as a Tool of Evidence in Criminal Trials," 1982 *Utah L. Rev.* 41, 57 n.82.

46. For a case where a U.S. district judge questioned whether the science of fingerprinting was adequately developed to satisfy the *Daubert* test, see *United States v. Llerla Plaza,* 179 F.Supp.2d 492 (E.D. Pa. 2002).

47. 412 U.S. 291 (1973).

48. 470 U.S. 753 (1985).

49. Dodd, "DNA Fingerprinting in Matters of Family and Crime," 26 *Med. Sci. L.* 5 (1986).

50. Morland, *An Outline of Scientific Criminology,* 59–60 (2nd ed. 1971). Jeffrey M. Prottas & Alice A. Noble, "Use of Forensic DNA Evidence in Prosecutors' Offices," 35 *J.L. Med. & Ethics,* 310, 311–13 (2007).

51. The law can be found in 42 U.S.C. § 14135a.

52. See, for example, Colo. Rev. Stat. § 16-5-401 (8)(a.5) (2006).

53. *Arturo Garcia-Torres v. Indiana, No. 64A03-0812-CR-630,* In App.Ct. (Sept. 30, 2009).

54. 523 U.S. 303.

55. *Schmerber v. California,* 384 U.S. 757, 764 (1966).

CHAPTER 14

THE PRETRIAL PROCESS

Chapter Outline

Chapter Objectives

After completing this chapter, you should
be able to:

- outline the process of a criminal case
  from discovery of the criminal act to
  preparation for trial.

- describe the two formal criminal
  charges that are filed against defendants
  in the United States.

- discuss the history, purpose, and
  procedures of grand juries, and contrast
  that with contemporary grand juries.

- describe and apply to fact scenarios the
  law of pretrial release of defendants.

- identify the material facts and legal
  issues in nearly all of the cases you
  read, describe the courts' analyses and
  conclusions in the cases, and demonstrate
  the ability to synthesize and think critically
  about the law of the subject.

INTRODUCTION

What follows is an outline of the basic process a case goes through, from before arrest to after trial. As previously mentioned, each state and the federal government have different processes. The federal process is used for illustration. Exhibit 14–1 provides a visual summary of the process. You may find it helpful to refer to it as you learn the different stages of the process.

DISCOVERY AND INVESTIGATION OF CRIMINAL ACTIVITY

The process begins when law enforcement officials learn of a crime that has been committed (or is to be committed). Police learn of criminal activity in two ways: They may discover it themselves, or a citizen may report such activity.

Once police are aware of criminal activity, the pre-arrest investigation begins. There are two objectives to this stage. First, police must determine whether a crime

Exhibit 14–1 VISUAL SUMMARY OF THE BASIC CRIMINAL PROCESS

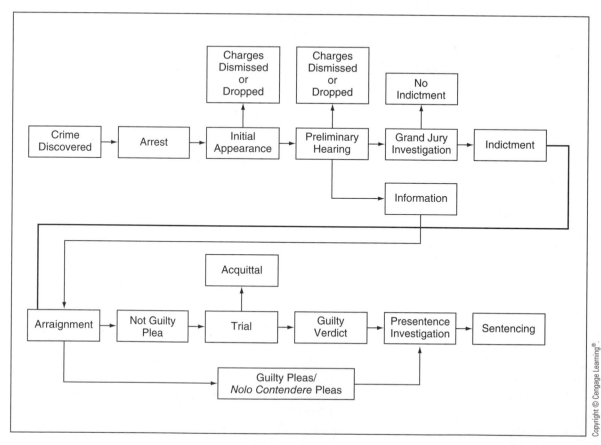

Copyright © Cengage Learning®.

has been committed. Second, if a crime has been committed, police attempt to gather sufficient evidence to charge and convict the person believed to have committed the crime.

ARREST

Once adequate evidence exists, an **arrest** is made in most cases. However, in some misdemeanor cases a defendant is asked to come to the police station, and an arrest is not made unless the defendant refuses. The arrest may be made without an arrest warrant in some situations. In others, an ex parte hearing may be held to determine if probable cause exists to believe that the person under investigation committed the crime. If so, the judge may issue an arrest warrant.

At the time of arrest, police ordinarily search the defendant. Once at the police station, the defendant is "booked." *Booking* consists of obtaining biographical information about the defendant (name, address, etc.), fingerprinting the defendant, and taking the defendant's photograph, commonly known as a "mug shot." The defendant is usually permitted to make a telephone call at this stage.

The defendant is then searched (sometimes deloused and showered) and held in jail until further arrangements are made. For minor offenses, the defendant may be able to post bail prior to appearing before a judge. In such cases, defendants are out of jail within hours. All others have to wait for a judge to set a bail amount at an initial appearance. During and after this stage, law enforcement investigation and gathering of evidence may continue.

arrest

■ The official taking of a person to answer criminal charges. This involves at least temporarily depriving the person of liberty and may involve the use of force. An arrest is usually made by a police officer with a warrant or for a crime committed in the officer's presence.

THE COMPLAINT

At this stage, a police officer, or in some instances a prosecutor, files a **complaint,** which acts as the charging instrument. Fed. R. Crim. P. 3 states: "The complaint is a written statement of the essential facts constituting an offense charged. It shall be made upon oath before a magistrate." The complaint need not be written upon personal knowledge. That is, an officer may use hearsay and circumstantial evidence in a complaint. Affidavits from those who have personal knowledge, such as witnesses and victims, are often attached to the complaint.

When a warrant is sought to arrest a defendant, the complaint is often produced in support of the request for a warrant. This occurs at the ex parte hearing mentioned earlier. Federal law requires that a warrant be issued if probable cause is established by the complaint and its accompanying affidavits. Upon the request of the government, a summons (an order to appear) may be issued rather than an arrest warrant.[1]

If the defendant was arrested without a warrant, the complaint serves as the charging document at the initial appearance or preliminary hearing.

For traffic violations and some lesser misdemeanors, the complaint acts as both a summons to appear in court and the charging document. In such cases the defendant appears in court on only one occasion, and the ticket is used in place of an information or indictment. See Exhibits 14–2 and 14–3.

complaint

■ A *criminal complaint* is a formal document that charges a person with a crime.

Exhibit 14–2 CRIMINAL COMPLAINT

AO 91 (Rev. 5/85) Criminal Complaint

United States District Court

_____ DISTRICT OF _____

UNITED STATES OF AMERICA

V.

CRIMINAL COMPLAINT

CASE NUMBER:

(Name and Address of Defendant)

I, the undersigned complainant being duly sworn state the following is true and correct to the best of my knowledge and belief. On or about _____ in _____ county, in the _____ District of _____ defendant(s) did,

(Track Statutory Language of Offense)

in violation of Title _____ United States Code, Section(s) _____. I further state that I am a(n) _____ and that this complaint is based on the following facts:

Continued on the attached sheet and made a part hereof: ☐ Yes   ☐ No

_____
Signature of Complainant

Sworn to before me and subscribed in my presence,

_____ at _____
Date   City and State

_____   _____
Name & Title of Judicial Officer   Signature of Judicial Officer

Source: http://www.uscourts.gov/uscourts/FormsAndFees/Forms/AO091.pdf

Exhibit 14–3   SUMMONS IN A CRIMINAL CASE

AO 83 (Rev. 5/85) Summons in a Criminal Case

United States District Court

_____ DISTRICT OF _____

UNITED STATES OF AMERICA

SUMMONS IN A CRIMINAL CASE

CASE NUMBER:

(Name and Address of Defendant)

  YOU ARE HEREBY SUMMONED to appear before the United States District Court at the place, date and time set forth below.

Place	Room
Before:	Date and Time

To answer a(n)
☐ Indictment   ☐ Information   ☐ Complaint   ☐ Violation Notice
☐ Probation Violation Petition

Charging you with a violation of Title _____ United States Code, Section _____.

Brief description of offense:

_____   _____
Signature of Issuing Officer   Date

_____
Name and Title of Issuing Officer

(continued)

Exhibit 14–3 *(continued)*

AO 83 (Rev. 5/85) Summons in a Criminal Case

RETURN OF SERVICE

| Service was made by me on:[1] | Date |

Check one box below to indicate appropriate method of service

☐ Served personally upon the defendant at: _____

_____

☐ Left summons at the defendant's dwelling house or usual place of abode with a person of suitable age and discretion then residing therein and mailed a copy of the summons to the defendant's last known address. Name of person with whom the summons was left:

_____

_____

☐ Returned unexecuted: _____

_____

_____

_____

I declare under penalty of perjury under the laws of the United States of America that the foregoing information contained in the Return of Service is true and correct.

Returned on _____   _____
              Date   Name of United States Marshal

                                  _____
                                  (by) Deputy United States Marshal

1) As to who may serve a summons see Rule 4 of the Federal Rules of Criminal Procedure

Source: http://www.nvd.uscourts.gov/Files/AO_083_0109.pdf

INITIAL APPEARANCE

After arrest, the defendant is taken "without unnecessary delay" before the nearest available federal magistrate.[2] In most cases this means that a defendant will be brought before the judge within 24 hours. However, if a defendant is arrested on a weekend, it may be the following Monday before the defendant has the initial appearance, unless a weekend session of court is held.

The first appearance is brief. If the arrest was executed under an arrest warrant, it is the duty of the presiding judge to make sure that the person arrested is the person named in the warrant. The defendant is also informed of various rights, such as the rights to remain silent and to have the assistance of counsel. If the defendant is indigent, the court will appoint counsel. The right to counsel is discussed more fully later. If the arrest was warrantless, an initial probable cause determination must occur.

In 1991, the United States Supreme Court examined the need for prompt probable cause determinations in warrantless arrest situations. In *County of Riverside v. McLaughlin*,[3] the Court held that persons arrested without a warrant must have a probable cause determination within 48 hours after arrest or quicker if reasonable. A defendant who asserts unreasonable delay, but was held less than 48 hours before a probable cause hearing was conducted, bears the burden of proving that the delay was unreasonable under the Fourth Amendment. If a defendant is held longer than 48 hours without a probable cause hearing, the burden of showing a bona fide emergency or other extraordinary circumstance falls on the government.

Time to gather additional evidence, ill will, or the fact that the defendant was arrested on a weekend are not sufficient to delay the probable cause determination longer than 48 hours.

Finally, a preliminary hearing date is set, and if the defendant is in jail, the court determines whether he or she should be released prior to trial.

PRETRIAL RELEASE AND DETENTION

In many cases, defendants are released prior to trial. A court may order many types of release, but the predominantly used methods are cash bail, surety bond, property bond, and personal recognizance.

Types of Release

The most obvious method of gaining release is to post **bail.** A defendant who has the resources may simply pay into the court the amount of the bail.

Whenever a third party, usually a professional bondsman, agrees to pay the bond for a defendant, a surety bond is created. The common practice is for the defendant to pay the surety 10 percent or more of the bond amount in exchange for the bondsman making the defendant's bail. The 10 percent is not refunded to the defendant after the case is concluded.

bail

■ The money or property given as security for a defendant's appearance in court. The money, often in the form of a bail bond, may be lost if the defendant released does not appear in court.

Some sureties require security (collateral) before a bond will be issued. Defendants may pledge cars, houses, or other property to obtain release. This is a property bond.

For many misdemeanors and a few felonies, a defendant may be released on personal recognizance. To gain such a release, a defendant need only promise to appear.

Regardless of the type of release, courts frequently impose conditions upon the defendant. Defendants who are arrested or caught intimidating witnesses or interfering with the judicial process may be jailed until trial.

Eighth Amendment

The Eighth Amendment proscribes the imposition of "excessive bail." This provision may be applicable to the states through the Fourteenth Amendment. The purpose of imposing money bail is to assure the defendant's appearance at trial, not to inflict punishment. Bail set higher than necessary to accomplish this purpose is deemed excessive.[4] In practice, courts have significant discretion in setting bail and are rarely reversed.

The Supreme Court has held that the mere fact that a defendant cannot pay the amount set by a court does not make it excessive. Additionally, the Court has stated that not all defendants have a right to bail. Defendants who are a danger to the community or unlikely to appear for trial may be held without bail.

The exact meaning of the Eighth Amendment has not been spelled out by the Supreme Court. Whether pretrial detention laws, especially those that create a presumption of detention, are constitutional remains to be seen.

Detention

The federal government (and presumably most states, if not all) provides for detention of some defendants prior to trial.

Pretrial detention may not be used to punish a person. To do so violates a person's due process right to be free from punishment without a fair trial. However, a defendant may be detained if there is reason to believe that he or she will not appear for trial or if he or she poses a threat to others.

In the federal system, the defendant is entitled to an adversary hearing concerning pretrial detention, and the government must prove by clear and convincing evidence that the defendant is either dangerous or unlikely to appear for trial.[5] The adversary hearing must be held at the initial appearance; or upon the motion of the defendant or the government, it may be continued.

Although the general rule is that the government bears the burden of proving that a defendant must be detained, there are exceptions. There are two classes of presumptions in the federal statute. One presumes that certain defendants will not appear for trial, and another presumes that certain defendants are a danger to the community. For example, defendants charged with crimes of violence who have a prior conviction for a crime of violence, which was committed while the defendant was released pending trial, are presumed to be dangerous to the community. It is also presumed that defendants charged with drug crimes that carry 10 years or more imprisonment will flee. These presumptions also apply to many other defendants.[6] The presumption is rebuttable, and the defendant has the burden of disproving it. Some question the constitutionality of such presumptions, and it remains to be seen whether such statutes will be reversed or upheld.

Many states have statutes that require detention of persons charged with crimes punishable by life imprisonment or death, provided that the proof of guilt is great.

PRELIMINARY HEARING

The defendant's second appearance before a judge is the **preliminary hearing.** How this stage is handled by the states varies significantly. At the preliminary hearing, the court determines if probable cause exists to believe the accused committed the crime. If probable cause is found, the defendant is "bound over" to the next stage of the process. The next stage is either trial or review by grand jury. If probable cause is not established, the defendant is released.

If indictment by grand jury is required, the case is bound over to the grand jury. The grand jury is not bound by the judge's decision that probable cause exists; it makes an independent decision whether to charge the defendant. If grand jury review is not required, the defendant is bound over for trial.

The purpose of the preliminary hearing is to have an impartial third party review the facts to be sure that probable cause exists. There is no constitutional requirement for a preliminary hearing.[7] However, many states do provide for preliminary hearings.

It is common to permit prosecutors to bypass the preliminary hearing either by submitting the case to a grand jury or by directly filing an information. Defendants often waive the preliminary hearing. In some states, prosecutors may demand a preliminary hearing over the objection of the defendant.

The preliminary hearing can be quite lengthy compared to a defendant's initial appearance. The hearing is adversarial. Witnesses are called, and the attorneys are allowed to make arguments. Rules of evidence are applied in modified form, so hearsay and illegally obtained evidence are often considered. Defendants have a right to counsel and may also be allowed to cross-examine the prosecution witnesses and to present defense witnesses. The right to counsel is a matter of federal constitutional law. The other two rights are granted by state laws. The preliminary hearing can be an important asset to both prosecution and defense, as it can serve as a source of discovery.

The preliminary hearing is different from the initial probable cause determination required by *County of Riverside v. McLaughlin.* The initial determination is constitutionally required, whereas the preliminary hearing is not. Further, although the same terminology is used (i.e., probable cause), less evidence is needed to satisfy the government's obligation at the initial determination than at the preliminary hearing. Probable cause at the initial hearing equates with the probable cause required to obtain a warrant, which is generally recognized as requiring less proof than does probable cause at the later preliminary hearing. Also in contrast is the fact that the probable cause hearing required by *County of Riverside* will likely be one-sided. That is, only the government will present evidence. Some states, however—such as California—permit defendants to present evidence at preliminary hearings.

preliminary hearing

■ The first court proceeding on a criminal charge, in federal courts and many state courts, by a magistrate or a judge to decide whether there is enough evidence for the government to continue with the case and to require the defendant to post bail or be held for trial.

Fed. R. Crim. P. 5 requires that the date for "preliminary examination" be scheduled at the defendant's initial appearance. It shall be held within 10 days of the initial appearance if the defendant is in custody and within 20 days if the defendant has been released.

In federal courts and in many states, probable cause may be founded upon hearsay evidence.[8] Motions to suppress illegally seized evidence are made after the preliminary hearing, so such evidence may be considered at the preliminary examination stage. If a grand jury has issued an indictment, the preliminary hearing may be dispensed within the federal system.[9] Many states have a similar rule.

THE FORMAL CHARGE

information

■ A formal accusation of a crime made by a proper public official such as a prosecuting attorney.

indictment

■ A sworn, written accusation of a crime, made against a person by a prosecutor to a *grand jury*.

grand jury

■ Persons who receive complaints and accusations of crime, hear preliminary evidence on the complaining side, and make formal accusations or indictments.

There are two formal charges: the **information** and the **indictment.** Informations are charges filed by prosecutors. Indictments are charges issued by grand juries. Once filed, an information or indictment replaces the complaint and becomes the formal charging instrument.

Indictment and Grand Jury

Purpose of the Grand Jury

In early American history, **grand juries** were used to guard against unfair and arbitrary government prosecutions and to preserve the reputation of persons investigated but not indicted. The Framers of the U.S. Constitution believed grand jury review so important that they stated in the Fifth Amendment: "[N]o person shall be held to answer for a capital, or otherwise infamous, crime, unless on a presentment or indictment of a Grand Jury."

Grand juries consist of 12 to 23 persons who are usually selected in the same method as petit juries (juries that determine guilt or innocence). Grand juries sit for longer periods of time and are called to hear cases as needed.

The primary objective of grand jury review is the same as that of the preliminary hearing: to determine whether there is probable cause to believe that a target of the investigation committed the alleged crime. The grand jury, therefore, was intended to protect individuals from unwarranted prosecutions. Because the grand jury proceedings are closed, individuals investigated but not charged are not subjected to the public humiliation and damage to reputation that often results from a more public investigation. The secondary objective of the grand jury has become its primary purpose, as defined by prosecutors: to facilitate investigation. See Exhibit 14–4.

Procedures of the Grand Jury

First, grand juries are closed. The public, including the defendant, is not entitled to attend. Second, the prosecutor runs the show before the grand jury, and the defendant has no right to present evidence or to make a statement. Third, the actions of grand juries are secret. Those who attend are not permitted to disclose what transpires. Defendants have no right to know what evidence is presented to a grand jury, unless it is exculpatory (tends to prove the defendant's innocence). Fourth, those who testify before the grand jury are not entitled to have counsel in the jury room.[10] In most states witnesses are permitted to

Exhibit 14–4 SUBPOENA TO TESTIFY BEFORE GRAND JURY

AO 106 (Rev. 5/85) Subpoena to Testify Before Grand Jury

United States District Court

DISTRICT OF _____

To

**SUBPOENA TO TESTIFY
BEFORE GRAND JURY**

SUBPOENA FOR:
☐ PERSON   ☐ DOCUMENT(S) OR OBJECT(S)

YOU ARE HEREBY COMMANDED to appear and testify before the Grand Jury of the United States District Court at the place, date, and time specified below.

PLACE	COURTROOM
	DATE AND TIME

YOU ARE ALSO COMMANDED to bring with you the following document(s) or object(s):[1]

☐ *Please see additional information on reverse*

This subpoena shall remain in effect until you are granted leave to depart by the court or by an officer acting on behalf of the court.

CLERK	DATE
(BY) DEPUTY CLERK	

This subpoena is issued on application of the United States of America	NAME, ADDRESS AND PHONE NUMBER OF ASSISTANT U.S. ATTORNEY

[1]If not applicable, enter "none"

(continued)

Exhibit 14–4 *(continued)*

AO 110 (Rev. 5/85) Subpoena to Testify Before Grand Jury

RETURN OF SERVICE[1]

RECEIVED BY SERVER	DATE	PLACE
SERVED	DATE	PLACE

SERVED ON (NAME)		

SERVED BY		TITLE

STATEMENT OF SERVICE FEES

TRAVEL	SERVICES	TOTAL

DECLARATION OF SERVER[2]

I declare under penalty of perjury under the laws of the United States of America that the foregoing information contained in the Return of Service and Statement of Service Fees is true and correct.

Executed on _____   _____

        Date   *Signature of Server*

                              _____

                              Address of Server

ADDITIONAL INFORMATION

(1) As to who may serve a subpoena and the manner of its service see Rule 17(d), Federal Rules of Criminal Procedure, or Rule 45(c), Federal Rules of Civil Procedure.
(2) "Fees and mileage need not be tendered to the witness upon service of a subpoena issued on behalf of the United States or an officer or agency thereof (Rule 45(c), Federal Rules of Civil Procedure Rule 17(d), Federal Rules of Criminal Procedure) or on behalf of certain indigent parties and criminal defendants who are unable to pay such costs (28 USC 1825, Rule 17(b) Federal Rules of Criminal Procedure)."

Source: http://www.uscourts.gov/uscourts/FormsAndFees/Forms/AO110.pdf

leave the proceeding to confer with counsel waiting directly outside. Because statements made to a grand jury can be used later, the Fifth Amendment right to be free from self-incrimination is available to witnesses. Grand juries can overcome Fifth Amendment claims (refusals to testify) by granting witnesses immunity from prosecution. Also, witnesses may not refuse to testify because the inquiry is the result of illegally seized evidence. To permit refusal or exclusion would not further the objective of the exclusionary rule (to deter police misconduct) and would substantially interfere with the grand jury process.[11]

Grand juries possess the power to order people to appear, to subpoena documents, to hold people in contempt, and to grant immunity in order to procure testimony.

As a general proposition, prosecutors control grand juries. For the most part, grand juries convene only when called by the prosecutor. The prosecutor decides what witnesses need to be called and who should be given immunity. Nearly all people targeted (the person the prosecutor believes guilty) by prosecutors are indicted. Many criticize the grand jury system for this reason: The government has too much control over the grand juries. The argument is reasonable when one considers the historical purpose of grand jury review.

The proponents of abolishing the grand jury system argue that grand juries have not only lost their independence, but they also now act to the benefit of prosecutors by allowing discovery of information that may otherwise have been unavailable.

The Indictment

After a grand jury has completed its investigation, a vote on whether to charge is taken. In the federal system, grand juries consist of 16 to 23 people. At least 12 must vote for indictment.[12] In many cases indictments are sealed until the indicted defendant is arrested.

The Constitution requires that all federal prosecutions for capital and infamous crimes be by indictment. However, if a defendant waives the right to grand jury review, he or she may be charged by information. The waiver of indictment form used in federal court is shown in Exhibit 14–5. Crimes punishable by 1 year or longer in prison are "infamous."[13] A defendant may not waive indictment in federal capital cases. It is always proper to charge corporations by information, as imprisonment is not possible.

The United States Supreme Court has ruled that grand jury review is not a fundamental right; therefore, the Fifth Amendment requirement for indictment is not applicable against the states. However, many states have grand juries and require that serious charges be brought by indictment.

Indictments must be written and state in "plain and concise" terms the essential facts constituting the offense charged.[14] Indictments are liberally read, and technical errors do not make them invalid. However, an indictment must contain all the essential elements of the crime charged. If an indictment charges more than one crime, each crime must be made a separate count.[15] Jurisdiction must be noted, and the law upon which the charge is made must be cited. It was upon this indictment that Ted Bundy was prosecuted, convicted, and executed.

If a defendant believes that an indictment is fatally deficient, it may be attacked by a **motion** to **quash.** Indictments are not quashed because of technical errors. An example of a valid reason to quash is failure to allege an essential element of the crime

motion

■ A request that a judge make a ruling or take some other action.

quash

■ Overthrow; annul; completely do away with. *Quash* usually refers to a court stopping a subpoena, an order, or an indictment.

Exhibit 14–5   WAIVER OF INDICTMENT

AO 455 (Rev.5/85) Waiver of Indictment

United States District Court

_____ DISTRICT OF _____

UNITED STATES OF AMERICA
                V.

WAIVER OF INDICTMENT

CASE NUMBER:

I, _____, the above named defendant, who is accused of being advised of

the nature of the charge(s), the proposed information, and of my rights, hereby

waive in open court on _____ prosecution by indictment and con-
                                    Date
sent that the proceeding may be by information rather than by indictment.

_____
Defendant

_____
Counsel for Defendant

Before _____
        Judicial Officer

Source: http://www.uscourts.gov/uscourts/FormsAndFees/Forms/AO455.pdf

charged. It is not violative of the Fifth Amendment's Double Jeopardy Clause for a grand jury to issue a second indictment after the first has been quashed or dismissed.

In some jurisdictions, a prosecutor may refuse to prosecute, even though an indictment has been issued. In that situation, the prosecutor must assist the jury in preparing the document and must usually explain why a prosecution will not be maintained. In other instances, the prosecutor *must* pursue the case. The former situation represents federal law; that is, the decision on whether to prosecute falls within the purview of the federal prosecutor, who may properly refuse to sign an indictment and prosecute the case.[16]

sidebar

PLEA BARGAINING

Statistics vary, but it is widely accepted that approximately 90 percent of all felony cases are disposed of by guilty pleas. The number is probably higher for misdemeanors. There is no question that plea bargaining greatly reduces the amount of time expended on trials. Warren Burger, past Chief Justice of the United States Supreme Court, estimated that judicial resources in the United States would have to be doubled if only 20 percent of all criminal cases went to trial. This conclusion was largely a matter of simple math and has been criticized. In any event, plea bargaining is an important part of the criminal justice system. It is so important that the Supreme Court has stated that it "is not only an essential part of the process but a highly desirable part," *Santobello v. New York*, 404 U.S. 257, 261 (1971).

In *Boykin v. Alabama*, 395 U.S. 238 (1969), it was announced that all defendants who plead guilty do so voluntarily and knowingly, the latter term meaning that the defendant understands the rights that are waived by entering a plea of guilty.

The plea negotiation involves the defendant and the prosecutor. Judges do not participate in plea negotiations. After a bargain is reached, it is presented to the trial court. The court may then accept the agreement and sentence the defendant accordingly. With good cause, the court may also reject the agreement. Some states permit defendants to withdraw their guilty pleas if the judge rejects the bargain. In others the judge has the discretion of allowing the defendant to withdraw the guilty plea or sentencing the defendant contrary to the bargain.

Sources: Burger, "The State of the Judiciary," 56 *A.B.A. J.* 929 (1970) and Note, "Is Plea Bargaining Inevitable?" 97 *Harv. L. Rev.* 1037 (1984).

Information

The second formal method of charging someone with a crime is by information. Informations are filed by prosecutors without grand jury review. The current trend is away from indictments and toward charging by information.

If a defendant has been initially charged by complaint, the prosecutor must independently review the evidence and determine whether a prosecution is warranted. If not, a prosecutor may file a nolle prosequi. If so, the information is filed.

Informations serve the same function as indictments. Under the federal rules, informations must take the same form as indictments. They must be plain, concise, and in writing. All essential elements, as well as the statute relied upon by the government, must be included.[17] (See the sample criminal information in Chapter 4.) As is true of indictments, informations must be filed with the appropriate court.

Defendants may seek to have defective informations quashed or dismissed. The rules regarding defectiveness are the same for informations as for indictments. Technical errors are not fatal.

ARRAIGNMENT

After the formal charge has been filed, the defendant is brought to the trial court for **arraignment.** This is the hearing at which the defendant is read the formal charge and is asked to enter a **plea.**

Defendants may plead guilty, not guilty, or nolo contendere. By pleading guilty a defendant admits all the charges contained in the charging document, unless a plea agreement has been reached with the government. A **plea agreement,** also known as a *plea bargain*, is the product of negotiations between the prosecutor and the defendant. It is common for the prosecution to dismiss one or more charges of a multi-count charge or to reduce a charge in exchange for a defendant's plea of guilty. Judges are not permitted to participate in plea negotiations and a judge's involvement, including urging a defendant to plead guilty, can be cause for a reversal of a conviction.[18]

Plea bargaining is an important aspect of criminal procedure. More than 90 percent of all felony cases are disposed of by pleas of guilty. Most guilty pleas are the result of plea bargaining.

By pleading guilty, defendants waive a host of rights. The right to a jury trial and to be proven guilty beyond a reasonable doubt are two of the rights waived by a guilty plea. Due to the significance of such waivers, courts must be sure that guilty pleas are given knowingly and voluntarily. To be knowing, a defendant must understand his or her rights and that he or she is waiving them by making the plea. The plea must be free of coercion or duress to be voluntary. Of course, the inducement of a plea bargain is not coercion.

The court must also find that a factual basis exists before a plea of guilty can be accepted. This means there must be sufficient facts in the record to support the conclusion that the defendant committed the crime. A defendant has no right to plead guilty to a crime he or she did not commit. The factual basis may be established by the testimony of the investigating officer or by the defendant recounting what transpired. Once the plea is taken, the court will either impose sentence or set a future date for sentencing.

If a defendant enters a not-guilty plea, the court will set a trial date. In some instances, courts will set a pretrial schedule, which will include a pretrial conference date and a deadline for filing pretrial motions.

Finally, a plea of nolo contendere may be entered. *Nolo contendere* is a Latin phrase that translates to "I do not contest it." The defendant who pleads nolo contendere neither admits nor denies the charges and has no intention of defending himself or herself.

Nolo contendere is treated as a plea of guilty. That is, the government must establish that a factual basis exists to believe the defendant committed the offense, and the court accepting the plea must be sure that the plea is made voluntarily and knowingly. In most jurisdictions a defendant may plead nolo contendere only with the court's approval. This is true in the courts of the United States.[19]

The advantage of a no-contest plea over a guilty plea is that the no-contest plea cannot be used in a later civil proceeding against the defendant, whereas a guilty plea may be used. If the case is not disposed of by a plea of guilty or nolo contendere, the parties begin preparing for trial.

PRETRIAL ACTIVITY

Discovery

Discovery refers to a process of exchanging information between the prosecution and defense. Discovery is not as broad in criminal cases as in civil.

The amount of discovery that should be allowed is heavily debated. Those favoring broad discovery contend that limited discovery leads to "trial by ambush," which is not in the best interests of justice. The purpose of a trial is to discover the truth and achieve justice, not to award the better game player. Proponents of this position claim that unexpected evidence at trial is inefficient, costly, and unfair. It is inefficient because trials often have to be delayed to give one party time to prepare a response to the unexpected evidence. Such tactics lead to time problems for the parties as well as the trial court. They may also be unfair. Evidence that was once available may not be so at trial. If the party surprised at trial had known about the unexpected evidence, other contrary evidence could have been secured and a proper defense or response could have been prepared.

Finally, it appears unfair to subject defendants to the possibility of surprise when the government is insulated from certain surprises. For example, affirmative defenses must be specially pled. Intent to rely on alibi and insanity defenses must be provided to the government in most jurisdictions, often with strict enforcement of time requirements. The purpose of these rules is to prevent surprises to the government at trial. Those who support expanded discovery feel that it is unfair to place such requirements upon defendants, but not upon the government.

Those opposed contend that expansive discovery increases the likelihood that defendants will manipulate the system. In particular, defendants might intimidate government witnesses. Additionally, opponents contend that it is easier for a defendant to skillfully plan his or her testimony, even if false, if a defendant knows the government's entire case. For example, if a defendant originally planned to assert an alibi but finds out through discovery that the government has a witness placing him at the location of the crime, he has been provided an opportunity to change his defense. Today, discovery in criminal proceedings is quite limited in many jurisdictions, including federal courts. A few states have enlarged what information may be obtained prior to trial.

discovery

■ The formal and informal exchange of information between the prosecution and the defense.

What follows is an examination of the federal rules, as well as constitutional requirements for discovery.

Bill of Particulars

One method that defendants have to obtain information about the government's case is through a **bill of particulars.** The purpose of bills of particulars is to make general indictments and informations more specific. Fed. R. Crim. P. 7(f) allows district courts to order prosecutors to file a bill of particulars.

Bills of particulars are not true discovery devices. If the charging instrument is sufficiently clear and detailed, the court will not grant a defense motion for particularization of the charge. A bill of particulars is intended to provide a defendant with details about the charges that are necessary for the preparation of a defense and to avoid prejudicial surprise at trial.[20] The test is not whether the indictment is sufficiently drawn; the question is whether the information is necessary to avoid prejudice to the defendant.

bill of particulars

■ A detailed, formal, written statement of charges or claims by a plaintiff or the prosecutor (given upon the defendant's formal request to the court for more detailed information).

Statements of the Defendant

Fed. R. Crim. P. 16(a) (1) (A) states that upon request the government must allow the defendant to inspect, copy, or photograph all prior relevant written and recorded statements made by the defendant. This includes testimony that defendants give before grand juries—an exception to the rule of secrecy of grand jury proceedings.

Prosecutors are required to allow inspection of all statements made by the defendant that are in the possession of the prosecution or that may be discovered through due diligence. Hence, if a defendant makes a statement to an arresting officer and the statement is recorded or reduced to writing, the prosecutor must allow defense inspection even though the statement may be in the possession of the officer and not the prosecutor.

In addition to recorded statements and writings, the government is required to inform the defendant of "the substance of any oral statement that the government intends to offer in evidence." This means that statements made by a defendant that are summarized by the police (or other government agent), but not verbatim or signed by the defendant, are also discoverable. However, such evidence is discoverable only if the prosecution intends to use it at trial. This is not true of written and recorded statements of a defendant.

Criminal Record of the Defendant

Fed. R. Crim. P. 16 also requires prosecutors to furnish a copy of the defendant's criminal record to the defendant. This includes not only the records known to the prosecutor but also those that can be discovered through due diligence.

Documents and Tangible Objects

Under Rule 16, defendants are also entitled to inspect and copy photographs, books, tangible objects, papers, buildings, and places that are in the possession of the government if:

1. The item is material to preparation of the defendant's defense, or
2. The item is going to be used by the government at trial, or
3. The item was obtained from, or belongs to, the defendant.

The situations in which this rule might apply are countless. For example, if the police take pictures of the scene of a crime, this provision allows the defendant to view and copy those pictures prior to trial. Or, if the police seize a building that was used to manufacture drugs, the defendant can invoke this rule to gain access to the premises.

This section of Rule 16 has a reciprocal provision. That is, defendants must allow the government to inspect and copy defense items. However, the rule is not as broad for government discovery. Defendants only have to permit inspection and copying of those items intended to be used at trial.

Scientific Reports and Tests

All scientific reports and tests in the possession of the government (or that can be discovered through due diligence) must be turned over to the defendant, if requested.

This provision includes reports and conclusions of mental examinations of the defendant, autopsy reports, drug tests, fingerprint analysis, blood tests, DNA (genetic) tests, ballistic tests, and other related tests and examinations.

The defendant must accord the government reciprocity, if requested. For example, if a defendant undergoes an independent mental examination, the government is entitled to review the report of the evaluator prior to trial.

Statements of Witnesses/Jencks Act

Many jurisdictions require that the prosecution, and in some the defense, provide a list of intended trial witnesses. It is common to require additional information about expert witnesses, such as background and reports they have prepared.

In the federal system, defendants are not entitled to inspect or copy statements of prosecution witnesses prior to trial. However, a federal statute, commonly known as the Jencks Act,[21] permits a defendant to review a prior written or recorded statement after the witness has testified for the government. Reviewing such statements may prove important to show that a witness is inconsistent, biased, or has a bad memory.

This procedure often causes trial delay, as defendants usually request time between direct examination and cross-examination to review such statements. For this reason, some federal prosecutors provide such information prior to trial. The Jencks Act is a matter of federal statutory law and does not apply in state criminal prosecutions.

Depositions

A **deposition** is oral testimony given under oath, not in a court. In civil procedure, depositions are freely conducted. Upon notice to a party or subpoena to a witness, an attorney can call a person to testify prior to trial. This is not so in criminal practice.

Fed. R. Crim. P. 15 allows depositions only when "exceptional circumstances" exist. Expected absence of a witness at trial is an example of an exceptional circumstance. If such a circumstance is shown, the deposition may be ordered by the trial court, and the deposition may be used at trial. Of course, both the defendant and government have the opportunity to question the witness at the deposition.

deposition

■ The process of taking a witness's sworn out-of-court testimony. The questioning is usually done by a lawyer, and the lawyer from the other side is given a chance to attend and participate.

Brady Doctrine

Although most discovery occurs under the authority of statutes and court rules, the Constitution also requires disclosure of information by the government in some situations. In *Brady v. Maryland*, the Supreme Court announced what is now referred to as the Brady doctrine.

Obviously, *Brady* applies to both state and federal prosecutions. Note that only exculpatory evidence must be provided. Evidence that tends to prove a defendant's innocence is exculpatory. *Brady* does not stand for the proposition that prosecutors must reveal incriminating evidence to defendants. Failure to disclose to a defendant will result in reversal of a conviction if there is a reasonable probability that the likelihood of a different result is great enough to undermine confidence in the outcome of the trial.[22]

BRADY V. MARYLAND
373 U.S. 83 (1962)

Petitioner and companion, Boblit, were found guilty of murder in the first degree and were sentenced to death. . . . Their trials were separate, petitioner being tried first. At his trial Brady took the stand and admitted his participation in the crime, but he claimed that Boblit did the actual killing. And, in his summation to the jury, Brady's counsel conceded that Brady was guilty of murder in the first degree, asking only that the jury return that verdict "without capital punishment." Prior to the trial petitioner's counsel had requested the prosecution to allow him to examine Boblit's extrajudicial statements. Several of those statements were shown to him; but one dated July 9, 1958, in which Boblit admitted the actual homicide, was withheld by the prosecution and did not come to petitioner's notice until after he had been tried, convicted, and sentenced, and after his conviction had been affirmed.

Petitioner moved the trial court for a new trial based on the newly discovered evidence that had been suppressed by the prosecution. Petitioner's appeal from a denial of that motion was dismissed by the Court of Appeals without prejudice to relief under the Maryland Post Conviction Procedures Act. . . . The petition for post-conviction relief was dismissed by the trial court; and on appeal the Court of Appeals held that suppression of the evidence by the prosecution denied petitioner due process of law and remanded the case for a retrial of the question of punishment, not the question of guilt. . . .

We now hold that the suppression by the prosecution of evidence favorable to an accused upon request violates due process where the evidence is material either to guilt or to punishment, irrespective of the good faith or bad faith of the prosecution.

[This principle] is not punishment of society for misdeeds of a prosecutor but avoidance of an unfair trial to the accused. Society wins not only when the guilty are convicted but when criminal trials are fair; our system of the administration of justice suffers when any accused is treated unfairly. An inscription on the walls of the Department of Justice states the proposition candidly for the federal domain: "The United States wins its point whenever justice is done its citizens in the courts." A prosecution that withholds evidence on demand of an accused which, if made available, would tend to exculpate him or reduce the penalty helps shape a trial that bears heavily on the defendant. That casts the prosecutor in the role of an architect of a proceeding that does not comport with standards of justice.

In most situations, disclosure at trial will satisfy *Brady*. However, if disclosure at trial would prejudice a defendant, pretrial disclosure may be constitutionally required. As is sometimes the case with Jencks Act materials, prosecutors may provide such information prior to trial as a courtesy.

In a case related to *Brady*, the Supreme Court found that it is violative of due process for prosecutors to use perjured testimony or to deceive juries. This is true even if the perjury was unsolicited by the prosecuting attorney. As such, a prosecutor has a duty to correct any testimony of a witness that he or she knows is false.[23]

Although *Brady* and related cases are law in both state and federal prosecutions, the other discovery rules differ. Be sure to check local law to determine what your client has a right to discover.

Freedom of Information Laws

The federal government and most, if not all, states have statutes requiring the public disclosure of files, documents, and other information in the possession of the government.[24] The federal statute is known as the Freedom of Information Act (FOIA).[25]

There are nine exemptions to the federal FOIA. If a request for information falls into one of the nine exemptions, the government may withhold disclosure. Otherwise, disclosure is mandated.

One of the exemptions provides that law enforcement records may be withheld if disclosure will:

1. Interfere with enforcement proceedings.
2. Deprive a person of a fair trial or an impartial adjudication.
3. Constitute an unwarranted invasion of personal privacy.
4. Disclose the identity of a confidential source.
5. Disclose investigative techniques and procedures.
6. Endanger the life or physical safety of law enforcement personnel.

The FOIA is not a discovery device. It is a statute of general applicability, and any person may request inspection or production of documents under its authority. The purpose of the FOIA, which is unrelated to litigation, is the promotion of democracy by having an informed citizenry; it keeps the governors accountable to the governed.

Even though the FOIA was not specifically intended to be used for discovery in litigation, it does not foreclose that use. However, although the FOIA may be used to obtain information, it is not intended to displace or supplement the recognized forms of discovery.[26] Nor shall the process of obtaining information through the FOIA be cause for delaying a criminal proceeding. Therefore, requests for information under the FOIA are separate from a defendant's discovery requests in a criminal case.[27]

Hence, defendants may seek information under the FOIA, but such requests are not part of the criminal discovery process, and criminal proceedings will not be delayed to wait for such requests to be answered or disputes over disclosure to be adjudicated.

The same principles apply to other disclosure laws. For example, the federal Privacy Act[28] provides that individuals have a right to discover the contents of files containing information about them. Again, requests for information under this law are aside from, not in addition to, criminal discovery rules.

Reciprocal Discovery

The Fifth Amendment's freedom from self-incrimination clause, as well as due process, greatly limits what can be expected of defendants in discovery. Requiring defendants to give notice of affirmative defenses, such as alibi and insanity, is common and constitutional. Many jurisdictions also expect defendants to provide witness lists, pretrial statements of the witnesses, and to detail expert testimony and reports that will be offered at trial.

Motion Practice

In both civil and criminal practice, a motion is a request made to a court for it to do something. In most cases a party that files a motion is seeking an order from the court. Generally, when a person desires something from a court, a formal motion must be filed and copies sent to opposing counsel. On occasion, oral motions are made. This is most common during trials and hearings. Some of the most common motions are discussed here.

Motion to Dismiss/Quash

If a defendant believes that the indictment or information is fatally flawed, the appropriate remedy is a motion to dismiss. In some jurisdictions, this would be called a motion to quash. Examples of fatal flaws in the charging instrument are as follows: the court lacks jurisdiction; the facts alleged do not amount to a crime; an essential element is not charged; or the defendant has a legal defense, such as double jeopardy.

If the form of the charging instrument is attacked, courts often permit prosecutors to amend the charge rather than dismissing it entirely. Dismissal of an indictment or information does not mean that the defendant cannot be recharged. A person is not in "jeopardy" under the Fifth Amendment until later in the proceeding.

Motion to Suppress

You have already learned that evidence obtained in an unconstitutional manner may not be used at trial. Objection at trial to the admission of such evidence is one method of excluding such evidence. Another is by way of a motion to suppress prior to trial.

A separate hearing is conducted prior to trial to determine whether the motion to suppress should be granted. Defendants may testify at suppression hearings, and their testimony may not be used against them at trial.[29] To allow a defendant's testimony from a suppression hearing to be used at trial would place the defendant in a position of choosing between the right to suppress evidence and the right to be free from self-incrimination. The best alternative is to allow the defendant to testify and to prohibit that testimony from being used later.

Who has the burden of proof in suppression hearings varies by jurisdiction and on what the defendant wishes to be suppressed. For example, most jurisdictions place the burden of proving that a search pursuant to a warrant was unconstitutional on the defendant. The opposite is true if there was no warrant; the government bears the burden of proving the propriety of the search. Most jurisdictions also place the burden of proving that a confession was voluntary upon the prosecution.

Motion for Change of Venue

Venue means "place for trial." In state criminal proceedings, venue usually lies in the county where the crime occurred. In federal proceedings, venue lies in the district where the crime occurred. Many federal crimes are interstate in character, and the charges may be filed in any district where the crime took place.

Fed. R. Crim. P. 21 permits transfer of a case from one district to another if "the defendant cannot obtain a fair and impartial trial" at the location where the case is pending. In addition, a district judge may transfer a case if it is most convenient for the defendant and witnesses.

Pretrial publicity of criminal matters may be cause to transfer a case (change venue in state proceedings). If a defendant receives considerable negative media coverage, it may be necessary to try the defendant in another location. Several factors are taken into consideration when a defendant moves for a change of venue due to excessive negative publicity, including the total amount of coverage, whether media attention had increased or waned since the case first became public, the length of time between first coverage and trial, the extent to which the coverage itself directly accused or implied guilt, and the nature of the facts that had been brought to light.

The early 2000s witnessed some of the largest and most costly financial scandals in U.S. history. Millions of people lost money and the economies of many nations suffered as a result of corruption in the accounting, banking, investment, energy, and other industries. Enron, one of the United States' largest corporations, found itself bankrupt in 2001. Jeffrey Skillings, its president and CEO, was charged and convicted, among others, as having lied to shareholders and others about the financial status of the company pre-bankruptcy. The case generated considerable attention around the world. Believing he could not be given a fair trial in Houston, Texas, the site of Enron's headquarters and where the charges were filed, he sought a change of venue. The trial court denied his motion. Eventually, the Supreme Court heard his case.

SKILLINGS V. U.S.
561 U.S. __ (2010)

In November 2004, Skilling moved to transfer the trial to another venue; he contended that hostility toward him in Houston, coupled with extensive pretrial publicity, had poisoned potential jurors. To support this assertion, Skilling, aided by media experts, submitted hundreds of news reports detailing Enron's downfall; he also presented affidavits from the experts he engaged portraying community attitudes in Houston in comparison to other potential venues.

The U.S. District Court for the Southern District of Texas, in accord with rulings in two earlier instituted Enron-related prosecutions, denied the venue-transfer motion. Despite "isolated incidents of intemperate commentary," the court observed, media coverage "ha[d] [mostly] been objective and unemotional," and the facts of the case were "neither heinous nor sensational." Moreover, "courts ha[d] commonly" favored "effective voir dire . . . to

(continued)

ferret out any [juror] bias." Pretrial publicity about the case, the court concluded, did not warrant a presumption that Skilling would be unable to obtain a fair trial in Houston. . . .

Following a 4-month trial and nearly five days of deliberation, the jury found Skilling guilty of 19 counts, including the honest-services-fraud conspiracy charge, and not guilty of 9 insider-trading counts. The District Court sentenced Skilling to 292 months' imprisonment, 3 years' supervised release, and $45 million in restitution. . . .

The Sixth Amendment secures to criminal defendants the right to trial by an impartial jury. By constitutional design, that trial occurs "in the State where the . . . Crimes . . . have been committed." Art. III, § 2, cl. 3. See also Amdt. 6 (right to trial by "jury of the State and district wherein the crime shall have been committed"). The Constitution's place-of-trial prescriptions, however, do not impede transfer of the proceeding to a different district at the defendant's request if extraordinary local prejudice will prevent a fair trial—a "basic requirement of due process". . . .

When does the publicity attending conduct charged as criminal dim prospects that the trier can judge a case, as due process requires, impartially, unswayed by outside influence? Because most cases of consequence garner at least some pretrial publicity, courts have considered this question in diverse settings. We begin our discussion by addressing the presumption of prejudice from which the Fifth Circuit's analysis in Skilling's case proceeded. The foundation precedent is *Rideau* v. *Louisiana*, 373 U.S. 723 (1963).

Wilbert Rideau robbed a bank in a small Louisiana town, kidnaped three bank employees, and killed one of them. Police interrogated Rideau in jail without counsel present and obtained his confession. Without informing Rideau, no less seeking his consent, the police filmed the interrogation. On three separate occasions shortly before the trial, a local television station broadcast the film to audiences ranging from 24,000 to 53,000 individuals. Rideau moved for a change of venue, arguing that he could not receive a fair trial in the parish where the crime occurred, which had a population of approximately 150,000 people. The trial court denied the motion, and a jury eventually convicted Rideau. The Supreme Court of Louisiana upheld the conviction.

We reversed. "What the people [in the community] saw on their television sets," we observed, "was Rideau, in jail, flanked by the sheriff and two state troopers, admitting in detail the commission of the robbery, kidnapping, and murder." "[T]o the tens of thousands of people who saw and heard it," we explained, the interrogation "in a very real sense *was* Rideau's trial—at which he pleaded guilty." We therefore "d[id] not hesitate to hold, without pausing to examine a particularized transcript of the *voir dire*," that "[t]he kangaroo court proceedings" trailing the televised confession violated due process.

We followed *Rideau* 's lead in two later cases in which media coverage manifestly tainted a criminal prosecution. In *Estes* v. *Texas*, 381 U.S. 532, 538 (1965), extensive publicity before trial swelled into excessive exposure during preliminary court proceedings as reporters and television crews overran the courtroom and "bombard[ed] . . . the community with the sights and sounds of" the pretrial hearing. The media's overzealous reporting efforts, we observed, "led to considerable disruption" and denied the "judicial serenity and calm to which [Billie Sol Estes] was entitled."

Similarly, in *Sheppard* v. *Maxwell*, 384 U.S. 333 (1966), news reporters extensively covered the story of Sam Sheppard, who was accused of bludgeoning his pregnant wife to death. "[B]edlam reigned at the courthouse during the trial and newsmen took over practically the entire courtroom," thrusting jurors "into the role of celebrities." Pretrial media coverage, which we characterized as "months

SKILLINGS V. U.S. *(continued)*

[of] virulent publicity about Sheppard and the murder," did not alone deny due process, we noted. But Sheppard's case involved more than heated reporting pretrial: We upset the murder conviction because a "carnival atmosphere" pervaded the trial.

In each of these cases, we overturned a "conviction obtained in a trial atmosphere that [was] utterly corrupted by press coverage"; our decisions, however, "cannot be made to stand for the proposition that juror exposure to . . . news accounts of the crime . . . alone presumptively deprives the defendant of due process." Prominence does not necessarily produce prejudice, and juror *impartiality*, we have reiterated, does not require *ignorance*. . . .

First, we have emphasized in prior decisions the size and characteristics of the community in which the crime occurred. In *Rideau*, for example, we noted that the murder was committed in a parish of only 150,000 residents. Houston, in contrast, is the fourth most populous city in the Nation: At the time of Skilling's trial, more than 4.5 million individuals eligible for jury duty resided in the Houston area. Given this large, diverse pool of potential jurors, the suggestion that 12 impartial individuals could not be empaneled is hard to sustain. . . .

Second, although news stories about Skilling were not kind, they contained no confession or other blatantly prejudicial information of the type readers or viewers could not reasonably be expected to shut from sight. Rideau's dramatically staged admission of guilt, for instance, was likely imprinted indelibly in the mind of anyone who watched it. . . .

Finally, and of prime significance, Skilling's jury acquitted him of nine insider-trading counts. Similarly, earlier instituted Enron-related prosecutions yielded no overwhelming victory for the Government. . . .

[therefore, the trial court's decision to not change venue was upheld]

Because of the First Amendment free press issue, judges are generally prohibited from excluding the press or public from hearings.[30] In some instances judges may order the attorneys involved in a case not to provide information to anyone not involved in the proceeding.

Motion for Severance

Fed. R. Crim. P. 8 permits two or more defendants to be charged in the same information or indictment if they were involved in the same crime. That rule also permits joinder of two offenses by the same person in one charging instrument, provided they are similar in character or arise out of the same set of facts.

In some situations, severance of the two defendants may be necessary to assure fair trials. For example, if two defendants have antagonistic defenses, severance must be granted. Defenses are *antagonistic* if the jury must disbelieve one by believing the other. For example, if Defendant A denies being at the scene of a crime, and Defendant B claims that they were both there, but also claims that A forced him to commit the crime, their defenses are antagonistic.

If a defendant is charged with two or more offenses, it may be necessary to sever them to have a fair trial. For example, if a defendant plans to testify concerning one charge and not the other, severance is necessary.

Motion in Limine

Prior to trial, both the defendant and the prosecution may file motions in limine. This is a request that the court order the other party not to mention or attempt to question a witness about some matter. A motion in limine is similar to a motion to suppress, except that it encompasses more than admission of illegally seized evidence.

For example, if one anticipates that the opposing counsel will attempt to question a witness about evidence that is inadmissible under the rules of evidence (e.g., hearsay), a motion in limine may be filed to avoid having to object at trial. This is important, as often a witness may blurt out the answer before an attorney has had an opportunity to object. In addition, knowing whether the judge will permit the admission of evidence prior to trial helps an attorney to plan the case.

Other Motions

A variety of other motions may be filed. If the prosecution fears that revealing information required under a discovery rule will endanger the case or a person's life, a motion for a protective order may be filed. In such cases the trial court reviews the evidence in camera and decides if it is necessary to keep it from the defendant. If so, the judge will enter a protective order so stating.

Motions for continuance of hearings and trial dates are common. In criminal cases, courts must be careful not to violate speedy trial requirements.

If two defendants have been charged jointly, one or both may file a motion for severance of trial. If defense counsel believes that the defendant is not competent to stand trial, a motion for mental examination may be filed.

Pretrial Conference

Sometime prior to trial, the court will hold a pretrial conference. This may be weeks or only days before trial.

At this conference the court will address any remaining motions and discuss any problems the parties have. In addition, the judge will explain his or her method of trying a case, such as how the jury will be selected. The next stage is trial.

EXTRADITION AND DETAINERS

extradition

■ One country (or state) giving up a person to a second country (or state) when the second requests the person for a trial on a criminal charge or for punishment after a trial.

If wanted persons are located outside the jurisdiction where they are, or will be, charged, **extradition** is one method of securing their presence in the charging jurisdiction. *Extradition* is the surrender of a person from one jurisdiction to another where the person has been charged or convicted of a crime.

Extradition usually occurs under the provisions of a treaty. Extradition includes transfers between states, as well as between nations. Extradition, especially international, is as much a political decision as a legal one.

Pursuant to the Uniform Interstate Criminal Extradition Act, which has been adopted by 47 states,[31] the request for extradition is made between governors. If a governor determines that the person sought should be delivered, an arrest warrant is issued by that governor.

Once seized, the arrestee is brought before a judge and may file a petition for writ of habeas corpus. During the proceedings, release on bail is permitted, unless the crime charged is one punishable by death or life imprisonment in the state where the crime was committed. If the person sought is under charge in the sending state, the governor may order his or her surrender immediately or may wait until the prosecution and punishment are completed in the first state.

Generally, the guilt or innocence of the accused may not be considered by the governor or courts during the proceedings; that issue is left to the requesting jurisdiction. It is the obligation of the governor and courts of the sending state to be sure that the correct person is seized and that proper procedures are followed.

Defendants may waive extradition. This waiver must be made in court, and defendants must be informed of their rights, including habeas corpus, for waivers to be valid.

The law permits arrests by police officers from outside a state in hot-pursuit situations. If an arrest is made in hot pursuit, the officer is to bring the accused before a local court, which is to order the defendant held, or released on bail, until an extradition warrant is issued by the governor.

The Supreme Court has held that the exclusionary rule does not exclude persons who have been illegally seized from trial. In *Frisbie v. Collins*, 342 U.S. 519 (1952), the fact that Michigan police officers kidnapped a defendant from Illinois and returned him to Michigan, disregarding extradition laws, did not affect the court's jurisdiction to try the defendant. The same result was reached in a case in which international extradition laws were not followed.[32] Today, if the government's conduct in seizing a defendant were outrageous or shocking, there is a possibility that a court would bar prosecution.[33]

You may recall from discussion of double jeopardy earlier in this text that the Fifth Amendment's Double Jeopardy Clause does not prevent two sovereigns from charging an individual for the same crime or two crimes arising from the same facts. Accordingly, one state may grant immunity to an individual and then extradite that individual to another state to be tried for the immunized crime.

A **detainer** is a request (or order) for the continued custody of a prisoner. For example, suppose federal charges are pending against a Utah prisoner. The United States would issue a detainer requesting that Utah hold the prisoner after his or her sentence is completed, so that the United States may take custody. This situation does not raise jurisdictional issues, as federal authorities have nationwide jurisdiction. As to interstate detention, the detainer is used in conjunction with extradition.

Pursuant to the Interstate Agreement on Detainers, a state may request the temporary custody of a prisoner of another state in order to try the person. Once the trial is completed, the prisoner is returned, regardless of the outcome. If the prisoner is convicted, a detainer is issued and he or she is again returned after the sentence is completed in the sending state.

The Agreement also provides that prisoners are to be notified of any detainers against them. Further, if a state issues a detainer for a prisoner, that prisoner may

detainer

■ A warrant or court order to keep a person in custody when that person might otherwise be released. This is often used to make sure a person will serve a sentence or attend a trial in one state at the end of a prison term in another state or in a federal prison.

request to be temporarily transferred to that state for final disposition of that case. A request for final disposition by a prisoner is deemed a waiver of extradition to and from the sending state. Also, it is deemed a waiver of extradition to the receiving state to serve any resulting sentence after the sentence in the sending state is completed.

It is a common practice for jail and prison officials to conduct warrant checks before releasing or transferring prisoners. The importance of this practice was highlighted by the tragic events leading to the death of 6-year-old Jake Robel. On February 20, 2000, a local jail in Missouri released Kim Davis. Within hours of his release, Davis carjacked an automobile owned by Christy Robel. Christy's son, Jake Robel, was in the automobile at the time Kim Davis stole the car. Ms. Robel attempted to remove her son from the car, but he became entangled in the seatbelt and her pleas to Kim Davis to stop were ignored. She was dragged for a short distance before she lost her grip of the car. Tangled in the seatbelt and hanging out of the car, Jake Robel was dragged five miles by Kim Davis while driving at speeds reaching 80 miles per hour. Jake was dead by the time Kim Davis was forced to stop the vehicle. It was discovered that there was an outstanding warrant for the arrest of Kim Davis when he was released and that a warrants check had not been conducted by jail officials. Kim Davis was subsequently convicted of second-degree murder and sentenced to life imprisonment. In response to the records check oversight, Missouri enacted "Jake's Law," a statute requiring records checks of individuals scheduled for release from jails and prison in Missouri.

REMOVAL

Congress has provided that, in certain circumstances, criminal cases may be removed from state courts to federal courts. Removal is premised upon the principle that certain cases are more properly adjudicated in a federal, rather than state, court. The purpose of removal is to preserve the sovereignty of the federal government by assuring a fair trial to particular criminal defendants. Otherwise, the states could interfere with the functioning of the federal government by harassing federal officials through criminal proceedings.

28 U.S.C. § 1442 provides that a federal official sued in state court, whether the action is civil or criminal, may remove the case to the federal district court where the action is pending, if the suit concerns the performance of his or her official duties. Similarly, 28 U.S.C. § 1442(a) provides for removal of cases, civil or criminal, filed against members of the U.S. armed forces for actions taken in the course of their duties. 28 U.S.C. § 1443 provides for removal of certain civil rights cases.

Removal of criminal cases is the same as for civil: The defendant must file a notice of, and petition for, removal.[34] Improperly removed actions are remanded to the state court from which they came.[35]

Ethical Considerations

LAWYER COMPETENCE AND COMPUTERS

Section 1.1 of the ABA Model Rules of Professional Conduct require attorneys to provide competent representation. Section 1.6 requires attorneys to maintain the confidences of their clients. There are obvious applications of these rules. An attorney may not, for example—and with few exceptions—reveal the content of a client's statements, such as a confession, to any person. The rule is clear. How far an attorney must go in protecting client information from theft and unintended disclosures is not. The advent of mass data storage and the use of the Internet to access client information have raised new questions about the obligation to preserve client confidentiality.

Must an attorney lock client files when they are not in use? May an attorney send confidential information by e-mail? May confidential data be stored on a mass storage device? If so, must it be encrypted? The State Bar of Arizona addressed just such a question in 2005 where it held that lawyers must take reasonable and competent steps to avoid disclosure of client confidences through theft or accidental disclosure. The Arizona bar went further by requiring attorneys who do not have the technical expertise to ensure the confidentiality of client data to secure the services of a computer security expert. This ruling, of course, requires a financial investment in the security expert as well as in software and hardware.

The ABA has not gone as far as the Arizona bar in its interpretation of Sections 1.1 and 1.6. In 1999, it interpreted these rules to not require encryption, or other increased security, of e-mail correspondence containing client information. However, as state bar authorities increase their expectations and as computer theft and crime increases, the likelihood increases that ABA will elaborate a more sophisticated and security conscious set of rules.

Source: John D. Comerford, "Competent Computing: A Lawyer's Ethical Duty to Safeguard the Confidentiality and Integrity of Client Information Stored on Computers and Computer Networks," 19 *Geo. J. Legal Ethics* 629 (2006).

Web Links

Directory of Attorneys

For a listing of attorneys, try one of these two sites: Martindale-Hubbell at http://www.martindale.com/ or http://lawyers.findlaw.com

Key Terms

arraignment

arrest

bail

bill of particulars

complaint

deposition

detainer

discovery

extradition

grand juries

indictment

information

motion

plea

plea bargain (plea agreement)

preliminary hearing

quash

Review Questions

1. For what two reasons may a defendant be detained prior to trial?

2. What is the difference between an indictment and an information?

3. What are the purposes of indictments and informations?

4. If a defendant needs more information than appears in the indictment to prepare a defense, what should be done?

5. What advantage does a plea of nolo contendere have over a guilty plea?

6. Kevin has been charged with murder. He believes a weapon that the prosecutor plans on using at trial was unconstitutionally seized from his home. How can he raise this issue prior to trial?

7. Place the following in the proper order of occurrence: preliminary hearing; formal charge; initial appearance; arraignment; trial; and complaint.

8. What is the Brady doctrine?

9. When is removal from state to federal court allowed?

10. What is extradition?

Problems & Critical Thinking Exercises

1. What is the historical purpose of the grand jury? Many feel that grand juries should be abolished. Why?

2. Discovery in civil cases is very broad. Fed. R. Civ. P. 26 permits discovery of anything "reasonably calculated to lead to the discovery of admissible evidence." Should discovery in criminal cases be broader? Explain your position.

3. Do you believe that indictment by grand jury should be incorporated? Explain your position.

Endnotes

1. Fed. R. Crim. P. 4.
2. Fed. R. Crim. P. 5.
3. 500 U.S. 44 (1991).
4. *Stack v. Boyle,* 342 U.S. 1 (1951).

5. 18 U.S.C. § 3142(f).

6. 18 U.S.C. § 3142(e), (f).

7. *Gerstein v. Pugh,* 420 U.S. 103 (1975).

8. Fed. R. Crim. P. 5.1; 18 U.S.C. § 3060.

9. 18 U.S.C. § 3060(e).

10. *United States v. Mandujano,* 425 U.S. 564 (1976).

11. *United States v. Calandra,* 414 U.S. 338 (1974).

12. Fed. R. Crim. P. 6.

13. *Ex parte Wilson,* 114 U.S. 417 (1884). *See also* Fed. R. Crim. P. 7.

14. Fed. R. Crim. P. 7(c).

15. Fed. R. Crim. P. 8(a).

16. *See United States v. Cox,* 342 F.2d 167 (5th Cir.), *cert. denied,* 381 U.S. 935 (1965).

17. Fed. R. Crim. P. 7(c).

18. See *United States v. Davila,* U.S. (2013)

19. Fed. R. Crim. P. 11.

20. *United States v. Diecidue,* 603 F.2d 535 (5th Cir.), *cert. denied,* 445 U.S. 946 (1979).

21. 18 U.S.C. § 3500.

22. *Smith v. Cain,* 564 U.S.(2012).

23. *Mooney v. Holohan,* 294 U.S. 103 (1935).

24. See Daniel Hall, *Administrative Law: Bureaucracy in a Democracy,* 4th ed., ch. 10 (Upper Saddle River, NJ: Pearson: Prentice Hall, 2009), for a more thorough discussion of the Freedom of Information Act.

25. 5 U.S.C. § 552.

26. *John Doe Corp. v. John Doe Agency,* 493 U.S. 146 (1989).

27. *North v. Walsh,* 881 F.2d 1088 (D.C. Cir. 1989).

28. 5 U.S.C. § 552(a).

29. *Simmons v. United States,* 390 U.S. 377 (1968).

30. *Richmond Newspapers, Inc. v. Virginia,* 448 U.S. 555 (1980).

31. Rhonda Wasserman, "The Subpoena Power: *Pennoyer's* Last Vestige," 74 *Minn. L. Rev.* 37 (1989).

32. *Ker v. Illinois,* 119 U.S. 436 (1886).

33. *See United States v. Toscanino,* 500 F.2d 267 (2d Cir. 1974).

34. 28 U.S.C. § 1446.

35. 28 U.S.C. § 1447.

CHAPTER 15

TRIAL

Chapter Outline

Chapter Objectives

After completing this chapter, you should be able to:

- identify and explain, in sequence, the various steps and procedures of trial.

- list, describe, and identify the landmark cases discussed in the book for the constitutional rights possessed by defendants at trial, such as the right to a public, speedy, jury trial, counsel, to remain silent, to cross-examine witnesses, and to confront accusers.

- identify the material facts and legal issues in nearly all of the cases you read, describe the courts' analyses and conclusions in the cases, and demonstrate the ability to synthesize and think critically about the law of the subject.

TRIAL RIGHTS OF DEFENDANTS

The Right to a Jury Trial

A trial is a method of determining guilt or innocence. In medieval England, trials by ordeal, combat, and compurgation were used.

To demonstrate how trials have changed, consider trial by ordeal. Trial by ordeal was considered trial by God; that is, God determined the person's guilt or innocence. There were two ordeals: by water and fire. Two water ordeals were used. In the first the accused was thrown into a body of water. If he sank he was adjudged innocent, and if he floated he was guilty. In the second water ordeal, the accused's arm was submerged in boiling water. The defendant had to survive this unhurt to be proven innocent. The fire ordeal was similar, the accused having to walk over fire or grasp hot irons.

Trial as we know it today finds its roots in the Magna Carta (1215), which guaranteed free men trial by their peers. Unlike juries today, those juries comprised people who knew the facts of the case. The concept of trial by a jury of one's peers was of great importance to the colonists of the United States and made its way into the Constitution of the United States.

The Sixth Amendment to the U.S. Constitution reads, in part, "[i]n all criminal prosecutions, the accused shall enjoy the right to a speedy and public trial, by an impartial jury of the State and district wherein the crime shall have been committed." The Sixth Amendment is fully applicable against the states via the Fourteenth Amendment. See exhibit 15-1 for an illustration of the trial rights found in the Sixth Amendment.

The Sixth Amendment has been interpreted to mean that defendants have a right to a jury trial for all offenses that may be punished with more than six months' imprisonment. Most crimes that have as their maximum punishment less than six months are "petty offenses," and there is no right to trial by jury.[1]

Note that the term "most" is used. Some argue that when fines become large enough, one is entitled to a jury trial, regardless of the amount of time one could be sentenced to spend in jail. In addition, it is argued that crimes that are moral in nature and subject the defendant to ridicule and embarrassment justify trial by jury, even when the punishment is less than six months' imprisonment. The same question is raised concerning crimes that were indictable at common law. The Supreme Court has not answered these questions, and the lower courts that have addressed these issues are split.

The maximum penalty allowed determines if a crime is petty, not the actual sentence. For example, if a crime is punishable by from three months to one year in jail, the defendant is entitled to a jury, even if the trial judge routinely sentences those convicted to three months for the offense. Some crimes do not have a legislatively established punishment, such as contempt. In such cases the issue is whether the defendant is sentenced to more than six months in jail. If so, the defendant is entitled to a jury.

Although the right to a jury trial for nonpetty offenses nearly always attaches, there are a few exceptions. There is no right to a jury in military trials. In addition, those appearing in juvenile court (delinquency proceedings) are not entitled to a jury trial.[2] Of course, juveniles who are tried as adults are entitled to the same rights as adults, including the right to have a jury trial.

Juries sit as fact finders. A defendant may be entitled to have a jury decide guilt or innocence, and as you learn in the next chapter, there is also a right to have juries decide the facts that are essential to passing sentence. Some jurisdictions have juries actually impose sentence, or make a sentence recommendation to the trial court; however, this is not usually the practice and there is no federal constitutional reason for it.

The Supreme Court has held that there is no constitutional requirement for 12 jurors.[3] Nor does the Constitution require juror unanimity. There is a limit to how small a jury may be and how few jurors must concur in a verdict. In one case, the Supreme Court found a law unconstitutional that required trial by six jurors and permitted conviction with a vote of five to one.[4]

It is common for six-person juries to be used for misdemeanors. However, a unanimous verdict is constitutionally required for conviction. If a 12-member jury is used, it is constitutional to permit conviction upon a concurrence of 9 or more jurors.

A defendant cannot be penalized for choosing to proceed to trial rather than pleading guilty. In *United States v. Jackson*, 390 U.S. 570 (1968), the Supreme Court found that a statute making the death penalty available for those who were tried and not for those who pled guilty was violative of the Sixth Amendment. An interesting question that has received considerable attention from the Supreme Court in recent years is exactly what facts must be found by a jury. As you will learn in the next chapter, the responsibility of juries extends beyond the guilt decision. They must also find all facts that are essential to the sentencing decision.

The Right to a Public Trial

The Sixth Amendment also guarantees the right to a public trial. This guarantee applies throughout the trial, from openings to return of the verdict; it also applies to many pretrial hearings, such as suppression hearings. The presence of the public is intended to keep prosecutions "honest." As the Supreme Court stated in *Estes v. Texas*, 381 U.S. 532 (1965): "History has proven that secret tribunals were effective instruments of oppression."

The right to a public hearing does not mean that everyone who wishes to attend has to be permitted in. The trial judge is responsible for maintaining order in the courtroom and may require the doors to be shut once all seats have been filled. Also, a disruptive citizen may be removed.

The defendant's right to a public trial is not absolute. Trial judges, acting with extreme caution, may order that a hearing be conducted in private. Facts that support excluding the public are rare. An example of when exclusion of the public may be justified is when an undercover law enforcement agent testifies, and public exposure would put the officer's life in jeopardy.

If a court closes a hearing (or trial) without justification, the defendant is entitled to a new hearing, regardless of whether the defendant was actually harmed. The 1998 First Circuit Court of Appeals case, *United States v. DeLuca*, addressed both the presumption of innocence and the right to a public trial in what are rather unusual circumstances.

Generally members of the press have no greater right to attend a hearing than do other members of the public. However, many judges provide special seating for reporters.

UNITED STATES V. DELUCA
137 F.3d 24 (1st Cir. 1998)

[Defendants were tried and convicted of extortion. Because of fears of juror tampering and intimidation, the trial judge ordered that the identity of the jurors be kept anonymous. The judge also permitted the U.S. Marshal to screen trial spectators. The defendants appealed several issues, including whether an anonymous jury violates the presumption of innocence and whether the screening violated the Sixth Amendment right to a public trial.]

A. THE ANONYMOUS JURY EMPANELMENT

Appellants first contend that the decision to empanel an anonymous jury constituted an abuse of discretion. . . . We disagree.

Although the empanelment of an anonymous jury should be recognized as an extraordinary protective device, especially if it tends to suggest that the jurors may have something to fear from the accused, thereby conceivably encroaching upon the presumption of innocence, it is a permissible precaution where (1) there are strong grounds for concluding that it is necessary to enable the jury to perform its factfinding function, or to ensure juror protection; and (2) reasonable safeguards are adopted by the trial court to minimize any risk of infringement upon the fundamental rights of the accused.

Our review takes into account not only the evidence available at the time the anonymous empanelment occurred, but all relevant evidence introduced at trial. We conclude that the record as a whole affords sufficient foundation for empaneling an anonymous jury both as a prudent safety precaution and a means of ensuring unfettered performance of the factfinding function.

First, the record links appellants to organized crime, a factor which strongly indicated that clandestine "outside" assistance might be brought to bear in any effort to intimidate or punish jurors. Moreover, Ouimette's capacity and readiness to enlist criminal confederates in jury tampering plans was supported by actual precedent. See *Ross*, 33 F.3d at 1520 (court may consider "defendant's past attempts to interfere with the judicial process"); *United States v. Tutino*, 883 F.2d 1125, 1132–1133 (2d Cir. 1989).

Second, both Ouimette and DeLuca Sr. have long been involved in violent crimes, including robbery, assault with a dangerous weapon, larceny in a dwelling, and conspiracy to commit murder, not to mention their violent extortions in the instant case.

Third, appellants also attempted to tamper with witnesses and to suborn perjury in the instant case. DeLuca Sr. and Ouimette, through intermediaries, pressured prospective prosecution witnesses, Paula Coppola and Robert Buehne, to perjure themselves, and offered $5,000 to another prospective government witness, David Duxbury, to abscond prior to trial. Thereafter, when Duxbury nevertheless showed up at a pretrial hearing, Ouimette told an associate: "If we can't get [Duxbury], we'll get one of his kids." See *United States v. Edmond*, 311 U.S. App. D.C. 235, 52 F.3d 1080, 1091–1092 (D.C. Cir. 1995) (noting that a general preparedness to obstruct the judicial process may serve as indirect evidence of readiness to engage in jury tampering as well); *United States v. Aulicino*, 44 F.3d 1102, 1116 (2d Cir. 1995) (same).

Fourth, both Ouimette and DeLuca were confronting mandatory lifetime sentences upon conviction, which surely provided a strong inducement to resort to extreme measures in any effort to influence the outcome of their trial. See *Ross*, 33 F.3d at 1520. Moreover, their trial was prominently and extensively covered by local print and electronic media (e.g., several lengthy front-page stories in the

(continued)

Providence Journal), to the degree that any public disclosure of the jurors' identities would have enhanced the practicability, hence the likelihood, of efforts to harass, intimidate, or harm the jurors.

Finally, the district court adopted prudent measures designed to safeguard defendants' constitutional rights by informing the members of the jury that their identities would not be disclosed, so as to ensure that no extrajudicial information could be communicated to them during trial, either by the public or by media representatives. Thus, the court explained, the constitutional right of each defendant to a jury trial, based exclusively on the evidence, would be preserved.

In our view, the district court thereby satisfactorily averted any unacceptable risk of intrusion upon the constitutional rights of the individual defendants by diverting juror attention from the possible perception that anonymous empanelment was a safeguard against defendants' dangerousness. Accordingly, given the demonstrated need, coupled with the cautionary instruction fashioned by the district court, the anonymous jury empanelment did not constitute an abuse of discretion.

B. THE PROCEDURAL IMPEDIMENTS TO COURTROOM ACCESS BY SPECTATORS

The United States Marshal, acting sua sponte on the first day of trial, established a screening and identification procedure whereby each would—be spectator was required to present written identification before being allowed to enter the courtroom. Deputy marshals examined whatever written identification was presented, then recorded the type of identification and the bearer's name, address and birth date. The recorded information was retained by the United States Marshal for use in determining whether the bearer had a criminal background or any connection with a defendant on trial, such as might indicate a courtroom security risk. On the second day of trial the district court ratified the

spectator screening procedure over appellants' objections.

Appellants contend on appeal that the screening procedure violated their Sixth Amendment right to a public trial. . . .

The Sixth Amendment right to a public trial enures to the benefit of the criminal justice system itself as well as the defendant, by enhancing due process, encouraging witnesses to come forward, and enabling the public at large to confirm that the accused are dealt with fairly and that the trial participants properly perform their respective functions. Due to the important individual rights and public interests at stake, an alleged violation of the Sixth Amendment right to a public trial resulting from a "total" closure is not subject to "harmless error" analysis. Nevertheless, the Sixth Amendment right to a public trial is not absolute and must on occasion yield to competing interests in the fair and efficient administration of justice.

The government initially urges, as a matter of law, that the Sixth Amendment right to a public trial was never implicated in the present case because the challenged screening procedure effected neither a total nor a partial closure. According to the government, a "closure" occurs only if the trial court unconditionally excludes persons from the courtroom, but not if it simply imposes universal preconditions on courtroom access which have the incidental effect of barring only those persons who elect not to comply. To cite an obvious example, magnetometer screenings are designed to prevent armed spectators from entering the courtroom, yet no one would suggest that conditioning spectator access on submission to reasonable security screening procedures for dangerous weapons violates the Sixth Amendment right to a public trial. Furthermore, the government correctly notes, no authority squarely holds that such "universal" preconditions to courtroom access constitute a Sixth Amendment "closure." Cf. *Brazel*, 102 F.3d at 1155

UNITED STATES V. DELUCA *(continued)*

(assuming, arguendo, that similar identification procedure amounted to "partial" closure). We need not opt for the broad rule urged by the government, however, since the security screening procedure utilized below amounted at most to a permissible "partial" closure.

Although we have yet to rule on the matter, cf. *Martin v. Bissonette*, 118 F.3d 871, 874 (1st Cir. 1997), several other courts of appeals have held that the Sixth Amendment test laid down in *Waller*, 467 U.S. at 48, need be less stringent in the "partial" closure context; that is to say, a "substantial reason," rather than an "overriding interest," may warrant a closure which ensures at least some public access. These courts essentially conclude that a less stringent standard is warranted in the "partial" closure context provided the essential purposes of the "public trial" guarantee are served and the constitutional rights of defendants are adequately protected. As yet, no court of appeals has held otherwise.

Unlike the "total" closure in *Waller*, 467 U.S. at 42, which excluded all persons (other than court personnel, witnesses, parties and trial counsel) throughout the entire suppression hearing, the screening and identification procedure employed below effected at most a "partial" closure, as it (1) barred only those would-be spectators who opted not to submit written identification, and (2) presumably may have "chilled" attendance by some potential spectators who opted not to present themselves at the courthouse. Cf. *Woods*, 977 F.2d at 74 (finding "partial" closure where members of defendant's family were excluded while particular witness testified). Moreover, the district court supportably found that members of the general public, as well as members of the defendants' families, attended throughout the seven-day trial, as did credentialed representatives of the print and electronic media, see *Douglas v. Wainwright*, 714 F.2d 1532, 1541

(11th Cir. 1983) (noting that media presence and coverage renders court order one for "partial" closure rather than total, by increasing the likelihood that witnesses with material evidence who are unknown to the parties may learn of perjured testimony through media reports even though they themselves do not attend the trial), vacated and remanded. . . .

Relying on the requirement that a closure be "no broader than necessary" to promote the asserted justification, *Waller*, 467 U.S. at 48, appellants suggest, alternatively, that (1) the anonymous empanelment and partial sequestration adequately addressed any legitimate security concerns, see *supra* Section II.A, or (2) the court could have resorted to less restrictive security measures, such as installing magnetometers immediately outside the courtroom. In addressing these contentions, we note at the outset that since the spectator-screening procedure resulted at most in a "partial" closure, the government was not required to establish that it furthered a "compelling" interest but simply a "substantial" one. See, *e.g., Osborne*, 68 F.3d at 98–99.

Although anonymous empanelment and partial sequestration may afford jurors significant protections beyond the confines of the courtroom, prophylactic procedures of an entirely different nature may be required to safeguard against attempts to intimidate jurors and witnesses in the performance of their courtroom responsibilities. These difficult judgments are matters of courtroom governance which require "a sensitive appraisal of the climate surrounding a trial and a prediction as to the potential security or publicity problems that may arise during the proceedings[.]" Thus, in our view an appellate court should be hesitant to displace a trial court's judgment call in such circumstances. ("The trial court's choice of courtroom security procedures requires a subtle reading of the immediate atmosphere and a prediction of potential

(continued)

risks—judgments nearly impossible for appellate courts to second-guess after the fact."); see also *United States v. Brooks*, 125 F.3d 484, 502 (7th Cir. 1997) ("The decisions of a district court concerning security in the courtroom are reviewed deferentially."); *Elledge v. Dugger*, 823 F.2d 1439, 1456 (11th Cir. 1987) ("We generally defer to a trial court's discretion in courtroom-security decisions."); cf. In re *San Juan Star Co.*, 662 F.2d 108, 117 (1st Cir. 1981) (noting that appellate court "must defer to the [district] court's . . . close familiarity with the nature of the [trial] publicity involved").

As the Eleventh Circuit acknowledged recently in relation to another spectator-screening procedure, given their many coincident duties trial judges cannot be expected to scan their courtrooms efficiently on a continuous basis for spectators whose very demeanor might represent an attempt to intimidate a witness or juror. See *Brazel*, 102 F.3d at 1155 (addressing "fixed stares" directed at witnesses by courtroom spectators). Similarly, in the circumstances presented here we cannot agree that prudent identification procedures suitably focused at deterring would-be trial spectators who may pose unacceptable risks—either to the security of the courtroom or the integrity of the factfinding process—need be held in abeyance pending evidence of an actual attempt to influence or harm a witness or juror in the case on trial. Therefore, though we cannot endorse the unilateral action by the United States Marshal, we hold that it did not strip away the substantial deference due the district court's subsequent assessment that the screening procedures were warranted.

These appellants either were directly associated with prior efforts to obstruct fair factfinding through untruthful trial testimony, or were found to possess the present means as well as ample inducement (viz., avoidance of potential life sentences) to sponsor similar efforts in the case at bar, see *supra* Section II.A. Moreover, the challenged spectator-screening procedure was reasonably designed to respond to these concerns, as it plainly alerted would-be spectators that their courtroom conduct would be closely monitored, thereby efficiently focusing the desired deterrent effect principally upon those most likely to impede a fair and orderly trial—particularly appellants' criminal associates. Thus, the challenged screening procedure represented a permissible response to defendants' demonstrated capacity and motivation to undermine the administration of justice at their trial.

Finally, as the district court supportably found, their extensive criminal histories (not to mention the violent criminal activity alleged in the pending indictment) generated realistic concerns that appellants might circumvent normal courtroom security procedures, as by attempting to coerce or bribe authorized personnel to facilitate the introduction of weapons into the courtroom or elsewhere in the courthouse.

In our view, therefore, the district court order ratifying these screening procedures adequately addressed and significantly minimized the demonstrated potential for harassment and intimidation of jurors and witnesses by would-be trial spectators, for many of the same reasons that warranted the anonymous empanelment and partial jury sequestration. See *supra* Section II.A. Although any courtroom closure represents a serious undertaking which ought never be initiated without prior judicial authorization, we conclude that the partial closure in this case did not contravene the Sixth Amendment, given the strong circumstantial and historical evidence that precautionary security measures were well warranted and the essential constitutional guarantees of a public trial were preserved.

The Right to Confrontation and Cross-Examination

The Sixth Amendment also contains a right to confront one's accusers. This means that a defendant has the right to cross-examine the witnesses of the prosecution. Each state drafts its own rules of evidence; however, it may not enact a rule of evidence that conflicts with a defendant's right to confrontation.

For example, a state procedure permitting government witnesses to refuse to identify themselves was found violative of the Sixth Amendment.[5] The Supreme Court reasoned that the procedure was invalid because it did not permit the defendant to conduct his or her own investigation into the credibility of government witnesses.

Statutes allowing victims to testify remotely, such as by closed-circuit television, also raise confrontation issues. However, the Supreme Court has stated that the Confrontation Clause does not per se prohibit child witnesses in child abuse cases from testifying outside the defendant's physical presence by one-way closed-circuit television. Before such a procedure is used, however, the court must examine the facts of the case and determine that remote testimony is necessary.[6] Failure to make such a finding (e.g., the child fears the defendant) can lead to reversal.[7]

The Confrontation Clause does not give defendants carte blanche to probe any area on cross-examination. If a state can show a compelling reason, it may prohibit cross-examination of a subject. For example, rape shield laws prohibit defendants from inquiring into a rape victim's sexual background in most cases. Courts have affirmed such laws, finding that the protection of the rape victims from unwarranted personal attacks is a legitimate reason to limit defense cross-examination.

The Confrontation Clause also restricts the government's use of hearsay evidence. *Hearsay* is a statement made by a person out of court that is intended to *prove the matter asserted.* To prove the matter asserted means, in plain language, that the out of court statement must prove, or support, the matter fact that the attorney is trying to make. For example, in a trial of Samuel for murder, it is hearsay for him to testify that a third person, Ambrose, told him that he observed Samuel commit the murder because the purpose of the testimony is to prove the matter asserted, e.g. Samuel committed the murder. The prosecutor in this instance must find and call Ambrose to testify.

There are exceptions to the hearsay rule, and hearsay is commonly admitted in civil trials. However, the Confrontation Clause limits the admissibility of hearsay in criminal trials. To be admissible, it must be shown that the (1) witness is unavailable at trial and (2) the defendant had a prior opportunity to examine the witness. This standard was announced by the Court in *Crawford v. Washington,* a case where a wife's statement to police that incriminated her husband had committed a crime was determined to be inadmissible because she was unavailable at trial to the prosecutor because of the marital privilege. The Court limited its Confrontation Clause protection to hearsay—evidence that is introduced to prove the matter asserted. Since the matter at hand in *Crawford* was intended to prove the guilt of the husband, the wife's incriminating statements to the police were excluded. As you will learn in a moment, the exception for non-testimonial statements will prove significant in a later case.[8]

The Confrontation Clause implicitly includes a right of a defendant to be at the trial. This right includes the entire trial, from selection of the jury to return of the verdict. It also includes many pretrial matters, such as suppression hearings. Of course, defendants have a right to be present at both sentencing and probation revocation hearings. Although the right to be present during one's trial is fundamental, it may be lost by disruptive behavior.

There is a long and widely accepted exception to evidence and Confrontation Clause rules that permits purely scientific evidence to be admitted through a report. Unless a defendant had evidence to challenge the validity of such a test, courts in most states and in the federal system admit scientific reports without requiring the scientist or lab attendant to testify. The Supreme Court appeared to have altered this long-standing practice in two cases, *Melendez-Diaz* and *Bullcoming*.

Note that a strongly worded dissent by four justices criticized the majority for setting aside over two hundred years of evidentiary law that permitted the admission of scientific testing through authenticated reports, citing the concern that the requirement of having analysts testify in all cases where scientific reports are introduced will be burdensome, expensive, and often difficult to implement.

MELENDEZ-DIAZ V. MASSACHUSETTS
577 U.S. 305 (2009)

The Massachusetts courts in this case admitted into evidence affidavits reporting the results of forensic analysis which showed that material seized by the police and connected to the defendant was cocaine. The question presented is whether those affidavits are "testimonial," rendering the affiants "witnesses" subject to the defendant's right of confrontation under the Sixth Amendment.

In 2001, Boston police officers received a tip that a Kmart employee, Thomas Wright, was engaging in suspicious activity. The informant reported that Wright repeatedly received phone calls at work, after each of which he would be picked up in front of the store by a blue sedan, and would return to the store a short time later. The police set up surveillance in the Kmart parking lot and witnessed this precise sequence of events. When Wright got out of the car upon his return, one of the officers detained and searched him, finding four clear white plastic bags containing a substance resembling cocaine. The officer then signaled other officers on the scene to arrest the two men in the car—one of whom was petitioner Luis Melendez-Diaz. The officers placed all three men in a police cruiser. During the short drive to the police station, the officers observed their passengers fidgeting and making furtive movements in the back of the car. After depositing the men at the station, they searched the police cruiser and found a plastic bag containing 19 smaller plastic bags hidden in the partition between the front and back seats. They submitted the seized evidence to a state laboratory required by law to conduct chemical analysis upon police request.

Melendez-Diaz was charged with distributing cocaine and with trafficking in cocaine in an amount between 14 and 28 grams. At trial, the prosecution placed into evidence the bags seized from Wright and from the police cruiser. It also submitted three "certificates of analysis" showing the results of the forensic analysis performed on the seized substances. The

MELENDEZ-DIAZ V. MASSACHUSETTS *(continued)*

certificates reported the weight of the seized bags and stated that the bags "[h]a[ve] been examined with the following results: The substance was found to contain: Cocaine." The certificates were sworn to before a notary public by analysts at the State Laboratory Institute of the Massachusetts Department of Public Health, as required under Massachusetts law.

Petitioner objected to the admission of the certificates, asserting that our Confrontation Clause decision in *Crawford* v. *Washington*, 541 U.S. 36 (2004), required the analysts to testify in person. [the objection was overruled and the defendant was convicted.] . . .

There is little doubt that the documents at issue in this case fall within the "core class of testimonial statements" . . . The "certificates" are functionally identical to live, in-court testimony, doing "precisely what a witness does on direct examination. . . .

In short, under our decision in *Crawford* the analysts' affidavits were testimonial statements, and the analysts were "witnesses" for purposes of the Sixth Amendment. Absent a showing that the analysts were unavailable to testify at trial *and* that petitioner had a prior opportunity to cross-examine them, petitioner was entitled to " 'be confronted with' " the analysts at trial. . . .

Respondent claims that there is a difference, for Confrontation Clause purposes, between testimony recounting historical events, which is "prone to distortion or manipulation," and the testimony at issue here, which is the "resul[t] of neutral, scientific testing. . . . Nor is it evident that what respondent

calls "neutral scientific testing" is as neutral or as reliable as respondent suggests. Forensic evidence is not uniquely immune from the risk of manipulation. According to a recent study conducted under the auspices of the National Academy of Sciences, "[t]he majority of [laboratories producing forensic evidence] are administered by law enforcement agencies, such as police departments, where the laboratory administrator reports to the head of the agency." And "[b]ecause forensic scientists often are driven in their work by a need to answer a particular question related to the issues of a particular case, they sometimes face pressure to sacrifice appropriate methodology for the sake of expediency." A forensic analyst responding to a request from a law enforcement official may feel pressure—or have an incentive—to alter the evidence in a manner favorable to the prosecution.

Confrontation is one means of assuring accurate forensic analysis. . . .

Confrontation is designed to weed out not only the fraudulent analyst, but the incompetent one as well. Serious deficiencies have been found in the forensic evidence used in criminal trials. One commentator asserts that "[t]he legal community now concedes, with varying degrees of urgency, that our system produces erroneous convictions based on discredited forensics." . . .

The Sixth Amendment does not permit the prosecution to prove its case via *ex parte* out-of-court affidavits, and the admission of such evidence against Melendez-Diaz was error.

In spite of the strongly worded dissent, the Court reaffirmed *Melendez-Dias* in the 2011 case *Bullcoming v. New Mexico*, where the use of a surrogate lab technician who testified on behalf of the technician who conducted a blood alcohol test was invalidated by the Court as contrary to the Confrontation Clause. The Court found that the analyst who conducted the test had to testify at trial or be available pretrial to testify and be subjected to cross-examination by the defendant.[9]

What appeared to be clear and settled law was dealt a confusing blow in 2012. In a 5-4 decision with no one rationale commanding a majority of justices, the Court decided in *Williams v. Illinois*[10] that the testimony of a forensic DNA expert who testified that the DNA of semen taken from a vaginal swab of a rape victim and analyzed at a private lab, Cellmark, which matched the defendant, was admissible. This expert did not conduct the testing and most likely had never been in the Cellmark lab.

Because the justices were divided, it is difficult to identify exactly how they distinguished the case from *Crawford, Melendez-Diaz,* and *Bullcomings.* But a few ideas can be extracted from the opinions. First, the testing occurred before the defendant had been identified as a suspect. The DNA profile had been built in order to identify an unknown rapist. Accordingly, the profile was not aimed at the defendant. Accordingly, the important purpose of enabling defendants to cross-examine witnesses "against them" would not have been satisfied by prohibiting the expert's testimony.

Second, the expert's statements were not hearsay. She didn't testify to prove the matter asserted—that is, she didn't testify as to the testing or the contents of the testing report. The Court summarized the expert's testimony as such:

> In order to assess petitioner's Confrontation Clause argument, it is helpful to inventory exactly what Lambatos said on the stand about Cellmark. She testified to the truth of the following matters: Cellmark was an accredited lab; the ISP occasionally sent forensic samples to Cellmark for DNA testing; according to shipping manifests admitted into evidence, the ISP lab sent vaginal swabs taken from the victim to Cellmark and later received those swabs back from Cellmark; and, finally, the Cellmark DNA profile matched a profile produced by the ISP lab from a sample of petitioner's blood. Lambatos had personal knowledge of all of these matters, and therefore none of this testimony infringed petitioner's confrontation right.

Third, the case was tried before a judge. The law assumes that judges have a better understanding of the law and are better at categorizing evidence and not considering it for purposes beyond what is permitted than jurors. In this case the expert's testimony was not admitted to prove that the quality of the testing and the judge is presumed to have not considered it for such purposes. Whether the decision would have been different if the case had been tried before a jury is unclear. But it easy to imagine that many jurors would interpret the testimony as proving the guilt of the defendant. The full impact of this decision will be revealed in the years to come.

The Presumption of Innocence/Burden of Proof

One of the most basic rights underlying the right to a fair trial is the presumption of innocence. All those accused must be proven guilty by the government. Criminal defendants have no duty to defend themselves and may remain silent throughout the trial. In fact, the government is prohibited from calling defendants to testify, and defendants cannot be made to decide whether they will testify at the start of the trial.[11] The fact that a defendant chooses not to testify may not be mentioned by the prosecutor to the jury. Defendants may testify in their own behalf. If so, they are subject to full cross-examination by the prosecutor. The Fifth Amendment right to be free from self-incrimination is discussed more fully in Chapter 9.

The standard imposed upon the government in criminal cases is to prove guilt **beyond a reasonable doubt.** A doubt that would cause a reasonable or prudent person to question the guilt of the accused is a reasonable doubt. Although not precisely quantified, beyond a reasonable doubt is greater than the civil preponderance (51 percent likely) and less than absolute (100 percent confidence of guilt). See the standards of proof graphic in Chapter 12 to refresh your understanding of the different standards that are employed in criminal law. The prosecution must prove every element of the charged crime beyond a reasonable doubt. The reasonable doubt standard is an important feature of the accusatorial system of the United States and is required by due process.[12] A juror must vote for acquittal if he or she harbors a reasonable doubt.

To further the presumption of innocence, judges must be careful not to behave in a manner that implies to a jury that a defendant is guilty.

The court and government must be careful not to create a physical setting that implies guilt. The Supreme Court has stated that the presence of a defendant at a jury trial in prison clothing is prejudicial.[13] In the *Young* case, a federal appellate court reviewed the use of "prisoner docks" for a Sixth Amendment violation. Similarly, a criminal defendant also has a right to be free from appearing before the jury in handcuffs or shackles.

The government's needs are balanced against the defendant's, however. In *Holbrook v. Flynn*, 475 U.S. 560 (1986), the Court stated that not all practices that single out the defendant are excessively prejudicial. The Court held that some prejudice may exist. The question is whether there is unacceptable prejudice that is not justified by governmental necessity. Using this standard, the Court allowed a conviction to stand where the defendant objected to the presence of four police officers in the first row of the spectator gallery, directly behind the defendant, during trial.

Trial judges also have a responsibility to monitor private conduct in the courtroom to ensure unacceptable unfairness to the defendant does not happen. For example, spectators are not permitted to express opinions about the case to jurors. Whether more subtle behaviors, such as wearing a button with a photo of the victim, are unacceptably prejudicial remains to be seen.[14]

This right to be free of restraint is not absolute. Judges have the authority to take whatever measures are necessary to assure safety in the courtroom and to advance the administration of justice. Accordingly, a defendant who is disorderly may be expelled from the trial. However, before exclusion is ordered the court should consider other alternatives. Defendants who are threatening may be restrained, and those who verbally interfere with the proceeding may be gagged.[15]

The Right to Speedy Trial

All criminal defendants have a right to a speedy trial. It is the Sixth Amendment, as extended by the Fourteenth Amendment to the states, that guarantees speedy trial. This right has a history dating back to at least the Magna Carta.

To date, the United States Supreme Court has not set a specific number of days within which trial must be conducted. Rather, the Court said in *Barker v. Wingo* that four factors

beyond a reasonable doubt

■ The level of proof required to convict a person of a crime. Precise definitions vary, but moral certainty and firm belief are both used. Beyond a reasonable doubt is not absolute certainty. This is the highest level of proof required in any type of trial.

Exhibit 15–1   SIXTH AMENDMENT TRIAL RIGHTS

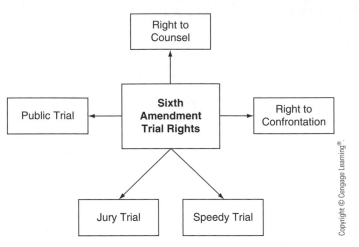

Copyright © Cengage Learning®

must be considered when determining if a defendant has enjoyed a speedy trial. First, the length of the delay; second, the reason for the delay; third, whether the defendant has asserted the right to a speedy trial; fourth, how seriously the defendant was prejudiced.[16]

Time for speedy trial begins once the defendant is arrested or formally charged.[17] If a defendant is charged by sealed indictment, speedy trial does not start until the indictment has been opened.

Dismissal with prejudice is the remedy for violation of speedy trial. That is, the charge is dismissed and may not be refiled by the prosecutor.

All the states and the national government have enacted speedy trial acts. The Speedy Trial Act of 1974[18] is the federal statute. That act requires that individuals be formally charged within 30 days from the date of arrest and tried within 70 days of the filing date of the information or indictment, or of the date the defendant had the initial appearance before the court that will try the case, whichever is later.

YOUNG V. CALLAHAN
700 F.2d 32 (1st Cir. 1983)

[The Court included a footnote which stated that a *prisoner dock* is "a box approximately four feet square and four feet high. It is open at the top so that the defendant's head and shoulders can be seen when he or she is seated. The dock is placed typically at the center of the bar enclosure which separates the spectator's section from that portion of the courtroom reserved for trial principals. The dock is usually fifteen to twenty feet behind counsel table, and is sometimes on a raised platform."]

YOUNG V. CALLAHAN *(continued)*

In January of 1979 appellant was tried in Massachusetts Superior Court on one count of assault and battery with a dangerous weapon and two counts of murder. The jury returned a guilty verdict on the assault and battery but was unable to reach a verdict on the two murder indictments. In a new trial in February of 1979, appellant was found guilty of second-degree murder on both counts. These convictions were affirmed by the Massachusetts Supreme Judicial Court. . . .

Prior to appellant's second trial, counsel moved that he be allowed to sit at counsel table rather than in the prisoner's dock on the grounds that "forcing him to sit in the prisoner's dock would deprive him of his constitutional rights to a fair trial, to the presumption of innocence, to access to counsel, non-suggestive eyewitness identifications, and due process of law." That motion was accompanied by an affidavit from appellant's trial counsel averring, based on his own observations and those of corrections officers during appellant's two years of incarceration and on appellant's conduct at the first trial, that "allowing [appellant] to sit at counsel table will not present any hazards to the orderly judicial process or to the security of its personnel," and that the trial of the case would involve a substantial amount of testimony concerning acts and conduct of the appellant over a several-day period and would thus "require consultation with the defendant." . . .

In once again evaluating for constitutional error the confinement of an accused to the prisoner's box, we reiterate . . . that such confinement, like appearance in prison attire, is a "constant reminder of the accused's condition" which "may affect a juror's judgment," eroding the presumption of innocence which the accused is due. . . .

The prisoner's dock, like other physical restraints, should thus be employed only when "the trial judge has found such restraint reasonably necessary to maintain order" and when cured by an instruction to the "jurors that such restraint is not to be considered in assessing the proof and determining guilty."

To avoid prejudice by having a trial before a defendant has had an opportunity to prepare a defense, the statute provides that trial shall not occur for 30 days, unless the defendant consents to an earlier date.

The statute specifies certain delays that are excluded from computing time for purpose of speedy trial. A few of the periods excluded by the Speedy Trial Act of 1974 are when the defendant is a fugitive; when trial is delayed because an issue is on appeal; when delays are caused by motions of the parties; and when delays result from mental examinations of the defendant.

The Speedy Trial Act of 1974 gives the trial court the discretion to decide whether violation of its provisions justifies a dismissal with or without prejudice. Factors that must be considered are the seriousness of the offense, the reason for delay, other facts of the case, and the impact of reprosecution on the administration of justice.[19]

Because the United States Supreme Court has not established specific time requirements for speedy trial, each state has its own time requirements. Of course, states must comply with the requirements of *Barker v. Wingo*. Most states have speedy trial provisions in their constitutions, which are similar, if not identical, to the Sixth Amendment. Other states set their speedy trial requirements out in statute or court rules. Time requirements differ, but trial within six months is common.

The Right to Counsel

The Sixth Amendment to the U.S. Constitution provides that "in all criminal prosecutions, the accused shall enjoy the right . . . to have the Assistance of Counsel for his defense." The right to counsel is one of the most fundamental rights guaranteed to criminal defendants and is fully applicable to the states.

The right to the assistance of counsel is found not only in the Sixth Amendment but also in the Fifth and Fourteenth Amendments. These alternative sources are discussed later in the particular contexts within which they apply.

Indigency

It has always been clear that criminal defendants are entitled to retain the attorney of their choice. It was not until 1923 that the United States Supreme Court recognized a constitutional right to appointed counsel for indigent defendants in *Powell v. Alabama*, 287 U.S. 45 (1923).

In the *Powell* case (commonly known as the Scottsboro case), nine young black males were charged with the rape of two white girls. Within one week of arrest, the defendants were tried. Eight of the "Scottsboro boys" were convicted and sentenced to death. The defendants appealed, claiming that they should have been provided counsel. The Supreme Court agreed.

However, the right to appointed counsel in *Powell* was not founded upon the Sixth Amendment, but upon the Fourteenth. The Court reasoned that the absence of counsel deprived the defendants of a fair trial, and, accordingly, violated the defendants' due process rights. This decision was narrow: It applied only to capital cases where the defendant was incapable of preparing an adequate defense and did not have the resources to hire an attorney.

The due process right to counsel was subsequently extended to all situations in which a defendant would not have a fair trial in the absence of defense counsel. Whether counsel was required depended on each particular case's "totality of facts." If denial of counsel was "shocking to the universal sense of justice," then the defendant's right to a fair trial, as guaranteed by the Fourteenth Amendment, was violated.[20] The Court refused to extend the right to counsel to all state criminal proceedings. Cases that involve complex legal issues or a defendant of low intelligence are the types of situation that required the appointment of counsel under the *Betts* due process standard.

In 1938 the Court decided *Johnson v. Zerbst*, 304 U.S. 458 (1938), which held that the Sixth Amendment guarantees a right to counsel. The Sixth Amendment right to counsel was found to be broader than the right to counsel announced in *Powell*, as it applied to all criminal prosecutions. However, *Zerbst* did not apply to state proceedings. Eventually, the Sixth Amendment right to counsel was extended to all state felony proceedings, in *Gideon v. Wainwright*.

GIDEON V. WAINWRIGHT
372 U.S. 335 (1963)

Petitioner was charged in Florida state court with having broken and entered a poolroom with intent to commit a misdemeanor. This offense is a felony under Florida law. Appearing in court without funds and without a lawyer, petitioner asked the court to appoint counsel for him, whereupon the following colloquy took place:

THE COURT: Mr. Gideon, I am sorry, but I cannot appoint Counsel to represent you in this case. Under the laws of the State of Florida, the only time the Court can appoint Counsel to represent a defendant is when that person is charged with a capital offense. I am sorry, but I will have to deny your request to appoint Counsel to defend you in this case.

THE DEFENDANT: The United States Supreme Court says I am entitled to be represented by Counsel.

Put to trial before a jury, Gideon conducted his defense about as well as could be expected from a layman. He made an opening statement to the jury, cross-examined the State's witnesses, presented witnesses in his own defense, declined to testify himself, and made a short argument "emphasizing his innocence to the charge contained in the Information filed in this case." The jury returned a verdict of guilty, and petitioner was sentenced to five years in the state prison. Since 1942, when *Betts v. Brady*, 316 U.S. 455, was decided by a divided Court, the problem of a defendant's federal constitutional right to counsel in a state court has been a continuing source of controversy and litigation in both state and federal courts. . . . Since Gideon was proceeding in forma pauperis, we appointed counsel to represent him and requested both sides to discuss in their briefs and oral arguments the following: "Should this Court's holding in *Betts v. Brady* . . . be reconsidered? . . .

Governments, both state and federal, quite properly spend vast sums of money to establish machinery to try defendants accused of crime. Lawyers to prosecute are everywhere deemed essential to protect the public's interest in an orderly society. Similarly, there are few defendants charged with crime, few indeed, who fail to hire the best lawyers they can get to prepare and present their defenses. That government hires lawyers to prosecute and defendants who have the money to hire lawyers to defend are the strongest indications of the widespread belief that lawyers in criminal courts are necessities, not luxuries. The right of one charged with crime to counsel may not be deemed fundamental and essential to fair trials in some countries, but it is in ours. From the very beginning, our state and national constitutions and laws have laid great emphasis on procedural and substantive safeguards designed to assure fair trials before impartial tribunals in which every defendant stands equal before the law. This noble idea cannot be realized if the poor man charged with crime has to face his accusers without a lawyer to represent him. . . . The Court in *Betts v. Brady* departed from sound wisdom upon which the Court's holding in *Powell v. Alabama* rested. Florida, supported by two other States, has asked that *Betts v. Brady* be left intact. Twenty-two states, as friends of the Court, argue that *Betts* was "an anachronism when handed down" and that it should now be overruled. We agree. . . . Reversed.

Subsequently, the right to counsel was again extended to encompass all criminal cases punished with a jail term. Whether the crime is labeled a misdemeanor or felony is not dispositive of the right-to-counsel issue.[21] In the 2002 case, *Alabama v. Shelton*, the Supreme Court extended the right again. In *Shelton*, the right to counsel was found for a convictee who was sentenced to imprisonment, even though the entire sentence was suspended to probation.

In some cases, it may be to the prosecution's advantage for a defendant to have counsel, even though a sentence of imprisonment is not available for a first conviction, but is available for subsequent convictions. This is because a sentence may not be enhanced to include jail time based on a prior conviction where the defendant possessed a right to, but was denied, counsel.[22] For example, the penalty for first-offense drunk driving is not punished by a term in jail; however, subsequent violations are. If Jack is arrested and convicted without counsel for his first offense, he may not be sentenced to jail time for his second drunk driving conviction, because he did not have counsel during his first trial.

To qualify for appointed counsel, a defendant does not have to be financially destitute. It need only be shown that the defendant's financial situation will prevent him or her from being able to retain an attorney. An indigent defendant does not have a right to choose the appointed attorney; this decision falls within the discretion of the trial court. See Exhibit 15–2 for a summary of when the right to counsel attaches.

Exhibit 15–2 THE RIGHT TO COUNSEL

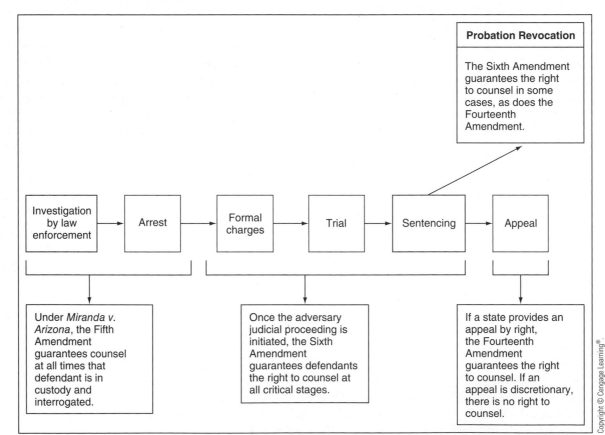

Copyright © Cengage Learning®.

ALABAMA V. SHELTON
535 U.S. 654 (2002)

This case concerns the Sixth Amendment right of an indigent defendant charged with a misdemeanor punishable by imprisonment, fine, or both, to the assistance of court-appointed counsel. Two prior decisions control the Court's judgment. First, in *Argersinger v. Hamlin*, 407 U.S. 25, 92 S. Ct. 2006, 32 L.Ed.2d 530 (1972), this Court held that defense counsel must be appointed in any criminal prosecution, "whether classified as petty, misdemeanor, or felony," . . . "that actually leads to imprisonment even for a brief period," . . . Later, in *Scott v. Illinois*, 440 U.S. 367, 373–374, 99 S. Ct. 1158, 59 L.Ed.2d 383 (1979), the Court drew the line at "actual imprisonment," holding that counsel need not be appointed when the defendant is fined for the charged crime, but is not sentenced to a term of imprisonment.

Defendant-respondent LeReed Shelton, convicted of third-degree assault, was sentenced to a jail term of 30 days, which the trial court immediately suspended, placing Shelton on probation for two years. The question presented is whether the Sixth Amendment right to appointed counsel, as delineated in *Argersinger* and *Scott*, applies to a defendant in Shelton's situation. We hold that a suspended sentence that may "end up in the actual deprivation of a person's liberty" may not be imposed unless the defendant was accorded "the guiding hand of counsel" in the prosecution for the crime charged.

After representing himself at a bench trial in the District Court of Etowah County, Alabama, Shelton was convicted of third-degree assault, a class A misdemeanor carrying a maximum punishment of one year imprisonment and a $2000 fine . . . He invoked his right to a new trial before a jury in Circuit Court. . . . where he again appeared without a lawyer and was again convicted. The court repeatedly warned Shelton about the problems self-representation entailed, see App. 9, but at no time offered him assistance of counsel at state expense.

The Circuit Court sentenced Shelton to serve 30 days in the county prison. As authorized by Alabama law, however, . . . the court suspended that sentence and placed Shelton on two years' unsupervised probation, conditioned on his payment of court costs, a $500 fine, reparations of $25, and restitution in the amount of $516.69.

Shelton appealed his conviction and sentence on Sixth Amendment grounds. . . .

. . . A suspended sentence is a prison term imposed for the offense of conviction. Once the prison term is triggered, the defendant is incarcerated not for the probation violation, but for the underlying offense. The uncounseled conviction at that point "result[s] in imprisonment. . . . This is precisely what the Sixth Amendment, as interpreted in *Argersinger* and *Scott*, does not allow. . . .

Satisfied that Shelton is entitled to appointed counsel at the critical stage when his guilt or innocence of the charged crime is decided and his vulnerability to imprisonment is determined, we affirm the judgment of the Supreme Court of Alabama. *It is so ordered.*

Effective Assistance of Counsel

Defendants are entitled not only to have an attorney but also to receive the "effective assistance of counsel." On appeal, defendants may challenge their convictions by claiming that at a lower level (trial or appellate) they did not have effective counsel.

To succeed with such a claim, two facts must be shown. First, the representation must be extremely inadequate. Second, the defendant must show that he or she was actually harmed by the lack of adequate counsel. So, if an appellate court determines that a defendant would have been convicted with the best of attorneys, the defendant's claim of inadequate counsel fails.

A Sixth Amendment claim of ineffective assistance of counsel can take many forms. Incompetence of counsel is often claimed, but rarely successful. Attorneys are expected to make the legal and tactical decisions of the defense. The fact that defense counsel rendered incorrect legal advice is not determinative. The issue is whether the defendant's representation was shockingly substandard.

A defendant has a right to the "undivided loyalty" of defense counsel. Hence, it is common to have ineffective assistance of counsel claims where one attorney is representing codefendants. In *Cuyler v. Sullivan*, 446 U.S. 335 (1980), it was held that an ineffective assistance of counsel claim based upon an alleged conflict of interest will succeed only if the defendant can show that the conflict "adversely affected" his or her rights.

Also, the accused has a right to confer with counsel to prepare a defense. If a court denies a defendant access to his or her counsel, a Sixth Amendment claim may be made.

Governmental eavesdropping on a defendant's conversation with his or her counsel is also improper and violative of the Sixth Amendment.

The Right to Self-Representation

In *Faretta v. California*, 422 U.S. 806 (1975), the right to self-representation was established. The Supreme Court recognized that the assistance of trained legal counsel is essential to preparing and presenting a defense. However, in balance, the Court found that a defendant's right of choice has greater importance. Therefore, defendants may choose to act as their own counsel (pro se), even though the decision increases the probability of a conviction.

The record must clearly show that a defendant who has chosen to proceed pro se has done so voluntarily and knowingly. The defendant "must be made aware of the dangers and disadvantages of self-representation." Whether the defendant possesses any legal training or education is not relevant.

Trial judges are permitted to appoint "standby counsel" for trial. This attorney attends the trial and is available to counsel the defendant or take over the defense, if necessary. The Court later approved the practice of appointing standby counsel over the objection of the defendant. This is routinely done in felony cases in which the defendant has opted to proceed pro se.

The right to self-representation is not absolute. A defendant who engages in disruptive behavior during the proceeding may be relieved of pro se status. Standby counsel, if appointed, may be ordered to complete the trial.

The Scope of the Right

Through *Gideon*, the right to counsel in criminal prosecutions was extended to the states. *Argersinger* made it clear that counsel must be provided in all cases in which the defendant is sentenced to actual imprisonment. But when does the right begin?

The United States Supreme Court has stated that the Sixth Amendment right to counsel applies to all critical stages of a criminal prosecution. This definition requires that a "prosecution" be initiated before the right to counsel, under the Sixth Amendment, attaches. Accordingly, the Sixth Amendment does not apply to juvenile proceedings, nor to administrative hearings such as parole determination and revocation.

The right starts whenever the "adversary judicial proceeding" is initiated. Police contacts prior to the initiation of an adversary judicial proceeding are not covered by the Sixth Amendment.

In determining what constitutes a critical stage, courts focus on "whether substantial rights of the defendant may be affected." The greater the contact between the prosecutor and the defendant, the more likely the event is at a critical stage.

The first critical stage is normally the initial appearance or the arraignment. Courts have also determined that a defendant may be entitled to counsel at a police lineup, sentencing, preliminary hearing, and during a probation revocation hearing. Once charges are filed, all interrogations of the defendant by the government are critical stages.

The Sixth Amendment is not the only constitutional provision assuring counsel. The Fifth Amendment's right to be free from self-incrimination also guarantees counsel in some instances, as does the Fourteenth Amendment's Equal Protection and Due Process Clauses.

TRIAL PROCEDURE

Voir Dire

The first stage of trial is the **voir dire.** This is a French phrase that translates "look speak" (to speak the truth). Voir dire is also known as *jury selection.*

The process of selecting a jury differs among the jurisdictions. In all jurisdictions, prospective jurors are asked questions bearing upon their individual ability to serve fairly and impartially. Each state differs in how this information is obtained. In many, the judge is responsible for asking most of the questions. In others, the judge makes only a few brief inquiries, and the lawyers do most of the questioning.

There are two ways of eliminating a juror. First, if one of the attorneys believes that a juror could not be fair and impartial, the juror can be **challenged for cause.** If the judge agrees, the juror is released. An unlimited number of jurors may be eliminated for cause.

In addition to challenges for cause, a juror may be eliminated by a party using a **peremptory challenge.** Each party is given a specific number of peremptory challenges at the start of the trial and may strike jurors until that number is exhausted. A party is free to eliminate, without stating a reason, any potential juror. However, a juror may not be eliminated because of race.[23]

In the federal system, both defendant and prosecutor have 20 peremptory strikes in death cases and 3 in misdemeanors; in noncapital felony cases the defendant gets 10 and the government 6.[24] States have similar rules. The authority of the parties to use peremptory challenges is nearly absolute. Two limitations exist, though—the use of a challenge to eliminate a prospective juror for race and sex. Such criteria violate the Fifth and Fourteenth Amendments' equal protection guarantees.[25] Other than these

voir dire examination

■ (French) "To see, to say"; "to state the truth." The preliminary in-court questioning of a prospective witness (or juror) to determine competency to testify (or suitability to decide a case). [pronounce: vwahr deer]

challenge for cause

■ A formal objection to the qualifications of a prospective juror or jurors.

peremptory challenge

■ The automatic elimination of a potential juror by one side before trial without needing to state the reason for the elimination.

limitations, parties often go to great lengths to try to understand the psychological profile of venireman. When resources permit, experts are retained who make recommendations about whether venireman should be retained or struck using models that predict how a prospective juror will react to the facts of the case.

In addition to challenging individual jurors, entire jury panels may be challenged. For example, a defendant may challenge the method used to select prospective jurors if the method does not select individuals who represent a fair cross section of the community. In many instances, these challenges concern race or ethnicity.

Preliminary Instructions

The next stage in the trial proceeding is for the judge to give preliminary instructions to the jury. The trial judge explains to the jury what its obligation is and gives a brief introduction to the law and facts of the case. The judge may read the formal charge verbatim to the jury or may summarize its contents.

The presumption of innocence is explained, and the judge admonishes the jury not to discuss the case prior to deliberating. Jurors are told not to read newspaper articles or watch television reports concerning the trial. In rare cases, it may be necessary to keep the jurors' identities secret and to conduct the voir dire in private. Threat to the safety of the jurors is an example of such an instance. This method is to be used cautiously, as it encroaches upon First Amendment rights of media and of the defendant to a public trial. Moreover, when using this method, the trial judge should be careful not to prejudice the jury. If the reason for secrecy is a perceived threat, the judge should instruct the jury as to another reason, such as concern over pretrial publicity.[26]

Opening Statements

After the judge has given the preliminary instructions, the parties address the jury. These statements are commonly known as *opening statements*. The purpose of opening statements is to acquaint the jury with the basic facts of the case. Opening statement is not the time for counsel to argue the law; only the facts expected to be presented should be mentioned.

In some cases the defense attorney may be permitted to wait until after the prosecution has put on its case before giving an opening. Because the purpose of opening statements is to present the facts surrounding the charge to the jury, opening statements are often waived in bench trials.

The Prosecution's Case in Chief

The United States employs an adversarial system of adjudication. In adversarial systems, the parties take the lead, not the court, in the development of the facts and theories of the case. At trial the parties are responsible for introducing the evidence, calling and examining the witnesses, and presenting theories to juries. Judges occasionally ask questions of witnesses and even less often, call witnesses. Historically jurors have been expected to sit silently during trials. They do not call or questions witnesses. In recent years there has been a small movement in the direction of jury participation. Arizona, Florida, and a few other states, for example, now permit jurors to ask questions of witnesses. State rules vary in how this happens. It is common, for example, to require questions to be submitted to the Court for review. In some jurisdictions the parties are permitted to review and object to questions. It is common for the judge to ask the questions that are approved.

Because the government has brought the charges, it puts its case on first. This consists of calling witnesses to testify and producing exhibits.

All jurisdictions have rules of evidence that govern procedure and the admissibility of evidence. The Federal Rules of Evidence are used in the federal courts, and many states have modeled their rules after the federal ones.

Many evidentiary questions can be resolved prior to trial through a motion **in limine.** Those arising during trial are handled through **objections.** Any time an attorney believes that a question, statement, or action of the opposing lawyer is improper, he or she may object. The court will then rule on the objection, and the trial will continue. In some instances the attorneys will want to argue the objection outside the hearing of the jury. In such cases a **sidebar** may be held, or the judge may order that the jury be removed until the matter is resolved.

The Confrontation Clause assures the defendant the right to cross-examine the prosecution's witnesses. Normally, cross-examination is limited to matters raised during the prosecution's direct examination. The defense also has the right to review an exhibit before it is shown to the jury.

The Supreme Court has held that prosecutors may not call defendants to testify. While a defendant may assert the privilege and refuse to testify once called, the Court has found that to demand this of a defendant creates an appearance of guilt. Furthermore, prosecutors may not refer to a defendant's failure to testify in closing arguments. Of course, a prosecutor may cross-examine a defendant who chooses to testify. However, in the 2013 case *Salinas v. Texas,*[27] the Supreme Court held that a defendant's silence in response to a question during a voluntary interview by police may be mentioned by a prosecutor as evidence of guilt to a jury.

Directed Verdict and Judgement of Acquittal

After the government has rested (finished its case), the defendant may move for a directed verdict or, as it is also known, a judgement of acquittal. Upon such motion the trial judge reviews the evidence presented by the government. If the evidence to support a conviction is insufficient, the judge will enter a directed verdict favoring the defendant. A directed verdict may never be entered favoring the government.

The prosecution's evidence is insufficient if reasonable persons could not conclude that the defendant is guilty. If the trial court grants a motion for directed verdict, the jury never deliberates and is discharged. Directed verdicts are rarely granted, as most judges prefer to have the jury return a verdict.

The Defense Case

If the motion for directed verdict is denied, the defense may put on its case. The defendant is not required to put on a defense, and juries are instructed not to infer guilt by the absence of a defense.

---

in limine

■ (Latin) "At the beginning"; preliminary. A motion in limine is a (usually pretrial) request that prejudicial information be excluded as trial evidence.

objections

■ A claim that an action by your adversary in a lawsuit (such as the use of a particular piece of evidence) is improper, unfair, or illegal, and you are asking the judge for a ruling on the point.

sidebar

■ An in-court discussion among lawyers and the judge that is out of the hearing of witnesses and the jury. Sidebar conferences are usually *on* the record.

If a defendant chooses to present a defense, the rules are the same as for the prosecution. The defendant may call witnesses and introduce exhibits, as limited by the rules of evidence. Defense witnesses are subject to cross-examination by the prosecutor. Defendants do not have to testify but may choose to do so. If a defendant does testify, he or she is subject to cross-examination by the prosecutor.

Rebuttal

After the defense has concluded, the prosecution may call rebuttal witnesses in an effort to disprove the evidence of the defense. No new issues may be raised during rebuttal. The defense is then permitted to rebut the prosecution's rebuttal evidence.

Closing Arguments

After the evidentiary stage of the trial has concluded, the parties present their closing arguments. The length of closing arguments is left to the discretion of the trial judge.

Attorneys may argue both the facts and the law during closing arguments. However, an attorney may not argue law different from what the judge will express to the jury as controlling in the case. Closing arguments give the parties an opportunity to summarize the evidence and explain their positions to the jury.

Attorneys must not make incorrect factual or legal statements to the jury. Objections to such statements may be made. If an objection is sustained, the jury will be instructed by the judge to disregard the statement. Prosecutors must be especially careful not to make inflammatory remarks about the defendant or defense counsel. Such remarks, if extreme, can lead to mistrial.

Final Instructions

After closing arguments are completed, the judge will instruct the jury. Through these instructions the judge explains the law to the jury. The information contained in the judge's instructions includes the prosecutorial burden, the standard of proof, the elements of the charged crime, how to weigh and value evidence, and rules for reaching a verdict.

Jury Deliberations and Verdict

After receiving its instructions, the jury goes into deliberations. Jury deliberations are secret in all cases.

Generally, no person has contact with the jury when it is deliberating. If the jury has a question for the judge, it is escorted into the courtroom where all the parties may hear the question. Some judges, but not all, permit juries to take the exhibits and instructions with them into the jury room.

As mentioned earlier, juror unanimity is not required when twelve jurors are empanelled. As few as nine jurors may support a guilty verdict. This is not true, however, in capital cases where a unanimous vote is required. Unanimity is also required if only six jurors sit in judgement.

On occasion, a jury may communicate to the judge that a verdict cannot be reached. Some courts will then give the jury an "*Allen* charge," an instruction encouraging jurors in the minority to reexamine their position. The charge gets its name from *Allen v. United States*, 164 U.S. 492 (1896), wherein the Supreme Court approved its use. Courts must be careful with such charges, but they are not violative of the U.S. Constitution. However, some states have banned the *Allen* charge.

In the event of a **hung jury,** the court will declare a mistrial and set a new trial date. Due to the expense and inconvenience of trying cases a second time, plea bargains are often reached.

hung jury

■ A jury that cannot reach a verdict (decision) because of disagreement among jurors.

If a verdict is reached, the parties are summoned to the courtroom and the jury verdict is read. The parties may request that the jury be polled. **Polling the jury** involves asking each juror how he or she voted. If there has been an error, the judge may order the jury to return to deliberations or may declare a mistrial.

polling the jury

■ Individually asking each member of a jury what his or her decision is. Polling is done by the judge, at the defendant's request, immediately after the verdict.

Jurors have an obligation to follow the law, as interpreted by the trial judge, when rendering a verdict.[28] Trial judges instruct jurors in this obligation. Further, the trial judge is not to instruct the jury, nor the parties to encourage the jury in closing arguments, to disregard the law. This rule affects defense, not prosecution. That is, if a law (defining a crime or punishment) is harsh or unfavorable, defendants have an interest in arguing that a jury should disregard the law and acquit, notwithstanding guilt. This is not permitted in most, if not all, jurisdictions. Accordingly, a defendant has no right to insist that a jury be instructed that it has the authority to nullify the law.[29]

In 2012 a professor in Manhattan was charged with obstructing justice for standing outside a courthouse with a sign that read "Jury Information" and distributed pamphlets encouraging jurors who disagree with a law to disregard it and acquit the defendants charged under it. The charges were dismissed by the trial court, finding that his general pleas were not intended to influence jurors in specific cases, as required by the statute.[30] The case also raises First Amendment Free Speech questions.

In reality, though, juries can and may disregard the law—-even though unlawful. When a jury retires, its deliberations are secret; and each juror, while feeling bound by the law, also feels bound by personal conscience. A jury does not have to support its verdict with a statement of its findings and conclusions. An acquittal, even if the result of nullification, is valid. Accordingly, although the trial judge may comment on the evidence to the jury before it retires to deliberate, a judge may not instruct a jury that the government has met its burden and that the jury must return a guilty verdict.[31]

JNOV/New Trial

If the jury returns a verdict of guilty, the defendant may move for a judgement notwithstanding the verdict, or **JNOV.** This is similar to a directed verdict, in that the defendant is asserting that the evidence is insufficient to support a guilty verdict.

In addition to JNOV, a defendant may file a motion for a new trial. The common-law equivalent of a motion for a new trial was the *writ of error coram nobis. Coram nobis* is still recognized in a few states.

JNOV

■ A request by a defendant convicted by a jury for the court to set aside the verdict as unsupported by the evidence.

The motion for a new trial is different from the JNOV because the defendant is not claiming that the evidence was insufficient, but rather that the trial was flawed. For example, if a defendant believes that evidence was admitted that should have been excluded and that he or she was denied a fair trial because of the admission of the evidence, he or she may file a motion for new trial. A motion for new trial may also be made because of new evidence discovered after trial.

Ethical Considerations

DISCLOSING INTENDED CLIENT PERJURY

As you have learned, attorneys have an obligation to zealously represent their clients. They also have a duty to be loyal to their clients and not to disclose the content of their client's statements. There are limits to these responsibilities, however. For example, the ABA Model Rules of Professional Responsibility allow (but do not require) an attorney to reveal client information, if such a disclosure will prevent death or substantial injury to another, will prevent the client from committing fraud that will lead to substantial financial harm to another, and in other specific situations (see Rule 1.6). Note, however, that an attorney may not disclose a client's confession for past acts or a statement of intention to commit a lesser crime.

A particularly thorny issue concerns client perjury. Model Rule 3.3 addresses this topic.

As provided in the ABA rules an attorney may not intentionally use false evidence. As such, an attorney may not call a witness that he or she reasonably believes will commit perjury. If a witness surprises an attorney on the stand by testifying falsely on material (important) facts, the attorney has an obligation to take "remedial" measures to correct the misinformation. Any remedial measure is acceptable—including inter alia, informing the court, calling a contrary witness, and questioning the witness further. In cases where notifying the court is the only solution open to an attorney, the court will react by instructing the jury to ignore the testimony, receiving more evidence on the subject; or, if the prejudice cannot be remediated, by declaring a mistrial.

The situation is more challenging if the perjury is committed by a client. The governing rule specifically distinguishes client perjury in criminal cases from civil cases. Defense attorneys may refuse to question a witness, other than the defendant, about matters where perjury is reasonably expected or to otherwise offer evidence that is reasonably believed to be false. If an attorney believes a client intends to commit perjury, the attorney has an obligation to attempt to dissuade the client. This is known as the remonstration requirement. In the remonstration, the attorney is to emphasize that the client has a legal obligation to testify truthfully, that the

Ethical Considerations *(continued)*

judge can consider a defendant's perjury at sentencing, that perjury can be prosecuted, that such perjury could hurt the defense case, and that defense counsel may withdraw if the client continues.

If the client is not dissuaded, it is generally agreed that an attorney must withdraw if he or she has knowledge of the client's intended perjury. If the attorney has only a reasonable belief, however, withdrawal is optional. Even when withdrawal is sought, it is not always granted. This is because of the prejudice to the defendant, both in front of the jury—who may be suspicious of the sudden, mid-trial change—and because it leaves a defendant without counsel at a critical time in the proceedings. Even if a motion to withdraw is denied, the attorney remains obligated not to present false evidence. To solve this conundrum, many jurisdictions have developed the "narrative" solution. In these cases, the attorney advises the client to call him- or herself to the witness stand. The attorney then questions the client in such a manner that the specific false evidence is not adduced; but instead, the door is opened for the client to provide testimony in narrative form. References to the false evidence are then omitted from the attorney's closing statements. While this method has been criticized by the ABA and Supreme Court of the United States as a passive form of introducing false evidence, many jurisdictions have seen it as the compromise position that allows defense attorneys to remain loyal to their clients while not presenting false evidence. While no solution has presented itself, there is no doubt that a better one needs to be identified.

⌐ Web Links

Famous Trials

Professor Linder of the University of Missouri at Kansas City has an interesting and fun Web site. Information on famous trials can be found there, as can legal jeopardy and golf! http://www.law.umkc.edu/faculty/projects/ftrials/ftrials.htm

Key Terms

beyond a reasonable doubt	JNOV	sidebar
challenged for cause	objections	voir dire examination
hung jury	peremptory challenge	
in limine	polling the jury	

Review Questions

1. What rights are encompassed by the Confrontation Clause?

2. What is the standard of proof in criminal cases? Define that standard.

3. How soon after arrest must a defendant be tried to comply with the Sixth Amendment's speedy trial clause?

4. What is jury nullification? May a prosecutor ask a jury to nullify? May defense counsel?

5. Distinguish challenging a prospective juror for cause from using a peremptory challenge.

6. Does a defendant have a right to self-representation?

7. What must a defendant show on appeal to be successful with a claim of ineffective assistance of counsel at trial?

Problems & Critical Thinking Exercises

1–4. Does each of the following defendants have a right to a jury trial? Explain your answer.

1. A juvenile delinquency proceeding has been initiated against John because of his involvement with drugs. For more than a year he has been dealing drugs, a crime punishable by as much as five years in prison in his state.

2. Jane is charged with simple assault. In her state that crime is punishable by a maximum fine of $2,500 and 12 months imprisonment. However, the judge assigned to her case has never sentenced a person to more than four months and customarily suspends that sentence to probation.

3. Nick is 16 years old. He is charged with murder in state trial court. Murder in his state is punished with life imprisonment or death.

4. Norm, an officer in the military, has been charged with raping a female officer. Rape is punished with 10 years to life imprisonment in the military.

Endnotes

1. *Baldwin v. New York*, 399 U.S. 66 (1970).
2. *McKeiver v. Pennsylvania*, 403 U.S. 528 (1971).
3. *Williams v. Florida*, 399 U.S. 78 (1970).
4. *Burch v. Louisiana*, 441 U.S. 130 (1979).
5. *Smith v. Illinois*, 390 U.S. 129 (1968).
6. *Maryland v. Craig*, 497 U.S. 836 (1990).
7. *Cumbie v. Singletary*, 991 F.2d 715 (11th Cir. 1993).
8. *Crawford. v. Washington*, 541 U.S. 36 (2004).
9. 564 U.S. ___ (2011).
10. 567 U.S. ___ (2012).

11. *Brooks v. Tennessee*, 406 U.S. 605 (1972).

12. *Johnson v. Louisiana*, 406 U.S. 356 (1972).

13. *Estelle v. Williams*, 425 U.S. 501 (1976).

14. *See Carey v. Musladin*, 549 U.S. ___ (2006).

15. *Stewart v. Corbin*, 850 F.2d 492 (9th Cir. 1988).

16. *Barker v. Wingo*, 407 U.S. 514 (1972).

17. *United States v. Marion*, 404 U.S. 307 (1971).

18. 18 U.S.C. § 3161.

19. 18 U.S.C. § 3162.

20. *Betts v. Brady*, 316 U.S. 455 (1942).

21. *Argersinger v. Hamlin*, 407 U.S. 25 (1972).

22. *Burgett v. Texas*, 389 U.S. 109 (1962).

23. *Batson v. Kentucky*, 476 U.S. 79 (1986).

24. Fed. R. Crim. P. 24(b).

25. *Batson v. Kentucky*, 476 U.S. 79 (1986) and *J.E.B. v. Alabama*, 511 U.S. 127 (1994).

26. *United States v. Locascio*, 6 F.3d 924 (2d Cir. 1993).

27. 570 U.S. __ (2013).

28. *See United States v. Avery*, 717 F.2d 1020 (6th Cir. 1983).

29. *United States v. Newman*, 743 F. Supp. 533 (M.D. Tenn. 1990).

30. Benjamin Weiser, Jury Statute Not Violated By Protestor, Judge Rules, *The New York Times*, April 19, 2012.

31. *See Sparf v. United States*, 156 U.S. 51 (1895); *United States v. Martin Linen Supply Co.*, 430 U.S. 564 (1977).

SENTENCING AND APPEAL

Chapter Objectives

After completing this chapter you should be able to:

- describe and apply to fact scenarios the laws of punishment, including the constitutional limitations of punishment.
- describe the sentencing process and identify the constitutional rights defendants possess at sentencing.
- connect and apply the various forms of punishment to the objectives of criminal justice.
- identify and describe the law of appeals and postconviction relief.
- identify the material facts and legal issues in nearly all of the cases you read, describe the courts' analyses and conclusions in the cases, and demonstrate the ability to synthesize and think critically about the law of the subject.

SENTENCING

After conviction, sentence must be imposed. For many misdemeanors and nearly all infractions, sentence is imposed immediately. For felonies and some misdemeanors, a future sentencing date is set.

In most cases, sentence is imposed by the trial judge. A few jurisdictions provide for a jury sentence recommendation, and even fewer actually permit the jury to impose sentence. Juries always plays a role in deciding whether death should be imposed. In some states, a jury recommendation is required before death can be imposed. In all jurisdictions, due process and jury trial right empower juries to find the facts, called an aggravating factor, that are required in capital cases.

The legislature determines how a crime should be punished. Legislatures normally set ranges within which judges may punish violators. In recent years there has been a substantial movement to limit the discretion of judges. This has been done in the federal system and many states.

The right of the legislative branch in this area is curbed by the Eighth Amendment, which prohibits "cruel and unusual punishment." The protection of the Eighth Amendment has been extended to state proceedings through the Fourteenth Amendment. However, legislatures enjoy wide discretion in deciding how to punish criminals.

Sentencing Procedure

The Presentence Investigation/No Right to Counsel

After a defendant is determined guilty, a sentencing date is set. For most felonies and misdemeanors the date will be set far enough in the future to permit the probation officer to complete a presentence investigation.

The investigation typically begins with an interview of the defendant. Information concerning the defendant's drug habits, criminal history, family, employment history, education, medical and psychological problems, and personal finances is obtained. The defendant is also permitted to give his or her version of the facts surrounding the offense. There appears to be no right to counsel during this interview,[1] although most courts and probation officers permit attorneys to attend. The Seventh Circuit Court of Appeals held that the Sixth Amendment right to counsel does not apply at presentence interviews by probation officers. The court reasoned that because probation officers are neutral judicial employees, and not law enforcement officers, interviews conducted by them are not critical stages of an *adversarial* proceeding.[2] The Seventh Circuit, like other courts that have considered the issue, thus determined that the presentence interview is a neutral, nonadversarial meeting between the probation officer and the defendant. This is so even though the defendant may be in custody and admissions could lead to greater punishment.

Three facts support the conclusion that there is no right to counsel during a presentence investigation interview. First, the objective of the interview is to gather information to assist the sentencing court, not to establish that the defendant committed a crime. Second (and related to the first), a probation officer is not, strictly speaking, a law enforcement officer. Third, the questions asked at the interview are routine, and defense counsel can properly advise the client of his or her rights before the interview occurs.

In addition to conducting an interview of the defendant, the probation officer will obtain copies of vital documents, such as the defendant's "rap sheet" and relevant medical records. The probation officer will attempt to verify the information provided by the defendant through these documents and other investigatory processes.

When the probation officer has completed the investigation, a presentence report is prepared. This report reflects the information discovered during the investigation and is used by the court in determining what sentence should be imposed. Often, the prosecutor and law enforcement officers involved in prosecuting the defendant, family members of the defendant, and the victim of the crime are permitted to make statements that are incorporated into the report.

There is no constitutional right to the preparation of a presentence report; however, most jurisdictions have followed the lead of the federal government, which requires a presentence report unless the record contains information sufficient to enable the meaningful exercise of sentencing discretion.[3]

In the federal system, the defendant is entitled to review the presentence report prior to sentencing. This is true in most states as well, but the right is not absolute. For example, the recommendation of the probation officer may be kept confidential.[4]

At the sentencing hearing, the defendant may disprove factual statements contained in the report. To this end witnesses may be called and exhibits introduced.

The Sentencing Hearing

The next stage in the process is the sentencing hearing. Sentencing hearings are adversarial. Witnesses may be called, other evidence introduced, and arguments made. In most instances the hearing is before a judge, not a jury, and accordingly the rules of evidence are relaxed. When the hearing is before a jury, such as in capital cases, the rules of evidence are fully effective. This is a critical stage under the Sixth Amendment, and therefore there is a right to counsel. As is true for defendants at earlier stages of the process, convictees are entitled to more than a warm body; they are entitled to effective assistance of counsel. To prove ineffective assistance of counsel, it must be shown that the attorney's representation fell below an objective standard of reasonableness and that the defendant was actually prejudiced. The following case, which involves the sentencing of a man for a brutal rape and murder, is an example of ineffective counsel at sentencing.

SEARS V. UPTON
561 U.S. ___ (2010)

PER CURIAM

In 1993, a Georgia jury convicted Sears of armed robbery and kidnaping with bodily injury (which also resulted in death), a capital crime under state law. During the penalty phase of Sears' capital trial, his counsel presented evidence describing his childhood as stable, loving, and essentially without incident. Seven witnesses offered testimony along the following lines: Sears came from a middle-class background; his actions shocked and dismayed his relatives; and a death sentence, the jury was told, would devastate the family. Counsel's mitigation

SEARS V. UPTON *(continued)*

theory, it seems, was calculated to portray the adverse impact of Sears' execution on his family and loved ones. But the strategy backfired. The prosecutor ultimately used the evidence of Sears' purportedly stable and advantaged upbringing against him during the State's closing argument. With Sears, the prosecutor told the jury, "[w]e don't have a deprived child from an inner city; a person who[m] society has turned its back on at an early age. But, yet, we have a person, privileged in every way, who has rejected every opportunity that was afforded him."

The mitigation evidence that emerged during the state postconviction evidentiary hearing, however, demonstrates that Sears was far from "privileged in every way." Sears' home life, while filled with material comfort, was anything but tranquil: His parents had a physically abusive relationship, and divorced when Sears was young, he suffered sexual abuse at the hands of an adolescent male cousin, his mother's "favorite word for referring to her sons was 'little mother fuckers,'" and his father was "verbally abusive," and disciplined Sears with age-inappropriate military-style drills. Sears struggled in school, demonstrating substantial behavior problems from a very young age. For example, Sears repeated the second grade, and was referred to a local health center for evaluation at age nine. By the time Sears reached high school, he was "described as severely learning disabled and as severely behaviorally handicapped."

Environmental factors aside, and more significantly, evidence produced during the state postconviction relief process also revealed that Sears suffered "significant frontal lobe abnormalities." Two different psychological experts testified that Sears had substantial deficits in mental cognition and reasoning—*i.e.*, "problems with planning, sequencing and impulse control,"—as a result of several serious head injuries he suffered as a child, as well as drug and alcohol abuse. Regardless of the cause of his brain damage, his scores on at least two standardized assessment tests placed him at or below the first percentile in several categories of cognitive function, "making him among the most impaired individuals in the population in terms of ability to suppress competing impulses and conform behavior only to relevant stimuli." The assessment also revealed that Sears' "ability to organize his choices, assign them relative weight and select among them in a deliberate way is grossly impaired." From an etiological standpoint, one expert explained that Sears' "history is replete with multiple head trauma, substance abuse and traumatic experiences of the type expected" to lead to these significant impairments.

Whatever concern the dissent has about some of the sources relied upon by Sears' experts—informal personal accounts,—it does not undermine the well-credentialed expert's assessment, based on between 12 and 16 hours of interviews, testing, and observations, that Sears suffers from substantial cognitive impairment. Sears performed dismally on several of the forensic tests administered to him to assess his frontal lobe functioning. On the Stroop Word Interference Test, which measures response inhibition, 99.6% of those individuals in his cohort (which accounts for age, education, and background) performed better than he did. On the Trail-Making B test, which also measures frontal lobe functioning, Sears performed at the first (and lowest) percentile. Based on these results, the expert's first-hand observations, and an extensive review of Sears' personal history, the expert's opinion was unequivocal: There is "clear and compelling evidence" that Sears has "pronounced frontal lobe pathology."

Further, the fact that Sears' brother is a convicted drug dealer and user, and introduced Sears to a life of crime, actually would have been consistent with a mitigation theory portraying Sears as an

(continued)

SEARS V. UPTON *(continued)*

individual with diminished judgment and reasoning skills, who may have desired to follow in the footsteps of an older brother who had shut him out of his life. And the fact that some of such evidence may have been "hearsay" does not necessarily undermine its value—or its admissibility—for penalty phase purposes.

Finally, the fact that along with this new mitigation evidence there was also some adverse evidence is unsurprising, given that counsel's initial mitigation investigation was constitutionally inadequate. Competent counsel should have been able to turn some of the adverse evidence into a positive—perhaps in support of a cognitive deficiency mitigation theory. In particular, evidence of Sears' grandiose self-conception and evidence of his magical thinking, were features, in another well-credentialed expert's view, of a "profound personality disorder." This evidence might not have made Sears any more likable to the jury, but it might well have helped the jury understand Sears, and his horrendous acts—especially in light of his purportedly stable upbringing.

Because they failed to conduct an adequate mitigation investigation, *none* of this evidence was known to Sears' trial counsel. It emerged only during state postconviction relief.

Unsurprisingly, the state postconviction trial court concluded that Sears had demonstrated his counsel's penalty phase investigation was constitutionally deficient. . . .

What is surprising, however, is the court's analysis regarding whether counsel's facially inadequate mitigation investigation prejudiced Sears. . . .

A proper analysis of prejudice under Strickland would have taken into account the newly uncovered evidence of Sears' "significant" mental and psychological impairments, along with the mitigation evidence introduced during Sears' penalty phase trial, to assess whether there is a reasonable probability that Sears would have received a different sentence after a constitutionally sufficient mitigation investigation.

[Accordingly the Court remanded the case for a full analysis of whether the ineffective assistance of counsel at sentencing actually prejudiced the outcome of the sentence. Be aware that Justices Scalia and Thomas issued a sharply worded dissent in this case.]

In most instances, sentencing facts are established by preponderance of the evidence and are found by the sentencing judge. In rare instances, however, clear and convincing evidence or proof beyond a reasonable doubt is required. Death cases are an example. This issue has also arisen in the context of sentence enhancements. For example, due process requires that any fact that increases the penalty for a crime beyond the prescribed statutory maximum, other than the fact of a prior conviction, must be submitted to a jury and proved beyond a reasonable doubt. So, a sentencing scheme that increases the punishment for racially motivated second-degree murder beyond the limits set by the second-degree murder statute is invalid unless the racial motive is proved to the jury beyond a reasonable doubt.[5]

One issue that has received considerable attention, and contradictory treatment, from the Supreme Court in recent years is the use of **victim impact statements** at sentencing. A *victim impact statement* is an oral or written statement to the sentencing judge explaining how the crime has affected the victim and, possibly, the victim's family. In 1987 the Supreme Court handed down *Booth v. Maryland*, 482 U.S. 496

victim impact statement

■ At the time of sentencing, a statement made to the court concerning the effect the crime has had on the victim or on the victim's family.

(1987), wherein it invalidated a state statute requiring sentencing judges to consider victim impact statements in capital cases. The Court determined that the use of victim impact statements could prejudice the proceeding by injecting irrelevant, but inflammatory, evidence into the sentencing determination.

Only four years later, though, the Supreme Court overruled *Booth* in *Payne v. Tennessee*. Thus, victim impact evidence may be admitted, even if it is not related to the facts surrounding the crime. The decision concerning admissibility must be made on a case-by-case basis, and it is a violation of due process to admit evidence that is so prejudicial that the sentencing becomes fundamentally unfair.

On the other side of the coin, defendants are generally allowed to present nearly any evidence at sentencing. This right is constitutionally mandated in capital cases; the Supreme Court has said that a state cannot preclude a defendant from proffering evidence in support of a sentence less than death.[6]

PAYNE V. TENNESSEE
501 U.S. 808 (1991)

In this case we reconsider our holdings in *Booth v. Maryland* . . . that the Eighth Amendment bars the admission of victim impact statement evidence during the penalty phase of a capital trial.

The petitioner, Pervis Tyrone Payne, was convicted by a jury on two counts of first-degree murder and one count of assault with intent to commit murder in the first degree. He was sentenced to death for each of the murders, and to 30 years in prison for assault.

The victims of Payne's offenses were 28-year-old Charisse Christopher, her 2-year-old daughter Lacie, and her 3-year-old son Nicholas. The three lived together . . . across the hall from Payne's girlfriend, Bobbie Thomas. On Saturday, June 27, 1987, Payne visited Thomas's apartment several times in expectation of her return from her mother's house in Arkansas, but found no one at home. One visit, he left his overnight bag, containing clothes and other items for his weekend stay, in the hallway outside Thomas's apartment. With the bag were three cans of malt liquor.

Payne passed the morning and early afternoon injecting cocaine and drinking beer. Later, he drove around the town with a friend in the friend's car, each of them taking turns reading a pornographic magazine. Sometime around 3 P.M., Payne returned to the apartment complex, entered the Christophers' apartment, and began making sexual advances toward Charisse. Charisse resisted and Payne became violent. A neighbor who resided in the apartment directly beneath the Christophers heard Charisse screaming, "'Get out, get out,' as if she were telling the children to leave." The noise briefly subsided and then began "horribly loud." The neighbor called the police after she heard a "bloodcurdling scream" from the Christopher apartment. . . .

When the first police officer arrived at the scene, he immediately encountered Payne, who was leaving the apartment building, so covered with blood that he appeared to be "sweating blood." The officer confronted Payne, who responded, "I'm the complainant." . . . When the officer asked, "What is going on up there?" Payne struck the officer with the overnight bag, dropped his tennis shoes, and fled.

Inside the apartment, the police encountered a horrifying scene. Blood covered the walls and floor

(continued)

PAYNE V. TENNESSEE (continued)

throughout the unit. Charisse and her children were lying on the floor in the kitchen. Nicholas, despite several wounds inflicted by a butcher knife that completely penetrated through his body from front to back, was still breathing. Miraculously, he survived. . . . Charisse and Lacie were dead.

Charisse's body was found on the kitchen floor on her back, her legs fully extended. . . . None of the 84 wounds inflicted by Payne were individually fatal; rather, the cause of death was most likely bleeding from all of the wounds. She had suffered stab wounds to the chest, abdomen, back, and head. The murder weapon, a butcher knife, was found at her feet. Payne's baseball cap was snapped on her arm near her elbow. Three cans of malt liquor bearing Payne's fingerprints were found near her body, and a fourth empty was on a landing outside the apartment door.

Payne was apprehended later that day. . . .

[T]he jury returned guilty verdicts against Payne on all counts.

During the sentencing phase of the trial, Payne presented the testimony of four witnesses, his mother and father, Bobbie Thomas, and Dr. John T. Huston, a clinical psychologist specializing in criminal court evaluation work. Bobbie Thomas testified that she met Payne at church, during a time when she was being abused by her husband. She stated that Payne was a very caring person, and that he devoted much time and attention to her three children, who were being affected by her marital difficulties. She said that the children had come to love him very much and would miss him, and that he "behaved just like a father that loved his kids." She asserted that he did not drink, nor did he use drugs, and that it was generally inconsistent with Payne's character to have committed these crimes. . . .

The State presented the testimony of Charisse's mother, Mary Zvolanek. When asked how Nicholas

had been affected by the murder of his mother and sister, she responded:

> He cries for his mom. He doesn't seem to understand why she doesn't come home. And he cries for his sister Lacie. He comes to me many times during the week and asks me, Grandma, do you miss Lacie. And I tell him yes. He says, I'm worried about my Lacie.

In arguing for the death penalty during closing argument, the prosecutor commented on the continuing effects of Nicholas's experience, stating:

> But we do know that Nicholas was alive. And Nicholas was in the same room. Nicholas was still conscious. His eyes were open. He responded to the paramedics. He was able to follow their directions. He was able to hold his intestines in as he was carried to the ambulance. So he knew what happened to his mother and baby sister. . . .
>
> Somewhere down the road Nicholas is going to grow up, hopefully. He's going to want to know what happened. And he is going to know what happened to his baby sister and mother. He is going to want to know what type of justice was done. He is going to want to know what happened. With your verdict, you will provide the answer. . . .

In the rebuttal to Payne's closing argument, the prosecutor stated:

> You saw the videotape this morning. You saw what Nicholas Christopher will carry in his mind forever. When you talk about cruel, when you talk about atrocious, and when you talk about heinous, that picture will always come into your mind, probably throughout the rest of your lives.

. . .

No one will ever know about Lacie Jo because she never had a chance to grow up. Her life was taken from her at the age of two years old. . . . His mother will never kiss [Nicholas] good night or pat him as he goes off to bed, or hold him and sing him a lullaby. [Petitioner's attorney] wants you to think about a good reputation, people who love the defendant and things about him. He doesn't want you to think about the people who loved Charisse Christopher, her mother, and daddy who loved her. The people who loved little Lacie Jo, the grandparents who are still here. The brother who mourns for her every single day and wants to know where his best little playmate is. He doesn't have anybody to watch cartoons with him, a little one. These are the things that go into why it is especially cruel, heinous, and atrocious, the burden that child will carry forever.

The jury sentenced Payne to death on each of the murder counts. The Supreme Court of Tennessee affirmed the conviction and sentence. . . .

We granted certiorari . . . to reconsider our holdings in *Booth* . . . that the Eighth Amendment prohibits a capital sentencing jury from considering "victim impact" evidence relating to the personal characteristics of the victim and the emotional impact of the crimes on the victim's family. . . .

Under our constitutional system, the primary responsibility for defining crimes against state law, fixing punishments for the commission of these crimes, and establishing procedures for criminal trials rests with the States. The state laws respecting crimes, punishments, and criminal procedure are of course subject to the overriding provisions of the United States Constitution. . . .

Within the constitutional limitations defined in our cases, the States enjoy their traditional latitude to prescribe the method by which those who commit murder should be punished. . . . The states remain free, in capital cases, as well as others, to devise new procedures and new remedies to meet felt needs. Victim impact evidence is simply another form or method of informing the sentencing authority about the specific harm caused by the crime in question, evidence of a general type long considered by sentencing authorities. [The] *Booth* Court was wrong in stating that this kind of evidence leads to the arbitrary imposition of the death penalty. In the majority of cases, and in this case, victim impact evidence serves entirely legitimate purposes. In the event that evidence is introduced that is so unduly prejudicial that it renders the trial fundamentally unfair, the Due Process Clause of the Fourteenth Amendment provides a mechanism for relief. . . . Courts have always taken into consideration the harm done by the defendant in imposing sentence, and the evidence adduced in this case was illustrative of the harm caused by Payne's double murder.

We are now of the view that a State may properly conclude that for the jury to assess meaningfully the defendant's moral culpability and blameworthiness, it should have before it at the sentencing phase evidence of the specific harm caused by the defendant. "[T]he State has a legitimate interest in counteracting the mitigating evidence which the defendant is entitled to put in, by reminding the sentencer that just as the murderer should be considered an individual, so too the victim is an individual whose death represents a unique loss to society and in particular to his family." . . . By turning the victim into a "faceless stranger at the penalty phase of a criminal trial" . . . *Booth* deprives the State of the full moral force of its evidence and may prevent the jury from having before it all the information necessary to determine the proper punishment for a first-degree murder.

The present case is an example of the potential for such unfairness. The capital sentencing jury heard testimony from Payne's girlfriend that they met at church, that he was affectionate, caring, kind to her children. . . . Payne's parents testified that he

(continued)

PAYNE V. TENNESSEE (continued)

was a good son, and a clinical psychologist testified that Payne was an extremely polite prisoner and suffered from a low IQ. None of this testimony was related to the circumstances of Payne's brutal crimes. . . . The Supreme Court of Tennessee in this case obviously felt the unfairness of the rule pronounced in *Booth* when it said "[i]t is an affront to the civilized members of the human race to say that at sentencing in a capital case, a parade of witnesses may praise the background, character and good deeds of the defendant (as was done in this case), without limitation as to relevancy, but nothing may be said that bears upon the character of, or the harm imposed, upon the victims." . . .

We thus hold that if the State chooses to permit the admission of victim impact evidence and prosecutorial argument on that subject, the Eighth Amendment erects no per se bar.

Punishing Acquitted Crimes

Historically, judges have held considerable discretion in sentencing. The rules of evidence are relaxed, and judges may hear evidence that is otherwise inadmissible. Victim impact evidence, family history, medical history, mental health history, employment history, and criminal history are examples of the type of evidence that is considered at sentencing.

Additionally, the nature of the crime committed and the particular manner in which it was committed are considered. In some cases, evidence concerning the nature and manner of the offense may include evidence of other crimes that were committed in conjunction with the offense under sentence. An interesting question concerns whether a defendant may have a sentence increased for acquitted crimes. This issue was before the Supreme Court in *United States v. Watts* (1997).[7] Police discovered both cocaine and guns in a search of Watts's property, and he was subsequently charged and tried for possession of cocaine and possession of a gun in relation to a drug offense. The jury convicted him of the former charge and acquitted him of the latter charge. At sentencing, however, the trial judge found that Watts did use the gun in relation to a drug offense and, accordingly, increased his sentence for the cocaine possession conviction.

On appeal, the Supreme Court affirmed the sentence enhancement. The Court stressed that judges have historically had significant discretion in sentencing and that the enhancement was not punishment for an acquitted offense, but instead was an enhanced punishment for the manner in which the defendant committed the crime of conviction. Also important are the differing standards of proof between conviction and sentencing. Conviction requires a finding beyond a reasonable doubt, while sentencing requires proof by preponderance of the evidence. The high standard of proof for conviction, according to the Court, means that an acquittal cannot be interpreted as a finding of fact. An acquittal means that the government has not proved its case, not that the defendant did not commit the act in question. However, for reasons to be discussed, the status of *Watts* is unknown.

Proving Facts for Sentencing

In a practice similar to that of using acquitted crimes to enhance a sentence, judges have historically used facts not presented to the trial jury to increase sentences. If there is a plea of guilty, the judge must find that the essential elements of the crime were committed. This usually involves a recitation of the facts by the defendant. If there has been a trial, the judge is armed with the findings of the jury; or in the case of a bench trial, of the trial judge. Once the facts have been established at trial, whether by confession or a finding of fact, additional evidence must be received at sentencing. However, that evidence is limited to the facts that are relevant to the sentencing decision. For over 150 years, trial judges routinely found facts, often by a preponderance of the evidence, at sentencing hearings. Judges have always been restricted by jury decisions. That is, they cannot refind facts that have been decided by trial juries. For example, if a jury finds a defendant guilty of possession of a specific amount of cocaine, a sentencing judge is prohibited from increasing the sentence because the judge finds that the defendant possessed a greater amount of cocaine.

However, judges would commonly find other facts that affected the final sentence—for example, whether a defendant possessed a weapon while engaged in a drug deal in a case where the defendant was charged only with dealing drugs, not possession of the weapon. Often these facts were proved by the preponderance standard.

In recent years, however, a new body of law has developed around the Sixth Amendment's jury trial right. In short, these cases require that all findings that are used to support the sentence must be heard by a jury and found to be true beyond a reasonable doubt.[8] In *Blakely*, the defendant had been charged with first-degree kidnapping. He and the state reached a plea agreement that reduced the charges to second-degree kidnapping involving domestic violence and the use of a firearm. Pursuant to the plea agreement, the state recommended a sentence of between 49 and 53 months. The judge, however, found that the crime involved deliberate cruelty and enhanced the sentence to 90 months. After the defendant objected, the judge conducted a three-day fact hearing on the deliberate cruelty question. The judge again sentenced the defendant to 90 months, having found deliberate cruelty following the hearing.

The Supreme Court reversed, finding that it was not possible for the judge to justify the enhanced sentence solely because of the facts admitted in the guilty plea. While the defendant admitted to kidnapping and the use of a gun, he did not provide evidence that he acted with deliberate cruelty. Accordingly, the judge had to find facts the trial jury was not charged with determining. This effort is proved by the judge's need to conduct a three-day sentencing hearing. Because the Sixth Amendment guarantees individuals the right to have all facts essential to sentencing heard by a jury, using the reasonable doubt standard, the trial judge erred. Whether the judge had charged the trial jury to make the deliberate cruelty finding or had empaneled a jury at sentencing to make the finding, the sentence would not have violated the Sixth Amendment. Similarly, in the 2007 *Cunningham* case, the Court invalidated a California law that created an upper range of 12 years in prison for the crimes covered by the jury's verdict but allowed the judge to sentence the offender to an additional four years for facts the judge could find, by preponderance of the evidence, at a sentencing hearing. Later, in the discussion of the federal sentencing guidelines, you may read an excerpt of the Supreme Court's decision *United States v. Booker* wherein the right to have facts decided by a jury under the Sixth Amendment was used to invalidate the mandatory nature of the federal sentencing guidelines. The relationship between *Booker* and *Watts* is not clear. *Watts* may be overruled altogether. At the least, *Booker* demands that the conduct for which the defendant was acquitted be found by a jury before a judge may rely upon them at sentencing.

In capital cases the Supreme Court has specifically held that the aggravating circumstances that must be found to impose death have to be found by a jury and beyond a reasonable doubt.[9] Judges may still be empowered to decide whether to impose death or another punishment, but death is only an option to the judge if the jury finds an aggravating factor. Some states have delegated only the aggravating factor decision to juries, as required, and others have handed the jury both the aggravating factor and the sentencing decision.

Forms of Punishment

The legislature determines what type of sentence may be imposed; judges impose sentences.

Capital Punishment

Clearly the most controversial punishment is the death penalty. In early American history, capital punishment was commonly used. During the nineteenth century, use of the death penalty greatly declined. Today, more than half the states provide for the death penalty, and its use has regained popular support. Although the number of inmates actually executed every year is small, the number is increasing.

The contention that the death penalty is inherently cruel and unusual and therefore violative of the Eighth Amendment has been rejected. However, the Court has struggled, as have state courts and legislatures, with establishing standards for its use.

In *Furman v. Georgia*, 408 U.S. 238 (1972), the Court held that the death penalty cannot be imposed under a sentencing procedure that creates a substantial risk of being implemented in an arbitrary manner. It found that Georgia's law permitted arbitrary decisions and so declared it void. *Furman* required that the sentencer's discretion be limited by objective standards to eliminate unfairness—specifically, to eliminate racial and other bias from death sentence decisions.

States responded to *Furman* in various ways. Some chose to eliminate discretion entirely by mandating capital punishment for certain crimes. The Supreme Court invalidated mandatory capital punishment laws in *Locket v. Ohio*, 438 U.S. 586 (1978). In *Locket* the Court held that individualized sentencing was constitutionally required. The Court stated that any law prohibiting a sentencer from considering "as a mitigating factor, any aspect of a defendant's character or record and any circumstances of the offense that the defendant proffers as a basis for a sentence less than death" creates an unconstitutional risk that the "death penalty will be imposed in spite of factors which may call for a less severe penalty."[10]

However, Georgia's new death penalty legislation was upheld in *Gregg v. Georgia*, 428 U.S. 153 (1976). The new law provided that the jury must find, in a sentencing hearing separate from the trial, an aggravating circumstance before the death penalty could be imposed. The statute enumerated possible aggravating circumstances. By requiring a jury to find an aggravating circumstance, arbitrariness is believed to be lessened. Indeed, today the decision to impose death must be made by a unanimous jury, and defendants must be given the opportunity to present mitigating evidence. A statute that mandates death in all cases is invalid. A statute may, however, require death if a jury finds that the mitigating factors do not outweigh the aggravating factors.[11]

Furman, Gregg, Locket, and their progeny stand for the principle that a sentencing statute cannot totally eliminate discretion, nor grant so much discretion that the death penalty can be imposed arbitrarily. These concepts of individualized sentencing and minimized discretion in sentencing are somewhat antithetical. The Supreme Court itself recognizes that a tension exists between the two goals and has struggled to establish procedures and standards to successfully implement them. "Experience has shown that the consistency and rationality promised in *Furman* are inversely related to the fairness owed the individual when considering a sentence of death. A step toward consistency is a step away from fairness."[12]

The death penalty issue has been divisive to the Court. Some justices have so strongly believed that the death penalty is unconstitutional (either inherently or as administered) that they have refused to acquiesce to notions of stare decisis on the issue. Justice Thurgood Marshall, for example, dissented in every capital punishment case, including both denials of petitions of certiorari and cases under review, because of his firmly held belief that capital punishment was unconstitutional.

Until 1994, Justice Harry Blackmun held that the death penalty was not inherently unconstitutional. However, in *Callins v. Collins*, he made the following statement.

Courts are in the very business of erecting procedural devices from which fair, equitable, and reliable outcomes are presumed to flow. Yet, in the death penalty area, this Court, in my view, had engaged in a futile effort to balance these constitutional demands, and now is retreating not only from the *Furman* promise of consistency and rationality, but from the requirement of individualized sentencing as well. Having virtually conceded that both fairness and rationality cannot be achieved in the administration of the death penalty . . . the Court has chosen to deregulate the entire enterprise, replacing, it would seem, substantive constitutional requirements with mere aesthetics, and abdicating its statutorily and constitutionally imposed duty to provide meaningful judicial oversight to the administration of death by the States. From this date forward, I no longer shall tinker with the machinery of death. For more than 20 years I have endeavored—indeed, I have struggled—along with a majority of this Court, to develop procedural and substantive rules that would lend more than the mere appearance of fairness to the death penalty endeavor. Rather than continue to coddle the Court's delusion that the desired level of fairness has been achieved and the need for regulation eviscerated, I feel morally and intellectually obligated simply to concede that the death penalty experiment has failed. It is virtually self-evident to me now that no combination of procedural rules or substantive regulations ever can save the death penalty from its inherent constitutional deficiencies. The basic question—does the system accurately and consistently determine which defendants "deserve" to die?—cannot be answered in the affirmative. It is not simply that this Court has allowed vague aggravating circumstances to be employed . . . relevant mitigating evidence to be disregarded . . . and vital judicial review to be blocked. . . . The problem is that the inevitability of actual, legal, and moral error gives us a system that we know must wrongly kill some defendants, a system that fails to deliver the fair, consistent, and reliable sentences of death required by the Constitution. . . . Perhaps one day this Court will develop procedural rules or verbal formulas that actually will provide consistency, fairness, and reliability in a capital-sentencing scheme. I am not optimistic that such a day will come. I am more optimistic, though, that this Court eventually will conclude that the effort to eliminate arbitrariness while preserving fairness "in the infliction of [death] is so plainly doomed to failure that it—and the death penalty—must be abandoned altogether." . . . I may not live to see that day, but I have faith that eventually it will arrive. The path the Court has chosen lessens us all. I dissent.[13]

---

sidebar

THE DEATH PENALTY MORATORIUM MOVEMENT

Although most Americans support the death penalty, polling also reveals majority support for a moratorium until fairness issues are addressed. Specifically, concerns about wrongly convicted prisoners and a possible racial bias in administering the penalty have led many conservatives who support the death penalty to join with death penalty abolitionists in support of a moratorium. The movement has had moderate success. Illinois governor George Ryan imposed a moratorium on imposing death in 2000. In the same year, the New Hampshire legislature became the first state legislature to abolish the punishment since 1965. Although the governor subsequently vetoed this bill, it is evidence of a new attitude about the death penalty. Death penalty abolitionist movements have come and gone in United States history. Why has the movement picked up steam now?

According to Jeffrey Kirchmeier, many events are fueling this movement, including the following:

- Sister Helen Prejean's book and subsequent movie, *Dead Man Walking*. Kirchmeier likens *Dead Man Walking's* impact on the death penalty abolitionist movement to that of Harriet Beecher Stowe's *Uncle Tom's Cabin* on the antislavery movement.

- The criticism of Supreme Court Justices Blackmun and Powell, as well as that of many other judges.

- The 1997 American Bar Association statement urging a moratorium on the death penalty.

sidebar *(continued)*

- New technologies leading to the discovery of wrongly convicted and sentenced individuals. Between 1973 and 2002, 99 prisoners were released from death row after new technology proved their innocence or at least established the absence of proof beyond a reasonable doubt.
- New research indicating that innocent persons are executed.
- A good economy and declining crime rate during the 1990s.
- Considerable media attention regarding cases where prisoners who had been sentenced to death were later set free.
- Many states adding the possibility of life without parole.[14]

The moratorium in Illinois continued until 2011, when capital punishment was abolished by statute. During this period several other states abolished the penalty. Connecticut followed suit in 2012, leaving capital punishment as an alternative, although not exercised in every state where it may be imposed, in 32 states.

One decision that bothered Justice Blackmun was *McCleskey v. Kemp*, 481 U.S. 279 (1987), wherein the Court refused to set aside a death sentence even though the defendant presented reliable statistical data supporting the conclusion that race continues to be a significant factor in the application of capital punishment. The Court held that statistical evidence could not be used to invalidate an entire sentencing scheme; rather, the burden falls on each individual defendant to prove that race was a factor in his or her sentence. Justice Blackmun argued that the Court was thereby abandoning the *Furman* requirement of consistency and rationality.

sidebar

CAPITAL PUNISHMENT IN THE UNITED STATES

In 2013, the laws of 32 states and the federal government authorized capital punishment. Alaska, Connecticut, Hawaii, Illinois, Iowa, Maine, Massachusetts, Michigan, Minnesota, New Jersey, New Mexico, New York, North Dakota, Rhode Island, Vermont, West Virginia, and Wisconsin were the states without the death penalty. Also, there was no death penalty in the District of Columbia.

By 2013 more than 3,125 people were awaiting execution, compared to 3,625 in 1999. In 2012, 43 individuals were executed. Hundreds of new inmates

(continued)

sidebar *(continued)*

receive death sentences every year, although the total number sentenced to death has declined since 1999. Between 1976 (*Furman* decision) and 2012 in the United States, 1,331 people were executed. Texas leads in the number of people executed; 497 people were executed there between 1977 and 2012. Virginia, with the second-highest state, executed 110 during that period.

Executions, 1930–2009

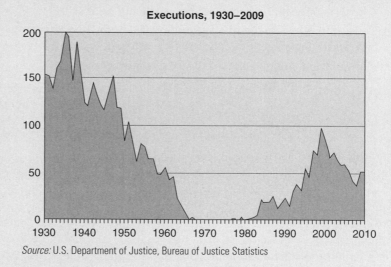

Source: U.S. Department of Justice, Bureau of Justice Statistics

Lethal injection is the method of execution employed in all states today, but state laws also provide for electrocution, gassing, hanging, and firing squad. Although the numbers vary by year, it is typical for more than a decade to pass between sentence and the imposition of death. Of those executed in 2012, 56% were white, 34% black, 8% Hispanic, and 2% "other."

Sources: Death Penalty Information Center and Amnesty International, *Facts About the Death Penalty*, 2013, and Bureau of Justice Statistics, Capital Punishment Statistics, 2011.

The definition of cruelty is an evolving concept. Electrocution, lethal injection, hanging, and shooting are all approved methods of executing a prisoner. Other methods, such as starvation, would not pass constitutional muster. In 2008, the Supreme Court decided that Kentucky's lethal injection process was constitutional in *Baze v. Rees*.[15]

The Eighth Amendment has been interpreted to prohibit sentences that are disproportionate to the crime committed. In this vein, the Supreme Court has held that capital punishment may not be imposed for the crime of raping an adult woman.[16] In *Kennedy v. Louisiana*, 558 U.S. 1 (2008) the long-standing question whether child rapists could be put to death was answered in the negative.

KENNEDY V. LOUISIANA
558 U.S. 1 (2008)

Petitioner's crime was one that cannot be recounted in these pages in a way sufficient to capture in full the hurt and horror inflicted on his victim or to convey the revulsion society, and the jury that represents it, sought to express by sentencing petitioner to death. At 9:18 A.M. on March 2, 1998, petitioner called 911 to report that his stepdaughter, referred to here as L. H., had been raped. He told the 911 operator that L. H. had been in the garage while he readied his son for school. Upon hearing loud screaming, petitioner said, he ran outside and found L. H. in the side yard. Two neighborhood boys, petitioner told the operator, had dragged L. H. from the garage to the yard, pushed her down, and raped her. Petitioner claimed he saw one of the boys riding away on a blue 10-speed bicycle.

When police arrived at petitioner's home between 9:20 and 9:30 A.M., they found L. H. on her bed, wearing a T-shirt and wrapped in a bloody blanket. She was bleeding profusely from the vaginal area. Petitioner told police he had carried her from the yard to the bathtub and then to the bed. Consistent with this explanation, police found a thin line of blood drops in the garage on the way to the house and then up the stairs. Once in the bedroom, petitioner had used a basin of water and a cloth to wipe blood from the victim. This later prevented medical personnel from collecting a reliable DNA sample.

L. H. was transported to the Children's Hospital. An expert in pediatric forensic medicine testified that L. H.'s injuries were the most severe he had seen from a sexual assault in his four years of practice. A laceration to the left wall of the vagina had separated her cervix from the back of her vagina, causing her rectum to protrude into the vaginal structure. Her entire perineum was torn from the posterior fourchette to the anus. The injuries required emergency surgery.

At the scene of the crime, at the hospital, and in the first weeks that followed, both L. H. and petitioner maintained in their accounts to investigators that L. H. had been raped by two neighborhood boys. One of L. H.'s doctors testified at trial that L. H. told all hospital personnel the same version of the rape, although she reportedly told one family member that petitioner raped her. L. H. was interviewed several days after the rape by a psychologist. The interview was videotaped, lasted three hours over two days, and was introduced into evidence at trial. On the tape one can see that L. H. had difficulty discussing the subject of the rape. She spoke haltingly and with long pauses and frequent movement. Early in the interview, L. H. expressed reservations about the questions being asked:

> "I'm going to tell the same story. They just want me to change it. . . . They want me to say my Dad did it. . . . I don't want to say it. . . . I tell them the same, same story."

She told the psychologist that she had been playing in the garage when a boy came over and asked her about Girl Scout cookies she was selling; and that the boy "pulled [her by the legs to] the backyard," where he placed his hand over her mouth, "pulled down [her] shorts," and raped her.

Eight days after the crime, and despite L. H.'s insistence that petitioner was not the offender, petitioner was arrested for the rape. The State's investigation had drawn the accuracy of petitioner and L. H.'s story into question. Though the defense at trial proffered alternative explanations, the case for the prosecution, credited by the jury, was based upon the following evidence: An inspection of the side

(continued)

yard immediately after the assault was inconsistent with a rape having occurred there, the grass having been found mostly undisturbed but for a small patch of coagulated blood. Petitioner said that one of the perpetrators fled the crime scene on a blue 10-speed bicycle but gave inconsistent descriptions of the bicycle's features, such as its handlebars. Investigators found a bicycle matching petitioner and L. H.'s description in tall grass behind a nearby apartment, and petitioner identified it as the bicycle one of the perpetrators was riding. Yet its tires were flat, it did not have gears, and it was covered in spider webs. In addition police found blood on the underside of L. H.'s mattress. This convinced them the rape took place in her bedroom, not outside the house.

Police also found that petitioner made two telephone calls on the morning of the rape. Sometime before 6:15 A.M., petitioner called his employer and left a message that he was unavailable to work that day. Petitioner called back between 6:30 and 7:30 A.M. to ask a colleague how to get blood out of a white carpet because his daughter had "'just become a young lady.'" At 7:37 A.M., petitioner called B & B Carpet Cleaning and requested urgent assistance in removing bloodstains from a carpet. Petitioner did not call 911 until about an hour and a half later.

About a month after petitioner's arrest L. H. was removed from the custody of her mother, who had maintained until that point that petitioner was not involved in the rape. On June 22, 1998, L. H. was returned home and told her mother for the first time that petitioner had raped her. And on December 16, 1999, about 21 months after the rape, L. H. recorded her accusation in a videotaped interview with the Child Advocacy Center.

The State charged petitioner with aggravated rape of a child under La. Stat. Ann. §14:42 (West 1997 and Supp. 1998) [which provided for death or life imprisonment at hard labor. Kennedy was

convicted and a sentencing hearing was conducted, at which the jury heard about prior unreported child rapes the defendant had committed. He was sentenced to death].

The Eighth Amendment, applicable to the States through the Fourteenth Amendment, provides that "[e]xcessive bail shall not be required, nor excessive fines imposed, nor cruel and unusual punishments inflicted." . . . The Amendment "draw[s] its meaning from the evolving standards of decency that mark the progress of a maturing society." This is because "[t]he standard of extreme cruelty is not merely descriptive, but necessarily embodies a moral judgment. The standard itself remains the same, but its applicability must change as the basic mores of society change.

Applying this principle, we held in *Roper* and *Atkins* that the execution of juveniles and mentally retarded persons are punishments violative of the Eighth Amendment because the offender had a diminished personal responsibility for the crime. The Court further has held that the death penalty can be disproportionate to the crime itself where the crime did not result, or was not intended to result, in death of the victim. In *Coker*, 433 U.S. 584, for instance, the Court held it would be unconstitutional to execute an offender who had raped an adult woman. And in *Enmund* v. *Florida*, 458 U.S. 782 (1982), the Court overturned the capital sentence of a defendant who aided and abetted a robbery during which a murder was committed but did not himself kill, attempt to kill, or intend that a killing would take place. On the other hand, in *Tyson* v. *Arizona*, 481 U.S. 137 (1987), the Court allowed the defendants' death sentences to stand where they did not themselves kill the victims but their involvement in the events leading up to the murders was active, recklessly indifferent, and substantial . . . .

In these cases the Court has been guided by "objective indicia of society's standards, as

KENNEDY V. LOUISIANA *(continued)*

expressed in legislative enactments and state practice with respect to executions." *Roper*, 543 U.S., at 563; see also *Coker*, *supra*, at 593–597 (plurality opinion) (finding that both legislatures and juries had firmly rejected the penalty of death for the rape of an adult woman); *Enmund*, *supra*, at 788 (looking to "historical development of the punishment at issue, legislative judgments, international opinion, and the sentencing decisions juries have made"). The inquiry does not end there, however. Consensus is not dispositive. Whether the death penalty is disproportionate to the crime committed depends as well upon the standards elaborated by controlling precedents and by the Court's own understanding and interpretation of the Eighth Amendment's text, history, meaning, and purpose. . . .

In 1925, 18 States, the District of Columbia, and the Federal Government had statutes that authorized the death penalty for the rape of a child or an adult. See *Coker*, *supra*, at 593 (plurality opinion). Between 1930 and 1964, 455 people were executed for those crimes. See 5 Historical Statistics of the United States: Earliest Times to the Present, pp. 5–262 to 5–263 (S. Carter et al. eds. 2006) (Table Ec343–357). To our knowledge the last individual executed for the rape of a child was Ronald Wolfe in 1964. . . .

. . . 44 States have not made child rape a capital offense. As for federal law, Congress in the Federal Death Penalty Act of 1994 expanded the number of federal crimes for which the death penalty is a permissible sentence, including certain nonhomicide offenses; but it did not do the same for child rape or abuse. . . .

The evidence of a national consensus with respect to the death penalty for child rapists, as with respect to juveniles, mentally retarded offenders, and vicarious felony murderers, shows divided opinion but, on balance, an opinion against it. Thirty-seven jurisdictions—36 States plus the Federal Government—have the death penalty. As mentioned above, only six of those jurisdictions authorize the death penalty for rape of a child. Though our review of national consensus is not confined to tallying the number of States with applicable death penalty legislation, it is of significance that, in 45 jurisdictions, petitioner could not be executed for child rape of any kind. That number surpasses the 30 States in *Atkins* and *Roper* and the 42 States in *Enmund* that prohibited the death penalty under the circumstances those cases considered.

[The Court recognized that there was a small trend in the direction of reinstituting death for child rape in several states. But the Court found the trend inconclusive.]

As we have said in other Eighth Amendment cases, objective evidence of contemporary values as it relates to punishment for child rape is entitled to great weight, but it does not end our inquiry. "[T]he Constitution contemplates that in the end our own judgment will be brought to bear on the question of the acceptability of the death penalty under the Eighth Amendment. . . .

Consistent with evolving standards of decency and the teachings of our precedents we conclude that, in determining whether the death penalty is excessive, there is a distinction between intentional first-degree murder on the one hand and nonhomicide crimes against individual persons, even including child rape, on the other. The latter crimes may be devastating in their harm, as here, but "in terms of moral depravity and of the injury to the person and to the public," they cannot be compared to murder in their "severity and irrevocability. . . ."

[The Court also discussed how imposing death could cause a rise in underreporting of the crime and could increase the number of raped children who are murdered. For the above reasons, the Court held that child rapists may not be punished with death.]

Although the text was included in your excerpt, be aware that the Court was careful to note that the decision was limited to crimes against the person, not crimes against the State (e.g., terrorism, treason).

In another case it was decided that a person may not be put to death for aiding in a felony that results in murder, unless there was an intent to kill.[17] In 2005, the Supreme Court extended the protection from capital punishment to individuals who are under the age of 18 when they commit their capital crimes.[18]

In 1986, the Supreme Court stated that defendants who are incapable of understanding why they are being executed because of insanity may not be executed until they regain their faculties.[19] In *Atkins v. Virginia*[20] (2002) the Court applied similar reasoning to reach the same conclusion about individuals who are cognitively disabled.

**commutation
of sentence**

■ Changing a criminal
punishment to one less
severe.

pardon

■ A president's or
governor's release of a
person from punishment
for a crime.

reprieve

■ Holding off on enforcing
a criminal sentence for a
period of time after the
sentence has been handed
down.

sidebar

EXECUTIVE CLEMENCY, PARDONS, AND REPRIEVES

In most states and the federal government, the chief executive (i.e., the governor or the president) possesses several powers concerning criminal convictions and sentences. One such power is executive clemency. To forgive or, more commonly, to reduce a punishment is clemency. To reduce a prisoner's sentence from death to life imprisonment is clemency. The reduction of a sentence is also known as **commutation of sentence.** Commutation is used when the executive believes a person guilty, but also believes the sentence is too harsh. In 1993 the Supreme Court ruled that prisoners sentenced to death who claim to have new evidence of their innocence do not possess the right to federal review in all instances. The court indicated that executive clemency is the fail-safe to guard against unwarranted executions.

The **pardon** is similar to commutation of sentence in that both relieve a person of punishment. However, the pardon is different in one important respect: it also relieves the defendant of the conviction. With the pardon, the conviction is erased and treated as though it never occurred. Pardons are used when the executive believes there was an error concerning the defendant's guilt.

Finally, a **reprieve** is a stay or delay of execution of sentence. Reprieves are used to give the executive or a court the opportunity to further review the case.

The governor has the sole authority to grant clemency in 31 states. In 10 states, clemency boards have the final authority. In seven states, clemency boards make recommendations to their respective governors. In Rhode Island, the governor can grant clemency only with the consent of that state's senate.

Sources: Janice Brown, "Note: The Quality of Mercy," 40 *UCLA L. Rev.* 327 (1992), citing Deborah Leavy, "Note, A Matter of Life or Death: Due Process Protection in Capital Clemency Proceedings," 90 *Yale L.J.* 889, 895–96 (1981).

Corporal/Physical Punishment

The Eighth Amendment limits the use of physical punishment. Punishment is not, however, unconstitutional simply because it involves pain. The issue is whether the pain is excessive. Pain is excessive when it exceeds the quantity necessary to achieve a legitimate penological purpose, such as rehabilitation or retribution. Generally, hard labor is not per se cruel.[21] If the labor is beyond the physical limits of the inmate, or involves unnecessary pain, it is unconstitutional.

Whipping has been held both constitutional[22] and unconstitutional[23] by lower courts. The Supreme Court has not decided the issue.[24]

Solitary confinement may be used in some circumstances, such as when a prisoner is disruptive or is highly dangerous. The use of prolonged solitary confinement for other prisoners is of questionable constitutionality.

The basic medical and nutritional needs of inmates must be satisfied by the government. Deliberately disregarding the medical or nutritional needs of inmates, or in some other manner imposing cruel or unusual punishment, can lead to liability under 42 U.S.C. § 1983.

sidebar

RACE AND COCAINE

When Congress established the penalties for powder and rock cocaine crimes (possession, distribution) in the 1980s, it was assumed that rock cocaine was more dangerous and as such, the punishment for rock cocaine crimes was more severe than for powder cocaine crimes. In the years that followed the experience of law enforcement personnel, courts, and drug treatment experts brought that assumption into question. Even more, a racial disparity was discovered. Rock cocaine proved to be more commonly used by African Americans and powder cocaine by European Americans. Therefore, African Americans, mostly men, were disproportionately represented in the prison population for cocaine offenses. The problem was recognized by the United States Sentencing Commission, and subsequently Congress, at the urging of President Barack Obama, enacted the Fair Sentencing Act of 2010.[25] The Act amended the Controlled Substances Act to harmonize powder and rock cocaine offenses punishments.

The Supreme Court has said that the Eighth Amendment is to be interpreted consistent with society's evolving standards of decency. Therefore, although some courts have approved sterilization, and many states are considering chemical castration of men who commit sexual assault, there is a possibility that such practices could be found inconsistent with the Eighth Amendment.

Incarceration

Restraint is an effective method of dealing with dangerous persons. Incarceration serves this purpose, and in some cases the offender is also rehabilitated. Regrettably, because rehabilitation is rare and (contrary to popular belief) prison conditions are often poor, many offenders leave prison angry, no more educated or employable, and occasionally more dangerous.

Nevertheless, incarceration continues to be the most common method of punishing violent offenders. Offenders may be committed to prisons, camps, or local jails. Those sentenced to short terms (one year or less) are usually housed in a local jail. Individuals sentenced to longer terms are committed to prisons.

Like capital punishment, the Eighth Amendment's prohibition of cruel and unusual punishments establishes boundaries. The cruelty provision impacts the conditions of confinement. This subject is discussed later, in this book.

The principle of keeping punishments proportional to crimes is not significant to incarceration as a form of punishment. The Court has given legislatures wide berth when setting terms of imprisonment for all crimes. Some justices, such as Antonin Scalia, reject the notion of proportionality altogether and as was famously suggested by Justice Stevens, Justice Scalia would permit life imprisonment for a parking ticket. *Harmelin v. Michigan*[26] is an example. The Court, in a divided opinion, upheld life imprisonment with no possibility of parole for possession of cocaine.

The Court has recognized a few limits for defendants of special populations. In the 2010 case *Graham v. Florida*, for example, the Court held that a juvenile may not be sentenced to life imprisonment without parole for a non-homicide crime. The Court extended this reasoning to murder by juveniles in *Miller v. Alabama*.

MILLER V. ALABAMA
567 U.S. ___ (2012)

JUSTICE KAGAN DELIVERED THE OPINION OF THE COURT.

In November 1999, petitioner Kuntrell Jackson, then 14 years old, and two other boys decided to rob a video store. En route to the store, Jackson learned that one of the boys, Derrick Shields, was carrying a sawed-off shotgun in his coat sleeve. Jackson decided to stay outside when the two other boys entered the store. Inside, Shields pointed the gun at the store clerk, Laurie Troup, and demanded that she "give up the money." Troup refused. A few moments later, Jackson went into the store to find Shields continuing to demand money. At trial, the parties disputed whether Jackson warned Troup that "[w]e ain't playin'," or instead told his friends, "I thought you all was playin'." When Troup threatened to call the police, Shields shot and killed her. The three boys fled empty-handed.

Arkansas law gives prosecutors discretion to charge 14-year-olds as adults when they are alleged to have committed certain serious offenses. [The defendant was convicted and sentenced to life imprisonment without the possibility of parole. The sentencing court noted that the punishment was the only one available to it.]

The cases before us implicate two strands of precedent reflecting our concern with proportionate punishment. The first has adopted categorical bans on sentencing practices based on mismatches between the culpability of a class of offenders and the severity of a penalty. So, for example, we have held that imposing the death penalty for nonhomicide crimes against individuals, or imposing it on mentally retarded defendants, violates the Eighth Amendment. See Kennedy v. Louisiana, 554 U. S. 407 (2008); Atkins v. Virginia, 536 U. S. 304 (2002). Several of the cases in this group have specially focused on juvenile offenders, because of their lesser culpability. Thus, Roper held that the Eighth Amendment bars capital punishment for children, and Graham concluded that the Amendment also prohibits a sentence of life without the possibility of parole for a child who committed a nonhomicide offense. Graham further likened life without parole for juveniles to the death penalty itself, thereby evoking a second line of our precedents. In those cases, we have prohibited mandatory imposition of capital punishment, requiring that sentencing authorities consider the characteristics of a defendant and the details of his offense before sentencing him to death. Here, the confluence of these two lines of precedent leads to the conclusion that mandatory life-without-parole sentences for juveniles violate the Eighth Amendment.

To start with the first set of cases: Roper and Graham establish that children are constitutionally different from adults for purposes of sentencing. Because juveniles have diminished culpability and greater prospects for reform, we explained, "they are less deserving of the most severe punishments." Those cases relied on three significant gaps between juveniles and adults. First, children have a " 'lack of maturity and an underdeveloped sense of

responsibility,' " leading to recklessness, impulsivity, and heedless risk-taking. Second, children "are more vulnerable . . . to negative influences and outside pressures," including from their family and peers; they have limited "contro[l] over their own environment" and lack the ability to extricate themselves from horrific, crime-producing settings. And third, a child's character is not as "well formed" as an adult's; his traits are "less fixed" and his actions less likely to be "evidence of irretrievabl[e] deprav[ity]. . . .

Our decisions rested not only on common sense—on what "any parent knows"—but on science and social science as well. In Roper, we cited studies showing that " '[o]nly a relatively small proportion of adolescents' " who engage in illegal activity " 'develop entrenched patterns of problem behavior.' . . . and in Graham, we noted that "developments in psychology and brain science continue to show fundamental differences between juvenile and adult minds"—for example, in "parts of the brain involved in behavior control." We reasoned that those findings—of transient rashness, proclivity for risk, and inability to assess consequences— both lessened a child's "moral culpability" and enhanced the prospect that, as the years go by and neurological development occurs, his " 'deficiencies will be reformed.' . . .

Roper and Graham emphasized that the distinctive attributes of youth diminish the penological justifications for imposing the harshest sentences on juvenile offenders, even when they commit terrible crimes. Because " '[t]he heart of the retribution rationale' " relates to an offender's blameworthiness . . .

Most fundamentally, Graham insists that youth matters in determining the appropriateness of a lifetime of incarceration without the possibility of parole. . . .

But the mandatory penalty schemes at issue here prevent the sentencer from taking account of

(continued)

MILLER V. ALABAMA *(continued)*

these central considerations. By removing youth from the balance— by subjecting a juvenile to the same life-without-parole sentence applicable to an adult—these laws prohibit a sentencing authority from assessing whether the law's harshest term of imprisonment proportionately punishes a juvenile offender. That contravenes Graham's (and also Roper's) foundational principle: that imposition of a State's most severe penalties on juvenile offenders cannot proceed as though they were not children. . . .

Graham, Roper, and our individualized sentencing decisions make clear that a judge or jury must have the opportunity to consider mitigating circumstances before imposing the harshest possible penalty for juveniles. By requiring that all children convicted of homicide receive lifetime incarceration without possibility of parole, regardless of their age and age-related characteristics and the nature of their crimes, the mandatory sentencing schemes before us violate this principle of proportionality, and so the Eighth Amendment's ban on cruel and unusual punishment.

Shaming

Using shame to punish has a long history, memorialized in the Nathaniel Hawthorne book, and film of the same name, *The Scarlet Letter*. Shaming was a common punishment in colonial America but declined in popularity in favor of imprisonment. Judges, citizens, and sometimes offenders, disillusioned with prison as a form of punishment, are increasingly returning to shaming. Consider the following examples:

- A federal judge ordered a mail thief to stand in front of a post office in San Francisco for 8 hours wearing a sign that read "I stole mail. This is my punishment." The sentence was upheld on appeal.[27]

- A woman who regularly drove onto a sidewalk to avoid a school bus was ordered to stand on a public street wearing a sign that read "Only an idiot would drive on a sidewalk to avoid a school bus."[28]

- Drunk drivers have been required to put license plates on their cars that identify them as having been convicted of DUI.

- Sexual offenders are required to register with local law enforcement after release and their locations are made known to the general public.

- A woman was required to place an advertisement in her local newspaper declaring that she purchased drugs in the presence of her children.

- One judge offered thieves probation is they permitted their victims to take one item each from the offenders' homes.

- A man who was convicted of assaulting his wife was ordered to allow her to spit in his face.[29]

indeterminate sentence

■ A sentence having a minimum and maximum, with the decision of how long the criminal will serve depending on the criminal's behavior in prison and other things.

Indeterminate and Determinate Sentencing

The **indeterminate sentence** gives corrections officials the greatest amount of control over an inmate's sentence. Under an indeterminate sentence, the judge sets a minimum and maximum period to be served, and the corrections agency determines the actual date of release. Once common in the United States, indeterminate sentencing has fallen into disfavor.

In **determinate sentencing** schemes, the sentencing judge is given discretion to set a fixed sentence from within a range set by the legislature. The determinate sentence is fixed, and there is no possibility of early release.

Definite and Indefinite Sentencing

Unlike determinate sentencing, with definite sentencing the sentencing judge has no discretion. Rather, the legislature establishes the specific penalty to be imposed for each crime, and there is no possibility of early release. Definite sentencing reduces sentencing disparity. However, it is criticized for not allowing the particular facts of each case to be taken into consideration.

Indefinite sentencing incorporates both judicial and corrections agency discretion. It is the antithesis of definite sentencing. The sentencing judge is given a range from which to impose sentence, and the corrections agency is delegated the authority to grant early releases.

Presumptive Sentencing

In many instances, when a legislature gives the sentencing judge discretion, it also establishes a *presumptive sentence*. That is, the legislature states what sentence should be imposed from within a range, absent **aggravating circumstances** or **mitigating circumstances.** Circumstances upon which the judge relies to increase the presumptive sentence are aggravating; those used to justify a sentence below a presumption are mitigating.

If a judge deviates from a presumptive sentence, the aggravating or mitigating circumstances justifying the departure must be made part of the record. For example, an assault statute may call for one to three years' punishment with a presumptive sentence of 18 months. If the judge sentences the defendant to more or less than 18 months, the reasons must be reflected on the record. Of course, even when deviating from a presumption, the sentencing judge must remain within the statutory limits.

What constitutes an aggravating or mitigating circumstance is often expressed in the statute. Examples of aggravating circumstances are injury, torture, or death of the victim; use of a weapon during commission of the crime; whether the crime involved a child; and whether the defendant violated a trust. Examples of mitigating circumstances are physical disability of the defendant; the defendant's having dependents; a crime committed in a non-violent manner; and the defendant's acting in good faith.

Suspended Imposition of Sentence

For some misdemeanors and infractions, judges are sometimes permitted to *suspend imposition of sentence* (SIS), also known as *diversion*. SIS is one of many forms of community-based correction, a term that refers to several varieties of nonincarceration correctional programs, such as probation, restitution, halfway houses, and parole. (Some of these other forms of community-based correction are discussed later.)

SIS is different from suspended sentencing. In SIS, a judge not only withholds sentencing the defendant but also refrains from entering a judgement of conviction

determinate sentence

◼ An exact penalty set by law.

aggravating circumstances

◼ Actions or occurrences that increase the seriousness of a crime, but are not part of the legal definition of that crime.

mitigating circumstances

◼ Facts that provide no justification or excuse for an action, but that can lower the amount of moral blame and thus lower the criminal penalty or civil damages for the action.

until some future date. If the defendant complies with imposed conditions until that date, the prosecution is dismissed and the defendant is freed from having a criminal record. Suspended sentences, in contrast, involve conviction and imposition of sentence, but the defendant is relieved of actually serving the sentence so long as conditions are satisfied.

Where available, SIS is usually limited to non-violent misdemeanors and infractions and is available to first-time offenders only.

Concurrent and Consecutive Sentencing

If a defendant is already serving a sentence for another crime, or is convicted of two related crimes, the sentencing judge may impose **concurrent sentences** or **consecutive sentences.** If two sentences are concurrent, it is said that they "run together." That is, a defendant who receives two 5-year sentences will actually spend 5 years incarcerated. If the sentences are consecutive, the defendant will spend a total of 10 years incarcerated.

Parole

After committing a defendant to a correctional institution, the judge loses control and responsibility over that defendant, unless a statute provides otherwise. In many states, **parole** is available to prison inmates. *Parole*, an early release from prison, is used to encourage inmates to stay out of trouble and engage in rehabilitative efforts while in prison. Parole decisions are made by corrections officials (i.e., a parole board). Similar to probation, an offender must comply with certain conditions while on parole. Conditions routinely include not possessing a gun; not contacting witnesses, judge, jurors, or prosecutors associated with the offender's conviction; and not becoming involved in further criminal activity. Violation of a condition of parole may result in recommitment to prison.

Parole has fallen into disfavor in recent years. The result has been to limit the availability of parole in many situations. Parole has been eliminated for those convicted of crimes against the United States.

The Federal Guidelines

In November 1987, the Federal Sentencing Guidelines became effective. The guidelines are a milestone in federal criminal law. Their purpose is twofold: (1) to reduce sentencing disparity and (2) to achieve "honesty in sentencing."[30] Prior to the Guidelines, judges were given a large penalty range from which a defendant could be sentenced. The result of this discretion was that defendants similarly situated were often sentenced very differently. One goal of the Guidelines is to reduce such disparity in sentencing.

The second goal, honesty in sentencing, concerns parole. Prior to the Guidelines, defendants could be released on parole, in some cases, after only one-third of the imposed sentence had been served. In addition, prisoners complained that parole was arbitrarily and inconsistently applied. Accordingly, Congress eliminated parole, and the guidelines now reflect the time that will be served, less 54 days of good time that may be earned yearly (after the first year).

To achieve the first goal—the reduction of sentencing disparity—the Guidelines greatly limit the discretion of the judge in sentencing. To determine what sentence

---

concurrent sentences

■ Prison terms that run at the same time.

consecutive sentences

■ An additional prison term given to a person who is already convicted of a crime; the additional term is to be served after the previous one is finished.

parole

■ Early release from prison or jail. Parole is usually granted with conditions such as requiring the parolee to refrain from communicating with the victim of the crime that led to the confinement and remaining free of criminality while on parole. If the conditions of parole are violated, parole may be revoked and the parolee may be returned to confinement to complete the original sentence.

should be imposed, the offender's criminal history category and offense level must be determined. The criminal history category is simply determined by the number of prior convictions of the offender.

Finding an offender's offense level is more complex. First, the crime is assigned a base offense number. That number is then increased by "specific offense characteristics." Adjustments to this figure are then made for mitigating or aggravating circumstances. This final figure is the offense level.

Once the criminal history category and offense level are determined, the court looks to the sentencing table. This table provides a small range (the top figure never exceeds 25 percent of the bottom figure) from which the judge is to sentence the defendant. Only in rare instances may a judge deviate from the proscribed sentencing range.

The Guidelines continue to permit judges to suspend sentences to probation for offenses at the low end of the sentencing table. For offenses just above the probation cutoff, judges may sentence an offender to probation, provided some form of confinement is ordered, such as house arrest or community confinement. There is also a third layer of offenses, for which the judge may order a "split sentence." This is where one-half or more of the sentence must be served in prison, and the remaining amount may be served in another form of confinement.

sidebar

A SENTENCING STORY

Sentencing a defendant today is much different from years ago, as evidenced by the following sentence, allegedly handed down by the infamous Judge Roy Bean, imposed upon a defendant in 1881. In addition to the many other limitations in judge's sentencing authority that have evolved since 1881, the racist comments in this sentencing would be found to violate the judicial code of ethics as well as the Fifth and Fourteenth Amendments' equal protection standards in the contemporary United States.

Jose Manuel Miguel Xavier Gonzales, in a few short weeks it will be spring. The snows of winter will flee away, the ice will vanish, and the air will become soft and balmy. In short, Jose Manuel Miguel Xavier Gonzales, the annual miracle of the year's awakening will come to pass—but you won't be here.

The rivulet will run its purling course to the sea, the timid desert flowers will put forth their tender roots, the glorious valleys of this imperial domain will blossom as the rose—still you won't be here to see.

From every treetop some wild woods songster will carol his mating song, butterflies will sport in the sunshine, the busy bee will hum happily as it pursues its accustomed vocation, the gentle breeze will tease the tassels of the wild grasses, and

(continued)

all nature—Jose Manuel Miguel Xavier Gonzales—will be glad but you. You won't be here to enjoy it because I command the sheriff or some other officer or officers of this country to lead you out to some remote spot, swing you by the neck from a nodding bough of some sturdy oak, and let you hang until you are dead.

And then, Jose Manuel Miguel Xavier Gonzales, I further command that such officer or officers retire quickly from your dangling corpse, that the vultures may descend from the heavens upon your filthy body, until nothing shall remain but the bare, bleaching bones of a cold-blooded, copper-colored, blood-thirsty, throat-cutting, sheep-herding, murdering son of a bitch. See Shawn E. Tuma, Law in Texas Literature: Texas Justice—Judge Roy Bean Style, 21 Review of Litigation 551, 563 (2002) for an alternative, but also colorful, account of the sentence.

The Guidelines have been the subject of much controversy. Federal judges themselves have been very critical of the Guidelines. Many contend that the reason judges are complaining is simply their loss of authority. Though this may be true, there also appear to be problems caused by the rigidity of the Guidelines.

The drafters of the Guidelines knew that all factors that should be considered in sentencing could not be anticipated (or quantified). As such, provisions are made to permit deviation from the Guidelines. However, deviation is rarely permitted. This practice has led to some absurd results. For example, one 21-year-old honor student, with no prior record, was sentenced to 10 years in prison for his involvement in one drug transaction.[31] At least one federal district judge has resigned because of dissatisfaction with the guidelines.

The guidelines were mandatory for nearly 20 years, surviving many constitutional challenges. Then, in 2005, the Supreme Court decided that the mandatory nature of the guidelines violated the Sixth Amendment's jury trial requirement in *United States v. Booker*.

UNITED STATES V. BOOKER
543 U.S. 220 (2005)

JUSTICE STEVENS DELIVERED THE OPINION OF THE COURT IN PART.

The question presented in each of these cases is whether an application of the Federal Sentencing Guidelines violated the Sixth Amendment. In each case, the courts below held that binding rules set forth in the Guidelines limited the severity of the sentence that the judge could lawfully impose on the defendant based on the facts found by the jury at his trial. In both cases the courts rejected, on the basis of our decision in *Blakely v. Washington*, 542 U.S. _____ (2004), the Government's recommended application of the Sentencing Guidelines because the proposed sentences were based on additional

UNITED STATES V. BOOKER (continued)

facts that the sentencing judge found by a preponderance of the evidence. We hold that both courts correctly concluded that the Sixth Amendment as construed in *Blakely* does apply to the Sentencing Guidelines. In a separate opinion authored by Justice Breyer, the Court concludes that in light of this holding, two provisions of the Sentencing Reform Act of 1984 (SRA) that have the effect of making the Guidelines mandatory must be invalidated in order to allow the statute to operate in a manner consistent with congressional intent.

Based upon Booker's criminal history and the quantity of drugs found by the jury, the Sentencing Guidelines required the District Court Judge to select a "base" sentence of not less than 210 nor more than 262 months in prison. See United States Sentencing Commission, Guidelines Manual §§ 2D1.1(c)(4), 4A1.1 (Nov. 2003) (hereinafter USSG). The judge, however, held a post-trial sentencing proceeding and concluded by a preponderance of the evidence that Booker had possessed an additional 566 grams of crack and that he was guilty of obstructing justice. Those findings mandated that the judge select a sentence between 360 months and life imprisonment; the judge imposed a sentence at the low end of the range. Thus, instead of the sentence of 21 years and 10 months that the judge could have imposed on the basis of the facts proved to the jury beyond a reasonable doubt, Booker received a 30-year sentence. . . .

It has been settled throughout our history that the Constitution protects every criminal defendant "against conviction except upon proof beyond a reasonable doubt of every fact necessary to constitute the crime with which he is charged." *In re Winship*, 397 U.S. 358, 364 (1970). It is equally clear that the "Constitution gives a criminal defendant the right to demand that a jury find him guilty of all the elements of the crime with which he is charged." *United States v. Gaudin*, 515 U.S. 506, 511 (1995).

These basic precepts, firmly rooted in the common law, have provided the basis for recent decisions interpreting modern criminal statutes and sentencing procedures. . . .

In *Apprendi v. New Jersey*, 530 U.S. 466 (2000), the defendant pleaded guilty to second-degree possession of a firearm for an unlawful purpose, which carried a prison term of 5-to-10 years. Thereafter, the trial court found that his conduct had violated New Jersey's "hate crime" law because it was racially motivated, and imposed a 12-year sentence. This Court set aside the enhanced sentence. We held: "Other than the fact of a prior conviction, any fact that increases the penalty for a crime beyond the prescribed statutory maximum must be submitted to a jury, and proved beyond a reasonable doubt." The fact that New Jersey labeled the hate crime a "sentence enhancement" rather than a separate criminal act was irrelevant for constitutional purposes. As a matter of simple justice, it seemed obvious that the procedural safeguards designed to protect Apprendi from punishment for the possession of a firearm should apply equally to his violation of the hate crime statute. Merely using the label "sentence enhancement" to describe the latter did not provide a principled basis for treating the two crimes differently.

In *Ring v. Arizona*, 536 U.S. 584 (2002), we reaffirmed our conclusion that the characterization of critical facts is constitutionally irrelevant. There, we held that it was impermissible for "the trial judge, sitting alone" to determine the presence or absence of the aggravating factors required by Arizona law for imposition of the death penalty. "If a State makes an increase in a defendant's authorized punishment contingent on the finding of a fact, that fact—no matter how the State labels it—must be found by a jury beyond a reasonable doubt." Our opinion made it clear that ultimately, while the procedural error in Ring's case might have been harmless because the

(continued)

UNITED STATES V. BOOKER *(continued)*

necessary finding was implicit in the jury's guilty verdict, "the characterization of a fact or circumstance as an 'element' or a 'sentencing factor' is not determinative of the question 'who decides,' judge or jury," . . .

In *Blakely v. Washington*, 542 U.S. _____ (2004), we dealt with a determinate sentencing scheme. . . .

For reasons explained in *Jones, Apprendi*, and *Ring*, the requirements of the Sixth Amendment were clear. The application of Washington's sentencing scheme violated the defendant's right to have the jury find the existence of "'any particular fact'" that the law makes essential to his punishment. . . .

If the Guidelines as currently written could be read as merely advisory provisions that recommended, rather than required, the selection of particular sentences in response to differing sets of facts, their use would not implicate the Sixth Amendment. We have never doubted the authority of a judge to exercise broad discretion in imposing a sentence within a statutory range. Indeed, everyone agrees that the constitutional issues presented by these cases would have been avoided entirely if Congress had omitted from the SRA the provisions that make the Guidelines binding on district judges; it is that circumstance that makes the Court's answer to the second question presented possible. For when a trial judge exercises his discretion to select a specific sentence within a defined range, the defendant has no right to a jury determination of the facts that the judge deems relevant.

The Guidelines as written, however, are not advisory; they are mandatory. . . .

[The Court concluded by invalidating the mandatory provision of the statute and thereby rendering the guidelines advisory. Judges, of course, remain obligated to sentence offenders within the statutory range and to refer to the advice of the guidelines.]

The impact of *Booker* on sentencing has not been significant. The vast majority of convictees have continued to be sentenced within the ranges established by the guidelines after *Booker* was decided. The patterns of sentencing, even within the guidelines, were largely unchanged. Also, differences in sentencing (e.g., by region) that existed before *Booker* continued post-*Booker*.[32]

The federal government was not the first to enact sentencing guidelines. At least two states, Minnesota and Washington, were using guidelines when the federal version became law. It is probable that more jurisdictions will contemplate similar reform in the future.

sidebar

PRISONS IN THE UNITED STATES

Lack of space in United States prisons is an ever-increasing concern. Most prisons are overcrowded, often housing double or triple the intended capacity; this leads to serious problems for both prison administrators and inmates. If prison conditions are extremely bad, an inmate may succeed in an Eighth Amendment lawsuit against prison authorities.

The total number of adults under local, state, and federal correctional supervision was 6.98 million in 2011, representing 1 out of every 34 adults in the United States. Of these individuals, 1,504,150 were in prison. The remainder were on probation, parole, or incarcerated in jail. About 1 in 200 people in the United States were incarcerated. The years 2010 and 2011 were the first ones since 1972 that the number of people in prison declined. The number of men in prison and jail is fourteen times greater than women, the number of African-American men is seven times greater than white men, and the number of African-American females is three times greater than white females. Over 128,000 inmates, 165 of federal and 7% of state, were housed in privately operated facilities in 2010.

Sources: Correctional Populations in the United States, 2011 and Prisoners in the United States, 2010. Bureau of Justice Statistics (2010/2011).

Probation and Revocation

A popular alternative to incarceration is probation, also known as a **suspended sentence.** Probation is not always an alternative and is rarely available for crimes that are punished with life imprisonment or death. While on probation, the defendant is released from custody, but must comply with conditions imposed by the court during the probationary period. Each defendant is placed under the supervision of a probation officer during this period. The probation officer is an officer of the court, not of the corrections system.

Typical conditions of probation include a requirement of steady employment, refraining from other unlawful conduct, not carrying a firearm or other weapon, and not leaving the jurisdiction of the court. A judge may tailor conditions to fit the circumstances of each case. For example, a child molester may be prohibited from obtaining employment that requires working around children.

Some judges make consent to search by a probation officer a condition of probation. This may include search of the person as well as property. In some cases, judges impose the search requirement independently; in others, the defendant and prosecutor stipulate to the searches through a plea agreement. In either situation, are there limits to this authority? May a probation officer search a probationer at any time, in any manner, and without any cause to believe that mischief is afoot? Further, can a defendant who is facing incarceration as an alternative give meaningful consent to such a condition? This is the subject of the *Consuelo-Gonzalez* case, in which the court decided that probationers are entitled to full Fourth Amendment protection as to law enforcement officers generally. Searches by police officers of probationers must satisfy the usual Fourth Amendment requirements.

suspended sentence

■ A sentence (usually "jail time") that the judge allows the convicted person to avoid serving (usually if the person continues on good behavior, completes community service, etc.).

UNITED STATES V. CONSUELO-GONZALEZ
521 F.2d 259 (9th Cir. 1975)

Consuelo-Gonzalez appeals from a conviction under 21 USC § 841(a)(1) for possession of heroin with intent to distribute. We reverse.

Between November 15, 1972, and December 18, 1972, agents of the Federal Bureau of Narcotics and Dangerous Drugs received information from four different sources that Virginia Consuelo-Gonzalez was actively engaged in the importation and sale of heroin. A check of the records at the United States Attorney's Office on December 12, 1972, revealed to the agents that Virginia Consuelo-Gonzalez had previously been convicted of heroin smuggling under the name of Virginia Cardenas and was currently on probation. At this time, the agents were also apprised that it was a condition of Consuelo-Gonzalez's probation that she submit her person and property to search at any time upon request by a law enforcement officer. On December 14, 1972, an independent verification was made of the fact that Virginia Cardenas and Virginia Consuelo-Gonzalez were one and the same person; and on December 19, 1972, the agents reconfirmed the probationary status and condition that she submit to search.

On the morning of December 19, 1992, . . . federal and local law enforcement officers approached the Consuelo-Gonzalez residence for purposes of conducting a search of the premises. When they arrived, they found the front door of the house ajar. The agents knocked on the door and waited for Consuelo-Gonzalez to appear. When she did so, the lead agent showed her his identification, informed her that he was aware of her probation and the conditions which had been attached to it, and indicated his intention to enter the residence and conduct a search. Consuelo-Gonzalez responded to his request by stepping back and saying "Sure, search my purse." Upon entering the house, the lead agent made a cursory search of her handbag to determine whether it contained weapons. None were found.

The handbag was then placed beside a chair in which Consuelo-Gonzalez was asked to sit.

A thorough search of Consuelo-Gonzalez's person and residence was then commenced. In the bedroom, the agents found a narcotics injection outfit in a dresser; and on a shelf in the living room they discovered a paper sack containing a bundle of notebook papers with brown debris on them. Both of these items were seized. A second search of Consuelo-Gonzalez's handbag revealed two coin purses, inside of which the agents found two white paper bindles and seven rubber condoms containing a total of 11.7 grams of brown powder, later proven to be heroin. This evidence was also seized, and subsequently used to provide the basis for the present conviction.

In a timely and appropriate manner, counsel for Consuelo-Gonzalez moved to suppress this evidence. However, the trial judge denied the motion to suppress, relying specifically upon the authorization to search which had been made a condition of the probation. . . . Thereafter, defendant was found guilty of possession of heroin with intent to distribute. . . .

In this appeal, defendant asserts that the trial court erred in failing to suppress the evidence on the ground that the condition of probation requiring her to "submit to search of her person or property at any time when requested by a law-enforcement" officer was improper and thus could not serve to make the search lawful. It is argued that the Fourth Amendment requires this result.

While we are not prepared to embrace the full reach of defendant's argument, we do believe that the condition employed in the instant case is not in keeping with the purposes intended to be served by the Federal Probation Act. It is our view that, even though the trial judge has very broad discretion in fixing the terms and conditions of probation, such terms must be reasonably related to the purposes

UNITED STATES V. CONSUELO-GONZALEZ *(continued)*

of the Act. In determining whether a reasonable relationship exists, we have found it necessary to give consideration to the purposes sought to be served by probation, the extent to which the full constitutional guarantees available to those not under probation should be accorded probationers, and the legitimate needs of law enforcement. Having done so, we have concluded that Consuelo-Gonzalez could have been required to submit her person and property to search by a probation officer. We have further concluded that any search made pursuant to the condition included in the terms of probation must necessarily meet the Fourth Amendment's standard of reasonableness. . . .

Although it is doubtful that any formulation of a condition relating to the search of a probationer's person or property can be drafted that will provide unambiguous guidance to both the probationer and the probation officer, it is suggested that the following condition would properly reflect the views expressed herein:

> That she submit to search of her person or property conducted in a reasonable manner and at a reasonable time by a probation officer.

. . . [W]e hold that the search in this case was improper and that the motion to suppress should have been granted. . . .

The guiding principle which has emerged in construing the Probation Act is that the only permissible conditions are those that, when considered in context, can reasonably be said to contribute significantly both to the rehabilitation of the convicted person and to the protection of the public. . . .

This guiding interpretive principle plainly suggests the manner in which the Act's administration should be accommodated to the constitutional guarantees of the Bill of Rights. While it must be recognized that probationers, like parolees and

prisoners, properly are subject to limitations from which ordinary persons are free, it is also true that these limitations in the aggregate must serve the ends of probation. . . . [I]t is necessary to recognize that when fundamental rights are curbed it must be done sensitively and with a keen appreciation that the infringement must serve the broad purposes of the Probation Act. This burden cannot be avoided by asserting either that the probationer has voluntarily waived his rights by not objecting in a proper manner to the conditions imposed upon him or that he must accept any condition the court "deems best" as a consequence of being "in custody."

Turning to the Fourth Amendment rights that Consuelo-Gonzalez insists were infringed, two things are obvious. The first is that some forms of search by probation officers are not only compatible with rehabilitation, but, with respect to those convicted of certain offenses such as possession and distribution of narcotics; are also essential to the proper functioning of a probationary system. The second is that the condition imposed on Consuelo-Gonzalez literally permits searches which could not possibly serve the ends of probation. For example, an intimidating and harassing search to serve law enforcement ends totally unrelated to either her prior conviction or her rehabilitation is authorized by the terms of the condition. Submission to such searches should not be the price of probation. A probationer, like the parolee, has the right to enjoy a significant degree of privacy. . . .

Probation authorities also have a special and unique interest in invading the privacy of probationers. This special and unique interest does not extend to law enforcement officers generally. . . . Inasmuch as the search of Consuelo-Gonzalez's residence and handbag occurred neither during the course of a probation visit by a probation officer nor

(continued)

UNITED STATES V. CONSUELO-GONZALEZ *(continued)*

pursuant to a proper warrant, the evidence must be suppressed. . . .

[I]t may well be necessary during the course of a probation visit to conduct a pat-down search for weapons or contraband, to examine the probationer's arms to ascertain whether drugs are being used, or take the probationer into custody. When done reasonably and humanely by probation officers, no question concerning the appropriateness of their actions should arise. Moreover, a thorough search of a probationer's residence incident to, or following, a probation visit is not dependent upon the establishment of probable cause. A reasonable belief on the part of the probation officer that such a search is necessary to perform properly his duties is sufficient. As we said [in a prior case], this belief may be based on a "hunch" having its origin in what the probation officer has learned or observed about the behavior and attitude of the probationer.

Probationers are also protected by the Fourth Amendment's reasonableness requirement in regard to searches by probation officers. However, the standards are lowered, as the public has a greater interest in searching the probationer and the probationer has a lessened expectation to privacy. Also, probation officers do have a penal objective; in fact, they should have the welfare of their probationers in mind.

Therefore, probation officers may search a probationer's person or property with reasonable grounds; no warrant is required, although the search must be conducted in a reasonable manner. These conclusions have also been reached by the Supreme Court.[33] As a condition of probation, a search condition must be reasonably related to the probation, or it is invalid. Therefore, if a person is convicted of embezzlement, a condition providing for searches of the person would be unreasonable. The result would, of course, be different if the offense were possession of a firearm or drugs.

Finally, any other condition of probation that encroaches upon a constitutional guarantee is suspect. For example, a condition that restricts free speech is unconstitutional in most circumstances.[34] However, the right to travel freely and to bear arms are examples of constitutionally preserved rights that are commonly restricted during probation and parole.

A defendant who violates a condition of probation may be disciplined. Generally, the decision about whether any action should be taken for a violation is made by the probation officer. If a violation is extreme, the probation officer may file a petition to revoke probation. The sentencing court then holds a **revocation hearing.** If the petition is granted, the defendant is taken off probation and incarcerated.

At the revocation hearing, the defendant may be entitled to counsel. As a general rule, the right is not found in the Sixth Amendment, as the "critical stages" of trial have passed. In one rare case, the Supreme Court held that a Sixth Amendment right to counsel did exist at a revocation hearing. In *Mempa v. Rhay*, 389 U.S. 128 (1967),

revocation hearing

■ The due process hearing required before the government can revoke a privilege it has previously granted.

the trial judge withheld sentencing, placed the defendant on probation, and did not pronounce sentence until after the defendant violated his probation and then had it revoked. Because the revocation hearing turned out to be the defendant's sentencing hearing, where there is a right to counsel under the Sixth Amendment, the Court found that the Sixth Amendment applied.

The Due Process Clauses of the Fifth and Fourteenth Amendments may also provide a right to counsel at a revocation hearing. If a substantial question of law or fact must be resolved at the hearing, counsel must be appointed for the indigent defendant so that the issues can be fully explored and developed. If revocation is obvious, though, counsel need not be allowed.

Community Service

One alternative to incarceration for non-violent offenders is community service. In such a program, a defendant's sentence is suspended and the completion of a stated number of community service hours is a condition of the defendant's probation.

In most instances, the probation officer works with the probationer to find an appropriate job. However, the judge may require that a specific job be performed.

The requirements of community service range from unskilled to professional. For example, a judge may require that a professional, such as a physician or attorney, work in a clinic that provides services to the poor. The same person may be expected to pick up trash from local roads. Clearly, the former makes best use of the defendant's skills and benefits the community the most.

Restitution

The purpose of restitution is to compensate the victim, not to punish the offender. As such, restitution is not a substitute for other forms of punishment.

Restitution is limited to the actual amounts resulting from the offenses convicted.[35] Said another way, restitution is limited to losses resulting from the specific conduct that formed the basis of the conviction.[36] However, an agreement between the government and the defendant to pay a higher amount may be constitutional.[37]

Restitution may be made a condition of probation. A probationer's refusal to pay restitution can result in a revocation of probation. However, when a fine or restitution is imposed as a condition of probation, and "the probationer has made all reasonable efforts to pay . . . yet cannot do so through no fault of his own, it is fundamentally unfair to revoke probation automatically without considering whether adequate alternative methods of punishing the defendant are available."[38]

Fines

Unlike the goal of restitution, the purpose of a fine is to punish the offender. Accordingly, restitution monies are paid to victims, and fines end up in the public treasury. Fines are a common method of punishing misdemeanants. Serious crimes are frequently punished with both a fine and incarceration. Any fine imposed must be reasonable; that is, the amount must be within the financial means of the offender. Excessive fines are prohibited by the Eighth Amendment.

It is a violation of equal protection to sentence individuals without means to pay a fine to longer periods of incarceration than those received by individuals who can pay a fine. In *Williams v. Illinois*,[39] a defendant was sentenced to a maximum one year in prison and a $500 fine for petty theft. Illinois statute provided that if at the end of the year, the fine (and court costs) were not paid, the defendant was to remain in jail for a time to satisfy the debt. This sentence was calculated at $5.00 per day. The Court found that because Williams was indigent, the statute violated the Equal Protection Clause by improperly sentencing defendants according to economic status. Of course, a defendant who has the financial means to pay a fine, and does not, may have probation revoked or incarceration increased.

Forfeiture

Forfeitures are similar to fines in that they involve the taking of property and money to punish defendants. A forfeiture is, however, not directed at the defendant's pocketbook in general, as is a fine. Rather, forfeiture focuses on taking the property owned by a defendant that is in some manner connected with the crimes. Automobiles, airplanes, or boats used to transport drugs are an example. Forfeiture has become an increasingly popular tool amongst law enforcement agencies.

Procedurally, forfeiture may occur within and as part of a criminal proceeding. In addition, many laws permit forfeiture to occur in a separative in rem civil proceeding. Most statutes allow law enforcement officers to make seizures based upon probable cause, to be immediately followed by the filing of a forfeiture proceeding.[40] Of course, seizure can also occur later in the proceedings. Under federal law, if a seizure was proper (i.e., based upon probable cause), the burden of proof falls on a claimant to establish that the property is not subject to seizure. The claimant must prove this by a preponderance of the evidence.[41]

Under federal law, forfeiture is provided for in several instances, including violations of the Racketeer Influenced and Corrupt Organizations Act (RICO) and under the so-called drug kingpin statute, the Continuing Criminal Enterprise law.[42]

There are limits to the use of forfeiture. In *United States v. James Daniel Good Real Property*,[43] the Supreme Court determined that the Due Process Clause requires the government to provide notice and a preseizure hearing when it intends to forfeit real property, unless exigent circumstances justify an immediate seizure. There is no requirement of preseizure notice in cases where property can disappear. The Court stated that in cases where property is movable, immediate seizure, without notice or a hearing, is necessary to "establish the court's jurisdiction over the property" and to guard against someone absconding with the property.

A critical issue concerns the relationship between the crime and the property forfeited. Forfeiture of all property associated with a crime can be troubling. Forfeiting a boat that was purchased with drug money and is used to transport drugs from Colombia to the United States is not problematic. But is it constitutionally sound to forfeit a home because one joint of marijuana is discovered inside? Does the Eighth Amendment's Excessive Fines Clause limit the use of forfeitures? In *Austin*, the Supreme Court examined this issue.

AUSTIN V. UNITED STATES
509 U.S. 602 (1993)

In this case, we are asked to decide whether the Excessive Fines Clause of the Eighth Amendment applies to forfeitures of property under 21 U.S.C. §§ 881(a)(4) and (a)(7). We hold that it does and therefore remand the case for consideration of the question whether the forfeiture at issue here was excessive.

On August 2, 1990, petitioner Richard Lyle Austin was indicted on four counts of violating South Dakota's drug laws. Austin ultimately pleaded guilty to one count of possessing cocaine with intent to distribute and was sentenced by the state court to seven years' imprisonment. On September 7, the United States filed an in rem action in the United States District Court for the District of South Dakota seeking forfeiture of Austin's mobile home and auto body shop under 21 U.S.C. §§ 881(a)(4) and (a)(7) [these laws provide for the forfeiture of property in drug cases]. Austin filed a claim and an answer to the complaint.

On February 4, 1991, the United States made a motion, supported by an affidavit from Sioux Falls Police Officer Donald Satterlee, for summary judgment. According to Satterlee's affidavit, Austin met Keith Engebretson at Austin's body shop on June 13, 1990, and agreed to sell cocaine to Engebretson. Austin left the shop, went to his mobile home, and returned to the shop with two grams of cocaine which he sold to Engebretson. State authorities executed a search warrant on the body shop and mobile home the following day. They discovered small amounts of marijuana and cocaine, a .22 caliber revolver, drug paraphernalia, and approximately $4,700 in cash. In opposing summary judgment, Austin argued that forfeiture of the properties would violate the Eighth Amendment. The District Court rejected this argument and entered summary judgment for the United States.

The United States Court of Appeals for the Eighth Circuit "reluctantly agree[d] with the government" and affirmed. . . . Although it thought that "the principle of proportionality should be applied in civil actions that result in harsh penalties," . . . and that the Government was "exacting too high a penalty in relation to the offense committed . . . the court felt constrained from holding the forfeiture unconstitutional." . . .

Austin contends that the Eighth Amendment's Excessive Fines Clause applies to in rem civil forfeiture proceedings. . . . In [an earlier case] we held that the Excessive Fines Clause does not limit the award of punitive damages to a private party in a civil suit when the government neither has prosecuted the action nor has any right to receive a share of the damages. . . . The Court concluded that both the Eighth Amendment and § 10 of the Bill of Rights of 1689, from which it derives, were intended to prevent the government from abusing its power to punish . . . and therefore "that the Excessive Fines Clause was intended to limit only those fines directly imposed by, and payable to, the government." . . .

We found it unnecessary to decide . . . whether the Excessive Fines Clause applies only to criminal cases. . . . The United States now argues that

> any claim that the government's conduct in a civil proceeding is limited by the Eighth Amendment generally, or by the Excessive Fines Clause in particular, must fail unless the challenged action, despite its label, would have been recognized as a criminal punishment at the time the Eighth Amendment was adopted.

• • •

It further suggests that the Eighth Amendment cannot apply to a civil proceeding unless that

(continued)

AUSTIN V. UNITED STATES *(continued)*

proceeding is so punitive that it must be considered criminal. . . .

Some provisions of the Bill of Rights are expressly limited to criminal cases. . . . The text of the Eighth Amendment includes no similar limitation.

Nor does the history of the Eighth Amendment require such a limitation. Justice O'Connor noted in *Browning-Ferris*: "Consideration of the Eighth Amendment immediately followed consideration of the Fifth Amendment. After deciding to confine the benefits of the Self-Incrimination Clause of the Fifth Amendment to criminal proceedings, the Framers turned their attention to the Eighth Amendment. There were no proposals to limit that Amendment to criminal proceedings. . . ."

The purpose of the Eighth Amendment, putting the Bail Clause to one side, was to limit the government's power to punish. . . . The Cruel and Unusual Clause is self-evidently concerned with punishment. The Excessive Fines Clause limits the Government's power to extract payments, whether in case or in kind, "as punishment for some offense." . . . "The notion of punishment, as we commonly understand it, cuts across the division between civil and criminal law." . . . "It is commonly understood that civil proceedings may advance punitive and remedial goals, and conversely, that both punitive and remedial goals may be served by criminal penalties." . . . Thus, the question is not, as the United States would have it, whether forfeiture . . . is civil or criminal, but rather whether it is punishment.

In considering this question, we are mindful of the fact that sanctions frequently serve more than one purpose. We need not exclude the possibility that a forfeiture serves remedial purposes to conclude that it is subject to the limitations of the Excessive Fines Clause. We, however, must determine

that it can be explained as serving in part to punish. . . . We turn, then, to consider whether, at the time the Eighth Amendment was ratified, forfeiture was understood at least in part as punishment and whether forfeiture under §§ 881(a)(4) and (a)(7) should be so understood today.

Three kinds of forfeiture were established in England at the time the Eighth Amendment was ratified in the United States: deodand, forfeiture upon conviction for a felony or treason, and statutory forfeiture. . . . Each was understood, at least in part, as imposing punishment.

▪ ▪ ▪

The First Congress passed laws subjecting ships and cargos involved in customs offenses to forfeiture. . . . Indeed, examination of those laws suggests that the First Congress viewed forfeiture as punishment. . . . It is also of some interest that "forfeit" is the word Congress used for fine. . . .

We turn next to consider whether forfeitures under 21 U.S.C. §§ 881(a)(4) and (a)(7) are properly considered punishment today. We find nothing in these provisions or their legislative history to contradict the historical understanding of forfeiture as punishment. . . .

The legislative history of § 881 confirms the punitive nature of these provisions. When it added subsection (a)(7) to § 881 in 1984, Congress recognized "that the traditional criminal sanctions of fine and imprisonment are inadequate to deter or punish the enormously profitable trade in dangerous drugs." . . . It characterized the forfeiture of real property as "a powerful deterrent." . . .

We therefore conclude that forfeiture under these provisions constitutes "payment to a sovereign as punishment for some offense," . . . and, as such, is subject to the limitations of the Eighth Amendment's Excessive Fines Clause.

The *Austin* Court held that the Eighth Amendment's Excessive Fines Clause applies to civil in rem forfeiture proceedings. Accordingly, a forfeiture must be proportional to the offense. A fine or forfeiture that is grossly larger than the underlying offense is excessive and violative of the Eighth Amendment. The fine at issue in *United States v. Bajakajian* is an example of an excessive fine.

UNITED STATES V. BAJAKAJIAN
524 U.S. 321 (1998)

JUSTICE THOMAS DELIVERED THE OPINION OF THE COURT:

Respondent Hosep Bajakajian attempted to leave the United States without reporting, as required by federal law, that he was transporting more than $10,000 in currency. Federal law also provides that a person convicted of willfully violating this reporting requirement shall forfeit to the government "any property . . . involved in such offense." 18 U.S.C. § 982 (a)(1). The question in this case is whether forfeiture of the entire $357,144 that respondent failed to declare would violate the Excessive Fines Clause of the Eighth Amendment. We hold that it would, because full forfeiture of respondent's currency would be grossly disproportional to the gravity of his offense.

On June 9, 1994, respondent, his wife, and his two daughters were waiting at Los Angeles International Airport to board a flight to Italy; their final destination was Cyprus. Using dogs trained to detect currency by its smell, customs inspectors discovered some $230,000 in cash in the Bajakajians' checked baggage. A customs inspector approached respondent and his wife and told them that they were required to report all money in excess of $10,000 in their possession or in their baggage. Respondent said that he had $8,000 and that his wife had another $7,000, but that the family had no additional currency to declare. A search of their carry-on bags, purse, and wallet revealed more cash; in all, customs inspectors found $357,144. The currency was seized and respondent was taken into custody.

A federal grand jury indicted respondent on three counts. Count One charged him with failing to report, as required by 31 U.S.C. § 5316 (a)(1)(A), that he was transporting more than $10,000 outside the United States, and with doing so "willfully," in violation of § 5322 (a). Count Two charged him with making a false material statement to the United States Customs Service, in violation of 18 U.S.C. § 1001. Count Three sought forfeiture of the $357,144 pursuant to 18 U.S.C. § 982 (a)(1), which provides: "[A] person or an agent or bailee of the person shall file a report . . . when the person, agent, or bailee knowingly—" (1) transports, is about to transport, or has transported, monetary instruments of more than $10,000 at one time—"(A) from a place in the United States to or through a place outside the United States. . . ." 31 U.S.C. § 5316(a).

"The court, in imposing sentence on a person convicted of an offense in violation of § . . . 5316, . . . shall order that the person forfeit to the United States any property, real or personal, involved in such offense, or any property traceable to such property." 18 U.S.C. § 982 (a)(1).

Respondent pleaded guilty to the failure to report in Count One; the Government agreed to dismiss the false statement charge in Count Two; and respondent elected to have a bench trial on the forfeiture in Count Three. After the bench trial, the District Court found that the entire $357,144 was subject to forfeiture because it was "involved in" the offense. The court also found that the funds were not

(continued)

connected to any other crime and that respondent was transporting the money to repay a lawful debt. The District Court further found that respondent had failed to report that he was taking the currency out of the United States because of fear stemming from "cultural differences": Respondent, who had grown up as a member of the Armenian minority in Syria, had a "distrust for the Government." Although § 982 (a)(1) directs sentencing courts to impose full forfeiture, the District Court concluded that such forfeiture would be "extraordinarily harsh" and "grossly disproportionate to the offense in question," and that it would therefore violate the Excessive Fines Clause. The court instead ordered forfeiture of $15,000, in addition to a sentence of three years of probation and a fine of $5,000—the maximum fine under the Sentencing Guidelines—because the court believed that the maximum Guidelines fine was "too little" and that a $15,000 forfeiture would "make up for what I think a reasonable fine should be."

The United States appealed, seeking full forfeiture of respondent's currency as provided in § 982 (a)(1). The Court of Appeals for the Ninth Circuit affirmed.

The Eighth Amendment provides: "Excessive bail shall not be required, nor excessive fines imposed, nor cruel and unusual punishments inflicted." U.S. Const., Amdt. 8. This Court has had little occasion to interpret, and has never actually applied, the Excessive Fines Clause. We have, however, explained that at the time the Constitution was adopted, "the word 'fine' was understood to mean a payment to a sovereign as punishment for some offense." The Excessive Fines Clause thus "limits the government's power to extract payments, whether in cash or in kind, 'as punishment for some offense.'" Forfeitures—payments in kind—are thus "fines" if they constitute punishment for an offense.

We have little trouble concluding that the forfeiture of currency ordered by § 982 (a)(1) constitutes punishment. The statute directs a court to order forfeiture as an additional sanction when "imposing sentence on a person convicted of" a willful violation of § 5316's reporting requirement. The forfeiture is thus imposed at the culmination of a criminal proceeding and requires conviction of an underlying felony, and it cannot be imposed upon an innocent owner of unreported currency, but only upon a person who has himself been convicted of a § 5316 reporting violation. The United States argues, however, that the forfeiture of currency under § 982 (a)(1) "also serves important remedial purposes." The Government asserts that it has "an overriding sovereign interest in controlling what property leaves and enters the country." It claims that full forfeiture of unreported currency supports that interest by serving to "dete[r] illicit movements of cash" and aiding in providing the Government with "valuable information to investigate and detect criminal activities associated with that cash." Deterrence, however, has traditionally been viewed as a goal of punishment, and forfeiture of the currency here does not serve the remedial purpose of compensating the Government for a loss. . . . Although the Government has asserted a loss of information regarding the amount of currency leaving the country, that loss would not be remedied by the Government's confiscation of respondent's $357,144. . . .

Traditional in rem forfeitures were thus not considered punishment against the individual for an offense. . . . The forfeiture in this case does not bear any of the hallmarks of traditional civil in rem forfeitures. The Government has not proceeded against the currency itself, but has instead sought and obtained a criminal conviction of respondent personally. The forfeiture serves no remedial purpose, is designed to punish the offender, and cannot be imposed upon innocent owners.

§ 982 (a)(1) thus descends not from historic in rem forfeitures of guilty property, but from a

UNITED STATES V. BAJAKAJIAN *(continued)*

different historical tradition: that of in personam, criminal forfeitures. Such forfeitures have historically been treated as punitive, being part of the punishment imposed for felonies and treason in the Middle Ages and at common law. Although in personam criminal forfeitures were well established in England at the time of the Founding, they were rejected altogether in the laws of this country until very recently.

The Government specifically contends that the forfeiture of respondent's currency is constitutional because it involves an "instrumentality" of respondent's crime. According to the Government, the unreported cash is an instrumentality because it "does not merely facilitate a violation of law," but is "the very sine qua non of the crime." . . .

Acceptance of the Government's argument would require us to expand the traditional understanding of instrumentality forfeitures. This we decline to do. Instrumentalities historically have been treated as a form of "guilty property" that can be forfeited in civil in rem proceedings. In this case, however, the Government has sought to punish respondent by proceeding against him criminally, in personam, rather than proceeding in rem against the currency. It is therefore irrelevant whether respondent's currency is an instrumentality; the forfeiture is punitive, and the test for the excessiveness of a punitive forfeiture involves solely a proportionality determination.

Because the forfeiture of respondent's currency constitutes punishment and is thus a "fine" within the meaning of the Excessive Fines Clause, we now turn to the question of whether it is "excessive."

The touchstone of the constitutional inquiry under the Excessive Fines Clause is the principle of proportionality: The amount of the forfeiture must bear some relationship to the gravity of the offense that it is designed to punish. . . . Until today, however, we have not articulated a standard for determining whether a punitive forfeiture is constitutionally excessive. We now hold that a punitive forfeiture violates the Excessive Fines Clause if it is grossly disproportional to the gravity of a defendant's offense.

The text and history of the Excessive Fines Clause demonstrate the centrality of proportionality to the excessiveness inquiry; nonetheless, they provide little guidance as to how disproportional a punitive forfeiture must be to the gravity of an offense in order to be "excessive." Excessive means surpassing the usual, the proper, or a normal measure of proportion. The constitutional question that we address, however, is just how proportional to a criminal offense a fine must be, and the text of the Excessive Fines Clause does not answer it.

Nor does its history. The Clause was little discussed in the First Congress and the debates over the ratification of the Bill of Rights. As we have previously noted, the Clause was taken verbatim from the English Bill of Rights of 1689. That document's prohibition against excessive fines was a reaction to the abuses of the King's judges during the reigns of the Stuarts but the fines that those judges imposed were described contemporaneously only in the most general terms. Similarly, Magna Charta—which the Stuart judges were accused of subverting—required only that amercements (the medieval predecessors of fines) should be proportioned to the offense and that they should not deprive a wrongdoer of his livelihood:

"A Free-man shall not be amerced for a small fault, but after the manner of the fault; and for a great fault after the greatness thereof, saving to him his contenement; (2) and a Merchant likewise, saving to him his merchandise; (3) and any other's villain than ours shall be likewise amerced, saving his wainage." Magna Charta, 9 Hen. III, ch. 14 (1225), 1 Stat. at Large 6–7 (1762 ed.).

(continued)

UNITED STATES V. BAJAKAJIAN *(continued)*

None of these sources suggests how disproportional to the gravity of an offense a fine must be in order to be deemed constitutionally excessive. We must therefore rely on other considerations in deriving a constitutional excessiveness standard, and there are two that we find particularly relevant. The first, which we have emphasized in our cases interpreting the Cruel and Unusual Punishments Clause, is that judgments about the appropriate punishment for an offense belong in the first instance to the legislature. The second is that any judicial determination regarding the gravity of a particular criminal offense will be inherently imprecise. Both of these principles counsel against requiring strict proportionality between the amount of a punitive forfeiture and the gravity of a criminal offense, and we therefore adopt the standard of gross disproportionality articulated in our Cruel and Unusual Punishments Clause precedents. In applying this standard, the district courts in the first instance, and the courts of appeals, reviewing the proportionality determination *de novo*, the amount of the forfeiture to the gravity of the defendant's offense. If the amount of the forfeiture is grossly disproportional to the gravity of the defendant's offense, it is unconstitutional.

Under this standard, the forfeiture of respondent's entire $357,144 would violate the Excessive Fines Clause. Respondent's crime was solely a reporting offense. It was permissible to transport the currency out of the country so long as he reported it. Section 982 (a)(1) orders currency to be forfeited for a "willful" violation of the reporting requirement. Thus, the essence of respondent's crime is a willful failure to report the removal of currency from the United States. Furthermore, as the District Court found, respondent's violation was unrelated to any other illegal activities. The money was the proceeds of legal activity and was to be used to repay a lawful debt. Whatever his other vices, respondent does not fit into the class of persons for whom the statute was principally designed: He is not a money launderer, a drug trafficker, or a tax evader. See Brief for United States 2–3. And under the Sentencing Guidelines, the maximum sentence that could have been imposed on respondent was six months, while the maximum fine was $5,000. Such penalties confirm a minimal level of culpability.

The harm that respondent caused was also minimal. Failure to report his currency affected only one party, the Government, and in a relatively minor way. There was no fraud on the United States, and respondent caused no loss to the public fisc. Had his crime gone undetected, the Government would have been deprived only of the information that $357,144 had left the country. The Government and the dissent contend that there is a correlation between the amount forfeited and the harm that the Government would have suffered had the crime gone undetected. We disagree. There is no inherent proportionality in such a forfeiture. It is impossible to conclude, for example, that the harm respondent caused is anywhere near - 30 times greater than that caused by a hypothetical drug dealer who willfully fails to report taking $12,000 out of the country in order to purchase drugs.

Comparing the gravity of respondent's crime with the $357,144 forfeiture the Government seeks, we conclude that such a forfeiture would be grossly disproportional to the gravity of his offense. It is larger than the $5,000 fine imposed by the District Court by many orders of magnitude, and it bears no articulable correlation to any injury suffered by the Government. . . .

▪ ▪ ▪

For the foregoing reasons, the full forfeiture of respondent's currency would violate the Excessive Fines Clause. The judgment of the Court of Appeals is Affirmed.

Similarly, even though forfeiture may be characterized as civil, the exclusionary rule applies to bar illegally seized evidence in quasi-criminal forfeiture cases.[44] This is contrary to the rule that the exclusionary rule is not applied in civil and administrative cases.

Modern Sentencing Alternatives

In recent years, many new alternatives to incarceration have been developed. Such alternatives are actually forms of probation, and, as such, are administered by courts and probation officers.

For the non-violent criminal, work release is an alternative. While in these programs the offender lives in a jail, but is permitted to leave jail to work. Work release has many advantages. The defendant continues to earn a living. This is particularly important if the defendant has dependents. Also, it is good for the self-esteem of offenders; they continue to feel a useful part of the community. The final advantage is true of many sentencing alternatives: the cost to the public is lower because the offender is often required to pay, in whole or part, for participation in the program.

For those convicted of some alcohol and drug offenses, courts have turned to alcohol and drug treatment over imprisonment. These programs vary greatly. For first-time drunk driving convictions, offenders may be required to do one or more of the following, in addition to traditional conditions of probation:

1. Participate in an alcohol treatment program, such as Alcoholics Anonymous.
2. Report for periodic urine or blood tests to detect the presence of alcohol.
3. Take a drug such as Antabuse, which makes a person ill if alcohol is ingested.
4. Participate in a defensive/safe-driving school.

If a defendant has a previous drunk driving conviction, he or she is likely to receive some "executed time" or jail time, in addition to some or all of the previously listed conditions. A few courts have tried a form of shock treatment. For example, a defendant may be required to meet with drunk drivers who are responsible for killing someone and discuss that experience. In another example, at least one judge has required that a drunk driver work in a hospital emergency room so that the defendant would be exposed to alcohol-related injuries and deaths.

First-time drug users may also be placed on probation, subject to conditions similar to those previously listed: periodic urinalysis or blood screening and drug counseling and treatment. This form of probation is not available to drug dealers.

Two other forms of probation that may be used independently or mixed with one or more of the others are house arrest and halfway houses. If a defendant is sentenced to house arrest, he or she may not leave the home without prior permission of the probation officer, except in emergencies.

Today, the use of electronic shackles makes enforcement of house arrests easier. These devices are attached to the probationer's leg; and through the transmission of a radio signal, it can be determined if the defendant is at home.

Halfway houses are minimum security homes located in the community. Generally they serve two groups of offenders: those making the transition from prison to the community and those who need some confinement, but not jail or prison.

halfway house

■ A facility in which persons recently discharged from a rehabilitation center or prison live for a time and are given support and assistance in readjusting to society at large.

Halfway houses are commonly used in conjunction with work release programs. The residents are given some freedom to leave the home but are restricted in their travel. Often such homes provide drug and alcohol counseling and treatment and vocational training.

Yet another community-based correction program is the boot camp or "shock incarceration" program. Boot camps are gaining in popularity as a method of reforming youthful offenders. As of early 1994, nearly 30 states were operating prison boot camps.[45]

The typical boot camp experience involves 90 to 180 days of "rigid military-training atmosphere followed by intensive community supervision." Boot camp programs are usually limited to first-time offenders who have been sentenced to a term of imprisonment. Most programs are designed to accommodate individuals sentenced to prison, but a growing number of jails are using boot camps as an alternative to traditional confinement.[46]

This is not by any means an exhaustive list of alternative punishments. The list is limited only by the U.S. Constitution and the imagination of judges. For example, one Florida judge required those convicted of drunk driving to place bumper stickers on their cars warning of their convictions. This requirement was upheld by the Florida Court of Appeals.[47]

Habitual Offender Statutes

habitual offender statutes

■ Laws that may apply to a person who has been convicted of as few as two prior crimes (often violent or drug-related crimes) and that greatly increase the penalties for each succeeding crime.

The career criminal or repeat offender is now subject to extreme penalty in most jurisdictions. These statutes are referred to as *recidivist* or **habitual offender laws.**

Most statutes provide for an increased penalty if a defendant has been convicted of a stated number of felonies, often three, within a certain period of time, such as 10 years. These are popularly known as the "three strikes and you're out" laws.

To prevent unfair prejudice to the defendant, the jury usually does not know about the habitual criminal charge until it has reached a verdict in the underlying charge. So, if Pam is charged with murder and of being a habitual criminal, the jury would initially know only of the murder charge. If the jury comes back with an acquittal, the habitual criminal charge is dismissed. If the verdict is guilty, the jury is then told that it must also determine if the defendant is an habitual criminal. This is known as a bifurcated procedure.

To prove the habitual criminal charge, the prosecutor will introduce court records reflecting the prior convictions and, in some instances, call the prosecutors involved in the prior convictions to attest that the defendant was indeed convicted.

sidebar

ANOTHER SENTENCING STORY

Willie Smith was convicted of the extortion and assault of a 93-year-old woman confined to a wheelchair. He was also convicted of resisting arrest, counterfeiting food stamps, and mugging.

sidebar *(continued)*

During sentencing, the trial judge told the defendant that he was irritated by the defendant's constant claims of police brutality and left the bench, approached the defendant, and punched him in the nose. While the defendant was on the floor of the courtroom, the judge kicked and punched him. The judge then returned to the bench and stated to the defendant, "That, Mr. Smith, is a sample of real, honest-to-goodness police brutality."

Habitual criminal laws have been attacked as violative of the Double Jeopardy Clause. Such claims have not been successful, as they are not considered a second punishment of one of the earlier offenses. Rather, evidence of a criminal record provides a reason to increase the penalty for the most recent offense.

POSTCONVICTION REMEDIES

Technically, motions for new trials are postconviction remedies. Other than such motions, there are two major methods of attacking a conviction or other decision at the trial level: appeal and habeas corpus.

Appeal

The Constitution of the United States does not expressly confer a right to appeal.[48] Regardless, every state provides for appeal either through statute or constitution. Once a state establishes a right to appeal, the U.S. Constitution requires that appellate procedure not violate the Fourteenth Amendment's Due Process or Equal Protection Clauses.

Appeals from federal district courts go to the U.S. Courts of Appeals (circuit courts). From there, appeal is taken to the Supreme Court of the United States. In state cases, appeal is taken to the state intermediate appellate court, if any. Appeal from that court is taken to the state high court, usually named the Supreme Court of the state. All issues, federal and state, are heard by those courts. Issues of state law may not be appealed any further. If the defendant wishes to appeal a decision of the state high court concerning an issue of federal law, the appeal is taken to the United States Supreme Court.

Filing the Appeal

Because the right to appeal is purely statutory, it may be lost if it is not timely filed. The federal rules require that appeals be filed within 10 days of the date of judgement.[49] The government is given 30 days in those instances where it may appeal.

Appeals from state courts to the United States Supreme Court must be filed within 90 days of the entry of judgement.[50]

Procedures vary, but it is common to require the appellant to file several documents to begin the appeal. The first document is a notice or petition of appeal. This simply informs all the parties, as well as the trial judge, that the case is being appealed. A designation of record will also be filed by the parties. Through this document, the parties select the portions of the trial record that they desire to be sent to the appellate court. A statement of issues that must be resolved on appeal may also be filed by the appellant. Finally, a filing fee must be paid. Appellants who cannot afford it may seek relief from the filing fee requirement.

After the necessary documents are filed, the parties brief the issues for the appellate court. The appellate court, in its discretion, may hear oral arguments.

Because the penalty for untimely filings is harsh (dismissal of the appeal), most courts recognize constructive filings. This is particularly true for incarcerated defendants who rely on counsel or prison officials in preparing or filing an appeal.

Note that most jurisdictions provide for the possibility of bail pending appeal. This is most often available in misdemeanor cases; however, it may be granted in felony cases also.

The Scope of Review

To avoid unnecessary delay, only **final orders** may be appealed. Therefore, erroneous pretrial decisions are not corrected until appeal is taken, after the case is completed. Orders that may not be reviewed until after final judgement are those relating to the suppression of evidence, discovery, and the sufficiency of the charging instruments.

There are a few exceptions to the final judgement rule. The most prominent exception is the collateral order doctrine. Under this doctrine, orders that are independent of the criminal case may be immediately appealed. The appeal proceeds concurrently with the underlying criminal case.

Appeals taken from ongoing litigation (where no final order has been issued) are called **interlocutory appeals.** Orders holding a defendant incompetent to stand trial, denying bail, and denying a defendant's double jeopardy claim have been held collateral and immediately appealable.[51] Certain orders that occur after judgement, such as revocation of probation, are also immediately appealable.

Remember, cases are not retried on appeal. Appellate courts review the record for errors of law, not fact. That means the appellate court will not examine the evidence and substitute its judgement for that of the trial court (or jury). However, the court will examine the record to make sure that sufficient evidence exists to support the judgement. So long as sufficient evidence can be found, the appellate court will not reverse, even if it would have decided the case differently. Issues of law are reviewed anew (de novo).

Not every error warrants reversing the trial court. Only when an error prejudices the defendant is reversal required. An error is prejudicial if there is a possibility that it changed the outcome of the case. If not, it was **harmless error.** The appellant bears the burden of proving that he or she was prejudiced by the error of the trial court.

---

final judgement (order)

■ The last action of a court; the one upon which an appeal can be based.

interlocutory appeal

■ The *Interlocutory Appeals* Act (28 U.S.C. 1292 (1948)) is a federal law that provides for an appeal while a trial is going on if the trial judge states in writing: (1) A legal question has come up that directly affects the trial. (2) There are major questions as to how that point of law should be resolved. (3) The case would proceed better if the appeals court answers the question.

harmless error

■ A trivial mistake made by a judge in the procedures used at trial, or in making l-egal rulings during the trial.

Some error is so violative of the Constitution that it is irrebuttably presumed prejudicial, so reversal is automatic. An order denying defense counsel at trial is never harmless error.[52]

Prosecution/Defense Appeals

Because of the Double Jeopardy Clause, defendants have a broader right to appeal than does the government. A defendant who is tried and convicted is free to appeal any factual or legal error. However, this right may be limited by a requirement of *preservation*. To satisfy this rule, the defendant must raise the issue at the trial level. This gives the trial judge an opportunity to avoid error.

Failure to raise the issue results in a waiver. For example, a defendant who does not challenge the sufficiency of an indictment at the trial level may not raise the issue for the first time before the appellate court. The same is true of evidentiary matters. The defendant must object to the admission of evidence that he or she believes should be excluded, so as to preserve the issue for appeal.

The prosecution has a limited right to appeal. Because of the prohibition on trying a person twice for the same offense, the government has no right to appeal acquittals. However, most states permit the government to appeal certain orders issued before jeopardy attaches. Orders dismissing charging instruments, suppressing evidence prior to trial, and releasing the defendant before trial may be appealed. These interlocutory appeals do not violate the Fifth Amendment's Double Jeopardy Clause, because jeopardy does not attach until a jury has been impaneled or the first witness is sworn in a nonjury trial. See Chapter 9 for a more thorough discussion of double jeopardy and appeals.

The Right to Counsel on Appeal

There is no Sixth Amendment right to counsel on appeal. The Sixth Amendment right begins once a defendant is charged and continues, at all critical stages, through trial and sentencing. In some instances, it is in effect at probation revocation. It does not ever include appeals.

The right to counsel on appeal can be found, however, in the Equal Protection Clause of the Fourteenth Amendment. The Supreme Court said, in *Douglas v. California*,[53] that indigent defendants convicted of a felony have a right to appointed counsel on appeal, provided that the appeal is by right. *By right* means that the defendant's appeal must be heard by the appellate court. Most, if not all, states have provided for appeal by right.

If an appeal is discretionary, the Equal Protection Clause of the Fourteenth Amendment does not compel the state to provide counsel.

As is true at trial, the defendant is entitled to effective counsel. The appointed attorney has an ethical obligation to zealously pursue the defendant's appeal. Because of the large number of frivolous appeals, the Supreme Court has stated that an appointed attorney may be allowed to withdraw. However, the following must be done: first, the attorney must request withdrawal from the appellate court; second, a brief must be filed explaining why the attorney believes the appeal to be wholly without merit. In that brief, all potential issues must be outlined for the court's review. If the appellate court agrees that there are no valid issues, the attorney may withdraw. If the court finds an issue that has some merit, the lawyer must continue to represent the defendant.

Habeas Corpus

Both the states and federal governments have habeas corpus relief. Here we discuss federal habeas corpus relief, particularly federal habeas corpus in state criminal proceedings. Although habeas corpus relief is available at any stage of a criminal proceeding, most habeas corpus petitions are filed after conviction. The discussion here is limited to such postconviction petitions.

Through habeas corpus proceedings, an individual may attack the lawfulness of confinement, whether it be substantive or procedural in nature. Further, the conditions of confinement and the lawfulness of an imposed punishment may be reviewed by a habeas court.

History

Translated, *habeas corpus* means "you have the body." In action, the writ is used to order someone who has custody of another to bring that person before the court. Any person who believes that he or she is being detained illegally may use the writ to gain his or her freedom. Because of the significant power of the writ, it has come to be known as the "Great Writ of Liberty."

The writ has ancient origin, dating back as far as the twelfth century. Habeas corpus was often used to enforce provisions of the Magna Carta. The success of the writ in protecting liberty in England influenced the drafters of the U.S. Constitution. The result is Article I, § 9, clause 2, which states: "The Privilege of the Writ of Habeas Corpus shall not be suspended unless when in Cases of Rebellion or Invasion the Public Safety may require it."

Federal habeas corpus is important in criminal law because it is used to challenge state court convictions. That is, if a defendant believes that his or her federal constitutional rights were violated in a state court, he or she may attack the conviction through federal habeas corpus.

Habeas corpus has had congressional authorization since 1789. The first statute made habeas corpus available only to federal prisoners. This was changed by the Habeas Corpus Act of 1867, which extended habeas corpus to any person "restrained of his or her liberty in violation of the constitution, or of any treaty or law of the United States." The 1867 act continues to be in effect, with some modifications.

Scope of Review

The current habeas corpus statutes are found at 28 U.S.C. §§ 2241–2255. Section 2254 provides habeas corpus relief to state prisoners. Under § 2255, federal prisoners are to move to vacate or set aside their sentences, in a procedure nearly identical to § 2254. Relief under this section must be sought before a federal prisoner can bring habeas corpus. Even then, the statute states that habeas corpus shall not be issued if the prisoner was unsuccessful with a § 2255 claim, unless that proceeding was "inadequate or ineffective." A biased judge is an example of when habeas corpus may be issued after a § 2255 motion has been denied.

The federal courts continued to have little involvement with state proceedings, even after the 1867 act extended the reach of federal habeas corpus to state prisoners. This was largely due to Supreme Court decisions limiting the review of federal habeas corpus to questions of jurisdiction.

The scope of review was enlarged in *Brown v. Allen*, 344 U.S. 443 (1953), in which it was held that federal habeas corpus could be used to relitigate all issues of federal law. This decision significantly increased the power of federal habeas corpus and resulted in increased intervention of federal courts in state criminal proceedings.

The Supreme Court has since narrowed habeas corpus relief by decision. For example, a state prisoner may not use federal habeas corpus to relitigate Fourth Amendment claims (search and seizure), provided the defendant was provided a "full and fair litigation" in state court. Also, the Court has emphasized that the purpose of habeas corpus is to provide relief to persons imprisoned in violation of the laws of the United States, not to relitigate or correct factual errors. Accordingly, a claim of innocence, even when supported by new evidence, is not alone sufficient to confer habeas jurisdiction upon a court. An independent constitutional claim must be made for a court to examine such a petition.[54]

Exhaustion of Remedies

Before a state prisoner can seek the aid of a federal court, he or she must satisfy certain procedural requirements. First, the defendant must use all means available in the state system to correct the alleged error. This is the doctrine of **exhaustion of remedies.** Section 2254(b) states:

> An application for a writ of habeas corpus in behalf of a person in custody pursuant to the judgment of a State court shall not be granted unless it appears that the applicant has exhausted the remedies available in the courts of the State, or that there is either an absence of available corrective process or the existence of circumstances rendering such process ineffective to protect the rights of the prisoner.

The remedies that must be exhausted depend on what is available in the state system, such as motions for new trial, state habeas corpus relief, and appeals. Of course, if no remedy is available, the defendant may immediately petition for habeas corpus relief.

If a remedy is available, but it would be futile to exhaust it, habeas corpus may be brought without exhaustion. For example, assume State Supreme Court has previously addressed the legal issue raised by the defendant, and its decision is contrary to the defendant's claim. Unless there is reason to believe that the court will reconsider its decision, there is no need to exhaust this remedy. Excessive delay in the state proceedings may also be a basis for bringing habeas corpus before the state remedies have been exhausted, provided the state does not have a remedy for such delays (e.g., mandamus).

The fact that a defendant has failed to timely appeal (or file a motion for new trial, etc.) does not mean that habeas corpus is unavailable. The question is: Are state remedies available? If a defendant has missed the right to appeal under state law, and no other remedy is available, then habeas corpus may be used to resolve his or her federal constitutional claims. However, defendants who deliberately bypass state procedures may be denied habeas relief.[55]

exhaustion of remedies

■ A person must usually take all reasonable steps to get satisfaction from a state or federal government before seeking judicial relief.

The Custody Requirement

The Habeas Corpus Act speaks of prisoners "in custody." However, this has been interpreted to include all wrongful restraints of liberty. The Supreme Court has said that persons who are subject to "restraints not shared by the public generally" are entitled to habeas corpus protection, even though they may not be in the physical custody of the government.

Under this interpretation, persons placed on probation and parole have been held to be in custody, as have defendants released on bail.[56] Habeas corpus protection is also available to a defendant who has served his or her entire sentence, because the restraint of liberty includes not only incarceration but also collateral loss of civil liberties (e.g., right to carry a weapon), injury to reputation, and the possibility of an increased penalty for a later conviction.

A defendant who is lawfully detained may use habeas corpus to challenge his or her sentence if he or she believes it is excessive. Also, if he or she was convicted of several crimes and was sentenced to consecutive sentences, he or she need not wait until the lawful sentence expires before petitioning for habeas corpus. It appears that an invalid sentence may be attacked even though it runs concurrently with a valid sentence. Again, the collateral effects of the conviction are the rationale.

Procedure

The following rules were established by the United States Supreme Court to implement 22 U.S.C. § 2254.[57] The petition for habeas corpus relief is filed in the federal district within which the prisoner is being held. The petition shall name the person who has custody of the applicant as the respondent. Indigent persons may file a motion to proceed in forma pauperis, which relieves such persons from paying the filing fee.

Immediately after the petition is filed, the district judge will examine the petition. If the petition is "plainly" invalid, the court will dismiss it. If not, the court will direct the respondent to answer the petition.

Counsel may be appointed and discovery is available, with leave of the district court. After the petition has been answered and appropriate discovery conducted, the district court may hold an evidentiary hearing and issue an opinion or rule from the record without a hearing. Habeas corpus decisions may be appealed.

The Right to Counsel

To date, the Supreme Court has not found a constitutional right to the assistance of counsel in preparing and presenting a petition for habeas corpus.

In some instances the district court may have to hold an evidentiary hearing. It is possible that in such instances a due process right to counsel exists to assure that the hearing is fair. The issue is not of critical importance presently, because federal habeas corpus rules require the appointment of counsel for such hearings. Additionally, the rules give the district court the discretion to appoint counsel earlier, if necessary.

Although there may be no right to counsel, there is a right to "access to the courts." Therefore, prisoners must be furnished with paper, pens, stamps, and access to a law library. Further, unless a prison provides adequate legal assistance to its prisoners, so-called jailhouse lawyers may not be prohibited from assisting other inmates in the preparation of legal documents.

Ethical Considerations

ATTORNEY DISCIPLINE BY THE NUMBERS

According to the American Bar Association, there were 1,380,528 attorneys in the United States in 2010. In that year, the state bar authorities collectively received 118,054 complaints against attorneys, 82,316 of those complaints were investigated, and 4,426 attorneys were charged after probable cause of a violation was found. Also in that year, 1,574 attorneys were privately sanctioned and 3,791 were publicly sanctioned in the United States in 2010 Of those attorneys who were sanctioned, 503 were involuntarily disbarred, 290 consented to disbarment, 1,969 had their practices suspended, 991 received a public censure, and 563 were placed on probation.

Today, many states have online databases that permit attorney discipline records to be investigated. These databases often indicate whether an attorney has been disciplined; and if so, the nature of the violation, the date, and the discipline imposed.

Source of filings data: American Bar Association, Center for Professional Responsibility, Survey on Lawyer Discipline Systems (2012).

Web Links

Punishment and Sentencing

Information and documents about trials, sentencing, appeals, and punishment can be found at *http://truTV.com*

There is much information about the death penalty on the Internet. Here are a few sites:

http://www.deathpenaltyinfo.org/

http://www.prodeathpenalty.com/

http://www.aclu.org/capital/

http://web.amnesty.org/

Key Terms

aggravating circumstances
commutation of sentence
concurrent sentences
consecutive sentences
determinate sentencing
exhaustion of remedies
final orders

habitual offender laws
halfway houses
harmless error
indeterminate sentence
interlocutory appeals
mitigating circumstances
pardon

parole
reprieve
revocation hearing
suspended sentence
victim impact statement

Review Questions

1. What is a presentence investigation? Who conducts the investigation, and what is its purpose?

2. What are aggravating and mitigating circumstances in sentencing?

3. What is the final judgement rule?

4. Does a defendant have a right to appointed counsel on appeal?

5. What is habeas corpus?

6. Distinguish harmless from prejudicial error.

7. May victim impact evidence be considered by sentencing courts?

8. Which of the following punishments has the Supreme Court held to be inherently cruel and unusual?
   a. Death by hanging
   b. Death by starvation
   c. Flogging
   d. Solitary confinement
   e. Imprisonment without lighting or a bed

9. Differentiate a suspended imposition of sentence from a sentence suspended to probation.

Problems & Critical Thinking Exercises

1–4. Kevin, an attorney, has been indicted for embezzlement. After his preliminary hearing, he filed a motion to suppress a confession he believes was illegally obtained. A hearing was conducted and the trial court granted his motion. The evidence was vital to the prosecution.

Kevin's attorney has also requested that the trial be continued because he claims that Kevin is not competent to stand trial. The judge ordered a mental evaluation, held a hearing, and found Kevin competent to stand trial.

The defense also requested that the court order a number of police officers to submit to depositions prior to trial. The court denied the motion.

At trial, the defendant objected to the introduction of a document that he believed was unconstitutionally obtained during a search of his office. The judge overruled the objection and admitted the confession into evidence.

Answer the following questions using these facts.

1. The prosecution strongly believes that the documents that were suppressed are admissible. The prosecutor objects on the record to the judge's order and then appeals the issue after Kevin is acquitted. What should be the outcome on appeal?

2. Kevin disagrees with the trial court finding of competency. What is his remedy?

3. Believing that Kevin cannot have a fair trial without the depositions, his attorney filed an interlocutory appeal seeking an order from the appellate court requiring the trial judge to provide for the depositions. What should be the outcome?

4. Kevin appealed the trial court's decision denying his motion to suppress the document. The appellate court affirmed the trial court, and Kevin filed a habeas corpus petition in federal court claiming that his federal constitutional rights were violated by admission of the evidence. What should be the outcome?

Endnotes

1. The Supreme Court has not yet answered this question. *See also United States v. Rogers*, 921 F.2d 957 (10th Cir. 1990), *cert. denied*, 111 S. Ct. 113 (1991).

2. *United States v. Jackson*, 886 F.2d 838 (7th Cir. 1989).

3. Fed. R. Crim. P. 32(c)(1).

4. Fed. R. Crim. P. 32(c)(3).

5. *Apprendi v. New Jersey*, 530 U.S. 466 (2000).

6. *Eddings v. Oklahoma*, 455 U.S. 104 (1982).

7. *United States v. Watts*, 519 U.S. 148 (1997).

8. *See Apprendi v. New Jersey*, 530 U.S. 466 (2000); *Blakely v. Washington*, 542 U.S. 296 (2004); *United States v. Booker*, 543 U.S. 220 (2005); and *Cunningham v. California*, _____ U.S. (2007).

9. *Ring v. Arizona*, 536 U.S. 584 (2002).

10. *Locket v. Ohio*, 438 U.S. at 604–05.

11. *See Kansas v. Marsh*, 548 U.S. (2006).

12. *Callins v. Collins*, 510 U.S. 1141 (1994) 114 S. Ct. 1127, 1132 (1994) (Blackmun, J., dissenting).

13. 114 S. Ct. at 1129–30.

14. All the data appearing before this endnote in this sidebar was taken from Jeffrey Kirchmeier, "Another Place Beyond Here: The Death Penalty Moratorium Movement in the United States," *73 U. Colo. L. Rev.* 1 (2002).

15. 553 U.S. 35 (2008).

16. *Coker v. Georgia*, 433 U.S. 584 (1977).

17. *Enmund v. Florida*, 458 U.S. 782 (1972).

18. *Ford v. Wainwright*, 477 U.S. 399 (1986).

19. *See Roper v. Simmons*, 543 U.S. 551 (2005).

20. 536 U.S. 304.

21. *Pervear v. Commonwealth*, 72 U.S. (5 Wall) 475 (1867); *Wing Wong v. United States*, 163 U.S. 228 (1896); *Kehrli v. Sprinkle*, 524 F.2d 328 (10th Cir. 1975).

22. *Delaware v. Cannon*, 55 Del. 587, 190 A.2d 574 (1963).

23. *Jackson v. Bishop*, 404 F.2d 571 (8th Cir. 1968).

24. For a thorough discussion of the constitutionality of whipping, *see* Daniel E. Hall, "When Caning Meets the Eighth Amendment: Whipping Offenders in the United States," 4 *Widener J. Pub. L.* 403 (1995).

25. 21 *U.S.C.* 841(b)(1).

26. 501 U.S. 957 (1991).]

27. United States v. Gementera, 379 F.3d 596 (9th Cir. 2004).

28. Laura Edwins, *10 Weird Criminal Sentences*, The Christian Science Monitor. Found on May 15, 2013 at csmonitor.com

634   Part II Criminal Procedure

29. All the examples with the exception of the first and second come from Jan Hoffman, *Crime and Punishment: Shame Gains Popularity, The New York Times*. January 16, 1997. Found at http://www.nytimes.com/1997/01/16/us/crime-and-punishment-shame-gains-popularity.html?pagewanted=all&src=pm

30. Breyer, "The Federal Sentencing Guidelines and the Key Compromises Upon Which They Rest," 17 *Hofstra L. Rev.* 4 (1988).

31. Federal Judges Association, *In Camera* (Dec. 1990).

32. Final Report on the Impact of the *United States v. Booker* on Federal Sentencing, United States Sentencing Commission, March 2006.

33. *Griffin v. Wisconsin*, 483 U.S. 868 (1987).

34. *Porth v. Templar*, 453 F.2d 330 (10th Cir. 1971).

35. *United States v. Green*, 735 F.2d 1203 (9th Cir. 1984).

36. *Hughey v. United States*, 495 U.S. 411 (1990).

37. *Phillips v. United States*, 679 F.2d 192 (9th Cir. 1982).

38. *Bearden v. Georgia*, 461 U.S. 660, 668–69 (1983).

39. 399 U.S. 235 (1970).

40. *See*, for example, 21 U.S.C. § 881.

41. 19 U.S.C. § 1615.

42. *See* 21 U.S.C. § 853.

43. 114 S. Ct. 492 (1993).

44. *One 1958 Plymouth v. Pennsylvania*, 380 U.S. 693 (1965).

45. *The Growing Use of Jail Boot Camps: The Current State of the Art* (Washington, DC: National Institute of Justice, October 1993).

46. Belinda McCarthy & Bernard McCarthy, *Community-Based Corrections*, 2nd ed. (Belmont, CA: Brooks/Cole, 1991), p. 128.

47. *Goldschmitt v. State*, 490 So. 2d 123 (Fla. Dist. Ct. App.), *review denied*, 496 So. 2d 142 (Fla. 1986).

48. *McKane v. Durston*, 153 U.S. 684 (1894).

49. Fed. R. Crim. P. 37.

50. Supreme Ct. R. 11.1.

51. W. Lafave & J. Israel, *Criminal Procedure* § 26.2(c). (Hornbook Series; St. Paul, MN: West, 1985).

52. *Gideon v. Wainwright*, 373 U.S. 335 (1963).

53. 372 U.S. 353 (1963).

54. *Herrera v. Collins*, 113 S. Ct. 853 (1993).

55. *Fay v. NOIA*, 372 U.S. 391 (1963).

56. *Jones v. Cunningham*, 371 U.S. 236 (1963); *Hensley v. Municipal Court*, 411 U.S. 345 (1973).

57. *See Rules Governing Section 2254 Cases in the United States District Courts* (February 1989). These rules also contain the forms necessary to petition for habeas corpus relief in the district court of the United States.

APPENDIX A

The Constitution of the United States of America

We the People of the United States, in Order to form a more perfect Union, establish Justice, insure domestic Tranquility, provide for the common defence, promote the general Welfare, and secure the Blessings of Liberty to ourselves and our Posterity, do ordain and establish this Constitution for the United States of America.

ARTICLE I

Section 1.

All legislative Powers herein granted shall be vested in a Congress of the United States, which shall consist of a Senate and House of Representatives.

Section 2.

1) The House of Representatives shall be composed of Members chosen every second Year by the People of the several States, and the Electors in each State shall have the Qualifications requisite for Electors of the most numerous Branch of the State Legislature.

2) No Person shall be a Representative who shall not have attained to the age of twenty-five Years, and been seven Years a Citizen of the United States, and who shall not, when elected, be an Inhabitant of that State in which he shall be chosen.

3) Representatives and direct Taxes shall be apportioned among the several States which may be included within this Union, according to their respective Numbers, which shall be determined by adding to the whole Number of free Persons, including those bound to Service for a Term of Years, and excluding Indians not taxed, three fifths of all other Persons. The actual Enumeration shall be made within three Years after the first Meeting of the Congress of the United States, and within every subsequent Term of ten Years, in such Manner as they shall by Law direct. The Number of Representatives shall not exceed one for every thirty Thousand, but each State shall have at Least one Representative; and until such enumeration shall be made, the State of New Hampshire shall be entitled to chuse three, Massachusetts eight, Rhode Island and Providence Plantations one, Connecticut five, New York six, New Jersey four, Pennsylvania eight, Delaware one, Maryland six, Virginia ten, North Carolina five, South Carolina five, and Georgia three.

4) When vacancies happen in the Representation from any State, the Executive Authority thereof shall issue Writs of Election to fill such Vacancies.

5) The House of Representatives shall chuse their Speaker and other Officers; and shall have the sole Power of Impeachment.

Section 3.

1) The Senate of the United States shall be composed of two Senators from each State, chosen by the Legislature thereof, for six Years; and each Senator shall have one Vote.

2) Immediately after they shall be assembled in Consequence of the first Election, they shall be divided as equally as may be into three Classes. The Seats of the Senators of the first Class shall be vacated at the Expiration of the Second Year, of the second Class at the Expiration of the fourth Year, and of the third Class at the Expiration of the sixth Year, so that one third may be chosen every second Year; and if Vacancies happen by Resignation, or otherwise, during the Recess of the Legislature of any State, the Executive thereof may make temporary Appointments until the next Meeting of the Legislature, which shall then fill such Vacancies.

3) No Person shall be a Senator who shall not have attained to the Age of thirty Years, and been nine Years a Citizen of the United States, and who shall not, when elected, be an Inhabitant of that State for which he shall be chosen.

4) The Vice President of the United States shall be President of the Senate, but shall have no Vote, unless they be equally divided.

5) The Senate shall chuse their other Officers, and also a President pro tempore, in the Absence of the Vice President, or when he shall exercise the Office of the President of the United States.

6) The Senate shall have the sole Power to try all Impeachments. When sitting for that Purpose, they shall be on Oath or Affirmation. When the President of the United States is tried, the Chief Justice shall preside: And no Person shall be convicted without the Concurrence of two thirds of the Members present.

7) Judgment in Cases of Impeachment shall not extend further than to removal from Office, and disqualification to hold and enjoy any Office of honor, Trust or Profit under the United States: but the Party convicted shall nevertheless be liable and subject to Indictment, Trial, Judgment and Punishment, according to Law.

Section 4.

1) The Times, Places and Manner of holding Elections for Senators and Representatives, shall be prescribed in each State by the Legislature thereof; but the Congress may at any time by Law make or alter such Regulations, except as to the Places of chusing Senators.

2) The Congress shall assemble at least once in every Year, and such Meeting shall be on the first Monday in December, unless they shall by Law appoint a different Day.

Section 5.

1) Each House shall be the Judge of the Elections, Returns and Qualifications of its own Members, and a Majority of each shall constitute a Quorum to do Business; but a smaller Number may adjourn from day to day, and may be authorized to compel the Attendance of absent Members, in such Manner, and under such Penalties as each House may provide.

2) Each House may determine the Rules of its Proceedings, punish its Members for disorderly Behaviour, and, with the Concurrence of two thirds, expel a Member.

3) Each House shall keep a Journal of its Proceedings, and from time to time publish the same, excepting such Parts as may in their Judgment require Secrecy; and the Yeas and Nays of the Members of either House on any question shall, at the Desire of one fifth of those Present, be entered on the Journal.

4) Neither House, during the Session of Congress, shall, without the Consent of the other, adjourn for more than three days, nor to any other Place than that in which the two Houses shall be sitting.

Section 6.

1) The Senators and Representatives shall receive a Compensation for their Services, to be ascertained by Law, and paid out of the Treasury of the United States. They shall in all Cases, except Treason, Felony and Breach of the Peace, be privileged from Arrest during their Attendance at the Session of their respective Houses, and in going to and returning from the same; and for any Speech or Debate in either House, they shall not be questioned in any other Place.

2) No Senator or Representative shall, during the Time for which he was elected, be appointed to any civil Office under the Authority of the United States, which shall have been created, or the Emoluments whereof shall have been encreased during such time; and no Person holding any Office under the United States, shall be a Member of either House during his Continuance in Office.

Section 7.

1) All Bills for raising Revenue shall originate in the House of Representatives; but the Senate may propose or concur with Amendments as on other Bills.

2) Every Bill which shall have passed the House of Representatives and the Senate, shall, before it become a Law, be presented to the President of the United States; If he approve he shall sign it, but if not he shall return it, with his Objections to that House in which it shall have originated, who shall enter the Objections at large on their Journal, and proceed to reconsider it. If after such Reconsideration two thirds of that House shall agree to pass the Bill, it shall be sent, together with the Objections, to the other House, by which it shall likewise be reconsidered, and if approved by two thirds of that House, it shall become a law. But in all such Cases

the Votes of both Houses shall be determined by Yeas and Nays, and the Names of the Persons voting for and against the Bill shall be entered on the Journal of each House respectively. If any Bill shall not be returned by the President within ten Days (Sunday excepted) after it shall have been presented to him, the Same shall be a Law, in like Manner as if he had signed it, unless the Congress by their Adjournment prevent its Return, in which Case it shall not be a Law.

3) Every Order, Resolution, or Vote to which the Concurrence of the Senate and House of Representatives may be necessary (except on a question of Adjournment) shall be presented to the President of the United States; and before the Same shall take Effect, shall be approved by him, or being disapproved by him, shall be repassed by two thirds of the Senate and House of Representatives, according to the Rules and Limitations prescribed in the Case of a Bill.

Section 8.

1) The Congress shall have Power To lay and collect Taxes, Duties, Imposts and Excises, to pay the Debts and provide for the common Defence and general Welfare of the United States; but all Duties, Imposts and Excises shall be uniform throughout the United States;

2) To borrow Money on the credit of the United States;

3) To regulate Commerce with foreign Nations, and among the several States, and with the Indian Tribes;

4) To establish an uniform Rule of Naturalization, and uniform Laws on the subject of Bankruptcies throughout the United States;

5) To coin Money, regulate the Value thereof, and of foreign Coin, and to fix the Standard of Weights and Measures;

6) To provide for the Punishment of counterfeiting the Securities and current Coin of the United States;

7) To establish Post Offices and post Roads;

8) To promote the Progress of Science and useful Arts, by securing for limited Times to Authors and Inventors the exclusive Right to their respective Writings and Discoveries;

9) To constitute Tribunals inferior to the supreme Court;

10) To define and punish Piracies and Felonies committed on the high Seas, and Offenses against the Law of Nations;

11) To declare War, grant Letters of Marque and Reprisal, and make Rules concerning Captures on Land and Water;

12) To raise and support Armies, but no Appropriation of Money to that Use shall be for a longer Term than two Years;

13) To provide and maintain a Navy;

14) To make Rules for the Government and Regulation of the land and naval Forces;

15) To provide for calling forth the Militia to execute the Laws of the Union, suppress Insurrections and repel Invasions;

16) To provide for organizing, arming, and disciplining, the Militia, and for governing such Part of them as may be employed in the Service of the United States, reserving to the States respectively, the Appointment of the Officers, and the Authority of training the Militia according to the discipline prescribed by Congress;

17) To exercise exclusive Legislation in all Cases whatsoever, over such District (not exceeding ten Miles square) as may, by Cession of particular States, and the Acceptance of Congress, become the Seat of the Government of the United States, and to exercise like Authority over all Places purchased by the Consent of the Legislature of the State in which the Same shall be, for the Erection of Forts, Magazines, Arsenals, dock-Yards, and other needful Buildings;—And

18) To make all Laws which shall be necessary and proper for carrying into Execution the foregoing Powers, and all other Powers vested by this Constitution in the Government of the United States, or in any Department or Officer thereof.

Section 9.

1) The Migration or Importation of such Persons as any of the States now existing shall think proper to admit, shall not be prohibited by the Congress prior to the Year one thousand eight hundred and eight, but a Tax or Duty may be imposed on such Importation, not exceeding ten dollars for each Person.

2) The Privilege of the Writ of Habeas Corpus shall not be suspended unless when in Cases of Rebellion or Invasion the public Safety may require it.

3) No Bill of Attainder or ex post facto Law shall be passed.

4) No Capitation, or other direct, Tax shall be laid, unless in Proportion to the Census or Enumeration herein before directed to be taken.

5) No Tax or Duty shall be laid on Articles exported from any State.

6) No Preference shall be given by any Regulation of Commerce or Revenue to the Ports of one State over those of another; nor shall Vessels bound to, or from, one State, be obliged to enter, clear or pay Duties in another.

7) No Money shall be drawn from the Treasury, but in Consequence of Appropriations made by Law; and a regular Statement and Account of the Receipts and Expenditures of all public Money shall be published from time to time.

8) No Title of Nobility shall be granted by the United States: And no Person holding any Office of Profit or Trust under them, shall, without the Consent of the Congress, accept of any present, Emolument, Office, or Title, of any kind whatever, from any King, Prince or foreign State.

Section 10.

1) No State shall enter into any Treaty, Alliance, or Confederation; grant Letters of Marque and Reprisal; coin Money; emit Bills of Credit; make any Thing but gold and silver Coin a Tender in Payment of Debts; pass any Bill of Attainder, ex post facto Law, or Law impairing the Obligation of Contracts, or grant any Title of Nobility.

2) No State shall, without the Consent of Congress, lay any Imposts or Duties on Imports or Exports, except what may be absolutely necessary for executing its inspection Laws: and the net Produce of all Duties and Imposts, laid by any State on Imports or Exports, shall be for the Use of the Treasury of the United States; and all such Laws shall be subject to the Revision and Controul of the Congress.

3) No State shall, without the Consent of Congress, lay any Duty of Tonnage, keep Troops, or Ships of War in time of Peace, enter into any Agreement or Compact with another State, or with a foreign Power, or engage in War, unless actually invaded, or in such imminent Danger as will not admit of Delay.

ARTICLE II

Section 1.

1) The executive Power shall be vested in a President of the United States of America. He shall hold his Office during the Term of four Years, and, together with the Vice President, chosen for the same Term, be elected, as follows:

2) Each State shall appoint, in such Manner as the Legislature thereof may direct, a Number of Electors, equal to the whole Number of Senators and Representatives to which the State may be entitled in the Congress: but no Senator or Representative, or Person holding an Office of Trust or Profit under the United States, shall be appointed an Elector.

The Electors shall meet in their respective States, and vote by Ballot for two Persons, of whom one at least shall not be an Inhabitant of the same State with themselves. And they shall make a List of all the Persons voted for, and of the Number of Votes for each; which List they shall sign and certify, and transmit sealed to the Seat of the Government of the United States, directed to the President of the Senate. The President of the Senate shall, in the presence of the Senate and House of Representatives, open all the Certificates, and the Votes shall then be counted. The Person having the greatest Number of Votes shall be the President, if such Number be a Majority of the whole Number of Electors appointed; and if there be more than one who have such Majority, and have an equal Number of Votes, then the House of Representatives shall immediately chuse by Ballot one of them for President; and if no Person have a Majority, then from the five highest on the List the said House shall in like Manner chuse the President. But in chusing the President, the Votes shall be taken by States, the Representation from each State having one Vote; a quorum for this Purpose shall consist of a Member or Members from two thirds of the States, and a Majority of all the States shall be necessary to a Choice. In every Case, after the Choice of the President, the Person having the greatest Number of Votes of the Electors shall be the Vice President. But if there should remain two or more who have equal Votes, the Senate shall chuse from them by Ballot the Vice President.

3) The Congress may determine the Time of chusing the Electors, and the Day on which they shall give their Votes; which Day shall be the same throughout the United States.

4) No Person except a natural born Citizen, or a Citizen of the United States, at the time of the Adoption of this Constitution, shall be eligible to the Office of President; neither shall any Person be eligible to that Office who shall not have attained to the Age of thirty-five Years,

and been fourteen Years a Resident within the United States.

5) In Case of the Removal of the President from Office, or of his Death, Resignation, or Inability to discharge the Powers and Duties of the said Office, the Same shall devolve on the Vice President, and the Congress may by Law provide for the Case of Removal, Death, Resignation or Inability, both of the President and Vice President, declaring what Officer shall then act as President, and such Officer shall act accordingly, until the Disability be removed, or a President shall be elected.

6) The President shall, at stated Times, receive for his Services, a Compensation, which shall neither be increased nor diminished during the Period for which he shall have been elected, and he shall not receive within that Period any other Emolument from the United States, or any of them.

7) Before he enter on the Execution of his Office, he shall take the following Oath or Affirmation:—"I do solemnly swear (or affirm) that I will faithfully execute the Office of President of the United States, and will to the best of my Ability, preserve, protect and defend the Constitution of the United States."

Section 2.

1) The President shall be Commander in Chief of the Army and Navy of the United States, and of the Militia of the several States, when called into the actual Service of the United States; he may require the Opinion, in writing, of the principal Officer in each of the executive Departments, upon any Subject relating to the Duties of their respective Offices, and he shall have Power to grant Reprieves and Pardons for Offenses against the United States, except in Cases of Impeachment.

2) He shall have Power, by and with the Advice and Consent of the Senate, to make Treaties, provided two thirds of the Senators present concur; and he shall nominate, and by and with the Advice and Consent of the Senate, shall appoint Ambassadors, other public Ministers and Consuls, Judges of the supreme Court, and all other Officers of the United States, whose Appointments are not herein otherwise provided for, and which shall be established by Law: but the Congress may by Law vest the Appointment of such inferior Officers, as they think proper, in the President alone, in the Courts of Law, or in the Heads of Departments.

3) The President shall have Power to fill up all Vacancies that may happen during the Recess of the Senate, by granting Commissions which shall expire at the End of their next Session.

Section 3.

He shall from time to time give to the Congress Information of the State of the Union, and recommend to their Consideration such Measures as he shall judge necessary and expedient; he may, on extraordinary Occasions, convene both Houses, or either of them, and in Case of Disagreement between them, with Respect to the Time of Adjournment, he may adjourn them to such Time as he shall think proper; he shall receive Ambassadors and other public Ministers; he shall take Care that the Laws be faithfully executed, and shall Commission all the Officers of the United States.

Section 4.

The President, Vice President and all Civil Officers of the United States, shall be removed from Office on Impeachment for, and Conviction of, Treason, Bribery, or other high Crimes and Misdemeanors.

ARTICLE III

Section 1.

The judicial Power of the United States, shall be vested in one supreme Court, and in such inferior Courts as the Congress may from time to time ordain and establish. The Judges, both of the supreme and inferior Courts, shall hold their Offices during good Behaviour, and shall, at stated Times, receive for their Services, a Compensation, which shall not be diminished during their Continuance in Office.

Section 2.

1) The judicial Power shall extend to all Cases, in Law and Equity, arising under this Constitution, the Laws of the United States, and Treaties made, or which shall be made, under their Authority;—to all Cases affecting Ambassadors, other public Ministers and Consuls;— to all Cases of admiralty and maritime Jurisdiction;— to Controversies to which the United States shall be a party;—to Controversies between two or more States;— between a State and Citizens of another State;— between Citizens of different States;—between Citizens of the same State claiming Lands under Grants of different States, and between a State, or the Citizens thereof, and foreign States, Citizens or Subjects.

2) In all Cases affecting Ambassadors, other public Ministers and Consuls, and those in which a State shall be Party, the supreme Court shall have original Jurisdiction. In all the other Cases before mentioned, the supreme Court shall have appellate Jurisdiction, both as to Law and Fact, with such Exceptions, and under such Regulations as the Congress shall make.

3) The Trial of all Crimes, except in Cases of Impeachment, shall be by Jury; and such Trial shall be held in the State where the said Crimes shall have been committed; but when not committed within any State, the Trial shall be at such Place or Places as the Congress may by Law have directed.

Section 3.

1) Treason against the United States, shall consist only in levying War against them, or in adhering to their Enemies, giving them Aid and Comfort. No Person shall be convicted of Treason unless on the Testimony of two Witnesses to the same overt Act, or on Confession in open Court.

2) The Congress shall have Power to declare the Punishment of Treason, but no Attainder of Treason shall work Corruption of Blood, or Forfeiture except during the Life of the Person attainted.

ARTICLE IV

Section 1.

Full Faith and Credit shall be given in each State to the public Acts, Records, and judicial Proceedings of every other State. And the Congress may by general Laws prescribe the Manner in which such Acts, Records and Proceedings shall be proved, and the Effect thereof.

Section 2.

1) The Citizens of each State shall be entitled to all privileges and Immunities of Citizens in the several States.

2) A Person charged in any State with Treason, Felony, or other Crime, who shall flee from Justice, and be found in another State, shall on Demand of the executive Authority of the State from which he fled, be delivered up, to be removed to the State having Jurisdiction of the Crime.

3) No Person held to Service of Labour in one State, under the Laws thereof, escaping into another, shall, in Consequence of any Law or Regulation therein, be discharged from such Service or Labour, but shall be delivered up on Claim of the Party to whom such Service or Labour may be due.

Section 3.

1) New States may be admitted by the Congress into this Union; but no new State shall be formed or erected within the Jurisdiction of any other State; nor any State be formed by the Junction of two or more States, or Parts of States, without the Consent of the Legislatures of the States concerned as well as of the Congress.

2) The Congress shall have power to dispose of and make all needful Rules and Regulations respecting the Territory or other Property belonging to the United States; and nothing in this Constitution shall be so construed as to Prejudice any Claims of the United States, or of any particular State.

Section 4.

The United States shall guarantee to every State in this Union a Republican Form of Government, and shall protect each of them against Invasion; and on Application of the Legislature, or of the Executive (when the Legislature cannot be convened) against domestic Violence.

ARTICLE V

The Congress, whenever two thirds of both Houses shall deem it necessary, shall propose Amendments to this Constitution, or, on the Application of the Legislatures of two thirds of the several States, shall call a Convention for proposing Amendments, which, in either Case, shall be valid to all Intents and Purposes, as Part of this Constitution, when ratified by the Legislatures of three fourths of the several States, or by Conventions in three fourths thereof, as the one or the other Mode of Ratification may be proposed by the Congress; Provided that no Amendment which may be made prior to the Year One thousand eight hundred and eight shall in any Manner affect the first and fourth Clauses in the Ninth Section of the first Article; and that no State, without its Consent, shall be deprived of its equal Suffrage in the Senate.

ARTICLE VI

1) All Debts contracted and Engagements entered into, before the Adoption of this Constitution, shall be as valid

against the United States under this Constitution, as under the Confederation.

2) This Constitution, and the Laws of the United States which shall be made in Pursuance thereof; and all Treaties made, or which shall be made, under the Authority of the United States, shall be the supreme Law of the Land; and the Judges in every State shall be bound thereby, any Thing in the Constitution or Laws of any State to the Contrary notwithstanding.

3) The Senators and Representatives before mentioned, and the Members of the several State Legislatures, and all executive and judicial Officers, both of the United States and of the several States, shall be bound by Oath or Affirmation, to support this Constitution; but no religious Test shall ever be required as a Qualification to any Office or public Trust under the United States.

ARTICLE VII

The Ratification of the Conventions of nine States, shall be sufficient for the Establishment of this Constitution between the States so ratifying the Same.

ARTICLES IN ADDITION TO, AND AMENDMENT OF, THE CONSTITUTION OF THE UNITED STATES OF AMERICA, PROPOSED BY CONGRESS, AND RATIFIED BY THE SEVERAL STATES, PURSUANT TO THE FIFTH ARTICLE OF THE ORIGINAL CONSTITUTION

AMENDMENT I (1791)

Congress shall make no law respecting an establishment of religion, or prohibiting the free exercise thereof; or abridging the freedom of speech, or of the press; or the right of the people peaceably to assemble, and to petition the Government for a redress of grievances.

AMENDMENT II (1791)

A well regulated Militia, being necessary to the security of a free state, the right of the people to keep and bear Arms, shall not be infringed.

AMENDMENT III (1791)

No Soldier shall, in time of peace be quartered in any house, without the consent of the Owner, nor in time of war, but in a manner to be prescribed by law.

AMENDMENT IV (1791)

The right of the people to be secure in their persons, houses, papers, and effects, against unreasonable searches and seizures, shall not be violated, and no Warrants shall issue, but upon probable cause, supported by Oath or affirmation, and particularly describing the place to be searched, and the persons or things to be seized.

AMENDMENT V (1791)

No person shall be held to answer for a capital, or otherwise infamous crime, unless on a presentment or indictment of a Grand Jury, except in cases arising in the land or naval forces, or in the Militia, when in actual service in time of War or public danger; nor shall any person be subject for the same offence to be twice put in jeopardy of life or limb; nor shall be compelled in any criminal case to be a witness against himself, nor be deprived of life, liberty, or property, without due process of law; nor shall private property be taken for public use, without just compensation.

AMENDMENT VI (1791)

In all criminal prosecutions, the accused shall enjoy the right to a speedy and public trial, by an impartial jury of the State and district wherein the crime shall have been committed, which district shall have been previously ascertained by law, and to be informed of the nature and cause of the accusation; to be confronted with the witnesses against him; to have compulsory process for obtaining witnesses in his favor, and to have the Assistance of Counsel for his defence.

AMENDMENT VII (1791)

In Suits at common law, where the value in controversy shall exceed twenty dollars, the right of trial by jury shall be preserved, and no fact tried by a jury, shall be otherwise re-examined in any Court of the United States, than according to the rules of the common law.

AMENDMENT VIII (1791)

Excessive bail shall not be required, nor excessive fines imposed, nor cruel and unusual punishments inflicted.

AMENDMENT IX (1791)

The enumeration in the Constitution, of certain rights, shall not be construed to deny or disparage others retained by the people.

AMENDMENT X (1791)

The powers not delegated to the United States by the Constitution, nor prohibited by it to the States, are reserved to the States respectively, or to the people.

AMENDMENT XI (1798)

The Judicial power of the United States shall not be construed to extend to any suit in law or equity, commenced or prosecuted against one of the United States by Citizens of another State, or by Citizens or Subjects of any Foreign State.

AMENDMENT XII (1804)

The Electors shall meet in their respective states and vote by ballot for President and Vice-President, one of whom, at least, shall not be an inhabitant of the same state with themselves; they shall name in their ballots the person voted for as President, and in distinct ballots the person voted for as Vice-President, and they shall make distinct lists of all persons voted for as President, and of all persons voted for as Vice-President, and of the number of votes for each, which lists they shall sign and certify, and transmit sealed to the seat of the government of the United States, directed to the President of the Senate;—The President of the Senate shall, in the presence of the Senate and House of Representatives, open all the certificates and the votes shall then be counted;—The person having the greatest number of votes for President, shall be the President, if such number be a majority of the whole number of Electors appointed; and if no person have such majority, then from the persons having the highest numbers not exceeding three on the list of those voted for as President, the House of Representatives shall choose immediately, by ballot, the President. But in choosing the President, the votes shall be taken by states, the representation from each state

having one vote; a quorum for this purpose shall consist of a member or members from two-thirds of the states, and a majority of all the states shall be necessary to a choice. And if the House of Representatives shall not choose a President whenever the right of choice shall devolve upon them, before the fourth day of March next following, then the Vice-President shall act as President, as in the case of the death or other constitutional disability of the President—The person having the greatest number of votes as Vice-President, shall be the Vice-President, if such number be a majority of the whole number of Electors appointed, and if no person have a majority, then from the two highest numbers on the list, the Senate shall choose the Vice-President; A quorum for the purpose shall consist of two-thirds of the whole number of Senators, and a majority of the whole number shall be necessary to a choice. But no person constitutionally ineligible to the office of President shall be eligible to that of Vice-President of the United States.

AMENDMENT XIII (1865)

Section 1.

Neither slavery nor involuntary servitude, except as a punishment for crime whereof the party shall have been duly convicted, shall exist within the United States, or any place subject to their jurisdiction.

Section 2.

Congress shall have power to enforce this article by appropriate legislation.

AMENDMENT XIV (1868)

Section 1.

All persons born or naturalized in the United States and subject to the jurisdiction thereof, are citizens of the United States and of the State wherein they reside. No State shall make or enforce any law which shall abridge the privileges or immunities of citizens of the United States; nor shall any State deprive any person of life, liberty, or property, without due process of law; nor deny to any person within its jurisdiction the equal protection of the laws.

Section 2.

Representatives shall be apportioned among the several States according to their respective numbers, counting the whole number of persons in each State, excluding Indians not taxed. But when the right to vote at any election for the choice of electors for President and Vice-President of the United States, Representatives in Congress, the Executive and Judicial officers of a State, or the members of the Legislature thereof, is denied to any of the male inhabitants of such State, being twenty-one years of age, and citizens of the United States, or in any way abridged, except for participation in rebellion, or other crime, the basis of representation therein shall be reduced in the proportion which the number of such male citizens shall bear to the whole number of male citizens twenty-one years of age in such State.

Section 3.

No person shall be a Senator or Representative in Congress, or elector of President and Vice-President, or hold any office, civil or military, under the United States, or under any State, who, having previously taken an oath, as a member of Congress, or as an officer of the United States, or as a member of any State legislature, or as an executive or judicial officer of any State, to support the Constitution of the United States, shall have engaged in insurrection or rebellion against the same, or given aid or comfort to the enemies thereof. But Congress may by a vote of two-thirds of each House, remove such disability.

Section 4.

The validity of the public debt of the United States, authorized by law, including debts incurred for payment of pensions and bounties for services in suppressing insurrection or rebellion, shall not be questioned. But neither the United States nor any State shall assume or pay any debt or obligation incurred in aid of insurrection or rebellion against the United States, or any claim for the loss or emancipation of any slave; but all such debts, obligations and claims shall be held illegal and void.

Section 5.

The Congress shall have power to enforce, by appropriate legislation, the provisions of this article.

AMENDMENT XV (1870)

Section 1.

The right of citizens of the United States to vote shall not be denied or abridged by the United States or by any State on account of race, color, or previous condition of servitude.

Section 2.

The Congress shall have power to enforce this article by appropriate legislation.

AMENDMENT XVI (1913)

The Congress shall have power to lay and collect taxes on incomes, from whatever source derived, without apportionment among the several States, and without regard to any census or enumeration.

AMENDMENT XVII (1913)

The Senate of the United States shall be composed of two Senators from each State, elected by the people thereof, for six years; and each Senator shall have one vote. The electors in each State shall have the qualifications requisite for electors of the most numerous branch of the State legislatures.

When vacancies happen in the representation of any State in the Senate, the executive authority of such State shall issue writs of election to fill such vacancies: *Provided,* That the legislature of any State may empower the executive thereof to make temporary appointments until the people fill the vacancies by election as the legislature may direct.

This amendment shall not be so construed as to affect the election or term of any Senator chosen before it becomes valid as part of the Constitution.

AMENDMENT XVIII (1919)

Section 1.

After one year from the ratification of this article the manufacture, sale, or transportation of intoxicating liquors within, the importation thereof into, or the exportation thereof from the United States and all territory subject to the jurisdiction thereof for beverage purposes is hereby prohibited.

Section 2.

The Congress and the several States shall have concurrent power to enforce this article by appropriate legislation.

Section 3.

This article shall be inoperative unless it shall have been ratified as an amendment to the Constitution by the legislatures of the several States, as provided in the Constitution, within seven years from the date of the submission hereof to the States by the Congress.

AMENDMENT XIX (1920)

The right of citizens of the United States to vote shall not be denied or abridged by the United States or by any State on account of sex.

Congress shall have power to enforce this article by appropriate legislation.

AMENDMENT XX (1933)

Section 1.

The terms of the President and Vice President shall end at noon on the 20th day of January, and the terms of Senators and Representatives at noon on the 3d day of January, of the years in which such terms would have ended if this article had not been ratified; and the terms of their successors shall then begin.

Section 2.

The Congress shall assemble at least once in every year, and such meeting shall begin at noon on the 3d day of January, unless they shall by law appoint a different day.

Section 3.

If, at the time fixed for the beginning of the term of the President, the President elect shall have died, the Vice President elect shall become President. If a President shall not have been chosen before the time fixed for the beginning of his term, or if the President elect shall have failed to qualify, then the Vice President elect shall act as President until a President shall have qualified; and the Congress may by law provide for the case wherein neither a President elect nor a Vice President elect shall have qualified, declaring who shall then act as President, or the manner in which one who is to act shall be selected, and such person shall act accordingly until a President or Vice President shall have qualified.

Section 4.

The Congress may by law provide for the case of the death of any of the persons from whom the House of Representatives may choose a President whenever the right of choice shall have devolved upon them, and for the case of the death of any of the persons from whom the Senate may choose a Vice President whenever the right of choice shall have devolved upon them.

Section 5.

Sections 1 and 2 shall take effect on the 15th day of October following the ratification of this article.

Section 6.

This article shall be inoperative unless it shall have been ratified as an amendment to the Constitution by the legislatures of three-fourths of the several States within seven years from the date of its submission.

AMENDMENT XXI (1933)

Section 1.

The eighteenth article of amendment to the Constitution of the United States is hereby repealed.

Section 2.

The transportation or importation into any State, Territory or possession of the United States for delivery or use therein of intoxicating liquors, in violation of the laws thereof, is hereby prohibited.

Section 3.

This article shall be inoperative unless it shall have been ratified as an amendment to the Constitution by conventions in the several States, as provided in the Constitution, within seven years from the date of the submission hereof to the States by the Congress.

AMENDMENT XXII (1951)

Section 1.

No person shall be elected to the office of the President more than twice, and no person who has held the office of President, or acted as President, for more than two years of a term to which some other person was elected President shall be elected to the office of the President more than once. But this Article shall not apply to any person holding the office of President when this Article was proposed by the Congress, and shall not prevent any person who may be holding the office of President, or acting as President, during the term within which this Article becomes operative from holding the office of President or acting as President during the remainder of such term.

Section 2.

This Article shall be inoperative unless it shall have been ratified as an amendment to the Constitution by the legislatures of three-fourths of the several States within seven years from the date of its submission to the States by the Congress.

AMENDMENT XXIII (1961)

Section 1.

The District constituting the seat of Government of the United States shall appoint in such manner as the Congress may direct:

A number of electors of President and Vice President equal to the whole number of Senators and Representatives in Congress to which the District would be entitled if it were a State, but in no event more than the least populous State; they shall be in addition to those appointed by the States, but they shall be considered, for the purposes of the election of President and Vice President, to be electors appointed by a State; and they shall meet in the District and perform such duties as provided by the twelfth article of amendment.

Section 2.

The Congress shall have power to enforce this article by appropriate legislation.

AMENDMENT XXIV (1964)

Section 1.

The right of citizens of the United States to vote in any primary or other election for President or Vice President, for electors for President or Vice President, or for Senator or Representative in Congress, shall not be denied or abridged by the United States or any State by reason of failure to pay any poll tax or other tax.

Section 2.

The Congress shall have power to enforce this article by appropriate legislation.

AMENDMENT XXV (1967)

Section 1.

In case of the removal of the President from office or of his death or resignation, the Vice President shall become President.

Section 2.

Whenever there is a vacancy in the office of the Vice President, the President shall nominate a Vice President who shall take office upon confirmation by a majority vote of both Houses of Congress.

Section 3.

Whenever the President transmits to the President pro tempore of the Senate and the Speaker of the House of Representatives his written declaration that he is unable to discharge the powers and duties of his office, and until he transmits to them a written declaration to the contrary, such powers and duties shall be discharged by the Vice President as Acting President.

Section 4.

Whenever the Vice President and a majority of either the principal officers of the executive departments or of such other body as Congress may by law provide, transmit to the President pro tempore of the Senate and the Speaker of the House of Representatives their written declaration that the President is unable to discharge the powers and duties of his office, the Vice President shall immediately assume the powers and duties of the office as Acting President.

Thereafter, when the President transmits to the President pro tempore of the Senate and the Speaker of the House of Representatives his written declaration that no inability exists, he shall resume the powers and duties of his office unless the Vice President and a majority of either the principal officers of the executive department or of such other body as Congress may by law provide, transmit within four days to the President pro tempore of the Senate and the Speaker of the House of Representatives their written declaration that the President is unable to discharge the powers and duties of his office. Thereupon Congress shall decide the issue, assembling within forty-eight hours for that purpose if not in session. If the Congress, within twenty-one days after receipt of the latter written declaration, or, if Congress is not in session, within twenty-one days after Congress is required to assemble, determines by two-thirds vote of both Houses that the President is unable to discharge the powers and duties of his office, the Vice President shall continue to discharge the same as Acting President; otherwise, the President shall resume the powers and duties of his office.

AMENDMENT XXVI (1971)

Section 1.

The right of citizens of the United States, who are eighteen years of age or older, to vote shall not be denied or abridged by the United States or by any State on account of age.

Section 2.

The Congress shall have power to enforce this article by appropriate legislation.

AMENDMENT XXVII (1992)

No law varying the compensation for the services of the senators and representatives shall take effect, until an election of representatives shall have intervened.

APPENDIX B

Selected Excerpts from the Model Penal Code

PART I GENERAL PROVISIONS

Article 1. Preliminary

§ 1.04. Classes of Crimes; Violations.

(1) An offense defined by this Code or by any other statute of this State, for which a sentence of [death or of] imprisonment is authorized, constitutes a crime. Crimes are classified as felonies, misdemeanors or petty misdemeanors.

(2) A crime is a felony if it is so designated in this Code or if persons convicted thereof may be sentenced [to death or] to imprisonment for a term which, apart from an extended term, is in excess of one year.

(3) A crime is a misdemeanor if it is so designated in this Code or in a statute other than this Code enacted subsequent thereto.

(4) A crime is a petty misdemeanor if it is so designated in this Code or in a statute other than this Code enacted subsequent thereto or if it is defined by a statute other than this Code which now provides that persons convicted thereof may be sentenced to imprisonment for a term of which the maximum is less than one year.

(5) An offense defined by this Code or by any other statute of this State constitutes a violation if it is so designated in this Code or in the law defining the offense or if no other sentence than a fine, or fine and forfeiture or other civil penalty is authorized upon conviction or if it is defined by a statute other than this Code which now provides that the offense shall not constitute a crime. A violation does not constitute a crime and conviction of a violation shall not give rise to any disability or legal disadvantage based on conviction of a criminal offense.

(6) Any offense declared by law to constitute a crime, without specification of the grade thereof or of the sentence authorized upon conviction, is a misdemeanor.

(7) An offense defined by any statute of this State other than this Code shall be classified as provided in this Section and the sentence that may be imposed upon conviction thereof shall hereafter be governed by this Code.

§ 1.05. All Offenses Defined by Statute; Application of General Provisions of the Code.

(1) No conduct constitutes an offense unless it is a crime or violation under this Code or another statute of this State.

(2) The provisions of Part I of the Code are applicable to offenses defined by other statutes, unless the Code otherwise provides.

(3) This Section does not affect the power of a court to punish for contempt or to employ any sanction authorized by law for the enforcement of an order or a civil judgment or decree.

§ 1.12. Proof Beyond a Reasonable Doubt; Affirmative Defenses; Burden of Proving Fact When Not an Element of an Offense; Presumptions.

(1) No person may be convicted of an offense unless each element of such offense is proved beyond a reasonable doubt. In the absence of such proof, the innocence of the defendant is assumed.

(2) Subsection (1) of this Section does not:

   (a) require the disproof of an affirmative defense unless and until there is evidence supporting such defense; or

(b) apply to any defense which the Code or another statute plainly requires the defendant to prove by a preponderance of evidence.

(3) A ground of defense is affirmative, within the meaning of Subsection (2)(a) of this Section, when:

(a) it arises under a section of the Code which so provides; or

(b) it relates to an offense defined by a statute other than the Code and such statute so provides; or

(c) it involves a matter of excuse or justification peculiarly within the knowledge of the defendant on which he can fairly be required to adduce supporting evidence.

(4) When the application of the Code depends upon the finding of a fact which is not an element of an offense, unless the Code otherwise provides:

(a) the burden of proving the fact is on the prosecution or defendant, depending on whose interest or contention will be furthered if the finding should be made; and

(b) the fact must be proved to the satisfaction of the Court or jury, as the case may be.

(5) When the Code establishes a presumption with respect to any fact which is an element of an offense, it has the following consequences:

(a) when there is evidence of the facts which give rise to the presumption, the issue of the existence of the presumed fact must be submitted to the jury, unless the Court is satisfied that the evidence as a whole clearly negatives the presumed fact; and

(b) when the issue of the existence of the presumed fact is submitted to the jury, the Court shall charge that while the presumed fact must, on all the evidence, be proved beyond a reasonable doubt, the law declares that the jury may regard the facts giving rise to the presumption as sufficient evidence of the presumed fact.

(6) A presumption not established by the Code or inconsistent with it has the consequences otherwise accorded it by law.

§ 1.13. General Definitions.

In this Code, unless a different meaning plainly is required:

(1) "statute" includes the Constitution and a local law or ordinance of a political subdivision of the State;

(2) "act" or "action" means a bodily movement whether voluntary or involuntary;

(3) "voluntary" has the meaning specified in Section 2.01;

(4) "omission" means a failure to act;

(5) "conduct" means an action or omission and its accompanying state of mind, or, where relevant, a series of acts and omissions;

(6) "actor" includes, where relevant, a person guilty of an omission;

(7) "acted" includes, where relevant, "omitted to act";

(8) "person," "he" and "actor" include any natural person and, where relevant, a corporation or an unincorporated association;

(9) "element of an offense" means (i) such conduct or (ii) such attendant circumstances or (iii) such a result of conduct as

(a) is included in the description of the forbidden conduct in the definition of the offense; or

(b) establishes the required kind of culpability; or

(c) negatives an excuse or justification for such conduct; or

(d) negatives a defense under the statute of limitations; or

(e) establishes jurisdiction or venue;

(10) "material element of an offense" means an element that does not relate exclusively to the statute of limitations, jurisdiction, venue or to any other matter similarly unconnected with (i) the harm or evil, incident to conduct, sought to be prevented by the law defining the offense, or (ii) the existence of a justification or excuse for such conduct;

(11) "purposely" has the meaning specified in Section 2.02 and equivalent terms such as "with purpose," "designed" or "with design" have the same meaning;

(12) "intentionally" or "with intent" means purposely;

(13) "knowingly" has the meaning specified in Section 2.02 and equivalent terms such as "knowing" or "with knowledge" have the same meaning;

(14) "recklessly" has the meaning specified in Section 2.02 and equivalent terms such as "recklessness" or "with recklessness" have the same meaning;

(15) "negligently" has the meaning specified in Section 2.02 and equivalent terms such as "negligence" or "with negligence" have the same meaning;

(16) "reasonably believes" or "reasonable belief" designates a belief which the actor is not reckless or negligent in holding.

Article 2. General Principles of Liability

§ 2.01. Requirement of Voluntary Act; Omission as Basis of Liability; Possession as an Act.

(1) A person is not guilty of an offense unless his liability is based on conduct which includes a voluntary act or the omission to perform an act of which he is physically capable.

(2) The following are not voluntary acts within the meaning of this Section:

(a) a reflex or convulsion;

(b) a bodily movement during unconsciousness or sleep;

(c) conduct during hypnosis or resulting from hypnotic suggestion;

(d) a bodily movement that otherwise is not a product of the effort or determination of the actor, either conscious or habitual.

(3) Liability for the commission of an offense may not be based on an omission unaccompanied by action unless:

(a) the omission is expressly made sufficient by the law defining the offense; or

(b) a duty to perform the omitted act is otherwise imposed by law.

(4) Possession is an act, within the meaning of this Section, if the possessor knowingly procured or received the thing possessed or was aware of his control thereof for a sufficient period to have been able to terminate his possession.

§ 2.02. General Requirements of Culpability.

(1) *Minimum Requirements of Culpability.* Except as provided in Section 2.05, a person is not guilty of an offense unless he acted purposely, knowingly, recklessly or negligently, as the law may require, with respect to each material element of the offense.

(2) *Kinds of Culpability Defined.*

(a) *Purposely.*

A person acts purposely with respect to a material element of an offense when:

(i) if the element involves the nature of his conduct or a result thereof, it is his conscious object to engage in conduct of that nature or to cause such a result; and

(ii) if the element involves the attendant circumstances, he is aware of the existence of such circumstances or he believes or hopes that they exist.

(b) *Knowingly.*

A person acts knowingly with respect to a material element of an offense when:

(i) if the element involves the nature of his conduct or the attendant circumstances, he is aware that his conduct is of that nature or that such circumstances exist; and

(ii) if the element involves a result of his conduct, he is aware that it is practically certain that his conduct will cause such a result.

(c) *Recklessly.*

A person acts recklessly with respect to a material element of an offense when he consciously disregards a substantial and unjustifiable risk that the material element exists or will result from his conduct. The risk must be of such a nature and degree that, considering the nature and purpose of the actor's conduct and the circumstances known to him, its disregard involves a gross deviation from the standard of conduct that a law-abiding person would observe in the actor's situation.

(d) *Negligently.*

A person acts negligently with respect to a material element of an offense when he should be aware of a substantial and unjustifiable risk that the material element exists or will result from his conduct. The risk must be of such a nature and degree that the actor's failure to perceive it, considering the nature and purpose of his conduct and the circumstances known to him, involves a gross deviation from the standard of care that a reasonable person would observe in the actor's situation.

(3) *Culpability Required Unless Otherwise Provided.* When the culpability sufficient to establish a material element of an offense is not prescribed by law, such element is established if a person acts purposely, knowingly or recklessly with respect thereto.

(4) *Prescribed Culpability Requirement Applies to All Material Elements.* When the law defining an offense prescribes the kind of culpability that is sufficient for the commission of an offense, without distinguishing among the material elements thereof, such provision shall apply to

all the material elements of the offense, unless a contrary purpose plainly appears.

(5) *Substitutes for Negligence, Recklessness and Knowledge.* When the law provides that negligence suffices to establish an element of an offense, such element also is established if a person acts purposely, knowingly or recklessly. When recklessness suffices to establish an element, such element also is established if a person acts purposely or knowingly. When acting knowingly suffices to establish an element, such element also is established if a person acts purposely.

(6) *Requirement of Purpose Satisfied if Purpose Is Conditional.* When a particular purpose is an element of an offense, the element is established although such purpose is conditional, unless the condition negatives the harm or evil sought to be prevented by the law defining the offense.

(7) *Requirement of Knowledge Satisfied by Knowledge of High Probability.* When knowledge of the existence of a particular fact is an element of an offense, such knowledge is established if a person is aware of a high probability of its existence, unless he actually believes that it does not exist.

(8) *Requirement of Wilfulness Satisfied by Acting Knowingly.* A requirement that an offense be committed wilfully is satisfied if a person acts knowingly with respect to the material elements of the offense, unless a purpose to impose further requirements appears.

(9) *Culpability as to Illegality of Conduct.* Neither knowledge nor recklessness or negligence as to whether conduct constitutes an offense or as to the existence, meaning or application of the law determining the elements of an offense is an element of such offense, unless the definition of the offense or the Code so provides.

(10) *Culpability as Determinant of Grade of Offense.* When the grade or degree of an offense depends on whether the offense is committed purposely, knowingly, recklessly or negligently, its grade or degree shall be the lowest for which the determinative kind of culpability is established with respect to any material element of the offense.

§ 2.03 Causal Relationship Between Conduct and Result; Divergence Between Result Designed or Contemplated and Actual Result or Between Probable and Actual Result.

(1) Conduct is the cause of a result when:

(a) it is an antecedent but for which the result in question would not have occurred; and

(b) the relationship between the conduct and result satisfies any additional causal requirements imposed by the Code or by the law defining the offense.

(2) When purposely or knowingly causing a particular result is an element of an offense, the element is not established if the actual result is not within the purpose or the contemplation of the actor unless:

(a) the actual result differs from that designed or contemplated, as the case may be, only in the respect that a different person or different property is injured or affected or that the injury or harm designed or contemplated would have been more serious or more extensive than that caused; or

(b) the actual result involves the same kind of injury or harm as that designed or contemplated and is not too remote or accidental in its occurrence to have a [just] bearing on the actor's liability or on the gravity of his offense.

(3) When recklessly or negligently causing a particular result is an element of an offense, the element is not established if the actual result is not within the risk of which the actor is aware or, in the case of negligence, of which he should be aware unless:

(a) the actual result differs from the probable result only in the respect that a different person or different property is injured or affected or that the probable injury or harm would have been more serious or more extensive than that caused; or

(b) the actual result involves the same kind of injury or harm as the probable result and is not too remote or accidental in its occurrence to have a [just] bearing on the actor's liability or on the gravity of his offense.

(4) When causing a particular result is a material element of an offense for which absolute liability is imposed by law, the element is not established unless the actual result is a probable consequence of the actor's conduct.

§ 2.04. Ignorance or Mistake.

(1) Ignorance or mistake as to a matter of fact or law is a defense if:

(a) the ignorance or mistake negatives the purpose, knowledge, belief, recklessness or negligence required to establish a material element of the offense; or

(b) the law provides that the state of mind established by such ignorance or mistake constitutes a defense.

(2) Although ignorance or mistake would otherwise afford a defense to the offense charged, the defense is not available if the defendant would be guilty of another offense had the situation been as he supposed. In such case, however, the ignorance or mistake of the defendant shall reduce the grade and degree of the offense of which he may be convicted to those of the offense of which he would be guilty had the situation been as he supposed.

(3) A belief that conduct does not legally constitute an offense is a defense to a prosecution for that offense based upon such conduct when:

(a) the statute or other enactment defining the offense is not known to the actor and has not been published or otherwise reasonably made available prior to the conduct alleged; or

(b) he acts in reasonable reliance upon an official statement of the law, afterward determined to be invalid or erroneous, contained in (i) a statute or other enactment; (ii) a judicial decision, opinion or judgment; (iii) an administrative order or grant of permission; or (iv) an official interpretation of the public officer or body charged by law with responsibility for the interpretation, administration or enforcement of the law defining the offense.

(4) The defendant must prove a defense arising under Subsection (3) of this Section by a preponderance of evidence.

§ 2.05. When Culpability Requirements Are Inapplicable to Violations and to Offenses Defined by Other Statutes; Effect of Absolute Liability in Reducing Grade of Offense to Violation.

(1) The requirements of culpability prescribed by Sections 2.01 and 2.02 do not apply to:

(a) offenses which constitute violations, unless the requirement involved is included in the definition of the offense or the Court determines that its application is consistent with effective enforcement of the law defining the offense; or

(b) offenses defined by statutes other than the Code, insofar as a legislative purpose to impose absolute liability for such offenses or with respect to any material element thereof plainly appears.

(2) Notwithstanding any other provision of existing law and unless a subsequent statute otherwise provides:

(a) when absolute liability is imposed with respect to any material element of an offense defined by a statute other than the Code and a conviction is based upon such liability, the offense constitutes a violation; and

(b) although absolute liability is imposed by law with respect to one or more of the material elements of an offense defined by a statute other than the Code, the culpable commission of the offense may be charged and proved, in which event negligence with respect to such elements constitutes sufficient culpability and the classification of the offense and the sentence that may be imposed therefor upon conviction are determined by Section 1.04 and Article 6 of the Code.

§ 2.06. Liability for Conduct of Another; Complicity.

(1) A person is guilty of an offense if it is committed by his own conduct or by the conduct of another person for which he is legally accountable, or both.

(2) A person is legally accountable for the conduct of another person when:

(a) acting with the kind of culpability that is sufficient for the commission of the offense, he causes an innocent or irresponsible person to engage in such conduct; or

(b) he is made accountable for the conduct of such other person by the Code or by the law defining the offense; or

(c) he is an accomplice of such other person in the commission of the offense.

(3) A person is an accomplice of another person in the commission of an offense if:

(a) with the purpose of promoting or facilitating the commission of the offense, he

(i) solicits such other person to commit it; or

(ii) aids or agrees or attempts to aid such other person in planning or committing it; or

(iii) having a legal duty to prevent the commission of the offense, fails to make proper effect so to do; or

(b) his conduct is expressly declared by law to establish his complicity.

(4) When causing a particular result is an element of an offense, an accomplice in the conduct causing such

result is an accomplice in the commission of that offense, if he acts with the kind of culpability, if any, with respect to that result that is sufficient for the commission of the offense.

(5) A person who is legally incapable of committing a particular offense himself may be guilty thereof, if it is committed by the conduct of another person for which he is legally accountable, unless such liability is inconsistent with the purpose of the provision establishing his incapacity.

(6) Unless otherwise provided by the Code or by the law defining the offense, a person is not an accomplice in an offense committed by another person if:

   (a) he is a victim of that offense; or

   (b) the offense is so defined that his conduct is inevitably incident to its commission; or

   (c) he terminates his complicity prior to the commission of the offense and

      (i) wholly deprives it of effectiveness in the commission of the offense; or

      (ii) gives timely warning to the law enforcement authorities or otherwise makes proper effort to prevent the commission of the offense.

(7) An accomplice may be convicted on proof of the commission of the offense and of his complicity therein, though the person claimed to have committed the offense has not been prosecuted or convicted or has been convicted of a different offense or degree of offense or has an immunity to prosecution or conviction or has been acquitted.

§ 2.07. Liability of Corporations, Unincorporated Associations and Persons Acting, or Under a Duty to Act, in Their Behalf.

(1) A corporation may be convicted of the commission of an offense if:

   (a) the offense is a violation or the offense is defined by a statute other than the Code in which a legislative purpose to impose liability on corporations plainly appears and the conduct is performed by an agent of the corporation acting in behalf of the corporation within the scope of his office or employment, except that if the law defining the offense designates the agents for whose conduct the corporation is accountable or the circumstances under which it is accountable, such provisions shall apply; or

   (b) the offense consists of an omission to discharge a specific duty of affirmative performance imposed on corporations by law; or

   (c) the commission of the offense was authorized, requested, commanded, performed or recklessly tolerated by the board of directors or by a high managerial agent acting in behalf of the corporation within the scope of his office or employment.

(2) When absolute liability is imposed for the commission of an offense, a legislative purpose to impose liability on a corporation shall be assumed, unless the contrary plainly appears.

(3) An unincorporated association may be convicted of the commission of an offense if:

   (a) the offense is defined by a statute other than the Code which expressly provides for the liability of such an association and the conduct is performed by an agent of the association acting in behalf of the association within the scope of his office or employment, except that if the law defining the offense designates the agents for whose conduct the association is accountable or the circumstances under which it is accountable, such provisions shall apply; or

   (b) the offense consists of an omission to discharge a specific duty of affirmative performance imposed on associations by law.

(4) As used in this Section:

   (a) "corporation" does not include an entity organized as or by a governmental agency for the execution of a governmental program;

   (b) "agent" means any director, officer, servant, employee or other person authorized to act in behalf of the corporation or association and, in the case of an unincorporated association, a member of such association;

   (c) "high managerial agent" means an officer of a corporation or an unincorporated association, or, in the case of a partnership, a partner, or any other agent of a corporation or association having duties of such responsibilities that his conduct may fairly be assumed to represent the policy of the corporation or association.

(5) In any prosecution of a corporation or an unincorporated association for the commission of an offense included within the terms of Subsection (1)(a) or

Subsection (3)(a) of this Section, other than an offense for which absolute liability has been imposed, it shall be a defense if the defendant proves by a preponderance of evidence that the high managerial agent having supervisory responsibility over the subject matter of the offense employed due diligence to prevent its commission. This paragraph shall not apply if it is plainly inconsistent with the legislative purpose in defining the particular offense.

(6) (a) A person is legally accountable for any conduct he performs or causes to be performed in the name of the corporation or an unincorporated association or in its behalf to the same extent as if it were performed in his own name or be half.

    (b) Whenever a duty to act is imposed by law upon a corporation or an unincorporated association, any agent of the corporation or association having primary responsibility for the discharge of the duty is legally accountable for a reckless omission to perform the required act to the same extent as if the duty were imposed by law directly upon himself.

    (c) When a person is convicted of an offense by reason of his legal accountability for the conduct of a corporation or an unincorporated association, he is subject to the sentence authorized by law when a natural person is convicted of an offense of the grade and the degree involved.

§ 2.08 Intoxication.

(1) Except as provided in Subsection (4) of this Section, intoxication of the actor is not a defense unless it negatives an element of the offense.

(2) When recklessness establishes an element of the offense, if the actor, due to self-induced intoxication, is unaware of a risk of which he would have been aware had he been sober, such unawareness is immaterial.

(3) Intoxication does not, in itself, constitute mental disease within the meaning of Section 4.01.

(4) Intoxication which (a) is not self-induced or (b) is pathological is an affirmative defense if by reason of such intoxication the actor at the time of his conduct lacks substantial capacity either to appreciate its criminality [wrongfulness] or to conform his conduct to the requirements of law.

(5) *Definitions.* In this Section unless a different meaning plainly is required:

    (a) "intoxication" means a disturbance of mental or physical capacities resulting from the introduction of substances into the body;

    (b) "self-induced intoxication" means intoxication caused by substances which the actor knowingly introduces into his body, the tendency of which to cause intoxication he knows or ought to know, unless he introduces them pursuant to medical advice or under such circumstances as would afford a defense to a charge of crime;

    (c) "pathological intoxication" means intoxication grossly excessive in degree, given the amount of the intoxicant, to which the actor does not know he is susceptible.

§ 2.09 Duress.

(1) It is an affirmative defense that the actor engaged in the conduct charged to constitute an offense because he was coerced to do so by the use of, or a threat to use, unlawful force against his person or the person of another, which a person of reasonable firmness in his situation would have been unable to resist.

(2) The defense provided by this Section is unavailable if the actor recklessly placed himself in a situation in which it was probable that he would be subjected to duress. The defense is also unavailable if he was negligent in placing himself in such a situation, whenever negligence suffices to establish culpability for the offense charged.

(3) It is not a defense that a woman acted on the command of her husband, unless she acted under such coercion as would establish a defense under this Section. [The presumption that a woman, acting in the presence of her husband, is coerced is abolished.]

(4) When the conduct of the actor would otherwise be justifiable under Section 3.02, this Section does not preclude such defense.

§ 2.10. Military Orders.

It is an affirmative defense that the actor, in engaging in the conduct charged to constitute an offense, does no more than execute an order of his superior in the armed services which he does not know to be unlawful.

§ 2.11. Consent.

(1) *In General.* The consent of the victim to conduct charged to constitute an offense or to the result thereof

is a defense if such consent negatives an element of the offense or precludes the infliction of the harm or evil sought to be prevented by the law defining the offense.

(2) *Consent to Bodily Harm.* When conduct is charged to constitute an offense because it causes or threatens bodily harm, consent to such conduct or to the infliction of such harm is a defense if:

  (a) the bodily harm consented to or threatened by the conduct consented to is not serious; or

  (b) the conduct and the harm are reasonably foreseeable hazards of joint participation in a lawful athletic contest or competitive sport; or

  (c) the consent establishes a justification for the conduct under Article 3 of the Code.

(3) *Ineffective Consent.* Unless otherwise provided by the Code or by the law defining the offense, assent does not constitute consent if:

  (a) it is given by a person who is legally incompetent to authorize the conduct charged to constitute the offense; or

  (b) it is given by a person who by reason of youth, mental disease or defect or intoxication is manifestly unable or known by the actor to be unable to make a reasonable judgment as to the nature or harmfulness of the conduct charged to constitute the offense; or

  (c) it is given by a person whose improvident consent is sought to be prevented by the law defining the offense; or

  (d) it is induced by force, duress or deception of a kind sought to be prevented by the law defining the offense.

§ 2.13. Entrapment.

(1) A public law enforcement official or a person acting in cooperation with such an official perpetrates an entrapment if for the purpose of obtaining evidence of the commission of an offense, he induces or encourages another person to engage in conduct constituting such offense by either:

  (a) making knowingly false representations designed to induce the belief that such conduct is not prohibited; or

  (b) employing methods of persuasion or inducement which create a substantial risk that such an offense will be committed by persons other than those who are ready to commit it.

(2) Except as provided in Subsection (3) of this Section, a person prosecuted for an offense shall be acquitted if he proves by a preponderance of evidence that his conduct occurred in response to an entrapment. The issue of entrapment shall be tried by the Court in the absence of the jury.

(3) The defense afforded by this Section is unavailable when causing or threatening bodily injury is an element of the offense charged and the prosecution is based on conduct causing or threatening such injury to a person other than the person perpetrating the entrapment.

Article 3. General Principles of Justification

§ 3.01. Justification an Affirmative Defense; Civil Remedies Unaffected.

(1) In any prosecution based on conduct which is justifiable under this Article, justification is an affirmative defense.

(2) The fact that conduct is justifiable under this Article does not abolish or impair any remedy for such conduct which is available in any civil action.

§ 3.02. Justification Generally: Choice of Evils.

(1) Conduct which the actor believes to be necessary to avoid harm or evil to himself or to another is justifiable, provided that:

  (a) the harm or evil sought to be avoided by such conduct is greater than that sought to be prevented by the law defining the offense charged; and

  (b) neither the Code nor other law defining the offense provides exceptions or defenses dealing with the specific situation involved; and

  (c) a legislative purpose to exclude the justification claimed does not otherwise plainly appear.

(2) When the actor was reckless or negligent in bringing about the situation requiring a choice of harms or evils or in appraising the necessity for his conduct, the justification afforded by this Section is unavailable in a prosecution for any offense for which recklessness or negligence, as the case may be, suffices to establish culpability.

§ 3.03. Execution of Public Duty.

(1) Except as provided in Subsection (2) of this Section, conduct is justifiable when it is required or authorized by:

  (a) the law defining the duties or functions of a public officer or the assistance to be rendered to such officer in the performance of his duties; or

(b) the law governing the execution of legal process; or

(c) the judgment or order of a competent court or tribunal; or

(d) the law governing the armed services or the lawful conduct of war; or

(e) any other provision of law imposing a public duty.

(2) The other sections of this Article apply to:

(a) the use of force upon or toward the person of another for any of the purposes dealt with in such sections; and

(b) the use of deadly force for any purpose, unless the use of such force is otherwise expressly authorized by law or occurs in the lawful conduct of war.

(3) The justification afforded by Subsection (1) of this Section applies:

(a) when the actor believes his conduct to be required or authorized by the judgment or direction of a competent court or tribunal or in the lawful execution of legal process, notwithstanding lack of jurisdiction of the court or defect in the legal process; and

(b) when the actor believes his conduct to be required or authorized to assist a public officer in the performance of his duties, notwithstanding that the officer exceeded his legal authority.

§ 3.04. Use of Force in Self-Protection.

(1) *Use of Force Justifiable for Protection of the Person.* Subject to the provisions of this Section and of Section 3.09, the use of force upon or toward another person is justifiable when the actor believes that such force is immediately necessary for the purpose of protecting himself against the use of unlawful force by such other person on the present occasion.

(2) *Limitations on Justifying Necessity for Use of Force.*

(a) The use of force is not justifiable under this Section:

(i) to resist arrest which the actor knows is being made by a peace officer, although the arrest is unlawful; or

(ii) to resist force used by the occupier or possessor of property or by another person on his behalf, where the actor knows that the person using the force is doing so under a claim of right to protect the property, except that this limitation shall not apply if:

(1) the actor is a public officer acting in the performance of his duties or a person lawfully assisting him therein or a person making or assisting in a lawful arrest; or

(2) the actor has been unlawfully dispossessed of the property and is making a re-entry or recaption justified by Section 3.06; or

(3) the actor believes that such force is necessary to protect himself against death or serious bodily harm.

(b) The use of deadly force is not justifiable under this Section unless the actor believes that such force is necessary to protect himself against death, serious bodily harm, kidnapping or sexual intercourse compelled by force or threat; nor is it justifiable if:

(i) the actor, with the purpose of causing death or serious bodily harm, provoked the use of force against himself in the same encounter; or

(ii) the actor knows that he can avoid the necessity of using such force with complete safety by retreating or by surrendering possession of a thing to a person asserting a claim of right thereto or by complying with a demand that he abstain from any action which he has no duty to take, except that:

(1) the actor is not obliged to retreat from his dwelling or place of work, unless he was the initial aggressor or is assailed in his place of work by another person whose place of work the actor knows it to be; and

(2) a public officer justified in using force in the performance of his duties or a person justified in using force in his assistance or a person justified in using force in making an arrest or preventing an escape is not obliged to desist from efforts to perform such duty, effect such arrest or prevent such escape because of resistance or threatened resistance by or on behalf of the person against whom such action is directed.

(c) Except as required by paragraphs (a) and (b) of this Subsection, a person employing protective force may estimate the necessity thereof under the circumstances as he believes them to be when the force is used, without retreating, surrendering possession, doing any other act which he has no legal duty to do or abstaining from any lawful action.

(3) *Use of Confinement as Protective Force.* The justification afforded by this Section extends to the use of confinement as protective force only if the actor takes all reasonable measures to terminate the confinement as soon as he knows that he safely can, unless the person confined has been arrested on a charge of crime.

§ 3.05. Use of Force for the Protection of Other Persons.

(1) Subject to the provisions of this Section and of Section 3.09, the use of force upon or toward the person of another is justifiable to protect a third person when:

  (a) the actor would be justified under Section 3.04 in using such force to protect himself against the injury he believes to be threatened to the person whom he seeks to protect; and

  (b) under the circumstances as the actor believes them to be, the person whom he seeks to protect would be justified in using such protective force; and

  (c) the actor believes that his intervention is necessary for the protection of such other person.

(2) Notwithstanding Subsection (1) of this Section:

  (a) when the actor would be obliged under Section 3.04 to retreat, to surrender the possession of a thing or to comply with a demand before using force in self-protection, he is not obliged to do so before using force for the protection of another person, unless he knows that he can thereby secure the complete safety of such other person; and

  (b) when the person whom the actor seeks to protect would be obliged under Section 3.04 to retreat, to surrender the possession of a thing or to comply with a demand if he knew that he could obtain complete safety by so doing, the actor is obliged to try to cause him to do so before using force in his protection if the actor knows that he can obtain complete safety in that way; and

  (c) neither the actor nor the person whom he seeks to protect is obliged to retreat when in the other's dwelling or place of work to any greater extent than in his own.

§ 3.06. Use of Force for the Protection of Property.

(1) *Use of Force Justifiable for Protection of Property.* Subject to the provisions of this Section and of Section 3.09,

the use of force upon or toward the person of another is justifiable when the actor believes that such force is immediately necessary:

  (a) to prevent or terminate an unlawful entry or other trespass upon land or a trespass against or the unlawful carrying away of tangible, movable property, provided that such land or movable property is, or is believed by the actor to be, in his possession or in the possession of another person for whose protection he acts; or

  (b) to effect an entry or re-entry upon land or to retake tangible movable property, provided that the actor believes that he or the person by whose authority he acts or a person from whom he or such other person derives title was unlawfully dispossessed of such land or movable property and is entitled to possession, and provided, further, that:

    (i) the force is used immediately or on fresh pursuit after such dispossession; or

    (ii) the actor believes that the person against whom he uses force has no claim of right to the possession of the property and, in the case of land, the circumstances, as the actor believes them to be, are of such urgency that it would be an exceptional hardship to postpone the entry or re-entry until a court order is obtained.

(2) *Meaning of Possession.* For the purposes of Subsection (1) of this Section:

  (a) a person who has parted with the custody of property to another who refuses to restore it to him is no longer in possession, unless the property is movable and was and still is located on land in his possession;

  (b) a person who has been dispossessed of land does not regain possession thereof merely by setting foot thereon;

  (c) a person who has a license to use or occupy real property is deemed to be in possession thereof except against the licensor acting under claim of right.

(3) *Limitations on Justifiable Use of Force.*

  (a) *Request to Desist.* The use of force is justifiable under this Section only if the actor first requests the person against whom such force is used to desist from his interference with the property, unless the actor believes that:

    (i) such request would be useless; or

(ii) it would be dangerous to himself or another person to make the request; or

(iii) substantial harm will be done to the physical condition of the property which is sought to be protected before the request can effectively be made.

(b) *Exclusion of Trespasser*. The use of force to prevent or terminate a trespass is not justifiable under this Section if the actor knows that the exclusion of the trespasser will expose him to substantial danger of serious bodily harm.

(c) *Resistance of Lawful Re-entry or Recaption*. The use of force to prevent an entry or re-entry upon land or the recaption of movable property is not justifiable under this Section, although the actor believes that such re-entry or recaption is unlawful, if:

(i) the re-entry or recaption is made by or on behalf of a person who was actually dispossessed of the property; and

(ii) it is otherwise justifiable under paragraph (1)(b) of this Section.

(d) *Use of Deadly Force*. The use of deadly force is not justifiable under this Section unless the actor believes that:

(i) the person against whom the force is used is attempting to dispossess him of his dwelling otherwise than under a claim of right to its possession; or

(ii) the person against whom the force is used is attempting to commit or consummate arson, burglary, robbery or other felonious theft or property destruction and either:

(1) has employed or threatened deadly force against or in the presence of the actor; or

(2) the use of force other than deadly force to prevent the commission or the consummation of the crime would expose the actor or another in his presence to substantial danger of serious bodily harm.

(4) *Use of Confinement as Protective Force*. The justification afforded by this Section extends to the use of confinement as protective force only if the actor takes all reasonable measures to terminate the confinement as soon as he knows that he can do so with safety to the property, unless the person confined has been arrested on a charge of crime.

(5) *Use of Device to Protect Property*. The justification afforded by this Section extends to the use of a device for the purpose of protecting property only if:

(a) the device is not designed to cause or known to create a substantial risk of causing death or serious bodily harm; and

(b) the use of the particular device to protect the property from entry or trespass is reasonable under the circumstances, as the actor believes them to be; and

(c) the device is one customarily used for such a purpose or reasonable care is taken to make known to probable intruders the fact that it is used.

(6) *Use of Force to Pass Wrongful Obstructor*. The use of force to pass a person whom the actor believes to be purposely or knowingly and unjustifiably obstructing the actor from going to a place to which he may lawfully go is justifiable, provided that:

(a) the actor believes that the person against whom he uses force has no claim of right to obstruct the actor; and

(b) the actor is not being obstructed from entry or movement on land which he knows to be in the possession or custody of the person obstructing him, or in the possession or custody of another person by whose authority the obstructor acts, unless the circumstances, as the actor believes them to be, are of such urgency that it would not be reasonable to postpone the entry or movement on such land until a court order is obtained; and

(c) the force used is not greater than would be justifiable if the person obstructing the actor were using force against him to prevent his passage.

§ 3.07. Use of Force in Law Enforcement.

(1) *Use of Force Justifiable to Effect an Arrest*. Subject to the provisions of this Section and of Section 3.09, the use of force upon or toward the person of another is justifiable when the actor is making or assisting in making an arrest and the actor believes that such force is immediately necessary to effect a lawful arrest.

(2) *Limitations on the Use of Force*.

(a) The use of force is not justifiable under this Section unless:

(i) the actor makes known the purpose of the arrest or believes that it is otherwise known by or cannot reasonably be made known to the person to be arrested; and

(ii) when the arrest is made under a warrant, the warrant is valid or believed by the actor to be valid.

(b) The use of deadly force is not justifiable under this Section unless:

(i) the arrest is for a felony; and

(ii) the person effecting the arrest is authorized to act as a peace officer or is assisting a person whom he believes to be authorized to act as a peace officer; and

(iii) the actor believes that the force employed creates no substantial risk of injury to innocent persons; and

(iv) the actor believes that:

(1) the crime for which the arrest is made involved conduct including the use or threatened use of deadly force; or

(2) there is a substantial risk that the person to be arrested will cause death or serious bodily harm if his apprehension is delayed.

(3) *Use of Force to Prevent Escape from Custody.* The use of force to prevent the escape of an arrested person from custody is justifiable when the force could justifiably have been employed to effect the arrest under which the person is in custody, except that a guard or other person authorized to act as a peace officer is justified in using any force, including deadly force, which he believes to be immediately necessary to prevent the escape of a person from a jail, prison, or other institution for the detention of persons charged with or convicted of a crime.

(4) *Use of Force by Private Person Assisting an Unlawful Arrest.*

(a) A private person who is summoned by a peace officer to assist in effecting an unlawful arrest, is justified in using any force which he would be justified in using if the arrest were lawful, provided that he does not believe the arrest is unlawful.

(b) A private person who assists another private person in effecting an unlawful arrest, or who, not being summoned, assists a peace officer in effecting an unlawful arrest, is justified in using any force which he would be justified in using if the arrest were lawful, provided that (i) he believes the arrest is lawful, and (ii) the arrest would be lawful if the facts were as he believes them to be.

(5) *Use of Force to Prevent Suicide or the Commission of a Crime.*

(a) The use of force upon or toward the person of another is justifiable when the actor believes that such force is immediately necessary to prevent such other person from committing suicide, inflicting serious bodily harm upon himself, committing or consummating the commission of a crime involving or threatening bodily harm, damage to or loss of property or a breach of the peace, except that:

(i) any limitations imposed by the other provisions of this Article on the justifiable use of force in self-protection, for the protection of others, the protection of property, the effectuation of an arrest or the prevention of an escape from custody shall apply notwithstanding the criminality of the conduct against which such force is used; and

(ii) the use of deadly force is not in any event justifiable under this Subsection unless:

(1) the actor believes that there is a substantial risk that the person whom he seeks to prevent from committing a crime will cause death or serious bodily harm to another unless the commission or the consummation of the crime is prevented and that the use of such force presents no substantial risk of injury to innocent persons; or

(2) the actor believes that the use of such force is necessary to suppress a riot or mutiny after the rioters or mutineers have been ordered to disperse and warned, in any particular manner that the law may require, that such force will be used if they do not obey.

(b) The justification afforded by this Subsection extends to the use of confinement as preventive force only if the actor takes all reasonable measures to terminate the confinement as soon as he knows that he safely can, unless the person confined has been arrested on a charge of crime.

Article 4. Responsibility

§ 4.01. Mental Disease or Defect Excluding Responsibility.

(1) A person is not responsible for criminal conduct if at the time of such conduct as a result of mental disease or defect he lacks substantial capacity either to appreciate the

criminality [wrongfulness] of his conduct or to conform his conduct to the requirements of law.

(2) As used in this Article, the terms "mental disease or defect" do not include an abnormality manifested only by repeated criminal or otherwise antisocial conduct.

§ 4.02. Evidence of Mental Disease or Defect Admissible When Relevant to Element of the Offense; [Mental Disease or Defect Impairing Capacity as Ground for Mitigation of Punishment in Capital Cases].

(1) Evidence that the defendant suffered from a mental disease or defect is admissible whenever it is relevant to prove that the defendant did or did not have a state of mind which is an element of the offense.

(2) Whenever the jury or the Court is authorized to determine or to recommend whether or not the defendant shall be sentenced to death or imprisonment upon conviction, evidence that the capacity of the defendant to appreciate the criminality [wrongfulness] of his conduct or to conform his conduct to the requirements of law was impaired as a result of mental disease or defect is admissible in favor of sentence of imprisonment.]

§ 4.03. Mental Disease or Defect Excluding Responsibility Is Affirmative Defense; Requirement of Notice; Form of Verdict and Judgment When Finding of Irresponsibility Is Made.

(1) Mental disease or defect excluding responsibility is an affirmative defense.

(2) Evidence of mental disease or defect excluding responsibility is not admissible unless the defendant, at the time of entering his plea of not guilty or within ten days thereafter or at such later time as the Court may for good cause permit, files a written notice of his purpose to rely on such defense.

(3) When the defendant is acquitted on the ground of mental disease or defect excluding responsibility, the verdict and the judgment shall so state.

§ 4.04. Mental Disease or Defect Excluding Fitness to Proceed.

No person who as a result of mental disease or defect lacks capacity to understand the proceedings against him or to assist in his own defense shall be tried, convicted or sentenced for the commission of an offense so long as such incapacity endures.

§ 4.05. Psychiatric Examination of Defendant with Respect to Mental Disease or Defect.

(1) Whenever the defendant has filed a notice of intention to rely on the defense of mental disease or defect excluding responsibility, or there is reason to doubt his fitness to proceed, or reason to believe that mental disease or defect of the defendant will otherwise become an issue in the cause, the Court shall appoint at least one qualified psychiatrist or shall request the Superintendent of the ___ Hospital to designate at least one qualified psychiatrist, which designation may be or include himself, to examine and report upon the mental condition of the defendant. The Court may order the defendant to be committed to a hospital or other suitable facility for the purpose of the examination for a period of not exceeding sixty days or such longer period as the Court determines to be necessary for the purpose and may direct that a qualified psychiatrist retained by the defendant be permitted to witness and participate in the examination.

(2) In such examination any method may be employed which is accepted by the medical profession for the examination of those alleged to be suffering from mental disease or defect.

(3) The report of the examination shall include the following: (a) a description of the nature of the examination; (b) a diagnosis of the mental condition of the defendant; (c) if the defendant suffers from a mental disease or defect, an opinion as to his capacity to understand the proceedings against him and to assist in his own defense; (d) when a notice of intention to rely on the defense of irresponsibility has been filed, an opinion as to the extent, if any, to which the capacity of the defendant to appreciate the criminality [wrongfulness] of his conduct or to conform his conduct to the requirements of law was impaired at the time of the criminal conduct charged; and (e) when directed by the Court, an opinion as to the capacity of the defendant to have a particular state of mind which is an element of the offense charged.

If the examination can not be conducted by reason of the unwillingness of the defendant to participate therein, the report shall so state and shall include, if possible, an opinion as to whether such unwillingness of the defendant was the result of mental disease or defect.

The report of the examination shall be filed [in triplicate] with the clerk of the Court, who shall cause copies to be delivered to the district attorney and to counsel for the defendant.

§ 4.08. Legal Effect of Acquittal on the Ground of Mental Disease or Defect Excluding Responsibility; Commitment; Release or Discharge.

(1) When a defendant is acquitted on the ground of mental disease or defect excluding responsibility, the Court shall order him to be committed to the custody of the Commissioner of Mental Hygiene [Public Health] to be placed in an appropriate institution for custody, care and treatment.

(2) If the Commissioner of Mental Hygiene [Public Health] is of the view that a person committed to his custody, pursuant to paragraph (1) of this Section, may be discharged or released on condition without danger to himself or to others, he shall make application for the discharge or release of such person in a report to the Court by which such person was committed and shall transmit a copy of such application and report to the prosecuting attorney of the county [parish] from which the defendant was committed. The Court shall thereupon appoint at least two qualified psychiatrists to examine such person and to report within sixty days, or such longer period as the Court determines to be necessary for the purpose, their opinion as to his mental condition. To facilitate such examination and the proceedings thereon, the Court may cause such person to be confined in any institution located near the place where the Court sits, which may hereafter be designated by the Commissioner of Mental Hygiene [Public Health] as suitable for the temporary detention of irresponsible persons.

(3) If the Court is satisfied by the report filed pursuant to paragraph (2) of this Section and such testimony of the reporting psychiatrists as the Court deems necessary that the committed person may be discharged or released on condition without danger to himself or others, the Court shall order his discharge or his release on such conditions as the Court determines to be necessary. If the Court is not so satisfied, it shall promptly order a hearing to determine whether such person may safely be discharged or released. Any such hearing shall be deemed a civil proceeding and the burden shall be upon the committed person to prove that he may safely be discharged or released. According to the determination of the Court upon the hearing, the committed person shall thereupon be discharged or released on such conditions as the Court determines to be necessary, or shall be recommitted to the custody of the Commissioner of Mental Hygiene [Public Health], subject to discharge or release only in accordance with the procedure prescribed above for a first hearing.

(4) If, within [five] years after the conditional release of a committed person, the Court shall determine, after hearing evidence, that the conditions of release have not been fulfilled and that for the safety of such person or for the safety of others his conditional release should be revoked, the Court shall forthwith order him to be recommitted to the Commissioner of Mental Hygiene [Public Health], subject to discharge or release only in accordance with the procedure prescribed above for a first hearing.

(5) A committed person may make application for his discharge or release to the Court by which he was committed, and the procedure to be followed upon such application shall be the same as that prescribed above in the case of an application by the Commissioner of Mental Hygiene [Public Health]. However, no such application by a committed person need be considered until he has been confined for a period of not less than [six months] from the date of the order of commitment, and if the determination of the Court be adverse to the application, such person shall not be permitted to file a further application until [one year] has elapsed from the date of any preceding hearing on an application for his release or discharge.

§ 4.09. Statements for Purposes of Examination or Treatment Inadmissible Except on Issue of Mental Condition.

A statement made by a person subjected to psychiatric examination or treatment pursuant to Sections 4.05, 4.06 or 4.08 for purposes of such examination or treatment shall not be admissible in evidence against him in any criminal proceeding on any issue other than that of his mental condition but it shall be admissible upon that issue, whether or not it would otherwise be deemed a privileged communication [,unless such statement constitutes an admission of guilt of the crime charged].

§ 4.10. Immaturity Excluding Criminal Conviction; Transfer of Proceedings to Juvenile Court.

(1) A person shall not be tried for or convicted of an offense if:

(a) at the time of the conduct charged to constitute the offense he was less than sixteen years of age [, in which case the Juvenile Court shall have exclusive jurisdiction]; or

(b) at the time of the conduct charged to constitute the offense he was sixteen or seventeen years of age, unless:

    (i) the Juvenile Court has no jurisdiction over him, or,

    (ii) the Juvenile Court has entered an order waiving jurisdiction and consenting to the institution of criminal proceedings against him.

(2) No court shall have jurisdiction to try or convict a person of an offense if criminal proceedings against him are barred by Subsection (1) of this Section. When it appears that a person charged with the commission of an offense may be of such an age that criminal proceedings may be barred under Subsection (1) of this Section, the Court shall hold a hearing thereon, and the burden shall be on the prosecution to establish to the satisfaction of the Court that the criminal proceeding is not barred upon such grounds. If the Court determines that the proceeding is barred, custody of the person charged shall be surrendered to the Juvenile Court, and the case, including all papers and processes relating thereto, shall be transferred.

Article 5. Inchoate Crimes

§ 5.01. Criminal Attempt.

(1) *Definition of Attempt.* A person is guilty of an attempt to commit a crime if, acting with the kind of culpability otherwise required for commission of the crime, he:

    (a) purposely engages in conduct which would constitute the crime if the attendant circumstances were as he believes them to be; or

    (b) when causing a particular result is an element of the crime, does or omits to do anything with the purpose of causing or with the belief that it will cause such result without further conduct on his part; or

    (c) purposely does or omits to do anything which, under the circumstances as he believes them to be, is an act or omission constituting a substantial step in a course of conduct planned to culminate in his commission of the crime.

(2) *Conduct Which May Be Held Substantial Step Under Subsection (1)(c).* Conduct shall not be held to constitute a substantial step under Subsection (1)(c) of this Section unless it is strongly corroborative of the actor's criminal purpose. Without negativing the sufficiency of other conduct, the following, if strongly corroborative of the actor's criminal purpose, shall not be held insufficient as a matter of law:

    (a) lying in wait, searching for or following the contemplated victim of the crime;

    (b) enticing or seeking to entice the contemplated victim of the crime to go to the place contemplated for its commission;

    (c) reconnoitering the place contemplated for the commission of the crime;

    (d) unlawful entry of a structure, vehicle or enclosure in which it is contemplated that the crime will be committed;

    (e) possession of materials to be employed in the commission of the crime, which are specially designed for such unlawful use or which can serve no lawful purpose of the actor under the circumstances;

    (f) possession, collection or fabrication of materials to be employed in the commission of the crime, at or near the place contemplated for its commission, where such possession, collection or fabrication serves no lawful purpose of the actor under the circumstances;

    (g) soliciting an innocent agent to engage in conduct constituting an element of the crime.

(3) *Conduct Designed to Aid Another in Commission of a Crime.* A person who engages in conduct designed to aid another to commit a crime which would establish his complicity under Section 2.06 if the crime were committed by such other person, is guilty of an attempt to commit the crime, although the crime is not committed or attempted by such other person.

(4) *Renunciation of Criminal Purpose.* When the actor's conduct would otherwise constitute an attempt under Subsection (1)(b) or (1)(c) of this Section, it is an affirmative defense that he abandoned his effort to commit the crime or otherwise prevented its commission, under circumstances manifesting a complete and voluntary renunciation of his criminal purpose. The establishment of such defense does not, however, affect the liability of an accomplice who did not join in such abandonment or prevention.

Within the meaning of this Article, renunciation of criminal purpose is not voluntary if it is motivated, in whole or in part, by circumstances, not present or apparent at the inception of the actor's course of conduct, which increase the probability of detection or apprehension or which make more difficult the accomplishment of the criminal purpose. Renunciation is not complete if it is motivated by a decision to postpone the criminal conduct until a more advantageous time or to transfer the criminal effort to another but similar objective or victim.

§ 5.02. Criminal Solicitation.

(1) *Definition of Solicitation.* A person is guilty of solicitation to commit a crime if with the purpose of promoting or facilitating its commission he commands, encourages or requests another person to engage in specific conduct which would constitute such crime or an attempt to commit such crime or which would establish his complicity in its commission or attempted commission.

(2) *Uncommunicated Solicitation.* It is immaterial under Subsection (1) of this Section that the actor fails to communicate with the person he solicits to commit a crime if his conduct was designed to effect such communication.

(3) *Renunciation of Criminal Purpose.* It is an affirmative defense that the actor, after soliciting another person to commit a crime, persuaded him not to do so or otherwise prevented the commission of the crime, under circumstances manifesting a complete and voluntary renunciation of his criminal purpose.

§ 5.03. Criminal Conspiracy.

(1) *Definition of Conspiracy.* A person is guilty of conspiracy with another person or persons to commit a crime if with the purpose of promoting or facilitating its commission he:

(a) agrees with such other person or persons that they or one or more of them will engage in conduct which constitutes such crime or an attempt or solicitation to commit such crime; or

(b) agrees to aid such other person or persons in the planning or commission of such crime or of an attempt or solicitation to commit such crime.

(2) *Scope of Conspiratorial Relationship.* If a person guilty of conspiracy, as defined by Subsection (1) of this Section, knows that a person with whom he conspires to commit a crime has conspired with another person or persons to commit the same crime, he is guilty of conspiring with such other person or persons, whether or not he knows their identity, to commit such crime.

(3) *Conspiracy With Multiple Criminal Objectives.* If a person conspires to commit a number of crimes, he is guilty of

only one conspiracy so long as such multiple crimes are the object of the same agreement or continuous conspiratorial relationship.

(4) *Joinder and Venue in Conspiracy Prosecutions.*

(a) Subject to the provisions of paragraph (b) of this Subsection, two or more persons charged with criminal conspiracy may be prosecuted jointly if:

(i) they are charged with conspiring with one another; or

(ii) the conspiracies alleged, whether they have the same or different parties, are so related that they constitute different aspects of a scheme of organized criminal conduct.

(b) In any joint prosecution under paragraph (a) of this Subsection:

(i) no defendant shall be charged with a conspiracy in any county [parish or district] other than one in which he entered into such conspiracy or in which an overt act pursuant to such conspiracy was done by him or by a person with whom he conspired; and

(ii) neither the liability of any defendant nor the admissibility against him of evidence of acts or declarations of another shall be enlarged by such joinder; and

(iii) the Court shall order a severance or take a special verdict as to any defendant who so requests, if it deems it necessary or appropriate to promote the fair determination of his guilt or innocence, and shall take any other proper measures to protect the fairness of the trial.

(5) *Overt Act.* No person may be convicted of conspiracy to commit a crime, other than a felony of the first or second degree, unless an overt act in pursuance of such conspiracy is alleged and proved to have been done by him or by a person with whom he conspired.

(6) *Renunciation of Criminal Purpose.* It is an affirmative defense that the actor, after conspiring to commit a crime, thwarted the success of the conspiracy, under circumstances manifesting a complete and voluntary renunciation of his criminal purpose.

(7) *Duration of Conspiracy.* For purposes of Section 1.06(4):

(a) conspiracy is a continuing course of conduct which terminates when the crime or crimes which are its object are committed or the agreement that they be committed is abandoned by the defendant and by those with whom he conspired; and

(b) such abandonment is presumed if neither the defendant nor anyone with whom he conspired does any overt act in pursuance of the conspiracy during the applicable period of limitation; and

(c) if an individual abandons the agreement, the conspiracy is terminated as to him only if and when he advises those with whom he conspired of his abandonment or he informs the law enforcement authorities of the existence of the conspiracy and of his participation therein.

§ 5.04. Incapacity, Irresponsibility or Immunity of Party to Solicitation or Conspiracy.

(1) Except as provided in Subsection (2) of this Section, it is immaterial to the liability of a person who solicits or conspires with another to commit a crime that:

(a) he or the person whom he solicits or with whom he conspires does not occupy a particular position or have a particular characteristic which is an element of such crime, if he believes that one of them does; or

(b) the person whom he solicits or with whom he conspires is irresponsible or has an immunity to prosecution or conviction for the commission of the crime.

(2) It is a defense to a charge of solicitation or conspiracy to commit a crime that if the criminal object were achieved, the actor would not be guilty of a crime under the law defining the offense or as an accomplice under Section 2.06(5) or 2.06(6)(a) or (b).

§ 5.05. Grading of Criminal Attempt, Solicitation and Conspiracy; Mitigation in Cases of Lesser Danger; Multiple Convictions Barred.

(1) *Grading.* Except as otherwise provided in this Section, attempt, solicitation and conspiracy are crimes of the same grade and degree as the most serious offense which is attempted or solicited or is an object of the conspiracy. An attempt, solicitation or conspiracy to commit a [capital crime or a] felony of the first degree is a felony of the second degree.

(2) *Mitigation.* If the particular conduct charged to constitute a criminal attempt, solicitation or conspiracy is so inherently unlikely to result or culminate in the commission of a crime that neither such conduct nor the actor presents a public danger warranting the grading of such offense under this Section, the Court shall exercise its power under Section 6.12 to enter judgment and impose sentence for a crime of lower grade or degree or, in extreme cases, may dismiss the prosecution.

(3) *Multiple Convictions.* A person may not be convicted of more than one offense defined by this Article for conduct designed to commit or to culminate in the commission of the same crime.

§ 5.06. Possessing Instruments of Crime; Weapons.

(1) *Criminal Instruments Generally.* A person commits a misdemeanor if he possesses any instrument of crime with purpose to employ it criminally. "Instrument of crime" means:

(a) anything specially made or specially adapted [sic] for criminal use; or

(b) anything commonly used for criminal purposes and possessed by the actor under circumstances which do not negative unlawful purpose.

(2) *Presumption of Criminal Purpose from Possession of Weapon.* If a person possesses a firearm or other weapon on or about his person, in a vehicle occupied by him, or otherwise readily available for use, it shall be presumed that he had the purpose to employ it criminally, unless:

(a) the weapon is possessed in the actor's home or place of business;

(b) the actor is licensed or otherwise authorized by law to possess such weapon; or

(c) the weapon is of a type commonly used in lawful sport.

"Weapon" means anything readily capable of lethal use and possessed under circumstances not manifestly appropriate for lawful uses which it may have; the term includes a firearm which is not loaded or lacks a clip or other component to render it immediately operable, and components which can readily be assembled into a weapon.

(3) *Presumptions as to Possession of Criminal Instruments in Automobiles.* Where a weapon or other instrument of crime is found in an automobile, it is presumed to be in the possession of the occupant if there is but one. If there is more than one occupant, it shall be presumed to be in the possession of all, except under the following circumstances:

(a) where it is found upon the person of one of the occupants;

(b) where the automobile is not a stolen one and the weapon or instrument is found out of view in a glove compartment, car trunk, or other enclosed customary depository, in which case it shall be presumed to be in the possession of the occupant or occupants who own or have authority to operate the automobile;

(c) in the case of a taxicab, a weapon or instrument found in the passenger's portion of the vehicle shall be presumed to be in the possession of all the passengers, if there are any, and, if not, in the possession of the driver.

§ 5.07. Prohibited Offensive Weapons.

A person commits a misdemeanor if, except as authorized by law, he makes, repairs, sells, or otherwise deals in, uses or possesses any offensive weapon. "Offensive weapon" means any bomb, machine gun, sawed-off shotgun, firearm specially made or specially adapted for concealment or silent discharge, any blackjack, sandbag, metal knuckles, dagger, or other implement for the infliction of serious bodily injury which serves no common lawful purpose. It is a defense under this Section for the defendant to prove by a preponderance of evidence that he possessed or dealt with the weapon solely as a curio or in a dramatic performance, or that he possessed it briefly in consequence of having found it or taken it from an aggressor, or under circumstances similarly negativing any purpose or likelihood that the weapon would be used unlawfully. The presumptions provided in Section 5.06(3) are applicable to prosecutions under this Section.

PART II DEFINITION OF SPECIFIC CRIMES

Offenses Involving Danger to the Person

Article 210. Criminal Homicide

§ 210.0. Definitions.

In Articles 210–213, unless a different meaning plainly is required:

(1) "human being" means a person who has been born and is alive;

(2) "bodily injury" means physical pain, illness or any impairment of physical condition;

(3) "serious bodily injury" means bodily injury which creates a substantial risk of death or which causes serious, permanent disfigurement, or protracted loss or impairment of the function of any bodily member or organ;

(4) "deadly weapon" means any firearm, or other weapon, device, instrument, material or substance, whether animate or inanimate, which in the manner it is used or is intended to be used is known to be capable of producing death or serious bodily injury.

§ 210.1. Criminal Homicide.

(1) A person is guilty of criminal homicide if he purposely, knowingly, recklessly or negligently causes the death of another human being.

(2) Criminal homicide is murder, manslaughter or negligent homicide.

§ 210.2. Murder.

(1) Except as provided in Section 210.3(1)(b), criminal homicide constitutes murder when:

(a) it is committed purposely or knowingly; or

(b) it is committed recklessly under circumstances manifesting extreme indifference to the value of human life. Such recklessness and indifference are presumed if the actor is engaged or is an accomplice in the commission of, or an attempt to commit, or flight after committing or attempting to commit robbery, rape or deviate sexual intercourse by force or threat of force, arson, burglary, kidnapping or felonious escape.

(2) Murder is a felony of the first degree [but a person convicted of murder may be sentenced to death, as provided in Section 210.6].[1]

§ 210.3. Manslaughter.

(1) Criminal homicide constitutes manslaughter when:

(a) it is committed recklessly; or

(b) a homicide which would otherwise be murder is committed under the influence of extreme mental or emotional disturbance for which there is reasonable explanation or excuse. The reasonableness of such explanation or excuse shall be determined from the viewpoint of a person in the actor's situation under the circumstances as he believes them to be.

(2) Manslaughter is a felony of the second degree.

---

[1] The brackets are meant to reflect the fact that the Institute took no position on the desirability of the death penalty. …

§ 210.4. Negligent Homicide.

(1) Criminal homicide constitutes negligent homicide when it is committed negligently.

(2) Negligent homicide is a felony of the third degree.

§ 210.5. Causing or Aiding Suicide.

(1) *Causing Suicide as Criminal Homicide.* A person may be convicted of criminal homicide for causing another to commit suicide only if he purposely causes such suicide by force, duress or deception.

(2) *Aiding or Soliciting Suicide as an Independent Offense.* A person who purposely aids or solicits another to commit suicide is guilty of a felony of the second degree if his conduct causes such suicide or an attempted suicide, and otherwise of a misdemeanor.

§ 210.6. Sentence of Death for Murder; Further Proceedings to Determine Sentence.

(1) *Death Sentence Excluded.* When a defendant is found guilty of murder, the Court shall impose sentence for a felony of the first degree if it is satisfied that:

  (a) none of the aggravating circumstances enumerated in Subsection (3) of this Section was established by the evidence at the trial or will be established if further proceedings are initiated under Subsection (2) of this Section; or

  (b) substantial mitigating circumstances, established by the evidence at the trial, call for leniency; or

  (c) the defendant, with the consent of the prosecuting attorney and the approval of the Court, pleaded guilty to murder as a felony of the first degree; or

  (d) the defendant was under 18 years of age at the time of the commission of the crime; or

  (e) the defendant's physical or mental condition calls for leniency; or

  (f) although the evidence suffices to sustain the verdict, it does not foreclose all doubt respecting the defendant's guilt.

(2) *Determination by Court or by Court and Jury.* Unless the Court imposes sentence under Subsection (1) of this Section, it shall conduct a separate proceeding to determine whether the defendant should be sentenced for a felony of the first degree or sentenced to death. The proceeding shall be conducted before the Court alone if the defendant was convicted by a Court sitting without a jury or upon his plea of guilty or if the prosecuting attorney and

the defendant waive a jury with respect to sentence. In other cases it shall be conducted before the Court sitting with the jury which determined the defendant's guilt or, if the Court for good cause shown discharges that jury, with a new jury empaneled for the purpose.

In the proceeding, evidence may be presented as to any matter that the Court deems relevant to sentence, including but not limited to the nature and circumstances of the crime, the defendant's character, background, history, mental and physical condition and any of the aggravating or mitigating circumstances enumerated in Subsections (3) and (4) of this Section. Any such evidence not legally privileged, which the Court deems to have probative force, may be received, regardless of its admissibility under the exclusionary rules of evidence, provided that the defendant's counsel is accorded a fair opportunity to rebut any hearsay statements. The prosecuting attorney and the defendant or his counsel shall be permitted to present argument for or against sentence of death.

The determination whether sentence of death shall be imposed shall be in the discretion of the Court, except that when the proceeding is conducted before the Court sitting with a jury, the Court shall not impose sentence of death unless it submits to the jury the issue whether the defendant should be sentenced to death or to imprisonment and the jury returns a verdict that the sentence should be death. If the jury is unable to reach a unanimous verdict, the Court shall dismiss the jury and impose sentence for a felony of the first degree.

The Court, in exercising its discretion as to sentence, and the jury, in determining upon its verdict, shall take into account the aggravating and mitigating circumstances enumerated in Subsections (3) and (4) and any other facts that it deems relevant, but it shall not impose or recommend sentence of death unless it finds one of the aggravating circumstances enumerated in Subsection (3) and further finds that there are no mitigating circumstances sufficiently substantial to call for leniency. When the issue is submitted to the jury, the Court shall so instruct and also shall inform the jury of the nature of the sentence of imprisonment that may be imposed, including its implication with respect to possible release upon parole, if the jury verdict is against sentence of death.

Alternative formulation of Subsection (2):

(2) *Determination by Court.* Unless the Court imposes sentence under Subsection (1) of this Section, it shall conduct a separate proceeding to determine whether the

defendant should be sentenced for a felony of the first degree or sentenced to death. In the proceeding, the Court, in accordance with Section 7.07, shall consider the report of the presentence investigation and, if a psychiatric examination has been ordered, the report of such examination. In addition, evidence may be presented as to any matter that the Court deems relevant to sentence, including but not limited to the nature and circumstances of the crime, the defendant's character, background, history, mental and physical condition and any of the aggravating or mitigating circumstances enumerated in Subsections (3) and (4) of this Section. Any such evidence not legally privileged, which the Court deems to have probative force, may be received, regardless of its admissibility under the exclusionary rules of evidence, provided that the defendant's counsel is accorded a fair opportunity to rebut any hearsay statements. The prosecuting attorney and the defendant or his counsel shall be permitted to present argument for or against sentence of death.

The determination whether sentence of death shall be imposed shall be in the discretion of the Court. In exercising such discretion, the Court shall take into account the aggravating and mitigating circumstances enumerated in Subsections (3) and (4) and any other facts that it deems relevant but shall not impose sentence of death unless it finds one of the aggravating circumstances enumerated in Subsection (3) and further finds that there are no mitigating circumstances sufficiently substantial to call for leniency.

(3) *Aggravating Circumstances.*

   (a) The murder was committed by a convict under sentence of imprisonment.

   (b) The defendant was previously convicted of another murder or of a felony involving the use or threat of violence to the person.

   (c) At the time the murder was committed the defendant also committed another murder.

   (d) The defendant knowingly created a great risk of death to many persons.

   (e) The murder was committed while the defendant was engaged or was an accomplice in the commission of, or an attempt to commit, or flight after committing or attempting to commit robbery, rape or deviate sexual intercourse by force or threat of force, arson, burglary or kidnapping.

   (f) The murder was committed for the purpose of avoiding or preventing a lawful arrest or effecting an escape from lawful custody.

   (g) The murder was committed for pecuniary gain.

   (h) The murder was especially heinous, atrocious or cruel, manifesting exceptional depravity.

(4) *Mitigating Circumstances.*

   (a) The defendant has no significant history of prior criminal activity.

   (b) The murder was committed while the defendant was under the influence of extreme mental or emotional disturbance.

   (c) The victim was a participant in the defendant's homicidal conduct or consented to the homicidal act.

   (d) The murder was committed under circumstances which the defendant believed to provide a moral justification or extenuation for his conduct.

   (e) The defendant was an accomplice in a murder committed by another person and his participation in the homicidal act was relatively minor.

   (f) The defendant acted under duress or under the domination of another person.

   (g) At the time of the murder, the capacity of the defendant to appreciate the criminality [wrongfulness] of his conduct or to conform his conduct to the requirements of law was impaired as a result of mental disease or defect or intoxication.

   (h) The youth of the defendant at the time of the crime.

Article 211. Assault; Reckless Endangering; Threats

§ 211.0. Definitions.

In this Article, the definitions given in Section 210.0 apply unless a different meaning plainly is required.

§ 211.1. Assault.

(1) *Simple Assault.* A person is guilty of assault if he:

   (a) attempts to cause or purposely, knowingly or recklessly causes bodily injury to another; or

   (b) negligently causes bodily injury to another with a deadly weapon; or

   (c) attempts by physical menace to put another in fear of imminent serious bodily injury.

Simple assault is a misdemeanor unless committed in a fight or scuffle entered into by mutual consent, in which case it is a petty misdemeanor.

(2) *Aggravated Assault.* A person is guilty of aggravated assault if he:

   (a) attempts to cause serious bodily injury to another, or causes such injury purposely, knowingly or recklessly under circumstances manifesting extreme indifference to the value of human life; or

   (b) attempts to cause or purposely or knowingly causes bodily injury to another with a deadly weapon.

Aggravated assault under paragraph (a) is a felony of the second degree; aggravated assault under paragraph (b) is a felony of the third degree.

§ 211.2. Recklessly Endangering Another Person.

A person commits a misdemeanor if he recklessly engages in conduct which places or may place another person in danger of death or serious bodily injury. Recklessness and danger shall be presumed where a person knowingly points a firearm at or in the direction of another, whether or not the actor believed the firearm to be loaded.

§ 211.3. Terroristic Threats.

A person is guilty of a felony of the third degree if he threatens to commit any crime of violence with purpose to terrorize another or to cause evacuation of a building, place of assembly, or facility of public transportation, or otherwise to cause serious public inconvenience, or in reckless disregard of the risk of causing such terror or inconvenience.

Article 212. Kidnapping and Related Offenses; Coercion

§ 212.0. Definitions.

In this Article, the definitions given in section 210.0 apply unless a different meaning plainly is required.

§ 212.1. Kidnapping.

A person is guilty of kidnapping if he unlawfully removes another from his place of residence or business, or a substantial distance from the vicinity where he is found, or if he unlawfully confines another for a substantial period in a place of isolation, with any of the following purposes:

   (a) to hold for ransom or reward, or as a shield or hostage; or

   (b) to facilitate commission of any felony or flight thereafter; or

   (c) to inflict bodily injury on or to terrorize the victim or another; or

   (d) to interfere with the performance of any governmental or political function.

Kidnapping is a felony of the first degree unless the actor voluntarily releases the victim alive and in a safe place prior to trial, in which case it is a felony of the second degree. A removal or confinement is unlawful within the meaning of this Section if it is accomplished by force, threat or deception, or, in the case of a person who is under the age of 14 or incompetent, if it is accomplished without the consent of a parent, guardian or other person responsible for general supervision of his welfare.

§ 212.2. Felonious Restraint.

A person commits a felony of the third degree if he knowingly:

   (a) restrains another unlawfully in circumstances exposing him to risk of serious bodily injury; or

   (b) holds another in a condition of involuntary servitude.

§ 212.3. False Imprisonment.

A person commits a misdemeanor if he knowingly restrains another unlawfully so as to interfere substantially with his liberty.

§ 212.4. Interference with Custody.

(1) *Custody of Children.* A person commits an offense if he knowingly or recklessly takes or entices any child under the age of 18 from the custody of its parent, guardian or other lawful custodian, when he has no privilege to do so. It is an affirmative defense that:

   (a) the actor believed that his action was necessary to preserve the child from danger to its welfare; or

   (b) the child, being at the time not less than 14 years old, was taken away at its own instigation without enticement and without purpose to commit a criminal offense with or against the child.

Proof that the child was below the critical age gives rise to a presumption that the actor knew the child's age or acted in reckless disregard thereof. The offense is a misdemeanor unless the actor, not being a parent or person in equivalent relation to the child, acted with knowledge that his conduct would cause serious alarm for the child's safety, or in reckless disregard of a likelihood of causing such alarm, in which case the offense is a felony of the third degree.

(2) *Custody of Committed Persons.* A person is guilty of a misdemeanor if he knowingly or recklessly takes or entices any committed person away from lawful custody when he is not privileged to do so. "Committed person"

means, in addition to anyone committed under judicial warrant, any orphan, neglected or delinquent child, mentally defective or insane person, or other dependent or incompetent person entrusted to another's custody by or through a recognized social agency or otherwise by authority of law.

§ 212.5. Criminal Coercion.

(1) *Offense Defined*. A person is guilty of criminal coercion if, with purpose unlawfully to restrict another's freedom of action to his detriment, he threatens to:

   (a) commit any criminal offense; or

   (b) accuse anyone of a criminal offense; or

   (c) expose any secret tending to subject any person to hatred, contempt or ridicule, or to impair his credit or business repute; or

   (d) take or withhold action as an official, or cause an official to take or withhold action.

It is an affirmative defense to prosecution based on paragraphs (b), (c) or (d) that the actor believed the accusation or secret to be true or the proposed official action justified and that his purpose was limited to compelling the other to behave in a way reasonably related to the circumstances which were the subject of the accusation, exposure or proposed official action, as by desisting from further misbehavior, making good a wrong done, refraining from taking any action or responsibility for which the actor believes the other disqualified.

(2) *Grading*. Criminal coercion is a misdemeanor unless the threat is to commit a felony or the actor's purpose is felonious, in which cases the offense is a felony of the third degree.

Article 213. Sexual Offenses

§ 213.0. Definitions.

In this Article, unless a different meaning plainly is required:

(1) the definitions given in Section 210.0 apply;

(2) "sexual intercourse" includes intercourse per os or per anum, with some penetration however slight; emission is not required;

(3) "deviate sexual intercourse" means sexual intercourse per os or per anum between human beings who are not husband and wife, and any form of sexual intercourse with an animal.

§ 213.1. Rape and Related Offenses.

(1) *Rape*. A male who has sexual intercourse with a female not his wife is guilty of rape if:

   (a) he compels her to submit by force or by threat of imminent death, serious bodily injury, extreme pain or kidnapping, to be inflicted on anyone; or

   (b) he has substantially impaired her power to appraise or control her conduct by administering or employing without her knowledge drugs, intoxicants or other means for the purpose of preventing resistance; or

   (c) the female is unconscious; or

   (d) the female is less than 10 years old.

Rape is a felony of the second degree unless (i) in the course thereof the actor inflicts serious bodily injury upon anyone, or (ii) the victim was not a voluntary social companion of the actor upon the occasion of the crime and had not previously permitted him sexual liberties, in which cases the offense is a felony of the first degree.

(2) *Gross Sexual Imposition*. A male who has sexual intercourse with a female not his wife commits a felony of the third degree if:

   (a) he compels her to submit by any threat that would prevent resistance by a woman of ordinary resolution; or

   (b) he knows that she suffers from a mental disease or defect which renders her incapable of appraising the nature of her conduct; or

   (c) he knows that she is unaware that a sexual act is being committed upon her or that she submits because she mistakenly supposes that he is her husband.

§ 213.2. Deviate Sexual Intercourse by Force or Imposition.

(1) *By Force or Its Equivalent*. A person who engages in deviate sexual intercourse with another person, or who causes another to engage in deviate sexual intercourse, commits a felony of the second degree if:

   (a) he compels the other person to participate by force or by threat of imminent death, serious bodily injury, extreme pain or kidnapping, to be inflicted on anyone; or

   (b) he has substantially impaired the other person's power to appraise or control his conduct, by administering or employing without the knowledge of the other person drugs, intoxicants or other means for the purpose of preventing resistance; or

(c) the other person is unconscious; or

(d) the other person is less than 10 years old.

(2) *By Other Imposition.* A person who engages in deviate sexual intercourse with another person, or who causes another to engage in deviate sexual intercourse, commits a felony of the third degree if:

(a) he compels the other person to participate by any threat that would prevent resistance by a person of ordinary resolution; or

(b) he knows that the other person suffers from a mental disease or defect which renders him incapable of appraising the nature of his conduct; or

(c) he knows that the other person submits because he is unaware that a sexual act is being committed upon him.

§ 213.3. Corruption of Minors and Seduction.

(1) *Offense Defined.* A male who has sexual intercourse with a female not his wife, or any person who engages in deviate sexual intercourse or causes another to engage in deviate sexual intercourse, is guilty of an offense if:

(a) the other person is less than [16] years old and the actor is at least [4] years older than the other person; or

(b) the other person is less than 21 years old and the actor is his guardian or otherwise responsible for general supervision of his welfare; or

(c) the other person is in custody of law or detained in a hospital or other institution and the actor has supervisory or disciplinary authority over him; or

(d) the other person is a female who is induced to participate by a promise of marriage which the actor does not mean to perform.

(2) *Grading.* An offense under paragraph (a) of Subsection (1) is a felony of the third degree. Otherwise an offense under this section is a misdemeanor.

§ 213.4. Sexual Assault.

A person who has sexual contact with another not his spouse, or causes such other to have sexual conduct with him, is guilty of sexual assault, a misdemeanor, if:

(1) he knows that the conduct is offensive to the other person; or

(2) he knows that the other person suffers from a mental disease or defect which renders him or her incapable of appraising the nature of his or her conduct; or

(3) he knows that the other person is unaware that a sexual act is being committed; or

(4) the other person is less than 10 years old; or

(5) he has substantially impaired the other person's power to appraise or control his or her conduct, by administering or employing without the other's knowledge drugs, intoxicants or other means for the purpose of preventing resistance; or

(6) the other person is less than [16] years old and the actor is at least [four] years older than the other person; or

(7) the other person is less than 21 years old and the actor is his guardian or otherwise responsible for general supervision of his welfare; or

(8) the other person is in custody of law or detained in a hospital or other institution and the actor has supervisory or disciplinary authority over him.

Sexual contact is any touching of the sexual or other intimate parts of the person for the purpose of arousing or gratifying sexual desire.

§ 213.5. Indecent Exposure.

A person commits a misdemeanor if, for the purpose of arousing or gratifying sexual desire of himself or of any person other than his spouse, he exposes his genitals under circumstances in which he knows his conduct is likely to cause affront or alarm.

§ 213.6. Provisions Generally Applicable to Article 213.

(1) *Mistake as to Age.* Whenever in this Article the criminality of conduct depends on a child's being below the age of 10, it is no defense that the actor did not know the child's age, or reasonably believed the child to be older than 10. When criminality depends on the child's being below a critical age other than 10, it is a defense for the actor to prove by a preponderance of the evidence that he reasonably believed the child to be above the critical age.

(2) *Spouse Relationships.* Whenever in this Article the definition of an offense excludes conduct with a spouse, the exclusion shall be deemed to extend to persons living as man and wife, regardless of the legal status of their relationship. The exclusion shall be inoperative as respects spouses living apart under a decree of judicial separation. Where the definition of an offense excludes conduct with a spouse or conduct by a woman, this shall not

preclude conviction of a spouse or woman as accomplice in a sexual act which he or she causes another person, not within the exclusion, to perform.

(3) *Sexually Promiscuous Complainants.* It is a defense to prosecution under Section 213.3, and paragraphs (6), (7) and (8) of Section 213.4 for the actor to prove by a preponderance of the evidence that the alleged victim had, prior to the time of the offense charged, engaged promiscuously in sexual relations with others.

(4) *Prompt Complaint.* No prosecution may be instituted or maintained under this Article unless the alleged offense was brought to the notice of public authority within [3] months of its occurrence or, where the alleged victim was less than [16] years old or otherwise incompetent to make complaint, within [3] months after a parent, guardian or other competent person specially interested in the victim learns of the offense.

(5) *Testimony of Complainants.* No person shall be convicted of any felony under this Article upon the uncorroborated testimony of the alleged victim. Corroboration may be circumstantial. In any prosecution before a jury for an offense under this Article, the jury shall be instructed to evaluate the testimony of a victim or complaining witness with special care in view of the emotional involvement of the witness and the difficulty of determining the truth with respect to alleged sexual activities carried out in private.

Offenses Against Property

Article 220. Arson, Criminal Mischief, and Other Property Destruction

§ 220.1. Arson and Related Offenses.

(1) *Arson.* A person is guilty of arson, a felony of the second degree, if he starts a fire or causes an explosion with the purpose of:

  (a) destroying a building or occupied structure of another; or

  (b) destroying or damaging any property, whether his own or another's, to collect insurance for such loss. It shall be an affirmative defense to prosecution under this paragraph that the actor's conduct did not recklessly endanger any building or occupied structure of another or place any other person in danger of death or bodily injury.

(2) *Reckless Burning or Exploding.* A person commits a felony of the third degree if he purposely starts a fire or causes

an explosion, whether on his own property or another's, and thereby recklessly:

  (a) places another person in danger of death or bodily injury; or

  (b) places a building or occupied structure of another in danger of damage or destruction.

(3) *Failure to Control or Report Dangerous Fire.* A person who knows that a fire is endangering life or a substantial amount of property of another and fails to take reasonable measures to put out or control the fire, when he can do so without substantial risk to himself, or to give a prompt fire alarm, commits a misdemeanor if:

  (a) he knows that he is under an official, contractual, or other legal duty to prevent or combat the fire; or

  (b) the fire was started, albeit lawfully, by him or with his assent, or on property in his custody or control.

(4) *Definitions.* "Occupied structure" means any structure, vehicle or place adapted for overnight accommodation of persons, or for carrying on business therein, whether or not a person is actually present. Property is that of another, for the purposes of this section, if anyone other than the actor has a possessory or proprietory interest therein. If a building or structure is divided into separately occupied units, any unit not occupied by the actor is an occupied structure of another.

§ 220.2. Causing or Risking Catastrophe.

(1) *Causing Catastrophe.* A person who causes a catastrophe by explosion, fire, flood, avalanche, collapse of building, release of poison gas, radioactive material or other harmful or destructive force or substance, or by any other means of causing potentially widespread injury or damage, commits a felony of the second degree if he does so purposely or knowingly, or a felony of the third degree if he does so recklessly.

(2) *Risking Catastrophe.* A person is guilty of a misdemeanor if he recklessly creates a risk of catastrophe in the employment of fire, explosives or other dangerous means listed in Subsection (1).

(3) *Failure to Prevent Catastrophe.* A person who knowingly or recklessly fails to take reasonable measures to prevent or mitigate a catastrophe commits a misdemeanor if:

  (a) he knows that he is under an official, contractual or other legal duty to take such measures; or

  (b) he did or assented to the act causing or threatening the catastrophe.

§ 220.3. Criminal Mischief.

(1) *Offense Defined*. A person is guilty of criminal mischief if he:

  (a) damages tangible property of another purposely, recklessly, or by negligence in the employment of fire, explosives, or other dangerous means listed in Section 220.2(1); or

  (b) purposely or recklessly tampers with tangible property of another so as to endanger person or property; or

  (c) purposely or recklessly causes another to suffer pecuniary loss by deception or threat.

(2) *Grading*. Criminal mischief is a felony of the third degree if the actor purposely causes pecuniary loss in excess of $5,000 or a substantial interruption or impairment of public communication, transportation, supply of water, gas or power, or other public service. It is a misdemeanor if the actor purposely causes pecuniary loss in excess of $100, or a petty misdemeanor if he purposely or recklessly causes pecuniary loss in excess of $25. Otherwise criminal mischief is a violation.

Article 221. Burglary and Other Criminal Intrusion

§ 221.0. Definitions.

In this Article, unless a different meaning plainly is required:

(1) "occupied structure" means any structure, vehicle or place adapted for overnight accommodation of persons, or for carrying on business therein, whether or not a person is actually present.

(2) "night" means the period between thirty minutes past sunset and thirty minutes before sunrise.

§ 221.1. Burglary.

(1) *Burglary Defined*. A person is guilty of burglary if he enters a building or occupied structure, or separately secured or occupied portion thereof, with purpose to commit a crime therein, unless the premises are at the time open to the public or the actor is licensed or privileged to enter. It is an affirmative defense to prosecution for burglary that the building or structure was abandoned.

(2) *Grading*. Burglary is a felony of the second degree if it is perpetrated in the dwelling of another at night, or if, in the course of committing the offense, the actor:

  (a) purposely, knowingly or recklessly inflicts or attempts to inflict bodily injury on anyone; or

  (b) is armed with explosives or a deadly weapon.

Otherwise, burglary is a felony of the third degree. An act shall be deemed "in the course of committing" an offense if it occurs in an attempt to commit the offense or in flight after the attempt or commission.

(3) *Multiple Convictions*. A person may not be convicted both for burglary and for the offense which it was his purpose to commit after the burglarious entry or for an attempt to commit that offense, unless the additional offense constitutes a felony of the first or second degree.

§ 221.2. Criminal Trespass.

(1) *Buildings and Occupied Structures*. A person commits an offense if, knowing that he is not licensed or privileged to do so, he enters or surreptitiously remains in any building or occupied structure, or separately secured or occupied portion thereof. An offense under this Subsection is a misdemeanor if it is committed in a dwelling at night. Otherwise it is a petty misdemeanor.

(2) *Defiant Trespasser*. A person commits an offense if, knowing that he is not licensed or privileged to do so, he enters or remains in any place as to which notice against trespass is given by:

  (a) actual communication to the actor; or

  (b) posting in a manner prescribed by law or reasonably likely to come to the attention of intruders; or

  (c) fencing or other enclosure manifestly designed to exclude intruders.

An offense under this Subsection constitutes a petty misdemeanor if the offender defies an order to leave personally communicated to him by the owner of the premises or other authorized person. Otherwise it is a violation.

(3) *Defenses*. It is an affirmative defense to prosecution under this Section that:

  (a) a building or occupied structure involved in an offense under Subsection (1) was abandoned; or

  (b) the premises were at the time open to members of the public and the actor complied with all lawful conditions imposed on access to or remaining in the premises; or

  (c) the actor reasonably believed that the owner of the premises, or other person empowered to license access thereto, would have licensed him to enter or remain.

Article 222. Robbery

§ 222.1 Robbery.

(1) *Robbery Defined.* A person is guilty of robbery if, in the course of committing a theft, he:

    (a) inflicts serious bodily injury upon another; or

    (b) threatens another with or purposely puts him in fear of immediate serious bodily injury; or

    (c) commits or threatens immediately to commit any felony of the first or second degree.

An act shall be deemed "in the course of committing a theft" if it occurs in an attempt to commit theft or in flight after the attempt or commission.

(2) *Grading.* Robbery is a felony of the second degree, except that it is a felony of the first degree if in the course of committing the theft the actor attempts to kill anyone, or purposely inflicts or attempts to inflict serious bodily injury.

Article 223. Theft and Related Offenses

§ 223.0. Definitions.

In this Article, unless a different meaning plainly is required:

(1) "deprive" means: (a) to withhold property of another permanently or for so extended a period as to appropriate a major portion of its economic value, or with intent to restore only upon payment of reward or other compensation; or (b) to dispose of the property so as to make it unlikely that the owner will recover it.

(2) "financial institution" means a bank, insurance company, credit union, building and loan association, investment trust or other organization held out to the public as a place of deposit of funds or medium of savings or collective investment.

(3) "government" means the United States, any State, county, municipality, or other political unit, or any department, agency or subdivision of any of the foregoing, or any corporation or other association carrying out the functions of government.

(4) "movable property" means property the location of which can be changed, including things growing on, affixed to, or found in land, and documents although the rights represented thereby have no physical location. "Immovable property" is all other property.

(5) "obtain" means: (a) in relation to property, to bring about a transfer or purported transfer of a legal interest in the property, whether to the obtainer or another; or (b) in relation to labor or service, to secure performance thereof.

(6) "property" means anything of value, including real estate, tangible and intangible personal property, contract rights, choses-in-action and other interests in or claims to wealth, admission or transportation tickets, captured or domestic animals, food and drink, electric or other power.

(7) "property of another" includes property in which any person other than the actor has an interest which the actor is not privileged to infringe, regardless of the fact that the actor also has an interest in the property and regardless of the fact that the other person might be precluded from civil recovery because the property was used in an unlawful transaction or was subject to forfeiture as contraband. Property in possession of the actor shall not be deemed property of another who has only a security interest therein, even if legal title is in the creditor pursuant to a conditional sales contract or other security agreement.

§ 223.1. Consolidation of Theft Offenses; Grading; Provisions Applicable to Theft Generally.

(1) *Consolidation of Theft Offenses.* Conduct denominated theft in this Article constitutes a single offense. An accusation of theft may be supported by evidence that it was committed in any manner that would be theft under this Article, notwithstanding the specification of a different manner in the indictment or information, subject only to the power of the Court to ensure fair trial by granting a continuance or other appropriate relief where the conduct of the defense would be prejudiced by lack of fair notice or by surprise.

(2) *Grading of Theft Offenses.*

    (a) Theft constitutes a felony of the third degree if the amount involved exceeds $500, or if the property stolen is a firearm, automobile, airplane, motorcycle, motorboat or other motor-propelled vehicle, or in the case of theft by receiving stolen property, if the receiver is in the business of buying or selling stolen property.

    (b) Theft not within the preceding paragraph constitutes a misdemeanor, except that if the property was not taken from the person or by threat, or in breach of a fiduciary obligation, and the actor proves by a preponderance of the evidence that the amount involved was less than $50, the offense constitutes a petty misdemeanor.

(c) The amount involved in a theft shall be deemed to be the highest value, by any reasonable standard, of the property or services which the actor stole or attempted to steal. Amounts involved in thefts committed pursuant to one scheme or course of conduct, whether from the same person or several persons, may be aggregated in determining the grade or the offense.

(3) *Claim of Right*. It is an affirmative defense to prosecution for theft that the actor:

(a) was unaware that the property or service was that of another; or

(b) acted under an honest claim of right to the property or service involved or that he had a right to acquire or dispose of it as he did; or

(c) took property exposed for sale, intending to purchase and pay for it promptly, or reasonably believing that the owner, if present, would have consented.

(4) *Theft from Spouse*. It is no defense that theft was from the actor's spouse, except that misappropriation of household and personal effects, or other property normally accessible to both spouses, is theft only if it occurs after the parties have ceased living together.

§ 223.3. Theft by Unlawful Taking or Disposition.

(1) *Movable Property*. A person is guilty of theft if he unlawfully takes, or exercises unlawful control over, movable property of another with purpose to deprive him thereof.

(2) *Immovable Property*. A person is guilty of theft if he unlawfully transfers immovable property of another or any interest therein with purpose to benefit himself or another not entitled thereto.

§ 223.3. Theft by Deception.

A person is guilty of theft if he purposely obtains property of another by deception. A person deceives if he purposely:

(1) creates or reinforces a false impression, including false impressions as to law, value, intention or other state of mind; but deception as to a person's intention to perform a promise shall not be inferred from the fact alone that he did not subsequently perform the promise; or

(2) prevents another from acquiring information which would affect his judgment of a transaction; or

(3) fails to correct a false impression which the deceiver previously created or reinforced, or which the deceiver knows to be influencing another to whom he stands in a fiduciary or confidential relationship; or

(4) fails to disclose a known lien, adverse claim or other legal impediment to the enjoyment of property which he transfers or encumbers in consideration for the property obtained, whether such impediment is or is not valid, or is or is not a matter of official record.

The term "deceive" does not, however, include falsity as to matters having no pecuniary significance, or puffing by statements unlikely to deceive ordinary persons in the group addressed.

§ 223.4. Theft by Extortion.

A person is guilty of theft if he obtains property of another by threatening to:

(1) inflict bodily injury on anyone or commit any other criminal offense; or

(2) accuse anyone of a criminal offense; or

(3) expose any secret tending to subject any person to hatred, contempt or ridicule, or to impair his credit or business repute; or

(4) take or withhold action as an official, or cause an official to take or withhold action; or

(5) bring about or continue a strike, boycott or other collective unofficial action, if the property is not demanded or received for the benefit of the group in whose interest the actor purports to act; or

(6) testify or provide information or withhold testimony or information with respect to another's legal claim or defense; or

(7) inflict any other harm which would not benefit the actor.

It is an affirmative defense to prosecution based on paragraphs (2), (3) or (4) that the property obtained by threat of accusation, exposure, lawsuit or other invocation of official action was honestly claimed as restitution or indemnification for harm done in the circumstances to which such accusation, exposure, lawsuit or other official action relates, or as compensation for property or lawful services.

§ 223.5. Theft of Property Lost, Mislaid, or Delivered by Mistake.

A person who comes into control of property of another that he knows to have been lost, mislaid, or delivered under a mistake as to the nature or amount of the property or the identity of the recipient is guilty of theft if, with purpose to deprive the owner thereof, he fails to take reasonable measures to restore the property to a person entitled to have it.

§ 223.6. Receiving Stolen Property.

(1) *Receiving.* A person is guilty of theft if he purposely receives, retains, or disposes of movable property of another knowing that it has been stolen, or believing that it has probably been stolen, unless the property is received, retained, or disposed with purpose to restore it to the owner. "Receiving" means acquiring possession, control or title, or lending on the security of the property.

(2) *Presumption of Knowledge.* The requisite knowledge or belief is presumed in the case of a dealer who:

  (a) is found in possession or control of property stolen from two or more persons on separate occasions; or

  (b) has received stolen property in another transaction within the year preceding the transaction charged; or

  (c) being a dealer in property of the sort received, acquires it for a consideration which he knows is far below its reasonable value.

"Dealer" means a person in the business of buying or selling goods including a pawnbroker.

§ 223.7. Theft of Services.

(1) A person is guilty of theft if he purposely obtains services which he knows are available only for compensation, by deception or threat, or by false token or other means to avoid payment for the service. "Services" includes labor, professional service, transportation, telephone or other public service, accommodation in hotels, restaurants or elsewhere, admission to exhibitions, use of vehicles or other movable property. Where compensation for service is ordinarily paid immediately upon the rendering for such service, as is the case of hotels and restaurants, refusal to pay or absconding without payment or offer to pay gives rise to a presumption that the service was obtained by deception as to intention to pay.

(2) A person commits theft if, having control over the disposition of services of others, to which he is not entitled, he knowingly diverts such services to his own benefit or to the benefit of another not entitled thereto.

§ 223.8. Theft by Failure to Make Required Disposition of Funds Received.

A person who purposely obtains property upon agreement, or subject to a known legal obligation, to make specified payment or other disposition, whether from such property or its proceeds or from his own property to be reserved in equivalent amount, is guilty of theft if he deals with the property obtained as his own and fails to make the required payment or disposition. The foregoing applies notwithstanding that it may be impossible to identify particular property as belonging to the victim at the time of the actor's failure to make the required payment or disposition. An officer or employee of the government or of a financial institution is presumed: (i) to know any legal obligation relevant to his criminal liability under this Section, and (ii) to have dealt with the property as his own if he fails to pay or account upon lawful demand, or if an audit reveals a shortage or falsification of accounts.

Article 224. Forgery and Fraudulent Practices

§ 224.0. Definitions.

In this Article, the definitions given in Section 223.0 apply unless a different meaning plainly is required.

§ 224.1. Forgery.

(1) *Definition.* A person is guilty of forgery if, with purpose to defraud or injure anyone, or with knowledge that he is facilitating a fraud or injury to be perpetrated by anyone, the actor:

  (a) alters any writing of another without his authority; or

  (b) makes, completes, executes, authenticates, issues or transfers any writing so that it purports to be the act of another who did not authorize that act, or to have been executed at a time or place or in a numbered sequence other than was in fact the case, or to be a copy of an original when no such original existed; or

  (c) utters any writing which he knows to be forged in a manner specified in paragraphs (a) or (b).

"Writing" includes printing or any other method of recording information, money, coins, tokens, stamps, seals, credit cards, badges, trademarks, and other symbols of value, right, privilege, or identification.

(2) *Grading*. Forgery is a felony of the second degree if the writing is or purports to be part of an issue of money, securities, postage or revenue stamps, or other instruments issued by the government, or part of an issue of stock, bonds or other instruments representing interests in or claims against any property or enterprise. Forgery is a felony of the third degree if the writing is or purports to be a will, deed, contract, release, commercial instrument, or other document evidencing, creating, transferring, altering, terminating, or otherwise affecting legal relations. Otherwise forgery is a misdemeanor.

§ 224.5. Bad Checks.

A person who issues or passes a check or similar sight order for the payment of money, knowing that it will not be honored by the drawee, commits a misdemeanor. For the purposes of this Section as well as in any prosecution for theft committed by means of a bad check, an issuer is presumed to know that the check or order (other than a postdated check or order) would not be paid, if:

(1) the issuer had no account with the drawee at the time the check or order was issued; or

(2) payment was refused by the drawee for lack of funds, upon presentation within 30 days after issue, and the issuer failed to make good within 10 days after receiving notice of that refusal.

§ 224.8. Commercial Bribery and Breach of Duty to Act Disinterestedly.

(1) A person commits a misdemeanor if he solicits, accepts or agrees to accept any benefit as consideration for knowingly violating or agreeing to violate a duty of fidelity to which he is subject as:

   (a) partner, agent or employee of another;

   (b) trustee, guardian, or other fiduciary;

   (c) lawyer, physician, accountant, appraiser, or other professional adviser or informant;

   (d) officer, director, manager or other participant in the direction of the affairs of an incorporated or unincorporated association; or

   (e) arbitrator or other purportedly disinterested adjudicator or referee.

(2) A person who holds himself out to the public as being engaged in the business of making disinterested selection, appraisal, or criticism of commodities or services commits a misdemeanor if he solicits, accepts or agrees to accept any benefit to influence his selection, appraisal or criticism.

(3) A person commits a misdemeanor if he confers, or offers or agrees to confer, any benefit the acceptance of which would be criminal under this Section.

Offenses Against the Family

Article 230. Offenses Against The Family

§ 230.1. Bigamy and Polygamy.

(1) *Bigamy*. A married person is guilty of bigamy, a misdemeanor, if he contracts or purports to contract another marriage, unless at the time of the subsequent marriage:

   (a) the actor believes that the prior spouse is dead; or

   (b) the actor and the prior spouse have been living apart for five consecutive years throughout which the prior spouse was not known by the actor to be alive; or

   (c) a Court has entered a judgment purporting to terminate or annul any prior disqualifying marriage, and the actor does not know that judgment to be invalid; or

   (d) the actor reasonably believes that he is legally eligible to remarry.

(2) *Polygamy*. A person is guilty of polygamy, a felony of the third degree, if he marries or cohabits with more than one spouse at a time in purported exercise of the right of plural marriage. The offense is a continuing one until all cohabitation and claim of marriage with more than one spouse terminates. This section does not apply to parties to a polygamous marriage, lawful in the country of which they are residents or nationals, while they are in transit through or temporarily visiting this State.

(3) *Other Party to Bigamous or Polygamous Marriage*. A person is guilty of bigamy or polygamy, as the case may be, if he contracts or purports to contract marriage with another knowing that the other is thereby committing bigamy or polygamy.

§ 230.2. Incest.

A person is guilty of incest, a felony of the third degree, if he knowingly marries or cohabits or has sexual intercourse with an ancestor or descendant, a brother or sister of the whole or half blood [or an uncle, aunt, nephew or niece of the whole blood]. "Cohabit" means to live together under the representation or appearance of being married. The relationships referred to herein include blood relationships without regard to legitimacy, and relationship of parent and child by adoption.

§ 230.4. Endangering Welfare of Children.

A parent, guardian, or other person supervising the welfare of a child under 18 commits a misdemeanor if he knowingly endangers the child's welfare by violating a duty of care, protection or support.

§ 230.5. Persistent Non-Support.

A person commits a misdemeanor if he persistently fails to provide support which he can provide and which he knows he is legally obliged to provide to a spouse, child or other dependent.

Offenses Against Public Administration

Article 240. Bribery and Corrupt Influence

§ 240.0. Definitions.

In Articles 240–243, unless a different meaning plainly is required:

(1) "benefit" means gain or advantage, or anything regarded by the beneficiary as gain or advantage, including benefit to any other person or entity in whose welfare he is interested, but not an advantage promised generally to a group or class of voters as a consequence of public measures which a candidate engages to support or oppose;

(2) "government" includes any branch, subdivision or agency of the government of the State or any locality within it;

(3) "harm" means loss, disadvantage or injury, or anything so regarded by the person affected, including loss, disadvantage or injury to any other person or entity in whose welfare he is interested;

(4) "official proceeding" means a proceeding heard or which may be heard before any legislative, judicial, administrative or other governmental agency or official authorized to take evidence under oath, including any referee, hearing examiner, commissioner, notary or other person taking testimony or deposition in connection with any such proceeding;

(5) "party official" means a person who holds an elective or appointive post in a political party in the United States by virtue of which he directs or conducts, or participates in directing or conducting party affairs at any level of responsibility;

(6) "pecuniary benefit" is benefit in the form of money, property, commercial interests or anything else the primary significance of which is economic gain;

(7) "public servant" means any officer or employee of government, including legislators and judges, and any person participating as juror, advisor, consultant or otherwise, in performing a governmental function; but the term does not include witnesses;

(8) "administrative proceeding" means any proceeding, other than a judicial proceeding, the outcome of which is required to be based on a record or documentation prescribed by law, or in which law or regulation is particularized in application to individuals.

§ 240.1. Bribery in Official and Political Matters.

A person is guilty of bribery, a felony of the third degree, if he offers, confers or agrees to confer upon another, or solicits, accepts or agrees to accept from another:

(1) any pecuniary benefit as consideration for the recipient's decision, opinion, recommendation, vote or other exercise of discretion as a public servant, party official or voter; or

(2) any benefit as consideration for the recipient's decision, vote, recommendation or other exercise of official discretion in a judicial or administrative proceeding; or

(3) any benefit as consideration for a violation of a known legal duty as public servant or party official.

It is no defense to prosecution under this section that a person whom the actor sought to influence was not qualified to act in the desired way whether because he had not yet assumed office, or lacked jurisdiction, or for any other reason.

§ 240.2. Threats and Other Improper Influence in Official and Political Matters.

(1) *Offenses Defined.* A person commits an offense if he:

(a) threatens unlawful harm to any person with purpose to influence his decision, opinion, recommendation, vote or other exercise of discretion as a public servant, party official or voter; or

(b) threatens harm to any public servant with purpose to influence his decision, opinion, recommendation, vote or pecuniary benefit as consideration for exerting special influence upon a public servant or procuring another to do so. "Special influence" means power to influence through kinship, friendship or other relationship, apart from the merits of the transaction.

(2) *Paying for Endorsement or Special Influence*. A person commits a misdemeanor if he offers, confers or agrees to confer any pecuniary benefit receipt of which is prohibited by this Section.

Article 241. Perjury and Other Falsification in Official Matters

§ 241.0. Definitions.

In this Article, unless a different meaning plainly is required:

(1) the definitions given in Section 240.0 apply; and

(2) "statement" means any representation, but includes a representation of opinion, belief or other state of mind only if the representation clearly relates to state of mind apart from or in addition to any facts which are the subject of the representation.

§ 241.1. Perjury.

(1) *Offense Defined*. A person is guilty of perjury, a felony of the third degree, if in any official proceeding he makes a false statement under oath or equivalent affirmation, or swears or affirms the truth of a statement previously made, when the statement is material and he does not believe it to be true.

(2) *Materiality*. Falsification is material, regardless of the admissibility of the statement under rules of evidence, if it could have affected the course or outcome of the proceeding. It is no defense that the declarant mistakenly believed the falsification to be immaterial. Whether a falsification is material in a given factual situation is a question of law.

(3) *Irregularities No Defense*. It is not a defense to prosecution under this Section that the oath or affirmation was administered or taken in an irregular manner or that the declarant was not competent to make the statement. A document purporting to be made upon oath or affirmation at any time when the actor presents it as being so verified shall be deemed to have been duly sworn or affirmed.

(4) *Retraction*. No person shall be guilty of an offense under this Section if he retracted the falsification in the course of the proceeding in which it was made before it became manifest that the falsification was or would be exposed and before the falsification substantially affected the proceeding.

(5) *Inconsistent Statements*. Where the defendant made inconsistent statements under oath or equivalent affirmation, both having been made within the period of the statute of limitations, the prosecution may proceed by setting forth the inconsistent statements in a single count alleging in the alternative that one or the other was false and not believed by the defendant. In such case it shall not be necessary for the prosecution to prove which statement was false but only that one or the other was false and not believed by the defendant to be true.

(6) *Corroboration*. No person shall be convicted of an offense under this Section where proof of falsity rests solely upon contradiction by testimony of a single person other than the defendant.

§ 241.2. False Swearing.

(1) *False Swearing in Official Matters*. A person who makes a false statement under oath or equivalent affirmation, or swears or affirms the truth of such a statement previously made, when he does not believe the statement to be true, is guilty of a misdemeanor if:

(a) the falsification occurs in an official proceeding; or

(b) the falsification is intended to mislead a public servant in performing his official function.

Offenses Against Public Order and Decency

Article 250. Riot, Disorderly Conduct, and Related Offenses.

§ 250.1. Riot; Failure to Disperse.

(1) *Riot*. A person is guilty of riot, a felony of the third degree, if he participates with [two] or more others in a course of disorderly conduct:

(a) with purpose to commit or facilitate the commission of a felony or misdemeanor;

(b) with purpose to prevent or coerce official action; or

(c) when the actor or any other participant to the knowledge of the actor uses or plans to use a firearm or other deadly weapon.

(2) *Failure of Disorderly Persons to Disperse Upon Official Order.* Where [three] or more persons are participating in a course of disorderly conduct likely to cause substantial harm or serious inconvenience, annoyance or alarm, a peace officer or other public servant engaged in executing or enforcing the law may order the participants and others in the immediate vicinity to disperse. A person who refuses or knowingly fails to obey such an order commits a misdemeanor.

§ 250.2. Disorderly Conduct.

(1) *Offense Defined.* A person is guilty of disorderly conduct if, with purpose to cause public inconvenience, annoyance or alarm, or recklessly creating a risk thereof, he:

   (a) engages in fighting or threatening, or in violent or tumultuous behavior; or

   (b) makes unreasonable noise or offensively coarse utterance, gesture or display, or addresses abusive language to any person present; or

   (c) creates a hazardous or physically offensive condition by any act which serves no legitimate purpose of the actor.

"Public" means affecting or likely to affect persons in a place to which the public or a substantial group has access; among the places included are highways, transport facilities, schools, prisons, apartment houses, places of business or amusement, or any neighborhood.

(2) *Grading.* An offense under this section is a petty misdemeanor if the actor's purpose is to cause substantial harm or serious inconvenience, or if he persists in disorderly conduct after reasonable warning or request to desist. Otherwise disorderly conduct is a violation.

§ 250.4. Harassment.

A person commits a petty misdemeanor if, with purpose to harass another, he:

(1) makes a telephone call without purpose of legitimate communication; or

(2) insults, taunts or challenges another in a manner likely to provoke violent or disorderly response; or

(3) makes repeated communications anonymously or at extremely inconvenient hours, or in offensively coarse language; or

(4) subjects another to an offensive touching; or

(5) engages in any other course of alarming conduct serving no legitimate purpose of the actor.

§ 250.5. Public Drunkenness; Drug Incapacitation.

A person is guilty of an offense if he appears in any public place manifestly under the influence of alcohol, narcotics or other drugs, not therapeutically administered, to the degree that he may endanger himself or other persons or property, or annoy persons in his vicinity. An offense under this Section constitutes a petty misdemeanor if the actor has been convicted hereunder twice before within a period of one year. Otherwise the offense constitutes a violation.

§ 250.6. Loitering or Prowling.

A person commits a violation if he loiters or prowls in a place, at a time, or in a manner not usual for law-abiding individuals under circumstances that warrant alarm for the safety of persons or property in the vicinity. Among the circumstances which may be considered in determining whether such alarm is warranted is the fact that the actor takes flight upon appearance of a peace officer, refuses to identify himself, or manifestly endeavors to conceal himself or any object. Unless flight by the actor or other circumstances makes it impracticable, a peace officer shall prior to any arrest for an offense under this Section afford the actor an opportunity to dispel any alarm which would otherwise be warranted, by requesting him to identify himself and explain his presence and conduct. No person shall be convicted of an offense under this Section if the peace officer did not comply with the preceding sentence, or if it appears at trial that the explanation given by the actor was true and, if believed by the peace officer at the time, would have dispelled the alarm.

Article 251. Public Indecency

§ 251.1. Open Lewdness.

A person commits a petty misdemeanor if he does any lewd act which he knows is likely to be observed by others who would be affronted or alarmed.

(1) *Prostitution.* A person is guilty of prostitution, a petty misdemeanor, if he or she:

   (a) is an inmate of a house of prostitution or otherwise engages in sexual activity as a business; or

   (b) loiters in or within view of any public place for the purpose of being hired to engage in sexual activity.

"Sexual activity" includes homosexual and other deviate sexual relations. A "house of prostitution" is any place where prostitution or promotion of prostitution is regularly carried on by one person under the control, management or supervision of another. An "inmate" is a person who engages in prostitution in or through the agency of a house of prostitution. "Public place" means any place to which the public or any substantial group thereof has access.

(2) *Promoting Prostitution.* A person who knowingly promotes prostitution of another commits a misdemeanor or felony as provided in Subsection (3). The following acts shall, without limitation of the foregoing, constitute promoting prostitution:

   (a) owning, controlling, managing, supervising or otherwise keeping, alone or in association with others, a house of prostitution or a prostitution business; or

   (b) procuring an inmate for a house of prostitution or a place in a house of prostitution for one who would be an inmate; or

   (c) encouraging, inducing, or otherwise purposely causing another to become or remain a prostitute; or

   (d) soliciting a person to patronize a prostitute; or

   (e) procuring a prostitute for a patron; or

   (f) transporting a person into or within this state with purpose to promote that person's engaging in prostitution, or procuring or paying for transportation with that purpose; or

   (g) leasing or otherwise permitting a place controlled by the actor, alone or in association with others, to be regularly used for prostitution or the promotion of prostitution, or failure to make reasonable effort to abate such use by ejecting the tenant, notifying law enforcement authorities, or other legally available means; or

   (h) soliciting, receiving, or agreeing to receive any benefit for doing or agreeing to do anything forbidden by this Subsection.

(3) *Grading of Offenses Under Subsection (2).* An offense under Subsection (2) constitutes a felony of the third degree if:

   (a) the offense falls within paragraph (a), (b) or (c) of Subsection (2); or

   (b) the actor compels another to engage in or promote prostitution; or

   (c) the actor promotes prostitution of a child under 16, whether or not he is aware of the child's age; or

   (d) the actor promotes prostitution of his wife, child, ward or any person for whose care, protection or support he is responsible.

Otherwise the offense is a misdemeanor.

(4) *Presumption from Living off Prostitutes.* A person, other than the prostitute or the prostitute's minor child or other legal dependent incapable of self-support, who is supported in whole or substantial part by the proceeds of prostitution is presumed to be knowingly promoting prostitution in violation of Subsection (2).

(5) *Patronizing Prostitutes.* A person commits a violation if he hires a prostitute to engage in sexual activity with him, or if he enters or remains in a house of prostitution for the purpose of engaging in sexual activity.

(6) *Evidence.* On the issue whether a place is a house of prostitution the following shall be admissible evidence; its general repute; the repute of the persons who reside in or frequent the place; the frequency, timing and duration of visits by non-residents. Testimony of a person against his spouse shall be admissible to prove offenses under this Section.

§ 251.3. Loitering to Solicit Deviate Sexual Relations.

A person is guilty of a petty misdemeanor if he loiters in or near any public place for the purpose of soliciting or being solicited to engage in deviate sexual relations.

§ 251.4. Obscenity.

(1) *Obscene Defined.* Material is obscene if, considered as a whole, its predominant appeal is to prurient interest, that is, a shameful or morbid interest, in nudity, sex or excretion, and if in addition it goes substantially beyond customary limits of candor in describing or representing such matters. Predominant appeal shall be judged with reference to ordinary adults unless it appears from the character of the material or the circumstances of its dissemination to be designed for children or other specially susceptible audience. Undeveloped photographs, molds, printing plates, and the like, shall be deemed obscene notwithstanding that processing or other acts may be required to make the obscenity patent or to disseminate it.

(2) *Offenses.* Subject to the affirmative defense provided in Subsection (3), a person commits a misdemeanor if he knowingly or recklessly:

   (a) sells, delivers or provides, or offers or agrees to sell, deliver or provide, any obscene writing, picture, record or other representation or embodiment of the obscene; or

(b) presents or directs an obscene play, dance or performance, or participates in that portion thereof which makes it obscene; or

(c) publishes, exhibits or otherwise makes available any obscene material; or

(d) possesses any obscene material for purposes of sale or other commercial dissemination; or

(e) sells, advertises or otherwise commercially disseminates material, whether or not obscene, by representing or suggesting that it is obscene.

A person who disseminates or possesses obscene material in the course of his business is presumed to do so knowingly or recklessly.

(3) *Justifiable and Non-Commercial Private Dissemination.* It is an affirmative defense to prosecution under this Section that dissemination was restricted to:

(a) institutions or persons having scientific, educational, governmental or other similar justification for possessing obscene material; or

(b) non-commercial dissemination to personal associates of the actor.

(4) *Evidence; Adjudication of Obscenity.* In any prosecution under this Section, evidence shall be admissible to show:

(a) the character of the audience for which the material was designed or to which it was directed;

(b) what the predominant appeal of the material would be for ordinary adults or any special audience to which it was directed, and what effect, if any, it would probably have on conduct of such people;

(c) artistic, literary, scientific, educational or other merits of the material;

(d) the degree of public acceptance of the material in the United States;

(e) appeal to prurient interest, or absence thereof, in advertising or other promotion of the material; and

(f) the good repute of the author, creator, publisher or other person from whom the material originated.

Expert testimony and testimony of the author, creator, publisher or other person from whom the material originated, relating to factors entering into the determination of the issue of obscenity, shall be admissible. The Court shall dismiss a prosecution for obscenity if it is satisfied that the material is not obscene.

Briefing and Analyzing Cases

Decisions of courts are often written and are commonly referred to as *judicial opinions* or cases. These cases are published in law reporters so they may be used as precedent. Many cases appear in this text for your education. Your instructor may also require that you read other cases, often from your jurisdiction. The cases included in your book have been edited, citations have been omitted, and legal issues not relevant to the subject discussed have been excised. There is a common method that students of the law use to read and analyze, also known as briefing, cases.

Most judicial opinions are written using a similar format. First, the name of the case appears with the name of the court, the cite (location where the case has been published), and the year. When the body of the case begins, the name of the judge, or judges, responsible for writing the opinion appears directly before the first paragraph. The opinion contains an introduction to the case, which normally includes the procedural history of the case. This is followed by a summary of the facts that led to the dispute, the court's analysis of the law that applies to the case, and the court's conclusions and orders, if any.

Most opinions used here are from appellate courts, where many judges sit at one time. After the case is over, the judges vote on an outcome. The majority vote wins, and the opinion of the majority is written by one of those judges. If other judges in the majority wish to add to the majority opinion, they may write one or more *concurring opinions*. Concurring opinions appear after majority opinions in the law reporters. When a judge who was not in the majority feels strongly about his or her position, he or she may file a dissenting opinion, which appears after the concurring opinions, if any. Only the majority opinion is law, although concurring and dissenting opinions are often informative.

During your legal education you may be instructed to "brief" a case. Even if your instructor does not require you to brief cases, you may want to, as many learners understand a case better after they have completed a brief. Here are suggestions for reading and understanding cases.

First, read the case. Don't take notes during your first reading. Get a "feel" for the case—the facts, the Court's tone, and the outcomes.

Second, brief the case. What follows is a suggested briefing format.

A common format for briefing judicial decisions is IRAC. The acronym represents Issue, Rules, Analysis, and Conclusion. It is recommended that you employ a modified form of IRAC that adds the facts of the case, hence FIRAC.

Begin your brief by identifying the most important and material **FACTS** of the case. Not all facts mentioned by the court are material to the issue you are studying. It is possible for a court to reference an immaterial fact, or more likely, it had to address more legal issues than you have read about and, accordingly, it is included facts that could be material to a separate legal issue. Remember, you are reading cases that have been edited and pared down to the topic you are studying.

Identify the legal **ISSUE** in the case. Issue spotting is a very important legal skill. The issue is the legal question the court is answering. The facts of the case give rise to and frame the legal issue(s) of the case.

What **RULE**(s) applies to the issue you have identified? The rules are the laws, from whatever source, that guide the analysis. The rules come in many forms. The law that directly applies to the issues and facts is known as doctrinal law. But other process rules may apply as well, such as the rules of statutory or constitutional interpretation and stare decisis. Often, some knowledge of the law, or least a good intuition, is needed to identify an issue. This is one of the challenges of being a legal neophyte.

ANALYZE the case, applying the law to the facts of the case. Remember, the law is "blind." The politics and social dimensions of cases are immaterial. Like Mr. Spock on *Star Trek,* engage in objective, logical (legal) analysis, and leave your personal opinions out of the mix. Often during analysis, new legal issues will emerge. Be prepared to add them to your analysis. See the example below for an example of how this happens.

Draw a **CONCLUSION**. Students often want to jump the "final answer." What is important is that you can identify and frame an issue and analyze the problem. Your final conclusion is less important (unless you are a judge!). In most cases, your conclusion won't be about guilt or innocence. It will be about the application of a law to a set of facts.

The figure above shows the sequence of the analysis. A simple example of the application of the FIRAC model follows.

Example: Gun Possession in the Home

Facts:

MegaTown enacts an ordinance making it a misdemeanor punished by as much as one year in jail and a fine of $10,000 for the possession of a handgun in the home. One evening, A. Sih, a resident of MegaTown, phoned the police to report a noise in her home. She invited the two officers who were dispatched to her residence to come into her home to search for possible intruders. While they didn't find an intruder, they discovered a handgun sitting on a table in the living room. They issued Ms. Sih a citation for possession of the firearm in violation of city ordinance. Subsequently, she pled guilty and was sentenced to sixty days in jail and a $100 fine.

Issue:

May MegaTown forbid the possession of handguns in the home?

Rules:

The Second Amendment to the U.S. Constitution provides that a "well regulated Militia, being necessary to the security of a free state, the right of the people to keep and bear Arms, shall not be infringed."

This is an example of where some knowledge of the law is necessary in order to identify the issue. One would have to know, at some level, that there is a protection of gun ownership to know to turn to the Constitution.

Additionally, as an issue is researched, new legal issues often emerge. In this case, for example, you would learn as you read the Supreme Court's cases that an issue that must be addressed is whether the Second Amendment applies against the States or just against the Federal government, as was the Framers' intention at the time of the adoption of the Bill of Rights. This analysis requires the application of a new rule, the Fourteenth Amendment's Due Process Clause (which is used to "incorporate" or apply the Bill of Rights to the States).

Analysis:

1) The Second Amendment right to bear arms is independent of the Militia Clause.

2) There is considerable evidence that possession of a handgun in the home for personal security is "deeply rooted" in U.S. and English history. The Framers of the Constitution, both Federalists and Anti-Federalists, considered gun ownership important to freedom. Attempts to disarm the colonists by the King of England were met with hostility. At the time of the adoption of the Second Amendment, the states commonly protected the right through their constitutions and the Framers purposely replicated those protections in the U.S. Constitution.

3) Accordingly, the right to possess a handgun in the home is a fundamental right intended to be protected from governmental intervention.

4) Rights that are fundamental and necessary to an ordered liberty are incorporate and apply against the states under the 14th Amendment. Initially, this wasn't true (*Barron ex rel. Tiernan* v. *Mayor of Baltimore*, 7 Pet. 243 (1833)), but years after the adoption of the Fourteenth Amendment, the Court decided that some rights may apply against the states (see *Hurtado v. California* (1884) and *Chicago, B. & Q. R. Co. v. Chicago* (1897)).

5) Because it is fundamental and necessary to an ordered liberty, the right is incorporated under the Fourteenth Amendment and applies against the States (which includes localities).

You will want to cite the cases, statutes, and constitutional provisions that stand for the principles you are advancing.

Conclusion:

MegaTown's ordinance violates the Second Amendment's right to bear arms and Ms. Sih's conviction must be overturned.

Note: this example is an amalgam of two Supreme Court decisions, *McDonald v. Chicago* (2010) and *Washington, D.C. v. Heller* (2008).

GLOSSARY

accessory   A person who helps to commit a crime without being present. An accessory before the fact is a person who, without being present, encourages, orders, or helps another to commit a crime. An accessory after the fact is a person who finds out that a crime has been committed and helps to conceal the crime or the criminal.

actus reus   (Latin) An act. For example, an *actus reus* is a "wrongful deed" (such as killing a person) which, if done with mens rea, a "guilty mind" (such as *malice aforethought*), is a crime (such as *first-degree* murder).

admission   A voluntary statement that a fact or a state of events is true.

adversary system   The system of law in the United States. The judge acts as the referee between opposite sides (between two individuals, between the state and an individual, etc.) rather than acting as the person who also makes the state's case or independently seeks out evidence.

affirmative defense   A defense that is more than a simple denial of the charges. It raises a new matter that may result in an acquittal or a reduction of liability. It is a defense that must be affirmatively raised, often before trial or it is lost.

aggravating circumstances   Actions or occurrences that increase the seriousness of a crime, but are not part of the legal definition of that crime.

alibi   (Latin) "Elsewhere"; the claim that at the time a crime was committed a person was somewhere else. [pronounce: *al*-eh-bi]

appellate court   A higher court that can hear appeals from a lower court.

arraignment   The hearing at which a defendant is brought before a judge to hear the charges and to enter a plea (guilty, not guilty, etc.).

arrest   The official taking of a person to answer criminal charges. This involves at least temporarily depriving the person of liberty and may involve the use of force. An arrest is usually made by a police officer with a warrant or for a crime committed in the officer's presence.

arson   The malicious and unlawful burning of a building.

assault   An intentional threat, show of force, or movement that could reasonably make a person feel in danger of physical attack or harmful physical contact. It can be a crime or tort.

attempt   An effort to commit a crime that goes beyond preparation and that proceeds far enough to make the person who did it guilty of an "attempt crime." For example, if a person fires a shot at another in a failed effort at murder, the person is guilty of *attempted murder.*

bail   The money or property given as security for a defendant's appearance in court. The money, often in the form of a bail bond, may be lost if the defendant released does not appear in court.

battered woman syndrome   Continuing abuse of a woman by a spouse or lover, and the resulting physical or psychological harm.

battery   An intentional, unconsented to, physical contact by one person (or an object controlled by that person) with another person. It can be a crime or a tort.

beyond a reasonable doubt   The level of proof required to convict a person of a crime. Precise definitions vary, but moral certainty and firm belief are both used. Beyond a reasonable doubt is not absolute certainty. This is the highest level of proof required in any type of trial.

bill of attainder   A legislative act pronouncing a person guilty (usually of treason) without a trial and sentencing the person to death and attainder. This is now prohibited by the U.S. Constitution.

bill of particulars   A detailed, formal, written statement of charges or claims by a plaintiff or the prosecutor (given upon the defendant's formal request to the court for more detailed information).

Bill of Rights   The first 10 amendments (changes or additions) to the U.S. Constitution.

breach of the peace   A vague term for any illegal public disturbance; sometimes refers to the offense known as "disorderly conduct." It is defined and treated differently in different states.

bribery   The offering, giving, receiving, or soliciting of anything of value in order to influence the actions of a public official.

brief   A written document filed with a court through which a party presents a legal claim, legal theory, supporting authorities, and requests some form of relief.

burden of going forward (production)   The requirement that one side in a lawsuit produce evidence on a particular issue or risk losing on that issue.

burden of persuasion   The requirement that to win a point or have an issue decided in your favor in a lawsuit you must show that the weight of evidence is on your side, rather than "in the balance" on that question.

burden of proof   The requirement that to win a point or have an issue decided in your favor in a lawsuit, you must show that the weight of evidence is on your side rather than "in the balance" on that question.

burglary   Unlawfully entering the house of another person with the intention of committing a felony (usually theft).

castle doctrine   An exception to the Retreat Doctrine, one has no obligation to retreat from his or her home before using deadly force to repel an intruder.

certiorari   (Latin) "To make sure." A request for certiorari (or "cert." for short) is like an appeal, but one that the higher court is not required to take for decision. It is literally a writ from the higher court asking the lower court for the record of the case.

chain of custody   The chronological list of those in continuous possession of a specific physical object. A person who presents physical evidence (such as a gun used in a crime) at a trial must account for its possession from time of receipt to time of trial in order for the evidence to be "admitted" by the judge. It must thus be shown that the *chain of custody* was unbroken.

challenge for cause   A formal objection to the qualifications of a prospective juror or jurors.

civil liberties   Political liberties guaranteed by the Constitution and, in particular, by the Bill of Rights, especially the First Amendment.

clear and present danger   A test of whether or not speech may be restricted or punished. It may be if it will probably lead to violence soon or if it threatens a serious, immediate weakening of national safety and security.

co-conspirator's rule   The principle that statements by a member of a proven conspiracy may be used as evidence against any of the members of the conspiracy.

common law   The legal system that originated in England and is composed of case law and statutes that grow and change, influenced by ever-changing custom and tradition.

commutation of sentence   Changing a criminal punishment to one less severe

compensatory damages   Damages awarded for the actual loss suffered by a plaintiff.

complaint   A *criminal complaint* is a formal document that charges a person with a crime.

concert of action rule   The rule that, unless a statute specifies otherwise, it is not a conspiracy for two persons to agree to commit a crime if the definition of the crime itself requires the participation of two or more persons. Also called *Wharton Rule* and *concerted action rule.*

concurrent jurisdiction   Two or more jurisdictions or courts possessing authority over the same matter.

concurrent sentences   Prison terms that run at the same time.

confession   A voluntary statement by a person that he or she is guilty of a crime.

consecutive sentences   An additional prison term given to a person who is already convicted of a crime; the additional term is to be served after the previous one is finished.

consent   Voluntary and active agreement.

conspiracy   A crime that may be committed when two or more persons agree to do something unlawful (or to do something lawful by unlawful means). The agreement can be inferred from the persons' actions.

constructive   Inferred, implied, or presumed from the circumstances.

contempt   A willful disobeying of a judge's command or official court order. Contempt can be *direct* (within the judge's notice) or *indirect* (outside the court and punishable only after proved to the judge). It can also be *civil contempt* (disobeying a court order in favor of an opponent) or *criminal contempt.*

contract An agreement that affects or creates legal relationships between two or more persons. To be a *contract,* an agreement must involve at least one promise, consideration, persons legally capable of making binding agreements, and a reasonable certainty about the meaning of the terms.

conversion Any act that deprives an owner of property without that owner's permission and without just cause.

corporate liability The liability of a corporation for the acts of its directors, officers, shareholders, agents, and employees.

corpus delicti (Latin) "The body of the crime." The material substance upon which a crime has been committed; for example, a dead body (in the crime of murder) or a house burned down (in the crime of arson).

court of general jurisdiction Another term for trial court; that is, a court having jurisdiction to try all classes of civil and criminal cases except those that can be heard only by a court of limited jurisdiction.

court of limited jurisdiction A court whose jurisdiction is limited to civil cases of a certain type, or that involve a limited amount of money, or whose jurisdiction in criminal cases is confined to petty offenses and preliminary hearings.

court of record Generally, another term for trial court.

criminal law The branch of the law that specifies what conduct constitutes crime and establishes appropriate punishments for such conduct.

criminal procedure The rules of procedure by which criminal prosecutions are governed.

culpable Blamable; at fault. A person who has done a wrongful act (whether criminal or civil) is described as "culpable."

damages Money that a court orders paid to a person who has suffered damage (a loss or harm) by the person who caused the injury (the violation of the person's rights).

deadly weapon Any instrument likely to cause serious bodily harm under the circumstances of its actual use. Such things as a fan belt used to choke a man and a fire used to burn an occupied house have been called *deadly weapons* by courts.

deposition The process of taking a witness's sworn out-of-court testimony. The questioning is usually done by a lawyer, and the lawyer from the other side is given a chance to attend and participate.

detainer A warrant or court order to keep a person in custody when that person might otherwise be released. This is often used to make sure a person will serve a sentence or attend a trial in one state at the end of a prison term in another state or in a federal prison.

deter To discourage; to prevent from acting.

determinate sentence An exact penalty set by law.

diminished capacity The principle that having a certain recognized form of *diminished mental capacity* while committing a crime should lead to the imposition of a lesser punishment or to lowering the degree of the crime.

discovery The formal and informal exchange of information between the prosecution and the defense.

discretion The power to act within general guidelines, rules, or laws, but without either specific rules to follow or the need to completely explain or justify each decision or action.

DNA printing Comparing body tissue samples (such as blood, skin, hair, or semen) to see if the genetic materials match. The process is used to identify criminals by comparing their DNA with that found at a crime scene, and it is used to identify a child's parent. Most states allow its use as evidence.

double jeopardy A second prosecution by the same government against the same person for the same crime (or for a lesser included offense) once the first prosecution is totally finished and decided. This is prohibited by the U.S. Constitution.

due process The *due process* clauses of the Fifth and Fourteenth Amendments to the U.S. Constitution require that no persons be deprived of life, liberty, or property without having notice and a real chance to present their side in a legal dispute.

duress Unlawful pressure on what a person would not otherwise have done. It includes force, threats of violence, physical restraint, etc.

Durham rule The principle, used in *Durham v. U.S.* (214 F.2d. 862 (1954)), that defendants are not guilty of a crime because of insanity if they were "suffering from a disease or defective mental condition at the time of the act and there was a causal connection between the condition and the act."

element A basic part. For example, some of the *elements* of a cause of action for battery are an intentional, unwanted physical contact. Each of these things ("intentional," "unwanted," etc.) is one "element."

embezzlement   The fraudulent and secret taking of money or property by a person who has been trusted with it. This usually applies to an employee's taking money and covering it up by faking business records or account books.

entrapment   The act of government officials (usually police) or agents inducing a person to commit a crime that the person would not have committed without the inducement.

ex post facto law   (Latin) After the fact. An *ex post facto* law is one that retroactively attempts to make an action a crime that was not a crime at the time it was done, or a law that attempts to reduce a person's rights based on a past act that was not subject to the law when it was done.

exclusionary rule   "The exclusionary rule" often means the rule that illegally gathered evidence may not be used in a criminal trial. The rule has several exceptions, such as when the evidence is used to impeach a defendant's testimony and when the evidence was gathered in a good-faith belief that the process was legal.

exhaustion of remedies   A person must usually take all reasonable steps to get satisfaction from a state or federal government before seeking judicial relief.

exigent circumstances   A situation where law enforcement officers must act so quickly to prevent the destruction of evidence, the successful flight of a suspect, or serious injury or death to any person, that there isn't time to obtain a warrant. Warrantless searches that occur when exigent circumstances exist are valid.

extortion   To compel, force, or coerce; for example, to get a confession by depriving a person of food and water. To get something by illegal threats of harm to person, property, or reputation. The process is called *extortion*.

extradition   One country (or state) giving up a person to a second country (or state) when the second requests the person for a trial on a criminal charge or for punishment after a trial.

false imprisonment   The unlawful restraint by one person of the physical liberty of another.

false pretenses   A lie told to cheat another person out of his or her money or property. It is a crime in most states, though the precise definition varies.

federalism   A system of political organization with several different levels of government (for example, city, state, and national) coexisting in the same area, with the lower levels having some independent powers.

felony-murder rule   The principle that if a person (even accidentally) kills another while committing a felony, then the killing is murder.

fighting words   Speech that is not protected by the First Amendment to the U.S. Constitution because it is likely to cause violence by the person to whom the words are spoken.

final judgement (order)   The last action of a court; the one upon which an appeal can be based.

first-degree murder   The highest form of homicide. The killing of another person with malice and premeditation, cruelty, or done during the commission of a major felony is typically murder in the first degree.

foreseeable   The degree to which the consequences of an action *should* have been anticipated, recognized, and considered beforehand. *Not* hindsight.

forfeiture   A deprivation of money, property, or rights, without compensation, as a consequence of a default or the commission of a crime.

forgery   Making a fake document (or altering a real one) with intent to commit a fraud.

fruit of the poisonous tree doctrine   The rule that evidence gathered as a *result* of evidence gained in an illegal search or questioning cannot be used against the person searched or questioned even if the later evidence was gathered lawfully.

general intent   The desire to commit a prohibited act but not the outcome of that act.

grand jury   Persons who receive complaints and accusations of crime, hear preliminary evidence on the complaining side, and make formal accusations or indictments.

habitual offender statutes   Laws that may apply to a person who has been convicted of as few as two prior crimes (often violent or drug-related crimes) and that greatly increase the penalties for each succeeding crime.

halfway house   A facility in which persons recently discharged from a rehabilitation center or prison live for a time and are given support and assistance in readjusting to society at large.

harmless error   A trivial mistake made by a judge in the procedures used at trial, or in making legal rulings during the trial.

hearsay   A statement about what someone else said (or wrote or otherwise communicated). *Hearsay evidence* is evidence, concerning what someone said outside of a court proceeding, that is offered in the proceeding to prove the truth of what was said. The *hearsay rule* bars the admission of hearsay as evidence to *prove the hearsay's truth* unless allowed by a hearsay exception.

hung jury   A jury that cannot reach a verdict (decision) because of disagreement among jurors.

identity theft   The act of assuming another person's identity by fraud.

in limine   (Latin) "At the beginning"; preliminary. A motion in limine is a (usually pretrial) request that prejudicial information be excluded as trial evidence.

independent source   The general rule that if new evidence can be traced to a source completely apart from the illegally gathered evidence that first led to the new evidence, it may be used by the government in a criminal trial.

indeterminate sentence   A sentence having a minimum and maximum, with the decision of how long the criminal will serve depending on the criminal's behavior in prison and other things.

indictment   A sworn, written accusation of a crime, made against a person by a prosecutor to a *grand jury*.

inevitable discovery rule   The principle that even if criminal evidence is gathered by unconstitutional methods, the evidence may be admissible if it definitely would have come to light anyway.

inference   A fact (or proposition) that is *probably* true because a true fact (or proposition) leads you to believe that the inferred fact (or proposition) is also true.

inferior court   A court with special, limited responsibilities, such as a probate court.

information   A formal accusation of a crime made by a proper public official such as a prosecuting attorney.

injunction   A judge's order to a person to do or to refrain from doing a particular–thing.

intentional   Determination to do a certain thing.

interlocutory appeal   The *Interlocutory Appeals* Act (28 U.S.C. 1292 (1948)) is a federal law that provides for an appeal while a trial is going on if the trial judge states in writing: (1) A legal question has come up that directly affects the trial. (2) There are major questions as to how that point of law should be resolved. (3) The case would proceed better if the appeals court answers the question.

interpret   Studying a document *and* surrounding circumstances to decide the document's meaning.

interrogation   Questioning by police, especially of a person suspected or accused of a crime. A *custodial interrogation* involves a restraint of freedom, so it requires a *Miranda* warning. A routine *investigatory interrogation* involves no restraint and no accusation of a crime.

intervening cause   A cause of an accident or other injury that will remove the blame from the wrongdoer who originally set events in motion.

irresistible impulse   The loss of control due to insanity that is so great that a person cannot stop from committing a crime.

JNOV   A request by a defendant convicted by a jury for the court to set aside the verdict as unsupported by the evidence.

judicial review   A higher court's examination of a lower court's decision.

jurisdiction   The geographical area within which a court (or a public official) has the right and power to operate. Or the persons about whom and the subject matters about which a court has the right and power to make decisions that are legally binding.

kidnapping   Taking away and holding a person illegally, usually against the person's will or by force.

knowingly   With full knowledge and intentionally; willfully.

larceny   Stealing of any kind. Some types of larceny are specific crimes, such as larceny by trick or grand larceny.

legal cause   The proximate cause of an injury; probable cause; cause that the law deems sufficient.

legal impossibility   A person who is unable to commit a crime because of legal impossibility cannot be convicted of a crime he or she intends or attempts.

legislative history   The background documents and records of hearings related to the enactment of a bill.

lineup   A group of persons, placed side by side in a line, shown to a witness of a crime to see if the witness will identify the person suspected of committing the crime. A *lineup* should not be staged so that it is suggestive of one person.

M'Naghten rule   A principle employed in some jurisdictions for determining whether criminal defendants had the capacity to form criminal intent at the time they committed the crime of which they are accused. The M'Naghten rule is also referred to as the M'Naghten test or the right-wrong test.

malicious (criminal) mischief   The criminal offense of intentionally destroying another person's property.

manslaughter   A crime, less severe than murder, involving the wrongful but nonmalicious killing of another person.

mayhem   The crime of violently, maliciously, and intentionally giving someone a serious permanent wound. In some states, a type of aggravated assault. Once, the crime of permanently wounding another (as by dismemberment) to deprive the person of fighting ability.

mens rea   (Latin) A state of mind that produces a crime.

merger of offenses   When a person is charged with two crimes (based on exactly the same acts), one of which is a lesser included offense of the other. The lesser crime *merges* because, under the prohibition against double jeopardy, the person may be tried for only one crime.

mitigating circumstances   Facts that provide no justification or excuse for an action, but that can lower the amount of moral blame and thus lower the criminal penalty or civil damages for the action.

Model Penal Code   A proposed criminal code prepared jointly by the Commission on Uniform State Laws and the American Law Institute.

motion   A request that a judge make a ruling or take some other action.

motive   The reason why a person does something.

National Crime Information Center   Computerized records of criminals, warrants, stolen vehicles, etc.

necessity   Often refers to a situation that requires an action that would otherwise be illegal or expose a person to tort liability.

negligence   Under the MPC, a defendant acts negligently when the resulting harm or material element of a crime occurs because of the defendant has taken a substantial and unjustifiable risk, even if the risk is not perceived, so long as the risk involves a gross deviation from the standard of conduct that a law-abiding person would observe.

nolle prosequi   (Latin) The ending of a criminal case because the prosecutor decides or agrees to stop prosecuting. When this happens, the case is "nolled," "nollied," or "nol. prossed."

objection   A claim that an action by your adversary in a lawsuit (such as the use of a particular piece of evidence) is improper, unfair, or illegal, and you are asking the judge for a ruling on the point.

omission   Failing to do something that should be done.

ordinance   A local or city law, rule, or regulation.

overbreadth doctrine   A law will be declared void for *overbreadth* if it attempts to punish speech or conduct that is protected by the Constitution and if it is impossible to eliminate the unconstitutional part of the law without invalidating the whole law.

pardon   A president's or governor's release of a person from punishment for a crime.

parole   Early release from prison or jail. Parole is usually granted with conditions such as requiring the parolee to refrain from communicating with the victim of the crime that led to the confinement and remaining free of criminality while on parole. If the conditions of parole are violated, parole may be revoked and the parolee may be returned to confinement to complete the original sentence.

peremptory challenge   The automatic elimination of a potential juror by one side before trial without needing to state the reason for the elimination.

perjury   Lying while under oath, especially in a court proceeding. It is a crime.

plain view doctrine   The rule that if police officers see or come across something while acting lawfully, that item may be used as evidence in a criminal trial even if the police did not have a search warrant.

plea bargain (plea agreement)   Negotiations between a prosecutor and a criminal defendant's lawyer, in the attempt to resolve a criminal case without trial.

plea   The *defendant's* formal answer to a criminal charge. The defendant says: "guilty," "not guilty," or "nolo contendere" (no contest).

police power   The government's right and power to set up and enforce laws to provide for the safety, health, and general welfare of the people.

polling the jury   Individually asking each member of a jury what his or her decision is. Polling is done by the judge, at the defendant's request, immediately after the verdict.

precedent   Prior decisions of the same court, or a higher court, that a judge must follow in deciding a subsequent case presenting similar facts and the same legal problem, even though different parties are involved and many years have elapsed.

preliminary hearing   The first court proceeding on a criminal charge, in federal courts and many state courts, by a magistrate or a judge to decide whether there is enough evidence for the government to continue with the case and to require the defendant to post bail or be held for trial.

presumption A presumption *of law* is an automatic assumption required by law that whenever a certain set of facts shows up, a court must automatically draw certain legal conclusions.

principal A person directly involved with committing a crime, as opposed to an accessory.

principle of legality The procedural side of due process, which requires that criminal laws (and punishments) be written and enacted before an act may be punished.

probable cause The U.S. Constitutional requirement that law enforcement officers present sufficient facts to convince a judge to issue a search warrant or an arrest *warrant*, and the requirement that no warrant should be issued unless it is more likely than not that the objects sought will be found in the place to be searched or that a crime has been committed by the person to be arrested.

prostitution A person offering her (in most states, his or her) body for sexual purposes in exchange for money. A crime in most states.

provocation An act by one person that triggers a reaction of rage in a second person. *Provocation* may reduce the severity of a crime.

proximate cause The "legal cause" of an accident or other injury (which may have several actual causes). The *proximate cause* of an injury is not necessarily the closest thing in time or space to the injury, and not necessarily the event that set things in motion, because "proximate cause" is a legal, not a physical concept.

punitive damages Damages that are awarded over and above compensatory damages or actual damages because of the wanton, reckless, or malicious nature of the wrong done by the plaintiff.

purposely Intentionally; knowingly.

quash Overthrow; annul; completely do away with. *Quash* usually refers to a court stopping a subpoena, an order, or an indictment.

racketeer influenced and corrupt organizations act (19 U.S.C. 1961). A broadly applied 1970 federal law that creates certain "racketeering offenses" that include participation in various criminal schemes and conspiracies, and that allows government seizure of property acquired in violation of the act.

rape The crime of imposing sexual intercourse by force or otherwise without legally valid consent.

receiving stolen property The criminal offense of getting or concealing property known to be stolen by another.

recklessness Indifference to consequences; indifference to the safety and rights of others. Recklessness implies conduct amounting to more than ordinary negligence.

record on appeal A formal, written account of a case, containing the complete formal history of all actions taken, papers filed, rulings made, opinions written, etc.

regulation Law created by governmental administrative agencies.

reprieve Holding off on enforcing a criminal sentence for a period of time after the sentence has been handed down.

retreat to the wall The doctrine that before a person is entitled to use deadly force in self defense, he or she must attempt to withdraw from the encounter by giving as much ground as possible.

revocation hearing The due process hearing required before the government can revoke a privilege it has previously granted.

robbery The illegal taking of property from the person of another by using force or threat of force.

rules of court Rules promulgated by the court, governing procedure or practice before it.

scienter (Latin) Knowingly; with guilty knowledge. [pronounce: si-*en*-ter]

second-degree murder Murder without premeditation.

self-defense Physical force used against a person who is threatening the use of physical force or using physical force.

separation of powers Division of the federal government (and state governments) into legislative (lawmaking), judicial (law interpreting), and executive (law carrying out) branches.

shield laws A state law that prohibits use of most evidence of a rape (or other sexual crime) victim's past sexual conduct at trial.

showup A pretrial Identification procedure in which only one suspect and a witness are brought together.

sidebar An in-court discussion among lawyers and the judge that is out of the hearing of witnesses and the jury. Sidebar conferences are usually *on* the record.

sodomy A general word for an "unnatural" sex act or the crime committed by such act. While the definition varies, *sodomy* can include oral sex, anal sex, homosexual sex, or sex with animals.

solicitation Asking for; enticing; strongly requesting. This may be a crime if the thing being urged is a crime.

sovereign immunity The government's freedom from being sued. In many cases, the U.S. government has waived immunity by a statute such as the Federal Tort Claims Act; states have similar laws.

specific intent An intent to commit the exact crime charged or the precise outcome of the act, not merely an intent to commit the act without an intention to cause the outcome.

stalking The crime of repeatedly following, threatening, or harassing another person in ways that lead to a legitimate fear of physical harm. Some states define *stalking* more broadly as any conduct with no legitimate purpose that seriously upsets a targeted person, especially conduct in violation of a protective order.

standing A person's right to bring (start) or join a lawsuit or to raise a particular issue because he or she is directly affected by the issues raised.

stand-your-ground A law that enables a person to use deadly force to repel an attack without first retreating.

stare decisis (Latin) The doctrine that judicial decisions stand as precedents for cases arising in the future.

statute A law passed by a legislature.

statute of limitation Federal and state statutes prescribing the maximum period of time during which various types of civil actions and criminal prosecutions can be brought after the occurrence of the injury or the offense.

statutory construction Guidelines employed by judges in the interpretation of statutes that have developed and evolved over hundreds of years.

statutory rape The crime of having sexual intercourse with a person under a certain state-set age, regardless of consent.

strict liability crimes Crimes or offenses in which mens rea or criminal intent is not an element. Such offenses include regulatory crimes, petty offenses, and infractions.

strict liability Guilt of a criminal offense even if you had no criminal intention (mens rea).

subornation of perjury The crime of asking or forcing another person to lie under oath.

suspended sentence A sentence (usually "jail time") that the judge allows the convicted person to avoid serving (usually if the person continues on good behavior, completes community service, etc.).

tax evasion The deliberate nonpayment or underpayment of taxes that are legally due. Criminal tax evasion has higher fines than civil fraud and the possibility of a prison sentence upon the showing of "willfulness."

tax fraud The deliberate nonpayment or underpayment of taxes that are legally due.

terrorism The definition of terrorism is the subject to ongoing debate. However, one federal statute defines it as activities that involve violence or acts dangerous to human life that are violations of law and appear to be intended to intimate or coerce a civilian population, to influence a policy of government by intimidation or coercion, or to affect the conduct of government through mass destruction, assassination, or kidnapping. 18 U.S.C. §2331.

tort A civil (as opposed to a criminal) wrong, other than a breach of contract.

transactional immunity Freedom from prosecution for all crimes related to the compelled testimony, so long as the witness tells the truth.

transferred intent The principle that if an unintended illegal act results from the intent to commit a crime, that act is also a crime.

trial court A court that hears and determines a case initially, as opposed to an appellate court; a court of general jurisdiction.

use immunity Freedom from prosecution based on the compelled testimony and on anything the government learns from following up on the testimony.

vagueness doctrine The rule that a criminal law may be unconstitutional if it does not clearly say what is required or prohibited, what punishment may be imposed, or what persons may be affected. A law that violates due process of law in this way is *void for vagueness.*

vicarious liability Legal responsibility for the acts of another person because of some relationship with that person.

victim impact statement At the time of sentencing, a statement made to the court concerning the effect the crime has had on the victim or on the victim's family.

voir dire examination (French) "To see, to say"; "to state the truth." The preliminary in-court questioning of a prospective witness (or juror) to determine competency to testify (or suitability to decide a case). [pronounce: vwahr deer]

INDEX

Note: page numbers followed by e indicate exhibits